WHITHORN AND ST NINIAN

This book is for Daphne Brooke, Jean Comrie, Rosemary Cramp and Lis Graham

WHITHORN AND ST NINIAN

The Excavation of a Monastic Town, 1984–91

Peter Hill

With contributions from

Ewan Campbell, Amanda Cardy, Ray Chadburn, Jane Clarke, Derek Craig, Rosemary Cramp, Anne Crone, Donald Davidson, Brenda Dickinson, Sheila Hamilton-Dyer, Nicholas Holmes, Fraser Hunter, Jacqui Huntley, Dorothy Lunt, Finbar McCormick, S. Metcalfe, Martin Millett, Jo Moran, Eileen Murphy, Andrew Nicholson, Dave Pollock, Elizabeth E.J. Pirie, Jennifer Price, Damien Ronan, M.E. Watts

THE WHITHORN TRUST
SUTTON PUBLISHING

First published in the United Kingdom in 1997 by
Sutton Publishing Limited
Phoenix Mill · Far Thrupp · Stroud · Gloucestershire

Reprinted 1998

Copyright © The Whithorn Trust and individual contributors per The Whithorn Trust

All rights reserved. No part of this publication may be reproduced, stored in a retrieval system, or transmitted, in any form or by any means, electronic, mechanical, photocopying, recording or otherwise, without the prior permission of the publishers and copyright holder(s).

British Library Cataloguing in Publication Data

Hill, Peter
Whithorn and St. Ninian: The Excavation of a Monastic Town, 1984–91
I. Title
941.495

ISBN 0 7509 0912 9

Typeset in 10/11 Times
Typesetting and origination by
Sutton Publishing Limited
Printed in Great Britain by
WBC Ltd, Bridgend

CONTENTS

Foreword	ix
Acknowledgements	x
Preface	xii
Chapter 1 Background and Speculations	1
The historical sources	1
The site and its setting	4
Previous excavations at Whithorn Priory	8
The 1984–1991 excavations	11
The early monasterium	11
The Northumbrians in Galloway	16
The church, shrine and miracles of St Nynia	19
Whithorn in the ninth century	20
The Lords of Galloway and the reform of the Gallovidian church	22
The monastic town	24
Chapter 2 The Development of the Site	26
Period I ?–730 AD	26
Period II: The Northumbrian minster *c.* 730–845 AD	40
Period III *c.* 845–1000 x 1050 AD	48
Period IV *c.* 1000 x 1050–1250	55
Period V *c.* 1250–1600	60
Period VI *c.* 1600–present	65
Chapter 3 Period I: The Early Centuries *c.* 500–*c.* 730 AD	67
Introduction	67
The inner precinct	74
The south sector	118
Chapter 4 The Northumbrian Minster *c.* 730–845 AD	134
Introduction	134
The development of the Northumbrian minster	139
Detailed descriptions	164
Chapter 5 Period III: The Minster Restored *c.* 845–1000 x 1050 AD	183
Introduction	183
Phase 1	186
Phase 2	194
Phase 3	201
Chapter 6 Period IV: Diverse Arts: The Monastic Town, *c.* 1000 x 1050–1250 x 1300 AD	210
Introduction	210
The southern sector	217
The eastern part of the central sector	227
The inner precinct	232
The displaced debris	237
Chapter 7 Period V: Priory and Town, *c.* 1250–1600 AD	251
Introduction	251
Phase 1	255
Phase 2	257
Phase 3	259
Phase 4	260
Phase 5	264
The southern sector	267

Chapter 8 After the Reformation	271
Introduction	271
Phase 1 *c.* 1600–1750	271
Phase 2 *c.* 1750–1900	271
Phase 3	276
Chapter 9 The Museum Garden and Fey Field Trenches	277
The Museum Garden	277
Phase 1	277
Phase 2	285
Phase 3	286
The Fey Field	287
The eastern part of the trench	287
Phase 1	288
Phase 2	289
Phase 3	289
Phase 4	289
Phase 5	289
Phase 6	289
The western end of the trench	291
Chapter 10 The Finds	292
Introduction	292
The Roman finds	293
The Samian ware	293
The Roman coarse wares	293
The Roman glass	294
The Tesserae	296
The Roman coin	296
The Early Medieval imports	297
The Early Medieval vessel glass	297
Additional Early Medieval vessels	314
The Dark Age ceramics	315
Distribution and chronology	322
The Early Medieval window glass	326
The coins	332
The Early Medieval coins	332
The later medieval and post-medieval coins	345
Distribution and economic implications	351
The hand-built Dark Age pottery	358
The glass rings	358
The amber	359
The non-ferrous metals	360
The copper alloy	360
The lead	389
The gold and silver	397
Moulds, crucibles and related metalworking debris	400
The iron	404
Nails	405
Structural ironwork	410
Dress fittings and riding equipment	417
Tools	421
The sculptured stones	433
The jet, shale and cannel coal	441
The stone	443
The architectural stone	443
The stone tiles	445
The graffiti and gravestone	447
The stone artefacts	447
The utilised stones	464
Exotic, imported and transformed stones	468
The antler	474
The waste	475

Comb making debris	478
Combs	480
Other artefacts	485
Strategrighic groupings	492
The bone and horn artefacts	495
The leather	499
The textiles	509
The wooden artefacts	510
The later medieval pottery	510
Chapter 11 The Environmental Material	519
The human bones	519
The late medieval cemetery	519
Introduction	519
Demography	519
Body build	522
Health status/life-style	524
Tumours	547
Developmental/congenital	547
Miscellaneous conditions	549
Non-metric traits	550
Archaeological notes	551
Cause of death	551
Summary	551
The Period I graveyard	552
Introduction	552
Demography	552
Body build	553
Health status/life-style	553
Developmental/congenital	555
Non-metric traits	556
Descriptions of individual skeletons	556
The 'central grave'	556
Summary/conclusions	556
Period II	556
The internal burials	557
The external burial	557
The children's cemetery	557
The bundle of bones	559
The cremation	560
The human dentitions	562
Introduction	562
Age	563
Pathological conditions	568
Summary	591
The 9th-century carbonised plant remains	592
Introduction	592
Results and discussion	592
The dendrochronological evidence	595
Introduction	595
Results	596
The radiocarbon dates	596
Soil Samples	598
Analysis of the diatoms in Sample 1	600
The bird and fish bones	601
Introduction	601
The fish	602
The birds	602
The animal bones	605
Introduction	605
General results	605
The Northumbrian midden	607
Cattle	608

Sheep/goat	610
Pig	610
Other domesticates	611
Wild animals	613
Appendix 1 The Provenance of the Early Christian Inscriptions of Galloway	614
Appendix 2 Metalwork and Sculpture: design and patronage in *c.* 900 AD	621
Bibliography	624
Concordance of stratigraphic units	639

Plate section

Plate I General view of Whithorn from the north-west with the Isle of Whithorn in the upper right corner.
Plate II Aerial view of the excavation in the Glebe Field from the south-west with the parish church and ruined priory to the left and the town to the right.
Plate III The *Latinus* stone
Plate IV **Period I** features in the eastern part of the Glebe Field viewed from the north. The special grave (**I/18**) is in the lower left corner and the hearth of Building I/1 in the centre.
Plate V Experimental reconstruction of a twelfth century house based on the evidence from Building IV/7.
Plate VI Excavation in progress in 1991 with the pebble covers of Graves I/68 and I/80 in the foreground, and log-coffin burials (Graves I/74–78) cutting the **Period I/3** roadway beyond.
Plate VII The **Period II** burial chapel from the east, during the excavation of the coffins in the internal graves.
Plate VIII The **Period II** church from the west showing the foundation trenches of the two oratories (1 and 2) framed by the sockets of the later arcade posts, and with the Period II/1 enclosure wall to the right.
Plate IX Early medieval window glass
Plate X Early medieval vessel glass
  Key to Plates IX and X

Foreword

When the Whithorn Trust began its excavations in 1986, it could hardly have foreseen the enormous efforts involved in seeking to uncover the origins of the 'Cradle of Christianity in Scotland'. The wealth of material uncovered between 1986 and 1991 has fully justified its work. This volume is the culmination of much labour and does credit to all those members of Peter Hill's team who have striven so effectively to dig up and interpret the vast quantities of material and artefacts brought to light. It is important to pay tribute also to the Local Authorities who have given considerable financial assistance over the years in their generous support of this academic project. All are to be congratulated on the successful completion of a daunting task. Some may have wished to see it finished at an earlier date, but the production of a work of true scholarship is more important than the speed of its delivery.

As the present chairman of the Whithorn Trust and the last surviving ex-Provost of the Royal Burgh of Whithorn, it gives me great pleasure to welcome a remarkable account of the continuous occupation of this historic site for a period of more than 1500 years. The story has for too long been little known to scholars, and it is my hope that book will give rise to more research and bring renewed interest in the history of the area.

Whithorn's motto is 'Resurgam'. Perhaps this volume will help to stimulate such a renewal.

TONY GRAHAM
Whithorn
Christmas 1996

Acknowledgements

The Whithorn excavations have involved massive investments of time, money and enthusiasm by numerous agencies and individuals, and it would be impossible to acknowledge all who have contributed.

The excavation season spanned some 155 weeks in 1984 and 1986–91, and hundreds of skilled excavators, trainees and enthusiasts have contributed to its successful completion. I am grateful to Jane Clarke, Karina Kucharski, Jenny Lee, Jo Moran, Andrew Nicholson, Damien Ronan, Lindsay Ross, and Chris Russell-White who worked as supervisors in 1986–91; to Annemarie Gibson, Mary Kemp, David Reed and Lindsay Ross who managed the 1984 trenches; to Alan James for regular metal detection monitoring; to all the excavators, but especially Terry Brawls, Ray Chadburn, Michelle Crichton, Simon Dick, Ian McGregor and Dave Murray; to numerous volunteers from the Universities of Durham, Glasgow, Liverpool and elsewhere; to the large local team recruited through the Community Programme and Employment Training Scheme, and to Les Pearce and Alf McHallum, who co-ordinated it; to Charles Thomas and numerous other visiting colleagues who have contributed ideas, possibilities and cautions; and especially to Dave Pollock, my Assistant Director, whose special skills have unravelled many of stratigraphic enigmas encountered, and whose drawings have enriched the project and this book

The analysis of the stratigaphy and finds has been a challenging, irksome and, ultimately, satisfying process, and I am indebted to Jane Clarke, Karina Kucharski, Jo Moran, Andrew Nicholson, Dave Pollock and Damien Ronan for the preparation of the excavation archive; to Joann Rogerson, Alastair Penman and Kate Vine for assisting with the processing of the finds; to Packard Harrington for overseeing the computer record; to Andy Wiles and Martha Maguire for technical advice on the reconstructions of the **Period II** buildings; to Ted and Tom Dowling, Cath Haig, Alex Higgins, David Kerr, Irma and Davy McLauchlin, Andrew Nicholson, Sarah Petrie, Damien Ronan and Sylvia Stevenson for illustrations of the finds; to John Pickin and Alison Reid for curatorial advice; to Alan McFarlane and Tom Gray for photographs; to Liz Slater (Glasgow University), Janey Cronin (Durham University), Katherine Lovell and William Murray (National Museums of Scotland), Richard Welander (Historic Scotland), and Jim Spriggs, Sonia O'Connor and Eric Patterson (York Archaeological Trust) for the conservation and X-radiography of the finds; to Fraser Hunter, Jim Tait and Paul Wilhew (National Museums of Scotland), and John Hunter (the University of Bradford), for the analysis of metal and glass objects; to Bill Cormack, Leslie Alcock, Jonathon Wooding, and many others for discussions about the finds; to the numerous specialists who have contributed to Chapters 10 and 11, and to Dennis Gallacher, Robin Murdoch, and Joann Rogerson for their archival reports on the clay-pipes and post-medieval glass and pottery; and particularly to Jean Comrie, Finds Officer, and Fay Templeton, Computer Operator, whose enthusiasm and industry have underpinned the programme of post-excavation work.

The preparation of this report has been a protracted and challenging process, and I am grateful to Leslie Alcock, Richard Bailey, Daphne Brooke, Rosemary Cramp, Lesley Ferguson, John Hume, Christopher Morris and Noel Fojut for comments upon a preliminary draft; to Derek Craig for giving free access to his unpublished doctoral research; to Daphne Brooke and Richard Oram for advice on historical problems; to Simon Brooke and Jim Wilson for computing advice and troubleshooting; to Catherine Craig and Senga Mitchell for checking the bibliography; to Kenneth and Liz Palmer for editorial comments; to Dianne Boe, Pete Heywood and John Slaven for preparing the final proofs; and particularly to Andrew Nicholson for his unstinting assistance over the years, to Damien Ronan for his fine illustrations, and to Richard Bryant for his support and editorial advice.

The excavation has attracted widespread public interest, and I am indebted to Cathy Aitken, Catherine Craig, Simon Lee and Patricia Shorthouse who have managed the visitor facilities; to Biddie Melville, Senga Mitchell, Alastair Spence and numerous other site guides; to Duncan Ross and the staff and residents of Penningham House for a uniquely spicy contribution to the guiding team; to Lynn Bell and the Directors of the Tristran Trading Company for managing the Trust's trading arm; and to Anne Black for orchestrating and implementing a successful programme of media exposure. I am particularly grateful to the Friends of the Whithorn Trust who have provided funds, volunteers, rock-cakes and enthusiasm, as well as supporting the Trust's research through a series of scholarly publications and the annual Whithorn Lecture inaugurated in 1992.

The main excavation trench lies within the glebe of Whithorn, and I am grateful to the minister and session of St Ninian's Priory Church, and to Alan Cowe and the General Trustees of the Church of Scotland for their enthusiastic collaboration over the years. The Whithorn Trust was established in 1986, and has been ably chaired by the Very Reverend Peter Brodie, Professor Rosemary Cramp, and Councillors Bob Robinson, Jack Cameron and Tony Graham. Sadly neither Peter Brodie nor Bob Robinson has survived to see the publication of this book. The excavation has been overseen by the Trust's Research Committee, and I am indebted to its members, and to Rosemary Cramp, Leslie Alcock, John Hume, Richard Bailey and Tony Graham who have chaired its meetings. The 1984 excavation was undertaken by the Central Excavation Unit (Scotland) and I am grateful to Noel Fojut and Historic Scotland for entrusting me with such an exciting project. Continuing support for the Whithorn Trust by Historic Scotland has been provided by John Hume, Noel Fojut and Doreen Groves, and by Bill Baron and Mickie Lyons, successive custodians of the Priory Museum. The complex problems of administration and financial management have been handled ably by John Baldwin, Sarah-Jane Bannerman, Jackie Beatson, Janet Butterworth, Annemarie Gibson, Dorothy Hodgson, Donna Hoodless, Yvonne Miller and Christine Wilson, and I am grateful to them for their help; to Jandy Stevenson, David Main and Jackie Rennie for committed and inspired accountancy support; and to Alastair Geddes, Clive Hartley, Alec Haswell, Leslie Jardine, Donald McIntyre, Ian Smith and the other officials of Wigtown District Council, Dumfries and Galloway Regional Council, and Dumfries and Galloway Council who have worked so hard for the success of the project.

The Whithorn Trust's research has been funded by a wide range of institutions and individuals, and I am grateful to them all, and hope the results have justified their support. The principal sponsors of the Trust's operations have been the General Trustees of the Church of Scotland, the Presbytery of Wigtown and Stranraer, the Roman Catholic Diocese of Galloway, the Bishops' Conference of Scotland, the Roman Catholic Church in Scotland, the Scottish Episcopal Church, the Church of Scotland Women's Guild, Dumfries and Galloway Regional Council, Wigtown District Council, Dumfries and Galloway Council, the Manpower Services Commission (Community Programme), the Training Commission (Employment Training), the European Regional Development Fund, the Friends of the Whithorn Trust and Friends of the Whithorn Trust (Stirling Branch), the Edinburgh Friends Ceilidh Committee, the Scottish Tourist Board, the Scottish Development Agency, the National Museums of Scotland, Historic Scotland, the Society of Antiquaries of Scotland, the Society of Antiquaries of London, the Dumfriesshire and Galloway Field Naturalist and Antiquarian Society, the Glasgow Archaeological Society, the Jennie S Gordon Memorial Foundation, the Hunter Archaeological Trust, the Mouswald Trust, the Russell Trust, the Columba Trust, the Orcome Trust, the Clark Charitable Trust, the Caram Trust, the Williamson Trust, the Rosemary Cramp Fund, the Adam Maitland Charitable Trust, the Royal Bank of Scotland, the Clydesdale Bank, the Bank of Scotland, the T.S.B. Foundation for Scotland, the Prudential Corporation, Cadbury Schweppes, Glaxochem Ltd, Swan Construction, Britoil, the Hepworth's Iron Company plc (Hepworth's Heritage Communication Award), the Glasgow Herald (1987 Archaeological Communication Award), William Grant and Sons (Glenfiddich Award 1990 and 1992), the Universities of Glasgow, Durham, and Liverpool, Bill Cowan, the Marquis of Bute, Digby Felix, and Joan McGavin. The former Councils of Wigtown District and Dumfries and Galloway Region have been the most generous and consistent sponsors, and I hope that their courageous investment in the antiquity of Whithorn will produce appropriate dividends to the people of the region in future years. I am particularly grateful to the Hunter Archaeological Trust, the Mouswald Trust and the Friends of the Whithorn Trust who funded a two week extension to the final excavation season, during which some of the most significant early deposits were recorded, and which brought the operation to a successful conclusion. The publication of this volume has been supported by generous grants from Historic Scotland and the Esmé Fairbairn Trust.

The people of Whithorn and the surrounding countryside have been obliging hosts to the varied band of diggers, scholars, administrators and others who have infested the area over the past ten years. They have fed and housed us, shared our triumphs, condemned our extravagances, explored our eccentricities, and united with us in researching and reasserting the role of Whithorn in the history of European Christianity and civilization: my particular and warm thanks are due to them for a thousand kindnesses.

Preface

In the five hundredth and sixty fifth year of our Lord's incarnation, when Justin the Less received the helm of the Roman Empire after Justinian, there came into Britain from Ireland a priest and abbot, distinguished by his monastic dress and way of life, by name Columba, to preach the word of God to the provinces of the Northern Picts, that is to say, to those which are separated from the southern regions by steep and rugged mountain ridges. For these southern Picts, who have their sees in the same mountains, had long before, as the story goes, forsaken the error of idolatry and received the faith of truth, when the word was preached to them by Nynia, a most reverend bishop and holy man of the nation of Britons, who had been regularly instructed at Rome in the faith and mystery of the truth; whose episcopal see, distinguished by the name and by the church of St. Martin the bishop, where he himself, together with many other saints, rests in the body, the English nation has just now begun to govern. The place, which belongs to the province of the Bernicians, is called in the vernacular At the White House, because he there built a church of stone in a manner to which the Britons were not accustomed.

(Bede *Historia Ecclesiastica Gentis Anglorum* III iv, trans. MacQueen 1990)

The publication of the Ecclesiastical History of the English Nation in 731 AD introduced the civilised world to the story of Bishop Nynia, a remarkable man, and Whithorn, the remarkable place where he had lived and died. Other historical sources, though less concise, provide little additional reliable information about Nynia's missionary work, the stone church he built, the character of the original Christian community at Whithorn, and most critically his chronology. These questions continue to excite controversy and the views of three recent protagonists illustrate the range of possible interpretations. Professor John MacQueen (1990, 86–7) infers that there was an extant late-Roman Christian settlement at Whithorn, and argues that Nynia, a British bishop consecrated in Rome between 400 and 450 AD, introduced a monastic community modelled on exemplars in the Western Empire. Professor Charles Thomas also infers that there was a Roman settlement in or near Whithorn, to which Nynia was appointed bishop in the fifth century, perhaps *c* 431. He denies the existence of a fifth century monastery, but detects a wave of Gaulish influence in the sixth century, which introduced the cult of St Martin, and was followed by the absorption of Irish monastic ideas and practices in the seventh century (1992, 19–20). Dr Alan MacQuarrie dates St Ninian's mission to a period a hundred or so years later, and sees his church as 'a territorial or regional episcopate, as yet unaffected by the Irish monastic organisation introduced into Scotland by Saint Columba in 563' (1987, 23–4).

Excavations by Historic Scotland in 1972–1984 (Tabraham 1979, Hill 1984), and by the Whithorn Trust since 1986, have identified a remarkable sequence of archaeological deposits to the west of Whithorn Priory, which have revealed a detailed record of the development of a large fragment of the site from *c* 500 AD. This new evidence is insufficiently precise to distinguish between an episcopal settlement and a monastic community, nor does it resolve the chronological problems of the Ninianic traditions. It does however provide a detailed picture of the evolving organisation, economy and cultural contacts of the community focused upon the church built by St Ninian, which preserved his relics and traditions, and exploited them to make Whithorn one of the great centres of the medieval church. This has provided rare insight into the organization of a major *monasterium* of the early church, and simultaneously charts the evolution of the town of Whithorn as a thriving community fuelled by the cult of St Ninian, and originating in the Early Middle Ages. This book is thus more concerned with the enduring symbiosis of the community and its patron, than with the historical problems of his life, context and missionary activity.

The archaeological record at Whithorn encompasses two distinct strands of evidence. The first comprises clear structural, artefactual, stratigraphic and chronological data, which are fairly simple to interpret and have been presented in a series of interim reports produced by the Whithorn Trust. A parallel strand of evidence includes large numbers of displaced artefacts, 'wall-less' earth-floored buildings disguised by mud, and other archaeological enigmas. I have adopted somewhat unconventional procedures to realize the potential of this material, and these methods may be too irregular for stratigraphic purists. I believe them to be justified by the richness of the picture that emerges when the concrete and enigmatic strands of evidence are combined.

The archaeological evidence is presented in Chapters 3–11, and I have attempted to integrate it with the extant historical and archaeological evidence to produce a new history of Whithorn, which is summarized in Chapter 2. This contains much that is new, some controversial and some speculative. It is proposed in the expectation that continuing excavation and improved techniques can and will transform what is laid out.

PETER HILL
Tonderghie
Christmas 1996

CHAPTER 1
Background and speculations

Peter Hill

Section 1: Background Information

1.1. THE HISTORICAL SOURCES

The historians and historiography

I, Nennius, pupil of the holy Elvodug, have undertaken to write down some extracts that the stupidity of the British cast out; for the scholars of the Island of Britain had no skill and set down no record in books. I have therefore made a heap of all that I have found, both from the Annals of the Romans and from the Chronicles of the Holy Fathers, and from the Irish and the English, and out of the tradition of our elders. Many learned scholars and copyists have tried to write but somehow they have left the subject more obscure ...

(Historia Brittonum)

Historia Brittonum was compiled in the early ninth century and tells nothing of Whithorn, but the honesty of the preface epitomises the problems faced by those seeking the truth about Bishop Nynia. Whithorn lay within a British area, and the problem lies with the Britons' failure to preserve their own history, leaving the task to other and potentially hostile people. Whithorn is thus invisible in British sources and, like Nennius, historians must rely upon English and Irish records.

Whithorn is undocumented for most of the period before the mid-twelfth century, save for an interlude in 731–802 AD when the Northumbrian bishopric is recorded in some detail. The Northumbrians seem to have invested considerable resources in the development of their new episcopal centre and the promulgation of the cult of St Nynia, which would probably have been lost without this intervention. There are no other reliable contemporary accounts of Galloway in this period, apart from the inscriptions at Kirkmadrine in the Rhinns (pp 11-2, 617-9) and the evidence from Whithorn is thus critical to the history of the region. The meagre historical framework has been enhanced greatly by studies of sculptures and place names, which are exploited in Chapter 2.

This section reviews the principal written sources and identifies their relationships with the evidence from the excavation. This is followed by an examination of some Irish evidence, which poses separate problems, but reveals a distinct perspective of Whithorn.

Whithorn: the principal historical sources. There are four principal written sources for the early history of Whithorn:

1. The inscription on the *Latinus* stone (p 615, Appendix 1) is the earliest text and the only contemporary reference to the early Christian community. It makes no mention of Bishop Nynia and no overt reference to *Candida Casa* (but see Thomas 1992a) and its precise meaning is controversial (pp 615-7).

2. The two references to Whithorn in Bede's *Historia Ecclesiastica Gentis Anglorum* (hereafter *HE*) completed at Jarrow in 731 AD. The first (*III.iv*, p xii) deals primarily with Nynia and his church, while the second (*V.xxiii*, p 16) records the establishment of a new Northumbrian diocese and the appointment of Pecthelm as bishop.

3. A verse life in Latin – *Miracula Nynie Episcopi* (the Miracles of Bishop Nynia, hereafter *Miracula*) written at Whithorn, probably in the late eighth century. Copies of *Miracula* and an acrostic verse – *Hymnus Sancti Nynie Episcopi* – were sent to the Northumbrian scholar Alcuin at Aachen, and these verses, preserved in Bamberg, and Alcuin's letter of thanks (Dümmler 1895, 431) comprise a trilogy of late eighth century Whithorn texts.

4. A prose life in Latin – *Vita Niniani* (the Life of Ninian, hereafter *Vita*) probably written by Ailred of Rievaulx, between 1154 and 1160 (MacQueen 1990, 17).

The last three accounts (2, *HE*, 3, *Miracula* and 4, *Vita*) have been published on several occasions and are most readily accessible in the second edition of Professor MacQueen's *St Nynia* (1990). They have been used extensively in attempts to create a history of St Ninian, but less frequently to explore the history of Whithorn in later periods. Professor MacQueen has made a particular study of the textual relationships between them (1961, 1990 and 1991) identifying two lost texts: an original prose version (PV) and a rather later Anglo-Saxon version (AV) used by Ailred.

The two passages in *Historia Ecclesiastica* have different evidential qualities. The report of the appointment of Pecthelm as the first Northumbrian bishop of *Candida Casa* (*HE V.xxiii*) can be treated as reliable and factual, as may the references to his successors in subsequent annals (p 19). Bede's brief account of Bishop Nynia (p xii) records a tradition some 200–300 years old, and this is implicit in Bede's own expression *ut perhibet* – 'so the story goes' (MacQueen 1990, 12). This account is generally considered to have been an interpolation which sits uneasily within the chapter dealing with Columba. Bede may have received this information from his correspondent, Pecthelm, the newly appointed bishop of *Candida Casa,* and it may thus have been derived from the original prose life (PV) inferred by MacQueen. *Historia Ecclesiastica* was distributed widely and almost certainly gave these traditions a prominence that they had not enjoyed previously. Their inclusion can be viewed as intentional propaganda for the new Northumbrian centre linked to the comprehensive redevelopment of the *monasterium* taking place at the same time (pp 40-1, 134-5).

Miracula and *Vita* have different evidential qualities again and both are pre-eminently manifestos of their own times. *Miracula* is a verbose, stylised work simultaneously displaying its author's erudition and literary limitations. Its primary purpose seems to have been the promotion of the eighth century cult centre and the therapeutic services it offered (pp 19-20). It is thus a contemporary product of the great establishment illustrated in Figure 2.12, and has contributed some of the evidence on which this reconstruction is based.

Vita is a profoundly political statement which exploits the Ninianic traditions to assert the primacy of Rome and orthodox practices as an instrument of ecclesiastical reform. It was written by the abbot of a the great Cistercian Abbey of Rievaulx during a bitter conflict between the Cistercian houses of northern England and the people of Galloway, whose adherence to old customs was impeding the progress of reform (pp 22-3). The contemporary archaeological remains (pp 55-60) can be interpreted as the *monasterium* or monastic town occupied by these stubborn *indigenes*, an otherwise mute party to the propaganda war.

Vita includes a perplexing topographical account of Whithorn, which is described as

> . . . . situated on the shore of the ocean, and, extending far into the sea on the east, west and south sides, is closed in by the sea itself, while only on the north is a way open to those who would enter.
>
> (*Vita Niniani III*)

This description fits the Isle of Whithorn much better than Whithorn itself (Figure 1.4), implying that the author had never visited the inland site, although he perhaps knew the coastal Isle, or had viewed it from the sea. *Vita* may thus have been written without direct knowledge of Whithorn and current, local traditions. Aelred's source was an earlier life in unpolished language (*barbario scriptu*) perhaps the life in Old English (AV) inferred by MacQueen (p 1, 1961, 5–6; 1990, 11).

Miracula and *Vita* present slightly different selections of stories in a slightly different order (Table 1.1). The problems of Nynia's visits to Rome and Tours; his conversion of the Picts and the affliction and cure of King Tudwall have been discussed widely elsewhere (e.g. Chadwick 1950, Radford 1950, MacQueen 1961, 1990; MacQuarrie 1987, Brooke 1989, Thomas 1992a) and, save for their controversial chronological evidence (p xii), are not immediately germane to Whithorn. The remaining elements are more pertinent and can be divided into two groups. An 'early' group includes the accounts of Nynia's life, miraculous deeds, death and burial, and comprises two sub-groups. The first contains the elements common to both sources: 1 – the construction of the church and its dedication to St Martin; 2 – the miracles of the leeks, cattle rustler and falsely accused priest; and 3 – the death and burial of Bishop Nynia. The miracle of the leeks (*VII* in both sources) portrays Nynia in an overtly monastic context, which has sometimes been seen to conflict with this episcopal rank. The early *monasterium* (pp 27-30) provides an appropriate context for this and the other miracles in the group, which are described briefly below (pp 14-5). The second sub-group includes two stories from *Vita* (*IX* and *X*) omitted from *Miracula*. The adventures of the mischievous schoolboy (*Vita X*) stand apart from the other 'early' material and seem more closely linked to the Finian stories contributed by Irish sources (p 3). Bishop Ninian is less important to the plot than his staff of office, suggesting a common purpose with the otherwise-dissimilar episode of the 'divine umbrella' (*Vita IX*). This tells how Ninian habitually carried a book of psalms and would periodically pause to study or sing from it, conveniently protected from rain by divine power. On one occasion, when travelling with his colleague Plebia, he was distracted 'by some unlawful thought' and the rain penetrated the 'umbrella' wetting the book. These stories seem to focus on non-corporeal relics – a staff and a water-stained book – which were, perhaps, venerated at his shrine at Whithorn. Both have a distinctly Irish flavour and may have been included in the lost, common source (PV) of *Vita* and *Miracula*, or were, perhaps, much later accretions from the tenth-twelfth centuries when Irish influences seem to have been strong (pp 59-60).

The second, '*Northumbrian*' group comprises the miracles associated with the tomb or relics of the saint, in which the actors bear Anglo-Saxon names. These seem to reveal a specific and unusual therapeutic regime with strong classical links, and are discussed in Section 2.3 (pp 19-20).

Miracula	Vita
	Prologue
	Preface
I Introduction	**I** Introduction
II Nynia's trip to Rome and his consecration there	**II** Ninian visits Rome, returns via St Martin at Tours
III His return to Britain and conversion of the Picts	**III** He chooses his see at Whithorn, builds a stone church and dedicates it to St Martin
IV His construction of *Candida Casa*, the dedication to St Martin, and its popularity with the sick	**IV** The divine punishment and miraculous cure of King Tudwal
V The punishment and miraculous cure of King Tudvael who had expelled him	**V** The miraculous acquittal of the priest accused of fornication
VI The miraculous acquittal of a priest accused of fornication	**VI** The conversion of the Picts
VII A miraculous growth of vegetables	**VII** The miraculous growth of leeks and other herbs
VIII The death and resurrection of a cattle rustler	**VIII** The death and resurrection of the cattle rustler
IX The death of Nynia	**IX** Ninian's qualities and a mishap with his 'divine umbrella' in the company of Plebia
X The cure of a paralytic boy at the tomb	**X** A delinquent schoolboy takes the saint's staff and flees by boat to Scotia
XI The cure of a man with elephantiasic leprosy at the tomb	**XI** The death of Ninian and his burial in a stone sarcophagus beside the altar of his church
XII The cure of a blind woman at the tomb	**XII** The cure of a malformed boy
XIII A miraculous vision granted to a priest at the tomb	**XIII** The cure of a man afflicted with scab
XIV Miracles, omitted from the poem, and the special qualities of Nynia, including his meditation in a cave	**XIV** The cure of Deisuit, the blind girl
	XV The miraculous cure of two lepers at a spring (or font) in the 'city'

Table 1.1 The contents of *Miracula* and *Vita*

The Irish sources. William Skene assembled a group of Irish texts purporting to describe a great sixth century monastery where young Irish Christians congregated for instruction (1887, 45–9). This material was reviewed by P.A.Wilson in 1964 who found that most of it had no discernible connection with Whithorn and should '. . . make us pause before claiming on behalf of the early Gallovidian church that she was the nursery of a numerous body of early Irish ecclesiastics.'

One of Skene's texts survived this review, and Wilson found tantalising additional evidence in its support. This fine tale of intrigue and romance is reproduced below. It survives in an eleventh century compilation of Irish liturgical verse (*Liber Hymnorum*) and no earlier versions have been traced. The story is located at Whithorn by the statement: 'Mugint made this hymn in Futerna' but it contains an overt anachronism. *Futerna* is almost certainly an Irish rendering of *hwit erne*, the Anglian name for *Candida Casa*, which is, itself, unlikely to have been coined before the late seventh century (pp 37, 130). The potential for confusion and modification in the five hundred years between the events and the earliest surviving record is patent.

> Mugint made this hymn in Whithorn. The cause: that is, Finnian of Moville went out to learn with Mugint, and Rioc and Talmach and some others with him. Drust king of Britain then, and he had a daughter, that is, Drusticc her name, and he gave her for reading to Mugint. And she loved Rioc and said to Finnian; I would give you all the books which Mugint has for writing, if you were to give Rioc in marriage to me. And Finnian sent Talmach to her that night in the form of Rioc; and he knew her, and from that Lonan of Treoit was conceived and born. But Drusticc thought that Rioc was the father of her son; but it is false, because Rioc was a virgin. Then Mugint was angry, and sent a certain boy to the church and said to him: Whoever comes first to you in the church tonight, strike him with an axe. He said it for this reason because Finnian usually reached the church first. However, that night at the Lord's instigation, Mugint himself came to the church first: and the boy struck him, as the prophet said; 'His sorrow shall be turned on his own head, and his iniquity shall descend on his neck'. And then Mugint said 'parce' because he thought that enemies were laying waste the people: or it might be for this reason that he made this hymn, that his crime might not be visited upon the people.
> (*Liber Hymnorum*, trans. MacQueen 1990, 42)

Its authenticity is supported by an even later text, a life of Bishop Finnian, collected in the fourteenth century by John of Tynemouth (Wilson 1964, 172–3). This gives Finnian an Irish ancestry and rehearses a more plausible romance in which the princess falls for Finnian, without the intricacies of Mugint's version. It is of particular interest in its description of Finnian's early training in Ireland and his 'Welsh' (i.e. British) name – *Winnin*. This training was interrupted when Bishop *Nennio* and his retinue arrived at the monastery of Nendrum on Island Mahee in Strangford Lough in a fleet of ships and carried him away to continue his education at *Magnum Monasterium*. Wilson

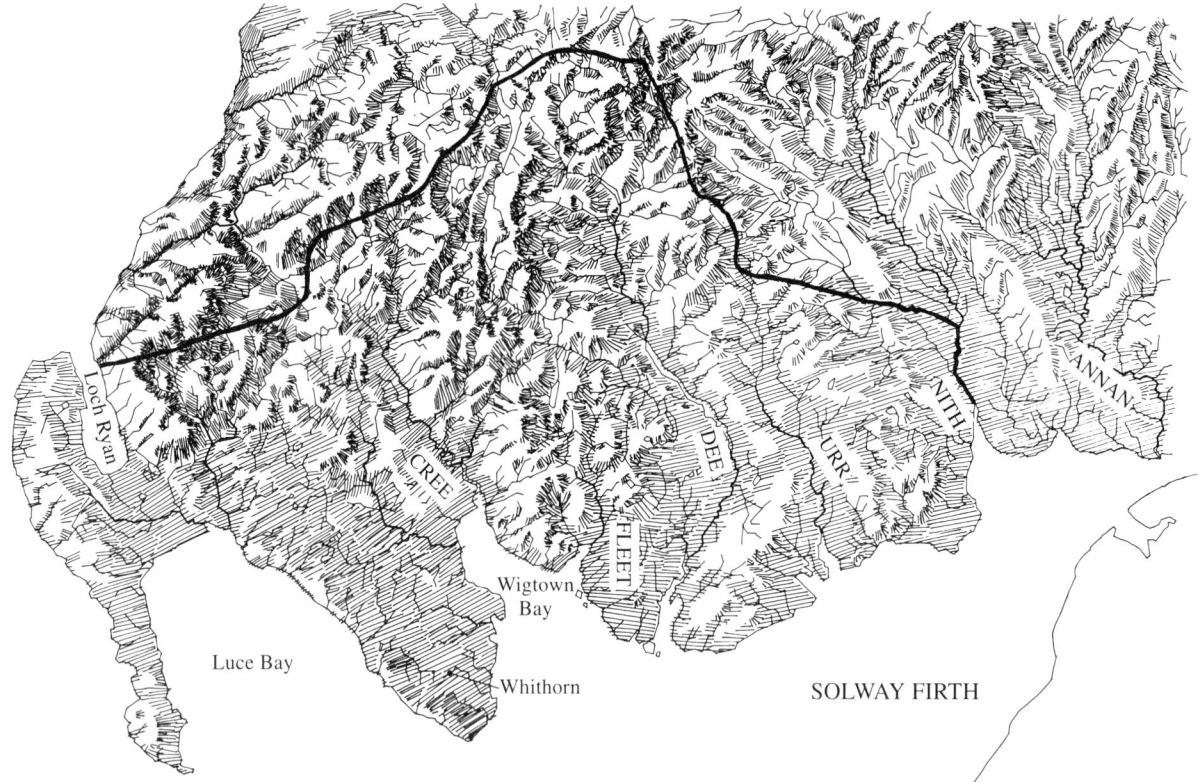

1.1 The modern boundary and topography of Galloway.

considered that the life contained authentic early elements, despite the problems of its late date and uncertain provenance, providing clear evidence of an early-sixth century monastery in south-west Scotland presided over by a bishop named Nennio (1964, 177). He did not see this as a challenge to the fifth century date of Nynia's mission, finding a solution in the Irish martyrologies which identify two distinct figures with that name. The earlier was known as *Nennio Sen* (Old Nynia) and the later as *Nennio* (Gorman) or *Moninnsen o Manistir* (Tallaght). *Nennio Sen* could thus have been the fifth century builder of *Candida Casa* and apostle of the Picts, while a successor, *Nennio/Moninnsen o Manistir*, ruled the sixth century *monasterium* and was responsible for the training of Finnian, Drusticc and their companions. Wilson has thus demonstrated that Irish writers were probably aware of a *monasterium* at Whithorn and of one or more bishops named *Nennio*. This awareness did not extend to the church – *Candida Casa* – nor, probably, to the dedication to St Martin; both being important components of the cult transmitted by the Northumbrians.

The excavation has now revealed an early-sixth century settlement at Whithorn which may have been the part of the *Magnum Monasterium*. The implications of this discovery and the ramifications of Finnian's increasingly convoluted biography are discussed in Section 2.1.

1.2 WHITHORN: THE SITE AND ITS SETTING

Galloway: land, sea and people. Galloway is a poorly-defined area which has meant different things to different people at different times. It can best be defined as encompassing the former counties of Wigtownshire and the Kirkcudbrightshire, bounded by Ayrshire to the north and the River Nith to the east (Figure 1.1). It has long been believed that the name derives from the Gall-Gaidhil, a footloose and ferocious people recorded from the early seventh century in Ireland, Scotland and, latterly, Galloway. The evidence – and particularly the place-name evidence of early sources – was recently reviewed by Daphne Brooke (1991a), who effectively refuted this long-standing association. This leaves the name unexplained. Brooke identifies three linguistic strands in which an original name has been adjusted to the British (*Galwit, -with, -wyth* or *-weth*), English (*Galweg, -wei, -wey*) or, possibly, Irish (*Galwad, -wath, -wal* or *-wall*) tongues. The prefix – *Gal* – is consistent and Brooke postulates a common origin with the *Coit Celidon* of the *Historia Brittonum*. The strong evidence for Gaulish contact in the fifth/sixth century (p 12, Thomas 1992a and b, 1994, 197–208) invites the speculation that it derives from *Gallus* (a Gaul), borrowed by the Irish as *Gall* (Thomas 1990) and only later widened to describe other foreigners such as the Gall-Gaidhil (the foreign Gaels).

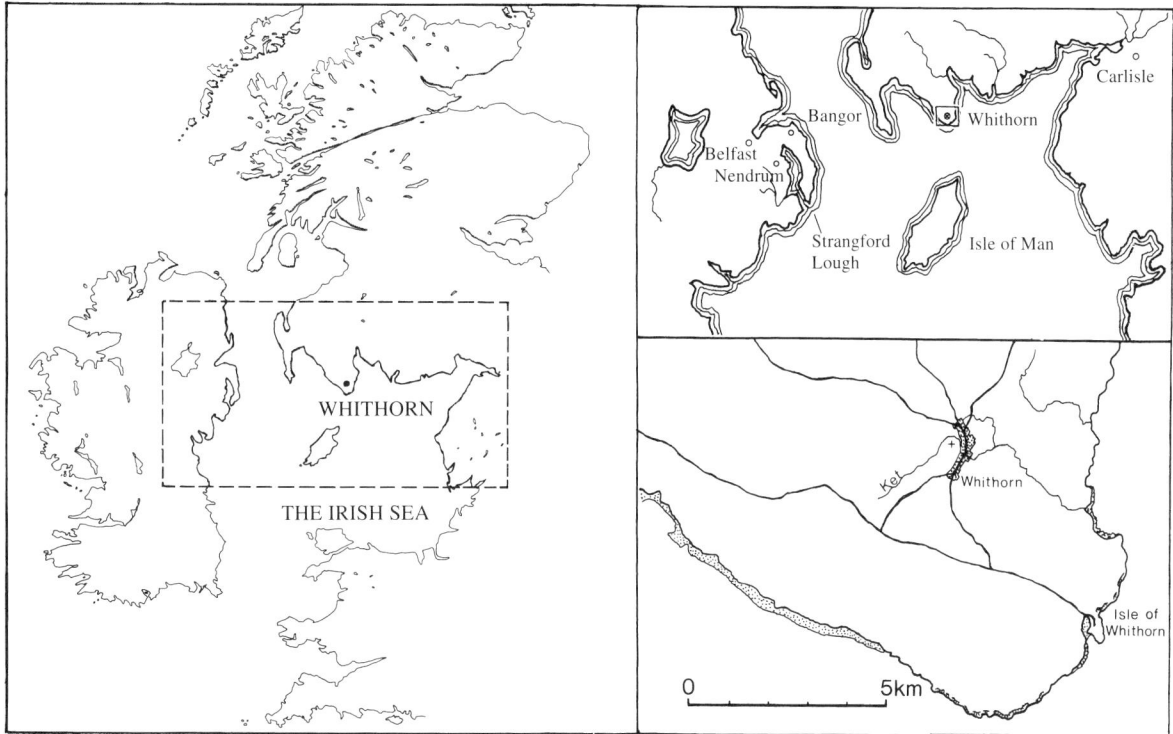

1.2 The location of Whithorn.

The area probably had greater cohesiveness to its own inhabitants but sadly they have left no definitive statement of its extent and its meaning to them. The latter is, perhaps, best expressed in the twelfth-thirteenth century dynasty of the Lords of Galloway (pp 22-3). This fiercely independent family struggled to resist the incorporation of the region to the increasingly powerful Kingdom of Scotland for more than 100 years. The final debacle saw a rising led by Thomas, the disinherited, illegitimate son of Alan who was the last in line of the Lords of Galloway. This short-lived and brutally suppressed rising had widespread support from the people and clergy, and was perhaps the last occasion when Galloway was seen as a people, rather than an area defined by lines on a map.

Physically the region is limited by mountains to the north and the Irish Sea to the south. The sea, viewed from my window, is now usually deserted except for occasional leisure craft cruising the coast or crossing to the Isle of Man. The infrequency of this traffic reflects the recent transformation of communication and economic systems which has severed close seaborne links formerly enjoyed by the older inhabitants of the area. Machars housewives, for example, used to sail to Liverpool on shopping trips in the earlier part of this century, and a system of coastal trading survived until the 1950's. Bishop Nennio's cruise to Strangford Lough (p 3) may not be historically accurate, but does not diminish the implicit acceptance that a Galloway bishop should travel to an Irish lough with a fleet of ships.

Whithorn and the Isle. The Isle of Whithorn lies 5.5 km to the south-east of Whithorn Priory on a rugged stretch of the coastline (Figure 1.2). The island is now joined to the mainland forming an enclosed bay with a gently sloping beach, but place names show that the harbour – *Port Wyterne* (1326, RMS ii, 460), *Portquhiterne* (1447, RMS ii) – and Isle – *insula de Port Witerne* (1326, RMS i App. i), *insula de Porthquhitirn* (1451, RMS ii) – were formerly distinguished, and probably still separated by water. The harbour combines a gently shelving beach with a secure anchorage, and was described in the seventeenth century as 'a very advantageous port in which ships of great burthen may be in safety in time of storm' (Sympson 1692 in Mackenzie 1841). It is still used by fishing boats and leisure craft.

Aelred's description of *Candida Casa* fits the Isle better than Whithorn (p 2) and has encouraged previous authorities to see it as the true site of Nynia's church (e.g. Simpson 1935, 1950). A large promontory fort at the south end of the Isle and a ruined chapel to the north have both been seen as possible sites for this foundation. This claim is no longer entertained by most scholars, but still has local adherents, and there is increasing evidence of a close symbiosis between inland Whithorn and the Isle. The relationship was so close that early map makers confused the two locations, portraying Whithorn as a coastal town. A place-name indicates that the bishop possessed a large farm on the landward side of the bay in the ninth/tenth century (p 53), while artefacts and commodities excavated at

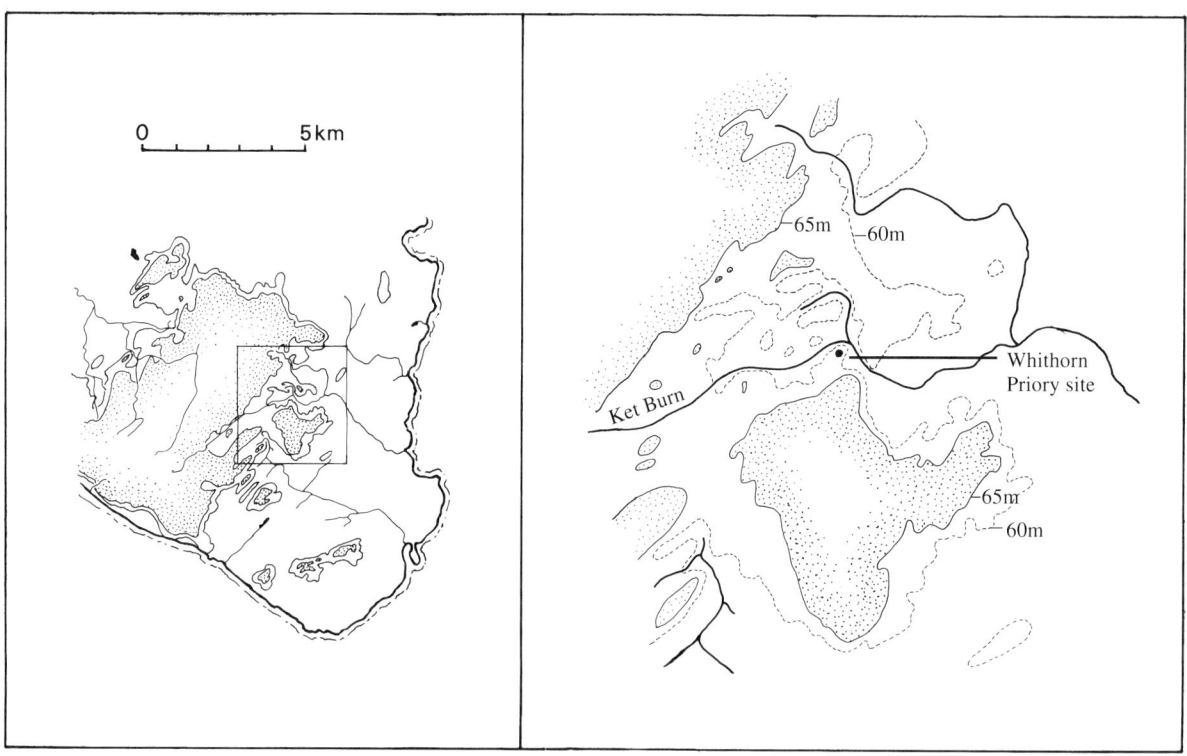

1.3 High ground in the southern Machars screening the early *monasterium* from wide visibility.

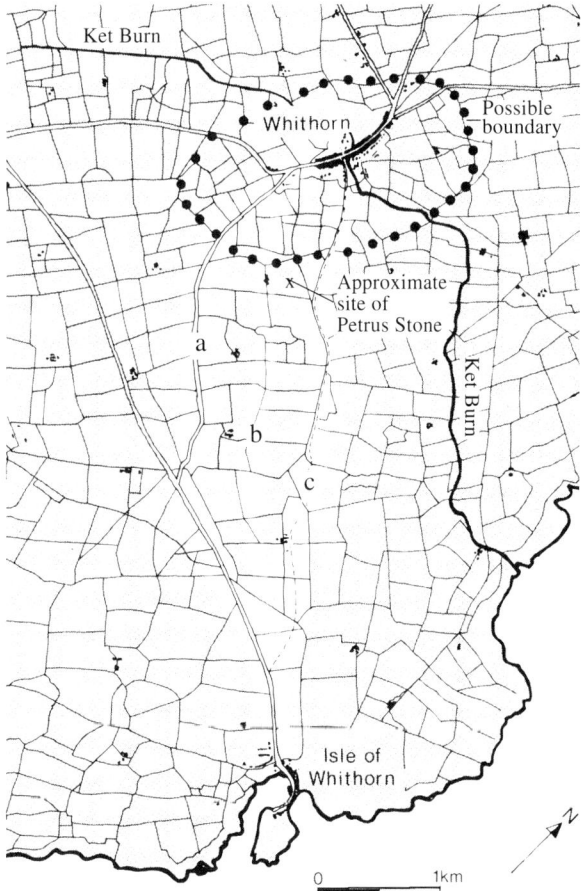

1.4 Early and modern routes connecting Whithorn and the Isle of Whithorn.

Whithorn attest marine trade from the early-sixth century if not before, which presumably passed through the Isle. The Isle was owned by the Priory in the late middle ages and a royal charter of 1491-2 (RMS ii 2075) granted the priory the customs of the goods carried in its own ships, which were listed as leather, wool, skins, cloth and fish in a charter of confirmation of 1499 (RMS ii 2486). These exports were probably the principal elements of outward trade from the early middle ages, with the possible exception of wool and cloth in the sixth and seventh centuries (p 37). Three possible routes between Whithorn and the Isle are illustrated in Figure 1.4. The modern road (**a**) swings to the south-west and is less direct than two alternative routes, a ridgeway (**b**) indicated by field boundaries and a little-used path (**c**) entering Whithorn along the King's Road, which is the most likely early route. The *Petrus* stone originally stood close to the latter two routes (Appendix 1) and may have marked the putative boundary sketched on Figure 1.4 (pp 37-8).

Whithorn. Whithorn preserves a pristine high-late medieval plan with a broad market-street, George St, closed at either end by constricted gateways, the Port and St John's Port (Figure 1.4). The houses lining the street generally display nineteenth century frontages, but behind them are the carefully measured burghage plots of a planned medieval town. The modern parish church and medieval priory occupy a slight eminence to the west of the town. They are connected by a narrow road, Bruce St or the Pend, which enters the main street through the late medieval priory gatehouse, now much-modified. Field walls indicate a possible early boundary enclosing both the town and priory (Figure 1.4), which could have delimited the *suburbana* of the early *monasterium* (p 35).

The origins of the town are poorly documented and the earliest charter of 1326 AD, only survives in a transumpt of 1451 AD (RMS ii 460). This royal charter by Robert I (RMS i App i) confirms an earlier grant by Edward Bruce, perhaps *c*. 1310, itself confirming privileges granted, or already extant, in the reign of Alexander III (1249–86 AD). This charter confirmed the grant to the Priory of the 'vill of Whithorn, which is called the Clachan, which Edward Bruce had given it as a free burgh'. A subsequent confirmation of the grant of free barony of 1459 (RMS ii,) specified that 'the burgesses and inhabitants have full power to sell wine and wax, and may have a cross and market one day a week, and a fair once a year on the eve of St Ninian's day, and for three days immediately after'. Clachàn is a Gaelic word for a settlement, usually associated with a church, and perhaps pertains to a brief period in the thirteenth century when the inhabitants were displaced from the **Period IV** *monasterium* (p 56) and, possibly, resettled along the Bruce Street/King's Road route to the Isle. The excavation has revealed a sketchy picture of the physical evidence for the separation of the priory and town in the thirteenth-fourteenth centuries (pp 60-2, Figures 2.22-23), which could be made more precise by further examination of the boundary between them.

The various elements of Whithorn integrate so well, feel so right and fit the inhabitants so exactly that it is difficult to envisage it without buildings, people and history. The other major settlements in Galloway are situated at nodes of communication and trade, and are, with few exceptions, either sited by natural harbours and landing places, or linked to the sea by navigable rivers. Whithorn has no such links and it is impossible to envisage an economic reason for its location until it had been established as a cult centre which generated sufficient activity to drive the economy. Thus stripped of buildings the site of the priory has a single striking characteristic – its obscurity. The kirk tower should be a prominent landmark but is invisible from almost all directions until one reaches the edge of the wide, shallow basin of the Ket Burn. The only chink in this low but effective screen is the narrow valley which leads the Ket eastwards to Wigtown Bay. This obscurity can be clarified by highlighting the ground between the 60 and 65 m contours to outline a central southern Machars plateau with the Ket basin concealed on its eastern margin (Figure 1.3). The Priory lies on the eastern side of this basin where it is protected by rising ground to the south-east. The Ket basin still contains a group of drained and partly-drained lochans, but would originally have been an inhospitable, watery place of lochans and bogs, subject to severe seasonal flooding.

The obscure situation of Whithorn is emulated by Kirkmadrine in the Rhinns which has produced a small, but remarkable, group of sculptures (Appendix 1). The kirk stands on a low knoll in the centre of an upland basin surrounded by rising ground on the east, south and west and effectively hidden by level ground to the north. Two gaps in this screen give glimpses of Luce Bay to the east and the Irish Channel to the west.

Site topography. The low eminence crowned by the priory is usually termed a hill in this account, but this is a rather grandiose description for a minor drumlin rising 6.0 m (19') or so (59.0–65.0 m OD) above the surrounding terrain (Figure 1.5). It is formed of ancient Silurian sedimentary rocks comprising greywackes, mudstones and shales, steeply folded by tectonic stresses into arches (anticlines) and troughs (synclines). Successive phases of glaciation have scoured away the softer younger rocks over the Silurian strata and torn away the weaker parts (usually the synclinal arches) of the underlying pleated sediments leaving jagged parallel ridges of the harder rock. The intervening troughs are coated with a gritty boulder clay deriving from rocky debris picked up by the glacier and macerated at the base of the moving ice. Exotic hard rocks, transported by the ice from outcrops to the north and west, were mixed with the debris of local rocks in this till, and appear from time to time in the archaeological record in stone structures and as artefacts.

The hill was originally far more rugged than it is today with three pronounced rocky ridges, two (**A** and **B**) defining the shoulders, and the third (**C**) half way down the slope on the south side. The ridges have been greatly modified over the centuries and builders have been quite capable of digging the rock away to provide secure foundations and level floors. The rock has, in turn, provided a useful building material. The greywacke fractures into blocks and slabs used for walls and paving, while the shales are readily smashed into thin platelets used to surface floors and paths. Local greywackes and siltstones were used for roof tiles in post-medieval buildings (pp 445-7), and all the local rock types were used for artefacts which exploited their specific properties.

The Ket Burn now runs in a rock-cut channel to the north of the priory, turning sharply to the south at the east end of the hill, and continuing through a tunnel beneath George St, eventually rejoining its natural bed to the east of the town. The gradient is shallow and would have been even gentler before the artificial channel was dug. The excavation of the low-lying ground in the **Glebe Field** (Figure 1.6) revealed layers of waterborne silt, interleaved with structural remains and cut by drains (Figure 6.7). Diatoms preserved in the silt indicate it was deposited in a shallow, probably muddy, pool or a shallow sluggish stream (pp 598-601). The former makes better topographical sense and these layers thus mark cycles of flooding, drainage and occupation. Roughly 1.5 m of silt accumulated in the lowest part of the trench and the accumulation is probably deeper still in the ground to the east. The uppermost silts lie at 58.3 m OD and the water surface would have been higher still. Any ground

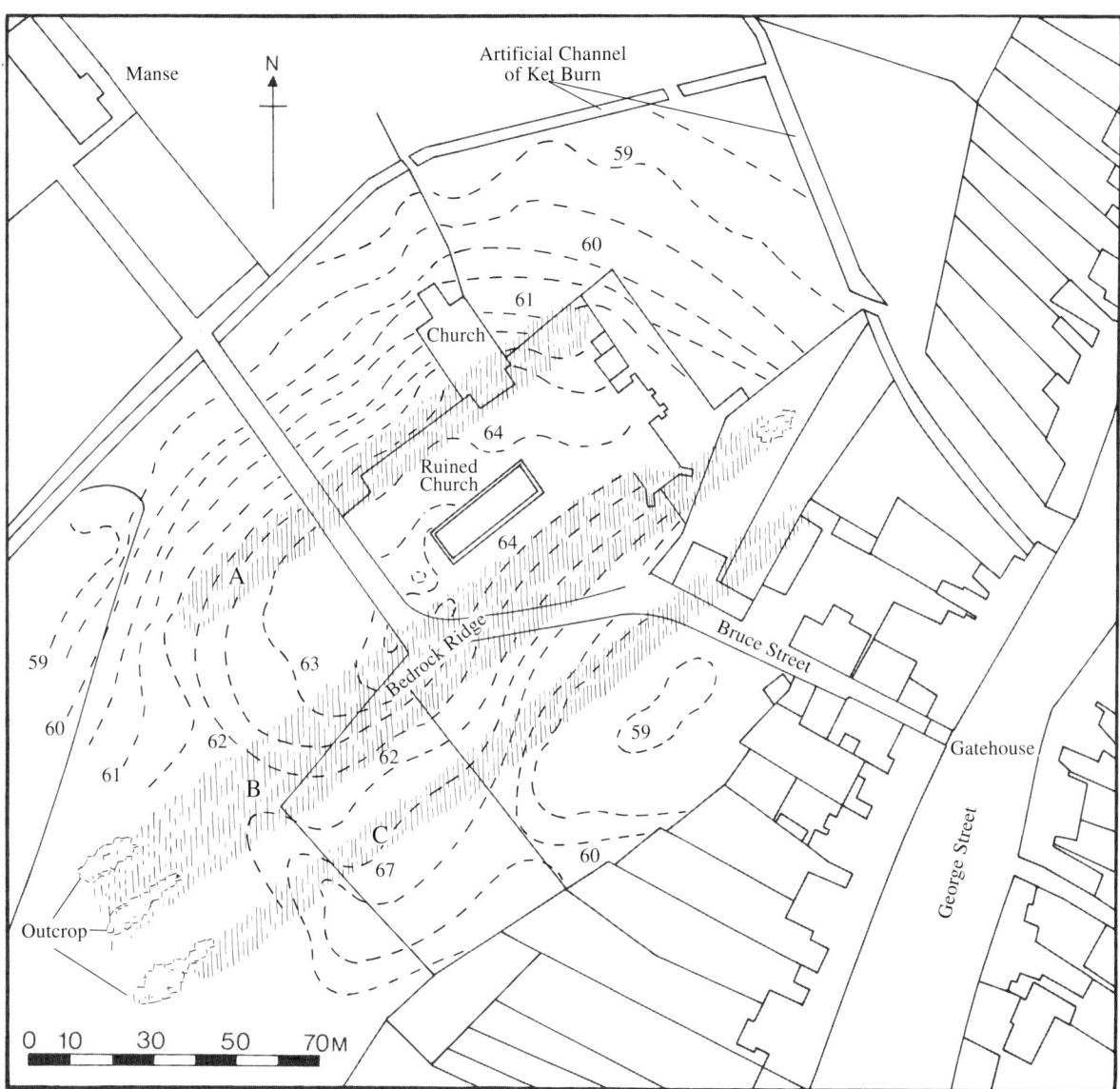

1.5 Modern topography of Whithorn Priory and projected extent of bedrock ridges.

below c. 60.0 m OD would have been flooded in the later-twelfth century, and the hill would have been surrounded on three sides by water (e.g. Figure 2.20). The uppermost deposit of silt dried out without the need for major drains in c. 1260 AD (p 227), and the canalisation of the Ket may date from this time, even if the present-day channel is less ancient.

1.3 PREVIOUS EXCAVATIONS AT WHITHORN PRIORY

Archaeologists have been as interested as historians in the origins and development of Whithorn, and four major campaigns of excavation at Whithorn are described briefly below. These excavations have produced important evidence of the original Christian community and tantalising hints of an early building and burial ground at the east end of the Priory church. Few artefacts have been recorded from the excavations in and around the Priory suggesting that this part of the hill was unoccupied or, more probably, was distanced from the messy activities of manufacture and day to day subsistence, which are richly attested in the **Glebe Field** to the south. The negative evidence thus supports the identification of the east end of the hill as the probable location of the original church, its possible successors and the other 'public buildings' appropriate to an early medieval *monasterium*.

William Galloway. In the late 1880's the Marquess of Bute commissioned a local architect, William Galloway, to carry out a programme of recording and restoration at Whithorn (Figure 1.6a). The work concentrated upon the crypts at the east end of the

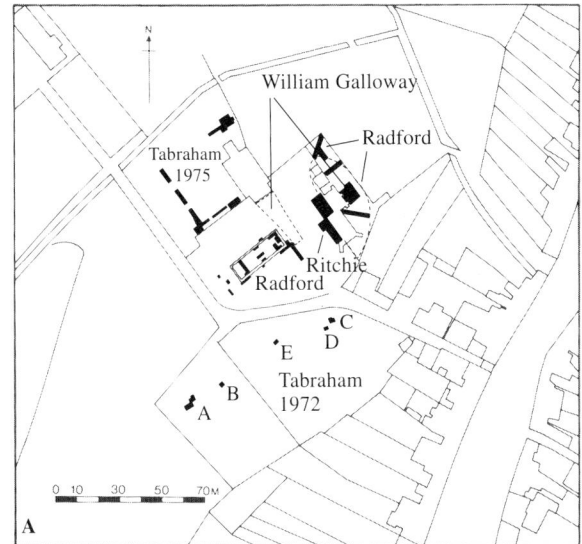
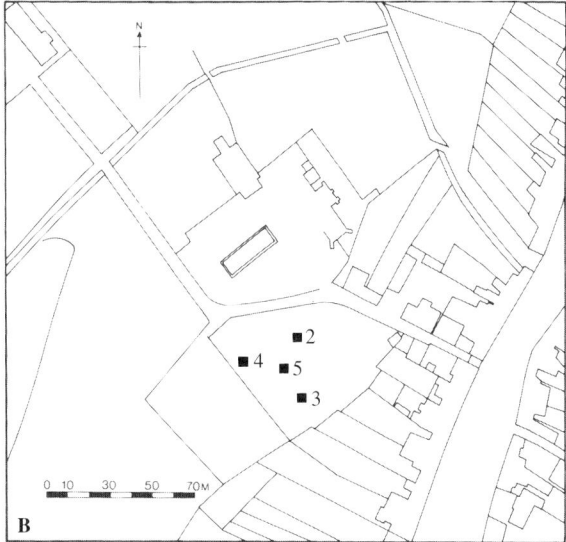

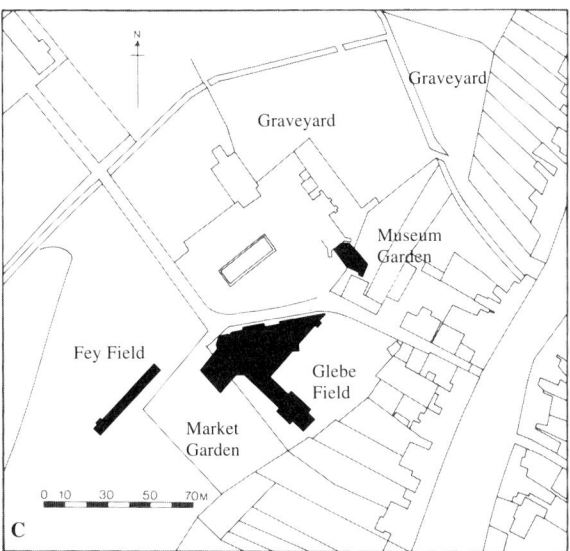

1.6 Previous and current excavations at Whithorn. A Excavations by Galloway, Radford, Ritchie and Tabraham. B 1984 trial excavation. C Excavations by the Whithorn Trust 1986-91.

church, but included the recording of structural remains underlying the path to the present day church. His discoveries were not formally reported although notebooks and other records survive among the Bute muniments, while McGibbon and Ross used his drawings (Figure 12.2) as the basis for their plan of the Priory. Originals and copies of some drawings are preserved in the photographic and drawing archives held by the National Monuments Archive of Scotland and these give hints of the work involved and the quality of the recording. The photographic archive includes a tattered photograph of Galloway's stonemasons posing with a local policeman, and excavation to the south of the crypt in 1989–90 revealed the wooden subframe of a winch, and produced mason's debris from the reconstruction and discarded boots (pp 286-7). Galloway's workmen uncovered two important pieces of evidence. The most significant discovery was the massive, roughly-shaped pillar of local greywacke – the *Latinus* stone – bearing the only contemporary, written evidence of the original Christian community at Whithorn (p 1. Appendix 1). The other major discovery was a rectangular, stone-walled building, exposed when rubble was cleared from the east side of the crypts. The three surviving walls lay beyond the east wall of the crypts and were aligned on the long axis of the priory church. The building was tentatively identified by Galloway as a Lady Chapel and the walls were capped with new masonry as part of his restoration work. The significance of this building remained unrecognised until Radford's excavations in 1949.

C A R Radford, 1949–51, 1953. In November 1948 C A Ralegh Radford launched a programme of research at Whithorn with a trial excavation of St Ninian's chapel at the Isle of Whithorn. This ambitious campaign encompassed excavations at Whithorn Priory, St Ninian's Cave and the chapel at the Isle. This was a period of great archaeological advances, achieved by precisely-targeted research excavations of short duration and published with exemplary promptness. By the end of a month's excavation in July 1949 Radford had demonstrated that the chapel at the Isle was a thirteenth century construction without Early Christian precursors, and had identified Whithorn Priory as the true home of the original Christian community. This followed the re-excavation of the 'Lady Chapel' exposed by Galloway's workmen where he observed patches of a 'coarse cream mortar of poor quality' daubed upon the outer face of the clay-bonded rubble walls (Figure 2.1). He believed this forged a close link with the stone church reported by Bede, inferring that: 'a church of stone in this connection must mean a plastered or lime-washed building', and claiming (1950, 119):

I have little doubt that these walls at the east end of the Priory Church are the remains of the church of St Martin built by S. Ninian or one of his immediate successors, the church in which his body lay through the earlier centuries.

Radford was later to question his original identification and concluded in his final report on the Whithorn campaign that the plastered building

. . . was one of the smaller oratories and that the great church lay elsewhere, probably on the summit, where early remains would have been planed off by the twelfth-century builders. (1957, 181)

This revised interpretation accords better with the model of the development of the *monasterium* outlined in Chapter 2, but evidence for the use of lime at an early date (p 81) supports Radford's view that the building was part of the early ecclesiastical centre. The stone founds and clay bonding are, however, most closely paralleled by the plinth of the clay-walled burial chapel built in the early eighth century (pp 166-8), and the building may thus have been part of a range of Northumbrian buildings, which included the principal church (Figure 2.11, pp 40-44).

The discoveries at Whithorn and the Isle were a powerful challenge to the enduring claim that Ninian's original monastic foundation was located at the Isle of Whithorn, and helped to establish a new orthodoxy in Ninianic studies, which prevailed until MacQuarrie's reassessment of the chronology was published in 1987 (p xii).

Radford also excavated a series of trenches in and around the nave of the cathedral (Figure 1.6a). His hopes of finding the remains of an earlier church were disappointed as the site had been levelled leaving scant trace of early medieval occupation. He was, nevertheless, able to elucidate the architectural history of this complex and fragmentary building, which remains the definitive account (Radford 1957, 133–151).

P R Ritchie, 1957–67. The third series of excavations began accidentally when a stone-lined grave beneath the quire was exposed during repairs to the crypts. Subsequent excavations by P R Ritchie extended over a period of eleven years, exposing the graves of many of the thirteenth-fourteenth century bishops and priors of Whithorn, and produced a rich collection of liturgical objects including pyxes, patens, rings and the magnificent twelfth century copper gilt crozier illustrated on the cover of this book.

Ritchie's narrow trench (Figure 1.6a) proved that early medieval deposits had survived beneath the quire of the church although they had been destroyed to the east by the foundations of the crypts. The original ground surface rose to the west and was cut by a group of oriented graves truncated by the foundations of the crypt. The graves seem to have been simple without evidence of stone or timber lining. Overlying deposits, possibly of early medieval date, were covered by levelling material, probably deposited during the construction of the twelfth century church. A group of simple – possibly timber-lined – graves were dug into this material and had been disturbed by the carefully-constructed stone graves of the thirteenth-fourteenth century prelates, in turn disturbed by the rebuilding of the crypts in *c*. 1500.

The results have still to be published, although there is a summary description in the Scotsman Weekend Magazine of 4th May 1963 (Cruden 1963), while colleagues who penetrated the screens surrounding the excavation have assimilated their impressions into their own published works. Radford, for example, describes a cemetery of oriented long cists surrounding a tiny plastered oratory, among which lay an inscribed stele – the *Latinus* stone (1967, 110). Ritchie's discoveries must have triggered this addition to his 1957 account. Thomas, similarly, recalls evidence of a cremation cemetery and wheel-thrown pottery in the lowest levels (e.g. 1992a, 19) indicative of a Roman phase of occupation with critical implications for the interpretation of the origins of the Christian community at Whithorn (pp 292-3).

C J Tabraham, 1972 and 1975. The first three Whithorn campaigns had concentrated upon the ruins of the priory church and had, between them, covered most of the ground at the east end of the building (Figure 1.6a). In 1972 C J Tabraham extended the enquiry to the fields to the south of the church and the research reported here is a direct consequence of this initiative. The smallest field to the west of Bruce Street had been a market garden for about a century, and the proprietors had leased the adjacent **Glebe Field** from the General Trustees of the Church of Scotland. The market garden closed in 1971 and the owners of the two pieces of ground began to explore plans for their redevelopment. Tabraham excavated five small trenches (**A–E**; 1979, 30–34) in these two fields, demonstrating the survival of extensive stratified deposits up to 1.5 m deep. Dating evidence was sparse, but he felt able to speculate that features recorded in the sub-soil might be early medieval, and that the area had considerable archaeological potential. In light of these discoveries the **Glebe Field** was scheduled as an Ancient Monument and the **Market Garden** was purchased by the Crown Estates to assure the preservation of the archaeological remains.

Three of Tabraham's trenches (**C–E**) were later subsumed in the large area examined by the Whithorn Trust in 1986–91, and a fourth (B) was so close that we can usefully reinterpret what was found. Walls recorded in trenches **C** and **D** can now be identified as the corner of a late medieval building (pp 262-3, Figure 7.8) demolished in *c*. 1500. A deep hollow in the floor of Trench **E** was a seventh century log-coffin burial (81.02). The disturbed soil in Trench **B** was probably the result of cultivation in the fourteenth century (p 257, Figure 7.5), while the underlying hollows could represent the robbing of an eighth century enclosure wall. Trench **A** revealed a ditch (0.9+ m deep) and bank aligned north-west/south-east which may have been part of the outer boundary of the late-seventh century *monasterium* (Figure 2.6).

Tabraham returned to Whithorn in 1975 and, after opening an inspection trench in the south part of the Glebe Field, turned his attention to the small field beside the kirk bounded by the kirkyard, Bruce St and the Ket Burn (Figure 1.6a; 1979, 34–38). The main effort was directed on trenches beyond the north-west wall of the kirkyard, which revealed the stone founds of the north range of the cloister, built directly upon the northern ridge of bedrock. Three trenches downslope to the NW were not excavated fully, although walls and burnt deposits were recorded in a trench at the foot of the slope.

1.4 THE 1984–1991 EXCAVATIONS

The 1984 excavation in the Glebe Field. The current series of excavations was initiated in 1984. The previous decade had seen a number of proposals to redevelop the **Glebe Field** and the most recent identified it as a suitable site for sheltered housing. The development seemed appropriate and the Inspectorate of Ancient Monuments decided that further excavation was necessary to inform its response to a formal planning proposal. An ambitious scheme to examine ten 5 m square trenches was frustrated rapidly when archaeological features were found directly below the turf in the first four trenches (2–5; Figure 1.6b). Continuing excavation revealed a densely-populated medieval graveyard in the northern part of the field disturbing deep early medieval deposits. Undisturbed sub-soil was reached in parts of each of the four trenches by the end of the five week season, and the overlying deposits had revealed a stratified sequence spanning 1500 years and including sixth/seventh century graves, a securely-dated Northumbrian boundary wall, and traces of an extensive 'Hiberno-Norse' settlement (Hill 1984, 1985). The importance of these discoveries was widely recognised and a suitable alternative site was found for the sheltered housing scheme which was completed in 1987.

Subsequent excavation has shown that Whithorn can be a thoroughly difficult site, but this first season was blessed by a co-operative archaeological record, ideally-located trenches, skilled collaborators and perfect weather. The spirit of Bishop Nynia seemed close.

Three of the areas opened in 1984 have since been subsumed by the 1986–91 excavation trench and the fourth (Trench 5) touches upon its edge. The records of 1984 excavation have been engrossed with those of subsequent years to provide an integrated archive of all the excavation findings from 1984–91 (below).

Excavations by the Whithorn Trust, 1986–1991. The Whithorn Trust was established in May 1986 and the Trust's research programme was initiated with a 10 week excavation in July–September of the same year. The first trench was intended to provide a transect of the south slope of the hill, and was gradually extended in 1987–91 to encompass the northern part of the **Glebe Field** and a small area on the east side of the **Market Garden** (Figure 1.6c). An exploratory trench was opened in the **Fey Field** in 1987 (Chapter 9) and a small area behind the Priory Museum was examined in 1989/90 (Chapter 9). Work has since continued on the north side of the hill (Pollock 1992, 1995) and this report has been modified to exclude speculations which have been disproved by this excavation, but which is not otherwise mentioned. The results have been published in a series of interim statements (Hill 1987a, 1988a, 1990a and 1992a), supported by supplementary reports (Hill 1988b, 1991b) and articles addressing specific issues (1991a, 1992b, Hill and Kucharski 1990, Cardy and Hill 1992, Hill and Pollock 1992).

The excavation has produced a large body of data encompassing some 11,212 archaeological contexts and 42,800 finds or groups of finds. The contexts have been assembled into 677 coherent groups representing, for example, a building, a line of graves or a suite of rubbish deposits. These groups are known as Blocks, and correspond with the 'Sets' used by other excavators. Blocks are usually referred to by their unique numbers, which are used as markers in the text and to give an approximate provenance in the finds catalogues. Fuller details are accessible in the excavation archive. The site sequence is frequently complex and has been divided into six Periods, sub-divided into Phases, in turn split into Stages. The quality of the dating evidence is variable and I have attempted to distinguish well- and poorly-dated horizons by using, for example, '*c*. 550 AD' for a well-dated horizon, 'later-sixth century' for one that is less secure, and sixth/seventh century for one that is less secure still.

Section 2: Speculations

2.1 THE EARLY *MONASTERIUM*

Whithorn and Western Galloway in the later fifth and early sixth centuries. Charles Thomas (1992a and b, 1994) has drawn attention to the singularity of the inscribed stones from Whithorn and Kirkmadrine; and the fifth–sixth century remains from Whithorn are most readily interpreted by a model which accommodates both sites. Both occupy obscure inland sites but are close to landing places (the Isle of Whithorn and the head of Luce Bay) which were probably nodes in the early medieval trading system (Hodges 1982, Alcock 1990). Both sites have produced 'extended Latinate' inscriptions (Thomas 1992a, 1994). The Kirkmadrine stones have close continental parallels (Thomas 1992a, 9) and the Constantinian Chi-rho on the *Latinus* stone (Appendix 1, pp 615-6) establishes a continental link in conjunction with the potentially indigenous, possibly 'Irish', kindred of *Barrovadus* (p 13). One of the Kirkmadrine stones commemorates two *sacerdotes*, a term embracing the senior ecclesiastical ranks of *presbyter* (priest) and *episcopus* (bishop), while the lost Curghie stone records a *subdiaconus* an obscure, lower rank of the clerical orders. Whithorn was ruled at an unknown date in the fifth or sixth century by a British bishop, Nynia, who was possibly succeeded by his namesake Nennio in the earlier sixth century. *Miracula* attests an unnamed *presbyter* responsible for baptisms as a junior colleague of Bishop Nynia at Whithorn (pp 14-5). The names (*Viventius, Ventidius, Mavorius, Florentius*) on the stones from the Rhinns of Galloway are accepted by Thomas (1992a) as 'continental' and invite comparison with the less-securely documented 'continental' bishops (*Auxilius, Iserninus, Secundinus and Benignus*) associated with St Patrick by Irish hagiographers (Dumville 1993, 89–105). The Rhinns monuments have been ascribed to the fifth, sixth and seventh centuries (Radford and Donaldson 1957, 46–7), but Collingwood (1938, 285–9) and Craig (1992, 205) have argued for a rather briefer span, while Dark (1992) has demonstrated the potential shortcomings of the epigraphic criteria used to date early Christian monuments. Thomas' estimated date of 500 AD + is, nevertheless, well-informed, offering a probable period for these monuments. *Viventius* and *Mavorius* may have been successive bishops, and might thus have ministered in the Rhinns for several decades before the erection of their joint memorial. Craig has established that the Kirkmadrine stones stood in what was probably their original position until the early nineteenth century (Appendix 1) and, while they could have marked an isolated, rural burial ground, they make greater sense as the ritual focus of a *monasterium*, identified by the proclamation – *Initium et Finis* – inscribed on one of the stones. The Curghie stone suggests there may have been a third *monasterium* in the southern Rhinns, and this finds support in a speculative interpretation of later, Anglian place names (p 17).

Thomas has argued that the Rhinns stones commemorate a group of émigré Gaulish clerics who introduced the cult of St Martin to Galloway and, perhaps, established a monastic community (1992b, 7–8). The excavation at Whithorn has revealed a broadly contemporary *monasterium* with parallel evidence of continental influence encompassing imported artefacts, new technologies, exotic plants and, perhaps, a therapeutic regime originating in the classical world (pp 19–20). Historians have argued that we need agonise no longer about the respective contributions of the clerical and monastic orders to these communities (Blair and Sharpe 1992). We can thus identify an important phase in the evangelisation of Galloway, which was strongly influenced from Gaul and, perhaps, originated there. We can identify the sites of two episcopal *monasteria*, and the general location of a third centre near Curghie. We cannot be certain that these were missionary churches and evidence of an earlier missionary phase at Whithorn may await discovery (pp 26-7).

The existence of two potentially-episcopal centres in Wigtownshire in the early medieval period has bedevilled Charles Thomas' attempts to identify sub-Roman dioceses in Northern Britain modelled on the relatively large sees of Late Roman Britannia (e.g. 1971, 16–17). Thomas dismisses an alternative, North African, model 'where virtually every village had its separate bishop' (1992a, 18) and questions (1971, 19–20) Kathleen Hughes, translation of the Irish texts (1966, 50, below) which suggests it may have obtained in Ireland.

Synodus episcoporum. The critical Irish evidence comes from a corpus of canons – *Synodus episcoporum* – extant in the seventh century and purportedly originating in a fifth century synod of Bishops Patrick, Auxilius and Iserninus. This is of immediate importance to our understanding of the evangelisation of Galloway, while the Gallovidian evidence helps to authenticate the canons. The canons were accepted for many years as an authentic product of the Patrician church of the mid- to late-fifth century, but were reassigned by Binchy (1962, 45–9) to the later-sixth and seventh centuries. Hughes saw them as a product of the earlier sixth century with occasional interpolations of later date (1966, 50). This date is accepted in one recent review (Dumville 1993, 175–8), though questioned by other scholars. Whether originating in the fifth, sixth or seventh century, the canons are still closer to Nynia's time than the Ninianic texts compiled by the Northumbrians in the eighth century (pp 1-2, 18), and they record the practicalities of ecclesiastical management rather than the symbol-laden traditions of hagiography. *Synodus episcoporum* presents a convincing picture of a young church in a country which is still largely pagan, and explores the problems of integrating the ecclesiastical structure with the secular hierarchy of a complex society, while maintaining the separation required by the adoptions of new standards. *Synodus* ruled, for example, that the clergy serving the new churches should shave their heads and wear Roman tunics to distinguish them from the non-Christian population and, similarly, that their wives should be veiled. These regulations present a valuable reminder of the problems which would have faced the two ecclesiastical centres in Wigtownshire, and the obscurity of their sites may have helped to ensure the separation that was so clearly needed.

Hughes' revised dating of the canons depended upon the advanced organisational structure they revealed. This required fully-staffed, hierarchical churches and monasteries that had advanced beyond a primitive level. She considered these features to be inappropriate to a first generation missionary church (Hughes 1966, 44–5). The *subdiaconus* commemorated at Curghie indicates the existence of a thoroughly hierarchical church in the Rhinns of Galloway, while the new evidence from Whithorn records the rapid development of a large and

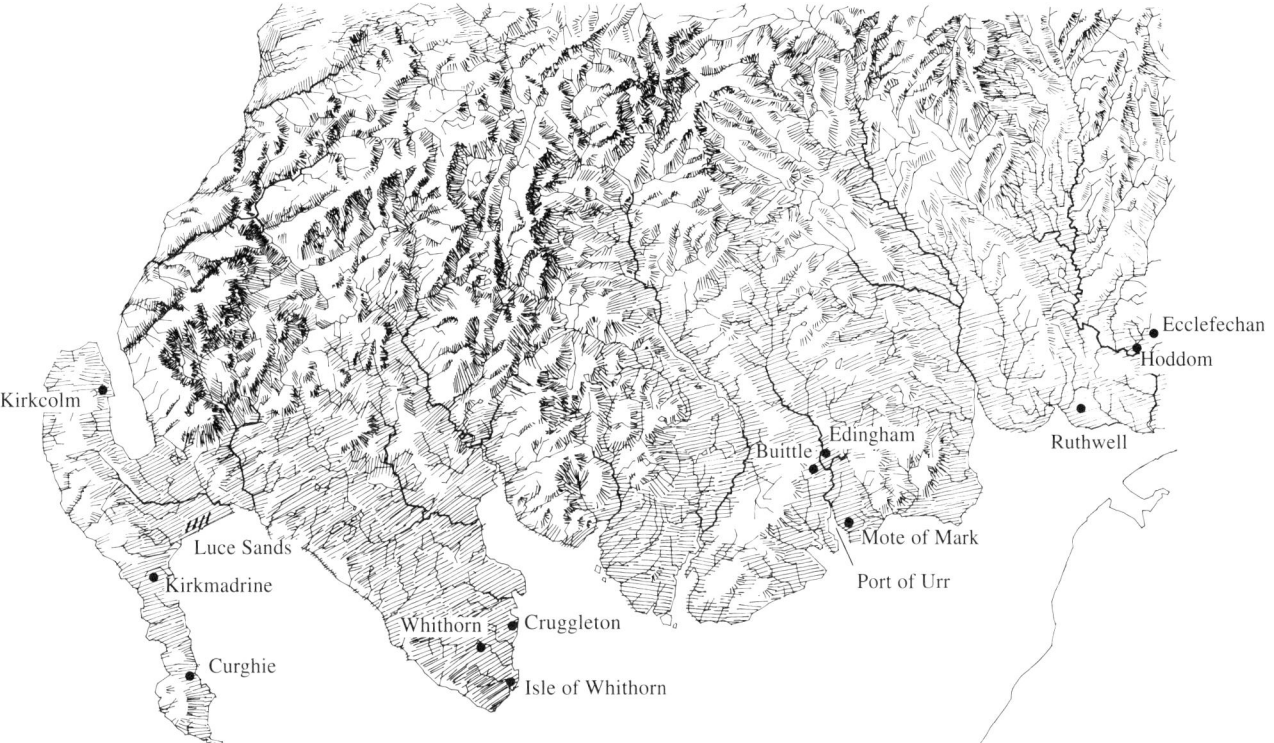

1.7 The principal early Christian centres, trade nodes and secular strongholds in early Galloway.

organised *monasterium* without a definable 'primitive' phase (pp 27-30). This indicates that the canons could relate to an early phase of ecclesiastical activity in a potentially similar social and economic environment, and so supports Hughes' preferred early-sixth century date.

Information in *synodus episcoporum* about the numbers of clerics needed to serve the major episcopal churches helps to explain the size of the early *monasterium* at Whithorn. The canons show that seven clerical grades were established and, if there were several clerics in each of the lower ranks, a 'chapter' of perhaps 15–20 may be envisaged. Some of these clerics may have had wives and families, and they were presumably supported by servants, farm-workers and artisans. This would have amounted to a sizeable population whether or not the *monasterium* was shared with a monastic community.

The indications that Whithorn and Kirkmadrine were both episcopal seats in *c*. 500 AD is fully explained by the canons in *Synodus episcoporum* and subsequent Irish collections (Charles-Edwards 1992). Hughes again:

> The canons quite unambiguously show a church under the rule of bishops. Each bishop held authority within his own *paruchia* and could not exercise his functions in the *paruchia* of another bishop. . . . The *paruchia* seems to have been coterminous with the *plebs*; it was the land inhabited by a particular group of people, possibly the *sept* or even the *tuath*, for the bishop had a number of churches in his diocese in which he was expected to officiate on occasions.
>
> (Hughes 1966, 50)

The *túath* was frequently a small territory, perhaps 10 to 15 miles across, and occupying a coherent geographical unit such as a river valley or stretch of coast (Charles-Edwards 1992, 64–65). No detailed information has survived concerning the early medieval tribes of Galloway, although the territories of some British kindreds, sometimes coterminous with later parishes such as Carnmoel/Kirkinner, can be identified from later records (Brooke 1995). The Machars and Rhinns are geographically distinct and, if the Irish pattern territories obtained, are likely to have been occupied by different tribes, and would thus have required their own episcopal churches. One contemporary group can be identified. *Latinus* seems to have been a member of the kindred of *Barrovadus* a name with close Irish parallels (Thomas 1992a 10), and may have been sufficiently powerful to endow a fifth century church at Whithorn (pp 26-7; Thomas 1992a).

Locations and relationships. The obscure locations of Whithorn and Kirkmadrine are matched by other early ecclesiastical centres in south-west Scotland, including Ecclefechan, Hoddom, Ruthwell and, perhaps, Edingham (Figure 1.7). This distinctive characteristic was shared by St Martin's monastery at Marmoutier as described by Sulpicius Severus:

> The place was so secluded and remote that it had

all the solitude of the desert. On one side it was walled in by the rock face of a high mountain, and the level ground that remained was enclosed by a gentle bend of the River Loire. There was only one approach to it, and that a very narrow one.

(The Life of St Martin X; Hoare 1980, 24)

Sulpicius' life of St Martin was widely distributed and was a popular text in the insular church. It is, thus, an attractive speculation that the sites of the ecclesiastical centres in south-west Scotland were chosen to accord with this 'Marmoutier formula'. Sulpicius was slightly disingenuous in his description of the remoteness of the monastery, for it lay a mere two miles from Tours, and Martin commuted between this rural retreat and his episcopal duties in the town. A similar pattern of separation and proximity is evident at Stirling, where a putative foundation of bishop Nynia (St Ninian's Old Kirk, formerly Eccles) lies a mile and half from the supposed early medieval centre on Castle Rock (Duncan 1975, 39–40; Brooke 1989), and at the Irish centres linked tenuously with Patrick and his continental colleagues:

Armagh was founded within two miles of Emain Macha, the ancient capital of Ulster. . . . Auxilius church at Killashee was near to Dún Ailline, capital of North Leinster, Secundinus' church at Dunshaughlin was about six miles from Tara and two from Lagore.

(Hughes 1966, 76)

It is impossible to identify equivalent centres of secular power in south-west Scotland with precision. The most likely candidate in the south Machars is the ancient stronghold of Cruggleton, perched on high cliffs some two miles to the north-east of Whithorn. The name Cruggleton restates the same word – hill – in three different tongues (Brooke 1991c, 318): *cruc* (Brythonic), *hyl* (English) and *dun* (Gaelic). The site emerges historically in the twelfth century as the Machars base of the Lords of Galloway, but excavation has demonstrated that it was occupied in the early and later years of the first millennium (Ewart 1985), and it may have been a power centre throughout this period. Kirkmadrine can be linked tentatively with *Rhionydd*, famed as one of the three national thrones of Britain in an early Welsh triad (Watson 1926, 34), and perhaps located at the head of Loch Ryan. The name is derived from *Rerigonium* recorded by Ptolemy and means 'very royal (place)' (Rivet and Smith 1979, 447). Edingham lies some 2 km from the Anglian centre at Buittle and 9 km from the early medieval fort at the Mote of Mark (Brooke 1987a).

The role of communications and trade in this locational formula is easier to identify and both Whithorn and Kirkmadrine are conveniently close to natural harbours, which seem to have been nodes in the early medieval trade network. The enduring symbiosis of Whithorn and the Isle is outlined above (pp 5-6). Kirkmadrine lies some 3 km from the sands at the head of Luce Bay, which have produced a range of exotic material, identifying it as a probable, early medieval *emporium*. Edingham, likewise, lies 7 km inland from the Port of Urr (Brooke 1987, Fig 2).

A final element is harder still to identify. The common people have left few records, and there is no stratum of abandoned settlements to show where they lived. Place-names are currently the most secure guide. The quality of this evidence is such that there is little information for the start of the early medieval period, but a picture emerges with increasing clarity as new linguistic groups settled in the area (pp 16-17, and 53-4). We must thus assume that the early ecclesiastical centres were sensibly located to exploit and serve the indigenous people, but cannot yet explore this relationship in any detail.

There thus seems to have been a common formula underlying the siting of the principal ecclesiastical centres in south-west Scotland. All maintained the seclusion of Marmoutier, and two – Whithorn and Hoddom – were similarly sited in the bends of rivers, ...if the Ket can be so distinguished. Their spatial relationships with secular power centres is difficult to establish, but closer links are evident with the nodes of communication and trade. Contact with the centres of trade and secular power seems to have been counterbalanced by the separation needed to maintain the integrity of the new ideas and customs, and we might expect to find other *monasteria* no closer than 2 km to the secular centres and, perhaps, slightly further – but not too far – from the commercial nodes.

The Miracles of Bishop Nynia. It is seldom wise to expect historical truth from the miraculous incidents recorded in the *vitae* of saints, but they can still provide valuable information. The model outlined above of a late fifth/early sixth century episcopal *monasterium* provides a realistic setting for the small *corpus* of miracle stories relating to Nynia's life at Whithorn (p 2). These are:

1. The miracle of the vegetables. This story relates how Nynia sat down to eat with the brethren but discovered there were no green vegetables (*Miracula VII*) or possibly leeks (*Vita VII*). The brother who was in charge of the gardens said that the seed had only been planted that day, but Nynia sent him out where he found 'all kinds of plants sprouting from the seed in the ground, springing up and growing to full verdure'. This story is compatible with the artefactual indications of communal life (pp 28-9) and the botanical evidence of the cultivation of culinary or medicinal herbs at an early date (pp 123-4, 127). *De Poenitentia* (1) gives a nearly-contemporary reference to the consumption of garden herbs in *monasteria* (p 16). The miraculous growth may strain our credibility, but its circumstances are supported by archaeological, botanical and documentary evidence.

2. The miracle of the Presbyter accused of unchastity. A priest 'who performed the office of baptist' was accused of fathering a child. Nynia caused the infant to speak and point out his true father so exculpating the priest (*Miracula VI, Vita V*). This reference to a cleric with specified pastoral duties is a significant neighbour to the miraculous vegetables, implying the coexistence of communal, 'monastic' life and clerical duties.

3. The miracle of the cattle rustlers. Nynia was staying with a neighbour during a visit to an outlying cattle herd to bless the beasts. Rustlers came in the night, but were miraculously paralysed, while their leader was killed by a bull. Nynia released the rustlers and restored their leader to life. The site of the miracle was marked by a bull's hoof print imprinted in the solid rock (*Miracula VIII*) at a place known as *Farres Last* (Old English, glossed in Latin as *tauri vestigium* – the bull's footprint) in the twelfth century (*Vita VIII*). The recent publication of a horse's hoof print and a group of backward-looking horses, carved on an outcrop at Eggerness to the north of Garlieston (Morris and van Hoek 1987, 35–8) provides an appropriate, local, petroglyphic context, though sadly of the wrong species. A second carving on the same farm displays three more animals, including a stag (Morris and van Hoek 1987, Fig. 4), and a bull's print may yet be discovered. Nynia's activities in Central Scotland reveal an allegorical involvement with wild bulls, suggesting conflict with – and the conquest of – a pagan bull cult (Brooke 1989, 25–6). The Eggerness carvings could reflect a pagan cult indicating that he might have encountered similar problems in Galloway. Cattle bones predominated in the earlier groups of faunal remains from the excavation (pp 605–6, Tables 11.54–6), adding plausibility to this tale of an outlying cattle ranch.

These three, simple tales could all have been based on real incidents, though transformed by the passage of time and the hagiographers' art. They portray bishop Nynia as a gentle and kindly man, reflecting, perhaps, how he was remembered by the community he led.

Winnin, Uinniau and Finian: the problems and potential of the Irish connection. The Irish accounts of St Finnian's education at Whithorn (pp 3–4) are of particular interest as he was later to be the mentor of Columcille, establishing a possible ideological link between Whithorn and Iona. The evidence rehearsed above reveals some of the problems in authenticating this material. A linguistic study (Dumville 1984, 207–14) has added a further dimension by identifying the purportedly Irish Finnian with the British bishop, Uinniau, who had corresponded with Gildas and has been credited with the authorship of a particularly severe penitential code. Dumville's assessment of Uinniau's career and the subsequent distortions of his ancestry are summarised in a later paper:

> Uinniau, shown by his name to be a Briton, was resident in Ireland in the middle of the sixth century. We have a penitential attributed to him and fragments of a letter which Gildas wrote in reply to a request from Uinniau for advice on certain problems of monastic discipline. What happened to memory of him in Ireland is a warning of what may lurk beneath the surface of other Gaelic hagiological evidence. Before *ca* 700 he had been naturalised in two widely separated Irish locations: at Clonard in Meath he became a saint of a local tribe, moccu Telduib; at Moville (Mag Bile) in Co. Down he was adopted by moccu Fiatach, Dal Fiatach, one of the principal peoples of the Ulaid. Uinniau thus became an Irishman, or rather two Irishmen, with two localisations, two pedigrees and therefore separate identities, and two different sixth-century chronologies.
> (Dumville 1993, 56)

This gives two figures (technically three); the British *Uinniau*, resident in Ireland, and the derivative, Irish *Finnian*, sent from Ireland to train in Britain, who reappears as the tutor of Columcille and the supposed founder of Moville and Clonard. A third figure, identified by Wilson as *Winnin* (1964, 168) must be added to Dumville's two. *Winnin* was reputedly buried at Kilwinning, Ayrshire, and is linked to south-west Scotland by the dedication of the church at Kirkgunzeon, Stewartry (Cherchwinni 1159 x 81; Kirkewinnen 1174 x 99; Kirkewynnyn 1175 x 85 and Kyrkgunni 1185–1200, Brooke 1983, 70). Wilson has argued that the life collected by John of Tynemouth may have originated at Kilwinning, where a lost Irish life had been adapted to record the local cult (1964, 169). Wilson's paper predated Dumville's study and assumes that *Winnin* was originally the Irish *Finnian* rather than *vice versa*, and so fails to explore the identification of *Finnian* (the Whithorn student) with *Uinniau*, the correspondent of Gildas and author of the Penitential.

If there is only one figure behind the triple personae of *Uinniau/Finian/Winnin*, and some at least of the traditional tales are genuine, a coherent story could be forged, linking the early- to mid-sixth century *monasterium* at Whithorn, the mid- to late-sixth century monastic movement in Ireland and, consequently, to Columcille's Iona. Whithorn could thus have been the archetype of a rapidly expanding monastic movement extending *inter alia* to Aidan's Lindisfarne; to the 'Irish' monastery of Malmesbury, which was later to supply the first Northumbrian bishop of Whithorn; and to the European houses founded by Columbanus, his Irish colleagues and their successors.

The penitentials. The convoluted biography of *Uinniau/Finian/Winnin* introduces a second group of documents, which are potentially germane to the early medieval *monasterium* at Whithorn. These are the penitentials which prescribe the penances appropriate for specific offences, outlining a moral code for Christians, and revealing some of the problems and tensions of communal life. They provide rare insight to the details of daily life specifying, *inter alia*, penitential diets and the meagre supply of hay for a penitent's bedding. The penitential ascribed to *Uinniau* may thus reflect his training at Whithorn, his mature response to it, and the influence of his contemporaries. This takes the teachings of the church a step further than the canons of the missionary church (*Synodus episcoporum*) and prescribes an austere regime of personal morality for the Christian laity. Its Pauline approach to the flesh is so pronounced that Hughes concluded the denial of pleasures to the laity would have been a strong argument for them to join monasteries. This attitude is manifest in Finnian's dealings with the wanton Drusticc (p 3), whose behaviour foreshadows the lax morals of the Gallovidians which incensed the Cistercians in the twelfth century (p 23).

The penitential ascribed to Gildas (*De Poenitentia*, Bieler and Binchy 1963) is less immediately linked to Whithorn, but is perhaps of greater value to our interpretation. It prescribes a set of rules for the communal life of monks and clerics that might have been applied at Whithorn in the mid-sixth century. Gildas was a senior ecclesiastic, who probably lived in Wales, and is principally remembered for a work of polemical history – *De Excidio Britonnum*, the Ruin of Britain – recording the parlous state of the British secular and ecclesiastical rulers in about 540 AD. He seems to have omitted monks from his excoriations (DEB 26:4) and, perhaps, held the monastic movement in special regard. The penitential is a model of common sense and humanity, and gives wise advice on personal relationships among the community. For example;

> One who sees any of his brethren violate the commands of the abbot ought not to conceal the fact from the abbot, but he ought first to admonish the offender to confess alone to the abbot the wrong he is doing. Let him be found not so much an informer as one who truly practices the rule.
> *De Poenitentia, 27*

Many of the penances involve dietary restrictions. Monks who committed lesser offences should go without their supper. One such regulation records:

> But if on account of drunkenness someone is unable to sing the psalms, being benumbed and speechless, he shall be deprived of his supper
> *De Poenitentia, 10*

This is a salutary reminder that over-indulgence was not confined to warriors, and provides a possible 'monastic' context for the sherds of drinking vessels from the excavation. More serious offences (sexual activity and theft) attracted a rigorous regime:

> He shall have bread without limitation and a titbit fattened slightly with butter on Sunday; on other days a ration of dry bread and a dish enriched with a little fat, garden vegetables, a few eggs, British cheese, a Roman half-pint of milk in consideration of the weakness of the body in this age, also a Roman pint of whey or buttermilk for his thirst, and some water if he is a worker. He shall have his bed meagrely supplied with hay. . . .
> *De Poenitentia, 1*

This was specifically aimed at presbyters and deacons in monastic orders. A monk of lower rank should do a similar penance with an increased ration of bread, while a worker should have

> . . . a Roman pint of milk and another of whey and as much water as the intensity of his thirst requires.
> *De Poenitentia, 2*

The rule is flexible. For:

> He who willingly has been defiled in sleep, if the monastic house is abundantly supplied with beer and flesh, shall make a standing vigil for three hours of the night if his health is strong. But if it has poor fare, standing as a suppliant he shall sing twenty-eight or thirty psalms or make satisfaction with extra work.
> *De Poenitentia, 22*

Circumstances, the austerity of the rule and the strictness with which it was applied must surely have varied over the years at Whithorn. We might expect to see a dim reflection of the evolving regime in the archaeological remains, and the transition from the liberal common sense of Gildas to the austerity of Uinniau might well show in a decreasing supply of luxury goods.

2.2 THE NORTHUMBRIANS IN GALLOWAY

> The provinces of the Northumbrians, whose king is Ceowulf, now have four dioceses with resident bishops; Wilfrid in the church of York, Oethiwald in that of Lindisfarne, Acca in that of Hexham, Pecthelm in the church called Candida Casa, where recently the number of the lay faithful has increased, and which in consequence has been promoted to a see with him as first bishop
> (*HE V xxiii*)

The establishment of the *Northumbrian* bishopric at Whithorn was reported by Bede in his résumé of the state of the English church in 731 AD (*V.xxiii*, above), while his earlier account of Bishop Nynia (*III.iv*; p xii) records the acquisition of the diocese by the northern Northumbrian province of Bernicia. These are the only written records of the expansion of Northumbria into Galloway, and are insufficiently explicit to establish how control was gained, and from whom it was wrested. *HE V.xxiii* implies that this was a relatively recent development, but the precise time scale is unclear. Northumbrian expansion to the north had been arrested following the battle of Nechtansmere in 685 AD, but a reference to the acquisition of Kyle in Ayrshire in 750 AD points to continuing territorial expansion in the west. Archaeological evidence indicates that the

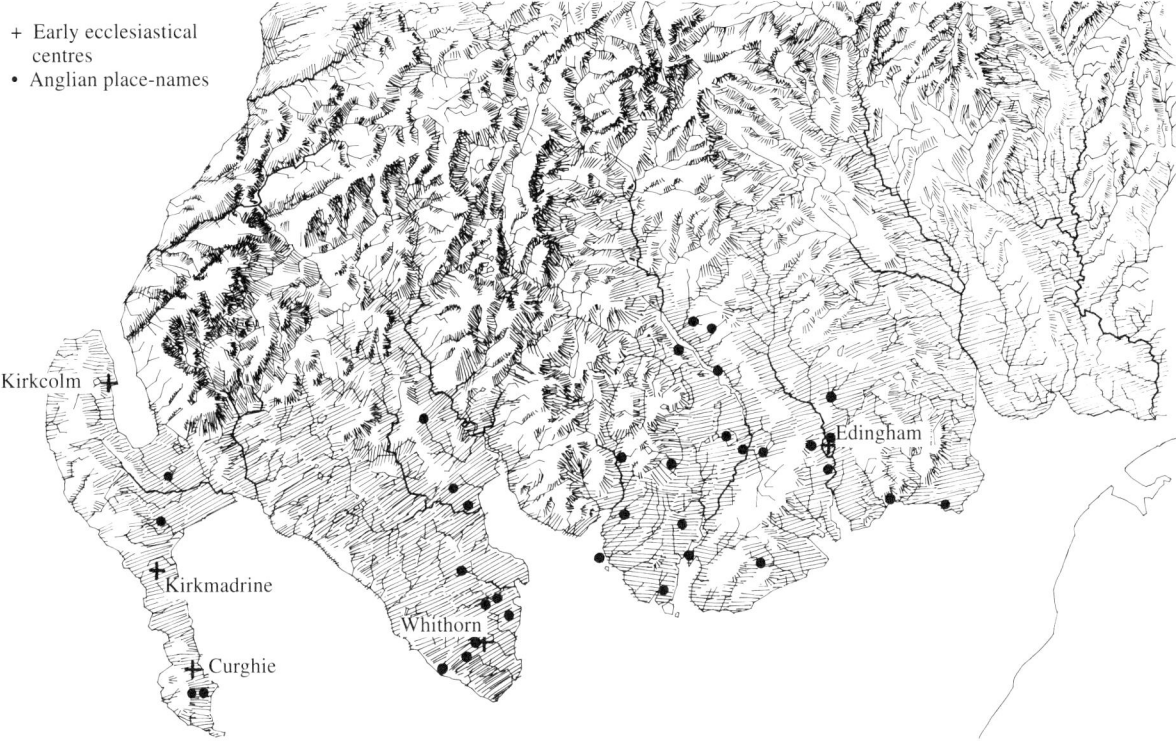

1.8 Early ecclesiastical centres and Anglian place-names in Galloway

Northumbrians may have gained control of Whithorn in the closing years of the seventh century (p 37). Place-names (Figure 1.8) reveal limited settlement by English speakers in south-west Scotland (Brooke 1991c, Illus 2), but concentrations and gaps in the distribution of names indicate the settlement of discrete blocks of land or estates, presumably leaving the intervening areas in the hands of their original owners. The distribution of the Northumbrian settlements is reminiscent of the dispersed territories of the great landed families in the late middle ages, won by dynastic marriage, political intrigue and the vicious exploitation of mortgage agreements. Military conquest and subsequent colonisation would, perhaps, have produced a less sharply focused distribution of names.

It is probably sensible to view the Northumbrian expansion westwards as a process spanning a period of fifty or more years rather than an event for which a single date can be specified. The Anglian settlements in the eastern parts of the region may already have been consolidated before the west was won. The involvement of the church adds a further dimension. Bede states (*HE III.iv*) that the English had acquired the diocese of St Martin, and this may have different connotations from the conquest of a geographical area or ethnic grouping. Three of the four areas with *Anglian* names in Wigtownshire can be correlated with the ecclesiastical *foci* – Whithorn, Kirkmadrine and Curghie – revealed by fifth–sixth century Latinate monuments. An isolated Anglian name – *Rintsnoc* – in the north Rhinns has been tentatively identified with the church at Kirkcolm (Brooke 1991c, 310) where traces of an enclosure reveal a possible early *monasterium*. The clusters of *Anglian* names might thus mark the estates of *monasteria* encompassed by the diocese of St Martin in the later-seventh or early-eighth century. The largest concentration is in the south Machars, suggesting that Whithorn controlled the most lands and may thus have been the most powerful of these sites.

The establishment of new Anglian names reveals comprehensive resettlement within these discrete areas, and *Miracula* and *Vita* (below) name four people – *Pethgils, Plecgils, Deisuit* and *Adelfrid* - who may have been among the new settlers. Two farms to the south-west of Whithorn give a glimpse of the tenurial arrangements that may have obtained. Carleton lies on the cliff tops to the WSW of Whithorn and overlooks the Irish Sea. The name derives from *ceorl tun* (OE) or *karl tun* (ON) and may be either Anglian or Scandinavian, but the meaning, the ceorl's settlement, is similar in both tongues. The local pronunciation – *Chiaultun* – favours an Anglian origin. A *ceorl* was a free peasant landholder owing duty to none but the king or, perhaps in this instance, to the bishop. Finberg (1964, 144–60) has remarked that Carlton/Charlton names are often found in close proximity to estate centres. The farm of Kidsdale lies further to the east and was among the lands forfeited by the 9th Earl of Douglas to the crown in 1455 AD. Detailed accounts survive for the next fifty years and show that this farm was tenanted by *coloni* paying their rents directly to their superior, rather than on the manorial system obtaining elsewhere (Brooke 1995). Although the name of this farm is Scandinavian, the uncommon form of agricultural tenancy may have originated with the free peasantry of the Anglian settlements.

The faunal remains from the excavation provide another strand of evidence, and reveal a marked change in animal husbandry between the seventh and eighth/ninth centuries, which may be equated tentatively with the new settlements, and perhaps with new tenurial arrangements, as both groups of bones were probably the produce of the ecclesiastical estates. Cattle bones dominate the earlier bone assemblage, which is similar to broadly contemporary groups from Celtic (British, Pictish and 'Scottish') sites in Scotland (Table 11-56), while the Northumbrian groups show increased numbers of sheep and the introduction of domestic fowl and geese.

The *Northumbrian* settlement of south-west Scotland is poorly documented and has not received much scholarly notice. Jackson (1955, 84) envisaged a 'scattered upper crust of landlords [rather] than a really thick settlement of peasants' while Duncan concluded that the evidence was slight 'because it [Northumbrian settlement] was always slight' (1975, 65). Brooke's review of the place-name evidence (1991c) and the excavation results from Whithorn affirm that the evidence is there, if hitherto obscured, and is sufficiently strong to identify Northumbrian enclaves, perhaps corresponding to the estates of the existing *paruchia* of St Martin.

The establishment of the bishopric at Whithorn. The creation of the new *Northumbrian* diocese, the choice of Whithorn as its centre, and the appointment of Pecthelm as the first bishop, were probably an appropriate response to the undocumented circumstances that gave Northumbria influence or control in Galloway and to the political aspirations of the Northumbrian church. These seem to show an unaccustomed regard for the sensibilities of the Britons; and *Historia Ecclesiastica* and *Miracula* record the assimilation of the traditional history of Whithorn by the Northumbrian church and its adaptation to address contemporary priorities. This process is marked by the unreserved adoption of Nynia as an acceptable patron, despite his British ancestry; by the literary exploitation of the name *Candida Casa* as a symbol of light; by the addition of a new corpus of miracles with Anglian beneficiaries and; perhaps most potently, by the restoration or continuance of the episcopal succession. The success of the Northumbrian *propaganda* is attested by the retrospective interest of Irish hagiographers (pp 3-4) and the circulation of the new Whithorn texts among English and continental scholars (e.g. MacQueen 1990, 7), while the high-late medieval cult of St Ninian records its endurance (Brooke 1987b). The absorption and re-presentation of the historical traditions is closely matched by the physical transformation of the *monasterium* at the start of **Period II**, when it was comprehensively redeveloped, while retaining and embellishing extant ritual *foci*. The establishment of the new episcopal seat provides an appropriate historical context for these radical changes; and the combined historical and archaeological evidence provides a compelling picture of the exploitation of tradition to achieve political control.

Two late sources report an association between Whithorn and Bishop Acca of Hexham (709–732). A tradition that he was briefly the bishop of Whithorn following his expulsion from Hexham in *c.* 732 is unlikely, but a twelfth century report by Richard of Hexham that he was involved in the preparation of the new see (Raine 1864, 35) is more plausible. The redevelopment of the *monasterium* would have been a complex business requiring the recruitment and maintenance of a large team of skilled craftsmen and the acquisition of the necessary building materials. These works may well have started before the appointment of the new bishop (p 136), and the whole project would have been a major administrative undertaking. Hexham was the nearest Northumbrian diocese and may formerly have encompassed the Northumbrian territories in southwest Scotland. The involvement of Bishop Acca is thus not only likely, but virtually inescapable. Acca had been Bishop Wilfrid's chaplain, and after his appointment as bishop, extended and embellished Wilfrid's church at Hexham, gathered relics of the apostles and martyrs, collected a library, and trained the community in church music (*HE V.xx*). His association with Wilfrid would have given him valuable experience in the acquisition and management of the estates required to support the dignity of the church. The excavation has provided a glimpse of the grand building scheme undertaken at Whithorn. Coloured window glass attests the embellishment of the new ecclesiastical buildings (pp 326-30), and the careful planning of gateways and access routes (pp 46-7), perhaps mirrors the complexity of the crypts at Hexham (Gilbert 1974, plan 1). The church at Hexham, despite all the problems of its interpretation (e.g. Gilbert 1974), provides an appropriate model for what may have been built on the crown of the hill at Whithorn.

Pecthelm was a respected senior member of the church. He had been a monk and deacon under Abbot Aldhelm at Malmesbury, had corresponded with Bede and is credited as the source of two miracle stories in *Historia Ecclesiastica* (*HE V.xiii* and *xviii*). His erudition is indicated by a letter from Bishop Boniface asking his advice upon an obscure point of canonical law (Haddan and Stubbs 1871, 310). The monastery of Malmesbury was named after its Irish founder, Maildhub, and the extensive writings of his successor, Aldhelm, combine a strong element of Irish scholarship with a wordy literary style acquired at Canterbury (Mayr-Harting 1991, 192). Aldhelm was subsequently appointed as Bishop of Sherborne and was instrumental in persuading his British neighbours in Dumnonia to adopt the Roman system of calculating Easter (Stenton 1947, 63–4). This cosmopolitan background would have given Pecthelm valuable experience in dealing with the British and Irish churches, which may well have influenced his appointment. The links between Whithorn and Malmesbury are probably reflected by the wordy literary style of *Miracula* and, perhaps, by the use of clay for the walls of the *Northumbrian* burial chapel (p 45).

Pecthelm's successors are well-documented until 802 AD, when the records falter and a last bishop – Heathored – is named in 833 x 836 AD (p 21). Much less is known of them than of Pecthelm, but there is sufficient evidence to show them playing an active role as suffragans of York (Craig 1992, 48–51).

Pecthelm	? x 731 – 735
Frithuwold	735 – 762 x 764
Pehtwine	762 x 764 – 776 x 777
Ethelbert	777 – 789
Badwulf	790 x 791 – 802+
Heathored	? 833 x 836 ?

Table 2.3: The Northumbrian bishops of Whithorn

2.3 THE CHURCH, SHRINE AND MIRACLES OF ST NYNIA: THE HEALING TRADITION AT WHITHORN

The early sources (*HE*, *Miracula* and *Vita*, pp 1-3) give three accounts of the church built by Nynia, that potentially describe a standing building revered by the *Northumbrian* community. Bede's succinct report of a stone-built church is unhelpful, although there is now evidence that it could be accurate (p 28). *Miracula* gives a slightly longer description, but the architectural detailing is implausible and the account should probably not be taken at face value. Aelred provides no details of the building and had probably not visited Whithorn (p 2).

Descriptions of the shrine are more revealing. *Miracula* and *Vita* recount a series of miracles associated with the shrine of St Nynia, and the original documentary source can be partly reconstructed by combining the two (pp 2-3). The beneficiaries in three of the four stories have Anglian names and the miracles probably took place in the eighth century during the Northumbrian supremacy. The accounts in *Miracula* and *Vita* are subtly different. *Miracula* gives clear descriptions of the symptoms of infantile paralysis, elephantiasic leprosy and blindness that suggest the stories are based on case histories prepared by a trained observer, perhaps a physician. *Vita* probably draws on the same source, but alters the descriptions of the symptoms to exploit the allegorical symmetry of the problem and the cure. They also differ in their descriptions of the shrine where the miracles took place. *Miracula* focuses upon the tomb, which seems to have played an important therapeutic role, while *Vita* credits the miracles to the saint's relics in two instances, to the tomb and 'soil' in a third, and to a spring or font (*fons*) in the fourth. These differences reverse the literary characteristics of the two works, for while *Miracula* is still wordy, its descriptions are clear, and *Vita*, though written with clarity, obscures the details with allegory.

The *Northumbrian* section of *Miracula* can thus be seen as a potentially-factual account of a healing centre, and three cures are described in sufficient detail to characterise the therapy offered. The most circumstantial account records the cure of Pethgils, who was brought to the church by his parents after a long illness and carried to the 'sacred tomb in the chapel'. His parents prayed for a cure and then, as night fell, left the boy lying 'at the tomb', bolting the doors of the shrine behind them. The bishop (Nynia) entered at midnight and touched the boy's head, releasing a stream of healing energy that corrected his misaligned feet and removed the numbness from his body.

The blind woman, Deisuit, was also brought to the church by her parents after prolonged suffering. The account of her cure is obscured by the pleonasm of the poem, but seems to be similar to the treatment of Pethgils. She arrived:

> . . . weighed down by her long sleep at the place where the saint's body is held prisoner by the hollowed out interior of the rock, she prostrated herself . . .

and prayed that the *long night* should be brightened and then

> . . . with her whole body flung down, she pressed against the earth with her forehead and lay in the hollowed out cave. She jumped up and dazzling light filled her eyes as darkness fled away . . . [and began] . . . to cross on foot the famous shrine . . .

The third cure was also effected at the tomb. Adelfrid came

> . . . to the tomb, in which the saintly bishop rests in the body in the furrowed marble . . .

gave a detailed account of his symptoms and prayed for relief which was speedily granted.

The fourth *Northumbrian* miracle recorded by *Miracula* also occurred at the shrine, and records a vision of the Christ child granted to a priest celebrating mass at the altar. The priest was named Plecgils and had returned to his native land and the 'familiar walls' of Whithorn after a period abroad. He could have been the boy who was cured of paralysis if the prefixes *Plec-* and *Peht-* were confused.

> So the day had come on which he entered the temple and stood at the altar, a suppliant in prayer, where the bishop Nyniau . . . rests in the body in the tomb . . .

The descriptions of the shrine are slightly ambiguous. It was located within a lofty church, possibly in a separate chapel, while the tomb and grave seem to have been distinct entities, although located in the same place. This indicates that the bones had been disinterred and translated to a shrine built above ground or, perhaps, the sarcophagus described by Ailred (*Vita XI*), which was also used as an altar. The original grave, which was apparently dug into rock, remained an object of veneration and, if the cure of Desuit is accepted at face value, played an important therapeutic role.

The tomb and relics were still revered as distinct entities in the late middle ages and the Treasurers' Account for August 9th 1506 states that the tomb or *ferter* was located in the outer kirk or nave of the cathedral. The evidence of continuity is now sufficiently strong (Chapter 2) to infer that the tomb of the eighth century miracles was the same as the *ferter* or tomb honoured eight hundred years later, and that it probably lay within the nave of the twelfth century church (p 56, Figure 2.20). This inferred location helps to explain the layout of the *inner precinct* of the **Period I** *monasterium* (pp 27-40, Figures 2.2-7) and the reconstructed *Northumbrian minster* is centred upon it (Figures 2.9-12).

The miraculous cures point to a specialised therapy focused upon the tomb, which was most effective during a solitary nocturnal vigil. These contrast with most contemporary miracles, which were achieved by contact either with the primary relics (the bones and other corporeal remains) or with secondary or non-corporeal relics such as clothing, dust from the grave or water in which the bones had been washed. The Whithorn miracles seem to reflect a different therapeutic tradition rooted in classical medicine and specifically in the cult of Asklepios. Jackson (1988, 145) gives a summary of the treatment offered:

> Each individual, whether attempting to avert illness, giving thanks for continued good health or seeking a cure for some disease or disability, was required to perform the cleansing rite on arrival at the sanctuary . . . After these preliminaries, overseen by the priests, those who had come as suppliants were led to the *abaton*, a 'sacred dormitory' adjacent to the temple, in which they passed the night, or occasionally, part of the day. This was 'incubation', the temple sleep, through which Asklepios effected their cure. He generally appeared as a dream vision and either healed directly or gave instructions which the patient remembered on waking and carried out accordingly . . . On some occasions the god's dream message was so cryptic that it required the interpretative assistance of the priests, who would then prescribe an appropriate remedy, normally drugs, or a regimen of diet, bathing and exercise . . .

A group of stone columns at the Asklepian sanctuary at Epidaurus recorded a number of cures naming the patient, describing the condition and then the cure. These are similar in style and content to the cures in *Miracula*, and it is probable that Whithorn offered a Christianised version of the Asklepian therapy of incubation. It was adapted by the early Christian church and its progress in the Mediterranean world has been studied by Hamilton (1906). It is a long step to *Northumbrian* Whithorn, but incubation could have been part of the package of exotic ideas introduced in the late-fifth/early-sixth century.

The presence of trained observers is implicit in the accurate recording of symptoms and case histories, and divine intervention was probably supported by appropriate medical care. The healing cult dominates the *Northumbrian* section of the *Miracula*, and its promotion seems to have been one of the principle aims of the author. The account of the church in Chapter IV shows his ardour in this cause:

> This is the house of the Lord, which many are eager to visit, for many who have been afflicted with a disease of long-standing hurry there. They eagerly accept the ready gifts of health-bringing healing, and they grow strong in all their limbs by the power of the saint.

The descriptions of the shrine and healing cult have important archaeological implications. The buildings of the *monasterium* could include an infirmary for the sick and accommodation for their families and retainers. Similarly the descriptions of the shrine, and particularly the reverence of an open, rock-cut tomb, demonstrate that the large timber church in the **Glebe Field** cannot have been the principal *Northumbrian* church, and consequently that the two early 'shrines' it encompasses (pp 134-5) are unlikely to have been dedicated to St Nynia. There is, surprisingly, some archaeological evidence of medical treatments. An early latrine pit contained a range of seeds appropriate to the treatment of gastric disorders (p 124), seeds from a later pit may have been the remains of a herbal compress for a wound (p 127) and a possible surgeon's knife was found in a *Northumbrian* deposit (p 163).

2.4 WHITHORN IN THE NINTH CENTURY

The *Northumbrian minster* at Whithorn underwent a crisis in the mid-ninth century, culminating in a fire that destroyed the surviving buildings (pp 162-4). The ecclesiastical buildings were restored in **Period III**, but the material culture and economic life of the community had been transformed (pp 185-6). Equivalent economic changes in this period have been discerned at other *Northumbrian* monasteries (Cramp Pers. Comm.), but the transformation of Whithorn was defined with uncommon clarity and was linked with a series of coin finds offering unusual chronological precision (pp 136, 352-5). The striking picture of decay, destruction and restoration, perhaps by new masters, invites a brief exploration of the three documentary references to Galloway and Whithorn in the middle part of the ninth century (*c.* 830–880), the political circumstances in the world beyond, and their correlation, if any, with the archaeological evidence.

There are few contemporary records of Northumbria in the ninth century, and students have had to rely upon histories compiled in the twelfth and thirteenth centuries (Dumville 1987). These present a chronological framework for the *Northumbrian* kings and Archbishops of York, which seems incompatible with the numismatic evidence, and a new chronology, reconciling the historical and numismatic information (Pagan 1969), has been widely, though not universally, accepted (Metcalfe 1987a *passim*). This highly-specialised debate is of immediate relevance to Whithorn as the events of the mid-ninth century can be related to the development of *Northumbrian* currency. Precise dates are, however, elusive and these events cannot be correlated exactly with the military campaigns and political upheavals recorded elsewhere.

The last reliable contemporary references to Northumbrian Whithorn are in episcopal lists, which name Heathored as the bishop of *Candida Casa* (Dumville 1987, 49–51). These lists of English bishops were brought up to date in the early ninth century (805 x 814 AD) and the northern entries were periodically updated for a further forty or so years. Heathored's name was entered on the second occasion of updating (833 x 836 AD), while Archbishop Uigmund of York was the only new, northern bishop, named when the list was again updated in 840 x 845. This could mean that Heathored remained bishop or that the compiler had lost contact with Whithorn. The two horizons can be correlated with the archaeological sequence. The first horizon (833 x 836 AD) overlaps with the numismatic date (835+ AD) for the end of a series of coins associated with the use of the church (p 136). A second group of coins, which was deposited within the derelict church during the crisis, included later issues (pp 353-4), mostly of Aethelred II (*c*. 841–849 AD) and Archbishop Uigmund (*c*. 837–850 AD), but perhaps dating to the opening years of the 840s, as coins of the second reign of Aethelred II (*c*. 843–849 AD) predominated in a third group of coins ascribed to **Period III** (pp 353-4). The coins from the floor of the church may thus correlate with the third revision of the episcopal lists in 840 x 845 AD and, perhaps, predate the usurpation of Redwulf, which interrupted the reign of Aethelred II. This usurpation indicates a phase of dynastic conflict and, perhaps, civil war in Northumbria, which is one of the possible causes of the burning of Whithorn.

The last reliable record of Whithorn in 833 x 836 AD coincided with an aggressive Viking campaign in Ireland beginning in 832 AD when Armagh was raided on three occasions. Previous raids, while ruthless, had been on a relatively small scale and were concerned more with plunder than conquest. The new campaigns involved larger fleets, which over-wintered at coastal strongholds such as Wexford, Waterford, Limerick and Dublin. The principal targets seem to have been the great monasteries, but Irish annals record that whole regions were laid waste. The peoples of Ireland failed to unite against this threat and internecine conflicts continued unabated. The first warfleets were Norwegian (known to the Irish as the finn-gaill), but in 851 AD a Danish fleet (the dubh-gaill) joined the fray and plundered the Norwegian base at Dublin. A separate Viking campaign in central Scotland resulted in a massive slaughter of Picts and Scots in 839 AD and seems to have created an unaccustomed sense of national cohesion leading ultimately to the genesis of the Kingdom of the Scots (Broun 1994) whose first king, Cinéad (Kenneth) mac Alpín, ruled from *c*. 841–858 AD. The history of Northumbria in this period is far from clear. Later traditions claimed that the Northumbrians had assisted the Picts against Cinéad, who later raided the northern parts of Northumbria, burning Melrose and Dunbar (Kirby 1987, 13–14). The burning of Whithorn might record a similar, undocumented, punitive campaign against the Northumbrians of south-west Scotland.

There are no records of Viking raids in Galloway, but a relatively late and unreliable source (Anderson 1978, 195–6) records that Alpín, father of Cinéad, died in Galloway in 841 AD after he had 'entirely destroyed and devastated' it (Anderson 1908, 270n). This dubious record is supported by the circumstantial evidence of a place on the eastern shore of Loch Ryan named *Leac-* or *Lacht-Alpin* (Alpín's gravestone), now marked by the farms of Meikle and Little Laight (Figure 2.17; Brooke 1995). Alpín is a somewhat problematical figure known principally because of his famous son. He is not recorded in the Irish annals and is imperfectly connected to the genealogies of the Scottish kings (Smyth 181–2). Smyth concludes that Cinéad was an independent Scottish warlord, who fought his way to supremacy in the aftermath of the defeat of the Picts and Scots in 839 AD. If so Alpín may also have been a freebooting warlord and his warband was presumably inherited by his son who used it to good effect in the year of his death. Alpín's supposed raid on Galloway probably dates to the period of crisis at the end of **Period II**, but might conceivably have been the cause of the fire, given the intrinsic flexibility of the dating evidence. It is of far greater value as a symbol of the political turmoil of this period, and a reminder that the Vikings were not the only warbands seeking plunder and advancement. Brooke (1995) has speculated that the Gallgaidhil warriors recorded in the Annals of Ulster as fighting in Ireland in 856, 857 and 859 AD were mercenaries from Galloway. Alpín and the Gallgaidhil add a strong hint of Gaeldom to the story that is supported by some of the finds from **Period III** (pp 50-2).

The final documentary reference to Whithorn, again comes from a late and potentially unreliable source. It occurs in Symeon's *Historia Ecclesiae Dunelmensis* (II xii; Arnold 1882, 67) compiled at Durham in the early twelfth century, and records the peregrinations of a small group of refugees from Lindisfarne, after it was sacked for the second time in 875 AD. The party included the bishop, Eardulf, and abbot, Aenred, and they brought with them the coffin of St Cuthbert and the Gospel book – the Lindisfarne Gospels – in its jewelled case. They finally reached Cumbria and, in despair, determined to sail to Ireland, but were driven back by a storm which washed the Gospels overboard. They continued their journey on foot arriving at a place called the White House or *Huuiterne*, where the Gospels were discovered some three miles from the shore after an unusually low tide. There are no extensive mud flats in the vicinity of Whithorn, and this miraculous recovery fits better with the topography of the eastern parts of the Solway estuary. This incident thus seems more appropriate to the diocese of *Candida Casa* than to Whithorn itself, but hints that this area was more peaceful than other parts of war-torn Northumbria (Brooke 1995). This episode probably occurred in around 882 AD, by which time the burnt ecclesiastical buildings at Whithorn had been restored and a new settlement established (p 89).

This review has failed to achieve a clear picture of the history of Whithorn and Galloway and the archaeological record is rather simpler to read. The burning of the buildings at Whithorn could have resulted from an unrecorded Viking incursion, the imperfectly-documented raid of Alpín, the vengeance of his son Cinéad or a hypothetical Northumbrian civil war; it could equally have been an accident. The preceding crisis mirrors the troubles in Ireland, and perhaps Northumbria, while the subsequent restoration suggests a new political alliance in Galloway, prepared to restore the *Northumbrian* ecclesiastical buildings, but with new Scandinavian and Irish traits in its material culture. That Whithorn, or its diocese, may have been viewed as a haven by the refugees from Lindisfarne is a measure of the success of this alliance, which seems to have steered Galloway into a prolonged period of independence.

2.5 THE LORDS OF GALLOWAY AND THE REFORM OF THE GALLOVIDIAN CHURCH

The **Period IV** deposits record a new settlement, which replaced the restored Northumbrian *minster* of **Period III** in the earlier eleventh century (p 211). This seems to have restored a 'Celtic' organisational pattern which, perhaps, originated in Ireland (p 55). This settlement survived into the later-thirteenth century, despite the supposed reform of the Gallovidian church in the mid-twelfth century, presenting a potential paradox. This can be explained in part by the turbulent history of the Lords of Galloway and their relationships with the fiercely independent inhabitants of the region, in part by the allegiances and duties of the new bishops, and in part by the conservatism which was by now strongly evident in western Galloway. The following summary is based on Chapters 4–6 in Brooke's *Wild Men and Holy Places* (1995).

The Lords. In the earlier twelfth century the region was ruled by Fergus, Lord of Galloway, who was first recorded in 1136 AD. Fergus undoubtedly had pretensions to independence from Scotland and sometimes described himself as the King of Gallovidians, although Scottish and English documents referred to him as lord (*dominus*), ruler (*regulus*) or prince (*princeps*). He maintained his autonomy by judicious diplomatic juggling with the Kings of England and Scotland, but a miscalculation in 1160 AD led to his downfall at the hands of Malcolm IV, who raided Galloway thrice, and 'encouraged' Fergus to retire as a canon to Holyrood Abbey. He was succeeded by two of his sons, Gilbert and Uchtred, who divided his domain between them. Uchtred ruled in eastern Galloway and introduced a series of well-documented measures including the settlement of new Anglo-Normans from Cumbria and the support of the new reformed church with grants of land and benefices. Gilbert took control of the western part of Galloway, which he probably ruled from Cruggleton Castle. His rule is virtually undocumented, suggesting that he was content to let old ways prevail and leave his estates in the hands of their traditional occupiers. Both brothers continued their father's dangerous dance with the Kings of England and Scotland, maintaining a precarious independence, while feuding intermittently with each other. In 1174 AD Uchtred was besieged and captured by Gilbert's son Malcolm, who demonstrated his victory by blinding and castrating him and cutting out his tongue. Brooke views this butchery as a traditional rite symbolically destroying the potency of a vanquished leader, and epitomising the conservatism of western Galloway and its triumph over the reforming east. Uchtred died shortly afterwards and was succeeded by his son, Roland, who continued his father's reforms in the eastern parts of Galloway. Gilbert died on January 1st 1185 and Roland swiftly took revenge for his father, invading Gilbert's territories, slaying the rich and powerful, and occupying their lands. This might have been the cause of the burning of Whithorn at the end of **Period IV/4** (pp 211-6). Roland died in 1200 AD and was succeeded by his son, Alan, who still struggled to maintain autonomy, establishing himself as a powerful sea-borne warlord. He died in 1234 AD without legitimate male heirs and Alexander II, following feudal law, supported the tripartite division of Galloway amongst his three legitimate daughters and their husbands. The 'community' of Galloway launched a counter claim in an attempt to maintain the integrity of the region, while accepting the suzerainty of the King of Scotland. This led to an abortive uprising in 1235 AD in support of Alan's illegitimate son Thomas, which was brutally suppressed. This is of particular interest as the Gallovidian churches seem to have played an important role in articulating the aspirations of the 'community' of Galloway. Order was restored by Walter Comyn, Earl of Mentieth, whose forces looted the monasteries, killing the prior and sacristan of Tongland Abbey, and sacking the Abbey of Glenluce. The fate of Whithorn is unrecorded, but the dynastic troubles of 1234–5 AD coincided with a disputed episcopal election between the canons' candidate,

Odo, and one Gilbert, elected by the 'clergy and people', and supported successfully by the Scottish king. Walter Comyn was apparently based at Cruggleton Castle and the uprising, its violent aftermath and the appointment of a new, unwanted bishop would have been an appropriate context for the reorganisation of the long-lived community at Whithorn attested by the transition from **Period IV** to **Period V** although this was probably later (p 255).

The bishops. The appointment of a new bishop of Whithorn – Gilla-Aldan – was recorded in a papal letter of 1128 AD in which he was addressed as bishop-elect and instructed to seek consecration from Thurstan, Archbishop of York. This appointment has been seen to mark the restoration of the lapsed, Northumbrian see, and has been variously ascribed to David I or Fergus of Galloway. The archaeological and sculptural evidence of ecclesiastical continuity commends an alternative view that Gilla-Aldan was the first-recorded of a long line of post-Northumbrian bishops (pp 52-3). He is a poorly-documented figure (Watt 1991 i, 24), but his Gaelic name conforms with contemporary Gallovidian fashions, and he can be viewed as a local leader of the indigenous church. Gilla-Aldan died in 1152 and was replaced in 1153 by Christian, an ardent reformer, apparently closely associated with the Cistercian Abbey of Holme Cultram in Cumbria, and an active collaborator in Uchtred's reforms in eastern Galloway. As a supporter of Uchtred, Christian may well have felt a sense of unease in the company of Gilbert and his apparent absence from the diocese after 1174, is, perhaps, unsurprising. The see was vacant for three years following his death in 1186 and his successor, John, an appointee of the Angevin court, ruled until 1206, dying while a monk at Holyrood in 1209. His successor, Walter, had been Alan of Galloway's chamberlain, but his appointment was, again, mediated by the English court. The disputed succession of 1234-5 is of importance as the popular candidate seems to have prevailed against the wishes of the canons.

Reform and defamation. The reformation of the church in Galloway was perhaps initiated by a visit to Fergus in 1139 by Malachy O'Moore, the papal legate to Ireland, and passionate advocate of the Cistercian rule. A Cistercian monastery was established at Dundrennan in 1142 and a daughter house at Soulseat in 1148. Visitations to Dundrennan from the mother house at Rievaulx brought the abbot, Ailred, to Galloway, and produced some of the first circumstantial, if biased, descriptions of the people of Galloway. The Gallovidians had already attracted adverse comment from the Cistercian and Augustinian houses of northern England. Fergus had provided a contingent of local warriors who participated in the Scottish invasion of Northumbria in 1137 AD, and were unkindly remembered by the local chroniclers for their barbarity. Their morals at home attracted similar opprobrium, and through such oft-repeated slanders Galloway gained an unwelcome reputation for backwardness, slack morals and barbarity. Ailred's biographer, Walter Daniel was to comment:

> It is a wild country where the inhabitants are like beasts, and is altogether barbarous. Truth there has nowhere to lay its head. . . . There chastity founders as often as lust wills, and the pure are only so far removed from the harlot that the more chaste will change their husbands every month, and a man will sell his wife for a heifer
>
> (Powicke 1950)

The campaign of vilification has significant implications for the interpretation of the archaeological evidence. It attests a local population with a strong sense of identity, seemingly loyal to the House of Galloway, and deeply resistant to change. The marital irregularities were rooted in ancient Celtic institutions of concubinage and customary marriage, pointing to the survival of pagan practices despite almost six hundred years of local Christianity.

The reformed and unreformed communities at Whithorn. The **Period IV** settlement is undocumented, but is identifiable as a monastic town originating in the remodelled *monasterium* of **Period III/3**. A community of Premonstratensian canons was probably established in about 1177 AD, although the documentation is somewhat contradictory, and Fergus, who died in 1161 AD, was remembered in the obituary of Prémontré as a founder of the priory. The crucial reference is in the Annals of Maurice of Prato which states under the year 1177 AD 'about this time Christian, Bishop of Candida Casa, in Galloway, a province of Scotland, changed the canons regular of his cathedral church into Premonstratensians. For which reason he is named in the obituary of Prémontré as founder of that church' (Radford 1950, 104). Scott (1988, 41) has inferred the survival the Anglian *minster* and suggested it may have been organised on Irish lines. He speculates further that Gilla-Aldan, might, like Malachy, have combined the offices of bishop and abbot. This would not have been acceptable canonically to Bishop Christian and so, in due course, a prior was appointed to rule the community. The new archaeological evidence fits this thesis well, and we may suggest that the senior members of the **Period IV** community were converted into Premonstratensians, perhaps under the leadership of a new prior from Soulseat. This may have been achieved with a minimum of fuss and without requiring any immediate changes to the organisation of the settlement.

One unreformed community in Galloway is documented. Ailred witnessed an unseemly incident at Kirkcudbright, which points to the survival of a celticised Anglian *minster* still involved in teaching or clerical training (Oram 1988). A bull had been given to the church in alms, but a group of clerics 'called in the Pictish language *Scollofthes*' resolved to have some fun (presumably bull baiting) and led the bull into the walled churchyard. They were upbraided by their elders, but one sniggered, challenged the authority of St Cuthbert, and released the bull. Needless to say the bull immediately gored him through the shins and the assembled company raised their voices in praise of St Cuthbert. The *scolocs* were a junior order of pre-reform Scottish monasteries and were frequently associated with *célidé* (Culdee) communities between the Forth and Moray firths (Robertson 1853). Some of these groups survived the twelfth century reforms and they were later converted into Augustinian communities with varying degrees of success (Cowan and Easson 1976). There is no reason to argue that Kirkcudbright was a *célidé* house, but this tale gives an authentic account of a pre-reform community, which is now matched by the archaeological evidence from Whithorn. The *inner precinct* of the late twelfth century establishment (Figure 2.21) would have been an equally appropriate place for the bullbaiting episode.

Implications. This précis of Gallovidian history from *c.* 1128 to 1235 AD has concentrated upon specific issues potentially bearing upon the survival of the **Period IV** settlement into the thirteenth century. There are grounds to question previous accounts, which see the appointment of Gilla-Aldan *c.* 1128, the construction of the cathedral in the mid-twelfth century, the composition of Ailred's *Vita Niniani* and the establishment of the Premonstratensian Priory as successive stages in a coherent programme of ecclesiastical reform in Galloway. An alternative interpretation is that Gilla-Aldan was elected by the pre-reform community of clergy and people, that the cathedral was designed to serve the needs of the unreformed community at Whithorn (p 56), and that it was converted to the Premonstratensian order to provide a veneer of respectability in the face of critics from beyond the region. Gilla-Aldan's three successors may all have been political appointees of the English Court (Oram 1991), and both John and Walter supplemented their incomes by working as suffragans in the Diocese of York. Bishop Christian's allegiances did not lie with the conservative faction in western Galloway, and he may have absented himself from the diocese in the latter part of his reign. There is thus little evidence that these early bishops of *Candida Casa* need have had any great impact on the population of Whithorn. Cruggleton Castle was one of the principal strongholds of the Lords of Galloway, and Whithorn was thus extremely close to one of the principal centres of secular power which was, perhaps, a focus of Gallovidian conservatism. Popular conservatism is evident in support for the Galloway dynasty and the behaviour that incensed Ailred and his Cistercian colleagues: Whithorn was, perhaps, the natural spiritual focus for these sentiments.

2.6 THE MONASTIC TOWN

What eloquence could sufficiently extol the beauty of this church and the innumerable wonders of what we may call its city? For city is the proper word to use, since [Kildare] earns the title because of the multitudes who live there; it is a great metropolitan city. Within its outskirts, whose limits were laid out by St. Brigid, no man need fear any mortal adversary or any gathering of enemies; it is the safest refuge among all enclosed towns of the Irish

Cogitosus (trans. De Paor 1976, 29)

The title of this book proclaims Whithorn as a monastic town and a consistent thread of urbanism pervades the archaeological results, despite the apparent rural seclusion of the site today. This is, for example, evident in Finbar McCormick and Eileen Murphy's surprise at the evidence for the consumption of suckling pigs and a trade in cat skins in the twelfth century (pp 610-1) and in the *comparanda* from urban excavations, which are cited extensively in Chapter 10. The reconstruction drawings in Chapter 2 show the potential scale of the settlement in the early-sixth, seventh, eighth and twelfth centuries. The associated phase plans chart the evolution of a church-centred *monasterium* for some 700 or more years from *c.* 500 to *c.* 1250 and the subsequent development of the Priory and town after they achieved separate identities in the thirteenth or fourteenth century.

There is nothing new in the concept of the monastic town, and the description of Kildare in the seventh century can be supplemented from other sources. Archaeological evidence has previously been somewhat sparse, encouraging at least one authority on early medieval economics to question the urban role of early ecclesiastical centres (Hodges 1982, 47–9). A study of early Irish sources has widened the enquiry by examining the symbolism of the eternal city which underlies the organisation of early ecclesiastical sites, and their evolving proto-urban role as ceremonial centres (Doherty 1985), while parallel morphological studies have identified a consistent pattern of 'monastic towns' occupying double curvilinear enclosures with a market to the east of the church (Swann 1985).

The problems of identifying towns in Scotland, plotting their origins and understanding their economies have been confronted by Spearman (1988) who quotes Reynolds' definition of a town as a permanent settlement in which a significant proportion (but not necessarily a majority) of its population lives off trade, industry, administration and other non-agricultural occupations (Reynolds 1977, ix–x). Spearman concludes that we must rely on archaeological evidence for trade, industry and social structure to identify pre-Charter towns, ideally supported by the witness of contemporary opinion (1988, 96). Whithorn satisfies these simple archaeological conditions from an early date and finds support in the picture of a thriving community evinced by *Miracula* and *Vita. Vita*, in particular, records the cure of two lepers at a spring (*fons*) in the city (*in civitate*) reminding us that, as an episcopal seat, Whithorn would have ranked with other regional centres as a *civitas*, a step above the lowlier *urbs* (Campbell 1979, 36–7; Alcock 1988a, 33).

The archaeological and historical evidence from Whithorn go some way to meeting the more stringent criteria of urban status outlined by Biddle in 1976. These comprise:

1. defences
2. a planned street system
3. a market
4. a mint
5. legal autonomy
6. a role as a central place
7. a relatively large and dense population
8. a diversified economic base
9. plots and houses of urban types
10. social differentiation
11. a complex religious organisation
12. a judicial centre.

Whithorn was undoubtedly a central place with a diversified economic base and a complex religious organization. The population was certainly dense and was probably relatively large, while regular planning is evident from an early date with successive, sometimes well-defined 'street' systems. The buildings are not closely paralleled, but as they were intermittently used for 'urban' crafts and did not include accommodation for livestock, might be considered of 'urban type'. Social differentiation is difficult to demonstrate, but can be inferred from the sporadic evidence of burial, tentatively in the sixth/seventh century, with certainty in the eighth/ninth, and inferentially in the tenth/eleventh century (p 52).

It is most unlikely that Whithorn had a mint, but the evidence of manufacture and trade identifies it as a probable market centre from the early- to mid-sixth century, and coins indicate an unusually early monetary economy in the eighth/ninth centuries. The site is indefensible and its security probably relied on its obscure location, the protection of local people and, perhaps, on mercenary settlers in the later ninth/tenth centuries (pp 53-4). We may infer legal autonomy in ecclesiastical matters at a local or regional level, and Whithorn would undoubtedly have been a judicial centre, albeit confined to ecclesiastical affairs.

The identification of Whithorn as an epsicopal *monasterium* helps to explain the recurrent urban traits evident from the early-sixth century. This would have been a populous, hierarchical institution, probably in close contact with the secular authorities, and striving to maintain a role as a ceremonial centre. It is unsurprising that it attracted craftsmen and enjoyed close trading and cultural links with other areas, nor that it should reveal archaeological evidence of careful planning. The ecclesiastical and commercial interests of this community seem to have been closely entwined and deeply interdependent. The settlement existed, in part, to serve the cult, which, in turn, generated the economic activity that maintained the community. Neither could have survived alone, and this is evident in the rapid decline in the status of Whithorn, following the banning of pilgrimage in the late sixteenth century. This is reflected archaeologically by the cessation of activity in the **Glebe Field** and its gradual reversion to agricultural use (Chapter 8).

The term 'monastic town' has been retained in deference to past studies employing it, which will be enhanced by the new evidence from Whithorn. The word 'monastic' is, however, potentially misleading and this is, in effect, a study of the urban aspects of a *monasterium*, *minster* or, perhaps, *ecclesia*.

CHAPTER 2
Whithorn transformed

Peter Hill

The evidence from the excavation is detailed in Chapters 3–11 and this section summarises the results, presents a series of speculative phase plans and attempts to integrate this new material with the historical evidence to produce a more detailed picture of the development of this crucially important site than has ever been possible before.

Period I (?–730 AD)

The origins and character of the early Christian community at Whithorn present what is perhaps the greatest challenge to understanding the site. The excavations conducted by the Whithorn Trust have not resolved these problems, but have provided a considerable body of new evidence, which brings resolution closer and indicates where the answers may be found. They have, however revealed a detailed picture of the evolution of the site over a period of more than two hundred years in the sixth, seventh and early eighth centuries. This shows the expansion of settlement from an original focus at the east end of the hill to encompass a large area to the south-west. By the mid- sixth century this area was rigorously organised with an *inner precinct* accommodating graves and 'shrines' and an outer, residential area. A large assemblage of finds records considerable prosperity, widespread, evolving trading contacts and sophisticated and innovative technological skills.

Thomas describes how Bede had 'inevitably flattened a three-century sequence into a single temporal plane' (1992a, 20) and the variations in current interpretations (pxii) show, if nothing else, the range of ways in which the historical palimpsest can be decompressed. The excavation has revealed a uniquely decompressed and broadly reliable sequence of events. It is effectively unique, as most comparable, excavated sites of this period present archaeological records as compressed (or flattened) as Bede's history or have been examined on too small a scale to elucidate a coherent structural evolution.

The problems of the early history of Whithorn and Galloway are outlined in **Chapter 1**. The only reliable, contemporary texts are the inscriptions on the *Latinus* and *Petrus* stones and Kirkmadrine monuments. All other sources are secondary and the 'facts' in them have potentially been modified during their transmission from original events. Much *Nynianic* material reflects the traditions of his missionary activities beyond Galloway and has no immediate relevance to Whithorn. *Miracula* and *Vita* are primarily of value for glimpses of a rural *monasterium* ruled by a bishop (pp 14-5); the identification of cult objects – an episcopal staff and a water-stained book (p 2) – and revered places – a hoof-marked stone and, perhaps, a cave – and, in particular, for recording the healing cult, focused on the saint's tomb (pp 19-20). Despite their problems, the Irish sources locate Whithorn and Nynia in a geographically and historically coherent context, and invite the use of canons, penitentials and other contemporary records to supplement the archaeological evidence.

The archaeological sequence has three principal sub-divisions, termed **A–C** to distinguish them from the stratigraphic phases (**0–4**) described in Chapter 3:

A – Origins. The earliest material comprises the fragmentary deposits ascribed to **Phase 0** (pp 74-6) and a handful of Roman finds (pp 292-7). The principal feature is a broad roadway traversing the excavated area, which must have been earlier than the late-fifth century, but cannot be dated with greater precision. The road might have led from the Isle of Whithorn to a fourth or fifth century church or settlement at the east end of the hill (Figure 2.1). The Roman finds were scattered throughout the earlier medieval deposits and all could have been introduced to the site in post-Roman times. The specialists reporting on these finds have, however, argued that they reflect occupation of Roman date, which may have been the settlement required by Thomas' model of a sub-Roman diocese. A fragment of a flask or stemmed cup (Vessel 82, pp 314-5, Figure 10.11) typifies the problems posed by this material. It could be Late Roman or post-Roman and has both Mediterranean and Frankish parallels. It is manifestly a significant find, but provides new possibilities rather than answers. The *Latinus* stone is generally ascribed to the mid-fifth century and so probably pertained to the latter part of this ill-defined period, although a slightly later date would place it at the beginning of the following phase,

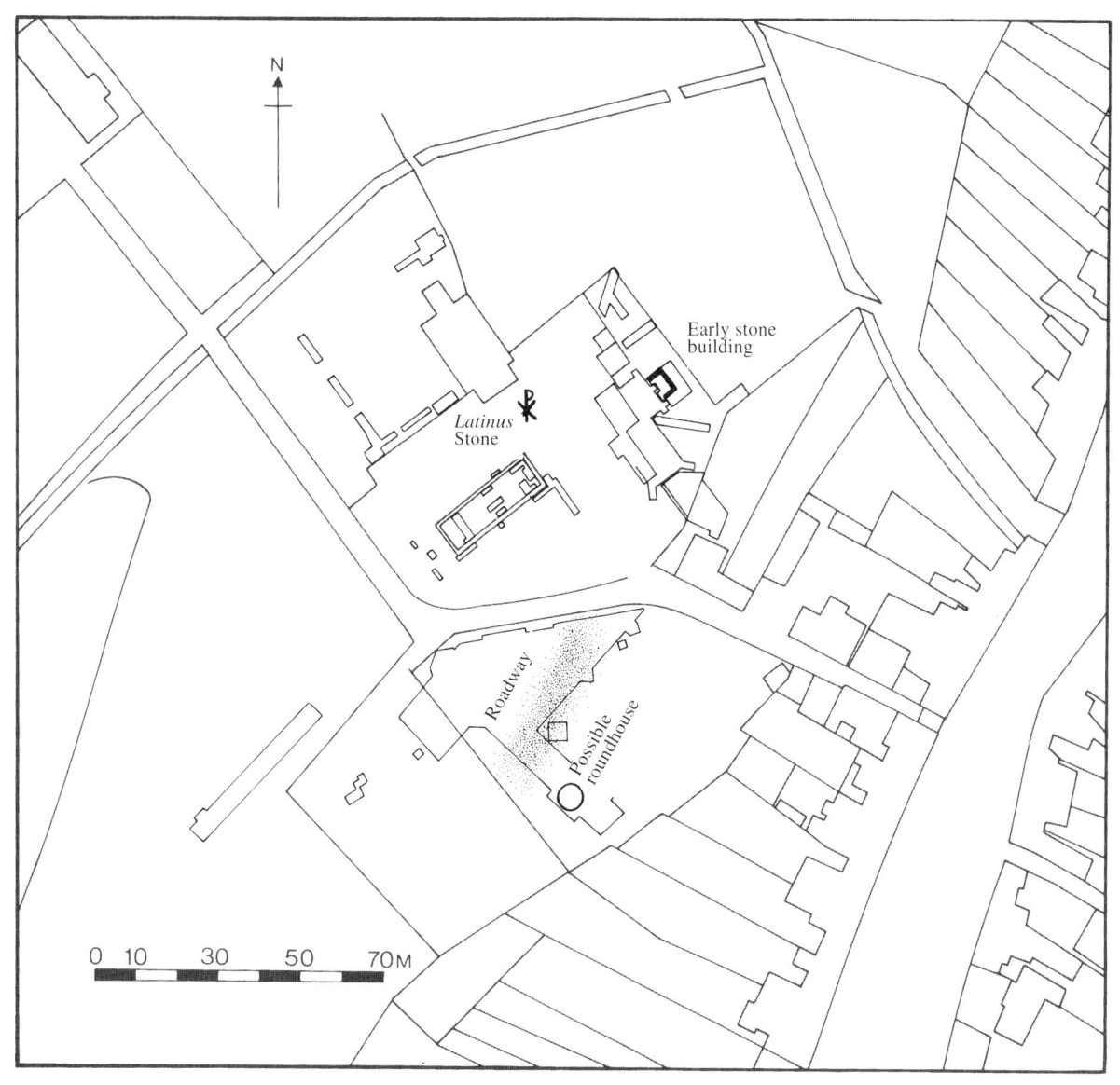

2.1 General plan of undated early features **(Period I/0)**.

for which it would have been an appropriate proclamation (p 28).

There is a long-lived and multi-faceted debate (e.g. Thomas 1992a, 16–17) about the identification of Whithorn with a place named Λουκοπιβια or Λουκοπιαβια in Ptolemy's geography and *Lucotion* or *Lucocion* in the Ravenna Cosmography (Rivet and Smith 1979, 389–90). The suffix **leuco-* means bright, shining or white in Celtic (Rivet and Smith 1979, 388) and is effectively identical to the Latin *Candida* in *Candida Casa* and the Old English *Hwit* in *Hwitærn*. An alternative meaning **luco-* (marsh) has not found favour, but would have been appropriate to the original topography of Whithorn outlined above (pp 7-8). The Roman finds from the excavation make this problematical identification marginally more plausible, but, given the absence of structural remains, it must remain unproven.

B – The first *monasterium*. The **Phase 1** deposits record intensive activity beyond an enclosure around a presumed focus at the east end of the hill. The sequence began in *Stage 1* with the cultivation of the ground beyond the enclosure using a mouldboard plough studded with protective plough pebbles. Construction work in *Stage 2* scattered builders' debris over the northern part of the main trench and was followed by the erection of small, sub-rectilinear buildings in *Stage 3*. Relatively large groups of debris accumulated during this time producing sherds of *amphorae*, indicating the consumption of wine, and distinctive glass vessels, including Germanic claw beakers and shallow bowls of possible Late Roman origin. Widely-scattered smelting and smithying waste included Haematite ore. *Stage 3* was followed by two further stages (*4* and *5*) in which the small buildings were replaced. An enclosed graveyard came into use in *Stage 5* indicating a westwards extension of the *inner precinct*, which became concrete as the developed *monasterium* (**C**) in **Phase 2**.

All the evidence points to this as a phase of colonisation, perhaps merely the expansion of an existing settlement onto unoccupied ground, but possibly the occupation of a new site by a large and energetic group with a coherent set of objectives. The establishment of a twelfth century Cistercian house in a suitably-fertile, 'desert' place offers an appropriate model for the successive activities. We may infer that the first priority of the settlers was to cultivate food (*Stage 1*), while the execution of a major building project required the location and preparation of lime (p 81) and the importation and smelting of iron ore and the subsequent smithying of nails and other necessary fittings. These materials were not used in the simple stake-walled buildings of *Stages 3–5* and point to the construction of a sophisticated, mortared and, perhaps, limewashed building in the vicinity. There is, of course, no proof that this was the stone church referred to by Bede, but these finds give substance to his account. Attention then shifted to the humbler buildings erected in *Stage 3*, and their subsequent replacements must mark the passage of some time. It is impossible to establish the extent to which Whithorn was truly 'deserted' at the beginning of this phase, but the obscurity of its location (pp 6-7 Figure 1.3) was, perhaps, an important factor in its choice for this new or expanded settlement and, probably, church.

The complex, sometimes confusing, chronological evidence is discussed in Chapter 3 (pp 69, 130). The end of this phase can be ascribed with confidence to *c.* 550 AD, but the initial cultivation and subsequent construction work are less easy to date and could pertain to the closing years of the fifth century or opening decades of the sixth. New evidence will be required to give greater precision.

The **Phase 1** settlement is illustrated in Figure 2.2. This shows terraces of small stake-walled buildings lying beyond an enclosure around the east end of the hill. This was represented by a ditch in the excavated area, which has been extrapolated to encompass the early building examined by Radford (pp 9-10) and the Museum Garden trench, where there was no ditch. The enclosure is centred upon the crossing of the high-medieval cathedral and might thus have been focused on the *Latinus* stone, which was found nearby (pp 614-6). The terraces of small buildings foreshadow the rectilinear plan of the eighth century Northumbrian monastery (Figures 2.9 and 10) and the early *monasterium* may thus have been modelled upon a classical urban or military plan that contrasts with the curvilinear design obtaining in later phases (e.g. Figure 2.6). Cemeteries were located outside Roman settlements in classical society and the *Stage 5* burials, close to the core of the community, may thus mark an important change in attitudes, perhaps *c.* 520 x 540 AD.

One of the most striking features of this phase is the range of sophisticated rural technologies employed. The plough pebbles are the earliest known examples by many centuries (pp 464-6) and, while the pebbles are local, the idea of inserting them into the sole and landside of a mouldboard plough may have originated beyond Britain. The lime technology evident in *Stage 2* seems equally exotic to early medieval Galloway and may not have survived elsewhere in post-Roman Britain. Similarly, while smelting technology may have been available in fifth/sixth century Galloway, the haematite ore was undoubtedly imported and it would have been more economical to smelt it at its source and import the bloom. The iron-working technology may thus have been a carefully guarded asset. All three technologies might conceivably have been available in Galloway or could have survived in post-Roman Britannia. They may, however, represent lost skills, needed for the establishment of the *monasterium* and construction of the church, which were introduced or reintroduced as part of the same movement, which brought a community of Gaulish clerics to the Rhinns of Galloway (p 12).

The finds are listed in Chapter 3 and described and discussed in Chapter 10. The most significant objects are the imported pottery and glass vessels, which attest contacts with Mediterranean markets and could have included the personal possessions of the putative émigrés. Successive groups of imports can be identified providing a unique insight onto the development of early medieval trade (pp 323-4), and arguing against the hypotheses that only one cargo of imported luxuries had reached northern Britain (e.g. Thomas 1988b, 22, Fig. 5) and that the imports were confined to a brief period in the sixth century. The Haematite and lime came from earlier deposits than these imports indicating that a coastal trade in commodities was established before the long-range trade in luxury goods. Other groups of finds are of equal interest, and early rubbish spreads record a range of craft activities (pp 83-9). Crucibles, for example, reveal the use of bronze rather than the quaternary copper-alloys of later periods (p 403) demonstrating another link with the Roman world. Other 'continental' finds include a silver hinge, perhaps from a casket (pp 397-8) and, possibly, herb seeds from an early latrine (p 124).

The plough pebbles are potentially the most significant finds. It has recently been suggested that these were an Irish invention of the thirteenth century (Brady 1988), but the numerous examples from Whithorn were securely stratified in contexts spanning the later-fifth/early-sixth to mid-ninth centuries (pp 464-6). They may thus have been part of a package of exotic technologies and ideas introduced to Whithorn in the late-fifth century. There is a possible association between plough pebbles and early *monasteria* in Scotland (Old Melrose and St Blanes, Isle of Bute; Hill and Kucharski 1990). The pebbles indicate the use of mouldboard ploughs drawn by large teams of horses or oxen and such equipment would have been beyond the resources of many medieval cultivators. There are numerous instances of organisational strategies by

CHAPTER 2

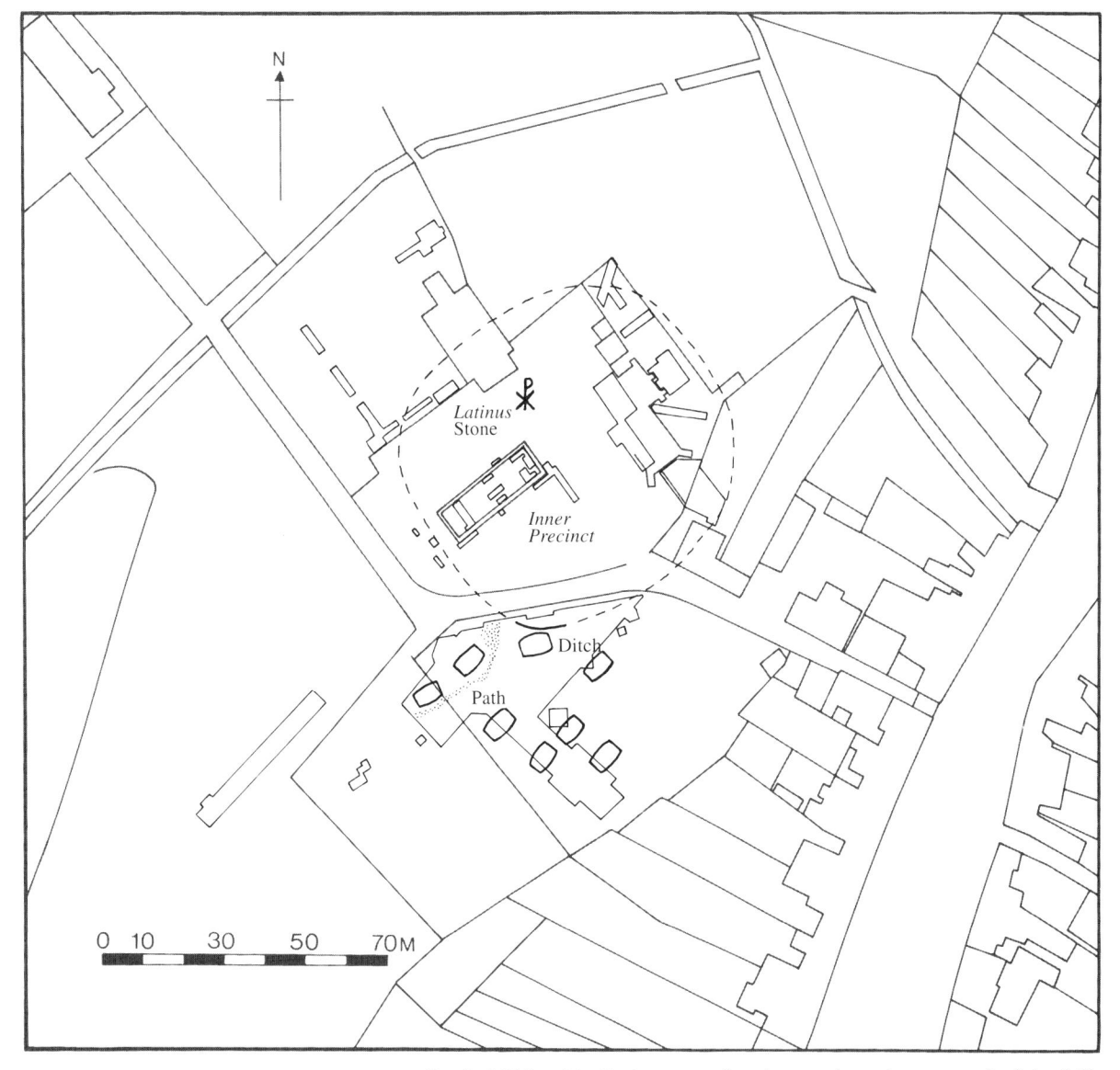

2.2 General plan of early *monasterium* (**Period I/1**) with ditch extrapolated to enclose the east end of the hill.

which a plough and team were owned jointly by several people or contributed by the landowner on a share-cropping basis. The communal labour and corporate wealth of a monastery would have obviated these problems. Mouldboard ploughs allow the cultivation of heavier clay soils, which defeated the less substantial ards previously used. This technology, if truly new, would have allowed a new *monasterium* to bring new ground into cultivation without encroaching on the fields of existing communities. Other examples from Scotland and Ireland may reflect the diffusion of this technology from the same unknown origin; from Whithorn; or from other, primary centres. The Irish examples are concentrated in northern Leinster (Brady 1988, 55) in an area between the monasteries of Moville and Clonard, which claimed Finnian as their founder. These finds cannot be associated with specifically 'monastic' cultivation, but may reflect contact with south-west Scotland between *c*. 500 and 850 AD.

Fragments of two large millstones from relatively early contexts may have originated in this phase (pp 460-1). They are indistinguishable from Romano-British millstones from the north (p 461) and might have come from an unknown Roman mill in the vicinity, but this should indicate the presence of a large military installation or a sophisticated population centre, perhaps a small town, for which there is little evidence (pp 294-7). The millstones, though of 'Roman' type, were, perhaps, manufactured for use in a mill constructed by the early *monasterium*, when still in contact with Roman technology. This is supported by the distribution of querns, which were rare until the latter part of **Period III**, arguing that food was previously prepared, and possibly eaten communally (pp 459-60).

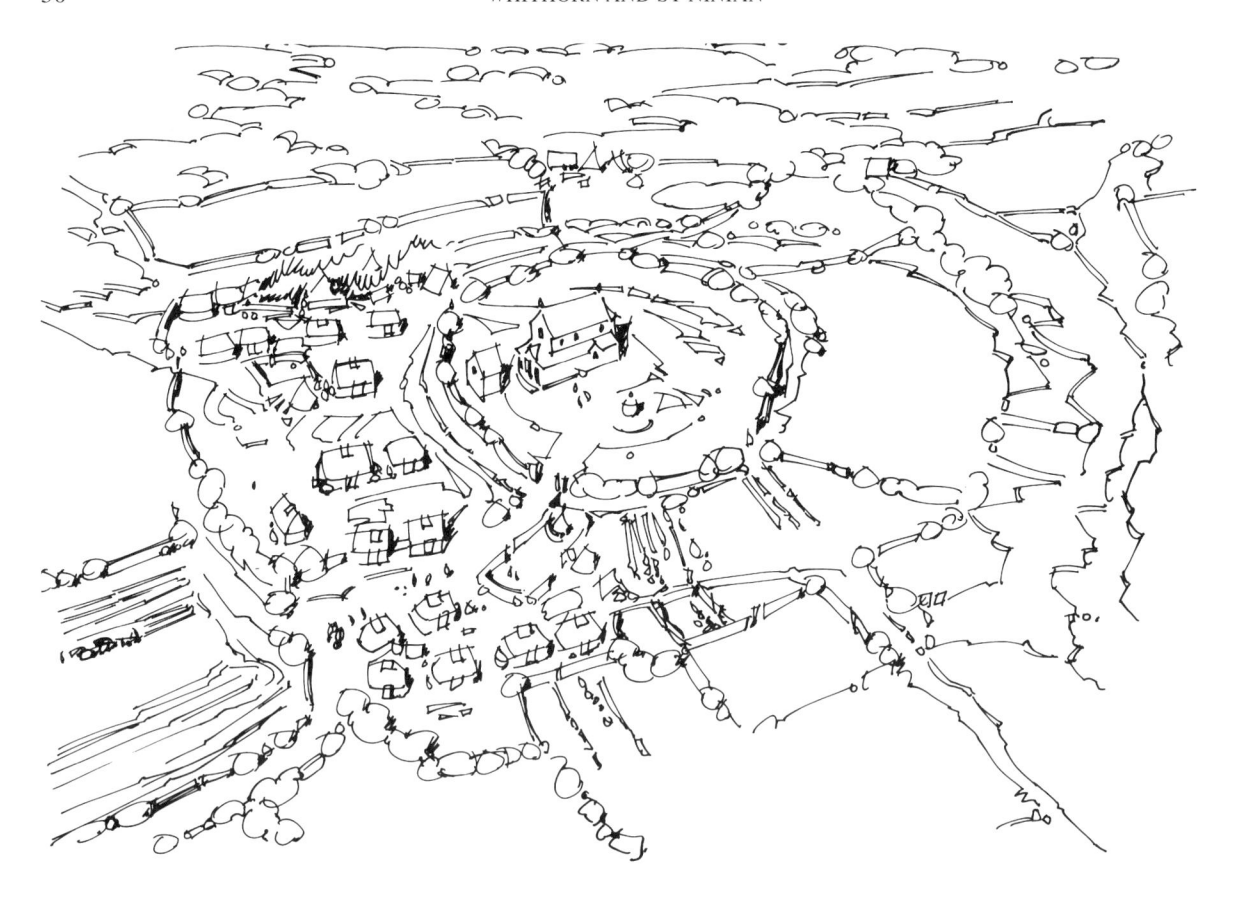

2.3 Speculative reconstruction of early *monasterium* (**Period I/1**) in the earlier-sixth century.

The buildings are another important group of artefacts for which there are no close parallels. This is perhaps due to the favourable circumstances which allowed the identification of their relatively insubstantial stake walls. Without this critical evidence they would have been represented solely by small oval building platforms, which *are* matched on contemporary settlements at Glastonbury Tor (Rahtz 1971) and Longbury Bank (Campbell and Lane 1993, Fig. 3) and perhaps at Tintagel (Thomas 1993, Plate 4). Glastonbury Tor has recently been re-identified as a *monasterium* (Rahtz 1993, 59–60); Longbury Bank is interpreted as an undefended high-status settlement (Campbell and Lane 1993, 66), but might also have been a *monasterium* named as *Eccluis guinniau* (the White Church) in the Llandaff charters (Campbell and Lane 1993, 55–59, 65); and Tintagel, formerly interpreted as a monastery (Radford 1935), is now viewed as a seasonal royal stronghold (Thomas 1993, 85–9).

A speculative reconstruction of the early-sixth century *monasterium* is presented in Figure 2.3. This assumes that the dense settlement of small buildings extended beyond the limited area examined and that the inhabitants were colonising a largely unexploited landscape. The enclosure surrounds a stone-built church at the east end of the hill. The founder's tomb lies to the west of the church and was subsequently to become the focus of community. These structures and their precise locations are, of course, conjectural, but are part of a model of continuous evolution extending to the Reformation. The peripheral area includes industrial workshops, attested by the abundant ironworking debris, and gardens for the cultivation of medicinal and culinary herbs, for which there is convincing botanical evidence (p 124). The ground beyond is being tilled by a plough team pulling a mouldboard plough.

C – The developed monasterium. The third subdivision of **Period I** comprises the successive buildings, graves and shrines of **Phases 2–4**, which conform to a double, curvilinear enclosure system originating in the final stages of **Phase 1** and surviving without major change until the site was transformed in the early eighth century. This plan corresponds with the physical remains of a large group of monastic and potentially monastic sites in Western Britain and Ireland (Swan 1985, Blair 1992, Fig. 10.2) and the internal details can be correlated with literary descriptions of monastic arrangements prior to the reforms of the twelfth century (below). While Whithorn preserves what seems to be an early 'monastic' plan it remains appropriate to term it a *monasterium* as there are no secure descriptions of a contemporary monastic community, and Whithorn

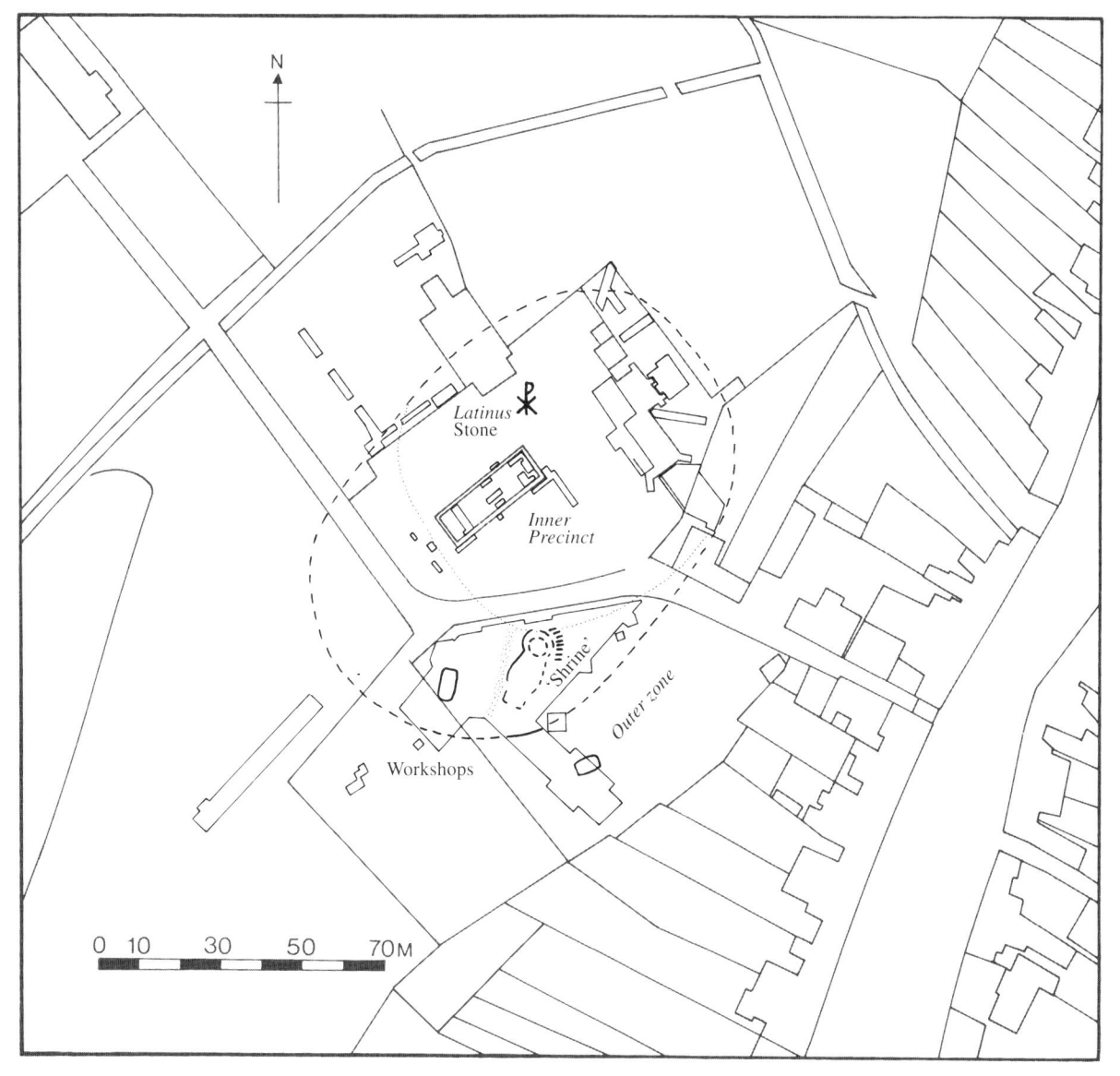

2.4 General plan of the developed *monasterium* in **Period I/2** with possible inner boundary extrapolated to enclose the east end of the hill.

may have continued to function as an episcopal seat. The dating evidence is rehearsed in Chapter 3. The *termini* of this phase can be dated confidently to *c*. 550 AD and *c*. 730 AD, but the intervening developments cannot be dated with precision, though their relative chronology is reliable.

The evolution of the *monasterium* in **Phases 2–4** is illustrated in Figures 2.4, 5 and 6. The *inner precinct* had been extended westwards by the beginning of **Phase 2** and the new boundary was marked by a shallow ditch in the **Glebe Field**, which probably continues on the north side of the hill (Pollock 1995). This has been linked to the inferred **Phase 1** boundary (Figure 2.2) to define a conjectural inner enclosure. There was probably a second boundary enclosing the buildings in the *outer zone*, but this can only be identified in **Phase 4** (Figure 2.6) and may have lain slightly beyond the excavated area in **Phases 2** and **3**. In all three phases the *inner precinct* revealed burials, associated with curvilinear 'shrines'; open space and 'industrial' debris, while the *outer zone* contained small sub-rectilinear buildings and somewhat different 'domestic' waste (p 68). The latter area was probably fairly densely settled throughout this period, despite the scarcity of buildings depicted on Figures 2.4 and 2.5.

The consistent design of the settlement throughout this phase must reflect an organisational system appropriate to the community and its position in society. The sparse historical records of Whithorn do not aid the interpretation of these remains, but the evidence from Ireland is potentially applicable (p 12). The historical sources are generally vague about the internal arrangements of monasteries, but present a consistent picture of their symbolic organisation. A monastery would include a consecrated precinct

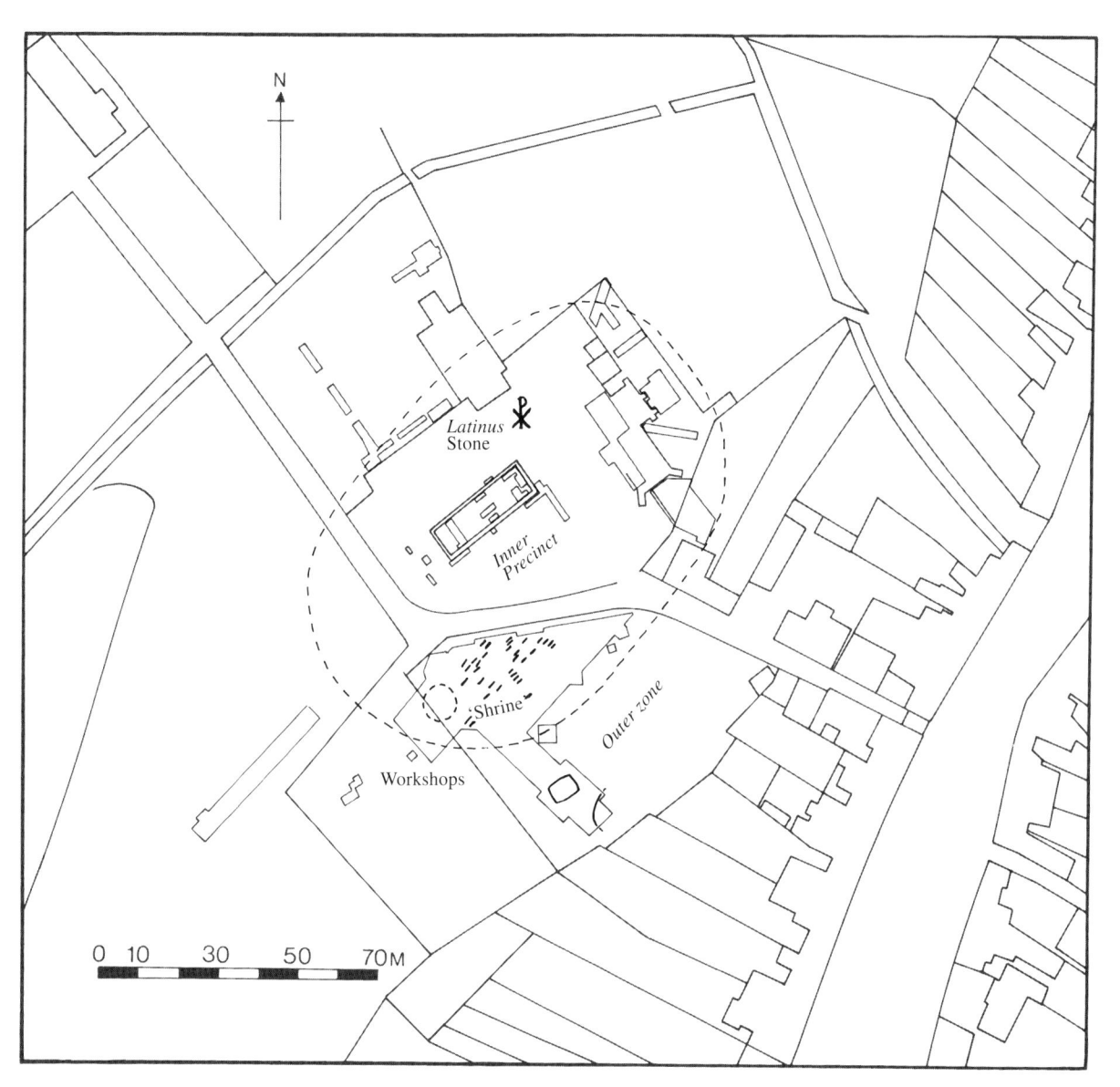

2.5 General plan of the developed *monasterium* in **Period I/3**.

known as a *termon* (from the Latin *terminus*) subdivided into zones of increasing sanctity. The holiest – *sanctissimus* – contained the relics of the saints, a surrounding area was deemed suitable for clerics and monks, while lay men and women occupied an outer zone (Hughes 1966, 148). This organisational system could extend into the countryside beyond the monastery, which was farmed by married lay members of the community known as *munachs*. The monks and clerics were not necessarily celibate and some kindreds in Ireland turned themselves and their lands into monasteries ruled by hereditary abbots. References to churches are relatively numerous and many centres may have had more than one church. Cemeteries, sometimes focused on a founders' grave, were probably close to the church. The cumulative evidence of the *Penitentials* indicates that meals were eaten communally and this was, perhaps, the primary purpose of the 'great houses' (*magna domus, tech mór*) recorded in Irish texts and, perhaps, exposed by excavation at Iona (Barber 1981, 358). Other accounts refer to guesthouses, possibly set apart from the main monastic buildings, and schoolhouses, although these need not have been specially designed buildings (Hughes and Hamlin 1977, 75). There are numerous references to the separate cells or houses occupied by abbots or founding saints, but less is known of the accommodation of the other members of the community, although they may have slept in cubicles within the 'great house' (Macdonald 1984, 284–9; 1981 310–11). The barns, mills, smithies and other functional buildings required to service these relatively large communities are mentioned anecdotally in saints' lives, but there is little information about their locations.

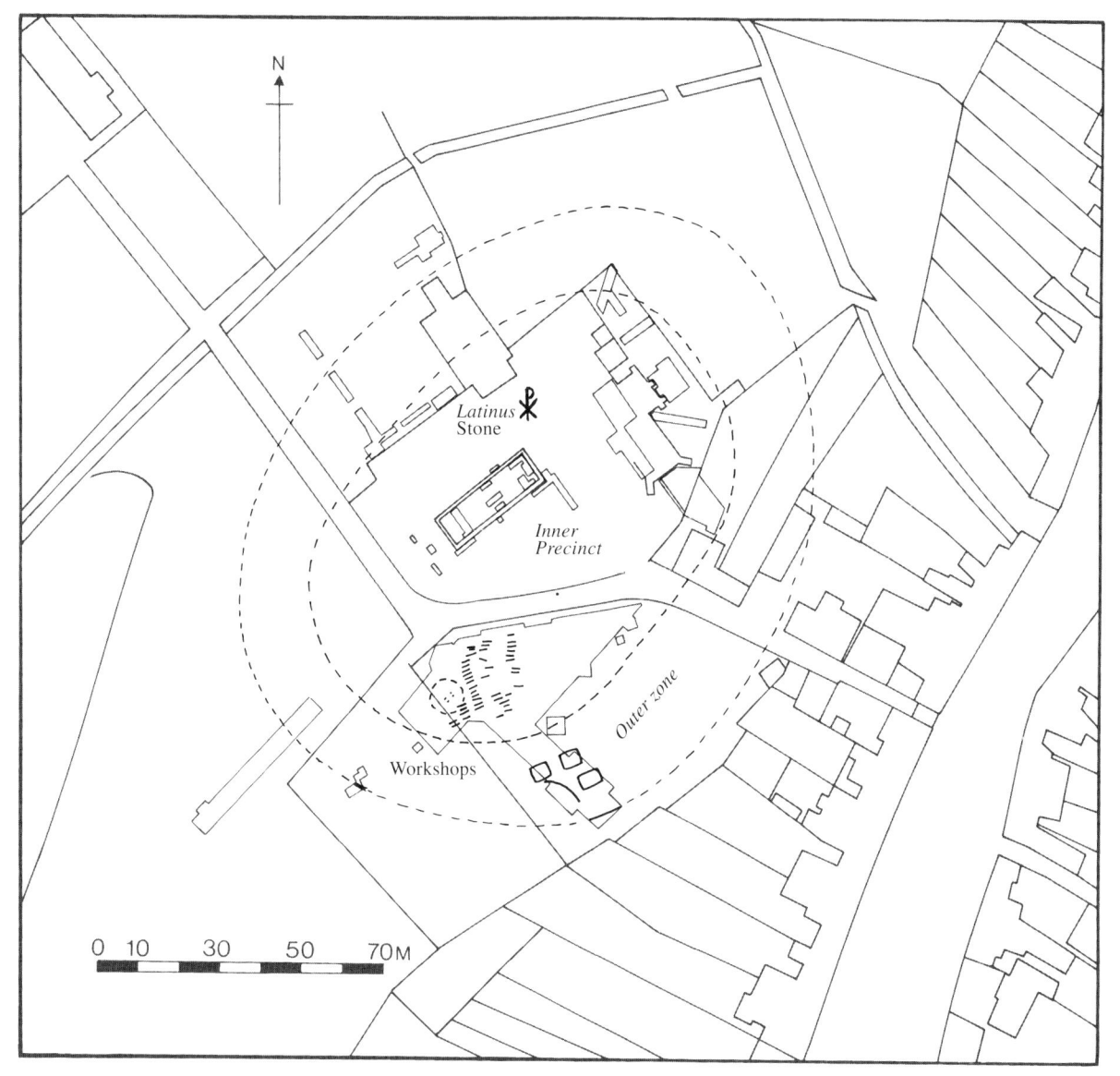

2.6 General plan of the developed *monasterium* in the latter stages of **Period I/4**, perhaps *c.* 700 AD.

The double curvilinear design of Whithorn offers rare physical evidence of the inner area of a sixth-seventh century *monasterium*. The '*inner precinct*' (pp 67–8) probably corresponds to one of the inner shells of the *termon*, perhaps the *sanctior* surrounding the *sanctissimus*. The residential '*outer zone*' may have accommodated a monastic, clerical or mixed community, while the insubstantial 'outer' boundary may have defined another zone within the *termon*. Other 'typical' monastic buildings – the refectory, kitchens, 'great house', *scriptorium*, guesthouse and schoolhouse – are missing, but may lie in unexcavated parts of the site. The structures required to store and process the food needed by the community are similarly unrepresented, but recent excavations at Hoddom, Dumfriesshire (Lowe 1991) have demonstrated that these may lie in an outer zone, in an area which has still to be examined at Whithorn. We may similarly infer that the *monasterium* commanded sufficient resources to feed a sizeable population, perhaps, combining its own produce with food renders from outlying estates. The putative boundary illustrated in Figure 1.4 may have delimited a *suburbana* cultivated by lay members of the community equivalent to the Irish *manachs*, while the estates may be indicated by the Anglian and Scandinavian place-names surrounding Whithorn (pp 16-8, 53-4).

The *inner precinct* was characterised by the evolving graveyard; the three 'shrines'; the isolated buildings of **Phase 2**; an area of open space and; occasional deposits of industrial debris and rubbish including valuable, 'high status', objects. Irish sources again help to elucidate these diverse features. O'Brien (1992) has examined the gradual process by which the Irish church gained control of burial as a route to the souls and purses of the laity. Burial grounds had previously been located on tribal boundaries, where they sometimes served a dual purpose as burial places and as markets. The church promulgated explicit 'blackmail' against the promiscuous burial of Christian with pagans (O'Brien 1992, 135) until the principle of burial in consecrated ground prevailed. Other sites in Britain reveal a consistent pattern with burials clustered around a 'special grave', which sometimes developed into a church or chapel and, were sometimes abandoned (Thomas 1971, 48–90; James 1992). Whithorn has revealed a somewhat different sequence. The church was probably built some time before the first burials, but a special grave still seems to have been required as the focus for the new graveyard (pp 94-6). Doherty (1980, 81–4) records a parallel process in which fairs (the *óenach*) previously held on tribal boundaries were gradually alienated by the major monasteries. This may explain the rich finds and workshop debris from the *inner precinct*, which foreshadow the arrangements of the eleventh-thirteenth centuries when this zone was used as a market (pp 237-48), but the Irish evidence is considerably later recording a process that began in the ninth century. The areas of unused ground fringing the evolving graveyard may have been part of a designated open space to the west of the principal church and variously known as the *platea* or *plateola*. Herity has concluded (1984) that the *plateolae* of hermitages were claustral areas used by the hermits, while the *plateae* of larger monasteries were public spaces used *inter alia* for the presentation of gifts and the display of public statements such as the Cross of the Scriptures at Clonmacnois. The Irish evidence indicates consistently that the principal church and saint's tomb lay to the east of this open area so corresponding with the arrangements inferred at Whithorn (Figure 3.1).

The three successive 'shrines' do not seem to have close parallels. Though superficially dissimilar, they were all circular or sub-circular and of similar size and shared a common design with an inner element and an outer boundary. The earliest 'shrine' was linked closely to the evolving **Phase 2** graveyard, while its successor conditioned the location of some of the **Phase 3** graves and was respected by the **Phase 4** burials. The latest shrine may have been erected with a similar mortuary role in mind, but this was unfulfilled due to the transformation of the site at the start of **Period II**. The closest parallel is, perhaps, a cemetery at Arfryn, Bodedern, Anglesey where a fenced, levelled, surfaced, circular area was associated with quasi-radial burials (White 1972), but the problematical, damaged monument at the Catstane, Midlothian (Cowie 1978, Rutherford and Ritchie 1974) displays some similarities to the **Phase 2** 'shrine', though potentially slightly earlier in date. Anglesey is one of the areas in western Britain with evidence for Gaulish influence in the later- fifth/sixth century (Thomas 1994, fig 12.4), while the Catstane bears a name – VETTA – which was potentially Latin or Iberian (Rutherford and Ritchie 1974, 185). These graveyard *foci* and the Whithorn 'shrines' may thus have been an adaptation of an exotic, continental prototype. Insular burial practices, however, reveal alternative, possible local prototypes (Thomas 1971, 58–67). A pre-Christian tradition of ditched, circular graves in Ireland survived into the seventh century. Tírechán records an example from Armagh in a Christian context:

> the days of mourning for the king's daughters came to an end, and they buried them . . . and they made a round ditch (*fossam rotundam*) after the manner of a *ferta*, because this is what the heathen Irish used to do, but we call it a *relic*.
> (Bieler 1979, 145)

This is of particular interest to Whithorn because the tomb of St Ninian revered in the late middle ages was sometimes known as the *ferter*. This may demonstrate a direct link with the early church, although it could equally derive from the English *feretory*, a shrine, reliquary or bier (Grant and Murison 1956, 60). These parallels present two possible ancestries for the Whithorn 'shrines' neither of which is necessarily apposite.

The *outer zone* presents relatively few interpretative problems. The challenging archaeological record revealed a sequence of small sub-rectilinear buildings associated with external latrine pits and spreads of 'domestic' debris. This part of the *outer zone* was prone to flooding, which made it temporarily uninhabitable, but occupation doubtless continued in better-drained areas. It is unlikely that all the buildings present were recognised and their density was probably greater than the phase plans suggest. The locations of successive buildings indicated an enduring, if poorly-defined, boundary system with a radial division within the outer annulus. Two of the buildings contained two chambers; a large one with a central hearth or stove, which was perhaps the living room, and a smaller one, which may have been for sleeping. If so the sleeping area was, perhaps, only large enough for one person or a married couple if Whithorn adhered to the relaxed rule obtaining from time to time in Irish communities (Hughes 1966 *passim*).

The **southern sector** encompassed roughly a fortieth of the *outer zone* and contained between one and three buildings during **Period I**. The *outer zone* thus had sufficient space for 120 buildings and would, perhaps, be over-sparsely populated with less that fifty. Each of these may have accommodated a single person, but could have held more, and the *monasterium* was thus of appropriate size for a community of between 50 and 200. This estimated population can be compared with the eighty monks at Marmoutier at the end of the fourth century recorded by Sulpicius Severus (pp 13-4), the 105 houses destroyed at Clonmacnois in 1179 (Edwards 1990, 113) and the similar population suggested by the eleventh-twelfth century remains at Whithorn (p 57).

The predominance of 'domestic' debris and the

restricted range of finds from the *outer zone* throughout **Period I** contrast with the more varied assemblages and distinctive groups of workshop debris associated with the similar clusters of twelfth-thirteenth century buildings in the same area (pp 222–7). This indicates that the **Period I** buildings were not used as workshops and, perhaps, that their inhabitants had a limited range of possessions. We can usefully recall Sulpicius Severus' description of the community at Marmoutier where:

> No one possessed anything of his own; everything was put into the common stock. The buying and selling which is customary with most hermits was forbidden to them. No craft was practised there except that of the copyist, and that was assigned to the younger men. The older ones were left free for prayer.

and it is worth noting that the only *stylus* from **Period I** came from an early deposit in this area (p 122). The relative abundance of fragments of glass vessels does not conflict with this view. Admittedly Martin's followers forswore wine, except when sick, but the *Penitential* of Gildas shows that it was an offence to be too drunk to sing the psalms but not, apparently, to drink (p 16). Bede's *Life of Cuthbert* provides a complementary picture for the mid-late seventh century. Cuthbert's abstinence was sufficiently unusual to merit attention (VI, Webb and Farmer 1965, 51) and he had the happy gift of making water taste of wine.

The *boundaries* surrounding and separating the different zones of activity in **Period I** were insubstantial at best and were only recognised when post-excavation work was well advanced. This late discovery probably reflects the expectation that the *vallum monasterii* should be a substantial boundary on the scale of the 2.5 m deep ditch at Iona (Barber 1981, fig. 10). Historical sources demonstrate that this is not necessarily true (Hughes and Hamlin 1977, 54–5). Giraldus Cambrensis observed an enclosure marked by a withy hedge at Kildare in the twelfth century; the monastery of Oundle was surrounded by a great thorn hedge in the early eighth century (*Eddius' Life of Wilfrid* 67, Webb and Farmer 1965, 181); and St Serf's monastery at Culross was purportedly enclosed by a hedge (*Vita Kentigerni* VI, Forbes 1874, 44, 172). The monasteries of Bangor in County Down and Caernarvonshire preserve the name *bancor* – the wattle enclosure. Successive boundaries in the **southern sector** were marked *inter alia* by lines of stakes, a band of stones and a narrow path (pp 130–1, Figure 3.42). There seems to have been no formal boundary between the *inner precinct* and *outer zone* for most of the period, but the graves in the former area and buildings in the latter were separated by a strip of unoccupied ground. The insubstantial radial division in the *outer zone* (p 131) seems to have been long-lived and suggests a formality in the organisation of the outer, residential area, which is less evident in the array of other features. A chordal boundary within the *inner precinct* can be discerned for much of the period and survived into the **Period II** as a line of posts or stones. Internal chordal divisions are evident in the monastery of Kiltiernan, Co Galway (Hodges 1982, Fig. 7), while Hughes and Hamlin's reconstruction drawing of the tenth century monastery of Nendrum (1977, Fig. 5) shows radial boundaries in the outer zones and examples survive with unusual clarity on the secular settlement at Corrofin, Co. Clare (Edwards 1990, Fig. 20).

The developed *monasterium* is reconstructed in Figure 2.7 The settlement is still focused upon the church and founder's tomb, and the original *inner precinct* survives as a special area, although no longer delimited by a ditch. This zone is indicated by the arrangement of large timber buildings appropriate to the public functions of the *monasterium*. The ditch marking the western extension to the *inner precinct* is still evident, though not regularly maintained, and the outer boundary is marked partly by wattles and partly by a hawthorn hedge. The enlarged *inner precinct* contains two circular 'shrines' to either side of a roadway leading southwards towards the ridgeway route to the Isle (Figure 1.4). The crown of the hill, accommodates a market with craftsmen's booths and livestock pens. At other times this area would have served as a ceremonial open space, variously appropriate for meditation, public gatherings and the display of gifts to the *monasterium*. The *outer zone* contains groups of small stake-walled building divided by radial wattle fences. These provide the proper segregation of different elements of the population, allowing the coexistence of monks, nuns, clerics, penitents, schoolboys, married *manachs* and craftsmen. One of these 'quarters' is used by craftsmen whose workshops come close to the *inner precinct* and their debris spreads into it. The ground beyond the outer boundary is used intensively for the cultivation of vegetables and herbs, and the penning of animals for slaughter or milking. This area is bounded by an outer group of buildings, modelled on those found at Hoddom (Lowe 1991), which includes a horizontal mill, driven by the sluggish waters of the Ket, a corn-drying kiln and a smokehouse for curing meat and fish. Beyond lies the *suburbana* with large fields tilled with the mouldboard ploughs (maintained in the workshop area pp 464-6), and water meadows providing grazing for the *monasterium's* herds. The latter are sufficiently large to require a specialised dairy producing the whey, buttermilk and cheese of the penitents' diet (p 16). Other members of the community have a more varied diet including pork, somewhat ancient beef (pp 608-9) and, probably, fish (p 79).

The finds. The large assemblages of finds from the developed *monasterium* are listed in Chapter 3 and described and discussed in Chapter 10. The most significant objects are undoubtedly the sherds of glass cones of Group E (pp 310-3, 324-5), which transform our understanding of technology and trade in Western Britain in the early medieval period. This bold claim requires elaboration. Sherds of glass

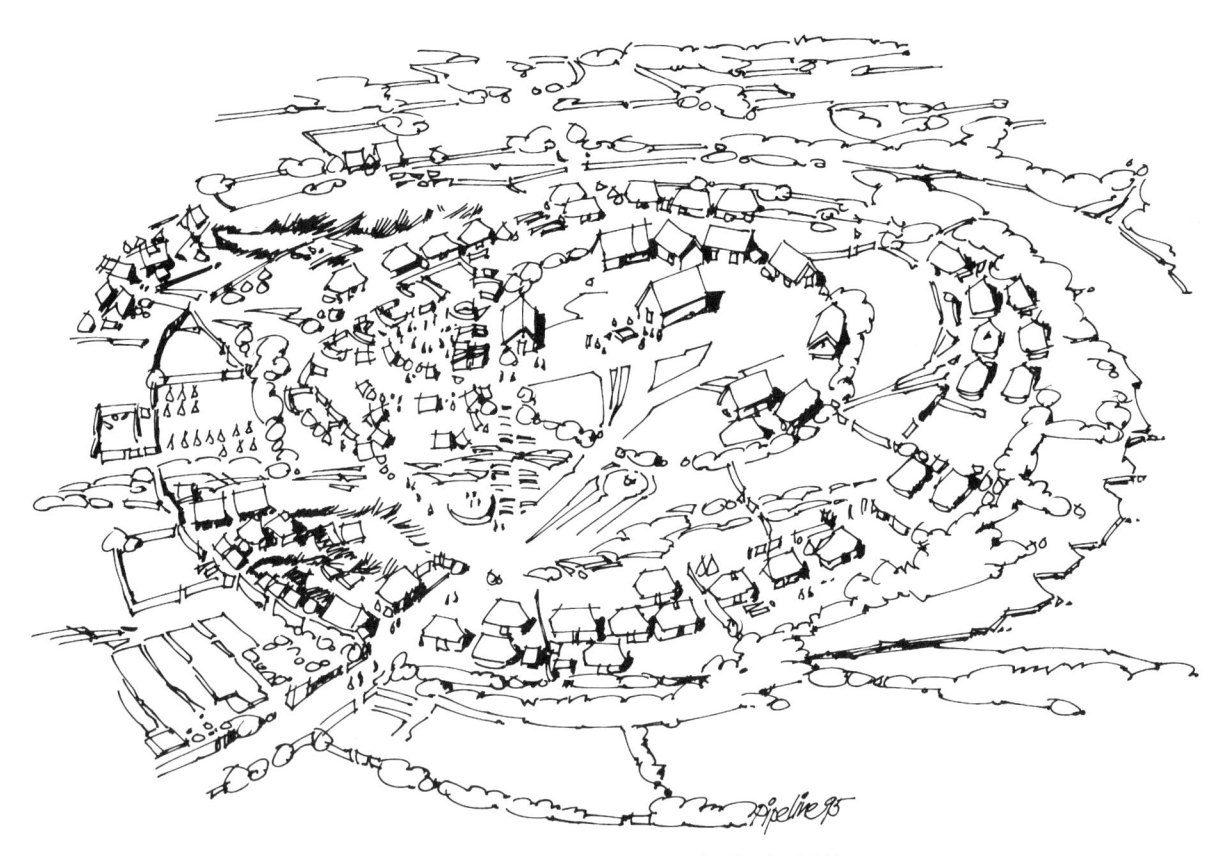

2.7 Speculative reconstruction of the developed *monasterium* in **Period I/4**.

vessels are an important element of early medieval assemblages pointing to the status of the inhabitants and their trading contacts with the continent. Modern studies can trace their origins to Harden's report on the glass from Dinas Powis, which was interpreted as cullet, imported from Gaul for the manufacture of jewellery (Harden 1963). This material was re-examined by Ewan Campbell (1991), who found that individual vessels could be partly reconstructed, establishing that the vessels rather than scrap glass had been imported. The Group E vessels are unparalleled both in Britain and abroad, and evince techniques of manufacture and decoration, which distinguish them from other groups (p 310). The model of continental manufacture and distribution along the western seaways would require that Whithorn was the sole destination of a batch of vessels manufactured in an unique fashion. It is more economical to conclude that these vessels were made at Whithorn, or in the immediate vicinity, in emulation of vessels from elsewhere, but without the expertise to perfect the rims and the finish off the decorative white trails. This interpretation is supported by the distribution of the Group E vessel sherds (pp 101, 310, 325) and by broadly contemporary chunks of folded and fused glass vessels, apparently of this type, discarded during recycling (pp 314, 227). It is, as yet, unsupported by complementary evidence of glass-making, and the high temperature kiln required to make the vessels has not been identified. The Group E vessels probably date to a brief period in the later sixth century when former trade contacts with the Mediterranean had been broken and new links with Gaul had still to be forged (pp 324-6). If so, the supply of glass vessels from elsewhere had, perhaps, ceased temporarily and the community had mustered the essential skills to make its own drinking vessels. The implications are that western Britain still commanded the technical resources to manufacture sophisticated objects, if pushed by necessity, and, perhaps, that other vessels which are unparalleled in continental assemblages may have originated in Western British workshops. It is pleasing that this unsuspected technological potential was first identified at Whithorn, and it would be even more pleasing to find British vessels among continental assemblages, reversing the long-standing assumption of an inward trade in luxuries paid for with leather, cloth, metals and other commodities.

There are other important groups of finds, whose significance is enhanced by the relative precision of the stratified sequence. There is, for example, a sequence of dress pins and brooches (pp 362-4, 417-9) while a number of fine objects, unparalleled in Britain, suggest distant contacts (pp 360, 398). Two swivel knives are of particular interest, as they are specifically Anglo-Saxon or Norse objects, and predate other early examples from the British Isles (p 429), contributing to the picture of Whithorn's extensive and precocious contacts. E ware pottery had been used for cooking suggesting a link with Dalkey Island off Dublin and Samson in the Scilly Isles, which have been interpreted as trading places or merchant's stop-over points (pp 319-20). This could imply that merchants brought their wares to Whithorn in the earlier-seventh century, or perhaps, that the community was sufficiently sophisticated to use these vessels for cooking rather than storage. A group of workshop debris, which accumulated in the western part of the *inner precinct* in the closing decades of this period, included a gold ingot and piece of gold wire, a rosette mould and copper alloy scrap (pp 115-7), while adjacent contexts produced crucible fragments with evidence of silver working (p 403). Earlier deposits in the same area produced smithying and metalworking debris (pp 107-9) and the main concentration of Group E glass (pp 101, 310). These attest the diversity of crafts at Whithorn in the later-sixth to early-eighth centuries and indicate the location of the workshop area illustrated in Figure 2.7.

Economic indicators. Bones were generally poorly-preserved in the **Period I** deposits and the two groups of seeds examined are highly specialised (pp 124, 127). The slender information can be supplemented to some extent by artefacts. There were thus few fish bones and only one – a salmon vertebra – was identifiable, but deep sea fishing is, nevertheless, indicated by fish-hooks and possible line weights. One large deposit of animal bones from the western part of the *inner precinct* produced a distinctively northern Celtic mix of animals, dominated by cattle and with strikingly few bones of goat and sheep (pp 605-7, Table 11.56). This may explain the rarity of spindle whorls and wool heckles from the sixth and seventh century deposits, which argues that textiles were manufactured elsewhere and were, perhaps, imported in this period.

Cultural change. There are two major changes during the latter part of **Period I** indicating, at least, the impact of new cultural influences and, perhaps, significant events in the history of Galloway. The effect in both cases is clear, but the cause remains uncertain.

The first change occurred during **Phase 3** and saw the replacement of the lintel graves, which predominated in **Phase 2**, with log-coffin burials. Comparable log coffin burials are sparse and the closest published parallel is at Scotch Street, Armagh (Lynn 1988), which revealed one log-coffin (**G**). A group of trench-like features (**7, 12, 15**), considered too long to have been graves, are similar in size and shape to many of the log burials at Whithorn, and may have been part of an analogous cemetery. An intact log coffin from Quernmore, Cumbria, is preserved in Lancaster Museum, and hints that this is a trait of the Irish Sea 'province' rather than a specifically Irish one. Pebble and cobble settings overlying three log-coffin burials are paralleled by three graves at Dunmisk, Co. Tyrone (Ivens 1989). This evidence is slim, but could mark the replacement in **Phase 3** of an indigenous tradition of lintel graves with new burial practices originating in Ireland. The change probably dates to the earlier, seventh century and coincides broadly with the importation of E ware from Gaul and the earliest large groups of comb-making debris (p 493). Arciform crosses, possibly associated with the seventh century shrine (p 102), may have pertained to this phase. These are paralleled at the monastery of Maughold on the Isle of Man (p 440), while comparable designs are widespread in Ireland, where some have been linked with early pilgrimage routes (Harbison 1991, 191–5). These diverse elements point to changes in ritual practice in the earlier-seventh century with parallels elsewhere in the Irish Sea 'province'. The evidence seems too weak to infer conquest and settlement by an undocumented Irish group and is, perhaps, more a reflection of changing spheres of influence uniting lands around the Irish Sea.

The second change saw the introduction of buildings with opposed timber-framed doorways in the late-seventh or early-eighth century (pp 130, 138-9). Although similar in size to the earlier stake buildings, these pertain to an architectural tradition that prevails in the *Northumbrian* buildings of **Period II** and can be seen in broadly contemporary monastic buildings at Hartlepool (Daniels 1988). They may thus mark the arrival of Anglian monks or clerics some decades before the establishment of the Northumbrian bishopric in *c*. 730 AD. This could have been a minor movement or the acquisition by Northumbria of the *monasterium* and its estates (p 17). Many scholars (e.g. Higham 1993, 111) date the Northumbrian expansion into south-west Scotland to the early seventh century, but Smyth has proposed a later date (1984, 24–27). He cites the appearance of mercenary Britons in Irish wars in 682–709 AD as evidence for the conquest of British territory, and surmises that the endowment of Wilfrid's church at Ripon in 671–678 followed closely upon the overthrow of the British kingdom of Rheged. Wifrid's endowment included 'the consecrated places in various parts which the British clergy had deserted when fleeing the hostile swords' of the Northumbrians (Eddius Stephanus, *Life of Wilfrid XVII*, Webb and Farmer 1983, 123–4). The coincidence between the early ecclesiastical centres in Wigtownshire and areas of Anglian settlement has already been remarked (p 17) and could reflect a similar endowment, perhaps in favour of the diocese of Hexham. There is thus an appropriate historical background for a gradual Northumbrian advance westwards, culminating with the acquisition of territories in western Galloway in *c*. 700 AD.

This is an appropriate point to introduce the *Petrus* stone, which formerly stood on the high ground to the south-east of the *monasterium*. This stone may

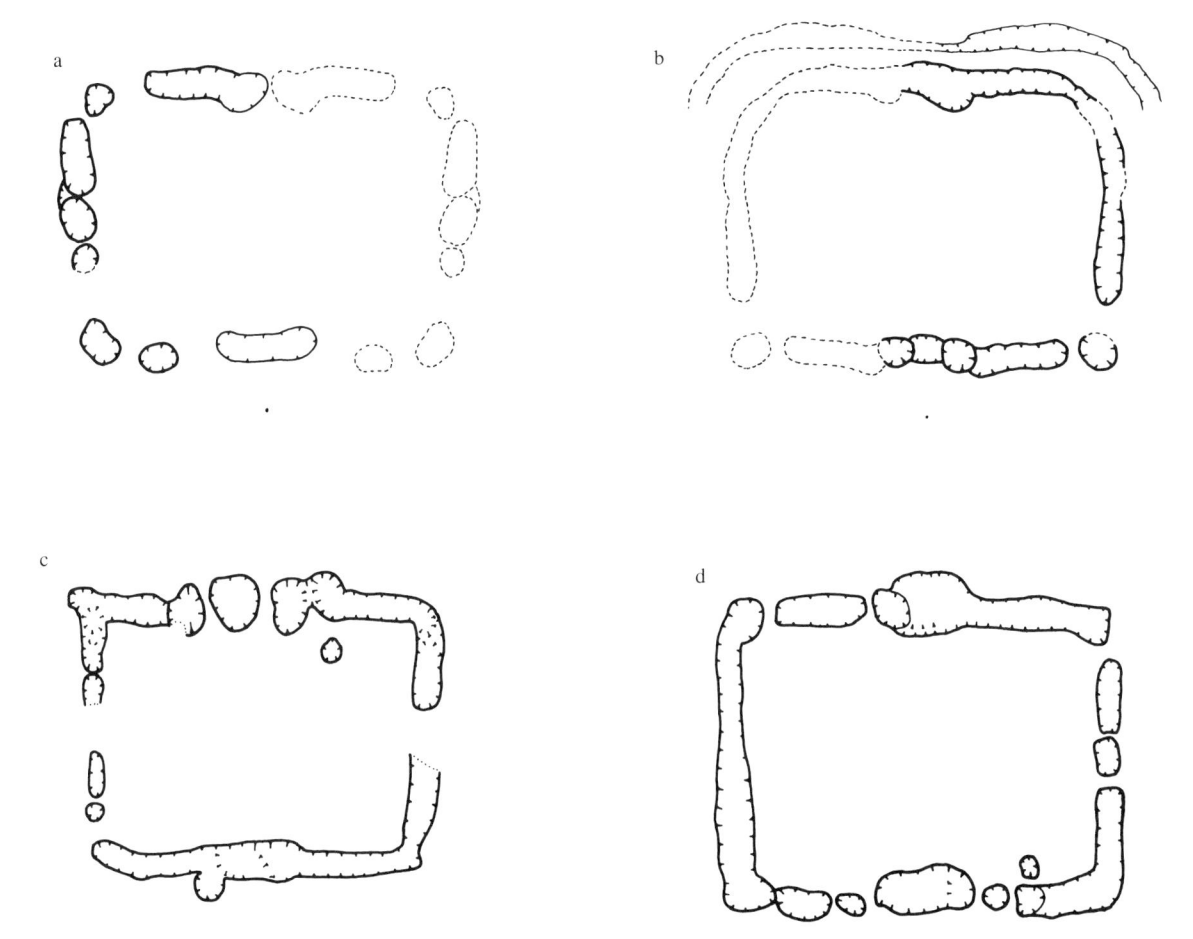

2.8 Small buildings from Whithorn and Church Close, Hartlepool (after Daniels 1985). **a**: Whithorn I/21; **b**: Whithorn II/12; **c**: Hartlepool X; **d**: Hartlepool VIII.

have marked an outlying oratory, the monastic boundary or a cemetery (p 616), and Craig has identified its approximate original location (Appendix 1; 1992, 191–6). The stone displays three potentially-contradictory elements: **a** a symmetrically placed, carefully-executed, stemmed, cross-of-arcs reminiscent of a *flabellum* or ritual fan; **b** an irregularly-placed inscription of three lines reading LOCI/PETRIAPU/STOLI; and, **c** a damaged, dressed face from which an earlier inscription or design may have been removed (p 617; Macalister 1936, 320). This last (**c**) seems to be the earliest event (p 617) and was followed by the execution of the stemmed cross to which the inscription was appended. Three 'cultural' influences may thus be discerned. The earliest is represented by the damaged dressed face, which could have borne a vertical inscription. Its cultural or ideological message is irrecoverable, but the violence of its removal – to quote Macalister – argues that it was no longer welcome. The next is the stemmed cross, now paralleled by the arciform cross fragments from the excavation, as well as those from Maughhold and Ireland. The final element is the inscription proclaiming the *locus* of Peter the Apostle. This can probably be attributed directly or indirectly to the Northumbrians, and almost certainly reflects the popularity of the cult of St Peter following the triumph of the Roman party at the Synod of Whitby. Thomas, for example, has suggested that it records the acquisition of a Petrine relic from the monastery of St Peter at Wearmouth (1992a, 19), arguing that it post-dates the re-establishment of the see by Pecthelm (1992a, 10). The inferred sequence of events hints that the stone was used by successive masters of Whithorn to proclaim their authority. Craig suggests that it stood beside the old road from Whithorn to the Isle, and it perhaps marked the putative boundary illustrated in Figure 1.4. Its message would thus have been an important preliminary notice to sea-borne pilgrims and other travellers. This proclamatory function does not conflict with the suggestions that the stone was associated with an oratory and cemetery, which may well have been the 'chapel on the hill' venerated by pilgrims in the later middle ages (Radford 1956, 179–80).

Conclusions. There is still no certain evidence of a Late Roman settlement on the site, and the clearest picture is of a *de novo* settlement dating to the later-fifth/early-sixth century. We have thus been unable to substantiate the models proposed by Professors

Thomas and MacQueen (above). It should perhaps follow that the apparent absence of early-fifth century activity at Whithorn should lead us to question other claims of evangelical activity in Scotland in this period which are linked with the name of Nynia. This is by no means safe. Absence of evidence is not evidence of absence, and there are sufficient unresolved enigmas among the **Phase 0** features to allow for the possibility of settlement in the fifth century if not before.

The sequence of structures and finds recording the early *monasterium* fits well the model of the foundation of a monastery in a 'desert place'. We may speculate that the colonists spent the first few years constructing a church, and establishing an appropriate economic basis, here marked by the cultivation with which the sequence starts. They had probably brought some goods with them, perhaps the 'Roman' bowls and claw beakers, but other, bulkier, supplies (lime and iron ore) had first to be located and then processed. These materials were clearly not needed for the simple sub-rectilinear, stake and wattle buildings erected in *Stage 3* and, in the context of Whithorn and her traditional history, it is safe to infer that they were used in the construction of a church. The combined evidence of the imported artefacts and 'exotic' technologies from Whithorn, and the continental names and ecclesiastical ranks from the Rhinns form a coherent package identifying the western empire, and most probably western Gaul, as the origin of the settlers. *Synodus episcoporum* provides an eloquent and appropriate commentary on the early years of a missionary church which is appropriate to the evidence from Wigtownshire, despite its Irish origins and uncertain date.

The British bishops, Patrick and Nynia, were subsequently credited with evangelisation on a national scale, but the picture of a gradual advance, *tuáth* by hard won *tuáth* is, perhaps, more convincing and one which perfectly accommodates the twin centres of Whithorn and Kirkmadrine in the cantankerously different Machars and Rhinns (pp 11-2). There is no trace of the Kirkmadrine *sacerdotes* in the popular history of Galloway or the annals of the Scottish church. This may in part reflect the plague in 549/50, which seems to have disrupted the transmission of reliable historical information, but it may also reflect a conscious revisionist decision to replace the commemorations of the original continental missionaries with the Celtic saints identified in early church dedications. The violent reworking of the left face of the *Petrus* stone suggests a similar revision at Whithorn (p 38).

Nynia may have a double identity as two separate persons of this name are recorded in potentially-reliable Irish sources (p 4). The discovery of waste lime among the earliest deposits gives unsuspected support to the traditional association of Nynia with a shining white, stone-built church and it is reasonable to link the earlier Nynia with this putative, primary building. The mission to the Picts may have been somewhat later, as MacQuarrie has argued (1987, 23–4), and would perhaps be more appropriate to the second Nynia of the Irish martyrologies. If so, his only named colleague, *Plebia*, can be ascribed to this secondary phase of missionary activity, and the monasteries they established on either side of Mount Bannog (Brooke 1989) were perhaps daughter houses of Whithorn and modelled, possibly upon a smaller scale, upon the early *monasterium*. We may thus endorse MacQueen's suggestion, based on *Miracula III*, that

> . . . monasteries founded by Nynia in Pictavia 'which now (i.e. in the eighth century) flourish with an excellent company of monks' may hint that records linking these houses to their founder were at that time in existence.

and dispute the suggestion that North British monasteries were necessarily of Irish type, modelled upon Iona, and later than 563 AD. The new archaeological evidence might be deemed sufficient to identify Whithorn as the prototype for the mid-sixth century Irish monasteries and, with a little dextrous manipulation of the evidence, *Uinniau/Finnian/Winnin* (p 15) can be viewed as the apostle of the Whithorn system. While this is plausible, it is probably too simplistic, and it is wiser to conclude that close contacts led to mutual development.

John Morris confidently equates the spread of monasticism with the introduction of agricultural improvements, citing recurrent references to ploughs, water mills and corn driers in the *Lives* of early saints (1973, 431–4). This case is intrinsically flawed by anachronistic and allegorical distortions in the sources, but is a reasonable inference in the light of the far-flung contacts of the Christian world; the potentially large monastic communities requiring a regular supply of food; and, most importantly, the discipline of communal labour, which provided an ideal context for collaborative innovations. The plough pebbles give strong support to this thesis and may prove to be a reliable indicator of the dissemination of new ideas and the mobility of individual artisans, potentially linking early Christian communities in Britain, Ireland and Europe.

The *monasterium* had adopted its distinctive and long-lived double-oval plan by the mid-sixth century and may well mark the adaptation of the organisation of secular settlement to ecclesiastical ends. The same solution may have been adopted on other monastic sites in Western Britain, but Whithorn is presently the only site where this can be assigned with confidence to such an early date. The subsequent development of the site has been charted in considerable detail. It reveals a lack of major change, suggesting stability and perhaps a twinge of conservatism, and Whithorn was perhaps no longer at the forefront of ecclesiastical affairs. The community has left no mark on the relatively numerous Irish records of the later-sixth and seventh centuries, and no traditions survive to supplement the slim corpus of Niniana. The change of burial rite during **Phase 3** indicates a major cultural change, and the community may have come under the sway of a northern Irish monastery at this juncture. This can be tentatively equated with the ecclesiastical site – perhaps an eremitical hermitage – at Ardwall Isle (Thomas 1966, 1967), which seems to show strong Irish characteristics in its early development. The subsequent architectural changes of the late-seventh century suggest a second takeover, this time by Northumbria. The fact that both changes left the overall design of the monastery unchanged suggests that this was widely accepted as appropriate in the contemporary milieux of northern and western Britain.

Period II: The Northumbrian *minster* c. 730–845 AD

The publication of Bede's *Ecclesiastical History* in 731 AD initiated a period of seventy years when there is a reliable historical framework for Whithorn, while contemporary written sources (pp 1-3) give some insight to the operation of the cult of St Nynia (pp 19-20), the community's intellectual attainments (below, MacQueen 1991), and its place in the Christian world. The records falter in 802 AD and fail completely in the mid-ninth century marking the beginning of a period of profound historical obscurity. This lasted until the early-twelfth century when William of Malmesbury observed that:

> (Pecthelm's) successors were Frithwald, Pehtwine, Ethelbert, Baldwulf. And beyond these I find no more anywhere, for the bishopric soon failed since it was as I have said the farthest shore of the Angles, and open to the raidings of Scots and Picts . . .
> *Gesta Pontificum* (Hamilton 1870, 257; trans. Anderson 1908, 53).

This reveals the depth of the shadow which fell over Whithorn and has led many authorities to conclude that the bishopric was extinguished until a new bishop, Gilla-Aldan, was elected in *c*. 1128 AD. It can now be demonstrated that this was a false impression, and the restoration and continuing development of the site in the later-ninth to twelfth centuries are described in Chapters 5 and 6.

Miracula has proved a troublesome source of Ninianic 'facts' (pp 1-3), but provides a wealth of circumstantial evidence about *Northumbrian* Whithorn and its aspirations. The therapeutic regime of the healing cult centred on St Nynia's tomb is discussed above (pp 19-20) and this must have made a significant contribution to the economy of Whithorn, aided, no doubt, by the hyperbolic promotion in *Miracula* (p 20). MacQueen (1991) has identified the interest in numerology which underlies this poem and the acrostic hymn written by the same author. *Miracula* incorporates phrases from various classical Christian poems and relies heavily on Anglo-Latin poetry and, particularly, the works of Aldhelm and Bede's metrical life of St Cuthbert (Levison 1940, 283-4). Both these works were probably included in the library at Whithorn and were, perhaps contributed by Bishop Pecthelm, who had trained under Aldhelm and was a friend of Bede. Future research exploiting Strecker's copious footnotes in *Monumentae Germaniae historica* (1923) will surely identify other texts and *florilegia* available to the author at Whithorn. The personal names here and in *Vita* may record some of the Anglian settlers of Galloway (pp 16-8) of whom one at least, *Pethgils*, may have been an Anglo-Pict, perhaps from a family displaced from eastern central Scotland following the battle of Nechtansmere in 685 AD. *Miracula* provides secure evidence of a *Northumbrian* monastic community at Whithorn, recording that after his miraculous cure (p 19), Pethgils '. . . . received the tonsure and lived a long time within our walls . . . .' (*Miracula* X, MacQueen 1990, 97). This community is also documented by Alcuin's letter of 782 x 804 AD, which was addressed '*fratris Deo serventibus*' (Dümmler 1895, 431; Hamilton 1870, 256). There is, thus sufficient contemporary written evidence to identify a successful eighth century cult centre, ruled by a bishop, accommodating a community of monks, and surrounded by an enclave of Anglian settlements (pp 16-8). This establishment was the immediate successor to the **Period I** *monasterium*, but, as a thoroughly Anglian institution, it is proper to describe it as a *minster* (Foot 1992).

Excavation in the **Glebe Field** and **Museum Garden** has revealed rich evidence of the *Northumbrian minster*, including a range of ecclesiastical buildings and what may have been the guest quarters to the south. Associated finds include a large group of Northumbrian coins, which gives considerable chronological precision to the later phases of development (pp 136, 352-5). The sequence began with the radical transformation of the **Period I** *monasterium* in the early-eighth century (probably *c*. 730 AD) and was followed by a period of intensive modification and redesign ending in the 760s or 770s. A subsequent phase of stability, lasting until the fourth decade of the ninth century, was followed by a brief 'crisis' culminating with the burning of the surviving buildings in *c*. 845 AD, which coincided with a period of political turmoil in northern Britain and Ireland (pp 20-2). The restoration of the *minster* shortly afterwards marks a new period of activity in which many aspects of the site were transformed (pp 48-55, Chapter 5).

The chronology of this period depends largely upon stratified coins, which give greater precision than is available at most other times, but are nevertheless intrinsically problematical (pp 352-5). There are parallel uncertainties in the historical records. It is, for example, suggested that the redevelopment of the site coincided with the appointment of bishop Pecthelm, but neither event is dated precisely. Pecthelm was already installed by 731 AD and Bede reported this as a recent event. A single coin from the chapel (p 136) and dendrochronological data from timbers used at the end of **Period I** (p 130) indicate that **Period II** commenced in the second or third decade of the

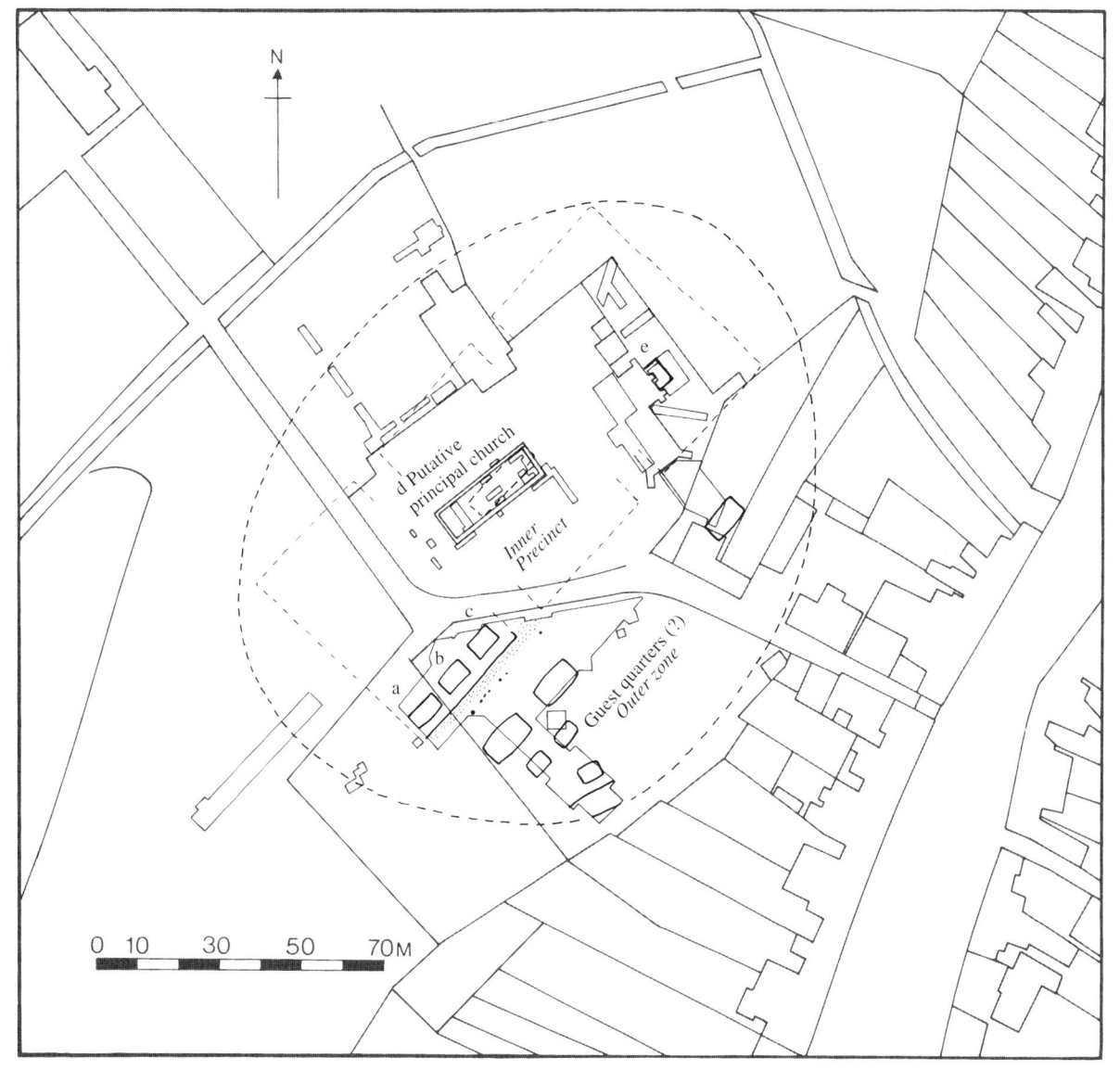

2.9 General plan of early Northumbrian *minster* (**Period II/2**) with hypothetical outer boundary, *inner precinct* and principal church.

eighth century. The correspondence is close, but not exact. Similar problems at the end of the period are discussed above (pp 20-22).

The development of the *minster* can be expressed in three speculative phase plans (Figures 2.9, 10 and 11), although the range of ecclesiastical buildings revealed six distinct structural phases (Figure 4.2). Figure 2.9 shows the site shortly after redevelopment had begun. The outer boundary of the **Period I** *monasterium* continued to delimit the site and seems to have remained in use for most of **Period II**. Three small structures (**a–c**) encompassing the **Period I** 'shrines', comprised two timber oratories (**a** and **b**) and a stone-founded burial enclosure (**c**). These were bounded by a low stone wall, reconstructed here as the south side and south-east angle of a rectangular enclosure. A wall exposed on the crown of the hill in 1993 (Pollock 1995) may have been the north side of this enclosure. Two similar enclosures have been depicted to the east, surrounding the crown of the hill and its eastern flank. The central enclosure is centred upon the inferred position of the founder's tomb (pp 20, 34; Figure 2.3), indicated here by a conjectural church (**d**), modelled on the excavated building, but potentially rather larger and more elaborate (p 15). The eastern enclosure surrounds the building (**e**) examined by Radford (pp 9-10), which may have pertained to this period (p 10). It is suggested that the three enclosures delimit a complex of ecclesiastical buildings, corresponding symbolically with the *inner precinct* of the **Period I** *monasterium*, but probably enlarged to emphasise the enhanced status of the *minster* and to accommodate the new bishop and his *familia*. There is, as yet, no physical evidence for the central and eastern enclosures, but this speculative reconstruction is supported by the range of large

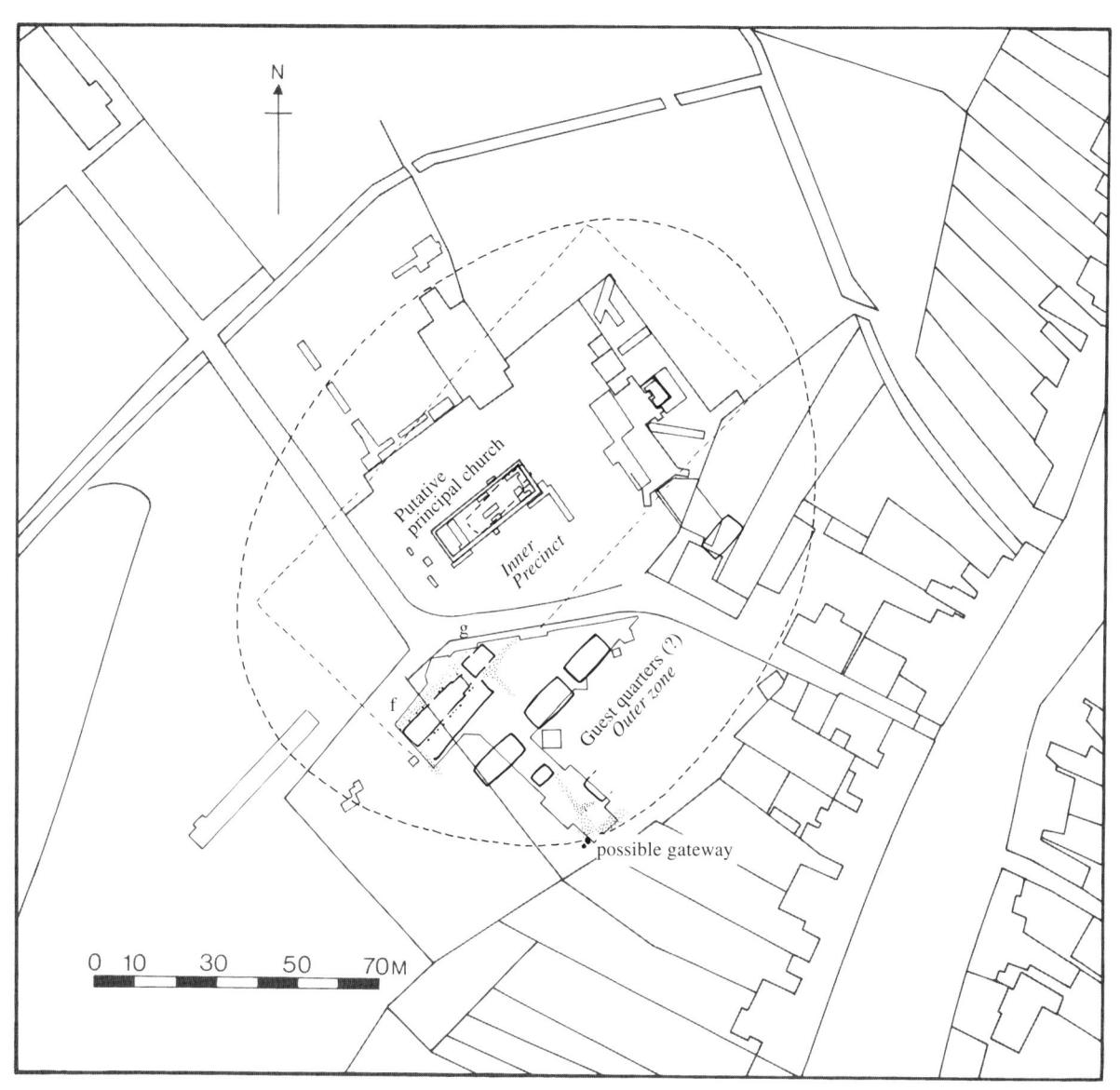

2.10 General plan of the Northumbrian *minster* in *c*. 800 AD after redevelopment in **Period II/4**.

timber buildings to the south. These extend eastwards to the **Museum Garden** and, perhaps, beyond, and the regularity of the planning argues that the *inner precinct* will also have extended this far. The central enclosure was probably the most important, accommodating the principal church and founder's tomb, which were the focus of the healing cult outlined in Chapter 1 (pp 19-20). The other two enclosures could have had specific functions, accommodating, for example, the monks and nuns of a double monastery, or segregating secular and ecclesiastical graveyards. Parallel ranges of large and small timber buildings to the south of the *inner precinct* were separated from the boundary wall by a strip of unoccupied ground. This unoccupied area produced most of the large assemblage of eighth and ninth century coins (pp 352-5, Figures 10.41-3) suggesting that it was a contact zone between the corporate wealth of the *minster* and the individual wealth of laity, and hence that the halls and small buildings may have been the guest quarters.

Figure 2.10 shows a reconstruction of the *minster* at a later date, perhaps *c*. 800 AD. The essential framework of the original *Northumbrian* foundation survives, but individual elements have been greatly modified and the three enclosures have been merged to form a single *inner precinct*. The two oratories (Figure 2.9 **a** and **b**) have now been united and adapted to form a large timber church (**f**), while the primary burial enclosure (**c**) has been rebuilt as a clay-walled burial chapel (**g**). This building seems to have been a gateway controlling access to the *inner precinct*, and was linked by a discontinuous pathway to a possible gate in the outer boundary. The preceding decades had seen various changes to the access routes within the *inner precinct*, suggesting

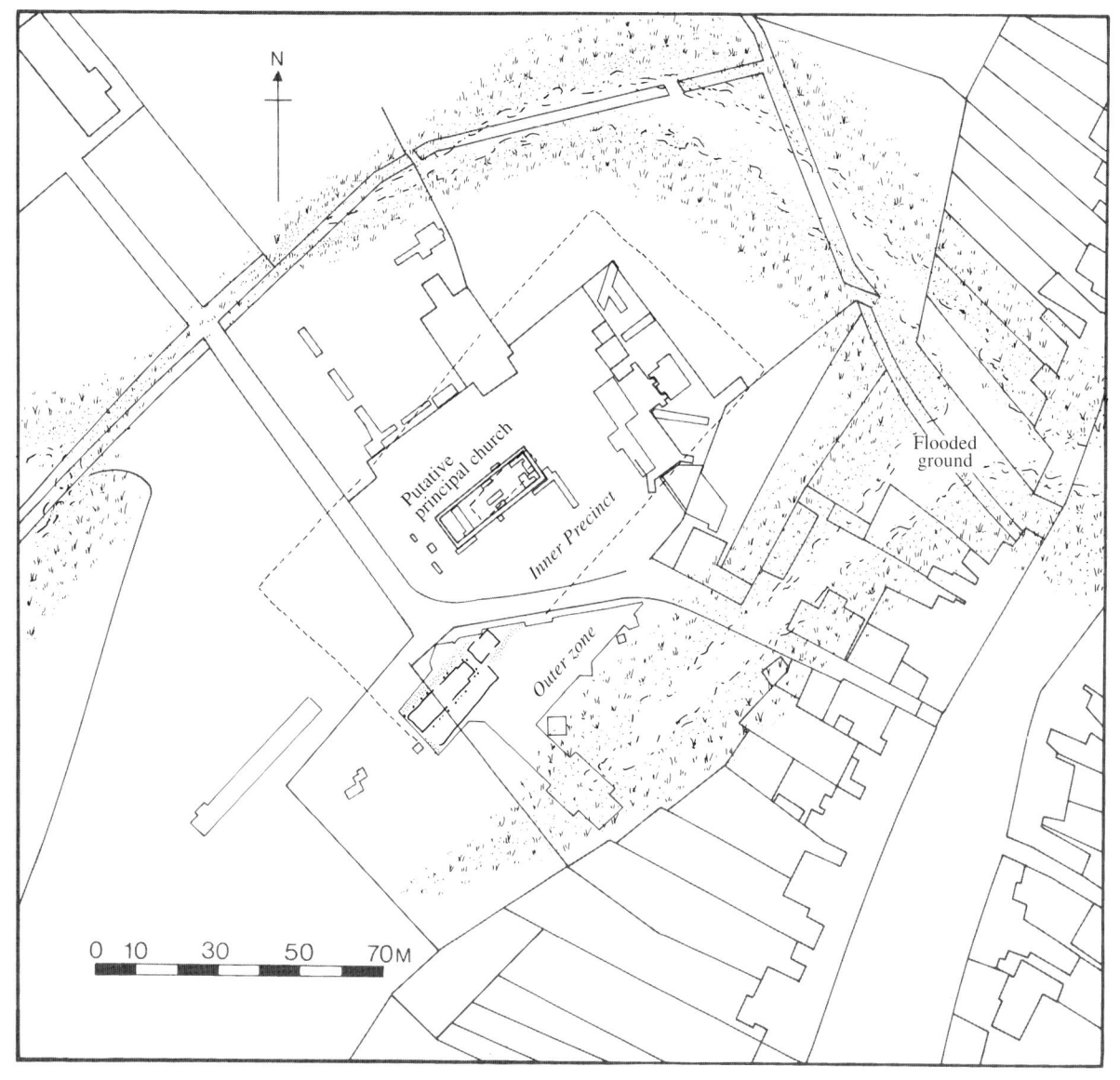

2.11 General plan of the Northumbrian *minster* in the mid-ninth century (**Period II/7**), perhaps *c*. 840 AD.

experimentation with the flow of pilgrims around the ritual *foci* (Figure 2.13). The ranges of halls and small buildings had been rebuilt in the later eighth century, but their function was probably unchanged.

The third drawing (Figure 2.11) shows the *minster* during the crisis of the mid-ninth century. The church has been stripped of its liturgical fittings and was used, *inter alia*, for processing and storing grain (pp 162-4). The chapel remains, though it was perhaps poorly maintained, but the 'guest-quarters' have either been dismantled or left to decay. The drainage system has broken down and the low-lying ground has flooded, obscuring the outer boundary and cutting off access from the south and east.

Figure 2.12 presents a speculative reconstruction of Whithorn in the late-eighth century, showing the regularly-planned, rectilinear *minster* fitting snugly within the oval enclosure of the earlier *monasterium*.

Detailed examination may reveal a certain degree of artistic licence, but this writer feels the reconstruction is more likely to be under-populated than the reverse, and, if anything, less regimented than the excavated evidence would suggest. The *minster* is still focused upon the founder's tomb, now housed in an appropriately 'lofty' church. There is ample accommodation for lay visitors in the halls shown in the foreground, but we have the authority of *Miracula* that 'many are eager to visit' (X, p 20). Approach roads to the south and west lead to the lands occupied by Anglian settlers, to the Isle of Whithorn and, thence, to the world beyond. The monastic community does not figure strongly in this reconstruction, due largely to the want of archaeological evidence. It may have occupied the more secluded and exposed north flank of the hill, where it would have been segregated from worldly

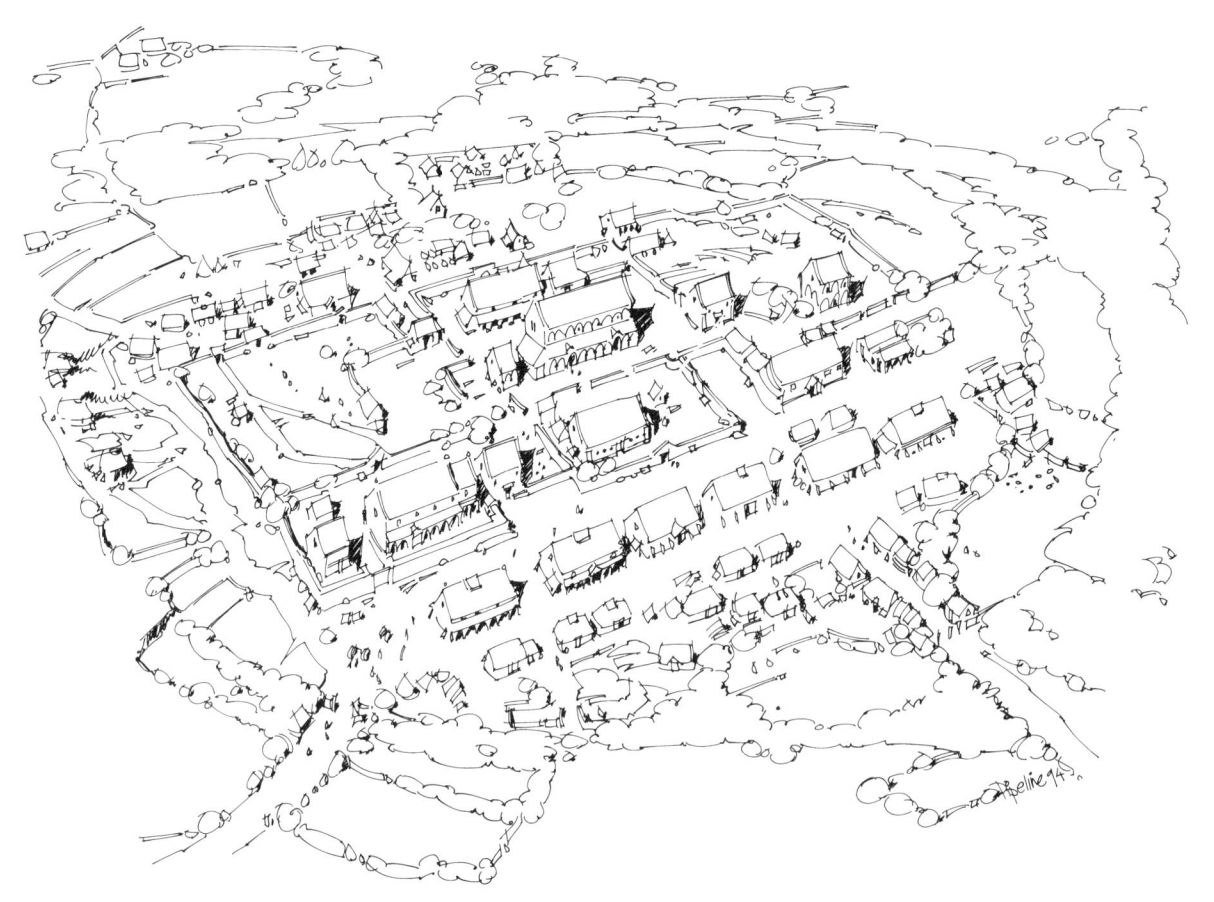

2.12 Speculative reconstruction of the Northumbrian *minster* in the later- eighth century.

contact with the laity to the south. The reconstruction also omits the necessary buildings for storing and processing the produce from the ecclesiastical estate, which perhaps, as at Hoddom (Lowe 1991), lay beyond the inner area depicted and could have survived with little change from the preceding period (Figure 2.7).

Architectural aspects. All the buildings were rectangular with opposed doorways in their long walls, and all but the chapel were built of timber. They conform reasonably closely with a distinctive, early medieval architectural tradition, which unites a wide range of Anglo-Saxon settlements and was, perhaps, derived from Romano-British buildings (James *et al.* 1984). Other cultural elements may have been incorporated, but there is no equivalent *corpus* of early medieval British or Scottish buildings with which they may be compared. Roundhouses still seem to have prevailed in Ireland at this time, although rectilinear buildings appeared in eastern Ulster in the eight/ninth century (Edwards 1990, 26), but these have more in common with the **Period IV** houses (pp 55-6).

The timber walls of three buildings rested on stone plinths. In two instances (the **Phase 4** church and Hall II/9b) the stones had been inserted to support decaying wall timbers in the course of running repairs, but the third (II/15) was a new building, and could mark the introduction of timber-frame construction, which is also evident in the **Period III** church (pp 186-7).

The **church** is an unique building without close parallels, which is unsurprising in the light of its distinctive structural history (Chapter 4). Its '*Northumbrian*' context seems to be beyond question, but it was erected in a period when Northumbrian churches were increasingly built of stone, while timber churches were described as being 'in the Scottish tradition' (*more Scottorum*). The large timber church at Whithorn might thus reflect Irish or British influence, but *comparanda* are few and there are none of equivalent size (Harbison 1982, 624-7). The most diagnostic features are, perhaps, the opposed doorways in the long walls, built at various stages in the development of the building. Early Irish churches seem always to have been entered through a single doorway in the west gable (Hare and Hamlin 1986, 133), and the same design is evident in the putatively-Irish chapel at Ardwall Isle (Thomas 1966, 1967). Written descriptions of Irish churches are rare and tend towards ambiguity (Harbison 1982, 624–7). The most apposite of these is Cogitosus' description of St Brigit's church at Kildare (Bieler 1963, 28), which is sufficiently elastic to be correlated with the completed church of **Phase 3**. This does not, however, establish any coherent linkage between Whithorn and Kildare, and it is surely sensible to treat the Whithorn church as *sui generis* until more appropriate *comparanda* are discovered.

The church seems to have developed around a monument at the centre of an earlier 'shrine'. This was removed when the fittings of the church were dismantled in the mid-ninth century, but its position was indicated by two sockets, one marking its original position and the second its replacement in the same place after its temporary removal in what seems to have been a hunt for relics. This continuing reverence for a pre-existing ritual focus complements the other evidence of the adoption, adaptation and absorption of Whithorn's ancient plan by the Northumbrian church.

The construction sequence began with the erection of two timber oratories in **Phases 1** and **2**, which were joined to form a bicameral church in **Phase 3**. The focal monument stood in the western part of the eastern oratory and was to lie between an eastern 'chancel' and a western 'nave' throughout the subsequent evolution of the building. A fragmentary structure at the east end of the nave has been interpreted as an altar, and altars in this position are known from other early English churches (Parsons 1986, 105–7). The altar was moved eastwards after the 'relic hunt' and had been dismantled before the fire of *c.* 845 AD. Debris in the immediate vicinity included a fourth century Roman coin and a slightly earlier sherd of Central Gaulish Samian (pp 162-4). These finds were insulated from the underlying fifth/sixth century surface by deposits comprising the floor of the building, and could have been relics associated with the cult honoured by the church. If so the Northumbrians were venerating distinctively Roman objects, which would have been appropriate to a third or fourth century saint.

The church was flanked by rows of vertical posts, which were renewed or resited on several occasions. They are not paralleled elsewhere, but can be interpreted as arcades supporting extended caves (p 149, Figure 4.12). They could also have been freestanding pylons aligned with other boundaries of posts and stones (Figure 4.1). They might bear some obscure relationship to the skeuomorphic pilaster strips at the churches of Deerhurst, Barton-on-Humber and Earls Barton (Rodwell 1986, 171–174), or to the 'assembly of planks' comprising the 'extensive portico' of the seventh century Irish chapel described in *Hisperica Famina* (Harbison 1982, 626).

The **burial chapel**. The burial chapel was as singular as the church. It had thick clay walls supported by a wide stone plinth, and was probably roofed with shingles. There are numerous parallels for clay-walled construction among more recent vernacular buildings in Galloway and elsewhere, but there are no contemporary examples of this economical and practical technique of construction. Clay-walling is often associated with humble dwellings, but the chapel was enriched with at least two windows of coloured glass (pp 167, 327) and contained five burials, seemingly of high-status (p 557). The answer to this puzzle may lie in scattered human bones found among the debris of the mid-ninth century fire (p 169). These suggest the chapel was used for the storage or display of bodies, and the widely-acknowledged insulating properties of clay walling would have maintained an even, cool temperature inhibiting rapid decay. The chapel seems to have served as a gateway to the western part of the *inner precinct*, and would therefore have been an appropriate temporary mortuary for deceased members of the laity awaiting burial in the consecrated ground within.

The east end of the building contained four well-preserved graves, one of which had virtually obliterated an earlier burial. All four contained coffins, three of which were chests with iron fittings and locks (pp 412-5). The skeletons were poorly preserved, but all were adult and seem to have been well-nourished. Two were male and one female, though markedly robust (p 557). The first three graves probably pertained to the initial phases in the development of the *minster*, and could, for example, have contained the bodies of Bishop Pecthelm and perhaps the leaders of the putative, pre-existing Anglian community (pp 37, 40). The remaining two burials (including the female) were somewhat later, and the coffins were still relatively intact when the chapel was burnt in the mid-ninth century. The coffins are described as 'chest coffins' and are paralleled in other Anglo-Saxon cemeteries (p 415), but locks are surprising fittings for coffins, and they could have been domestic chests reused when their owners died (pp 412-3).

The ground to the east of the chapel revealed a graveyard, densely populated with infants and young children. These were far too young to have been members of the ecclesiastical community and must have come from the lay population of the area. The situation of this graveyard could reflect reverence for those buried in the chapel, or it may have been deemed appropriate for the very young to be buried at the gateway to the inferred area of consecrated ground.

The chapel has been described as a *mausoleum* (e.g. Blair 1992, 262), and similar co-axial churches and *mausolea* or crypts have been recorded at Repton, Wells, Glastonbury, and, perhaps, St Oswald's Priory, Gloucester (Blair 1992, 252–3, Heighway and Bryant 1986). A *mausoleum* has, however, a specialised meaning as a building-shaped tomb, and the Whithorn chapel seems to have had a more dynamic function as a gateway and, perhaps, a mortuary chapel. Its glass windows indicate its importance and probably reflect the status of those buried within. Its unusual construction suggests a special function, perhaps as a cool chamber for the temporary repose of the dead. If so, the novel method of construction may have been introduced, along with the new bishop, from south-western England, where cob or wychert buildings and a warmer climate

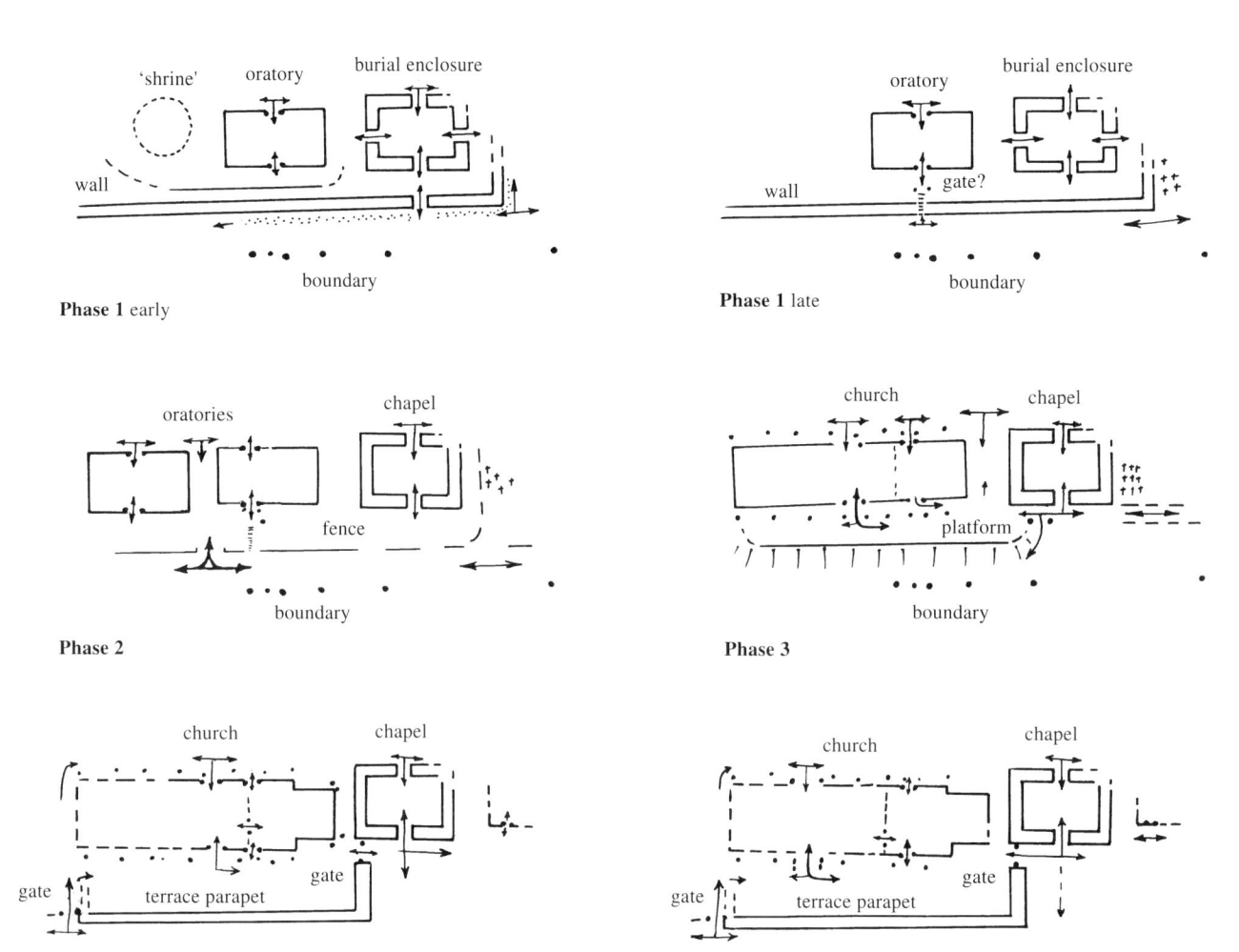

2.13 Schematic drawing of the evolving patterns of access to the *Northumbrian* ecclesiastical buildings in the eighth and ninth centuries.

may already have suggested this solution to an irksome problem.

The **halls** are interpreted as a range of guest quarters on the bases of the coins and food debris from the unoccupied ground to the north (pp 42, 160-2). They may also have been the source of scattered needles, knives, strap ends, dress pins and other personal ornaments from the same area (pp 363, 418-9). These finds argue against their use as barns or byres but are, perhaps, equally compatible with occupation by members of the ecclesiastical community.

The **small buildings**. The small buildings are of particular interest as they conform to two distinct traditions. They can, for example, be seen as a stage in an evolving sequence of small sub-rectilinear buildings at Whithorn, absorbing the current fashion of timber construction and opposed doorways. They can equally be viewed as an new design, directly modelled on the buildings at Hartlepool (pp 37-8,

Figure 2.8). The sequence of small buildings began in the closing years of **Period I** (pp 139-43), pointing to a phase of Northumbrian occupation before the appointment of Pecthelm and the transformation of the site (pp 139-43), and continued into **Period III**, when timber walling was superseded by wattle or wicker, a new pattern of internal features prevailed and a single doorway, still in the long wall, was held to suffice, and, perhaps, found less draughty. The finds from the small *Northumbrian* buildings were similar to those from the halls and did not help to identify their function.

Space and boundaries. The development of the northern part of the site evinced a long history of changing paths, barriers, gateways and enclosed spaces suggesting experimentation with the movement of people around and within the *inner precinct* (Figure 2.13). The excavated fragment is too small to identify the symbolic significance of these arrangements, but seems sufficiently strong to infer that there was one. The reports of three design consultants, who have aspired to enhance the facilities for visitors at Whithorn, offer an appropriate analogy for these attempts to identify the best point of entry, the most inspiring sequences of experiences, and the most profitable locations for tills and donation boxes.

The finds. The paucity of debris from the church, chapel and pathways indicates that the site was carefully maintained for most of the eighth century. Standards seem to have deteriorated in the ninth century and slipped further during the mid-ninth century crisis. As a result, artefacts and other debris were concentrated in the later deposits and generally reflect the specialised functions of this fragment of the *minster* and its component buildings. The coins (pp 332-44), window glass (pp 326-32) and 'chest coffins' (pp 412-5) have already been discussed briefly and are specifically Northumbrian or Anglo-Saxon in origin. The other main source of finds was the debris which was scattered on the unoccupied ground between the halls and the ecclesiastical buildings, which produced other diagnostic pieces including strap ends, and ball-headed pins from female head-dress (pp 363, 373-4). The assemblage shows no evidence of contacts beyond Northumbria, indicating that life within the enclave was thoroughly Northumbrian. Mid-ninth century deposits in the church included a small group of objects potentially relating to its ecclesiastical use, and a larger group of debris which had apparently accumulated after the fittings were removed (pp 162-4).

One of the most striking finds is a broken, cross-marked, sandstone vessel (SE14.9), perhaps a ritual *mortarium* for preparing the host (p 437). This object seems to have been imported from northern England and serves as a reminder of the paucity of Northumbrian sculptures from Whithorn. The large collection in the Priory Museum includes only four sculptures of the eighth or ninth centuries (Radford and Donaldson 1984, nos 4, 6, 10 and 36; Craig 1992, nos 3–6), and common Northumbrian forms and motifs such as free-armed cross heads and plant scroll sculpture are unrepresented in western Galloway (Craig 1992, 208). This may partly reflect the lack of suitable sandstones in this area, but perhaps also records the character of the local Northumbrian church and the ways in which it communicated its authority. A group of compass-drawn graffiti on paving leading to the chapel may have pertained to the latter part of **Period II** or the first two phases of **Period III** (pp 155, 439-41). These might have been inspired by seventh century arciform crosses, perhaps still displayed in the church, and there are related designs on two of the sculptures (Craig 1992, Nos 4 and 5 [/36]) in the Priory Museum. The Northumbrians may thus have adopted existing sculptures, along with other features of the earlier *monasterium*, developing these motifs in their own sculptures.

Environmental evidence. The Northumbrian layers produced two important groups of bones and seeds. A large group of animal bones, dumped between one of the halls and the terrace surrounding the church (pp 160-1, 607-8), included prime cuts of beef, haunches of roe venison, domestic fowl, geese and oysters. This might be viewed in several ways. It can, for example, be seen as a sample reflecting the regional diet of Galloway in the late-eighth/early-ninth century. It may, however, be argued that this was debris from a feast consumed in the adjacent hall. The species present, and in the case of cattle their age, correspond with the food renders specified by contemporary charters (p 608), and the animals may thus have been the produce of the ecclesiastical estate. Two groups of carbonised cereal grains from the floor of the church probably accumulated after the liturgical fittings had been removed. One deposit seems to have been the residue from sieving grain and the former chancel may have been used for grain processing, perhaps exploiting the draft through the opposed doorways to give an *ad hoc* winnowing floor. The second group from the nave comprised fully-processed grain. Six-rowed barley predominated in both samples. The associated weed species indicate the cultivation of a range of soils (pp 592-5), and the grain could have come from scattered fields on the estate, or from a large field encompassing varied soils. The level ground immediately to the west of the hill in the Fey Field (Figure 1.5) would, perhaps have produced these species. The ground beyond the church was ploughed at roughly the same time (pp 190-2), confirming that the pebble-studded mouldboard ploughs remained in use. Two unbroken millstones from a pit inside the church might have been buried ritually, or were, perhaps, hidden to deny the use of the mill to potential invaders (p 159). Fishbones include salmon, *Gadidae*, eel, herring and shark or ray (pp 602-3).

The economy. The excavation has exposed a specialised fragment of what seems to have been a highly-organised settlement, and the economic evidence is unlikely to be representative. There is thus little evidence of manufacture or trade for most of the period, while the bones and seeds may reflect atypical circumstances, though they are welcome witnesses to the ecclesiastical estates, and perhaps *demesne* fields surrounding the *minster*. The coins record a more sustained economic activity, and are interpreted as evidence of a contact zone between secular visitors and the ecclesiastical community (pp 352-5). The 'mortuary' chapel and healing cult suggest the quality of the transactions which may have taken place. Burial dues were an important element in the economies of early ecclesiastical centres, and the healing cult would, doubtless, have led to further payments. It is implicit in this interpretation that the lay visitors were accustomed to cash transactions and had the means to pay. This would suggest that coinage was already circulating within the Anglian enclaves of Galloway by the mid-eighth century, and this is supported by coin finds from Barhobble (Cormack 1990) and Luce Sands (Cormack 1965, Metcalf 1987, n 42).

Conclusions. The excavation has revealed a large fragment of the Northumbrian *minster*, which probably included a relatively unimportant part of the *inner precinct* of ecclesiastical buildings and what may have been part of the guest quarters. The construction of the *minster* was broadly contemporary with the appointment of the first Northumbrian bishop of *Candida Casa*, both indicating the establishment of an ecclesiastical bridgehead in western Britain. There is clear evidence in both the archaeological and historical records for the absorption and adaptation of pre-existing elements of the site and its traditions. The finds and the place-names in the surrounding countryside indicate that Whithorn lay within an enclave of Anglian settlement, and there is little evidence of contact with the neighbouring Britons. Similarly, though ideally located for commerce with Ireland, there was no evidence for Irish contacts, and the absence of Northumbrian coins from Irish sites (Metcalf 1992, 92–6) suggests this was a period of relative isolation. This contrasts with the seventh century when imports, such as E ware; motifs, such as arciform crosses; and ritual practices, such as log coffin burials, point to the active exchange of goods and ideas around the Irish Sea (p 37, e.g. Griffiths 1992, 63–5). This must cast doubt on the efficacy of Whithorn as a bridgehead, and its founders' original objectives may not have been achieved. The period ended in crisis and destruction, which almost certainly reflect the complex political circumstances of the mid-ninth century (pp 20-2).

Period III (*c*. 845–1000 x 1050 AD)

Period III records the restoration of the *monasterium* after the fire which marked the end of **Period II**, and encompasses subsequent developments over a period of some 150–200 years. There are no reliable contemporary records of Whithorn or Galloway in this period, although the continuing evolution of the region is reflected by a new stratum of Scandinavian place-names, a large and informative group of sculptures, and a smaller and rather less informative collection of portable artefacts. The principal debates about this undocumented period concern the fate of the ecclesiastical centre at Whithorn and the extent of Scandinavian and Gaelic influences. Some writers have concluded that Galloway was conquered by the Vikings and entered the second millennium as a Norse earldom, while others hold that Galloway was conquered by *Gall Gaidhil* of mixed Gaelic and Viking ancestry. This literature and the sparse evidence for a Norse earldom have been reviewed by Cowan (1991), who finds much confusion and little substance, while Brooke (1991a) has challenged the toponymic link between Galloway and the *Gall Gaidhil*. Both look towards the evidence from the excavation in the hope that it will throw new light upon an undoubtedly difficult period.

The excavation has made a major contribution to these debates, demonstrating that some ecclesiastical buildings were restored after the debacle of the mid-ninth century and that settlement continued throughout the undocumented period. This restored settlement provides a context for the sculptured crosses of the Whithorn School (pp 52-3), which in turn affirm ecclesiastical continuity, and support the identification of the settlement as a *minster* or *monasterium*. The finds include a handful of tenth century objects of Norse type, but these are too few to justify the claims of Viking dominion, while specifically Irish material is sparse until the end of the period. The most significant group of material was, perhaps, the waste from the manufacture of antler combs, which appeared at the start of the period and continued to accumulate until the late twelfth century. The production of combs is generally considered to be an urban industry (pp 474, 493) and, while other evidence for manufacture and trade in **Period III** was sparse, this marks an important stage in the development of Whithorn as a monastic town.

Period III encompassed three principal phases of activity (Figures 2.14–16), each sub-divided into several episodes (Chapter 5). **Phase 1** (Figure 2.14) saw the reconstruction of the chapel and the erection of a new timber church on a stone plinth to the west. This restoration may have extended to other ecclesiastical buildings in the *inner precinct* of the Northumbrian *minster*, which is outlined on the phase drawing. The low-lying ground was, by now, flooded and a new settlement of small sub-rectilinear wattle buildings was erected on the level higher ground to the south of the church and chapel. The church was demolished at the beginning of **Phase 2** (Figure 2.15) and a cluster of wattle buildings was erected over its remains, while new, slightly smaller buildings replaced the **Phase 1** structures to the south. The demolition of the church suggests that the ritual complex had contracted and it may have been reorganised. The organisation of the settlement was transformed in **Phase 3** (Figure 2.16). The new settlement comprised a densely-packed band of buildings, running across the excavated area at 45° to the former *Northumbrian* buildings, and enclosed by successive discontinuous shallow ditches, which might have been associated with boundary hedges. These seem to delimit the perimeter of a new curvilinear enclosure centred on the west end of the hill, which survived, much adapted, until the end of **Period IV**, and restored the curvilinear *inner precinct* and concentric *outer zone* of the **Period I** *monasterium*.

The inferred principal church and founder's shrine lie beyond the projected line of the enclosure and may have been excluded intentionally from the *inner precinct* of the new *monasterium*. The **Phase 3** remains might therefore mark a double rejection of the physical structure of the *Northumbrian minster* and of the carefully-articulated cult of Bishop Nynia

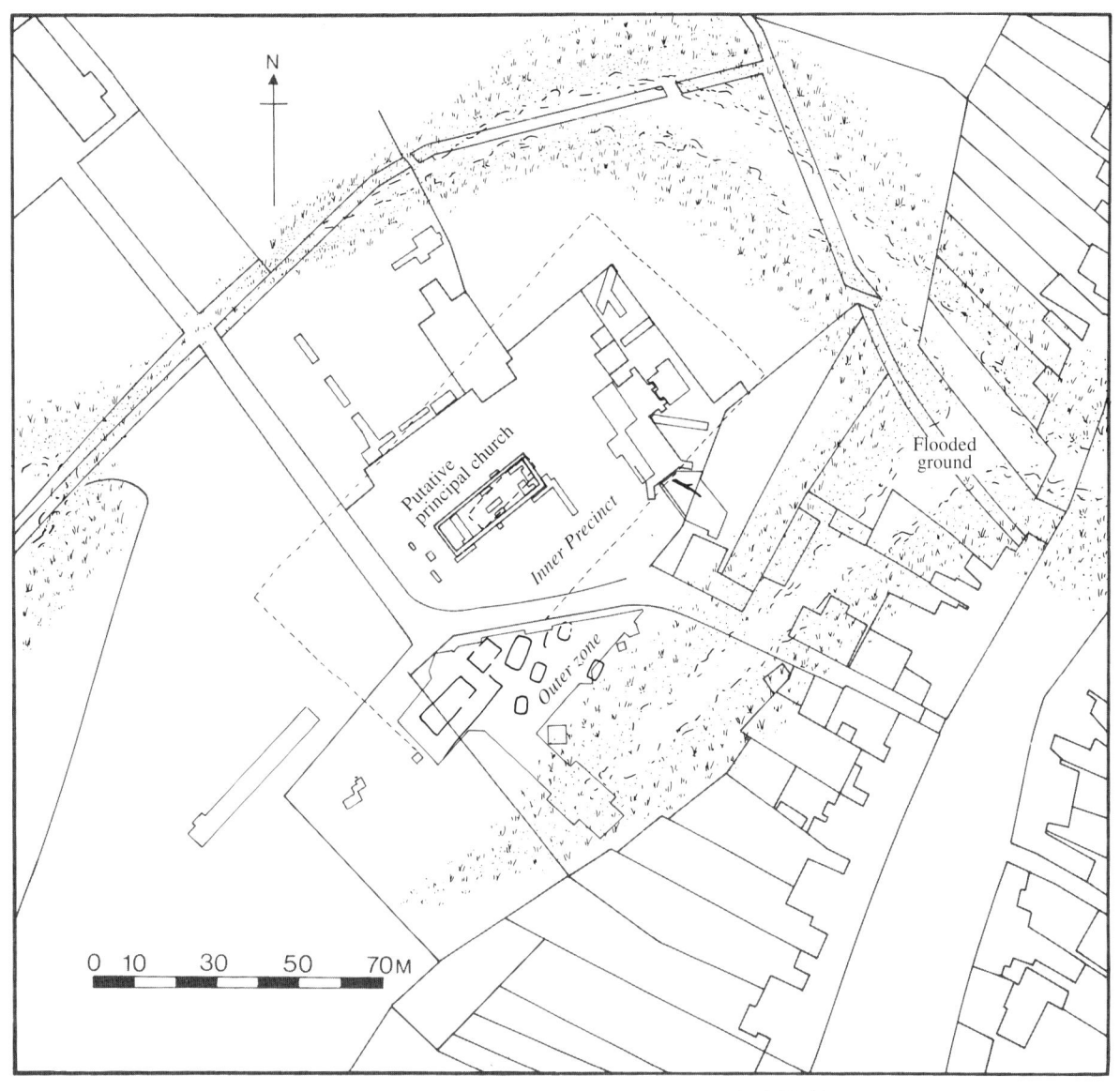

2.14 General plan of the restored *minster* in the later-ninth century (**Period III/1**).

transmitted by *Northumbrian* authors. The beginning of **Phase 3** is therefore the logical conclusion to the history of *Northumbrian* Whithorn, and indicates a possible political watershed in the affairs of Galloway (pp 23-4, 54-5).

The beginning of the **Period III** was dated with considerable precision to the mid-ninth century (pp 136, 354), but the chronology of subsequent developments was problematical and there is no sure evidence for dating the transition to **Period IV**. A securely-stratified ring pin dates **Phase 2** to the early- to mid-tenth century (pp 369, 623), and an insecurely-stratified coin hints that this phase may have ended in the late tenth century (p 198). This implies that **Phase 3** pertained to the later-tenth/earlier-eleventh century. The number of *stages* of rebuilding and other activity encompassed by the period offer tenuous support for this imperfect chronology.

The small buildings were broadly similar to those built in **Period I**, but they were distinguished by details of construction and the arrangement of internal features. There were two principal types of building. One group had earth floors and were generally without hearths, and the other displayed a wider range of fittings including paving, pits, and hearths associated with large posts. The hearth lay close to the back of the building, abutting its transverse axis, with paving and a pit in the same half of the floor. Comb-making debris was restricted to specific buildings in the **central sector**, while the larger **Phase 2** buildings in the **northern sector** produced several spindle whorls and a slightly greater number of ornaments and personal items. These differences of design and debris probably reflect the functions of the buildings, and of different parts of the site, but are insufficient to distinguish between male or female; clerical or monastic; or

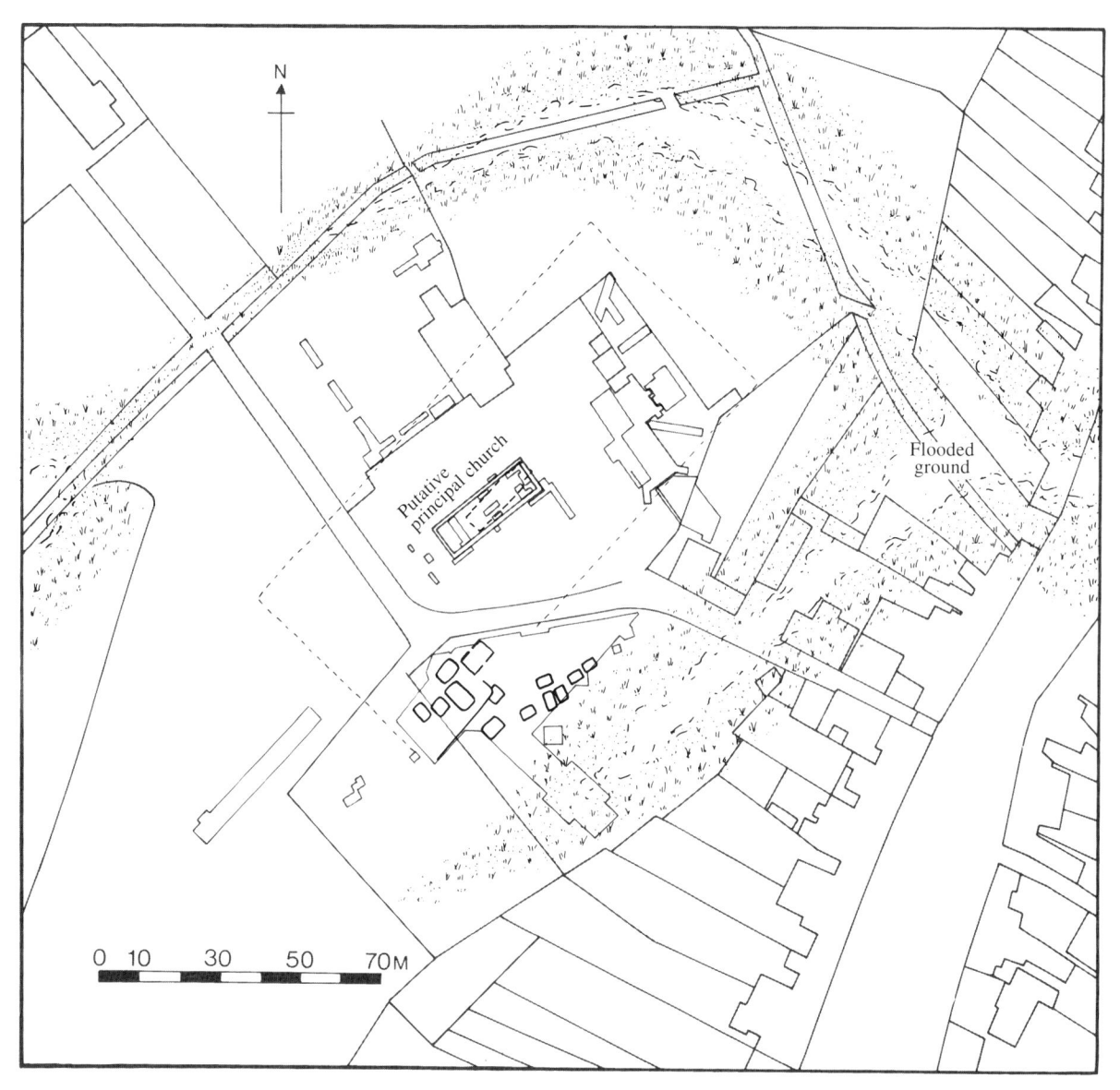

2.15 General plan of the restored *minster* in the tenth century (**Period III/2**).

secular and ecclesiastical occupation. The **Period IV** buildings were different in design (pp 55-6, 216-7), and the evidence for an Anglo-British alliance in **Period III** (p 52) suggests the **Period III** houses may have been 'Anglo-British', perhaps combining elements of the small buildings of **Periods I** and **II**.

The finds. The **Period III** buildings produced relatively small, specialised and somewhat austere groups of finds, but debris scattered on the southern margin of the settlement produced a wider range of materials, including ironworking debris and animal bones. The **Period III** deposits had been severely disturbed by later buildings and graves, and many significant finds from this time (indicated with an * in the following account) had been displaced into later contexts. These, and the relatively small group of securely stratified objects, revealed a surprisingly clear picture of the evolving economic and cultural influences affecting the *monasterium*. Early deposits produced a final group of stycas indicating continuing contact with Northumbria for a decade or so after the fire, but the latest issues in the styca series were scarce, suggesting that this had diminished some time before the fall of York to the Danes in 867 AD. The coins are the only overtly Northumbrian objects, and other characteristic items such as dress pins seem to have been replaced with new types at the start of **Period III**. The sole exception is a copper-alloy strap end (BZ19.6), politely-described as 'devolved', which may have been made in the neighbourhood in emulation of the earlier Northumbrian pieces. The only Anglo-Scandinavian objects are fragments of two ninth century antler combs* (AR70.2 and 3, pp 482-3) and two broken glass finger rings* of tenth century type (GS05.5 and 6). Specifically Norse objects comprise a tenth century needle case*

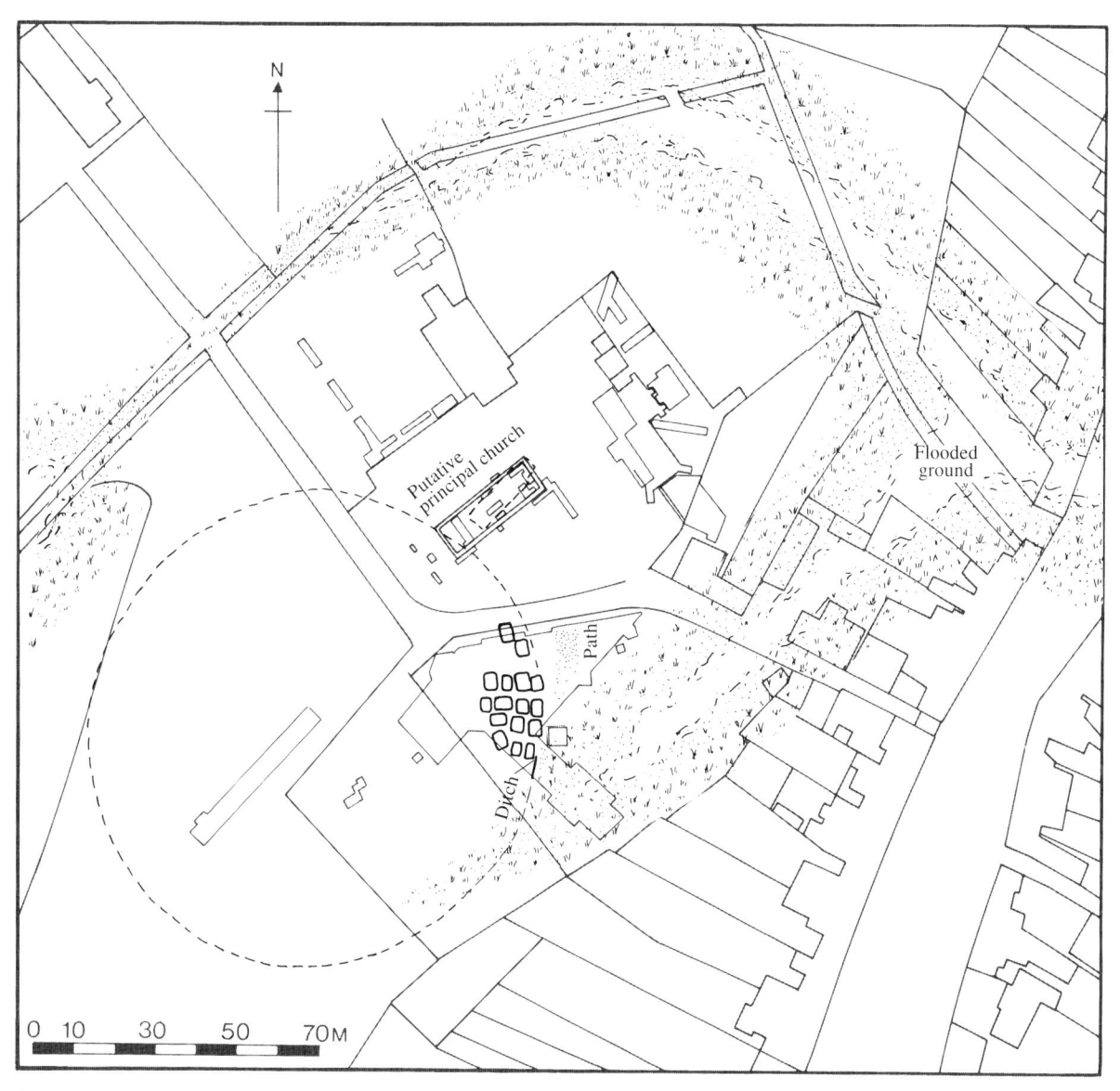

2.16 General plan of the replanned *monasterium* of **Period III/3**, perhaps dating to the later-tenth or earlier-eleventh century.

(BZ30.62), a fragment of a steatite bowl (SE50.14), an ornamental weight* probably of the tenth century (LD5.16), a fishing weight of tenth/eleventh century type (SE50.10), a piece of silver ring money of the later- tenth/eleventh century (SR17), and a copper alloy strip with Ringerike-style decoration of the mid-eleventh century (BZ35.9). An early tenth century buckle* (BZ18.4) displays 'Celtic' features, but the *comparanda* are mostly from pagan Norse burials, and were perhaps made for Norse patrons by Celtic craftsmen (pp 621-3). This group of buckles is closely linked to a leather offcut* (LR16.1) with incised designs on both sides, which may have been a craftsman's trial piece (pp 502, 621). An unfinished, hammer-headed cross slab* of the tenth/eleventh century (SE14.7) has similar Gaelic- or Celtic-Norse affinities (Bailey 1980, 182-3), although the Wigtownshire examples (p 436) do not coincide with known areas of Scandinavian settlement. These pieces are distinct from a slightly later group of Irish/Norse objects including a series of ring pins spanning the tenth-twelfth centuries (pp 369-70), a Tafl board* (SE23.3), and a finely-carved antler handle* of the tenth/eleventh century (AR74.14). Specifically Irish objects were relatively rare, comprising a needle-headed ring pin (BZ15.4) from the start of **Period III**, a knobbed ball-headed pin* (BZ13.5) dating to the later tenth/early eleventh century, and a small group of Souterrain-Ware sherds, probably pertaining to **Phase 3** (pp 201, 358). A tenth century buckle with stylised animal head terminals* (BZ18.6) could also be Irish, although 'Insular' is a safer classification. The most significant finds are the decorated leather off-cut, the hammer-headed cross and the Tafl board, which were probably made at Whithorn, as they are unlikely trade goods. The

Souterrain Ware was, perhaps, too unlovely to have been traded, and suggests the presence of Ulstermen during **Phase 3**.

These diagnostic artefacts indicate continuing Anglian and Anglo-Scandinavian contacts in the later-ninth and, perhaps, earlier-tenth centuries with Scandinavian influence in the tenth century, but not apparently before. The leather offcut and hammer-headed cross indicate that 'Celtic/Norse' craftsmen were working at Whithorn in the tenth century (pp 621-3). The gradual appearance of Irish and Irish/Norse finds in the later- tenth century marks a new zone of contact which lasted until the end of **Period IV**. This picture of evolving cultural contacts contrasts with the continuity evident in the design of the buildings, which indicates a stable population developing without strong influences from elsewhere, and argues against the intrusion of new ethnic groups. The gradual shift towards Irish/Norse objects and the late appearance of specifically Irish material is potentially significant, and may be correlated cautiously with the organisational changes of **Phase 3**.

Other finds reveal changing customs and new economic contacts, but are less culturally specific. These include amber beads, which appear towards the beginning of **Period III**, and indicate long range contact with the Baltic (p 359). Beads, still awaiting specialist study, indicate further Irish and Scandinavian links. Grooved, smoothed and incised slabs (SE54) seem to have been standard domestic equipment (pp 467-8), while querns reappear, indicating that food was no longer prepared, nor perhaps eaten, communally (pp 459-60). The absence of plough pebbles may, similarly, mark the end of communal cultivation (pp 466). The animal bones dumped beyond the settlement (Tables 11.54-5) show a similar range of species to the *Northumbrian* samples, although without the prime young beef enjoyed previously (Table 11.58).

The evidence of sculptures and place-names offers a useful supplement to the information from the excavation. The distinctive sculptures of the 'Whithorn School' of crosses present valuable and relatively-uncontroversial evidence of a new pattern of ecclesiastical organization in the Machars, and of a high-status burial ground at Whithorn itself. Their cultural and chronological implications are more problematical and must be discussed before their other ramifications can be explored. It is generally agreed that these sculptures were designed and manufactured at Whithorn in the tenth and, perhaps, earlier-eleventh centuries, and incorporate a range of features paralleled in northern England (Craig 1992 *passim*). They reveal a mastery of interlaced ornament derived from Hiberno-Saxon patterns, while the use of monumental slabs is essentially a western British trait. In his classic study of the sculptures of Galloway, Collingwood rose to the challenge posed by these diverse 'cultural' features, suggesting that the 'Whithorn master' had been apprenticed in Derbyshire (specifically at Bakewell) before taking over the workshop of an Anglo-Cumbric sculptor at Whithorn (1923, 220-1). Others have remarked the absence of a range of forms and designs commonly used in Viking Age sculptures of northern England and the Isle of Man (e.g. Craig 1991, 51), and view these sculptures as a pre-eminently western British phenomenon rooted in the tradition of slab monuments.[1] Craig has followed Simpson in seeing a link in the design of the disk-heads of these sculptures with the cross-of-arcs on the *Petrus* stone (p 441, Appendix 1). The new finds of seventh century arciform crosses and the potentially-imitative ninth century *graffiti* reveal the importance and endurance of these designs at Whithorn and would seem to strengthen this case. The distribution of the sculptures spans areas of British and Anglian settlement, which commends the view that they mark the fusion of British and Anglian features with the potent cross-of-arcs design, which had proclaimed Whithorn's Christianity for some three hundred years. Despite the stylistic links with north-western England, this 'school' is in essence *sui generis*, and the sculptures seem to mark a phase of independent development in the Machars, aware of the world beyond; influenced by it, perhaps, but definitely not led.

The chronology of the sculptures depends upon art-historical considerations, and few scholars will commit themselves to close dating. It is, however, reasonable to assume that the sculptures record a developing school of work spanning some fifty or more years and centred upon the mid- to late-tenth century (p 623). This imprecise chronology corresponds with the equally-imprecise dating of the **Period III** remains, but we can still speculate that the *floruit* of the sculptures corresponds broadly with **Phase 2**, possibly extending into **Phase 3**, but not, perhaps, into **Period IV**.

There are roughly twenty crosses of this type from Whithorn (Craig 1992, 212) and comparable concentrations of Viking Age sculptures, notably at Govan, Llantwit Major and Merttiyr Mawr (Davies 1994) have been interpreted as evidence for lay patronage of favoured churches, reflected by expensive high-status graveyard monuments. It is not immediately clear why a burst of lay patronage should have caused the contraction of the ecclesiastical buildings evident in **Phase 2**, unless the western part of the *inner precinct* was cleared to accommodate new burials and the associated prestigious monuments.

The outlying crosses of the Whithorn School are confined to the Machars (Figure 2.17), but extend into the western parts of the area, which were still probably occupied and ruled by British kindreds. Craig (1992, 212–4) has demonstrated that these broadly coincide with later parish centres, and argues that they marked churches of the estate centres attached to a collegiate *minster* at Whithorn, possibly with the rights of baptism and burial. The cross slabs may thus record the establishment of burial rights on private estates, acting as burial licences issued to

---

[1] This carries the authority of Professor Rosemary Cramp in an unpublished lecture to the Friends of the Whithorn Trust in 1987

A

Meikle Laight

● Anglian place-names
■ Scandinavian place-names

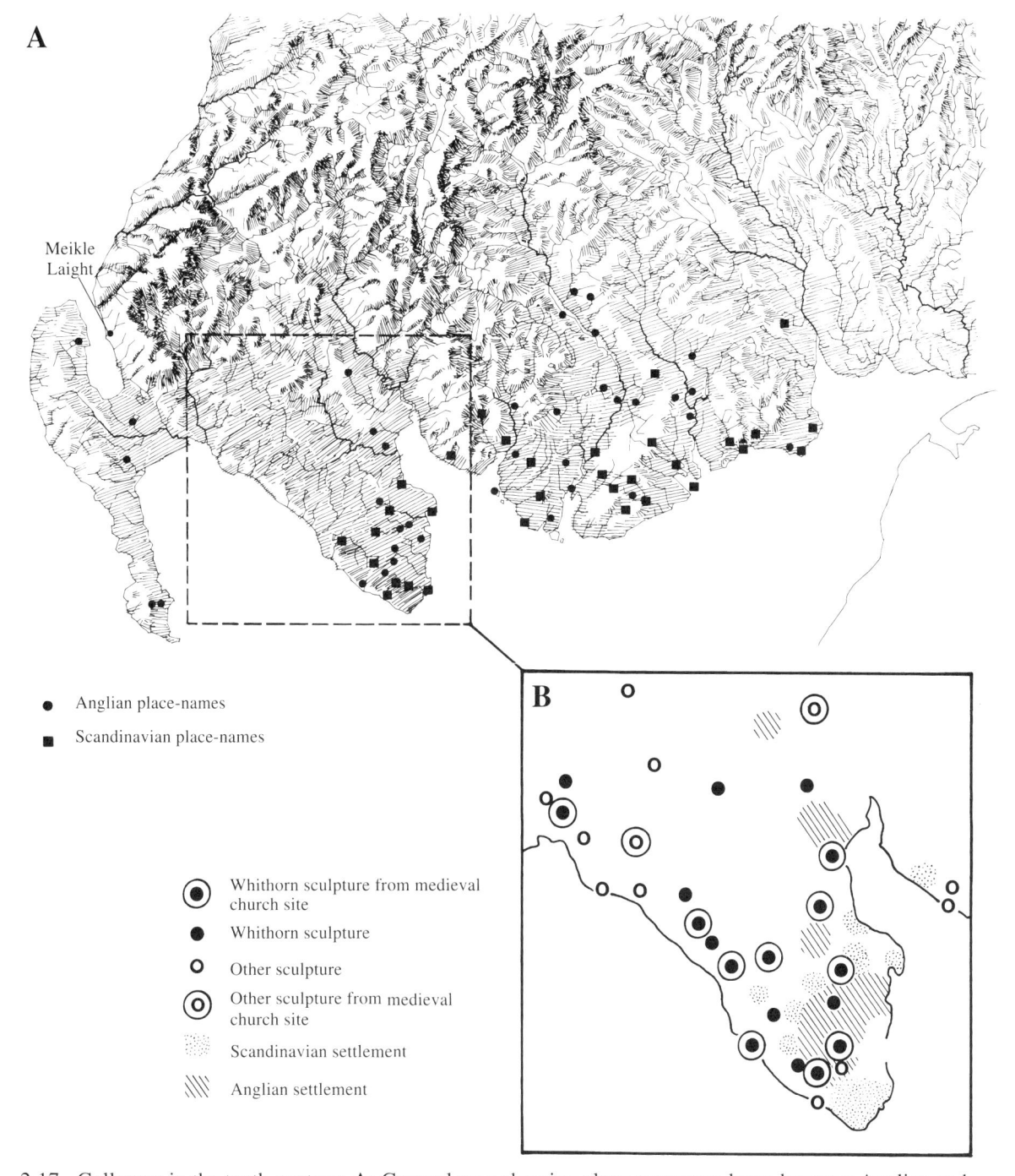

B

⊙ Whithorn sculpture from medieval church site
● Whithorn sculpture
○ Other sculpture
⊚ Other sculpture from medieval church site
⋮ Scandinavian settlement
▨ Anglian settlement

2.17 Galloway in the tenth century. **A**: General map showing close correspondence between Anglian and Scandinavian place-names (after Brooke 1991c). **B**: The Machars showing approximate areas of Anglian and Scandinavian settlement, and locations of sculptures (after Craig 1991).

dependencies by the centre of ecclesiastical administration in the area. This presents a strong argument that the episcopal succession had continued after the crisis of the mid-ninth century (pp 20-2, 40), as the duties of a bishop specified in canon law include the consecration of priests and chrism, and the dedication of churches and burial grounds. The south Machars must therefore have been served by a bishop from elsewhere (Oram 1991, 83–4), or else we must infer, following Barrow (1981, 67), that the ancient line of bishops was maintained. A place-name on the mainland adjacent to the Isle of Whithorn gives valuable support. Surviving today as Bysbie Mill and Bysbie Cottage, medieval name forms include *Biskeby* (1305, CDS ii) and *Biscobu* (1466, CPL xii), preserving Old Norse *biscop-byr*, the Bishop's farm (Brooke 1991c, 322; 1995). This name was probably coined in the later-ninth or tenth century, and points to a settlement of Norse speakers in the immediate vicinity. This Bishop's farm occupied a strategic site controlling trade and other contacts with the world beyond, and is the earliest evidence of the territorial link between Whithorn and the Isle, inferentially operating from the early-sixth century (p 6).

Other place-names reveal limited settlement by Scandinavians in the Machars in about 900 AD (Fellowes-Jensen 1991; Brooke 1991c, 321–3; 1995, Hill 1991a). Most of these lie on the fringes of the Anglophone *Northumbrian* enclave around Whithorn (pp 16-8, Figure 1.8) and occupy some of the best land in the area (Figure 2.17). The Scandinavian settlements seem too sparse to have been won by conquest, and the settlers may thus have been mercenaries brought in to defend the enclave and coastal belt. The inferred history of the *Northumbrian* enclave (pp 17, 47) and the proximity of the new settlements to Whithorn suggest that this political decision was taken by the ecclesiastical authorities, but perhaps at the expense of the Anglian farmers who may have surrendered some of their best land. Fellowes-Jensen has argued that the settlers were Danes and ascribes their arrival to the period between the visit of the Lindisfarne refugees in *c*. 882 AD (pp 21-2) and the treaty of 927 AD between King Athelstan and the Scots and Strathclyde Britons (1991, 80). The finds from Whithorn are, perhaps, slightly later and more Norse than Danish, but are fully compatible with Scandinavian settlement in the earlier- tenth century. Craig has noted that there are no sculptures of the Whithorn School in the south-eastern coastal parishes of the south Machars (1991, Fig. 4.6) and these gaps may have coincided with areas of Scandinavian settlement (Figure 2.17). If so we may speculate that the mercenaries remained pagan, and this could explain a layer of cremated human bones deposited beside the east wall of the chapel towards the end of **Phase 1** (p 189), and an earlier burial of disarticulated human remains (pp 559-60). Both are reminiscent of the broadly-contemporary pagan Viking burial at St Cuthbert's church in Kirkcudbright and of related finds from parish churchyards at Michael, Braddan, Maughold, Malew and Jurby on the Isle of Man (Scott 1983).

Conclusions. The archaeological evidence of reconstruction and continuing occupation, supported by sculptural and other evidence presented above, refutes the impression given by the failure of the historical records, which led William of Malmesbury and subsequent historians to conclude that this marginal centre had been extinguished. Whithorn almost certainly survived as an ecclesiastical centre, and circumstantial evidence argues that the episcopal succession was maintained throughout the undocumented period. The distribution of the sculptures of the Whithorn School suggests that the authority of Whithorn, though strong and with considerable local support, was now confined to the Machars. Comparable groupings of sculptures around Gatehouse of Fleet, Kirkcudbright and Carsphairn identify three other individualistic ecclesiastical centres within the former *Northumbrian* diocese (Craig 1991 Fig. 4.3). Kirkcudbright survived as a 'celticised *minster*' or collegiate church until *c*. 1160 AD (pp 23-4), and there may have been similar isolated institutions in the other districts.

The artefacts present a picture of evolving cultural contacts, but there is no evidence of major ethnic changes during **Period III**. The beginning of the period was, however, marked by radical changes in the material culture and economy of the site, which suggest that a new alliance was forged after the mid-ninth century crisis to restore the Northumbrian *minster* and preserve its endowments. The Anglian farmers and the survivors of the ecclesiastical community must have been among the parties involved, as their language survived phonetically until the high middle ages, while the coins show continuing *Northumbrian* contact after the crisis. They may not, however, have been the dominant partner, as the Scandinavian settlers were probably granted some of their best land. The chronology of these new settlements remains uncertain and there is no evidence for them before the tenth century, but the Scandinavians may still be seen as partners in the defence of the Machars and, possibly, patrons of the craftsmen working at Whithorn. The sculptures of the 'Whithorn School' indicate a resurgence of British culture and argue that the Britons, still occupying their ancient territories around the Anglian enclave, had reasserted themselves. The handful of exotic objects from the excavation must be viewed against the background of this strong evidence of indigenous control, and the Britons were perhaps the dominant partner in the alliance.

Craig has identified one stone – Whithorn 8 (Radford and Donaldson 1984, No. 7) – as the prototype of the Whithorn School. This straight-shafted, disk-headed cross with keyhole armpits is decorated with narrow-band interlace, on one side only. Craig argues that this was a major monument, which had been set up in a prominent position against a wall (1992, 217–8). Taking this argument a stage further, we may interpret this cross as a powerful cultural statement by the new alliance encompassing the western British tradition of slab monuments and an Anglian talent for interlace, and reinterpreting the cross-of-arcs design from Whithorn's past.

Collingwood believed that the Whithorn sculptures indicated a period of peace and prosperity in the Machars (1923, 226–7), and this is endorsed by the apparent stability of the evolving **Period III** settlement and the hints of urban trade evinced by antler waste and other finds. The piece of ring money and a coin of Eadgar (p 335) show that Whithorn participated in the bullion economy of the Irish Sea province in the tenth century, but not seemingly in its wars, which left hoards of unretrieved bullion and coins scattered over eastern central Ireland and north-western England (Graham-Campbell 1992; Dolley 1966, Map 3). Troubles are more readily identified in the later-ninth century when the deposition of the Talnotry hoard *c*. 875 AD (Graham-Campbell 1992, 111; 1976, 118, 127) hints at unrest, perhaps also manifested by the burning of buildings at Whithorn at the end of **Phase 1.4** (pp 184-5).

The transformation of the restored *minster* in

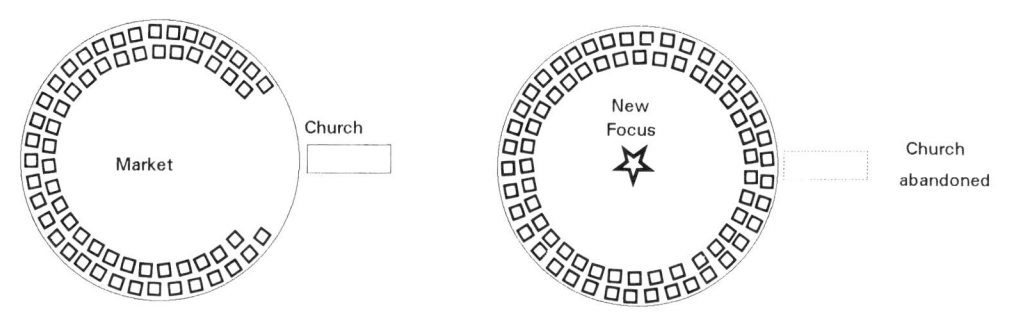

2.18 Alternative models for the organization of the **Period III/3** *monasterium*.

Phase 3 perhaps followed the *floruit* of the Whithorn School sculptures and, on the slim evidence of the Souterrain Ware and related finds (pp 51), may reflect the Irish influence, which seems to have prevailed in **Period IV** (pp 55-6). There seem to be two ways of interpreting the new *monasterium* (Figure 2.18). It might, for example, have followed a new plan in which the residential buildings were grouped around a market or *plataea*, intentionally sited to the west of the church and founder's tomb, in accord with the model proposed by Herity (p 34, 1984). It might, equally, reflect a return to the design of the **Period I** *monasterium*, but with a new ritual focus lying to the west of the original centre. In both instances it is reasonable to infer that the new design was essentially 'Celtic' and, potentially, Irish. A similar pattern has been noted by Hamlin on at least two sites in Ulster (Devenish and Movilla, Yates 1983, 54–5), and Souterrain Ware is concentrated in eastern Ulster (Edwards 1990, 73–5), as are possible parallels for the sub-square buildings of **Period IV** (below). Ulster – and specifically Counties Down and Antrim – is thus an attractive source for the new organisational ideology apparent in **Phase 3**, although the evidence of the buildings argues that it was adopted by the extant Anglo-British community rather than being imposed by new settlers.[2]

The **Period III** sequence is of vital importance to the history of Galloway, representing the first part of the archaeological bridge which now spans the undocumented centuries. It is of equal significance in providing a coherent context for the sculptures of the 'Whithorn School', which hold the key, however obscure, to the culture and aspirations of the Machars in the tenth century. Together they proffer a picture of independence and prosperity, which must be recognised by historians of this dynamic period of state formation.

Period IV (*c.* 1000 x 1050–1250 x 1300)

Period IV saw a major expansion of the **Period III/3** *monasterium*, which was initiated and facilitated by draining the flooded ground to the south, east and north. New buildings erected on the reclaimed ground and on the slightly higher ground to the east adhered to the extant curvilinear plan and were probably bounded by a new enclosure – perhaps a hedge – lying slightly beyond the excavated area in the **Glebe Field**, but passing through the **Museum Garden** trench where pits and a cobbled road marked a possible boundary. The earlier enclosure now formed the *inner precinct* and was approached by radial paths leading from the buildings in the *outer zone*. It was left open for most of this phase and abundant finds suggest that it was used *inter alia* as a market.

Period IV spans roughly two hundred years from the eleventh century until the mid- to later-thirteenth century, and encompasses the early-twelfth century horizon when Galloway re-emerges from historical obscurity after almost three hundred years of silence. Unsurprisingly the region's affairs had been transformed in the intervening period, and a strong, possibly dominant, Gaelic element had been added to the alliance of Northumbrians, Britons and Scandinavians, which seems to have maintained the independence of the region until the early-eleventh century. The **Period IV** remains were subtly different to those of **Period III**, revealing marked Hiberno-Norse, though still potentially Gaelic, characteristics. The buildings were, again, the critical indicator and, though still small and constructed of wattle or wicker, evinced a new shape and new internal plan, marking the end of the long sequence of sub-rectilinear buildings originating in the late-fifth/early-sixth century. The new buildings were sub-square,[3] with a single doorway in the gable wall connected by paving to a hearth in the middle of the floor. The best-preserved of these buildings (IV/7) is strikingly similar to one of the building types from Hiberno-Norse Dublin (Murray 1983), though somewhat smaller. The shape, size and internal arrangements of the buildings are matched closely at Whitefort, County Down (Waterman 1956a), and comparable, though larger, structures have been excavated at Ballywee (Lynn

---

[2] Whithorn was for a long time believed to have been the town of *Hvitsborg* visited by Kari Solmundarsson after the battle of Clontarf (1014; Magnusson and Palsson 1960). This does not really work and Whitburgh, Berwickshire is a better candidate (Hill 1991a, 41): sadly so, as the **Period III/3** *monasterium* is of approximately the right date.

[3] Sub-square is, perhaps, a new and unfamiliar term. It is used here to describe a more-or-less square building with rounded corners.

1974) and Craig Hill, County Antrim (Waterman 1956b). This suggests the general direction from which the new influence came and is supported by the artefacts, which include series of stick-pins and combs, closely or exactly paralleled at Dublin and other Irish sites (pp 364-7, 480-5). It is unsafe to push these parallels too far, as the *corpus* of Irish material is dominated by the rich finds from Dublin, while there are few equivalent Scottish sites with comparable eleventh-twelfth century buildings and assemblages of artefacts. The small size of all the buildings distinguishes them from most of the parallels on Irish sites, and perhaps reflects social contrasts between the putatively-ecclesiastical inhabitants of Whithorn and the secular communities in Ireland.

The strong archaeological indications of Hiberno-Norse influence conform with documentary evidence, which shows extensive use of Gaelic personal and place-names in the twelfth and thirteenth centuries, while the dedication of churches to Columban saints reveals a new association between Galloway and Iona. The introduction of Gaelic place-names has been ascribed to the tenth-eleventh century on linguistic grounds (Jackson 1958, 277–9), while Brooke argues that the new Columban dedications date to the eleventh century (Brooke 1995). This Gaelic horizon thus corresponds reasonably closely with the organisational changes of **Period III/3** and the cultural change at the beginning of **Period IV**. Gaelic influence is thus a predictable feature of this period, although it is somewhat surprising that the archaeological evidence should be so markedly Irish. The most unexpected aspects of **Period IV** are, however, the lack of any clear evidence for the impact of the ecclesiastical reforms of the twelfth century, and the apparent survival of a pre-reform community into the later-thirteenth century. The explanation for the apparent conflict between the historical evidence of reform and archaeological evidence of continuity, probably lies with the increasing evidence of commerce as the settlement evolved and, perhaps, with the conservatism now evident in western Galloway (pp 22-4). Thus, what may, in the eleventh century, have been a monastic community, supplementing its income from the manufacture of combs, had developed by the late twelfth century into an industrious trading centre with specialised craft quarters grouped around a central market place. These commercial interests were perhaps so strong that the inhabitants were prepared to thole the reformation of the church as long as their tenurial and mercantile privileges were not infringed. It may seem perverse to term this apparently commercial community a monastery, but the settlement conformed to the pre-existing 'monastic' design, and a continuing, if undocumented, role as a cult centre, perhaps brought trade to an otherwise unlikely site for a market. This evidence of commerce invites the identification of the **Period IV** settlement as a *monastic town*, which displays a range of urban characteristics, while maintaining the physical organisation of a monastery. The *outer zone* was depopulated at the end of **Period IV**, and the displaced inhabitants may have been resettled beyond the ecclesiastical precinct. A new settlement is dimly visible as the *Clachan* of Alexander III's reign (1249–86 AD), before re-emerging as the Burgh of *Wyterne* in the early fourteenth century (p 7).

The cathedral. The high medieval cathedral dates to the mid-twelfth century, and was probably constructed under the patronage of Fergus of Galloway (p 22) in emulation of new churches built by royal patrons elsewhere. It was thus an important element in the organisation of the settlement during the later stages of **Period IV**, and is illustrated in Figure 2.21, which reconstructs the monastic town in the later-twelfth century. The church lies in the *outer zone* fitting neatly between the projected lines of the inner and outer boundaries. This may have been a coincidence as it occupies the inferred site of the tomb of St Ninian (p 20), and perhaps replaced an extant building of which no trace has yet been recognised. It may however reflect renewed reverence for the shrine, which lay beyond the perimeter of the **Period III/3** monastery, and may thus no longer have been central to the life of the community (pp 54-5).

Little survives of the twelfth century cathedral, which was extensively remodelled in the thirteenth century, but it seems to have been a simple cruciform church with a short nave (Radford 1957, 146–50). Radford has cited the churches of Penmon, Anglesey; Bangor; St Mary on the Rocks, St Andrews and Killaloe, Co. Clare as parallels, commenting:

> These indications point to a building of a type widely adopted in the twelfth and early thirteenth centuries as the principal church of those Celtic communities which had avoided assimilation into one of the reformed Orders and retained their status as houses of secular canons or collegiate churches. These churches were often cruciform with a short nave which might be either aisleless, as here, or aisled. They often have a disproportionately long eastern arm in which the stalls of the canons' quire seem to have been placed.
>
> (Radford 1957, 184)

This observation accords well with the new evidence and hints that the new church was designed to meet the needs of the existing 'monastic' community rather than the somewhat different requirements of the reformed church. The latter were probably reflected by subsequent modifications. The eastern arm of the church was probably extended *c*. 1200 to provide for the elaborate rituals and quire liturgies of the Premonstratensian canons, while the underlying crypts were perhaps designed for the veneration of St Ninian's relics (Fawcett 1985, 89–90). The nave was extended at an unknown date in the thirteenth century, presumably to accommodate the enlarged secular congregation from the nascent town (Figure 2.22).

The evolving plan of the monastic town in **Period IV** can be summarised in two drawings (Figures

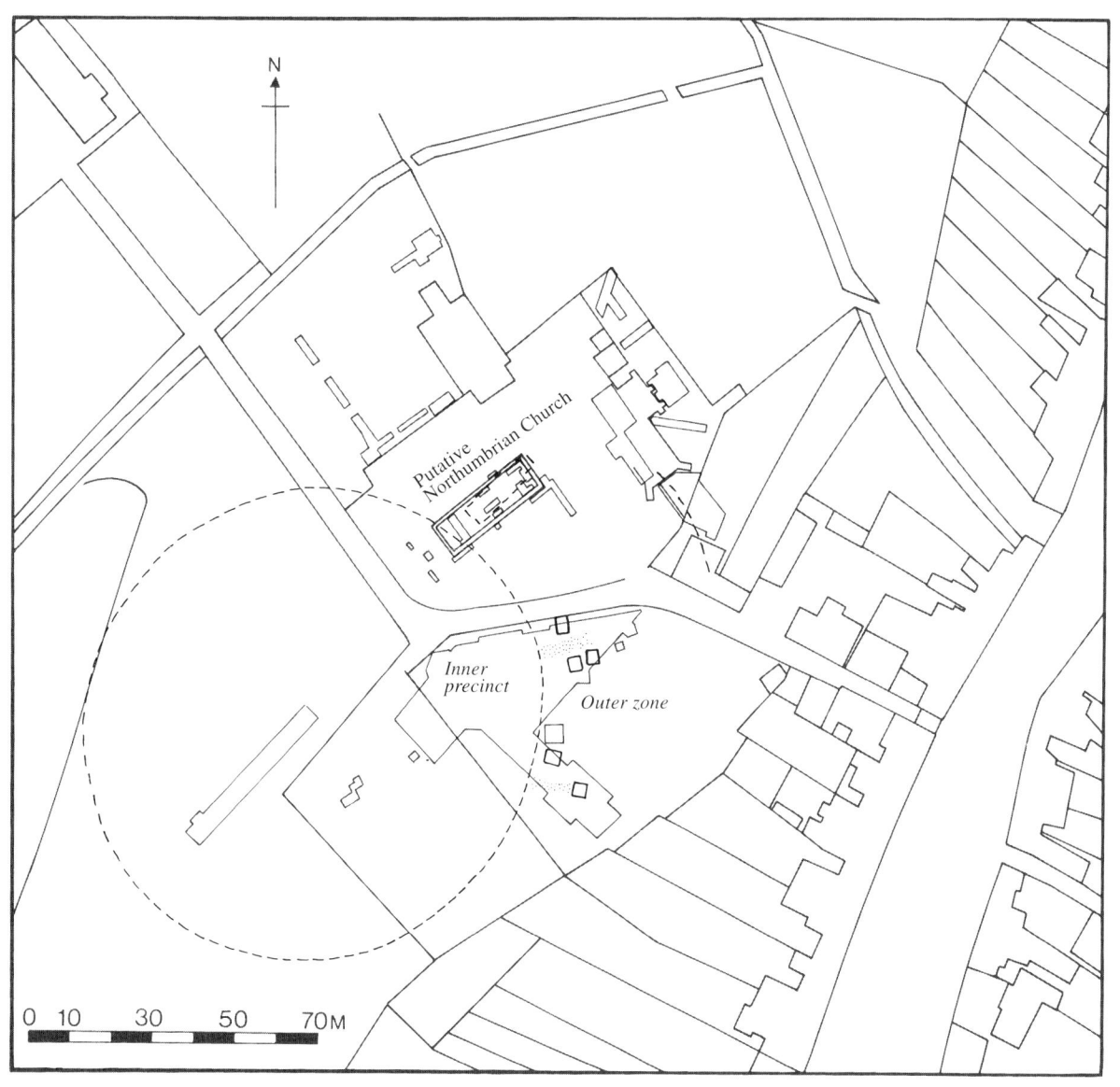

2.19 General plan of the **Period IV** settlement in the later-eleventh or earlier-twelfth century.

2.19 and 20), despite the far fuller structural sequences described in Chapter 6. Figure 2.19 shows the settlement in the later-eleventh century following the drainage and reoccupation of the flooded ground at the foot of the hill. The small buildings in the *outer zone* are linked by radial paths to the new *inner precinct*, which corresponds with the **Period III/3** enclosure, and may still have been delimited by a hedge. The outline of the inferred, principal, *Northumbrian* church is included, but it may have been ruinous at this time. The *outer zone* contains sufficient room for some 120–150 buildings and so corresponds with the numbers of buildings recorded on broadly contemporary Irish sites (p 34).

Figure 2.20 shows the settlement in the early-thirteenth century after the construction of the church and the renewed flooding of the lowlying ground in the later-twelfth century (p 224). Settlement has expanded temporarily into the *inner precinct*, perhaps due to pressures on space caused by the flooding of parts of the *outer zone*, and now extends into the **Fey Field**. The outer boundary would have been partly flooded, and the inner boundary may have fallen into disuse. This phase ended with the burning of the buildings (p 224), and the settlement subsequently reverted to the earlier pattern with the *inner precinct* left unoccupied.

Figure 2.21 shows a speculative reconstruction of the monastic town at about the same time. The Romanesque cathedral is still under construction, and is surrounded by an encampment for the builders, and the necessary workshops. The shape of the earlier *monasterium* is nevertheless still clearly visible, and the former pattern of life continues relatively unaffected by the new construction programme. The

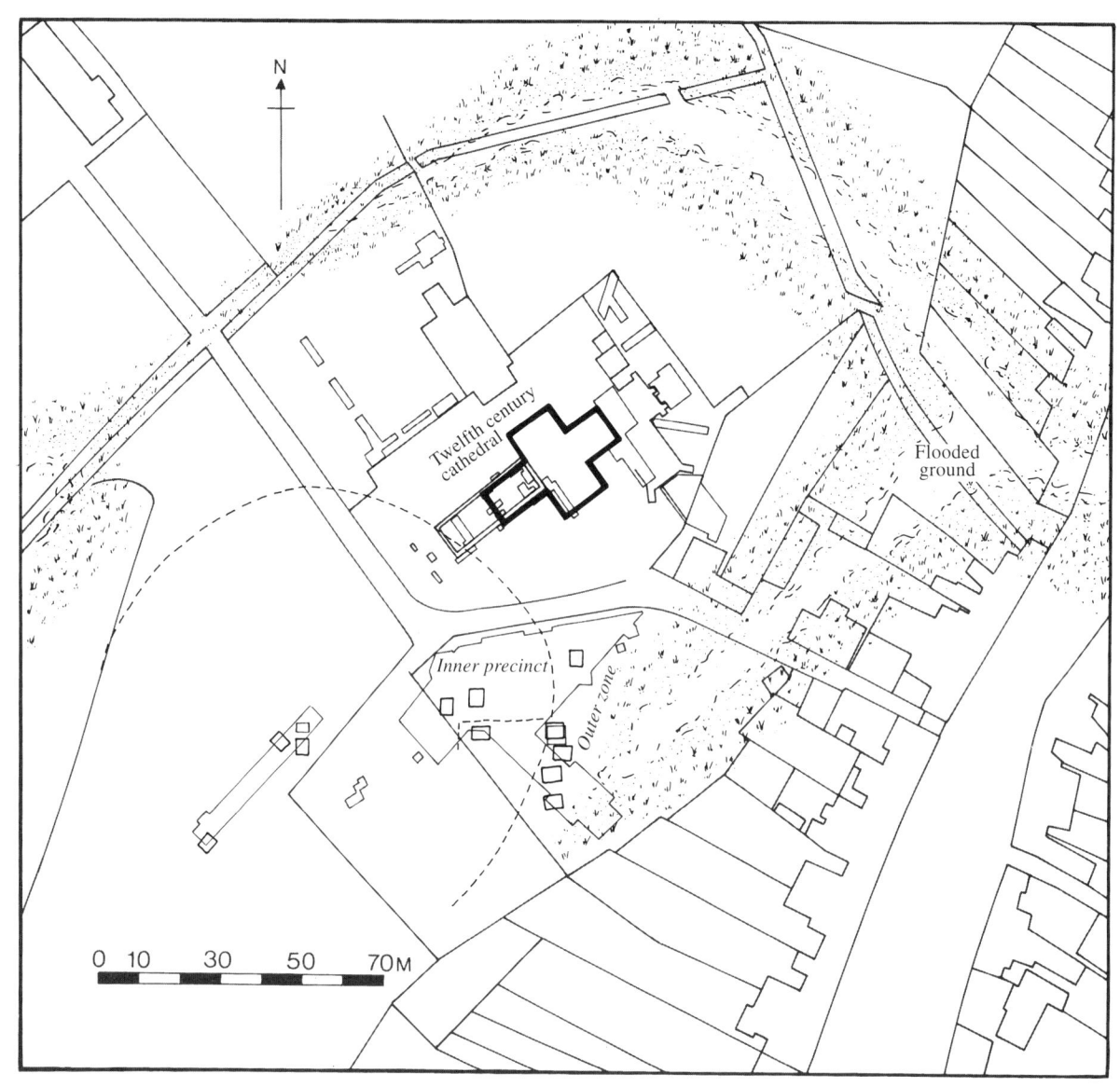

2.20 General plan of the settlement in the latter part of **Period IV**, probably later-twelfth or earlier-thirteenth century.

inner precinct lies to the west of the new church and is divided into quarters by walls, hedges and a road. The south-east quarter accommodates a market with temporary booths and a few more permanent buildings. Buildings have also encroached on the two northern quarters impinging upon an earlier graveyard marked by upright stones (Pollock 1995). The buildings are concentrated in the parts of the *outer zone* adjacent to the market, and other parts of this area are, as previously, used for gardens. A road leads southwards, maintaining the essential link with the Isle of Whithorn, while the flooded Ket basin has blocked access from the north and east. The inner and outer boundaries are marked by hedges, which are not necessarily maintained with care, but are sufficiently vigorous to maintain the appearance of old divisions, no longer respected universally. The scene is pictured in high summer. An autumn view would have shown more evidence of the cattle that were still an important factor in the economy, and whose hides contributed to the wealth of the community.

The **Period IV** deposits produced a rich body of archaeological evidence, which had been greatly disorganised by later burials and cultivation. Detailed sequences were recorded in separate southern and south-eastern parts of the *outer zone*, and fragmentary stratified deposits survived in the *inner precinct*. These revealed a potentially reliable framework, within which the wider body of disturbed evidence can be accommodated. The finds from all three areas reveal similar qualities, starting with relatively sparse and unvaried assemblages, and becoming progressively more numerous and varied during the course of the period. Both areas of the *outer zone* produced clear evidence of craft specialisation. This was particularly clear in the south-east part of the *outer zone*, which remained the focus of comb manufacture as in **Period III**. There was probably a direct link between this

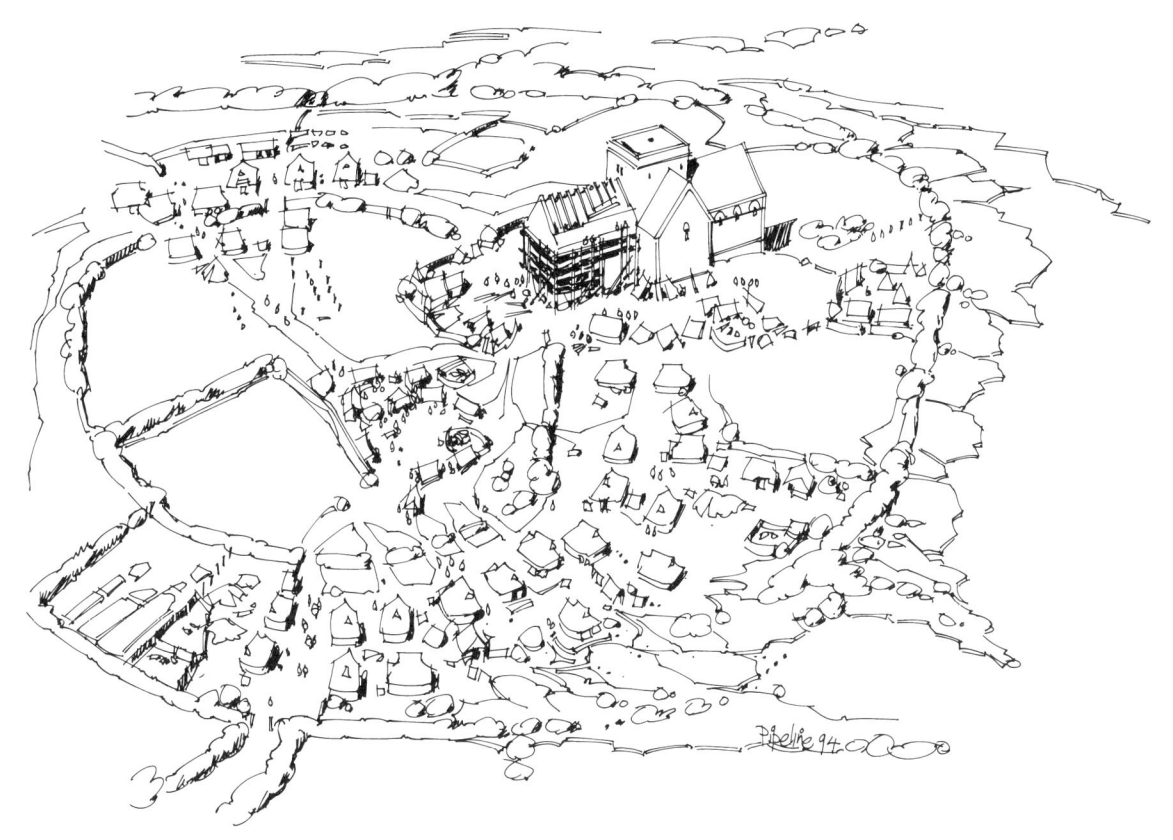

2.21 Speculative reconstruction of the *monastic town* in the late-twelfth century.

domestic industry (pp 493-5) and a large dump of antler waste in the adjacent part of the *inner precinct*. One of the buildings here seems to have been used for the repair of combs (p 494, Figure 10.136), and a later structure may have been a smithy (pp 229-30). A concentration of weaving tensioners, faceted and pierced antler tines, lead whorls and other objects points to later use for weaving (pp 242-3, Figures 6.29 and 10.133); and crucibles, tools, commodities and other finds identify a goldsmith's workshop in the vicinity, possibly practicing enamelling (pp 239-40, 404, Figures 6.24, 10.88).

The **southern sector** offered different, but complementary evidence. The first three building phases (*Stages 2–4*) revealed no evidence of specialised craftwork. Comb-making debris made a brief appearance in *Stage 5*, while the end of *Stage 6* produced evidence of shoemaking, leatherwork and the preparation of cat and, possibly bird, skins (pp 222-3). Subsequent deposits here (pp 224-6) included a concentration of shears fragments, indicating a cloth-working shop (pp 244, 246, Figure 6.36); heavy tools from a smithy (Figure 10.116); and debris from copper alloy casting (p 404, Figure 10.88), and fine metalwork (p 240).

This clear pattern of specialised workshops in the *outer zone* helps to explain the abundant finds from the disturbed ground in the *inner precinct* (Table 6.41), which produced concentrations of glass *tesserae*, copper-alloy scrap, farrier's debris, and possible writing implements (styli and prickers). These may either mark workshops in the *inner precinct* or dumps of debris originating in the workshops in the *outer zone*. Needles, awls and punches, concentrated on the outer margin of the area (Figure 6.26 and 27), indicate booths or workshops; and other randomly-scattered finds (knives, stick-pins, spindle-whorls, gaming pieces and pottery) suggest other activities in this area of open ground (pp 237-48). Lead weights indicate that the *inner precinct* was used by traders from the start of the period, while scattered coins show that this continued into the thirteenth century (pp 355-6). Weights were absent from the *outer zone* and coins scarce (pp 246-7) suggesting that trading was confined to the *inner precinct*. There are significant omissions from the large group of finds from this area. Crucibles and related debris were scarce, there was relatively little ironworking debris, and large hones were absent. This suggests that forges, furnaces and related structures were confined to the *outer zone*.

Conclusions. Period IV a records a distinct cultural phase in the history of Whithorn with pervasive Gaelic features, perhaps originating in Ireland, and revealing enduring Irish links. The introduction of a new type of building at the beginning of the period argues for the displacement of the former, possibly Anglo-British, inhabitants, and the establishment of a new, potentially Hiberno-Norse or Irish, community.

This may have coincided with the new involvement of Iona with Galloway, marked by the dedication of churches to St Coman of Elo, St Aed Macbric, St Bride, St Cormac and St Cummene. It is noteworthy that comparable dedications are found in districts of Argyll associated with the *Gall Gaidhil*, but not in areas then controlled by the Kings of Scotland (Brooke 1995), and this may have been the time when Whithorn acquired estates in Kintyre (McKerral 1950). This would have been an appropriate point for the incorporation of the putatively Irish elements of the Ninianic cult (p 2). The new Columban dedications are absent from the Machars, and Whithorn was perhaps involved in the undocumented process by which the Lords of Galloway acquired many of the Northumbrian territories in Galloway (Brooke 1991c, 313). The new cathedral built in the mid-twelfth century was apparently designed to meet the needs of the extant community, which seems to have maintained its tenurial rights until the later-thirteenth century, despite the appointment of reforming bishops in the second half of the twelfth century (p 23). The establishment of the Premonstratensian community *c.* 1177 AD has left no immediate impact on the archaeological record of the **Glebe Field**, although it was, perhaps, reflected by the remodelling of the eastern arm of the cathedral *c.* 1200 AD. This may be explained in two ways. The upper ranks of the extant community may have been converted into Premonstratensians, perhaps under the leadership of a new prior; or a new group might have been introduced, establishing their house on the unexcavated ground to the north of the church. The fortunes of Whithorn seem to have been linked closely with those of the House of Galloway, and the burning of the settlement in the later twelfth century and its depopulation in the thirteenth could reflect the vengeance of Roland in 1185 AD (p 22) and the suppression of the popular uprising in 1235 AD (pp 22-3).

We can achieve a tentative picture of the pre-Reform community by conflating the archaeological evidence from Whithorn, the territorial implications of the Whithorn School sculptures (pp 52-3), and the anecdotal evidence from Kirkcudbright (pp 23-4). The changes at the beginning of **Period III/3** and **Period IV** indicate the reform of the old Anglo-British *minster*, and a new hierarchy of senior clerical and junior scholastic orders was, perhaps, introduced. We may follow Scott (1988, 41) in inferring that it was ruled by a single person combining the offices of bishop and abbot, while its *paruchia* may have encompassed the Machars, corresponding with the distribution of Whithorn School sculptures and the later Deanery of Farnes. This new community became increasingly commercial, processing raw materials, especially antler, leather and, perhaps, wool from the hinterland. Coins were scarce until the thirteenth century (p 356) and a barter economy may have prevailed, although there are two rare Hiberno-Norse coins from Whithorn (pp 335-6). The cultural contacts indicated by the finds look consistently westwards in the early part of the period, but new eastern influences are evident in the later-twelfth century with the appearance of Red Gritty Ware pots and a wider range of local fabrics in the early-thirteenth (pp 511-4).

Galloway seems to have been a melting-pot of different peoples in this period. Celtic kindreds of British origin still dominated extensive territories in the Machars, and both here and elsewhere in the region the survival of phonetically-correct Anglian and Scandinavian place-names shows that these languages also survived. Roland introduced new Anglo-Norman tenants, while the widespread Gaelic names suggest a predominantly Scottish peasantry.

The **Period IV** sequence might be relatively unexceptional on an equivalent southern English *minster*, but is effectually unique in the north, apparently recording a Celtic reform of the old Northumbrian *minster*, the rapid development of a monastic town, resistance to the reforms of the twelfth century, and finally, the separation of the church and town at the opening of **Period V**.

Period V (*c.* 1250 x 1300–*c.* 1600)

Period V encompasses a period of about three hundred years from the mid- to late-thirteenth century to the Reformation in the late-sixteenth century. The archaeological record was dominated by a densely populated graveyard to the south of the cathedral for much of this time, but features on the periphery of the graveyard revealed a new curvilinear enclosure system centred upon the cathedral (Figure 2.22). The new enclosure initially contained buildings which may have replaced the **Period IV** settlement, but these were relatively short-lived, and the former inhabitants had probably moved to a new settlement by the early-fourteenth century. The original enclosure had fallen into decay by the end of the thirteenth century and the wall was incorporated into an earthen bank marking the backlands of the town in the mid-fourteenth century. The archaeological record changed in the second half of this period (**Period V/3–5**). The graveyard contracted in *c.* 1400 and was abandoned by the mid-fifteenth century. The contracted burial ground was skirted by a broad roadway probably leading from the Priory gatehouse to the west door of the cathedral, which would have been used for processions on important feast days. The west end of the cathedral was remodelled at the end of the fifteenth century, and the **Glebe Field** produced scattered builders' debris, a masons' workshop, and the ephemeral remains of workers' temporary accommodation. The **Museum Garden** excavation revealed the foundations of the new crypt constructed during this operation. Continuing change in the early-sixteenth century saw the construction of a large building to the east of the roadway which is identified tentatively as the Commendator's house.

The graveyard revealed ten stages of development encompassing some 1,470 burials in the **Glebe Field** and 124 in the **Museum Garden**. These have

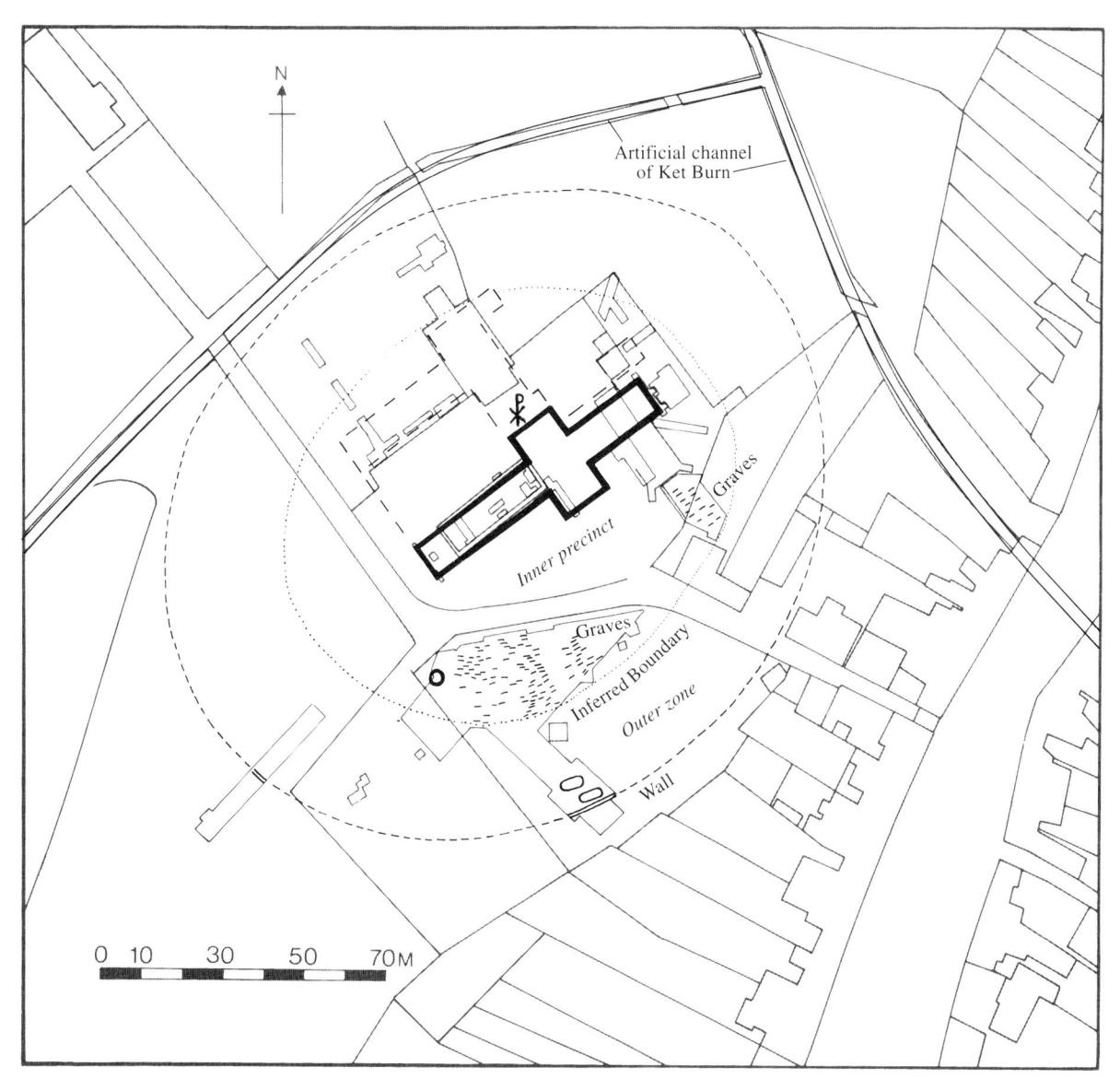

2.22 General plan of the ecclesiastical site in the earlier-fourteenth century (**Period V/1**), possibly prior to the formal establishment of the town.

revealed a detailed picture of the population in the fourteenth and earlier-fifteenth centuries, despite the poor preservation of many skeletons and the extensive disturbance of many graves (Chapter 11). The graves were dug into the *inner precinct* and eastern part of the *outer zone* of the **Period IV** monastic town displacing thousands of finds and contributing to a stratigraphic nightmare, partly unravelled in Chapters 6 and 7, but recurring in the discussions of finds in Chapter 10. These problems were exacerbated by recent cultivation which had disturbed many of the **Period V** deposits. Large numbers of finds were, nevertheless, recovered, including a large assemblage of coins offering considerable chronological precision to the sequence and presenting a picture of a peripatetic 'market' on the fringe of the graveyard (pp 355-7). Other notable finds include two pilgrim's badges (pp 394-5), a large assemblage of pottery (pp 511-8) and interesting groups of pins, brooches and buckles, continuing the series of such finds from earlier periods (Chapter 10).

The evolving plan of the Priory and the adjacent parts of the town can be summarised in three drawings (Figures 2.22–24). Figure 2.22 shows the site at the end of the thirteenth century. The drainage has been improved and the flooded ground is now dry, suggesting that the new Ket channel has been dug (pp 7-8). The new enclosure is centred on the cathedral, and has an outer boundary marked by a stone wall which was exposed in the **Glebe** and **Fey Fields**. The successive graveyards of **Period V/1** (Figure 7.2) generally seemed to respect an archaeologically-invisible division indicating an inner boundary, perhaps marked by a hedge. The function of a small, circular stone-founded building to the west of the graves is uncertain. Although it is paralleled by a

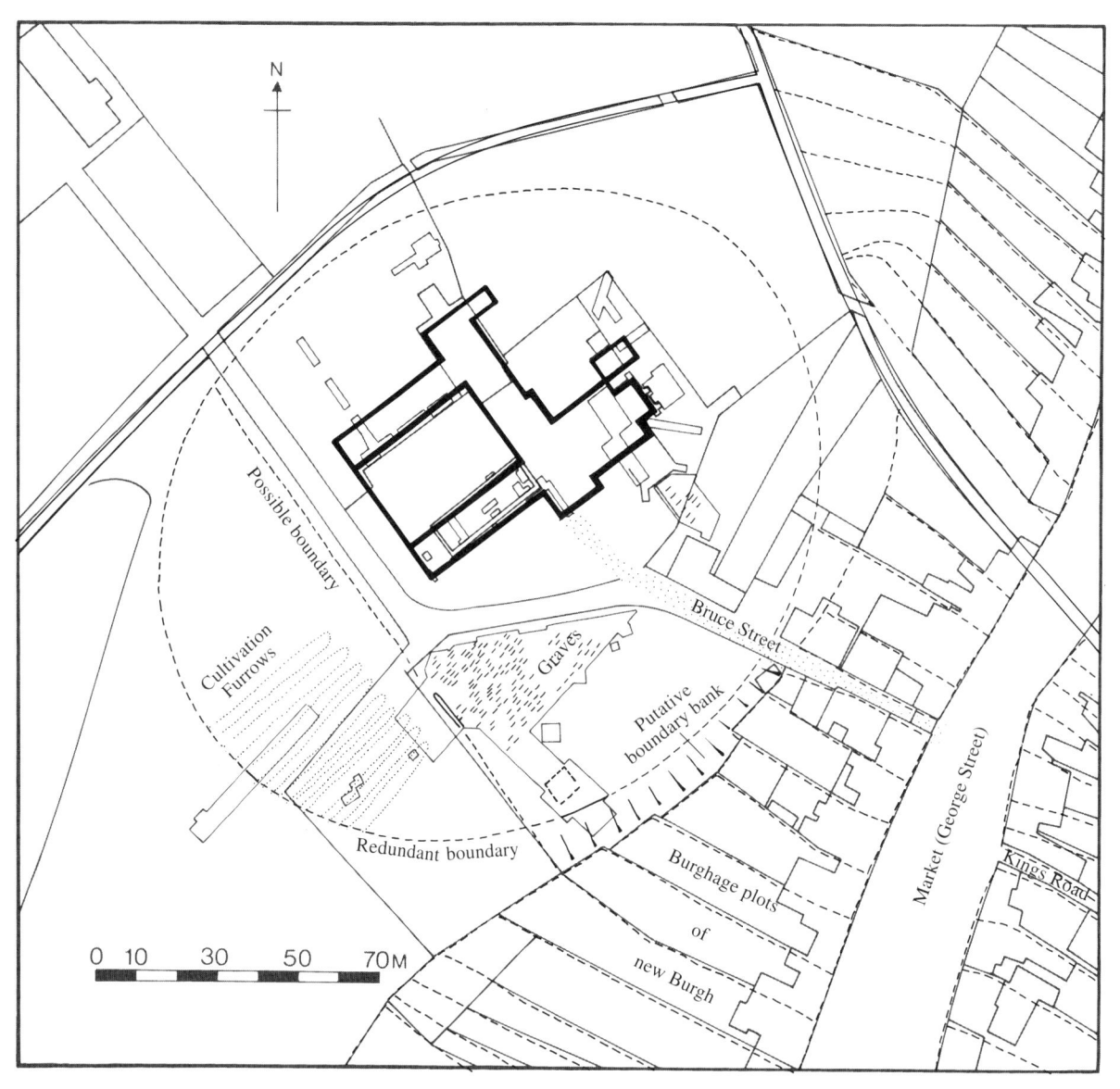

2.23 General plan of the ecclesiastical site and adjacent parts of the planned town in the later-fourteenth century (**Period V/2**).

storehouse at Crossraguel, and by a putative kiln at Nendrum, it seems to have had stained glass windows suggesting a grander function, and it could have served as a temporary mortuary analogous to the **Period II** chapel (p 45). Two buildings (one somewhat dubious) are depicted beside the boundary in the *outer zone* of the enclosure. These were, perhaps, similar to the last building erected in **Period IV** (IV/16, p 227) marking a return to the sub-rectilinear plan prevailing in **Periods I–III**, and continuing the tradition of wattle construction. Their position and arrangement is reminiscent of the **Period I** *monasterium* (Figure 2.6) and the monastic town of **Period IV** (Figures 2.19–20), but they were, perhaps, inappropriate accommodation for the Premonstratensian canons. The eastern and western arms of the cathedral have been extended. The east end was probably refurbished *c.* 1200 AD, while the nave was enlarged at an unknown date in the thirteenth century.

Figure 2.23 shows the Priory and part of the nascent town in the later-fourteenth century. The southern part of the derelict outer boundary has been replaced by a bank marking the backlands of the town, which nevertheless bends eastwards avoiding the curvilinear ecclesiastical precinct. The putative inner boundary has disappeared and a new ditched boundary on the line of the modern field wall separates the evolving graveyard from cultivated ground in the **Fey Field** and **Market Garden**. The remains of a stone-walled building in the former *outer zone* have been included, although this was probably ruinous by this time. The plan of the Priory buildings is based on fragmentary remains recorded by Galloway (pp 8-9) and Tabraham (1979), and follows Radford and Donaldson (1984). Bruce Street is now seen as the principal access route leading from the broad market street to the south crossing of the cathedral.

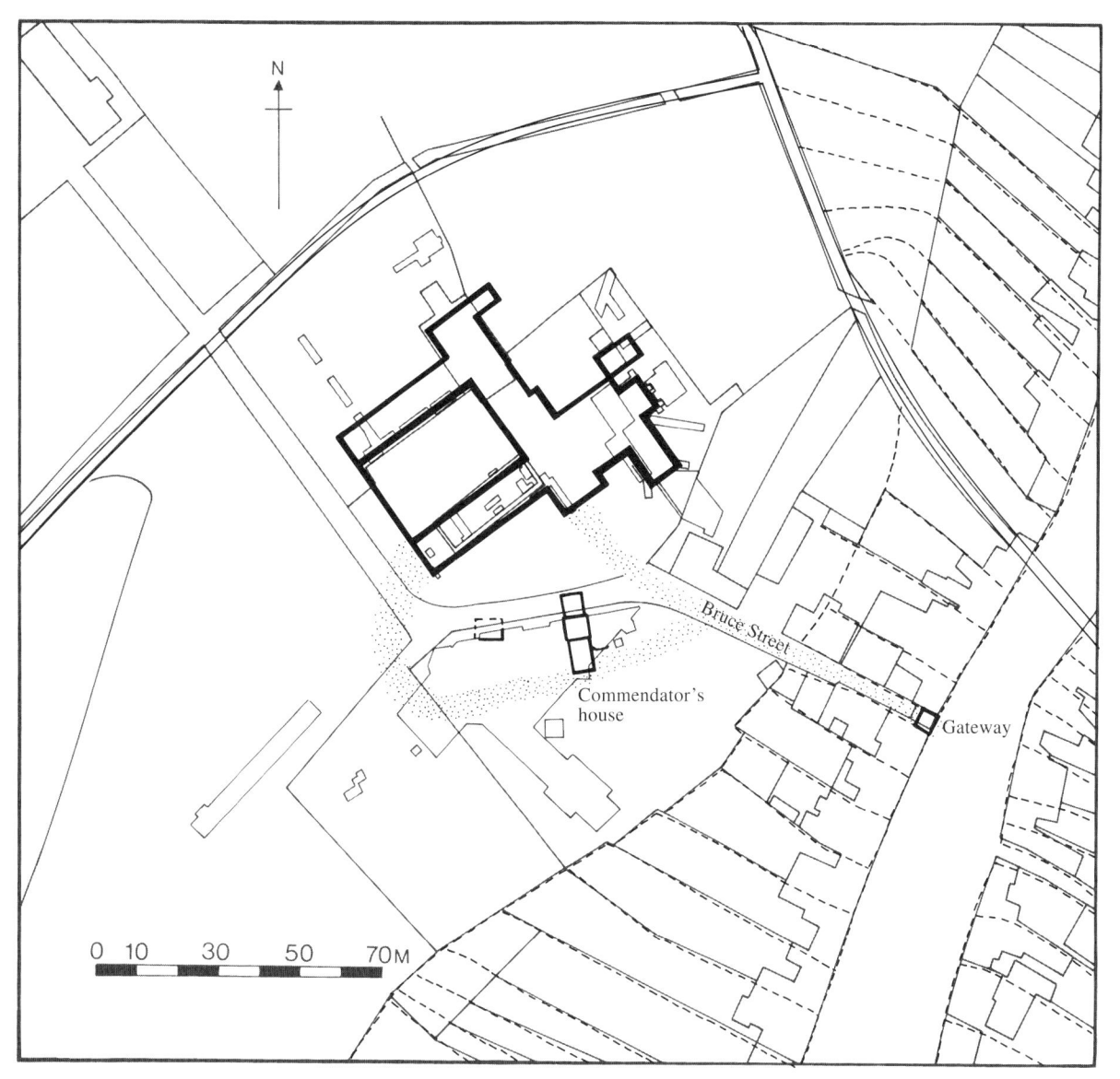

2.24 General plan of the Priory and town in the mid-sixteenth century (**Period V/5**).

Figure 2.24 shows the site in the early- to mid-sixteenth century. The graveyard has moved to a new, unknown position, perhaps to the south-east of the cathedral, and a new roadway branches from Bruce Street leading to the west door of the cathedral. The ground between the two roads is occupied by a substantial stone building, interpreted as the Commendator's house, with an outbuilding in a compound to the west. The east end of the cathedral has been extensively modified, and a new side chapel has been built over enlarged, barrel-vaulted crypts. The former enclosure has been omitted from the drawing as there was little evidence of activity in the ground between the Commendator's house and the backlands of the town, which now seem to have been the principal boundary.

The historical background. The priory and town of Whithorn are poorly documented, and their history is only recorded in documents which survive elsewhere. This means that, while the succession of bishops and priors, and their political relationships are relatively well known, the circumstantial details of the layout and management of the ecclesiastical centre and its estates are virtually unrecorded. The sole written records of a major programme of building work in the late- fifteenth/early- sixteenth century are, thus, two entries in the Treasurer's Accounts for 1491 and 1502 recording royal donations of 'drink silver' to the masons. The disputed election of 1235 AD (pp 22-3) and subsequent documents are of interest as they record the numbers of canons which fluctuated from twenty-two in 1235 AD to twelve in 1408, and around twenty in the earlier- sixteenth century (Dilworth 1994, 8), which contrast with the rather larger 'monastic' populations postulated in earlier periods (pp 34, 57). The history of this period is not otherwise immediately germane to the archaeological

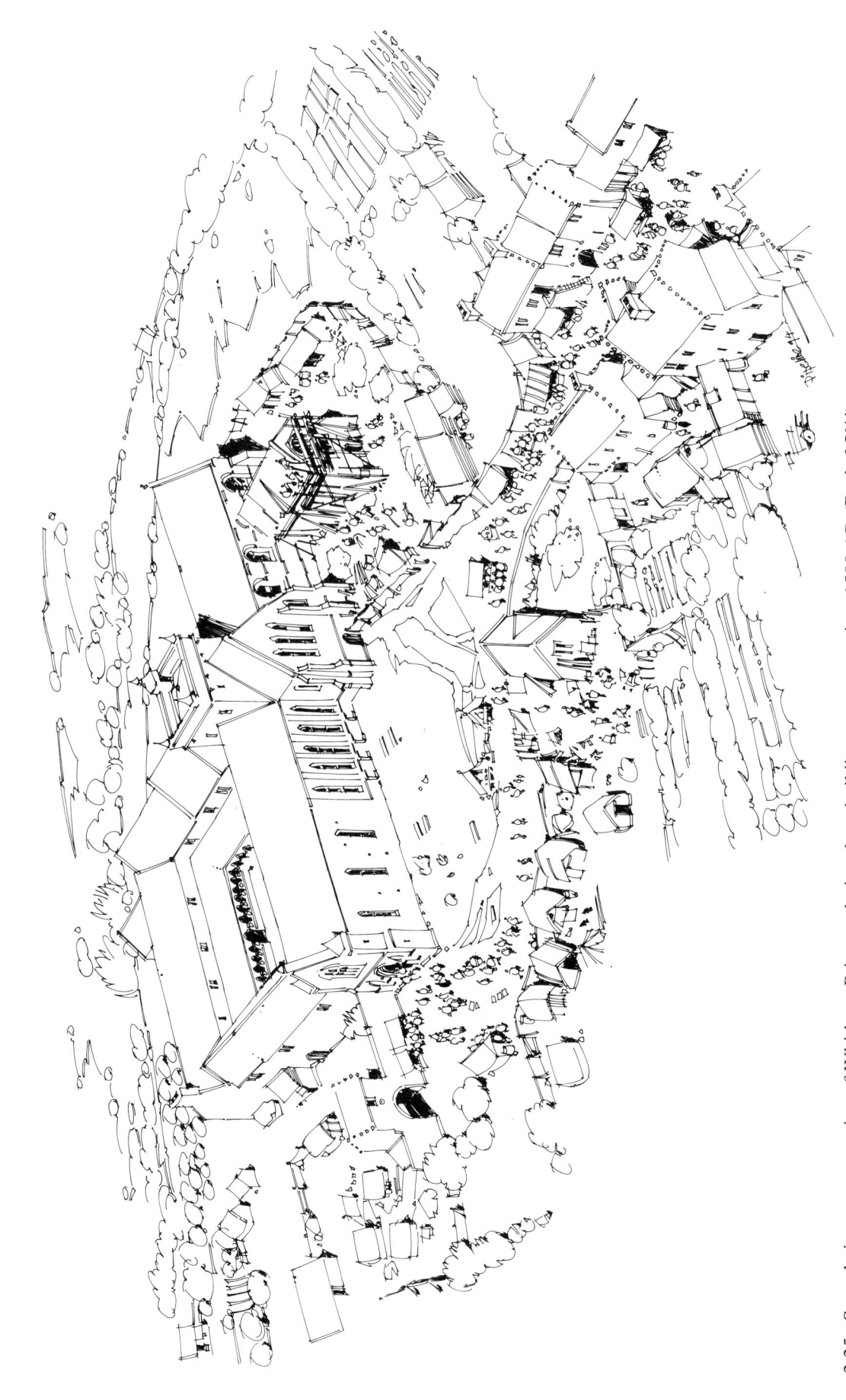

2.25 Speculative reconstruction of Whithorn Priory during the rebuilding programme in c 1500 AD (**Period V/4**).

results, and is discussed elsewhere (Radford 1950, Donaldson 1950, Dilworth 1994, Brooke 1995).

Period V may seem relatively insignificant when compared to earlier periods, but nevertheless records a vital stage in the evolution of Whithorn in which its ecclesiastical and urban aspects were separated physically. This process was revealed by somewhat fragmented deposits in the south part of the **Glebe Field**, and this account is intentionally imprecise due to the ambiguities of the archaeological record. There are, thus, two possible points when the population may have shifted to the new town. The earlier is at the end of **Period IV** when the new enclosure system was laid out and the former buildings were abandoned. This probably took place in the middle years of the thirteenth century – the evidence is ambiguous – and would, perhaps, have been an appropriate consequence of the suppression of the conservative faction in Galloway following the failed rising of 1235 AD (p 22). This move may have been formalised by arrangements in the time of Alexander III (1249–86 AD) recorded in the transumpt charter of 1326 AD (p 7). The new buildings within the **Period V** enclosure (Figure 2.22) might, however, indicate that the former organisational system had been restored. This is supported by coins suggesting that the *inner precinct* served as a market until replaced by graves, when commercial activity shifted to the *outer zone* (pp 356-7). This hypothesis would date the critical change to the early- to mid-fourteenth century, indicating that the charters of *c.* 1310 and 1326 AD (p 7) truly recorded the establishment of the new town. This problem is left unresolved in the confident expectation that future excavation of the backlands boundary and the adjoining sector of the **Period V** *outer zone* should provide the organisational and chronological precision that the current excavations have failed to deliver. The large numbers buried over a relatively brief period in the early-thirteenth to mid-fifteenth centuries attest a large local population. Many, doubtless, lived on farms but others, perhaps the majority, will have come from the new town.

The delineation of a new curvilinear enclosure, sub-divided into an *inner precinct* and *outer zone* in the later-thirteenth century, is noteworthy. It would be unsurprising to find the shadows of such a plan from an earlier period surviving as boundaries and roads (e.g. Swann 1985), but this was a new system involving a major shift in focus, which may be seen as a reflection of the conservatism of western Galloway (pp 22-4).

Period VI (*c.* 1600–present)

The long history of intensive occupation and redevelopment in the **Glebe Field** seems to have ended with the Reformation and by the present century it had reverted to the cultivation with which the sequence began in **Period I/1.1**. There was little evidence of activity during the seventeenth century, although coins were still lost on the roadway, which presumably remained in use. The Commendator's house remained standing, though perhaps in disrepair, and by the end of the century had been refurbished as the manse, and was the largest house in the town. The manse underwent major renovations in the eighteenth century when a new western wing was added, causing severe damage to the underlying deposits. The ground to the south was brought into cultivation at roughly the same time resulting in further disturbance of the **Period IV** and **V** remains. A new manse was built to the north-west of the church in the early-nineteenth century, but the old building remained in use, and was occupied *inter alia* by a minister's widow and a school. It was demolished in the late-nineteenth century.

The Priory, meanwhile, had fallen into disrepair. Various 'yairdis within the precincts and closage of the abbacie' were leased to a schoolmaster in 1633 (Radford and Donaldson 1951), but architectural fragments from the town show that it had become a quarry for builders. The nave of the cathedral survived as the parish kirk, undergoing major refurbishment when it was restored as the cathedral by Bishops Hamilton and Sydserf in the early seventeenth century, and again after the collapse of a new western tower, still standing in 1684 (Radford and Donaldson 1951). It was replaced by a new kirk in 1822 built over the reredorter of the Priory. The graveyard now surrounded the nave of the old cathedral, and seems to have occupied a curvilinear enclosure, corresponding broadly with the *inner precinct* of the early *monasterium* (Figure 2.2). The eastern part of this enclosure was demolished during the restoration of the crypts, but had been recorded by William Galloway (pp 8-9), while fragments of the wall and gateway were exposed in the **Museum Garden** trench (p 286).

Figure 2.26 shows the site in *c.* 1800 AD. The west wing has been added to the manse and the ground to the south is under cultivation. The west wall of the **Glebe Field** had apparently been built in the seventeenth century and cultivation in the **Fey Field** and, perhaps, the **Market Garden** was indicated by shallow cultivation ridges and scattered eighteenth and nineteenth century debris. The old kirk is shown in its final form, while the known fragments of the kirkyard have been extrapolated to show its possible shape and extent.

Period VI brings this long story to a close. The Kirk, of course, survives and worship continues after more than fifteen hundred unbroken years. There is, however, a clear separation between the church and town, which is no longer, physically, a church-centred community whatever its spiritual allegiances. The Kirk now lies to one side of the town, attached umbilically by Bruce Street, but surrounded by graves and grassland, and with a northern vista of a rough landscape, which might have been familiar to the first Christian community. The process by which this somewhat isolated position was achieved has been sketched out in the preceding pages, and will be

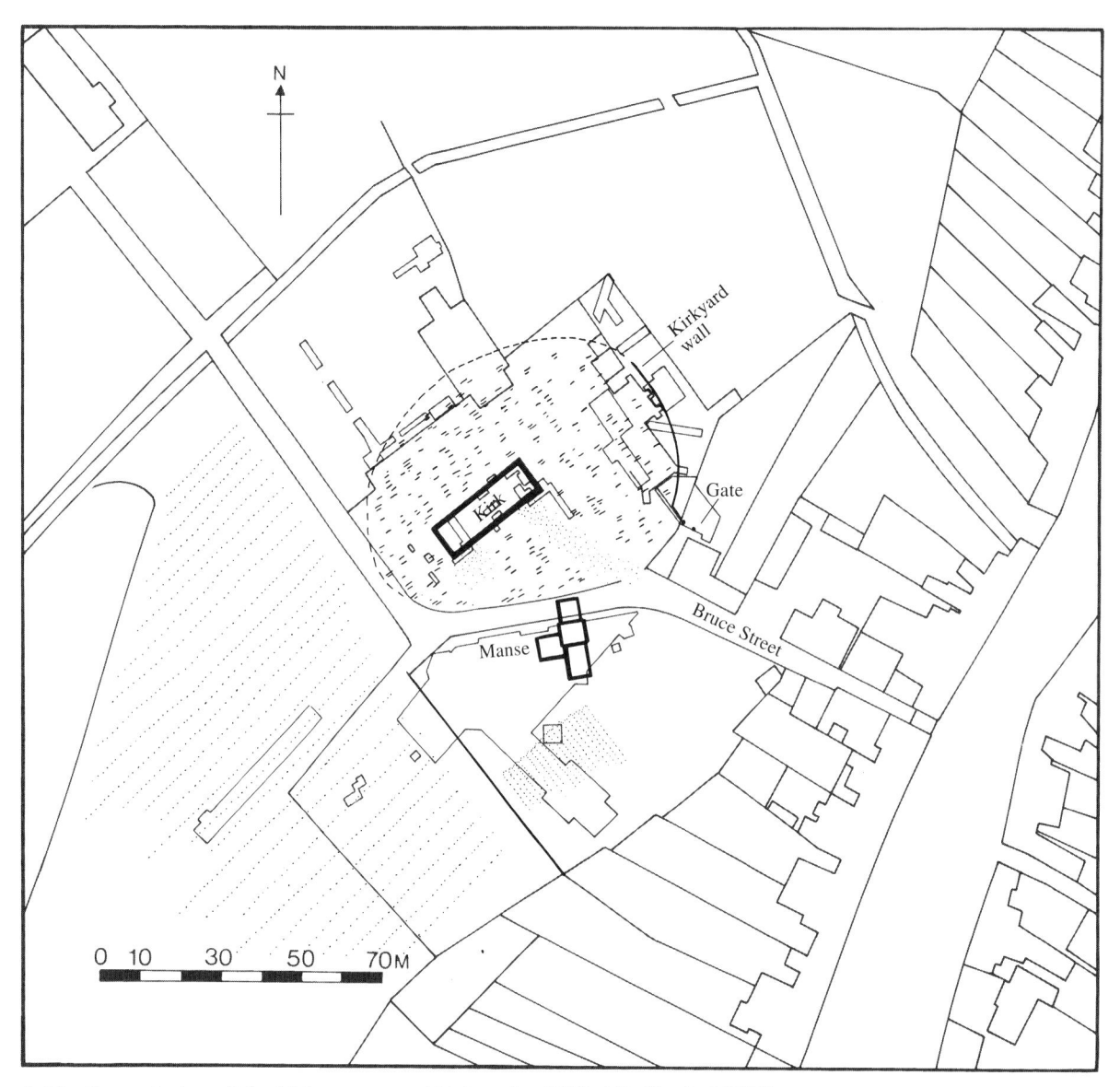

2.26 General plan of the kirk, manse and kirkyard *c* 1800 AD (**Period VI/2**).

seen as an accident of urban evolution, which has left Scotland's oldest town as a green field site. This has been an undisguised blessing for current and future archaeologists as a large part of the evolving settlement remains both well-preserved and accessible.

Postscript

The contents of this chapter have been detached from the descriptive chapters in order to segregate the archaeological 'facts' from the speculations they have engendered. The reconstruction drawings are, indeed, highly speculative, but the phase plans are rather less so. These depend on three assumptions; that the focus of the site lay on the crown of the hill in the vicinity of the nave of the twelfth century cathedral; that the excavated fragment is sufficiently large to predict the whole; and that symmetry will have balanced the known to the south-west with the unknown to the north-east. Successive previous publications (Hill 1984–1992) demonstrate that these conclusions are in no way the product of prior expectations, but have arisen after a long struggle with frequently-troublesome primary evidence. The dating is frequently more speculative than the phase plans, and could be improved by further analysis of the extant evidence, and by future excavation in the waterlogged areas where dendrochronology promises a precision which other techniques cannot reach. The wider implications of the sequence of structures, finds and organisational systems have largely been left unexploited.

CHAPTER 3

Period 1: The Early Centuries (*c*. 500–*c*. 730 AD)

Peter Hill, Jo Moran, Dave Pollock

Introduction

Topography. The **Glebe Field** revealed a detailed sequence of stratified fifth to early-eighth century remains, which are interpreted as parts of the *inner precinct* and *outer zone* of a *monasterium* (pp 30-5). This pattern emerged in the early part of **Period I** and was maintained in varying forms for the ensuing millennium. Earlier activity in **Phases 0** and **1** probably reflects the topography more than planning. The dominant features at this time were a ridge of bedrock to the north of a level area (the central plateau), bounded on the south by a second, less-pronounced, bedrock ridge. Successive level building stances were constructed by quarrying the northern ridge and building aprons to the south. These gradually extended southwards, and by the early eighth century the lower part of the ridge had been transformed into a level terrace backed by outcropping rock. This produced two distinct zones (the **northern** and **central sectors**) with distinct archaeological characteristics which conditioned developments until the eleventh century. The ground to the south of the lower bedrock ridge lay within the *outer zone* throughout **Period I,** and is termed the **southern sector**.

Excavation evidence 1984–1991. Period I remains were glimpsed in the trial excavation in 1984 (Hill 1984, 1985) and gradually exposed from 1987 onwards. The features in the **southern** and **central sectors** were excavated in 1987–1991, but the **northern sector** did not become available until the excavation of the *Northumbrian* ecclesiastical buildings was completed in June 1991. The archaeological evidence in the *inner precinct* and *outer zone* was radically different and there were few stratigraphic links between them. These two areas are described separately, as is the sparse evidence from the **Fey Field** and **Museum Garden** (Chapter 9).

The organisation of the *monasterium*. The shape of the settlement was consistent throughout **Period I** (Figure 3.1). There was always an *inner precinct*, which from the end of **Phase 1** contained graves, 'shrines' and open space. The evolving graveyard was generally kept clean, but the open ground produced spreads of *industrial* debris and scattered artefacts, perhaps, revealing sporadic use by craftsmen. Beyond lay a zone where small sub-rectilinear buildings with external latrines were associated with scattered *domestic* debris. A distinct industrial area in the western part of the *outer zone* was indicated by debris extending into the *inner precinct*. The boundaries and the arrangement of features indicate a curvilinear master plan in which the *inner precinct* was divided into zones by chords, while the *outer zone* was separated into radial segments. The boundaries and internal divisions were generally insubstantial, but their persistence reflects the enduring organisation of the site. The historical evidence and possible *comparanda* are discussed above (pp 11-16, 31-5).

Past excavations. Past excavations described above (pp 8-11) have revealed no certain stratified evidence of activity in the fifth to early-eighth centuries, and, apparently, few early finds, despite Ritchie's meticulous excavation and Radford's unsuccessful

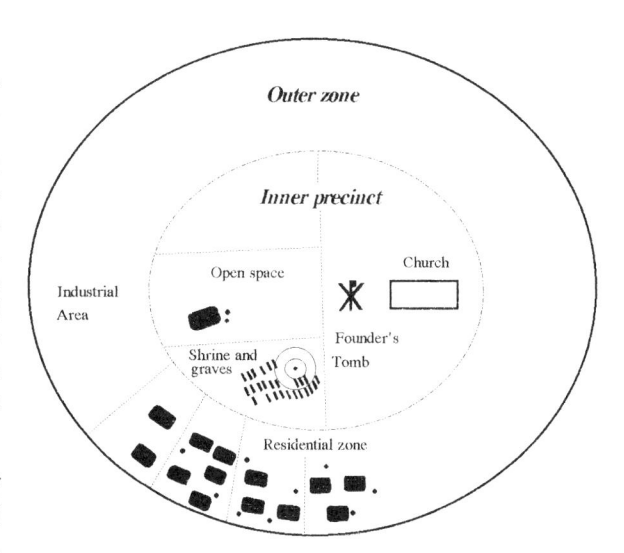

3.1 Schematic drawing of the organization of the developed *monasterium*.

search for early artefacts in the nineteenth century builders' debris. This negative evidence paradoxically identifies the eastern part of the hill as a likely location for the original church, its possible successors, and the other public buildings appropriate to an early *monasterium*.

Previous publications. Previous publications (Hill 1990, 1992a and b) have given an increasingly full and reliable account of the **Period I** remains, but all predate the recognition of the shape of the site, and should be treated with circumspection.

Phasing. The **Period I** features generally record a process of gradual evolution, and successive graveyards in the **northern** and **central sectors** demonstrate the most secure evidence of major change. This reveals a coherent framework for the evolution of the *inner precinct,* that unites stratigraphically remote parts of the trench in a reliable relative sequence. The artefacts add chronological and functional dimensions to the interpretation of the *inner precinct,* and provide a rough framework within which the stratigraphically-distinct *outer zone* can be correlated (pp 119-21). Five principal phases of activity in the *inner precinct* (**0–4**) and thirteen *stages* of development in the *outer zone* are described below, while their wider implications are discussed in Chapter 2 (pp 26-40).

Finds assemblages. The **Period I** features produced large assemblages of finds with important implications for the organisation of the settlement, and its chronology, economy and cultural contacts. There were three basic types of assemblage – '*domestic*', '*industrial*' and '*clean*'.

Domestic assemblages were characterised by a limited range of artefact types, generally with a large proportion of pottery, glass and flint. These assemblages can sometimes be identified as scatters around individual buildings, and are exemplified by the distributions of pottery and glass in the *outer zone* in the earlier-sixth and seventh centuries (Figures 10.21 and 24).

Industrial assemblages were characterised by a wide range of artefact types, including broken and serviceable tools, commodities (charcoal, burnt bone, scrap metal), and manufacturing waste. The richest *industrial assemblages* were the large rubbish deposits that accumulated in the western part of the *inner precinct* in **Phases 2** and **3** (e.g. Tables 3.18-20, 3.22 24), as illustrated by the distributions of stone tools associated with metalworking (Figure 10.116), copper alloy and lead scrap (Figure 10.70), debris from a goldsmith's shop (Figure 10.87), and glass sherds from a putative workshop (Figure 10.23). Significant groups of bronze-casting waste (Figure 10.86) occupied a wider area in the *outer zone* of the early-sixth century *monasterium*.

Clean assemblages were the easiest to characterise, but the hardest to identify. They record areas where waste was not disposed and where things were rarely lost. The **Phase 2** graveyard is the clearest example (Figure 3.12). This area seems to have been kept scrupulously clean, and most of the small group of finds from the graves can be identified as displaced *domestic* or *industrial* debris from underlying **Phase 1** deposits. Similar cleanness can be identified in **Phases 3** and **4**, though with increasing difficulty, as the graveyard expanded into areas strewn with earlier industrial debris.

These gain added clarity when compared with assemblages from similar environments in later periods. There were thus three opportunities to study the debris preserved when buildings in the low-lying ground were flooded in the late-seventh/early-eighth century (**Period I/4**), late-eighth/early-ninth century (**Period II**, pp 181-2) and mid- to late-twelfth century (**Period IV** *Stage 6/7*, pp 221-6). The circumstances were similar on each occasion, but the finds assemblages were radically different, revealing functional differences which cannot be attributed to chronological factors.

Charcoal and comminuted bone. Various **Period 1** deposits produced large groups of charcoal that were not associated with industrial or domestic hearths, nor with identifiable bonfires, ash or 'destruction' layers. Four samples revealed a predominance of roundwood from a variety of species (Table 3.1), and the charcoal is likely to have derived from charcoal stores, perhaps associated with the extensive ironworking recorded in **Period 1**. 'Stoves' in **Buildings 6** and **18** produced charcoal but no ash, suggesting that charcoal rather than wood was used for domestic fires. Scott cites broadly similar charcoal assemblages from Irish metalworking sites (1990, 167), and has located a single reference to a sack of charcoal in an eighth century law tract (1990, 185).

	1	2	3	4
Oak	*	*	*	*
Alder		*		*
Ash				*
Hazel	*	*	*	
Birch	*	*		*
Willow	*	*	*	
Rowan	*			
Pomoidae				*

Table 3.1. Charcoal from **Period I** deposits. (**1**) **Phase 1.6** charcoal spread; (**2**) Charcoal spread over *Structure 2*; (**3**) Fill of **Phase 1.6** pit (84.01); (**4**) **Phase 2** industrial debris (89).

The charcoal was frequently associated with substantial amounts of calcined bone, which was far less abundant in later periods. It is, perhaps, more contentious, but it too may have been a commodity which would have found ready use as a flux in iron smelting. Both seem to have been 'commodities' which had been manufactured elsewhere and were stored or used in the immediate vicinity of the excavated area.

Pottery and glass imports: chronological implications. The rich group of artefacts, and particularly the imported pottery and glass (pp 297-326), provides a valuable supplement to the otherwise sparse framework of absolute dates. Studies of imported early medieval pottery are relatively advanced and some types can be dated with precision. Whithorn provides valuable new stratigraphic information and significantly extends known distributions, but does not alter the extant picture radically (pp 315–22). Studies of imported glass vessels from western British sites are, perhaps, less advanced and depend on potentially-unreliable continental chronologies (Alcock Pers. Comm.). The detailed, stratified sequence of vessels from Whithorn is unparalleled and potentially offers a chronological framework for finds from other sites (pp 323-26).

The combined evidence from previous artefact studies, stratigraphy and spatial distributions allows the creation of a provisional chronology which is potentially precise. This chronology centres on the transition in the mid-sixth century from Mediterranean links to a Gaulish trade network. The Mediterranean 'trade package' included *amphorae* (B ware), fine table wares (A ware) and two types of glass bowls (Group A, pp 300–1). The distributions of sherds of the two predominant *amphora* types (B*i* and B*ii*) were spatially and stratigraphically distinct (Figures 3.11, 12, 10.21 and 22) as were sherds of two groups of glass bowls (pp 323–5). The *amphorae* were long-lived types, but the table wares reflected shifting fashions closely and can be dated with considerable accuracy. The Mediterranean imports to western Britain include fine wares from two production centres. Phocean Red Slipware, imported from the east Mediterranean, reveals a maximum date range of 475–550 with a *floruit* in the first quarter of the sixth century. African Red Slipware was imported from the Carthage region during a shorter period in the second third of the sixth century. The nine fine ware sherds from Whithorn were all African Red Slipware, and the absence of the earlier Phocean pottery hints that Whithorn was not linked to the earlier stage of Mediterranean trade. Four of the African Red Slipware sherds have been reused as rubbers or crayon and a fifth had been shaped into a disc, while three had been displaced into anachronous contexts. A sherd of one vessel (V2) was, however, associated with a spread of B*ii* *amphora* sherds pertaining to **Phase 1.6**. The form was current from *c*. 525–600, but the closest parallel comes from a pit in Carthage dating to *c*. 540-50 AD (pp 315-6), while the associated *amphorae* are unlikely to have been imported after *c*. 550 AD (p 316). This association was sufficiently secure to ascribe **Phase1.6** to the end of the second quarter of the sixth century, and the date *c*. 550 AD can be assigned to two associated early E ware vessels (V1 and V6), while providing a *terminus ad quem* for earlier B*i* amphorae and glass vessels, and a *terminus post quem* for subsequent finds of vessel glass and E ware pottery (pp 324–6). This horizon is incompatible with the mid-sixth century date (p 302, Evison 1982) ascribed to fragments of two 'Germanic' claw beakers (Vs 11 and 12, Figure 10.5) from earlier deposits (69.01 p 81; 56.02 Table 3.40). The sherds of both vessels were small and scattered, but both seem to originate in contexts preceding the earliest *amphora* sherds, and a date at the end of the fifth century or beginning of the sixth seems more appropriate.

Chronology. There is no secure historical framework for Whithorn in the fifth/sixth to seventh/early-eighth century, and the conflicting historical models (p xii) must be treated as hypotheses to be tested rather than established facts. The archaeological record contains two distinct interwoven strands of chronological evidence. The stratigraphy records separate sequences with twenty-three *stages* in the *inner precinct* and thirteen in the *outer zone* that provide a reliable progression from earliest to latest irrespective of the duration of **Period I**. An absolute dating framework of reliable calendar dates cannot yet be constructed, although one is potentially available if future excavations in the waterlogged deposits surrounding the site (pp 7–8) produce timbers suitable for tree-ring dating. Radiocarbon-dating was a valuable tool in establishing the original chronological framework for the site (Hill 1984, 1987a), but at most points in the sequence is less precise than the evidence available from stratigraphy and finds. The case for a closely-dated horizon *c*. 550 AD is presented above, and a second horizon *c*. 700 AD is indicated (but not proved) by the dendrochronology of timbers from the **southern sector** (p 130). The **Period II** deposits produced a large group of Northumbrian coins, which establishes a convincing late-eighth/ninth century chronology, and supports the inferred dating of the later **Period I** features (pp 136, 352–5).

The Buildings. The **Period I** deposits revealed twenty-three, small, sub-rectilinear buildings (**1–10, 12–24**). The buildings were simple, but have no close contemporaneous parallels (p 30), and are most readily understood within the context of similar structures from later periods at Whithorn. The remains of most of the buildings were ephemeral, and their discovery reflects the excellent preservation of early deposits over large parts of the site, and the skills of our excavators. The buildings displayed various recurrent features, and the whole group is perhaps rather more convincing than its individual members. All but one of the **Period 1** buildings were rectilinear or sub-rectilinear, and they were generally built in shallow hollows cut into the topsoil, or on platforms dug into outcropping rock. All the buildings probably had earth floors of fine silt, sometimes with a stony substrate, and several

Type	Name	Characteristics	Examples	Phase
1	Wicker buildings	Insubstantial walls, rounded corners, relatively deep earth floors supporting the base of the walls. Roofs probably integral and so probably rounded rather than pitched	4, 6, 7	Common in *Phase 1* and start of *Phase 2*
2	Stake-walled buildings	Substantial stake walls with angular/sub-angular corners. Frequently divided into small and large chambers with hearth or stove in larger chamber. Roofs possibly an independent framework, gabled	1, 17, 18, 20	One in *Phase 1*, common between *Phase 2* and *4a*
3	Timber-sill building	Walls possibly wattle with wands mortised into narrow timber sills. Angular bowed wall-line and angular corners. Earth floor	5	One example in *Phase 1*
4	Timber-framed wattle building	Principal structural elements were substantial, opposed, timber-framed doorways. Walls made of light wattle and/or spaced planks. Unilateral timber buttresses. Floors of earth or shale with rounded corners.	21, 24	Appear in *Phase 4b* continue in **Period II**

Table 3.2: **Period I** building types.

revealed evidence of an internal partition dividing a small apartment, sometimes with a rough stone floor, from a larger, sub-square room with an earth floor and a central hearth or stove.

All the buildings were of similar size and shape, but four distinct types are indicated by construction details (e.g., Figures 3.9-11, 37-43). Only one of the earlier buildings (**14**) had an identifiable doorway, and the surviving structural members were large and small stakes. These indicate two possible building styles. A few early buildings in the **northern sector** (*Type 1*) were principally defined by their floors, and the sporadic stakes marking the walls were small. They had rounded corners, and were probably built of relatively light wickerwork, perhaps with the roof woven integrally with the walls. The walls of a second group of buildings (*Type 2*) were marked by larger stakes, frequently set close together, and sometimes forming staggered double rows. Some had rounded corners, but these were less marked than in the wicker buildings of *Type 1*. These stake-walled buildings may have been sufficiently strong to support an independent roof structure. The walls of one building (**5**, *Type 3*) were based on narrow timber sills, probably supporting wattle work. The latest buildings (*Type 4*) incorporated large squared timbers, and the structure seems to rely upon substantial opposed timber-framed doorways. These probably reflect an Anglo-Saxon building tradition (pp 37, 138-9) and are paralleled at Church Close, Hartlepool (Daniels 1988).

The insubstantial wattle - and stake-walled buildings have no close parallels in the area. Rispain Camp, some 1.5 km to the west, revealed substantially-built roundhouses of the early 1st millennium (perhaps *c*. 200 AD), with floor areas in excess of 140 m² (Haggarty and Haggarty 1983). The Whithorn buildings were approximately a sixth of this size and no structural similarities were evident.

The graves. The *inner precinct* revealed 118 graves (**1–118**) spanning four distinct phases of burial (Figure 3.2). The earliest burials occupied the problematical **Phase 1.5** graveyard in the middle of the **central plateau** (pp 86-8), and the **Phase 2** graves mostly lay in disturbed ground to the west, south and east. The graveyard expanded into the **northern sector** in **Phases 3** and **4**, and the gradual accumulation of deposits here preserved the contemporary ground surfaces, and revealed valuable evidence of grave marking. There were two principal grave types – *lintel graves* and *log-coffin burials* - to which most of the burials can be ascribed, and which seem to have been chronologically distinct. The transition from *lintel graves* to *log coffin burials* occurred during **Phase 3**, and perhaps marks an important cultural horizon in the affairs of Whithorn (p 37). This possibly reveals the shifts of fashion, but may reflect the differing status of the two principal grave types, and thus of the populations buried. The considerable labour required to fashion a log coffin suggests that these were reserved for special burials. Lintel graves would have been much easier to construct, and may thus have been used for less privileged burials. This hypothesis is supported by the evidence from other sites. Lintel graves were widespread in western Britain, occurring in large numbers in many cemeteries. Log coffins are extremely rare (p 37), although this may partly reflect the difficulty of recognising the ephemeral evidence of decayed timber. A small group of log-coffin burials in the **Phase 1.5** graveyard (p 87) perhaps pertained to the end of **Phase 1** or **Phase 2**, although they were probably relatively late burials in this long-lived enclosure (pp 87, 105-7). The term *lintel grave* has been adopted in preference to *long cist*, but the distinction between these grave types is not clear cut - and depends to an extent on where in the country the graves are found. Representative graves are illustrated in Figure 3.3.

Lintel graves were lined with timber or stone, and covered with timber or stone lintels, usually covered with a relatively shallow layer of soil. The graves

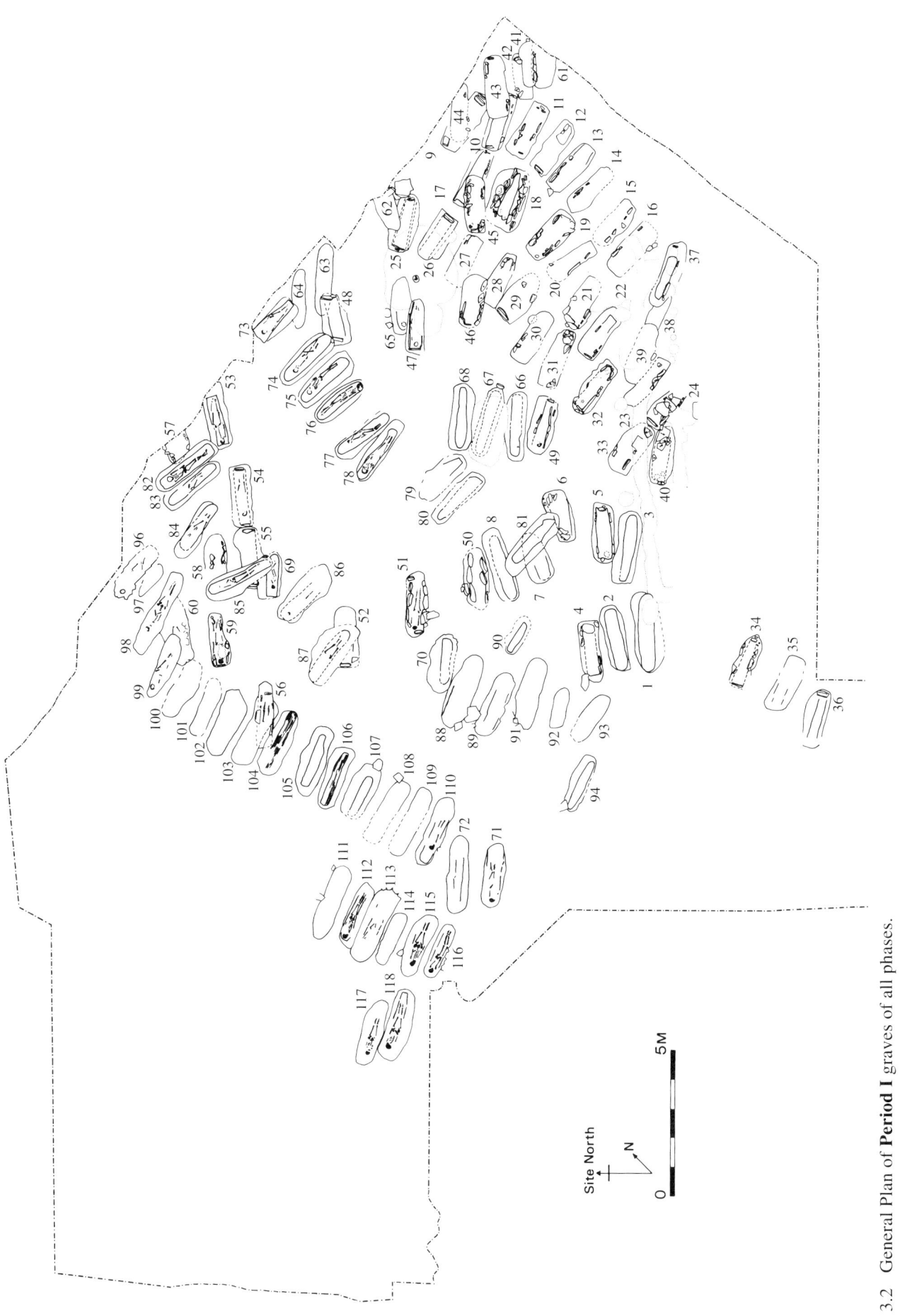

CHAPTER 3

3.2 General Plan of **Period I** graves of all phases.

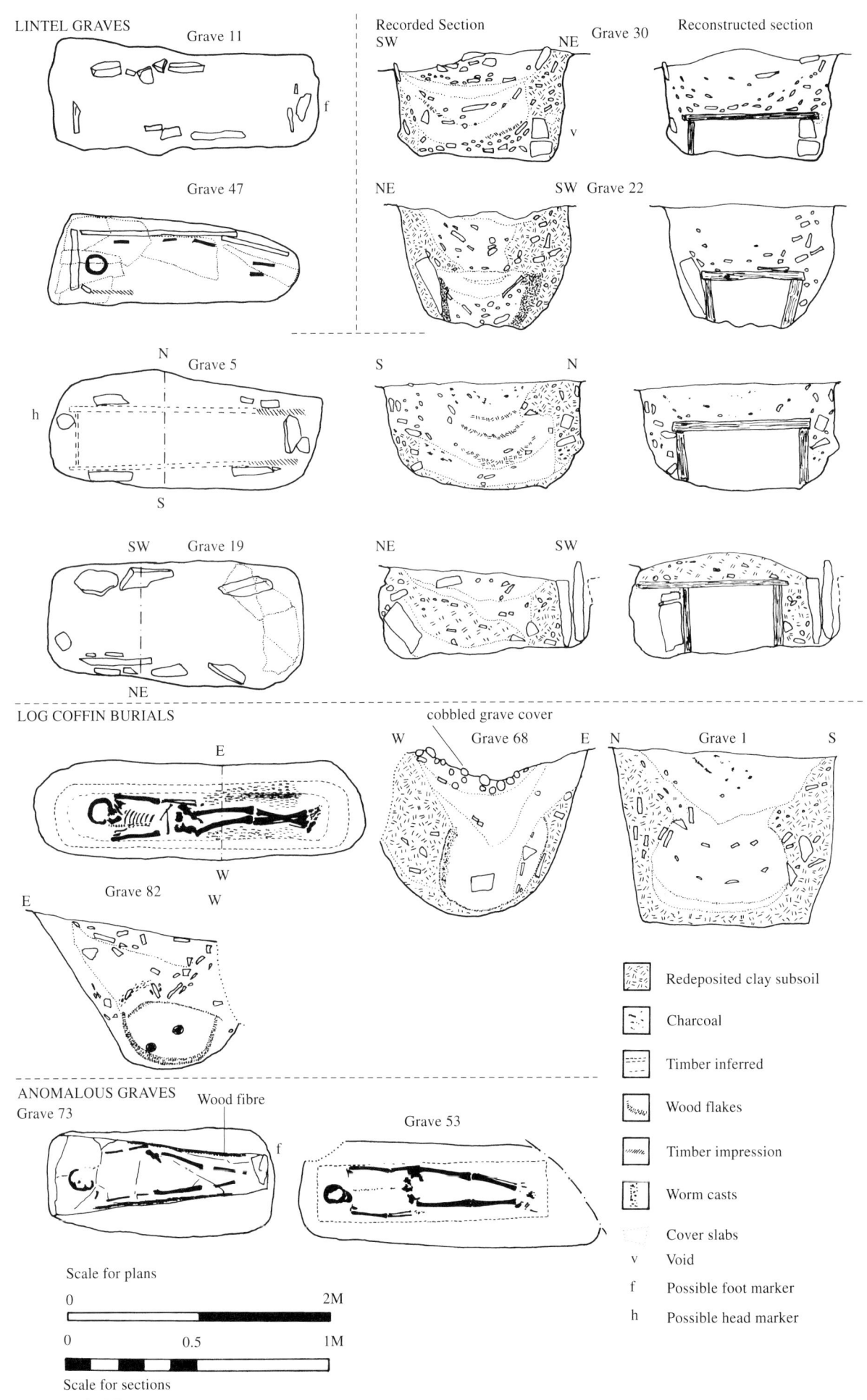

3.3 **Period I** grave types.

were not covered by mounds, and most of the soil dug from them must have been removed. Many graves were built of both timber and stone. The decay of the timber and consequent collapse of the grave structure made them appear very different from the stone-built graves, although they were originally similar in appearance, and served an identical function. There were three principal types of lintel grave:

> *Type 1* lintel graves had low side walls of timber or stone, and stone or timber lintels lying well below the ground surface (e.g. **30**). Graves with timber sides were frequently marked by lines of stones packed behind the wooden sides (e.g. **5** and **22**). A variant form (*Type 1a*) had dry stone walling, augmenting and levelling the side slabs.

> *Type 2* lintel graves had timber sides, separated and supported by stone slabs at the head and foot (e.g. **5**). These presumably supported timber lintels as cover stones were rare. The lintels lay some way below the ground surface.

> *Type 3* lintel graves had relatively high stone sides, indicating that the grave cover was flush with the ground surface, or close to it (e.g. **19**). The cover slabs did not generally survive. The 'focal' grave (**18**) in the **Phase 2** shrine was an unusually well built example of a *Type 3* lintel grave, and seems to have been specifically designed to receive successive burials. The other *Type 3* graves may also have accommodated special burials.

There was no consistent system of grave marking. A few graves had irregular stone kerbs flush with the ground, which had sometimes slumped below the surface when timber lintels decayed and the grave collapsed. A group of **Phase 3** graves (*Group A*, p 104) were covered with incomplete rectilinear settings of small slabs. Grave fills occasionally revealed slumping or staining at the head end which may indicate a marker post. Despite the general absence of recognisable markers, the graves were laid out in regular lines and rows, demonstrating that the positions of earlier burials were not forgotten.

Log coffin burials contained large coffins, apparently made from tree trunks, shaped, split and hollowed out. The coffins were circular in section and their ends were sometimes rounded. They were generally long (up to 2.6 m) and surprisingly narrow (as little as 0.2 m in diameter). The cavities within them must have been even smaller, and some of the surviving skeletons were laid on their sides, or twisted to accommodate the hips and shoulders (Figure 3.33). The larger coffins were probably extremely heavy, and it might have been difficult to bury them with dignity.

The coffins seem to have been highly durable. Their rounded tops and ends provided natural arch-formers for the overlying grave fill, and several survived as cavities long after the wood had decayed. These hidden cavities presented an unexpected hazard for later builders. The east wall of the *Northumbrian* church ran over one row of graves, two of which collapsed dragging the wall timbers downwards. Unidentifiable wood fibres survived in several graves, and the coffins in others were revealed by cavities, stains, worm-casts and the pattern of the soil and stones filling the graves.

The *log coffin burials* revealed a different system of grave marking. Two 'special' graves (**1** and **72**) were marked by posts at the head and foot, and were perhaps enclosed by light wattle fences (Figure 3.30). The heads of two others were marked by small granite boulders, and the foot of a third (**67**) was marked by a low stone slab. Four graves (**68, 80, 82** and **113**) were covered with pale granite and quartz pebbles (Table 3.3). One of these (**68**) was covered by two beds of pebbles (**68a** and **b**) separated by a layer of worm-sorted soil, and this grave probably enjoyed an enduring 'special' quality. The granite pebbles and rounded quartz came from beaches, and the abraded quartz pebbles probably came from stream beds. A similar range of stones was recovered from the displaced **Period I** metalworking debris (110, Table 3.35) used in the construction of the original *Northumbrian* ecclesiastical buildings. Enigmatic pebbles and other stones with calcium carbonate crusts or stains are discussed below (p 472). Most of the graves do not seem to have been marked, though the orderly rows of burials show that their positions were remembered.

Grave number	68a	68b	80	82	113	Total
Round quartz pebbles	32	47	477	15	139	*710*
Abraded quartz pebbles	64	98	944	73	169	*1348*
Granite pebbles and cobbles	239	520	679	17	55	*1510*
Pebbles with calcium carbonate	1	6	22	30	292	*351*
Total	*336*	*671*	*2122*	*135*	*655*	*3919*

Table 3.3. The composition of pebble and cobble grave covers

Other grave types. Two graves contained anomalous furnishings (Figure 3.3). **Grave 73** (**Phase 4.1**) had an unnailed trapezoid timber lining resting on a paved floor, and was, presumably, a variant form of lintel grave or long cist. **Grave 53** (**Phase 3.1**) contained an unnailed rectangular timber coffin or lining. Its phase suggests that it was a timber lining, and hence was the only all-timber lintel grave. A few graves revealed no evidence of coffins or lining, and could have been simple 'dug graves'.

The human remains. The skeletal remains in the **Period I** graves were generally poorly-preserved, and accordingly little is known of the population (pp 552-6). Preservation was particularly poor in the earlier graves in the south-east part of the site. Many graves here produced no remains, and only the tooth enamel survived in others. The skeletons in the **Phase 4** graves were generally better preserved, and included juveniles and adults of both sexes. The statures of nine skeletons could be estimated. Eight were male, and all but one were tall. The average male height of 176 cm (5' 9") contrasts with the shorter stature of the fourteenth to fifteenth century population (p 522). This indicates a well-nourished population that had reached its full genetic potential, and supports the hypothesis that log coffins were reserved for privileged members of society. The presence of a small number of females may indicate that this was a secular burial ground, although it could as easily have contained the monks and nuns of a double monastery.

Grave finds. The *inner precinct* produced a large assemblage of finds, which probably originated in well-stratified deposits, but had been greatly disturbed by the graves covering much of the area. The distributions of sherds of pottery and glass from specific vessels revealed a close, frequently exact, correlation between the finds from undisturbed deposits, and those from graves cutting through them (Figure 3.25). The finds from the graves cannot thus be the debris of the ritual graveside feasts as inferred at Tintagel Churchyard (Nowakowski and Thomas 1990, 15). Spreads of *industrial* debris disturbed by graves revealed similar patterns, and plough pebbles, which might have been deposited as 'white stones' (pp 472-3), generally corresponded with areas of earlier plough cultivation. Most of the finds from graves were thus probably displaced, and can frequently be reassigned to their original context.

This interpretation cannot be extended automatically to all the finds from the graves. Two fragments of 1st/2nd century glass bangles were probably intentional deposits, as may be a projectile point (IN75.1) and sherds of Samian pottery from two graves (**25** and **66**). Other finds which may have been intentional deposits, include knives (IN.66), flints, pins and 'white' pebbles of quartz and granite. Two **Phase 2** graves (**9** and **32**) produced iron objects with mineralised wood impressions which were probably the remains of decayed timber fittings, although there was inadequate evidence to reconstruct nailed timber coffins. Other possible furnishings are identified in Section 2.

The northern and central sectors: the archaeology of the *inner precinct*

INTRODUCTION

Excavation history. Period 1 deposits in the *inner precinct* were glimpsed during the trial excavation in 1984 (Hill 1984, 1985) and had been partly exposed by the end of 1989 (Hill 1990). The best preserved remain were, however, sealed beneath the *Northumbrian* church and related structures (pp 139-66), and were examined in the last four months of the 1991 excavation season. By this stage, plans for the restitution of the site and the start of a new phase of excavation were well advanced, and the earliest deposits in the north part of the **Glebe Field** were left unexcavated. A detailed plan of the unexcavated deposits has been lodged in the excavation archive.

Stratigraphy and phasing. The stratigraphic relationships of the **Period 1** features in the **central** and **northern sectors** record an eventful but coherent sequence, linking shallow, and frequently poorly-stratified features to the south with deeper, stratified deposits to the north (Figure 3.4). The stratigraphy was bound together by the successive graveyards of **Phases 2–4**, each displaying clearly defined sub-phases that give chronological depth to the diagram. The shallow deposits in the **central sector** had been disturbed by a brief episode of ploughing in the mid-ninth century (399.01 and 02, pp 190-2), displacing a small number of significant objects, which have nevertheless been included in distribution plots.

THE SEQUENCE

Phase 0

Phase 0 (Figures 2.1 and 3.5) records the earliest features, which were greatly disturbed by later activity. These produced no clear dating evidence, although they may be equated tentatively with a small group of Roman finds displaced into later contexts (pp 294-7).The principal feature was a broad roadway on the southern edge of the central plateau. This was the first of a series of roadways leading from the east end of the hill, and heading towards the Isle of Whithorn and perhaps the easier landing at Physgill Bay. A large prostrate stone slab on the upper slope of the northern bedrock ridge may have been natural, but could have been part of a slighted prehistoric monument.

The roadway (102) traversed the lower rock outcrop (Figure 3.5). Surface irregularities had been removed to provide a reasonably level surface, and the exposed rock was worn by prolonged use. The road was surfaced with pebbles which were covered by a thick layer of worm-sorted silt, indicating a period of disuse. Both layers had been disturbed by cultivation in **Phase 1.1**, and by the insecurely-dated **Phase 1** building (**1**) and boundary ditch to the east. The small group of finds from the roadway included a knife blade fragment (IN66.81), nail heads and a possible lead spindle whorl (LD03.1), but offers no firm dating evidence. The absence of metalworking waste and other debris confirms that the roadway preceded the industrial activity evident in **Phase 1**.

There was no other evidence of early activity in the *inner precinct,* and the absence of displaced earlier material (p 80) argues against extensive occupation of the plateau, although it cannot establish that there was no occupation. The **southern sector** revealed hints of cultivation predating the roadway, and a possible early building (*Stage 1* or *3* p 121): equivalent deposits have not been reached in the ground to the north. The distribution of Roman finds is discussed below (pp 121, 294-7).

CHAPTER 3

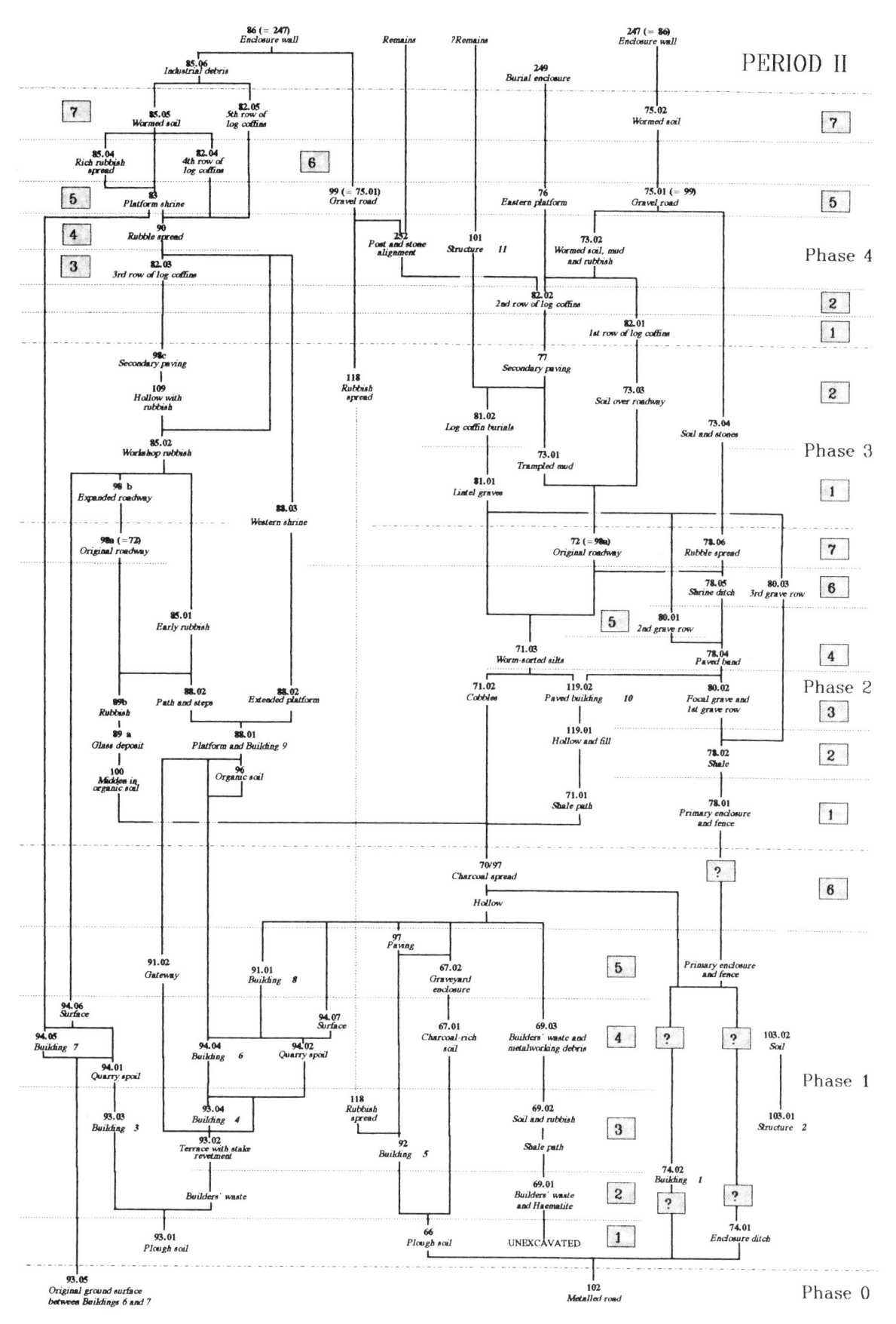

3.4 The stratigraphic sequence in the *inner precinct* in **Period I**.

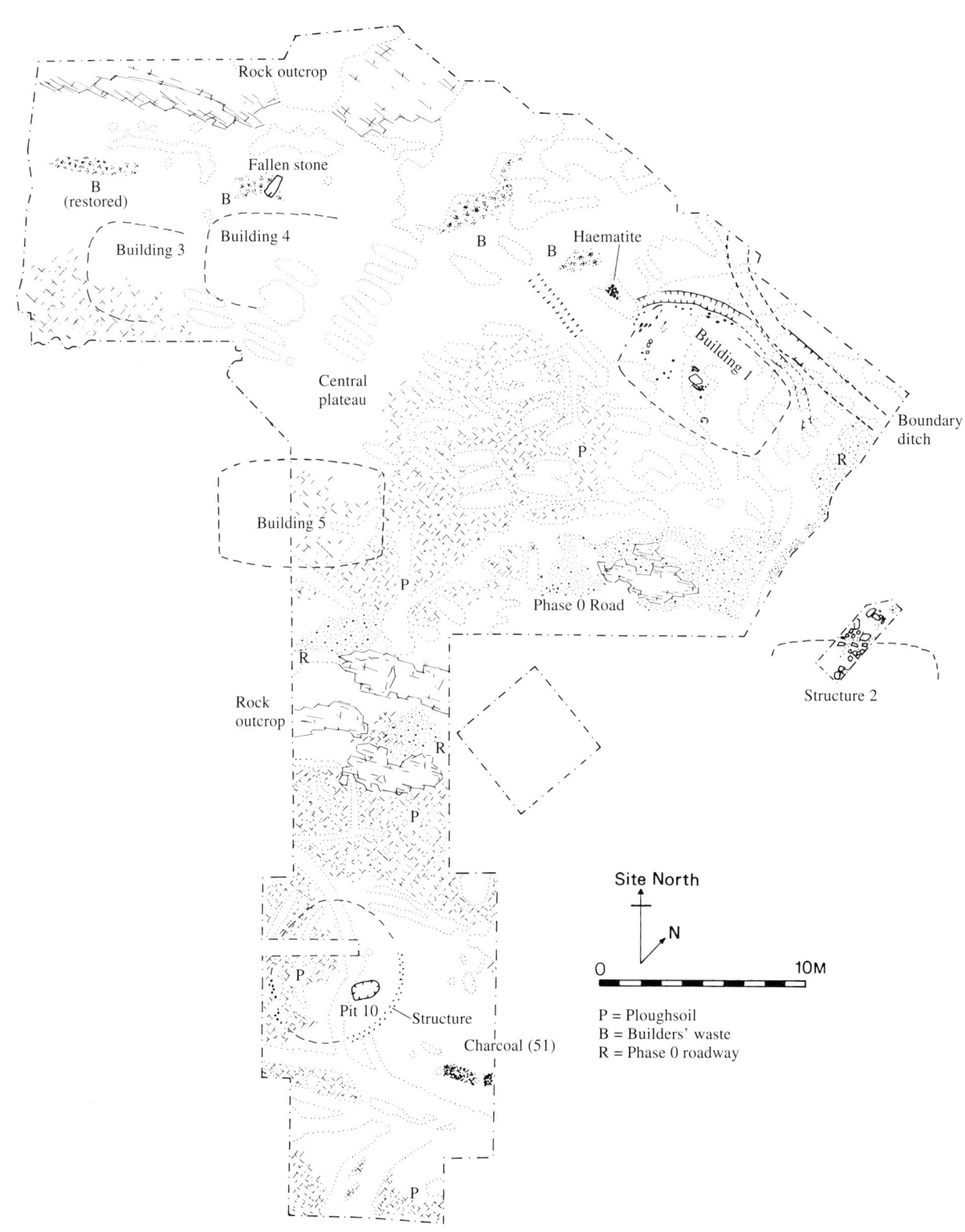

3.5 General plan of early structures and deposits ascribed to **Period I/0** and **Period I/1.1-.3**.

Phase 1

Phase 1 (Figures 2.2, 3.5 and 3.6) records the colonisation of the south side of the hill, and reveals the rapid expansion of settlement in the late-fifth/early-sixth century. Much of the evidence was fragmentary and insubstantial, but stratified deposits on the north side of the central plateau revealed six sub-phases (*Stages 1–6*) with which most of the features further to the south can be correlated. The **southern sector** revealed a similar sequences and the two areas can be correlated with considerable confidence, despite the weak stratigraphic links (pp 119-20). The boundary ditch at the east end of the central plateau was the most important single **Phase 1** feature (pp 27-30), but its chronological position is uncertain due to the shallow stratigraphy and scarcity of finds.

The sequence began in **Phase 1.1** with the cultivation of the better ground on the south side of the hill, and a subsequent accumulation of builders' debris in **Phase 1.2** points to the construction of a plastered and, possibly, mortared and lime-washed building in the vicinity. A spread of crushed Haematite from the north-east part of the site and a distinctive group of ironworking debris from the **southern sector** indicated iron smelting, and may reflect the manufacture of fittings for the new buildings. These deposits reveal a sophisticated use of the requisite technologies, and the knowledgeable exploitation of regional resources. The expansion of the original community in **Phase 1.3** was marked by the erection of simple cabins on the formerly ploughed ground. By this time the community was sufficiently prosperous to attract merchants with supplies of wine and luxury goods originating in the Mediterranean. The **Phase 1.3** cabins were replaced in **Phase 1.4** with slightly better-finished buildings. Increasing formality in the organisation of the settlement was indicated by the demarcation of a new graveyard in **Phase 1.5**. This seems to have remained a revered part of the *inner precinct* throughout **Period I**, and perhaps contained the graves of some of the founders of the community. The process of formalisation was complete by the end of **Phase 1**, and most of the clustered buildings seem to have been cleared from the *inner precinct* by **Phase 1.6**. A rich group of finds included a sequence of imported pottery and glass, providing a detailed picture of trade and contact in the first half of the sixth century, and perhaps the closing years of the fifth (pp 323-5).

This crucial period can be summarised in three phase drawings. Figure 3.5 shows the fragmentary features and deposits of **Phase 0** and **Phase 1.1–1.3**. **Building 1** and the boundary ditch are included as they are likely to have been contemporary with the *Stage 1* cultivation (p 80). Figure 3.6 illustrates the **Phase 1** settlement at its greatest extent, conflating the *Stage 4* buildings in the **northern sector**, the *Stage 5* buildings in the **southern sector**, and two poorly-stratified buildings (**2** and **5**) on the fringes of the **central sector**. This forms the basis for the general phase plan in Chapter 2 (Figure 2.2), and the speculative reconstruction of the *monasterium* in the early-sixth century (Figure 2.3). Figure 3.7 shows the **northern** and **central sectors** at the end of **Phase 1**. **Building 1** has been abandoned, and the boundary ditch is partly filled, while the new graveyard occupies the middle of the **central sector**. **Building 6** and, perhaps, **Buildings 5** and **7** remain standing, but the south side of **Building 8** has been dug away by the **Phase 1.6** hollow. The buildings in the **southern sector** (Figure 3.6) may have remained standing.

The chronology of **Phase 1** depends upon the inferred date of *c.* 550 for *Stage 6* (p 69) and a radiocarbon date of 1690±50bp (GU-2052, pp 596-7) from a detached structure (**2**, p 79), which hints that the sequence started in the late-fifth century. These dates indicate that **Phase 1** spanned a period of fifty or more years in the closing decades of the fifth century and first half of the sixth. There is insufficient evidence to date the boundary ditch and builders' debris with precision, and while both are likely to pertain to the beginning of this phase, they could be earlier (below p 81). They are, perhaps, unlikely to have been much later than 500 AD.

Unphased features: Building 1 and the boundary ditch (Figure 3.8). A curvilinear ditch at the east end of the central plateau was probably part of an enclosure around the east end of the hill, defining the boundary between the original *inner precinct* and the agricultural, residential and industrial activities to the south west. A fragmentary sub-rectilinear stake-walled building (**1**) immediately beyond the ditch was probably contemporary, although it was probably erected after the ditch had been dug. The ditch and building underlay the **Phase 2** shrine and graveyard, but their relationship to other **Phase 1** features cannot be established. The only finds came from the soil filling the ditch, although scattered *industrial* and *domestic* debris seems to have respected the building. The *Stage 1* ploughing did not extend this far east, suggesting that this ground may already have been occupied by the building and ditch. Despite the lack of stratigraphic links with other **Phase 1** deposits, the building and ditch were probably primary features maintained throughout the early stages of **Phase 1** (*Stages 1–4*).

The ditch. The ditch lay on the east side of the trench, and described a shallow curve, perhaps centred on the crossing of the high-medieval cathedral. The northern part ran down slope, but crossed the level ground to the south obliquely, and is thus unlikely to have been dug as a drain. The ditch was 1.0 m wide and 0.5 m deep, with steep sides and a flat base. There was no evidence of a bank, and the spoil from the ditch was probably removed. The ditch was partly filled with silt overlain by a thick layer of charcoal. The only other find was an unassigned sherd of vessel glass. The ditch seems to have been short-lived, but it marked a boundary which was respected by the **Phase 2** graveyard, and possibly retained its significance until the end of **Period 1**.

Building 1 had been severely disturbed by graves and other later features, but enough survived to identify an unusually substantial stake-walled building, probably occupying a shallow hollow cutting the topsoil. The principal features were a rectilinear stone hearth and scattered stake holes marking a bowed north-east wall and a straight wall to the north-west. The stake-holes of the north-east wall were large and deeply driven. The floor comprised lightly trampled gravelly subsoil overlain by fine silt, which probably represents an earth floor. Scattered stones in the north-west part of the building

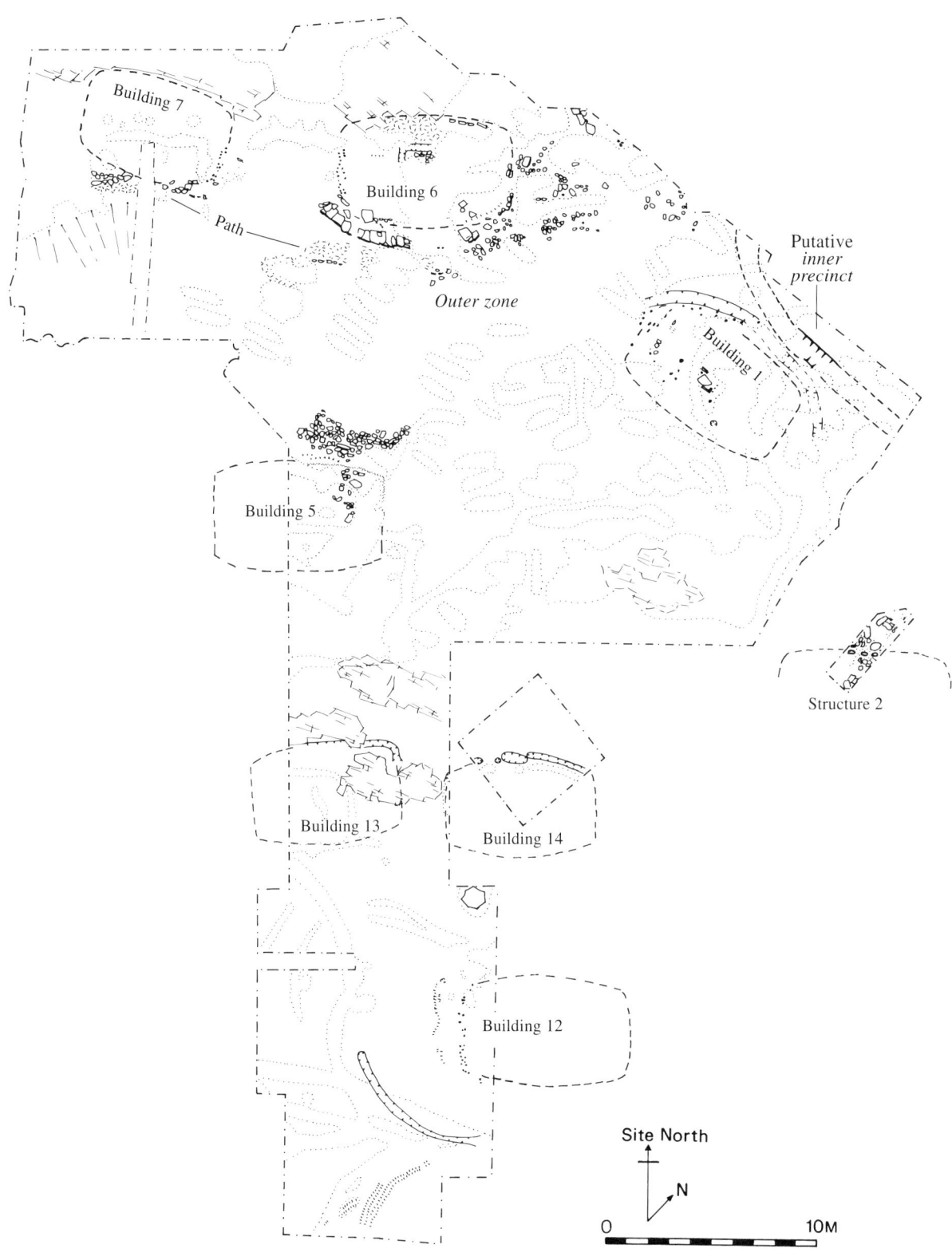

3.6 General plan of **Period I/1.4** structures and surfaces.

may have been a rough surface in a separate room, and an irregular line of stakes-holes marked a possible internal partition. A curvilinear drainage gully around the east side of the building touched the boundary ditch. They were probably broadly coeval, although their exact relationship was unclear. The northern part of the building was oversailed by a diffuse scatter of charcoal probably pertaining to *Stage 6*. The original shape of the building is uncertain, and the reconstructed outline (Figures 3.8 etc) is based on **Building 6**.

The only find from the building was a pronged, ring-headed, copper-alloy instrument (BZ24.11) from silt filling the drainage gully. This is a undoubtedly a

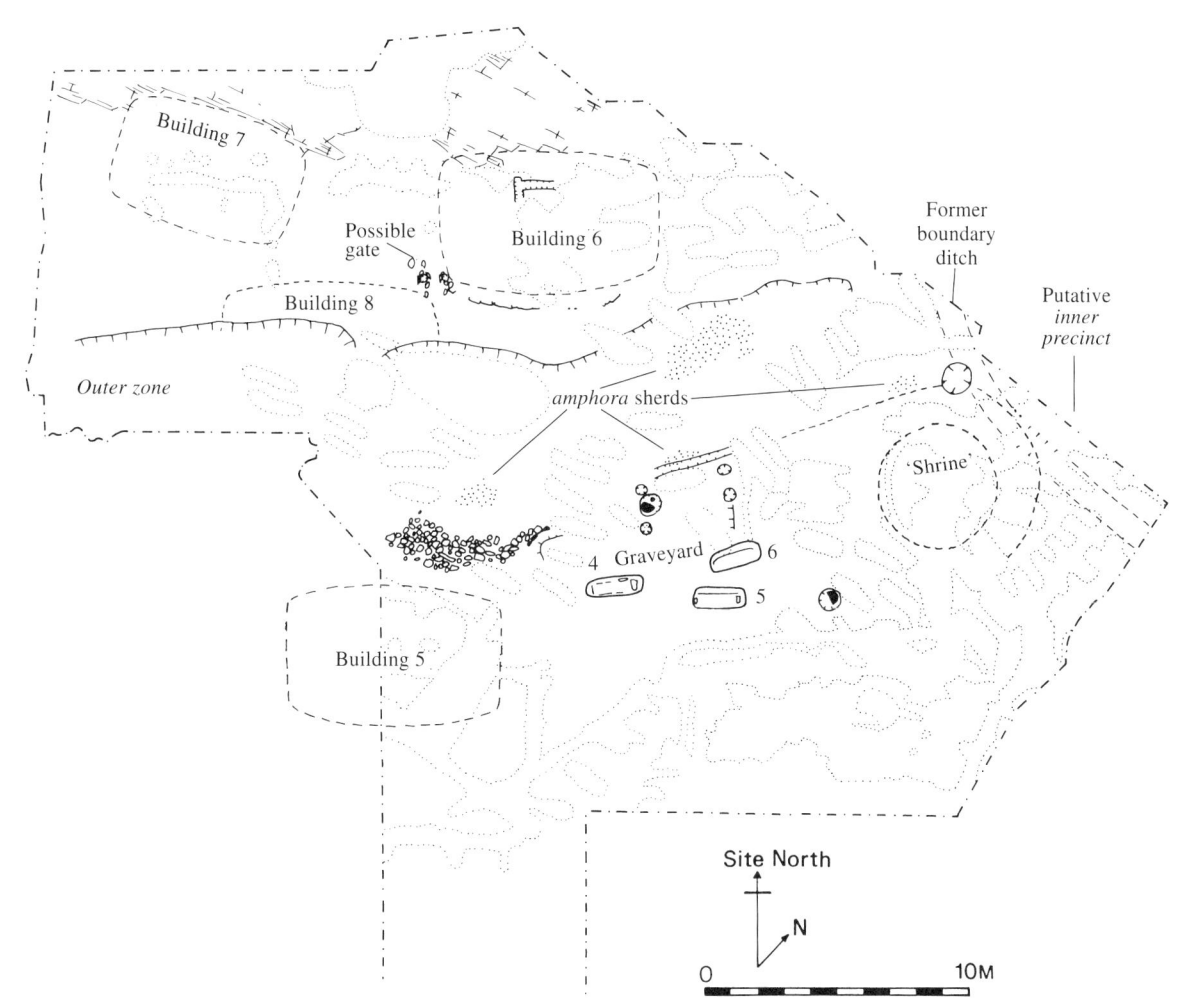

3.7 General plans of **central** and **northern sectors** in **Period I/1.5-.6**.

Roman type of artefact, and is similar to 'nail cleaners' from native sites in Scotland and from Early Christian sites in Ireland. These were clearly popular beyond the Empire, and some examples may have been produced by native bronze smiths after the end of the Roman occupation (p 377).

Adjacent deposits. The ground to the north of **Building 1** revealed a stratified sequence of surfaces, wormed soil and rubbish spreads with three principal phases of deposition (69.01–03) ascribed to *Stages 2–4* (below). The ground to the west (67.01) produced a scatter of metalworking debris, indicating ironwork and bronze-casting (Figure 10.86), and finds from graves to the south were probably part of the same rubbish spread. These, and other disturbed deposits in the vicinity, produced scattered sherds of glass vessels and B*i amphorae* (Vs 1 and 2) which may have been *domestic* debris associated with the building (Figure 3.8). These included scraps of three, possibly four, of the five Group A vessels with wheel-cut decoration (Vs 1, 4, 5 and, possibly, 3, p 300) and a possible squat jar of Group B or D (V54, pp 308-9). **Building 1** was probably built before debris had started to accumulate, and remained standing while rubbish spreads accumulated around it.

Structure 2 (Figure 3.8). The 1984 excavation (Trench 2) revealed an isolated structure (**2**, 103.01) to the south of **Building 1**, comprising an area of paving crossed by a beam slot (*c.* 0.15 m wide). The paving lay immediately south of the lower outcrop, and was laid in a level platform cutting into the bedrock. The paving was overlain by a layer of charcoal sealed by a thick layer of soil (0.2 m deep; 103.02), which must have been introduced from elsewhere, possibly to form a a cultivation plot. Thin section analysis (p 600) identified this as a 'cultivated midden soil'. The paving produced a sherd of a B*i amphora* (V1), and other sherds of this vessel were deposited in *Stage 3* contexts to the north. The charcoal comprised fragments of alder, birch, hazel and willow roundwood and more mature oak, and produced a radiocarbon date of 1690±50BP (GU 2052 pp 596-7). The structural features possibly comprise part of the north side of a building in a shallow stance cutting the bedrock ridge (Figure 3.6).

Phase 1: The stratified sequence

Stage 1

Stage 1 saw the cultivation of the western part of the central plateau, and probably of the low-lying

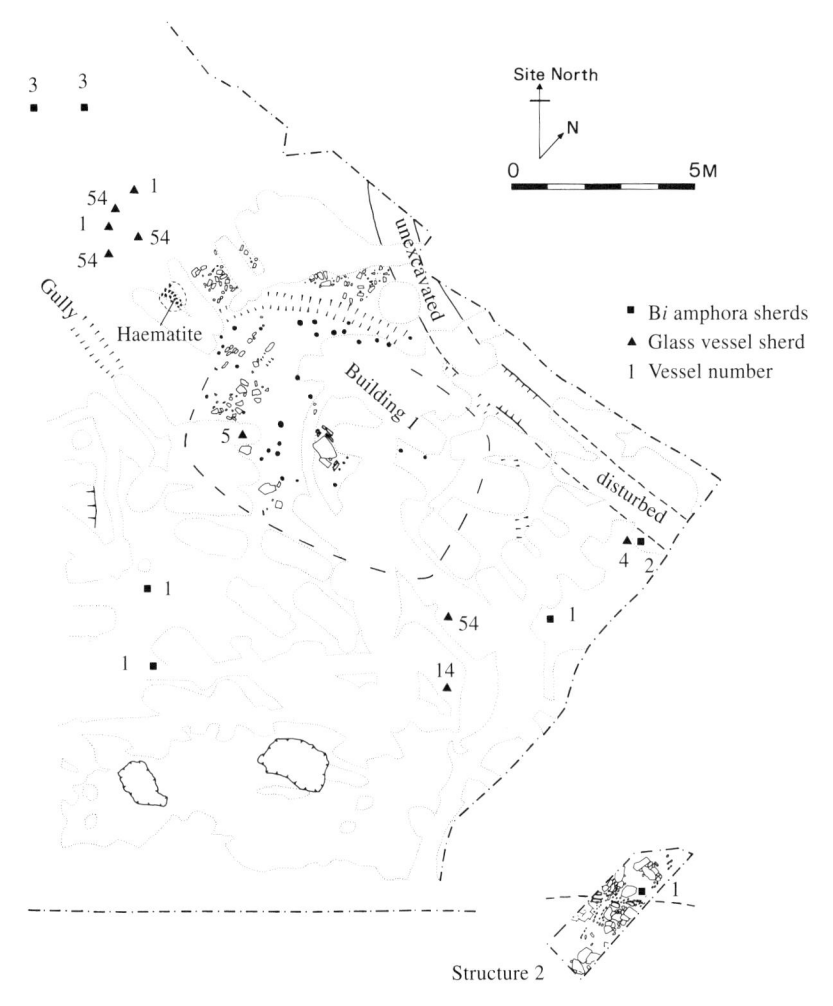

3.8 Detailed plan of early structures and ditch in the eastern part of the **central sector**.

ground in the **southern sector** (Figure 3.5). The ploughing did not extend to the east end of the central plateau, indicating that the boundary around the east end of the hill had already been established, although it may not yet have been marked by a ditch.

The cultivation (66, 105, 93.01) was represented by a churned, charcoal-rich clayey plough soil extending over most of the western part of the central plateau, and cutting into the foot of the northern slope. The use of a mouldboard plough was indicated by sporadic furrows oriented north-east/south-west, and confirmed by plough-pebbles from the ploughsoil, overlying wormed horizon, and intrusive graves (Figure 10.124a). The eastern limit of the cultivated ground was marked by a shallow gully, which may originally have joined the drain around **Building 1**. The ploughsoil was overlain by a worm-sorted layer indicating a period of fallow. The ploughing had disturbed the **Phase 0** roadway, but was otherwise the earliest event recognised.

The ploughsoil was only partly excavated, and the small group of finds (Table 3.4) was dominated by plough pebbles. The pebbles with flat facets may derive from the axle of a wheeled plough fore-carriage (Lerche 1970a, 144) rather than from the plough sole. The absence (or sparseness) of materials common in later deposits (iron-working debris, worked and unworked flints, iron artefacts), indicates that there was little debris in the area before **Period I**. The *amphora* sherd and glass fragments were probably derived from overlying deposits. The bowl sherd was, perhaps, domestic debris associated with **Building 3**.

Seven plough pebbles, six of quartz with flat facets, one of granite with a unilateral facet (SE51)
A corroded iron ring (IN30.5)
A sherd of a Group A glass bowl (V8)
Two featureless vessel glass sherds and one of group E2
A B*ii amphora* sherd (V2)
A chip of botryoidal Haematite (SE62.15)
A natural flint pebble and three **retouched** flints
Six lumps of glassy cinder (62gm)

Table 3.4: Finds from *Stage 1* ploughsoil (66, 105, 93.01)

Stage 2
Stage 2 (Figure 3.5) was marked by spreads of builders' waste on the sloping ground to the north of the **central plateau**, probably deriving from the construction of a plastered or mortared building in the vicinity. The waste comprised '*clastic lime*'

which survived as concreted lumps of grey lime, sometimes with an incomplete white crust of calcium carbonate. It included particles of clay, and so probably derives from carboniferous limestone, which had been burnt, pulverised and slaked. It was presumably intended as a component of cement, plaster or limewash, but had not been mixed with sand, although slightly later contexts produced fragments of these materials. The calcium carbonate crust shows that piles of unmixed lime had been exposed for some time, and the surface had gradually been converted to calcium carbonate by exposure to atmospheric CO_2. These piles were subsequently broken up and dumped on the slope below the bedrock ridge.

There are no carboniferous rocks in the vicinity of Whithorn, and limestone outcrops on the north Solway coast some 22 miles to the east are the closest possible source. It is uncertain where the lime was produced. It would have been more economical to burn it at its source, but later deposits produced both burnt and unburnt limestone, (pp 470-1) and it may have been imported for processing at Whithorn. Lime technology would have been readily available in Roman Britain, but was, perhaps, among the casualties of the collapse of the Roman economy in the fifth century. The lime may have come from a relatively local source, but the technologies of preparing it and using it have no known antecedents in early Galloway.

There were two deposits of waste. The larger group to the west was disturbed by building platforms dug in *Stages 3* and *4*, and the primary dump was recorded, but left *in situ*. Further debris to the west was displaced from the stance of **Building 7** (*Stage 4*), and scattered over the remains of **Building 3** (*Stage 3*). No lime was recovered from the adjacent *Stage 1* plough soil, indicating that it was deposited after cultivation had ceased. The second dump of *clastic lime* lay to the east among the stratified deposits (69.01) to the north of **Building 1**. This group overlay a cobble surface at the foot of the northern ridge, and extended some way up the slope. It included some 5.4 kg of 'clastic lime', and further lumps had been displaced into later graves.

There was no evidence that lime had been used in the excavated **Period 1** buildings, and it was probably associated with the construction of a building (or buildings) on the crown of the hill. The fact that lumps of abandoned plaster had been broken up before they were deposited means that this phase of construction cannot be correlated precisely with the in the sequence, and despite the stratigraphic evidence, could have preceded the *Stage 1* cultivation.

A discrete deposit to the south of the eastern group of 'clastic lime' comprised a cluster of chunks of massive Haematite (Figure 3.8). This had been disturbed by two later graves (**77** and **78**), and dispersed upwards into later **Period 1** deposits. 34 lumps weighing a total of 3,748 gm survived *in situ*, and a further 81 lumps weighing 5,982 gm had been displaced. The original deposit probably covered an area of *c.* 0.6 x 0.6 m, and contained at least 115 lumps weighing 9,730 gm. The most obvious use for the Haematite would have been iron smelting, but there was no related metalworking debris at this level, although the overlying deposits (Tables 3.9 and 21) and intrusive graves (pp 112-3) produced large groups of waste. It can be correlated tentatively with a group of metalworking debris in the **southern sector** (*Stage 4*, pp 122-3) post-dating a cultivated soil (*Stage 3*, p 122), potentially equivalent to the *Stage 1* cultivation on the central plateau. These deposits point to an episode of ironworking which probably involved smelting, and had left debris scattered widely over the southern part of the **Glebe Field**. This was probably the source of metalworking debris displaced into the **Phase 2** graves, and underlying the *Stage 5* graveyard. The focus of this activity perhaps lies in the unexcavated ground in the south part of the field.

The scattered clastic lime (69.01) produced a small sherd from the claw of a Germanic beaker (V12b) ascribed to the mid-sixth century, and a second fragment was found in a **Phase 4** context nearby (76). This date is incompatible with other evidence from this suite of deposits, suggesting either that the sherd was intrusive, or else that it was rather earlier (perhaps *c.* 500 AD) than is supposed. The only other find was a tanged Class C2 knife, possibly lost in its sheath (IN66.23). The absence of other imported pottery and glass indicates that *Stage 2* predated the arrival of the first goods of Mediterranean origin.

Stage 3

Stage 3 (Figure 3.5, 9 and 10) saw the erection of three buildings on the cultivated ground in the western part of the central plateau. Two (**3** and **4**) were built in hollows cutting the foot of the northern ridge, the third (**5**) lay in the middle of the plateau on the west edge of the trench. The structural remains were ephemeral, and the interpretation of '**Buildings**' **3** and **4** is tenuous. Three buildings (**12–14**) on the same alignment in the **southern sector** may have been erected at this time (Figures 3.6 and 38). The buildings produced few finds, but a broadly contemporary spread of debris (69.02) accumulated to the north of **Building 1**, while a complementary group of finds from debris overlying **Building 3** (94.01) probably pertained to this phase. These seem to have been part of an extensive rubbish accumulation on the northern slope, which produced the earliest securely-stratified groups of imported pottery and glass, and a wide range of industrial debris.

'**Building**' **3** (93.03) occupied a sub-circular scoop cutting the *Stage 1* ploughsoil at the foot of the northern ridge (Figure 3.9). The floor of the scoop revealed scattered stakeholes, a shallow sub-rectilinear gully and a shallow pit. These features probably represented fragments of a sub-rectilinear building, although its form and size cannot be established. The small group of finds included a sherd of a Group A bowl (V8) from undisturbed ground to the south of the putative building.

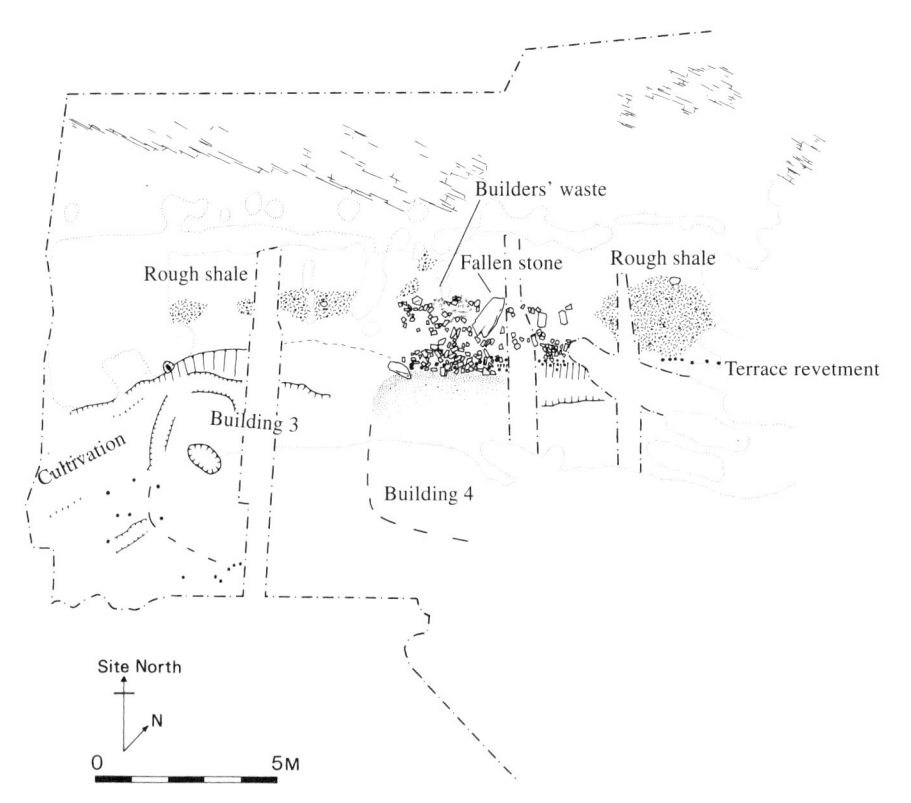

3.9 **Period I/1.3** buildings and associated deposits in the western part of the **northern sector**.

Building 4 (93.04) lay to the east of **Building 3**, and occupied a level platform cut through the *Stage 2* builders' waste into the foot of the northern ridge (Figure 3.9). The building was represented by an earth floor on rubble and shale foundations, with a rounded north-west corner comparable with later, and better-preserved, wattle-walled buildings. The southern part of the building was destroyed by a later hollow (91.02). The spoil from the platform was dumped behind a stake revetment, forming a terrace (93.02) immediately north of the building. The revetment was at least 9.0 m long and may have extended further to the east and west. This was the first of a series of boundaries on this alignment, which evolved into an important chordal division within the *inner precinct* of the **Period I** *monasterium*, and seems to have survived as the boundary of the ecclesiastical buildings in its *Northumbrian* successor (p 135).

The western part of the central plateau revealed a group of structural remains overlying the *Stage 1* cultivated soil, which probably represents a sequence of buildings, beginning in *Stage 3*, and surviving to the end of **Phase 1**. The most coherent elements were part of a sub-rectilinear building (92, **5**) and a paved surface (95) to the north. A stony layer beneath the paving may have been floor of a second building. The paving was probably laid against the enclosure around the *Stage 5* graveyard, while other features and deposits (118) in this area of shallow stratigraphy probably pertained to **Phases 3** and **4** (Table 3.24).

Building 5 (Figure 3.10) extended beyond the excavated area, and its southern side had been obliterated by a later *Northumbrian* hall (II/6). The north and east walls survived as narrow strips (0.1 m wide and 0.03 m deep) cut or pressed into the underlying soil, and probably representing timber sills, perhaps with drilled sockets for vertical wattle wands. The north wall line displayed three slightly angled segments. Fine silts to either side of the slot probably comprised a beaten earth floor and weathered daub from the walls. A shallow gully immediately beyond the wall, was sealed by silt, and was perhaps a naturally-formed eaves-drip. Paving at the east end of the building respected the walls, and may have been the floor of a small separate apartment, similar to examples in other buildings (pp 67-70).

Two sherds of glass from the floor of **Building 5**, and a concentration of sherds beyond the east wall (Figure 3.10), included fragments of three or four bowls, two of Group A (Vs 6 and 7) and one or two of Group D or A (V48 and, possibly V49), and a possible Anglo-Saxon cone or funnel beaker (V53). These were probably *domestic debris* associated with the building, and comprising a distinctively different assemblage to the broadly contemporary group associated with **Building 1** (pp 79-80). The predominance of bowls (or possible bowls) in both groups is significant, as is the absence of Group C and D cone sherds, while the different types of vessels in the two groups may identify successive cargoes of trade goods (pp 323-4).

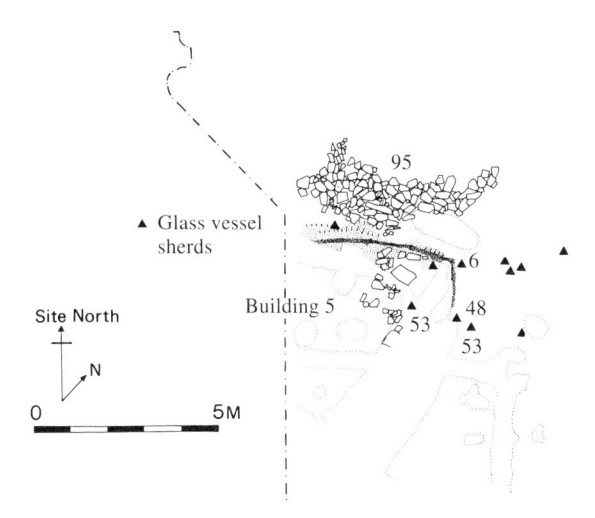

3.10 **Building I/5** and the adjacent paving showing distribution of displaced and stratified sherds of vessel glass.

The northern part of the **central plateau** produced two large groups of finds which probably pertain to *Stage 3*, although they were not directly associated with the buildings. The first group (**1**, 69.02) came from the undisturbed stratified deposits to the north of **Building 1**. The second group (**2**, 94.01), comprising debris overlying the remains of **Building 3**, was deposited at the start of *Stage 4*, but had probably accumulated on the ground to the north in *Stage 3*. Two large groups of finds (64.02 and 56.01/02, Tables 3.39 and 40) from the **southern sector** may have accumulated at roughly the same time.

Group 1. The eastern spread of builders' debris (69.01) was sealed by a shale surface covered by a layer of soil (69.02). This produced a wide range of finds, including sherds of pottery and glass which were the earliest securely-stratified imported objects (Table 3.5, Figures 3.8 and 11). The B*ii* amphora sherd was almost certainly intrusive, but other sherds of the B*i* amphora (V3) came from adjacent deposits, and probably originated in this deposit (Figure 3.11). The engraved glass sherd matches others from the vicinity of **Building 1**, and a second sherd (1b) came from an adjacent later context, as did the other sherds of the 'squat jar' (V54, Figure 3.8). Four of the nails (IN11) were unusually long, and have distinctive small square heads. The clastic lime was probably displaced from the underlying **Phase 1.2** deposit. The antler and copper alloy were matched in the larger **Group 2** assemblage, as was the small group of metalworking debris. The antler discoid may have been a partly-finished amulet for protecting cattle (p 491).

Two sherds of a B*i* amphora (V3)
A sherd of a B*ii* amphora (V1)
A sherd of engraved glass (V1a)
Two sherds of a possible Anglo-Saxon pale-green squat jar (V54 c and d)
Two featureless glass vessel sherds
A possible class C tanged knife (IN66.36)
Six nails

A broken copper alloy plate with a border of punched dots (BZ35.2)
A curved copper alloy strip (BZ38.1)
An antler tine and a burr trimmed to form a discoid (AR81.5)
Three **retouched** white flints
A siltstone discoid (SE20.3) and a quartz plough pebble (SE51)
Four lumps of clastic lime
Scraps of metalworking debris including a rare furnace wall fragment.

Table 3.5: finds from rubbish spread to north of **Building 1** (69.02)

Group 2a comprised debris from deposits overlying **Building 3**, which probably derived from the excavation of a new building stance immediately to the north at the start of *Stage 4*. There were two main layers. The lower layer of dirty clay probably derived from the boulder clay over the outcrop, while an overlying spread of rubble may have come from the bedrock itself. The large group of finds (Table 3.6) thus probably represents debris scattered over the northern slope. It included *clastic lime*, which presumably derives from *Stage 2* deposits, but the other finds probably date to *Stage 3*. It is a typical *industrial* assemblage, including antler working debris, scrap iron and copper-alloy stock, but with a possible *domestic* element indicated by the bead and glass vessel sherds, and perhaps the flints. The vessels comprise part of a possible bowl (V59), confirming the relatively early date of this form, and the earliest (V41) of a series of cones with horizontal trails from relatively early contexts in the *inner precinct* (pp 306-7). The large group of plough pebbles is the earliest of a series from this part of the site, which were disassociated from plough soil, and perhaps reflect the repair of ploughs in the vicinity. The group of metalworking debris is of particular interest due to the presence of slag and a relatively rare fragment of furnace wall. It contrasts with the distinctive debris of *Stage 4*, and almost certainly derives from different processes, perhaps smelting rather than smithying. The iron objects are characteristic scrap (pp 405, 432), while the loom weight, rubbing stone and scored slab are matched in other groups with metalworking debris (e.g. Table 3.35, pp 456, 458). The copper-alloy and lead point to other metalworking activities, while the tines indicate the manufacture and repair of handles. The piece of unburnt limestone may have been displaced from the deposits producing the clastic lime, and hints that the lime was burnt at Whithorn. The group is similar in many ways to larger groups of industrial debris which accumulated in the same area in **Phase 3**, and suggests that an industrial zone had already been established in the western part of the site at this relatively early date.

A B*i* amphora sherd (V2)
Sherds of a glass cone (V41) and possible bowl (V59)
Five unassigned glass vessel sherds (one of Group C, the others uncertain)
An amber-coloured wound glass bead (GS03.2)
Ten nails and fragments
Two possible iron wedges (IN53.1 and 2) and a hook (IN31.1)
An iron rivet (IN21.1), a strip (IN80.1), two plates (IN82.1 and 2),

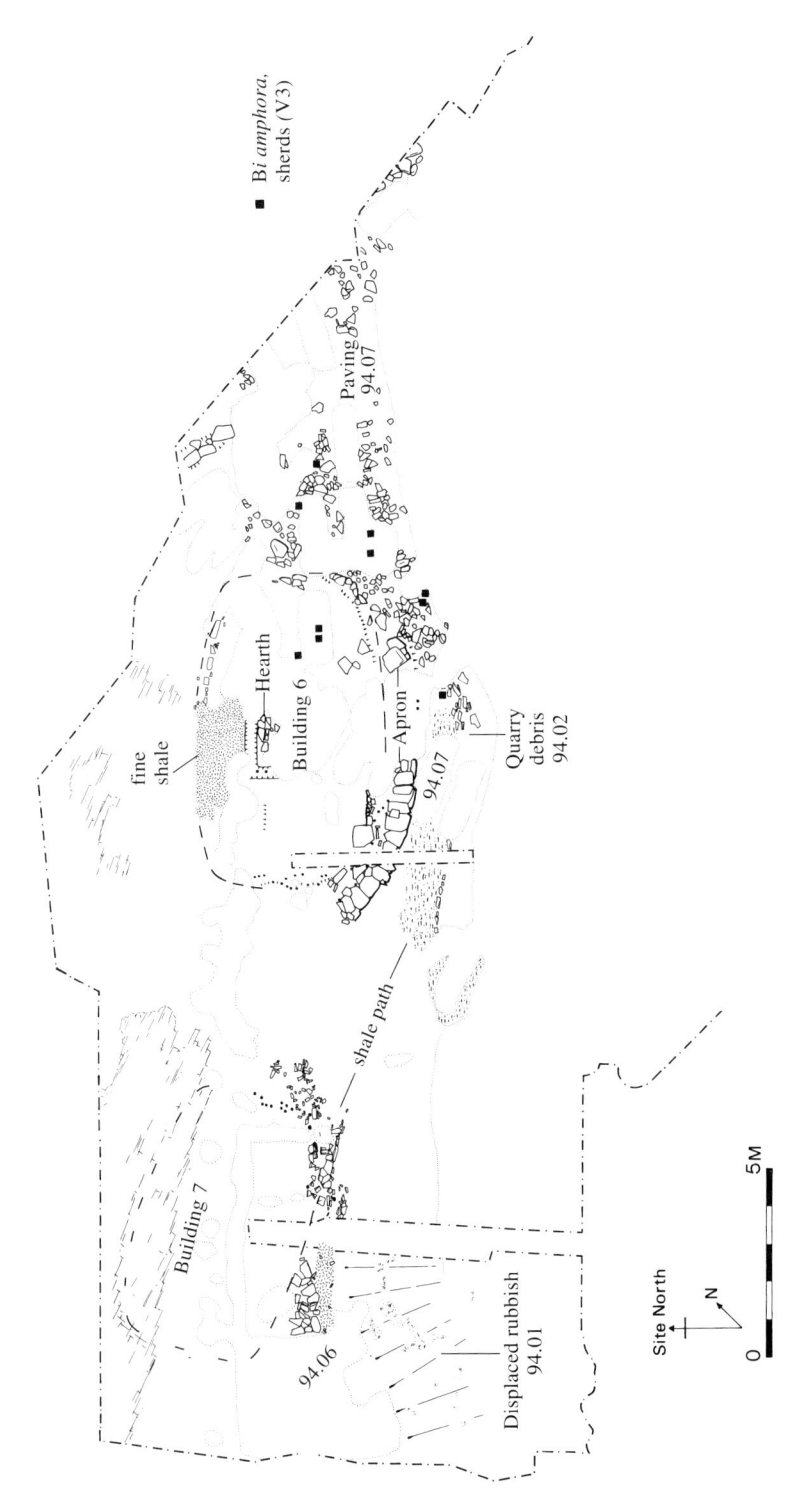

3.11 **Period I/1.4** buildings and associated surfaces and deposits in the **northern sector**.

two shaped bars (IN83.1 and 2) and four unidentified lumps (IN93.5–8)
Two rods or pieces of copper-alloy wire (BZ36.1 and 2) and five sheet fragments (BZ38.2–4)
A round-headed lead rivet (LD6.1) and three (?molten) nodules (LD12.1–3)
Three antler tines and a tine tip
Nine **retouched** flints and an **unretouched** waste flake
A greywacke 'loom weight' (SE29.4), a shaped rubbing stone (SE50.11) and an incised and scored slab (SE54.2)
Eleven plough pebbles (SE51)
A botryoidal Haematite polisher (SE62.12) and a sandstone hone blank (SE71.42)
A distinctive group of metalworking debris including:
    Six fragments of slag (SG3)
    A furnace floor fragment (SG35)
    A fragment of furnace wall fused to a hearth base (SG32)
    Nine tuyere core fragments (SG27)
A piece of unburnt limestone (SE59.4) and a large group of clastic lime (CO1)

Table 3.6: Possible *Stage 3* finds from debris overlying **Building 3** (94.01)

A second smaller group of finds (**Group 2b**, Table 3.7) came from equivalent deposits (94.02) abutting **Building 6**, which can be ascribed to *Stage 3* for the same reason. The *industrial* debris of **Groups 1** and **2a** is missing and the group suggests that pottery and glass may have been distinct, separate components of the rubbish spread. The group indicates that one B*ii* amphora (V3, p 318,) may have originated in *Stage 3*. The cone sherd is of an early type (pp 306-7).

Sherds of two B*i* amphorae (neck and rim of V2, and a fragmented body sherd of V3)
A B*ii* amphora sherd (V3)
A Group C cone beaker sherd (V44) and an unassigned vessel glass sherd
A plough pebble (SE51)
A piece of burnt limestone (SE60)
Three crucible fragments with traces of leaded brass (SG15.1)

Table 3.7: Finds from quarry debris abutting **Building 6** (94.02)

Stage 4
Stage 4 (Figures 3.6 and 11) followed the abandonment or demolition of **Buildings 3** and **4**, and saw the construction of two new buildings (**6** and **7**) on adjoining platforms further up the slope of the northern ridge. **Building 5** probably remained standing. The relatively small groups of finds from this phase included iron-working debris from the eastern part of the area. Pottery and glass were sparse, perhaps indicating an hiatus in supplies.

Building 6 (94.04, Figure 3.12) had been severely disturbed by later graves, but enough survived to identify a small sub-rectilinear stake-walled building with a central hearth, flanked by a substantial curvilinear stone revetment or apron. The building was erected on the platform behind **Building 4**, which was enlarged by quarrying the outcrop to the north, and dumping the displaced debris to the south. The stone apron extended this platform to the south, and was built around the eastern part of the earlier stake revetment (93.02). The apron comprised up to three courses of large slabs rising to the level of the shelf. The eastern part of the apron had been robbed, but its former position was marked by the edge of a paved surface extending to the east.

The building platform underlay the east end of the *Northumbrian* church, and revealed numerous stakeholes which could be of any date in the sixth to eighth centuries. The west wall of **Building 6** was marked by an irregular line of stakeholes on the lip of a shallow shelf, while the east and north walls were marked by internal stone kerbs apparently laid against the wattles. The western part of the north wall-line ran along solid rock, and wattling here may have been supported on a timber sill. Two small postholes towards the middle of the east wall were probably secondary features, possibly inserted to support sagging walls, or more probably the roof. The fire-cracked, heat-reddened slabs of a central hearth were enclosed by a shallow rectangular slot, which probably contained a horizontal timber frame, perhaps supporting a wattle and daub chimney, or a gantry to support cooking vessels. The final use of the hearth was marked by a spread of charcoal covered by a layer of clayey silt. These features were paralleled in **Building 18** in the **southern sector** (Figure 3.39). In both structures the charcoal was not associated with ash, suggesting that it was fuel rather than fire debris.

The ground beyond the apron was levelled up with a pile of rubble, capped with clay (94.02), which was probably quarry debris from the building platform. This was covered by a shale surface (94.07), which was probably part of a west/east path linking up with a similar surface to the south of **Building 7** (94.06). The shale was interleaved with paving to the east of **Building 6**, sealing the *Stage 2* builders' waste (69.01), and the shale and debris of *Stage 3* (69.02). Sherds of a B*i* amphora (V3, Figure 3.11) scattered in and around the building probably originated in the underlying debris (69.02, Table 3.5).

Building 7 (94.05, Figure 3.11) to the west of **Building 6**, occupied a shelf dug into the rock outcrop. The spoil from this excavation (94.01) was dumped over the remains of **Building 3**, extending the platform slightly to the south, and providing the foundations for the western part of the shale path (94.07). The building was revealed by a band of external paving analogous to the stone apron around **Building 6**, which gave a negative impression of the rounded south-east corner, and helped to identify a line of stake-holes as part of the east wall. The position of the north and west walls was indicated by a slight hollow in the bedrock. This area was occupied by the west end of the *Northumbrian* church, and no other **Phase 1** structural features can be identified.

Finds. The two buildings produced almost no finds, and those from the quarry spoil (94.01 and 94.02) probably derive from *Stage 3* (above). The shale path produced a small group of finds (Table 3.8). The bead and iron pin may have been contemporary losses, the other finds probably derive from the underlying displaced *Stage 3* debris.

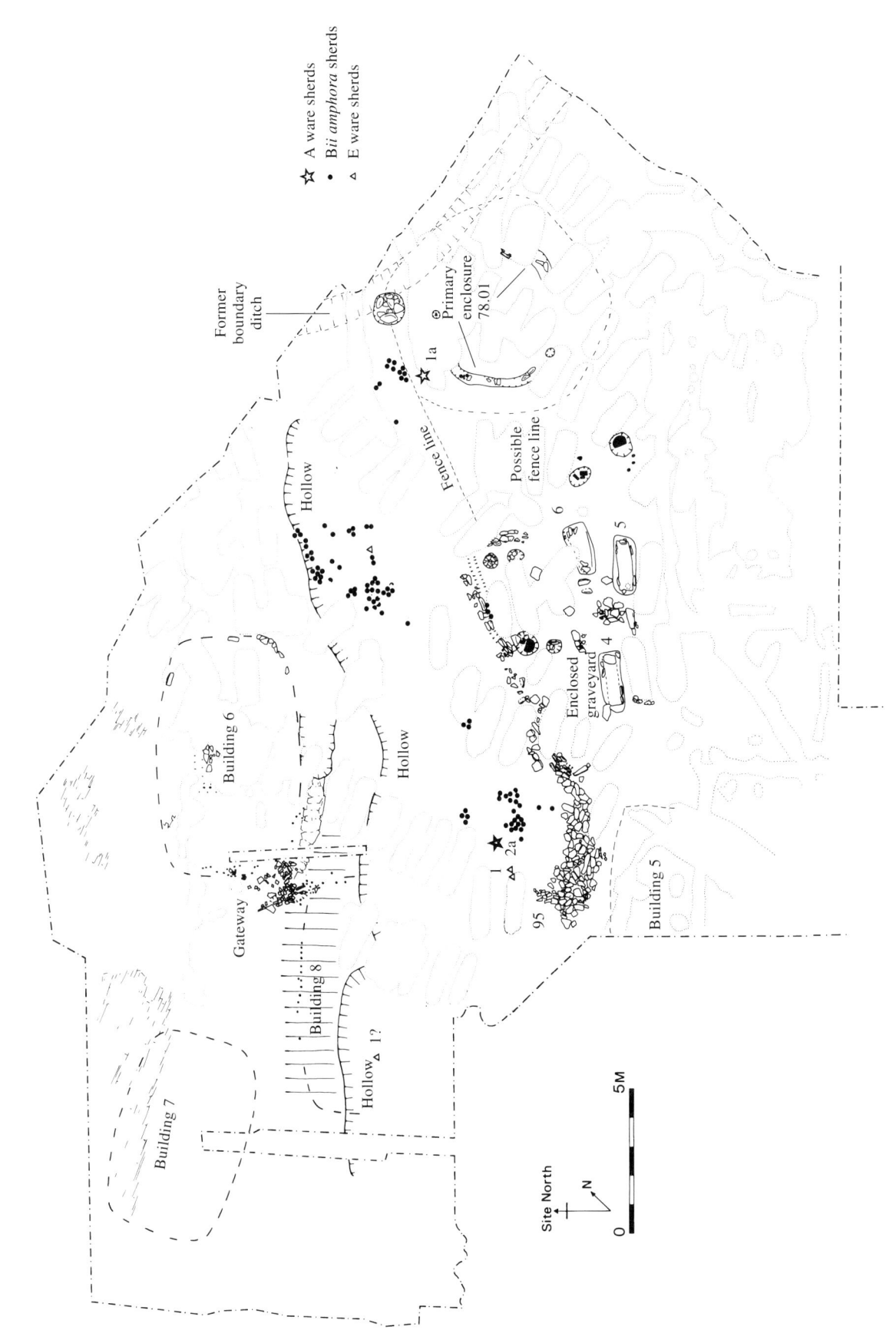

3.12 The **central** and **northern** sectors at the close of **Period I/1**, including buildings of *Stages 3-5*, *Stage 5* graveyard, *Stage 6* hollow and associated debris, and 'shrine' ascribed to **Period I/2.1**.

A small green glass bead (GS03.5)
A broken copper-alloy strip (BZ38.5)
An iron pin fragment (IN40.1)
An antler burr
A small group of metalworking debris including a lump of slag (SG03) and a tuyere fragment

Table 3.8: Finds from *Stage 4* shale path (94.06 and .07)

A concentration of debris (69.03) to the north of **Building 1** included iron working debris, smears of lime, and small slabs of sand. The lime and sand were probably the remains of sand plaster from which the lime had been leached, and may thus have been builders' waste from the repair of a plastered building at the east end of the hill. Related metalworking debris was scattered over the ground to the west (67.01), and displaced into the soil filling adjacent later graves (pp 112-3). There was however no trace of high-temperature working in the area and the debris presumably originates elsewhere. The group was characterised by fragments of toroid clay bellows-protectors fused to plano-convex 'hearth bottoms' of light glassy cinder (Group B), and vitreous cinder flecked with quartz. The pebbles are exotic to the site, and similar groups were associated with later groups of industrial debris (e.g. Tables 3.22 and 35), although their presence cannot be explained (pp 472-3). Other finds include a decorated copper-alloy strip paralleled at Dinas Powys (Alcock 1963, 109, fig. 19).

A ribbed handle from a B*misc. amphora* (V2)
An iron implement with a curved tip (IN78.1)
A nail
Forty-six quartz and granite pebbles
A distinctive group of metalworking debris including
    Three Group B hearths with trapped ceramic, one a bellows-protector
    A slag cake broken into nine chunks
    Vitreous cinder with embedded quartz
    Two glazed bung or tuyere fragments

Table 3.9: Finds from rubbish to the north of **Building 1** (69.03).

An abraded B*ii amphora* neck sherd (V2)
A copper-alloy strip with relief borders and a zig-zag pattern (BZ35.1)
An antler burr
A nail
A **retouched** flint
Two plough pebbles (SE51), one with a flat facet
A small group of metalworking debris including
    A Group B hearth fragment with a vestigial bellows-protector or tuyere
    Vitreous cinder with embedded quartz (217gm)
    A concentration of crystalline cinder (781 gm)

Table 3.10: Finds from rubbish to the west of **Building 1** (67.01).

Stage 5
Stage 5 (Figure 3.7) marks the final stage in the development of the terrace of **Phase 1** buildings on the north side of the central plateau, and was more a modification to *Stage 4* than a major change. Features in the centre of the central plateau probably represented an enclosed graveyard marked by massive timber monuments. The graveyard was respected by the *Stage 6* hollow, and was integral to the development of the *inner precinct* in **Phase 2**.

Building 8 (Figure 3.12). **Building 4** was probably demolished when **Building 6** was erected, and a replacement (**Building 8**) on the same stance was indicated by a sunken floor, and stakeholes marking the north and east walls. The east wall cut through the path to the south of **Building 6**. A gateway between the two buildings was indicated by a shallow construction slot oversailed by a spread of rubble. This respected the north-east corner of **Building 8** and the south-east corner **Building 6** which must thus have remained standing. The small group of finds (Table 3.11) was probably contaminated with later objects from **Phase 2**, which is the likely date of the Group E cone sherd and the lump of folded and fused vessel glass (pp 314, 324-5).

A sherd of a Group E cone (V77) and an unassigned sherd (Gp C5)
A lump of folded and fused vessel glass (FBa)
Two B*i amphora* sherds (V2e and V3j)
Two granite plough pebbles (SE51)

Table 3.11: Finds from gateway between **Buildings 6** and **8** (91)

The enclosed graveyard. The central part of the central plateau revealed an enigmatic group of features (67) including gullies, post-holes, paving, massive post-pits, and graves (Figure 3.12). The gullies demarcated the north side of an area avoided or respected by subsequent features for most of the remainder of **Period I**, and it thus seems to have been an enclosure, although no boundaries survived to the south, and there was no evidence of fencing. This 'enclosure' contained two rows of graves oriented on the northern boundary. These included three lintel graves (**4–6**) and five log coffin burials (**1–3**, **7** and **8**). Two log coffin burial on a different alignment can be ascribed with confidence to **Phase 4**, but there was insufficient stratigraphic evidence to interrelate the earlier burials. Evidence elsewhere indicated that the log coffin burials were later than the lintel graves, and this group has, accordingly been ascribed to **Phase 3.2** (Group D, pp 105-7), suggesting that the enclosed graveyard remained in use until the end of **Phase 3**. The three lintel graves are thus likely to have been the primary burials. The interpretative problems stem from the fact that this area seems to have enjoyed enduring respect, perhaps reverence, and was not intruded upon by later structures or debris, which would have provided stratigraphic and chronological detail. It is thus interpreted with considerable caution as an enclosed burial ground in use from the end of **Phase 1** until the end of **Phase 3**, which was probably remembered and respected, but no longer used, in **Phase 4**.

The graveyard is ascribed to *Stage 5* as it was respected by the *Stage 6* hollow, and overlay deposits probably pertaining to *Stages 1–4*. Cultivation in *Stage 1* was marked by churned clayey subsoil, recorded in section, and indicated by plough-pebbles from the graves. The ploughsoil was overlain by a layer of rough cobbling, which may have been part of a rough surface surrounding **Building 1** in *Stage 2* or *3*. This was covered by a deep deposit of charcoal-stained silty soil (67.01) which produced a small group of metalworking debris (Table 3.10), corresponding to the stratified group (69.03) to the north of **Building 1**, and so perhaps pertaining to *Stage 4*.

The north side of the enclosure was demarcated by a shallow gully broken by a possible inturned entrance, and the sides were indicated by truncated gullies to the west and east. These were insubstantial, but marked a long lived boundary, and perhaps abutted a wattle fence of which there was no concrete evidence. A large post-hole at the entrance could have supported a gate. The edge of this socket was clipped by a large post pit which had contained a large D-shaped timber (some 0.5 m in diameter). This seems to have been extracted, and the cast of the timber was covered by slabs in the upper fill of the pit. A second post-pit to the east of the graveyard revealed a similar massive D-shaped timber impression, and may mark the new site of the original timber. It is difficult to conceive of a structural role for these massive timbers, and they were perhaps appropriately-ornamented pylons – or a single pylon relocated – proclaiming the special quality of the graveyard. The interior revealed four post-holes, a patch of paving, and a clay-filled gully, possibly comprising gravemarkers and grave surrounds. The **Phase 2.1** shrine to the east of the graveyard (pp 92-4) may have been erected at this time, and is illustrated in Figure 3.12. It seems to have been surrounded by a fence (pp 94-5) aligned with the north side of the graveyard, and the graveyard and shrine may have been designed as a single structure, although this can only be perceived dimly, due to the truncation of its south side.

The finds from the graves (Table 3.12) are relatively uninformative and, with the possible exception of the finger ring from **Grave 4**, contained no furnishings.

A Group E glass vessel sherd (V68/69g)
A broken iron finger-ring (IN45.1)
Four quartz plough pebbles (SE51)
A small group of metalworking debris
Grave 4

A nail and two plough pebbles (SE51)
Grave 6

Table 3.12: Finds from potentially primary lintel graves (79.01) in **Phase 1.5** graveyard.

The north-east corner of the graveyard was probably abutted by paving (95), although it had been extensively damaged and its original extent is unknown. It was covered with patches of a distinctive sooty soil, and produced a small group of finds (Table 3.13) including joining base-sherds of an E ware beaker (V1, type E2). These were apparently earlier than the B*ii amphora* sherds and A ware deposited in *Stage 6* (Table 3.14), and so reveal a period, however brief, when all three pottery types were in use (p 324). The soil filling the eastern part of the gully (67.02) produced three sherds of a B*ii amphora* (V2) and a body sherd of a B*iv amphora* (V1). These are linked to finds in the *Stage 6* hollow, and indicate that the gully had silted up at this time. The only securely stratified find from the graveyard was an inner fragment of a large rotary mill stone (SE44.03) from the paving surrounding **Grave 1** (pp 105-7). The overlying mid-ninth century ploughsoil (399, Table 5.4) produced scattered sherds of B ware, E ware and vessel glass potentially deriving from the graveyard, but it otherwise seems to have been kept clean for the remainder of **Period 1** (Figures 10.22-24).

Two joining base-sherds of an E Ware beaker (V1)
An iron knife blade fragment (IN73.3) and a bent iron strip (IN81.1)
A **retouched** flint
A Group B hearth with a trapped bellows-protector fragment (SG30/42)

Table 3.13: Finds from *Stage 5* paving to north-west of graveyard (95)

Stage 6
Stage 6 (Figures 3.7 and 12) saw the excavation of a sinuous hollow, or series of hollows, along the northern edge of the central plateau. The hollow skirted the apron around **Building 6**, which presumably remained standing, but removed the south side of **Building 8**, and damaged the remains of the earlier buildings in this part of the site. The reason for digging the hollow is unclear. The spoil from it was removed, and may have been used as a building material, or to supplement a shallow cultivated soil elsewhere. It certainly did not improve the site's drainage, and successive, increasingly soggy deposits accumulated in it during the later phases of **Period 1**. Similarly, though it was later overlain by a paved road (72/98), it did not seem to have been dug for this purpose, as the earliest surface was a discontinuous and narrow shale path.

The floor of the hollow was covered with a layer of charcoal into which numerous sherds of pottery (and a few of glass) had been pressed (Figure 3.12). There was no evidence of burning *in situ*, and the charcoal, which survived in drifts on the northern edge of the hollow and was scattered widely to the south, possibly derived from a charcoal store scattered by a north wind (p 68). The finds from the eastern (70) and western (97) parts of the hollow are listed in Tables 3.14a and b. Both areas (and a detached deposit to the east) produced large numbers of B*ii amphora* sherds mostly deriving from two vessels (V1 and V2), which may originally have contained olive oil. The densest concentration of sherds in the east part of the hollow produced parts of both vessels. A second concentration to the west produced sherds from the upper part of Vessel 2, while sherds from the lower part of the *amphora* came from the eastern group and from a third concentration abutting the fence around the 'shrine'. It is thus clear that slabs of the two vessels were deposited in different parts of the area, and were subsequently smashed, scattered, and then smashed again. Fragments of Vessel 3 were more widely distributed, and two came from earlier contexts (94.02, *Stage 3* and 67.01 *Stage 4*), suggesting it was brought to the site before the other B*ii* vessels. The African Red Slipware sherd is the earliest securely-stratified example of this ware, and indicates a date of *c*. 550 (p 69). A sherd of a second A ware vessel (V1) lay within the fenced shrine (Table 3.15). The most surprising finds were two sherds of E ware, which is generally considered to postdate the Mediterranean *amphorae*. These, and two sherds of a beaker from the paving (95) adjacent to the western hollow, are a distinctive early type (p 320). One sherd might be dismissed as an intrusion; three are perhaps sufficient to confirm an overlap between the two wares. Two of the glass sherds (V1b and V54b) from the eastern group were probably displaced from earlier contexts (pp 79, 323-4), but the sherds of Vs 43 and 46 are among a series of early Group C cones decorated with horizontal trails. Two unassigned sherds display vertical trails (C4). The two beads belong to a sub-group common in the early stages of **Period 1**. The socketed adze and awl came from the charcoal-strewn surface to the south of the hollow. The other finds were less exceptional and the metalworking debris, antler and plough pebbles were probably displaced from underlying deposits. This was certainly the case with a tuyere fragment, which joins a smaller piece from the *Stage 4* dump (69.03). The flints were intermingled with the pottery and glass and were probably lost at the same time.

Despite the large number of *amphora* sherds this was primarily a *domestic* assemblage and the *industrial* component was small and possibly displaced. The *amphora* slabs were too incomplete and dispersed to mark the spots where complete vessels were broken and they had, perhaps, found a secondary use as *ad hoc* plates or containers. The floor of the hollow was disturbed by three later hollows (84.02, 119.01, 109) which corresponded with gaps in the scattered pottery and glass.

One B*i* amphora sherd (V1)
95 sherds of B*ii* amphora (37 of V1 and 58 of V2)
Two joining cross-marked B*ii* amphora sherds (V3)
A strap handle fragment of an E ware jug (Type E4, V6) and an unassigned E ware sherd
Sherds from four glass vessels (Vs 43, 46, 1b and 54b)
Six unassigned vessel sherds (2 of C4, 1 of C5, 1 of D1 and two of E2)
Two tiny green-blue glass beads (GS03.3 and 4)
A socketed iron adze (IN59) and a tanged awl (IN50.1)
An iron strip with a non ferrous rivet (IN79.1) and a nail head
A rolled copper-alloy tube (BZ35.3) and a rolled and folded strip (BZ38.7)
Six **retouched** and two **unretouched** flints
A sandstone smoothing stone (SE42.7)
Two plough pebbles (SE51)
An antler beam offcut
A small group of metalworking debris

Table 3.14a: Finds from eastern part of *Stage 6* hollow (70)

An abraded rim sherd of a large African Slipware plate (V2)
Forty-three sherds of B*ii* amphorae (three of V1 and forty of V2)
An unassigned vessel glass sherd of group C3
Three **retouched** flints
A nail shank
An iron artefact comprising two plates connected by rivets (IN78.2)
A small group of metalworking debris.

Table 3. 14b: Finds from western part of *Stage 6* hollow (97)

Phase 2

Introduction

Phase 2 (Figures 2.4, 3.13–16) saw the completion of the transformation of the *inner precinct*, which had begun in the closing stages of **Phase 1**, and the boundary between the *inner precinct* and the *outer zone* was now marked by a shallow ditch. The principal features in the *inner precinct* were a 'shrine' immediately to the west of the **Phase 1** ditch, and a graveyard which developed around it. This respected and absorbed the **Phase 1** burial ground, and by the end of **Phase 2** most of the central plateau was occupied by graves, while the ground to the north was, seemingly, disused. The relatively dense buildings of **Phase 1** were replaced by a single building which perhaps had a specialised function, and might for example have housed a *fossor* with specific responsibility for the adjacent graveyard. It was itself replaced by a second 'shrine' at the end of **Phase 2**, which later became the focus of the *Northumbrian* church. The **Phase 1** boundary probably continued to divide activities within the *inner precinct*, even though the ditch was not maintained, and was indeed oversailed by the **Phase 2** graveyard. The *outer zone* was occupied by sub-rectilinear stake-walled buildings aligned with the boundary ditch. The principal public buildings presumably lay at the east end of the hill.

The graveyard was kept scrupulously clean, but a rich group of finds from the ground to the north-west included a distinctive group of broken glass vessels (pp 99-101, 324-5), which may have been produced in an adjacent workshop. This initiated a period of industrial activity in the western part of the trench, that lasted until the end of **Phase 3**. The composition of the metalworking debris changed, indicating the introduction of new techniques. The artefactual evidence – particularly the pottery and glass – suggests that this was a period of economic isolation when former contacts with the Mediterranean world had ceased, and new links with Atlantic Europe had still to be forged.

The **Phase 2** remains in the *inner precinct* comprise two distinct groups with few stratigraphic links. The 'shrine' and graveyard in the south-east part of the area revealed seven stages of development, while the ground to the north displayed an independent evolution, with intense activity at the start of the phase and comprehensive disuse at the end. The two areas are described separately, both with internal sub-divisions into *stages*. The two areas can, however, be correlated to give a detailed, if somewhat subjective, picture of the evolution of the

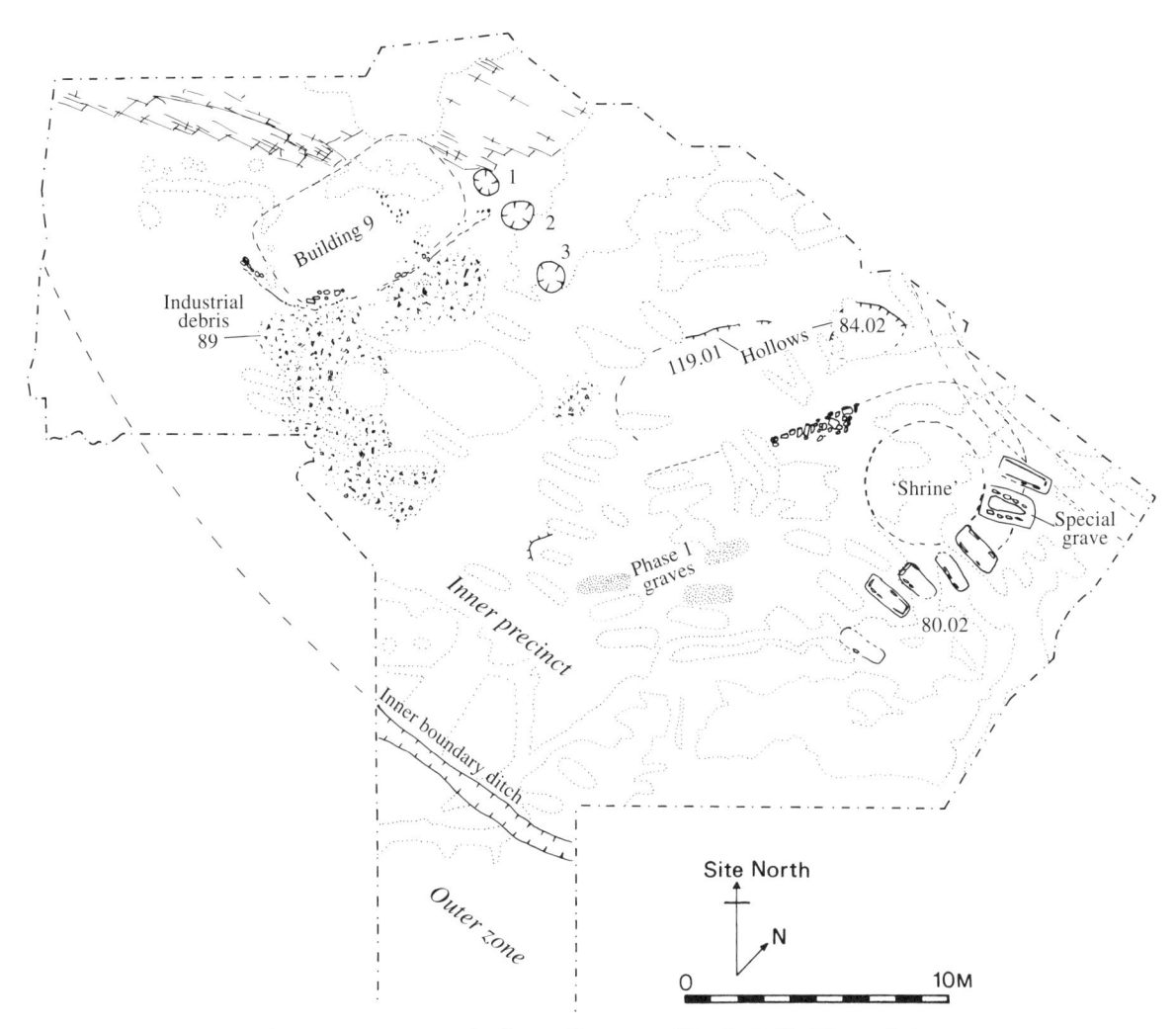

3.13 Speculative plan of the *inner precinct* in the earlier part of **Period I/2** (**Phase 2a**).

inner precinct (Figures 3.13–16). Figure 3.13 shows the *inner precinct* in the early part of **Phase 2**. A circular 'shrine' has been erected on the western margin of the **Phase 1** boundary ditch, and perhaps lay within a fenced enclosure linked to the earlier graveyard. A row of graves arcing around the eastern side of the shrine, included a 'special grave' apparently designed to receive successive burials (pp 94-6). Two hollows in the ground to the north seem to respect the fenced shrine. A new building (**9**) to the north-west is roughly aligned with the **Phase 1.6** graveyard, and is flanked by three putative latrine pits. Scattered rubbish to the south of the building included much of the Group E vessel glass, which was perhaps made at Whithorn (pp 310, 324-5). There was no evidence of high-temperature working, and the putative glass workshop may lie in the unexcavated ground to the south-east. Figure 3.14 shows the area at a slightly later stage. A band of paving has been laid against the fence around the shrine, but the special grave is still accessible. A possible building (**10**) has been erected in the hollow to the north of the **Phase 1/6** graveyard, and is linked by a paved path to the extant building (**9**). Figure 3.15 shows the area at a slightly later time. A new row of graves has been dug around the eastern part of the shrine, cutting into the earlier paving, and producing spoil which seals the 'special grave'. The north side of the shrine is now marked by a gently curving ditch, and the ground beyond is now unoccupied, and covered with a layer of mud and worm-sorted silt. **Building 9** is still depicted, although it may have been disused by this point. Figure 3.16 shows the *inner precinct* at the end of **Phase 2**. A new 'shrine' has been erected over the remains of **Building 9**, and although the original 'shrine' seems to have been slighted by a third row of lintel graves, the area is still respected by a new paved road. The new shrine had been severely damaged by later features, but may have had a paved surround, and was perhaps of similar size to its predecessor. A setting of four uprights of stone or timber at the centre of the shrine, may have included a monolith moved from the original shrine, which was subsequently to be the focus of the *Northumbrian* church. A single building (**15**) in the *outer zone* is oriented on the **Phase 2** boundary, and there may have been more buildings in this area.

The beginning of **Phase 2** follows the horizon dated *c.* 550 AD (p 69), and the **Phase 2** sequence possibly spanned the remainder of the sixth century.

The Phase 2 boundary 'ditch'. The boundary ditch

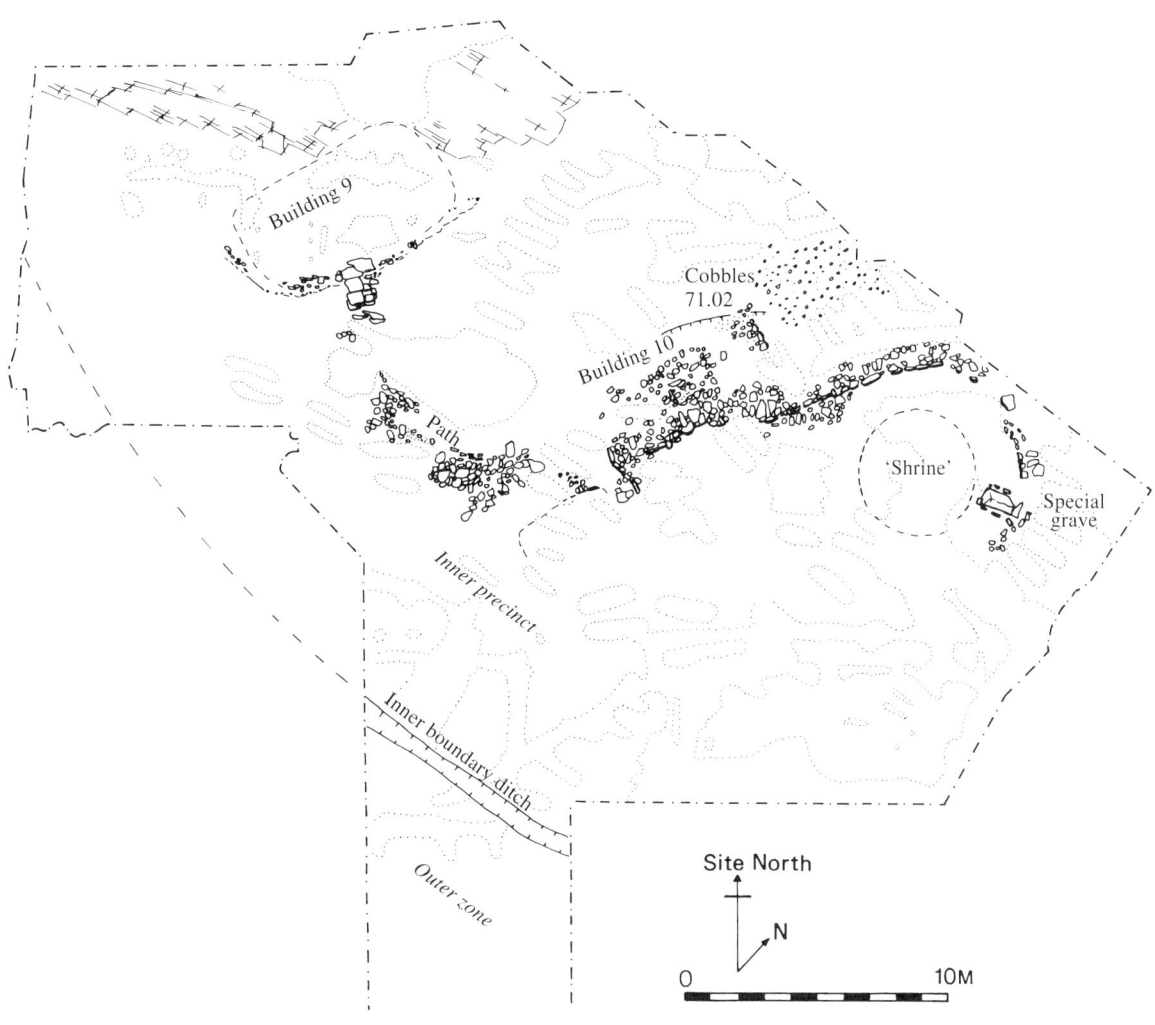

3.14 Speculative plan of the *inner precinct* during **Period I/2 (Phase 2b).**

(120) around the *inner precinct* crossed the shallow strata at the west end of the **central sector**, and was some 0.8 m wide, but only 0.15 m deep, barely penetrating the rock beneath the **Phase 1.1** ploughsoil. It had been truncated by a *Northumbrian* building (II/6). It is ascribed to **Phase 2** on the insubstantial grounds that it seems to have been respected by a small group of burials (80.03) possibly pertaining to the end of **Phase 2** (Figure 3.16), and was unlikely to have coexisted with **Building 5** (Figure 3.6). The only find was an iron bolt (IN22.1).

The Phase 2 shrine and graveyard. The **Phase 2** graveyard was exposed and partly excavated in 1988. For the next three years interest concentrated upon an lintel grave with a massive cover slab (**18**), which seemed to have been the focus for subsequent burials. The burial ground thus seemed to be an example of a 'developed cemetery' (Thomas 1971) in which the grave of a revered person attracted further burials in the expectation of sharing the founder's 'virtue' through proximity to his corporeal relics. It was unlikely to be the grave of Bishop Nynia, who was reputedly buried inside the church he built (*HE III.iv*), but might have contained the remains of another leader of the early church (Hill 1991b).

Excavation was completed in 1991, demonstrating that this interpretation was incorrect, and revealing a rather more complex monument, combining aspects of a special graveyard and outdoor 'shrine'. The graveyard had developed around a small timber-walled enclosure which may have surrounded a 'special' burial, a monument, or possibly both. This seems to have been contained by an outer fenced enclosure appended to the **Phase 1.5** graveyard (Figure 3.12). The supposed 'focal' grave lay between the inner and outer enclosures, had a removable cover slab, and had been used for successive burials. The outer enclosure was subsequently encompassed by a band of paving with a wide opening leading to the **Phase 1** graveyard. Later lintel graves disturbed the outer margin of the paving, and extended westwards to the south of the **Phase 1** graveyard. This elaborate composite monument was disturbed by new graves on a different alignment in **Phase 3**, but was avoided by the **Phase 4** burials, suggesting that appropriate respect had been restored. The **Phase 1** graveyard remained inviolate throughout **Phase 2**, and the new shrine and graveyard should probably be seen as logical appendage to it, rather than as a replacement. The complex is reconstructed in Figure 3.17, which

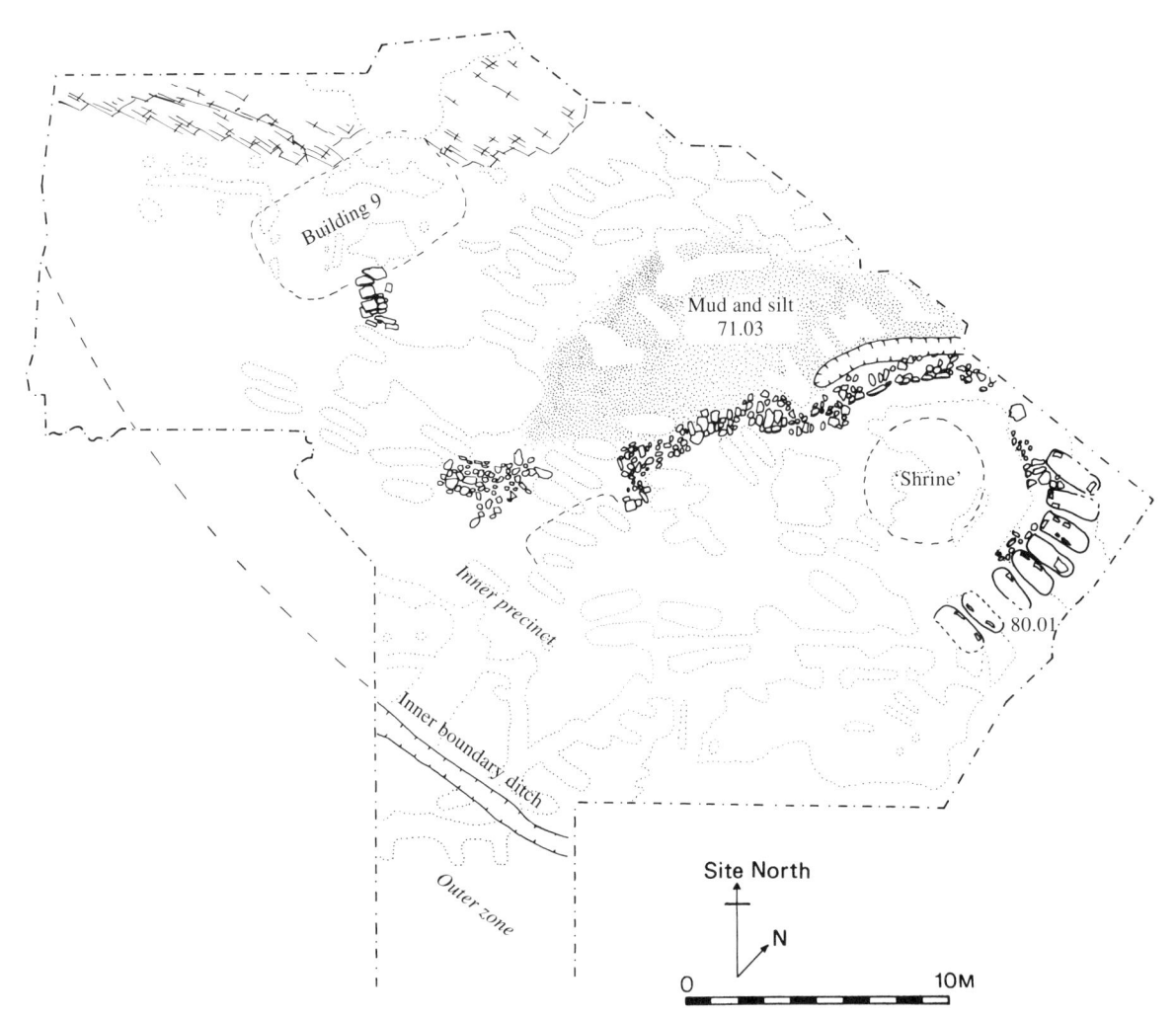

3.15 Speculative plan of *inner precinct* during **Period I/2** (**Phase 2c**).

conflates the proven and the conjectural to give an impression of the shrine in *Stage 4*.

The area had been damaged by later features, and the centre of the primary enclosure had been cut away by an eighteenth century drain. The graves were relatively unaffected, but the associated surfaces had been severely disturbed, particularly in the south-west part of the area. The northern part of the monument had, however, survived intact, and the sequence of features here may originally have been mirrored to the south. The evolution of the 'shrine' is sub-divided into seven stages correlating successive structural features (78.01–07) with the three rows of **Phase 2** lintel graves (80.01–03). The skeletons in the graves were poorly preserved, and most were represented solely by tooth enamel. The absence of small graves suggests that young children were buried elsewhere, but it is otherwise impossible to characterise the population. The 'shrine' seems to have been kept clean, and most of the finds from the graves can be attributed to earlier deposits.

Stage 1
The primary 'monument' was marked by a shallow groove defining an angular, possibly sub-square, enclosure, some 4.0 m wide. The groove disturbed the hearth in **Building 1**, re-emerging tenuously at the west end of the massive lintel grave (Figures 3.18 and 12). Sporadic packing stones suggested it had contained a plank wall, possibly supported by large stakes. Two truncated post-holes in disturbed areas to the north and south may have been part of the original enclosure. The enclosure lay immediately beyond the **Phase 1** ditch, and while this may have been fortuitous, the earlier boundary perhaps survived as a functional division within the *inner precinct*. Although this was the primary element of the **Phase 2** sequence it may have originated in **Phase 1.5**.

The primary enclosure remained a focal feature long after the slot had disappeared. The purpose and 'special' quality of the enclosure is uncertain. It may have surrounded a 'special' burial, and three graves were possible candidates. Grave **46** was a large lintel grave ascribed to **Phase 3** on the basis of its orientation. It had unusually large side slabs and the lost cover slab (or timbers) would have been flush with the ground surface. This design is similar to Grave **50** on the north side of the **Phase 1** graveyard,

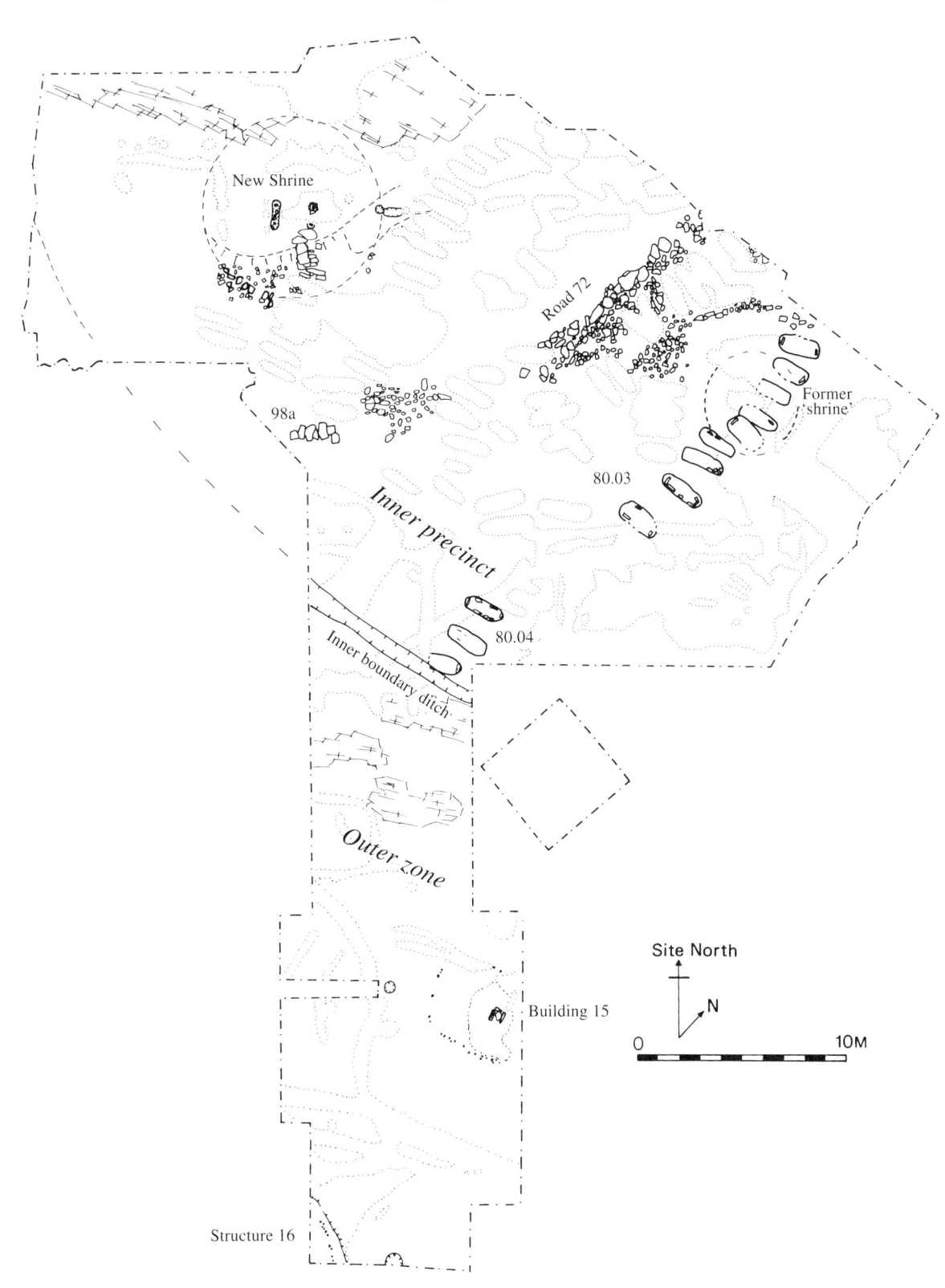

3.16 Speculative plan of the *inner precinct* and *outer zone* at the close of **Period I/2**.

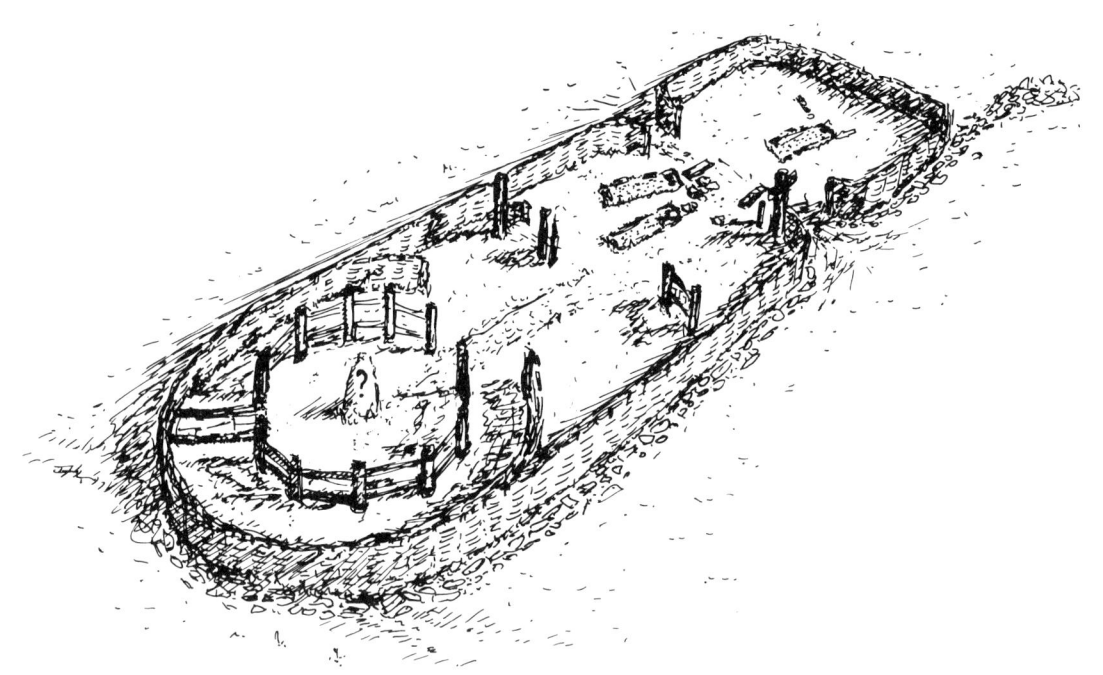

3.17 Speculative reconstruction of **Period I/2** shrine surrounding putative focal monument, and encompassing **Period I/5** graveyard.

and is a simplified version of the 'massive' grave (**18**) to the west. Two fragmentary lintel graves (**27** and **28**) oriented west/east (true orientation) lay within the enclosure, but are ascribed to the relatively late third row of **Phase 2** graves (80.03). None of these was located centrally, and all fit comfortably in the later burial phases assigned to them. It is more likely that the enclosure had surrounded a suitably-inscribed timber or stone pillar which may have been moved to the new shrine at the end of **Phase 2**. The enclosure had been severely disturbed by a Northumbrian clay-puddling pit and an eighteenth century drain, which would have obliterated the socket of a central pillar.

Stage 2
The eastern part of the enclosure was subsequently oversailed by a shale surface. This extended beyond the gully to the south-east and was, perhaps, a path leading to the putative central monument.

Stage 3
Stage 3 (Figures 3.18, 19) saw the excavation of three graves (**17–19**) on the eastern margin of the primary enclosure, cutting the *Stage 2* shale. Six others lintel graves (**20–24**) to the south-west were in the same row (80.02) and can be tentatively assigned to this phase.

The massive lintel grave (**18**) was unique in its construction and contents, and displayed a close relationship with the *Stage 1* enclosure, indicating that it was the primary element of this phase, while the other graves were probably secondary additions. The grave (**19**) immediately to the south-west may also have been 'special'; the other graves displayed no unusual features. Paving to the north associated with a gravel surface (78.03), indicated the position, of the outer fence and a possible curving fence to the south-west of the enclosure. Only two stakeholes can be ascribed to the outer fence, but its position was indicated by the successive layers of paving against its inner and outer edges (Figures 3.12, 18 and 20). This otherwise invisible fence-line was aligned with the north side of the **Phase 1.5** graveyard and was probably part of an apse-ended enclosure encompassing these graves and the new shrine (Figure 3.12 and 17). The pebbles were fine river gravel sand probably originated in alluvial clay, which may have been daubed on the fence.

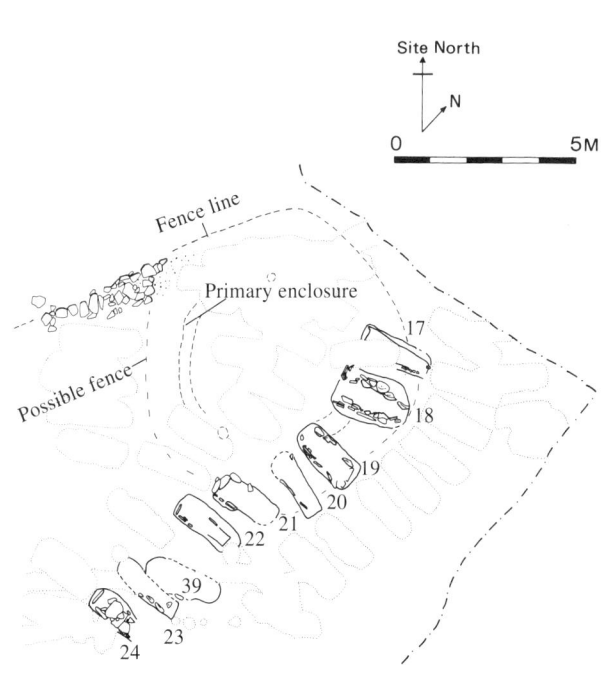

3.18 **Period I/2.3** 'shrine (*Stage 3*).

A Grave structure

B Grave with cover slab restored

C Final burial and related bone casts and fragments

D Displaced bones in fill of grave

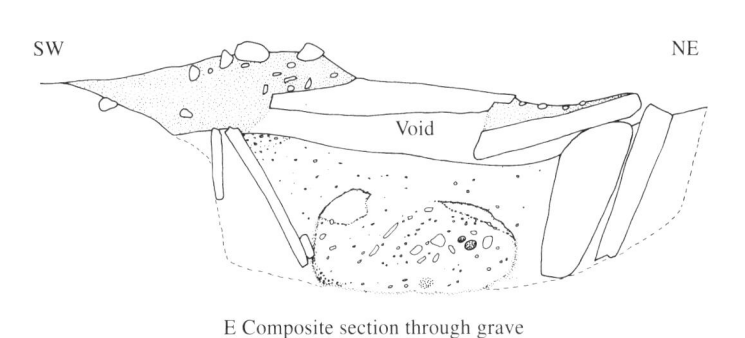

E Composite section through grave

3.19 Plans and section of special grave (**I/18**), and evidence of multiple successive burials.

The **special grave** (**18**, Figure 3.19) lay between the eastern margin of the primary enclosure and the outer fence, and though the plank wall may still have been standing when it was dug, a segment would have been removed by the grave cut. The grave occupied a large pit and was constructed with unusual care. The grave cover originally comprised a single thin slab of greywacke which rested on the tapering side walls of the grave. These had been carefully levelled so that the cover was flush with the ground surface. These supports were flanked by vertical slabs forming a regular kerb at ground level, and framing the cover slab. The cover stone was probably designed as a lid and a relatively thin slab was chosen to reduce the weight. This was perhaps a mistake, as the cover was subsequently broken and, a detached slab was moved to a new position at the foot of the grave.

The skeletal remains in the grave were poorly preserved, but the dentitions of four individuals survived, and there was enough skeletal evidence to infer the sequence of the burials, and to suggest the function of this exceptional grave. Two complete dentitions associated with spheroid cavities at the west end of the grave mark two skulls with articulated lower jaws, while scraps of bone and the casts of the arm and leg bones indicated the position of one articulated skeleton, and perhaps additional disarticulated bones. The casts of the skulls and bones were contained by a contorted cavity edged by compact stained soil, possibly representing a leather container which had buckled and eventually split. A fragmentary third dentition lay close to the articulated skulls on the floor of the grave, and a fourth dentition came from the grave fill immediately below the cover slab, which produced other fragments of displaced bone. The two displaced dentitions came from mature adults, the articulated ones from a young adult and a sub-adult (p 556). The presence of two skulls with articulated jaws indicates that the final body was buried before the soft tissues of the previous corpse had decayed, while the other dental remains indicate the grave had contained at least two previous burials, and hint that the remains of old burials were not fully removed when new bodies were entombed. Later graves disturbing earlier burials produced similar skeletal assemblages in which displaced skulls and long bones were sometimes placed carefully beside the new body. There were however no earlier burials in this area, and the massive lintel grave was apparently the first grave in this part of the site. The skeletal remains thus seem to represent successive burials, while the unusually solid construction of the grave, and the provision of a framed cover at ground level, suggest that it was specifically designed for this purpose. It occupied a prominent position, but was not the focus of the graveyard, and may have been a temporary tomb, drawing 'virtue' from the central enclosure, but containing bones destined for final interment elsewhere.

Stage 4
Stage 4 (Figure 3.20) was marked by a band of paving with an inner margin of large stones abutting the outer fence. The paving oversailed **Grave 17**, and abutted the west ends of **Graves 18** and **19**, continuing westwards along the northern edge of the **Phase 1** graveyard and overlying the south side of **Building 10** (p 98).

Stage 5
Stage 5 was represented by a second row of lintel graves (80.01) dug through the outer margin of the *Stage 4* paving (Figure 3.21). The north-east end of the row curved around the monument, suggesting that the outer fence remained standing and that the focus was still revered. The earlier graves and paving adjoining the original enclosure were covered by a thick layer of gravelly soil dug from the new graves. This formed a low mound concealing the cover of the massive grave and precluding further burials. The paving to the north was covered with red gravel including lumps of vein quartz which were perhaps intended to emphasise the ritual significance of the enclosure.

Stage 6
The continuing development of the outer enclosure was marked by a curving ditch around the northern perimeter of the paving (Figure 3.22). A third row of lintel graves (80.03) cannot be placed securely in the sequence, but possibly pertained to this phase. The row ran through the centre of the *Stage 1* enclosure indicating that its sanctity was not longer respected or perhaps that burial was now of greater significance than the original 'meaning' of the inner monument. It is also possible that the ritual focus had been transferred to the new shrine (88.03, p 102) overlying the remains of **Building 9**. This could have involved the movement of a monument or merely the transfer of reverence from one focus to another.

Stage 7
The final development of the 'shrine' was marked by a spread of rubble laid over the *Stage 6* ditch and spreading inwards over the earlier paving (Figure 3.28). The rubble abutted the paved road constructed at the end of **Phase 2**, reuniting the separate sequences in the 'shrine' and the ground to the north. The rubble was overlain by a 'kerb' of large stones on the inner edge of the ditch, which was perhaps the outer face of a wall dismantled in **Phase 4b** (p 116). This suggests that the shrine was still demarcated and respected in

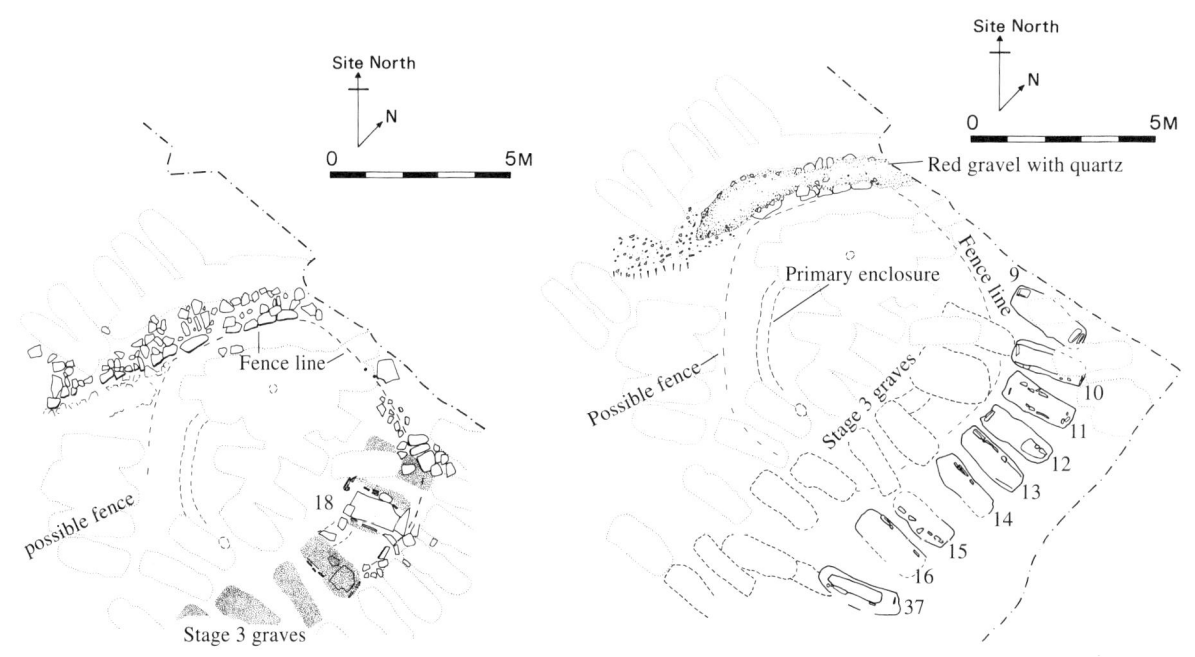

3.20 **Period I/2.4** 'shrine' (*Stage 4*).

3.21 **Period I/2.5** 'shrine' (*Stage 5*).

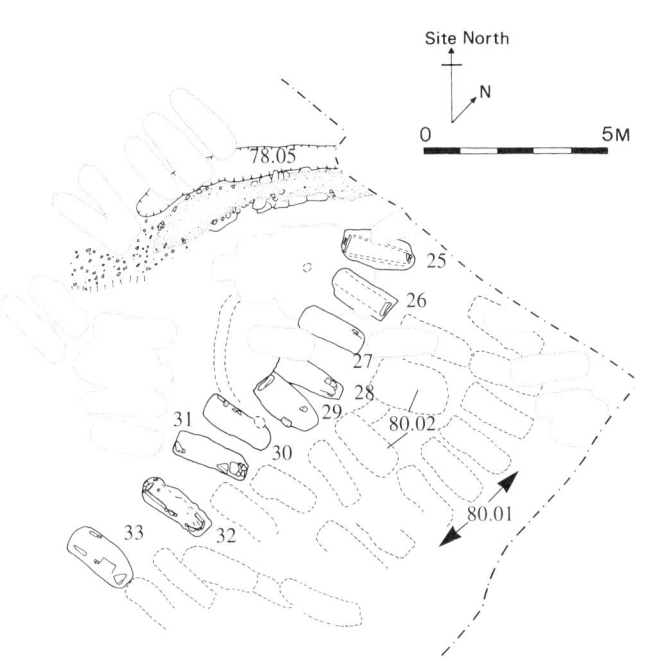

3.22 **Period I/2.6** graves cutting through earlier 'shrine' (*Stage 6*).

Phases 3 and **4a**, although the lack of subsequent structural modifications suggests it was now revered as a relic of the past, rather than as a dynamic feature of contemporary ritual life.

Finds
The **Phase 2** shrine produced very few finds, and is the archetypal example of a *clean assemblage*. This was emphasised by the large groups of *industrial* and *domestic* debris which accumulated to the west. The only finds groups which can be attributed to the use of the 'shrine' came from the area immediately within the *Stage 4* paving, and had perhaps accumulated in soil (78.07) at the foot of the fence (Table 3.15). The Haematite, *clastic lime* and metalworking debris were probably displaced from the underlying **Phase 1** deposits, but the flints and African Red Slipware sherd were perhaps contemporary losses. The concentration of flints is of interest, as they were not associated with other debris, and were perhaps used – and lost – here. The paving included a damaged, greywacke, rotary quern upper-stone (SE43.13) which is the earliest hand mill recovered, and perhaps originated in an earlier native settlement in the vicinity.

Four **unretouched** and seven **retouched** flints
A rim sherd of a small African Red Slipware bowl (V1a)
An unassigned sherd of vessel glass
A nail
A lump of massive Haematite and four small lumps of clastic lime
Scraps of metalworking debris (*c.* 50 gm)

Table 3.15: Finds from inner margin of paving surrounding **Phase 2** shrine (78.03 and 07)

Most of the small groups of finds from the **Phase 2** graves seem to have been displaced **Phase 1** debris. The graves to the south-east (80.01) produced scattered metalworking debris including pieces of Group B hearths with trapped bellows-protector fragments fused to glassy cinder, two tuyere nozzle fragments (SG 20), and small amounts of glassy and crystalline cinder. One grave (**14**) produced three crucible fragments (SG15.3–5), probably used for bronze and leaded brass, another (**23**) incorporated a broken sandstone slab with a possible ingot mould (SE45.2), and a third (**32**) produced a fragment of a clay pin-mould with traces of an unspecified copper alloy (SG17.2). These finds and other displaced objects, identify early metalworking here perhaps involving iron smelting or bloomwork, and the casting bronze nail-headed stick-pins (Figure 10.86). Two sherds of a squat jar (V54) belong with other fragments scattered around **Building 1** (p 79). Flints probably derive from surface debris.

'Grave furnishings' listed in Table 3.16 include probable furnishings from **Graves 9** and **32**, and possible furnishings from other graves, which cannot be sourced in earlier debris. The plough pebble from **Grave 13** is listed as it lay beyond the area cultivated in **Phase1.1**, and it was possibly buried as a talisman. Three other graves (**12, 14** and **34**) produced quartz or granite pebbles, possibly for the same reason. **Grave 25** produced a sherd of Samian ware and an unusual iron implement which had been wedged behind the footstone, and may have been placed there for luck. It was perhaps a large projectile point, more akin to a harpoon than an arrow. The finds from **Graves 9** and **23** indicate the presence of nailed wooden objects, neither reconstructable. The iron stick-pin from **Grave 32** is a rare item of personal dress, paralleled by a find from an early context in the **southern sector** (pp 122, 418-9).

A corroded nail and two shanks, one with mineralised wood
Two riveted copper-alloy plates (BZ37.1)
Grave 9

A quartz plough pebble (SE51)
Grave 13

A sandstone pebble with a pigment-stained hollow (SE50.8)
Grave 17

A weathered fragment of Central Gaulish bowl (F. 30) *c.* 165–200 AD (PY01:01)
A tanged, barbed iron implement (IN75.1)
Grave 25

A tube of rolled lead sheet, possibly a line weight (LD09.4)
Grave 27

A lump of smoothed red botryoidal Haematite (SE62.10)
Grave 31

A right-angled iron bracket with two nails (IN29.1)
Two opposed nails rusted together
Two bent nail shanks
An iron stick pin with a collar and a pierced, flat head (IN41.2)
Grave 32

Table 3.16: Possible furnishings from **Phase 2** graves (80.01–03)

The northern part of the inner precinct
The northern part of the *inner precinct* revealed five stages of activity (*i–v*) during **Phase 2**, and the

western part of the area produced large groups of industrial debris, perhaps originating in the adjacent part of the *outer zone*.

Stage i. **Building 6** seems to have continued in use briefly at the start of **Phase 2**, and **Building 7** may also have survived (Figure 3.7). A friable, organic soil (100) accumulated to the south, covering the floor of the **Phase 1.6** hollow. This was dissimilar to the worm-sorted silts recorded elsewhere, and closely comparable to the soil filling three latrine pits adjacent to **Building 9** in *Stage ii*. It was initially identified as peat, but possibly comprised human *faeces* and other organic waste. A small group of *domestic debris* from the organic soil spanning *Stages i* and *ii* is discussed below (Tables 3.17a and b).

Stage ii. Stage ii followed the abandonment of **Building 6**, and saw the erection of a new building (**9**) on an enlarged platform aligned with the **Phase 1** graveyard (Figures 3.13 and 23). The platform survived until the final stages of **Phase 4**, but the building may have been abandoned when a new building (**10**) was erected to the east in *Stage iii*, and seems to have been replaced by a shrine at the end of **Phase 2**. The remains of the building were ephemeral, and it was perhaps similar to other small sub-rectilinear houses of this period. Rubbish deposits filling the **Phase 1** hollow at the foot of the platform produced a remarkable group of *domestic and industrial* debris (Table 3.18). A similar group (Table 3.19) was recovered from a large hollow (119.01) dug through the **Phase 1.6** deposits to the east, which was probably contemporary, although the stratigraphic links between the two deposits had been severed by later disturbances.

Building 9 (88.01) occupied a relatively insubstantial platform oversailing the remains of **Building 8** and the western part of **Building 6**. A wattle revetment may have formed the south wall of the building, and scattered stakeholes on the platform revealed fragments of a possible north wall and a staggered double line of stake-holes marking the east wall or an internal partition. Three hemispherical pits to the east of the platform and an oval pit to the south were perhaps external latrines. They were filled with a friable organic soil which was perhaps equivalent to the waterlogged cess in the latrine pits in the **southern sector**. Friable, 'peaty' soil continued to accumulate around the platform, spreading over the remains of **Building 6**.

Stage iii saw the construction of a new building (**10**) abutting the north side of the **Phase 1** graveyard, and probably followed the abandonment of **Building 9**. A shale path with rubble foundations cut through the industrial debris led to a flight of stone steps ascending to the *Stage ii* platform, which seems to have been extended eastwards (88.02) at roughly the same time (Figure 3.24).

Building 10 was represented by a paved floor cutting the *Stage ii* hollow immediately north of the **Phase 1** graveyard (Figure 3.14). The south side of the building had been disturbed by a hollow containing the paving associated with the *Stage 4* shrine. The north-west corner displayed a characteristic rounded angle, indicating that it lay within a wattle building, although the north-east wall seems to have been straight with a rectangular north-east corner. A detached block of paving to the east may represent a separate apartment at the east end of the building. A cobbled surface further to the east (71.01) may have been contemporary or slightly earlier.

Stage iv records a period of inactivity in the northern part of the *inner precinct*, marked by a worm-sorted soil (71.03) overlying **Building 10**, the cobbles to the east (71.02), and the earlier remains (94.07) to the north (Figure 3.15). Patches of a similar soil overlay the *Stage iii* platform and industrial debris to the west. This phase of inactivity seems to have begun before the paving was laid around the shrine (*Stage 4*). The wormed soil produced few finds, but the continuing development of the shrine shows that activity continued in the *inner precinct*. There was no evidence of an equivalent period of disuse in the **southern sector**, and settlement probably continued in the *outer zone*.

Stage v saw the construction of a paved roadway (72) abutting the northern edge of the graveyard, and overlying the *Stage iv* soil (Figure 3.16, 28). The paving oversailed the ditch around the shrine, and was abutted by the final cobbling. The paving ran out to the west of the entrance to the **Phase 1.5**

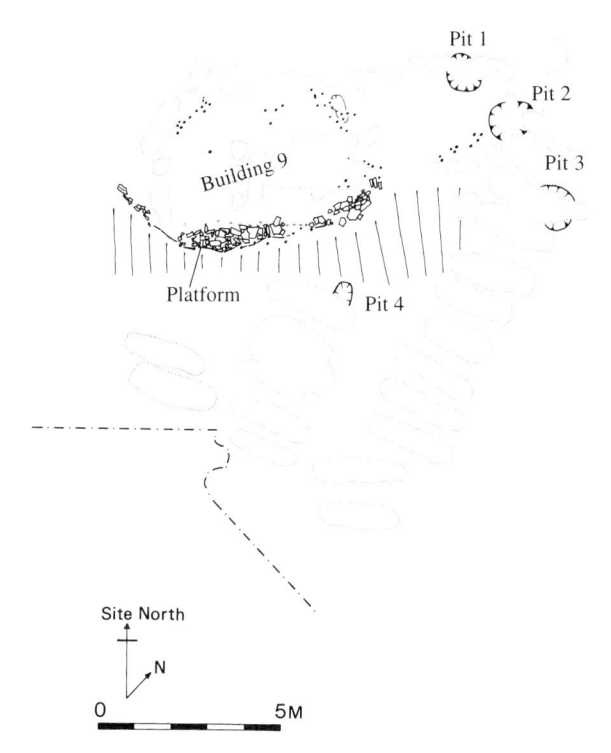

3.23 **Period I/2.2** building (**9**) in the **northern sector**.

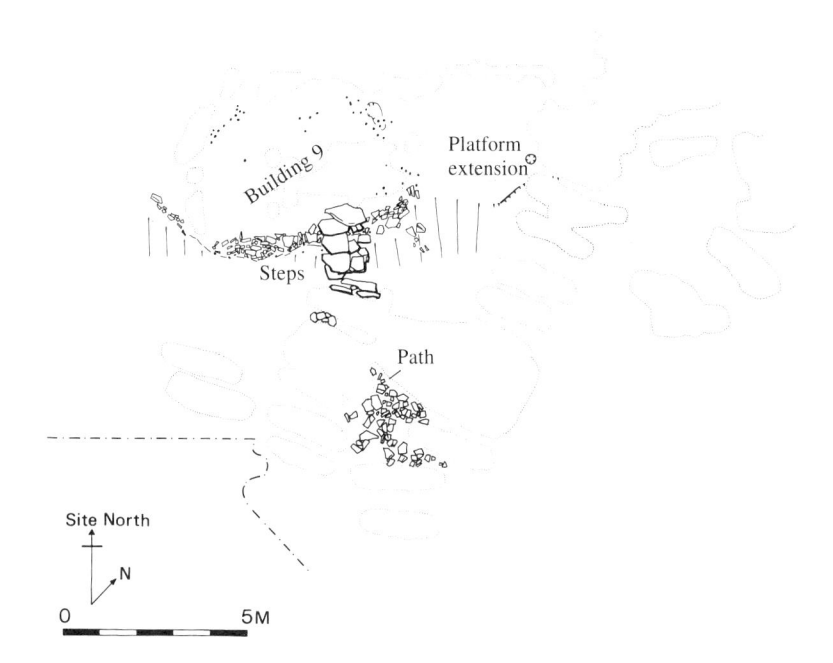

3.24 Path and steps approaching **Building 9 (Period I/2.3)**.

graveyard, but continued on the western edge of the trench, where it sealed the southern part of the rubbish deposits (89) to the south of the *Stage ii* building (**9**), and may have passed through a gateway between the *inner precinct* and the *outer zone*.

Finds assemblages
The **Phase 2** deposits in the northern part of the *inner precinct* produced a group of large, inter-related assemblages of finds. The most remarkable was the industrial debris (89) which accumulated to the south of **Building 9** in *Stage 2*, but an earlier group of *domestic debris* can be isolated, while the platform (88.01 and 02) produced a distinct group of displaced *industrial debris*. All these deposits had been disturbed by **Phase 4** graves (82.03–05), which produced identifiably displaced objects (Table 3.22). A large oval hollow (109) dug in **Phase 3** had punched a large hole in the **Phase 2** deposits.

The early 'peaty' deposits were strikingly 'clean', producing small groups of *domestic debris* (Table 3.17 a and b) including the fish hook and ceramic counter or playing piece. Both groups contain fragments of Group E cones, perhaps, the earliest of this short-lived type (pp 310-3, 324-5), and the two chunks of folded glass support the case that the Group E cones were made in the immediate vicinity (Figures 3.25 and 10.123). Vessel 47 belongs to an early group of Group C cones decorated with horizontal trails current in the closing stages of **Phase 1** (pp 307, 323-4), while Vessel 18 provides a valuable link with Dinas Powys and the Mote of Mark, where similar vessels have been found (p 303). Both may precede the manufacture of the Group E cones.

Sherds of two pale yellow Group E cones (Vs 73 and 78) and one unassigned vessel glass sherd
A B*i* amphora sherd (V1)

A large copper-alloy fish-hook for sea fishing (BZ27.1)
An iron bar with looped ends (IN25.1) and a nail shank
A scrap of glassy cinder (SG 01 (8gm),

Table 3.17a: Finds from 'peaty' soil (100) on floor of **Phase 1** hollow

Sherds of pale yellow (V47) and French Blue cones (V18b)
Two unassigned vessel glass sherds
Two broken lumps of folded, fused Group E vessel glass (FAa and b)
A sherd of burnished and rouletted black slipware (PY02:02)
A broken 'loom weight' (SE29.9)

Table 3.17b: Finds from 'peaty' soil (96) under and around **Building 9**

The *Stage ii* deposits produced four large groups of finds (Tables 3.18–21). The first comprised rubbish to the south of **Building 9**, which filled the **Phase 1.6** hollow, and spilled over onto the surrounding ground (89, Table 3.18). This deposit included several layers, but was generally poorly stratified. The B*ii* amphora and E ware sherds were probably displaced from **Phase 1** deposits, while the iron stick pin, beads, and perhaps the flints, may have been *domestic* waste. The large group of *industrial* debris comprised the antler, including two pieces of comb-making waste; the drawknife, possibly used for comb-making (p 429); the iron, possibly including scrap gathered for reworking; a group of metalworking debris; including the earliest Type 2 tuyere fragments; a large hone; an object blank of bitumen (p 443); and numerous sherds of Group E vessel sherds and other glass, linked to other finds from this area, and indicating the manufacture of vessels in the vicinity (pp 310, 324-5). The Group E sherds were confined to the basal layer of rubbish, confirming that these pertained to the start of this sequence, and probably represented a relatively brief phase of production. Part of a pebble-studded plough sole from the foot of the platform, and eight plough pebbles, suggest that ploughs were repaired in this putative workshop area.

Forty-three sherds of vessel glass including:
    Parts of two cones with vertical and horizontal trails (Vs 30, 31)
    Parts of a flask (V64) and jar (V65)
    Parts of five group E vessels (70, 71, 73, 74 and 79)
    Sixteen unassigned Group E sherds and eight unassigned sherds.
    A blue green glass bead and half of a second (G03.9 and 10).
    Fragments of orange glass (GS12)
Two sherds of Samian pottery (PY01)
Sherds of a B*ii amphora* (V2) and an E ware vessel (possible V6)
Two sherds of unidentified wheel-thrown pottery (PY07)
Nineteen iron objects, including
    A broken drawknife with a looped terminal (IN69.1)
    A club-headed stick-pin (IN41.3),
    Two bent pin fragments (IN40.2, 41.22)
    Six nails and fragments
    A clench plate and nail (IN20.2)
    Three strips (IN80.3 and 4, 81.2) and two plate fragments (IN82.4 and 5)
An iron disc with a square perforation (IN89.1)
A curved strip of copper-alloy binding (B37.2) and a folded strip (BZ38.8)
A large hone (SE 35.1)
Eight plough pebbles (SE 51) and part of a possible plough (SE51.1).
Seventeen pieces of antler comprising:
    Two burrs
    A broken beam fragment
    Two tines and a tine tip
    A tine segment and a comb plate trimming
    Four offcuts
    Five tine offcuts or trimming.
    One paring
Five **retouched** flints and a burnt flint
A squared block of bitumen, perhaps an object blank (SH06.1)
4 kg of metalworking debris including:
    a relatively large amount of glassy cinder (997gm)
    a relatively small amount of crystalline cinder (394gm)
    a chunk of tool-marked furnace lining (SG09)
    a small group of Type 2 tuyere fragments (SG20-24),
    two possible bellows protector fragments (SG31)
    possible bellows protector and tuyere fragments fused to hearth waste (SG30, SG42)

Table 3.18 Finds from **Phase 2** rubbish spread to the south of **Building 9** (89).

A second group (Table 3.19, 85.01) came from poorly-stratified, but relatively early deposits flanking the **Phase 3** shrine (85.01). These probably comprised debris from the upper part of the **Phase 2** rubbish spread (89, Table 3.18), perhaps contaminated with finds from the overlying **Phase 3** debris (85.02, Table 3.22). The iron, flints, antler, plough pebbles and metalworking debris were all matched in the underlying material, but Group E glass was unrepresented.

An abraded sherd of a large African Red Slipware plate (V2)
A thick iron needle (IN39.55)
A nail and three iron strip fragments (IN80.5–7)
Two pieces of antler
Sixteen **retouched** flints, a core and four **unretouched** flints
Fourteen plough pebbles (SE51)
A hone blank (SE71.17)
Eighteen pebbles and cobbles
    A relatively small group of metalworking debris including:
    A relatively small amount of glassy cinder (329gm)
    A relatively large amount of crystalline cinder (1484 gm)
    A Type 2 tuyere fragment
    Two bellows protector fragments fused to 'hearths'

Table 3.19. Finds from rubbish flanking the **Phase 3** shrine (85.01)

The third group (Table 3.20) came from the building platform of **Building 9** (88.01). This included a large group of specialised metalworking debris, but there was no evidence of industrial activity *in situ*, and it was probably derived from earlier industrial waste in the vicinity, which had been quarried to build the platform. The group shares features with the slightly later rubbish to the south (89) including antler waste, flints and plough pebbles, but not the Group E vessel glass. The relatively large group of metalworking debris is distinctively different with a large group of 'hearth bottoms' including four smithying hearths, a unique group of light, charcoal-rich, 'hearth' fragments and four slag-cake chunks. This was probably mostly smithying debris, apart from a rare fragment of slag. The enlarged platform of *Stage 3* (88.02) produced a second group of finds which probably derives in part from a similar source, and included similar items (antler, flints and plough pebbles). The Group E glass and the burnt vessel sherd probably came from the underlying 'peaty' layers. The group of metalworking debris was,

Primary Platform (88.01)

A quartz crystal with Haematite (SE58.13)
An unassigned E ware sherd
Two antler tine fragments
An antler burr used as a pad (AR81.13)
Two **retouched** flints, a core and a burnt flint
A broken iron long bracket (IN18.1)
A fragmentary granite rotary quern lower-stone (SE43.18)
Three plough pebbles (SE51)

Secondary Platform (88.02)

Sherds of a Group E cone (V80)
An unassigned Group E sherd
A burnt glass vessel fragment (GS01.4)
An antler tine tip and beam
Six **retouched** flints
Three nail fragments
Two hones (SE32.5 and 38.8)
Three plough pebbles

Metalworking debris

A large group including:
Similar quantities of glassy (789 gm)
and crystalline cinder (653gm)
Fragments of a tuyere and bellows protector
One piece of slag
Four Group D puddling hearths
Four charcoal-based 'hearths'
Thirteen classified and unclassified hearths and fragments
Four slag-cake fragments

A small group including:
Small quantities of glassy (80gm)
and crystalline cinder (209gm)
A tuyere plate fragment
Two pieces of slag
A ceramic pin mould fragment (SG17.1)

Table 3.20: Finds from **Phase 2.ii** building platform (88.01) and **Phase 2.iii** platform extension (88.02)

however, much smaller, and included a fragment of a ceramic pin mould which, with related displaced objects, identifies an early episode of bronze casting in the *outer zone* of the **Phase 1** *monasterium* (pp 402-3, Figure 10.86).

The fourth group came from the soil filling the large hollow to the north of the **Phase 1** graveyard (Table 3.21, 119.01). This was linked to the two more westerly groups by the glass and included a similar small group of scrap iron. A relatively large group of metalworking debris included two fragments of a large Type 1 tuyere block displaced from the underlying **Phase 1.4**, debris, and other finds, notably the Group B hearths and perhaps the slag-cake chunks, may also derive from the same earlier deposit.

A sherd of a pale green flask or stemmed cup frag (?4th–6th C GS01.3)
A Group E cone sherd (V69) and an unassigned Group C sherd (C3)
A tiny, fragmentary green bead (GS03.8)
Six nails and fragments
A tapering iron punch (IN50.35) and an iron rod (IN84.1)
Two **retouched** flints, a flint pebble and a burnt flint
A large group of metalworking debris including:
    A relatively large quantity of glassy cinder (848 gm)
    A small amount of crystalline cinder (84 gm)
    Hammerscale (SG13)
    A tuyere block fragment (SG28.2)
    Three Group B hearths, two with trapped tuyere or bellows protector fragments
    Two Group C smelting hearth fragments
    Eight slag-cake fragments (SG44, 45)
    Nine assigned and unassigned 'hearths'

Table 3.21: Finds from **Phase 2:ii** hollow (119.01) to north of **Phase 1** graveyard

The most significant finds from the **Phase 2** assemblages were the sherds of vessel glass, and the evidence is sufficiently clear to recreate the original assemblage by restoring displaced material from later contexts (Figures 3.25, 10.9 and 23). The early rubbish spread (89) produced fragments of eight glass vessels (Vs 30, 31, 64, 65, 70, 71, 73, 74 and 79), including five (70, 71, 73, 74, 79) of the fifteen Group E vessels (pp 312-3). The other vessels from 89 were of equal interest. Two (30 and 31) were Group C cones decorated with vertical and horizontal trails, and the other two (64 and 65) have kicked bases, and may have been a flask (64) and a jar (65). The only parallels for the flask come from western Ireland (pp 309-10). These came from slightly later layers than the Group E cones and can thus be seen as a marginally later group.

The character of the material in 89 is industrial rather than domestic, and the charcoal and calcined bone were probably sweepings from storage bins of commodities, rather than debris from domestic hearths (pp 68-9). The glass may also be seen as workshop debris rather than *domestic* debris. If so the glass workshop was probably close at hand. It would have required an efficient furnace and there was no evidence of such a structure in the trench. The white trails may explain why the broken vessels were discarded rather than being remelted. These would have muddied the metal, and untrailed sherds may have been removed for reworking. The metalworking debris and antler-working waste suggest that there may have been a cluster of workshops, in the *outer zone*. The rubbish spreads were generally located to the north of the road, and the workshops may have been sited on its north edge. The evidence of the later rubbish dumps (85.02, 109, 85.04, pp 107-9, 117) suggests that this workshop area continued in use until the late-seventh/early-eighth century, and perhaps expanded west from its original site. The lack of equivalent debris in the **Fey Field** trench (pp 287-91) suggests that industrial activity did not extend this far north.

The date of this deposit is of great interest and, for once, the evidence was reasonably clear. This suite of deposits overlay the crucial horizon (**Phase 1.6**) ascribed to c. 550 AD (p 69), and the earlier layers, including the concentration of Group E vessels, probably date to the later- sixth century, and perhaps to its third quarter. This is supported by a radiocarbon date of 1650 + 50 BP (GU-2058, p 597) from charcoal (alder, birch, ash, oak and *pomoideae*; Moffat 1985) on the edge of the rubbish spread. These deposits seem to have preceded the main phase of E ware importation. The single sherd of E ware is probably part of the vessel (V6) from the **Phase 1.6** debris (pp 321-2).

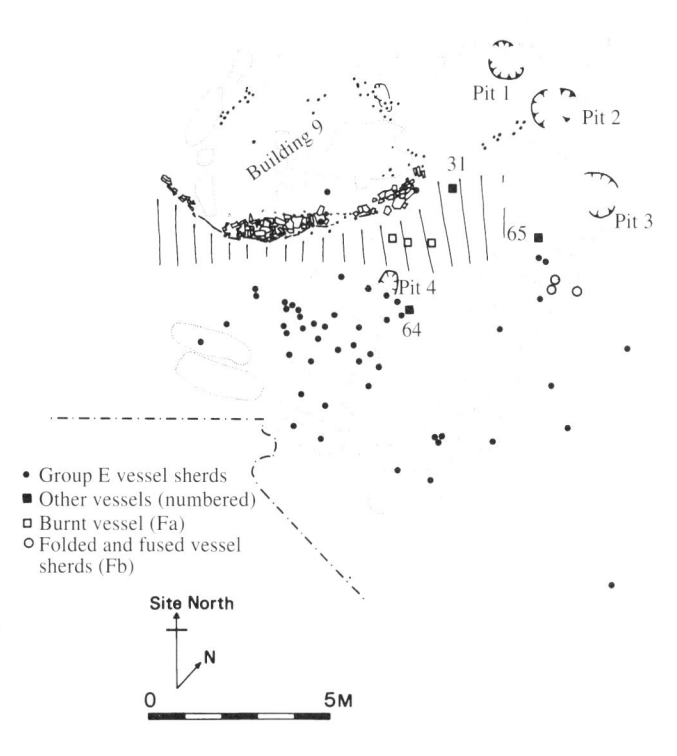

3.25 The distribution of Group E and other glass vessel sherds in deposits flanking **Building I/9** and from intrusive graves.

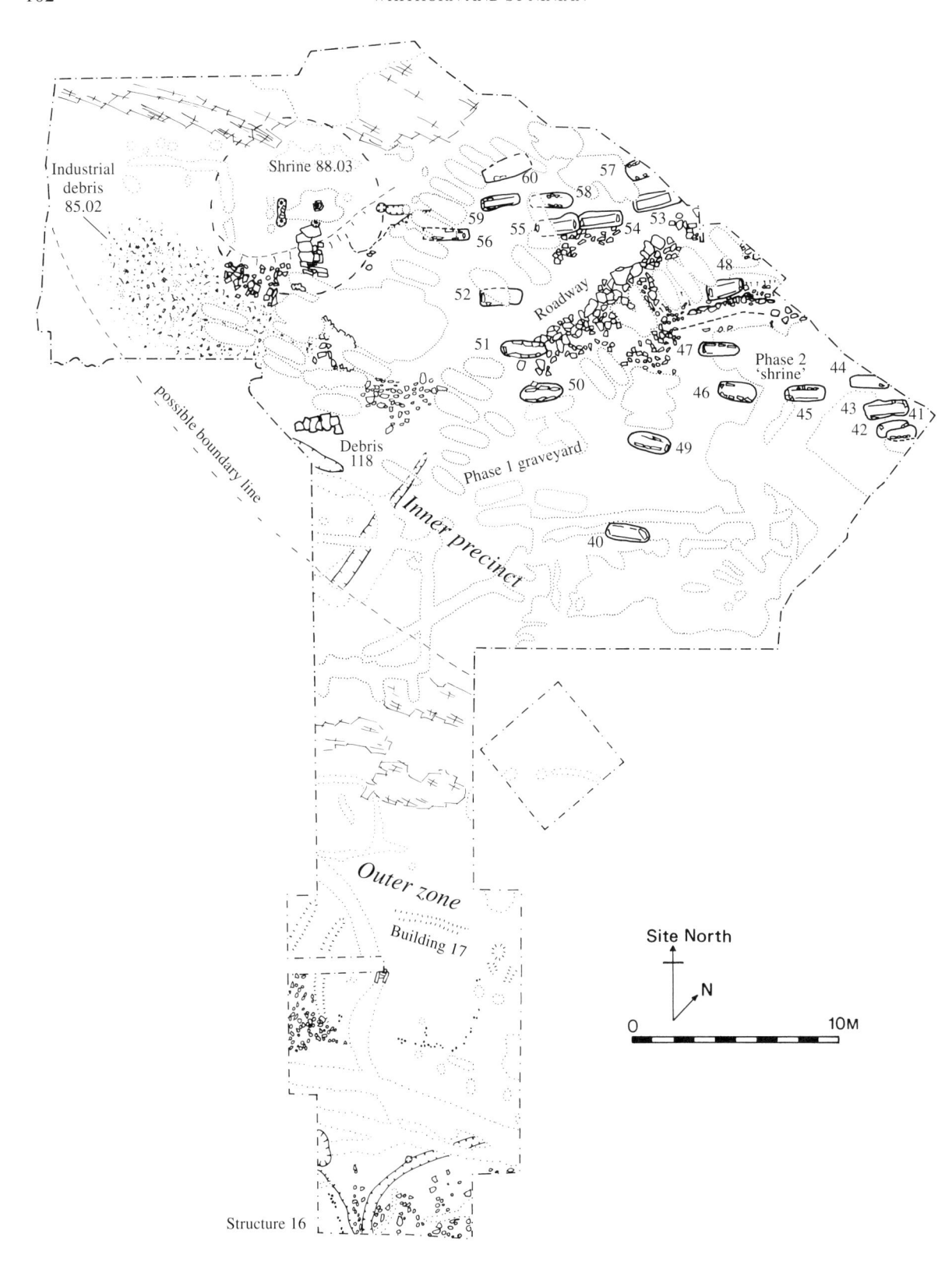

3.26 General plan of the *inner precinct* and *outer zone* in the earlier part of **Period I/3**.

Phase 3

Phase 3 saw the development of a new graveyard extending over much of the eastern part of the *inner precinct* (Figures 3.26 and 3.29), and impinging upon earlier boundaries and graves. The graves were oriented south-west/north-east (true orientation), and were concentrated to the east of a new shrine overlying the **Phase 2** platform. The burials oversailed the **Phase 1** enclosure, and the distinction between the original *inner precinct* and the ground to the west was perhaps no longer recognised. The paved road built at the end of **Phase 2** continued in use, and was patched and repaired, while a muddy layer accumulated to the north. Industrial debris in the western part of the *inner precinct* spread up to the foot of the new 'shrine'. This points to continuing industrial activity in the adjacent part of the *outer zone*, which may have been the source of abundant ironworking waste used in the construction of the *Northumbrian* buildings at the beginning of **Period II** (Table 3.35). Settlement probably continued to evolve in the *outer zone* where new buildings maintained the alignment of the **Phase 2** boundary.

The **Phase 3** graveyard contained lintel graves and log coffin burials (pp 70-73). Four of the log coffin burials disturbed earlier lintel graves, suggesting that all the log coffin burials may have been late, and all the lintel graves relatively early. This inference identifies two sub-phases (*Stages 1* and *2*). The change in burial practice probably dates to the early-seventh century, but its meaning is uncertain. It may reflect the imposition of an alien culture, the arrival of a new cultural group, or a change in the status of the graveyard (p 37).

Phase 3 deposits in the northern part of the *inner precinct* produced large groups of finds, including important groups of metalworking waste and related *industrial debris*. Almost all the pottery and glass had been displaced from earlier deposits, and there thus seems to be an hiatus in the supply of imported wares. A relatively late deposit (109) produced a small group of E ware sherds, which coincided broadly with the change in burial practice, and may mark a new phase in the site's economic relationships (pp 325-6).

Phase 3 was probably relatively short-lived and it can be assigned tentatively to the earlier-seventh century on the basis of relative chronology, although other dating evidence was sparse.

The 'shrine'. The **Phase 3** 'shrine' (88.03) comprised a regular, rectilinear setting of sockets for stones or posts on the extended platform (88.02) of **Phase 2.3**, one of which cut the upper tread of the stone steps (Figure 3.27). A band of stones at the foot of the platform had been severely disturbed by a **Phase 3.3** hollow and **Phase 4.6** graves, but may have been the remains of a paved surround of similar size to the penannular setting around the **Phase 2** shrine. The paving hints that the shrine was enclosed by a fence, and a hypothetical perimeter is included in the phase plans. The stratigraphy on the platform was shallow and greatly disturbed, and gives no detailed chronological evidence, other than that the shrine post-dated the stone steps, and was earlier than the *Northumbrian* church. It is ascribed to **Phase 3** on the bases of its shared orientation with the **Phase 3** graves, and the apparent respect accorded to it by the **Phase 4** burials. It may, indeed, have been erected in the closing stages of **Phase 2**, when late graves were dug through the inner enclosure of the original shrine, and the putative focal monument may have been transferred to the new shrine (Figure 3.18).

The identification of this simple structure as a shrine depends on circumstantial evidence spanning the following four hundred years. The core of the 'shrine' was a rectilinear setting of uprights (*A*, **1–4**) spanned by a line of sockets (*B*) oriented west/east. The platform underlay the west end of the Northumbrian church, and the central axes of the two original 'oratories' follow the socket line (*B*), while the central setting (*A*) lay in the south-west corner of the primary building (Figure 4.7). The north-east socket (**1**) seems to have been the ritual focus of the church, and probably contained a monolith, which seems to have dictated the siting of the altar when the oratories were joined to form a single church in **Period II/3**. It was temporarily removed after the fabric of the building was renovated in **Period II/4**, and a large pit was dug, possibly in pursuit of relics, which removed all but the base of the socket. The *monolith* was replaced in its original position, though at a higher level, and was incorporated in the centre of a wooden screen separating the chancel from the nave.

A small group of seventh century arciform crosses from this part of the site provides a second strand of evidence. Two crosses (SE14.14 and 18) had been incorporated in tenth century buildings overlying the

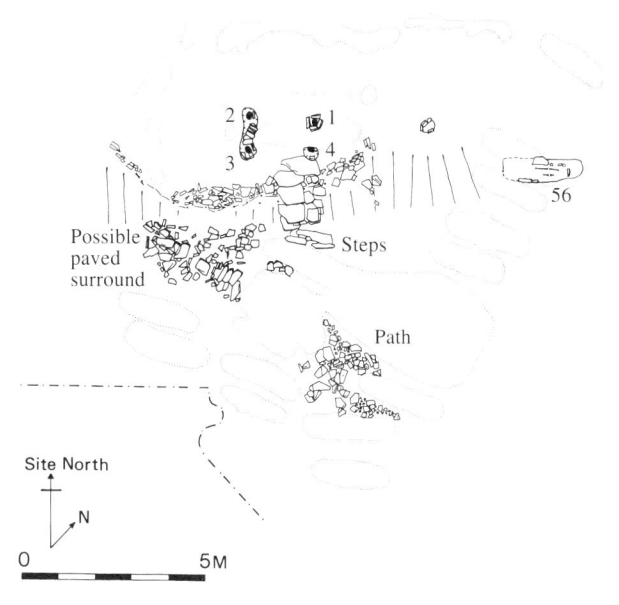

3.27 **Period I/3** shrine overlying **Building I/9**.

east end of demolished church, while a fragment of a third (SE14.16) was found in the soil filling a **Period 1 Phase 4** log coffin burial (**Grave 106**) to the east of the shrine. These seventh century crosses may have been the inspiration for a group of ninth century compass-drawn graffiti on paving stones outside the **Period II** burial chapel and **Period III/1** church (pp 155, 187, 439-41), and could have stood in the shrine.

This indicates that the 'shrine' was dedicated to a figure or concept which was equally attractive to the seventh century church and its potentially different *Northumbrian* successors. It was probably embellished with arciform crosses in the seventh century, which may have been incorporated as objects of veneration in the eighth century church. The *focal monolith* was probably large enough to dominate the church, and the surviving sculptures were perhaps too small to have achieved this. An appropriate inscription would have ensured the enduring reverence it seems to have attracted. The surviving structural evidence suggests that the shrine included timber posts, but the late-eighth century pit had caused too much damage to attempt a reconstruction of its original appearance. It lay some 8.0 m from the boundary of the *inner precinct*, and some 10.0 m to the north of the road, which probably led to the principal church. The underlying **Phase 2** building (**9**) may have accommodated a revered figure who was subsequently commemorated by the shrine.

Stage 1
Stage 1 was represented by lintel graves covering much of the eastern part of the *inner precinct*, but generally avoiding the **Phase 2.7** roadway (Figure 3.32) which separated two distinct groups of burials (*A* and *B*).

Group A comprised eight graves (**53–60**) in the eastern part of the **northern sector** with a single outlier (**52**) to the south. There were two clear strings of graves (**53–56** and **57–59**) with a second outlier (**60**) to the north. These may have been aligned with an insubstantial fence to the south, or a path to the north leading eastwards from the new shrine. The most westerly grave was cut into the foot of the extended platform (88.02) of **Building 9**, and may have abutted the putative fence around the new shrine. Five of the graves (**52, 54–56, 59**) were deep, well-defined *Type 2* lintel graves with large head- and foot-stones separating timber sides. Three (**57, 58** and **60**) were poorly defined *Type 1* graves with irregular stone linings, which may have been the packing behind timber side walls. The last grave (**53**) contained a unique coffin burial, apparently comprising an unnailed, rectilinear wooden chest some 1.75 m long, 0.4 m wide and at least 0.3 m deep (Figure 3.3). Three graves (**53, 54** and **59**) contained identifiable human bones. All were adult, but of uncertain sex.

Four of the burials (**53–55, 58**) had been covered with small stone slabs which slumped into the graves as the wooden covers decayed (Figure 3.29). A massive granite boulder was subsequently placed over the stones covering the head of **Grave 53** and the foot of **Grave 54**. It was probably set up as a grave-marker, but may have enjoyed additional ritual significance as it lay on the axial line of the 'shrine'. It was subsequently built into the south-east corner of the *Northumbrian* burial chapel, and may have been one of a group of extant monuments dictating the design of the *Northumbrian* buildings.

The *Group A* graves produced a small assemblage of finds including *clastic lime*, flints, B*i* and B*ii amphora* sherds, plough pebbles and metalworking debris which were probably displaced from underlying **Phase 1** deposits. The metalworking waste included fragments of a clay mould with traces of a lead alloy (SG17.03) and crucible (SG15.7), which probably originated in deposits of the earlier-sixth century (Figure 10.86, p 403). A copper alloy needle (BZ12.10) from **Grave 56**, and a worn glass bangle fragment of 1st/2nd century type (GS04.2) from **Grave 52**, may have been intentional deposits.

Group B comprised eleven graves (**40–50**) to the south of the **Phase 2.7** road, with an outlier (**51**) cutting the road surface. Although there was one possible string of graves (**44–46, 50**), the *Group B* burials were widely scattered and superficially show little order. This is probably illusory, and they generally seem to have filled gaps in and around the densely populated **Phase 1–2** graveyard. A few graves impinged upon earlier burials which were perhaps unmarked and forgotten. Two graves (**45** and **46**) were dug into the primary enclosure of the **Phase 2** shrine, which may mean this area was no longer revered, possibly because the focal monument had been moved. The group included three *Type 1* graves (**40, 47,** and **49**), with thin greywacke cover-slabs set below the ground surface, resting on relatively-low side walls of stone or timber; four *Type 3* graves (**45, 46** and **50**) with relatively high and massive side walls, presumably supporting covers close to the ground surface; and only two *Type 2* graves (**43** and **48**) with head and foot-stones separating timber side slabs. The remaining three graves (**41, 42** and **44**) were poorly defined, and may have been of *Type 1* or *2*. The graves were thus more varied than those in *Group A*, and this may mark a real distinction between the two groups, perhaps in date, or in the status of the people buried.

The graves produced a small group of finds which is consistent with their location in the 'clean' area of the **Phase 1–2** graveyard. A sherd of an E ware bowl (V4) from **Grave 51** probably derives from the adjacent **Phase 3.3** rubbish (109), and was perhaps deposited when the cover of the grave was removed. The most

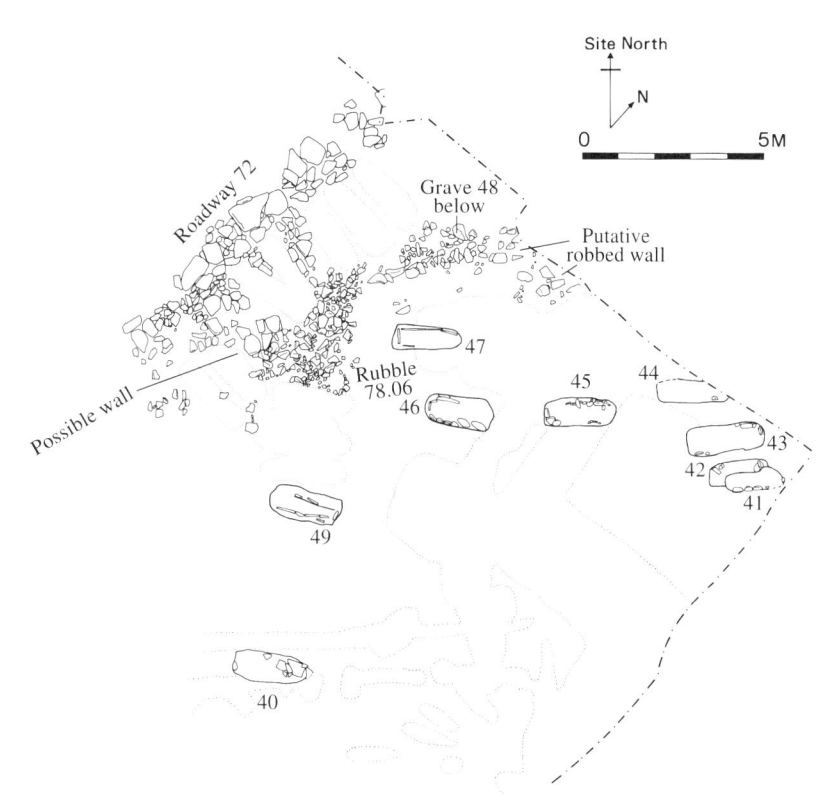

3.28 **Period I/3.1** lintel graves cut into **Period I/2** 'shrine', and broadly contemporary rubble and roadway to the north.

exceptional find was a small slab of greywacke with an incised cross and other graffiti (SE14.3) from the side wall of **Grave 45**. It is unlikely to have been a grave-marker, but could have originated in the **Phase 2** shrine. Two graves (**47** and **51**) produced skeletal remains, both of adults.

Stage 1: other deposits
There is no secure evidence of other activities in the *inner precinct* in the early part of **Phase 3**, although industrial debris probably continued to accumulate on its western fringe (Table 3.19), and a spread of metalworking debris (85.02, Table 3.22) oversailing the paved surround of the shrine, may have pertained to this stage. A thick deposit of trampled mud (73.01) accumulated in the trough to the north of the road. This produced a number of finds (Table 3.25) which may have been displaced from underlying layers, while metalworking waste was perhaps brought in as hard core.

Stage 2
Stage 2 saw the continued use of the graveyard to the south of the road, and was represented by twelve log coffin burials (**1–3**, **61–68**). Four further burials (**69–72**) lay to the north of the road, of which two (**71** and **72**) may have been special burials associated with the shrine. Industrial debris continued to accumulate in the western part of the *inner precinct*, and a large hollow filled with debris (109 Table 3.24) probably pertained to this stage. The graves fall into four groups (*C–F*).

Group C comprised eight graves (**61–68**) on the periphery of the **Phase 2** 'shrine'. These generally filled gaps between existing burials, although four (**61**, **62**, **63** and **65**) clipped the edges of earlier lintel graves. Three of the graves (**66–68**) occupied the northern half of the gap in the penannular paving of **Phase 2.4**. Five graves (**62**, **65**, **66**, **67**, and **68**) revealed clear evidence of log-coffins, and the others may have contained similar coffins. The foot of **Grave 67** was marked by a low stone slab, and the neighbouring grave to the north (**68**) was covered with two distinct layers of quartz and granite pebbles (Table 3.3). Most of the other graves had been disturbed, and revealed no evidence of marking. Two graves (**65** and **68**) produced fragmentary skeletal remains of which one was adult (**65**:*1649*).

Group D comprised the five log coffin burials (**1–3**, **7** and **8**) in the **Phase 1.5** graveyard. These cannot be distinguished stratigraphically from the other early burials in this area, and are ascribed to **Phase 3.2** on the bases of the burial type and, to a lesser extent, their orientation. Some or all of them could pertain to an earlier phase, although this would run counter to the evidence that log coffin burials replaced lintel graves in the middle of **Phase 3**.

Group D included two of the largest log coffins (**Graves 1** and **2**). The coffin in **Grave 1** was at least 2.6 m long and *c.* 0.5 m in diameter. Two large post-holes dug into the grave fill were associated with a fragmentary structure (**11**, 101) which may have been the remains of a building, but is more likely to

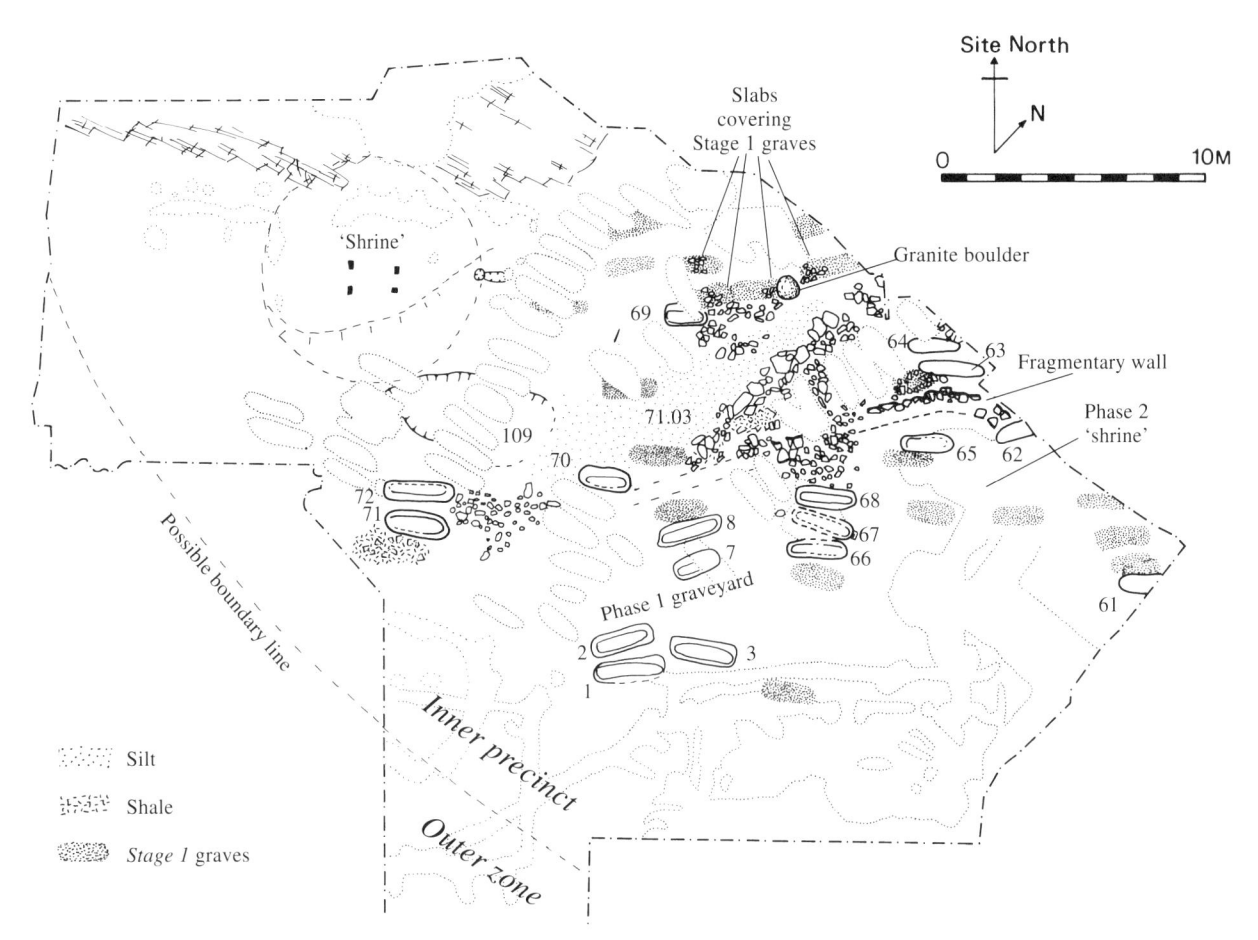

3.29 General plan of the *inner precinct* in **Period I/3.2** showing the first group of log-coffin burials, and features marking earlier lintel graves.

have been a long lived graveyard monument (Figure 3.30). The structure had been severely disturbed by successive *Northumbrian* halls. The surviving elements comprised two large post-sockets cutting the south side of the grave, a stone 'kerb' overlying **Grave 2**, and an area of paving at its east end surrounding a small post socket. The kerb and postholes were surrounded by charcoal, and overlain by a thick layer of fine river gravel. The western post-hole collapsed into the grave when the west end of the coffin decayed, but the eastern socket survived, and contained the impression of a rectangular timber. The 'kerb' possibly marked the outer margin of an insubstantial fence, and the paving and post-hole may have been the remains of an entrance to the enclosure. The gravel oversailed

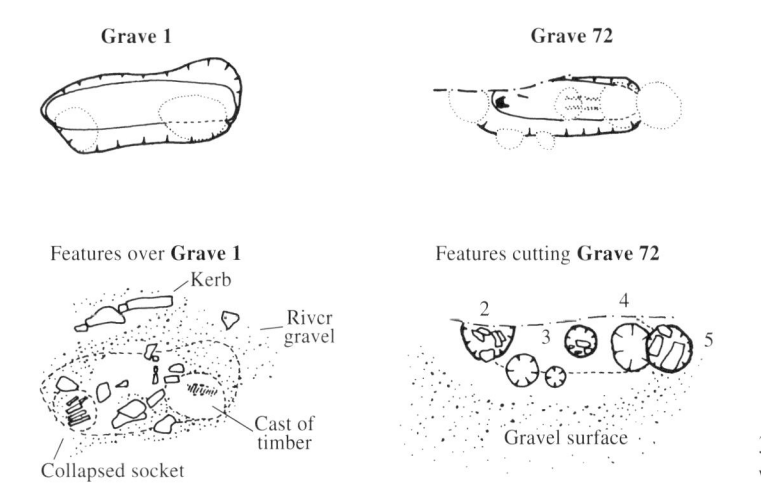

3.30 Possible grave markers associated with **Graves 1** and **72**

the 'kerb', but surrounded the surviving marker post. The paving included a fragment of a large millstone (SE44.03) and a joining fragment had been displaced into an overlying fourteenth century grave (pp 29, 460-1).

Group E comprised two small log coffin graves (**69** and **70**) to the north of the road. **Grave 69** lay immediately south of the southern string of lintel graves in *Group A*, and contained the fragmentary remains of a child. **Grave 70** was dug into the northern margin of the road.

Group F comprised two adjacent log coffin graves (**71** and **72**) dug into the northern side of the road, and lying some way to the west of the other **Phase 3** graves. The graves lay due south (site orientation) of the focus of the new shrine, and were perhaps placed here for ritual reasons. The soil filling the northern grave (**72**) was disturbed by a cluster of postholes which probably contained successive paired marker posts, analogous to those marking **Grave 1** (Figure 3.30). The final pair of posts was still standing in the mid- to late-eighth century, and formed part of an alignment of posts and, possibly, stones lying between the *Northumbrian* ecclesiastical buildings in the **northern range** and the potentially secular or domestic buildings to the south (pp 112, 135). The post-pair straddled an enduring north/south axis running through the opposed doorways of the church, and the buildings to the south. Later surfaces surrounding this grave gave a negative impression of an oval enclosure similar to the putative feature over **Grave 1**. The more southerly grave produced fragmentary remains of a large, but immature, individual.

Stage 2: Other deposits
Mud probably continued to accumulate to the north of the road in the eastern part of the **northern sector**, but cannot be distinguished stratigraphically from the *Stage 1* deposits. Two, successive deposits of *industrial debris* and *food waste* (85.02 and 109) immediately south of the new shrine probably pertained to this stage, and were the last large rubbish spreads to accumulate in the *inner precinct* during **Period I**, although a small group of specialised metalworking debris built up against the platform of the **Phase 4.5** shrine in **Phase 4.6** (Table 3.33).

The first group comprised a rich rubbish spread (85.02) to the south and west of the **Phase 2** platform (Figure 3.26). The eastern part of the deposit had been dug away by a later hollow (109) ascribed to *Stage 2*, and this already-confused area was further disturbed by log coffin burials in the later stages of **Phase 4**. The finds from the rubbish spread and intrusive graves are listed in Table 3.22, which reveals close similarities between the two groups. The discrepancies are easily explained. The graves penetrated the underlying **Phase 1** and **2** deposits which were respectively the source of the sherds of B*i* amphora and Group E vessel sherds. The graves also clipped the later rubbish (109) to the east, which was probably the source of the E ware sherds and anomalous metalworking 'hearths'. Antler and iron fittings (IN24) were discrete deposits in the central and western parts of the rubbish spread and so were not displaced into the graves.

The combined assemblage comprised *industrial debris* probably originating in a blacksmith's shop. The key finds were the large groups of nails and other iron scrap, and the large collection of hones and related implements (Figure 10.166). Other iron artefacts may also have been scrap, although the three chisels and the awl could have been workshop tools. The predominance of tine fragments among the antler finds suggests the manufacture and repair of antler handles for iron implements, and contrasts with the comb-making debris in the later deposit (109, Table 3.23). The staples, looped hasp, hinge and sliding bolt could have come from the upper part of a chest (pp 410-1). The two possible brooches were found together, and a large iron penannular brooch with spiral terminals (IN42.1), recovered during the removal of a baulk, perhaps originated in this deposit. The metalworking debris is unusual due to the low incidence of 'hearths' and hearth furniture (*tuyeres*), despite the relative abundance of cinder. Metalworking waste was perhaps separated into different categories, and this may thus merely represented the cinder waste of a smithy which deposited other waste elsewhere. The pebbles and cobbles are similar to those capping log coffin burials (Table 3.3), and mostly came from beaches and rivers. They were recurrently associated with industrial debris in this area and elsewhere, but no explanation can be offered for their presence (pp 472-3).

The second large group came from the soil filling a large oval hollow (109) to the south-east of the 'shrine', which cut the **Phase 2** path (88.02), and probably disturbed the north side of the **Phase 2–3** road. It was covered by a secondary paved surface (98c) laid at the end of **Phase 3**, and had been disturbed by at least three **Phase 4** graves (82.03; **107–109**). The finds group was relatively small, and contrasts in content and quality with the earlier group (85.02) to the east, through which the hollow was probably cut. The group included a few sherds of pottery and glass displaced from earlier deposits, but their scarcity shows that the soil dug from the hollow was removed from the site. The most important finds are the E ware sherds which mark the reappearance of imported pottery in the *inner precinct* after a long interval extending back to the end of **Phase 1**. The antler waste included comb-plate trimmings which are the earliest certain evidence for comb manufacture in this part of the site. The large stick pin seems to be unparalleled in Insular assemblages, and may have been a continental import.

a) Rubbish spread

A B*iv amphora* sherd (V1)

Six vessel glass sherds (V2b; two Group E,
  66/7 and 69/70; and two featureless)
A tinned copper-alloy chape (BZ30.1)

A striated lead washer (LD4.1)
Two folded pieces of lead sheet (LD11.1 and 2)
An iron staple (IN17.02), a looped hasp (IN24.3),
  a possible hinge (IN24.1), a staple attached
  to riveted strips (IN24.2) and a sliding bolt (IN33.1)
Three iron buckle, (IN44.1, 2, 20), two possibly brooches (2 and 20)
An iron chain link or hook (IN30.7)
A possible chisel (IN52.11)
A sickle blade fragment (IN55.1)
A possible Class C knife (IN66.37)
A possible iron fishhook (IN31.3)
Twenty-two nails and fragments
Seven iron strips (IN80.12-16, 81.04 and 5)

Two iron wire fragments (IN90.1 and 2)
Three iron lumps (IN93.14-16)
Two large hones (SE34. 4 and 5)
Four small hones (SE36.8; 38.2, 13 and 18)
A hone blank (SE71.23)
A well-finished sandstone smoother (SE42.13)
Nineteen pieces of antler including:
  Three burrs
  Twelve tine fragments
  Four offcuts
Fourteen plough pebbles (SE51)
Two smoothed, incised greywacke slabs (SE54.7 and 8)
Sixteen **retouched**, six **unretouched**
  and two burnt flints
Fifty-three pebbles and cobbles including five with CaCO3
Three pieces of burnt limestone (SE60)
A large group of metalworking debris including:
  Relatively large amounts of glassy (2174gm)
    and crystalline cinder (2821gm)
  A scrap of a Type 2 tuyere
  Two slag-cake chunks
  A notably small group of ' hearth' fragments:
  Two Group D puddling hearths
    and three related fragments

b) Intrusive graves

A B*iv amphora* neck sherd (V1)
Two B*i amphora* sherds (V2)
Two rim sherds of an E3 bowl (V3)
Thirty vessel glass sherds mostly of Group E

A large copper alloy tag end (BZ20.1)
A ring or buckle loop (BZ28.8)
A squashed copper-alloy stud (BZ34.5)
Two copper-alloy sheet fragments (BZ38.21, 25)
A nodular lump of lead (LD12.4)
A piece of lead with a cut edge (LD11.6)
Two iron rivets (IN21.3 and 4)

An S-shaped hook (IN31.5)
Two possible chisels (IN52.3 and 4)
An iron awl or punch (IN50.69)
An unidentified object (IN78.9)
A possible wool-comb tooth (IN62.2)
Fourteen nails and fragments
Five iron strip (IN80.24-26) and plate fragments (IN82.10
  and 11)

Six small hones (SE36.1, 37.1,2;38.16,23)

A sandstone smoother (SE42.9)

Five plough pebbles (SE51)

Twenty-one **retouched**, two **unretouched** and
  two burnt flints, and four flint pebbles

Small amounts of glassy (212gm)
  and crystalline cinder (125gm)
Two Type 2 Tuyere fragments

A relatively large group of 'hearth' fragments
  A Group D puddling hearth
  Two glassy hearths, one with fused bellows protector
    fragments
  Five Group C smelting hearth fragments

Table 3.22: Finds from **a**) main midden (85.02) to south of **Phase 2** platform and **b**) intrusive **Phase 4** graves (82.04–05, **111–118**)

Sherds of a B*i amphora* (V2) and an early E2 beaker (V1)
Rim sherds of two E ware bowls (E3, V3 and V4) and two
  unassigned sherds
Seven vessel glass sherds, including pieces of V24 and V73 (+
  FAc, C2d, C3, C5, E2bb)
Sherds of a 1st-3rd C prismatic glass vessel (GS 01.4) and a
  1st/2nd C convex vessel (01.2)
A large copper-alloy stick pin with an inverted crescent head
  (BZ14.7)
The front and back-plates of a small copper alloy strap end
  (BZ19.2)
A tubular copper alloy rivet surrounded by plaster (BZ34.1)
A fragment of tin-plated, copper-alloy sheet (BZ35.5)
An iron staple (IN17.21), a rectangular loop (IN29.2) and a
  penannular finger ring (IN45.2)
A tanged iron punch (IN50.50)
Two rectangular strips connected by two rivets (IN78.4)
Three nails and fragments, two iron strips (IN80.17 and 19), a bar
  (IN83.5), a rod (IN84.2) and a piece of looped wire (IN90.3).
A greywacke, 'loom-weight' fragment (SE31.5) and a large hone
  (SE35.10)
Thirteen pieces of antler including:

  Three coronets
  Two beam fragments and a beam segment
  A tine with a sawn base
  Three comb-plate trimmings
  Two offcuts and a tine offcut or trimming
A burnt flint and twenty-four **retouched** flints
Eleven plough pebbles (SE51)
Fourteen pebbles and cobbles
A relatively small group of metalworking debris including:
  A relatively large amount of glassy cinder (1133 gm)
  A small amount of crystalline cinder (61gm)
  Two Type 2 tuyere fragments
  Three Group C smelting hearths and a small group of
    varied 'hearth' fragments

Table 3.23a: Finds from **Phase 3.2** hollow (109) south-east of the **Phase 3** shrine.

Two sherds of vessel glass (V51 and Gp C4)
Opaque white Type 3a bangle fragment (1st/2nd C, GS04.04)
Two pieces of copper-alloy sheet (BZ38:18, 19)
Three nail shanks and a possible broken awl (IN50.33)

Half of a possible fly-wheel (SE50.15)
A granite plough pebble (SE51)
Four **retouched** flints

Table 3.23b: Finds from graves (**106–109**) cutting **Phase 3.2** hollow (109)

A gully cutting the north side of **Building 5** produced a related group of finds (Table 3.24), which includes earlier material, notably the glass sherds, potentially associated with the building (pp 82-3, 323-4). The metalworking debris and antler indicates that most of the material belongs with the larger group of finds from 109.

A rim sherd of small E1 jar (V16)
Pieces of four glass vessels (Vs 6, 48, 53d, 66/67d).
Six featureless vessel sherds and two of Gp C3
A silver hinge (SR19)
Four small rivulets of molten copper alloy waste (BZ39.1–4)
Three nail fragments and a broken clench plate (IN20.1)
An iron bar with opposed hook ends (IN65.1)
Tapering flat pointed object (IN65.2) and a blade fragment (IN73.1)
A concreted iron lump (IN93.2) Medium-grained, greywacke discoid (SE20.13)
Two fine-grained, sandstone hone blanks (SE71.5 and 16)
Thirteen quartz plough pebbles (SE51)
A segment removed from an antler tine or beam
A burnt flint and ten **retouched** flints
Nineteen rounded quartz pebble, ten granite pebbles, seven vein quartz fragments
Three pieces of quartz with $CaCO_3$
A small group of metalworking debris comprising:
    Glassy cinder (570 gm)
    Crystalline cinder (202 gm)
    Four Group C smelting hearth fragments (991 gm)
    Four miscellaneous 'hearths' (668 gm)

Table 3.24: Finds from features disturbing **Building 5** and surface to the east (118)

An unfinished disc made from African Red Slip ware (V3)
A sherd of B*i* amphora (V1) and three sherds of B*ii* amphora (V2)
A sherd of an early E ware beaker or jug (V6)
A Group C3 vessel glass sherd
An iron swivel knife fragment (IN 68.1)
A nail, a nail shank and an iron strip (IN80.9)
A greywacke 'loom weight' (SE29.5)
Five **retouched** flints, a core and a burnt flint
Six plough pebbles (SE51)
Eight 'pebbles'
A distinctive group of metalworking debris including:
    A crucible fragment with traces of bronze (SG15.6)
    A small quantity of glassy cinder (165 gm)
    A disproportionately large group of crystalline cinder (3593 gm)
    Two Type 2 tuyere fragments
    A Group B 'hearth' fused to a tuyere or bellows protector fragment
    A Group C smelting hearth and a small group of 'hearths' and fragments
A small group of animal bones

Table 3.25: Finds from **Phase 3** muddy deposit north of the paved road (73.01).

The muddy layer (73.01) north of the paved road in the eastern part of the area produced a third group of finds partly pertaining to **Phase 3** (Table 3.25). The sherds of pottery and glass were probably displaced from the underlying **Phase 1.6** deposits (Table 3.14a Figure 10.22), as was the crucible sherd (Figure 10.88). The most remarkable object is the broken swivel knife which is one of two seventh century examples from Whithorn, and one of the earliest from Europe (p 429). The disproportionate amount of crystalline cinder among the metalworking debris suggests it was introduced as hard core. Flints, plough pebbles and 'pebbles' were ubiquitous in the **Phase 3–4** rubbish spreads in the **northern sector**.

Phase 4

Phase 4 (Figures 2.6, 3.32 and 33) saw the development of a new graveyard to the north and west of the main burial ground of **Phases 1–3**, and revealed two distinct sub-phases, indicating a major reorganisation of the *monasterium* in *c*. 700 AD (pp 37-8). The new graves reverted to the west/east orientation (true) of the **Phase 2** burials, and most contained log-coffins. The changed orientation gives an impression of radical change, but the new graves caused minimal damage to the earlier burials in the southern part of the *inner precinct*, indicating a conscious decision to avoid disturbing earlier burials by extending the graveyard into the unoccupied ground to the north. This respect for extant burials also extended to the two 'shrines' and the marked 'special' grave (72) to the west of the main burial ground. Other features were disregarded. The first row of **Phase 4** graves (82.01) was dug through the roadway, and the irregular second row (82.02) was dug through the **Phase 3.1** graves in *Group A* and the western part of the **Phase 1.5** graveyard enclosure. The disturbance of the *Group A* graves may have been accidental. Their wooden lintels had already decayed, and the overlying slab markers had slumped into the graves, and were covered by a thick layer of worm-sorted soil. The new graves swung around **Grave 54** which was still clearly marked by the massive granite boulder at its head. A line of large posts and stones ran west/east across the north side of the **central sector**, marking a long-lived chordal boundary (252, p 112, Figures 3.32 and 33) within the *inner precinct*, which survived into **Period II**, when it may have separated ecclesiastical and secular zones (p 135). It is impossible to be certain when these were erected, due to the shallow stratification, but the alignment almost certainly originated in **Phase 4**, and probably preceded the major changes of *Stage 5*.

There was no evidence of other activity in the *inner precinct* during the first three stages of **Phase 4** (Figure 3.31). Muddy soil continued to accumulate at the foot of the northern slope, obscuring the earlier graves, and covering the paving (77, 98c) laid at the end of **Phase 3**. A relatively large group of metalworking debris from this soil was probably brought in as hard core to alleviate the muddiness which may also explain the loss of a small group of artefacts (Table 3.26).

The later stages of **Phase 4** saw a major redevelopment of the northern part of the area (Figure 3.32). A new curvilinear 'shrine' was built to the west of the **Phase 3** shrine, and a platform to the

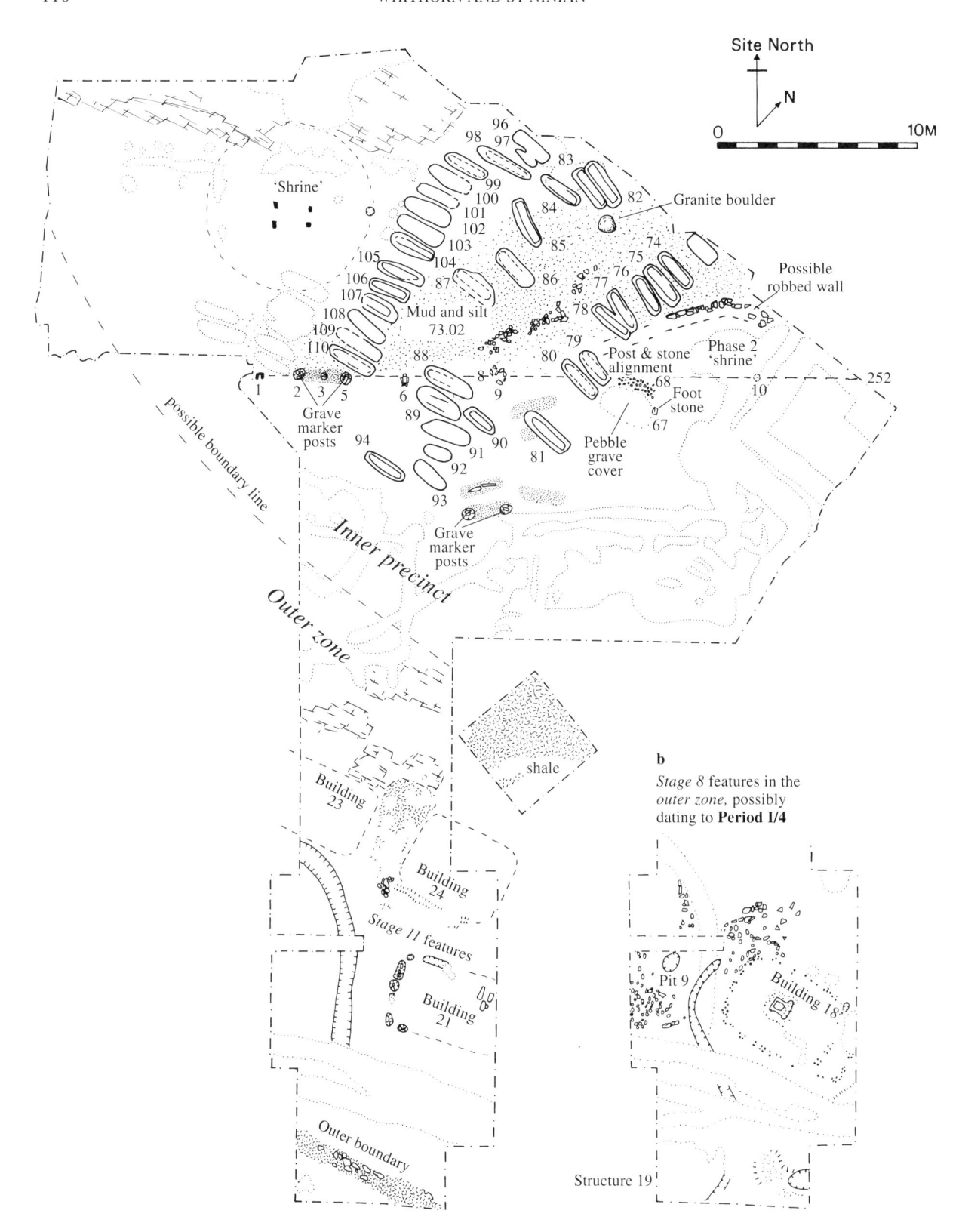

3.31 General plan of earlier **Period I/4** features in the *inner precinct* (*Stages 1-3*) and *outer zone* (*Stage 11*).

east possibly accommodated another new monument. A new gravel road was laid following the line of the earlier paved roadway. The graveyard continued to expand westwards, and two final rows of graves were dug after the construction of the new shrine. An important group of finds (Table 3.33) from the western part of the **northern sector** included a gold ingot and piece of gold wire, and was perhaps derived from a workshops in the adjacent part of the *outer zone*. The finds hint that the *monasterium* enjoyed new, probably wider, contacts. The array of ritual structures standing at the end of **Phase 4** seems

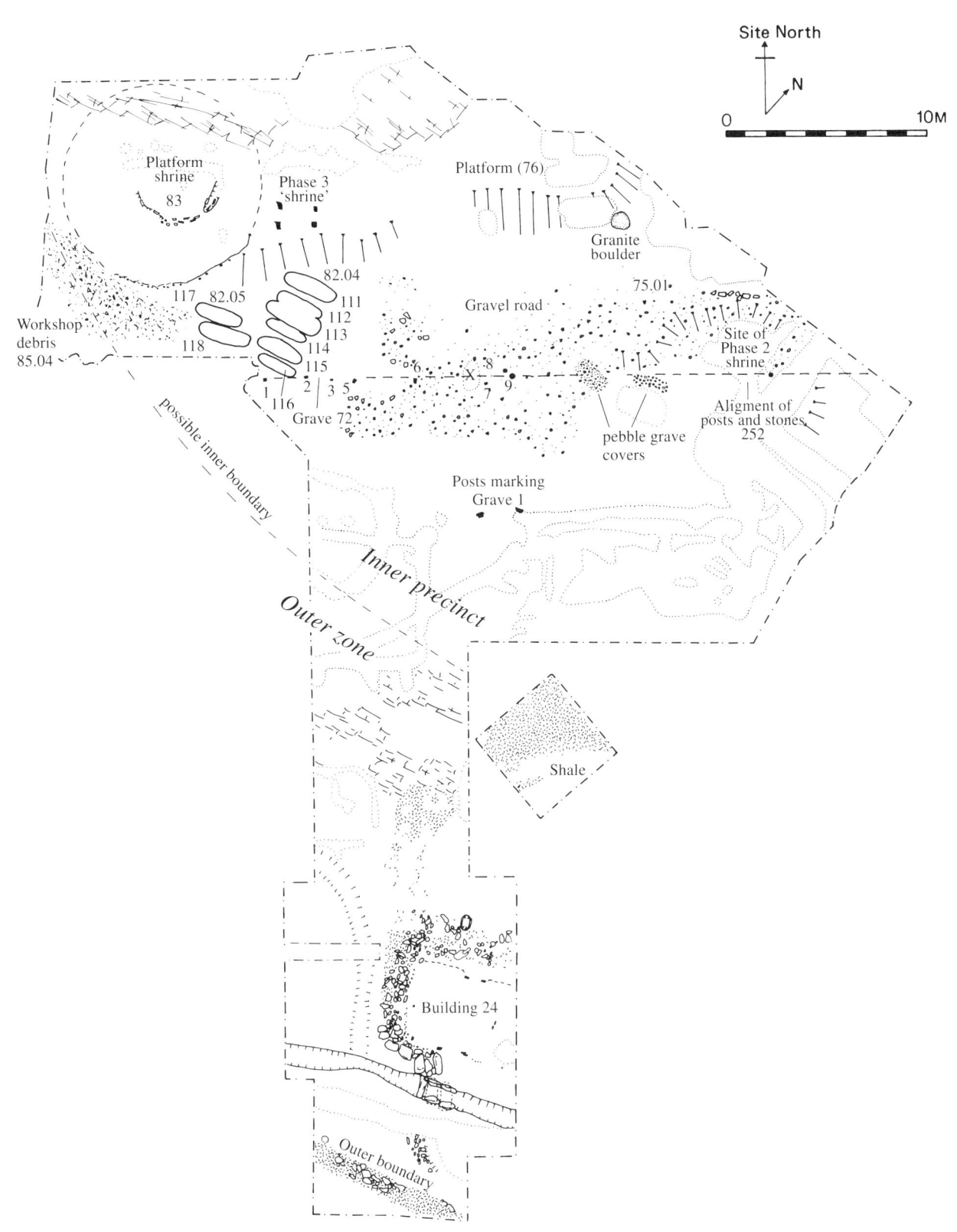

3.32 General plan of later **Period I/4** features in the *inner precinct* (*Stages 4-7*) and *outer zone* (*Stages 12-13*).

to have played a critical role in the siting of *Northumbrian* ecclesiastical buildings erected in the early stages of **Period II** (pp 134-5).

A long sequence of buildings in the *outer zone* was enclosed by an insubstantial outer boundary. During this phase the stake-walled buildings of **Phases 1–3** were replaced by buildings of similar size and shape, but built of timber and wattle (pp 37-8, 138-9). The natural drainage deteriorated, leading to periodic flooding and waterlogging in the low-lying ground, while the upper part of the site became increasingly muddy.

The phase can be ascribed tentatively to the second half of the seventh century and the first two or three decades of the eighth. Archaeological evidence suggests that **Phase 4** ends in the early-eighth century, and there is a good case for correlating the comprehensive redevelopment of the site at the start of **Period II** with the appointment of Pecthelm as bishop in *c.* 730 AD (pp 18-19, 40-41, 136). The beginning of the phase was not dated clearly, and the relative stratigraphic sequence provides the best gauge.

The post and stone alignment. The alignment comprised ten sockets for timbers and stones running east-west across the northern part of the **central sector**, and marking a line which was a critical boundary in the **Period II** *minster*. The most westerly socket (1) lay on the west edge of the trench, and was left unexcavated. The next four sockets (2–5) were cut into **Grave 72**, and may have had a dual role as grave and boundary markers (Figure 3.30). The earliest feature (4) was a shallow hollow with a rounded base at the foot of the grave. This was cut by the most easterly of three post-holes (2, 3 and 5), comprising the sockets (2 and 5) for two large timbers cutting the head and foot of the grave, and one for a smaller post (3) in between. The eastern post seems to have remained standing until the mid-eighth century and the upper part of the cavity left by the decayed timber was filled with late-eighth/early-ninth century rubbish (303, pp 160-3). The next feature to the east (6) comprised the packing for a rectangular stone slab abutting the face of the Northumbrian terrace. The packing lay at the base of a **Period III/3** pit (Figure 5.10, p 205), which may have been dug to extract the stone. It had apparently been inserted when the ground level was higher than in **Period II**, and was probably erected in **Period I/4**. The next feature was a large sub-rectilinear cavity (7) cutting into a **Phase 4.2** grave (**88**), and sealed by an early Northumbrian path (Figures 4.9 and 10). The cavity could have been left by the decay of a small log coffin, although none of the characteristic evidence was recorded. It could equally mark a solid piece of timber, perhaps serving as the socket for a post or stone. Any evidence would have been destroyed when the cavity and overlying deposits collapsed in **Period III** or **IV** (p 205). The next two sockets (8 and 9) lay some 1.5 m to the east. Both were cut into the **Phase 2.7** road, and the earlier of the two had disturbed the edge of a **Phase 3.1** grave (**51**). Both sockets were oversailed by the **Phase 4.5** road surface, which may have been laid around the uprights they contained. The earlier feature (8) seems to have contained a large timber, and had been disturbed by a larger shallow hollow with chock stones for a stone, perhaps similar to the granite boulder to the north. The last socket (10) lay to the east on the eastern margin of the **Phase 2.1** shrine, clipping the edge of a late **Phase 2** grave (**26**). The original socket had been severely damaged by a recut which disturbed the edge of a late-eighth century puddling pit (250.03, p 166). This later hole seems to have contained a slim stone, which had probably been displaced from the original socket. The cumulative stratigraphic evidence argues that the alignment originated in the earlier part of **Phase 4**, but probably not before, and was maintained until the later-eighth century. It may have marked the southern boundary of the **Phase 4.3–7** burials and, on the evidence of the enigmatic cavity (7), could have been erected towards the end of **Phase 4.2**. This suggests that it was originally intended to separate the burials and shrines to the north from the unused ground to the south, and that this symbolic distinction survived the transformation of the site at the start of **Period II** (p 135).

The sequence
The stratigraphy of the **Phase 4** features in the inner precinct was relatively straightforward (Figure 3.4). The burials seem to have expanded from east to west, and the five rows of log coffins (82.01–05) indicate five distinct stages (1–3, 6 and 7). The construction of the new shrine and associated features marks a sixth stage (5), and an underlying spread of rubble points to a brief episode of disrepair (Stage 4). The new constructions of Stage 5 are an important development dividing this period into two sub-phases (**Phase 4a** and **b**).

Stage 1
Stage 1 was represented by the first row of burials (82.01) comprising nine graves (**73–81**), of which eight (**74–81**) contained log coffins. The most northerly grave (**73**) was an unique burial with an un-nailed trapezoid timber lining resting on a paved floor (Figure 3.3). The graves to the north-east were dug through the southern side of the **Phase 2.7** road clipping the **Phase 3** graves on the northern perimeter of the **Phase 2** shrine. A detached pair of graves (**79** and **80**) to the south-west were dug into an empty space in the corner of the **Phase 1.5** graveyard. The last burial (**81**) lay 2.0 m to the south-west clipping the sides of two earlier burials (**6** and **8**) and destroying the east end of a third (**8**). The head of **Grave 78** was marked by a large granite cobble, and **Grave 80** was covered with assorted quartz and granite pebbles (Table 3.3) laid flush with the earlier paving. A thick layer of greywacke chips in the upper fill of **Grave 74** may represent a mound, which had slumped when the coffin decayed. A rickle of stones to the north-west of the graves (77) may have been the remains of an insubstantial boundary.

A compact group of graves (**74–78**) was overlain by the corner of the *Northumbrian* enclosure wall and associated path (Figure 3.33). The wall seems to have been plastered, and the coffins and skeletal remains were unusually well-preserved, perhaps because leached lime had counteracted the acidity of the soil. The skeletal remains comprise five tall robust adults of whom four were male. The high incidence of spinal anomalies indicated that they may have been related (p 554).

Most of the large group of finds from the graves (excavation archive) were probably derived from

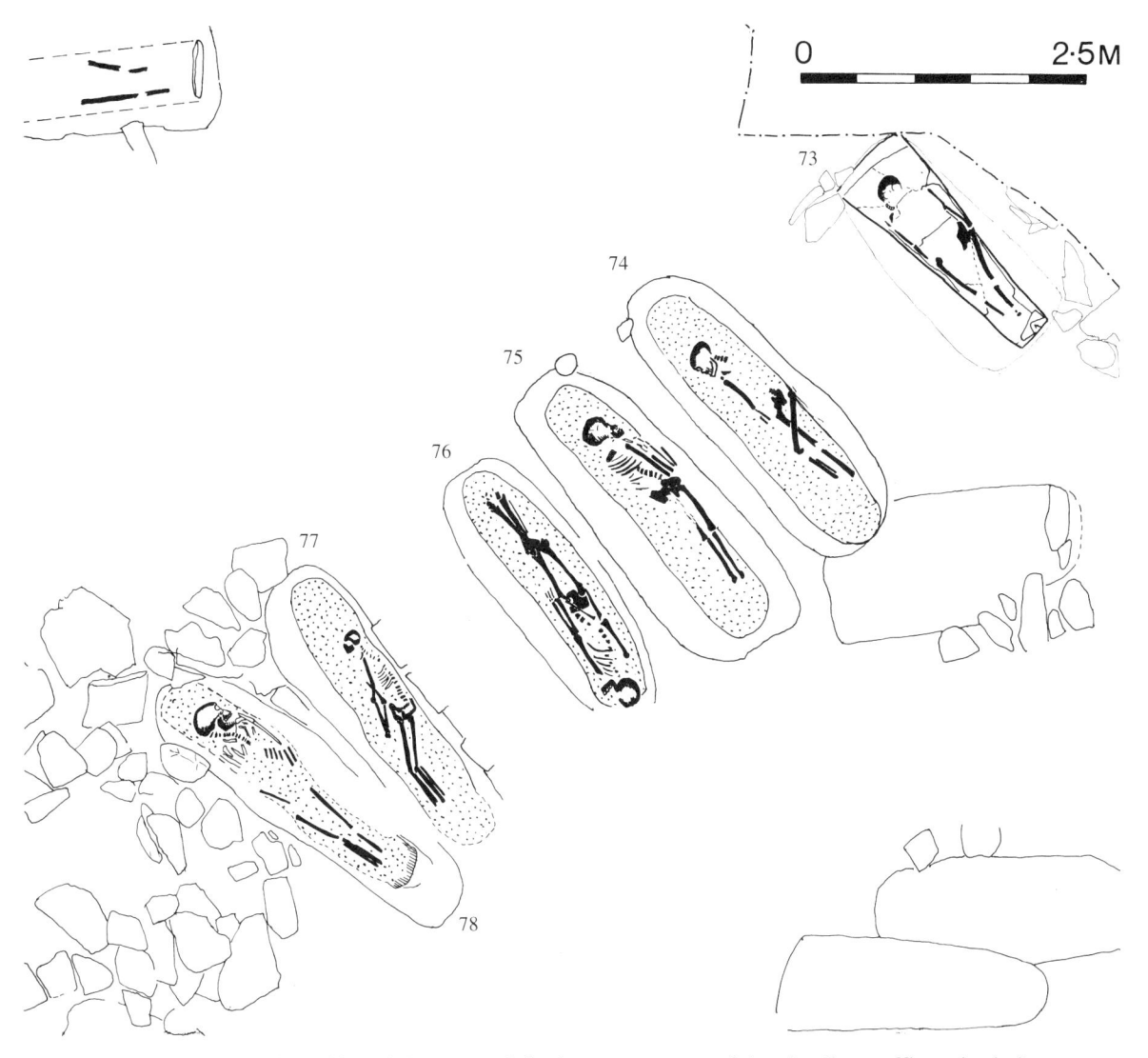

3.33 Well-preserved **Period I/4** burials (*Stage 1*) in the eastern part of the site (log-coffins stippled).

underlying deposits, and included massive Haematite and *clastic lime* displaced from the underlying **Phase 1.2** builders' waste. A copper-alloy wire-loop attached to a folded plate (BZ18.2) from **Grave 74** may have been an intentional deposit. A large group of metalworking debris from **Graves 77–80** included a large segment of a Group C smelting 'hearth' fused to a skin of furnace wall (**Gr 78**), a large lump (340 gm) of heated massive Haematite (**Gr 79**) and a chip of heated botryoidal Haematite (5.5 gm), which suggest that this was smelting waste. This concentration coincides spatially with the **Phase 1.2** cluster of unheated massive Haematite, but there was no evidence of *in situ* smelting, and the source of the finds from the graves cannot be identified.

Stage 2
Stage 2 was represented by an irregular row of thirteen graves (82.02, **82–94**), skirting the granite boulder at the head of **Grave 54**, and after a break between **Graves 87** and **88**, cutting into the western part of the **Phase 1.5** graveyard enclosure. Ten graves (**82–90, 94**) revealed clear evidence of log coffins: the remaining three were featureless. The most northerly grave (**82**) contained an unusually well-preserved log coffin (Figure 3.3) represented by dark wood fibre, which unfortunately could not be identified. This was overlain by the east wall of the Northumbrian burial chapel, which had perhaps shielded it from moisture. The neighbouring grave (**83**) was marked by an amorphous spread of quartz and granite pebbles (Table 3.3). A band of large stones overlying **Grave 88** had slumped into the hollow left after the coffin collapsed, but had probably marked the spine of the grave.

The finds from the graves (excavation archive) can generally be sourced in the underlying deposits, and included displaced pottery, glass, plough-pebbles, flints and metalworking debris. The most notable objects were two crucible fragments (SG15.8 and 9) from **Grave 86**, a dark blue glass tessera (GS05.1) and a small perforated silver bead (SR9) from **Grave 87**, part of a snaffle bit with a decorated terminal (IN49.1) from **Grave 89**, and a spiral copper-alloy ring (BZ15.1), probably from a ring pin, from **Grave 91**.

Stage 3

Stage 3 was represented by a regular row of sixteen graves (82.03, **95–110**) immediately to the east of the **Phase 3** shrine. The more northerly graves (**95–100**) were dug into the bedrock ridge where the row curved slightly eastwards, perhaps to avoid hard rock. The south end of the row stopped immediately to the north of the most westerly **Phase 3** grave (**72**), which was probably marked by posts at the head and foot (p 112). There was clear evidence of log coffins in nine of the graves (**98, 99, 102–107, 110**), and one (**108**) seems to have been a rare, dug grave. Two graves (**107** and **108**) may have been marked by footstones, while post-sockets at the heads of **Graves 102** and **103** may have contained markers, but might have been part of the **Phase 3** shrine.

The relatively large group of finds from the graves (excavation archive) probably comprised material displaced from the underlying structures and rubbish deposits of **Phases 1–3**. **Graves 106–109** were dug through a rubbish-filled **Phase 3** hollow (109, Table 3.24b). The most noteworthy finds are a clay pin-mould fragment (SG17.4) from **Grave 103**, probably originating in **Phase 1** debris (Figure 10.86), and a first/second century opaque white glass bangle fragment (GS04.4) from **Grave 108**, which may have been buried as a talisman. A fragment of an arciform cross (SE14.16) from **Grave 106** may have originated in the adjacent shrine (p 102). A possible iron wool heckle (IN62.1, **Grave 107**) is of interest as there was little evidence of wool processing in **Period I** (pp 424-5). A broken stone object (SE50.15) from **Grave 109** may have been part of a fly-wheel, displaced from the underlying industrial debris.

A muddy layer (73.02) to the east covered some of the *Stage 2* graves, and was subsequently overlain by the *Stage 5* roadway. This produced a relatively large group of finds (Table 3.26), which probably marks a spread of contemporary debris, although some pieces may have been displaced from earlier deposits. The metalworking debris is matched in the underlying layer (73.01, Table 3.25) and probably represents a single deposit brought in as hard-core. This possibly included the hones and scrap iron, but the knives and other implements may have been accidental losses which hint at craft activity on the muddy verge of the road. The crucible lid and mould fragment might have been displaced from earlier deposits, but could have derived from the fine metalworking shop evident to the west in **Phase 4.6** (pp 117, 403-4; Table 3.33). The two muddy layers were not clearly distinguished, but there was more displaced material in the 'earlier' deposit, and only one implement – a swivel knife – which might be ascribed to the later group.

Two unassigned E ware sherds
A chunk of fused and folded vessel glass (FBb)
An iron blade cased in copper-alloy with plated rivets (BZ30.3) and a detached rivet (BZ34.2)
A tapering copper alloy strip (BZ38.20)
A broken key or latch lifter (IN34.1)
A tanged iron gouge (IN52.10)
A class C3 knife blade (IN66.24) and a broken tanged knife (IN66.75)
A shaped, iron plate (IN78.6) and a looped iron bar (IN44.22)
An iron rivet (IN21.2)
Five nails and fragments
Three unidentified iron lumps
A large hone (SE35.6), a small hone (SE38.1) and two hone blanks (SE71.1 and 48)
Five **unretouched** and ten **retouched** flints
Four plough pebbles
A distinctive group of metalworking debris including
    A crucible lid with traces of silver (SG15.10)
    A grooved clay mould fragment with traces of leaded brass (SG17.5)
    A small quantity of glassy cinder (290 gm)
    A disproportionately large group of crystalline cinder (3665gm)
    A Type 2 tuyere fragment and a displaced Type 1 Tuyere block fragment (SG28.2)
    Two Group C smelting hearth fragments and
    A small group of other 'hearths' and fragments
A relatively large group of animal bones

Table 3.26: Finds from **Phase 4a** silt and mud deposits in the east part of the northern sector (73.02)

Stage 4

Stage 4 saw the decay of the western shrine represented by a spread of rubble (91) at the west end of the **northern sector**. The rubble oversailed the *Stage 3* graves, and was sealed by the *Stage 5* platform, and cut by subsequent graves of *Stages 6* and *7*. It was scattered around the **Phase 3** shrine and perhaps formed part of an outer bank of which no other trace remained. Most of the objects in the small group of finds (Table 3.27) were matched in the underlying rubbish spreads (85.02, 109) from which they were, perhaps, displaced. The comb is the earliest from the site, although there was earlier comb-making debris (p 493), while the mould fragment was probably displaced from earlier-sixth century debris (Figure 10.86). The sandstone slab is one of a small group of cupped stones from this area and may have contained oil or water for ritual aflutions (p 462).

The central portion of a Class B antler comb (AR71.1)
A sherd of a pale French Blue cone (V18) and a chunk of fused and folded vessel glass (FBe)
An iron awl or punch (IN50.68)
An iron strip (IN81.6), a flat fragment (IN82.9) and a possible clench plate (IN93.21)
Two nails and a shank
A large hone (SE34.2) and a broken bar hone (SE32.12)
A sandstone slab with a pecked oval hollow (SE49.2)
Five plough pebbles (SE51)
A burnt flint, one **unretouched** and nine **retouched** flints
A small group of metalworking debris including:
    A fragment of a clay mould with traces of leaded brass (SG17.6)
Two lumps of clastic lime and a scrap of plaster

Table 3.27 Finds from *Stage 4* rubble (90) surrounding **Phase 3** shrine

Stage 5

Stage 5 saw the comprehensive redesign of the northern part of the *inner precinct* (Figure 3.32). A new curvilinear shrine (83) was erected to the west of the **Phase 3** shrine, a low platform (76) was built over the *Stage 2* burials to the east, and the roadway was restored with a new gravel surface. These

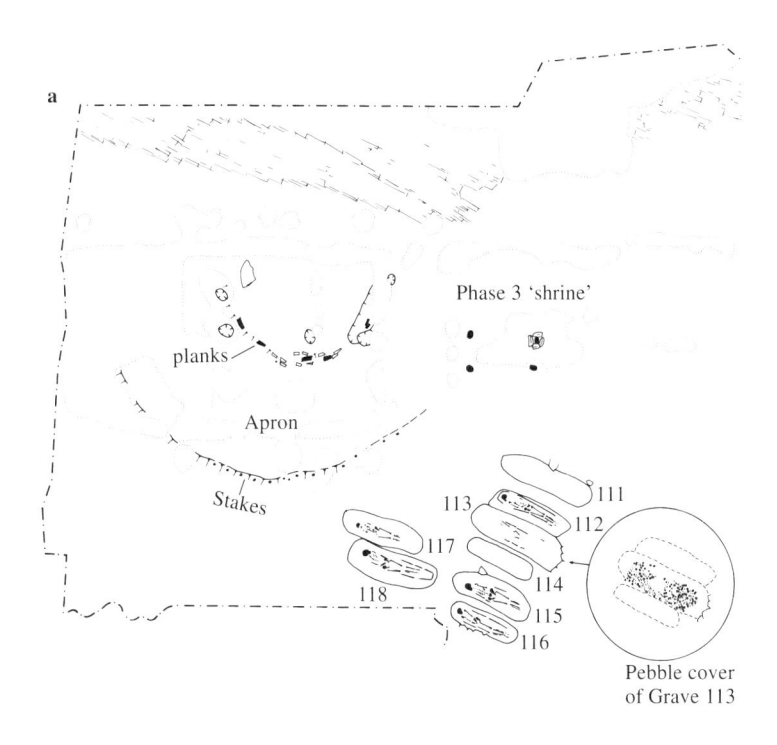

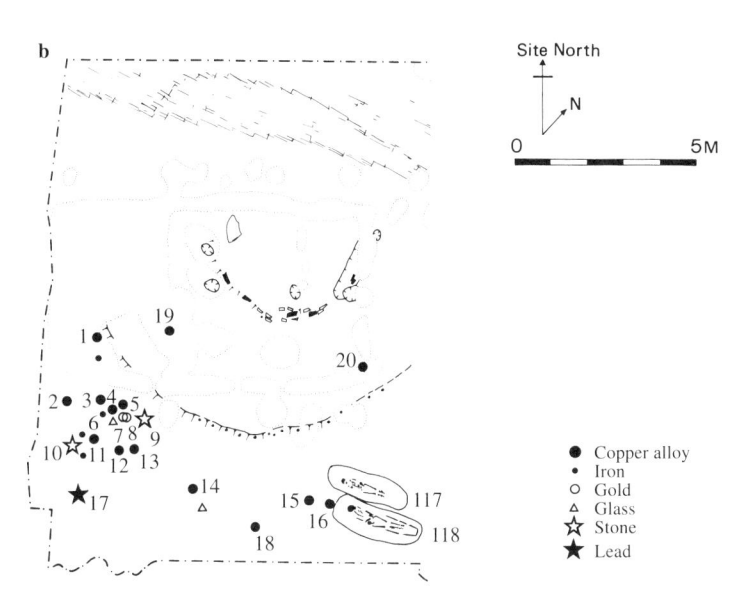

3.34 The **Period I/4.5** 'shrine' and related features. **a** The *Stage 5* shrine and burials of *Stages 6* and *7*. **b** Specialised workshop debris abutting the 'shrine' (listed p 117).

developments probably pertained to the closing decades of the seventh century or first decade of the eighth century, and were broadly contemporary with a group of new buildings and paths in the **southern sector** (*Stages 11–13*, pp 130-3), which marked a similar phase of renewal in the *outer zone*. This seems to have involved changes to the industrial area to the west of the site, and the finds groups from *Stage 5–7* contexts were sparse when compared to earlier groups.

The new western shrine (Figure 3.34) comprised a platform with an arc of upright timbers at the centre analogous to the primary enclosure of the **Phase 2** 'shrine'. The platform consisted an apron of soil contained by a wattle revetment, and overlying the *Stage 4* rubble. The north side of the platform was probably dug into the bedrock ridge, removing the **Phase 1** deposits. The platform and the enigmatic central structure remained intact when the first Northumbrian oratory was built to the east (pp 139-41).

The platform produced a large group of finds (Table 3.28). These were generally matched in the large **Phase 3** rubbish spread (85.02, Table 3.22) to the south, and the apron was probably constructed of soil quarried from an equivalent deposit beyond the trench.

A slotted antler handle (AR74.9)
Four sherds of vessel glass (V67, C2 and two unassigned)
A sherd of a bluish-green, prismatic 1st-3rd C vessel (GS01.3)
A flint pebble, a burnt flint, two **unretouched** and thirteen **retouched** flints
Two nails, four shanks and three nail heads
An iron hook attached to a perforated plate (IN31.4)

A possible iron wedge (IN80.23), a strip (IN80.22) and three
    unidentified lumps (IN93.22-24)
A piece of folded lead sheet waste (LD11.5)
Two small hones (SE38. 5 and 11) and a hone blank (SE71.33)
A granite smoothing stone (SE42.1)
Four plough pebbles (SE51)
Nineteen rounded and ten abraded angular quartz pebbles
An interesting group of metalworking debris including:
    A lump of massive Haematite (SE62.38)
    A tuyere nozzle and other tuyere fragments
    Two scraps of slag
    312 gm of crystalline cinder and 171 gm of glassy cinder
    Three slag cake segments
Scraps of baked clay and clastic lime

Table 3.28: Finds from platform of western *Stage 5* shrine (83)

The eastern platform (76) comprised an insubstantial mound overlying the *Stage 2* graves. This was probably associated with a scarp cut into the rock outcrop to the north, which removed the upper parts of the northern *Stage 3* graves. The Northumbrian burial chapel was built over the platform, and no evidence of a central focus had survived. The apron produced a small group of finds apparently displaced from **Phase 1** and **2** deposits in the vicinity.

A smashed sherd of a B*i amphora* (V3)
A claw beaker sherd (V12a)
A sandstone flake with a serrated edge (SE53.1)
A clay mould fragment with traces of an unspecific copper alloy
    (SG17.7)
A **retouched** flint
Three pebbles
Scraps of metalworking debris, clastic lime and daub

Table 3.29: Finds from eastern *Stage 5* platform (76)

The new gravel roadway (Figure 3.32) was laid on the line of the old paved road, which had probably remained an important access route, despite disturbance by graves and partial inundation with mud. A stone 'kerb' marking the north side of the **Phase 2** shrine was perhaps the base of a wall demolished before the new road was laid. The southern edge of the road had been disturbed by ploughing in the mid-ninth century. The eastern part of the road produced two distinct groups of finds. The first (Table 3.30) comprised material incorporated in the surface. Plough pebbles, pebbles and metalworking debris were common in this area, and were perhaps displaced from earlier layers. The sherd of window glass was stratified beneath the **Period II** deposits producing window sherds. Two partly-worked pieces of copper alloy could have been lost by a craftsman on the road or working in the vicinity. The second group (75.02, Table 3.31) came from a layer of worm-sorted soil overlying the road surface, and complements the assemblage from the underlying mud (73.02 Table 3.26). There was little displaced material. The possibly miscast copper-alloy object was perhaps related to the partly-worked pieces in the underlying surface, the bead may have been lost by a passer-by, and the knife and Haematite polisher recall the implements lost in the underlying mud. The third group (99, Table 3.32) came from the western part of the road and included finds from the surface and overlying soil. The E ware and vessel glass sherds were displaced from **Phase 1** and **2** deposits lying immediately beneath the roadway, and the metalworking debris and hones may derive from the rubbish spread to the north and west. The bucket mount, ringed pin and knife (the earliest of Class A p 427) were all potentially contemporary losses, and so complement the small groups of lost objects from the ground to the east. The ringpin (without its ring) can be tentatively reunited with the pin ring (BZ15.1) from the adjacent **Grave 91** (*Stage 2*, pp 114, 369). These finds point to a new pattern of use spanning the remainder of **Phase 4** (and perhaps starting rather earlier), in which waste was no longer scattered in the northern part of the *inner precinct*. The *outer zone* revealed a similar picture, and the broadly contemporary deposits of *Stages 11–13* were relatively clean (Table 3.47-54).

A rectangular-sectioned copper alloy bar with a hammered surface
    (BZ35.12) and a rod with a pinched end (BZ36.9)
A sherd of light green window glass (GS06.74)
A 'loom weight' (SE29.11)
A nail shank
Three plough pebbles (SE51)
A small group of metalworking debris including:
    A lump of heated botryoidal Haematite
    A possible furnace fragment
    Three Group C smelting hearth fragments
A small group of pebbles

Table 3.30: Finds from surface (75.01) of eastern part of *Stage 5* roadway

A domed copper-alloy stud with a short shank (BZ29.1)
A corroded piece of copper-alloy, perhaps a miscast animal head
    (BZ35.6)
An unassigned vessel glass sherd (GS02)
A biconical/drop-shaped bluish-green wound bead (GS03.1)
A complete Class C1 tanged iron knife (IN66.19) and an
    unidentified iron lump (IN93.26)
A botryoidal Haematite polisher (SE62.16)
A quartz plough pebble (SE51)
A **retouched** flint
A small group of pebbles
A scrap of glassy cinder (2 gm)

Table 3. 31: Finds from wormed soil (75.02) over eastern part of *Stage 5* roadway

A cube-headed copper-alloy ring-pin missing its ring (BZ15.2)
Three sherds of Group E glass vessels (two V69 or 70, one Group
    E2)
A base sherd of an early E ware beaker (E2, V1)
A possible iron bucket mount (IN57.1)
A complete tanged Class A knife (IN66.11)
A broken bar hone (SE32.10)
A quartz plough pebble (SE51)
A small group of metalworking debris

Table 3.32: Finds from western part of *Stage 5* road (99)

Stage 6
Stage 6 saw the continued development of the graveyard with a fourth row of log coffin burials (82.04, **Graves 111–116**) to the south of the **Phase 3** shrine (Figure 3.34). The graves were dug through the *Stage 4* rubble, disturbing the underlying rubbish deposits which had accumulated in **Phases 2** and **3**. Finds from these graves are listed in Table 3.22.

A shallow bank of debris (85.04, Table 3.33) abutting the platform of the new shrine, probably accumulated in *Stage 6* (Figure 3.38). The rubbish deposits in this area were poorly stratified and some objects, marked by asterisks, have been assigned to this group on the basis of their distribution, although technically ascribed to a lower layers (85.01 and 02). Finds locations are given in bold numerals. A concentration of objects included a gold ingot and a piece of gold wire, which were perhaps a craftsman's hoard concealed in a spread of workshop debris. Other finds indicate work in copper-alloy, and a workshop may lie nearby (Figure 10.70). A hollow cutting this material produced a lead cuboid-headed pin (LD09.11, **17**). The close association with the copper-alloy, gold and mould, supports the identification of this pin as a master from which moulds would have been made (pp 398-9). Adjacent deposits produced a tinned chape (BZ30.1, **19**, 85.02) and a copper-alloy buckle (BZ18.1, **20**, 85.05), which are included in the finds plot as they could have originated in this deposit. The Roman vessel sherd (**18**) is unlikely to have been displaced from a **Phase 0** context, and belongs with a group from this area which was, perhaps, introduced in the sixth and seventh centuries (p 297).

*A small gold ingot and length of gold wire (AU1 and 2, **7** and **8**)
*A cross-marked, bivalve, stone mould for a floral stud (SE46.1, **9**)
*A broken bead in reddish-brown glass (GS03.11, **6**)
*A rim sherd of a 1st/2nd century Roman cup or bowl (GS01.2, **19**)
A bramble-headed copper-alloy stick pin (BZ14.1, **13**)
A lobate copper-alloy strap end (BZ19.18, **4**)
*Three copper-alloy rod fragments (BZ36.3, **2**, 4, **3** and 6, **15**)
A folded copper alloy strip (BZ38.22, **1**) and three sheet fragments (BZ38.9, **14**, 23, **12** and 24, **5**)
A scrap of copper-alloy (BZ41.3, **11**) and a perforated plate (BZ37.5, **16**)
A small broken hone (SE37.3, **10**)
Two nails and a lump of iron
Two **retouched** flints and a burnt flint
A plough pebble (SE51)
A small and unexceptional group of metalworking debris

Table 3.33: Finds from debris (85.04) banked against the *Stage 5* shrine

Stage 7
Stage 7 was represented by a final row of burials comprising two graves (**117–8**) to the south-east of the new 'shrine' (Figure 3.34). Both graves revealed traces of timber coffins which were perhaps logs, although the evidence was inconclusive. The skeletons were relatively well preserved, having been shielded by the overlying *Northumbrian* terrace. Neither grave was marked, although the disturbed clayey soil filling them was clearly visible against the dark midden soil through which they were cut. The large groups of finds from the graves were probably displaced from these deposits and are listed in Table 3.22.

Patchy layers of silt (85.05) overlying the *Stage 5* shrine and the adjacent rubbish deposits, indicated a phase of disuse of the ground to the west of the graves. The small group of finds mostly came from the shrine, and was probably derived from the displaced debris in the platform. The copper-alloy buckle may have belonged with the *Stage 6* metalworking debris (85.04, Table 3.33) to the south.

Half of a flat rectangular copper-alloy buckle (BZ18.1)
Four sherds of early vessel glass (V21b, Gp C4 and E2 and one unassigned)
Five nails and fragments
A lump of massive Haematite (SE62, 145gm)
Two plough pebbles (SE51)
Two **retouched** flints
A small and unexceptional group of metalworking debris

Table 3.34: Finds from silts (85.05) overlying *Stage 5* platform and adjacent rubbish layers

Displaced Period I metalworking debris

The northern range of *Northumbrian* buildings was erected on a platform surfaced with an ashy soil incorporating a large assemblage of ironworking debris (Figure 4.7). This included a range of materials common in the **Phase 3–4** deposits, and was probably quarried from a dump of specialised waste in the industrial area in the western part of the *outer zone*. The waste was spread in and around the buildings, and may have been chosen because of the soft charcoal-rich texture, rather than for the lumps of cinder and other ironworking waste. The material listed in Table 3.35 came from a wide range of **Period II** contexts in which this material was either used or disturbed, and some *Northumbrian* objects may have been included. The critical components of this large assemblage were the Group C smelting 'hearths' and the fragments of Type 2 tuyeres. The numerous Group C hearths were matched in the later **Phase 3** deposits (109, 118 Tables 3.23 and 3.24), and Type 2 tuyeres became common at roughly the same time, while Group B hearths, which characterised earlier deposits, were virtually absent. The proportions of glassy and crystalline cinder were matched in the main **Phase 3** rubbish spread (85.02 Table 3.22), as was the large group of nails and other iron scrap. Complete iron tools and other objects were strikingly underrepresented. The hones are an unsurprising component of this metalworking group, but 'loom weights', smoothers, and smoothed and scratched slabs were recurrently associated with ironworking debris, and may also have been smithy equipment (Figure 10.116). Other finds were sparser than the iron-working waste, showing this to have been a more specialised group of debris than others listed above. The distinctive aquamarine sherds of Vessel 2 may have originated in the main **Period I/3** rubbish spread (85.02, pp 107-8), and were broadly contemporary with a second Group A vessel (V3). The small group of copper-alloy and lead finds included wire and sheet and had perhaps originated in workshops, while the plough pebbles and flints were also common finds in the rubbish spreads in the western part of the *inner precinct*. The large group of cobbles and pebbles gives further evidence that these were somehow related to the industrial activities in this area.

a) Ironworking debris and potentially related finds
Two iron punches, two awls and two tanged awls (IN50.02, 19, 37, 56, 78)
Seventeen nails and thirty-seven nail fragments
Sixteen strip and strap fragments (IN80.29-40, 43, 44; IN 81.8 and 9)
Six plate fragments (IN82.13-17, 19)
Fifteen unidentifiable iron lumps (IN93.36-39, 41-47, 51 and 52)
A broken large hone (SE35.12) and two broken small hones (SE36.22 and 38.10)
Smoothing stones of sandstone (SE42.5) and granite (SE42.8)
A broken greywacke 'loom weight' (SE29.10)
Two smoothed and scratched greywacke slabs (SE 54.11 and 12)
A piece of unburnt limestone and four pieces of burnt limestone
Two lumps of smoothed botryoidal Haematite (SE62.14 and 27)
A large group of metalworking debris (60,850 gm) comprising:

Glassy cinder	13879 gm (23%)
Crystalline cinder	12896 gm (22%)
Slag	721 gm (1%)
Bear	191 gm (<1%)
Ferrous concretion	1845 gm (3%)
Heated Haematite	55 gm (<1%)
Smithied iron debris	1731 gm (3%)
Group B hearths	206 gm (<1%)
Group C smelting hearths	6517 gm (11%)
Group D smithy hearths	7412 gm (12%)
Slag cake segments and chunks	3932 gm (6%)
Type 2 tuyere fragments etc	6047 gm (10%)
Furnace base with attached wall	869 gm (1%)

b) Other finds
A Bi *amphora* sherd (V1) and an African Red Slip Ware sherd (V3)
A body sherd of an E1 jar (V12) and an unassigned early medieval sherd (PY7.)
Nine sherds of vessel glass (Vs 2a and c, 53a, 73e, C3, D1 and three unassigned)
Two antler offcuts and a paring
A triangular sectioned copper-alloy ring (BZ23.1)
A piece of drawn or swaged copper-alloy wire (BZ32.1)
A nodular lump of molten copper-alloy waste (BZ39.7)
Three fragments of copper alloy (BZ41.4 and 5)
A sandstone slab with six ovoid ingot moulds with a small, compass-drawn design (SE45.3)
A lead disc, perhaps a nail head (LD6.34) and two fragments of lead sheet (LD11.9 and 10)
Fifteen plough pebbles (SE51)
Thirty-one **retouched**, nine **unretouched** and four burnt flints, and two flint pebbles
A large group of pebbles and cobbles comprising:
     238 rounded quartz pebbles
     157 abraded, angular, quartz pebbles
     158 granite pebbles and 12 cobbles
     68 greywacke and quartz pebbles and stones with Calcium carbonate

Table 3.35: Finds from displaced metalworking debris (110) used during construction of Northumbrian ecclesiastical buildings

A related group of debris (Table 3.36) was scattered over the **Period I** surface below and around the Northumbrian enclosure wall (Figure 4.7) sand was probably derived from this material.

Three sherds of vessel glass (one C2 the others unassigned)
A fragment of a copper-alloy tube (BZ35.4)
A greywacke spindle whorl (SE24.13)
An antler offcut and a tine fragment
Two **unretouched** and six **retouched** flints, and a burnt flint
A sub-circular iron ring (IN30.8) and a curved bar (IN83.6)
Three nails and fragments
Sixty-five pebbles and cobbles including nine with CaCO3
A relatively small, but distinctive group of metalworking debris including
     Glassy cinder (275gm), but no crystalline cinder

A fragment of a large tuyere block (SG25.5)
A possible furnace wall fragment (SG35)
A tuyere trapped in an unusual A/B 'hearth'
A Group C smelting hearth fragment
Three lumps of slag

Table 3.36: Finds from debris (85.06) underlying *Northumbrian* wall and path.

The southern sector: the archaeology of the *outer zone*

INTRODUCTION

The **southern sector** revealed a long sequence of of small sub-rectilinear buildings of the sixth to early-eighth centuries associated with outdoor latrine pits and distinctive '*domestic*' assemblage of artefacts. These represent an outer residential zone beyond the *inner precinct* of the *monasterium*. The evidence was clearest in the latter part of the period (*Stages 11* and *12*) when the buildings were enclosed by an outer boundary, and linked by paths (Figure 3.42). Similar arrangements probably obtained for much of this period, perhaps with an outer boundary lying slightly beyond the trench. A bedrock ridge on the northern margin of the area coincided with a neutral area separating the *inner precinct* from the *outer zone*, where there was little structural evidence and relatively few finds. There were no stratigraphic links between the two areas for most of **Period I**.

Successive contradictory interim statements (Hill 1988 a and b, 1990 a, 1992) record the interpretative problems posed by the perplexing sixth and seventh century deposits in the **southern sector**. The stake-walled buildings (**12, 15–20**) were not identified during the excavation, and were only revealed after detailed re-examination of the plan of the numerous stake-holes in the floor of the trench (Figure 3.35). Although these stakes had been driven from various levels, they were generally unrecognisable above the subsoil unless the wood was preserved. This had the effect of transforming a stratified record of superimposed structures into a palimpsest with the crucial evidence of the walls compressed onto a single surface (Figure 3.35). The buildings probably occupied shallow hollowed stances with earth floors. The ground around them was usually unsurfaced, and the later buildings were interleaved with layers of waterborne silt. The stratigraphic record was thus dominated by silts, some forming floors, others marking worm-sorted soils and flood deposits. The sequence elucidated is relatively reliable, if incomplete, but the area probably contained more buildings, and had a fuller history. The finds record is similarly imperfect. Some groups, particularly those from pits, were securely stratified, but others were probably contaminated with extraneous material, and **Period I** finds continued to be displaced until the twelfth/thirteenth century (e.g. Table 6.14).

no sign of a natural watercourse. Periodic flooding in the later years of **Period I** was marked by layers of waterborne silt interleaved with *laminae* of sand, charcoal and other debris (p 129). A thick deposit of silt covering the lower ground (Figure 6.7) recorded a phase of severe inundation in the mid- to late-seventh century, which probably flooded the low ground on north, east and south flanks of the hill (pp 7-8). The water-table had risen by some 0.2–3 m by the end of **Period I**, and the structural woodwork of the latest buildings was preserved (pp 130-3).

The southern sector sequence and possible links with the *inner precinct*. The stratigraphy of the **south sector** is illustrated in Figure 3.36. Distinct, inadequately-linked 'trees' in the south (S), centre (C) and north (N) reveal seventeen *stages* of development, of which the first three (*0–2*) pertain to **Phase 0** and the last three (*14–16*) to **Period II**. The remaining eleven stages (*3–13*) spanned the two hundred years or so of **Period I**. The final stage (*16*) records a prolonged phase of flooding lasting from the ninth century until the eleventh when occupation resumed at the start of **Period IV** (pp 219-21).

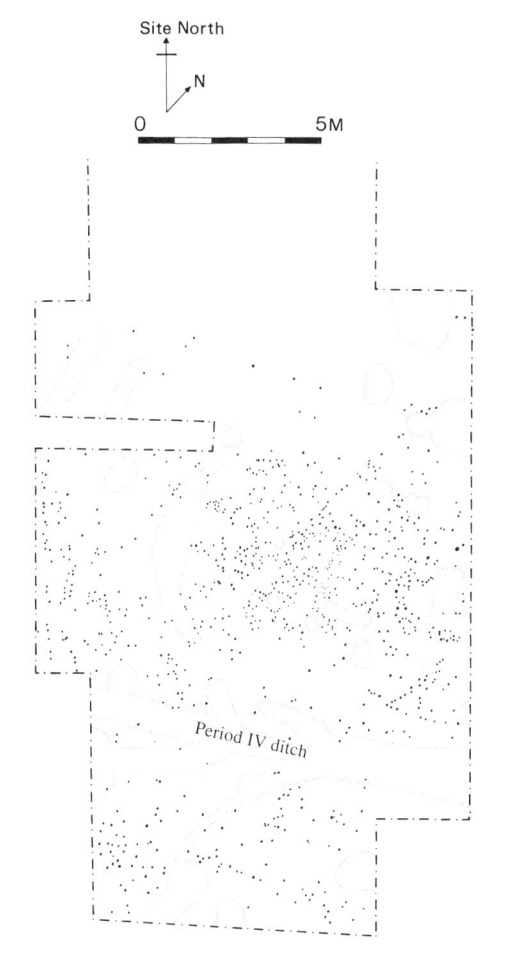

3.35 **Period I** stake-holes in the **southern sector**.

The stratigraphic difficulties were compounded by intermittent flooding. The modern manifestation of the ancient drainage problems (pp 7-8) is a fluctuating, seasonal water-table which sinks rapidly in late April/early May as transpiration increases, resurges in spells of wet weather, and is gradually restored to its winter level between August and November. Several site plans were made as the waters rose, and significant artefacts were recovered from 'cleaning contexts' (901) when the winter's slime was removed at the start of a new excavation season.

The **southern sector** provides an incomplete transect of the low ground between the Priory and the town (Figure 1.5 and 6). The lowest point of this trough lies some 5.0 m north of the south end of the trench, and was the natural position for successive drains cut between the seventh and thirteenth centuries (Figure 6.7). The largest of these (417), dug in the eleventh century, penetrated the sub-soil, destroying the stratigraphic links between the earlier deposits to either side. Other drains caused less damage, but had nevertheless disrupted the stratified deposits, and dispersed early finds into late contexts. This explains the intermittent disharmony between the features to either side of the disturbed area (e.g. *Stage 7*, pp 125-6).

The area was originally well-drained and there was

Stages 11–12	?=	**Phase 4**	Coherent plan (Figure 3.32), both areas affected by **Period II** buildings
Stages 8–10	?=?	**Phase 3.2**	Main deposits with E ware in both areas
Stage 7	???	**Phase 1.6**	B*ii amphora*, A ware, cone with or horizontal trails
		Phase 3	Building orientation
Stage 6	?=?	**Phase 2**	Building aligned with inner boundary, Group E2 vessel sherds
Stage 5	?=	**Phase 1.3–5**	Common orientation of buildings, B*i* vessels
Stage 4	?=	**Phase 1.2–4**	Iron working debris
Stage 3	?=	**Phase 1.1**	Both areas cultivated
Stage 2	=	**Phase 0**	Roadway common to both areas

Table 3.37. Possible links between *outer zone* and *inner precinct*

The **southern sector** produced a large collection of imported pottery and glass, including most of the types recovered from the more-securely-stratified deposits in the *inner precinct*. These demonstrate that the sequences were broadly contemporary, but too many of these finds had been displaced to allow the precise correlation of the two areas. The sequences are most readily related at the beginning and end of **Period I** (Table 3.37). The **Phase 0** roadway spanned both areas, and both had been cultivated with mouldboard ploughs after the road went out of use (Figure 3.5). Both areas subsequently produced distinctive iron working debris, indicating a link between *Stage 4* and **Phase 1.2–4**; and the first group of buildings in the **southern sector** (*Stage 5*, Figure 3.37) was aligned with the **Phase 1.3–4** buildings to the north (Figure 3.6). Subsequent links were less secure. Scattered sherds of Group E2 vessel glass from *Stages 3* to *7* (Figure 10.23, pp 313, 324-5) suggested a link with the earlier **Phase 2** deposits to the north (89 etc), while the *Stage 6* building (15) seems to have been

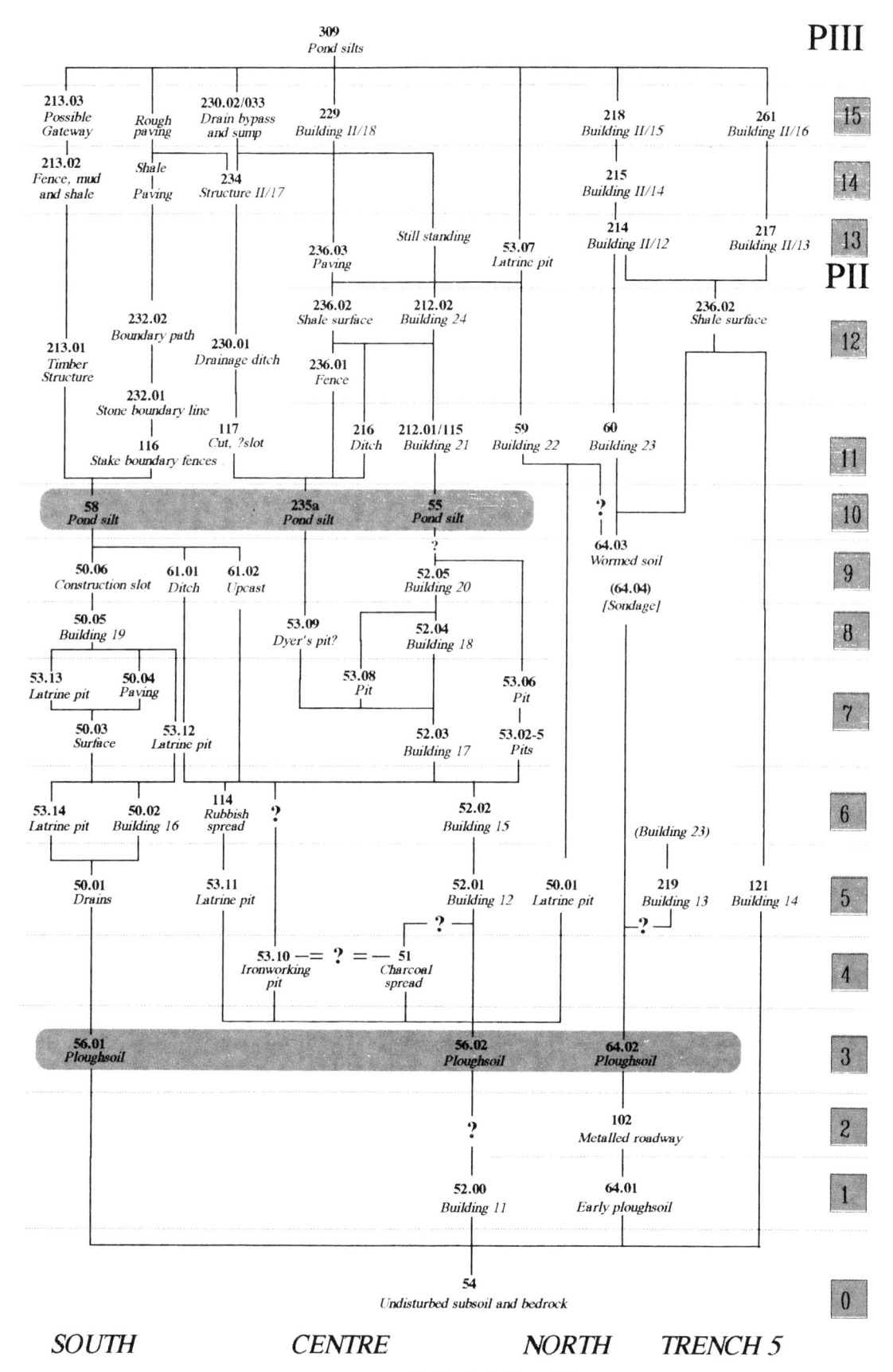

3.36 The stratigraphic sequence in the *outer zone* in **Periods I** and **II**.

aligned with the **Phase 2** boundary ditch (Figure 3.17). The evidence was less clear in *Stages 7–10*. *Stage 7* deposits in the south part of the area produced a distinctive group of finds comprising B*ii amphora*, A ware and horizontally trailed vessel glass. These indicated a link with **Phase 1.6** (pp 88-9), although the *inner precinct* sequence demonstrated that these finds should have been earlier than the Group E2 sherds from *Stage 6*, while the alignment of **Building 17** (*Stage 7*) hinted that it may have been built in **Phase 3**. The appearance of E ware suggests the equation of *Stages 8–9/10* in the **southern sector** with **Phase 3.2**, and perhaps the earlier part of **Phase 4**, in the *inner precinct*. The final stages (*11–12*) can be equated with the **Phase 4** features with confidence, as they shared a similar relationship to the **Period II** buildings, and can be linked to give an unusually coherent plan (Figure 3.32). *Stages 11* and *12* probably corresponded with the later part of **Phase 4**, and *Stages 9* and *10* may have overlapped with the earlier **Phase 4** features (Figure 3.31). *Stage 13* may have spanned **Periods I** and **II**.

The chronology of the sequence is generally imprecise, but follows that of the *inner precinct* (p 69) where links can be established. It is accordingly relatively reliable in the sixth century, and less so in the seventh. The earliest features may have been associated with Roman finds, which hint at activity in the second or third century (pp 292-7, Table 3.38). Timbers preserved in the later deposits provided valuable dendrochronological information (pp 595-6) giving an absolute date range in the later-eighth century for *Stage 14*, and a *terminus post quem* of *c.* 700 AD for the construction of **Building 24** in *Stage 12* (p 130).

THE SEQUENCE

The sequence in the **southern sector** is described without much equivocation despite the considerable difficulties outlined above. Almost all the stages have intrinsic interpretative problems, but the overall impression of an intensively occupied area, with sporadic and limited industrial activity, is reliable (c.f. Figures 10.24 and 70).

Stage 0
Stage 0 marks the beginning of the sequence with purportedly natural deposits, including bedrock, subsoil and fragments of an early soil (54). A small group of finds included three plough pebbles (SE51), a piece of vessel glass (V22d) and a fragmented antler beam. The pebbles were presumably dislodged during cultivation in *Stage 3*, while the glass must have been intrusive, illustrating the stratigraphic problems in the area. The antler beam was of unusual interest as it had been partly broken into segments appropriate for the manufacture of long Type B comb-plates, and so provides the earliest, if poorly stratified, evidence for comb manufacture (p 493, Figure 10.136a).

Stage 1
Stage 1 was represented by a vestigial cultivated soil (64.01, N) underlying the *Stage 2* roadway. A fragmentary stake-walled structure (**11**, *c.* 6.5 m in diameter) to the south, potentially pertained to this undated phase of activity, or its successor (*Stage 2*). It lay on the west side of the trench where the *Stage 3* ploughsoil survived, but there was no evidence of a floor cutting the ploughsoil, and it may thus have been earlier. It was defined by a shallow groove to the east, perhaps a drain or wall foundation, and an irregular arc of stake-holes to the south-west (Figures 3.5 and 38). The evidence was ephemeral, and the structure lacked both the deeply-set door posts needed to maintain the strength of round-buildings, and the internal post-rings associated with most Iron Age buildings of similar size. It may have been as a circular version of the stake-walled buildings of later phases, or could have been a small circular pen, without a sunken floor, built at a later date.

The area around the building produced six pieces of Roman glass and three of pottery, all displaced into later contexts (Table 3.37). Three of the pieces came from relatively early contexts (*Stage 3*), and a fourth, from a ditch (230.01) cutting the subsoil, was perhaps displaced from an equivalent level. These are similar to other Roman finds from the site, and while all may have been early medieval imports reflecting a 'reliquary' or medicinal interest in the past (p 293), these four (and some or all of the others) could, nevertheless, have derived from second-third century occupation, which was not otherwise evident (pp 292-7).

Period/ stage	Block	
I.3	(64.02)	A burnt sherd of the footring of a Samian vessel (PY01.7)
I.3	(64.02)	Dark green window glass chunk, probably Roman (GS01.13)
I.3	(56.02)	Small body sherd of Central Gaulish Samian (PY01.02)
I.6	(114)	Cast bluish-green matt-glossy window fragment (1st-3rd C, GS01.07)
I.10	(55)	Flat pale bluish-green vessel/window fragment, possibly Roman: joins b (GS01.09a)
	(901)	Flat pale bluish-green vessel/window fragment, possibly Roman: joins a (GS01.09b)
I.12	(230.01)	Flat bluish-green vessel or window fragment, possibly Roman (GS01.10)
III	(309.02)	Possibly Roman pottery sherd (PY02.06)
IV	(412)	Bluish-green cylindrical bottle fragment (1st-2nd, C GS01.05).

Table 3.38 Roman finds from the **southern sector**

Stage 2
Stage 2 was represented by the **Phase 0** roadway (102, N) which crossed the northern part of the area and provided a secure stratigraphic link with the *inner precinct* (p 74, Figure 3.5). The surface had been damaged by ploughing in *Stage 3*, and further disturbed by subsequent buildings.

Stage 3
Stage 3 saw the cultivation of the ground to the south of the bedrock ridge (Figures 3.5, 6.7)

Central part of area (56.02)

A sherd of Samian (PY01.02)
Eleven sherds of vessel glass including four scraps of V11, one C5; two E2 (d and j) and four unassigned.
A tapering copper-alloy rod (BZ36.10)
An iron stylus head with double lugs (IN64.1)
A plated, T-headed, collared iron stick pin (IN41.01)
Two unidentified iron objects (IN 78.9 and 10)

Three **retouched** flints
Six plough pebbles (SE51)
A small group of metalworking debris (972gm)

Southern part of area (56.01)

A tine tip and an antler offcut
One **unretouched** and nine **retouched** flints
Two plough pebbles (SE51)
A scrap of glassy cinder

Table 3.39: Finds from **Period I** plough soil in central (56.02) and southern parts (56.01) of the **southern sector**

represented by a mixed clayey soil with abundant charcoal and burnt bone, occasionally overlying broad, shallow furrows (56.01, 56.02, 64.02). An undulating silty upper deposit probably comprised a worm-sorted soil. Plough-pebbles (SE51, pp 464-6) indicated the use of a mouldboard plough, and intersecting patterns of displaced stones to the north (in 64.02) suggested cross-ploughing or several seasons of cultivation. The ploughing was probably contemporary with the **Phase 1.1** cultivation to the north (p 80), and should thus pertain to the later-fifth or early-sixth century.

The ploughsoil produced a relatively large group of finds divided between three areas (Tables 3.39 and 40) which have features in common, but important differences. The group from the southern part of the area (56.01) was probably the most securely stratified, and revealed few surprises. The plough pebbles were self explanatory, and the antler and flints perhaps derived from earlier activity in *Stage 1*. The group from the central part of the area (56.02) was more varied and problematical. The flints and plough pebbles were similar to those in the southern group, but the glass and metal objects were unparalleled here, and in the potentially contemporary ploughsoil in the *inner precinct* (Table 3.4). The four small sherds of a colourless claw beaker (Vessel 11) were dispersed in the ploughsoil, and are unlikely to have been intrusive (p 302), while the two Group E2 sherds were part of an interesting early group (pp 313, 324-5). The putative *stylus* is the only example from **Period I** (p 35), and the plated iron stick pin is the earliest such find (p 423), but broadly similar to one (IN41.02) from a **Phase 2** grave (80.03, **Gr 32**). The northern group (64.02) was probably contaminated by later debris, but included two of

A burnt sherd of the footring of a Samian vessel (PY01.7)
Two B*i amphora* sherds (V1 and V2)
Four vessel glass sherds (V22f, C2, C3 and C4)
A sherd of Roman window glass (GS01.13)
A copper alloy pellet (BZ40.01)
Two plough pebbles (SE51)
One **retouched** flint
A relatively large group of metalworking debris (2506gm) comprising four Group D 'smithy hearths'

Table 3.40: Finds from **Period I** plough soil in the northern part of the **southern sector** (64.02)

the earliest stratified Roman finds (PY02.1 and GS01.13), which could have derived from disturbed deposits of Roman date (pp 292-7).

Stage 4
Stage 4 marks an episode of industrial activity probably contemporary with **Phase 1.2–4** in the *inner precinct* (Figure 3.5). A thick spread of charcoal (51) lay over truncated clayey subsoil on the east side of the trench. This probably occupied the floor of a hollow cut through the *Stage 3* plough soil, that had otherwise been obliterated by the sunken floors of later buildings, and other intrusions. A charcoal-filled pit to the north-west was probably part of the same working area. The pit was sub-rectangular, and its floor was covered with a thick layer of charcoal. A shallow transverse groove on the floor probably indicated the position of a squared timber. Charcoal scattered over the ploughsoil to the west probably pertained to the same phase. The pit and charcoal spread perhaps lay on the periphery of a workshop area to the east that may have been the source of other metalworking debris dispersed through the overlying deposits (e.g. Table 3.45, Figure 10.86).

The pit and charcoal spread produced distinctive groups of metalworking debris dominated by the glassy cinder characterising smelting and bloom working, but without the crystalline waste of smithying (Table 3.41). The heated Haematite is a clear indicator of smelting. Fragments of bellows-protectors fused to glassy Group B hearths were characteristic early finds in the displaced metalworking debris in the *inner precinct*, and this example was possibly close to the original hearth or furnace. A stone mould and crucible indicate non-ferrous metalworking. The other finds include a relatively large group of vessel glass sherds, mostly unassigned, but with a piece of an early Group D vessel (V62) from the pit (pp 309, 324). The lead disc was too large to be a spindle whorl, and though its function is unknown, is one of a small group of lead objects from early contexts. The leather trimmings provided rare evidence of leather-working in **Period I** (p 500), while the discarded antler was matched in other early deposits, but did not point to any specific product.

Charcoal spread (51)

Three unassigned vessel glass sherds (one C5)

An antler beam fragment and an intact tine
A slotted antler handle (AR74.10)
A flint scraper
A perforated lead disc with a grooved edge (LD9.12)

A stone pin mould (SE47.)
A large amount of glassy cinder (1559gm)
Five lumps of smithied iron debris (458gm)
A possible heating tray fragment (SE26)

Two lumps of heated massive Haematite (41.5gm)

Pit (53.10)

Eight vessel glass sherds (one of V62, three of Group C6 a-c and four unassigned)
Two trimmings and two scraps of cattle hide (LR01 and 08)
An antler burr

A plough pebble (SE51)

Metalworking debris

A possible crucible fragment (SG15.11)
A large amount of glassy cinder (4148gm)
A small piece of smithied iron debris (27gm)
A fragment of a tuyere or bellows-protector fused to a Group B hearth fragment
A slag-cake segment (SG45)

Table 3.41: Finds from *Stage 4* charcoal spread (51) and pit (53.10)

Stage 5

Stage 5 (Figure 3.37) saw the erection of buildings in the southern (50.01), central (**12**, 52.01) and northern parts of the area (**13**, 219 and **14**, 121). The latter (**12–14**) shared the west/east alignment of the **Phase 1** buildings in the northern part of the *inner precinct* (*Stages 3* and *4*) which were perhaps broadly contemporary (Figure 3.6). Two latrine pits (**1** and **11**) can tentatively be ascribed to this time. One (**1**) produced valuable botanical evidence indicating the cultivation of exotic herbs and the use of medicinal remedies for gastric complaints.

Building 12 (52.01) was the earliest of a sequence of buildings (**15, 18, 20, 21** and **24**) in the central part of the area. Most of the building lay beyond the trench, but irregular double stake-lines marking the south and west walls were relatively prominent among the dense stake-holes here (Figure 3.35). The west wall had been disturbed by the sunken hearth of **Building 15**, and the north wall had probably been removed by later pits (53.02-06). A shallow cut penetrating the subsoil a metre to the west of the west wall, indicated a hollow building stance, and suggested that the building was *c.* 4.0 m wide. A deep curvilinear ditch to the south of the building clipped the shallow gully defining **Structure 11**. This produced an antler tine and a lump of heated smoothed massive Haematite (SE62.21) which was probably displaced from a *Stage 4* deposit, and may have been reused as a polisher (pp 471-2).

Building 13 (219) was indicated by a shallow gully cutting the boulder clay in a hollow in the bedrock ridge, and by a vestigial cut in the rock to the west. The remainder of the building had presumably been truncated by subsequent structures and the erosion of the shallow soil over the bedrock. It is assigned to this stage on the basis of its alignment (Figure 3.6). The only find was a fragment of the early claw beaker (V11d, pp 302, 323) from the gully.

Building 14 (121) lay to the east of the main trench, and was represented by a shallow rock-cut gully, a truncated floor surface, and a pair of post sockets

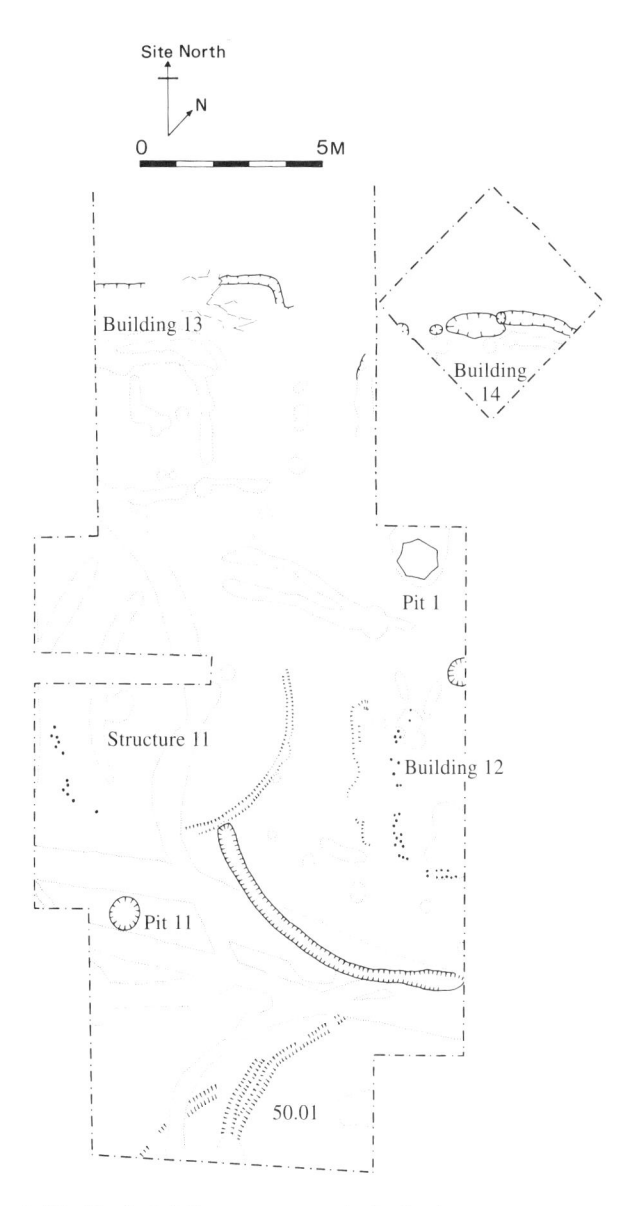

3.37 **Period I.5** structures and pits in the *outer zone* (*Stage 5*).

framing a doorway in the north wall. A vestigial cut into the bedrock in the main trench perhaps marked the north-west corner. These features were sealed by a shale surface, which was probably part of the path running between the *Stage 11–12* buildings (Figure 3.32, p 43). It is ascribed to this stage on the bases of its alignment (Figure 3.6) and its primary position in the Trench 5 sequence. The putative doorway was unique among the earlier **Period I** buildings (pp 69-70). There were no finds.

Pit 1 lay between **Buildings 12** and **14** and, though poorly stratified, produced a neck sherd of a B*i amphora* (V1) indicating that it was relatively early. Three further B*i* sherds from the ground to the north-west (Tables 3.40 and 46) may have been lost at the same time (Figure 10.21). Other finds included a plough pebble (SE51), two **retouched** flints, a nail head, and an iron cylinder enclosing a broken iron object (IN86.1).

The pit was cut into the bedrock through a vestigial ploughsoil, was lined with clay, presumably to retain its contents, and was filled with 'peaty', organic soil including lumps and strands of moss. A sample examined at Durham University (Groves 1990) contained seeds, fly puparia, mosses and abundant bran. These identified it as human faeces including fibre from coarsely-ground cereal and mosses used for cleansing. The clay-lining had originally suggested that the pit was a shallow well, but its contents argue that it was a latrine, and it was perhaps lined so that these could be collected and recycled, perhaps as manure.

The species identified are listed in Table 3.42. The plants include four edible species (coriander, dill, blackberry and black mustard), and two (redshank and fat hen) which have sometimes been used as food. Neither coriander nor dill is native to Britain, and both may have been introduced as herbs or spices by the Romans, although it is unknown whether these penetrated beyond the province of Britannia. These plants may thus have been introduced by the supposed new settlers (pp 12, 28) in the late-fifth/early- sixth-century and, as species of Mediterranean origin, it is appropriate that they were associated with a B*i amphora* sherd. They may have been used for cooking, although many modern recipes call for ground seeds, but both are acknowledged cures for wind and flatulence, and the seeds could have been imbibed as infusions. Mustard, chickweed and dog rose are also medicinal plants. Chickweed is an emollient and vulnerary, used externally for wounds and itching, and internally for rheumatism. Mustard is *inter alia* a diuretic and emetic, while the hips and seeds of dog rose are mildly laxative and diuretic, and are prescribed for constipation (Hoffman 1990). The predominance of species with medicinal properties appropriate to digestive problems, indicates that this was primarily a medicinal assemblage. A later pit produced a second group of potentially medicinal herbs (pp 127-8), though without the faecal indicators. These two deposits complement the historical evidence of healing practised at Whithorn (pp 19-20). Whether culinary or medicinal, the coriander, dill and mustard are likely to have been cultivated, and imply that there was a herb garden at Whithorn in the earlier-sixth century. The other species are not all natural neighbours, and were unlikely to have been growing in the vicinity of the pit. Sedges prefer wet ground, dog rose favours woods, hedges and scrubland, while bracken needs light acid soils. Fat hen, chickweed and red shank are all weeds of cultivation, and could have been included accidentally with the cereal. The mosses show a similar diversity of habitat and would have been gathered from scattered sites.

Pit 11 to the south west of **Building 12**, was lined with stakes, and filled with organic waste. This was covered with a flat stone overlain by layers of silt. The deposits over the stone had been disturbed by a *Stage 12* post-hole, but produced a small group of

SPECIES	COMMON NAME	NUMBER OF SEEDS/SPECIMENS	HABITAT (mosses)
A. Plant seeds			
Coriandrum sativum	coriander	18	
Anethum grave lens	dill	5	
Chenopodium album	fat hen	3	
Carex sp.	sedge	2	
Rubus fruticosus	blackberry	2	
Brassica nigra	black mustard	1	
Polygonum lapathifolium	red shank	1	
Rosa cf. canina	dog rose	1	
Stellaria media	chickweed	1	
B. Ferns			
Pteridium aquilinum	bracken	1	
C. Mosses			
Eurynchium sp.		9	
Pleurozium schreberi		6	Coniferous woodland, heathlands
cf. Rhytidiadelphus triquetrus		4	Woodlands
cf. Hyocomium flagellar		3	
Hypnum cupressiforme		2	Hedgebanks, heathland soils

Table 3.42 Botanical specimens from Pit 1 (53.01)

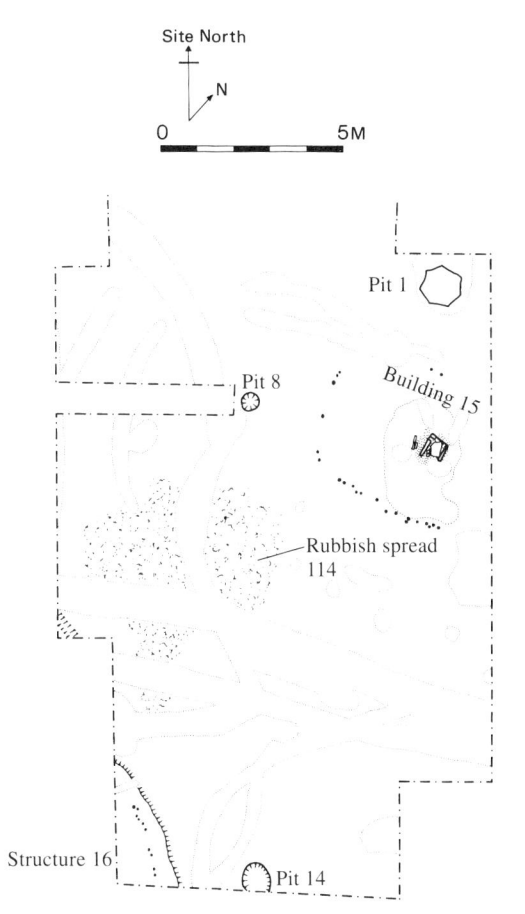

3.38 **Period I/6** structures, pits and deposits in the *outer zone* (*Stage 6*).

finds potentially pertaining to *Stage 5*, or the overlying *Stage 6* debris (114). This included an antler handle (AR74.1) and tine, two retouched flints, and three sherds of vessel glass, including a small piece of a Germanic palm cup (V9), and a neck sherd with self-coloured trails (V13). The last is similar to the claw beaker (V11) from the adjacent *Stage 3* plough soil. Three curving drains to the south (50.01) indicated that other buildings lay beyond the trench. These produced a few finds, including three unassigned vessel glass sherds and four flints.

Stage 6
Stage 6 (Figure 3.38) saw the construction of a new building (**15**) in the central part of the area, and a second structure (**16**) on a different alignment to the south. **Building 15** was oriented north-west/south-east in approximate alignment with the **Phase 2** boundary around the *inner precinct* (Figure 3.17). A spread of rubbish (114) to the west of **Building 15** included decayed animal bones, suggesting that this was a relatively squalid area with open latrines and rubbish scattered around the buildings.

Building 15 (52.02) occupied a shallow hollow cutting the north part of **Building 12** and the *Stage 3* plough soil to the west. The principal feature was a rectangular hearth surrounded by an earth floor of fine soil mixed with charcoal. These indicated the positions of the south and west walls of a building some 6.0 m long and 4.0 m wide. Charcoal scattered on the floor produced two unassigned splinters of vessel glass (one C5); there were no other finds.

'Structure' 16 (50.02) comprised a line of stakeholes in the south-west corner of the trench, flanked by a gully cutting the *Stage 3* ploughsoil. The only find was a cone rim sherd with horizontal trails (V39) indicating a possible link with the **Phase 1** deposits in the *inner precinct* (pp 307, 324). An adjacent latrine pit (53.14) was lined with stakes. The basal deposit comprised silt with *laminae* of sand, indicating periodic flooding. This was covered with a thick layer of organic debris, including cherry pits, in turn covered by further flood deposits of silt and sand. It produced a relatively large group of finds including wood and organic debris, four flints, three unassigned sherds of vessel glass, a rare fragment of worked leather (LR16.9), a crucible fragment with traces of bronze (SG15.12), and scraps of hammerscale (SG13).

The rubbish spread (114) included decaying and burnt animal bone and a small group of finds (Table 3.43) indicating limited craft activity. Three sherds of Group E2 vessel glass suggest a link with the earlier **Phase 2** deposits (89 etc pp 324-5) in the *inner precinct*. The small group of metalworking debris included smithying waste absent from the underlying *Stage 4* deposits. The well-used cold chisel could have been used for masonry, lettering or sculpture (p 423).

Seven sherds of vessel glass (V9e, C2h, C4, three E2[b, h, i], one unassigned)
A fragment of first-third century Roman window glass (GS01.11)
An iron chisel (IN52.5)
Four plough pebbles (SE51)
An antler coronet
A **retouched** flint
A small group of metalworking debris including:
    Glassy (155gm) and crystalline cinder (132gm)
    A furnace wall fragment
    A Group D smithy hearth

Table 3.43 Finds from *Stage 6* rubbish spread (114)

Stage 7
Stage 7 saw renewed activity over the whole area (Figure 3.39). **Building 15** was replaced with a larger building (17); new latrine pits (53.13, possibly, 53.02-05 and 12) were dug, and rough surfaces were laid over the earlier rubbish spread (114), and the ground to the south (50.03). The orientation of **Building 17**, and the inferred chronology of the preceding structures, provide insubstantial grounds for correlating *Stage 7* with **Phase 3** (Figure 3.26). Pottery from the south part of the area (p 126) suggested an earlier date in the sixth century, but these deposits may have been wrongly assigned to *Stage 7*.

Building 17 (52.03) was the largest building in the **southern sector**. Shallow gullies to the west, north

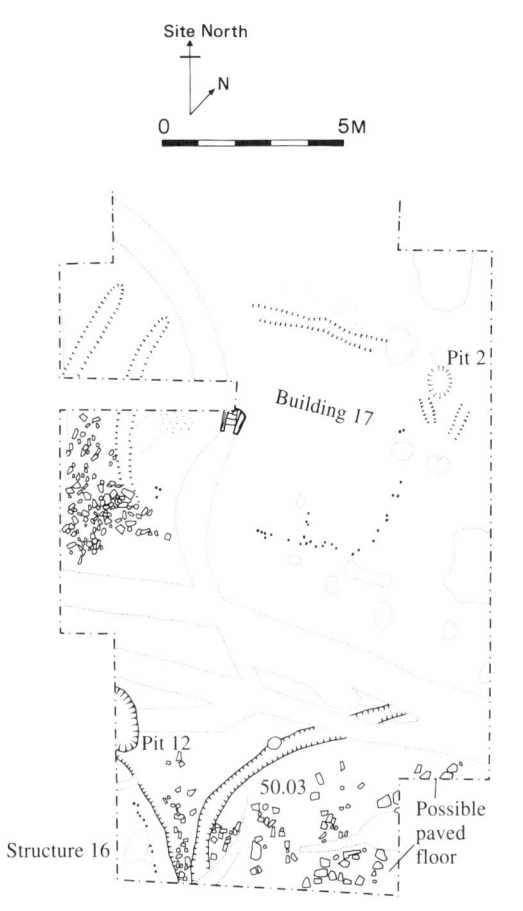

3.39 **Period I.7** structures, surfaces and pits in the *outer zone* (*Stage 7*).

and east delineated three sides of a sub-rectangular building stance with a sunken floor. Internal features comprised a patch of trampled gravel to the west, a small stone hearth slightly west of centre, and a patch of charcoal-rich soil marking an earth floor. These features helped to identify the south and east walls, and the south end of a north/south partition, among the relatively sparse stakeholes in this area. These revealed a large sub-rectangular stake-walled building some 7.5 m long and 5.5 m wide, with straight sides, curving end walls, and rounded corners. The partition separated a large apartment with a central hearth at the west end from a smaller room to the east. The floor of the building was relatively clean, but produced three unassigned sherds of vessel glass (two C4). The northern gully produced a nail-headed coper-alloy stick pin (BZ 14.3), similar to pins cast in the earlier-sixth century, and possibly displaced from an adjacent *Stage 4* deposit (Figure 10.86). Three unidentifiable lumps of corroded iron (IN93.29-31) and a turnshoe heel (LR22.3) probably derive from an unrecognised **Period IV** intrusion.

A cluster of intersecting shallow pits (53.02-06) immediately beyond the north-east corner of building probably pertained to this phase. They were shallower than the latrine pits in this area, and their function was unclear. The base of one pit (53.05) produced a polished ovoid cobble of black basalt with rubbed facets (SE41.1), and a large granite pebble. These may have been an intentional deposit, though of unknown meaning. The west end of **Building 17** was flanked by rough stone surface covering the *Stage 6* rubbish spread (114), which produced a faceted antler tine tip (AR77.1) and an abraded body sherd of an African Red Slipware plate (V2d). A similar surface (50.03) extended eastwards from the platform of **Building 16**. The latter had been disturbed by a curvilinear gully leading north-east to the natural drainage line, and enclosing paving which may have been the floor of another building. Pit 12 (53.12) lay on the west side of the trench, and was poorly stratified, but had been disturbed by a *Stage 9* ditch (61). A basal layer of gravel was covered by flat stones and timbers, including three pieces of oak, one an offcut growing in 376 x 498 AD (pp 595-6). The only other finds were the abraded rim and handle of a B*ii* amphora (V3) and a sherd of Group E2 vessel glass (E2g). The other pit (53.13) lay on the west side of the trench and contained successive deposits of woody debris, organic 'peaty' soil (producing cherry pits) and silt, suggesting that it was a periodically-flooded latrine. The finds included three antler beam sections (AR16) representing mid-stage comb-making (pp 478-9). A spread of gravel to the west was probably upcast when the pit was dug. Finds included scraps of metalworking debris, a hone blank (SE71.52), and a second abraded body sherd of an African Red Slipware plate (V2c). The paving between the two pits (50.03) produced a second sherd of the B*ii* amphora (V3b), a B*iv* amphora body sherd (V1), and a sherd from a pale blue-green glass vessel with self-coloured trails (V15). The later paving (50.04) produced a plough pebble and four flints. The pottery and glass finds probably date to the mid-sixth century (pp 69, 324) although these structures have been assigned to a rather later date (p 102). These finds suggest that the sequence of structures at the south end of the trench may all have pertained to **Phase 1**.

Stage 8
Stage 8 followed the abandonment of **Buildings 16** and **17**, and saw the erection of new buildings (**18** and **19**) in the central and southern parts of the area (Figure 3.40). The relatively small group of finds conformed to the model of domestic debris, and included a small group of E ware jar fragments (Vs 7 and 14) potentially dating to the earlier-seventh century (pp 319, 376). Additional finds from the *Stage 10* flood deposits were probably deposited in *Stages 8* and *9* (Table 3.45, p 129). The orientation of **Buildings 18** and **20** hinted that *Stages 8* and *9* pertained to the earlier part of **Phase 4** (Figure 3.31)

Building 18 was the most-clearly defined of the **Period I** stake structures in the **southern sector**, with irregular double rows of stake-holes revealing a sub-rectilinear building with rounded corners, straight sides and bowed ends. It was some 7.0 m long and 4.0 m wide, with an internal partition 1.2 m from the east end, separating a large chamber (5.8 m rather than being hearth debris. The stone slab seems to be *in situ*, and may have been used for the preparation of food, although similar objects from **Period I** contexts were often associated with metalworking debris (p 467). The original structure represented by the slots, may have been similar, with a wattle superstructure mortised into the horizontal timber frame.

The north-west corner of the building was abutted by rough paving which overlay the remains of **Building 17**. A curving ditch leading to the natural drainage point at the foot of the slope, probably pertained to this stage, but was too far from the building to have served as an eaves-drip trench. Most of the small group of finds came from the ditch which produced three flints, a broken hone (SE36.10), and sherds of an E ware jar (V14), a B*i* amphora (V1), a possible mould-blown Germanic palm cup (V10), and two sherds of unassigned vessel glass. A pebble surface north of the building produced a **retouched** flint and two unassigned vessel glass sherds, while the 'stove' produced a plough pebble and a fragment of an antler beam. This was a typical *domestic* assemblage, and included the earliest securely-stratified E ware from the **southern sector**.

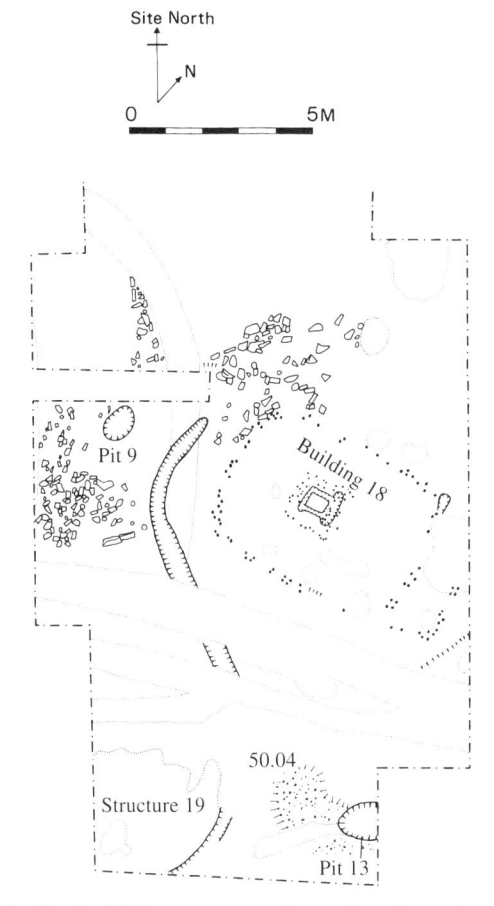

3.40 **Period I.8** structures, pits and surfaces in the *outer zone* (*Stage 8*).

× 4.0 m) from a smaller chamber (1.2 × 4.0 m). A stove or hearth in the middle of the large chamber was marked by a group of features comprising:

a – a rectilinear setting of three narrow depressions with a wider and longer one to the east which probably contained a horizontal timber frame.
b – stakeholes in the floor of the eastern timber slot, apparently inserted after the timber frame had been removed.
c – an irregular sub-square setting of stakes surrounding the timber frame.
d – spreads of charcoal filling the slots and concentrated around the structure.
e – patches of unfired yellow clay on the east and south sides, and a scatter of baked clay to the east
f – a thin, oval, slab of greywacke with a smoothed surface marked by deep scratches and scores (SE54.09).

These features represented a two phase structure. The remains of the later structure comprised the stakeholes, and the burnt and unburnt clay. These may have formed a wicker chimney coated with clay daub, the upper parts of which were baked, while the founds remained plastic. There was no hearth slab, and the fire was perhaps built in a fire basket, or on fire bars built into the chimney. There was no ash, and the charcoal probably derives from a fuel store,

Seeds	Whole	Frag
Rubus Fruiticosus (blackberry)	2824	*c.* 858
Sambucus nigra (elder)	22	27
Stachys arvensis (woundwort)	16	48
Conium maculatum (hemlock)	2	
Urtica urens (Small nettle)	2	*c.* 450
Ranunculus acris (Meadow buttercup)	1	
Other plant macrofossils		
Calluna vulgaris	2	
Gramineae indet. Glume base	1	
Wood fragments	*c.* 274	
Bark fragments		*c.* 330
Roots and stems	*c.* 151	

Table 3.44: Plant remains from *Stage 8* pit (53.09): both layer samples (after Heaton 1994)

A deep oval pit (53.09) to the west of the building, cut through the surface associated with **Building 17**, was sealed by the *Stage 10* silts, and so potentially pertained to this phase. The floor of the pit was covered by a thick deposit of blackberry pips, in turn overlain by a deep deposit of silt. Samples of the upper and lower fill were examined at Durham University (Heaton 1994) revealing a large number of seeds, representing a small number of species; wood, bark and other plant remains (Table 3.44). Preservation was good, but the two samples produced none of the faecal indicators (bran, mosses and fly puparia) present in Pit 1 (Table 3.42, p 124). Heaton noted that the blackberry pips were abraded and sometimes fragmented, concluding that these, and the heather and bark, were debris from dyeing. The other seeds and grasses were interpreted as 'environmental' plants growing in the vicinity of the pit, but they may also be considered as a medicinal assemblage, with different attributes to those in Pit 1 (p 124). Elder has been described as a 'veritable medicine chest' (Hoffman 1990, 197), and the bark, leaves, flowers and berries are all used as herbal medicine. The berries and flowers are recommended for colds, influenza and other respiratory disorders, while the berries are also used in the treatment of rheumatism. Woundwort – as its name suggests – is a vulnerary used directly on wounds in ointments and compresses, and taken internally as an infusion for cramps, joint pains, diarrhoea and dysentery. Hemlock, in moderation, is a powerful sedative, while nettle has astringent, diuretic and tonic properties, and is prescribed *inter alia* for eczema and haemorrhage. Meadow buttercup is the sole exception, and though poisonous to men and animals, does not seem to have medicinal properties. The predominance of species with medicinal properties is once again striking, and the pit may thus have contained a mixture of dyer's waste, waterborne silts and medicinal herbs. The latter were perhaps the remains of compresses for wounds or inflammations, combining the vulnerary virtues of woundwort, the astringent properties of nettle, and the sedative qualities of hemlock. Other finds from the pit included two vessel glass sherds (C3 and E2e), a rim sherd of an E1 jar (V7), an unassigned E ware sherd, and a broken spindle whorl (SE25.15), the last a rare find from **Period I** (p 450).

Structure 19 (50.05) lay to the south, sealing the remains of **Building 16**, and extending beyond the trench. The principal element was a trampled gravel surface overlain by small stone slabs. A clearly defined north edge can be linked tentatively with a line of undecayed stakes to produce a north wall line. Charcoal-stained clay in a trough to the north, may have been the remains of eroded daub from this wall. A curving slot cutting the floor, was probably a later intrusion, and was in turn cut by a later trench (50.06). The east end of this somewhat unconvincing building had been destroyed by later disturbances. The small group of finds included a flint core and four retouched flints, but no diagnostic material.

Stage 9
Stage 9 saw the replacement of **Building 18** with a new building (**20**) in a slightly different position (Figure 3.41). **Structure 19** was abandoned, and a ditch was dug in the south part of the site. These feature do not present a coherent picture, and probably mark successive phases of activity that cannot be distinguished stratigraphically.

Building 20 was similar to **Building 18**, but was less-clearly defined, and revealed no evidence of a partition or central hearth The best evidence was displayed on its north side, where stones abutting the wall covered the stakeholes of the earlier wall. This surface produced a displaced sherd of a mould-blown palm cup (V9h), there were no other finds.

Continuing activity to the south was marked by a drain (61.01) and a construction slot (50.06). The slot had stone packing along one side, which had been dislodged by later activity. Its purpose is

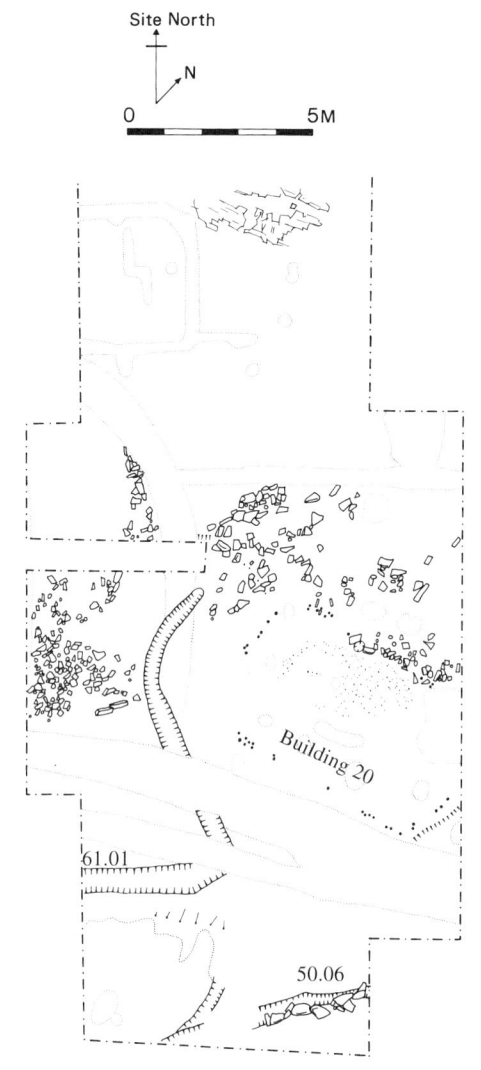

3.41 **Period I.9** structures, ditches and surfaces in the *outer zone* (*Stage 9*).

unknown. The drain was flanked by a spread of upcast gravel (61.02), and ran west/east, angling slightly to the north at the point where it probably merged with another drain, which had been obliterated by the deep eleventh century ditch (417). These features marked the final stages of a complex and confusing sequence of structural remains at the south end of the trench (Figure 3.41), which revealed no convincing buildings, but pointed to intensive structural activity in the sixth, and perhaps seventh, centuries, extending beyond the excavated area. The relatively small groups of finds from these two features included an abraded body sherd of a B*v* amphora (V1) from the construction slot (50.06), and three sherds of vessel glass from the upper fill of the ditch. These included sherds of a distinctive, pale, streaky wine-red vessel (V20b, pp 303-5) and a rim sherd of a pale amber cone of Group D (V56), the former probably dating to the later-seventh century (p 304). Other finds included waterlogged wood, an antler burr and tine, and scraps of displaced metalworking debris.

Stage 10

Stage 10 saw the flooding of the low-lying south and central parts of the **southern sector**, represented by a layer of silt (58, 55, 235) deposited by stagnant or slowly moving water (Figure 6.7 pp 598-601). The *Stage 9* drain had already silted up, and it was overlain by *laminae* of sand, clay and waterborne debris (charcoal, twigs etc). The sudden deterioration of the drainage must mark poor maintenance of the Ket Burn to the east (pp 7-8). The flood presumably rendered **Building 20** uninhabitable, and its floor revealed a shallow silt deposit. Silt deposits continued to accumulate on the west side of the trench in subsequent phases, and some of the finds from this area (Block 235), may have been deposited after others ascribed to this stage (Table 3.45).

Numerous finds were recovered while the *Stage 10* silts were being excavated (Table 3.45). Some of these may have been carried in by the floodwater, but many were probably scattered over and among the rough surfaces surrounding the *Stage 8–9* buildings, while others (the B and D ware) were perhaps displaced from earlier deposits by trampling animals. The assemblage had a more strongly marked '*industrial*' component than earlier groups from the area, but was still characterised by the relative abundance of pottery, glass and flints, distinguishing these groups. It can be contrasted usefully with the larger groups of debris from the **Phase 3** deposits in the western part of the *inner precinct* (pp 107-9, e.g. Table 3.22) in which the *domestic* element is small, and specialised industrial debris abundant. The comparative richness of this assemblage probably resulted in part from the flooding and puddling, which may have hidden objects (the cabochon and razor, for example) that would otherwise have been retrieved. A similar picture obtained in the twelfth century when this part of the site was again flooded (pp 222-6).

The group incorporated a number of significant finds despite the stratigraphic problems. The earlier types of imported pottery and glass were scarce or absent, and later types predominated. It contained the largest single group of E ware sherds – mostly from jars – revealing a spatial contrast to the *inner precinct* where bowls were more common (Figures 10.18 and 24). The glass sherds included a group of vessels with horizontally-trailed rims (Vs 33, 34, 36, 37), which were probably later than equivalent vessels from the *inner precinct* (p 309). One of these (V34), and a rare vessel with vertical running chevrons (23), are paralleled at the Mote of Mark (pp 305-6) and may represent a relatively late group of glass vessels associated with E ware pottery. Sherds of two Group D vessels (58 and 61) were members of a late group of undecorated cones (pp 309, 325-6). Distinctive opaque blue sherds (V52) from 235 may have been later that the other vessels (pp 308, 326). The swivel knife fragment is unusually early (p 429). The metalworking waste indicated non-ferrous and ferrous working in the vicinity, but much of it may have been displaced from the *Stage 4* deposits (51), which displayed common distinctive features (heated Haematite, crucible and heating tray fragments, glassy hearths with trapped tuyeres, and glassy cinder). The wood was probably waterborne debris.

Two B*i amphora* sherds (Vs 1 and 3)
A rim sherd of a D ware plate or bowl (V1)
Twenty E ware sherds comprising fragments of four jars (Vs 8, 10, 11 and 15), one bowl (V5) and ten unassigned sherds
Twenty-six sherds of early medieval vessel glass, including pieces of Vessels 3 (c), 9 (b and d), 11 (e), 20 (a) 23 (a and b), 26, 33, 34, 36, 37,52 (a and b) 58, 61 and 73 (g), nine unassigned sherds (one C2, three C3, three C4, two C6, one D1 and one E2) and a sherd of burnt amber vessel glass
A sherd of 'Roman' window or vessel glass (GS1.13)
A quartz cabochon (SE58)
A hooked iron bar (IN31.6)
A possible broken knife (IN73.5), a swivel knife fragment (IN68.2) and a drill bit (IN65.5)
A fragmentary iron object with a spiral terminal (IN78.12) and a tube (IN85.3), perhaps a mounting for a wooden shaft.
A nail and nail shank, two iron strips (IN80.27 and 28), and a tapering bar (IN83.7)
A broken copper-alloy needle (BZ12.2), a stick-pin shank with a zig-zag decoration (BZ14.6) and a razor blade (BZ24.6)
A thin piece of lead waste (LD10.1)
Two hones (SE34.7 and SE38.19) and a hone blank (SE71.38)
A greywacke discoid (SE20.8) and a broken sandstone disc (SE50.6)
A plough pebble (SE51)
Four pieces of antler comprising:
    a rare skull fragment with the antler sawn off
    a beam section
    two tine tips
Sixty-one pieces of flint including nineteen waste flakes, four cores, twenty-eight **retouched** flints, three tools and four burnt flints
A large group of wood including stakes, shavings and thorn twigs
A distinctive group of metalworking debris including:
    Two pieces of heated Haematite, one trapped in glassy cinder
    A small group of tuyere and bellows-protector fragments, two trapped in Group B hearths
    A heating tray fragment (SG26)
    Two crucible sherds with traces of 'copper alloy' (SG15.14 and), a mould fragment (SG17.8) and two bar moulds (SE45.1 and .5)
    Three slag cake chunks and segments
    A Group C smelting hearth fragment
    Glassy (1.187kg) and crystalline cinder (536gm)
A large collection of animal bones, among which burnt bone and tooth fragments predominated, indicating acidic conditions

Table 3.45: Finds from *Stage 10* waterborne silts (55, 58 and 235) in the **southern sector**, probably including scattered debris from earlier stages.

The unoccupied ground in the north part of the area produced a complementary group of finds (Table 3.46) which shared some elements, notably metalworking debris, and sherds of pottery and glass, but lacked the antler, flints, iron and copper alloy

A B*i amphora* sherd (V1f)
An E ware jar rim sherd (V11) and an unassigned jar base sherd (E19)
Four sherds of vessel glass (V60, Gp Ab, GpC4, one unassigned)
Two sherds of light green window glass (GS06.75–6)
Two nail shanks
A relatively large group of metalworking debris including:
    Eight 'hearth bottoms' and fragments
    Small quantities of glassy cinder (180 gm)
    Three tuyere fragments

Table 3.46. Finds from later deposits (64.03, 04; ?*Stages 4–10*) in north part of **southern sector**

artefacts found in the flooded ground. This group probably predated the *Stage 11* buildings, was sealed by the of *Stage 12* pathway, and probably accumulated over a relatively long period between *Stages 4* and *10*. The relative poverty of the group contributes to the impression that there was a sterile area between the *inner precinct* and the buildings in the *outer zone*. The two window glass sherds could have been displaced from the overlying **Period II** buildings, but one, included in a programme of analysis at Bradford University (Hold 1991), was of similar composition to much of the vessel glass.

Stages 11–15
Stages *11* and *12* saw renewed settlement following the flooding of *Stage 10*. A sequence of features at the south end of the trench probably marks an outer boundary, and successive ditches slightly to the north record attempts to deal with the drainage problems. There were few clear connections between the *Stage 11* structures, but a shale path laid at the start of *Stage 12* bound the area together with unusual clarity. *Stages 14* and *15* dated to **Period II**, but were a logical part of the depositional continuum and are included in the stratigraphic matrix (Figure 3.36). *Stage 13* possibly spanned both periods, recording a transitional phase contrasting with the radical transformation of the *inner precinct* (pp 139-43).

The waterlogged deposits of *Stages 12–15* preserved a group of structural timbers and other organic debris. Oak timbers from **Building 24**, the adjacent drain (230.01), the possible gateway (213.01) to the south, and an oak stake from **Structure II/17** (234), provided valuable dating evidence, and contributed to a dendrochronological master chart for 278–752 AD (pp 594-5). The timbers from the *Stage 11–12* features came from mature trees, at least one of which was more than 400 years old. All had been trimmed during conversion, and the outer sapwood was missing. This meant that the felling dates were uncertain, although parts of the growth period were precisely dated. The youngest timber from **Building 24** was an 'offcut' from a tree growing in 589 x 706 AD, which cannot have been felled before 716 AD, while the youngest, securely-stratified timber was growing in 356–681 AD, and cannot have been felled before 691 AD. An early timber from the structure at the south end of the trench (213.01) was growing in 563–695 AD, and cannot have been felled before 705 AD. These date-spans indicate that *Stage 12* is unlikely to be earlier than *c*. 700 AD, and was probably a decade or so later. The linked inferences that **Building 24** pertained to **Period I**, and that **Period II** began in *c*. 730 AD (pp 136) argue that the building was erected in the early-eighth century, perhaps *c*. 716 x 730 AD. *Stage 11* can thus be ascribed to *c*. 700 with reasonable confidence. The sapwood survived on a stake from **Structure II/17**, which came from a tree felled between 756 and 801 AD. *Stage 14* can thus be dated to the second half of the eighth century, providing a useful, if imprecise, *terminus ante quem* for *Stages 11–13*.

The finds from *Stage 11–13* contexts are listed in Tables 3.46-52. Most of the groups seemed to be relatively uncontaminated with displaced earlier material, and imported pottery and vessel glass were much rarer than in the underlying *Stage 10* deposits (Table 3.45). Only two E ware vessels, a carinated bowl (V2) and a jar (V9), can be ascribed to this phase with confidence, and the other E ware sherds were either unassigned, or ascribed to vessels occurring in earlier contexts (p 322). The strikingly small group of vessel glass included the rims of two undecorated Group D cones, one amber (V55, 236.01) and one blue-green (V63, 212.02), which were members of a potentially late group of vessels (pp 325-6); a sherd of a late stemmed beaker (V20, pp 303-5) and a sherd of a Group A bowl or cup with wheel-cut decoration (3a, 213), all potentially late types (pp 325-6). Other finds were more abundant, and concentrations of flints on the floor of **Building 21** and elsewhere (232, 212.02) indicate that it continued to be used. 'Shale' bangles appear for the first time (236 and 232). Leather-working waste from two ditches (216, Table 3.48 and 230.03, Table 4.26) was potentially a contamination from immediately adjacent twelfth century deposits (417.02 etc, Table 6.10), and other finds from these features may also have been intrusive.

Stage 11
Stage 11 (Figure 3.42) followed the flooding in *Stage 10*, and saw the demarcation of a new boundary in the south part of the trench, and the erection of a new timber-framed building (21, 212.01) overlying the remains of the stake-walled **Buildings 18** and **20**. A curving ditch to the west (216) indicated a new drainage system, probably joining a shallow drain to south of **Building 21**. Two poorly-preserved buildings (**22–23**) to the north were probably contemporary.

The outer boundary evolved rapidly during *Stage 11* (Figure 3.42a, b and c). It was initially marked by a line of stakes (116), probably supporting a wattle fence, and possibly lying on the outer margin of a shallow ditch. This was subsequently augmented, or replaced, with a carefully-constructed band of stones (232.01) some 1.0 m wide, similar to the basal course of a wall, but with no evidence for any superstructure (Figure 3.42b). Flooding deposited a layer of clayey silt to either side of the 'wall'. The 'wall' and silts were in turn covered by a narrow shale path flanked to the south by a shallow ditch. A sequence of post-holes and shale surfaces (213.01-03) beyond the boundary in the south-west corner of the trench may have been part of the north wall of a building or a gate associated with the *Stage 12* path.

Two lines of stake-holes on a similar alignment indicated earlier versions of the boundary, and probably preceded the deterioration of the drainage in *Stage 10*. These could have been the outer boundary of the *monasterium* in Stages *8* and *9* if the other features at the south end of the trench have been wrongly ascribed to this phase. Two clearly-defined, but unphased, lines of stake-holes lying at right-angles to the outer boundary in the central part of the area, indicated a radial division in the *outer zone*, which may have dictated the siting of the successive buildings on the east side of the trench, and was replaced by a fence in *Stage 12* or *13*.

Building 21 (212.01) overlay the remains of **Buildings 18** and **20**, and was represented by a sub-rectilinear setting of post-holes, revealing the western half of a timber-framed building. It probably had opposed doorways in the north and south walls, which had been virtually obliterated by the door-post sockets of **Building 24**. The timbers had been removed and the packing stones pushed over when **Building 24** was erected, and most of the floor was perhaps dug away at the same time. A puzzling group of features (115) at the east end of the building, included a rectangular pit, a broad gully edged with large stones, and scattered charcoal and patches of clay. These may have been part of this building, or of an earlier structure to the east. The finds (Table 3.47) were generally uninformative, although the E ware jar may have been contemporary loss.

a
A corroded iron pin (IN40.5)
A greywacke 'loom weight' (SE29.1)

b
A rim sherd of an E ware jar (V9) and an unassigned E ware sherd
A nail and iron plate fragment (IN82.12)
Three **retouched** flints, four **unretouched** waste flakes and a serrated quartz flake
A plough pebble (SE51)
A small group of metalworking debris

Table 3.47: Finds from **Building 21** (**a**, 212.01) and possible floor (**b**, 115)

Building 22 (59) lay to the north of **Building 21**, and was defined by a stone-packed foundation trench marking the south wall, and a fragmentary slot indicating the position of the east wall. The floor comprised a shallow silty hollow skirted by the shale path laid at the start of *Stage 12*. A stone-filled hollow in the east part of the floor was similar to the anomalous feature (115) in **Building 21**. The only find was a fragment of a tapering copper-alloy strip (BZ38.27).

'**Building**' **23** was indicated by a possible sunken floor on the north side of the ditch, which was skirted by the *Stage 12* path. Successive **Period II** buildings had disturbed this area, and no certain structural evidence survived.

The ditch (216) curved through the western part of the area, skirting **Buildings 21–23**. It was deepest to the north-west, and probably ran into a shallow west/east drain at the foot of the slope, which was obliterated by the *Stage 12* ditch. The area enclosed by the ditch revealed a spread of charcoal and patches of clay, but was otherwise featureless, and was unoccupied for the remainder of **Period I**, and throughout **Period II**. The floor of the ditch produced a small group of comminuted human bone, including

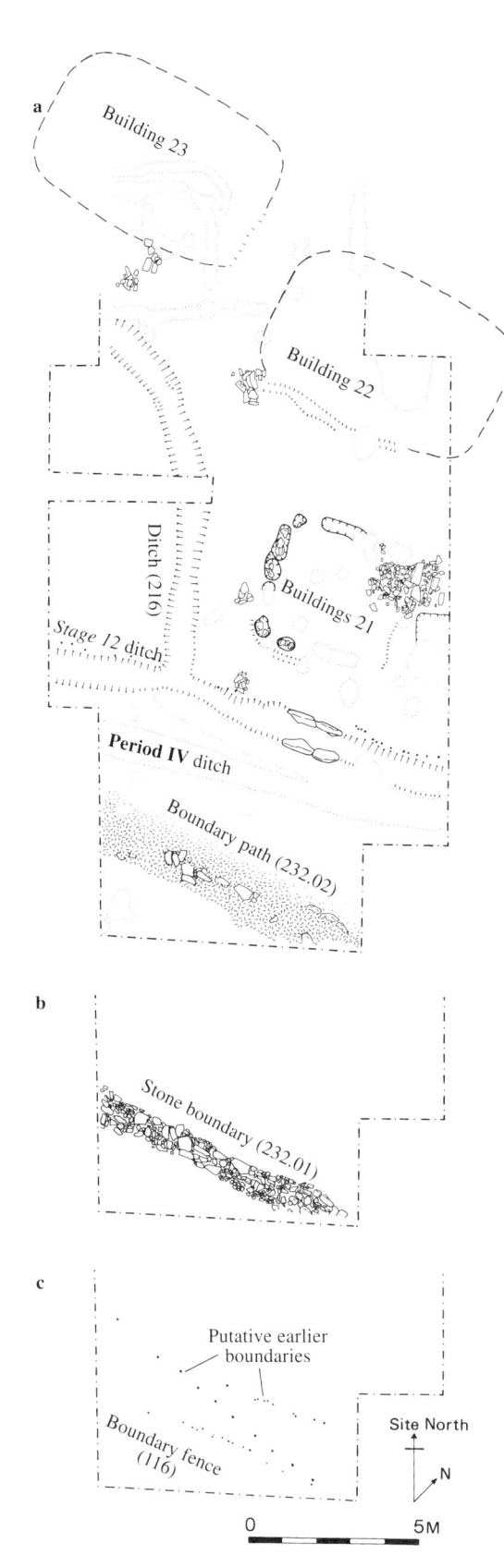

3.42 **Period I.11** structures, ditches and boundaries in the *outer zone* (*Stage 11*). **a** *Stage 11* buildings and shale boundary path. **b** Stone boundary underlying shale path. **c** Fence probably preceding stone boundary, and possible earlier stake boundary fences.

fragments of a skull and radius, apparently burnt after the soft tissue had decayed. This hints at ritual activity in the vicinity, perhaps linked to the charcoal spreads enclosed by the ditch. There is no ready explanation for the seemingly pagan practice of cremation in the residential zone of an unquestionably Christian site in the late-seventh/early-eighth century.

Five sherds of vessel glass (V35, C3, D1b and two unassigned)
Two droplets of molten lead (LD13.1 and 2)
A large rounded fire-damaged hone (SE35.13)
A sandstone hone blank (SE71.32)
Two antler burrs (AR04)
Three trimmings and three scraps of cattle hide (LR01, 08)
One **retouched** and five **unretouched** flints
A group of waterlogged wood including stakes, trimmings and chips
A small group of metalworking debris including:
    Glassy (355 gm) and crystalline cinder (151 gm)
A group of 'white stones' comprising thirty-eight quartz pebbles and four granite pebbles

Table 3.48: Finds from *Stage 11* ditch (216)

A post-built fence, running northwards from the outer boundary, and clipping the eastern side of the ditch, may have been constructed at the end of this phase. It redefined the possible radial boundary formerly marked by stakes, and respected by many of the **Period I** buildings.

Stage 12
Stage 12 saw the construction of a new building (**24**, 212.02) on the site of **Building 21**, and the excavation of a drainage ditch (230.01) to the south. A stone bridge adjacent to the doorway of the building, led to a new path joining with the extant path marking the outer boundary. The new path ran northwards, skirting **Buildings 22** and **23**, and oversailing the eastern edge of the *Stage 11* ditch. **Buildings 22** and **23** were probably dismantled during this phase, and the south wall of **Building 22** was cut by a latrine pit (53.07) located conveniently by the north door of **Building 24** (Figure 4.30).

Building 24 was unusually well preserved and, paradoxically, difficult to interpret. The structural remains were covered by a thick deposit of waterborne silt, and the building was first revealed as an untrampled sub-rectilinear shale surface surrounded by the *Stage 13* paving (Figure 4.30). A regular rectangular setting of large, dressed oak timbers, exposed as the shale was removed, framed the dismantled post-sockets of **Building 21**. Although the two groups of features could be integrated to form a coherent timber building fitting snugly inside the later paving, this was stratigraphically impossible because of the intervening layer of shale. It gradually became clear that the preserved timbers had protruded through the shale, while the dismantled posts were sealed by it, demonstrating the presence of two distinct buildings (**21** and **24**). The preserved posts of the later building comprised opposed plank-framed doorways, a line of slightly-angled posts along the south wall, and two possible ridge pole supports at either end of the floor. The south-west corner of the building was indicated by an external spread of charcoal-rich soil, but there was no clear physical evidence of the walls at ground level. The paradox was resolved when the underlying layers had been excavated, revealing the stake-holes and decaying stakes of insubstantial wattle walls. These corresponded with wavy lines in the shale 'floor', and were abutted by the *Stage 13* paving. The untrampled internal shale can thus be identified as the substrate of a beaten earth floor removed along with the overlying waterborne silts.

The building pertains to the architectural tradition prevailing in **Period II**. Its ground plan and reconstruction are illustrated in Figures 4.3, 4.4 and 4.30, and discussed below (pp 138–9).

Most of the finds from the building (Table 3.49) came from the shale substrate, but had perhaps been lost on the putative earth floor. They included a Group D sherd from an apparently late series of glass vessels (pp 325-6), and two large hones, which were perhaps appropriate to a workshop. A third small hone came from one of the post-holes.

An undecorated rim sherd of a blue-green cone (V63) and an unassigned sherd (C4)
A melon bead (GS03.12.)
One piece of iron (IN93.32)
A perforated phyllite flake (SE31.1)
A bar hone (SE32.1), a large rounded hone (SE35.3) and a broken small manufactured hone (SE36.2)
Two **retouched** and two **unretouched** flints
A small group of metalworking debris

Table 3.49: Finds from **Building 24** (212.02)

A probable latrine pit (53.07) beside the north door of the building contained opposed vertical slabs resting on a primary fill of organic debris. An oak plank (growing in 329 x 466 AD, pp 594-5) from the bottom of the pit may originally have rested on these supports. The pit was subsequently filled with gravelly soil which was oversailed by the *Stage 13* paving. The pit produced a sherd of a Group C cone (V22a), potentially displaced (p 305), four pebbles, and scraps of metalworking debris. Routine sieving of the organic debris produced none of the faecal indicators found in other latrine pits.

A drain (230.01) running west–east across the low ground to the south of **Building 24**, was probably dug at the start of *Stage 12*. Opposed upright slabs lining the ditch to the south of the doorway, probably supported a bridge of flagstones which was dismantled and moved to the west in **Period II** (pp 181-2). The bridge led to a narrow stone path which joined the shale marking the outer boundary. By the end of *Stage 12*, the ditch had become clogged with debris (Table 3.50, 230.01), which included large amounts of wood but few artefacts. The wood included planks, stakes, laths, chips, roundwood and trenails, indicating a woodworking shop in the vicinity, or perhaps upstream. Blackthorn twigs probably derive from a hedge.

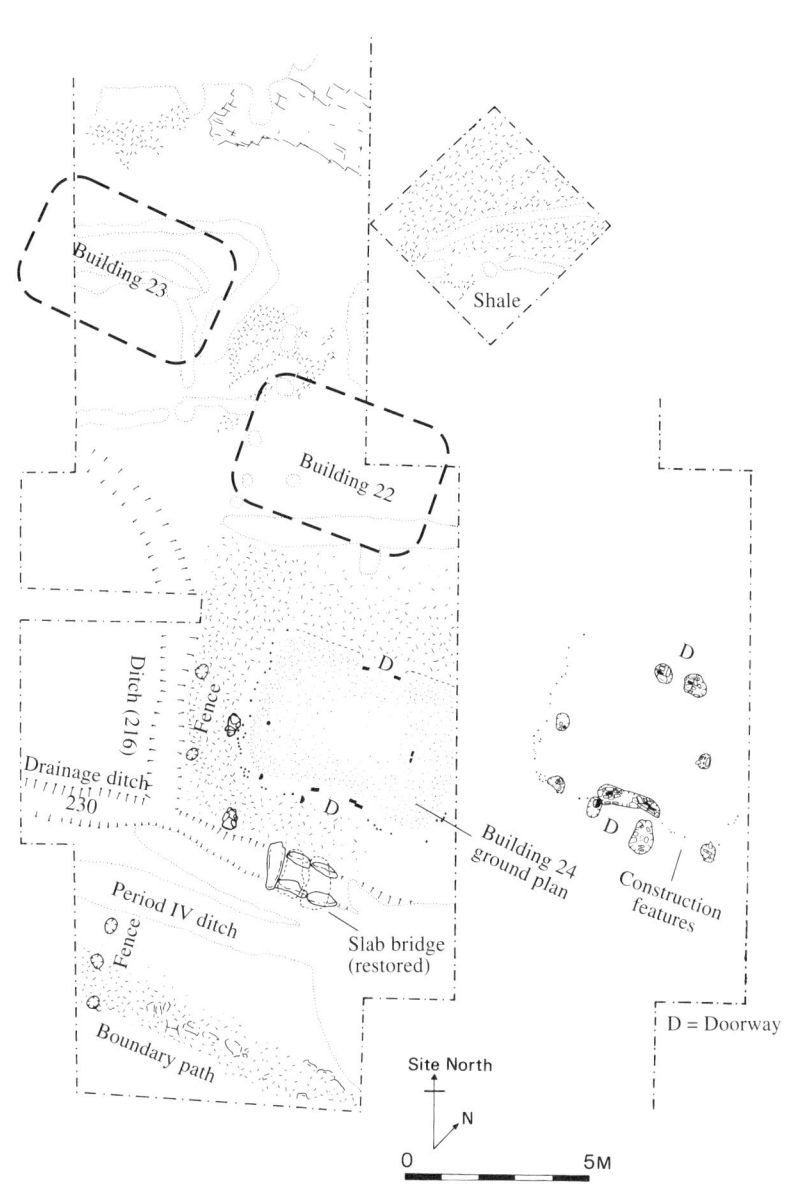

3.43 **Period I.12** structure, drains, boundaries and surfaces in the *outer zone* (*Stage 12*), and construction features of **Building 24** (inset).

A possibly Roman sherd of blue-green vessel or window glass (GS1.10)
One unascribed (C3) and an unassigned vessel glass sherd
A yellow sandstone socket stone (SE3.1)
A small broken manufactured hone (SE36.19)
A plough pebble (SE51)
A lead rod with opposed grooves on either side (LD11.7)
A copper-lead alloy waste nodule (BZ39.6)
A **retouched** flint
A small group of metalworking debris
A large group of wood comprising stakes, chips, laths and blackthorn twigs and including:
    An oak plank (growing 469 x 561AD, pp 594-5)
    Chips and fragments of oak (9), willow (1), hazel (1), ash (1) and alder (2)
    Hazel and willow roundwood
    Two oak trenails

Table 3.50: Finds from main ditch (230.01)

The finds from the path and fence (Table 3.51) included sherds of another late Group D vessel (V55, pp 325-6). and an E ware bowl (V2), not represented in earlier deposits, and so perhaps dating to the opening decades of the eighth century. The perforated discoid may have been used for making cord (p 452).

Seven joining fragments of a late E ware bowl (V2)
Vessel glass sherds from V22 (b) and V55
A well-finished 'shale' bangle fragment (SH01.2)
A greywacke discoid with three perforations (SE30.3)
A plough pebble
Three **retouched** flints
Nine quartz pebbles
Scraps of metalworking debris
Three eroded lumps of oak, possibly carpentry offcuts

Table 3.51: Finds from 'shale' path and fence (236)

One unassigned E ware sherd
A fragment of a well-finished 'shale' bangle (SH1.1)
Nine **retouched** flints
An antler burr
A small group of metalworking debris

Table 3.52: Finds from outer boundary and related silt layers (232)

CHAPTER 4

Period II: The Northumbrian *minster* (*c.* 730–845 AD)

Peter Hill, Jo Moran, Andrew Nicholson and Dave Pollock

4.1 INTRODUCTION

The beginning of **Period II** was defined by the construction of three parallel ranges of buildings in the **Glebe Field**, and its end by the fire which destroyed the church and burial chapel in the mid-ninth century. Both horizons were defined clearly and there were generally few problems in distinguishing **Period II** features from earlier and later deposits in the **Glebe Field**. A hall in the **Museum Garden** (pp 278-81) was aligned with the halls in the **Glebe Field**, and was probably broadly contemporary, while poorly-preserved ninth century features in this area were reliably dated by coins. **The Fey Field** has revealed no certain evidence of occupation in this period, although a large hollow at the west end of the trench might conceivably have been part of a sunken-floored building lying some way beyond the outer boundary (p 291).

The excavation revealed a large group of timber buildings of which the church was undoubtedly the most significant. The foundations of this building were dug into earlier shaly deposits, and it was recurrently surfaced and surrounded with layers of shale. This provided ideal circumstances for excavation, as the fill of post-holes and slots frequently preserved perfect casts of the structural timbers. Most of these features were excavated by emptying the casts of the timbers, which were sufficiently precise in several instances to identify radially-split planks. The timber casts are illustrated on the plans, which distinguish clear impressions (black) from less certain evidence (hatched). Similar techniques of excavation were used on most of the other building, although these had not been evolved fully when the small buildings in the **southern sector** were examined.

As in other periods, the interpretation infers light fences and wattle walls, indicated by flanking surfaces, but without foundations, stake- or post-impressions. These putative fences would have been supported on stakes driven through worm-sorted topsoil and into the frequently complex strata of **Period I** features, and would have been difficult to detect in either medium. These ghost features generally offer coherence to deposits in confusing juxtapositions, but are of different evidential quality to tangible structural remains.

Previous excavations. Previous excavations have revealed no certain evidence of the Northumbrian *minster*, although the building exposed by William Galloway and re-examined by Radford (pp 8-10) may have been part of a range of buildings including the principal *Northumbrian* church, although slightly askew to the alignment of other buildings of this period (Figures 2.9–11). The early burials excavated by Ritchie (p 10) were aligned with the Northumbrian buildings, and might thus have pertained to this period, but were also aligned with the **Period I/3** burials, and could have been earlier. Northumbrian coins are small and easy to miss, but it is probably significant that none have been found previously at Whithorn. This suggests that the zone of commercial activity identified in the **Glebe Field** (Figure 10.41), is complemented by coin-free areas elsewhere on the site, and specifically at the east end of the hill, and in the two fields to the north sampled by Tabraham in 1976, and by the Whithorn Trust in 1987 and 1992–3 (pp 287-91, Pollock 1993, 1995).

Previous reports. Previous interim reports are reliable in general outline, but not in detail. The greatest changes affect buildings in the **southern sector** (I/21 and I/24) formerly dated unequivocally to the Northumbrian period (e.g. Hill 1992 fig. 10), but now ascribed to the end of **Period I**, and the enigmatic features at the south end of the trench, now identified as part of the curvilinear outer boundary.

Continuity and change. The curvilinear **Period I** *monasterium* was replaced by a rigorously-planned rectilinear settlement at the beginning of **Period II**. The change seems radical, but there were strong links between the old and the new, which may be seen as a physical expression of the process of assimilation and transformation evinced by the written records (pp 18-21). Continuity in the excavated area was demonstrated by the siting of the ecclesiastical buildings in the **northern range** to encompass the

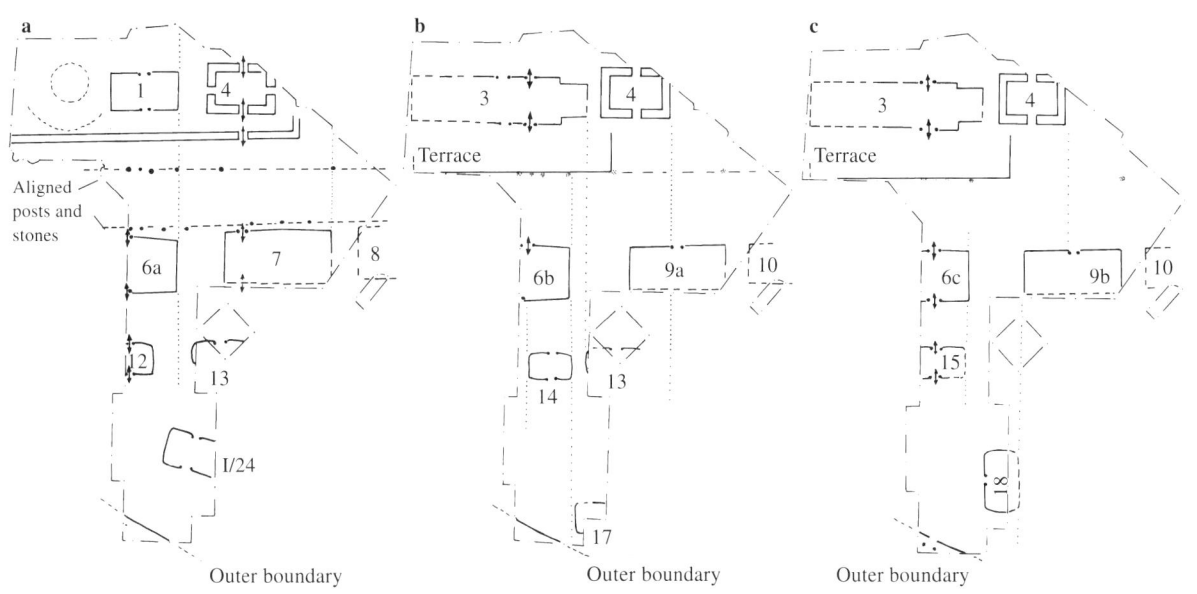

4.1 Evidence of planning in the **Period II** minster. **a** Earlier-eighth century. **b** Later-eighth century. **c** Earlier-ninth century. Dotted lines link aligned gables and doorways, arrows indicate co-axial doorways.

Period I shrines. The new buildings disregarded the burials of **Period I/3** and **1/4**, but avoided the 'special area' occupied by the **Period I/2** graveyard. The derelict **Period I/3** shrine was incorporated into the first of the new buildings, while the **Period I/4b** shrine to the west apparently remained standing. A stone-founded burial enclosure erected on the platform to the east (76) incorporated the massive granite boulder marking the **Phase 3** graveyard. The curvilinear outer boundary of the **Period I** *monasterium* seems to have been maintained for most of **Period II**. Possible continuity beyond the excavated area, and in particular on the putative site of the founder's tomb, is discussed in Chapter 2 (p 42).

Planning (Figure 4.1). The three ranges of buildings were aligned with each other, and with the row of posts and stones (252), which seems to have originated in **Period I/1.4** (p 112, Figure 3.32), but which may have been augmented in the early stages of **Period II**. This alignment seems to have marked part of the border of the ecclesiastical precinct, initially bounding the south side of an east/west path, and subsequently delimiting successive terraces to the south of the church. A second alignment of large posts some 7.0 m to the south, lay immediately to the north of the halls in the middle range, and included potentially-structural timbers associated with **Halls 6** and **7**, and the posts at the head and foot of Grave I/1. This may have been fortuitous, but it ran parallel to the earlier alignment, and perhaps reflected a linear boundary which was otherwise unmarked. The wide corridor between the two alignments was unoccupied throughout **Period II**, and the only features were paths linking the halls with the ecclesiastical buildings. The arcades framing the **Phase 3** church and its successors, may have had a similar dual role as structural members and colonnades framing vistas within the *minster*. A second series of planning axes linked the opposed doorways and gables of the buildings in the different ranges. There were minor shifts in the orientation of these axes during **Period II**, but they recurred too frequently to have been coincidental. Notable examples linked the opposed doorways of **Hall 6** and **Building 12**; the entrances of the **Phase 1** enclosure and burial enclosure, and the doorway of **Hall 7** (Figure 4.1a); and the opposed doors of the chancel, **Hall 6c** and **Building 15** in the latter part of the period (Figure 4.1c). The combined evidence indicates that the original buildings were laid out with considerable regularity which endured into the ninth century, despite minor changes in the orientation of the planning grid.

Stratigraphy, phasing and report structure. The stratigraphic relationships of the *Northumbrian* deposits are illustrated in Figure 4.2. Successive surfaces linked a long sequence of structural remains in the **northern sector** to less-well preserved halls in the **central sector**. The stratigraphy in the southern part of this area was shallow, and had been extensively disturbed. The **southern sector** revealed a succession of small timber buildings immediately south of the lower rock outcrop, with further structures interleaved with pond silts and rough surfaces on the lower ground. These were not linked stratigraphically with the remains to the north, but can be correlated tentatively with them on the bases of alignment and relative sequence.

The phase structure for **Period II** is based on the ecclesiastical buildings in the **northern sector**, which revealed rapid evolution over a relatively short period when there was little discernible change elsewhere. There were four principal elements in the **northern sector**. The church revealed seven distinct phases (**1–7**). The adjacent chapel had two structural phases, both closely linked with the evolution of the church, and with independent links to internal and external features. An area to the east of the chapel – the children's graveyard – revealed a sequence of burials, boundaries and buildings that continued into **Period III** and, though intermittently linked to the development of the chapel and church, was a discrete stratigraphic entity, and is described separately (pp 170-2, 187-9). The area between the ecclesiastical buildings and the halls to the south revealed successive boundaries, terraces and paths, interleaved with worm-sorted soils and, latterly, rubbish spreads. These features provided the principal links between the church, chapel and children's graves, and are the only connections between them and the middle range of halls. The buildings and other features in the **central** and **southern sectors** can be ascribed to three stages of development (Figures 4.30, 32 and 34), but are described separately.

Chronology. The **Period II** deposits produced a large group of coins representing the larger part of a numismatic sequence extending into the opening years of **Period III** (pp 332-4, 351-5). These revealed four critical chronological markers in **Period II**.

1. A Southumbrian sceat (Group 1: CN2:61), securely stratified on the floor of the **Phase 1** burial enclosure, is of a type usually dated 715–730 AD and should mean that **Phase 2** cannot be earlier than 715 AD, and was probably somewhat later. Metcalf has reattributed these coins to York and suggested they date to *c.* 710 AD, arguing that the Whithorn find was lost before the appointment of Pecthelm (1992, 93). The chronological discrepancy is slight, but hints that **Phase 1** may have preceded the establishment of the bishopric in *c.* 720–730 AD.

2. The renovation of the church in **Phase 4** preceded the deposition of a group (**2a**) of Northumbrian sceattas and an East Anglian penny of Beonna. The latter is closely dated to *c.*758-765, and is likely to have reached Northumbria in a relatively brief interlude in the issue of Northumbrian regnal coins (p 335). This commends the proposed date of *c.* 760 AD for the completion of the programme of renovations which is supported by the relatively late design of the associated sceattas (p 333). The coins were deposited at a relatively advanced stage of **Phase 4**, implying that **Phases 1–3** represented a period of rapid evolution lasting some twenty-thirty years in, perhaps 720 × 730–*c.* 750 AD.

3. Phase I stycas predominated in the large group of coins deposited between the ecclesiastical boundary and the halls, and this series ended shortly after the introduction of the Phase II stycas (pp 352-3), but before the first issues of Aethelred II and Archbishop Uigmund. This horizon seems to have marked the end of the long period of stability encompassed by **Phases 4–6**, offering a plausible date of *c.* 835–840 AD for the beginning of **Phase 7**, when changed circumstances seem to have prevailed.

4. A distinctive group of coins associated with the secular use of the church in **Phase 7** (pp 162-4) represents a specific phase of money supply during the reign of Aethelred II (*c.* 841–849 AD), while the subsequent fire possibly pertained to a period between the issues of the Type IIA stycas of Aethelred II and the Type IIC stycas of his second reign (pp 353-5). The inferred date of *c.* 845 AD (p 121) is unlikely to be refined by new excavation evidence, but will perhaps be modified as numismatic studies advance.

The appointment of Pecthelm as bishop and the putative preparation of the see by Bishop Acca offer an appropriate, historical context for the transformation of the *monasterium* at the start of **Period II**, but these events were not precisely dated (pp 40-1). The coin from the **Phase 1** burial enclosure indicated a slightly earlier date than the timbers from the **southern sector** (p 130). There were no other intrinsically datable finds from secure contexts pertaining to the early part of **Period II**. The renovations of **Phase 4** can be dated with some confidence to the mid-eighth century, and were probably complete by *c.* 760 AD. These mark the end of the rapid development of the ecclesiastical buildings, and there was little further change in the later-eighth and earlier-ninth centuries apart from the renewal and replacement of the external arcades of the church in **Phases 5** and **6**, and the rebuilding and repair of the halls and small buildings beyond. The coins suggested that the latter part of **Phase 4** and **Phases 5–6** spanned the period from *c.* 760 to *c.* 835–840 AD, indicating that each lasted for about 25 years. This allows the generation of a speculative chronology for the construction, renovation and subsequent repair of the church (Table 4.1). This accords reasonably well with the probable life of the ground-set timbers of the church and halls, which might have survived for some thirty–fifty years before requiring major repairs. The church, thus, required major renovation after thirty to forty years and the arcade was replaced some fifty years later. The halls revealed a similar pattern with three phases of construction or major repair within perhaps 120 years, indicating major refurbishments every forty years or so.

Phases 1 & 2	*Two oratories built*	?720–730 AD
Phase 3	*Oratories joined and first arcade erected*	735 AD
Phase 4	*Major renovation of church*	750–760 AD
Phase 5	*Doors moved and arcade repaired*	785 AD
Phase 6	*Arcade replaced*	810 AD
Phase 7	*Internal fittings removed, arcade decaying or removed*	835–840 AD
	Fire	845 AD

Table 4.1: Speculative chronology of the church building phases

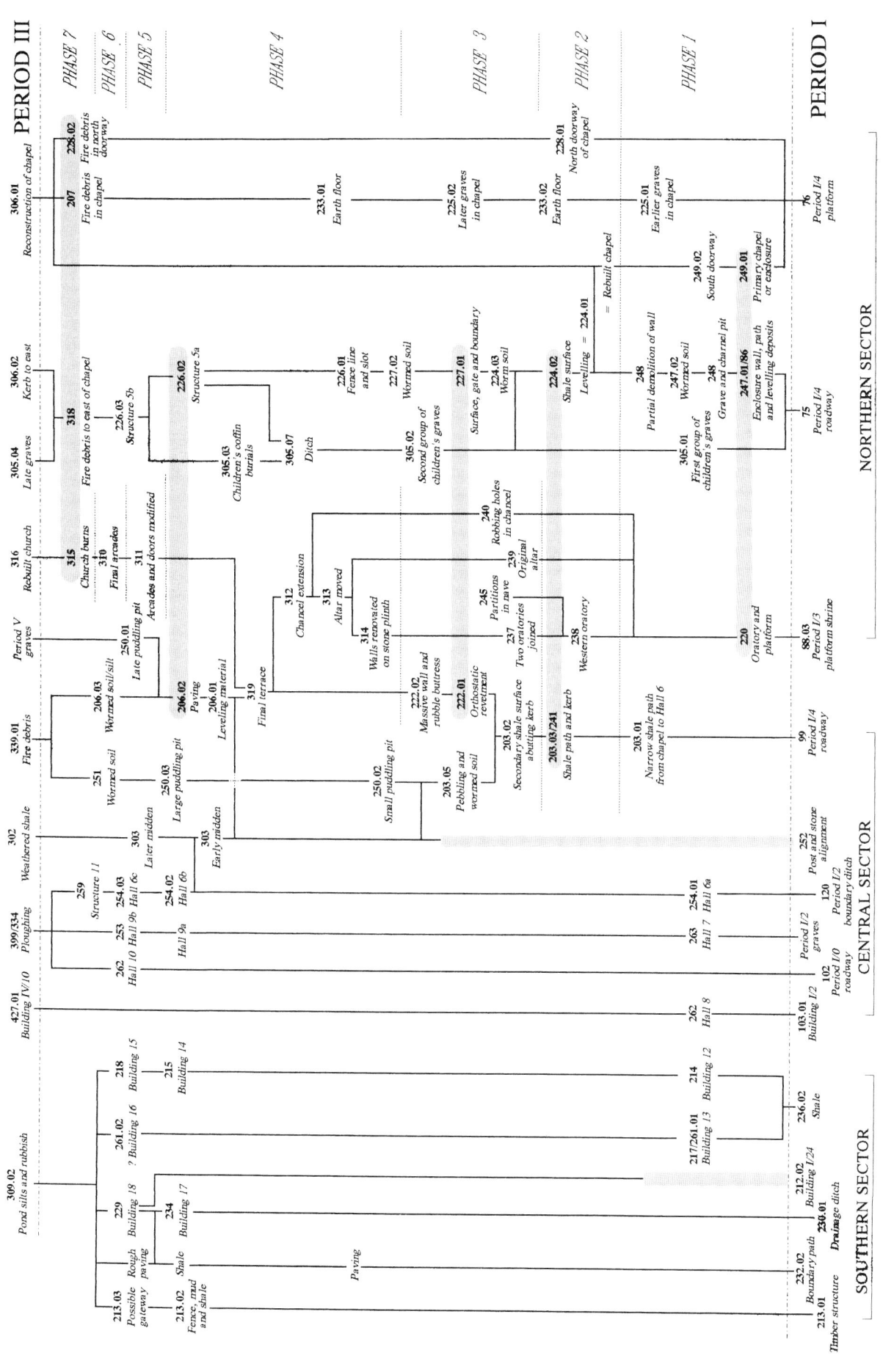

4.2 The stratigraphic sequence in **Period II**.

A stake-built structure (**II/17**, 234) at the foot of the slope included a lath from an oak felled between 756 and 801 AD (pp 130, 595-6). This was replaced by a similar structure (**II/18**, 299) lying slightly to the north, and was followed by renewed flooding which apparently lasted until the eleventh century. The dendro-chronological date suggested the first building was erected in **Phase 4** or **5**, and its successor may thus have pertained to **Phase 5** or **6**.

Finds. The earlier deposits of **Period II** were consistently clean, and almost all of the finds from them can be ascribed to displaced **Period I** debris. The picture changed in the later-eighth/earlier-ninth century when rubbish accumulated in the ground to the south of the ecclesiastical buildings, and changed again in the opening years of **Period III** with the appearance of new artefact types and the debris from a comb-making industry (Table 5.1). The fire of *c*. 845 AD was represented by rich destruction deposits in the church and chapel. Structural debris predominated in the chapel providing valuable information (pp 164-70), but was less evident in the church, although the finds from the floor indicated a range of activities after the removal of the ecclesiastical furnishings at the start of **Phase 7**. Other specialised assemblages included iron-bound timber chest/coffins (pp 412-5) and window glass (pp 326-32) from the chapel and children's graveyard, and the coins, which indicated a zone of commercial activity in the open ground between the halls and the ecclesiastical buildings (pp 351-5, Figures 10.41-43). Other finds, mostly from the unoccupied corridor in the **central sector**, encompassed a range of diagnostic objects, including club-headed pins (pp 363, 418) favoured by Anglo-Saxon women (p 362), and strap ends (pp 373-4), Table 5.1, Figure 10.98). A complementary group of functional objects included iron needles with punched eyes (p 417), iron wall-hooks (p 412) and lead waste (pp 396-7). The finds from the waterlogged deposits at the foot of the slope were disappointingly sparse (Tables 4.24–26) and, though organic materials were preserved, only wood and other botanical remains were recovered.

The assemblages of finds from **Period II** were unusually specialised, and were probably unrepresentative of the range of activities encompassed by the Northumbrian *minster*. This is unsurprising, as the excavated area represented a relatively small fragment of what seems to have been a large, organised settlement, and included part of the ritual area of the site where domestic and industrial debris would have been inappropriate.

Ashy soil quarried from a **Period I** dump of industrial debris (pp 117-8) had been used extensively in the construction of the early buildings in the **northern sector**, and the proportions of finds from various deposits indicated that different dumps or different parts of the same dump had been used. This material had been disturbed repeatedly by later features, displacing tuyere fragments, iron working debris and scrap iron into later deposits. These finds can generally be reassigned to **Period I** with confidence, but the iron objects listed in Table 3.35 may have included artefacts lost in **Period II**.

Architecture. Ancient ground surfaces survived over large parts of the site, and structural evidence was preserved which has allowed the tentative reconstruction of examples of all the building types recorded (Figures 4.4, 6, 8, 12, 23, 28, 31 and 33). The church and chapel are effectively unique, and the halls conform broadly to an architectural tradition which is widespread on Anglo-Saxon sites (James *et al* 1984), but have revealed rare evidence of internal linings and timber bracing. The small buildings seem to have few close parallels but, despite the incompleteness of much of the evidence, displayed distinctive architectural features, identifying them as a coherent group. This group comprised the small buildings in the third range, and related **Period I** and **II** buildings to the south (**I/21**, **I/24**, **II/17** and **II/18**). The plans of eight buildings (**I/21**, **I/24**, **II/12**, **II/13**, **II/14**, **II/15**, **II/17** and **II/18**) are restored in Figure

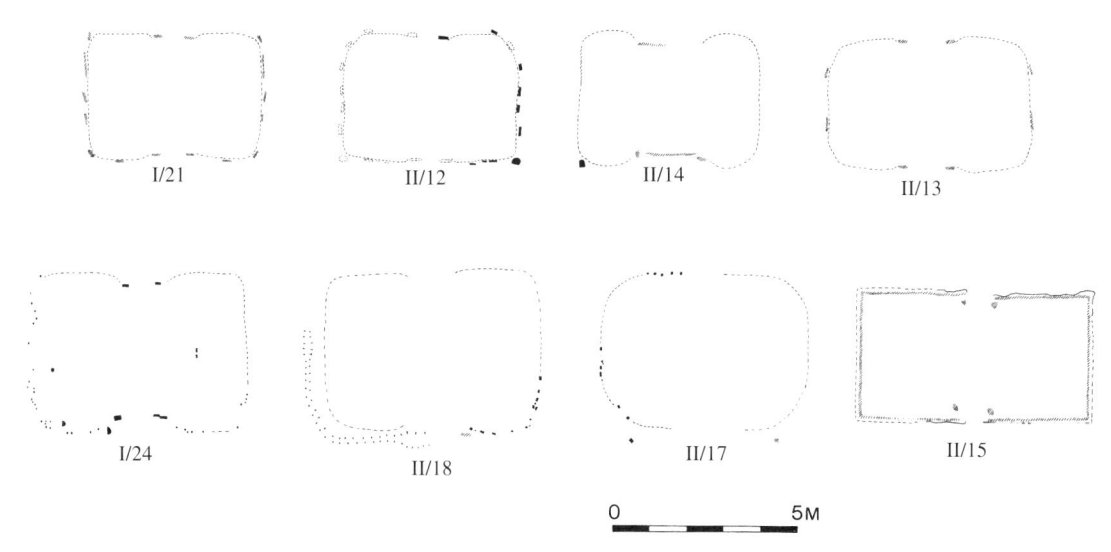

4.3 Reconstructed ground plans of selected small buildings of the eight and earlier-ninth centuries.

4.3, while the surviving construction features are illustrated in Figures 3.42, 3.43, 4.30, 32 and 34, and are described in the appropriate sections of the text. The excavated evidence obscures the uniformity of the buildings which is suggested by conjectural ground plans (Figure 4.3), produced by reconstructing unexcavated parts of buildings and restoring damaged or destroyed elements. Seven of these buildings conform to the same tradition, while the eighth (**II/15**), though resting on a stone sill or plinth, was of comparable scale, and possibly of similar construction above ground. All had (or may have had) opposed inset doorways, composed of vertical planks, in the long walls. The walls of at least three buildings included vertical planks of timber, most commonly recorded on the end walls. Five revealed evidence of continuous wattle walling, sometimes turned in behind the door frames to give a distinctive waisted or dumb-bell plan. Three or four buildings (**II/12, II/14, II/17** and probably **I/24**) had single corner posts lying beyond the curved wattle walling, and large stakes were similarly sited in a fifth (**II/18**). Five had shale surfaces, probably the substrates of unrecognised earth floors, but the interiors were generally featureless, and in contrast to the equivalent small buildings of **Periods I** and **III** and **IV**, with no evidence of hearths or other heating arrangements. Three reconstructions are illustrated in Figure 4.4, although not all the characteristic features are explained. Figures 4.4**a** and **b** show a reconstruction of **Building I/24** with alternative roofing systems. In one (**a**) the roof is supported by paired trusses resting on the opposed door-frames, while the other (**b**) uses a simpler conical arrangement of rafters appropriate to the small size of the building. The weight of the roof in both versions is borne by the wattle walls, the strength of which is increased by the rounded corners. The third reconstruction (**c**) addresses the particular problems posed by **Building II/12** in which a wattle lining was associated with external timbers. The building seems to have been longitudinally asymmetrical with a rounded corner to the north, and a square corner, marked by a free-standing post, to the south (Figures 4.3, 4.30). The timbers on the south side could have supported a wall-plate, but the absence of an equivalent member to the north, argues for a different structural regime, and the wall timbers are accordingly interpreted as rafter supports, while the opposed door frames are again seen as the supports of paired trusses.

The continuing evolution of this building style can be traced throughout **Period III**, although it seems to have been superseded by a similar, but different tradition in **Period IV**. A tentative link with the Anglian monastery at Hartlepool has been identified on the basis of the similarity in the plans of sub-surface features of **Buildings I/21** and **II/12** with Buildings VIII and X at Church Close (p 37, Figure 2.8). The rounded corners revealed by stakes and surface features at Whithorn can also be identified in the surface deposits of Period 2 at Hartlepool (Daniels 1988, Figures 26–9, Plate VIB). These are ascribed to

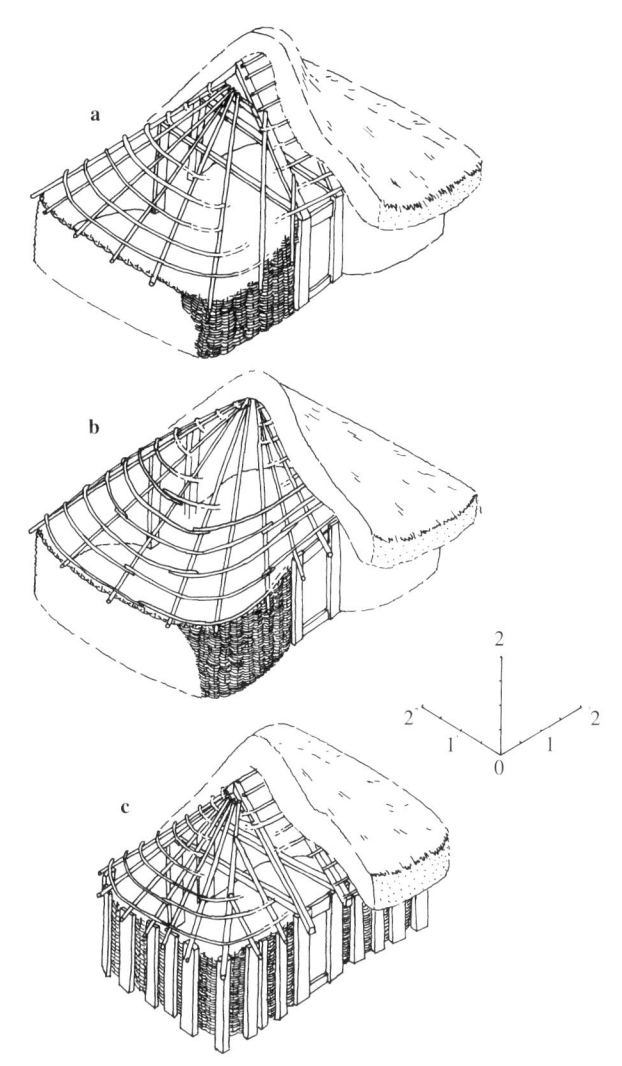

4.4 Speculative isometric reconstructions of **Buildings I/24** (**a** and **b**) and **II/12** (**c**).

the eighth century, and are thus broadly contemporary with the Whithorn structures.

4.2 THE DEVELOPMENT OF THE NORTHUMBRIAN *MINSTER*

Phase 1: Redevelopment

Phase 1 began with an ambitious building programme embracing most of the **Glebe Field** and extending east as far as the **Museum Garden** and possibly beyond (Figure 2.9). Three parallel ranges of buildings were erected, probably as part of a unified, planned development (Figure 4.5). The **northern range** comprised a small timber 'oratory' (1); a stone founded structure (4a) underlying the **Phase 2** burial chapel, but perhaps unroofed at this time; and the **Period I/4** 'shrine' (83, p 115), which probably remained standing. These were enclosed by a stone wall (86/247) turning north to the east of the burial enclosure. A narrow shale path on rubble foundations immediately beyond the wall ran west/east across the area, apparently branching to the north at the east end

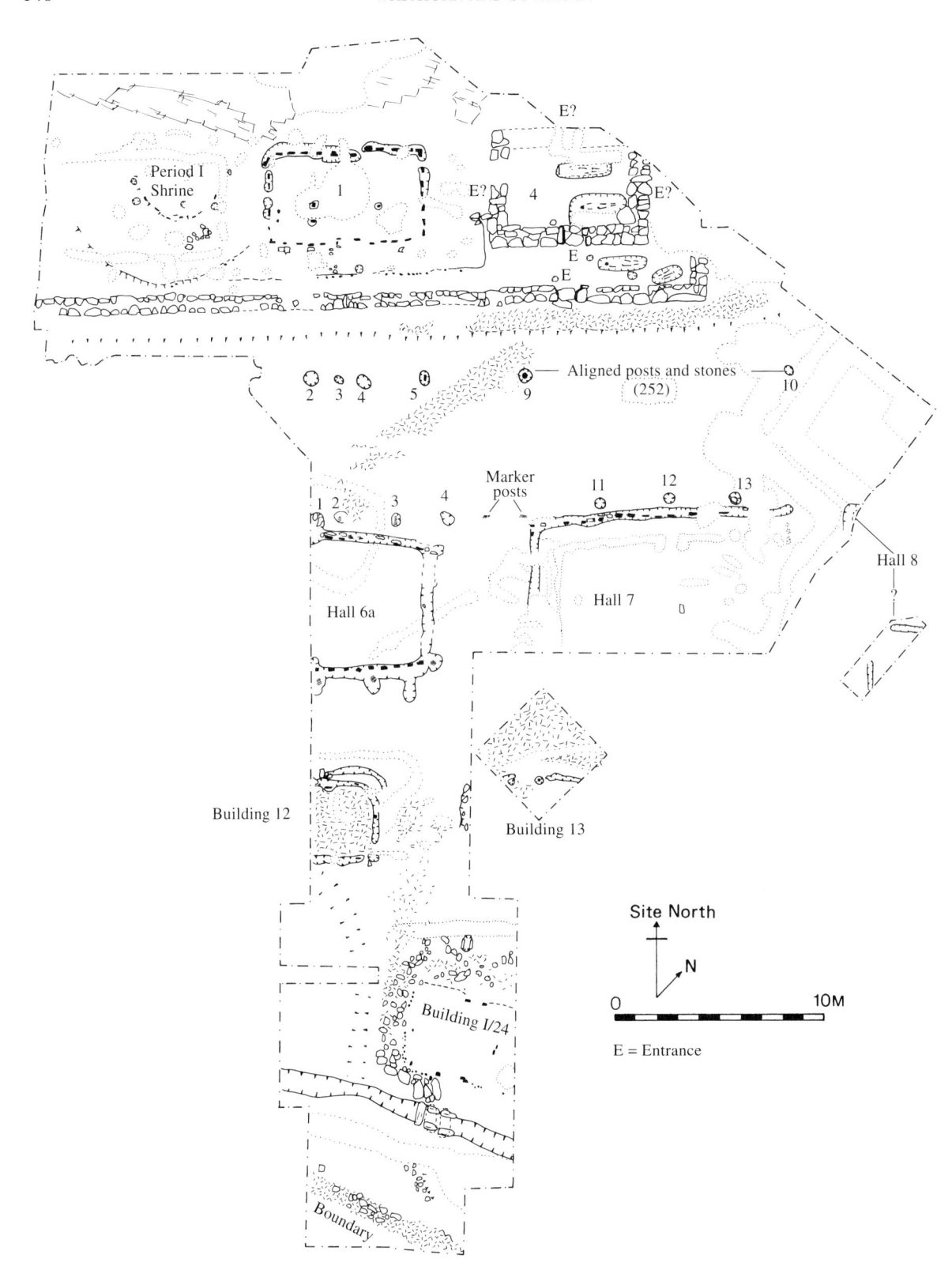

4.5 General plan of earlier **Period II** features encompassing **Phase 1** structures in the **northern sector** and *Stage 1* structures to the south.

of the enclosure. A range of halls was built some 10 m to the south of the enclosure, and a third range of smaller buildings was erected beyond them. **Building I/24** probably remained standing, and the shale path marking the curvilinear outer boundary seems to have continued in use.

The regularity of the planning was a striking feature of these buildings, suggesting the hand of a master architect whose grand design, somewhat matured, is reconstructed in Figure 2.12. Each of the large timber buildings might have taken some two man-years to build (Richard Hallam Pers. Comm.), and we may infer that a large, skilled, work-force was employed for much of this period, and would have been adequately supported by cooks, storekeepers, smiths and other craftsmen. Building processes were strikingly evident in the deposits of **Phases 1** and **2**, giving valuable evidence that the construction of the new *minster* probably spanned a period of several years. The chronological evidence (p 136) indicated that the developments in **Phases 1** and **2** lasted for a brief period of perhaps ten to fifteen years.

Stage 1: redevelopment
Stage 1 saw the construction of the enclosure wall, oratory and burial enclosure, and the preparation, but not completion, of a west–east path beyond (Figure 4.5 and 7). It is likely, though unprovable, that work had yet to start on the halls and other buildings to the south, and that this stage records a brief span of perhaps a year or so.

The primary oratory and platform. The **Phase 1** oratory was built on an extant shelf comprising the remains of **Building I/6** and the **Period I/3** shrine to the west. This was extended southwards by building a rectilinear platform revetted with stakes, which joined the southern edge of the **Period I/4.5** shrine. The eastern end of the platform was revetted with stone, and was keyed into the west wall of the burial enclosure. The platform was built of dumped rubble and shale, starting at the west end and gradually expanding eastwards. Work had already started on the construction of the oratory, and the spoil from the construction slots for the walls in the northern half of the building, was included in the rising platform. The soil to the west of the platform produced vestigial traces of wood shavings and bark, probably from the dressing of the structural timbers. The walls were erected after the platform had been built. The timbers in the northern part of the building were chocked into the construction trenches, but those to the south rested on the surface of the platform and were supported by stones built against their outer sides. Once the walls were complete, the platform, and floor were covered with a thick layer of ashy soil which surrounded the wall timbers, obscuring the construction slots.

The oratory was some 7.5 m long and 4.5 m wide, and was built of regularly-spaced timbers presumably mortised into a wall plate which supported the roof. L-shaped plank impressions in the north-east and south west corners probably represented pairs of narrow planks jointed together. An anomalous square timber at the north-east corner has been ascribed to the original structure, but makes better sense as a new timber inserted when the two oratories were joined in **Phase 3**. The spaces between the wall timbers may have been filled with slightly narrower timbers (*c.* 0.2–0.4 m wide) or narrow panels of wattling. There was, however, no evidence of a daub coating, despite the excellent survival of other deposits, which implies that planks were used. Opposed doorways some 0.5 m wide in the north and south walls had internal plank frames set parallel to the walls with hints of a timber sill in the south door. The doors were aligned with two post sockets on the lip of the platform, and a possible beam slot edged with stone on the outer edge of the path to the south. These could have supported a wooden stair leading south from the platform, and framed by the large posts cutting Grave I/72 (pp 106-7). The rough foundations of the path were unsurfaced to the east of the putative stair, suggesting that the original design was not completed.

A tentative reconstruction of the building is presented in Figure 4.6. The consistent size of the planking in the side and end walls indicates that both were load bearing, and argues for a hipped roof structure supported by trusses to either side of the doorway. This inference is supported by the locations of the arcade posts inserted in **Phase 3,** which followed a different arrangement from those flanking the **Phase 2** oratory, for which a gable roof has been postulated. The weight of the roof would have been spread by the wall-plates, allowing the relocation of the doorway in **Phase 2** (p 144), and the removal of part of the west wall in **Phase 3** (pp 146-8). The building conforms to the double-square ground plan prevailing in related Anglo-Saxon buildings, and falls within the sub-group in which the door width is added to each of the flanking squares (James *et al* 1984, 186).

The apron of the earlier shrine had been obscured by the construction of the new building platform, but the central timber setting probably remained standing for a while, and paving was laid beyond it. This paving was subsequently overlain by a thin spread of yellow clay that sealed the impressions of the arc of timbers which must already have been removed. The clay was similar to builders' debris from the construction of the **Phase 2** chapel, and, like that, may have been dumped at the beginning of **Phase 2**.

The primary burial enclosure. The walls of the **Phase 1** burial enclosure (249) were demolished to

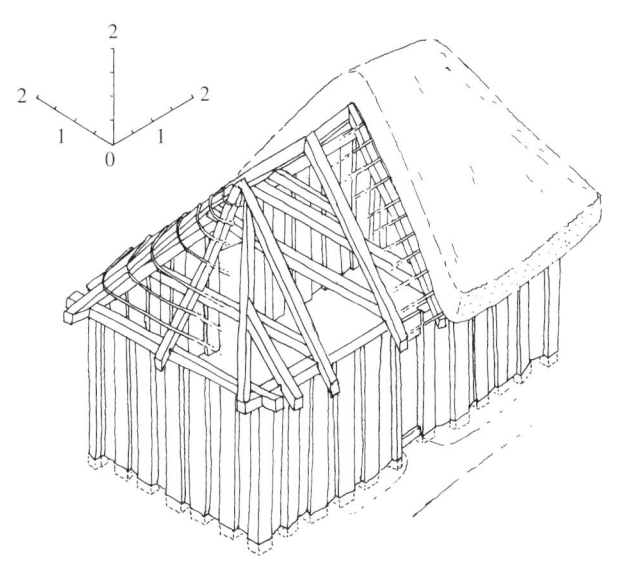

4.6 Isometric reconstruction of **Period I/1** oratory.

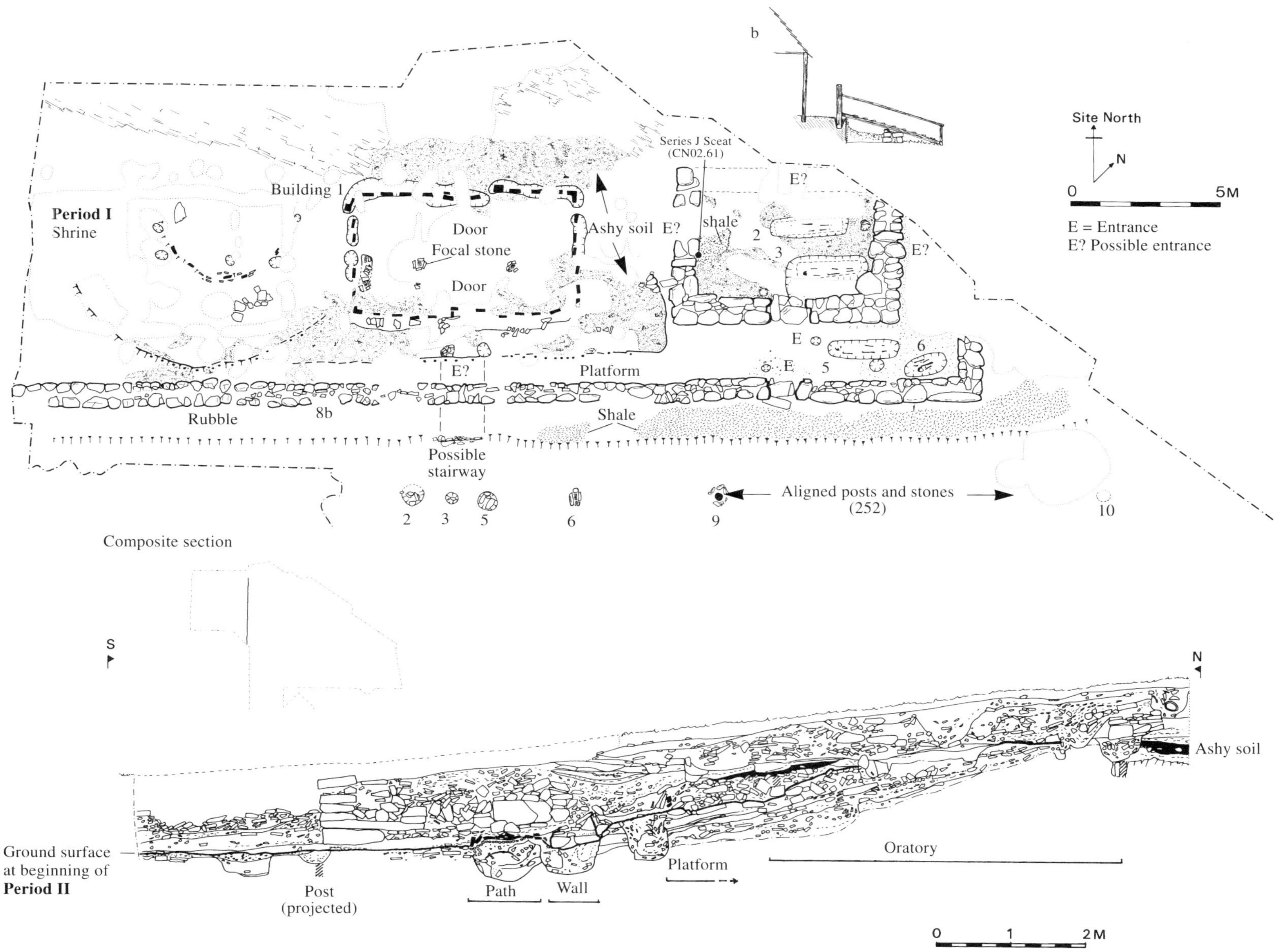

4.7 The **Period II/1** structures in the **northern sector**, displaced **Period I** metalworking debris ('ashy soil', 110) and speculative reconstruction of stair to **Building 1 (b)**.

foundation level and rebuilt at the start of **Phase 2**. The remains comprised the stone foundations of west, south and east walls, and a vestigal hollow in the rock indicating the position of a north wall (Figure 4.7). Single courses of large stones survived in the outer faces of the foundations, and up to three courses of the inner face were found on the south side. The foundations were thus of similar construction to the contemporary enclosure wall (see below). Through-stones in the foundations were matched by similar stones in the enclosure wall, and may also have marked entrances. Shallow foundation trenches had been dug for the south-west and south-east corners, but the remainder of the building lay directly over the **Period I/4.5** platform (76, Figure 3.32). Stones reveting the north end of the oratory platform had been keyed into the west wall, and the massive granite boulder overlying two **Period I/3.1** graves was built into the south-east corner (Figures 4.7 and 3.29). Whilst this may have been a sensible solution to an immovable obstacle, it may reflect the incorporation of an earlier monument for ritual motives. After the walls had been built, the interior of the structure was levelled with ashy soil, and surfaced with shale. The Southumbrian sceat (CN02.61) was recovered from a fragment of this surface abutting the west wall (pp 136, 335). The rest of the large group of finds from the building seem to have been derived from the displaced metalworking debris, and are included in the material listed in Table 3.35. Three burials in the eastern half of the enclosure (**Graves II/2, 3** and **4b**) probably pertained to this phase (pp 167-9).

The construction of the clay walls of the **Phase 2** chapel was revealed by spilled clay and the sockets for shuttering or scaffolding (pp 165), but there was no comparable evidence from the early building, and the character and height of the superstructure supported by the stone foundations was uncertain. The structural similarities with the enclosure wall indicated that it was not designed as a roofed building, and that the stone walls were relatively low, and had perhaps encased the base of a timber or wattle parapet. The three through-stones possibly marked symmetrical entrances in the west, south and east walls, and a similar entrance in the north wall may be inferred.

The enclosure wall and path. The enclosure wall (86/247.01) seems to have been built after the oratory was complete, as it overlay scattered metalworking debris (Table 3.36), which was presumably spilled while being carried to the new platform. The structure of the wall was somewhat enigmatic, and the excavators of the eastern and western parts drew different conclusions, perhaps because the wall was different in the two areas. The eastern part of the wall (247.01) had an outer face of large rocks, and an inner face of smaller stones with up to five courses surviving. Patches of alluvial clay survived in the core of the wall, and small river pebbles flanking the wall had probably eroded from it. It thus seems to have been built around an earth and clay core, and the stonework had tended to slump inwards as this eroded. This core could have supported a breastwork of planks or wattles, but no certain evidence was recorded. Demolition and decay deposits (248, p 144) included numerous fragments of 'clastic lime', plaster, and pieces of greywacke crusted with calcium carbonate, while slabs of sand indicated more plaster from which the lime had leached. These finds suggested that the outer face of the wall, or perhaps the breastwork, had been coated in a lime plaster, although none survived *in situ*. The wall was broken by a paved entrance aligned with the south entrance of the burial enclosure, and perhaps closed by a gate marked by a single post-hole. The western part of the wall (86) had a similar gap between the inner and outer faces, and more courses were again preserved on the inner face. It is likely that this part of the wall was never completed, and that the gap between the faces formed the seating for a timber breastwork. The clearest evidence for this hypothetical fence was presented by the **Phase 2** deposits which showed a clear break on this line. Rough rubble foundations marked a narrow path along the south side of the wall. The rubble was covered by a surface of shale in the eastern part of the area, but this was missing further west, and the path may not have been completed. The rubble and shale swung around the eastern angle of the wall, indicating that a path had originally run northwards along the east side of the enclosure.

Stage 2: modification and use
Stage 2 was represented by two burials to the south of the burial enclosure (Figures 4.7 and 29b), and possibly by the first phase of the children's graveyard to the east (pp 170-1). A new shale path was laid leading from the entrance through the enclosure to the north door of **Hall 6**, indicating that the range of halls had now been built.

A shallow grave between the chapel and the enclosure contained the remains of a middle-aged adult, probably buried in a log coffin (246, **Grave II/5**, SK 716). The grave fill produced fifty-five quartz pebbles, fifteen granite pebbles and a plough pebble. There was no obvious source for these in the underlying deposits, and they may have been scattered intentionally over the grave, as further examples survived on its southern edge (Figure 4.9). An adjacent shallow pit (246, **Grave II/6**) produced disarticulated human remains arranged in a loose bundle. These bones could have been displaced from a **Period I** grave, and reinterred perfunctorily in what was perhaps hallowed ground, but later groups of disarticulated human bones indicated unusual burial practices, of which this may have been an early example (pp 169, 189). The finds included two glass beads (GS03.13 and 14), and a perforated flake of phyllite (SE31.4) which might have been an amulet or bead. Both features were covered with a layer of worm-sorted soil.

A yellow shale path led from the entrance in the enclosure to the doorway of Hall 6 (Figure 4.5), establishing a stratigraphic link between the **northern** and **middle ranges**, and hinting that the halls had been completed some time after the ecclesiastical structures. This path was slightly later than the original east-west pathway, but probably preceded the blocking of the entrance and the dismantling of the wall in *Stage 3*, and indicated that access to the ecclesiastical buildings was obtained through the opposed entrances of the burial enclosure, perhaps in preference to the putative stairs (p 141) leading to the 'oratory' (1).

Stage 3: modification and decay
Stage 3 saw various modifications to the east part of the enclosure. The entrance was blocked with new walling, and the enclosed area to the south of the burial enclosure was covered with a thick layer of ashy soil. The upper part of the wall was demolished at roughly the same time, scattering small stones, plaster and soil over the path to the south and the ground to the east.

Phase 2: Redesign

Phase 2 (Figure 4.9) saw the comprehensive remodelling of the ecclesiastical buildings, and the enclosure and paths to the south. The principal events were the erection of a new oratory (**2**) to the west of the original building (**1**), and of a clay-walled chapel (**4**) on the remains of the **Phase 1** burial enclosure. The doorways of the original oratory seem to have been moved to the west, and a new wider west/east path was laid to the south. There was no evidence of change elsewhere, and these new buildings may be seen as a stage in the continuing development of the ecclesiastical precinct, and as minor modifications to the original design. They probably pertained to the 720s or early 730s (p 136).

The second oratory. The new oratory (**2**, 238) was built over the **Period I/4** shrine (83), some 2.3 m to the west of the original oratory. The site did not need much preparation, as most of the building occupied the platform dug into the slope for **Building I/7** and the apron of the **Period I/4** shrine. The building was slightly larger (8.2 × 4.5 m) than the **Phase 1** oratory, but otherwise of similar design although the doorways were less clearly defined. The construction sequence was relatively clear. Stave walls were erected with the planks set on the inner edges of discontinuous slots, and chocked with blocks of packing stones, similar to those on the south side of the earlier building. The ground to the south was then levelled up with rubble, apparently contained by the breastwork of the **Phase 1** enclosure, and a rough shale surface was laid to either side of the south wall. A shallow slot that probably contained a timber screen separating a relatively narrow aisle to the south from a slightly wider area to the north, may have been erected at this stage, but other internal features seem to have pertained to **Phase 3** (p 148). A tentative reconstruction of the **Phase 2** oratory is

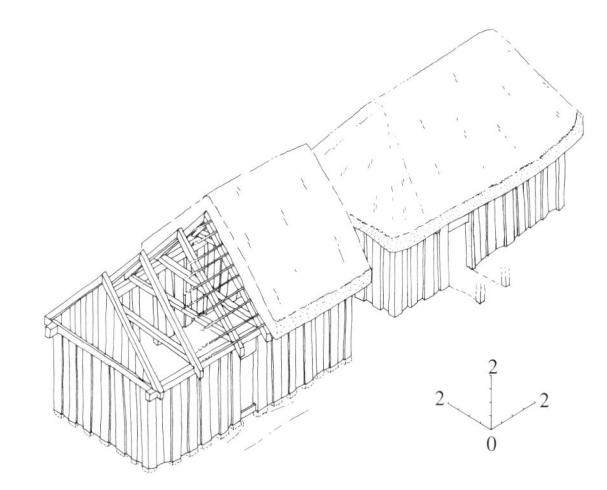

4.8 Isometric reconstruction of **Buildings 1** and **2** in **Period II/2**.

presented in Figure 4.8. The new building conformed to the same double-square plan as the **Phase 1** structure, but has been reconstructed with a gabled roof (Figure 4.8) to illustrate a coherent alternative to the hipped structure proposed for the building to the east. This speculation is supported by the positions of the arcade posts erected in **Phase 3**, which probably included paired settings (1/*8 and 4/11) flanking the gables (Figure 4.10).

The burial chapel. The new burial chapel (**4b**, 224) had clay walls resting on stone founds, and had at least two glass windows, one at the south end of the east wall, and the other at the east end of the south wall. It was surprisingly stable, and survived without major modification until *c*. 845 AD when it was severely damaged by fire (p 162). The construction, maintenance, use and destruction of the building formed a coherent unit spanning six phases (**2–7**), and is described below (pp 164-70). The chapel was built at the beginning of **Phase 2**, and was complete before the new shale path was laid to the south.

Paths, steps and boundaries. A new wider shale path (241, 203.02/.03) was laid to the south of the buildings in the **north range**. Part of the south side of the path was bordered with small stones which may have been laid against a light fence to the north of the alignment of posts and stones (252). The north side of the path oversailed the basal course of the outer face of the **Phase 1** enclosure, and was perhaps edged by a fence or breastwork. This putative fence-line was broken by two flights of steps leading to the platform and buildings to the north. The western flight was aligned with the east end of the new oratory, and comprised a lower tread of four paving stones, with two paving stones set into the slope to the north. A small cupped greywacke slab (SE49.3) lay beside these steps, with the hollow upwards and could have been used as a container for blessed water for ritual ablutions by people entering the ecclesiastical precinct on special occasions. It is one of a small group of similar objects from the same

CHAPTER 4

4.9 The **Period II/2** buildings, paths and fences in the **northern sector**.

general area and time (p 462). The eastern flight was more complex, and probably led to a new doorway in the south wall of the original oratory. The stairs were indicated by paired double post-holes linked by a paved tread on the edge of the **Phase 1** platform, and by a short stretch of stonework built over the **Phase 1** enclosure, which may have supported a timber stair with a gate at its head. It was aligned with new opposed doorways in the north and south walls of the original oratory, which were perhaps inserted at this time. These doorways continued in use until the beginning of **Period III/2**, and later renewals of the sockets had removed most of the evidence of the original features. The positions of the **Phase 2** doors were indicated by vestigial sockets for porches, subsequently framed by arcade posts in **Phase 3**. The **Phase 1** doorways may have been blocked by timbers slotted into the extant door frames. The stairway lay on a common axis linking the new doors of the original oratory with the opposed doorways of **Hall 6** and **Building 12** to the south, and passing between the large posts at the head and foot of Grave I/72. There was no evidence of a linking path, and this alignment perhaps provided a vista, rather than a route of access.

A shale surface (224.02), laid in front of the new chapel, extended to the inner edge of the partly-demolished enclosure wall and the outer edge of its northern return. This may have been bounded by an insubstantial fence dividing it from a distinct surface (203.03) immediately to the south, which overlay the demolition deposits, and formed the eastern part of the main pathway. The children's graveyard probably continued in use to the west of this possible fence.

Phase 3: The Church

Phase 3 (Figure 4.10) saw the modification to the two wooden oratories to form a bicameral timber church some 17.9 m long and 4.4–4.5 m wide. The west wall of the original oratory survived as a screen separating an eastern *chancel* from a western *nave*, and straddling a stone feature identified cautiously as an altar. The new building was flanked by large vertical timbers forming external arcades, and shale paths were laid on both sides of the building. The building platform was extended to the south, and contained by a stone revetment built over the remains of the **Phase 1** enclosure wall. The **Phase 2** pathway may have continued in use for a short while, but was covered by a rubble buttress when the revetment proved unstable. The revetment angled north towards the west wall of the chapel, where a timber gate controlled access between the new church and the open space and buildings to the south. The gateway was linked to stone lines marking a boundary to the south of the chapel, and a parallel fence to the north bounded the children's graveyard, which now extended to the east wall of the chapel. There was no evidence of change elsewhere, and the halls and small building beyond probably remained standing without needing major maintenance. The **Phase 3** deposits produced few finds other than displaced **Period I** debris used in the original construction of the ecclesiastical buildings. The phase, perhaps, began in *c*. 735 AD and lasted until *c*. 760 AD or slightly before (p 136).

Joining the two oratories. The two original oratories were probably of timber-frame construction with roofs supported on wall plates (pp 141, 144). The two buildings were not precisely aligned and the structural problems of uniting them are addressed by the reconstruction drawing in Figure 4.12. The alterations involved the dismantling of the eastern gable of the western oratory, the insertion of a new south doorway in the gap between the two buildings, and the construction of a linking roof. The removal of the gable was indicated by small pits (**a** and **b**) dug to remove the timbers in the south part of the wall, while two posts (**c** and **d**) immediately to the east, were probably inserted before it was dismantled, to support a truss jointed to the wall-plates of the north and south walls. Most of the west wall of the east building was left standing, and the wall plate was probably not affected, although the central wall timbers were removed, providing access between the nave and chancel, and allowing the construction of the altar in the gap. The new south doorway was well preserved, and was framed symmetrically by two posts in the south arcade. The door frame was probably mortised into a new wall plate lapped onto the end walls of the original buildings. External planks at 90° to the wall line have been interpreted as the supports for a gabled porch over the door. The evidence from the north side of the building was more problematical. A large square timber abutting the corner of the original oratory was probably inserted at this time to support a new wall-plate lapped onto the new truss to the west, and mortised onto a new wall timber in the gap between the two buildings. Two timbers inserted into the north east corner of the original oratory looked like one side of a door, but access would have been impeded by the adjacent arcade post, and they were probably replacement wall timbers. A narrow doorway in the west part of the new wall was indicated by a featureless post hole, and would have opened onto the gap between arcade posts 4 and 5. The opposed **Phase 2** doorways in the north and south walls of the western oratory probably continued to provide separate entrances to the chancel.

Internal features. The floor of the chancel had been severely disturbed, and revealed little evidence of internal furnishings. The **Period I** pillar stone was probably the principal ritual focus and, though visible from the nave, was still perhaps sacrosanct. Two large featureless pits (1 and 2, 240) at the east end of the building, dug at an unknown time in **Phase 3**, lay on the perimeter of the underlying shrine (pp 102-3), and possibly marked the positions of stone

147

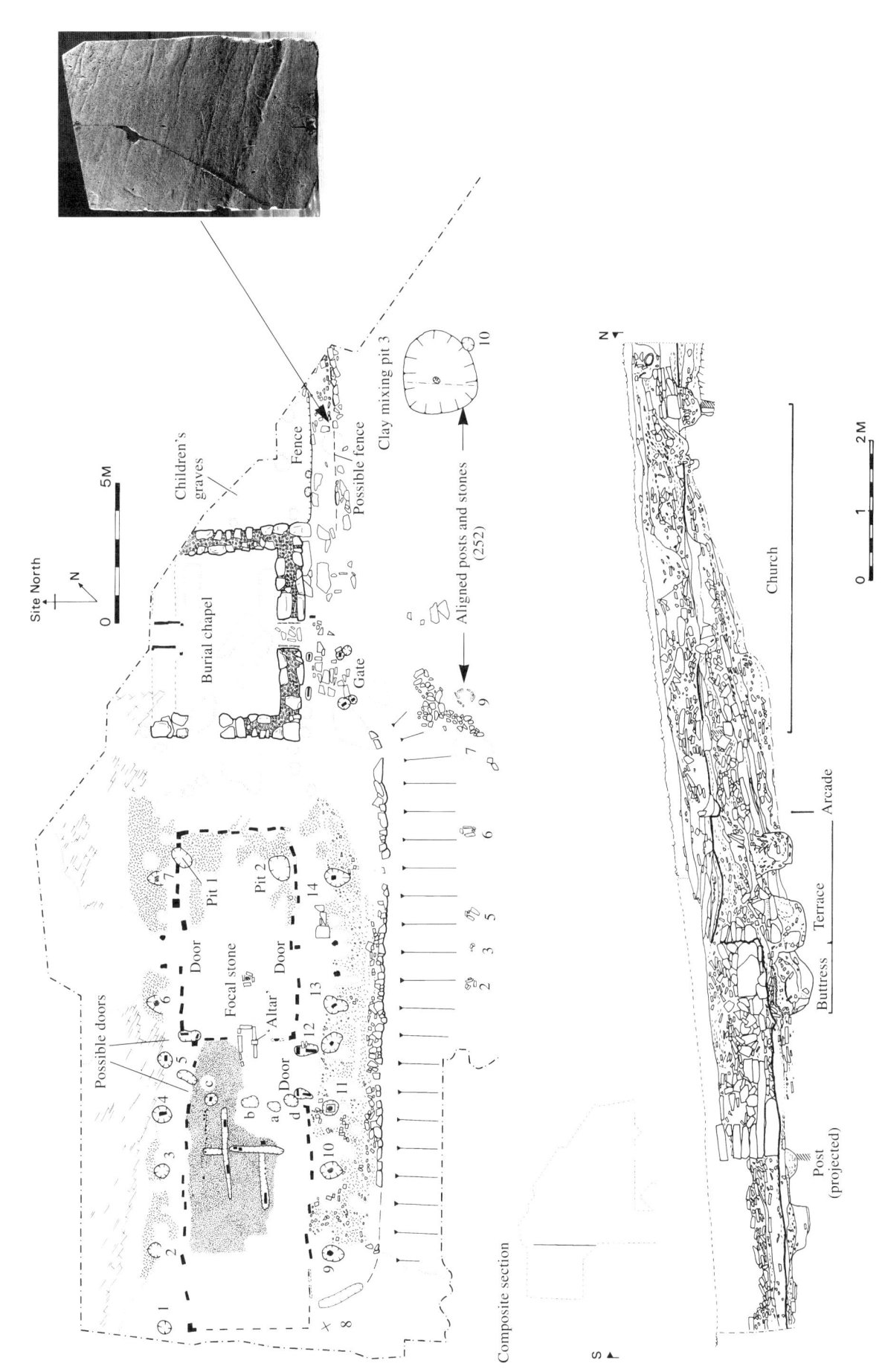

4.10 The **Period II/3** buildings, fences, paths and related features in the **northern sector**.

monuments moved, perhaps to the nave, during the reorganisation of the church. A large part of the floor of the nave survived, and revealed three narrow slots marking timber furnishings. The two earlier slots divided the nave longitudinally into three roughly equal segments, and were aligned with the south wall of the nave and the arcade beyond, though lying obliquely to the long axis of the church. Casts of vertical planks were identified in both slots, while packing stones indicated that they had contained continuous timber screens. The southern screen may have been erected in **Phase 2**. A later transverse slot respected the northern screen, but was cut through the southern slot. It possibly contained a screen, although the central part may have been a door, with a door post to the north and a timber sill to the south. A slight shelf associated with a line of stakeholes to the north of the north screen, respected the transverse slot, and may have been the remains of a secondary wattle screen. The screen timbers emerged through a shale surface which abutted the north wall and extended eastwards, abutting the north side of the 'altar' and the screen to the north. The shale had not been trampled and was probably the prepared base of an earth floor.

The 'altar' (239) was framed by the screen separating the chancel and nave, and would have been accessible from both chambers. It was dismantled in **Phase 4**, and parts of it were probably reused in the new altar built to the east. The surviving features (Figure 4.11a) comprised chockstones, stone holes, and stones knocked flat to form a level surface in **Phase 4** (Figure 4.11b). These features overlay the sockets of two timbers removed from the west wall of the **Phase 1** oratory, and an earlier socket forming the north-west corner of the **Period I** shrine (88.03). The floor of the altar was slightly sunken. An incomplete, speculative reconstruction (Figure 4.11c) infers that two vertical side slabs had been knocked flat in **Phase 4**, while an end slab, potentially fitting the original socket, had been moved to the new altar. These features might have formed a raised stone box, possibly with a table supported by the end slabs. The interpretation of this damaged feature as an altar is necessarily speculative, and depends principally upon the subsequent development of this part of the building, and the presumed ritual role of the inferred **Period I** pillar (pp 45, 102).

The timber arcades. **Phase 3** saw the erection of the first of a sequence of timber arcades flanking the north and south walls of the church. Most of the posts were replaced in later phases, disturbing the original features, but successive surfaces of shale and regular spacing patterns provided sufficient evidence to disentangle the sequence of posts (Figures 4.10, 13, 14, 19 and 20). Two relatively undamaged **Phase 3** sockets preserved the impressions of vertical circular or sub-circular timbers (*c.* 0.25–0.3 m diameter), and the remaining posts may have been similar. The sockets of the south arcade were cut into the slope beyond the church, and had level 'tails' to the south, indicating that the timbers were manoeuvred into place horizontally, before being hoisted up to the vertical. This would have allowed the prefabrication of horizontal tie beams linking the tops of the posts, and the absence of massive packing stones in the sockets indicated that they had supported a rigid structure, and did not have to counteract lateral thrust. All the sockets had basal padstones, and a stack of stones in one probably compensated for a miscalculation when digging the socket or preparing the timber. The bases of the posts must have been temporarily secured until the revetment to the south was complete, at which point they were encased by the rubble dumped behind it. The sockets of the northern arcade posts were shallower and difficult to identify among the numerous later sockets, but two had well-defined ramps to the north, indicating that these posts were erected in the same fashion as those in the south arcade.

The two arcades were parallel, and comprised fourteen paired posts (1/*8, 2/9, 3/10, 4/11, 5/12, 6/13, 7/14), of which *8 is a conjectural timber in a severely truncated area at the south-west corner of the building. The arcade posts remained in roughly the same positions until **Phase 6**, and the same numbering scheme is used for the replacement timbers and their sockets dug in **Phases 4** and **5**. The northern arcade was aligned with the north side of the burial chapel, and the southern arcade with a possible fence line to the south of the children's graveyard. Both encompassed the porches of the opposed chancel doorways, while the south arcade framed the new door into the nave. The western part of the church fitted neatly within this frame, but the

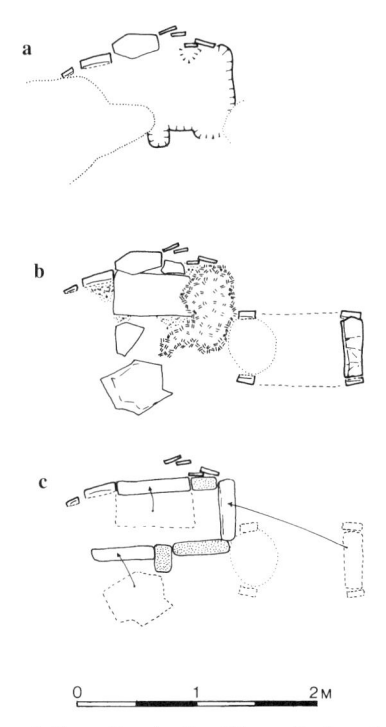

4.11 The putative altar in the **Phase 3** church. **a** Surviving stone holes and chock stones. **b** The dismantled **Phase 3** altar and its **Phase 4** replacement. **c** Reconstruction.

eastern part was markedly skewed, perhaps providing a covered approach to the south chancel door. The arcades were arranged differently in respect of the original buildings. The western building was framed by four pairs of posts, including two aligned with the gables, while the eastern building was framed by two pairs of posts. These differences could reflect appropriate responses to the gabled and hipped roofs postulated in the reconstructions in Figures 4.6 and 8. The last post pair (5 and 12) lay immediately west of the west wall of the eastern oratory, and was perhaps related to the new roof truss inserted when the buildings were joined. The arcades were built of large vertical timbers which probably supported a rigid superstructure and, while their foundations could have supported a considerable weight, they do not seem to have been required to resist thrust, and were

east end, but these could have been compensated for by adjusting the thickness of the thatch. The shuttered window in the nave wall is based on iron fittings and window glass recorded in the **Phase 7** fire debris on the north side of the building (Figure 4.21b, Table 4.7, pp 162-4). The reconstruction has nevertheless been relatively simple to devise, and the features excavated in the central part of the building mark essential foundations for a practical structural assembly.

The terrace and features to the east. The remodelling of the church ended with the construction of a level terrace revetted by a stone wall with curving terminals to the east and west (222.01). The revetment was constructed on a ledge cutting into the stump of the **Phase 1** enclosure wall and the edge of the **Phase 2** path beyond, and so

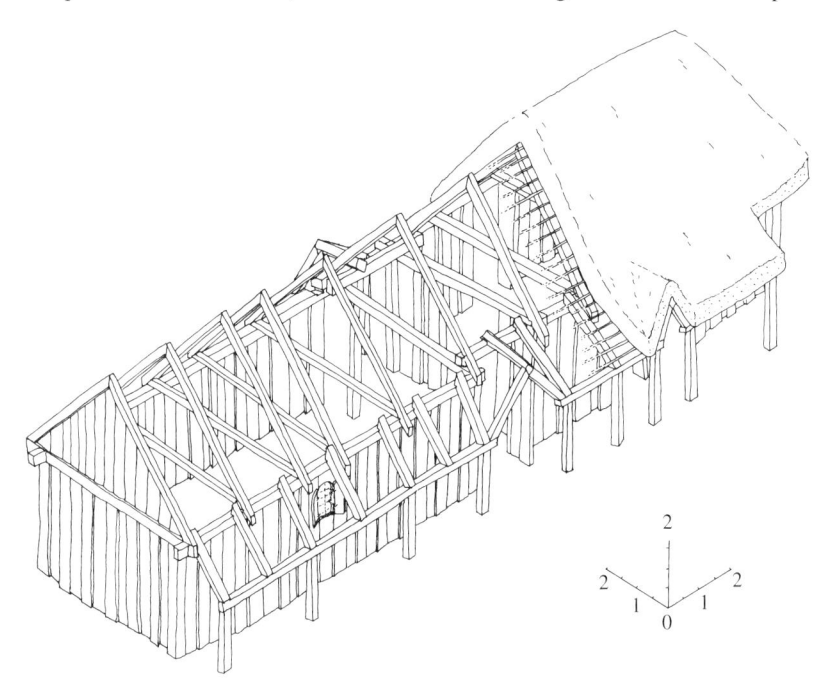

4.12 Isometric reconstruction of the **Phase 3** church.

thus unlikely to have been buttresses. The most probable structural role is as arcades carrying the weight of extended eaves, and so protecting the load-bearing timber walls from moisture, and hence decay. They could, however, have had a complementary, less-functional role as colonnades framing the church and outlining vistas within the *minster*.

The **Phase 3** church is reconstructed in Figure 4.12, which opts for a functional interpretation of the arcades. The weight of the roof is still borne by the wall-plates and plank walls, but the adjacent ends of the original oratories are now covered by a single roof carried by simple trusses. An alternative roofing system based on light Romanesque trusses is equally feasible. The asymmetry of the original buildings and the south-eastern arcade posts is reflected by slight irregularities in the pitch of the roof and eaves at the

preserving the line of the **Phase 1** boundary. The basal course comprised large stone slabs set on edge interspersed with poorly-built dry-stone walling. This was overlain by further dry-stone work, while the space behind was filled with rubble and shale as the revetment rose, burying the sockets of the arcade posts. This levelling material was capped with a rough shale surface extending from the revetment to the wall of the church, and a complementary shale surface was laid to the north of the church. An area of finer shale and a patch of paving between the south arcade and the east end of the chancel may have been the west end of a path linked to the similar surface in front of the burial chapel. The curved east end of the revetment led to a timber gateway immediately to the west of the chapel door, which was aligned with the south arcade. Two lines of stones to the east revealed a boundary (227.01) on the same line. The northern stone line had a straight southern edge possibly marking a fence or timber sill, while the southern line comprised larger stones dipping to the north. The form of this boundary was uncertain and it might have been a simple fence or an elaborated jointed structure continuing the line of the south arcade eastwards. A fragmentary paved path between the boundary and the children's graveyard, included a thin greywacke slab decorated with festoons of small compass-drawn circles (SE14:20, Figures 4.10 and 10.108).

Stage 2
Essential repairs. The orthostatic construction of the revetment was inappropriate for its role, and it began to lean outwards, opening crevasses in the shale surface, and threatening the stability of the south arcade, and potentially the church. This seems to have prompted the construction of a new and far more substantial revetment, but the project was abandoned before the new wall was completed, perhaps before it had risen above the first course. The new revetment was represented by shallow foundations cutting the **Phase 2** path, and an incomplete basal course of massive rocks. These were butted to the south by a bank of clay, possibly intended as a ramp up which the second course of rocks was to have been dragged. The partly-built wall seems to have been dismantled after the plan was changed. The smaller rocks were apparently removed, but the largest were left in place. The space behind the new wall was subsequently filled with a bank of rubble which served to stabilise the sagging revetment. Paving skirting the east end of this bank indicated a new pathway leading from the burial chapel to the north door of **Hall 6**, and passing between two of the boundary markers.

Finds. The **Phase 3** deposits produced a number of important objects (Table 4.2) although most of the finds were derived from displaced **Period I** metalworking debris. The dark green vessel sherd came from the western socket of the south door in the nave. It belongs to a Northern European or Scandinavian tradition of glass making, and the possible parallels from Britain are all from Anglo-Saxon sites (pp 314-5). It perhaps came from a vessel broken in **Phase 1** or **2**, and possibly used in one of the two oratories. The silver mount came from the east end of the foundation trench for the revetment wall, and could have originated in the rich debris that accumulated at the end of **Period I** (pp 115-7, 398). The ornament is paralleled on the leather binding of the Stonyhurst Gospels, and the mount may thus date to the late-seventh century. The ingot mould and Group A vessel sherd came from shale surfaces, but were potentially displaced from **Period I** deposits. The finds from the church included only three nails and no iron structural fittings, suggesting that trenails were used in the extensive joinery work at the start of the phase. The only other finds that may have been contemporary with the building were five retouched flints and a needle from the shale to the south of the church.

A sherd from a dark green seventh–ninth century glass vessel with bichrome rod ornament (GS01:1)
A sherd of wheel-decorated Group A glass (V2)
A silver mount with interlaced ornament, possibly for a scabbard or sheath (SR10)
An iron needle with a punched eye (IN39:9)
A sandstone slab with six ovoid ingot moulds and a small compass-drawn design (SE45:3)

Table 4.2: Select finds from **Phase 3** contexts.

Access and observance. The **Phase 3** revetment was cut into the **Phase 2** path which was completely blocked by the new wall and stone bank in *Stage 2*. The principal access route to the **Phase 3** church seems to have been the paved path running eastwards from the south door of the chancel. The south arcade perhaps marked a notional southern boundary to this path, while the gateway and putative fence presented a more practical barrier to the east. This could be interpreted as a segregated access route within the ecclesiastical precinct for the clergy approaching the chancel, but no independent route can be identified for others to reach the nave. The gateway seems to have controlled access to the ecclesiastical buildings from the ground to the south, but the absence of linking pathways suggested this was of limited importance. It is interesting that it did not open directly onto the south doorway of the chapel, which seems subsequently to have been an important route into the ecclesiastical precinct from the ground to the south. The shale surrounding the church indicated that this area was accessible, but the revetment may have blocked access from the south-west. A second west/east path probably ran along the outer side of the north arcade and the north wall of the chapel. Access between the ecclesiastical buildings and the ground to the south thus seems to have been limited during this phase, and the principal entrance to the ecclesiastical precinct may have lain further to the east.

The internal arrangements of the church continued to focus upon the stone pillar in the chancel, and its importance was now enhanced by visibility from the nave. Other monuments may have been moved, perhaps to the nave, at this time. The median position of the altar is paralleled in other early churches (p 45) although its orientation is unusual. The screens in the nave would have constricted a relatively small space, but possibly divided the congregation according to sex or status.

Phase 4: Renovation and Repair

Phase 4 saw a major programme of redesign and repair to the church, which was probably occasioned by the decay of the wall timbers, and also saw the relocation of the altar and the extension of the chancel. The terrace was enlarged and enclosed by a carefully-built stone revetment probably capped by a parapet wall (Figure 4.14). Coins from rubbish strewn beyond the wall, indicated that it was completed by *c.* 760 AD (p 136), and indicated a link with a pit to the east, which was used to mix clay for the repair of the burial chapel (pp 166, 353). A tentative correlation of the ecclesiastical buildings with those to the south is presented in Figure 4.16, which reconstructs the settlement plan after the completion of the renovations. There were virtually no stratigraphic links between the buildings in the **central** and **southern sectors**, but the inferred plan is supported by common alignments identified in Figure 4.1b. A possible pathway leading from the old, and seems to have required major repairs occasioned by the decay of the walls. Earth-set timbers are prone to decay at ground level, where alternate wetting and drying provides an ideal environment for insects, fungi and other biological activity. This seems to have endangered the church, and a radical remedy was adopted, in which the wall timbers were trimmed slightly above ground

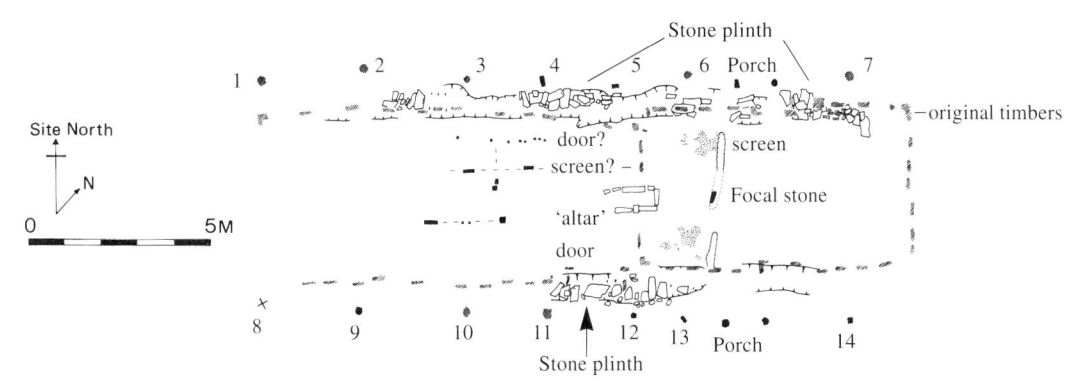

4.13 The stone plinths inserted below the church walls during repairs at the beginning of **Phase 4**.

chapel to the outer boundary, and passing between **Halls 6b** and **9**, seems to have joined a path immediately within the fenced perimeter. The alignment of posts and stones to the south of the ecclesiastical buildings seems to have been depleted at this time, although part of this boundary was now marked by the new terrace and parapet wall. The post sockets cutting Grave I/72 were sealed by the rubbish (303, pp 160-1) which accumulated after the terrace was complete, and it filled the cavity left as the eastern timber decayed. The sockets to the east of the terrace were sealed by the levelling for the new path to the south of the chapel. The possible alignment immediately north of the early halls (Figure 4.5) may also have fallen into disuse at this time, though still marked by the door of **Hall 6b**. This plan forms the basis of the reconstruction of the *minster* in Chapter 2 (Figure 2.12).

The renovation of the church. The comprehensive renovation of the church was demonstrated by features overlying the foundations of the earlier buildings, which lay at a slightly higher level, and had suffered far more damage from later activity. The west end of the building had been destroyed by fourteenth century cultivation (pp 226-7), the east end was seriously disturbed by fourteenth–fifteenth century graves, and a section of the south wall had been removed by the hollow stance of a late-nineteenth century greenhouse (p 276). The evidence was thus fragmented, and became more so in subsequent phases of development. There was no subsequent evidence of the walls, and the interpretation of **Phases 5** and **6** depends upon internal features and external sockets, and assumes that the **Phase 4** building remained standing.

The church was by now some thirty or so years level, and a stone damp course or sill was inserted beneath them (Figures 4.13 and 14). This repair work was marked by broad shallow troughs on the line of the north and south walls, with flat stones laid along their outer sides. The trenches were dug outside the building, and curved to avoid the extant arcade posts. The irregularity of the stonework indicated that the stones were wedged in beneath the wall timbers. The work must have been completed in short stretches, as the walls were still the principal support of the superstructure. The putative damp course and original wall timbers are illustrated in Figure 4.13. This reveals an intrinsic interpretative problem, as the stone footings on both sides lay beyond the original wall foundations, implying that the replaced walls would have been slightly splayed. A timber sill, or series of sills, jointed to the wall timbers would probably have been needed to ensure the stability of the building. The footings ran across the opposed doorways in the chancel and nave, but these probably remained in use, and the footings would have combined the roles of paving and drains. The arcades erected in **Phase 3** do not seem to have required repair, and apparently remained standing while the walls were renovated.

New internal arrangements. The interior of the church was redesigned shortly after the walls had been repaired, and a new wooden screen incorporating the pillar stone of the original 'shrine', was inserted in a narrow slot some 2.0 m east of the earlier screen (Figure 4.13). The renovated church would thus have had three chambers, with the altar lying between the nave and the middle chamber, while the former chancel was divided into two by the new screen and stone. The screens and possible door or gate in the nave would have added further

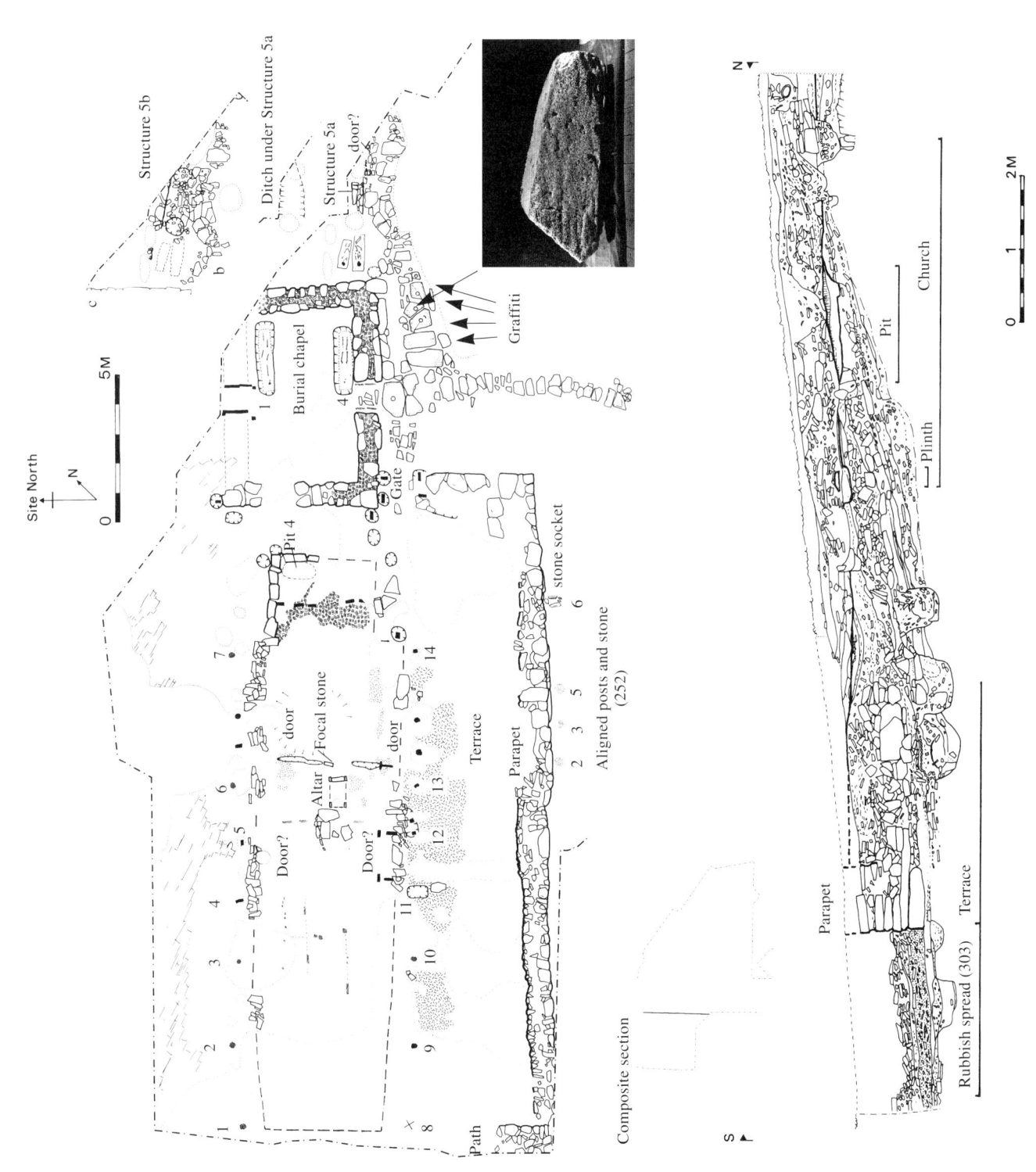

4.15 The buildings in the **northern sector** after the completion of the **Period II/4** renovations.

complexity to the internal arrangements and the way that the building was used.

The new internal arrangements did not last long, and a further series of changes transformed and extended the chancel (Figure 4.14 and 15). The initial stage of this operation saw the excavation of a large pit (**3**) centred upon the pillar stone, which involved the dismantling of the central part of the screen, and the removal of the stone from its socket (Figure 4.15a). There seems to have been no structural reason for this excavation, and the pit was perhaps dug in the course of a quest for relics, stimulated by a symbolic or written message inscribed on the stone. The pillar did not mark an early grave, and it is likely that nothing was found. The pit was subsequently backfilled with rubble, and capped with clay. The stone was then reinserted directly above its original socket, and the screen was replaced in a new groove cutting the clay. The precision with which the stone and screen were replaced, suggested that the timbers had been shaped to accommodate the stone.

The relocation of the altar. The **Phase 3** altar was dismantled at roughly the same time, and a new altar, probably using some of the original stones, was erected immediately to the west of the focal stone, oversailing the backfilled pit (Figure 4.15b). The new altar was dismantled at the start of **Phase 7**, but apparently comprised two upright stone slabs supporting a timber or stone table. The uprights were neatly chocked in place with small stones, which were all that survived when the west slab was removed. The space between the slabs revealed a thin bed of sand flecked with lime, that may have been the remains of a sandy plaster from which the lime has been leached. The **Phase 7** debris surrounding the remains of the altar produced a small group of anomalous objects that might have been associated with it (Figure 4.21b, Table 4.7, pp 162-4).

Extending and modifying the chancel. Additional modifications to the chancel were broadly contemporary with the relocation of the 'altar'. A large shallow hollow (*c*. 0.1 m deep) was dug between the opposed north and south doorways, clipping the edge of the clay covering **Pit 3**. This was covered with an earth floor of clayey silt. Its original purpose was obscure, and it subsequently seems to have been covered with a wooden floor (p 162). The chancel was extended eastwards at roughly the same time. The east wall of the **Phase 1** oratory overlay a row of log coffin burials (82.03) of which two had collapsed, dragging the wall timbers down, and de-stabilising this end of the church. There were two distinct stages in the construction of the extended east end of the chancel. The first stage was indicated by a clay floor extending beyond the original east wall, which may have lain within a temporary structure supported on timber sill beams. The clay respected the timbers in the north and south parts of the original east wall, which may have survived as an internal screen, broken by a central opening where

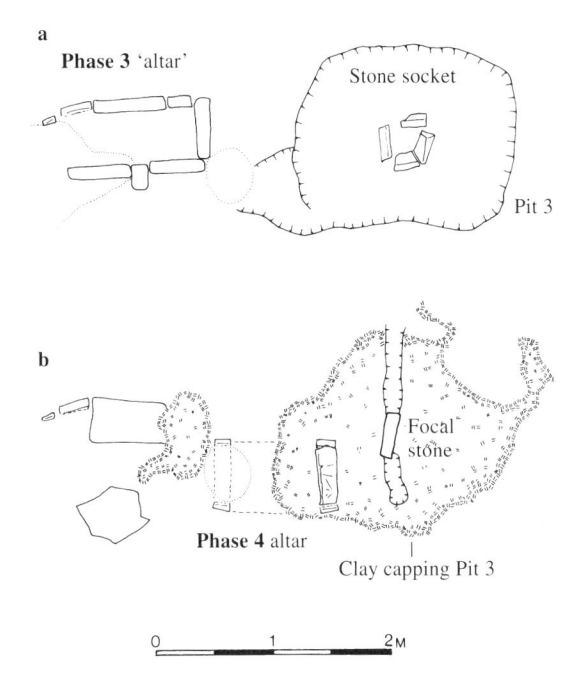

4.15 The relocation of the altar in **Phase 4**. **a** The **Phase 3** altar and pit to the east. **b** The new altar and screen, and replaced focal stone.

the clay sealed the earlier timber socket. A carefully-constructed stone plinth oversailing the clay marked the second stage of construction, and indicated the erection of permanent timber walls jointed into timber sill beams. The corners of the extended chancel were framed by external posts, possibly similar to the north and south arcades, but markedly closer to the walls. A large pit (**4**) in the north-east corner of the extended building may have been dug at the beginning of this programme of works and was perhaps a soakaway associated with ritual ablutions, identifying the extension to the chancel as a possible sacristy (p 158).

The end of the protracted restoration works was represented by a fresh surface of yellow shale laid around the walls of the church, and linked with the surface of the new terrace. This surface was cut by the sockets of new timbers renewing the nave porch, and of the later arcade and other features of **Phases 5** and **6**. The repairs seems to have been weather-tight, and the new internal arrangements survived without major changes for seventy or eighty years.

The new terrace. The terrace (319) was extended to the south shortly before the restoration and reorganisation of the church was complete. It was contained by a stone revetment built on a shallow shelf cutting the foot of the earlier slope, and lying immediately to the north of the alignment of posts and stones (252), and directly over the **Phase 2** kerb. The new wall was more substantial than its unstable predecessor, with a well-built outer face including large stones which may have been removed from the **Phase 3b** revetment (Figure 4.13). Freshly quarried rubble was piled behind the revetment after the first few course had been laid. The wall rising above this

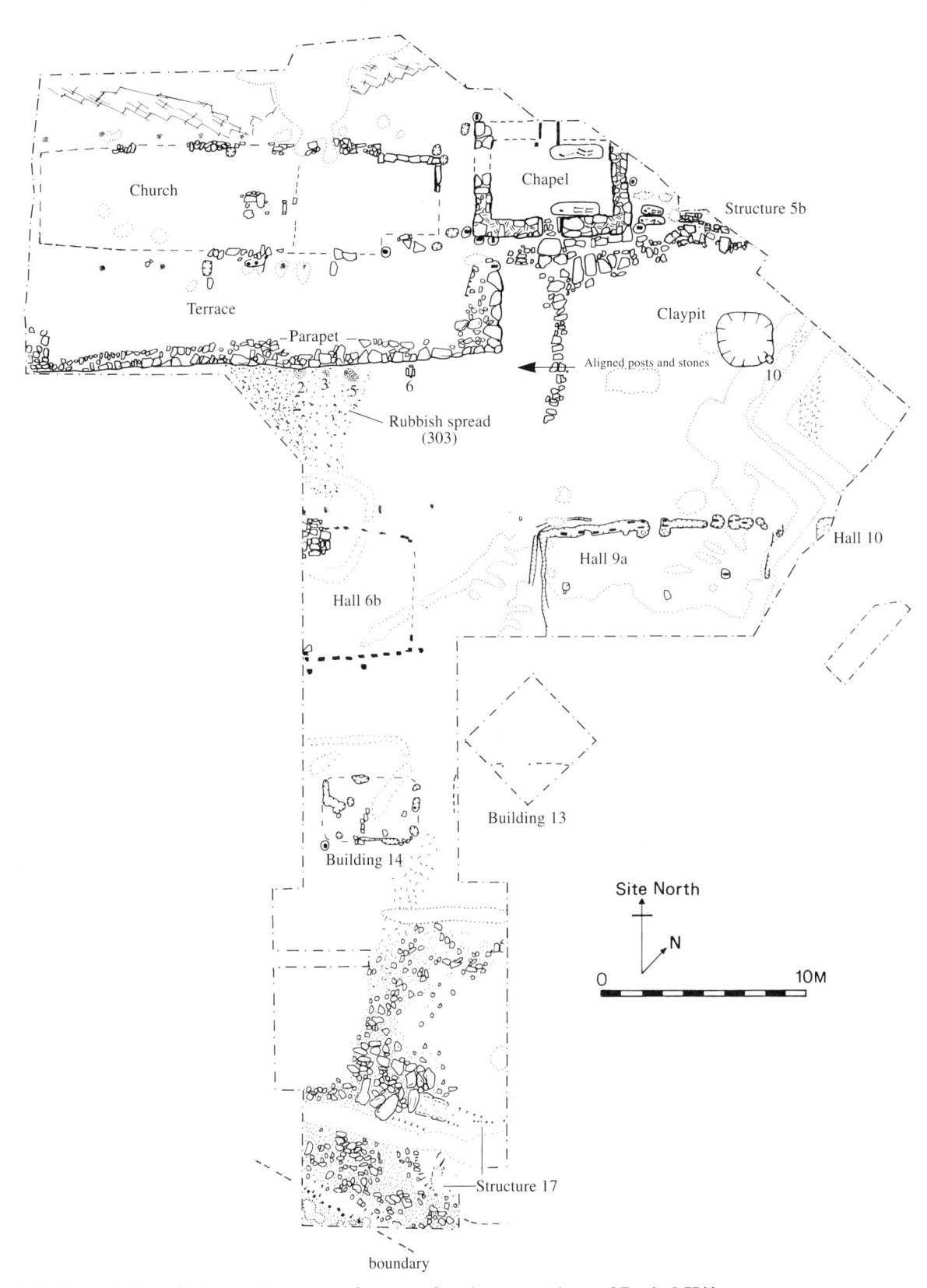

4.16 General plan of later-eighth century features after the renovations of **Period II/4**.

infill had a less-substantial rear face, indicating that the extended terrace was enclosed by a stone parapet. The completed terrace was surfaced with a thick layer of orange shale. The terrace had rectangular corners to the west and east. The western corner had been severely disturbed by fourteenth century cultivation, but a strip of paving marked a path which probably flanked the terrace, and perhaps the church beyond. A post-hole to the east of the path may have been one side of a gateway. The eastern return of the terrace was aligned with the west wall of the burial chapel, and had deep foundations which disturbed earlier remains here. A timber gate controlled access through the gap between the chapel and the terrace.

New paths. After the new terrace revetment was complete, the ground to the south of the chapel was levelled up with dumps of shale (206.01), and two new paved paths were laid (Figures 4.14 and 16). The earlier path led southwards from the south door of the chapel, veering to the west in the **central sector**, and probably passing through the gap between **Halls 6b** and **9**. This path was abutted by larger paving stones which resurfaced the existing path to the east, and were linked to a new structure (**5**) overlying the children's graves of **Phases 1–3**. These features were all later than the reconstruction of the church, and apparently continued in use thereafter. The paving slabs had been dressed with a pick and drag action to roughen their surfaces, presumably to give purchase in wet weather. A smoothed path was gradually worn leading eastwards from the door of the chapel. Four groups of compass-drawn graffiti were incised into this smoothed area, and then themselves worn by continuing traffic (pp 187, 439–41). A similar less-worn design was incised on a paving slab flanking the **Period III** church, and the entire group may have been executed in this phase, but is more likely to have pertained to the later phases of **Period II**.

Structure 5 (Figure 4.14 and 14c). The children's graveyard was overlain by structural features extending beyond the excavated area, which were probably the south-west corner of a building, but could have been a substantial boundary replacing the earlier fence (226.01) flanking the children's graveyard. These probably originated at the end of **Phase 3** or the start of **Phase 4**, and the latest structure may have survived until **Phase 7**. The sequence began with the excavation of a deep ditch (305.07) to the north of the **Phase 3** boundary, which had severely disturbed the underlying graves (Figure 4.14b). The first structure (**5a**, 226.02) was represented by a short stretch of narrow dry stone walling overlying the backfilled ditch, which may have been part of the plinth for a timber-framed building. Two post-holes, and stones bordering a possible timber sill to the east, indicated the position of a doorway. The posts and wall were abutted by the paving on the northern edge of the **Phase 4** path. The later building (**5b**, 226.03) was represented by a substantial dry-stone wall of three courses, flanked by two large post-pits dug through the earlier wall, and surrounded by irregular paving (Figure 4.14c). The west end of the wall had been virtually obliterated by later pits and graves, but may have been part of the south-west corner of a timber-framed building that replaced **Structure 5a**. Two burials in timber chests (305.03, Graves 53 and 54) were dug through the ditch and earlier children's graves, and were sealed by clay associated with the construction of **Structure 5b**. They are thus likely to have been contemporary with **Structure 5a**. The finds from the two 'buildings' included five nails and the tip of a light green window quarry with blue streaks (GS06.77).

Finds. The **Phase 4** deposits produced two distinct groups of finds. The first group comprised objects from the various construction deposits in the northern range, and was generally uninformative, although it produced a few interesting objects amongst displaced **Period I** metalworking debris. The second group comprised debris which accumulated against the terrace wall in **Phases 4–6**. Coins from this accumulation indicated the date of the **Phase 4** construction work (p 136), but it was generally impossible to distinguish other early objects deposited in the later-eighth century, from the material lost in the earlier-ninth century during **Phase 5** and **6** (pp 159-62, Table 4.4).

The construction deposits produced relatively few finds ascribable to **Period II**. Finds from the church included a small group of distinctive nails with small heads (IN11), while the fill of the pit (3) beneath the new altar, produced a sherd of pale blue window glass (GS06.14). A plated ornament of looped wire (IN90.4) from the floor of the extended chancel, perhaps came from a barrel padlock, and may have been associated with other lock fragments from **Pit 4** (p 158). The terrace produced a small group of finds probably displaced from earlier deposits elsewhere, and including a broken glass bead (GS03.16), a copper alloy chain link (BZ28.9), a broken shale finger-ring (SH02.1), a small tanged iron blade (IN66.59) and a piece of folded lead sheet waste (LD11.19). The levelling material in front of the chapel (206.01) produced a group of metalworking debris and other finds, most of which are likely to have originated in the displaced **Period I** industrial waste. It included four sherds of window glass: one deep blue (34), one deep green (122), and two joining pieces of very pale blue/colourless glass (27–8). These are of interest as the pale blue and deep green colours were not represented in the later groups associated with the chapel (Table 4.9), and could thus have been derived from a different building, or from windows that had been replaced before the fire. An underlying layer of worm-sorted soil (203.05) over the **Phase 2** surface (203.03), produced three other sherds of pale blue (22), pale turquoise (63) and purple glass (132), of which the last was, again, unique (Table 4.9), while soil overlying the **Phase 4** paving (206.03) produced two light green sherds (77 and 78) and one pale green (108).

Access and observance. The structural developments in **Phase 4** changed the patterns of communication among the ecclesiastical buildings, and indicated a major reorganisation of the ecclesiastical precinct. The terrace revetment abutted the extant alignment of posts and stones (252), and perhaps marked an intentional advance to the outer limit of the designated territory of the church. The parapet surrounded an enclosed space to the south of the church, that could only be entered from the church, or through the gateway at the south-west corner of the chapel. The new, possibly gated, path

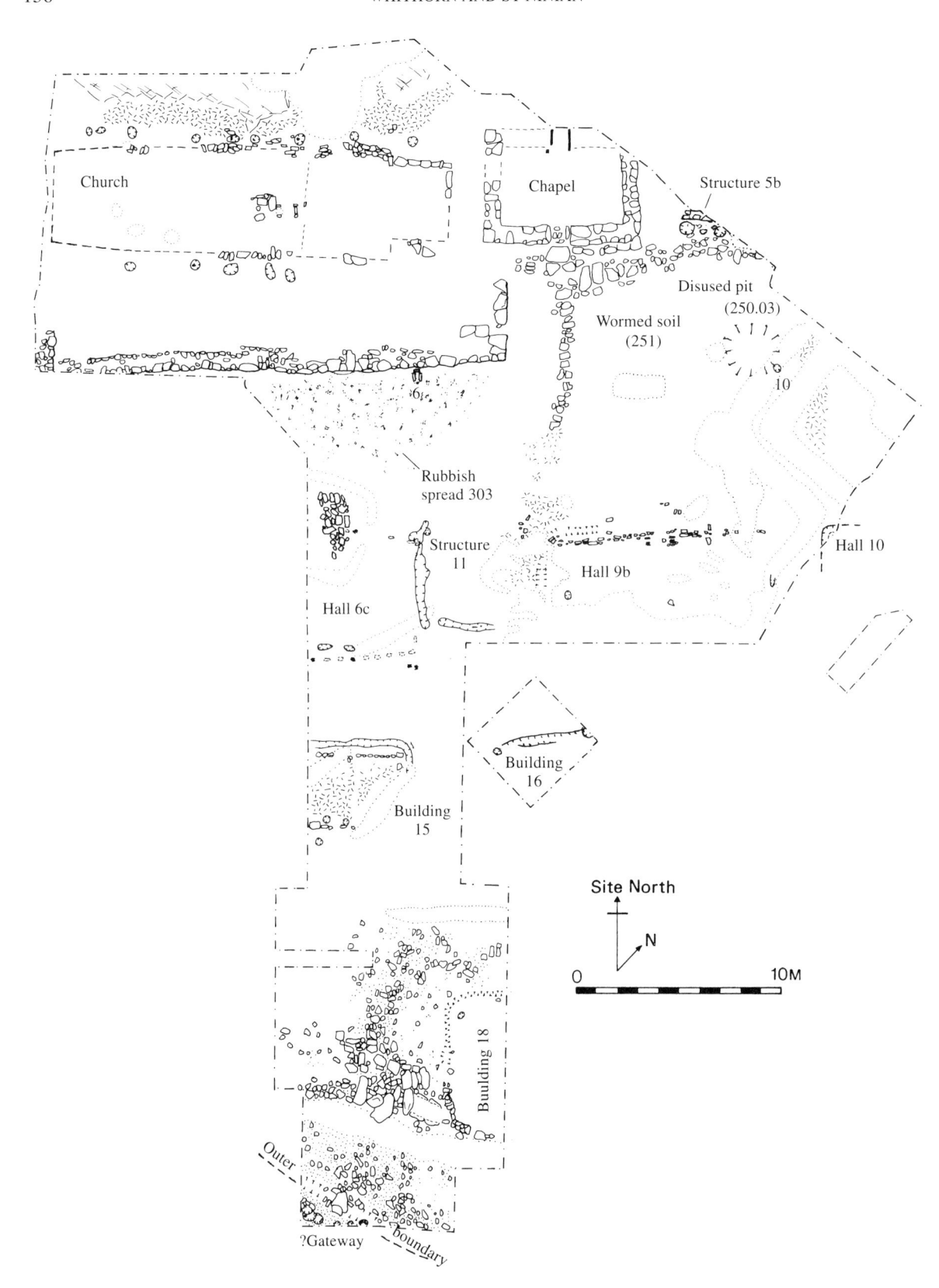

4.17 General plan of buildings, paths and related deposits in the earlier-ninth century.

indicated a new, controlled entrance at the west end of the church. The chapel, by contrast, seems to have been more accessible, and the paved path heading to the south indicated that it was an important entry point to the ecclesiastical precinct. The new structure overlying the children's graveyard suggested further redevelopment in the ecclesiastical precinct, and a new site would have had to be found for the burial of children.

The internal arrangements of the renovated church

had become increasingly complex, and there were now four distinct zones that replaced the simple, bicameral division of the **Phase 3** building, and perhaps reflected the elaboration of the rituals practised. The most important developments were the erection of the new screen and the movement of the altar. The screen effectively segregated the chancel from the nave, creating a private space at the east end of the church, probably with opposed doorways providing segregated access for the clergy. A second screen formed by the original east wall may have divided the chancel from a small sacristy. The altar now occupied a distinct zone at the east end of the nave, framed to the west by the screen of the **Phase 3** church and divided from the chancel by the new screen. It no longer linked the chancel and the nave, and was now located firmly to the west of the dividing screen, though retaining its former spatial relationship with the focal pillar stone.

Phases 5 & 6: Stability

The **Phase 4** programme of reconstruction ended *c*. 760 AD, and was followed by a period of comparative inactivity lasting for seventy to eighty years. The walls of the church do not seem to have required further repairs, although the nave doors were moved further to the west. Continuing maintenance saw the replacement of the arcade posts on two occasions, defining two further phases (**5** and **6**, Figures 4.19 and 20), both perhaps lasting for about twenty-five years (p 136). Fragmentary internal features revealed at least two phases of development within the church, which can be correlated tentatively with the external changes. The chapel revealed no evidence of further modification, although a relatively late clay-preparation pit (250.01) which was cut through the **Phase 4** path, indicated continuing repairs to the walls. The later halls (**6c, 9b** and **10**) of *Stage 3*, and a problematical building (**11**) of *Stage 4*, which probably pertained to this period, are described below (pp 175-8), as are potentially-contemporary small buildings (pp 178-82). Rubbish continued to accumulate beyond the terrace (pp 160-2), and a small group of late-eighth century coins and a large group of early-ninth century coins, point to continuing financial transactions in this area, ending abruptly in *c*. 835–840 (p 136). The absence of structural changes in this period contrasts with the numerous developments of **Phases 1–4**, and, though the *minster* probably continued to function smoothly, it perhaps lacked the vigour of the earlier-eighth century. Figure 4.17 shows the area in this period of stability correlating relatively late structures between which there were few stratigraphic links.

The church: unphased features. The church revealed a number of features which cannot be correlated precisely with the main sequence (Figure 4.18), but were nevertheless of interest, and produced a number of significant finds (Table 4.3). Most of these lay among the disturbed upper deposits reflecting the later stages in the development of the building, and most can be ascribed to **Phases 5** and **6**. There were six principal groups of features (**i–vi**).

Group i comprised four shallow sockets immediately within the north wall-line (1–4), and a fifth (5) in a similar position to the south. All were filled with charcoal-rich debris, and they could have been the sockets of timbers, or possibly stones, removed shortly before or after the fire. Two of the sockets (3 and 5) lay directly over important earlier timbers (the south-east corner of the **Phase 1** oratory and the large post erected beside its north-east corner in **Phase 3**). These features lay within the stake-lines in **Group ii**, and were apparently respected by a screen associated with the **Phase 4** altar. These features may merely have been dimples left as the underlying timbers decayed and the overlying soil slumped, but could have been the sockets for a timber arch. Two other sockets (1 and 2) lay between the stone 'sill' and the internal stake-lining, and one (2) was cut through the 'sill' stones. Their location immediately inside the wall line was matched by similar shallow sockets in **Hall 9** (Figure 4.32), and comparable features in Anglo-Saxon buildings elsewhere have been identified as cruck sockets (James *et al* 1984). This seems a plausible explanation, and later disturbances had perhaps removed complementary sockets on the opposite wall and elsewhere in the building.

Group ii comprised lines of stake-holes on the north (**a**) and south sides (**b**) of the building, and an intermittent line of small stone slabs (**c**) coinciding with the northern line of stakes. One of these slabs had been smashed by a driven stake, indicating that the stone sill and stakes were successive features, probably fulfilling similar roles. Both of the stake rows seem to have been aligned with the extended chancel of **Phase 4**, but ran across the **Phase 4** nave doorways and may thus have supported an internal wattle lining in the **Phase 5–6** church. The small stones on the north side of the church probably formed a plinth for horizontal timber sills, which could either have supported an internal timber or wattle lining, or the joists of a raised wooden floor. The plinth and stake line on the north side of the building lay immediately to the south of the putative cruck sockets, and may thus be viewed as successive internal linings in the **Phase 5** and **6** churches.

Group iii comprised an angled line of larger stakes (**d**) driven into the **Phase 4** clay floor at the east end of the chancel. These could have supported a relatively late screen, perhaps replacing the original east wall (p 154), but can also be interpreted as the wall of a **Period III** building (**III/15**, p 196).

Group iv comprised an arc of shallow, narrow dents and edge-set stones (**e**), straddling the west end of the **Phase 4** altar, and possibly extending as far as the stake wall-linings. Though insubstantial, this was clearly defined in the vicinity of the altar, and may be

4.18 'Unphased' features in the church (320), mostly dating to **Periods II/5** and **II/6**.

interpreted as the base of a curving plank screen or rail encompassing the altar. The two shallow sockets (4 and 5) occupying the north and south junctions of the screen and wattle linings, could have contained monumental stones, cruck blades, or perhaps an arch. A similar plank impression in a shallow socket (6), and three stake-holes to the west, hinted at another screen curving to meet the east end of the altar. This socket (6) produced a Phase II styca of Eanred (c. 837–841) which was probably deposited shortly after the plank was removed.

Group v comprised five pits (**4–8**) and a hollow (**9**):

Pit 4 lay in the north-east corner of the extended **Phase 4** chancel, and was filled with bones and stones in a matrix of dark soil. This was covered with a layer of clayey silt similar to the adjacent floor. The pit may have been a soakaway used for the disposal of water in which the communion vessels and other sacred objects and furnishings would have been ritually washed (Parsons 1986, 110–119). This interpretation supports the inference that there was a separate room at the east end of the chancel (p 153, Figure 4.14), which may thus have been a sacristy where liturgical objects were stored and washed ritually. The animal bones (Table 11.54) included a similar range of species to those from the main rubbish spread abutting the revetment (303, pp 607-8), but the bones of cattle feet were more common. The fish-bones included eel, salmon and herring, and the birds, fowl and goose. The rodent awaits identification, hopefully as an appropriately ecclesiastical mouse. The iron strips perhaps came from the broken lock, ornamental iron wire from which (IN90.4) was found in the adjacent clay floor (p 155).

Pit 5 lay immediately inside the **Phase 5** doorway into the nave, and was a deep flat-bottomed cut. The base of the pit contained undamaged upper and lower millstones, which had, perhaps, been buried ritually or hidden. The pit was cut through the floor of the **Phase 3** building, and was oversailed by **Phase 7** deposits.

Pits 6 and **7** lay to the west of **Pit 5** in the western part of the nave. Both were cut through the floor of the **Phase 3** building, but cannot be related to later developments because of subsequent disturbances. Neither produced any significant finds, but **Pit 6** was cut through a small hollow (**7**) filled with streaky clay, which produced an Aii styca of Aethelred II. This feature lay on the projected line of the southern stake lining and the streaky clay may have been the remains of daub. This coin indicated that the pit was later than the church, but its period and purpose were unknown.

Pit 8 was a hemispherical, clay-lined hollow lying in the middle of the west end of the nave. It was filled with burnt debris from the fire at the end of **Phase 7**. Although this was, perhaps, an appropriate position for a font, the base of the pit produced oyster shells, and it might have been used to store live shellfish in **Phase 7**.

'Pit' 9 was a shallow hollow immediately inside the southern stake line, which had been truncated to the west by the foundations of the greenhouse. An adjacent hollow produced a styca of Archbishop Eanbald II (830–835 AD). Both were oversailed by burnt deposits in **Phase 7**.

Group vi comprised a cluster of post-holes and a spread of burnt soil beside the north wall of the chancel. These could have pertained to a **Period III/2** building, or to a relatively late stage in the evolution of the church. The finds included a rare fragment of a side plate of a Class B comb (pp 482) from the burnt soil. The lead from the adjacent post-hole was a characteristic find for the end of **Period II**.

The finds are listed in Table 4.3. It is probably significant that these included a Phase 1b styca, an early Phase II styca and a third styca of Group A, which are appropriate to a brief numismatic horizon (pp 353-4). Other significant finds are discussed above, while related objects from the burnt deposits are listed in Table 4.7.

A wool comb tooth with 'bearded' head (IN62:04)
A possible tuyere plate inner fragment

A Shale bank associated with reconstruction of terrace.

Two iron strips (IN80.056 and 57), one (57) a possible perforated lock fitting
A piece of pale turquoise window glass with a grozed edge (GS06.65)
A **retouched** flint
A large group of bones including
 2,609 fragments of animal bone
 214 fragments of burnt bone
 32 pieces of bird bone.
 34 rodent bones
 c. 340 pieces and fragments of fishbone
Fragment of seashell including periwinkles and mussels
A small group of metalworking debris including hammerscale

B Pit 4

A complete sandstone mechanical mill lower stone (SE44.1)
A complete granite mechanical mill upper stone (SE44.2)
An angular unfractured natural flint pebble

C Pit 5

Twenty seven scraps of bone, including thirteen burnt
Four rounded, quartz pebbles (SE64)

D Pit 6

A styca of Aethelred II, *c.* 841–849. (Pirie IIAii, CN02.39)

E Clay flecked soil in small hole beside Pit 6

A styca of Eanred, *c.* 837–841. (Pirie IICi, CN02.44).

F post-pipe to north of altar

A square nail shank, possibly with non-ferrous plating and a nail head.
An unidentified iron lump (IN93.35)
A probable styca of Archbishop Eanbald II, 830–835 (CN02.35)

G Hollow 9 and an associated hollow in the nave

A Class B comb side plate with decoration & rivet holes (AR70.1)
A roe deer antler (AR87)
A **retouched** flat white flint
An unidentified iron fragment (IN93.34)

H Burnt material to the north of the chancel

A cut lump of waste lead (LD11.24)

I Post-hole to north of chancel

Table 4.3: Finds from poorly stratified features (320) associated with church

Phase 5: renewing the church arcades

Phase 5 saw the replacement of various posts in the north and south arcades, and the construction of a new porch, and probably a new doorway in the south side of the nave (311, Figure 4.19). A single post-hole with an unusually clear plank-impression on the north side of the building may represent one side of a similar porch here. The new arcade posts generally conformed to the existing pattern, and this seems to have been a phase of maintenance rather than redesign. New sockets were dug for posts 6 and 7 on the north side of the church, and the timbers in 1, 2 4 and 5 may not have required replacement. More of the timbers in the south arcade were replaced, and new sockets were dug for posts 11–14. No evidence survived of posts 8 and 9, while posts 3 and 10 were replaced by the new porches in the north and south walls.

The earlier 'unphased' internal features can be assigned tentatively to this time, and are included on

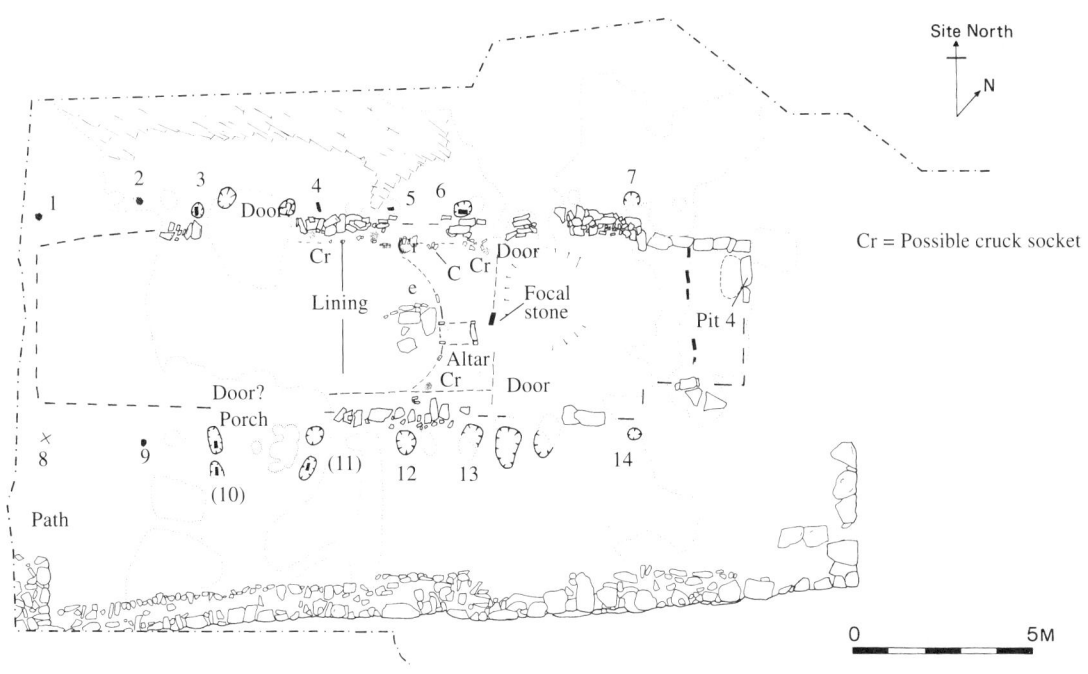

4.19 The **Period II/5** church.

the phase drawing. These comprised the putative cruck sockets (**Group i**), the stone plinth (**Group ii c**), and the arcing screen linked to the west end of the altar (**Group iv e**). These indicated that the church was still divided into four rooms or zones, with a putative sacristy to the east opening off the chancel. The altar still lay at the east end of the nave, and was now guarded by the arcing screen or rail, which had, perhaps, replaced the earlier screen. Both sides of the nave were now probably lined, perhaps with wattling, and the roof may have been rebuilt on crucks. Similar evidence was recorded in **Hall 9a** (pp 177-8), and the principles used in the reconstruction of this building (Figure 4.33), could have been applied in the church.

Phase 6: the final arcades

Phase 6 saw the erection of new arcades flanking the north and south walls of the church, while the ground to the north was resurfaced, sealing several of the earlier arcade sockets (310, Figure 4.20). The new arcades no longer maintained the pattern of their predecessors, and it is clear that a new design had been adopted. Two of the old post positions (5 and 6) survived, although new sockets were cut, perhaps due to their proximity to the long established chancel doorways. The new arcades displayed some regularity, especially on the north side of the building, and may be interpreted as two separate assemblies focused upon the chancel and nave doors respectively, and possibly reflecting the positions of new roof trusses. There was little evidence of change in the interior of the church, although the stake rows (**Group ii a** and **b**) suggested that the nave had been relined with wattling. The screen or rail associated with the altar may have been moved, and a new wattle screen may have been inserted between the chancel and sacristy.

The small group of finds included a possible domed lead weight (LD05.1) from a post-hole in the south arcade, and a piece of lead waste (LD11.23) from the surface to the north, both potentially deposited in **Phase 7**.

Finds

The ground between the ecclesiastical buildings and the halls to the south yielded a rich group of finds, most of which probably accumulated in the later part of **Phase 4**, and in **Phases 5** and **6**. The assemblage came from four distinct groups of contexts (303, 250.03, 251 and 399) with different circumstances of deposition.

The largest group came from a rubbish spread abutting the revetment of the **Phase 4** terrace (303, Table 4.4, Figures 4.16 and 18), and comprised large numbers of coins, animal bones, domestic artefacts and industrial debris. It was most unlikely that all the coins were in circulation at one time as their dates span some seventy-five years. The earlier coins were concentrated in a relatively small area at the west end examined in 1984 (Trench 4), while the later issues were more widely scattered (Figures 10.42 and 43) suggesting successive accumulations ending *c.* 835–840 AD. These could not be distinguished stratigraphically, and the few datable finds apart from the coins were of ninth century origin. The high proportion of dress fittings, ornaments and small implements is striking, and, with related groups from the **central sector**, identifies an area where female accoutrements were

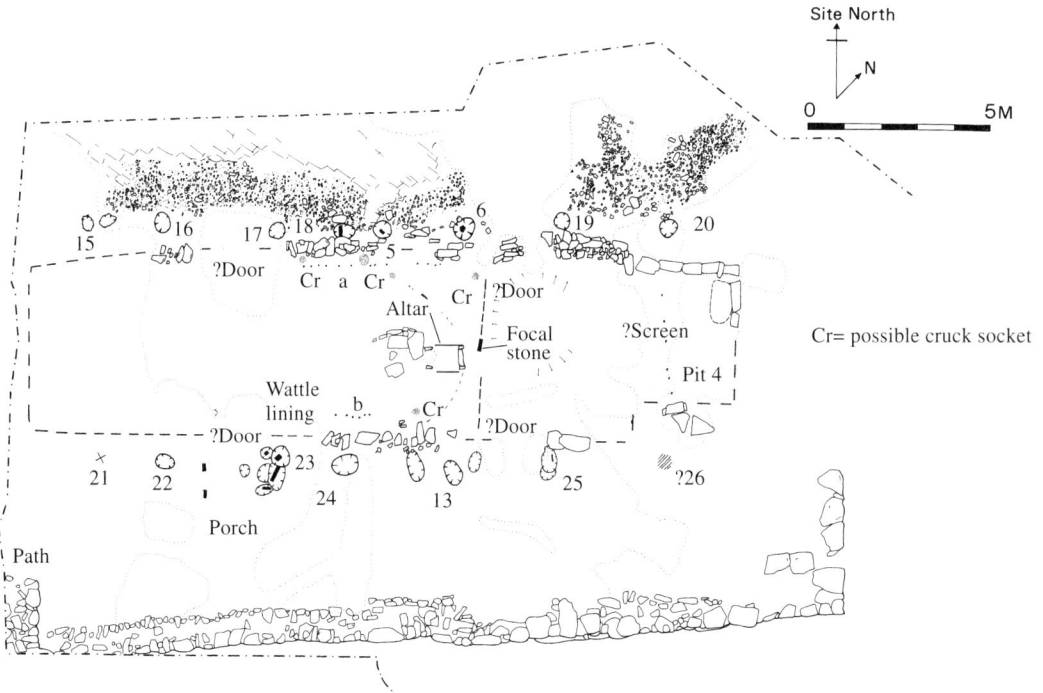

4.20 The **Period II/6** church.

deposited (Figure 10.98). These finds can be identified as domestic debris, but they revealed a range and intrinsic value, which contrast with the restricted finds from equivalent domestic groups from **Period I**, and the austere assemblages from the **Period III** buildings. There was a small component of *industrial debris* (the antler, lead sheet, metalworking waste and perhaps iron strips), but many of the objects seem to have been lost accidentally, as they were still serviceable. The most plausible origin was **Hall 6** to the south, and they could have been floor sweepings. The animal bones are discussed below (pp 607-8). There were two distinct groups with slightly different characteristics. The first group comprised relatively well preserved bones from a deep rubbish deposit excavated in 1984 (Trench 4 [303]), which coincided with the concentration of earlier coins. These revealed a predominance of high-meat yielding parts of the carcass, and butchery waste was rare. These may thus have been debris from the kitchen or table. The second group (303) was scattered over a larger area to the east, and was less well preserved. The relative proportions of the species were similar, but the dominance of high-meat yielding joints was less marked. The association of putative feasting debris and possible floor sweepings, may have reflected the function of the adjacent hall, but must be treated with caution, as it had perhaps built up over a period of sixty to seventy years.

Twenty-nine eighth and ninth century coins (**Group 2**, pp 352-3)
Two fragments of silver spillage (SR14 and 15)
A silver finger ring (SR1)
A gunmetal finger ring (BZ23.2)
Three ninth century copper-alloy pendant strap ends (BZ19.3, 4 and 5)
Two club-headed copper-alloy pins (BZ 13.1 and 2)
Two hemispherical bone playing pieces (BA15.2 and 3)
Four iron pins (IN40.7, 8, 55 and 56) including two plated pins with bulbous heads (55 and 56)
Two iron buckle pins (IN44.24 and 25)
An iron needle with a punched eye (IN39.4)
A perforated, axe-shaped, iron plate, possibly part of a bit (IN49.2)
Four iron knives (IN 66.7, 40, 60 and 61), including a possible surgeon's knife with a convex blade (60)
A wall hook (IN31.7) and two hook fragments (IN31.8 and 9)
An articulated iron chest hinge (IN24.4) and a possible hinge or hook fragment (IN26.1)
Three iron keys (IN34.3–4), one for a barrel padlock (3) and one for a sliding bolt lock (2)
A convex rectangular clench plate (IN20.3)
A broken perforated iron disc (IN89.2)
Two tapering iron strips (IN78.18 and 19), three strips (IN80.48–50) and a curved strip (IN81.10)
Thirty nails and fragments
A lead nail or rivet (LD06.29)
Two folded pieces of lead sheet (LD11.20 and 22) and a thin fragments with a cut edge (LD11.21)
Nine fragments of molten lead (LD12.7–15).
A greywacke spindle whorl (SE 28.8) and a small broken manufactured hone (SE36.4)
An antler burr (AR08), a beam fragment (AR14) and a beam segment (AR55)
Six **unretouched** and nine **retouched** flints
Numerous crumbs of baked clay (244 gm)
A small group of quartz (17) and granite (13) pebbles.
A small group of metalworking debris including:
   745 gm of glassy cinder
   634 gm of crystalline cinder
   Two crucible fragments, one with traces of bronze or brass (SG15.23 and 24)
   Three tuyere fragments
A large group of animal, bird and fish bones

Table 4.4: Finds from late-eighth/early-ninth century rubbish spread (303)

The second group of finds (251, Table 4.5) came from the worm-sorted soil overlying the surfaces to the south of the chapel, and can be ascribed safely to the later-eighth/early-ninth centuries. The needle, plated iron pin and bolt were characteristic finds of this period, but the plated head of a hunting arrow is rare at this time. The metalworking debris probably originated in the displaced **Period I** material. This small group of finds came from a relatively large area that remained open for some time. It seems to have been kept clean, and so contrasted with the ground to the west, where large quantities of rubbish were deposited (303, above). The objects were perhaps not retrieved because they lay concealed among the weeds and grass that colonised the soil.

A broken iron needle with a punched eye (IN39.3)
An iron pin with a square shank and a plated globular head (IN78.17)
An iron ring (IN30.10)
A tanged iron awl (IN50.3) and a Class A knife with a welded blade and back (IN66.1)
A plated socketed arrowhead (IN75.2)
An iron bolt (IN22.3) and a lynch pin with a looped end (IN25.2)
Eight nails and fragments
One unidentified iron lump (IN93.54)
Crumbs of daub and baked clay
A small group of metalworking debris comprising:
   Glassy cinder 349 gm
   Crystalline cinder 52 gm
   A tuyere nozzle fragment and six tuyere fragments

Table 4.5: Finds from wormed soil (251) over shale surfaces

The third group came from the large clay-puddling pit cutting though the surfaces to the south of the burial chapel (Table 4.6). Most of the finds came from the layer of worm-sorted soil (**B**) over the primary deposit of clay (p 166), which produced the small personal items and lead waste characterising this group of deposits. The coins indicated that this material had accumulated in the later-eighth century. The uppermost layer (**A**) had been disturbed by ploughing in the mid-ninth century, and the coin of Aethelred II was probably intrusive. The concentration of nail heads in the lower clay deposit is surprising, and perhaps indicates a component of the mixture being prepared (pp 165-6).

A styca of Aethelred II, 2nd reign (CN02.53)
A sherd of deep turquoise window glass (GS06.70)
A small iron staple (IN17.4)
A small group of pebbles

A Uppermost fill
A sceat of Eadberht (CN02.1) and styca of Aethelred I: 2nd reign (CN02.12)
An iron tack and a nail shank
A plated ball-headed iron pin (IN40.54)

A quadrilateral iron buckle including the buckle pin (IN44.3)
Three thin strips of iron (IN80.45–7)
Three lead waste fragments (LD11.16–18)
A **retouched** flint
Scraps of metalworking debris

B Middle silty deposit

A nail and four nail heads
A piece of molten lead (LD12.6)
A quartz plough pebble (SE51)
Scraps of metalworking debris

C Lower clay layer

Table 4.6: Finds from large clay-puddling pit (250.03)

A fourth group of finds came from the **Period III** ploughsoil in the **central sector** (399, Table 5.7), and probably included displaced debris from the halls and the ground to the north, as well as earlier material and a scatter of later finds. The cultivation has been ascribed to the opening stages of **Period III** (pp 190-2), and the large group of finds is discussed in Chapter 5 (pp 191-2), although most of it had probably accumulated in **Period II**.

Phase 7: Crisis and change

Phase 7 recorded a brief period of change which seems to have marked a crisis in the affairs of the *minster*, and culminated with the fire which destroyed the church, and damaged or destroyed the burial chapel. The fire has been adopted as a convenient stratigraphic horizon marking the end of **Period II**, but the crisis probably lasted for a short while thereafter, and was attested by the cultivation of the central plateau at the beginning of **Period III** (pp 190-2, Figure 5.6). Clear evidence of change was confined to the church, which was stripped of its internal fittings at the beginning of **Phase 7**, and seems to have been used subsequently as an outhouse or barn. The chapel probably remained in use as a gateway to the ecclesiastical precinct, and perhaps as a temporary mortuary, but the halls to the south must have been dismantled before the area was ploughed, and may already have fallen into disuse. The drainage system had probably broken down at about this time, flooding the low ground to the south and east of the hill (Figure 2.11). Coins provided a tight date range for the events in the **northern** and **central sectors** (pp 136, 356-9). The fire probably dates to *c.* 845 AD, and **Phase 7** apparently began some five-ten years previously in *c.* 835–840 AD.

The crisis has been inferred from the archaeological evidence of the stripping and reuse of the church, the cultivation of the central plateau, the flooding of the low ground, and the fire which destroyed the two surviving buildings. The case is strong, though not conclusive, and is supported by the picture of cultural and economic change in **Period III**. The existing organisation was undoubtedly disrupted, but the changes suggest a response to stress, rather than reorganisation, while the ensuing phase saw a partial restoration of the earlier buildings. The evidence of turmoil elsewhere in Scotland and Ireland, and the unreliable account of the devastation of Galloway by Alpín, provide a plausible historical context for the archaeological evidence (pp 20-22).

The 'deconsecrated' church. The 'deconsecration' of the church at the start of **Phase 7** saw the demolition of the altar, and probably the chancel screen and other internal fittings. Subsequent, 'secular' use was indicated by rubbish strewn on the floor, and preserved when the building burnt down (Figure 4.21b, Table 4.7). The altar seems to have been dismantled with some force. The stump of the upright slab at the east end had been shattered and its upper surface was subsequently discoloured by heat. The socket of the western upright slab had been disturbed by a later post hole. The absence of any burnt debris in the fill of the slot containing the screen and pillar stone, and in other features in the nave, indicated that these had also been removed before the fire. The putative cruck sockets (**Group i**, p 156) were however filled with burnt debris, suggesting that these timbers had survived the fire and were dismantled subsequently.

The west end of the chancel revealed a thick deposit of carbonised cereal grains and matted grasses, and probably represented debris from sieving a crop of barley (pp 592-5). It lay in the shallow hollow in the western part of the chancel, and was covered with a thin layer of silt, overlain by small, jumbled paving stones and charred timber. The silt may have been an earth floor laid over the sievings, and the stones could have been the remains of a raised floor. The charcoal was strewn in a lattice pattern, and was disturbed, suggesting that some timbers had been salvaged after the fire. Patches of carbonised cereal from the floor of the nave seem to have been fully processed grain which had perhaps been stored there (pp 592-5).

The fire was attested by burnt and charred deposits covering much of the floor of the church, and by the discoloration of the stone plinth of the north wall. The relative sparseness of debris and absence of fire-reddening on the south wall plinth, suggested that the building was not completely destroyed, and that damaged structural timbers had been salvaged from the ruins. There was no burnt debris in the sockets of the arcade posts, which may thus have decayed or been removed before the fire. The west end of the nave had been destroyed by fourteenth century cultivation, but the central part of the floor was covered in a thick deposit of orange ash, which produced numerous fragments of burnt and twisted animal bone, indicating that a deep deposit of food refuse had been burnt.

Finds from the floor of the church are listed in Table 4.7 and are divided into a group of exotic items potentially associated with the church (**A**), and a larger assemblage comprising fittings and potentially 'secular' debris from the floor (**B**). The distribution of the finds (Figure 4.21b) primarily reflected the

CHAPTER 4 163

4.21a Evidence of burning in the **northern sector** at the end of **Period II (Phase 7)**. **a** Fire debris in and around the church and chapel. **b** The distribution of artefacts on the floor of the 'deconsecrated' church.

areas of surviving deposits, but revealed a number of interesting groupings. The spread of ash in the centre of the nave produced a concentration of nails and two pairs of large interlinked staples which were perhaps the hinges of a window shutter beside the northern nave door. The bracket fragment and looped end may have been part of the simple suite of furnishings. Other finds from this area included the bone gaming counter, weaving tensioner, wedge and plated pin. A second group of finds surrounding the demolished altar included the Samian sherd, the rock crystal and Roman coin, which are reminiscent of the contents of a charm bag, but could have been associated with the altar (p 45). Scattered debris at the east end of the nave included the two copper alloy strips. The cross-marked fragment was perhaps part of a broken liturgical object, while the round-ended plate may have been the handle of a spoon. The three sherds of window glass were scattered on the north side of the nave. This sparse group contrasts with the large collection of window glass from the chapel (p 167), and hinted that the north side of the nave was originally glazed, perhaps with pale blue and light green quarries (Table 4.9F), but that the window or windows had been removed before the fire. The lead waste came from a restricted area to the south of the demolished altar. The coins were scattered throughout the building, and three additional coins from the 'unphased' internal features (320 Table 4.3) are included in Figure 4.21b, while two others (49 and 60) are omitted, as they came from identified, but unlocated spoil (Figure 10.42b).The coins seem to have marked a distinct phase of deposition which probably followed the removal of the internal furnishings, but may have preceded the accumulation of rubbish. The distinctive features of this group are discussed below (pp 353-4).

The group shared some features with the broadly contemporary spreads of debris to the south (Tables 4.4–6), but was in general distinct from these, and from the burnt debris deriving from the burial chapel. The coins, tools, charred cereal, animal bones and lead waste were the principal evidence of secular use, while the finds from the altar and the ground to the north west, were probably debris left after the ecclesiastical fittings were stripped at the start of **Phase 7**. There was surprisingly little evidence of structural fittings and other structural evidence was notably – but informatively – sparse. There was no fired clay, showing that the walls were not rendered, and no sign of roof tiles, lead sheeting or thatch. The droplets of lead came from a small patch on the floor of the nave, and were probably derived from a small fitting in the ceiling or roof which had melted in the fire. The relatively small number of nails contrasted with the larger group from the chapel and associated deposits (p 166), and suggested that the structural timbers were jointed and secured by trenails.

A coin of Constantius II or Constans (**a**, 347–8; CN1.1)
A sherd of Antonine Central Gaulish Samian pottery (**b**, PY01.5)
A quartz crystal (**c**, SE 58.11)
A tapering copper alloy strip with a round end (**d***, BZ 37.10)
A broken copper alloy strip with a cross motif and silver/niello inlay (**d***, BZ35.8)

A Potentially associated with altar or church.

Five stycas (CN2.30, 36, 40, 49 and 60; see **Group 4**, pp 353-4)
Three pieces of window glass (GS06, two pale blue, 15 and 16;one
  light green, 104)
A perforated disc or bead, possibly leaded glass (GS03.18)
Twenty nails, nineteen nail shanks and two nail heads
A group of structural fittings comprising:
  Two pairs of interlinked, looped staples (**e** and **f**, IN 24.5 and 6)
  A broken bracket or hinge fragment (**g**, IN24.8)
  A looped end with a broken shank (**h**, IN24.7)
  A plated fragment of a possible latch (**i**, IN27.1)
A plated club-headed iron pin or nail (**j**, IN40.59)
A corroded Class C1 knife blade (**k**, IN66.20)
A small broken iron hook (IN31.10)
A tapering iron point from a pin or tool (**l**, IN41.23)
An iron wedge (**m**, IN53.3)
An iron fishhook (**n**, IN56.1)
A two-pronged weaving tensioner (**p**, IN63.1)
Four iron strip fragments (IN80.52–55) and two plate fragments
  (**r**, IN82.22–3)
Three unidentifiable iron lumps (IN 93.56–8)
A possible dome-shaped bone gaming counter (**s**, BA15) and the
  butt end of a bone handle (**t**, BA14)
A copper alloy pellet (**u**, BZ40.2) and nine fragments of copper
  alloy (**v**, BZ41.6–14)
Four pieces of lead waste (LD11.25–28)
Five pieces of lead waste discoloured by heat (LD12.21–5)
Three molten lead fragments and *c*. 700 droplets of lead
  (LD12.16–20)
Two **unretouched** flints, four **retouched** flints, a flint nodule and
  a burnt flint
A small group of metalworking debris comprising:
  Glassy cinder 269 gm
  Crystalline cinder 163 gm
  A piece of non ferrous slag
  A tuyere nozzle fragment and two tuyere fragments

B Fittings and other debris from floor

Table 4.7: Finds from floor of **Phase 7** church and burnt debris (315). Bold letters mark locations on Figure 4.21b. * = imprecisely located.

4.3 DETAILED DESCRIPTIONS

The burial chapel

The burial chapel was erected at the start of **Phase 2**, and survived without major reconstruction until damaged or destroyed by fire in *c*. 845 AD. It was then rebuilt and may have remained standing for a century or more, offering clear evidence that the Northumbrian *minster* was restored rather than being replaced by an entirely different institution. The chapel and the structure which preceded it contained four or five coffin graves. The two later coffins (225.02) were only partly decayed at the time of the fire, and the intense heat charred the wood and caused their lids to collapse, creating deep hollows, which were filled with fire debris (207, Figures 4.21 and 27, Table 4.10). This, and related material from beyond the chapel (318, 305.04, 339, Tables 4.11–12, 5.2), produced valuable evidence of the superstructure and tantalising hints of the chapel's function. The debris included glass from at least two windows (Table

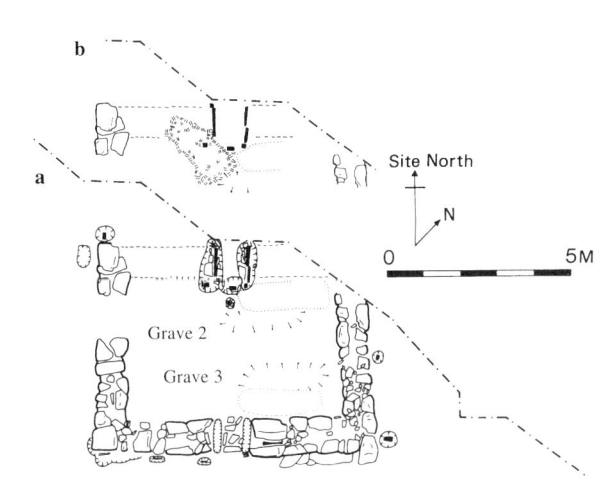

4.22 The **Period II/2** burial chapel. **a** Stone plinth and related construction features. **b** Timber casts in north doorway.

4.9), which indicated the high status of the chapel, and probably of the burials it contained.

The chapel had clay walls resting on stone foundations, an unusual method of construction at this time, which may hold the key to its function. Clay-walling is stable and long-lived as long as it is carefully maintained and protected from damp, the latter requiring a good overhang at the eaves, and a plinth of stone to counteract rising damp, and act as a splashback during heavy rain. Clay-walled buildings are well-insulated, and are cool in the summer and warm in the winter, while internal humidity is controlled naturally if the walls are maintained properly, and not clad with impermeable materials such as pebble dash or mortar (Wright 1991, *passim*). The chapel may have served as a temporary mortuary (pp 45, 170), and the clay walls would have ensured an optimum environment for the short-term storage of human remains. The provision of a stone plinth and the careful preparation of the clay (pp 165-6) showed that the builders were fully conversant with the practicalities of clay-walled construction, while the long life of the building attests their skills, and the care with which it was maintained. It is uncertain where this knowledge originated, as there are no certain antecedents in Galloway or Northumbria, while it called for different skills from those used in the contemporary timber buildings at Whithorn, and in the broadly-contemporary stone churches of Northumbria. The technical knowledge may have been introduced from south-west England by Pecthelm or members of his *familia* (pp 18-19), and this method of construction may have been employed because of its properties of temperature and humidity control.

The construction of the chapel. Deposits in and around the building gave a detailed picture of the construction of the walls and doors, and of site preparation and eventual tidying up (Figure 4.22 and 23). Much more can be inferred about the structure and use of the chapel from the burnt debris (Tables 4.10–12, 5.2), slightly later features, and the considerable literature about clay construction. The construction sequence began with the demolition of the **Phase 1** burial enclosure (pp 141-3). Shallow foundation trenches were then dug at the south-west and south-east corners, and the new stone plinth was erected over the foundations of the **Phase 1** walls. An unusually wide stone foundation at the east end of the south wall was overlain by walling of standard width. The plank frames of the north and south doorways were probably erected after the plinth was complete, although the rock-cut foundation slots for the north doorway (228.01) may have been dug previously. The timbers of the south door rested on the **Phase 1** foundation, and were chocked by the stones of the new threshold. Small rectangular posts in sockets abutting the stone founds of the walls, probably supported shuttering used in the construction of the clay walls, but may also have served as scaffolding, and could have remained after the building was complete. Two clay-filled post-holes immediately inside the north doorway were probably internal scaffolding or shuttering supports which had been removed when the construction work was complete. The ground beyond the south wall was levelled up with rubble and displaced **Period I** industrial debris, which covered the sockets of the shuttering supports. The clay superstructure was erected on the stone foundations, and packed around the wooden frames of the two doorways. Patches of clay were dropped on the newly levelled ground to the south. When the building was complete, a shale surface (224.02) was laid over the construction debris and levelling to the south of the building. This may have been enclosed by a light fence on the line of the derelict, buried **Phase 1** enclosure wall (Figure 4.9).

Building and finishing the walls. Clay buildings can either be made of prefabricated blocks, or else prepared clay can be laid directly on the walls, and moulded into shape while still plastic. The upper course of the stone plinth was bonded with clay, and the baked clay render from the interior walls had an

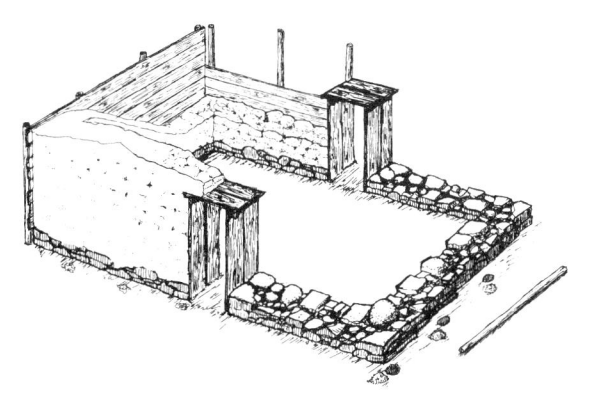

4.23 Reconstruction of the burial chapel during construction in **Period II/2**.

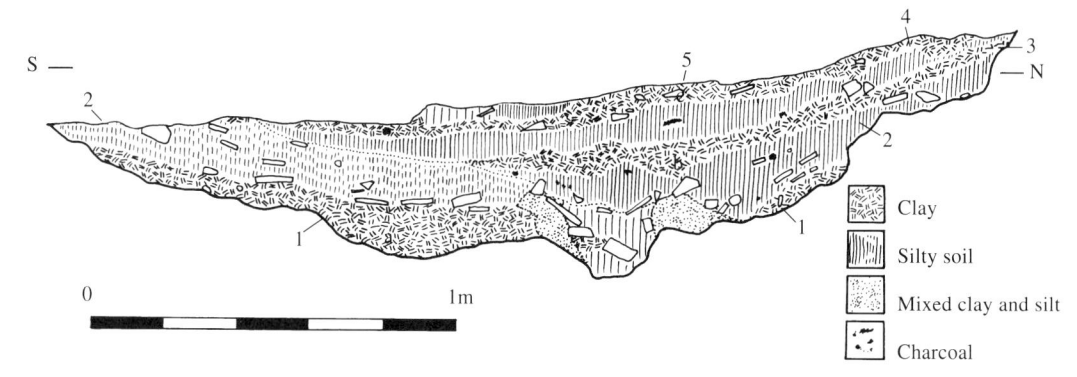

4.24 Section through the large clay-preparation pit (250.03).

undulating inner surface. These undulations are matched in surviving clay buildings at Claybiggings to the west of Carlisle, where the walls are built of layers of clay separated by straw. The walls of the chapel may thus have been built in layers of pre-shaped clay 'sausages', but without straw bedding of which there was no trace. The clay was, perhaps brought into the building, and packed against the shuttering which formed the outer face (Figure 4.23). Large amounts of an internal clay render survived in the fire debris filling the later graves (207, Table 4.10). The fabric was finer than the clay used for the walls, and it was probably prepared separately and to a different formula. The outer surface was smoothed and had a fine structure suggesting the use of a float.

The clay for the walls probably came from the alluvial deposits to the north of the hill, and would have had to be prepared before use. Clay (or cob, mud, adobe, pisé etc) buildings are known from many parts of the world, and every area seems to have had its own formula for mixing and preparing the clay. Common treatments (Harrison 1990) include the addition of fibre (frequently straw) and animal dung; weathering (exposure to rain and frost) or soaking (mixing with water in a pit); souring (leaving it to acidify to increase flocculation); and tempering or puddling (stirring it manually or by trampling). Three clay-preparation pits (250.01–03) survived a few metres to the east and south-east of the chapel (Figures 4.10 and 14). All three were later than the construction of the chapel, and were probably used to prepare clay when it was maintained. The eastern pit (250.01) was dug through the **Phase 4** paved path, and mostly lay beyond the trench. The other two pits were contiguous, comprising a small, relatively-early pit (250.02), cut by a slightly later and much larger one (250.03). Both cut the **Phase 2** shale path, and so must have been later than the construction of the chapel. The large pit contained three principal layers (Figure 4.24). The base was filled with a deposit of unmixed, or partly-mixed, yellow, blue-grey and red alluvial clays (1), which was probably an unused, partly-soured, and incompletely-puddled mix. A large post hole, apparently cut through the clay, probably post-dated, it but might have been a tethering post for an animal trampling it. The basal deposit was covered by a thick layer of clay-flecked silty soil (2) with *laminae* of darker silt and burnt bone, indicating a phase of disuse. The upper layer comprised two further deposits of orange (3) and yellow clay (4), separated by a second layer of silty soil (5). There was no obvious source for these layers which may have been associated with later repairs to the chapel. The middle silty layer (2) produced two coins – a sceat of Eadberht, *c.* 737–758. (Pirie Ai CN02.01) and a styca of the second reign of Aethelred I (*c.* 790–796 CN02.12). Other finds are listed in Table 4.6.

The roof and gables. The fire debris from the interior of the chapel (207) and associated deposits (318, 305.04, 339.01, Tables 4.10–12, 5.2), produced a limited range of materials, which were potentially derived from the roof and gables. There was only one small piece of lead and no burnt stone tiles, while the charred material within the building did not include straw or reeds. The most abundant finds were nails, and some 145 nails, nail heads and shanks were recovered, of which 76 were potentially complete. Most of the classifiable nails had flat round heads (IN01), and the group included an unusually high proportion of long nails (60–100 mm, Figure 4.25); with some thirty-three between 60 and 80 mm. The latter were an appropriate length for fixing double-nailed shingles to sarking boards attached to the rafters. The upper gable walls in surviving clay buildings are sometimes timber-clad, or filled with other materials to reduce the mass of the wall (e.g. Wright 1991, figs 2.7, 5.1, Gailey 1991 fig 51), and, as some twenty-three nails came

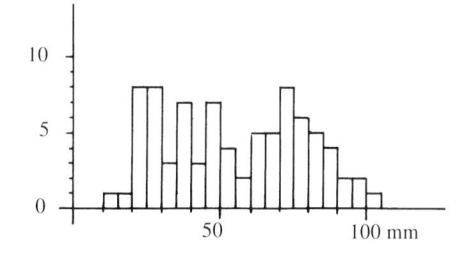

4.25 The lengths of complete nails from burnt deposits deriving from the burial chapel.

from the ground to the east, the upper gables of the chapel may have been shingled. The main timber framework of the roof was probably secured by trenails.

The floor. The chapel seems to have had an earth floor, which survived as scattered patches of clayey silt overlying the earlier shale and levelling deposits, and as deeper deposits filling the slumped graves (Figure 4.27a). The **Phase 1** graves seem to have been covered with two layers of flooring, each comprising a bed of stones overlain by fine silty soil. Similar layers of silt over the coffins in the later graves marked repairs to the floor after these had been buried. All of the finds from the floor (Table 4.8) could have derived from the underlying displaced industrial debris, except the sherd of window glass. The relative paucity of debris indicated that the building was kept clean consistently.

A sherd of strain-cracked, pale-green window glass ((GS06.110)
A nail and two nail shanks
Six rounded quartz pebbles and two granite pebbles
Scraps of metalworking debris

Table 4.8: Finds from earth floor in chapel (233)

The windows and doorways. Some one hundred and fourteen fragments of window glass were recovered from various deposits in and around the chapel (Figures 4.26, 10.25, Table 4.9 **A–E**), and most seem to have originated in two windows at the south end of the east wall, and east end of the south wall. A hundred and two sherds came from the fire debris and later contexts, and many of these were damaged by heat and some partly molten. Much of the glass from the east window had been affected, and the sherds were scattered, indicating that the window had exploded outwards during the fire. Some were still molten when they landed, and grains of sand were fused to the glass. The distribution of sherds shows that the east window included a range of blue, turquoise, green and dark brownish amber quarries (panes), and that the south window was similar, but without the rich light blue and amber colours (Table 4.9). The burnt debris produced no lead calmes and the only piece of molten lead (LD12.26) was too small to have supported all the glass. The glass quarries were thus probably held in a wooden frame, and one quarry (62) had minute scars where it had been pinned in place, while a second (122) bore an indentation from a possible calme or wood strip (p 329). There were, however, no small tacks among the deposits producing most of the glass (305.04, 318), and the quarries were perhaps held by grooved wood. Small sherds of window glass from earlier contexts (Table 4.9 **B**, and some of **E**) had perhaps fallen from their frames in **Phases 2–6**, but included pale blue, dark green, blue and purple fragments which were not matched in the later groups.

	A	B	C	D	E	F	G	H
Light blue	6	1	2	4	5	4	2	.
Pale blue/colourless		2						
Very pale blue/colourless			2					
Rich light blue	3							
Blue					2			
Deep blue	3	1	1		1			
Light turquoise	5							
Pale turquoise	16	1	1	1	2	1		
Turquoise	1			1				1
Deep turquoise blue	2		1				1	
Light green*	19	2	2	2	3	1	3	2
Pale green	4	1	1	6			2	
Deep green			1					
Dark green		1						
Pale olive green							1	
Dark brownish amber	7							
Purple					1			

Table 4.9: Distribution of window glass by colour.
A Chapel east window (post-fire contexts), **B** Chapel (pre-fire contexts), **C** Chapel south-east window, **D** Chapel interior (mostly post-fire), **E** Chapel surrounds (all contexts), **F** Church (all contexts), **G Central sector** (all contexts), **H Southern sector** (all contexts).
* Includes three pieces from **Period I** contexts.

The opposed north and south doorways were cased with vertical planks, erected before the clay walls were built, which presumably supported lintels carrying the weight of the overlying walling and roof. Posts on the inner side of the north doorway may have supported the frame for an inward-opening door hung on the east post. Paired posts outside the south door probably supported scaffolding or shuttering during the construction of the building, but may subsequently have framed a porch.

The internal graves (Figures 4.7, 14 and 27). The east end of the chapel contained five graves (**1–4, 4b**), two lying to the north and three to the south. The

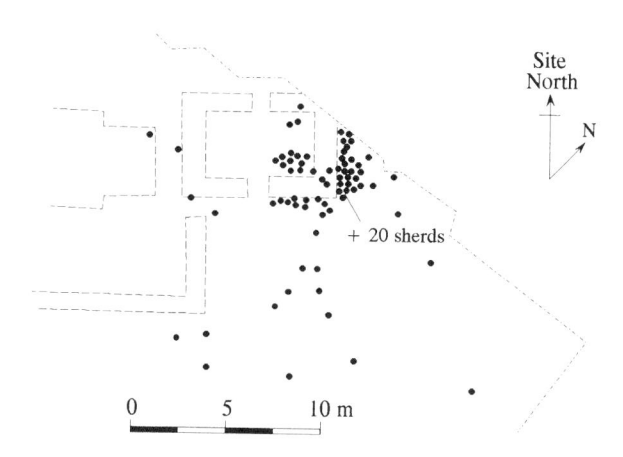

4.26 The distribution of window glass sherds in and around the **Period II** burial chapel.

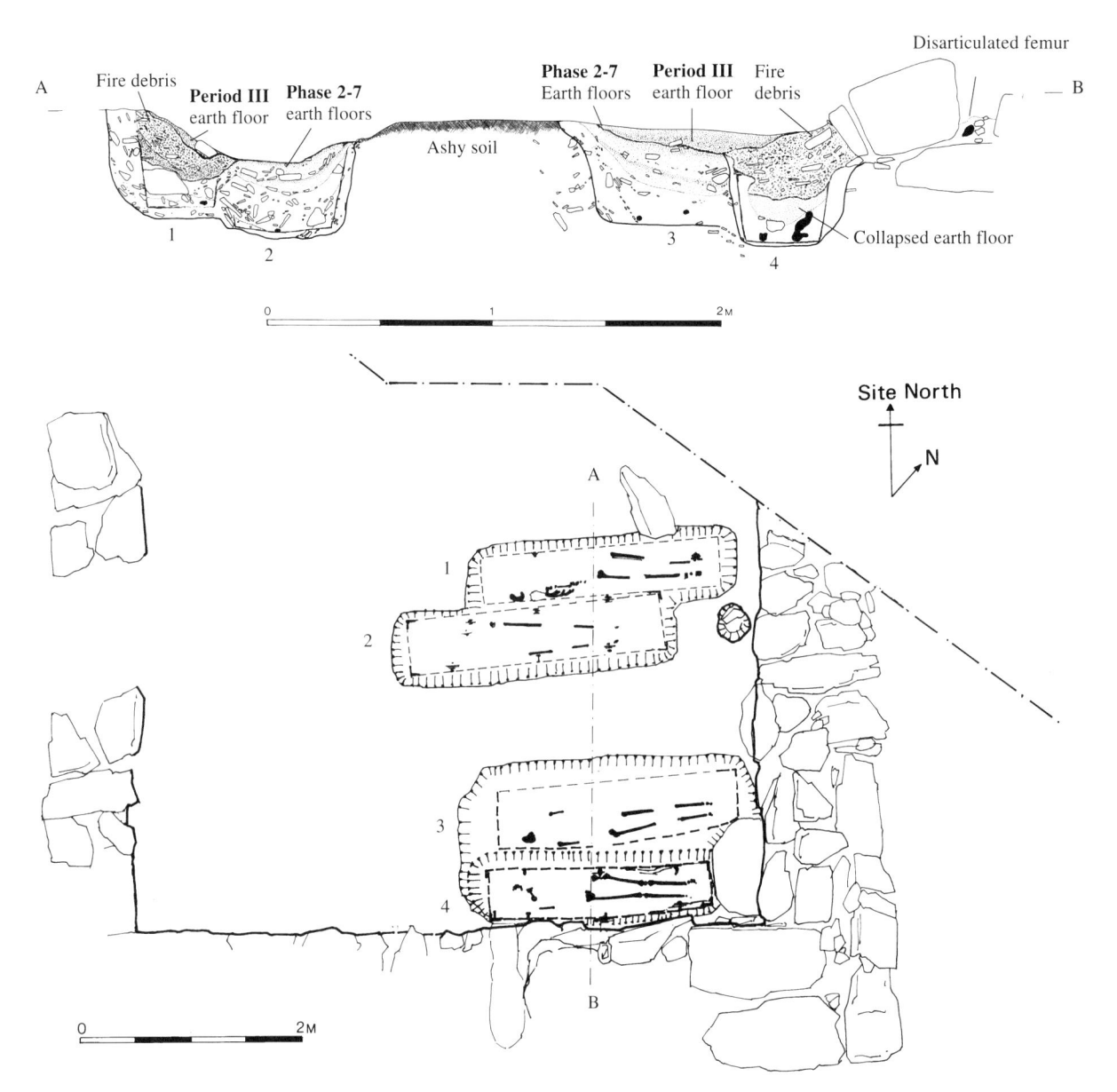

4.27 The **Period II** coffin burials within the burial chapel. **a** Section showing burials and overlying fire debris and earth floors of **Periods II** and **III**. **b** Plan of graves, coffin outlines and larger fittings (c.f. Figure 10.93).

earlier graves on either side were overlain by construction debris from the **Phase 2** chapel, and must have been primary burials in the **Phase 1** structure, dating to the earlier-eighth century, perhaps c. 710–730 AD. The later graves (**1** and **4**) post-dated the construction of the **Phase 2** chapel, and the coffins in them were only partly decayed when the building was destroyed by fire in c. 845 AD. They cannot be dated more closely within this period. The four well-preserved graves (**1–4**) contained wooden coffins, three with iron fittings (Chest/coffins 1, 2 and 4) and a fourth (3) of similar form, but with only one possible iron fitting. A late grave (**54**) in the adjacent children's graveyard contained a comparable, though smaller chest/coffin (5), while a **Phase 1** or **2** grave (**10**) may have contained a box or coffin (6) with a hinged lid. Three, possibly four, of these coffins had locks and/or keys, and two had been locked before they were buried. Locks seem somewhat inappropriate fittings for coffins, and these were perhaps domestic chests recycled as coffins when their owners had died. Parallels on other Northumbrian and Anglo-Saxon sites are relatively numerous (p 415), but the evidence at Whithorn was unusually well-preserved, allowing detailed reconstructions of three examples (pp 412-5, Figure 10.93).

The early graves (Phase 1)

Grave 2 lay on the north side of the chapel and contained the remains of a poorly-preserved adult skeleton of indeterminate sex (SK573), buried in a wooden chest with a full set of iron fittings (Chest/coffin 2, p 413). The coffin seems to have collapsed before the construction of the **Phase 2** chapel, and its west end was oversailed by clay from the construction phase. The foot of the coffin lay 1.4 m from the east wall of the chapel, and a post-socket beside the wall on the central axis of the grave might have contained a marker post.

A large sub-rectilinear pit, cut through the levelling material in the south-east corner of the structure, probably contained two adjacent burials (**3** and **4b**), perhaps interred at the same time. The northern burial (**3**) comprised the remains of a tall, early-middle-aged adult (probably male, SK 582) in a wooden chest or coffin (3), with a rounded iron plate which may have been a fitting. The southern half of the grave pit had been virtually obliterated by **Grave 4**, and no evidence of a coffin survived, but the bones of a tall young-adult male, arranged around the coffin in the later grave (**4**), may have been displaced from an original, southern burial (**4b**).

The later graves

Grave 1 lay in the north-east corner of the chapel, and contained the fragmentary remains of a robust middle-aged female in a wooden coffin (1) with a hinged lid, possibly secured by a lock (p 413). The coffin had partly decayed before the fire, and collapsed during it, or shortly afterward. The head of the grave was overlain by a heat-shattered slab of greywacke, which could have been the remains of an associated stone structure set into the floor of the chapel.

Grave 4 lay in the south-east corner of the chapel, and was dug into the south side of the **Phase 1** grave pit, clipping the side of **Grave 3**, and obliterating **Grave 4b**. It contained the skeleton of a tall, old or middle-aged adult (probably male, SK574) in a well-preserved chest coffin with iron fittings (4, p 413). The coffin had a locked draw-bolt lock, and the key, though found on the floor of the coffin, had probably been placed on the lid.

Disarticulated human bones. The chapel produced an interesting group of disarticulated human bones. Some were probably from earlier graves, but others seem to have derived from remains housed in the chapel when it was burnt. The most important group comprised calcined and charred human bones from the fire debris filling **Grave 4** (Figure 4.27). The coffin had been sealed by the beaten earth floor of the chapel, but had weakened and collapsed during the fire as the wood charred. The overlying debris included the fire-damaged bones of at least two individuals, chaotically distributed in a layer full of charcoal and nails, in turn sealed by heated clay render which had flaked from the walls. The condition of the bone fragments varied from unburnt, through blackened, to grey and white; and the calcined fragments had twisted, indicating that the bones were incompletely desiccated or 'green'. Individual bones displayed coherent patterns of heat discolouration, indicating that they had been intact when burnt, but had been fragmented and scattered before deposition in the collapsed grave: none of the fragments was articulated. These bones seem to have been stored or displayed in this part of the building, and might have derived from articulated or disarticulated bodies awaiting burial. Unburnt human bones from the grave derived from at least three individuals. These possibly included undamaged elements of the burnt bodies, but the bones of a tall young-adult male from the original fill of the grave, had probably been displaced from **Grave 4b**. The northern grave (**1**) produced a few additional burnt human remains. Other disarticulated human bones were found in other contexts within the chapel, of which the most singular was a particularly-robust right femur (probably of a 6' male) built into the stone plinth to the right of the south doorway (Figure 4.22).

The population in the chapel seems to have included two distinct elements. The first comprised the four burials in coffins, and probably a fifth (**4b**), subsequently displaced. These bodies were all robust and tall, suggesting that they were privileged members of society. They are likely to have been among the leaders of the ecclesiastical community, and could have included some of the bishops, although the presence of a female, albeit robust, precluded this as a universal interpretation. The disarticulated remains indicated less orthodox burial practices, which may have been germane to the function and construction of the building. There were two sub-groups. The first comprised the remains from the burnt debris. The bones of both individuals were still 'green', and perhaps came from cadavers or disarticulated remains which had been stored in the building. These were complemented by two burials of disarticulated remains in the surrounding ground, the earlier (**Grave 6**, 246, p 144) pertaining to the beginning of **Period II**, and the later (**Grave III/56**) to the earlier part of **Period III** (p 189). The second group comprised the disarticulated bones built into the walls. These are likely to have been intentional ritual deposits, perhaps emphasising the inferred mortuary role of the building.

Other finds. The assemblages of glass, nails, chest/coffins and human remains were not matched by other finds. The finds from the chapel and the late surfaces to the east are listed in Tables 4.10–14. The large quantities of glass, nails and clay render are identifiable as structural debris from the fire, and apart from these, the groups are small. Metalworking debris, and perhaps the awls and punches, can be attributed to the underlying displaced **Period I** debris (Table 3.35). Large groups of pebbles from graveyard contexts probably reflect ritual practices (pp 472-3), although there were no regular settings equivalent to the **Period I** grave covers. The function of the iron bolts is unclear, although they pertained to a small group concentrated in **Period II** contexts, and were perhaps used in the construction of the chapel. The absence of clay and clay render from the deposits to the east of

4.28 Speculative reconstruction of the burial chapel following the renovation of the adjacent church in **Period II/4**.

the chapel (318, 305.04, 305.06) was significant, indicating that the clay walls had survived the fire, although severely damaged internally. The handful of remaining objects included the fragment of copper-alloy filigree and the inscribed sandstone disc, which may have been associated with the activities in the chapel, but their paucity contributes to the impression that the building was kept clean, and had limited and highly-specialised functions.

A piece of copper-alloy filigree in the form of a Stafford knot (BZ330.5)
A fine-grained sandstone disc inscribed '18' (SE18.8)
Nine pieces of window glass (GS06.3, 21, 62, 99, 100, 115–8)
Large quantities of baked clay render
Forty nine nails (10 × 01, 2 × 02, 4 × 03, 1 × 10, 3 × 11, 3 × 12 and 26 × 14)
Thirty-eight nail shanks and three nail heads
A square shank (IN44.23), a tanged awl (IN50.5) and a tanged punch (IN50.51)
An iron strip (IN80.51)and a twisted bar (IN83.8)
An abraded neck sherd of a Biv amphora (V1)
Three quartz pebbles and two granite pebbles
A tiny nodule of copper-alloy waste (BZ39.8)
A small group of ironworking debris

Table 4.10: Finds from burnt debris (207) filling collapsed graves in burial chapel.

Thirty sherds of window glass (GS06.4, 26, 40–3, 46–53, 67., 72, 80–7, 111–2, 125–8)
Twelve nails (8 × 01, 1 × 02 and 3 × 14), three shanks and two heads
Two bolts (IN22.4 and 5) and a possible punch (IN50.57)
An unretouched flint

Table 4.11: Finds from burnt debris (318) to east of chapel

Thirty-six sherds of window glass (GS06.2, 17–9, 25, 29–31, 35–7, 44, 54–60, 71, 88–9, 90–8, 113, 114, 123, 129–30)
Eight nails (4 × 01, 1 × 02 and 3 × 14) and three shanks
An iron bolt (IN22.6) and a broken tool or nail shank (IN65.6)
A bent molten lump of lead (LD12.26, 21mm × 11mm × 2mm.)
Forty-seven rounded quartz pebbles, thirteen angular quartz pebbles and seventeen granite pebbles
A small group of metalworking debris
A crumb of baked clay and scraps of clastic lime and mortar
A **retouched** flint

Table 4.12: Finds from graveyard surface (and **Period III** graves) to the east of the chapel (305.04)

A small green/blue bead (GS03.16)
Three sherds of window glass (GS06.20,61 and 131)
Three nails and a nail shank
Ninety-six rounded quartz pebbles, twenty-eight angular quartz pebbles and twenty-five granite pebbles

Table 4.13: Finds from poorly stratified contexts (305.06) in children's graveyard

A nail (b) and an iron strip (a, IN80.41)
A fragmentary knife or saw with a broken tang (b, IN73.6)

Table 4.14: Finds from north doorway of chapel (228); a primary deposits, **b** fire debris.

Conclusions. The building and its contents are, it seems, unparalleled, and must be interpreted without recourse to archaeological *comparanda*. The critical features were **a**) the clay-walled construction, which was probably introduced from elsewhere, and may have been employed because of its environmental properties; **b**) the internal burials, apparently of high status; **c**) displaced bones suggesting the temporary storage of potentially-disarticulated human remains; **d**) the adjacent children's graveyard; and **e**) the patterns of access, that suggest that the chapel was an important entry point to the ecclesiastical precinct, particularly in **Phases 4–6** (Figure 2.13). The chapel may thus be seen as an important building, apparently serving as a gateway, and containing the graves of important, possibly revered figures. It may have been designed as a cool resting place for human remains awaiting burial in hallowed ground within the ecclesiastical precinct. These remains may have included disarticulated bodies, perhaps brought for burial from distant places. The absence of inappropriate finds suggests that this function lasted throughout **Period II**, while the restoration of the chapel (pp 187) indicated that this was maintained in the earlier part of **Period III**.

The children's graveyard

The children's graveyard to the east of the chapel was used for a relatively brief period of perhaps 30–40 years during **Phases 1–3** or **4**. It was subsequently overlain by successive structures (**5a** and **b**, p 155) associated with two later burials (305.03), and followed by further burials in **Period III** (pp 187-9). The development of the graveyard was linked intermittently with the structural remains in the **northern sector**, but is described separately as a distinct stratigraphic entity. The population is summarised in Tables 4.15 and 16, and is discussed at greater length in Chapter 11 (pp 561-3).

Early burials. The *Stage 1* path to the east of the **Phase 1** enclosure wall was disturbed by the first group of children's graves comprising some fourteen burials (305.01, **Graves II/7–20**, Figure 4.29a and b). The graves were densely packed, but were arranged in regular rows, and respected the enclosure wall to the west. They had been disturbed by a deep ditch (305.07) dug in **Phase 3** or **4**, and, as the

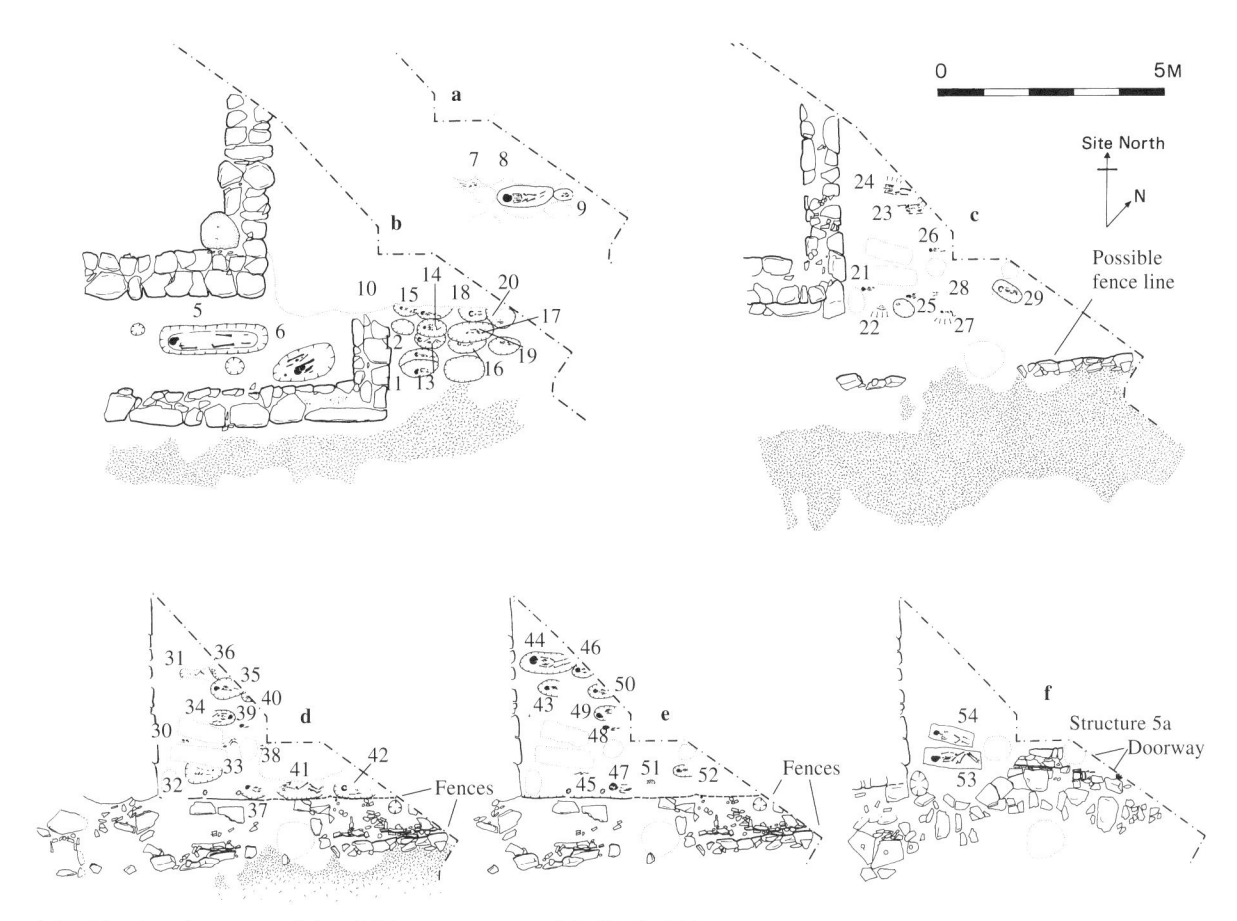

4.29 The development of the children's graveyard in **Period II**.
a and **b** Early burials (305.01) probably dating to **Phases 1** and **2**. **c**-**e** Successive waves of burials (305.02 W1-3) probably dating to **Phase 3**. **f** Late burials (305.03) possibly dating to **Phase 4**.

graveyard probably extended eastwards and northwards beyond the trench, the original population is likely to have been considerably larger. The more southerly graves were sealed by paving in **Phase 3**, and all the burials probably pertained to the relatively brief span of **Phases 1** and **2**. One of the earlier graves (**8**) contained a 4–7 year old, a second (**18**) contained an unspecific 'immature' skeleton and three others were too poorly preserved for identification. The remaining nine skeletons were either infants (*c.* 2 months–two years) or perinatal (< 2 months). One of the latter, aged between birth and six weeks (**Grave 10**), may have been buried in a wooden coffin, or box with a hinged lid (Chest coffin 6, p 419). The remaining finds from the graves are likely to have been displaced from earlier deposits.

The burials apparently pertained to the brief span, perhaps 10–15 years, of **Phases 1** and **2**, and the complete burial ground may have contained a far larger population. The dominance of perinatal and infant burials may have reflected the unusual circumstances of **Phases 1** and **2**, when the resident population is likely to have been augmented by a large construction crew and, perhaps, camp followers. The absence of older children could reflect the circumstances of a transient workforce whose other children had been left at home.

The later burials. The later burials (305.02) extended further to the east than the earlier graves, cutting into the deposits abutting the plinth of the burial chapel, and apparently obliterating the remains of the **Phase 1** enclosure wall. The graveyard seems to have respected a boundary aligned with the south wall of the burial chapel, and marked by a light fence (Figures 4.10, 29c and d). The graves probably pertained to **Phase 3**, and so spanned a period of perhaps 25–30 years in the mid-eighth century. The graveyard probably extended further to the north and east, and the original population is likely to have been considerably larger. The population showed a wider range and more even distribution of ages than in the earlier group (Tables 4.15 and 16), but the upper age limit still seems to have been about ten years. The remains in both phases displayed an

	Perinatal	Pe/Inf	Infant	Inf/Ch	Child	Young Juvenile	Uncertain/Immature
305.03					•	•	
305.02/W3	•••••	•	•		•	••	
305.02/W2	•••	••	••••	•	••	••	••••
305.02/W1	•	•	••	•	••	••	
305.01	••••••		•••			•	•••••

Table 4.16: Simplified distribution of children's graves by age

	Perinatal	Perinatal/Infant	Infant	Infant/Child	Child	Young Juvenile	Uncertain/'immature'
305.03					2–4 y **54**	6–10 y **53**	
305.02/W3	B–3 m **45, 51** B **49** 7m iu **50** Perinatal **52**	48	1–2 y **46**		5–6 y **44** 4–5 y **43**	6–8 y **47**	
305.02/W2	0–2m **35** 8m iu **32a** 7m iu **31**	32c 38	30–42m **34** 6–12 m **40a** 3–6m **32b** 2–4m **33**	39	3–6 y **37**	9–13 y **41** 6–10 y **30c, 40b**	**30a, 30b** **36, 42**
305.02/W1	B **29** 2m **14**	22	7–11m **21** 4–8m **26** 1 y + **12**	27	3–5 y **25** 1½–3½ y **28**	6–10 y **23, 24** 4–7 y **8**	**9, 12, 18,** **19, 20**
305.01	B–1½m **10** B **11, 15, 16** Premature **7**		2–6 m **17** Infant **13**				

Table 4.15: Distribution of children's graves by age. B = birth, iu = *in utero*, m = months, y = years. Graves **32** and **40** contained multiple burials.

unusually high incidence of *cribra orbitalia*, indicating that the children had been raised in unusually adverse circumstances (pp 562-3), and so contrasted with the robusticity of the adults buried in the chapel. The graves were numerous and it was generally difficult to identify individual grave cuts, but three 'waves' or stages of burials can be detected. The first wave (305.02/W1) comprised nine graves (**II/21–29**) scattered over the ground to the east of the chapel (Figure 4.29c). The second wave contained roughly twenty burials in thirteen graves (**II/30–42**, Figure 4.29d). There were two multiple burials. Grave 32 contained the remains of three, possibly four, perinatal and infant bodies, while Grave 30, though severely disturbed, seems to have contained a 6–10 year old and perhaps two other individuals. The former perhaps indicated an epidemic resulting in multiple deaths over a brief period. The third wave comprised some ten burials (II/43–52) apparently arranged in rows (Figure 4.29e) and with a similar age range.

The final Period II burials. The last two **Period II** burials (305.03, Graves 53 and 54) were inserted in the narrow space between **Structure 5** and the burial chapel, and probably pertained to the period of stability following the renovations of **Phase 4**. Both contained timber coffins and the one in Grave 54 had an incomplete set of iron fittings (Chest/coffin 5) including a locked sliding-bolt lock, and seems to have been a scaled down version of the chest/coffins in the adjacent chapel. Subsequent burials in **Period III** are described in Chapter 5.

The central and southern sectors

The **central** and **southern sectors** revealed parallel ranges of halls and small buildings, with other small buildings beyond, and included a short stretch of the putative outer boundary. One of the **Period I** buildings (I/24) seems to have survived in the area between the boundary and the third range of buildings, and was subsequently replaced by new buildings on the 'Northumbrian' alignment. The two ranges of buildings and the ground beyond posed different problems, and the three areas are described separately. There was, however, sufficient evidence to correlate the three areas into a coherent and potentially reliable sequence with four stages (**1–4**) expressed in three plans (Figures 4.30, 32 and 34). The final stage (**4**) was represented by a single, problematical structure (11) overlying one of the halls (Figure 4.34b). The surfaces and finds from the unoccupied corridor between the halls and the ecclesiastical buildings have been described above, as they were linked stratigraphically with the structures in the **northern sector**, but were more likely to have reflected activities in the halls than the ecclesiastical buildings.

The halls

A range of halls some 12.5 m to the south of the ecclesiastical buildings, was probably occupied for most of **Period II**, although no longer standing by the end of **Phase 7**. The halls lay in the southern half of the **central sector**, extending over the northern part of the lower rock outcrop. The shallow deposits here had been disturbed extensively by buildings in **Period III**, and graves in **Period V**, and had been confused further by ploughing in the mid-ninth century. The trench revealed parts of three buildings, described as halls, on account of their size, and to distinguish them from the smaller buildings to the south. The best preserved building (**Hall 6**) lay to the west, and revealed three phases of development on the same stance (**6a–c**). The second hall lay within the trench, but was incompletely preserved as its southern half overlay the outcrop, and most of the evidence here had been obliterated by **Period V** graves. The original hall (**7**) had been replaced by a new building (**9**) lying further to the south, but with similar stratigraphic problems. The third hall was represented solely by its north-west corner, and the

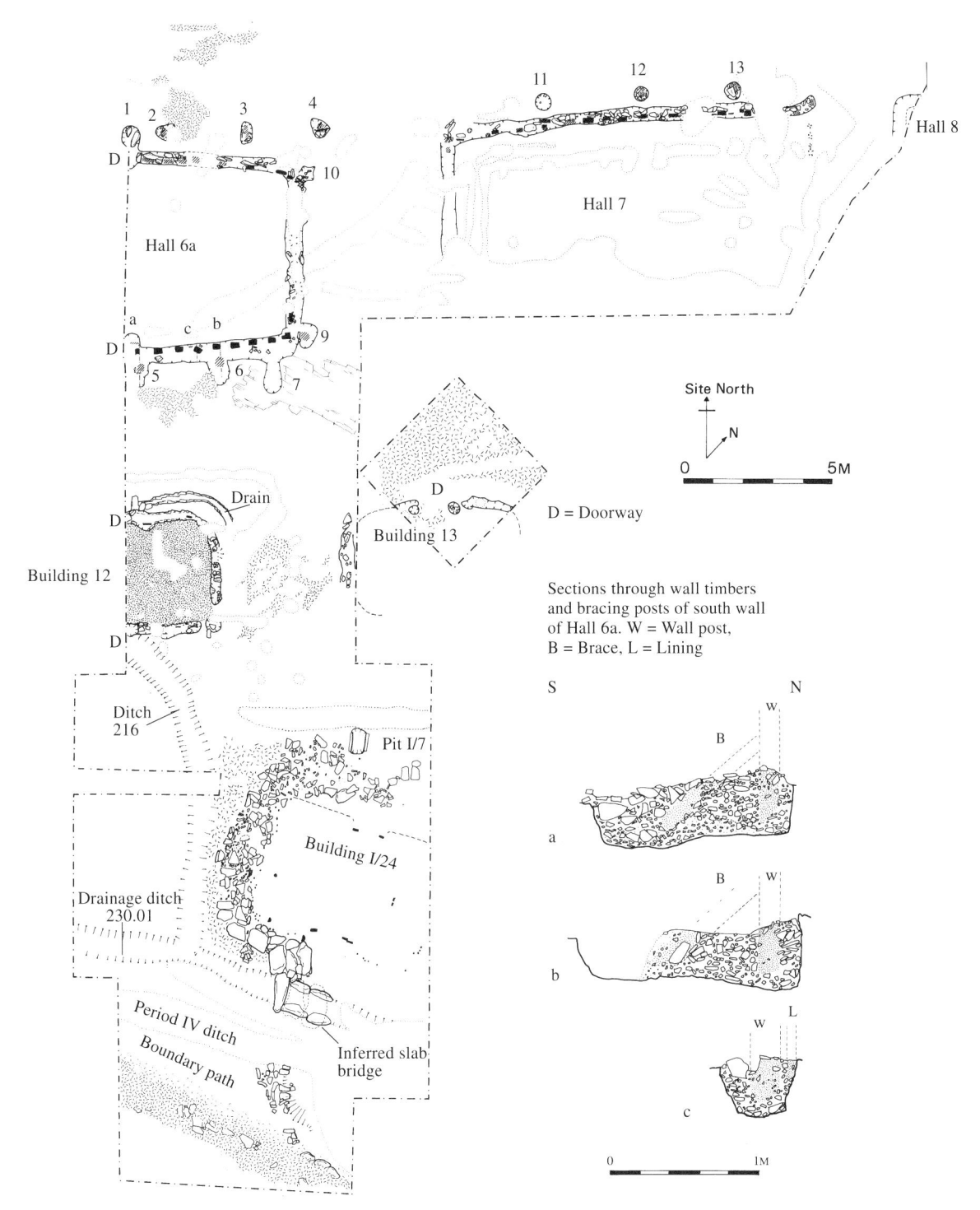

4.30 Early buildings and related features in the **central** and **southern sectors** (*Stages 1*, *i* and *a*).

remainder of the building is in an unexcavated area to the east. This building had also been resited, probably on the same occasion as the hall to the west. The north wall of a fourth hall on the same alignment has been identified in the **Museum Garden**, and there was sufficient room for a fifth hall of similar size in the intervening area (Figure 2.9). The original halls (**6a, 7** and **8**) were probably erected at the start of **Period II**, although they may have been built after the first ecclesiastical buildings (p 144). There was no evidence of change until **Phase 4**, and no major structural repairs were evident in the intervening thirty or forty years. A second stage of construction (**2**, Figure 4.32) perhaps dated to the later-eighth century, and saw the remodelling of **Hall 6** (**6b**), and the replacement of **Halls 7** and **8** with new buildings (**9** and **10**). A third stage, possibly dating to the end of the eighth or beginning of the ninth century, saw a major redesign of **Hall 6** (**6c**), and substantial repairs to

Hall 9 (**9b**). The latest structure was an incomplete building (**11**) marked by a wall trench cutting the east wall of **Hall 6**, and defining a fourth stage of construction (Figures 4.34).

Hall 6

Hall 6 lay in the western part of the **central sector**, and the opposed doorways in the north and south walls were bisected by the west side of the trench. The south side of the building oversailed the lower outcrop, and the foundations were cut deeply into the rock. The foundations on the north side of the building were cut through the boulder clay, intermittently exposing the surface of the underlying rock. The foundations of the original building (**6a**, *Stage 1*) were well preserved and revealed clear evidence of the wall timbers. Two subsequent structural phases (**6b** and **c**) were represented by paving at the north entrance, demonstrating that the original doorway was moved to the east. The original structure was probably modified on the first occasion (**6b**, *Stage 2*), but the final building was on a different alignment, and probably involved the replacement or substantial modification of the original structure.

Hall 6a (Figure 4.30) was erected towards the beginning of **Phase 1**, and seems to have survived unmodified until **Phase 4**. The trench containing the south wall was cut through rock, and was filled with broken rock and soil, preserving perfect impressions of the deeply-set spaced wall timbers, set close to the inner face of the trench. The timbers were squarer and more substantial than those used in the church, and should perhaps be seen as closely-spaced studs. The gaps between the posts at the west end of the wall were covered by a layer of trampled shale (Figure 4.32), indicating that these gaps were not filled with planks or wattle. An internal lining, perhaps of narrow vertical planks, was indicated by sporadic timber impressions and small edge-set stones on the inner margin of the trench (Figure 4.30c). The foundation trench of the north wall was cut though boulder clay, and the timbers set against the inner edge were chocked by large stones on its outer side. The timber impressions were less clear than to the south, but the timbers were probably similar in size and spacing. The east wall had been severely damaged by the west end of **Building 11**, but casts surviving at the south end, indicated that it had contained timbers similar to those forming the north and south walls. The south wall was flanked by three large rock-cut pits which had been excavated at the same time as the adjoining wall trench. Two of these (5 and 6) revealed clear evidence of steeply-raked posts (Figure 4.30a and b), and a similar timber may have been removed from the third pit lying (7) further to the east. The raking posts and wall timbers were both set into a shallow layer of broken rock, indicating that they were inserted at the same time. The posts were too steeply raked to have functioned as buttresses, and were probably braces supporting the south wall during the erection of the building, and potentially superfluous when it was complete. One (1) of the four large timbers on the north side of the building was probably vertical, and framed the east side of a porch, while a second (3) set at a shallow angle, was probably a buttress. The remaining two sockets (2 and 4) seem to have contained vertical timbers, which could have supported arcades protecting the building from the prevailing wind. All four timbers were aligned with three posts immediately to the north of **Hall 7**, and framed the south side of the unoccupied corridor in the northern part of the **central sector**. Two large post-holes (9 and 10) at either end of the east wall, were too close to the wall to have contained buttresses, and probably held vertical posts, perhaps related to the roof structure. The opposed doorways were obscured by the edge of the trench, but possibly comprised an inset, plank door-frame lying parallel to the walls, with a porch to the north, but not to the south. The interior had been extensively disturbed by later features, but revealed no evidence of a trampled surface, and may thus have had a raised wooden floor, although layers of silt removed during the examination of the building, could have been an unrecognised earth floor.

The hall is reconstructed in Figure 4.31. The roof is supported by collared trusses resting on wall plates mortised into the wall posts. The substantial timbers surviving in the east wall indicated that it was load-bearing, and it has accordingly been reconstructed with a wall-plate supporting a hipped roof. The gaps between the wall timbers have not been filled with timbers or wattles due to the evidence from the south wall, but a wattle lining has been inferred on the basis of stake holes in the north-east corner, and the traces of internal timbers recorded in section (Figure 4.30c). This would probably have been coated with daub, but the small quantities of clay recorded argue for a biodegradable mix which had left little trace. The posts immediately beyond the east wall are reconstructed as the supports for extended wall plates bearing the rafters at the angles of the hipped roof. The building is viewed from the south-east to show the most clearly-defined wall posts and their basal braces. This viewpoint obscures the northern porch which perhaps distinguished the north doorway as the principal entrance.

Hall 6b (Figure 4.32) was represented by a band of paving marking a new, or enlarged, north doorway. The paving covered the most westerly timber of the original north wall, but was laid around the next post to the east, showing that most of the original structure remained standing. The paving was bilaterally symmetrical, indicating that the door was moved eastwards rather than expanded. There was no clear evidence of complementary changes to the south door, where equivalent deposits had not survived, but the recurrent symmetry of these buildings argues for similar changes. The paving oversailed the shale path leading to the burial chapel, and was cut through a layer of ashy soil, which was probably part of the rubbish spread (303) to the north of the building. It is thus likely that **Hall 6b** pertained to **Phase 4** or **5**, and was later than the coins deposited in *c*. 760 AD (p 130).

Hall 6c (Figure 4.34) was represented by a second layer of paving in the north doorway, framing the same wall timber as the *Stage 2* surface. The paving was slightly skewed, and was aligned with a pair of small post sockets immediately inside the south wall, which probably marked a new inset doorway. A skewed wall timber adjacent to the eastern door socket indicated the modification of the south wall, and two shallow timber impressions at the east end of

An unidentifiable coin similar to an anachronous farthing of James III (CN3:29)
A curved copper-alloy needle fractured at the eye and point (BZ12.3)
An iron needle with a punched eye (IN39.6)
Three nail shanks
A diamond-shaped iron clench-plate (IN20.4)
An unfinished sandstone spindle whorl (SE28:10)
Four plough pebbles (SE51)
Two **retouched** flints, an **unretouched** flint and a burnt flint

Table 4.17: Finds from **Hall 6** (254.02)

Hall 7 lay some 4.5 m to the west of **Hall 6**, and is ascribed to *Stage 1* as it was oversailed by the path flanking **Hall 9** (Figure 4.34). The relationship between these two buildings was nevertheless

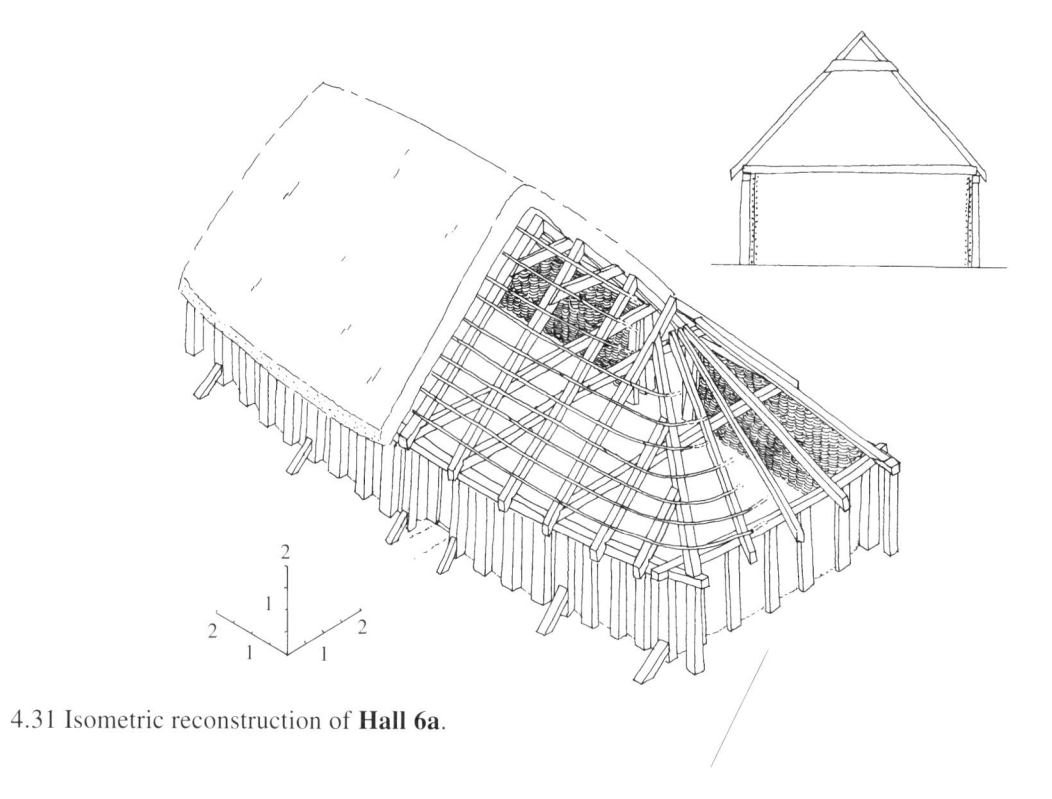

4.31 Isometric reconstruction of **Hall 6a**.

the wall may have been repositioned wall timbers moved from their original sockets. The alignment of the new doorways argues that the building had been rebuilt on a new orientation, while the absence of new ground-set wall timbers, suggests it was rebuilt on timber or stone sills.

The sparse finds from the hall (Table 4.17) included two needles and a spindle whorl, which are matched in other groups from the **central sector** (Figure 10.98), but otherwise indicated that the building was carefully-maintained and that debris was not allowed to accumulate. The copper-alloy needle and unidentified coin may have been intrusive, while the plough pebbles and flints may derive from earlier deposits. The large rubbish deposit (303, Table 4.4) immediately to the north could have originated in the building, and included a much wider range of material, suggesting that it was used *inter alia* for feasting (pp 160-1).

difficult to establish, and the fragmentary east wall seems to have been common to both. The building was 12.0 m long and perhaps *c*. 5.0 m wide. The south side of the building overlay the rock outcrop and no structural features had survived, but the slot containing the north wall was well-preserved, and revealed clear evidence of regular rectangular wall timbers chocked against the inner face by carefully-placed packing stones. The doorway lay some 2.5 m from the west wall, and comprised two large, square, deeply-set posts on the wall line, with a single off-set rectangular timber beyond. The south end of the west wall had been destroyed by drains associated with the eighteenth century manse, and the evidence surviving to the north was compromised by over-zealous excavation. The wall nevertheless seems to have comprised closely spaced timbers which were indicated by shallow dents filled with silt, recorded before the slot was excavated. The west wall had been severely damaged by later features, but seems to have been more substantial than the equivalent wall of **Hall 9** (Figure 4.32). **Hall 7** is thus likely to have been similar to **Hall 6**, with a hipped roof supported by four load-bearing walls. Three large holes (11-13) immediately north of the north wall, probably contained vertical posts which formed part of the southern alignment, but could have supported an arcade shielding the north wall from the prevailing winds.

The finds from the hall (Table 4.18) included a millstone fragment and chisel-marked slab from the packing, which probably pertained to **Period I** (pp 29, 465), but the needle and fragments of an iron vessel may reflect the use of the building. The raw clay from the north wall was probably derived from daub.

A sherd of early vessel glass (GpE2)
Five **retouched** flints and a natural flint pebble
Lumps of raw clay (210 gm)
A nail and nail shank and an iron staple (IN17.6)

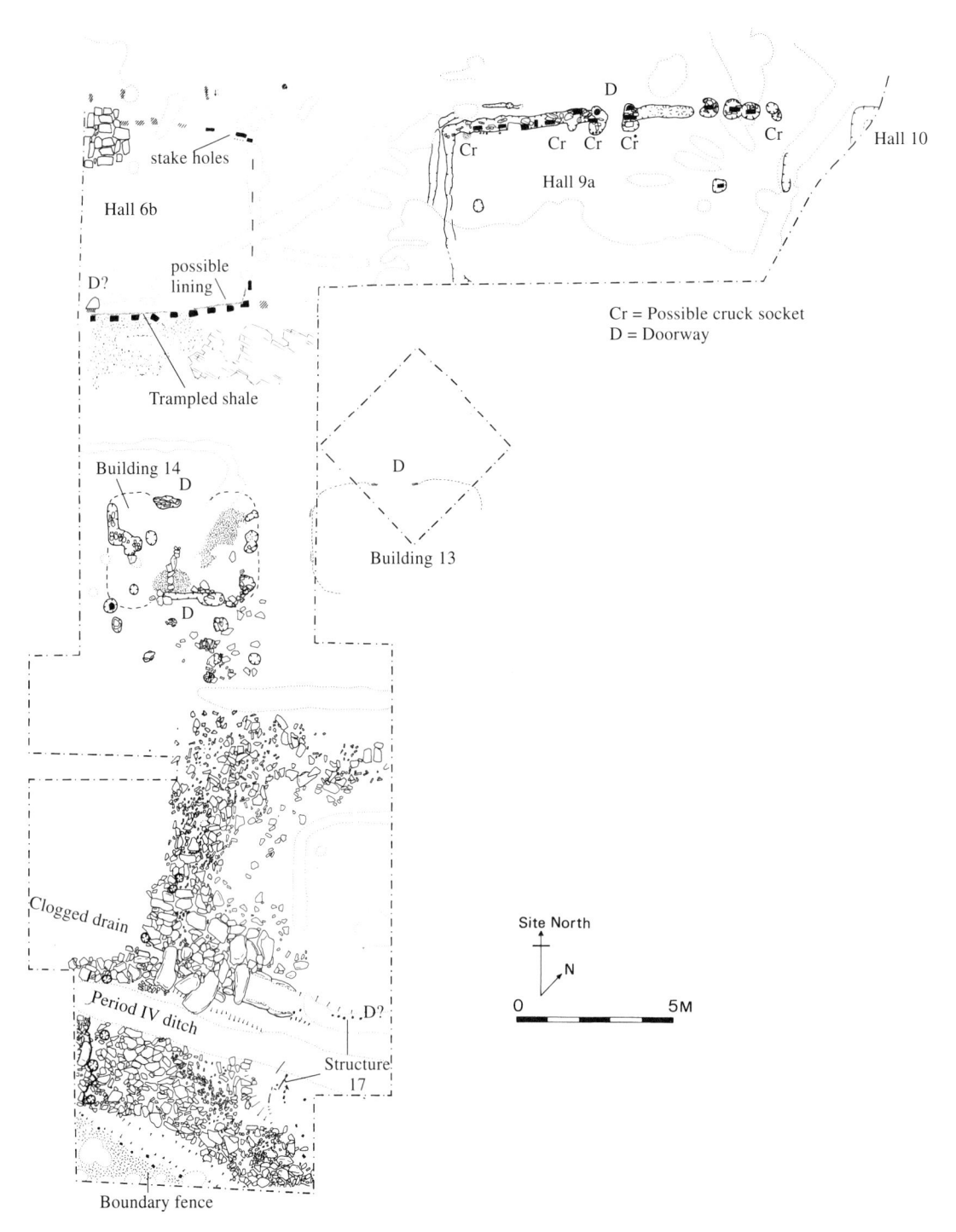

4.32 The **central** and **southern sectors** in *Stages 2, ii* and *b*.

A broken iron needle (IN39.74) and an unidentified object (IN78.21)
Four sheet fragments from an iron vessel (IN36.1)
An outer fragment of a large sandstone millstone (SE44:4)
A chisel-marked sandstone slab (SE75)
A small group of metalworking debris

Table 4.18: Finds from **Hall 7** (253)

Hall 9

Hall 9 lay some 6.0 m to the east of **Hall 6**, and was probably erected in *Stage 2*. The south part of the building oversailed the lower rock outcrop and had been virtually obliterated by later graves, while the east end had been severely damaged by an eighteenth century drain surrounding the west wing of the manse. Despite these problems, the building had a well-preserved north wall and door, and displayed interesting architectural features, suggesting the use of a different structural system from that in **Hall 6**. There were two structural phases, assigned to *Stages 2* and *3*, and probably dating to the later-eighth and earlier-ninth centuries. A shale path skirting the west wall of the building led from the chapel to the putative gateway in the outer boundary. A second path of pebbles and shale probably ran between the east wall and **Hall 10**.

Hall 9a (Figure 4.32) was some 11.2 m long and *c*. 5.0 m wide, conforming to the double-square design of related buildings (James *et al* 1984). Most of the structural evidence came from a shallow construction slot cutting the boulder clay, exposing the underlying rock, and containing a large part of the north wall. Spaced rectilinear timbers were set on the inner edge of the slot, and supported by stones placed behind them. The eastern quarter of the wall was marked by a line of post-holes, three of which revealed similarly-spaced timbers. The west wall was marked by a shallow narrow slot with no evidence of timbers or packing, while the fragmentary slot to the east produced no useful information. The doorway in the north wall comprised three pairs of timbers. The outer pair contained a round and a half-round timber, and the middle pair comprised rectangular balks of timber aligned with the western part of the wall. The sockets of the inner pair of posts were re-used in *Stage 3*, but possibly contained a pair of cruck-blades from frames spanning the middle of the building. Two shallow holes on the inner edge of the north wall slot, were perhaps the sockets of two further cruck blades, and an inset post-hole at the east end of the building may mark a third. Two post-holes on the inferred central axis of the building may have contained ridge supports, and a deep rock-cut slot in the foot of the later drain, may have contained a third in the centre of the eastern gable. Sporadic stake-holes on the inner margin of the north wall indicated a wattle screen possibly bending inwards around the putative cruck blades at the door. A shallow gully at the east end of the building was probably a drain marking the position of the overhanging eaves.

The building is reconstructed in Figure 4.33 which shows a gable roof supported by crucks and wall-plates, as inferred in other Anglo-Saxon buildings (James *et al* 1984). The wall-plates of the north and south walls are secured to the crucks by spur ties, and

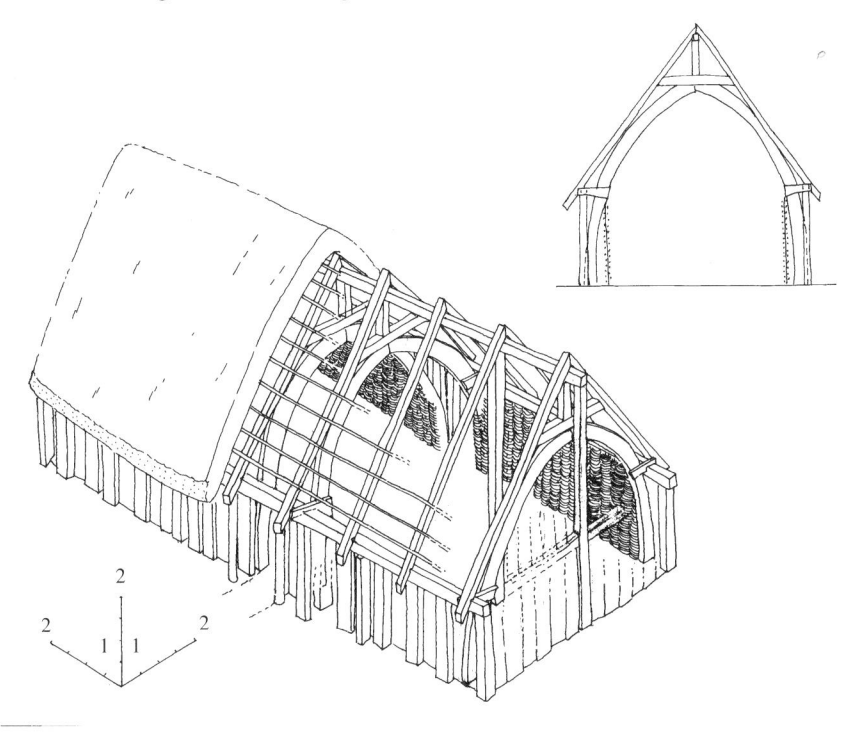

4.33 Isometric reconstruction of **Hall 9a**.

the ridge pole is supported by crown posts resting on collar beams over the crucks. The outer timber wall and inner wattle lining follow the pattern used in the reconstruction of **Hall 6**, although the evidence from the wall trench was inconclusive. The building is viewed from the north-west, and a gable post has been incorporated in the east wall on the basis of the evidence from the west end of the building. This was probably superfluous to the support of the roof structure, but could have been used to support the cruck-frames before the walls were built. It is reconstructed as the central member of a timber frame for an insubstantial wall of planks. The reconstructed building indicates that there was a major architectural change in *Stage 2*, which may also have been evident in the **Phase 5** church (p 160). This may have reflected the availability of suitable timber, and the new architectural style was probably less prodigal than the earlier tradition exemplified by **Hall 6**, though perhaps requiring managed woodland to provide suitable timbers for the cruck blades.

Hall 9b. The second phase of **Hall 9** was represented by sporadic stones covering the primary timber impressions on the north wall to form an irregular stone plinth, and indicating the repair of decaying wall timbers. The plinth was most complete to either side of the door where relatively regular footings may have supported sill beams. Further stones to the east overlay the earlier post holes, and may have been pads inserted below the timbers after their decaying bases had been trimmed off. The doorway was remodelled during this phase of repair. Narrow planks marked an inset door-frame parallel with the wall, and sandwiched between the sill beams and putative cruck blades. The four finds from the building were probably displaced from underlying deposits.

Halls 8 and **10** lay *c*. 3.0 m to the east of **Halls 7** and **9**, and were represented by two angled slots marking the north-west corners of successive buildings (Figure 4.30, 32 and 34). An isolated slot (262) in the 1984 trial trench (2) may have been part of the south wall of **Hall 8**, and a north/south slot to the south could have contained a fence aligned with the west gable, and flanking the path between **Halls 7** and **8**. A large pit dug in *c*. 1500 (601, Figure 7.8) exposed part of an extensive paved surface in the area to the east. This may have been the floor of this building, and well-preserved deposits have probably survived in this part of the site. No finds were recovered.

Building 11 (259, Figure 4.34 inset)

The latest building in the middle range was represented by a curving slot cutting the east gable of **Hall 6**, and a vestigial slot indicating a possible south wall. The ground enclosed by these features revealed two stone surfaces separated by a layer of silt, which were perhaps fragments of superimposed earth floors. These features were initially identified as an extension to **Hall 7**, but the united plan (not reproduced), though relatively convincing, is incompatible with the stratigraphic evidence. The remains thus seem to have been the latest building in the middle range, and could either have been the west end of an insubstantial hall replacing **Halls 6** and **9**, or more probably a small building, perhaps aligned north/south. The finds from the putative floors (Table 4.19) included an intrusive sherd of pottery, but the needles are characteristic of the **Period II** buildings and adjacent deposits (Figure 10.98).

Two iron needles, one broken (IN39.56), one with a punched eye (IN39.5)
A curved iron strip, perhaps a broken ring (IN81.11)
A sherd of red gritty ware (MP01)
A quartz plough pebble (SE51)
A small group of pebbles
An **unretouched** flint flake
Scraps of metalworking debris

Table 4.19: Finds from possible floors in **Building 11** (4a, 259)

The small buildings in the third range

The north part of the **southern sector** and the contiguous trial trench (5) excavated in 1984, revealed a range of small buildings aligned with the halls and ecclesiastical buildings to the north, and comprising parts four or five buildings, with three distinct phases of construction (*Stages i–iii*). The buildings in the main trench lay to the south of the lower bedrock ridge, and were not linked stratigraphically with the deposits to the north, while the 1984 trench was stratigraphically isolated. The buildings were dug into **Period I** deposits (64.01–04), and the small groups of finds from them included some redeposited material, as well as potentially contemporary objects (Tables 4.20–23). Spatial considerations suggested these buildings were ancillary to the halls to the north, but the finds were insufficiently sensitive to confirm this relationship, or identify its functional implications. The architecture of the buildings is discussed briefly above, and speculative reconstructions are presented in Figure 4.4.

Stage i saw the construction of two new buildings (**12**, 214 and **13**, 217/261.01) on the Northumbrian alignment, cut into the remains of **Buildings I/22** and **I/23**. The opposed doorways of **Building 12** were coaxial with the doors of **Hall 6a** and the secondary doorways of the **Phase 1** oratory beyond, and it was perhaps built in **Phase 1** or **2**. The two buildings shared the same alignment and were probably broadly contemporary.

Building 12 (214) lay on the west side of the main trench, and the doorway was bisected by the trench edge. The walls were contained by shallow slots, flanked to the north by a narrow rock-cut drain, bridged by paving stones immediately beyond the north door. Regularly-spaced clusters of packing stones in the eastern wall slot probably supported planks set against the inner side of the slot, as in the oratories and halls. A shale surface, possibly the substrate for an earth floor, preserved the outline of the wall, and had rounded corners, suggesting that the wall timbers were lined with wickerwork. The slots did not extend to the south-east angle where a corner post was contained in a distinct post-hole. A plank impression on the east side of the north doorway marked one side of an inset door-frame with timbers parallel to the walls. The south doorway was damaged by an intrusive post-hole, but was probably similar to the better-preserved doorway in **Building I/24**. The ground plan is reconstructed in Figure 4.3, and the construction features restored in Figure 2.8, are compared with one of the Hartlepool buildings. The building is reconstructed in Figure 4.4 and discussed above (pp 138-9).

The finds from the building are listed in Table 4.20. The wall hook and chain may have been internal fittings, while the knife and flint may have been lost during the use of the building. The other finds were probably displaced from earlier deposits.

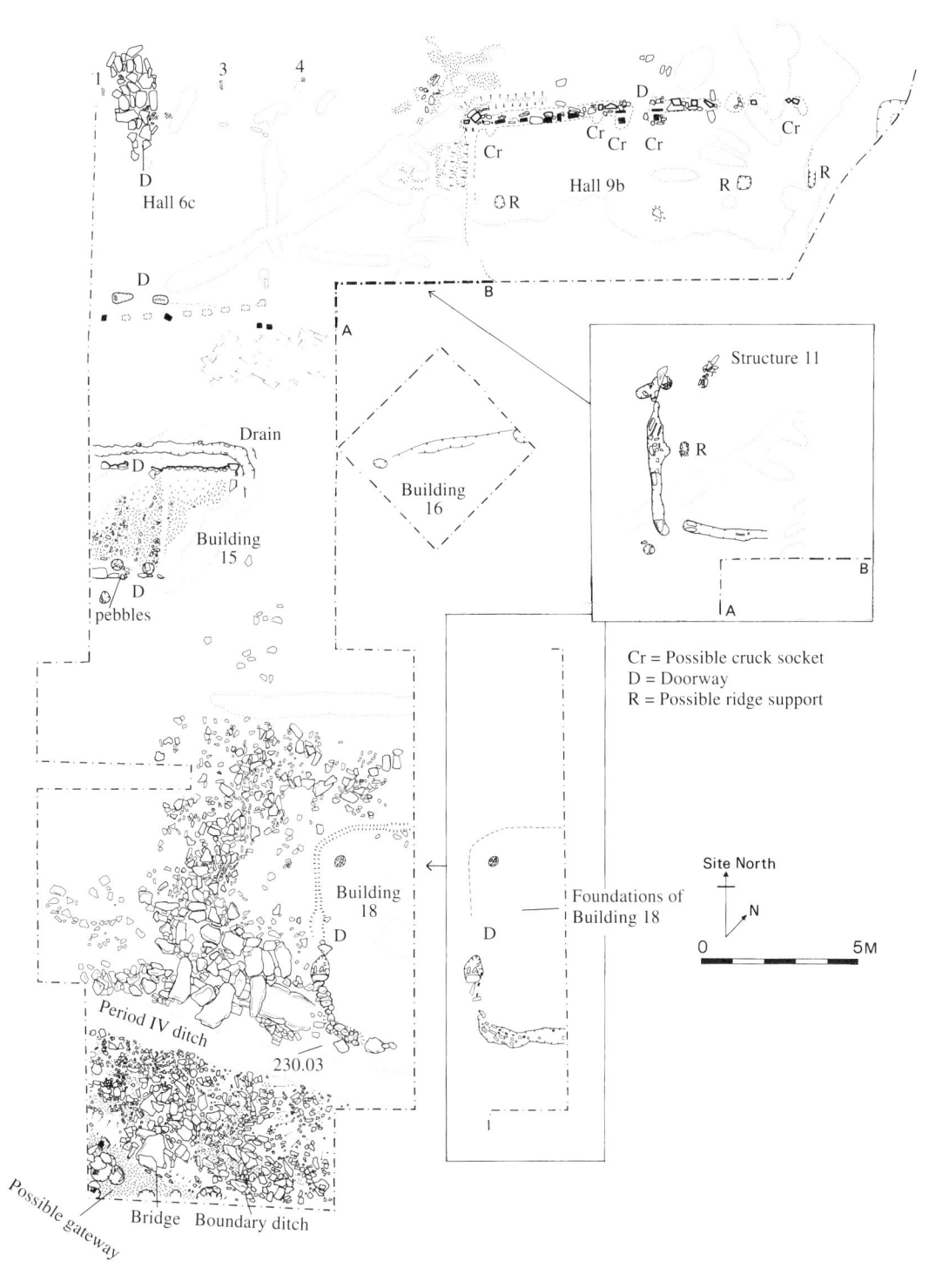

4.34 Late buildings and related features in the **central** and **southern sectors** in *Stages 3, 4, iii* and *c*.

An iron chain with a staple and a ring (IN30.1)
An iron wall-hook (IN31:11)
A probable tanged knife (IN66:76)
A natural flint pebble and a **retouched** flint
[A B*i* amphora sherd (V1)
A quartz plough pebble (SE51)
A small group of pebbles
A small group of metalworking debris]

Table 4.20: Finds from **Building II/12** (214). [ ] = potentially displaced finds.

Building 13 (217/261.01) lay 4.0 m to the east of **Building 12** on the same alignment, and was represented by middle parts of the bowed slots of the north wall, the sockets of an inset door-frame some 1.2 m wide, and a large part of the west wall slot, with characteristic spaced stone packing, mirroring the east wall of **Building 12**. The building was probably of similar size and design to its neighbours, and its ground plan is reconstructed in Figure 4.4. The finds (Table 4.21) were probably displaced from **Period I** deposits.

A curved iron strip with hammer marks (IN81:13)
[An unassigned sherd of vessel glass
A quartz plough pebble
A relatively large group of metalworking debris]

Table 4.21: Finds from **Building II/13** (217/261.01). [ ] = potentially displaced finds.

Stage ii was represented by a group of structural features overlying the eastern part of **Building 12** in the centre of the main trench (Figure 4.32), which probably represented a distinct later building (**14**), but could have been an annexe appended to **Building 12**. The surviving elements indicated that **Building 14** was a composite structure with wicker walls, timber door-frames, and external posts, perhaps supporting an extended porch. The most coherent feature was a doorway in the south wall, represented by a narrow slot for a timber sill which was respected by small paving stones. Two post-holes at the east end of the sill contained successive, deeply-set, rectilinear timbers, and an oblong socket to the north probably marked the equivalent element of a reversed, opposed doorway in the north wall. The interior revealed a patchy shale surface towards the centre of the building, and a spread of charcoal-rich soil to the west. The shale covered the south end of the east gable of the earlier building, and was in turn covered by a band of paving on the line of the old wall. This may represent a damp course inserted as in the **Phase 4** church, or could have been an internal feature of the distinct new building. The position of the walls was indicated by the door frames and internal surfaces, particularly a curving strip of paving to the east of the south door, which was probably laid within a curved wicker corner. Three shallow pits lying against the west wall were perhaps internal features.

Most of the finds (Table 4.22) came from the floor of the building, and may thus have been contemporary losses, probably in the final stages of its use. The tweezers are characteristic of domestic assemblages in **Periods II-IV** (p 377). The hone blank came from the paved strip, while the antler section derived from the comb making, and came from one of the pits on the east side of the building. The most important find was the broken cross-marked basin, which was wedged in the east socket of the south door. The fractured hollow could have been served as a pivot for the door, but displayed no sign of appropriate wear. This was almost certainly a Northumbrian liturgical fitting, perhaps a ritual mortar for preparing the host, and it may have been imported from northern England (p 437). Another piece of the fly-wheel came from a **Period I** grave (**109**), and it must have been displaced (p 114).

A broken coarse sandstone basin with a low relief cross (SE14:13)
Decorated copper alloy tweezers made from a folded strip (BZ24:4)
A broken iron blade (IN73.7) and an unidentifiable iron lump (IN93.60)
A neatly-coiled length of waste lead strip (LD11.30)
An antler beam section with a segment removed (AR19)
A broken sandstone fly-wheel (SE50.16)
A greywacke hone blank (SE71:4)
[A sherd of vessel glass (V20c)
A quartz plough pebble (SE51)
Scraps of metalworking debris]

Table 4.22: Finds from **Building II/14** (215). [ ] = potentially displaced finds.

Stage iii saw the construction of a new timber-framed building (**15**, 218) overlying the remains of **Buildings 12** and **14**, while a vestigial slot in the adjacent trial trench may have been the remains of a second building (**16**, Figure 4.34). The new building (**15**) was represented by an incomplete stone plinth of small stones enclosing a shale floor overlain by patches of yellow clay which may have been the vestiges of a clay floor, or perhaps daub fallen from the walls. Paired post sockets marked an inset door in the south wall. The western doorpost was surrounded by a bed of quartz and granite pebbles of ornamental or ritual significance. A later ditch had disturbed the ground to the north, where a matching opposed door may have lain. A narrow rock-cut drain around the northern side of the building, was similar to that around **Building 12**, and perhaps indicated the extent to which the roof overhung the walls. The stone plinth probably supported the timber sills of a timber-framed building, and this novel construction technique was unmatched on the site, despite the similarity of the stone 'plinths' inserted during running repairs to **Hall 9** and the **Phase 4** church. Despite the novelty of it foundations, the building was of similar size to its predecessors (Figure 4.3), and probably fulfilled a similar function within the *minster*.

Most of the finds came from the floor and were potentially contemporary waste, although the vessel glass and metalworking debris were probably displaced. The 'loom weight' and hone came from post holes and were presumably earlier. The most striking object was the silver pin, which does not seem to have Northumbrian parallels (pp 398-401). Pins and silver were, however, relatively common in the eighth–ninth century deposits to the north (Figure 10.98), and it could be a contemporary loss, perhaps of an old – and cherished – object.

A ball headed silver pin with radial grooves of seventh/eighth century type (SR6)
A bent copper-alloy hook (BZ27:3)
An iron punch/awl or pin (IN50:70)
A medium-grained greywacke 'loom weight' (SE29:3)
A large manufactured greywacke hone (SE33:2)
An angular flint pebble, two cores, three **unretouched** flakes and a scraper
  221 rounded quartz pebbles
  6 abraded angular quartz pebbles
  49 granite pebbles
  29 quartz pebbles with Calcium carbonate
[Three glass vessel sherds (V9g, Gp B1, Gp E2)
Scraps of metalworking debris]

Table 4.23: Finds from **Building II/15** (218). [ ] = potentially displaced finds.

Stage iv followed the abandonment of the *Stage iii* buildings, and was marked by a trampled surface of cobbles and shale, encompassing the remains of earlier buildings and surfaces. This was followed by a period of disuse, when the low-lying ground was flooded, which lasted until the beginning of **Period IV**.

The outer boundary and the southern part of the southern sector

The southern part of the **southern sector** revealed a sequence of surfaces and structures, interleaved with waterborne silt, and including a fragment of the curvilinear outer boundary of the *minster*. The crucial evidence came from the area at the south end of the trench beyond the main **Period IV** ditch (417). The deposits here were excavated under the disadvantageous circumstances of a rising water table at the end of the 1987 season, and have previously been interpreted as a building flanked to the north by a ditch (e.g. Hill 1990a, 16–17, Fig. 14). The identification of the outer boundary of **Period I/4** (Figure 3.42) prompted a reappraisal of these features, and the recognition that the curvilinear **Period I** boundary, now marked by a shallow ditch and wattle fence, probably remained in use until the latter part of **Period II**. A section through the boundary and overlying pond silts is illustrated in Figure 6.7, which reveals the insubstantiality of the remains.

Finds from this area were generally sparse, despite the moist conditions which preserved wood and other botanical remains, and most of the artefacts (predominantly sherds of vessel glass) were probably displaced from **Period I** deposits. This small assemblage can be contrasted with the rich and varied groups of debris that accumulated in the same area during **Periods I.10** (pp 129-30, Table 3.45) and **IV.6** (pp 222-4, Tables 6.10–11), and in the **central sector** at roughly the same time (Tables 4.4–6). This indicated that the area was kept relatively clean, and was perhaps little used.

Stage a. **Building I/24** has been ascribed to the final phase of **Period I** on the bases of its orientation and relationship to the earlier **Building I/21**, but seems to have remained standing in the opening years of **Period II**, and was perhaps one of many buildings in the *outer zone* to span both periods. The continuing occupation of **Building I/24** (Figure 4.30) after the abandonment of the other **Period I** buildings in the *outer zone*, was indicated by paving which surrounded the western half of the building, and oversailed the remains of **Building I/22**. A cross-marked slab (SE14.1) outside the north door of **Building I/24**, may have been a gravemarker displaced from the graveyard to the north, perhaps during the construction of the first **Period II** buildings. The abandonment of the building was followed by flooding, which deposited a layer of waterborne silt over its remains, and presumably reflected the rising water table which preserved its structural timbers (p 130).

Stage b presumably followed the desertion of **Building I/24**, and saw the erection of a new sunken-floored structure (**17**) dug through the clogged **Period I** drain (230.01) on the east side of the trench (Figure 4.32). The sides of the hollow were reveted with regular-squared oak stakes with vestigial traces of horizontal wands. A larger post immediately beyond the curved south-west corner, was reminiscent of the isolated corner posts of **Buildings 12** and **14**, and the structure can be reconstructed as a similar sub-rectilinear wattle-walled building (Figure 4.3), although its moist low-lying site seems an unwise choice for a sunken-floored dwelling. One of the stakes came from a tree felled between 756 and 801 AD (pp 595-6), and the structure may thus be ascribed to the later-eighth century, and correlated with the **Phase 4** and **5** buildings to the north.

A new path seems to have been laid at this time, rerouting the southern part of the earlier pathway which skirted **Building I/24** (Figure 4.30). The upper part of the clogged **Period I** drain was filled with stones, and overlain by paving including three massive slabs which had perhaps been moved from the redundant bridge to the south of **Building I/24**. The paving ran up to the edge of a shallow ditch on the line of the outer boundary. This now seems to have been marked by a fence, surviving as a line of stakes on the outer edge of the ditch. Post-holes marked a second fence to the west of the north/south path, and were abutted by a line of stones in the southern part of the trench, that may have been the base of a wall blocking access to the west.

The small group of finds from **Structure 17** is listed in Table 4.24. The flints, vessel glass and hearth were probably displaced. The wood shows a predominance of oak in contrast with the later group from **Building 18**, and included the chronologically-vital dated stake.

Three featureless sherds of vessel glass
Two **retouched** flints
A complex oval 'hearth' with a trapped tuyere nozzle fragment
A group of wood comprising:
  An oak offcut from a tree growing in 410–514 AD

An oak stake from a tree growing in 643–752, and felled
   756–801 AD
Six oak stakes
A reused alder post and an alder stake
A fragment of ash

Table 4.24: Finds from **Structure 17** (234)

Stage c saw the erection of a new building (**18**) overlying the remains of **Building I/24**, and clipping the north side of **Structure 17** (Figure 4.34). The remains probably comprised the western half of a sub-rectilinear wattle building aligned north/south. The surviving features were a shallow gully penetrating the shale substrate of **Building I/24**, and leading into a deeper crescentic slot cut into the floor of the **Period I** ditch. The south-east angle preserved a regular line of stakes with the characteristic curved corner of wattle buildings, and similar deep crescentic corners were identified in some of the **Period III** buildings to the north, and in other buildings on the north side of the hill (Pollock 1993, 13). The south side of a doorway in the west wall was indicated by a large post-hole, and the stakes curved inwards at this point, as in other buildings (Figure 4.3). A vestigial shale surface, perhaps the substrate of an earth floor, was recorded in section, but not recognised in plan. The ground plan of the building is reconstructed in Figure 4.3, and may mark a transitional stage between the timber and wattle buildings of **Period II**, and the wattle buildings prevailing in **Period III**. The **Period I** ditch was partly recut to form a drain to the south of the building, which destroyed a small part of **Building 17**, and was itself disturbed by a later stone-filled sump (230.03).

A new irregular surface of rough flags was laid in the area to the south of the **Period IV** ditch, oversailing **Structure 17**, but still respecting the shallow boundary ditch. This was now bridged by a large flagstone, indicating a possible pathway to the south-east, and straddled by a group of post-holes, which were perhaps the remains of successive gateways.

The small group of finds from **Building 18** is listed in Table 4.25. The glass sherd was probably displaced, and a similar vessel (18) was probably deposited at the beginning of **Period I/2** (p 303). The enigmatic granite object is the most striking of a small group of cupped stones from this period (p 462). Both objects came from the slot cutting the earlier ditch. The wood included a wider range of species than used in **Structure 17** (Table 4.24). The finds from the sump were problematical, and the group is probably contaminated with material from the adjacent **Period IV.6** deposits, which are the likely source of the leather offcut, and perhaps the lead rivet (Tables 6.10–12). The finds from the putative gateway (Table 4.27) were probably displaced from the underlying **Period I** deposits.

A rim sherd of a French blue glass vessel (V19)
A large roughly-shaped granite dome with a shallow hollow in its
   apex (SE49.4)
An interesting group of wood including
   Five stakes and two offcuts of willow
   Two laths and a stake of oak
   An ash lath
   Four stakes, a lath and three pieces of hazel
   Two pieces of *Pomoideae* roundwood
   An alder stake and a piece of worked roundwood

Table 4.25: Finds from possible **Building*** (229)

A round-shanked lead rivet (LD06.2)
A piece of rock crystal (SE58.12)
A greywacke fragment with parallel incised grooves (SE54.10)
A fragment of greywacke with a pecked groove around one end
   (SE7.13)
171 trimmings, offcuts and scraps of unidentified hide
One **unretouched** and six **retouched** flints
Scraps of metalworking debris
A large collection of wood including:
   Prunus sp. twigs
   Hazel (*Corylus av.*) twigs (eight, three chopped)
   Worked oak (*Quercus sp.*) including offcuts, laths and a
   damaged trenail
   A possible turning cone (*Corylus av.*)

Table 4.26: Finds from sump (230.03) to the south of **Building 18**

Vessel sherds from Vessels 3 (a) and 20 (d)
Two **retouched** and one **unretouched** flints

Table 4.27: Finds from gateway or building in south-west corner of trench (213)

Stage d saw the inundation of the low-lying ground, and as marked by a thick deposit of waterborne silt covering much of the **southern sector** (Figures 2.14, 6.7). This seems to have been a shallow muddy pool or sluggish stream (pp 598-601) which remained until the area was drained at the beginning of **Period IV**. It is impossible to date the beginning of this long phase of flooding with any precision. It has been ascribed to the latter part of **Period II** as an appropriate, but as yet unproven, time.

CHAPTER 5

Period III: The *minster* restored
c. 845 – 1000 x 1050 AD

Peter Hill, Jo Moran, Andrew Nicholson, Dave Pollock, Damien Ronan

INTRODUCTION

Period III saw the restoration of the *minster* after the fire which destroyed the **Period II** church and burial chapel, and was clearly defined by structural developments in the **northern** and **central sectors** which revealed a long sequence of frequently fragmentary buildings. The **southern sector** was flooded throughout this time, but produced a group of debris scattered beyond the settlement. The latter part of the period saw the restoration of the curvilinear design of the sixth/seventh century *monasterium*, and was followed in **Period IV** by the drainage of the flooded area and the expansion of settlement onto the reclaimed ground. This change can be identified stratigraphically with precision, though its date was much less certain, and is placed in the period *c.* 1000–1050 AD with due caution.

Past excavations. Past excavations have revealed no evidence of the **Period III** *minster* apart from the sculptures of the *Whithorn School* which were probably produced during the latter part of this period and may have marked a ritual focus, perhaps a high status graveyard. A number of these sculptures were discovered by William Galloway's workmen in the vicinity of the 'chapter house' (pp 619-20), which may have been their original position, but they may have been removed there during **Period V**.

Previous publications. Previous publications of the Whithorn Trust excavations (especially Hill 1990 and 1991a) record a confused picture in which the remains of **Periods III** and **IV** were still enmeshed. These are superseded by the present account.

Stratigraphy and phasing. Period III revealed three principal phases of activity sub-divided into ten *stages* (Figure 5.1). The successive, densely-clustered buildings revealed numerous stratigraphic relationships, many of which are omitted from the diagram for the sake of simplicity. There were few stratigraphic links between the **northern** and **central sectors**, and the correlations proposed are necessarily speculative. The pond silts in the **southern sector** can be linked tentatively with the **Phase 3** settlement, but otherwise revealed little activity (Figure 6.7). These are omitted from Figure 5.1, but included in Figures 4.2 and 6.1.

The buildings. Only two of the forty-two small buildings described below were identified during the excavation, and this accounts for the major discrepancies between this and previous reports. The apparent blindness of the excavation team is partly the result of the stratigraphic havoc wrought by the **Period V** graves, but is principally due to the nature and unfamiliarity of the evidence. The **Period III** buildings conformed to the enduring tradition of small sub-rectilinear structures of light construction, but were now erected without the post-holes and slots which framed the **Period II** buildings, or the stakeholes and gullies identifying their precursors in **Period I**. The new structures seem to have been built in shallow sub-rectilinear hollows in the topsoil, and only a few had deep sockets for structural supports. The walls probably comprised light wattling or wicker, and were indicated by internal and external surfaces laid against them, and in rare instances by bands of clay which had presumably eroded from daub coatings. The floors seem to have comprised beaten earth, sometimes resting on a substrate of cobbles, shale or heat-shattered greywacke. Excavation in 1992 and 1993 established that such earth floors could be identified with considerable precision (Pollock 1993), but in previous years the fine clayey silts of earth floors had been interpreted as worm-sorted soil marking episodes of disuse, and ascribed to hyperactive earthworms. A sample of one earth floor was included in a small group of thin-sectioned soil samples to examine the hypothesis that it was a wormed soil (Sample W4, pp 599-600). The 'invisible' **Period III** buildings were eventually revealed by the rounded corners marked by lines of angled stones and internal and external surfaces. Once isolated, these building made considerable sense of the confusing stratigraphic record, and many, though not all, can be treated with confidence. The earlier features had suffered particularly severe damage from subsequent buildings and graves, and a

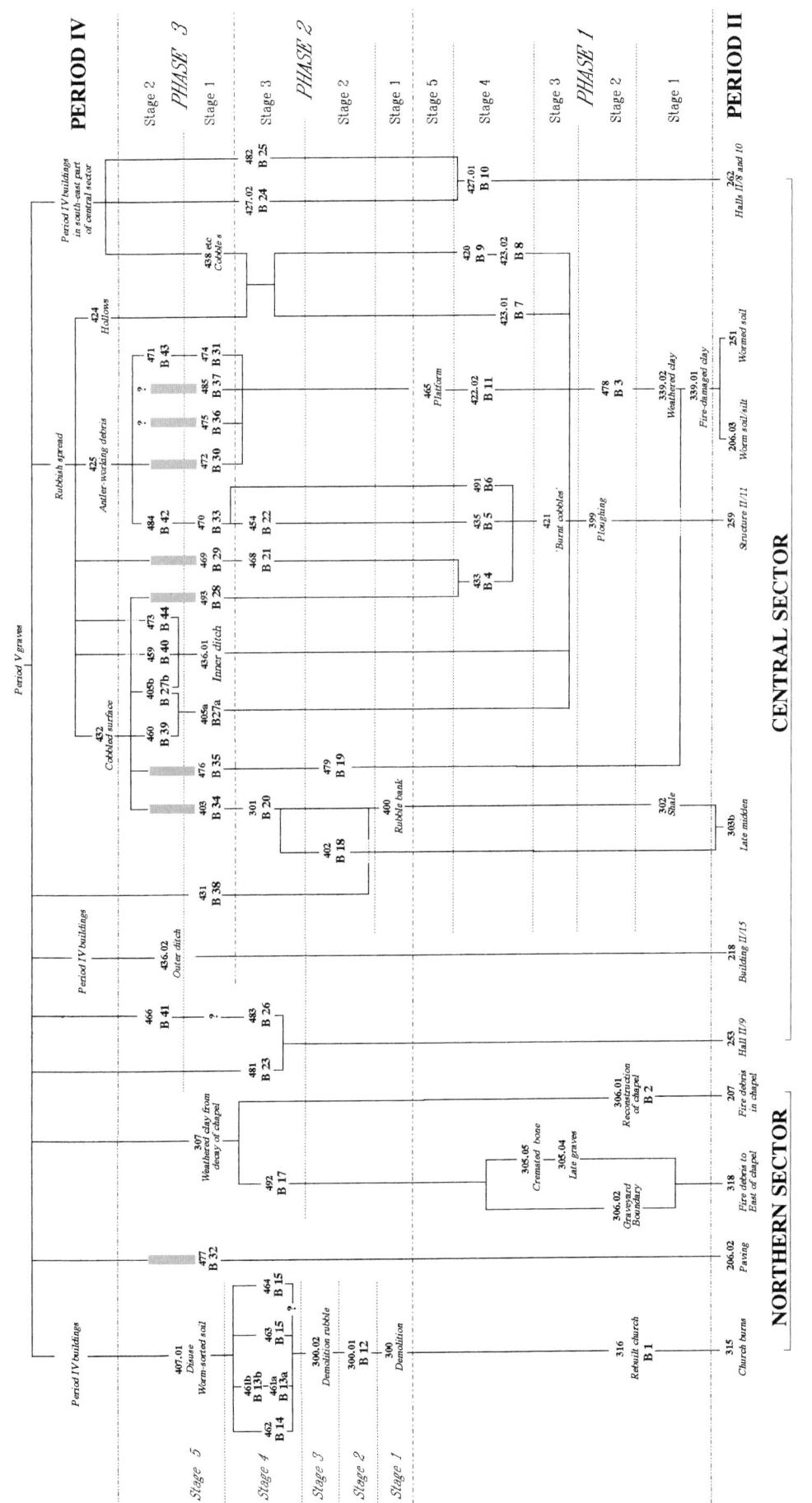

5.1 The stratigraphic sequence in **Period III**.

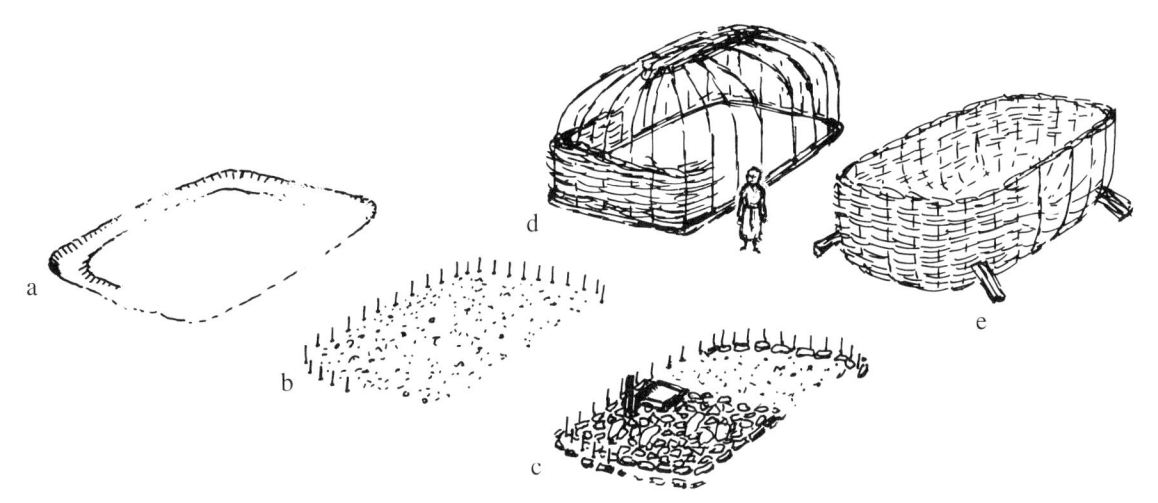

5.2 The inferred construction of the small buildings of **Period III/3**.
a Shallow sunken stance with deeper corners. **b** Prefabricated wicker walls set in stance subsequently floored with earth on stone bed. **c** Distinct paved and earth floor areas. **d** Prefabricated on wooden frame.
e Superstructure prefabricated up-side-down.

number of possible buildings have been identified which should be treated as informed speculations, rather than confirmed structures.

The general absence of post-holes, construction slots and deep stake-holes is one of the most striking features of these buildings and explains the use of the term 'wicker' to describe the walls. The **Period I** buildings in the **southern sector** had walls of substantial stakes which may have served as the wands of wattle panels, and the absence of large stake holes in the **Period III** buildings argues for a lighter, perhaps more closely-woven, style of wall. One building (27) seems to have been moved bodily between the two stages of **Period III/3**, and perhaps had a semi-rigid superstructure akin to a large, inverted basket. This would account for the absence of substantial structural members, while the shallow hollows in which the building were seated and the deeper corners would have served to stabilise the open part of the basket. The small size of most of the buildings means that large timbers would not have been needed to strengthen the wattle frame, and their principal interest lies in the distinctive arrangement of internal features and the potential invisibility of their remains. The construction features of a typical building of **Period III/3** (Figure 5.2) comprise (**a**) a shallow, sunken, sub-rectilinear building stance with deeper foundations for the corners, filled with stones and fine soil after the walls had been inserted (**b**). The distinctive floor plan (**c**) comprises paved and unpaved areas, with a hearth set in the paved part. Alternative sketches of the prefabrication of a building show upright (**d**) and inverted (**e**) modes.

Finds assemblages. Most of the assemblages of finds from **Period III** deposits seem to have been relatively uncontaminated with earlier material, despite the challenging stratigraphy and extensive disturbance of many deposits. Many of these groups came from earth-floored buildings, and the earth flooring seems to have been specially chosen, or prepared, from fine silt, and rarely produced material overtly derived from earlier deposits. The earth floors were probably kept clean while the buildings were occupied, and the finds perhaps reflect brief episodes of untidiness when the floors were renewed or the buildings fell into disuse. These assemblages were generally not sealed by clearly-defined layers, and many were potentially contaminated with objects from the overlying **Period IV** debris (Figures 6.23–39). Poorly-stratified and displaced finds add an extra dimension to the interpretation of **Period III**, and are discussed in **Chapter 2** (pp 50-2) and Appendix 2 (pp 621-3). Many of these finds had been displaced into fourteenth-fifteenth century graves covering much of the *inner precinct*, and the palimpsest of disorganised evidence is explored in the final section of Chapter 6 (pp 237-50).

The finds revealed a dramatic change in the material culture of the community, corresponding with the erection of the first buildings in **Phase 1.2**. Selected classes of finds illustrating this are listed in Table 5.1, and include a range of cultural, chronological, economic and functional indicators. Plated iron stick pins (**a**) and club-headed copper-alloy pins (**f**) seem to have been superseded by ring pins (**p**), and millstones (**c**) by querns (**r**, pp 459-60), while silver (**d**) possibly disappeared or became less common, and amber (**q**) and opaque white beads (**o**) were introduced. Stratified Northumbrian coins (**b, h** and **m**) spanned **Period II** and the earlier part of **Period III**, and revealed a coherent depositional sequence (pp 352-5), while spindle whorls became more common in **Period III**, and comb-making extensive. Needles and knives were evenly distributed, lead-working waste was concentrated in the ultimate **Period II** deposits, and locks and keys were absent from **Period III** contexts. The implications of these changes are discussed in Chapter 2, while their rapidity is evident from the lists of finds from the later stages of **Period II** and earlier part of **Period III**.

	a	b	c	d	e	f	g	h	i	j	k	l	m	n	o	p	q	r
Period III/1.3–3.2/	/	/	/	/	/	/	1	7	5	6	8	4	A	3	1	2	3
Period III/1.1-1.2 /	/	/	/	1	1	1	3	14	2	2	1	2	p	/	1	1	/
Period II	5	17	2	5	2	3	3	7	43	8	9	5	1	p	1	/	/	/

Table 5.1: Incidence of selected finds in **Periods II** and **III**
a = Plated iron stick pins, **b** = Phase I stycas, **c** = millstones, **d** = silver, **e** = wall hooks, **f** = club-headed copper alloy pins, **g** = locks and keys, **h** = Earlier Phase II stycas, **i** = lead working waste, **j** = knives, **k** = needles, **l** = spindle whorls, **m** = Later Phase II stycas **n** = comb-making debris, **o** = opaque white beads, **p** = ringed pins, **q** = amber, **r** = quern fragments.

A= Abundant, p = present

Phase 1

Phase 1 saw the reconstruction of the church and refurbishment of the burial chapel in the **northern sector**, while a parallel sequence of deposits in the **central sector** included a phase of cultivation followed by the construction of small wattle buildings and the introduction of a comb making industry (Figure 5.3). These developments seem to record the partial restoration of the **Period II** *minster*, but many of the cultural and economic aspects of the settlement had changed. Coins from the **central sector** indicated that the **Phase 1** developments spanned a relatively brief period in the later- ninth century (pp 189, 352-5). There were few links between the **northern** and **central sectors**, and the two areas are described separately.

The Northern Sector

The deposits in the **northern sector** had been severely damaged by later features, and only fragments of the **Phase 1** structures had survived. These comprised a stone-founded building erected on the site of the **Period II** church, and the burial chapel, which seems to have been rebuilt or restored. The ground to the east of the chapel was relatively undisturbed, and revealed a sequence of unusual burials.

The rebuilt church (**1**, 316). The rebuilt church was represented by fragmentary stone wall-footings to the south, north and west; opposed doorways in the north and south walls; a strip of paving at the west end of the building, and paved paths abutting the north and south walls (Figure 5.4). The position of the east wall was uncertain, but was perhaps indicated by a gap in the rubble which filled the building after it was demolished. The building was erected over the burnt remains of the **Period II** church, and had been more severely affected by later disturbances, including small buildings erected in **Phase 2**, the western part of the fourteenth–fifteenth century graveyard, and a greenhouse built in the late-nineteenth century.

The north wall was the best-preserved with up to seven surviving courses of small stones. The structure was relatively insubstantial and the 'walls' were probably the plinth for a timber superstructure of which there was no other evidence. The opposed doorways in the north and south walls were framed by internally-splayed timbers set in deep sockets cut into the remains of the chancel doors of the earlier building. A relatively large area of the floor was preserved beneath the rubble filling the demolished building (Figure 5.8). This surface had not been trampled, and the building is thus likely to have had a raised timber floor, presumably resting on joists supported by the stone plinth. The paved band at the west end of the building must therefore have lain at a lower level that the raised timber floor, and was perhaps, enclosed by a recessed wooden frame. The paving had been disturbed in **Phase 2**, and its original extent and shape was uncertain. One of the stones bore a carefully-executed design of intersecting compass-drawn circles (Figure 5.4.inset; SE14.17) forming a marigold or hexafoil cross. The paved path to the south of the building included a slab with a graffito of three compass-drawn circles, suggesting a link with the graffiti on the path to the south of the chapel (below). The demolition of the superstructure at the end of **Phase 1** was indicated by scattered charcoal on the floor, but the stone plinth remained standing, and a small building (**12**) seems to have been constructed within this shell at the beginning of **Phase 2** (p 195, Figure 5.3b).

The small group of finds from the church (Table 5.2) was relatively uninformative, and most of the objects were probably displaced from underlying deposits pertaining to the destruction of the earlier church in **Period II/7** (pp 162-4). The sceat of Eadberht came from shale levelling beneath the paving on the north side of the church and had presumably been displaced from an eighth century deposit. The styca of Aethelred II is one of a significant concentration of Group A coins from the church (pp 352-5). The strap end, from a poorly-stratified context to the north of the church, is a devolved version of the strap ends found in the main **Period II** rubbish spread (303, Table 4.4), and may have been a late variant of this type produced locally.

A sceat of Eadberht (CN02.3, *c*. 737–758, Pirie Aii)
A styca of Aethelred II (CN02.37, *c*. 841–9 NUM AD, Pirie IIAi)
A copper-alloy pendant strap-end with a possible stylised animal head (BZ19.6)
A broken, tanged knife blade (IN66.77)
A square sectioned iron point (IN51.1)
Two nails and four shanks
An iron rivet or nail shank (IN21.7)
A plated nail in mineralised wood
Three parallel iron strips (IN78.22) and a plate (IN82.25)
A driblet of molten lead (LD13.4)
Two **unretouched** flints
A group of pebbles
A relatively large group of metalworking debris

Table 5.2: Finds from rebuilt church of **Period III Phase 1** (316)

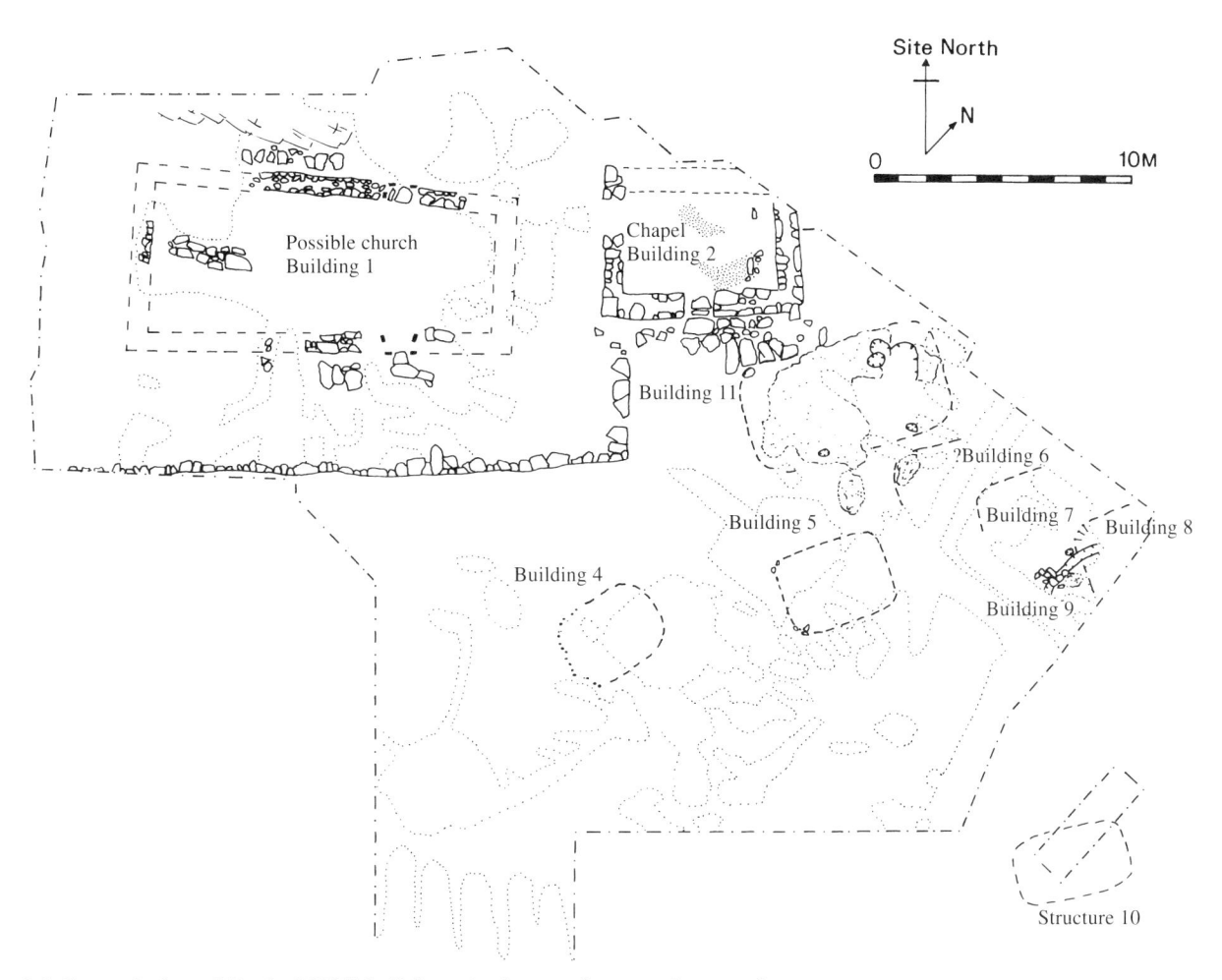

5.3 General plan of **Period III/1** buildings in the **northern** and **central sectors**.

It was not certain that the new building was in fact a church, and other ecclesiastical or secular functions are possible. The principal reason for interpreting it as a church was that it seems to have been a substantial, carefully constructed building which, though shorter, occupied a similar position to the **Period II** church. The marigold design on the paving lay on the central axis of the building, and may have had liturgical significance.

The rebuilt burial chapel (306, 308). The reconstruction of the chapel after the fire was demonstrated by the renewal of the east wall and south door (Figure 5.4), and later disturbances – notably the fourteenth–fifteenth century graveyard – may have removed equivalent evidence from other parts of the building. The new east wall was set in a shallow construction trench cutting into the graveyard soil, and overlying the stump of the earlier plinth. The new wall was slightly narrower than its predecessor and was bonded with yellow clay. The new south doorway was well-preserved. An external timber sill was abutted by the extant paving and a new threshold stone displayed the distinctive wear of an inward-opening door hung from the west side of the doorway. The sides of the doorway were lined with timbers contained in shallow slots. The eastern slot extended into the interior of the chapel, and revealed the casts of three planks. A new earth floor was represented by patches of clayey soil overlying the fire debris in the slumped **Period II** graves (Figure 4.21). A line of stones may have been the remains of a bench or some other fitting at the east end of the building. There were no new internal burials and no evidence that the positions of the earlier graves had been remembered.

A bank of clay and stones (308) abutting the eastern part of the south wall of the chapel may have been a buttress erected at this time. The paved path outside the chapel was repaired by laying small stones beside the buttress and new slabs to the east of the doorway. The path probably continued eastwards to join the paving to the south of the church and the group of compass-drawn graffiti (SE14.19, 21–4, pp 155, 439-41) may have been executed at this time. There was a similar design on a large paving stone flanking the church which could relate to the use of either or both of these buildings.

Period III burials. A line of rocks overlying the fire debris (318) to the east of the chapel, defined a boundary to the south of the former children's graveyard. This restored a long-lived boundary of **Period II**, and suggested that further buildings to

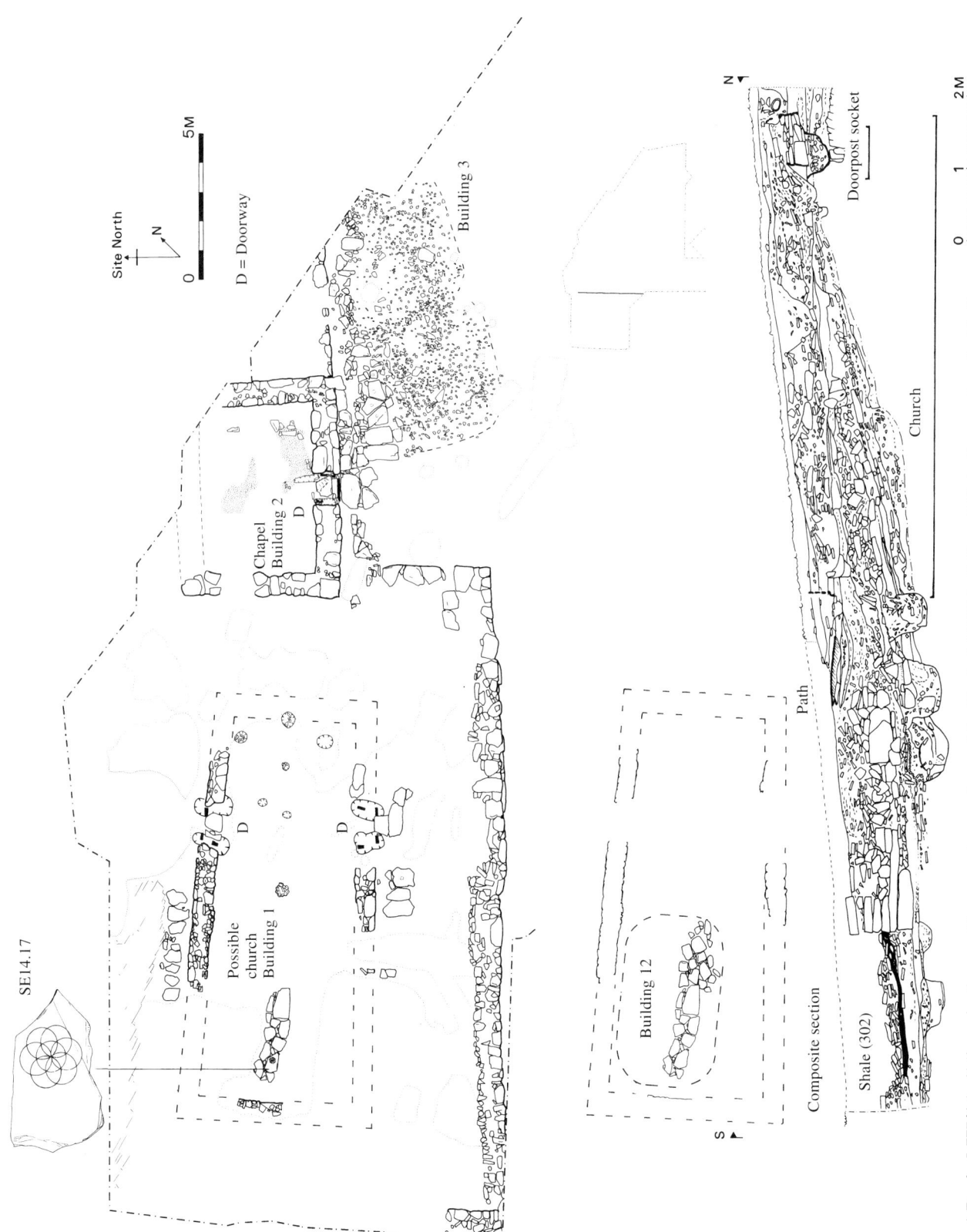

5.4 **Period III/1** buildings in the **northern sector** and possible **Period III/2** building (**12**) in the western half of the former church (inset).

The last burial comprised a spread of cremated human bone (305.05) scattered over a narrow strip of ground to the east of the chapel, but concentrated over the grave containing bundled bones (Figure 5.5b). Some 2002 gm of comminuted bone included the remains of at least four individuals, none obviously immature (p 560). Fragments of long bones displayed horizontal cracks indicating that they were burnt while 'green', and so derived from wholly or partially intact corpses rather than desiccated skeletons. The fragments were neither buried nor concealed, and they may have been contained in a bag placed beside the chapel, and had scattered as it disintegrated. The northern end of the scatter of bone was disturbed by a **Phase 2** building (**17**, 492). Cremation was an overtly pagan practice and this deposit may have reflected the changed cultural circumstances of the later-ninth century (p 54).

The central sector

Period II ended with the burning of the *Northumbrian* church and burial chapel in *c*. 845 AD, but there were no equivalent burnt deposits in the **central sector** which was perhaps unoccupied at this time. Although the archaeological evidence of subsequent developments had been severely compromised by later disturbances, a stratified deposit immediately to the south of the burial chapel revealed a coherent sequence of five *stages* with which the fragmentary remains to the south can be correlated tentatively. Despite the challenging stratigraphy, the finds from these remains were informative, and show that the function of this part of the site had changed radically by the time the first buildings were erected in *Stage 2*.

The **Phase 1** deposits produced a small group of Northumbrian coins including three stycas of the second reign of Aethelred II, and one of Osberht (pp 352-5) probably dating to the later 840s and 850s, and demonstrating that economic contact with Northumbria had been maintained after the crisis. The end of *Stage 4* was marked by burnt deposits in several of the buildings and on the surrounding ground. This apparently coincided with the deposition of the latest in the series of Northumbrian coins, although a few earlier coins were recovered from slightly later contexts. The burnt deposits could have been caused by an accidental fire, but might have resulted from renewed warfare in the sixth or seventh decade of the ninth century. The coins indicated that **Phase 1** spanned no more than twenty years or so in *c*. 845–865 AD, but later deposits produced scant dating evidence, and this inference cannot be substantiated.

Stage 1 followed the fire. Fire-damaged structural debris was cleared from the chapel, and a pile of clay scattered with charcoal and nails (339.01) was dumped on the stone path leading south. This clearance necessarily preceded the refurbishment of the chapel (306), but no construction debris survived

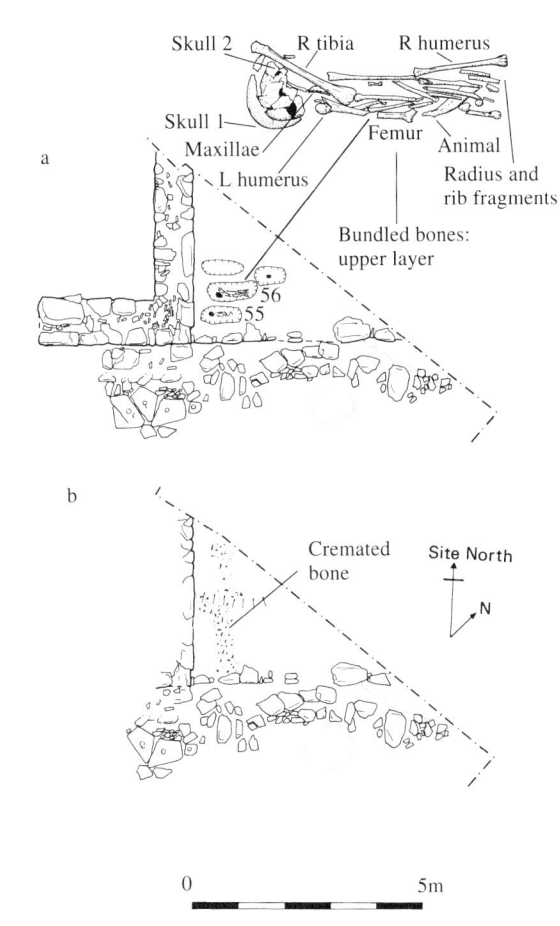

5.5a **Period III/1** burials to the east of the chapel. **a** Burials and adjacent pits. **b** Cremated human bone over burials.

the east had been restored – or perhaps remained standing – at this time. Two graves were dug through the burnt deposits in the angle between the boundary and the chapel (Figure 5.5a). The more southerly grave (**55**) contained the body of an infant of 8–12 months, with beads of amber (AM01.2) and shale (SH03.1) lying on its chest. The second burial (**56**) comprised a neat bundle of bones placed in a narrow hollow, and included parts of two adult humans and the forelimb of a cow (pp 559-60). Most of the bones came from an early-middle-aged female, and all the skeleton was present, except the right radius and a few ribs. The body was probably incompletely decomposed when the remains were buried, as some of the bones lay in anatomically correct relationships to each other. The second skeleton was represented by part of the skull and a few other bones, and was perhaps a young or early middle-aged male. The bones seem to have been placed in a perishable container or wrapped in cloth, and could thus have been brought to Whithorn from some distance. The presence of parts of two adults and a cow indicates a certain confusion when the bones were gathered, and they could have come from the scene of some catastrophe – war, plague or famine. Disarticulated human bones were, however, found in earlier deposits associated with the chapel (p 169), and this group could have reflected the continuance of practices established in **Period II**.

here, and the dumped clay was exposed long enough for a layer of worm-sorted soil to develop (339.02). This soil produced a styca of Archbishop Uigmund (Table 5.5) and a similar coin (CN02.46) from an overlying building (**3**, Table 5.6) may have been displaced from the same deposit. A discontinuous spread of shale (302) at the foot of the terrace oversailed the earlier rubbish spreads (II/303), and was interleaved with the dumped clay. This was untrampled, and seems to have weathered from the terrace, perhaps as a result of poor maintenance or sharp frosts.

The large group of finds from the fire debris shared features with the groups from the **Period II** rubbish spreads (Tables 4.4–6) and, to a lesser extent, with the burnt deposits in the church (Table 4.7). It included a wider range of objects than the fire debris from the floor of the chapel (Table 4.10), which was therefore unlikely to have been its source, although the nails may have come from the shingled roof of the building (pp 166-7). It included a marked concentration of knives and other small tools and scrap iron, and the smaller group of finds from the adjacent shale (Table 5.4) had similar features. Both groups contrasted with the assemblages of comb-making debris, hones and other finds from the marginally later buildings to the east (Tables 5.6, 9–12,14). These spreads of rubbish probably accumulated during the mid-ninth century crisis and were effectively contemporary with the ultimate **Period II** deposits, despite their ascription to the subsequent phase.

A tin-plated, club-headed copper alloy pin (BZ13.3) and a pin shank (BZ9.1)
A copper alloy button (BZ17.12) and a gilded, rolled ring (BZ28.10)
A broken copper-alloy rod (BZ36.12) and a folded strip (BZ38.29)
An iron pin (IN40.10)
A complete Class D knife (IN66.41) and a broken Class A2 knife (IN66.12)
A blade with a broken tang, possibly from shears (IN73.9)
A possible iron punch (IN50.58) and wedge (IN53.4)
A tapering iron point (IN65.7)
A riveted, U-shaped strip (IN78.23), five strip fragments (IN80.59, 81.14–16) and a broken bar (IN83.10)
Eleven nails, five shanks and four nail heads
An ovoid domed lead weight (LD5.2)
Eight pieces of lead waste (LD10.7, LD11.32–38) and four nodular fragments (LD12.27–30)
Three sherds of light green window glass (GS06.101–3)
Lumps of daub and baked clay
A small group of pebbles
A fairly small group of metalworking debris

Table 5.3: Finds from fire-damaged clay spread to south of chapel (339.01)

A spring and possibly-plated barrel-padlock lock-plate (IN33.3)
A possible iron awl (IN50.21)
An iron strip with two protruding nails (IN80.58)
A curved iron bar (IN83.9) and a corroded piece of iron (IN93.61)
An arrowhead point of white flint

Table 5.4: Finds from shale abutting Northumbrian terrace (302)

A Group Ci styca of Uigmund, Archbishop of York (*c.* 841–843/4 AD, CN02.48)

An iron wall-hook (IN31.12)
A short standard iron needle with a mispunched eye (IN39.9) and a broken pin (IN40.11)
A length of iron wire pinched at 6.5mm intervals (IN90.5)
An iron nail and two shanks
Four pebbles
A small group of metalworking debris.

Table 5.5: Finds from wormed soil over clay spread (339.02)

Stage 2 saw the construction of a large building (**3**) to the south of the chapel, and the ploughing of the ground beyond (Figure 5.6). The ploughing seems to have respected the south wall of the buildings and may therefore have been slightly later. **Building 3** (Figure 5.4) was represented by a scalloped hollow cutting the paving to the south of the chapel; a rough surface of cobbles filling this cut; and a thick layer of stony soil overlying the stones and shelving steeply to the south-east. These features can be interpreted tentatively as the floor of a large, sub-rectilinear, wattle-walled building, possibly with an internal division. The cobbles were probably hard-core trampled during construction, and covered by an earth floor when the superstructure was complete. A post at the west end of the floor emerged through the cobble sub-surface, and may have been a roof support. The north-west corner was abutted by small paving slabs that perhaps filled a gap where larger **Period II** slabs had been removed. The south-west corner had been disturbed by the revetment wall of a platform built at the end of **Phase 1** (465).

The floor produced a valuable group of finds (Table 5.6). A styca of Archbishop Uigmond and a sherd of window glass from the cobbles were probably displaced from the underlying layers, but the earth flooring produced a small group of antler and flints, two hones and a hone blank, which was strikingly different to the material from the underlying fire debris and associated deposits (Tables 5.3–5). The antler derives from the early stages of comb production (pp 475-80), and records the introduction of comb making to this part of the site within a few years of the end of **Period II**.

A Group IICi styca of Archbishop Uigmond of York (CN02.46, *c.* 837–41 AD)
A piece of pale turquoise window glass (GS06.66)
A banded quartz crystal (SE58.15)
Two nails
Two hones (SE35.4 and 36.17) and a hone blank (SE71.49)
An antler beam segment
Three antler comb tooth plate rough-outs
Four antler offcuts
A tine and a tine tip
A burnt flint, a core rejuvenation flake and two **retouched** flints
Twenty rounded quartz pebbles
Scraps of metalworking debris

Table 5.6: Finds from **Building 3** (478)

The ploughing (399) covered a large part of the **central sector** (Figure 5.6) and damaged the **Period II** features extensively. The northern margin of the ploughed area seemed to have skirted **Building 3** and the underlying fire debris (339), clipping the south edge of the rubbish spread flanking the terrace

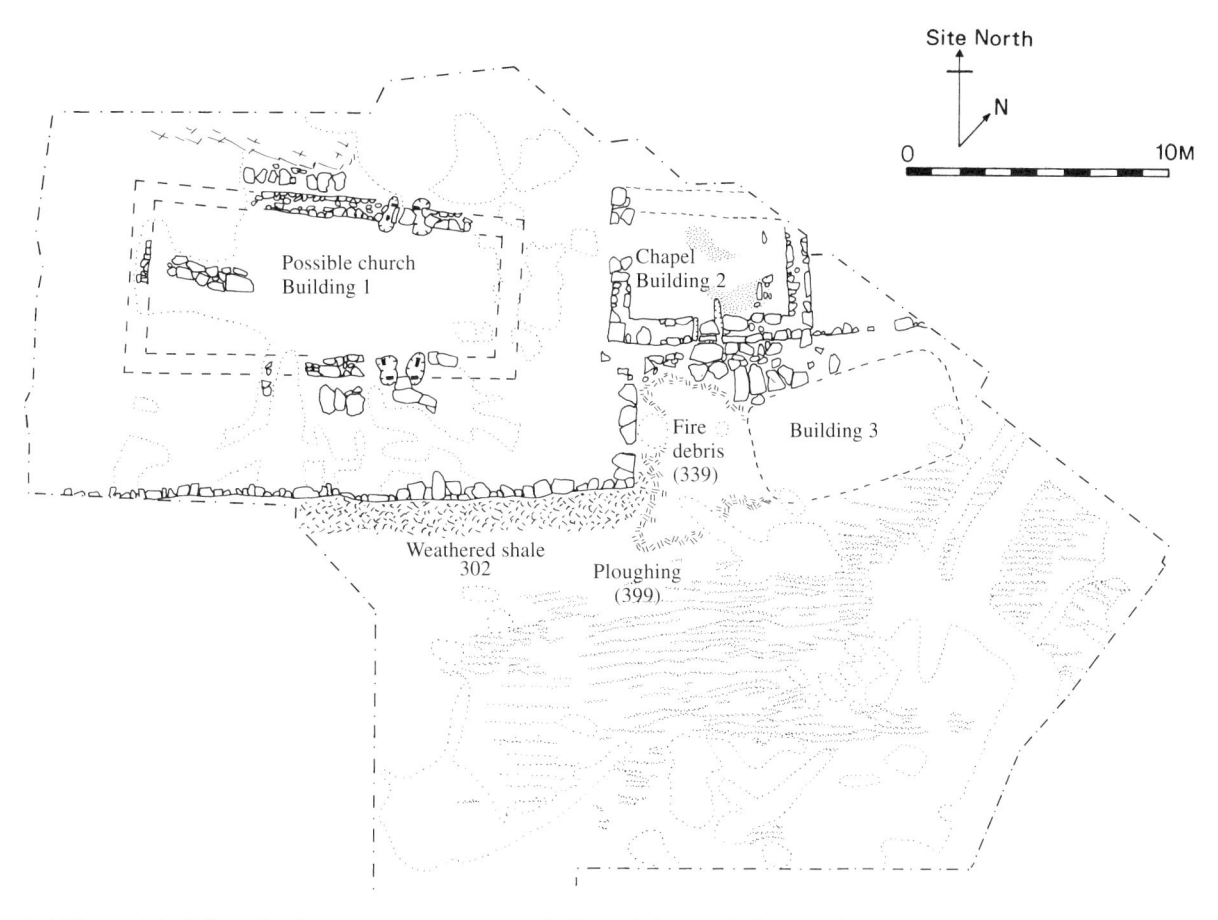

5.6 **Phase 1** buildings in the **northern sector** and **Phase 1.2** plough furrows in the **central sector**.

(II/303, pp 160-1). The southern edge was less clear, dying out by the southern rock outcrop. The plough furrows here had sometimes penetrated the fifth/sixth century ploughsoil of **Period I/1** (p 80), and the two phases of cultivation were difficult to distinguish.

The cultivated soil comprised complex undulating layers of shale and pebbles, interleaved with wormsorted soil. These were initially interpreted as furrows, but subsequently identified as partly-inverted sods cut from the compressed surfaces, wormed layers and debris which had accumulated in the **central sector** in **Periods I** and **II**. The inverted sods indicated the use of a mouldboard plough, which was confirmed by the recovery of fifty-one plough pebbles (SE51, pp 464-6). These were concentrated in the central and western part of this area where bedrock and the packing stones in earlier timber sockets had presumably knocked them from the plough. The survival, albeit sliced and inverted, of the earlier strata in the ploughsoil suggested that cultivation was confined to a single season. A worm-sorted soil overlying the cultivated ground in the eastern part of the area revealed a subsequent period of fallow, and equivalent deposits elsewhere had probably been removed by the sunken floors of later buildings.

The large group of finds from the ploughsoil (Table 5.7) may have included a small number of intrusive objects from the sunken floors of later buildings, but most of the material must have been displaced from earlier deposits. The sherds of imported pottery and vessel glass originated in domestic debris of **Period 1**, and are included in the distribution plots in Figures 3.8, 3.10 and 10.21-24. Many finds came from the area to the north of **Hall II/9**, and probably comprised a mixture of floor sweepings equivalent to the larger group flanking **Hall II/6** (303, pp 160-1), with scattered iron tools and waste from the *Stage 1* deposits (Table 5.3–4). Finds indicating the repair of copper alloy and lead vessels (the sheet fragments and lead rivet) might have come from either group. Both the coins came from the wormed soil over the ploughing, and belong with related issues from **Period III** contexts (pp 352-5). The miscast ball-headed pin and associated casting debris may have been displaced from the main **Period II** rubbish spread (II/303) which produced crucible sherds and possibly casting debris (Figure 10.87b). The small group of antler debris was probably intrusive, and may have originated in one of the small sunken-floored buildings of **Period III**. The flints were probably displaced from **Period I** deposits, as they were scarce in the **Period II** rubbish to the west (303) and absent from the wormed soil to the north (251, Table 4.5).

Four sherds of B*i* amphora (V1 and V3) and E ware (unassigned)
A sherd of Samian ware (PY01.6)
Ten sherds of early vessel glass (including pieces of Vs 4, 7, 9 and 53)
A Group Cii styca of Aethelred II (second reign, *c.* 843–9, CN02.57)
A nonsense styca of Group Di (CN02.59)
Sherds of pale blue (GS06.23) and pale green (GS06.120) window glass
A miscast ball-headed pin and casting waste (BZ14.8a and b)
A copper-alloy chain of eight extended-S links (BZ31.1)
A broken copper alloy mount (BZ35.7)
Two fragments of copper alloy sheet (BZ38.28 and 31), a fragment of rolled strip (BZ38.30) and a corroded lump (BZ41.15)
A tanged iron tool (perhaps a file or chisel, IN54.1) and a tanged punch or chisel (IN50.52)
An iron blade (IN73.10)
A broken standard iron needle with a punched eye (IN39.10)
An incomplete iron strap guide (IN45.4)
An iron clench plate (IN20.5)
A looped iron staple (IN17.34) and two bolts (IN22.7 and 8)
A right-angled hinge pivot (IN26.2)
Two iron strips (IN80.60 and 61), a curved strap fragment (IN81.17), two bars (IN83.11 and 12) and two unidentifiable lumps (IN93.62 and 63)
Eight nail fragments
A lead tack (LD6.51) and three fragments of lead waste (LD11.39, LD12.31–2)
A broken, decorated sandstone spindle whorl (SE28.5)
A botryoidal Haematite polisher (SE62.22)
Four flint pebbles, ten **unretouched** flints, twenty-two **retouched** flints and a burnt flint
One antler comb tooth-plate rough-out, an antler paring and an offcut junction.
Fifty-one plough pebbles (SE51)
A large group of pebbles and cobbles
A relatively small group of metalworking debris

Table 5.7: Finds from **Period III** ploughsoil (399, 333)

The precise position of the ploughing in the sequence was uncertain. It had disturbed the **Period II** halls, included displaced finds similar to those in the late **Period II** rubbish spreads, and was in turn overlain by the *Stage 3* cobbles and *Stage 4* buildings. It is ascribed to *Stage 2* as it seems to have avoided the burnt debris from the chapel and the overlying *Stage 2* buildings, but this relationship could have been illusory, and the ploughing may have preceded the fire at the end of **Period II** by a few years, although it is unlikely to have been earlier that the beginning of **Period II/7**.

Stage 3 was represented by a discontinuous band of angular fire-reddened stones overlying the plough soil, which had been extensively disturbed by the sunken floors of later buildings and fourteenth-fifteenth century graves. It had not been trampled and thus cannot have been a roadway. The small group of finds (Table 5.8) was dissimilar to those from the underlying **Period II** deposits, and probably pertained to **Period III**, although it lacked the manufacturing debris associated with the adjacent buildings. The link-ringed pin is a specifically Irish type, which hints at the cultural diversity of **Period III** (pp 50-2). Its introduction coincided with the end of a series of plated iron dress-pins from marginally earlier deposits (p 418).

A link-ringed, needle-headed copper alloy pin (BZ15.5)
A fragment of a copper alloy tube (BZ36.14)
A short standard iron needle with a punched eye (IN39.11)
A sherd of pale bluish-green Roman window or vessel glass (GS01.11)
A nail shank
A broken shale finger ring (SH02.2)
A small group of pebbles
Scraps of metalworking debris

Table 5.8: Finds from rubble surface (421)

Stage 4 saw the erection of new buildings in the **central sector** to the south of the *Stage 2* structure (Figure 5.7). The evidence was tenuous, as the insubstantial remains had been disturbed extensively by later features, and these buildings can at best be described as 'possible'. These structures lacked the internal features (hearths and paving) which survived in many of the **Phase 2** and **3** buildings, and were generally defined by vestiges of earth flooring and the underlying stony substrate, and particularly by the characteristic rounded corners. There were traces of eight possible buildings (**4–11**), none with a complete ground plan. The most easterly buildings (**7–9**) revealed at least two phases of construction, and several seem to have been destroyed by fire at the end of this stage.

Building 4 (433) to the west of **Building 5** in the middle of the **central sector**, was defined by a line of small stones marking a possible western wattle wall, and a spread of ash in the north-west corner of the floor. The north wall had been damaged by **Building 35**, and the sunken floor of **Building 29** had removed a large area in the east part of the building (Figure 5.8). No finds can be ascribed to the building.

Building 5 (435) lay some 5.0 m to the east of **Building 4**, and was overlain by four later buildings (**22, 30, 33, 43**). It was represented by a spread of fire-reddened stones with a clearly-defined, rounded, south corner and a fragment of the north-west wall marked by pitching slabs. The stones had not been trampled and were probably hard-core underlying an earth floor.

'Building' 6 (491) lay to the east of **Building 4** in an extensively disturbed area. A shallow hollow filled with burnt debris may have been the vestige of a sunken floor.

Building 7 (423.01) underlay the floor of the west wing of the eighteenth century manse, and was represented by a possible floor with a stony sub-stratum overlain by stony soil. The floor produced a small group of finds, perhaps reflecting the activities of a coppersmith (Table 5.9).

A fragment of rolled copper-alloy wire (BZ32.2)
Two fragments of copper alloy sheet with rivet holes (BZ37.11–2)
A nail
Two burnt flints

Table 5.9: Finds from **Building 7** (423.01)

Building 8 (423.02) lay to the south-east of **Building 7** and was represented by a sunken, dark-brown earth

5.7 Period III/1.4 buildings in the **central sector**.

floor with a rounded north-west corner. A post-hole on the edge of the floor may mark one side of a doorway in the west wall, and an adjacent pit may have been an internal feature. Most of the building lay in unexcavated ground to the east and south. The floor and pits produced an interesting group of finds (Table 5.10) including antler debris from the mid and late stages of comb production and, possibly, handle manufacture, while the hones indicate the maintenance of edged tools. The styca pertains to the late group of coins characterising **Period III** (p 354).

A styca of the second reign of Aethelred II (CN02.52, Pirie IICi, 843–9 NUM AD)
Two tapering strips of tin-plated leaded speculam (BZ37.8-9)
A nodular lump of copper-alloy (BZ39.14)
An iron bar (IN83.13) and a nail shank.
Two small hones (SE36.11 and 38.6), one broken (SE36.11)
An antler handle for a wittle tang (AR74.6)
A small group of antler-working debris including:
    Two segments and three tooth-plate rough-outs
    Three tine pieces and two tine tips
    Ten parings
Four **retouched** flints
Three pebbles and crumbs of metalworking debris

Table 5.10: Finds from area of **Building 8** (423.02)

'Building' 9 (420) was represented by a sequence of structural features and other deposits overlying **Buildings 7** and **8**, and possibly representing the north-west part of a poorly-preserved building with a door in the north-west wall. A shallow ditch indicated one side of a possible sub-rectangular building stance. The ditch was filled with silt which was covered by a spread of ash, the latter producing a large quantity of comb-making debris. This was in turn overlain by a band of paving, indicating the possible position of the doorway. This was oversailed by a layer of clayey soil with patches of burning, including scraps of daub which may have derived from the walls. The finds (Table 5.11) included an unusually large group of comb-making debris from all stages of production, which was concentrated immediately inside the putative doorway – a sensible, and well-illuminated place for delicate work. The numerous shavings and parings identified this as the actual working area, and indicated a contrast with other **Period III** buildings where these were rare. Further comb-making debris from the ground beyond the building (424, Table 6.33) was probably broadly contemporary. The coins from this area date the building with considerable precision (p 354, Figures 10.42 and 43), and so give valuable evidence for the date of the fragment of a Type F2 comb (p 486) and the opaque white bead.

An opaque, white glass bead (GS03.19)
A short standard iron needle with a punched eye (IN39.12) and a pin fragment (IN40.12)
A spiral terminal of an iron eye fitting (IN45.11)
Four nodular, copper-alloy fragments (BZ39.10–13)
Two **retouched** flints
A decorated antler comb side-plate of Type F2 (AR70.4)

A faceted antler gaming piece (AR75.2)
A large group of antler-working debris including:
   Three segments
   Eleven comb tooth-plate rough-outs
   Two comb tooth-plate trimmings
   Over 350 shavings and parings
   Four tine tips with sawn bases
   Nine offcuts and eight tine off-cuts or trimmings
Scraps of metalworking debris

Table 5. 11: Finds from **Building 9** (420)

Structure 10 (427.01) in the south part of one of the 1984 trial trenches **(2),** comprised a possible earth floor overlain by fire-reddened cobbles. The small group of finds from the floor included a retouched flint and a stone spindle whorl (SE25.11).

Building 11 overlay **Building 3** and was represented by a new floor of earth and stones, cut by postholes, and potentially associated with further postholes beyond (422.01). The building seems to have burnt down at the end of *Stage 4*, and islands of burnt debris were probably the remains of a rubbish-strewn floor (422.02). The building may have been *c.* 10.0 m long and perhaps 4.5–5.0 m wide. A group of shallow pits in the north-east corne were probably internal features. The finds from the floor (Table 5.12a) and overlying burnt deposits (Table 5.12b) included characteristic comb-making debris, which was probably deposited shortly before the fire.

Twelve fragments of copper-alloy (BZ41.16–27)
A curved iron strip, perhaps a drawn staple (IN81.18)
A natural flint pebble and two **retouched** flints
A sandstone hone blank (SE71.34)
A small group of antler-working debris comprising:
   Two comb tooth-plate rough-outs
   An antler paring
   Two off-cuts, a burr and a sawn tine

Table 5.12a: Finds from **Building 11** (422.01)

A nail
A folded piece of lead waste (LD11.40)
Two **unretouched** flints
Antler-working debris comprising:
   Two segments
   An antler comb tooth-plate rough-out
   Five parings
   Two tine tips
   Three offcuts

Table 5. 12b: Finds from ash over **Building 11** (422.02)

The burnt deposits. Five of the *Stage 4* buildings were associated with burnt deposits, suggesting that they were destroyed by fire. The floors of **Buildings 4, 5, 6** and **11** revealed patches of orange ash, and a layer of ash possibly marked the demise of **Building 9** (420). Two large spreads of ash to the south of **Building 11** (422.03) may either be external debris from the burning of this building, or internal deposits in the north-east corner of **Building 5** and the north-west corner of **Building 6**. An extensive spread of ash between **Buildings 4** and **5** (422.04) overlay a layer of silt which sealed the *Stage 2* cobbling. This produced a small group of finds (Table 5.13a) including a styca of Osberht and what appears to be a whistle mouthpiece made of antler (p 491). The styca was the latest in the series of Northumbrian coins and belongs with the small group of late coins from **Period III/1** (p 358). The absence of antler-working debris hinted that this craft was confined to the buildings to the east. The finds from the smaller ash deposit (Table 5.13b) were uninformative and included an intrusive sherd of twelfth century pottery.

A styca of Osberht (CN02.54, *c.* 849–855 NUM AD, Pirie IICi)
A sherd of pale green window glass (GS06.121)
An iron pin or piece of wire (IN90.6)
A probable whistle mouthpiece made of antler (AR81.6)
A square-sectioned iron punch (IN50.38)
A bent nail shank
An antler tine

Table 5.13a: Finds from ash between **Buildings 4** and **5** (422.04)

An iron tool shank (IN65.8) and a possible clench plate (IN93.65)
[A sherd of red gritty ware]

Table 5.13b: Finds from ash between **Buildings 5** and **11** (422.03)

Stage 5
Stage 5 saw the construction of an earth platform with a stone revetment (465) aligned with the **Phase 1** church (Figure 5.8). It overlay the remains of **Building 11** and the ash layers to the south, and the revetment was cut into the earth floor of the earlier building. A spread of clay at the foot of the wall was flanked by tumbled rocks, possibly deriving from the collapse or demolition of the revetment. The clay may have come from a daubed wattle wall, and the platform was covered in small stones which may have been a surface, or the foundation for the earth floor of a building. The finds (Table 5.14) included the earliest of a distinctive group of long iron staples or dog joiners (pp 408-9) and a small group of comb-making debris, which was perhaps displaced from the underlying building (**11**, Table 5.12).

Four bent long staples corroded together (IN18.2–5)
An iron pin fragment (IN40.13) and a corroded, sub-triangular plate (IN82.28)
Two comb, side-plate rough-outs and a tooth-plate rough-out
Three antler off-cuts

Table 5.14: Finds from **Phase 1.5** platform (465)

Phase 2

Phase 2 began with the demolition of the **Phase 1** church at an unknown date, possibly in the early-tenth century. A cluster of small sub-rectilinear buildings was built on the site of the church, and some nine new buildings were erected in the **central sector**. Two *stages* of construction were distinguished in both areas by stratigraphy, and the deposits in the **northern sector** revealed two further *stages* of demolition, and one of disuse. The **southern sector** was still flooded and revealed no evidence of activity. Chronological evidence was sparse, imprecise and sometimes poorly-stratified. The key finds were a securely stratified ring pin from the floor of a building in the **northern sector**, and a coin of Eadgar (959–75 AD), possibly associated with demolition deposits to the south of the chapel. These indicated that **Phase 2** probably pertained to the tenth century and ended c. 960 × 1000 AD.

The buildings were generally better-preserved than those of **Phase 1**, and revealed patterns of internal features which continued to evolve in **Phase 3**, and distinguished them from the buildings of **Periods II** and **IV**. The buildings in the **northern sector** were significantly larger than those to the south and produced small groups of tools and ornaments, while comb-making continued as a domestic craft in the **central sector**. There thus seems to have been a functional difference between the two areas, perhaps reflecting the occupations and status of the respective inhabitants.

The northern sector

The deposits overlying the **Phase 1** church in the **northern sector** had been extensively disturbed by later intrusions, leaving an irregular island of stratified material in the middle of the area, with isolated fragments beyond. This revealed a cluster of **Phase 2** buildings which may have extended further to the west where the equivalent deposits had been obliterated by later cultivation. Only one of the buildings (**13**) was well-preserved, and many finds from this area had probably been displaced into later graves. The corner of what may have been a similar building (**17**) to the east of the chapel probably pertained to this phase. The **Phase 2** remains revealed five stages of development.

Stage 1
The sequence began with the demolition of the timber superstructure of the **Phase 1** church (316). Scattered oak charcoal on the floor of the building indicated that some of the timbers were burnt *in situ*, but it was sometimes difficult to distinguish these deposits (300) from those associated with the destruction of the earlier church. The small group of finds (Table 5.15) included a group of square nail shanks from the vicinity of the former altar, but was uninformative about the structure of the demolished building.

A socketed iron object, perhaps a gouge (IN65.9)
An iron strip (IN80.62)
A nail and six square nail shanks

Table 5.15: Finds from demolition of **Phase 1** church (300)

Stage 2
Stage 2 saw renewed construction within the shell of the demolished church (Figure 5.3b). The paving at the west end of the church was partly removed and replaced with a cruder surface of slabs, which may have been the south part of the floor of a sub-rectilinear building (**12**) aligned west/east, and c. 6.0 m long and perhaps 3.5 m wide. Post holes cutting the burnt debris on the church floor to the east, may have supported a second structure of uncertain form. The small group of finds (Table 5.16) was uninformative, although the tweezers and comb-plate were characteristic finds of this period (p 377).

An pair of simple, flat tweezers made from copper-alloy strip (BZ24.1)
An antler comb-tooth-plate rough-out
A nail shank
Scraps of metalworking debris

Table 5.16: Finds from **Building 12** and associated deposits (300.01)

Stage 3
Stage 3 saw the partial demolition of the stone plinth of the church, spreading rubble (300.02) over the Stage 2 remains and beyond the walls (Figure 5.8). Most of this deposit was sterile, but the rubble under **Building 13** produced material probably deriving from the overlying floors (Table 5.17a).

Stage 4
Stage 4 saw the erection of four buildings (**13–16**) in shallow hollows cut into the Stage 3 rubble and the plinth of the **Phase 1** church (Figure 5.8). These formed a coherent, densely-packed group clustered around the east end of the burial chapel, and may have had interconnecting doorways. The only well-stratified, datable object was the ring pin from the rubble underlying **Building 13**, which was perhaps lost in the mid-tenth century. The buildings seem to have respected the chapel which possibly stood until the late- tenth century (p 198), and they may thus be ascribed to the mid- to late-tenth century with reasonable confidence. The finds offered little evidence of the specialised craft work evident in the smaller buildings in the **central sector**, but included personal ornaments and spindle whorls, which were less common there.

Building 13 lay within the island of stratified deposits, and was the best-preserved building in the northern cluster. The building was sub-rectangular (c. 4.0 wide and perhaps 6.0 m long) and oriented north/south. Postholes framed a doorway to the east, and a crescent of slanting stones indicated the position of the north-west corner of a sunken wattle or wicker wall. The floor revealed two phases of use. The original building (**13a**) had an earth floor which was later covered with paving comprising a central strip of large stones with smaller paving slabs to the north (**13b**). Flagstones to the east may have been a path leading to a door in the west wall of **Building 15**. An extension of the central paved strip westwards indicated the threshold of a door in the west wall, and the gap between these stones and the paved floor may have contained a timber doorsill.

An important group of finds (Table 5.17a and b) from the original earth floor and underlying rubble seems to have been uncontaminated by debris from the floor of the **Period II** church (Table 4.7), and shared features with the groups from the floors of other **Period III** buildings. The ring pin is widely paralleled in the Norse provinces of Western Britain,

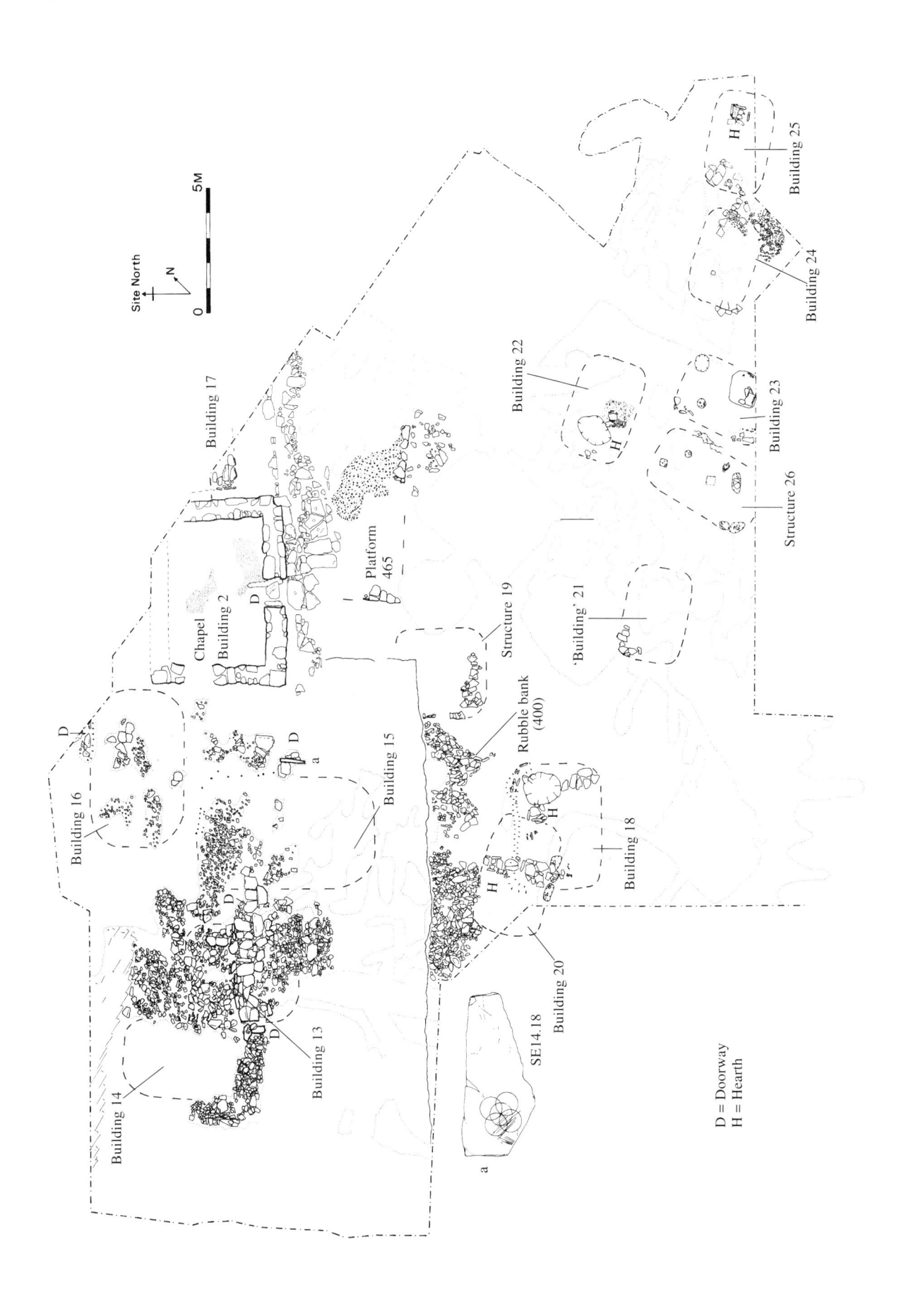

and may have been manufactured in Dublin: it can be ascribed tentatively to the second quarter of the tenth century (p 623). A relatively unworn sceat of Eadberht (CN02.5) was recovered from spoil from this deposit. Its presence here in relatively pristine state is difficult to explain (pp 353-4).

A plain copper-alloy ringed pin with a polyhedral head (BZ15.3)
An amber bead (AM01.1)
A round-headed lead rivet (LD06.3)
A fine-grained greywacke spindle whorl (SE24.2)
An improvised antler handle (AR74.13)
An iron nail and clench plate (IN20.6)
A natural flint pebble
Scraps of metalworking debris

a The rubble substrate (300.02/461)

A complete tanged Class A iron knife (IN66.3)
A nail
A natural flint pebble, a core (08) and an arrowhead point (16)
Two fragments of waste lead (LD12.33–4)
Scraps of metalworking debris

b The earth floor

Table 5.17: finds from floor of **Building13a** (461)

Building 14 immediately to the west of **Building 13**, was marked by a sub-rectilinear hollow dug through the rubble, a possible eastern wall-line, a rounded south-west corner cutting the rubble, and an earth floor. The building was probably *c.* 3.5 m wide and 6.0 m long, and may have coexisted with **Building 13a**, but was probably abandoned when the paved floor (**13b**) was laid. No finds can be assigned to it.

Building 15 to the east of **Building 13** had been severely disturbed by later graves, and the principal surviving feature was a massive stone doorsill with a socket for the south side of the door frame on its inner edge. The sill was abutted by fragments of internal and external paving, the former lying slightly higher than those outside. Large stake-holes driven into the clay floor in the chancel of the **Period II** church may have been part of the east and north walls, or possibly screens in the earlier church. The interior comprised an area denuded of rubble, overlain by a fragmentary floor of dark earth. The doorway faced the gap between the south-west corner of the burial chapel and the end of the terrace, suggesting that the chapel remained standing, although the parapet wall had probably been demolished (p 199). A fragmentary paved path between the west wall of the chapel and the east wall of the building led towards **Building 14**. The building was relatively large (perhaps *c.* 4.5 × 7. 0m), and was comparable to **Building 39** to the south, which had a similar featureless earth floor and massive door sill.

The door sill bore a compass-drawn arciform cross of five circles (SE14.18) on its west face, and may have been displaced from the paving in the **Phase 1** church (316), or was perhaps a free-standing monolith or grave marker (pp 102, 148). The finds from the floor area had been contaminated with high medieval and recent material, but included a few objects which were probably associated with this building (Table 5.18).

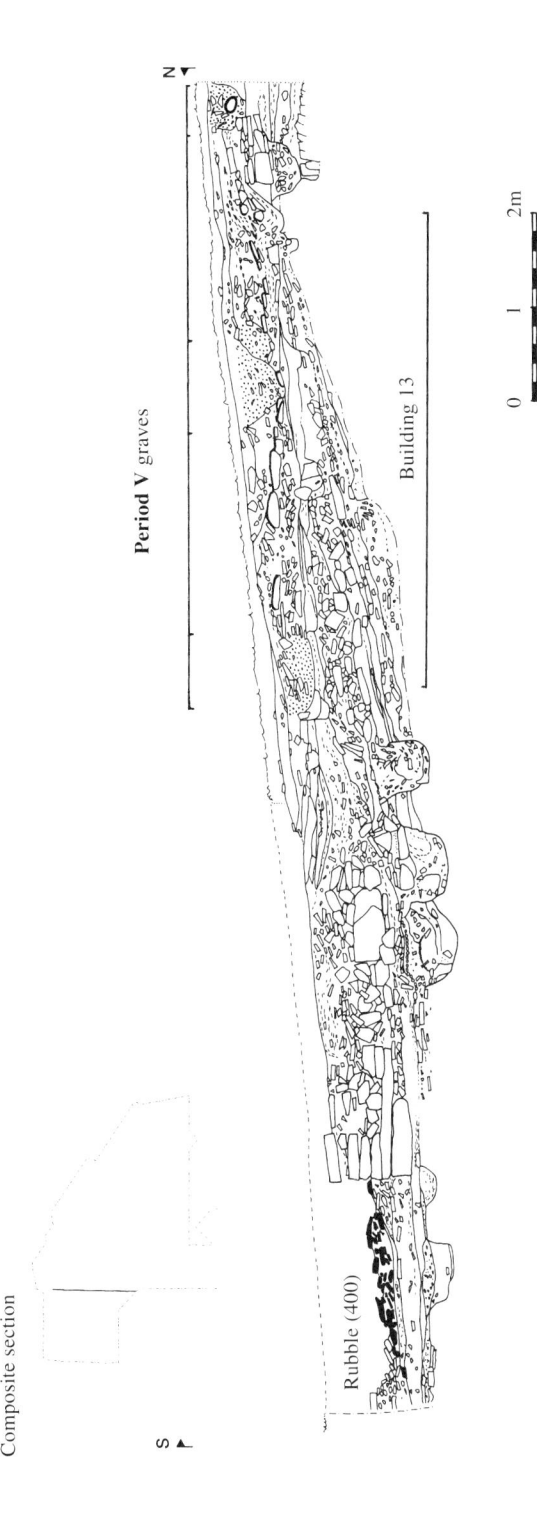

5.8 **Period III/2** buildings and related deposits in the **northern** and **central sectors**.

A copper-alloy pin shank (BZ09.2)
A burnt flint and two **unretouched** flints
A spindle whorl (SE25.6)
An iron bar (IN83.14)

Table 5.18: Selected finds from floor of **Building 15** (463)

Building 16 lay at the north end of the trench and was probably oriented west/east, although there was no certain evidence of the east and west walls. A doorway in the north wall was marked by a rock-cut slot, possibly containing a timber sill, and the socket for the west side of the door frame. An opposed doorway in the south wall would have opened onto the path to the east of **Building 15**. Successive shale and stone surfaces in the north part of the building were overlain by a paved strip including a broken arciform cross (SE14.14). This may have been a grave marker or a monolith, originating in the seventh century 'shrine', subsequently moved into the church, and only discarded after the last church was demolished (pp 102, 148, 437-9). These surfaces were overlain by a thick layer of soil which had been extensively disturbed by later graves, but which may have been an earth floor. It produced a small group of potentially early material (Table 5.19).

A broken arciform-cross slab (SE14.14)
A fiddle-key nail, two nails and two nail fragments
A fine-grained sandstone spindle whorl (SE26.6)
A shale bangle fragment (SH01.7)
An antler tine tip
An **unretouched** flint

Table 5.19: Finds from **Building 16** (464)

Stage 5
Stage 5 saw the temporary abandonment of the area marked by an accumulation of soil over **Building 13**, which contained jumbled stones and shale, and may have been ploughed. The disuse of this area apparently lasted until a relatively late stage in **Period IV** (pp 211-6), although it may have been part of an open market (pp 247-9). The finds (Table 5.20) are likely to have derived from the burnt debris in the **Period II** church (315, Table 4.7).

A lobed copper-alloy mount with a cross design (BZ22.1)
A broken, short, standard iron needle with a punched eye (IN39.13)
A nail shank
Four fragments of molten lead (LD12.35–38)
A burnt flint
Scraps of metalworking debris

Table 5.20: Finds from *Stage 5* plough soil in the **northern sector** (407.01)

Building 17 and the demise of the Northumbrian burial chapel. The rebuilt burial chapel seems to have remained standing throughout **Phase 1**, and perhaps survived until the end of **Phase 2**. Fourteenth–fifteenth century graves had penetrated the original floor, and little survived of the **Period III** building and the overlying demolition deposits. Clay walling had slumped over the paved path to the south of the chapel, and the overlying graves produced scraps of baked clay which had probably been displaced from this deposit. A penny of Eadgar (959–975, CN02.63) from the side of a grave which cut the clay spread, may have been deposited when the chapel walls collapsed. This hinted that the chapel had survived until the late-tenth century, but the coin was poorly stratified, and the date is unsupported by other evidence. Banks of eroded clay walling abutted the east wall and north-west corner of the chapel, but there was no other evidence of the substantial mass of clay which must have resulted from the decay of the chapel. The finds from the collapsed clay walling included four pieces of window glass (GS06), two light blue (5 and 6), one pale turquoise (64), and one deep turquoise (73); two plough pebbles (SE51); a nail shank; scraps of baked clay; and a small quantity of ironworking debris, the last probably deriving from the underlying seventh century deposits. This sparse assemblage contrasted with the groups from the debris of the mid-ninth century fire (Tables 4.10–12, 5.2), indicating that the roof had been removed, and that the nails and other iron fittings had been salvaged. The fragmentary evidence indicated that the burial chapel was maintained until the late tenth century, and was flanked by an east/west path leading to the clustered **Phase 2** buildings to the west. Maintenance lapsed towards the end of the tenth century. The walls collapsed and were covered by the layer of rubbish which accumulated in **Period IV**, and was disturbed and displaced by the **Period V** graves (pp 237-50).

Building 17 (492) was represented by paving in a shallow hollow to the east of the chapel, which may have been the south-west corner of a wattle building extending beyond the excavated area (Figure 5.8). The hollow was cut through the spread of cremated bone ascribed to **Phase 1**, while the paving was oversailed by the weathered clay marking the decay of the chapel, potentially at the end of **Phase 2**. The small group of finds produced no contemporary artefacts.

The central sector

The **central sector** revealed the remains of nine possible **Phase 2** buildings, and others may have been obliterated by later disturbances (Figure 5.8). Stratified deposits in the north-west part of the area included three buildings revealing two phases of construction (*Stages 2* and *3*). The ground to the east had been severely damaged by later buildings and graves, but revealed fragments of a further five buildings and a less-severely damaged seventh (**25**) on the south-east edge of the trench. All probably pertained to *Stage 3*. The only dateable stratified objects were Northumbrian stycas (CN02.34 and 56) from two buildings (**20** and **22**). These seem anachronous, and may have been displaced, or could have been votive deposits (p 200).

The stratified sequence in the north-west part of the central sector. The stratified **Phase 2** remains in the north-west part of the **central sector** provided the key to identifying and interpreting the poorly-stratified features further to the east. The relationships of two buildings (**18** and **20**) were clear indicating three *stages* of activity.

Stage 1
Stage 1 was represented by a pile of rubble (400) banked against the face of the Northumbrian terrace (Figure 5.8). This was probably derived from the parapet wall which may have been demolished when the **Phase 1** church was dismantled. The rubble covered the weathered shale (302) ascribed to **Phase 1.1**, and had been extensively disturbed by later buildings and graves. The finds (Table 5.21) revealed a wide chronological spread. The buckle probably pertained to **Phase 2**, but many of the other objects were matched in extensive spreads of **Period IV** debris in this area (pp 237-50, Figures 6.23–39, Tables 6.41–42), and were probably deposited in the twelfth and thirteenth centuries.

A tuyere nozzle fragment
Two antler tine tips
An incised greywacke slab (SE54.15)
A red sandstone smoothing stone (SE42.2)
A hone blank (SE71.30)
Two nails and a clench nail (IN19.4)
A figure-of-eight shaped hasp (IN24.9)
A needle blank with a flattened end (IN39.40)

a. From rubble (potentially early)

A **retouched** flint
A clay pipe stem
A sherd of white gritty ware (MP06)
Scraps of metalworking waste.

b. From rubble (potentially late)

A decorated tenth century D-ring buckle (BZ18.4)
A round-headed stick-pin of Type 3 (BZ14.9)
A possible chisel (IN52.6) and an iron drawknife (IN69.2)
A broken tanged knife (IN66.34)
A stone gaming counter (SE19.17) and spindle whorl (SE26.9)
A perforated bone artefact (BA10.3)
A sherd of white gritty ware (MP06)

c. Soil over and among rubble

Table 5.21: Finds from *Stage 1* rubble bank (400)

Stage 2
Stage 2 saw the erection of a small sub-rectangular building (**18**) some 3.5 m from the terrace, presumably on the edge of the rubble bank. The north wall was defined by a narrow stone-packed trench with rounded north-west and north-east corners. The south part of the building had been severely disturbed, but a patch of paving to the south-east indicated the wall-line. The building had the waisted dumb-bell shape characteristic of the small buildings of **Period II** (Figure 4.3), and was some 4.5 m long and roughly, 3.5 m wide. A large pit in the north-east corner was covered with paving which had presumably rested on wooden supports, and had slumped as these decayed. A hearth immediately to the west, lay 0.4 m from the north wall with its west side abutting the transverse axis of the building. A large post socket to the west of the hearth may have supported one side of a cooking gantry. A second paved area in the north-west corner of the building had been incorporated into a later building (**20**). It covered a layer of dark soil which may have been an original earth floor, and produced a concentration of comb-making debris (Table 5.22a). Most of the other finds came from the soil filling the pit (Table 5.22c) and, though potentially pertaining to this building, were probably derived from the overlying **Period IV** rubbish spreads which revealed concentrations of needles in this part of the site (Figure 6.26).

An antler beam section
An intact tine
A sawn tine tip
Four antler segments
Two antler off-cuts
Six comb tooth-plate roughouts
A nail head and four fragments of iron sheet (IN82.30)

a. Finds from possible earth floor under paving

A triangular iron plate (IN82.29)

b. Paving

A possible copper-alloy needle shank (BZ12.04)
Three nails and a clench nail and plate (IN19.5)
A standard iron needle with a punched eye (IN39.14)
An iron club-headed stick pin with a trilobate head (IN41.4)
Two **retouched** flints

c. Pit fill

Table 5.22: Finds from **Building 18** (402)

A second structure to the north-east (**19**) shared the east/west orientation of **Building 18**, and probably pertained to this stage. It was represented by a low wall set into the rubble bank, and a strip of paving at right angles to it overlying a shallow drain. Shale to the north and east oversailed the burnt debris from the chapel, and may have been a floor. This structure may have been a building, although its size and shape were uncertain. Most of the finds (the lead waste, nails, window glass and metalworking debris, Table 5.23) were matched in the underlying burnt debris (339, Table 5.3), and were probably derived from it. The possible file was one of a small group of tools from late-ninth/tenth century contexts in the vicinity of the terrace. The most interesting find was the quartzite cobble which was perhaps used to make beads (p 472).

A sherd of light blue window glass (GS06.7)
A possible iron file (IN54.2)
Three nails and a nail shank
A piece of lead waste (LD11.42)
A quartzite cobble with four, hollow drill scars (SE63.1)
A small group of pebbles
Scraps of metalworking debris

Table 5.23: Finds from **Structure 19**

Stage 3

Stage 3 followed the abandonment of **Building 18** which was replaced by a new building (**20**). **Building 20** (301) occupied a level stance cut into the rubble bank, and was approximately 3.0 m wide and possibly *c.* 4.5 m long. It presumably had wattle walls, but no trace survived. The sockets for a massive door-frame of rectangular timbers in the south wall, opened onto a narrow band of paving leading to a hearth close to the back wall. The paving was similar to the central band of paving in **Building 13b**, and the position of the hearth was matched in other buildings of **Phases 2** and **3**. The sparse finds included two nails, and two incised and grooved stone slabs (SE54.17 and 18) from the paving immediately south of the hearth. A styca of the second reign of Aethelred II (CN02.56) was found as the hearth was being removed. This was potentially anachronous, and it perhaps originated on the underlying **Phase 1** ground surface.

Phase 2 buildings in the central and south-east parts of the central sector (Figure 5.8). The central and south-eastern parts of the **central sector** revealed the fragmentary remains of five possible **Phase 2** buildings (**21–25**), and a concentration of post-holes which may have been the remains of a sixth structure (**26**). All were aligned with **Building 20** and are ascribed to *Stage 3*. The more fragmentary structures (**21–22**) can only be identified tentatively as 'buildings', although they made stratigraphic sense and displayed some of the characteristic features of broadly contemporary buildings.

'Building' 21 (468) occupied the north-west corner of a **Period II** hall (**II/7**), and was represented by the north-west corner of a sunken, paved floor flanked by angled slabs marking a possible wattle wall. The remainder of the building had been destroyed by **Building 41**. No finds can be ascribed to this building.

Building 22 (454) lay immediately south-west of **Building 21**, and was represented by a sunken stone hearth in an ash-filled hollow, and a large sub-circular pit to the north-east. The juxtaposition of a pit and hearth was matched in **Building 18**. The pit contained a layer of slumped flagstones, and may thus have been covered by a paved floor. Finds from the hearth and pit (Table 5.24) included a group of characteristic comb-making debris. The styca from the ash surrounding the hearth seems anachronous, and may have been displaced from an earlier context, or was perhaps an heirloom placed there for good luck.

A styca of Eanred (CN02.34, *c.* 830–835 AD)
An antler comb tooth-plate rough-out
A bent nail
Scraps of metalworking debris

a. Finds from the hearth

An antler base with attached skull fragment
Two antler segments
Six comb tooth-plate rough-outs
Five antler offcuts and a paring
A possible bung made from a faceted antler tine base (AR81.3)

b. Finds from pit

Table 5.24: Finds from **Building 22** (454)

Building 23 (481) lay on the south edge of the trench, and was represented by the stone-packed bedding trench of the west wall, and traces of a rounded north-west corner flanked by small paving stones. The floor revealed two pits (481.01 and 481.02) and a post-hole. The smaller pit (481.01) was sub-circular with vertical sides cut into the bedrock, and its regularity suggests it was intended to hold a circular container, perhaps a wooden tub or barrel. The larger pit was also dug into the bedrock, and its south side was covered by slumped flagstones indicating that it had been covered with paving resting on wooden supports. The position of the east wall was uncertain, and the building may either have been a relatively-large sub-square structure, or a smaller sub-rectilinear building aligned north-north-east/south-south-west. Most of the finds (Table 5.25) came from the large paved pit and included a small group of comb-making debris which may have accumulated on the floor of the building.

A nail
An antler beam section
A tine tip with a sawn base
An antler comb tooth-plate rough-out
Three antler off-cuts and two shavings
A burnt flint, an **unretouched** flint and a **retouched** flint
Scraps of metalworking debris

Table 5.25: Finds from **Building 23** (481)

Building 24 (427.02) lay on the south side of the trench in an area of shallow stratigraphy much damaged by graves. The building was represented by patches of internal paving, and an arc of paving abutting the south-west corner. A fragment of the east wall was indicated by small slanting stones abutted by paving, and overlain by dirty clay, presumably derived from clay daub. Unexcavated angled slabs on the floor of a later grave probably mark the north wall. A band of rubble and soil may mark the western part of the floor. A strip of fire-reddened stones under the building and immediately to the south, sealed the earth floor of **'Building' 10**. The building produced two small groups of finds. The first came from internal deposits (Table 5.26a), and the second from the stones beyond the building (Table 5.26b). These produced a range of artefacts characteristic of **Period III**, including the smoothed greywacke slab, opaque white glass bead and bone pin, while the quern was the earliest of a series from **Period III–V** contexts (pp 459-60). The faceted and pierced tine tip was matched in **Period IV** assemblages from this area (Figures 6.29 and 10.133), and the finds from the stone spread – including the enigmatic cog-like strip – probably pertained to these later accumulations.

A small bead of opaque white glass (GS03.20)
A segment of a granite, rotary-quern, upper stone (SE34.17)
A smoothed greywacke slab with pocks, scratches and grooves (SE54.19)
An unidentifiable iron lump (IN93.65)
Two **unretouched** flints

a. Finds from floor of **Building 24**

An antler tine section and a segment removed from an antler beam
A faceted and pierced antler tine tip (AR79.1)

A headless bone pin (BA11)
A spoked, pierced, curved copper-alloy strip (BZ30.6)

b. Finds from stones to the south of **Building 24**

Table 5.26: Finds from **Building 24** (427.02)

Building 25 (482) lay immediately to the west of **Building 24**, was incompletely excavated, and probably survives in good condition. A paved floor and post-hole at the west end of the building were excavated in 1984, and a hearth to the east was exposed in 1991. These were probably part of a sub-rectangular building similar to the more complete examples of **Phases 2** and **3**. No finds can be ascribed to this building.

Structure 26 was represented by a cluster of post-holes cutting the bedrock ridge to the west of **Building 23**, and possibly pertaining to this phase. No finds can be ascribed to this rather dubious structure.

Phase 3

Phase 3 saw the transformation of the site from the rectilinear plan established in **Period II** to a new curvilinear plan, which endured until the thirteenth century (Figure 5.9). This change foreshadowed the larger settlement of **Period IV**, but the design of the buildings indicated continuity from **Phase 2**, and **Phase 3** may thus be seen as a transitional stage between **Periods III** and **IV**. The new settlement comprised a dense group of small, sub-rectilinear buildings in the **central sector**, revealing two distinct building phases (*Stages 1* and *2*), which recorded a slight expansion of the settlement. Shallow, discontinuous ditches marked successive enclosures, and were perhaps associated with hedges. There was no evidence of activity in the **northern sector**, while the lowlying **southern sector** seems to have been flooded throughout this phase, although a large group of finds from the pond silts (Table 5.35) may have been rubbish discarded beyond the perimeter of the settlement.

The finds from the **Phase 3** buildings and related deposits were distinguished by their poverty, and contrast with those from the overlying **Period IV** rubbish deposits and buildings. The only diagnostic objects potentially ascribable to **Phase 3** were six sherds of coarse hand-built pottery, including Souterrain Ware which probably originated in the Antrim area of northern Ireland (pp 51, 358). There was no secure internal chronological evidence, and the date and duration of **Phase 3** can only be estimated from its stratigraphic relationships with earlier and later features, and the finds associated with them. These indicated that **Phase 3** pertained to the late-tenth/early-eleventh century, and it may have been relatively brief, as there were only two building phases. This dating is supported by the distribution of tenth and eleventh century coins from displaced or insecure contexts on the inner margin of the **Phase 3** buildings (pp 246, 356, Figures 6.38 and 10.45a).

The buildings. Although almost all the buildings had been damaged by later features, several were relatively well preserved and displayed features not seen in earlier structures. They shared the shallow, sunken sub-rectilinear stances of the earlier **Period III** buildings, and probably had similar wicker or wattle walls and earth floors. The floors in some buildings were divided into two distinct areas to either side of the transverse axis, one being paved while the other probably had an earth floor. Hearths were sited towards the rear of the building in the paved area and were sometimes associated with a single socket for a large post. One was abutted by a stone-framed slab, perhaps used in the preparation of food. The distinctive hearth position was matched in at least two **Phase 2** buildings (**16** and **20**), and is one of the diagnostic features of this group of structures. The end walls were frequently defined by bands of internal paving, termed 'packing walls', and perhaps laid to support the base of the wall. These tended to occur at the unpaved ends of the buildings, and the paving at the other end would have fulfilled the same structural role. Although the position of the doorways was usually unclear, the buildings probably had a single doorway set in one of the long walls. The two floor zones could have been separated by an internal partition, and might have comprised a cooking and living area with a paved floor and hearth, and a sleeping area insulated by its earth floor. The finds were insufficiently numerous and sensitive to distinguish different functional areas.

The boundary and boundary ditches (436, Figures 5.9–11). The boundaries of the successive **Phase 3** enclosures were defined by two insubstantial, discontinuous ditches, and by the dense buildings contained by them. The ditches were not linked stratigraphically, but the inner ditch pertained to *Stage 1*, while the outer ditch contained the slightly expanded *Stage 2* settlement. The inner ditch was represented by a segment in the west part of the area, a dubious segment in the centre, and a possible fragment on its north-east edge. The west segment was a shallow, round-bottomed cut which may have been cleaned out once or twice, and was subsequently oversailed by the *Stage 2* buildings. The central 'ditch' segment continued the line to the north-east, but was confused by the overlapping building stances, walls and door-frames of **Buildings 30** and **33**, and was probably never very substantial. The north-east ditch fragment was a vestigial round-bottomed cut truncated by later buildings and graves. The outer ditch lay some 3.5 m to the south-east of the inner boundary, and was less substantial, with a surviving fragment on the west margin of the trench possibly continuing as a shallow trough which cut the bedrock ridge in the southern part of the **central sector**. The ground further to the east had been severely disturbed, and a shallow ditch

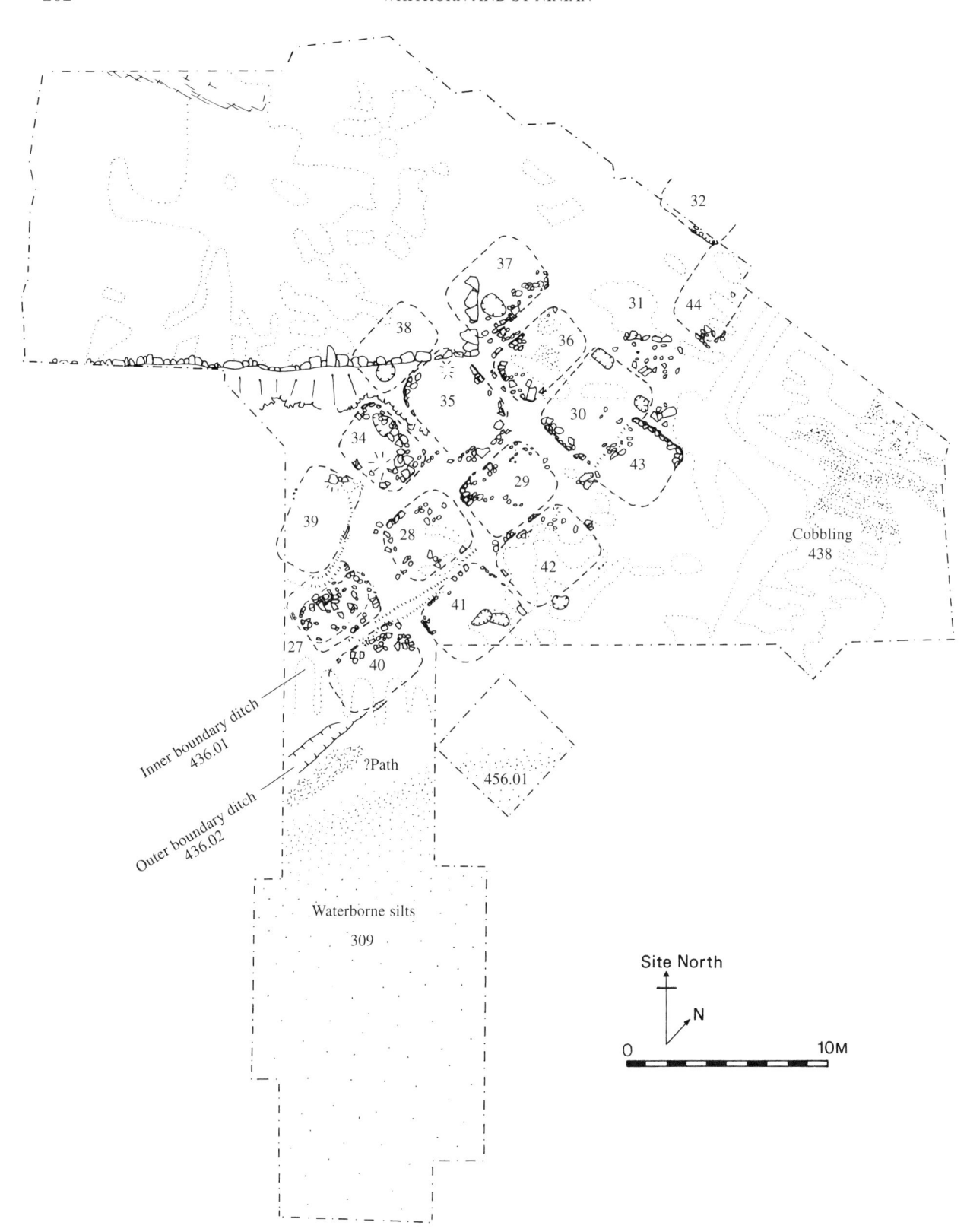

5.9 General plan of **Period III/3** buildings and related deposits.

here would have been obliterated by later features. The west segment of the ditch had been recut at least once, and was flanked to the south by a spread of upcast gravel which had been trampled to form a path. This was oversailed by pond silts, establishing a stratigraphic link between the **Phase 3** buildings in the **central sector** and the **Period IV** structures to the south.

The small groups of finds from the ditches (Table 5.27) were generally uninformative, but suggested that they were filled before much debris had accumulated. Some or all of the finds may derive from underlying deposits, although the group of staples from the inner ditch may derive from some unspecified contemporary activity.

An antler tine
A broken bone pin shank (BA09.1)
A sherd of light blue window glass (GS06.8)
Two long staples and a square staple, all bent at the ends (IN18.6–8)
An iron bar
A large broken, natural hone (SE35.11)
A plough pebble (SE51)

a. Finds from inner boundary ditch (436.01)

A **retouched** flint
A nail shank
Scraps of ironworking debris

b. Finds from outer ditch (436.02)

Table 5.27 Finds from **Phase 3** boundary ditches (436.01 and 02)

The insubstantiality and short life of these ditches belied the importance of the boundary they marked, which seems to have endured until the later-thirteenth century (pp 211-6). They may have been associated with hedges, which would have ensured this endurance, while leaving little archaeological evidence.

Stage 1
Stage 1 probably began with the marking out of the new curvilinear boundary, which was followed by the erection of six sub-rectilinear buildings (**27–32**) on its inner side. Five buildings to the north (**34–38**) were probably broadly contemporary with these, while a small building (**33**) to the south of the boundary perhaps marked expansion during *Stage 1*. The boundary and buildings overlay the **Phase 2** structures which must have decayed or been dismantled before construction started.

Building 27 occupied a shallow hollow cutting the floor of a **Period II** hall (**II/6**) in the west part of the **central sector**, and revealed two phases of construction pertaining to *Stages 1* and *2* respectively. The earlier building (**27a**, Figure 5.10) lay immediately to the north of the inner ditch, and was some 2.8 m wide and *c*. 4.0 m long. The south-west part of the building was paved, and a separate 'packing wall' marked the inner side of the north-east wall. The paving defined a rounded south corner, while occasional angled stones indicated the line of wattle walls. The hearth lay 0.6 m from the north-west wall, immediately to the west of the transverse axis of the building. A paving stone surrounded by low, edge-set slabs beside the hearth, and a large post socket at its west corner, seem to have been related domestic furnishings. The doorway probably lay at the centre of the south-west wall, although no traces survived. The north wall of the building was clipped by the south corner of **Building 39**. The finds (Table 5.28) included two antler segments indicating comb-making, but were otherwise uninformative.

Two antler segments and an off-cut
A nail and a wool-comb tooth (IN62.6)
A burnt flint
A tuyere fragment

Table 5.28 Finds from **Building 27a** (405)

'**Building**' **28** was represented a disturbed area between **Buildings 27** and **29**, which probably contained a similar building. Scattered paving preserved a dubious trace of the line of the north-west wall. No finds can be assigned to this building.

Building 29 lay 1.2 m to the south-west of **Building 30**, and was represented by a paved floor with a rounded west corner, and angled stones indicating the line of a north-eastern wattle wall. Small stones in the north-east corner were perhaps the substrate of an earth floor, while the rest of the eastern part of the floor had been destroyed by graves. The south-east side of the building oversailed the corner of **Building 21**. The reconstructed building was sub-square, measuring some 3.9 by 3.9 m. No finds can be assigned to this building.

Building 30 lay to the west of **Building 33**, and was relatively well preserved despite extensive damage to the centre of the floor. The building was sub-rectilinear, and measured some 5.2 by 4.5 m. The south-west end of the building was defined by a single course 'packing wall' abutted by fragments of a paved floor. Most of the south-east wall had been damaged by the sunken floor of **Building 42**, but traces of a ditch or sunken stance survived. The north-east wall survived in a hollow, cutting **Building 11** and the adjacent ash spreads, and was abutted by external paving. A sub-rectilinear pit in the north corner of the floor with an unidentifiable organic lining, was covered by a secondary surface of rough rubble. There was a second pit or large post-hole in the east corner. The central part of the building had been obliterated by later graves, a nineteenth century field drain, and an exploratory trench excavated in 1972. Most of the finds (Table 5.29) were securely-stratified in the rectangular pit and overlying surface, and included a small group of comb-making debris.

A domed copper-alloy stud with a short thick shank (BZ29.2)
A broken long iron staple (IN18.9)
A square-sectioned iron bar (IN65.10)
An antler coronet attached to fragments of the skull
Two antler comb-plate rough-outs
An antler off-cut (beam and tine)
An antler paring

Table 5.29: Finds from **Building 30** (472)

Building 31 (474) lay to the north-east of **Building 30** in the north-east part of the **central sector**. This area had been severely disturbed by graves, and the building was represented by a large amorphous hollow cutting earlier deposits, and possibly associated with scattered post-holes. No finds can be assigned to this building.

Building 32 (477) extended beyond the excavated area. The south-west wall was indicated by tipping stones leading to the west corner where the wall was contained by a stone packed slot. No finds can be assigned to this building.

cut into the **Period III** rubble bank (400) abutting the **Period II** terrace, and overlay the north-east corner of **Building 18** and the east wall of **Building 20**. Small, steeply-angled slabs marked wattle walls with rounded corners to the north and east, showing that

5.10 **Period III/3.1** buildings in the **central sector**.

Building 33 (470) occupied a shallow hollow immediately beyond the boundary, which was cut into the south-east corner of **Building 6**. The west part of the floor was paved, and the north-east corner was marked by slanting stones. The east part of the building had been destroyed by sumps associated with the west wing of the eighteenth century manse, and its south-west end had been removed by the sunken floor of **Building 43**. Paving protruding through the north-west wall indicated the position of a possible doorway. The building was probably c. 3.2 m long and at least 2.3 m wide. The paving included a damaged, granite rotary-quern lower-stone (SE43.16). No other finds can be assigned to this building.

Building 34 (403) occupied a sub-rectilinear stance

the building was 4.6 m long, while a possible west corner indicated a width of 2.9–3.0 m. The doorway was probably in the middle of the south-west wall, and may have been marked by stones on the edge of the pit in **Building 18**. New paving at the rear of the building had slumped into a shallow, oblong pit in the north quadrant of the floor. The west and possibly the south quadrants of the floor were unsurfaced. The small group of finds comprised scraps of animal bone, although some of the artefacts from the earlier pit (Table 5.22) may have been derived from this building.

Building 35 (476) lay immediately north-east of **Building 34** on a stance cut into the rubble bank abutting the **Period II** terrace. Angled slabs revealed a rounded west corner and parts of the north-west and south-west walls. The north-east and south-east walls were indicated by angled slabs and internal paving stones, possibly forming 'packing walls'. A large slab towards the middle of the south-east wall may mark the threshold of the door. An enigmatic cavity (252.06) underlying the north corner of the building is interpreted as part of a **Period I** alignment of posts and stones (252, p 112), and seems to have collapsed during the life of the building. A possible earth floor which had slumped over the collapsed pit produced a small group of finds (Table 5.30) including a rare iron fish hook. The window glass was almost certainly displaced from the underlying burnt debris from the chapel (Table 5.3), and the other objects may also derived from earlier deposits. The debris filling the cavity (252.06) included a sherd of possible Souterrain Ware (PY08.4), a sawn tine tip and a perforated bone spindle whorl (BA06.1). These were all appropriate to this period, and are likely to have come from the floor of the building.

A piece of light green window glass (GS06.105)
A corroded length of flat-sectioned copper alloy wire (BZ32.3)
A looped iron staple with an attached ring (IN24.10)
An unbarbed iron fish-hook (IN56.2)
An antler tine with a cut base

Table 5.30: Finds from **Building 35** (476)

Building 36 (475) lay immediately to the north-east of **Building 35**. The west corner of the building was marked by two curving bands of paving probably comprising an internal 'packing wall' and an external surface. An underlying surface of untrampled, rough cobbles (not illustrated) was probably the substrate of an earth floor, and indicated a slightly different wall line, suggesting that the building was shifted when the paving was laid. A gap in the paving on the north-west wall marked the position of a possible timber door sill. The small group of finds included scraps of bone and a greywacke slab incised with a dubious gaming board (SE23.5)

Building 37 (485) was represented by a possible paved floor associated with a large pit between **Building 36** and the burial chapel. Occasional slanting stones marked possible wall-lines to the north-east and south-east. No finds can be assigned to this building.

'Building' 38. A possible building (431) oversailing the **Period II** terrace to the north-west of **Buildings 34** and **35**, was indicated by two pits and a patch of a possible earth floor. One of the pits (431.01) exposed the socket of an earlier monolith (252.05, p 112) and may have been dug in order to remove it. The finds from the two pits included a possible Souterrain Ware rim sherd (PY08.2), a bone toggle (BA12), two nails and an antler tine.

Stage 2
Stage 2 saw the erection of a range of new buildings between the inner and outer boundary ditches (Figures 5.9 and 11). Some of the *Stage 1* buildings may have remained standing, but the north-west sides of the new buildings consistently oversailed the south-east walls of their predecessors which must have been replaced. **Building 27** was shifted slightly eastwards to make way for a new building (**39**) to the north, and other *Stage 1* buildings may also have been moved. These shifts need not have involved reconstruction as the conjectured wicker or wattle structures could have been moved bodily (pp 184-5), but the area was too severely disturbed to reveal the potentially ephemeral evidence for such movements. The overall plan makes greater sense if the *Stage 1* building plots continued to be occupied, and the outlines of hypothetical buildings are depicted in Figure 5.11. The ground to the south was still flooded, although the pond had still to reach its greatest extent (p 219).

Building 27b occupied a slightly difference stance than **Building 27a**, and oversailed the silt-filled inner ditch (Figure 5.11). The original superstructure seems to have been moved some 0.5 m to the east to allow the erection of **Building 39** to the north. The new building had an earth floor with irregular paving in its south-west end. The north-east wall was marked by a new 'packing wall', and patches of clay beyond it may have been derived from daub coating the wicker wall. The hearth was rebuilt in its original position. The small group of finds from soil overlying the floor (Table 5.31) included two tag-ends which were probably contamination from **Period V** graves.

Two copper-alloy tag ends (BZ20.4 and 5)
Two nails and two shanks
A bent iron pin (IN40.14)
A fragmentary cetacean bone.

Table 5.31: Finds from **Building 27b** (405)

Building 39 (460) lay between **Buildings 20** and **27** on a stance defined by a shallow ditch cutting the remains of earlier buildings. The principal feature was a doorway in the east wall, marked by a massive stone door sill flanked by two insubstantial post holes. Wattle walls were indicated by three stakeholes at the north end of the west wall, and by occasional angled stones towards the outer edge of the ditch. The building was roughly 5.0 m long and 3.5 m wide. It probably had an earth floor without internal furnishings, suggesting that it had a different function from the other *Stage 2* buildings. No finds can be assigned to the building.

Building 40 (459) lay between the boundary ditches on the southern bedrock ridge, and was represented by a stone-edged hearth in a shallow hollow, an area of paving to the north-east, and a shallow slot and possible post socket on the south wall. These features indicated a building some 3.5 m wide and perhaps 4.5 m long, with a door in the south-east wall, an incompletely paved floor and a hearth set against the back wall, immediately to one side of the transverse

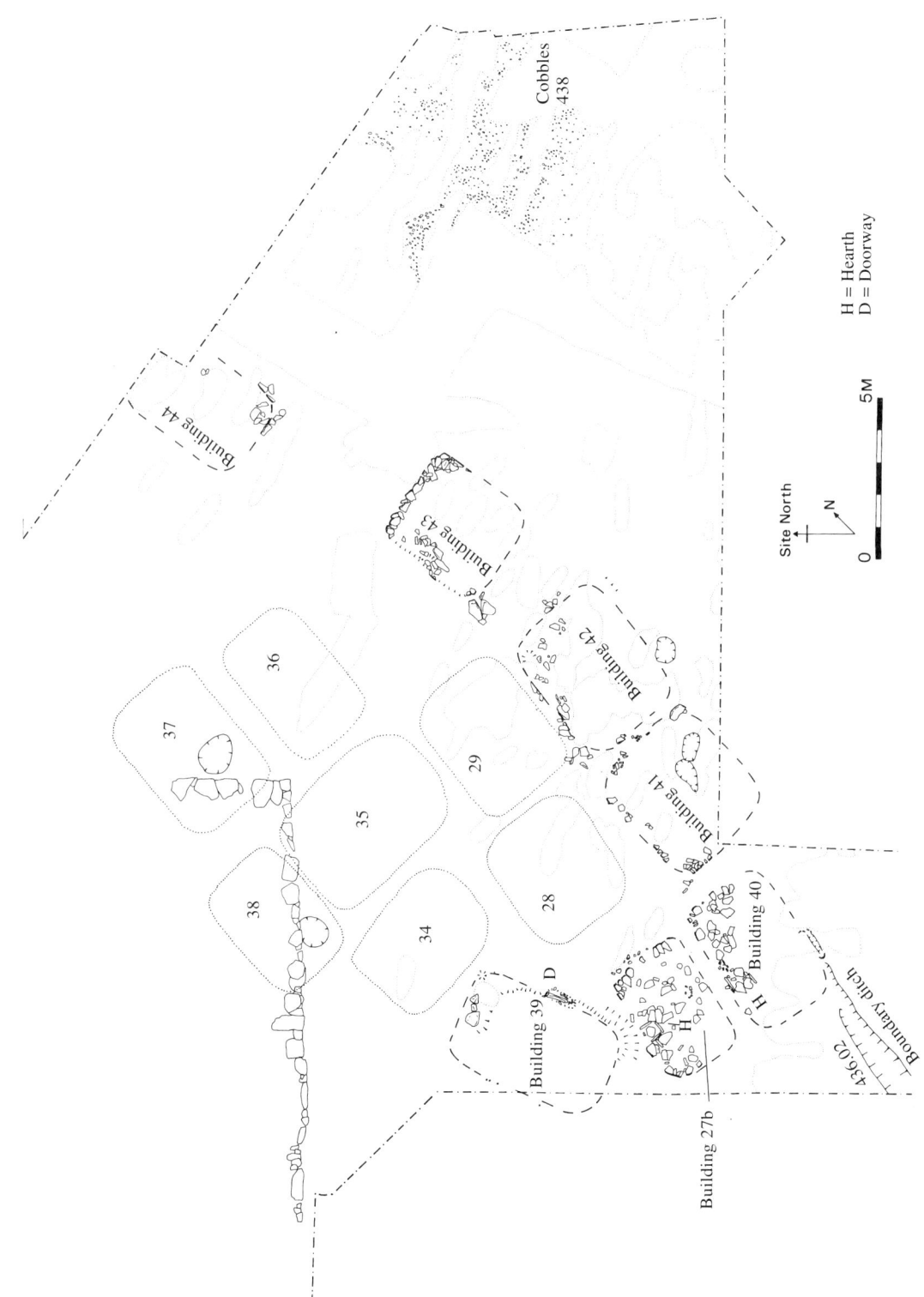

5.11 **Period III/3.2** buildings and related deposits in the **central sector**. Dotted lines mark *Stage 1* buildings still likely to have been occupied.

axis. A large post-socket immediately north-east of the hearth was matched in other broadly contemporary buildings. The paving and an overlying deposit of rubble produced a small group of finds, including a smoothed stone slab with possible mould impressions.

A D-shaped iron buckle (IN44.05)
A smoothed greywacke slab with two possible mould impressions (SE50.15)
A roe deer antler

Table 5.32: Finds from **Building 40** (459)

Building 41 (466) lay in severely disturbed ground over the bedrock ridge, immediately to the north-east of **Building 40**. It was represented by a curved band of stones indicating the rounded north-west part of the floor, and a post-hole, possibly marking one side of a doorway in the north-west wall. Two shallow pits in the south-east part of the floor may have been internal features. The pits produced a small group of finds (Table 5.33), including tweezers and an incised greywacke slab which were characteristic finds of this period.

A pair of copper-alloy tweezers made from a folded strip (BZ24.3)
An antler pin (AR73.1)
A fire-damaged smoothed, incised greywacke slab (SE54.21)
An unassigned sherd of early vessel glass
A **retouched** flint

Table 5.33: Finds from pits in **Building 41** (466)

Building 42 (484) occupied a severely damaged stance between **Buildings 41** and **43**, and was represented by a discontinuous hollow marking a possible north-west wall, and scattered paving which may have been the north-east part of the floor. A band of external paving indicated the north wall-line. A shallow rock-cut ditch to the south-east was probably part of the outer boundary, and the south-east wall probably lay on its inner margin. The building probably had a hollow floor which had removed the south-east part of **Building 21**. No finds can be assigned to the building.

Building 43 (471) lay to the north-east of **Building 42** oversailing the south-east wall of **Building 30** and the south-west part of **Building 33**. The well preserved north-east end of the building revealed a single course 'packing wall' with curving ends preserving the rounded corners characteristic of wicker walling. A post-hole and stone threshold, and two stakeholes on the lip of a shallow scoop indicated a doorway in the north-west wall. Slanting stones revealed the wall-line at the east corner, while external paving indicated the shape of the west corner. The south part of the building had been destroyed. The building was thus some 3.3 m wide and *c*. 4.0 m long. The finds (Table 5.34) came from a confusing feature encompassing the *Stage 1* boundary 'ditch', the south-east wall of **Building 30**, and the north-west wall of **Building 43**. This was cut into the **Period III** ploughsoil and related deposits, and some or all of the objects may have been displaced from earlier deposits.

A tapered, square sectioned iron punch (IN50.39)
A nail shank
A round lead rod (LD11.43)
Three antler comb-plate rough-outs
A segment removed from a beam or tine
An antler off-cut

Table 5.34: Finds from **Building 43** (471).

'**Building**' **44** (473) lay in the north-east part of the **central sector** and had been extensively disturbed. The sole surviving feature was a possible south corner of a wall marked by internal paving and external slabs. No finds can be assigned to the building.

The external road. An extensive cobble surface (438) in the south-east part of the **central sector** overlay the **Phase 1** buildings, and may represent a roadway beyond the **Phase 3** boundary, linked to the path at the north end of the **southern sector**. The small group of finds (Table 5.35) probably included objects displaced from underlying deposits, and the antler was probably derived from the extensive deposits associated with **Building 9**. The remainder of the group was similar to that from the **Period IV** cobbling in the north-west part of the **central sector** (p 232; Table 6.29), as both included finished or broken artefacts, while manufacturing debris was scarce.

A copper-alloy stick pin with a flattened club head (BZ14.40)
A faceted antler gaming piece (AR57.3)
A broken standard iron needle with a punched eye (IN39.15)
A possible iron buckle tongue (IN44.26)
A thistle-shaped piece of lead (LD09.13)
A small broken rounded hone (SE38.21)
A broken antler comb tooth-plate (AR67)
Three segments removed from tines or beams
Two tines and a tine tip
A fragment of antler beam

Table 5.35 Finds from **Phase 3** cobbling beyond boundary (438)

The southern sector: the flood deposits

The **southern sector** seems to have been flooded throughout **Period III**, but the deposits overlying the **Period II** buildings produced a large group of finds (Table 5.36) that is likely to have been debris scattered beyond the settlement in **Period III**. The waterborne silts produced few finds, but an overlying layer of rubble interleaved with silt (309.02) produced a large groups of animal bones, primary antler-working waste and metalworking debris. The antler was of interest as there was only one tooth-plate blank, and the group thus contrasts with the assemblages from the **Period III** and **IV** buildings, and with a larger, but broadly contemporary group that accumulated in the *inner precinct* at the beginning of **Period IV** (Table 6.30 and 31). A group of ornaments was perhaps concealed by the muddy soil and would otherwise have been retrieved. The amber, opaque white bead and shale bangle were all characteristic finds of this period (Table 5.1), while the gold ring hints that the austerity apparent in the other groups of **Period III** finds may have been illusory. The plated iron pin and ball-headed pin head are more characteristic of **Period II** (Table 5.1), and the assemblage perhaps included debris from the earlier-ninth century. Metalworking tools included six hones, two hone blanks and a rotary grindstone, and may have came from the workshop which produced the metalworking debris (Figure 10.166b). The flints merit notice. These were insulated from the underlying deposits by the ponds silts, and are unlikely to have come from a prehistoric scatter transported in turves. They are thus likely to have been used for an unknown purpose in **Period III** and complement the smaller groups from the buildings. Two sherds of red gritty ware (MP01) were probably intrusions from **Period IV** contexts. The metalworking waste included a distinctive, dense, 'hearth' attached to furnace walling (SG32) possibly from a slag-tapping furnace. The only other examples came from the **Period IV** stony bank in the **central sector** (Table 6.34). A significant feature of the group was the absence of organic materials which should have survived if the ground had not been drained at the start of **Period IV**. This large deposit seems to have been the source of much of the metalworking debris, antler and hones found in the earlier **Period IV** buildings erected on the drained ground.

A gold ring (AU4)
A plated head of a ball-headed pin (BZ13.7)
A blue glass bead (GS03.28) and a small decaying white bead (GS03.21)
A chunk of amber (AM02)
A shale bangle fragment (SH01.3)
A sherd of early medieval vessel glass (V11h)
Two sherds of red gritty ware (MP01)
Three nails and two shanks
Two staples (IN17.23 and 24)
A broken iron ring (IN30.11) and two hooks (IN31.13 and 14)
A plated, decorated iron pin (IN41.5) and two pins (IN41.24 and 25)
A worn Class C3 or D knife (IN66.39) and a broken swivel-knife blade (IN68.3)
A corroded iron bar (IN78.24) and a convex iron disc (IN88.1)
A spindle whorl (SE24.7)
Six hones, three large (SE32.9 and 11, SE33.6) and three small (35.2, 36.3 and 36.21)
Three hone blanks (SE71.13, 14 and 65)
A rotary grindstone fragment (SE39.4) and a perforated sandstone block (SE57.3)
A natural flint, six burnt flints, seventeen **retouched** and two **unretouched** flints
An interesting group of antler comprising:
　Four coronets, one with attached skull fragments
　Three beams
　Nine tines
　Four sections
　Six segments
　Eight tine tips
　One comb-plate rough-out
　A faceted tine tip and a pierced tine tip
　Eighteen offcuts
A group of metalworking debris including a dense furnace bottom with attached walling, and a lump of haematite

Table 5.36. Finds from hard-core (309.02/456.01) over pond silts

CHAPTER 6

Period IV: Diverse Arts: The Monastic Town
c. 1000 x 1050–1250 x 1300 AD

Peter Hill, Jo Moran, Andrew Nicholson, Dave Pollock, Damien Ronan

6.1 INTRODUCTION

Period IV saw the continued development of the **Period III/3** settlement with an *inner precinct* and *outer zone* apparently conforming to the curvilinear plan of the **Period I/2–4** *monasterium*, though occupying a more westerly position (Figure 2.19). The archaeological record was rich, but difficult to integrate, and encompassed distinct sequences of buildings in two parts of the *outer zone*, and a rich, but chaotically fragmented, picture of complementary activities in the *inner precinct*. The beginning of the period was clearly defined by the drainage and subsequent settlement of the flooded ground at the foot of the hill, and its end by the delineation of a new enclosure centred upon the cathedral. The finds included important and potentially diagnostic groups of pottery, stick-pins, combs and other artefacts, but most came from disturbed contexts, and their chronological potential cannot be realised. Recurrent evidence for specialised workshops and the large assemblage of manufacturing waste, tools and other artefacts indicated the increasingly commercial basis of the economy, and commends the identification of the settlement as a monastic town (pp 56, 247-8).

Previous excavations. Previous excavations in and around the cathedral have revealed features potentially pertaining to **Period IV**, notably the west wall of the original cathedral. These present a distinct picture complementing the current results, but of completely different quality.

Previous reports. The 1984 excavation revealed the west part of the best-preserved of the **Period IV** building (**7**) and sufficient artefacts and manufacturing debris to assess the economy, date and cultural contacts of the site in this period. The **Period IV** deposits in the **southern sector** were examined in 1986/7, and elsewhere in 1988, '89 and '91, when the overlying fourteenth–fifteenth century graves had been excavated. The 'shape' of the settlement was obscured until a late stage, and previous reports are flawed by linking the **Period IV** buildings with a notional road defined by the parallel boundary ditches of the **Period III/3** settlement. This evinced a picture of a proto-urban community flanking a road leading to a hypothetical eleventh–twelfth century church, which has been identified as an Hiberno-Norse trading post (Hill 1990, 1991a). Many of the economic and cultural conclusions remain valid, although the morphology of the settlement, and its possible origins as a tenth/eleventh century *monasterium* have been reassessed.

Stratigraphy and report structure. The stratigraphic relationships of the principal **Period IV** structures are illustrated in Figure 6.1. A large area in the **central** and **northern sectors** had been extensively disturbed by fourteenth–fifteenth century graves which severed the links between the stratified deposits in the **southern sector**, the west end of the **northern** and **central sectors**, and the south-east part of the **central sector**. Three stratigraphically-distinct areas are described separately in Sections 2–4, and a speculative phasing is presented below (pp 211-6, Figures 6.2–5). The **Period V** graves produced a huge group of finds displaced from **Period IV** deposits, which is discussed in Section 5.

Chronology. The chronology of these deposits was problematical and most of the intrinsically datable finds came from the disturbed deposits in the *inner precinct* (Table 6.42). These included a wide range of eleventh to thirteenth century artefacts, which would have provided a detailed chronological framework in more favourable circumstances. The buildings in the *outer zone* were generally fairly clean, and few diagnostic objects were securely stratified. The most reliable evidence was provided by a group of shoe fragments from the lowlying ground, dating to the second half of the twelfth century, preserved when the drainage deteriorated, and securely sealed by a thick deposit of waterborne silt (Figure 6.7). Pottery should have contributed to this picture, but most of

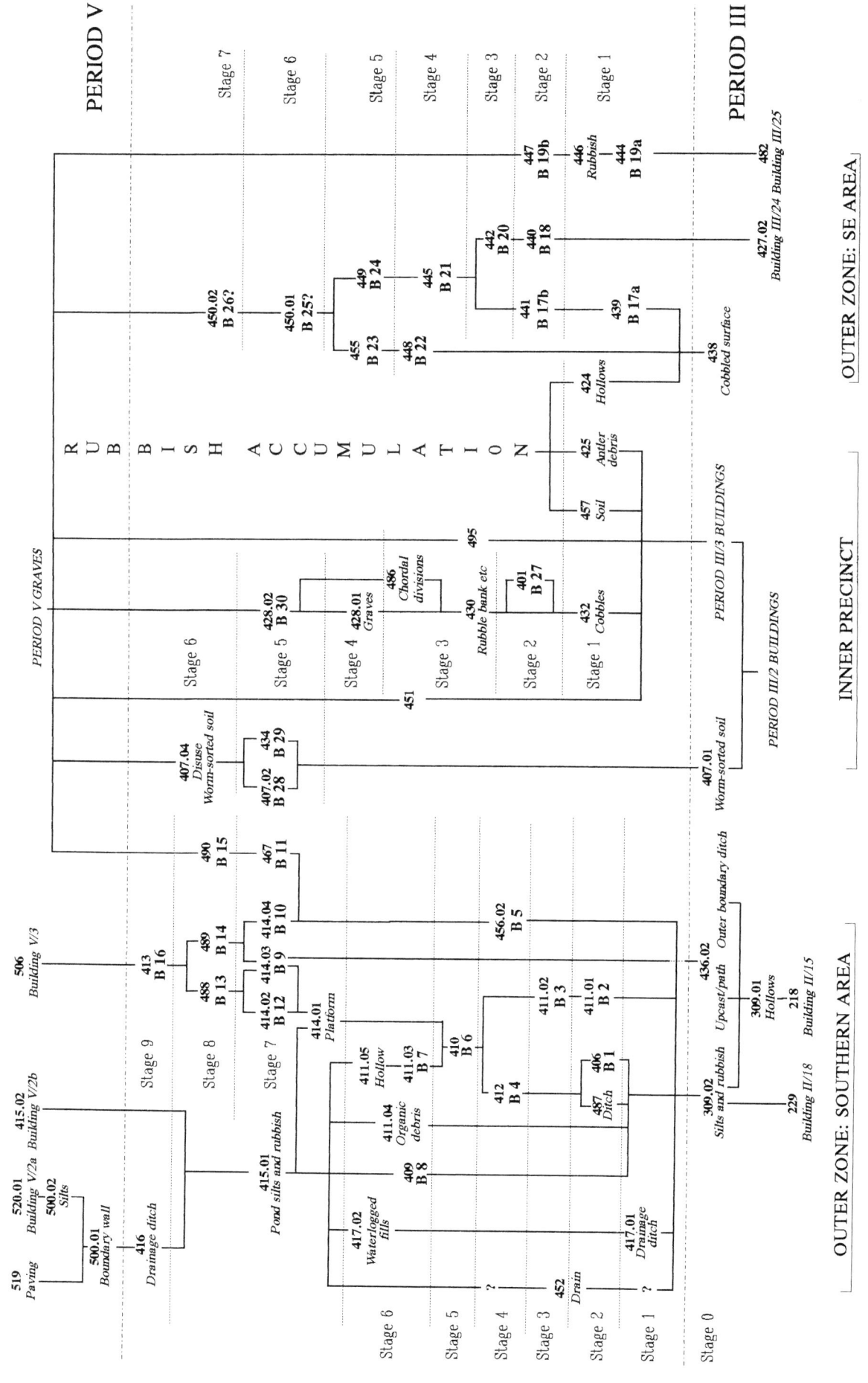

6.1 The stratigraphic sequence in **Period IV**.

the assemblage came from disturbed contexts in the *inner precinct*, and securely stratified finds from the *outer zone* were sparse. The ceramic sequence seems to have begun with red gritty ware, ascribed to the mid- to late-twelfth century (p 511), and continued with white gritty ware (MP06) and locally-manufactured, green-glazed oxidised wares. The spatial distributions of the three commonest fabrics differed (Figure 6.39), but the chronological implications are unclear, as most of the finds were displaced. It is inferred that most of the pottery from the *inner precinct* pertained to the rubbish spreads which accumulated before the first **Period V** burials, and this is an element in the complex argument for ascribing the latter to the later thirteenth century (p 253). The site produced an important group of stick pins, but only six of the forty-five examples came from secure contexts (pp 364-5). Coins were rare for most of this period and only four issues of the eleventh and twelfth centuries were recovered (pp 246, 355-6, Figures 6.38 and 10.45a). Thirteenth century coins were more abundant and, though mostly displaced, indicated that the *inner precinct* was used as a market until the late- thirteenth century. The chronology of **Period IV** thus pivoted upon the securely stratified group of shoe fragments from the **southern sector**, which is ascribed to the second half of the twelfth century (p 222). The deposition of this material was preceded by five phases of construction (*Stages 2–6*) and followed by three more (*Stages 7–9*). The end of this sequence can be associated tentatively with the deposition of a relatively-unworn penny of Henry III (p 227), and can thus be ascribed to *c*. 1260 AD. The **Period V** enclosure may have been built at the end of the thirteenth century (pp 289-90). The beginning of **Period IV** cannot be dated with any precision, and is ascribed with some caution to the first half of the eleventh century. A small group of radiocarbon dates do not conflict with the artefactual evidence and are discussed below (pp 596-8).

Phasing. The stratigraphic circumstances posed severe problems to the interpretation of the development of the site, which may be resolved by future excavations in less severely disturbed ground. It is nevertheless possible to suggest a tentative sequence illustrating the potential history of this rich area, and charting an important period in the economic development of Whithorn, which seems to have preceded the physical separation of the ecclesiastical site and the town (pp 55-65).

Phase 1 (Figure 6.2) was initiated by the desertion, and probably the dismantling of the **Period III/3** buildings, and the drainage of the flooded ground at the foot of the hill. New buildings were erected on the drained ground with doors facing towards the *inner precinct*. Other new buildings to the east opened onto a path leading radially from the *outer zone* to an open area in the *inner precinct* where antler-working debris was discarded. A pebbled surface to the west indicated a more-carefully maintained part of the *inner precinct*, and a single building (**IV/27**) cutting this surface, shared the radial orientation of the buildings beyond. The assemblages of finds from this phase were relatively small and of limited range. The stratified deposits in the *inner precinct* produced scattered implements and waste (Tables 6.29, 32 and 30) indicating the initiation of some of the craft activities revealed by the displaced material (Section 5). The southern buildings were strikingly clean, possibly because there were no workshops in this area, while those to the east produced debris from comb-making and implements indicating weaving.

Phase 2 (Figure 6.3) saw continued occupation in the *outer zone*, while the *inner precinct* was raised with rubble brought in to level the ground beyond the derelict *Northumbrian* terrace. The levelled area coincided with the densest concentration of displaced finds, and many of the nails, flints, pebbles and, perhaps, other finds could have been mixed up with the rubble. Fragmentary walls and ditches indicating chordal divisions within the *inner precinct* possibly pertained to this phase. Comb-production and possibly weaving continued in the south-eastern part of the *outer zone,* and there was clear evidence of a smithy (Figure 6.15). Comb-making now extended to the **southern sector**, while stratified finds from the *inner precinct* (Table 6.34a) indicated the continuing evolution of craft activities.

Phase 3 (Figure 6.3) was represented by two graves in the *inner precinct*, which apparently respected the **Phase 2** boundaries. Continuing settlement in the *outer zone* saw the replacement of the earlier buildings on one or more occasions, and the appearance of leather- and skin-working debris in the **southern sector**, while smithying, weaving and comb production continued in the south-eastern part of the *outer zone*. Securely-stratified crucible sherds from the **southern sector** (Tables 6.9 and 10) indicated the introduction of fine metalworking in silver, gold and copper alloys, probably in workshops further to the north-east. This seems to have continued in **Phases 4** and **5**, and can be linked with rich evidence from the displaced material in the *outer zone* (pp 239-40, Figure 6.24). Shoe fragments dated this phase to the second half of the twelfth century (p 222), and it closed with the deteriorating drainage which led to renewed flooding of the low-lying ground.

Phase 4 (Figure 6.4) saw a significant change in the organization of the site, with buildings reappearing in the *inner precinct*. The fragmented deposits in the **Glebe Field** revealed three possible buildings, and there were at least two others in the **Fey Field** pointing to extensive settlement in the *inner precinct*. The new buildings in the *outer zone* broadly conformed to earlier patterns, but their arrangement was now constrained by the flooded ground, and the most westerly building deviated from the established

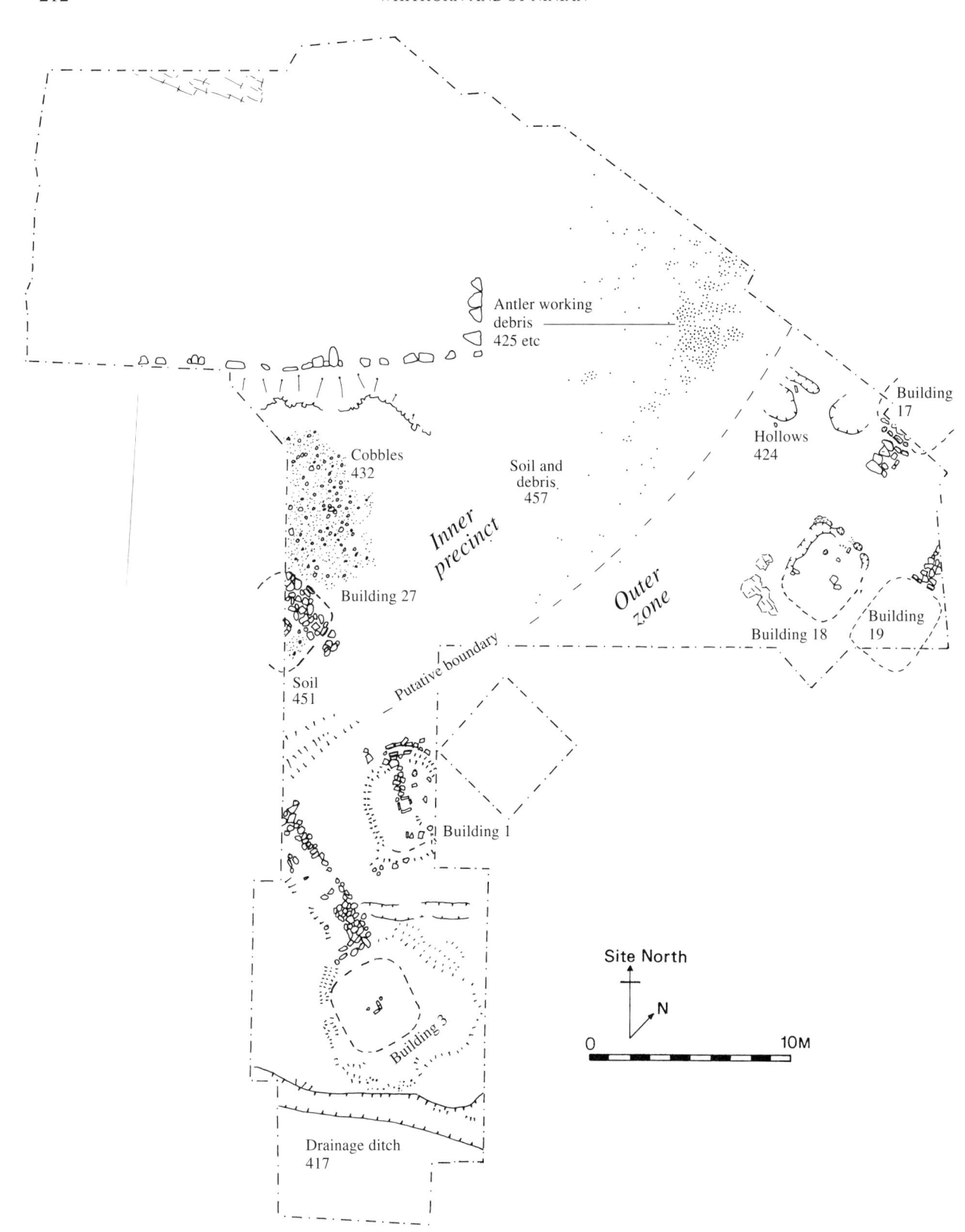

6.2 General plan of **Period IV/1** buildings and related deposits.

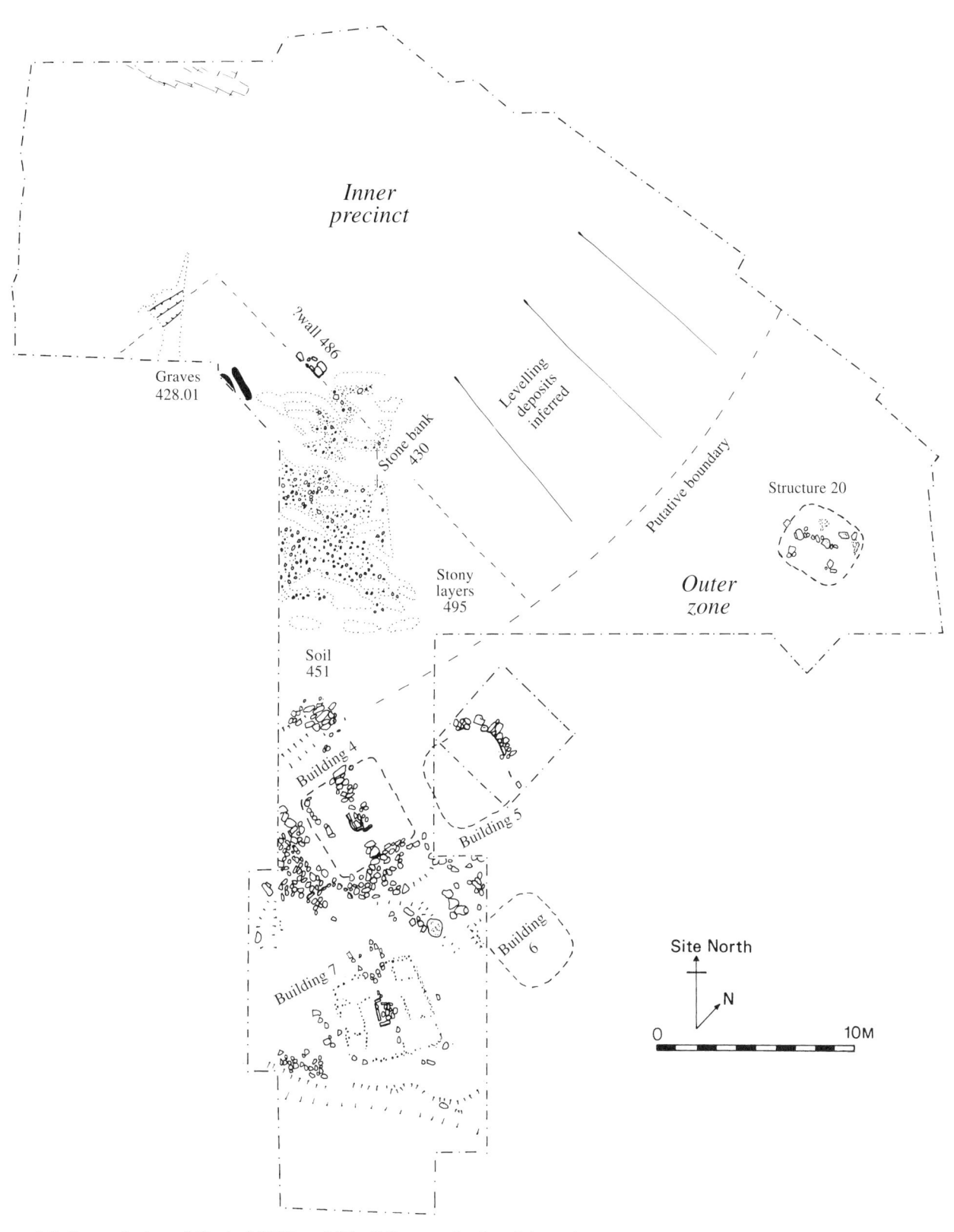

6.3 General plan of **Period IV/2** and **3** buildings and related deposits.

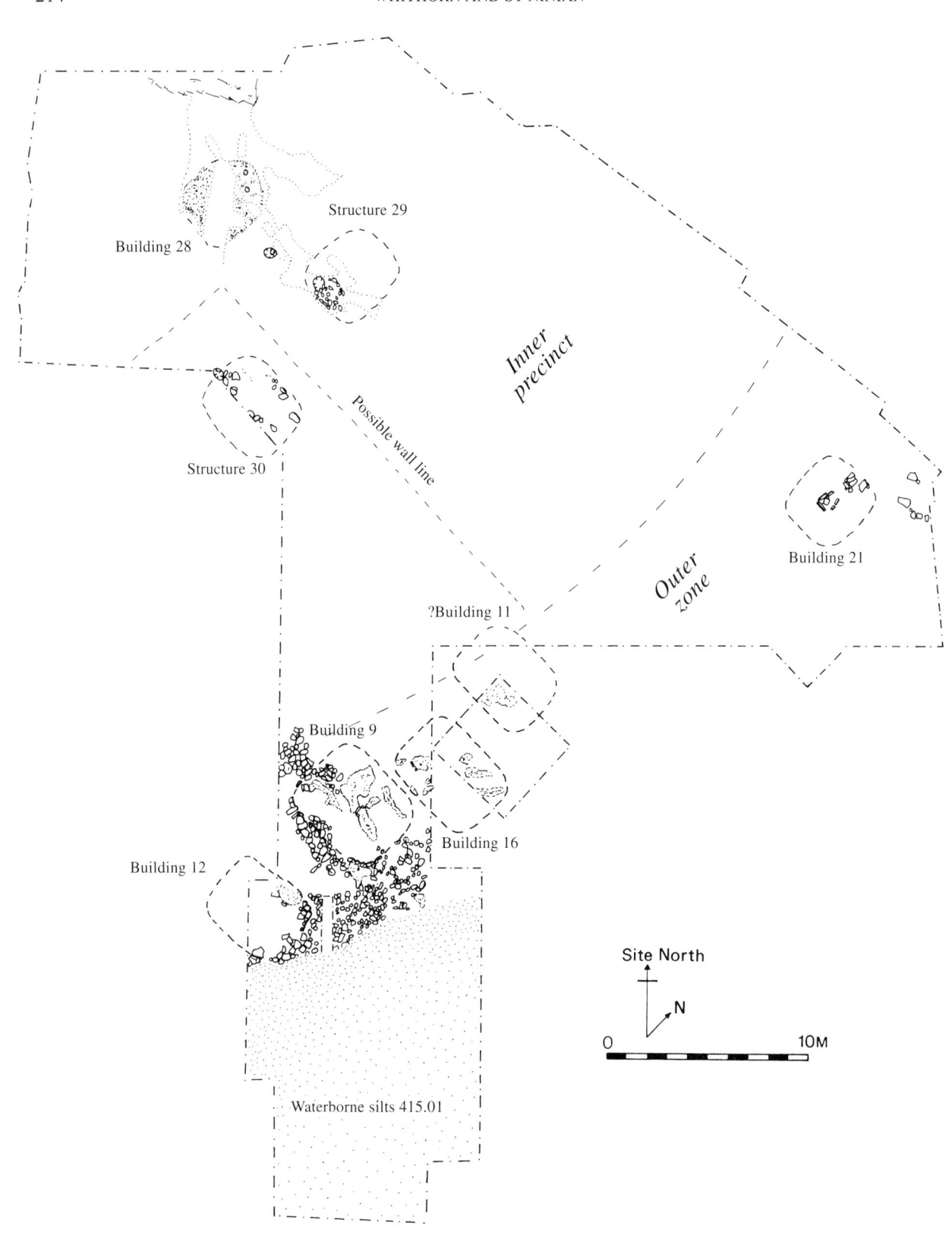

6.4 General plan of **Period IV/4** buildings and related spirits.

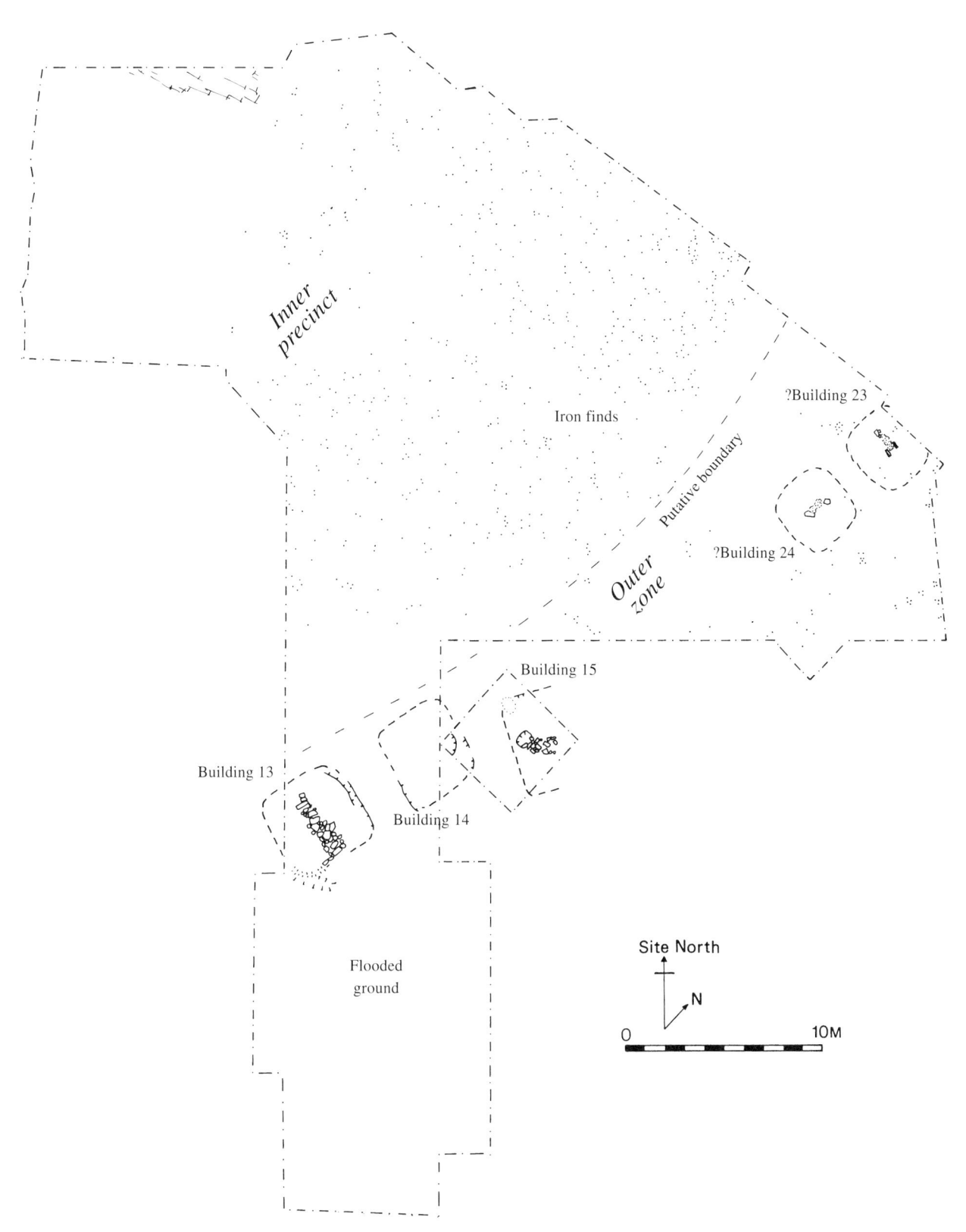

6.5 General plan of **Period IV/5** buildings and related deposits.

radial orientation. This phase seems to have ended with the burning of buildings in various parts of the site, which could have been accidental, but perhaps records an undocumented raid (p 22).

The finds from this phase show a number of interesting features. The structures produced two broken crosses (SE14.6 and 7, pp 435-6), both of rather earlier date. This may well have been coincidental, but could reflect the destruction of an earlier focus in the *inner precinct*, perhaps a graveyard dismantled to make way for the new buildings. The large groups of finds from the **southern sector** included two merels boards, an increased range of iron objects, and what were probably the latest stratified groups of antler-working debris (Tables 6.14 and 15). Drawknives and broken shears from the western part of the site indicated cloth-working and the production of combs, while comb-making and weaving in the south-east part of the *outer zone* were probably superseded by metalworking. Pottery was poorly linked to the buildings, but **Phase 4** may have seen the introduction of locally made oxidised wares, and this could have been the time when coins of David I, William the Lion and, possibly, Henry II were deposited in the *outer zone* (Figures 6.38 and 10.45b, pp 246, 356). This phase was unlikely to have been much earlier than the late-twelfth century, and almost certainly post-dated the establishment of the Premonstratensian community in *c.* 1177 AD (p 23).

Phase 5 (Figure 6.5) saw the reconstruction of the buildings in the *outer zone*, but not seemingly in the *inner precinct* where debris (*Stage 6*) accumulated over the remains of the building burnt at the end of **Phase 4**. The new buildings in the *outer zone* conformed to the plan of their predecessors, indicating the restoration of the **Phase 1–3** design with a densely-settled *outer zone* and unoccupied *inner precinct*. The plan of the settlement is manifestly incomplete and the dating evidence imprecise, but both seem to show the survival of the eleventh century settlement pattern into the thirteenth century. Comb-making seems to have ceased, perhaps in response to new forest laws curtailing the supply on antler. There was no precise dating evidence from this phase which may, nevertheless be ascribed to the earlier-thirteenth century on the bases of the evidence from **Phases 4** and **6**.

Phase 6 saw the construction of the last building (**16**, *Stage 9*) in the **southern sector** (Figure 6.12). The design of the building was novel, although the sub-rectilinear floor plan and opposed doorways were reminiscent of the small Northumbrian buildings of the eighth century. It can be linked tentatively with a new drainage ditch probably producing the thirteenth century leather, and the loss of a coin of Henry III (p 315), both consistent with a new phase of drainage in the mid-thirteenth century. It was no longer possible to identify contemporary stratified deposits in the *inner precinct*, but the thirteenth century coins from this area indicated that it continued to function as a market (Figures 6.38, 10.44a and 10.45b, pp 246, 356).

Finds assemblages. The **Period IV** finds assemblages can be divided into two groups. The first comprised the relatively small and coherent groups from the buildings and related contexts in the *outer zone*, which revealed a range of domestic and workshop debris, and became progressively richer and more varied, perhaps as a reflection of the increasing prosperity and commercial orientation of the inhabitants. The second group comprised the extremely large assemblage of finds from the *inner precinct*, most of which had been displaced into later graves and the overlying fifteenth and sixteenth century surfaces. The surviving fragments of stratified deposits (Tables 6.30, 6.32–37) hint at the original organisation of this material, and underpin the abundant evidence of craft workshops revealed by the distributions of stratified and displaced objects (Figures 6.24–39, 10.44, 45, 71, 88, 116, 133 and 136).

The buildings. Period IV saw the introduction of new styles of building linked to the long Whithorn tradition of small wattle structures. The earlier buildings (**1–3, 18**) were sub-rectilinear with single doorways in the narrow wall. These were superseded by a distinctive series of sub-square buildings, which continued until the penultimate stage of the period. Both types had similar patterns of internal arrangements with a paved strip leading from the doorway to a central hearth, and were generally without the adjacent 'furnishings' and internal pits characterising the **Period III** buildings. There was no transitional stage of development between the buildings of **Periods III** and **IV**, and the rapidity of the change suggests the arrival of new people with specific requirements of their living space. The remains of the buildings were frequently ephemeral,

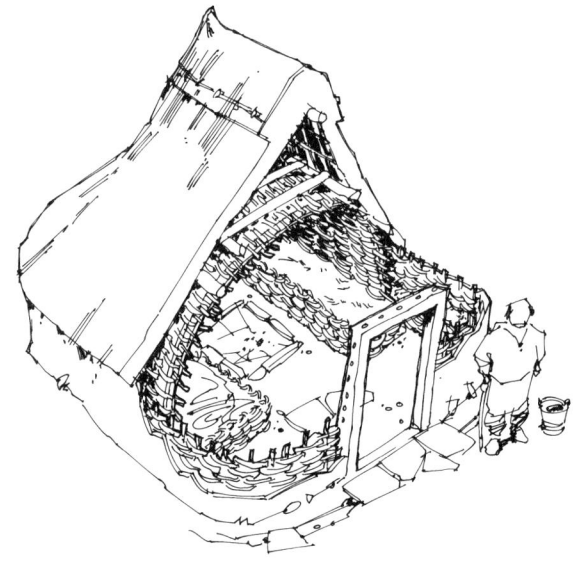

6.6 Speculative reconstruction of **Period IV** building.

but their essential characteristics of shape and internal design were consistent. A typical building is reconstructed in Figure 6.6 which illustrates the characteristic rounded corners of a wattle or wicker building, and infers a double skin roof supported by the domed basket-work.

The boundaries. The **Period IV** settlement preserved the shape and focus, but not the size, of its **Period III/3** predecessor, and the former outer boundary now marked the inner margin of the settled area, and was approached by paths leading from the buildings in the new *outer zone*. No evidence of a physical boundary survived in this disturbed area, but both the buildings and finds suggested that it continued to be demarcated, perhaps by a fence or hedge. An approximate line is indicated on the various plans of this period, but it is most clearly indicated by the distributions of specific artefacts (Figures 6.23–27). There was probably a new outer boundary lying beyond the excavated area in the **Glebe Field**, and thorn twigs from a silted drainage ditch at the foot of the hill (417, Table 6.10, p 223) could have been trimmed from a hedge, which may also have been the source of blackthorn and sloe seeds from an adjacent hollow (p 222, Table 11.45). A sunken road flanked by post pits in the **Museum Garden** (p 281) following the inferred perimeter of this boundary, which is also indicated by a vestigial earthwork in an unexcavated part of the **Fey Field**. The cathedral was probably built in the middle years of **Period IV**, and was sited between the conjectured inner and outer boundaries. The implications of this superficially unusual position are explored in Chapter 2, and a speculative reconstruction of Whithorn at this time is presented in Figure 2.21.

6.2 AND 3: THE *OUTER ZONE*

Introduction

Two disconnected areas of the outer, residential zone were excavated, both revealing intense and long-lived settlement. The first area described is the **southern sector** which lay beyond the boundary of the **Period III/3** settlement, and had been flooded for perhaps two hundred or more years. The second area in the south-east part of the **central sector** also lay beyond the **Period III/3** boundary, but overlay buildings of **Period III/1** and **2**.

6.2 THE SOUTHERN SECTOR

The lower part of the **southern sector** was flooded until the start of **Period IV**, and a thick layer of silt had accumulated over the remains of **Periods I** and **II**. The silt deposits became progressively shallower to the north, dying out at the foot of the bedrock ridge. The deep, soft silt to the south and the shallow rocky soil to the north presented two very different archaeological environments. The north part of the area was occupied by successive small buildings with paved floors and paved surrounds on stone platforms, and were generally defined by stone features linking a central hearth, paved-doorway, and a stone-lined drain beyond. Wall-lines have been inferred from the doorways, from the differences between 'internal' and 'external' surfaces, and from the assumption that hearths were sited centrally. Conditions in the ground to the south were completely different. Little evidence survived of the buildings erected after the pond silts had been drained, apart from the characteristic hearths, doorways and external entrance drains (e.g. **Building 3**, Figure 6.8). The drainage system deteriorated during *Stage 6*, restoring waterlogged conditions which preserved the stake walls of the latest buildings, and organic debris in the shallow gullies surrounding them. Subsequent flooding covered these remains with a second layer of waterborne silt, and the structural features were sandwiched between two thick layers of silt, uniform in colour and texture, among which silt-filled features were well camouflaged. Sections revealed several features which had not been identified in plan, and other unrecognised intrusive features probably account for occasional late artefacts from relatively early contexts. This problem was particularly acute in the southern part of the area, where some of the contents of twelfth (417) and thirteenth century ditches (416), and a fourteenth century pit (523.01) were confused by over-hasty excavation in the closing weeks of the 1986 excavation. The finds recovered during this operation have been ascribed to the latest context (523.01), and unfortunately included a tenth century leather trial piece (LR16.1) of particular significance (pp 50-52, 621-3). The west section of the south end of the trench (Figure 6.7) illustrates the ephemeral evidence of the outer boundary of **Periods I** and **II**; the thick silt deposits overlying it; the successive drains of the start and close of **Period IV**; the position of the robbed **Period V** boundary; and the tail of the bank which succeeded it in the fourteenth century.

The **southern sector** revealed a stratified sequence with some nine stages encompassing eight successive building phases (*Stages 2–9*). These presented a picture of gradual evolution in which buildings were replaced or repaired as required, and the earlier stages overlap to some extent. This sequence was reliable, but the absolute chronology is imprecise, as dateable artefacts were scarce, and most came from relatively late contexts. The two largest groups of finds came from the waterlogged deposits. The earlier group (Tables 6.10–12) accumulated as the drainage deteriorated, and included a securely stratified group of leather dating to the second half of the twelfth century. The second group (Table 6.18) came from the overlying pond silts and was concentrated on the edge of the flooded area, probably comprising debris from the adjacent buildings of *Stages 7–9*. Finds included a worn sterling of David I (*c.* 1140–50, CN03.1, p 345), perhaps lost in the late-twelfth century, and a varied group of pottery probably dating to the later-twelfth

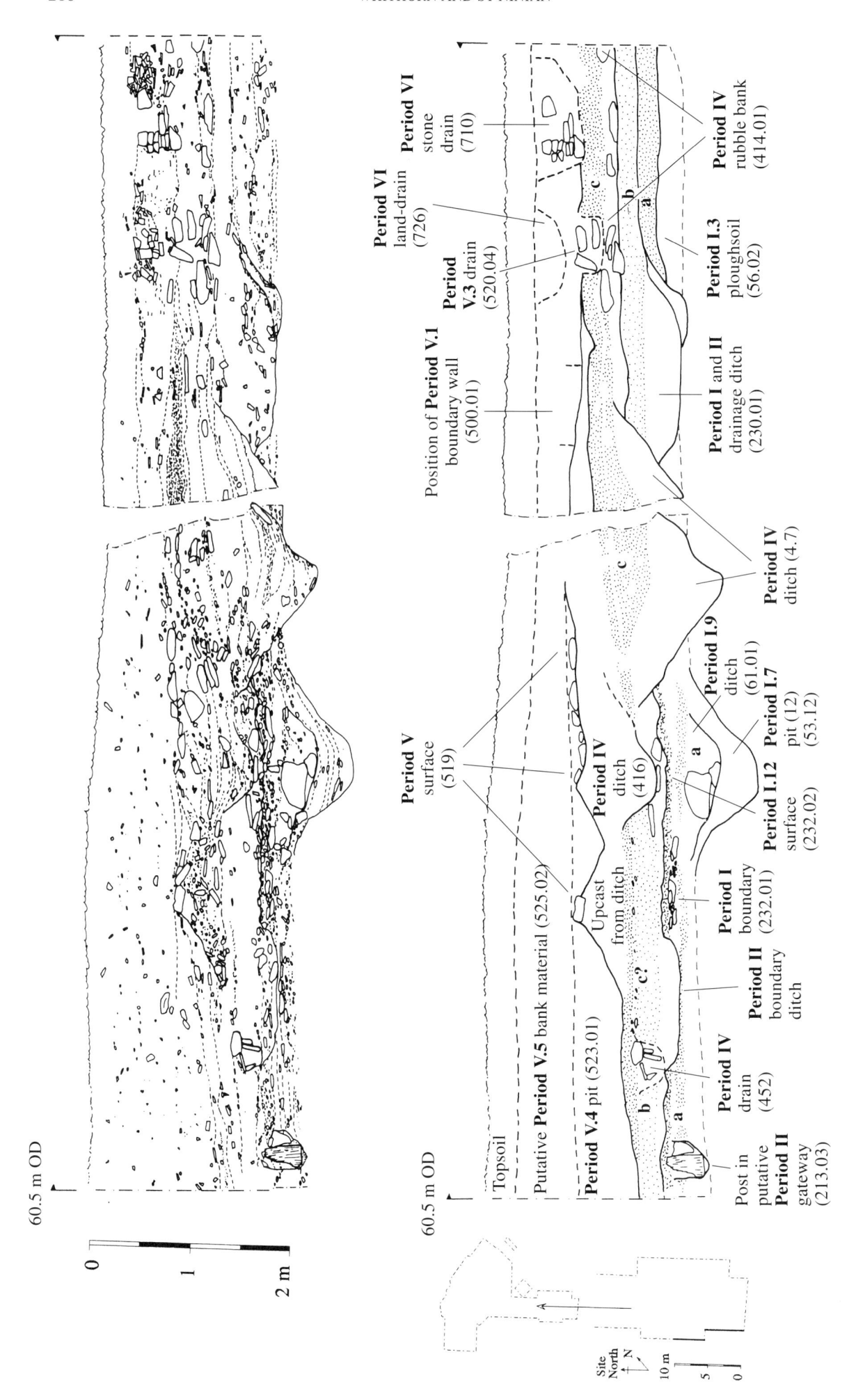

6.7 Recorded and schematic sections of the **southern sector** showing successive water-borne silt deposits and subsequent drainage ditches. Principal silt layers pertain to **Period I.10 (a)**, **Period III (b)** and **Period IV.7–8 (c)**.

and earlier-thirteenth centuries. An isolated patch of ash overlying the flood deposits produced a bent, but only slightly worn, penny of Henry III of 1248–50 (CN03.65), indicating that the area had been drained by the mid-thirteenth century. The **Period IV** deposits produced several ninth and tenth century objects, but most of the other finds were appropriate to the eleventh, twelfth and earlier- thirteenth centuries. Radiocarbon dates from *Stages 6* (**7**, 411.03) and *7* (**15**, 490) gave a similar chronological range (p 597).

Stage 0 encompassed developments between the inundation of the area towards the end of **Period II**, and the drainage which allowed it to be reoccupied at the beginning of **Period IV**. A uniform layer of silt in the southern part of the area indicated flooding throughout this period, while shallower deposits to the north marked the edge of a fluctuating pool. Diatoms indicated that the silts had formed in a shallow, muddy pool or slowly moving stream (pp 598-601), and thin-section analysis indicated periodic drying. The northern part of the area revealed a sequence of features and deposits interleaved with the pond silts, and probably pertaining to **Period III**. Early features included a hollow cutting the east end of the late stone-founded building (**II/15**, pp 180-1), and an area of disturbed ground to the east which may have been ploughed. There were no finds. These features were overlain by a pebble path immediately beyond the outer boundary of the **Period III/3** settlement, which was covered with silt and greatly churned about by animals during a subsequent re-advance of the pond. A large group of finds from the silt was probably deposited in **Period III**, and may have been debris strewn beyond the **Period III/3** boundary (Table 5.32). This was characterised by primary antler waste (p 493), ironworking debris, large hones and flints, and was probably the source of much of the material from the overlying structures (Tables 6.1–4).

Stage 1 saw the draining of the low-lying ground at the foot of the hill, which initiated **Period IV**, and probably involved digging a new channel for the Ket Burn across what is now George Street. A deep ditch (417, Figure 6.8) was subsequently dug across the lowest part of the **southern sector** cutting through the pond silts into the subsoil. The ditch was maintained until the mid- to late-twelfth century (*Stage 6*) when the low-lying ground was again flooded (pp 224–7). A small drain with stone sides and capping to the south (452) must have been constructed after the area was drained, and perhaps pertained to a phase when the main drain was blocked.

Stage 2 saw the erection of two buildings on the drained ground. **Building 1** (406) lay in the north part of the area some 3.0 m beyond the **Period III/3** boundary (Figure 6.8). A low construction platform was built over the silts, and a drain (478) was dug to the south, and the upcast dumped against the platform. The walls of the building were defined by a low

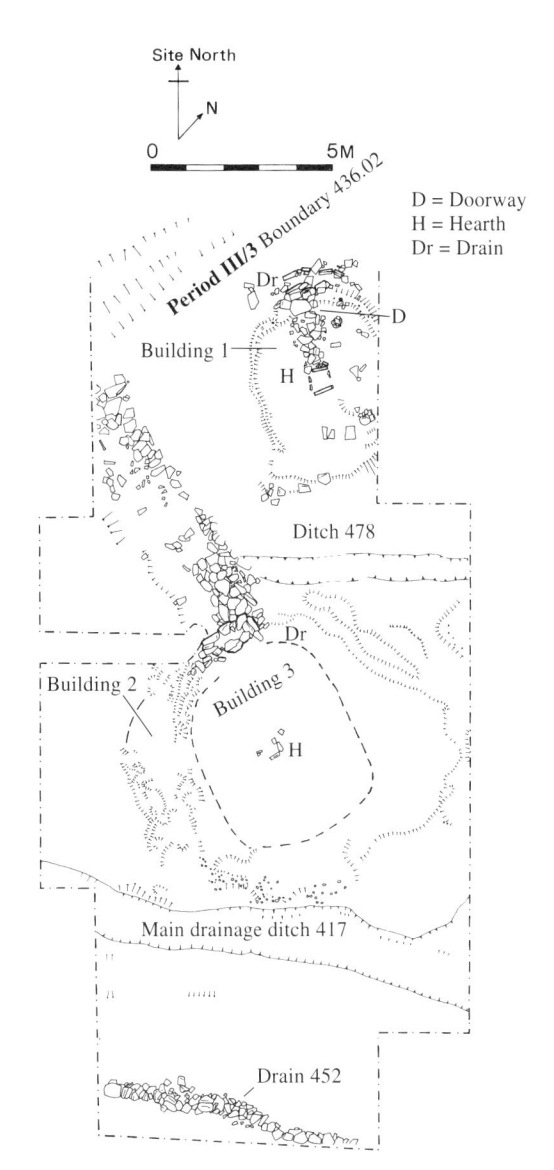

6.8 **Period IV.2** and **3** buildings and related features in the **southern sector**.

clayey bank, probably designed to support the wands while the walls were being built, but possibly including eroded daub. Five stake holes and the impression of a larger post survived in the rounded north-east corner. The south wall was damaged, but the building was probably sub-rectilinear (*c.* 4.0 m long and 3.5 m wide) with a floor area of *c.* 14 m². The doorway in the north wall was marked by a break in the clay bank, a stone threshold, and an external stone-edged drain, while a paved strip led from the door to a central hearth. The floor comprised dirty trampled clay with sporadic paving stones to the east and south. The small group of finds (Table 6.1) probably consisted largely of debris displaced from the underlying deposits (309.02, Table 5.32), and included characteristic 'massive hearth' fragments. The small size of the group of finds from the adjacent ditch (Table 6.2) indicated that the area was kept clean in the opening stages of **Period IV**.

An antler offcut
Two iron nails and a blunt tapering rod (IN78.30)

A small group of ironworking debris including two 'massive
  hearth' segments (SG61)
[An E ware jar body sherd (V9)]

Table 6.1. Finds from **Building 1** (406)

An antler tine and a beam fragment
A **retouched** flint

Table 6.2: Finds from *Stage 2* ditch (478)

A second building (**2**, 411.01) lay immediately to the north of the main drain. The sole surviving element was a curvilinear gully marking the west side of the building, while a slight dog-leg kink in the main ditch indicated the position of the south wall. The small group of finds from the gully (Table 6.3) was probably displaced from the underlying **Period III** debris (309.02, Table 5.32).

An iron bar fragment, possibly tanged (IN83.19)
A large broken hone (SE35.5)
An antler coronet
Two beam sections
A tine
Three segments removed from tines
Four antler offcuts
Two **retouched** and two **unretouched** flints

Table 6.3: Finds from **Building 2** and related deposits (411.01)

Stage 3 saw the erection of a new building (**3**, 411.02) over the remains of **Building 2** (Figure 6.8). It had been severely disturbed by later structures, and no trace survived of the walls, which had probably decayed in the dry conditions that prevailed. The surviving elements were a damaged hearth associated with a spread of ash, and a drain beyond the doorway, linked to shallow external gullies defining the approximate position of the building. Shallow scoops on the inner edge of the west gully may have been dug to remove the walls when the building was replaced. Spreads of ash under the paving in the overlying **Building 7** were probably debris on the floor when it was abandoned. A long sunken paved path led north-west from the doorway towards the *inner precinct*. The building may have been similar to **Building 1**, which probably remained standing. The ground to the west produced a scatter of debris (Table 6.4). The antler waste, flints and metalworking debris were probably derived from the underlying **Period III** rubbish (309.02, Table 5.32), although the concentration of tines is notable, but the stick-pin, chain and decorated plate may have been lost during the life of the building. The horse shoe was found outside the door, and was perhaps a talisman of good fortune, fallen on hard times.

A fragment of turquoise window glass (GS06.69)
The shank of an undifferentiated stick pin (BZ14.47)
A copper-alloy chain of four and half figure-of-eight links
  (BZ31.2)
An antler plate decorated with incised lines (AR76.3)
A burnt flint, four **unretouched** and two **retouched** flints
An iron horse shoe (IN48.2)
A small, broken, manufactured hone (SE36.23)
A plough pebble (SE51)
Three offcuts of cattle hide
A group of antler debris comprising:
  Four coronets, one with attached skull

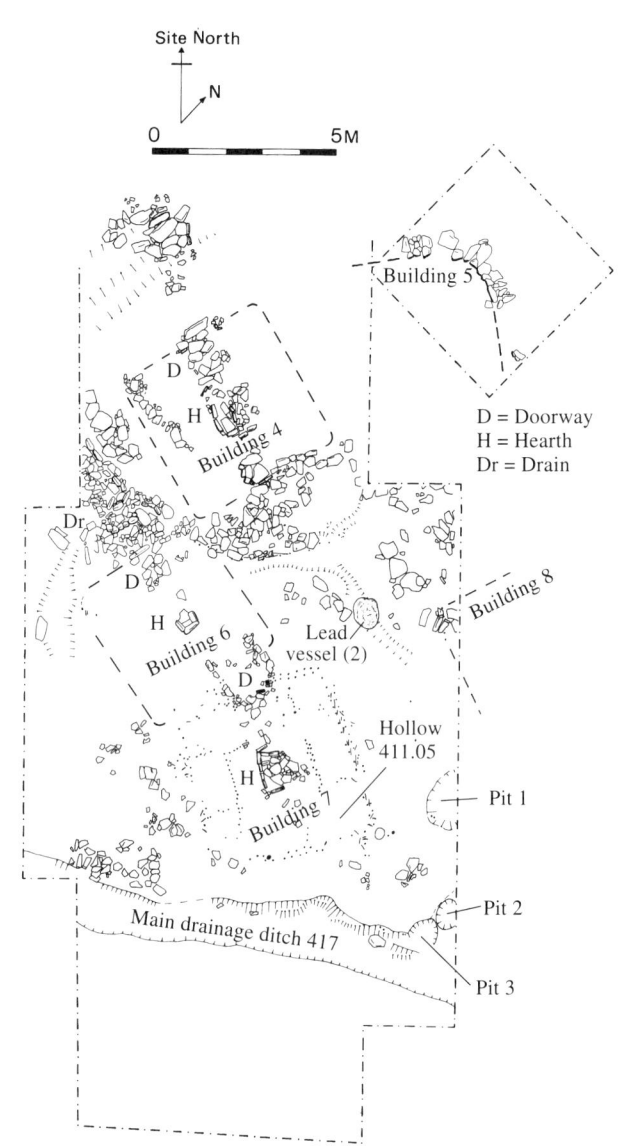

6.9 **Period IV.4-6** buildings and related deposits in the **southern sector**.

Three beam sections
Ten worked tines and a tine tip
One offcut
Scraps of metalworking debris

Table 6.4: Finds from **Building 3** (411.02)

Stage 4 saw the construction of a new building (**4**, 412) in the northern part of the area. It occupied a rubble platform with a curvilinear wattle revetment, which oversailed the *Stage 1* ditch and the west part of **Building 1** (Figure 6.9). The principal elements of the building were a stone door-sill, the sockets for the door frame, an irregular oblong hearth, and adjacent internal paving. Paving to the south-west and south-east indicated possible wall lines, while larger slabs to the west may have formed part of a paved area around the house. Slabs slumped into the **Period III/3** boundary ditch marked a path heading north-west from the door. Most of the finds (Table 6.5), including the gaming piece, came from the rubble platform, and were probably derived from earlier deposits, but the distinctive assemblage of antler pointed to a tine-based product, probably handles, also evident in the underlying **Period III** debris (309.02, Table 5.32). The piece of Roman glass, two iron needles, a putative iron brooch pin, a tine, a tine tip, and two unretouched flints from the hearth were probably contemporary losses. The smoothed and incised slab came from the paving in the south part of the floor, and was perhaps a piece of domestic equipment. The needles and punch offered a link with the artisanal debris in the *inner precinct* (Figures 6.26 and 27).

A 1st/2nd C Roman cylindrical bottle fragment (GS01.5)
A faceted antler tine gaming piece (AR75.1)
Two iron needles (IN39.18 and 57), one (18) with a punched eye, the other fine
A probable iron brooch pin (IN41.16)
An iron punch with a beaded head (IN50.62)
Two nail shanks
A smoothed greywacke slab with incisions and pocks (SE54.22)
A burnt flint, five **unretouched** and three **retouched** flints
A group of antler debris comprising:
  Two coronets
  Four worked tines
  A sawn tine with a groove worn at the upper end (AR81.9)
  Seven tine tips and three tine bases
  A segment removed from a beam
  Two offcuts
A small group of metalworking debris including two 'massive hearth' fragments (SG61)

Table 6.5: Finds from **Building 4** (412)

A second building (**5**) in the adjacent 1984 trench was indicated by an arc of paving and a possible paved threshold. The small group of finds (Table 6.6) from an internal pit included a quartzite spindle socket (SE 52.2), which could have been a displaced door pivot, or the bearing of a mill, or other machine. The lead disc is the earliest of a group of finds of uncertain function confined to this area (p 391).

A small perforated ovoid lead disc (LD02.2)
A greywacke bar hone (SE32.7)
A quartzite cobble with opposed spindle sockets (SE52.2)
Two antler offcuts
A core tool and three **retouched** flints

Table 6.6: Finds from **Building 5** (456.02)

Stage 5 saw the construction of a new building (**6**, 410) oversailing the remains of **Buildings 2** and **3** (Figure 6.9). The main elements were a small square hearth associated with an area of clay flooring, a possible stone door sill some 2.0 m to the north, and an entrance drain some 0.8 m beyond, linked to a shallow curving gully to the west of the building. A sunken paved path with a stone kerb to the east led north-west towards the *inner precinct*. The water table had begun to rise by the time the building was abandoned, and stakes surviving in the west and south walls, indicated that the building was some 4.0 m square. Paving was laid to the west of **Building 4** after the path to the new house was complete, showing that it remained standing.

The ground to the east of the building produced an interesting group of finds (Table 6.7), which seems to have been relatively uncontaminated with displaced earlier material. The antler-working debris included waste from the middle and later stages of comb production, and so differed from the earlier groups from the area (Tables 6.1–6). The relatively large group of tines may have been partly prepared for use as handles. Other finds included tools and personal ornaments. The pin is linked to a group from the *inner precinct* (pp 240-1, 500-1; Figure 6.26), while the gadrooned bead is a characteristic find of this period. An unusually small whorl (SE27.2) indicated the spinning of fine thread, and was linked to a cluster of finds to the north (Figure 6.29) The pecked ring boss was probably detached from a sculptured cross of the Whithorn School, and subsequently reworked (pp 436-7). The three sherds of red gritty ware (MP01) came from a relatively late silt deposit beside the path, and may have been deposited in *Stage 6*. The metalworking debris was probably displaced from the underlying **Period III** deposit.

A greywacke flake with a pecked ring boss from a sculptured stone (SE14.12)
Three sherds of red gritty ware (MP01)
A gadrooned blue glass bead (GS03.39)
A longitudinally-perforated antler handle with ring and dot decoration (AR47.8)
Three nails and a broken hook (IN31.7)
A faceted antler tine tip (AR77.8543)
A broken, nail-headed bone pin with projecting lugs (BA07.1)
A greywacke discoid (SE20.12)
Two spindle whorls (SE24.6 and 27.2)
Two hone blanks (SE71.11 and 26)
An interesting group of antler-working debris comprising:
  Three coronets
  Four intact tines
  Seven incomplete tines and a tine section
  Two tine tips and a tine base
  Eight segments removed from beams or tines
  Seven comb tooth-plate roughouts
  Six offcuts and a comb-plate trimming
An **unretouched** flint
A small group of metalworking debris

Table 6.7: Finds from **Building 6** (410)

Stage 6 records the final occupation of the southern part of the area before the drainage system broke down and the low-lying ground flooded. This phase is divided into two episodes. *Stage 6a* saw the construction of a square building (**7**, 411.03) with double stake walls immediately to the north of the main drain (Figure 6.9). Gravel thrown up from the base of the ditch had been piled beside the south wall, showing that the drain was still maintained when it was built. The drainage system had broken down before the building had decayed, and the rising watertable preserved the stakes of the walls and internal fittings at ground level. Stakes marking the corner of a second building to the east (**8**, 409) were similarly well-preserved, as was the revetment of the platform around **Building 4**. *Stage 6b* followed the deterioration of the drainage system, and was represented by shallow hollows cutting the remains of **Building 7**, and rough paving overlying the walls. These do not seem to have been the remains of a new building and their function was uncertain.

Building 7 was unusually well-preserved, but displayed a number of unusual characteristics. The three surviving corners were squarer than those of other buildings, and it was difficult to see how these could have been constructed of continuous wattling. The answer was suggested by the socket of a pulled post in the south-east corner, which might have supported separate panels forming the south and east walls. The interior contained a large central hearth flanked by wattle divisions. These may have been the remains of raised platforms analogous to those in contemporary Dublin buildings, although the floor continued to either side, and hence they could have been internal partitions. The doorway was framed with squared posts with the remains of a plank sill between. Irregular paving inside the door was matched in other buildings. The floor of the building was strikingly clean (Table 6.8), suggesting that it was carefully maintained, while debris accumulated around it.

A triangular cross-marked sandstone pendant (SE50.1)
An antler tine
A flint core
A hone blank (SE71.28)

Table 6.8: Finds from **Building 7** (411.03)

Building 8 lay mostly beyond the trench, and was represented by a fragment of the north-west corner surrounded by a shallow drain. The finds included sherds of a crucible with traces of leaded brass, bronze and silver (Table 6.9), giving secure stratified evidence of the fine metalworking in the *outer zone*, which was also evident in the adjacent ditch (Table 6.10) and overlying deposits (Table 6.18). These finds were linked to a larger group of displaced material lying to the north-east (pp 239-40, 396 Figures 6.24 & 10.88)

A plated hollow bar, perhaps a lynch pin or hinge (IN25.3)
An iron strip (IN80.66)
Three joining crucible body sherds with traces of leaded brass, bronze and silver (SG15.27)

Table 6.9: Finds from **Building 8** (409)

The ground between the buildings revealed a spread of organic debris (411.04) including wood, moss, plant-stems, faecal remains and leather, while pits to the south and east of **Building 7** produced further leather-working debris and plant remains. The adjacent ditch was filled with similar layers of organic debris and silt, which had probably accumulated towards the end of *Stage 6*, and the area was subsequently covered in a thick deposit of silt reflecting renewed flooding in *Stage 7* (Figure 6.7). Botanical samples from a *Stage 6a* pit and a *Stage 6b* hollow excavated in 1984 included seeds of Celery-leaved Crowfoot and Ivy-leaved Water Crowfoot, both species favouring shallow, often mineral rich, water with a muddy substrate. It was originally suggested (Cameron 1984) that these came from drainage ditches, and had been introduced with animal dung, but the subsequent discovery of the ditch a couple of metres from the sample spots, suggests they had grown in the immediate vicinity. The results of this analysis and of a third sample from the upper fill of the ditch are summarised in Table 11.45. All three samples produced similar results, and included seeds of plants favouring wet environments (Sedge and Cotton grass), damp meadow (Meadowsweet and Hemlock), grassland (Tormentil and Buttercup), cultivated ground (Stinking Mayweed and Corn Marigold), and disturbed nitrogen-rich sites such as dung heaps (Fat Hen, Stinging Nettle and Red Shank). Some species favour heavy clayey soil (Nipplewort, Mayweed and Chickweed), while others (Sheep's Sorrel) prefer lighter sandy soil. Some of the seeds from the pit and hollow (Table 11.45**E** and **F**) may have been introduced with dung, but the large group from the ditch (Table 11.45**G**), is likely to have been washed in, and indicates a mixture of meadow, grassland and cultivated ground in the relatively small catchment area to the west. The range of habitats was similar to that revealed by carbonised sievings from the floor of the **Period II** church (pp 592-5). The most interesting components were perhaps the seeds of hawthorn and sloe from the hollow, which may have been derived from an adjacent boundary hedge, and the absence of similar material in the upper fill of the ditch, suggested that the hedge was drowned in *Stage 7*. Bracken was present in all three samples and abundant in two. It has a wide variety of possible uses, and could have been used as thatch or animal litter, or may have been a residue from tanning. The mosses derive from a range of habitats, and were almost certainly gathered intentionally for specific purposes reflecting their insulatory and absorbent properties. The presence of fly *puparia* in two samples argues that they were used as toilet paper, although they, and the bracken, would have been equally serviceable as insulation sandwiched between the wattles of **Building 7**.

The large groups of finds from the *Stage 6* deposits (Tables 6.10–12) were marked by the superb preservation of bone and organic materials. The organic debris clogging the ditch was sieved comprehensively, but produced only a limited range of finds. The large group of leather included shoe fragments paralleled at Perth in contexts ascribed to the second half of the twelfth century (pp 502-8). Leatherworking waste was concentrated in the ditch, but was also recovered from the debris surrounding **Building 7** (Table 6.11), and in one of the pits to the south (Table 6.12), while a large group from the upper fill of an underlying **Period II** drain (230.03, Table 4.26) may also have pertained to this phase. **Building 7** could thus have been a cobbler's workshop even though the floor produced neither leather nor appropriate tools. The large leather assemblage included numerous strips and worked fragments, as well as worn turnshoe soles and fragments of uppers. No complete shoes were recovered, and the group seems to have been waste from a workshop where shoes were both made and repaired. There were no recognisable leatherworking tools among the finds from the area. A distinctive group of antler included two comb tooth-plate roughouts, but larger pieces predominated, and the presence of four semi-intact antlers was remarkable. This seems to have been a dump of large debris, including numerous beam fragments, analogous to the somewhat larger **Period III** group from the area (309.02, Table 5.32). The bones revealed a number of interesting features. The remains of at least six young cats included two skulls with skinning cuts, indicating the exploitation of catskins. The animals were small, and were perhaps slaughtered as soon as they reached full size (p 612). The pig bones revealed a marked preference for piglets culled at an uneconomic age, but doubtless tasty (p 611). Both features are matched in samples from Waterford, and suggest a prosperous urban economy. Fishbones were extremely scarce despite the good preservation, but this dearth was offset by abundant shellfish remains. The triangular pharyngeal bones of ballan wrasse are used Manx fisherman as amulets against drowning, and for the divination of favourable directions, presumably for fishing (Cubbon 1952), and this may explain their presence in the ditch. Plant remains included hazelnuts and other seeds (*c.* 22,000 fragments), numerous thorn twigs, stakes, worked and unworked wood. Other finds include a finely made handle for a small bow saw (pp 510-1), which would have been suitable for antler- or horn-working, a rare wooden jar lid, and scraps of lead-working waste. The crystal is one of a group from this part of the site (pp 240, 469-70), and may have been associated with the inferred fine-metalworking shop (Figure 6.24).

Four sherds of pottery (two MP01, one MP04 and one MP12.2)
An obsidian cabochon on a silver base with a rope twist border (SR5)
A quadrilateral shale bangle fragment (SH01.5)
A jar lid of willow (WD03.2)
A bow saw handle of yew wood (WD03.1)
A large bone needle or pierced pin (BA10.1)
A perforated pig fibula pin (BA10.5)
A piece of corroded copper-alloy wire (BZ32.5)
A simple pair of iron tweezers (IN74.1)
A wedge-shaped iron bar, perhaps a tool (IN65.14)
A broken iron blade (IN73.13)
A possible iron pin shank (IN78.31)
A sub-square iron disc with a possible stalk (IN88.2)
Four nails and a nail shank
A convex lead disc, probably an ingot formed in the base of a large crucible (LD10.5)
Two pieces of lead waste (LD11.49–50)
A piece of molten lead (LD13.6)
A possible stone gaming piece (SE19.9)
A spindle whorl (SE26.7)
A small natural greywacke hone (SE38.9)
An outer fragment of a sandstone rotary quern (SE43.12)
A quartz plough pebble (SE51)
A botryoidal haematite polisher (SE62.26)
A large, imperfect crystal of vein quartz and Haematite (SE58.18)
Two hone blanks (SE71.45 and 51)
A crucible base (SG15.28) and scraps of metalworking debris
A length of Z-spun woollen thread (TX01)
A large group of leather-working debris (2675 individual finds) including:
   1586 pieces of cattle hide (LR01, 662; LR05, 681; LR08, 243)
   Thirty-four pieces of sheep or goat hide (LR02, 7; LR06, 17; LR09, 10)
   Six pieces of deer hide (LR03, 3; LR10, 3)
   801 pieces of unidentifiable hide (LR04, 294; LR07, 254; LR11, 253)
   Four pieces of discarded leather (LR12)
   172 pieces of leather with evidence of working (LR13, 36; LR14, 22; LR15, 91; LR16, 23)
   Three turnshoe uppers (LR17) and twenty-five upper fragments (LR18)
   Eight turnshoe soles (LR19) and twelve sole fragments (LR20)
   Sixteen shoe fittings (LR22, rands, insoles, vamps, top-bands, clumps etc)
   Six strap fragments (LR24)
   Two possible discoid gaming pieces (LR25)
A group of antler-working debris comprising:
   Five antler coronets
   Four beams with intact tines
   Four beams with tines sawn off
   Two beam sections
   Two intact tines
   Two tines with sawn bases and cut tips
   A sawn tine base
   Two segments removed from antler beams
   Two comb tooth-plate roughouts
   A faceted tine tip (AR77.9)
   One antler offcut
Four scraps of mortar (CC05)
Four burnt flints, nine **unretouched**, nine **retouched** flints and a core
A large group of animal bones
A small group of bird bones comprising fowl (but no geese), a raven, a buzzard and a jay or magpie
Four fish bones comprising a shark or ray vertebra and three pharyngeal bones of ballan wrasse
Large numbers (5000+) of seashells comprising periwinkles (*c.* 70%) and limpets (*c.* 30%)

Table 6.10: Finds from silts in main ditch (417.02)

The finds from the waterlogged deposits surrounding **Building 7** (Table 6.11) included a small group of leather-working trimmings and large quantities of organic debris, including beds of mosses mixed with cherry pits and other seeds. The immediate environment was muddy, and apparently squalid, and this doubtless explains the survival of the most remarkable finds from the area – two large crumpled sheet-lead vessels (LD01.1 and 2, pp 390-1). These were recovered while the overlying silts of *Stage 8* (Table 6.18) were being removed, but their positions indicated that they had originally lain in the broad gullies around **Building 7**. The lead must have been valuable, even if the vessels were no longer needed, and they probably survived because they were lost when the ground flooded, and were subsequently covered by waterborne silts. The evidence of cat-skinning from the adjacent ditch provided a possible explanation for the use of these vessels and other finds in the assemblage. The cat skins would probably have been prepared by tawing in a mixture of alum and salt, and lead vessels would have ideal for steeping them, as they are more stable than iron or copper alloy, and would not have stained the skins. Such a trade in skins could account for the buzzard, raven and magpie or jay bones from the ditch, which might have been discarded when the feathers and skins were prepared for sale. There was little evidence of other artisanal activities, and comb-production in this area seems to have ceased temporarily.

A pair of gilded copper alloy tweezers (BZ24.2)
A copper-alloy pin shank or buckle pin in corroded iron (BZ30.9)

A tapering copper alloy strip (BZ38.35)
A heavy pale yellow glass ring fragment, possibly 10th C (GS04.5)
A fragment of a rotary stone abrader (SE50.5)
A bone pin with a flat expanded head (BA07.7)
An antler coronet
An antler tine and tine tip
A perforated leather disc (LR26.1)
A torn end of a leather tie belt (LR24.01)
Two trimmings of cattle hide (LR01)
Sixty-nine trimmings and scraps of unidentifiable leather
Two burnt flints, two **unretouched** and four **retouched** flints
A polished rose quartz pebble (SE58.8)
Scraps of metalworking debris

Table 6.11: Finds from waterlogged debris around **Building 7** (411.04)

Eleven trimmings and two offcuts of cattle hide and a scrap of unidentifiable leather
Scraps of glassy cinder

a. Finds from debris between **Building 7** and ditch (411.07)

Three trimmings, four offcuts and two scraps of cattle hide

b. Finds from Pit 2 (411.09)

Table 6.12: Finds from *Stage 6* debris and pit (411.07 and 09)

Stage 7 saw renewed construction in the north part of the area, while silts to the south attested intermittent flooding (Figure 6.7 and 10). The complex structural remains revealed four possible buildings and a bank of rubble to the south, which seems to have served jointly as a construction platform and a path. All the

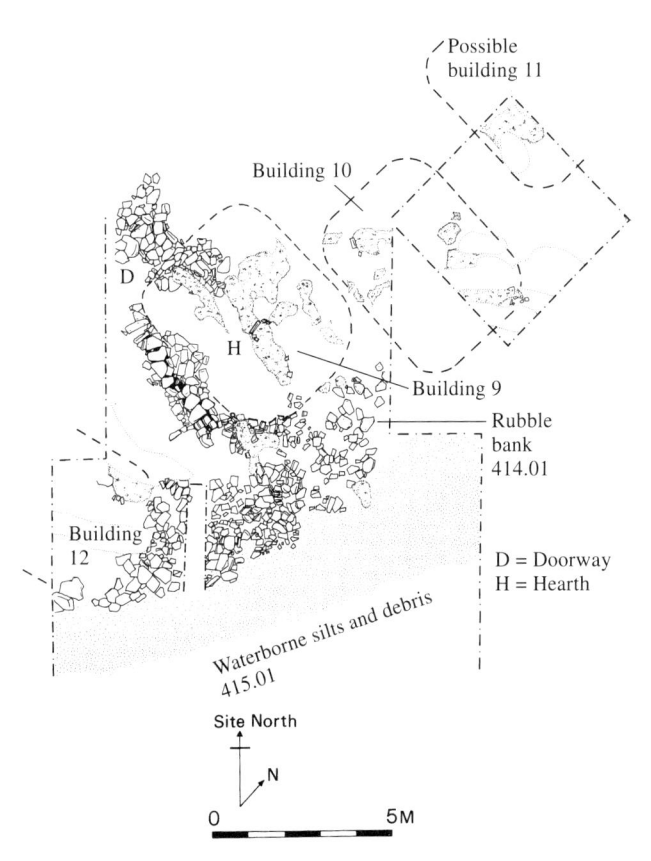

6.10 **Period IV.7** buildings and related deposits in the **southern sector**.

buildings had dirty clay floors overlain by thick deposits of orange ash.

The clearest building (**9**, 414.03) overlay the remains of **Building 4**. The floor revealed a small stone-edged hearth aligned with a sunken paved path to the north-west, which probably lay immediately beyond the doorway. A stone-lined drain covered with slabs probably indicates the alignment of the south-west side of the building. A possible wall line abutting the drain, and enclosing the floor and ash deposits, was respected by the rough surface to the south. The south-west 'wall' was crossed by paving, possibly marking a second doorway.

A second building to the east (**10**, 414.04, 456.03) was represented by ash in the main trench, and a sequence of ash deposits in the 1984 trial trench (**5**) to the east, overlying the remains of **Building 5**. A spread of ash in the north corner of Trench 5 indicated a third possible building (**11**, 467), probably extending to the south side of the **central sector**. A fourth building (**12**, 414.02), to the west of **Building 10**, extended westwards beyond the trench, and was represented by successive clay floor deposits and layers of ash, and by a possible wall-line indicated by the rubble bank to the east.

The ash deposits were the most distinctive feature of these buildings, and indicated that all were destroyed by fire. In **Buildings 10** and **12** the orange ash overlay layers of grey and black ash which might result from the collapse of a turf roof onto a layer of burning wood. The grey and black layers would thus represent a wood fire, possibly of internal screens and rafters, suffocated by the collapse of parts of a turf roof which smouldered gently to produce the distinctive oxidised orange ash. The wall lines were difficult to detect, but there was no charred wattling, suggesting that the fire was confined to the upper parts of the buildings. There were similar burnt structures in the *inner precinct* (Figure 6.19, pp 236-7) and **Fey Field** (p 290), and all may have been burnt at the same time, perhaps during an unrecorded raid in the later-twelfth or earlier-thirteenth centuries (p 22).

The large groups of finds from the buildings and related deposits (Tables 6.13–17) included a wider range of objects than in those from earlier structures in the **southern sector**. The most distinctive feature was the number and range of iron artefacts, and they were similar in this respect to later groups from the *inner precinct* (Tables 6.34, 36, 40). These indicated a range of craft activities and was probably linked with the adjacent segment of the *inner precinct*. The drawknife was one of a small group from the **Period IV** deposits (Figure 6.28), and was probably used in the manufacture of antler combs (pp 429, 478-80). The three possible shears fragments belong with a group concentrated in this part of the site, and identifying an area of cloth-working (Figure 6.36). A relatively complete example from a disturbed context to the north is of an early- to mid-thirteenth century type and is thus slightly later than the inferred late-twelfth century date of the *Stage 7* buildings. The tanged chisel is suitable for woodworking, and only two other examples are ascribed to **Period IV** (p 423), while the hones are part of a group concentrated in the *outer zone* (Figures 6.23 and 10.116b). The crucible sherd and tuyere fragments from **Trench 5** indicate the continuation of the fine metalworking established in *Stage 6,* and the iron punch may also have been a tool of this trade (Figure 6.27). The small groups of antler working debris in **Buildings 9** and **12** derived from the mid stages of comb production, and were complemented by the wider range of debris from the adjacent rubbish spreads (415.01, Table 6.18). The hammer-headed cross may have been displaced from an earlier graveyard when new buildings were erected in the *inner precinct* (p 216), while the merels board was the earliest certain example of a playing board from the site. The two stick pins were of different types, although their probable late-twelfth century date is unproblematical (pp 364-6), and the association with an ornamental bone pin in **Building 9** seems secure.

A possible iron chisel with a forged point (IN52.08)
A broken slab with a low-relief, hammer-headed cross (SE14.7)
A slab with a merels board incised on one face (SE23.1)
Two tines
A segment from an antler tine

Table 6.13: Finds from rubble bank (414.01)

[A sherd of early vessel glass (V11g)]
A conical bone spindle whorl (BA06.3)
The point of a polished bone pin (BA09.3)
A U-shaped staple (IN17.8)
An iron drawknife (IN69.4)
An Class D iron knife or shears blade (IN66.45)
A round-shanked lead nail (LD06.39)
A broken spindle whorl (SE26.12)
A small hone (SE36.12), a broken small hone (SE36.15) and a flake of a large hone (SE35.14)
A hone blank (SE71.47)
A group of antler comprising:
    Two burrs
    A tine, a tine tip and a tine base
    Four tine segments
    A tooth plate rough-out
    Two offcuts
One **retouched** and one **unretouched** flint

Table 6.14: Finds from **Building 12** (414.02)

A squared spatulate-headed copper-alloy stick pin (BZ14.14)
A broken bone pin with a flattened head with lobate projections (BA07.3)
A gadrooned blue glass bead (GS03.40)
A decorated comb side plate (AR69.4)
A possible iron buckle tongue with a flat hooked end (IN44.29)
A broken iron shears blade and the point of a second (IN72.1 and 2)
Three nails and a nail head
A perforated iron fragment (IN78.32) and a piece of perforated iron sheet (IN82.32)
A discoid stone gaming piece (SE19.16)
A hone blank (SE71.12)
A small group of antler-working debris comprising:
    Three worked tines and two tine segments
    A comb-plate rough-out
    An offcut
One **retouched** and one **unretouched** flint

Table 6.15: Finds from **Building 9** (414.03)

A sherd of local oxidised pottery (MP02/11)
An iron clog plate (IN47.1)
A tapered square-sectioned iron punch (IN50.41)
A complete Class D tanged knife (IN66.44)
A curved iron object (IN81.19)
A nail and a nail shank
One **retouched** and one **unretouched** flint

Table 6.16: Finds from **Building 10** (414.04)

A round-headed copper-alloy stick pin (BZ14.10)
A broken ovoid shale bangle (SH01.6)
An iron needle (IN39.59)
A plated iron strap retainer (IN45.5)
An iron clench plate (IN20.8)
Five nails
A small natural hone (SE28.30)
A rounded quartzite smoothing stone (42.11)
Three antler tine tips
A core, three burnt flints, one **unretouched** and four **retouched** flints
A small group of metalworking debris including:
    A crucible body sherd (SG15.29)
    Five tuyere fragments

Table 6.17: Finds from *Stage 7* ash deposits in 1984 trench (5, 456.03)

The waterborne deposits (415.01) beyond the rubble bank probably accumulated in *Stages 7–9,* and revealed a phase of flooding, perhaps lasting for 25–50 years, which ended with renewed drainage marking the transition from **Period IV** to **Period V** (p 227). The thick bed of waterborne silt lapped against the *Stage 7* rubble bank where *laminae* of ash indicated rubbish thrown from the adjacent buildings into the pond. The silts produced a relatively large group of finds (Table 6.18) which were concentrated on the edge of the flooded ground, and probably comprised debris from the adjacent buildings of *Stages 7–9*. This produced a small group of pottery including red and white gritty wares, perhaps of the later-twelfth century, and a range of green-glazed oxidised wares (MP02) probably dating to the earlier-thirteenth century. The sherds of reduced wares were probably intrusive, but one of the imported fabrics (MP17) was found in other early contexts. The assemblage included the last large group of stratified flints from the **southern sector**, and a final small group of antler-working debris from all stages of comb production, which complemented the more specific groups from the adjacent buildings (**9** and **12**, Tables 6.14 and 15). Metalworking debris pointed to non-ferrous metalworking in the vicinity, and complemented the evidence from adjacent and slightly earlier deposits, and from the displaced material to the north-east (Figures 6.24 and 10.88). A fragment of a tuyere block joined others from the south-east part of the *outer zone* (Table 6.26), while a grindstone, smoothing stone and hone blanks indicated the finishing of iron tools. The most noteworthy individual objects were the sterling of David I, the two lead vessels, a stylus, and two quadrilateral burnishers. The stylus is a ninth century type (p 378) which might have been displaced from a **Period II** context, and probably had a different function than the iron styluses from the displaced debris in the *inner precinct* (pp 243, 425, Figure 6.30). The burnishers were part of a small group (SE40) of finely-finished tools suggesting a specialised craft, perhaps the finishing of fine metalwork (pp 243, 456-8, Figure 6.30). The two lead vessels were probably associated with the underlying *Stage 6* building (7, p 223). This deposit and the adjacent buildings of *Stages 7–9* had been disturbed by the foundations of an early- to mid-fourteenth century building (V/3, pp 269-70), and numerous finds, including early pottery and two spatulate-headed copper-alloy stick pins (BZ14.16 and 13), similar to one from **Building 9** (*Stage 7*, Table 6.15), seem to have been displaced. Despite these problems the group was of considerable value, and probably spans the later-twelfth and earlier-thirteenth centuries.

A very worn Roxburgh sterling of David I (1140–50, CN03.1)
A decorated F3 comb side plate (AR70.9)
A broken Class F comb fragment (AR71.5)
A bone spindle whorl with a biconical perforation (BA06.2)
A bone pin fragment (BA09.2)
A copper alloy stylus (BZ25.1)
A copper alloy sheet fragment with angled sides (BZ37.13)
Forty-one sherds of pottery comprising:
   Seven sherds of red gritty ware (MP01)
   Ten sherds of white gritty ware (MP06)
   Local, glazed oxidised wares (MP02/1 × 2, /4 × 2, /5, /6 × 2, /7, /8, /9 × 3, /11 × 4, /12)
   Two sherds of local reduced wares (MP07/1 and /4)
   Sherds of MP17 (1) and MP33 (2)
A broken, tapering iron ring (IN30.12)
A possible iron wedge (IN53.6)
A barbed iron fish-hook with a looped shank (IN56.3)
Four nails and three shanks
A broken long staple (IN18.12)
A riveted iron strip and a broken object (IN78.28 and 29)
Two unidentifiable iron lumps (IN93.72 and 73)
Two large crumpled lead vessels (LD01.1 and 2)
A sub-rectangular perforated lead plate (LD02.1)
Two stone spindle whorls (SE24.9 and 26.5) and a discoid shale spindle whorl (SH04.1)
Two quadrilateral quartzite burnishers (SE40.3 and 4)
A fragment of a large sandstone rotary grindstone (SE39.1)
A small granite smoothing stone (SE42.12)
A large piece of heated smoothed massive Haematite (SE62.8)
Four hone blanks (SE71.8, 18, 50 and 64)
A small group of antler comprising:
   Two coronets
   A beam fragment
   An intact tine, two worked tines and a tine fragment
   Four comb tooth-plate rough-outs
   Five offcuts
Five burnt flints, twenty-two **retouched** and eleven **unretouched** flints
A relatively large group of metalworking debris including
   A thumb crucible with traces of brass or leaded brass (SG15.31)
   Pieces of two tuyere blocks (SG28.1 and 3)
   Four lumps of non-ferrous waste

Table 6.18: Finds from silts and interlaminated debris (415.01), *Stages 7–9*

Stage 8 saw the construction of at least two new buildings (**13** and **14**) which cut through the burnt material covering the *Stage 7* structures (Figure 6.11). A third building (**15**) was indicated by relatively late pits and paving in **Trench 5** to the east, although its form cannot be reconstructed.

Building 13 (488) was the best-preserved structure in this group. The north-east wall was indicated by a shallow trench cutting the ash deposits on the floor of

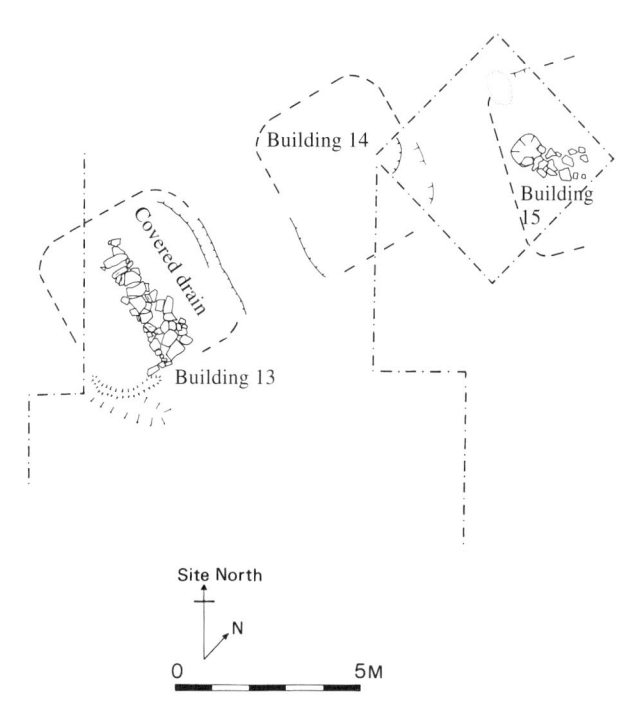

6.11 **Period IV.8** buildings in the **southern sector**.

Building 39, while a wider gully filled with soil and rubbish marked the south corner and part of the south-west wall. Both had probably been dug to support a pre-fabricated wattle wall, and a low bank of clay overlying the ditch fill was probably daub applied to the south west wall. The building was sub-square measuring some 4.0 × 4.0 m. The stone-lined drain flanking **Building 9** ran through the central axis of the floor, opening onto the lower ground to the south. It was covered with flagstones overlain by patchy clay flooring.

Building 14 (489) lay some 2.0 m to the west of **Building 13**. Shallow cuts through the *Stage 7* ash deposits marked wall trenches to the south-west and north-east, suggesting a building of similar size and construction to **Building 13**, with a large pit on the east side of the floor.

Building 15 (490) was indicated by a patch of paving and a pit on the west side of Trench 5. The position of the north-west wall was suggested by a shallow cut through the *Stage 7* ash in the north corner of the trench, and the building probably had a shallow sunken floor. It had been severely disturbed by later features.

The finds from these buildings are listed in Tables 6.19 and 20. The largest group came from **Building 13**. The clay floor produced the flint, knife, a crucible rim, and sherds of red gritty ware and an early oxidised local fabric, all of which are likely to have been contemporary losses. The merels board, rotary quern and hone were built into the drain, and perhaps pertained to *Stage 7*. The pit in **Building 14** produced another hone (SE 38.17), while all the finds from **Building 15** came from the pit. There was no antler-working debris, and these buildings may have post-dated the end of this long-lived industry, perhaps as a result of new forest laws.

Three sherds of red gritty ware (MP01)
Two sherds of local oxidised ware (MP02/1 and /9)
A decorated copper-alloy vessel handle (BZ30.74)
A mudstone slab with a merels board incised on each face (SE23.2)
A broken small manufactured hone (SE36.9)
A large, decorated rotary-quern upper-stone fragment (SE43.10)
A crucible rim sherd with traces of lead (SG15.30)
A tanged Class D knife (IN66.46)
A folded iron strip (IN78.33) and a piece of wire (IN90.7)
A nail and a small staple (IN17.25)
Four **unretouched** flints and a burnt flint

Table 6.19: Finds from **Building 13** (488)

A decorated sandstone spindle whorl (SE28.11)
A nail and a possible iron blade (IN73.14)
A hone blank (SE71.57)
A core, a burnt flint and an **unretouched** flint

Table 6.20: Finds from **Building 15** (490)

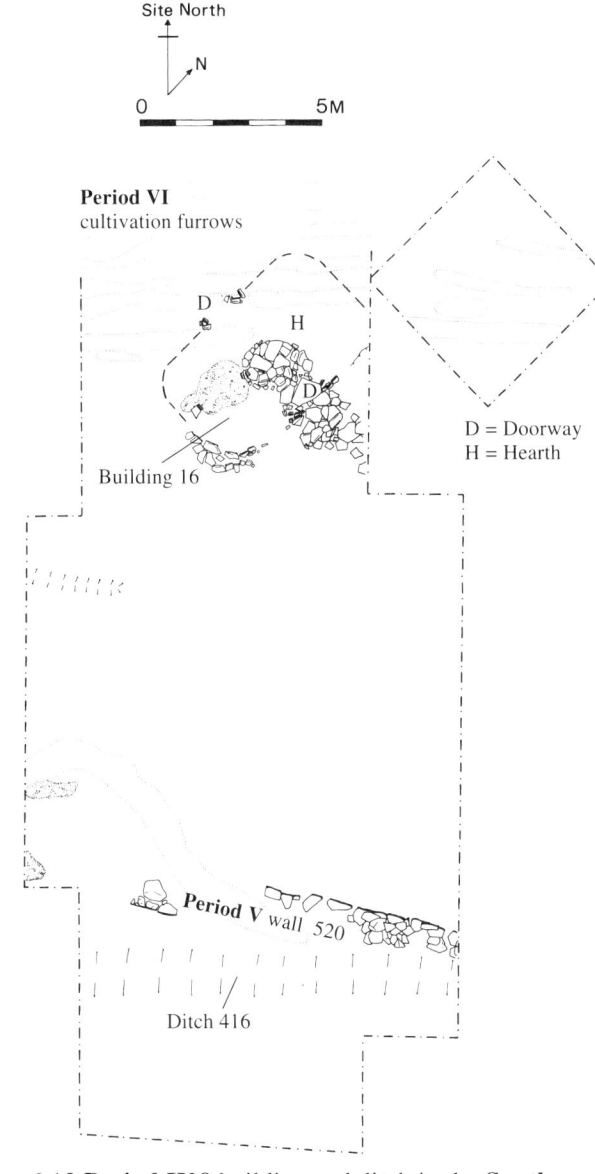

6.12 **Period IV.9** building and ditch in the **Southern sector**.

Stage 9 (Figure 6.12) saw the construction of a final building (**16**, 413) in the north part of the **southern sector**, and its abandonment probably marked the transition from **Period IV** to **Period V**. The drainage of the low-lying ground to the south possibly pertained to this phase, and was indicated by a ditch (416) cutting the silts at the foot of the slope. This was probably the source of a group of late-thirteenth century leather recovered after the removal of the **Period V** deposits, but before the ditch was recognised (pp 267-8, 500). A coin of Henry III (CN03.65) was deposited after the area was drained, and may have been lost *c.* 1260 AD, possibly at the end of this phase. The overlying **Period V** boundary is likely to have been rather later (pp 287-8), and the date of the transition from **Period IV** to **V** cannot be determined precisely.

Building 16 overlay the burnt remains of the *Stage 8* houses and, although severely disturbed by later features, seems to represent a new structural type. The principal features were opposed doorways some 1.0m wide and 3.3m apart, connected by a paved passage which joined a path beyond the south wall. The north-west, north-east and south-west walls were suggested by gaps in the underlying *Stage 7* ash, and a curved south corner was defined by external paving. The building thus seems to have been sub-rectilinear, and was some 5.8 long and 3.3 m wide. A spread of ash to the west of the passage way was probably the remains of domestic fire shortly before the building was abandoned. The finds (Table 6.21) included a copper-alloy pin from the ash, and a stone spindle whorl from the path. The pin was misappropriated from a temporary display in 1986, but the primary finds record indicated that it was crutch-headed, and may originally have been a ring pin.

A possible crutch-headed copper-alloy pin (BZ14.46)
A fine-grained sandstone spindle whorl (SE24.11)
A fiddle key nail
An **unretouched** flint

Table 6.21: Finds from **Building 16** (413)

6.3 THE EASTERN PART OF THE CENTRAL SECTOR

Introduction. The eastern part of the **central sector** revealed a sequence of **Period IV** features with seven stages of development. These had been severely damaged by fourteenth-fifteenth century graves, a sump outside a late-fifteenth century building (V/4), and the foundations and drains of a mid-eighteenth century extension to the manse (Figures 6.20 and 21). Distribution plots of the numerous dispersed finds (Figures 6.23–39, 10.71, 88, 133 and 136d) indicated the original richness of the deposits here, and allowed the identification of a range of craft workshops, some of which can be linked with surviving structures where diagnostic finds were recovered. The earlier layers revealed successive buildings recurrently associated with evidence of comb-making and other specialised crafts. The later features were too fragmented to be reconstituted into coherent structures, but superimposed hearths, hollows and surfaces indicated a sequence of structures as full as, possibly fuller than, in the less-disturbed **southern sector**, and produced rich group of finds revealing the continuing evolution of craft activities. The crucial objects were the debris from comb manufacture; pronged, socketed iron objects, identified as weaving tensioners; faceted and pierced antler tines, possibly fittings from upright looms; smithy waste and related objects; and, latterly, traces of fine metalworking. Flints were recurrently associated with comb-making waste, although specific tool kits have not been identified. The evidence of manufacture was so abundant that this may always have been a workshop area, the craftsmen living elsewhere. The eastern fringe of the area was not fully excavated, but the density of graves diminished here (Figure 6.20), and relatively undamaged deposits of **Period III** and **IV** probably survive in the ground to the south-east.

Stages 1 and *2* (Figures 6.13 and 14) saw the erection of two small buildings (**17** and **18**) aligned south-west/north-east, with doors to the north-east and south-west facing each other some 5.5 m apart. This gap, though partly blocked by a line of paving stones, probably marked a path leading south-east from the *inner precinct*.

Buildings 17a and **b**. Most of **Building 17** lay beyond the trench, but the doorway and external surfaces were well preserved, and had been reconstructed at least once. The earlier doorway (**17a**, 439, Figure 6.13) comprised a paved threshold flanked by two post-holes 0.9 m apart. The doorway was approached by a cobble path flanked to the south-east by a pile of flagstones and rubble, and to the north-west by a band of flagstones. This may have been a path or the footings of a wall, and included a worn and broken slab bearing an incised and encircled cross (SE14.2). The secondary door (**17b**, 441) had a raised sill of vertical slabs with a socket for the door-frame at one end (Figure 6.14). Gaps between the sill and the flush internal paving, and again between the sill and the lower external flags may have contained horizontal timber members of the door frame. A path of large flags leading south-west from the door was bedded in a layer of debris.

Building 18. The sub-rectilinear walls of **Building 18** (440) were defined by shallow gullies, which may have been dug to support prefabricated wattle walls, while a patch of charcoal-rich debris to the north may have been the remains of burnt walling. Two post-holes some 0.8 m apart marked a doorway in the north-east wall, and traces of a sill-beam socket survived on the south-east side of the doorway. A spread of burnt debris in the north part of the floor overlay a shallow pit and oversailed the wall gully. This may reflect either the ultimate use of the building or, perhaps, its destruction. The building was some 3.0 m wide and was one of the smallest structures identified.

Building 19. A third incompletely-excavated building (**19**) at the east end of the trench was represented by a fragmentary door sill aligned with the door of **Building 18** (Figure 6.14). A path leading to the north-east comprised two layers of paving (**19a**, 444 and **19b**, 447) separated by a layer of rubbish-strewn soil (446).

The finds from these features (Tables 6.23–24) are of particular interest because of the detailed evidence

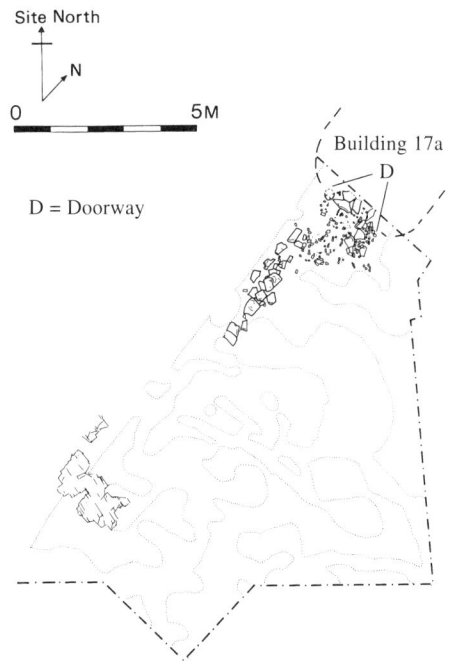

6.13 SE part of **central sector**: *Stage 1* buildings.

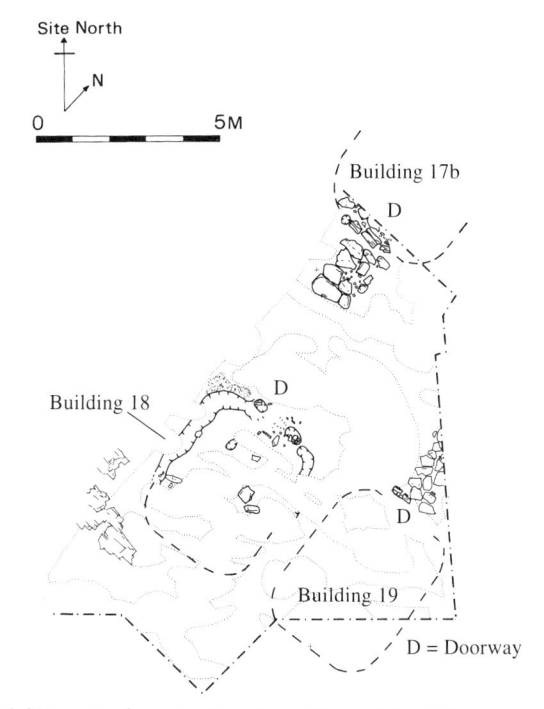

6.14 SE part of **central sector**: *Stage 2* buildings.

of the various stages of comb production, which seems to have been a domestic industry (pp 493-5). The gravel path (**a**) leading to **Building 17a** produced scraps of antler, suggesting that combs were made in the relatively well-lit doorway. The silt overlying the path (**b**) contained further comb-making waste, while the bead, knife and spindle whorl may have been lost in the muddy environment. The rubbish underlying the path to **Building 17b** (**d**) included large pieces of waste antler and a hasp that perhaps came from the door of **Building 17a**. The final deposit of silt overlying the *Stage 2* path (**e**) produced more comb-making debris and flints. The antler was mostly primary waste from the early and late stages of comb manufacture, and may be contrasted with the late stage waste from **Building 18** (Table 6.23), and the mid and late stage waste from the path to **Building 19** (Table 6.24). The rolled lead waste is the harbinger of a larger group from this area (Figure 6.31).

[An intrusive sherd of 16th C pottery (MP08)]
A faceted tine tip (AR77.05)
A comb-plate trimming and four antler parings

a. Finds from path

A sherd of early medieval vessel glass
An opaque white glass bead (GS03.22)
A broken Class C knife blade (IN66.35)
A broken spindle whorl (SE24.23)
A large natural hone (SE35.8)
A segment from an antler beam
Two smoothed tooth-plate roughouts
Two comb-plate trimmings
Two tine offcuts
Four **unretouched** and two **retouched** flints

b. Silt over path

A faceted antler tine tip (AR77.04)
An antler beam fragment and a tine offcut
An **unretouched** flint

c. Door post holes

A nail
A swivel hasp (IN24.11)
An iron strip (IN80.68), a broken perforated disc (IN89.3) and a lump (IN93.77)
Two antler coronets and a piece of beam
A burnt flint, two **unretouched** and four **retouched** flints
A tuyere block fragment

d. Debris under path to **Building 17b**

An iron knife blade tip (IN66.82)
A piece of rolled lead waste (LD11.51)
An antler tine section and seven parings
An **unretouched** and two **retouched** flints

e. Silt over paved path leading to **Building 17b**

Table 6.22 : Finds from paths leading to **Buildings 17a** and **17b** (439, 441)

The finds from **Building 18** are listed in Table 6.23. The wall slots and post-holes (**a**) produced a varied group of artefacts and comb-making debris, and displaced finds indicated that it was use for comb repairs (p 494, Figure 10.136e). The clench plates were of equal interest, and more examples were recovered from disturbed contexts in this area (Table 6.41). The smaller group of finds from the earth floor included a faceted and pierced tine implement, possibly part of a loom (pp 487-90, Figures 6.29 and 10.133), and scraps of primary waste from the late stages of comb production.

A Class G comb side plate (AR68.3)
A broken green glass bead (GS03.47)
A faceted antler tine tip (AR77.6)
A broken spindle whorl (SE26.13)
A shale bangle fragment (SH01.4)
A nail, a nail head and a small squared staple (IN17.26)
A clench plate and a broken clench plate (IN20.10 and 11)
A possible clench-plate strip with two perforations (IN20.9)
Three lumps of iron and mineralised wood (IN93.74–6)
A curved copper-alloy rod (BZ36.16)
A small group of antler-working debris comprising:
    A tine
    Two tine offcuts
    Two comb plate rough-outs
One **unretouched** and five **retouched** flints

a. Finds from wall trenches and internal post socket of **Building 18**

A faceted and pierced tine tip (AR79.4)
An antler offcut
A comb-plate trimming and a paring
Eight **unretouched** flints

b. Finds from silt floor of **Building 18**

Table 6.23: Finds from **Building 18** (440)

The debris overlying the earlier path to **Building 19** (Table 6.24) included a third group of comb-making debris, comprising primary waste from the mid and late stages of production. The building itself produced no finds, but the overlying displaced material included concentrations of needles (Figure 6.26), 'awls' (Figure 6.27), and weaving implements (Figures 6.29 and 10.33), which might have originated in it.

Two nails
A **retouched** flint and two **unretouched** flints
A small group of antler-working debris comprising:
    An intact tine and a tine fragment
    Two tine tips
    Two segments
    Six offcuts
    Two comb-plate trimmings

Table 6.24: Finds from debris between paving in path to **Building 19** (446)

Stage 3 (Figure 6.15) was marked by an accumulation of ash deposits overlying the earth floor of **Building 18** and interleaved with paving (442). These features possibly comprised the fragmentary remains of a structure (**20**), but no evidence of walls survived the increasingly pervasive damage by graves. The stratified finds (Table 6.25) included thick deposits of hammerscale platelets from the ash, pointing to a smithying hearth and anvil in the immediate vicinity, which may account for the tuyere block and nozzle fragments from adjacent *Stage 4* deposits (Table 6.26**d** and **e**). The displaced material from the immediate area produced other finds appropriate to a smithy, including a hammer head (IN65.19) and two other unidentified tools, scattered farrier's debris (Figure 6.33) and scrap iron (Figure 6.32). It is tempting to infer a link with the clench-plates recorded from the

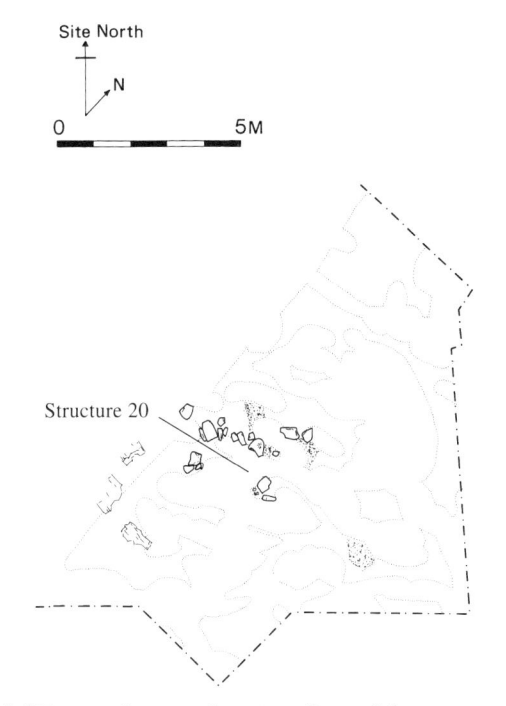

6.15 SE part of **central sector**: *Stage 3* features.

6.16 SE part of **central sector**: *Stage 4* structures.

underlying building, and more examples, including a strip of three plates, were recovered from the displaced debris from this part of the site (Table 6.42).

A broken Class F1 comb (AR71.7)
A broken spindle whorl (SE24.22)
A lump of iron (IN93.78)
A flint pebble, a **retouched** and three **unretouched** flints
An antler tine base and tip and a beam section
Two antler parings
c. 645 gm of hammerscale
c. 50 gm of glassy cinder and two 'hearth' fragments

Table 6.25: Finds from ash deposits in possible **'Structure' 20** (442)

Stage 4 (Figure 6.16) was represented by further, fragmentary structural remains (445, 448) associated with rich groups of finds. An island of undamaged material in the west part of the area included a well-built rectangular stone hearth (445) which probably lay at the centre of a building (**21**) oriented south-west/north-east, while paving to the north-east perhaps led to the doorway. The hearth was rebuilt on at least two occasions, indicating that the building had a relatively long lifespan.

The finds (Table 6.26) derived from five distinct groups of contexts (**a–e**), and included more comb making debris and a small group of smithy waste. An early silt floor deposit (**a**) and spread of ash (**b**) produced artefacts, but little waste. These were was overlain by a spread of rubbish (**c**) full of comb-making debris, which was, in turn, covered by a second layer of rubbish (**d**), including smithy waste related to the finds from an isolated pit to the east (**e**). The close proximity, though not technically the association, of a faceted and pierced tine tip and a weaving tensioner is noteworthy, and was matched in the adjacent structure (**22**, 448, Table 6.27), commending the identification of the worked tines as

components of looms (pp 487-90). These stratified finds indicated that *Stage 4* perhaps marked a phase of weaving in this area, offering a possible context for the larger group of displaced material (Figures 6.29 and 10.133). Metalworking debris included fragments of a tuyere block (SG28.3), and other pieces of it were recovered from the overlying graves and the *Stage 7–9* rubbish deposits (415.01) in the **southern sector** (Table 6.18). Smithying and comb-making may have alternated in this part of the site, but probably coexisted with other artisanal activities (Section 5).

A plated iron barrel padlock key (IN34.6)
A pronged and socketed weaving tensioner (IN63.2)
A possible knife blade fragment (IN80.69)
An antler comb tooth-plate

a. Silt floor:

Fragments of an iron pin (IN41.26) and plate (IN82.33)
A bone needle fractured at the eye (BA10.2)
Two antler tines

b. Ash deposits:

Two nails and an iron pin (IN 40.21)
A fragment of a granite rotary quern (SE43.8)
An antler tine and three tine tips
A faceted antler tine tip (AR77.7) and a faceted and pierced tine tip (AR79.5)
Four comb-plate trimmings and twenty parings
Two **unretouched** flints and three **retouched** flints

c. Rubbish spread overlying **a**) and **b**)

Two nails
A sandstone discoid (SE20.4)
A spindle whorl (SE24.14)
An antler burr and four beam offcuts
Two antler parings
A flint pebble, four **unretouched** flints, a core and two **retouched** flakes.

A small group of metalworking debris comprising:
   A tuyere block fragment (SG28.3)
   Three tuyere nozzle fragments
   Glassy and crystalline cinder

d. Rubbish deposit over c)

A sherd of white gritty ware (MP.06)
Another piece of tuyere block 3 (SG28.3)
Hearth bottom fragments

e. A pit to the east

Table 6.26.Finds from **'Building' 21** (445)

The second island of stratified deposits (448) to the east comprised a depressed cobbled area (**a**) with a spread of charcoal (**b**) to one side, overlain by paving and a possible earth floor (**c**). Generous minds will accept an identification as a fragmentary building (**22**). Most of the finds (Table 6.27) came from the putative earth floor, and complemented those from other structures in this area, indicating weaving and the later stage of comb production.

Three antler tines and a tine tip

a. and **b**. The cobbling and charcoal

A blue glass bead (GS03.31)
A nail
A sharp iron pin (IN40.22)
A two-pronged socketed weaving tensioner (IN63.3)
A faceted and pierced antler tine (AR79.6)
An antler comb tooth plate roughout
Two comb-plate trimmings
One **retouched** and two **unretouched** flints

c. The earth floor

Table 6.27: Finds from **Building 22** (448)

Stages 5–7. The uppermost deposits were highly fragmentary, but demonstrated continuing structural activity, and probably represented a new group of buildings, replaced at least once, and refurbished several times (Figure 6.17). The abundant industrial debris from this area (Section 5) indicates that these were primarily workshops, and the artisans may have lived elsewhere. Three stages have been identified to illustrate the potential longevity of settlement in this area, but the 'buildings' (**23–6**) are all conjectural. Hearths in the north part of the area (455) and on its west margin (449), had both been rebuilt at least once, and probably lay within buildings (**23** and **24**). The south-west hearth was overlain by rough cobbling sealed by a layer of silty loam (450 **a**) which also covered the north hearth, and perhaps comprised the floor of a third building (**25**). Two shallow hollows were then dug through this layer, and a second deposit of silt (450 **b**) accumulated or was laid down, which could have been the floor of a fourth building (**26**).

The finds from these deposits (Table 6.28) recorded the continuing evolution of activities in this area, and were of particular interest, as comb-making debris was absent from the latest deposits which may thus have been broadly contemporary with the latest finds groups in the **southern sector** (*Stages 8* and *9*). The antler from the earlier layers was derived from the middle stages of comb production. The group also included a rare well-stratified quadrilateral burnisher (pp 456-8) and a crucible with traces of brass, leaded brass and silver. Both were matched in the displaced material from this area (Table 6.42) and helped to identify a late phase of fine metalworking in the vicinity (pp 239-40, Figures 6.24, 10.88), with which the two copper-alloy strips may also have been associated (p 244). The iron needle is one of a group of coarse examples from this area (Figure 6.26b), and would have been suitable for darning or netting.

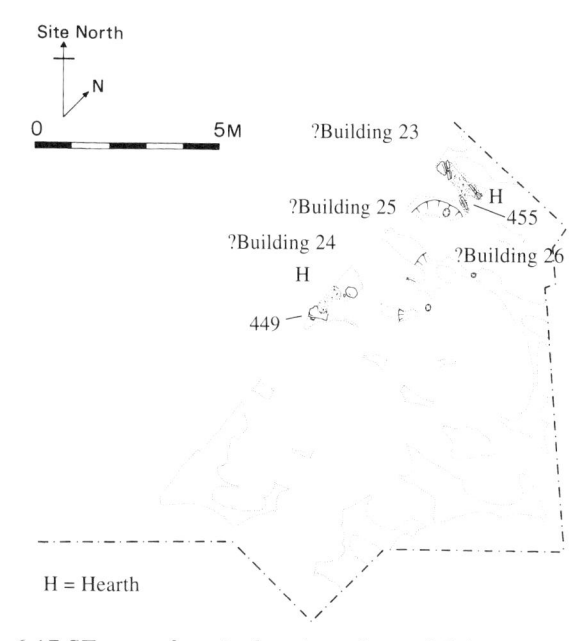

6.17 SE part of **central sector** : *Stage 5-7* features.

Four antler tines and four junctions of beam and tine
Seven antler shavings and parings
An iron pin (IN40.24) and a long coarse needle (IN39.58)

a. Cobbles under the N hearth (455)

A burnt flint
A tanged iron Class D knife (IN66.47)
A folded bronze strip (BZ38.36)

b. Ash associated with the SW hearth (449.02)

A small squared iron staple (IN17.27)
A small orange, glass bead (GS03.48)
A burnt flint and a **retouched** flint

c. Cobbles over SW hearth

An antler beam, tine-tip and tine off-cut
A faceted and pierced tine tip (AR79.13)
Four nail shanks
An iron pin fragment (IN40.23)
A tapering tanged iron bar, probably a tool (IN65.15)
A quartz plough pebble (SE51)

d. Soil over both hearths

A nail shank
A burnt flint, one **unretouched** and two **retouched** flints

e. The overlying cobbles

A quadrilateral quartzite burnisher (SE 40.6)
A large greywacke discoid (SE21.3)
Two burnt flints, a scraper and a **retouched** flint
A crucible fragment with traces of brass, leaded brass and silver (SG15.32)
Scraps of slag

f. The hollow cutting the cobbles

A fragment of a copper-alloy pin with a rounded expanded head (BZ41.28)

A curved, copper-alloy strip (BZ38.37).

g. The soil over the hollows

Table 6.28: Finds from possible **Buildings 23, 24** and **25** (449, 455 and 450)

6.4 THE *INNER PRECINCT*

Introduction. The rich **Period IV** deposits in the *inner precinct* had been devastated by the **Period V** graveyard and other intrusions (Figures 6.20 and 21), and only limited stratified evidence survived. The area seems to have been unoccupied by buildings for most of the period, and the most significant feature was a swathe of debris concentrated in a band some 10 m or so wide on the inner margin of the **Period III/3** boundary. Fragmentary stratified deposits on the western fringe of the **central sector**, and in isolated patches to the east, indicated the potential development of the area, while a narrow strip of undisturbed ground in the **northern sector** revealed a small group of relatively late structures overlying a graveyard, which seems to have been associated with chordal divisions in the *inner precinct*. Fragmentary surfaces interleaved with the buildings produced relatively little debris, suggesting that the central part of the *inner precinct* was kept relatively clean. This area produced a concentration of thirteenth century coins (Figures 6.38, 10.45a and 10.45b), and may have been a market flanked by workshops and dwellings. The fragmented stratified deposits revealed six *stages* of activity, while the finds (Section 5) suggested a rather more complex evolution.

Stage 1 (Figure 6.18a) was represented by a cobbled surface (432) overlying the **Period III** buildings (**III/27, III/39, III/34** and perhaps **III/28**) in the north-west part of the **central sector**, and lapping against the foot of the rubble bank (400, Figure 5.7). The cobbles were covered with a layer of worm-sorted soil which produced a small group of finds (Table 6.29) that was probably uncontaminated by extraneous material. It comprised small objects which could have been lost on open ground, and contrasted with the sparse assemblages from the buildings in the *outer zone*, the large group of antler-working waste to the east (Table 6.30 and 31), and the rich finds from the overlying *Stage 3* deposits (Tables 6.34 and 36). The comb side-plate is a relatively late type, while the lead weight is one of a group concentrated in the *inner precinct*, and pointing to commercial transactions before the widespread use of coinage was restored (Figure 6.38). Needles and punches were also concentrated in the *inner precinct* (Figures 6.26 and 27, pp 241-3), and these early stratified finds foreshadowed the much larger groups from the displaced material (Section 5).

A decorated Type F3 antler comb side-plate (AR70.7)
A copper-alloy strip (BZ38.33)
Four nails and two shanks

An iron punch (IN50.40)
A short standard iron needle with a punched eye (IN39.17)
Two pieces of iron sheet, probably from a vessel (IN36.2)
Two square-sectioned iron bars (IN83.16 and 17)
A conical lead weight (LD05.6)
An elongated piece of lead waste (LD11.44)
An **unretouched** flint flake.

Table 6.29: Finds from *Stage 3* cobbled surface (432)

The **Period III** buildings to the north-east were overlain by a spread of antler-working debris, animal bones and other rubbish (425.01, Figure 6.2), which may have been broadly contemporary with the cobbles, although the two deposits were not linked stratigraphically. This debris lay directly over the remains of **Buildings III/43** and **44**, and had been so severely disturbed by later graves that only fragments survived *in situ*. Distribution plots indicated that most of the antler-working debris from the later graves and overlying deposits originated in this rubbish spread (Figure 6.2, Tables 6.30 and 31). The limited range of finds in the undisturbed material (Tables 6.30) contrasted with the wide range from the graves (Table 6.42), demonstrating that the rubbish deposit was merely the first in a series in this area, which included concentrations of needles, awls, copper alloy and iron scrap (Figures 6.26, 24, 28 and 29). The antler is a primary deposit, containing a wide range of waste and recording all stages of comb production (pp 475-80). The rubbish overlying **Building III/43** included a concentration of faceted and pierced tines (AR79), and weaving tensioners (IN63, pp 242-3, 488, Figures 6.29 and 10.133), while comb-making debris predominated in the larger group overlying **Buildings III/31** and **44**. The assemblage of antler listed in Tables 6.30 and 31 seems large, but there were only forty discarded burrs, and no more than forty or fifty antlers may have been processed. The second largest group of antler-working debris (309.02; Table 5.32) was slightly earlier and, while comb-making and antler working continued until the final stages of **Period IV**, there was no subsequent evidence for the profligate disposal of potentially-usable antler. It may thus originally have been an undervalued commodity which was, perhaps, used with increasing economy as demand increased and supply diminished.

The small number and narrow range of the associated finds supported the inference that this was specialised rubbish which accumulated rapidly. The flints were of particular significance, since assemblages from the buildings to the south (Tables 6.22–28) indicated a consistent link between **retouched** flints and comb-making debris, which was, seemingly, belied by this particularly large group. The two lead rivets may have been intended for the manufacture or repair of sheet lead vessels (p 393), and the displaced material showed this was a continuing activity in the *inner precinct* (Figure 6.32). The hone blanks were the only tools, but the overlying graves produced a cluster of drawknives (Figures 6.28 and 10.136), which may have been used in the manufacture of combs (p 429). Comb making has been viewed as a seasonal activity confined to major markets, and practised by itinerant craftsmen.

Whithorn does not seem to have conformed to this model, and this spread of debris can be linked with some confidence to the *Stage 1* and *2* buildings (**17–19**) to the south (Tables 6.22–4), where comb-making seems to have been a domestic activity (pp 493-5).

A barrel padlock key (IN34.5)
A loop-headed pin for a brooch or buckle (IN41.15)
Two nails
A corroded iron lump (IN93.68)
Two lead rivets (LD06.5 and 30)
Two hone blanks (SE71.24 and 56)
Five burrs (four AR8, one AR10)
Three pieces of beam (two AR13 and one AR14)
Three beam fragments (AR15)
Five beam sections (one AR16 and four AR19)
Four intact tines (two AR20 and two AR22)
Eleven worked or broken tines (AR24–39)
Two tine sections (AR40), four tine tips (AR47, 49) and three tine bases (AR52, 53)
Six segments removed from antler beams (AR55/56)
Thirty comb-plates in varying stages of completeness
Seven comb-plate trimmings (AR84)
Thirty offcuts (AR82/83)
Seven tine offcuts of trimmings (AR85)
Sixty shavings or parings (AR86)
Two roe deer antlers (AR87)
A faceted tine tip (AR77.3)
A faceted and pierced tine tip (AR79.3)
A worked tine (AR81.13)
Four **unretouched** flints and a core

Table 6.30 : Finds from antler-working debris spread (425.01)

Thirty-five burrs (three AR4, four AR5, four AR6, seventeen AR8, two AR9, five AR10)
Three pieces of beam (two AR13 and one AR14)
Three beam fragments (AR15)
Six beam sections (four AR16 and two AR19)
Thirty-one intact tines (eleven AR20, two AR21, two AR22 and sixteen AR23)
Forty worked and broken tines (three AR24, fifteen AR26, four AR27, one AR31, two AR32, one AR33, seven AR34, one AR36 and six AR39)
Fourteen tine sections (thirteen AR40 and one AR43)
Thirteen tine fragments (twelve AR45 and one AR46)
Seventy-two tine tips (forty-five AR47, five AR48 and twenty-two AR49)
Ten tine bases (four AR51, three AR52 and three AR53)
Forty-one segments removed from antler beams (eighteen AR55, thirteen AR56 and ten AR57)
Ninety-one comb-plates in varying stages of completeness (AR58–66)
Six comb-plate trimmings (AR84)
Sixty offcuts (forty AR82 and twenty AR83)
Seven tine offcuts or trimmings (AR85)
Eleven shavings or parings (AR86)
Seven faceted tine tip (AR77.9–15) and two pierced tine tips (AR78.2 and 3)
Six faceted and pierced tine tips (AR79.8–13)

Table 6.31: Displaced antler from graveyard and other later contexts (N.B. combs and other objects are listed in Tables 6.41 and 42)

A patchy layer of soil overlying the **Period III** buildings in the middle of the **central sector** (457), produced an interesting group of finds (Table 6.32) which were probably the vestiges of the rubbish accumulation displaced into the later graves. This included the western fringe of the *Stage 1* antler spread, while the needle and lead weights were matched in the finds from the cobbles to the west (Table 6.29), and in the overlying displaced material (Figures 6.26 and 38). Although these finds could have been deposited in *Stage 1*, the deposit also produced pottery appropriate to the later stages of **Period IV** (Figure 6.39), while the bangle fragment may have been linked to jewellery manufacture in the later part of the period (p 240, Figure 6.24).

A worn opaque white 1st/2nd C bangle fragment (GS04.3)
Two sherds of pottery (MP01 and 2/11)
A short fine iron needle with a punched eye (IN39.16)
Two lead weights (LD05.4 and 5), one (4) with an incised cross on one face
An iron nail and a tack
A folded iron strip (IN80.63) and a corroded object (IN78.25)
A small group of antler comprising:
    Two burrs (AR8)
    Two segments removed from tines or beams (AR57)
    Two tooth-plates (AR65)
    A comb-plate trimming (AR84)
    Two parings (AR86)
    Two offcuts (AR82)
A flint core
A plough pebble (SE51)
A small group of pebbles and scraps of metalworking debris

Table 6.32: Finds from soil overlying **Period III/3** buildings in middle of **central sector** (457)

Two hollows (424) cutting the **Period III/1** buildings at the east end of the **central sector** possibly pertained to the early part of **Period IV**. The finds from the hollows and the surrounding surface (Table 6.33) included a few intrusive objects (parenthesised), but should otherwise have pertained to **Period III**, or an early stage of **Period IV**. The styca came from one of the hollows, and was probably displaced from a **Period III/1** context, while the antler comprised a primary deposit of mid and late stage comb-making debris which complemented other groups from the area, and could have originated in **Period III/1** (Tables 5.10 and 11) or **Period IV** (Table 6.30). The most singular find was the silver-plated copper-alloy bracelet, possibly relating to the fine-metalworking practised in this area at a somewhat later date.

[A sherd of green-glazed pottery (MP08)
A globule headed copper-alloy pin (BZ01.1) and a child's thimble (BZ11.3)]
A styca of Aethelred II's second reign (*c*. 843–9, Pirie IICi, CN02.51)
A silver-plated copper-alloy bangle (BZ30.7)
A corroded needle fragment (IN93.67)
Four nails shanks
A plano-convex lead discoid (LD10.6) and a molten droplet (LD13.5)
A fine-grained sandstone spindle whorl (SE26.2)
A small, naturally rounded hone (SE38.25) and a hone blank (SE71.2)
A **retouched** and an **unretouched** flint
A group of antler-working debris comprising:
    Two beam sections with segments removed
    Four sawn tines, a tine fragment and a tine tip
    A segment removed from a tine or beam
    Four tooth-plate rough-outs
    Six offcuts and two trimmings
    Three parings
Scraps of metalworking debris

Table 6.33 Finds from surface and fragmentary hollows (424) at the east end of the **central sector**

Stage 2 saw the construction of a building (**27**, 401) in the south-west corner of the **central sector**. The building was represented by a hearth flanked by a strip of paving which occupied a sunken stance cutting the *Stage 1* cobbles and extending beyond the excavated area (Figure 6.18b). A gap in the paving indicated the position of the south-east wall, and the doorway, of which no evidence survived, was probably located opposite to the hearth. No finds were associated with the building.

Stage 3 was represented by a spread of fire-reddened stones overlying the *Stage 1* surface (432), and oversailing the **Period III** rubble bank (400) and the northern part of **Building 27** (Figure 6.18c). A thick band of this rubble survived on the western side of the **central sector** and small islands further to the east showed that it was originally more extensive. The rubble covered the uneven ground beyond the Northumbrian terrace, and may have been spread to level this part of the *inner precinct*. Dark soil overlying and interlaminated with the stones produced a rich and distinctive group of finds (Table 6.34) which is of particular value in establishing a possible context for the displaced finds from the graveyard (Tables 6.41 and 42), and these finds are included in the distribution plots in Section 5. The rubble layer was relatively uncontaminated by later material, but the overlying soil, while generally predating the fourteenth–fifteenth graves, produced several anachronous finds (parenthesised), and probably contained other less diagnostic intrusions. The two groups (Table 6.34**a** and **b**) shared many features, but displayed differences which may reflect the evolving pattern of craft activities in the *inner precinct*. The potentially uncontaminated group (**a**) was dominated by nails and other iron objects which were mostly matched in the far larger group of displaced material. The two needle blanks are noteworthy, but other finds were sparse, and the low incidence of antler was remarkable in light of its abundance further to the east. The slightly larger group of potentially contaminated material (**b**) revealed a similar dominance of iron, but with a wider range of types, and small groups of lead and smelting debris, which were absent from the underlying material.

Fragmentary deposits to the south and east (451 and 495) produced further debris which had probably begun to accumulate at the same time, but similarly included anachronous finds from **Period V**. A stony band interleaved with dark soil (495) on the south side of the **central sector** was probably part of the same deposit as the rubble bank to the north-west (430), and may originally have spread over the rubbish in 457 (Table 6.32). The finds from this deposit (Table 6.35) included characteristic **Period IV** objects and pottery. A layer of dark soil (451) to the south of the rubble bank produced a small group of objects possibly pertaining to **Period IV**, though contaminated with sherds of later pottery (Table 6.36). The finds from both deposits are included in the distribution plots discussed in Section 5.

Stage 4 was represented by a two graves (428.01) oriented west/east (true orientation) associated with fragmentary stone walls and ditches (486) marking possible chordal division within the *inner precinct* (Figure 6.3). The head of one grave was marked by large squared post set in a deep post-hole, and the skeleton in it produced a radiocarbon date of 755+/-

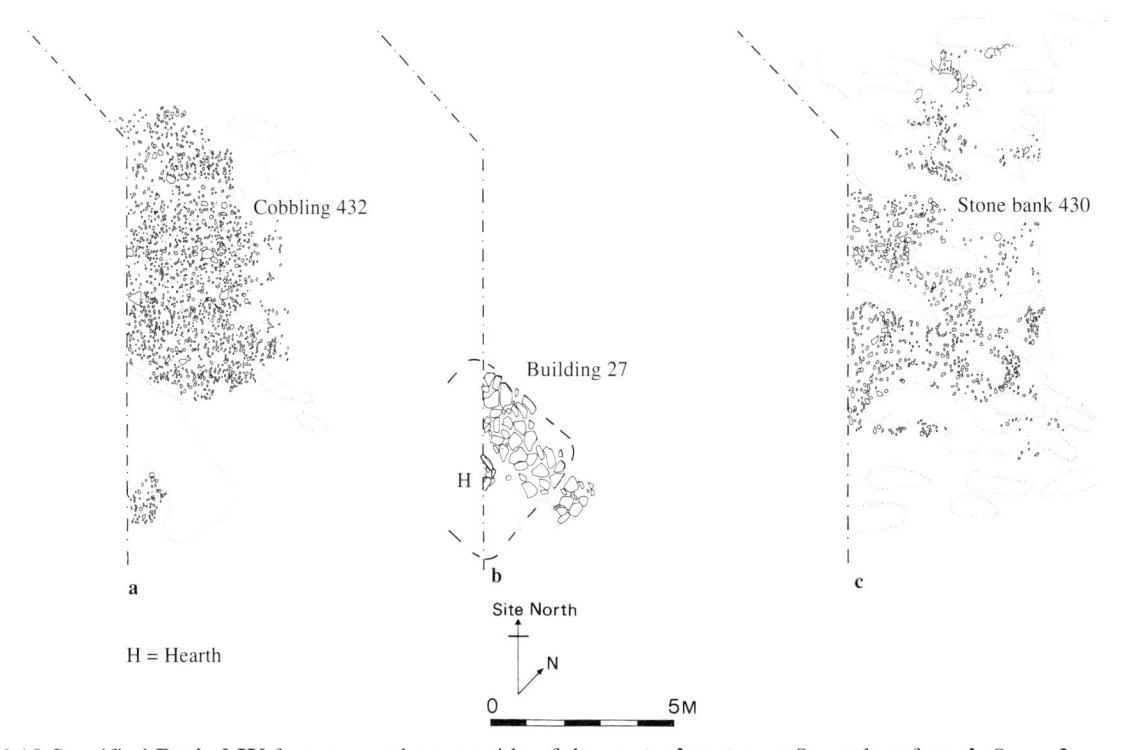

6.18 Stratified **Period IV** features on the west side of the **central sector**. **a** *Stage 1* surface. **b** *Stage 2* building. **c** *Stage 3* stone bank.

CHAPTER 6

a) Uncontaminated rubble and soil

[A greywacke roof tile (SE07.58)]

One sherd of red gritty ware (MP01
Two sherds of MP2/11 and one of MP2/55
One sherds of MP31 (unidentified French)

Two antler tines
An antler coronet with skull fragments (AR05)
A decorated F3 comb side-plate (AR69.03)
An undifferentiated copper-alloy stick pin
 with a Type 3 head (BZ14.25)
A piece of round copper-alloy wire (BZ32.4)
A triangular copper-alloy off-cut (BZ38.34)

Forty-one nails and fragments

Two spatulate iron needle blanks (IN 39.41, 42)
Three iron pins (IN40.16, 18 and 20)
A sub-ovoid iron buckle and tongue (IN44.6)
An iron punch or chisel (IN50.60)
An iron chisel (IN52.7)
A tapering iron rod, perhaps a tool (IN64.11)
A waisted bar with opposed hooked ends (IN65.11)
A square sectioned bar, perhaps a tool (IN65.12)
A broken Class D knife (IN66.42)
A curved, tanged iron blade (IN67.1)
An iron hook (IN31.16)
Two iron strips (IN80.64 and 65)

A quartzite polishing stone (SE 41.3)
A greywacke slab with three ingot moulds (SE 45.4)
A quartz plough pebble (SE 51)
A botryoidal Haematite polisher (SE 62.21)
A hone blank (SE 71.35)
Three **unretouched**, five **retouched** and one
 burnt flint
Scraps of iron working debris attached to dense slag

b) Potentially contaminated soil
[Two post-medieval pottery sherds]
[Three scraps of modern glass]
[A copper farthing of James III, 1465–6, CN03.22)]
[A worn penny of Edward I (1282–9 CN 03.74)]
[A plated 8-point iron rowel spur (IN46.1)]
[A greywacke roof tile (SE 07.52)]
[A phyllite roof tile (SE10.39)]
[One sherd of reduced ware (MP7/2)]
One sherd of white gritty ware (MP06)
Two sherds of MP2/11 and two of MP2/12
One sherd of MP17 (undated French)
One sherd of coarse pottery (MP05)

A stud-headed copper-alloy stick pin (BZ14.29)
A copper alloy pin shank (BZ09.4)
A grooved copper-alloy shank (BZ30.8)
A perforated copper alloy 'plug' with an octagonal boss (BZ30.72)
A black glass 'eye' bead (GS03.44)

Forty-nine nails and fragments
Two iron staples (IN18.10 and 11)
A hooked iron rod, possibly a door catch
 or snaffle bit fragment (IN 27.3)
A barrel padlock spring (IN33.6)
An iron pin (or piece of wire (IN40.17)
 and possible pin shank (IN40.19)
An iron buckle and tongue (IN44.27 and 40)
A tanged point, perhaps a punch (IN50.61)
An iron rod or tool (IN50.71)
A tapered iron strap end or tool (IN65.13)
An iron rod, possibly a catch (IN27.4)
A plated, socketed, arrowhead (IN75.3)
A broken iron Class A3 or D knife (IN66.4)
A possible iron bodkin (IN75.4)
An S-shaped iron hook (IN31.15)
Two iron bars (IN84.18 and 84.7)
An iron shank with a hammered, splayed, perforated end (IN78.26)
Two iron fragments (IN93.69 and 70)
A possible lead spindle whorl (LD03.3)
Two lead 'nails' (LD06.37 and 38)
A tapering lead tube (LD09.14)
An arciform cross fragment (SE14.15)
A siltstone discoid (SE20.2)

A hone blank (SE71.9)
Three **unretouched**, two **retouched** and one burnt flint
A piece of burnt limestone (SE60.17)
An interesting group of iron-working debris including rare furnace wall fragments

Table 6.34: Finds from *Stage 3* stone bank and associated soil (430). Anachronous finds are parenthesised.

80 bp (GU-2056), which is compatible with the associated chronological evidence (p 597). The finds from the graves (Table 6.37) were probably displaced from the underlying rubble (430, Table 6.34), while the small group associated with the chordal wall (Table 6.37) included a bronze strip with Ringerike style ornament, probably dating to the eleventh century.

Eight sherds of pottery (MP01 × 3, 02/1, 02/2, 02/11, 12/2 × 2)
A faceted and pierced antler tine (AR79.2)
Two Haematite polishers (SE62.11 and 12)
A lead rivet (LD06.4) and a piece of molten waste (LD12.39)
Eight nails and fragments
An antler burr
A relatively large group of pebbles (40)
Three burnt flints, seven **retouched** and five **unretouched** flints

Table 6.35: Finds from stony layers on south side of *inner precinct* (495)

A round-sectioned punch (IN50.59) and a tanged awl or fine
 punch (IN50.79)
A possible knife blade fragment (IN73.11)
Four nails and a U-shaped staple
A nodule of copper-alloy waste (BZ39.9)
An antler offcut
Scraps of metalworking debris
An **unretouched** flint
A large quartz crystal (SE58.20)

Table 6.36: Selected finds from soil to south of rubble bank (451)

A buckle pin (IN44.28)
Bent knife blade (IN66.68)
Two nails
A **retouched** flint.

Table 6.37: Finds from 428.01

A folded, riveted strip with eleventh century Ringerike-style
 interlace (BZ35.09)

A sherd of white gritty ware (MP06)
A **retouched** flint
Scraps of metalworking debris.

Table 6.38: Finds from walls in *inner precinct* (486)

Stage 5 (Figure 6.19, 4) was represented by structural remains in the **northern sector** comprising one certain building (**28**), a possible second (**29**), and a paved area which may have been the floor of a third (**30**). Further buildings in the vicinity – and elsewhere in the *inner precinct* – may have been destroyed by later disturbances. Scattered sherds of white gritty ware (MP06) indicated a broadly contemporary rubbish spread surrounding the buildings, oversailing the remains of the Northumbrian burial chapel, and concentrated over **Building III/16** to the north-west (Figure 6.39).

Building 28 (407.02) was defined by a sub-rectilinear spread of orange and black soil marking the scorched earth floor of a building oriented south-west/north-east, and some 4.5 m long and 3.5 m wide. Charred hazel roundwood from the west corner of the floor was probably the base of the wattle wall, sealed by the earth floor, and hence charred, rather than burnt, when the building was destroyed. A carbonised post to the south was probably burnt at the same time. Finds from the floor (Table 6.39) included a possible shears fragment matched in potentially contemporary buildings in the **southern sector** (**9** and **12**, Tables 6.14 and 15, Figure 6.36).

A possible line weight of rolled lead sheet (LD9.7)
A possible iron wedge (IN53.5)
A possible Class D knife or shears fragment (IN66.43)
Two nails
An unretouched flint
Scraps of metalworking debris

Table 6.39: Finds from floor of **Building 28** (407.02)

Structure 29 (434) was represented by a strip of paving flanked by gravel. A possible post-hole at one end hinted that this was a doorsill, possibly of a building lying to the north-east. The paving overlay a pit containing two human skulls of uncertain origin. There were no other finds.

Structure 30 (428.02) comprised a small area of paving covered with patches of ash and burnt soil, and oversailing the *Stage 4* graves. The paving included a broken low-relief cross (SE14.6) splashed with a drop of molten copper alloy, and a pock-marked greywacke 'anvil' stone (SE56.1). The only find from the ash was a broken decorated spindle whorl (SE28.12), although the later finds from the underlying rubble bank (400, Table 5.18), may have been associated with this phase of activity.

Patches of orange ash indicated two potentially

6.19 Fragmentary **Period IV** remains in the western part of the **northern sector**.

contemporary deposits isolated from the stratified remains in this area. One patch of ash (407.05) overlying a pebbled surface, produced a piece of folded lead waste (LD11.47), a chunk of a massive 'hearth' (SG61), and a small hone (SE38.14), while a pit (407.07) slightly to the north of **Structure 30**, was filled with orange ash, and produced two nails and a short-cross penny of Cnut (1016–1035, CN02.64). The coin is significantly earlier than the inferred late-twelfth century date of **Phase 5** (p 217), and both deposits could have pertained to **Period III** (p 356, Figures 6.38 and 10.45a). The truncated base of a pit (434.02) to the east of **Structure 29** produced an antler offcut and a disc spatulate headed stick pin (BZ14.20), the latter appropriate to a late stage in **Period IV**.

Stage 6 followed the fire marking the end of *Stage 5*, and was marked by a narrow strip of worm-sorted soil (407.04) overlying the remains of **Building 28**. The finds from this small area (Table 6.40) showed that debris continued to accumulate in the *inner precinct*, and perhaps extended further inwards than before. The drawknife is one of a group from the *inner precinct* (Figure 6.28), and may have been used in the production of combs (p 429).

A sherd of white gritty ware (MP06)
A broken, blue glass bead (GS03.30)
Two nails, three shanks and three heads
An iron clench plate (IN20.7)
A complete Class C3 knife (IN66.25) and a possible blade fragment (IN73.12)
A broken drawknife with a looped terminal (IN69.3)
A spindle whorl (SE24.1) and an unfinished spindle whorl (SE 28.6)
A burnt flint and a **retouched** flint
Scraps of metalworking debris

Table 6.40 Finds from the *Stage 6* soil in the **northern sector** (407.04)

6.5 THE DISPLACED DEBRIS

The **Period V** graves produced a huge group of finds, most of which were probably displaced from **Period IV** deposits, but including a small, but potentially-significant, group of objects from **Period III**, and smaller groups from **Periods I** and **II**. This complicated picture was further confused by objects derived from fourteenth-fifteenth century surface scatters, and intrusive material of later centuries. Although concentrated in the *inner precinct* of the **Period IV** settlement, the graves had also disturbed the deposits in the south-eastern part of the *outer zone*. There were significant differences between the finds displaced in the two areas, which are listed separately in Tables 6.41 and 42. The tables include all the finds from the graves (530–540) and related contexts (541–3, p 255), and encompass material which is demonstrably inappropriate to **Period IV**. Most of the components pertaining to **Period IV** can be identified by comparison with the assemblages from stratified deposits. Diagnostic finds included combs, copper-alloy and iron stick and ring pins, and red and white gritty wares. Less-diagnostic material included antler tine implements; lead nails, rivets and spindle whorls; stone spindle whorls and playing pieces; lead, iron and copper alloy scrap; iron, copper-alloy and bone needles; crucibles; Haematite polishers; and bone pins and spindle whorls. Other groups virtually confined to displaced graveyard contexts included a concentration of glass *tesserae* overlying **Building III/36**, iron wool comb teeth, stone flakes with serrated edges and lead weights. Objects contemporary with the graves are discussed below (pp 253, 360); miscellaneous post-medieval and recent finds can be accounted for by roots, rodents and related minor disturbances.

Distribution plots of finds from a range of stratified and disturbed contexts (Figure 6.2, 5, 23–39) provide considerable clarity, though open to varying interpretations. The extent of the graveyard is illustrated in Figure 6.20, which also depicts cultivation furrows of the fourteenth and eighteenth centuries, into which other finds had been displaced. Coherent clusters of related objects from these contexts (e.g. Figures 6.24, 26 and 34) indicated that the integrity of spatial distributions had survived despite the obliteration of *in situ* deposits, and the plots thus provide a reliable indication of the organization of activities within the damaged area, though lacking a vital chronological dimension. This evidence was, however, compromised by a group of eighteenth and nineteenth century features which involved the excavation and removal of both stratified and disturbed deposits (Figure 6.21). The west wing of the manse and the associated drains (**a**) had caused the most severe damage, and had virtually obliterated the evidence from an important sector of the *outer zone*. The graves surviving beneath the floor of this building preserved metalworking debris, including the iron draw-plate (p 424, Figures 6.24, 10.102) which is one of the most striking finds from this accumulation. Other features causing more limited damage included a late fifteenth century

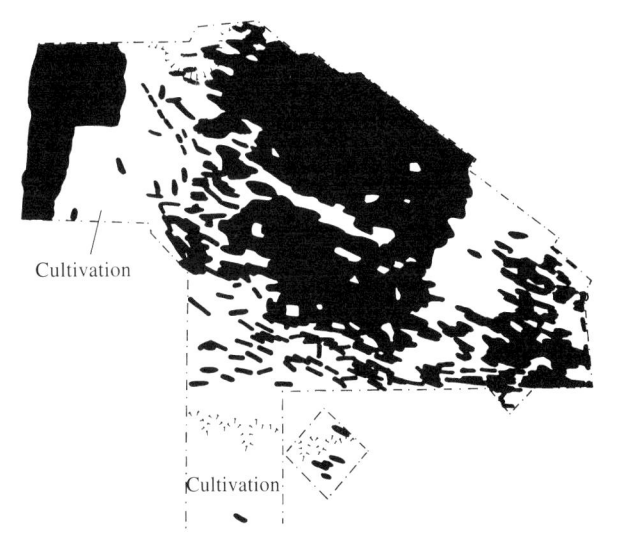

6.20: Graves and cultivation furrows of **Periods V** and **VI** disturbing **Period VI** deposits.

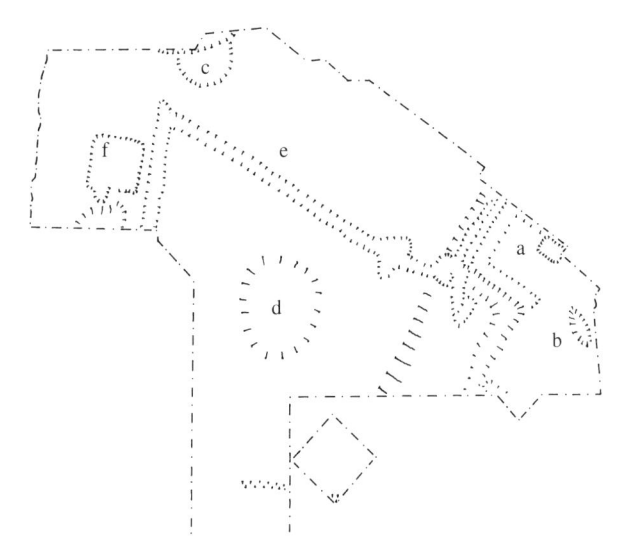

6.21: Later features cutting the graveyard and underlying deposits

sump (**b**), the sunken floor of **Building 5/1** (**c**, 507), a large hollow dug in the nineteenth century (**d**, 735), a deep land drain (**e**, 725), and a greenhouse (**f**, 747–754) on the east side of the **Market Garden**. All corresponded with gaps in the distributions of finds, but had probably not distorted the overall patterns.

Excavators are accustomed to the dislocation of their evidence, though perhaps not on this scale, but the processes are illustrated in Figure 6.22 to inform those less familiar with the problems of excavation and the peculiar contribution of earthworms (Darwin 1881). An originally-coherent sequence of deposits and finds (**a**) is disturbed by intersecting graves, redistributing the finds upwards and sideways (**b**). The worms, meanwhile, reorganise the material by ingesting fine silt and depositing it in worm casts on the surface, but leaving coarser materials behind. Eventually (**c**), and in this instance after the graveyard went out of use in the fifteenth century, the upper part of the deposit has been completely sorted by worm action, leaving a bed of indigestible grit, stones and artefacts below a thick, relatively sterile

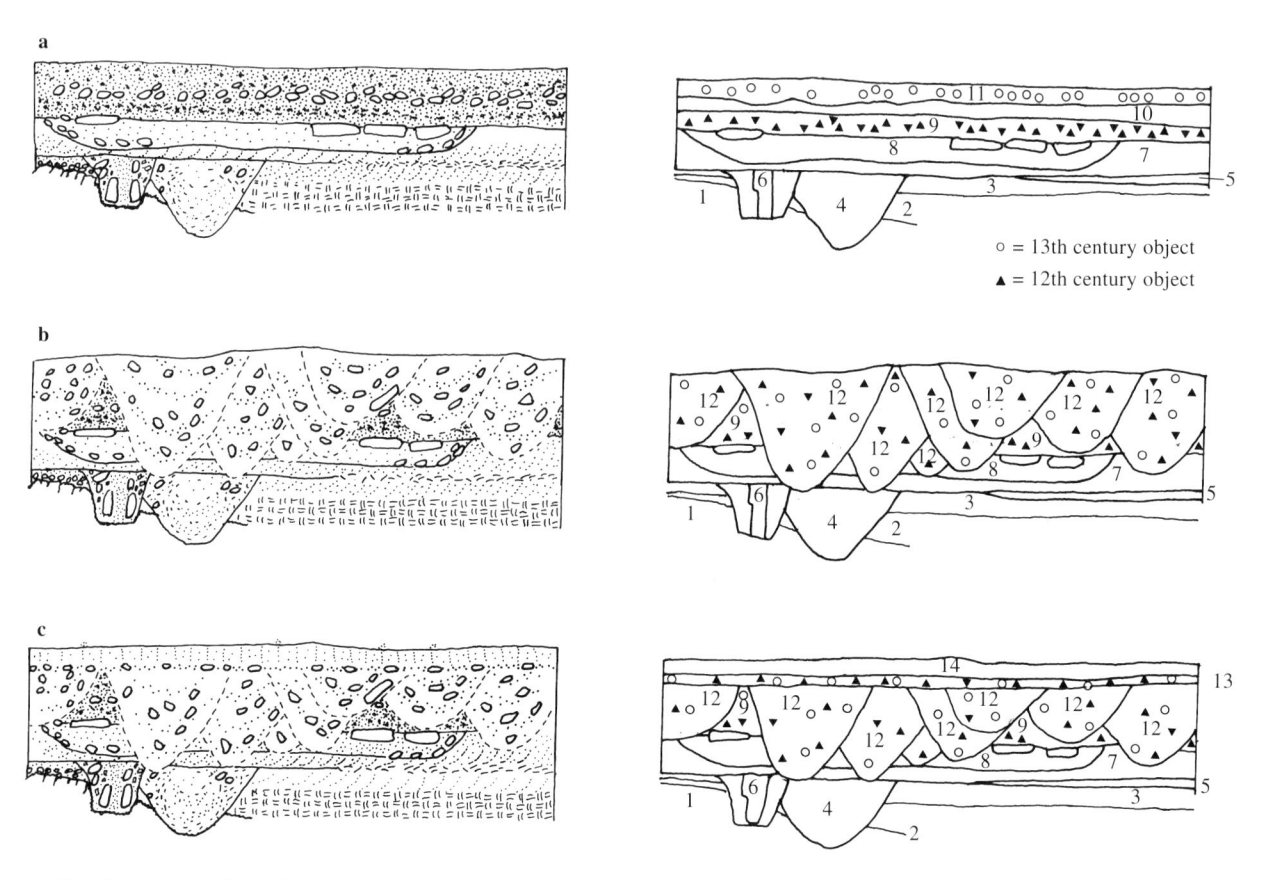

○ = 13th century object
▲ = 12th century object

6.22: Hypothetical section demonstrating the redistribution of **Period IV** debris.
a Stratified deposits in the *inner precinct* at the close of **Period IV**. **b** The same after extensive disturbance by **Period IV** graves. **c** The same after the upper material has been resorted by worms.

Key
1 Bedrock
2 Boulder clay
3 **Period I** cultivation
4 **Period I** grave
5 **Period II** surface
6 **Period II** construction slot
7 **Period III** cultivation
8 **Period III** building
9 **Period IV** early debris
10 **Period IV** stone spread
11 **Period V** late debris
12 **Period V** grave
13 **Period V** restratified 'surface'
14 Worm-sorted soil

layer of fine silt. The **Period IV** material had thus been redistributed into three stratigraphically-distinct horizons, excavated at different times and frequently in different years. One group, much fragmented, survived *in situ*; a second had been scattered into the graves; while a third had been converted by worm action into a stony layer which sealed the graveyard. The upward mobility of the **Period IV** debris only ended when a road was laid in the fifteenth century, though subsequent cultivation continued the processes of dispersal and restratification by worms.

The most numerous finds were nails, flints, pebbles and antler-working debris. The nails revealed a broad swathe of debris concentrated in the *inner precinct* (Figure 6.5), and linked with the surviving stratified material on the west side of the trench (430, Table 6.34). Many of these probably originated in rubbish brought in to level the uneven ground in the *inner precinct*, and some of the other finds may have been introduced at the same time. Antler displayed a totally different picture with a concentration of debris in the *inner precinct*, adjacent to the part of the *outer zone* where combs were manufactured. These finds indicated a workshop area spanning both zones (Figure 6.2), and similar patterns were displayed by potentially-later groups of copper-alloy scrap, *tesserae* and styluses (Figures 6.30 and 31). Flints were concentrated in the outer part of the *inner precinct* and south-eastern part of the *outer zone*, where numerous stratified finds account for the displaced material, although not explaining its use. Stratified deposits in the **southern sector** indicated that flint continued to be deposited until the closing stages of **Period IV**, but not subsequently, and these finds probably reflect activity in this phase. Pebbles were scattered densely over the central and eastern parts of the area, but were poorly represented in the stratified deposits. They may have been included in the **Period V** graves for ritual reasons (pp 472-3) and so are potentially irrelevant to the interpretation of the **Period IV** deposits.

Various groups of finds were concentrated in the *outer zone* and scarce or absent from the *inner precinct*, the clearest being hones, handles, and crucible fragments (Figures 6.23 and 24). Hones were concentrated in the *outer zone* and the only examples from the *inner precinct* were small. Some of the hones from the *outer zone* may have been displaced from the **Period III** debris surrounding the settlement (Table 5.36), but nevertheless indicate an enduring functional distinction with the heavier industries concentrated beyond the *inner precinct*. Handles of antler and bone revealed a similar pattern, although the meaning is less clear. A cluster in the south-east part of the *outer zone* included a finely carved tine with a broken tip (AR74.14) which might have been displaced from a **Period III** deposit, or could have been associated with combs repaired in **Building 18** (p 229). Crucible fragments (Figures 6.24, 10.88) were concentrated in the south-eastern part of the *outer zone*, and only three examples were recorded from the inner part of the *inner precinct*. EDXRF analysis revealed traces of silver, gold, and a

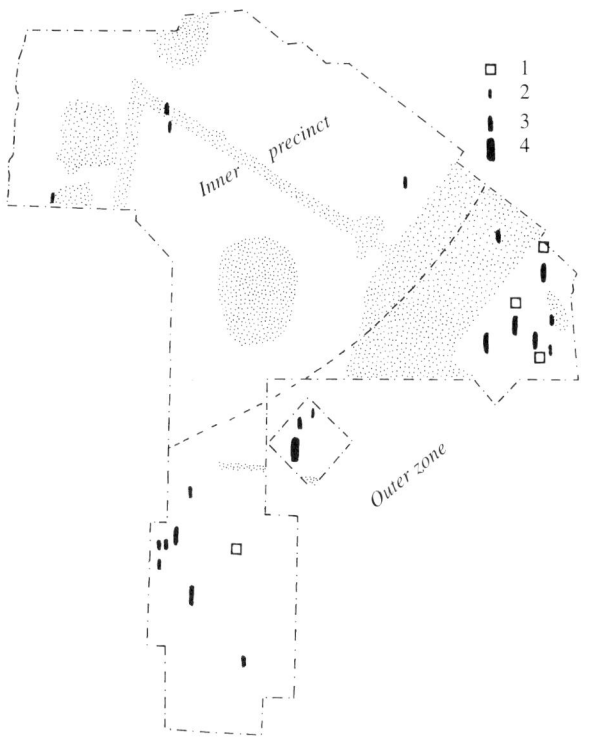

6.23 Hones and handles
1 = Antler and bone handles, 2 = Small hones, 3 = Large hones, 4 = Bar hone.

range of copper and lead alloys (p 404), establishing clear links between the stratified and displaced fragments, and indicating an area of fine metalworking in the *outer zone*, probably centred in the unexcavated ground to the south of the main trench. The distribution of crucible fragments overlapped with distinct scatters of lead and copper-alloy waste (Figures 6.31, 10.71), but coincided with scraps of nodular lead, one with a high-copper content, which were probably related production debris. Three other important finds – an iron draw-plate (**a**), strands of silver wire (**b**) and a piece of worked porphyry (**c**) – coincided with concentrations of crucible sherds, and may have been linked with the metalworking shops. The draw-plate (IN60.1) was used for making silver wire (p 424), and radiography revealed a cut halfpenny of Henry II or III (CN03.63) in the corrosion surrounding it. This indicated a date in the later-twelfth or mid-thirteenth centuries, and the coin could have been part of the craftsman's supply of bullion destined for reworking as wire. The silver wire came from a fragmentary stratified deposit close to the displaced draw-plate, and was probably destined for embroidery. It was narrower than the smallest hole in the drawplate, but might have been reduced in thickness by rolling between smoothed stones, after preliminary manufacture using a draw-plate. The piece of porphyry (**c**, SE58.26) which lay to the west of the draw-plate may have been a commodity used in the manufacture of jewellery, and both serpentine and marble are listed among the goldsmith's commodities described by Neckam in the late-twelfth century (pp

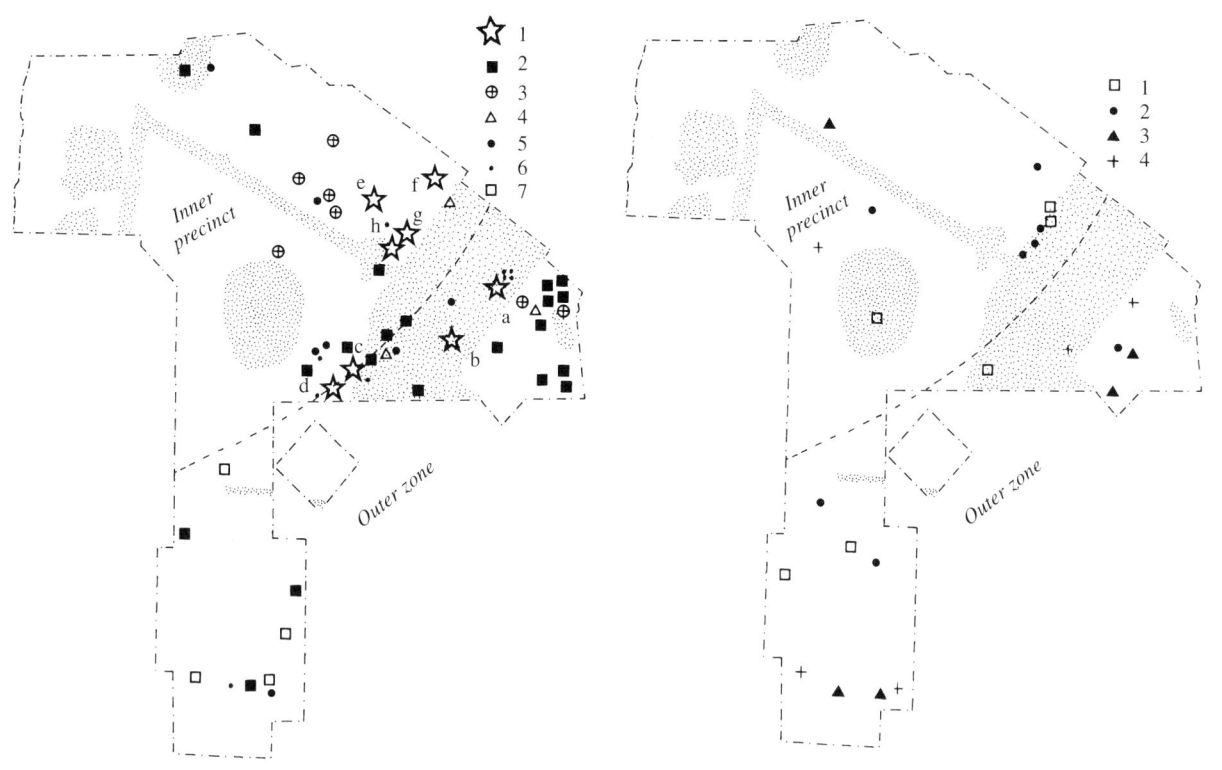

6.24 Crucible fragments and related finds
1= Special objects, 2 = Crucible fragments, 3 = *Tesserae*, 4 = Smoothed stone slabs, 5 = Haematite polishers, 6 = Nodular lead, 7 = Exotic qualrtz.

6.25 Bone artefacts
1 = Ornamental pin, 2 = Pin fragment, 3 = Headless pin, 4 = Needle or perforated pin.

469-70, Campbell 1991, 120–1). A silver ring (**d**, SR2) from the same area might have been part of a jeweller's stock, but lay on the skull of a **Period V** burial, and may have been a contemporary ear ring. A second cluster of objects from the *inner precinct* included a chopped fragment of a thirteenth century gold fillet (**e**, AU3), a piece of tenth/eleventh century ring money (**f**, SR13), a worn fragment of an opaque white glass bracelet of the first/second century (**g**, GS04.3), and a broken horse-bit decorated with gold leaf (**h**, IN49.4). The gold and silver may have been bullion destined for reworking, while the bracelet may have been an enameller's commodity linked to the *tesserae*. A second bangle fragment of an opaque red and yellow glass (GS04.01) from the same general area, is of similar date, and invites the same explanation. A group of exotic quartz crystals from the **southern sector** (SE58, pp 469-70) includes at least one (SE58.12) which seems to have been prepared as a gem, and all are likely to have been associated with this craft. Other finds potentially associated with these activities include burnishers (Figure 6.30), Haematite polishers (pp 471-2), burnt limestone (pp 470-1), and smoothed stone slabs (p 468). Stratified finds of crucibles, burnishers and Haematite polishers from the **southern sector** indicated that this phase of metalworking pertained to the later-twelfth century, supporting the earlier of the two possible dates for the draw-plate. The *tesserae* were predominantly of dark blue glass. The two examples from the *outer zone* coincided with crucible fragments with traces of silver and gold, and the entire group could be debris from a craft area spanning both zones. The *tesserae* were concentrated in the *inner precinct* some way from the crucible fragments, but are included in this plot as they were probably used in enamelling or the manufacture of jewellery. Some of the copper-alloy and lead waste may also have been scrap awaiting recycling (p 385, Figures 6.31, 10.71). The only mould fragment associable with the crucibles (SG17.9) came from an insecure context in the south-east part of the *outer zone*, and revealed traces of bronze or brass.

Bone artefacts displayed similar characteristics (Figure 6.25) with a marked concentration in the *outer zone,* which produced four out of five headless pins, four out of five 'needles', and half the ornamental pins and pin fragments. The distribution was potentially skewed by the differential preservation of bone, but examples were scarce in areas where human remains were well preserved. The distributions contrast with those of similar artefacts (stick pins and needles) made of other materials (Figures 6.35 and 24), and the headless pins and 'needles' were probably the tools of crafts restricted to the *outer zone*. The needles are larger than their metal equivalents, and would only have been suitable for working with coarse fabrics or, possibly, nets. Some of the headless pins had been worn to a high polish though long use, and these were probably weaving implements used to raise the warp and beat the weft down. A cluster of ornamental pins and pin

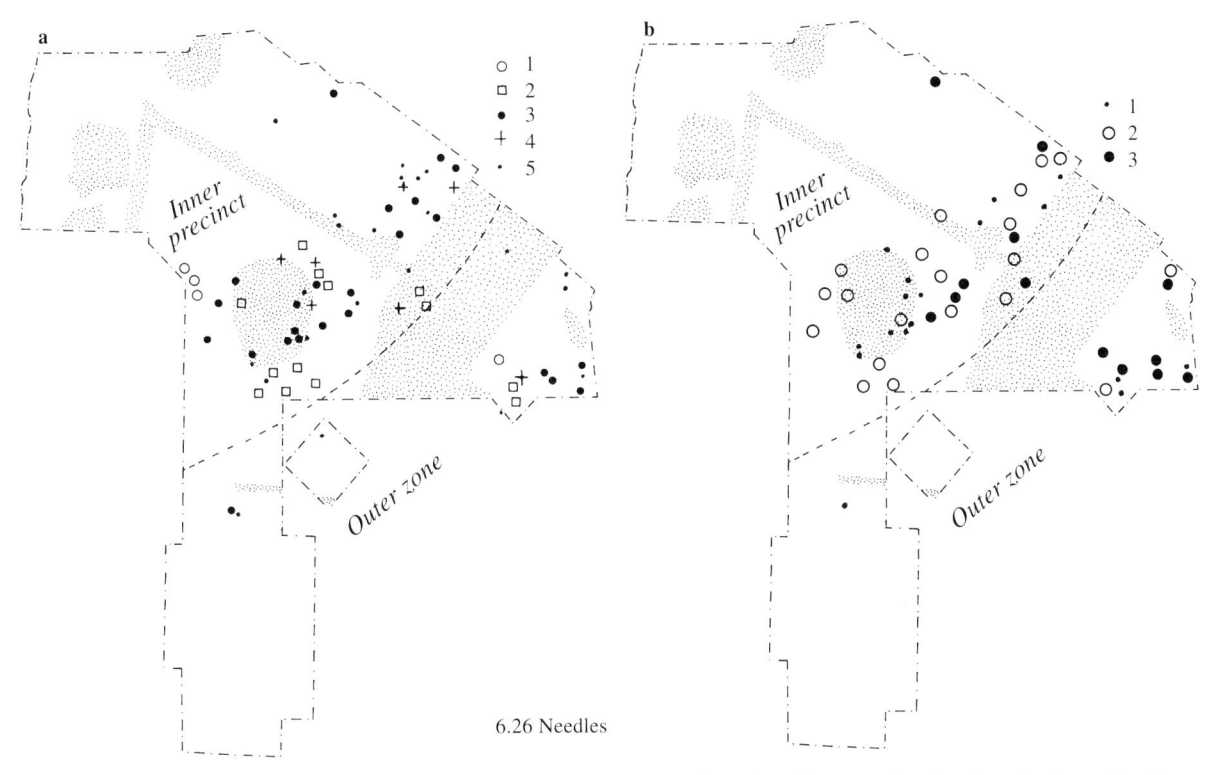

6.26 Needles
a Type. 1= Needle blanks, 2 = Copper-alloy needles, 3 = Iron needles with punched eyes, 4 = Iron needles with Y-eyes, 5 = Iron needle fragments.

b Function. 1 = Fine needle, 2 = Standard needle, 3 = Coarse needles.

fragments on the outer margin of the *inner precinct* lay in an area where manufacturing debris predominated, and possibly marked the site of a booth where pins were sold. The ornamental pins are paralleled in tenth-eleventh century deposits elsewhere (pp 496-7), and stratified examples from *Stage 5* and *7* contexts in the **southern sector** (Tables 6.7 and 15) probably pertained to the later part of this period, and seemed to have been contemporary with the series of stick pins.

Needles (Figures 6.26a and b) and 'awls' (Figure 6.27), displaying complementary distributions to those of hones, handles and crucible fragments, were concentrated within the outer margin of the *inner precinct*. This area produced the densest group of nails, and although the needles and 'awls' could have been included in the same random spread of rubbish, detailed examination revealed concentrations of specific types. The awls and punches included a cluster of tanged awls (Figure 6.28), isolated within a wider spread of tanged and untanged punches. Though similar in appearance to nails and only distinguished by radiography, the awls and punches have different functional implications, and the tanged awls might have been associated with the weaving implements concentrated in this area (Figures 6.29 and 10.133), although the functional implications are unclear. The punches hinted at similar functional differences, with a cluster of tanged punches to the west of the tanged awls, which could have been used for leather- or metalwork. Untanged punches in the *outer zone* coincided with the

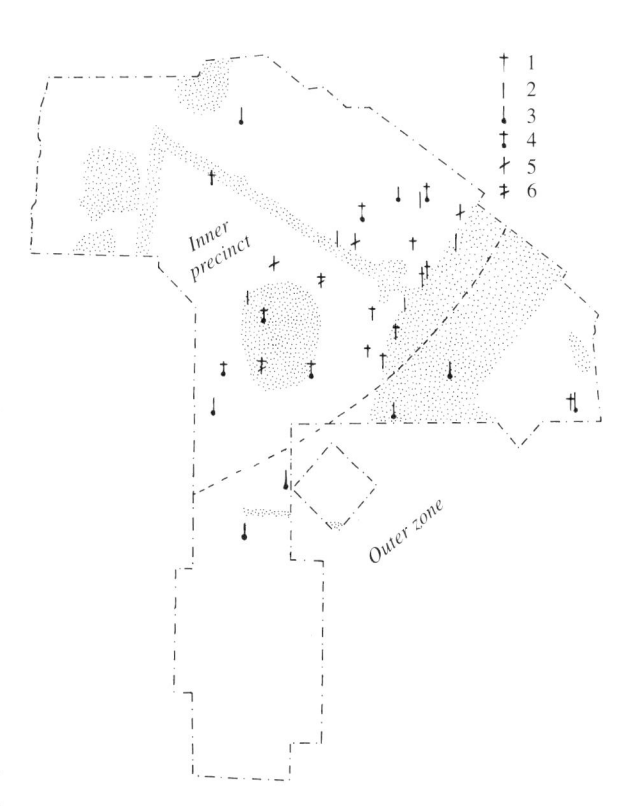

6.27: Awls and punches.
1= Tanged awl, 2 = Awl, 3 = Punch, 4 = Tanged punch, 5 = Awl or punch, 6 = Tanged awl or punch.

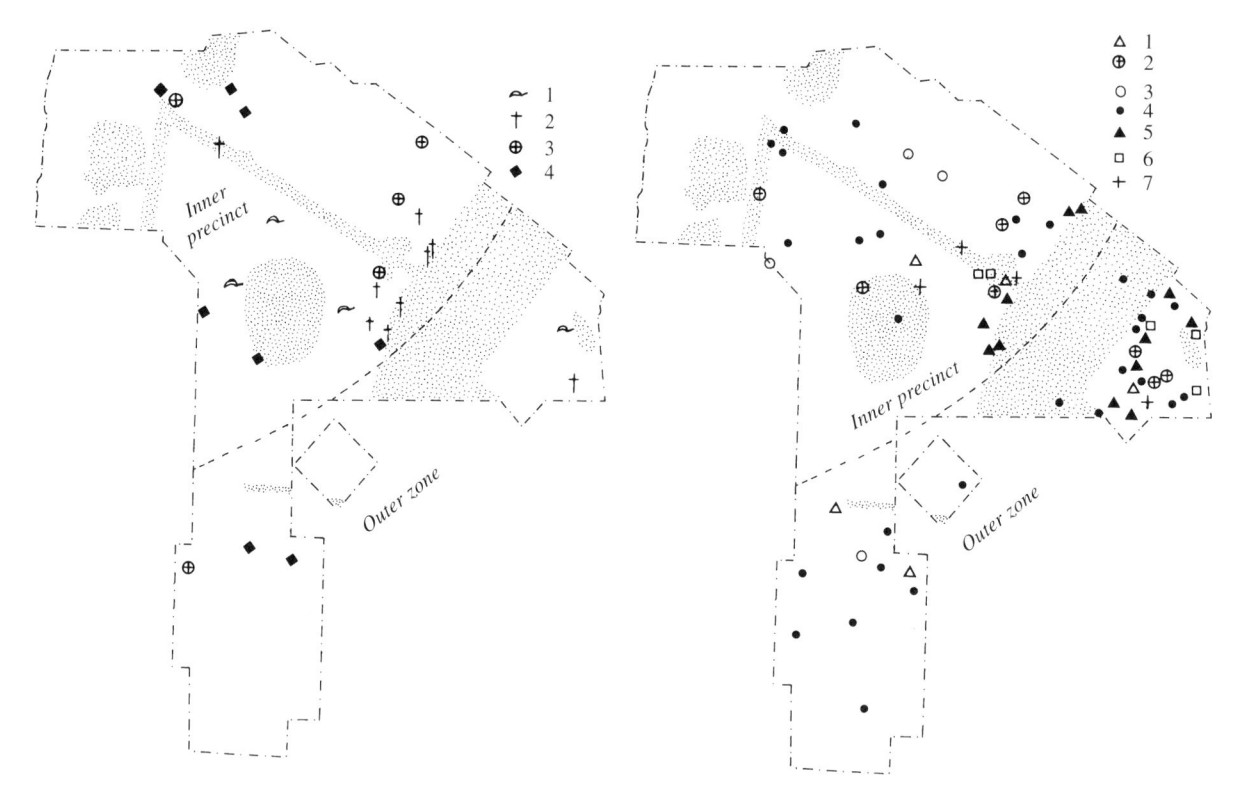

6.28 Miscellaneous tools
1= Curved blades, 2 = Tanged awls, 3 = Drawknives, 4 = Chisels and wedges.

6.29 Spinning and weaving implements
1 = Bone whorls, 2 = Lead whorls, 3= Very small whorls, 4 = Spindle whorls, 5 = Faceted and pierced tines, 6 = Weaving tensioners, 7 = Wool comb teeth.

crucible fragments, and may have been used in the decoration of metal objects. The needles revealed similar patterns with slight differences in the distributions of punched and Y-eyed examples, and a concentration of copper-alloy needles in the western part of the *inner precinct* (Figure 6.26a). An alternative distribution plot (Figure 6.26b) revealed concentrations of large coarse needles in the south-east part of the *outer zone* and fine needles in the western part of the **central sector**. The former coincided with concentrations of putative weaving equipment (Figure 6.29) and could have been used for darning or netting, though including two needles suitable for quilting. The fine needles would have been appropriate for embroidery or sewing fine cloth, and could mark a stall selling needles or, as some were broken, an embroiderer's or tailor's booth. Needles of standard size were more widely scattered in a belt on the outer margin of the *inner precinct*, and would have been suitable for sewing cloth or leather. The needles and 'awls' thus seem to indicate areas of specific craft activities within the *inner precinct*, while a group of coarse needles in the *outer zone* marked a possible workshop in **Building 19**. Both distribution plots encompass finds from the earlier stratified deposits, suggesting that these activities were established at the beginning of **Period IV**.

Similar patterns were displayed by other tool types with marked concentrations in the *inner precinct* (Figures 6.28). Scattered chisels and wedges in the western part of the area suggested stone or woodworking, while possible pruning hooks were concentrated in a relatively small area to the west of the main concentrations of debris. The small drawknives could have been used for leatherworking, but the group from the eastern part of the *inner precinct* coincided with the densest group of antler-working debris (425, Figure 6.2 and 10.136), and curved draw-knife cuts were identified on partly-worked comb tooth- and side-plates (pp 479-80). Assorted artefacts linked to the manufacture of thread and cloth revealed differing distributional characteristics (Figures 6.29). Spindle whorls were diffusely scattered in the *inner precinct* and *outer zone*, extending further to the north-east than most other categories of finds. These outliers might have been displaced from the **Period III** buildings in this area (**III/13–16**), but otherwise indicated spinning beyond the areas occupied by workshops in **Period IV**. Three unusually small whorls appropriate to spinning fine wool or flax (SE27, p 450) came from a restricted area in the *inner precinct*. The outer margin of the *inner precinct* revealed a tight group of wool-comb teeth associated with a pair of weaving tensioners, and two small groups of socketed and pierced tines which may have been used in looms (pp 487-90). Although these could have been debris from the adjacent part of the *outer zone*, which produced similar stratified and displaced finds, the close associations of related objects suggest that they mark workshops on the outer margin of the *inner precinct*. A cluster of lead spindle whorls from the same area spanning the *inner precinct* and *outer zone*, is intriguing as it contrasted with the more random distribution of other types of whorl. These

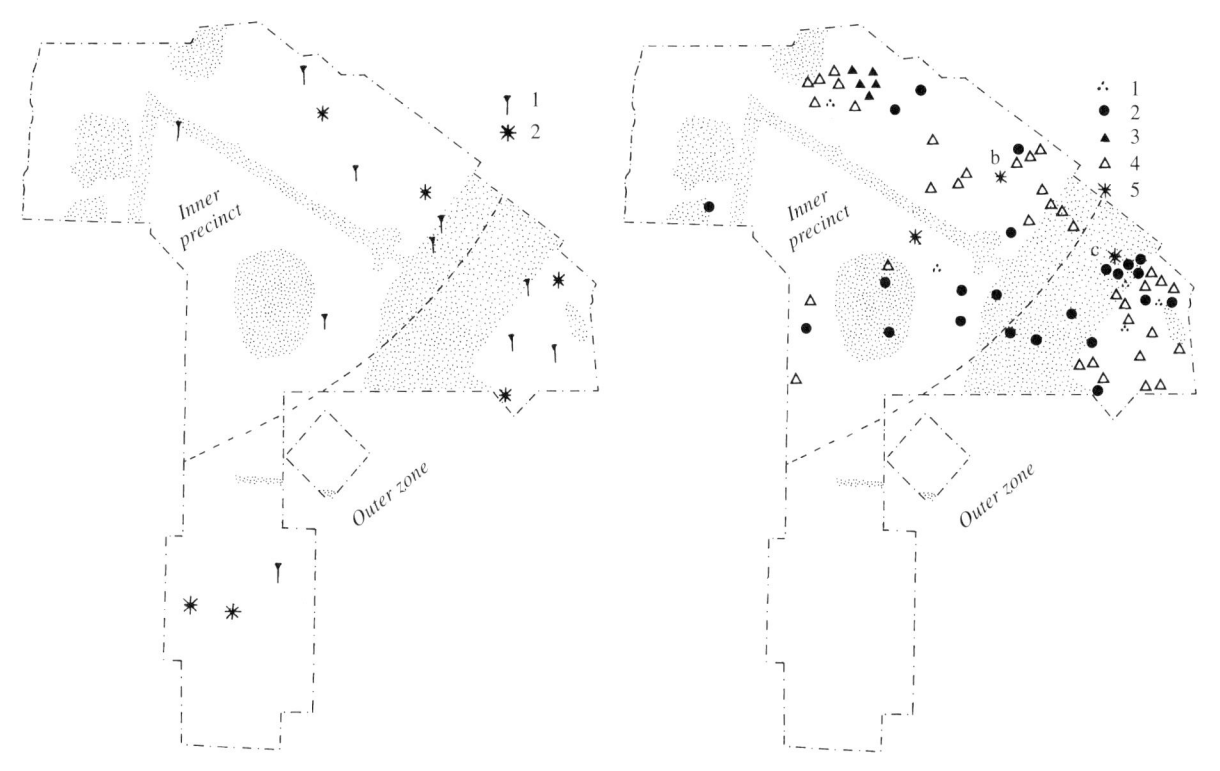

6.30 *Styluses* and burnishers
1= Stylus etc. 2 = Burnisher.

6.31 Lead and copper-alloy waste
1 = Burnt limestone, 2 = Lead strip and sheet,
3 = Nodular copper-alloy waste, 4 = Copper-alloy
strip and sheet, 5 = Lead-casting debris.

would have been suitable for spinning the stronger, more tightly-woven warp thread, and its production may thus have been a specialised activity in this 'weavers quarter'. Headless bone pins (BA08, Figure 6.25) give further evidence of weaving in this area. No loom weights were recorded here, and the only examples came from the **northern sector** where the **Period V** graves had disturbed the displaced **Period I** metalworking debris which was the source of other 'loom weights' (p 452). This indicates that the putative weaving equipment may have been used in horizontal looms.

The displaced material was densest on the eastern side of the trench, and encompassed several groups of finds spanning the *outer zone* and *inner precinct* (Figure 6.30 and 31). These could have derived from phases of activity when these areas were no longer distinguished, but might have derived from workshop areas spanning both zones, as indicated by the comb-making debris (Figures 6.2, 10.136). These finds included burnishers, styluses and prickers, pointing to sophisticated crafts, and potentially deriving from workshops in the vicinity, rather than random rubbish (Figure 6.30). The iron styluses and prickers came from the eastern part of the site, and would have been appropriate to marking out stone for dressing or sculpture, but styluses are among the goldsmith's tools listed in broadly contemporary documents (Campbell 1991, 120). A copper alloy stylus or pricker from a late context further to the west, and a ninth century stylus from the **southern sector** (415.02, Table 6.18) indicated writing and manuscript preparation (p 376). The finely-finished burnishers (pp 456-8) were scattered in a similar area, and two other examples from the **southern sector** were also loosely associated with fine-metalworking debris (415.01, Table 6.18). Their precise function is uncertain, although burnishers are included in inventories of broadly contemporary goldsmith's tools (Campbell 1991, 120).

Pieces of lead and copper-alloy waste were concentrated in a broad band in the eastern part of the site, and straddled the *inner precinct* and *outer zone* (Figure 6.31). Although the distributions of the two materials overlapped, the lead was concentrated to the south and west of the copper-alloy finds, and the two scatters indicated separate craft areas. A concentration of copper-alloy scrap overlying **Building III/16** in the north end of the trench was associated with a cluster of molten metal fragments, and the area produced two crucible sherds. One from a **Period V** grave, revealed traces of lead, while a second, with traces of bronze or brass, came from a later pit which produced more copper-alloy nodules, potentially displaced from the same workshop. Strip fragments predominated among the copper-alloy waste, and the sheet appropriate to the repair of vessels, was rare. The distribution of the copper-alloy objects is discussed at greater length below (pp 384-5, 404, Figures 10.71, 88) Sheet fragments were commoner among the lead finds (Table 10.6). These were

6.32 Iron scrap and lead nails
1 = Iron strips etc, 2 = Lead rivets and nails.

6.33 Farriers debris
1 = Horseshoe fragments, 2 = Fiddle-key nails.

frequently folded, which is a sensible way of storing scrap for recycling, and they may have been a commodity awaiting remelting rather than an indicator of lead sheet working in this area. Both distributions overlapped the concentration of crucible fragments in the *outer zone*, and would have been appropriate to the alloys of lead and copper which were produced (p 404). The plot includes fragments of burnt limestone which corresponded broadly with the scattered copper-alloy waste and *tesserae* (Figures 6.24 and 30). Limestone had to be imported (pp 470-1), and might have been used as a pigment or mordant, for liming to dissolve the hair from leather or hides, or as a glaze modifier in the production of glass or enamel. The spatial coincidence with *tesserae* and copper-alloy strips argues strongly in favour of the last option, and these finds might well be debris from an enameller's workshop. The earliest English formula for enamel employs lead oxide made by boiling lead and collecting the residue (Campbell 1991, 128), and this might explain the lead waste and crucible fragments with traces of lead. Three pieces of lead-casting debris comprised two casting plugs (**a** and **b**) and a plano-convex ingot (**c**) preserving the shape of a large round-based crucible. The last came from the early deposits in the east part of the site (424, Table 6.33), and could have pertained to **Period III** or the beginning of **Period IV**. These pieces indicated lead casting but there were no moulds or large crucibles from this area, and they are more likely to have been further scrap gathered for recycling. Iron scrap was distributed more randomly, but was concentrated in the *inner precinct* and virtually absent from the **southern sector** (Figure 6.32). This dispersed material probably included finds displaced from the **Period I** debris used in the construction of the **Period II** buildings (Table 3.35), and others may have been associated with the nails in the putative levelling material (430). Horseshoe fragments and the related fiddle-key nails (pp 407-8) revealed a less random distribution, with concentrations in the south-east part of the *outer zone* and western parts of the **central** and **northern sectors** (Figure 6.33). While possibly displaced, these may reveal farriers' workshops, accounting for the scattered cinder and 'hearths' from these areas. A concentration of ironworking debris in the south-eastern part of the *outer zone*, was associated *inter alia* with large hones, and can be linked with the smithying evident in **Structure 20** (pp 229-30). Stratified deposits on the west side of the trench produced scattered smelting debris, hinting at iron production in the unexcavated ground further west. Lead rivets and nails displayed a similar random distribution, though with a marked concentration in the *inner precinct* (Figure 6.32). These could have been used in the manufacture or repair of lead vessels (pp 390, 393), but the diffuse scatter does not identify a specific workshop, and contrasts with the restricted distribution of lead waste. Finds from early deposits indicate that this activity was established at the beginning of **Period IV**. Pieces of iron and copper-alloy wire displayed contrasting patterns, both with concentrations in the *inner precinct* lying in the middle of the trench, and distinct from other copper-alloy and iron finds (Figure 6.34). Both thus hint at workshops, and the copper-alloy wire could have been associated with the *tesserae* from the same area (Figure 6.24) as separate components of *cloisonné* enamels.

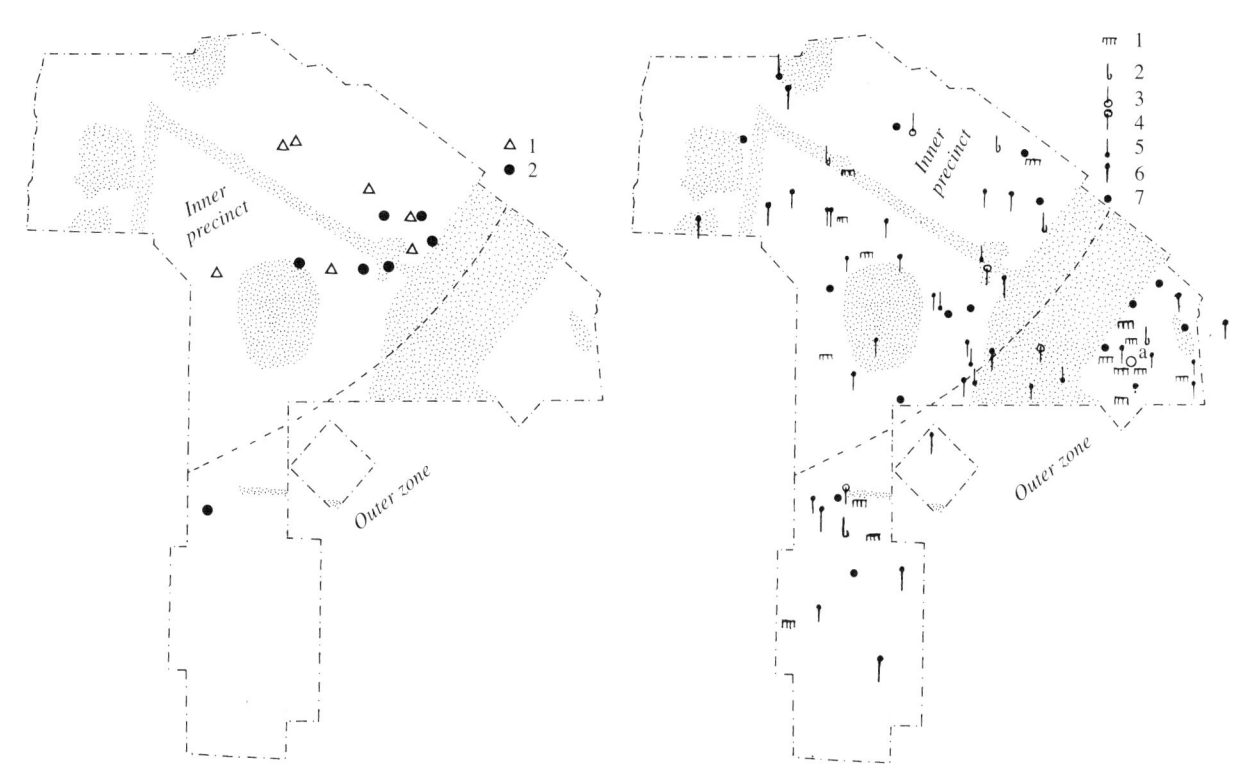

6.34 Copper-alloy and iron wire
1 = Copper-alloy wire, 2 = Iron wire.

6.35 Stick- and ring-pins, beads and combs
1 = Combs and fragments, 2 = Loop-headed iron pin, 3 = Iron ring pin, 4 = Copper-alloy ring pin etc, 5 = Iron stick pin, 6 = Copper-alloy stick pin, 7 = Bead.

Stick-pins, comb fragments and beads displayed patterns of distribution different to those of the manufacturing debris and implements (Figure 6.35). These finds spanned the *inner precinct* and *outer zone*, but had markedly western distributions, and were scarce in the richest areas of manufacturing debris in the eastern part of the site. A concentration of finds in the south-east part of the *outer zone* and coinciding with **Building 18**, included a range of comb fragments and a tenth-twelfth century finger ring of leaded glass (**a**). The comb fragments could have been debris from a workshop where combs were repaired (p 494). Despite the random overall distribution, specific types showed marked concentrations, with iron stick pins confined to a narrow belt in the outer part of the *inner precinct*, and loop-headed and ringed pins concentrated to the north. The iron stick-pins may thus have been stock produced in an adjacent smithy, perhaps **Structure 20**, possibly marking a booth where its products were sold. They might also have been associated with the fine metalworking in the area, and could have been brought here for plating. The stratified combs, beads and pins from the **southern sector** were probably domestic debris, and this may account for the finds from the south-eastern part of the *outer zone*. The finds from the *inner precinct* may have included stock lost from stalls, and stray losses by craftsmen and their customers. Knives and blade fragments displayed a similar random distribution, though largely confined to the *inner precinct* (Figure 6.36). Finds from the north-west part of the site could have

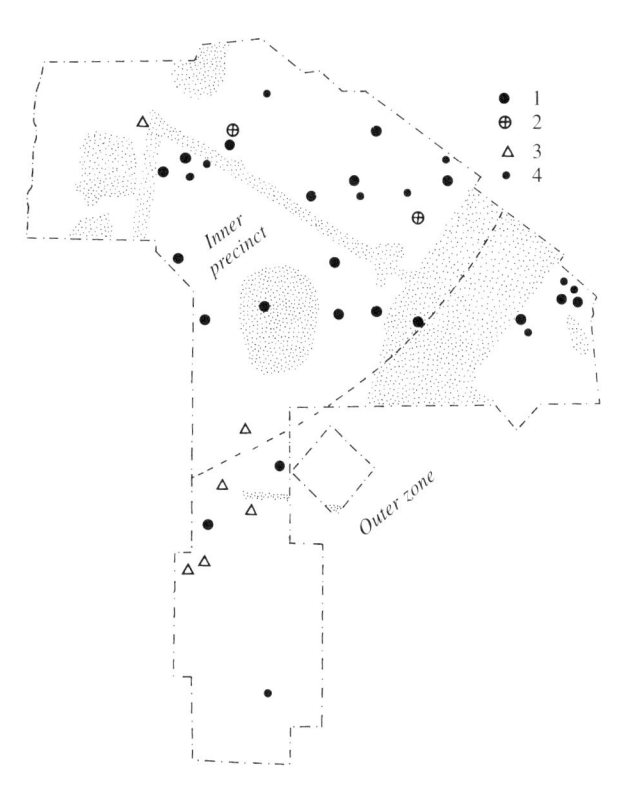

6.36 Knives and blades
1 = Knife, 2 = Swivel knife, 3 = Shears or fragment, 4 = Blade fragment.

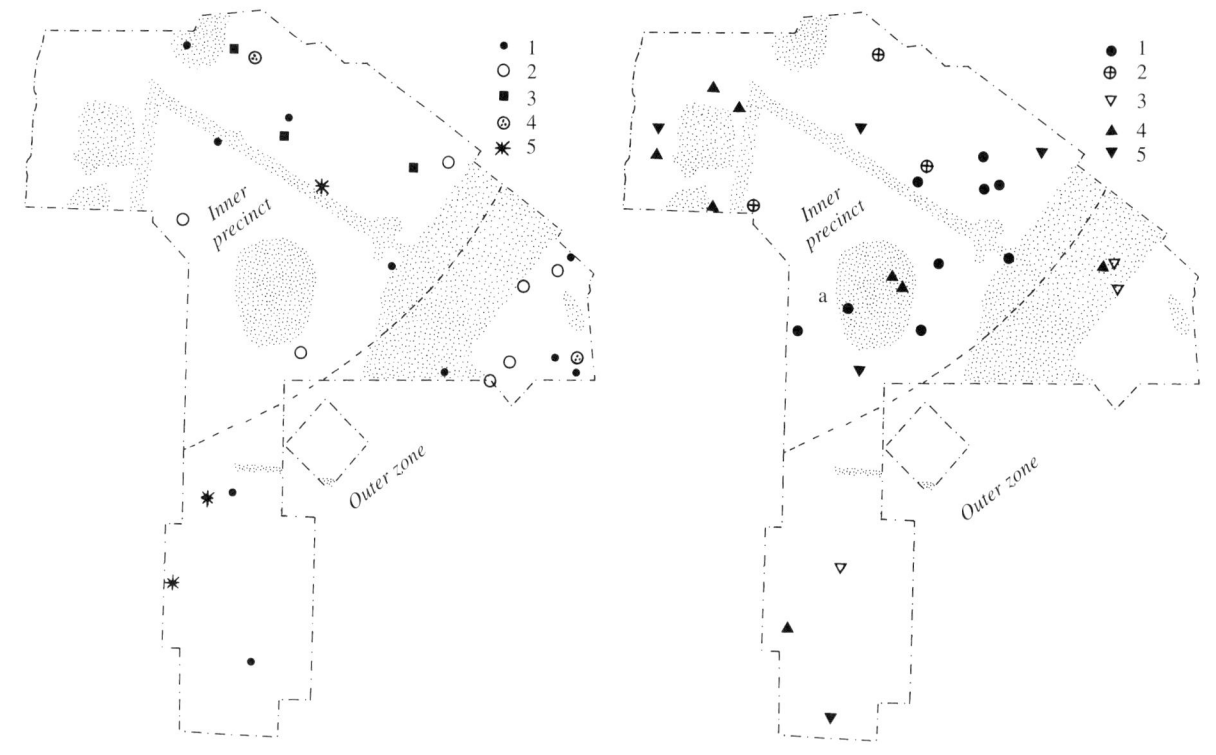

6.37 Miscellaneous stone artefacts
1 = Gaming piece, 2 = Discoid, 3 = Serrated flake implement, 4 = Multiply-perforated flake, 5 = Gaming board.

6.38 Coins and lead weights
1 = Lead weights, 2 = 10th and 11th C coins, 3 = 12th C coins, 4 = Coins of Henry III etc, 5 = Early issues of Edward I and Alexander III.

been displaced from the **Period III** buildings, and others might have been included in the spread of levelling debris (430). The group included two swivel knives and a possible surgical knife. Shears fragments were confined to late contexts in the western part of the site, identifying an area where cloth was worked, possibly as a domestic industry. The only intact example (**a**, IN72.3) came from a late context (617.02) on the periphery of the graveyard, but is identifiable as an early- to mid-thirteenth century type, broadly supporting the inferred period of the other examples. Stone gaming pieces and discoids were randomly distributed in the two zones, and there was sadly no correspondence between the former and a *tafl* board from the middle of the trench, and two merels boards from the **southern sector** (Figure 6.37). Three stone flakes with serrated edges from the north-eastern part of the *inner precinct* could have been used for combing pottery, although there was no other evidence for potting, while perforated discs may have been used for making cord (pp 452-3).

Coins and lead weights (Figure 6.38) displayed distinctive distribution patterns potentially indicating areas of trading activity. Four groups of coins are distinguished in Figures 6.38 and 10.45. Three coins of the later tenth and eleventh centuries from the north-eastern part of the *inner precinct* possibly pertained to **Period III**, and may thus have been lost on the inner margin of the **Phase 3** buildings (Figure 10.45a). The two, possibly three, twelfth century coins came from the *outer zone* where the cut halfpenny of Henry II or III may have been linked to silver-working. A broadly-contemporary coin of William the Lion was found nearby, and may also have been destined for reworking. Most of the thirteenth century coins came from the *inner precinct*, and were concentrated in the western part of the **northern sector** where other finds were sparse. This may thus have been the area where trading took place, while goods were manufactured in the peripheral workshops. These coins are divided into two groups. The coins of Henry III in the earlier group were demonetised in 1278/9, and were probably deposited in the closing years of **Period IV**. The second group comprises a penny of Alexander III and the earlier issues of Edward I. All were worn by circulation and were probably deposited in the fourteenth century (p 356). Lead weights were concentrated in the *inner precinct*, and were confined to a narrow belt slightly within its outer margin. The finds plotted include a decorated weight of the ninth/tenth century (**a**) displaced into the nineteenth century hollow, a second from the **Phase 1** surface (432, Table 6.29), and two from residual rubbish spreads (457, Table 6.32) underlying the graves in the **central sector**. These indicated that some or all of the weights pertained to a relatively early stage of deposition, potentially extending into **Period III**. The weights appear to have been a slightly ungenerous version of the Norse system based around the 24 g *øre* and 8 g *ertog* (pp 392-3), and may have been

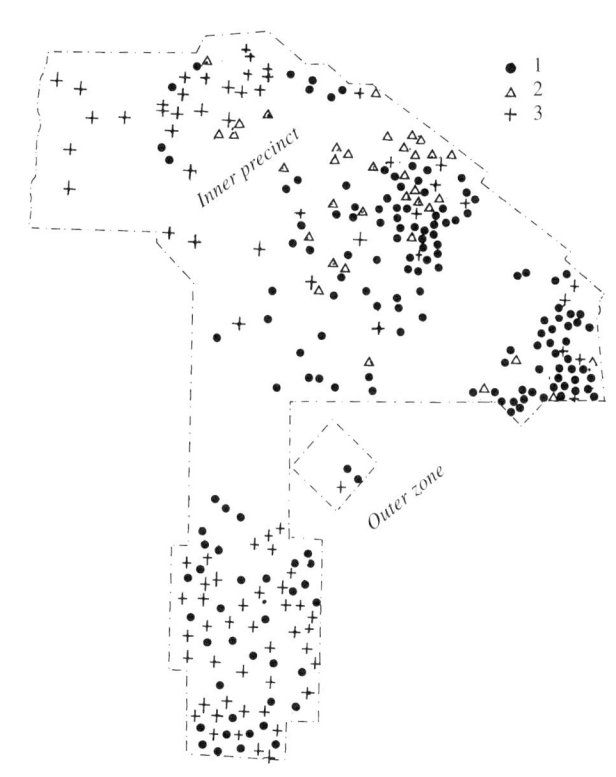

6.39 Early pottery
1 = Red gritty ware, 2 = Green-glazed jugs and jars (F. 2/11), 3 = White gritty ware.

scaled from a master set controlling transactions in the market at Whithorn. The group includes small weights appropriate to trading in small quantities of valuable commodities such as bullion, medicines or spices. The weights were concentrated in the area producing *tesserae* and copper-alloy wire, and might conceivably have been lost by a craftsman trading in bullion and jewellery.

The final plot (Figure 6.39) shows the contrasting distributions of the three commonest groups of twelfth and thirteenth century pottery. Sherds of globular, red gritty ware jars were concentrated in the eastern part of the site, where they spanned the *inner precinct* and *outer zone*. Sherds were notably scarce among the stratified deposits in the south-eastern part of the *outer zone*, and the pottery probably pertained to the later stages of **Period IV**. The distribution of white gritty ware was focused in the north-west part of the trench, and occasional stratified sherds suggested that deposition commenced in **Phase 4** slightly after the introduction of red gritty ware. The distribution extended into the **Fey Field** where red gritty ware was absent, and thus seems to reflect the organisational changes of this phase (p 291). A distinct scatter of sherds from early green-glazed, oxidised jars or jugs (MP2/11) was concentrated in the *inner precinct* on the north-east side of the trench. This fabric was found in a range of earlier contexts in the **southern sector**, and may have coexisted with red gritty ware. It seems to have been relatively long-lived and the numerous sherds from the **southern sector** have been omitted from the drawing in the interests of clarity. The differing distributions probably reflect a combination of chronological and functional factors, while the circumstantial evidence of a market in the *inner precinct* argues that they were associated with the preparation and sale of food and drink.

Conclusions. The **Period IV** finds record a vitally important stage in the economic development of Whithorn, and there were sufficient clues among the stratified deposits to make a confident assessment of the displaced material. The two excavated segments of the *outer zone* revealed a clear picture of evolving craft activities, and the displaced material probably reflects a similar, if more complex, evolution over the same period. Workshop areas spanning adjacent parts of the *outer zone* and *inner precinct* were revealed by the early deposits of comb-making debris, and subsequently by lead and copper-alloy waste, iron styluses and other objects. The distribution of crucible fragments and *tesserae* suggests a possible explanation. Crucible fragments and lead nodules were concentrated in the *outer zone*, and probably derive from furnaces in the adjacent unexcavated ground. The potentially-related debris from the *inner precinct* could have been derived from workshops where objects cast in this industrial area were finished, bullion traded and products sold. The awls, needles, putative weaving equipment and other specialised tools point to other overlapping workshop areas on the outer margin of the *inner precinct*, but there was no evidence of heavier industries, which may have been confined to specific areas in the *outer zone*. The coins hint that trading took place towards the centre of the *inner precinct*, while random scatters of knives, stick-pins, beads and combs could have been stray losses by craftsmen and their customers, or possibly stock lost from market stalls.

The combined evidence argues that the south side of the hill accommodated both dwellings and workshops, the latter extending into the outer part of the *inner precinct*. There was evidence for a wide range of crafts, some clearly visible, such as comb-making and fine metalwork, and others more conjectural (cord-weaving) or obscure (a cluster of curved blades). The thirteenth century coins suggest an inner area used by traders, and the earlier issues hint that this may have originated in latter part of **Period III**, perhaps in the late-tenth century. Intact deposits demonstrated that comb-making and weaving, and the activities associated with needles, punches and lead nails had been established at the beginning of **Period IV**, and these finds revealed distributions in which the distinction between the *inner precinct* and *outer zone* was clearly defined. Other crafts seem to have been introduced at a later date, and the distinction between the two zones, though still evident, seems to have become more blurred. This evolution accords well with the inferred division by a fence or hedge which may thus have been increasingly breached by craftsmen and traders with activities spanning both areas.

This postulated eleventh–thirteenth century market

emerges from a cocktail of evidence which had been both shaken and stirred during the subsequent development of this area. Intact deposits in the *outer zone* gave convincing evidence of craft specialisation, which can be extrapolated with confidence to explain the non-random distributions of specific finds in the *inner precinct*. The unexcavated ground to the south and west probably preserves a less compromised record of the evolving economic activities in **Period IV**; it should provide the chronological dimension missing from the present account, and may reveal the workshops from which so much debris had been dispersed.

Fourteen coins:
   Penny of Eadgar, *c*. 959–975 (CN02.63)
   Penny, phase III *c*. 1035–55, very slight wear (CN02.65)
   ALEXANDER III, penny, 2nd coinage, cB 1280–86+, fairly worn (CN03.03)
   HENRY III, penny of Ion at Bury St Edmunds, long cross, c2 1248 (CN03.64)
   HENRY III, penny of Walter at Canterbury, long cross, *c*5g 1251–71 (CN03.67)
   EDWARD I, penny of London, cIIa 1280, worn (CN03.69)
   EDWARD III, halfpenny of London, 2nd coinage 1335–43, very worn (CN03.83)
   EDWARD III, penny of Durham, probably pre-Treaty sF or G 1356–61 (CN03.85)
   JAMES II, penny of Edinburgh, crown groat coinage, tB 1451–*c*. 1460 (CN03.15)
   JAMES III?, billon penny, 1460–88, probably fairly worn (CN03.21)
   JAMES III, copper farthing, 1st issue 1465–6, moderate wear (CN03.26)
   JAMES III, copper forgery of a farthing, as 1st issue 1465–6 (CN03.28)
   JAMES IV, billon penny, 2nd issue, tII *c*. 1500–10, slight wear (CN03.33)
   CRVX PELLIT issue, tIa later 15th C, corroded (CN03.16)

A small collection of coal
Ten pieces (or groups) of decaying medieval window glass (GS07)
Nineteen sherds of green-tinged or iridescent window glass (GS81)
Thirteen sherds of modern window glass (GS82)
Ten groups of 17th–19th C bottle glass (GS09) and seven of recent fragments (GS10)
Nine copper-alloy pins with round, globular heads (BZ01.8, 9, 11–17); one with a flat head (BZ2.1); four with mushroom heads (BZ04.1–4); five with wire-wrapped heads (BZ03.3, 5–8) and eight large pins with wire-wrapped heads (BZ10.1–8), six (BZ10.1–6) found together; twenty-one pin shanks (BZ09.5, 7–8, 9, 11–26, 29)
A decorated copper-alloy annular brooch (BZ16.2) and a fragment of a possible second (BZ16.5)
Forty-two copper-alloy tag-ends (BZ20.8–11, 13, 15–24, 26–39, 41–47, 49–53, 62)
Three copper-alloy 6-petal studs (BZ21.2, 4 and 6)
Eight wire-loops (BZ33.1–8)
Two copper-alloy buckle pins (18.7 and 8), a broken 13/14 C quadrilateral buckle (BZ18.9), a 15 C figure of eight buckle (BZ18.10) and a quadrilateral buckle with a bezel (BZ18.11)
Two possible copper-alloy strap-ends (BZ19.9 and 14) and a piece of folded binding (BZ19.19)
A circular wire fish hook (BZ27.2)
A squashed, butted copper-alloy suspension ring (BZ28.1)
Three small rings, two certainly eyelets with textile (BZ28.6 and 7), one possibly so (BZ28.11)
A perforated copper-alloy dome (BZ29.3) and a small convex ring stud (BZ29.14)
A possible, hexagonal eyelet (BZ30.19), a dress fastener of rolled wire (BZ30.14), a tapering needle or pin (BZ30.12), a cast tracery fragment (BZ30.16), horseshoe-shaped strip with pierced terminals (BZ30.21), a possible ridged handle (BZ30.23) and a perforated rough disc (BZ30.22)
Two pieces of architectural sandstone waste (SE06)
Twenty-seven stone tiles and fragments (SE07–13)
The cut terminal of a decorated gold band of 13th C type (AU3)
A piece of diamond-sectioned silver ring money of the 10th/11th C (SR13)
Crushed fragments of amber (AM02.1)
Seven glass beads, two opaque white (GS03.23 and 27), one plain blue (GS03.32), half a dark green eye bead (GS03.45), half of a yellow bead (GS03.50) and a yellow glass ring bead (GS03.51)
A severely-weathered Ist/2nd C red and yellow glass bangle fragment (GS04.1)
Four blue glass *tesserae* (GS05.2, 5–7), a yellow *tessera* (GS05.12) and a dark red *tessera* (GS05.11)
A shale ring fragment (SH02.3) and a ring or bangle fragment (SH02.4)
An ornamental copper-alloy pin-head with a cut shank (BZ13.6)
Three stirrup-ringed crutch-headed pins (BZ15.6–8), one (8) without its ring.
Seven complete stick pins (BZ14.30, 32, 33, 41, 44 and 45) and a stick pin shank (BZ14.49)
Six copper-alloy needles and shanks (BZ12.7, 8, 10–13)
A copper-alloy razor blade (BZ24.7)
A tin-plated bar with a decorated head (BZ24.10)
Two copper-alloy points or awls (BZ25.5 and 6)
Six pieces of copper-alloy wire (BZ32.6–12)
A tubular copper-alloy rivet with hammered ends (BZ34.3)
A tapering copper-alloy rod (BZ36.17)
Five pieces of worked copper-alloy strip or sheet (BZ37.16, 17, 19, 20,21)
Sixteen pieces of waste strip and sheet (BZ38.43–47, 49, 56–9, 61–66)
Six pieces of nodular copper-alloy waste (BZ39.15–20) and four copper alloy fragments (BZ41.31, 41–3)
Three hundred and nineteen nails, and a hundred and forty-five heads and shanks
Seven staples, two square (IN17.28–9) and five U-shaped (IN17.9–13)
Five certain or possible long staples (IN18.13–17)
Three clench nails (IN19.10–12), a clench plate (IN20.13) and a rivet (IN21.8)
A broken tapering hinge (IN24.12)
An iron ring (IN30.14) and two linked rings (IN30.17)
Five hooks (IN31.18–22)
A spring-leaf padlock mechanism (IN 33.7)
A plated key (IN34.8), a plated 12th/13th C key (IN34.9) and a plated 13th/14th C key (IN34.7)
A rimmed iron plate (IN36.3)
Thirty iron needles, five Y-eyed (IN39.44–7, 49 and 51), ten with punched eyes (IN39.19–23, 25–8, 30 and 31) and fifteen broken (IN39.60–66, 69–71, 75, 76 and 79)
Nine iron pins (IN40.26–31, 33, 34, 36 and 37) and a plated, club-headed iron pin or nail (IN40.6)
A fragment of a plated iron club-headed stick pin (IN41.7), a stud-headed stick pin (IN41.10) and a possible third (IN41.8), a stick pin with a square-spatulate head and bent tip (IN41.11), an iron pin with a broken looped end (IN41.18) and a possible ringed-pin (IN41.19)
Half of an iron brooch or buckle with a pin (IN42.03)
Five iron buckle pins (IN44.31–35), five iron buckles (IN44.7–9, 11 and 12) and two possible buckles (IN44.21 and 41)
A belt guide (IN45.7), a strap retainer (IN45.6) and an hexagonal finger ring (IN45.3)
Three horseshoe fragments (IN48.3, 4 and 7)
Two bridle bits (IN49.3 and 4), one with foil decoration (4)
Twenty two awls, tanged awls and punches (IN50.6–11, 13, 25–28, 34, 42, 43, 53, 54, 65, 73–76)
A chisel (IN52.2), three chisels or wedges (IN52.12–14) and a possible file (IN54.3)
Six iron wool-comb teeth (IN62.9–14) and two weaving tensioners (IN63.4 and 5)
Seven possible iron *styli* or scribers (IN64.2, 4, 6, 7, 9, 10, 12)
Fifteen knives (IN66.5, 8, 14–16, 21, 26–28, 49–53 and 71), including a possible surgical knife (5)
Two pruning knives or hooks (IN67.2 and 3)

Two swivel knives (IN68.4 and 5)
Three drawknives with looped ends (IN69.6–8)
A possible iron razor blade (IN71.1)
Six blade fragments (IN73.15–17, 19, 20 and 23)
Four socketed hunting arrows (IN75.5–7, 13), one plated (5)
Part of a bifurcated candle holder (IN76.1)
A plated bifurcated strip with a tang (IN78.36), a possible socketed tool or arrowhead (IN78.37), a broken iron strip riveted to copper alloy plates (IN78.38) and a tanged fragment, perhaps of a tool (IN78.39)
Twenty-eight iron strip fragments (IN80.74–79,81, 82, 84–87, 91, 93–96, 98–105, 107–110), three curved strips (IN81.20, 21 and 23), nine plate fragments (IN82.35–42 and 46), six bars (IN83.20–22, 25–27), five rods (IN84.8, 10–13), a perforated disc (IN89.5), seven pieces of wire (IN90.9–14, 18) and twelve corroded lumps and fragments of iron (IN93.80–89, 91–3)
Two perforated lead discs (LD02.8 and 9) and a possible washer (LD04.3)
Five possible lead weights (LD05.7–11)
Three possible lead spindle whorls (LD03.6, 7 and 9)
Eight lead rivets (LD06.6–13), seven nails (LD06.31, 32, 43, 44, 46–48) and a tack (LD06.52)
A lead casting plug or waste bar (LD10.1) and an ovoid plug (LD10.2), fourteen pieces of lead sheet and strip waste (LD11.53–55, 57, 60, 64, 66 –69, 71–4), four pieces of nodular lead waste (LD12.40–41, 44 and 46), three lead pellets and two molten driblets (LD13.7–10 and 12)
A bi-convex bone spindle whorl (BA06.5) and a plano-convex bone spindle whorl (BA06.6)
Three bone pins, one with a thistle head and projecting lugs (BA07.1), one with a flattened club head (BA07.5), one with a nail head (BA07.4)
Five bone pin fragments (BA08.3, BA09.4, 5, 7 and 8), one (08.3) from a headless pin
A possible bone pin blank (BA11)
A small rounded bone bead (BA18)
A perforated bone fragment (BA13.1), a split worked bone (BA17), a hollowed bone (BA19.3) and a utilised bone sliver (BA19.2)
Four decorated comb side plates (AR69.1[F1], AR70.3[F1], 6[F1/3] and 8 [F3])
The centre of a broken Class F1 comb (AR71.2) and a broken Class F1/3 comb (AR71.3)
A faceted tine gaming piece (AR74.12) and a possible barrel-shaped gaming piece (AR75.6)
A slotted antler handle with ring and dot decoration (AR74.12)
Seven faceted tine tips (AR77.10–16) and two pierced tine tips (AR78.2 and 3)
Five faceted and pierced tine tips (AR79.7–10, 14)
An antler wedge (AR80.1)
A sawn tine with the cancellous tissue removed (AR81.1)
A tine with the base sharpened to a point (AR81.2)
A flat antler plate (AR81.11)
A fractured piece of antler with a screw thread (AR81.7)
A large cross-shaft fragment with interlace (SE14.9)
A sandstone fragment with an incised cross (SE18.5)
A slab with an incised *tafl* board (SE23.3)
Six possible stone gaming counters (small discoids, SE19.7, 8, 11, 14, 15, 21)
Two stone discoids (SE20.1 and 14), two large stone discoids (SE21.7 and 8) and a very large greywacke discoid (SE22.1)
Fourteen spindle whorls (SE24. 3, 16, 19 and 20; SE25. 4, 8 and 13; SE26.1, 3, 4 and 11; SE27.3, 4 and 6)
Three possible stone loom weights (SE29.2, 12 and 13)
Two stone discoids with multiple perforations (SE30.1 and 5)
Three small manufactured hones (SE36.13, 14 and 18) and a small natural hone (SE37.5)
Nine hone blanks (SE71. 6, 19, 20, 25 37, 40, 54, 61 and 63)
Two quadrilateral burnishers (SE40.1 and 2)
Two smoothed botryoidal Haematite polishers (SE62.17 and 18)
A rotary quern upper stone fragment (SE43.4)
A small stone ball (SE50.12)
Three sandstone flakes with serrated edges (SE53.3–5)
A smoothed sandstone slab (SE55.2)
Three 'exotic' stones – a red jasper pebble (SE58.7), a piece of banded rock crystal (SE58.14) and a banded quartzite pebble (SE58.34)
A large group of flints comprising:
  Seven pebbles (FT01)
  Seventeen burnt flints (FT22)
  Sixteen waste flakes with retouch (FT04)
  Eighty-three **unretouched** waste flakes (FT04)
  Two **retouched** core waste flakes (FT06)
  Nine **retouched** blade flakes (FT07)
  Seven cores (FT08)
  Five arrowhead points (FT16) and four other points
  Seven scrapers (FT09, 17)
  Two knives, a sickle tooth and a spurred implement
  Forty-two **retouched** flints (FT24)
An extremely large group of quartz and granite pebbles and vein quartz fragments (1199 individual finds and groups)
A numerous but insubstantial group of metalworking debris of which the important elements are:
  Two crucible fragments (SG15.34 and 50) including one with traces of lead (34) and one with traces of bronze and brass (50)
  Three pieces of non-ferrous waste (SG14)
  A small assemblage of dense Group 1 puddling hearths and other debris
  A piece of furnace floor with an attached wall fragment (SG63)
Small groups of fire-cracked stones (18, SE 76) and glazed sandstone pebbles and fragments (17, SE77)
Five pieces of burnt limestone (SE60)
A small group of small fragments of clay, daub and raw clay
A small group of mortar, clastic lime and chalk plaster

Three sherds of light blue window glass (GS06.9-11), one blue (GS06.32), one deep blue (GS06.38) and one light green (GS06.106)
One sherd of early medieval vessel glass (GS02)
Four plough pebbles (SE51)

Table 6.41 Finds from **Period V** graves and related contexts cutting **Period IV** deposits in the *inner precinct*

Five coins:
  CN03.02. WILLIAM THE LION, penny of Roxburgh, 2nd coinage, c2 c1180–95
  CN03.63: HENRY II or III?, cut halfpenny, probably short-cross, from x-ray of drawplate
  CN03.31. JAMES IV, forgery of a plack 1488–1513, fairly worn
  CN04.19: Copper halfpenny, probably 18th C, worn flat
  CN04.12: ELIZABETH II, new halfpenny 1980
One fragment of coal
Two sherds of green-tinged or iridescent window glass (GS81) under manse
One sherd of modern window glass (GS82) under manse
Three groups of 17th–19th C bottle glass (GS09) all under manse
Two pieces of architectural sandstone waste (SE06)
Four stone tiles and fragments (SE07–13)
Six copper-alloy pins with round, globular heads (BZ01); three with wire-wrapped heads (BZ03.1, 2 and 4) and four pin shanks (BZ09.3, 6, 10 and 27)
Five copper-alloy tag-ends (BZ20.7, 14, 25, 40 and 48)
A small butted copper-alloy suspension ring (BZ28.2)
A cast hollow copper-alloy foot with three projecting lobes (BZ30.17)
A copper-alloy disc with a ferrous stud (BZ30.13)
A stamped copper-alloy disc with an embossed motif (BZ30.20)
A broken, plated iron 15th C six-point rowel spur (IN46.2)
A plain silver ring (SR2)
A heavy, pale yellow glass ring fragment, possibly 10th C (GS04.6)
Two blue glass *tesserae* (GS05.3 and 4)
A shale bangle fragment (SH01.10)
Four complete stick pins (BZ14.23, 31, 36 and 38), a stick pin shank (BZ14.51) and a stirrup ring from a ringed pin (BZ15.9)
Two copper-alloy needles (BZ12.5 and 9), one fractured across at base of the eye (5) and one shank (9)
A copper-alloy chain of 24 small figure-of-eight links (BZ31.3)
A copper-alloy rivet with one hammered end (BZ34.5)
A straight-sided copper alloy strip with a rivet at one end (BZ37.15)

Ten pieces of waste strip and sheet (BZ38.41, 42, 48, 50, 51–55 and 60)
Two ovoid copper-alloy pellets or droplets (BZ40.4 and 6) and one copper alloy fragment (BZ41.40)
Fifty nails and a hundred and thirty-one heads and shanks
Three clench nails (IN19.6, 8 and 9) and four clench plates (IN20.14–17) including a strip of three plates (17)
A simple looped swivel ring (IN25.4)
A broken, plated iron drawer handle (IN28.1)
Two iron rings (IN30.13 and 16) and a flattened iron hook (IN31.23)
A U-shaped bar and double spring from a barrel padlock (IN33.04) and a barrel padlock key (IN34.10)
A possible triangular iron weight (IN35.1)
Seven iron needles, one Y-eyed (IN39.58), three with punched eyes (IN39.24, 29 and 32), two broken (IN39.67–68) and one possibly plated (IN39.78)
Two iron pins (IN40.32 and 35)
A loop headed pin (lacking ring or brooch IN41.17), a stud-headed stick pin (IN41.9) and a stick pin with a triangular head (IN41.12)
An iron buckle tongue (IN44.34) and a corroded iron D-ring buckle (IN44.10)
A probable belt guide (IN45.8)
Two horseshoe fragments (IN48.5 and 6)
A tanged awl (IN50.12) and three punches (IN50.44, 46 and 64)
An iron drawplate (IN60.01)
An iron wool comb tooth or pin (IN62.07)
A two pronged weaving tensioner (IN63.6)
Three possible iron *styluses* (IN64.3, 5 and 8)
Four probable tools (IN65.19, 21 and 22) including a possible hammer head (19)
A complete tanged Class C knife (IN66.22), a tanged pruning hook (IN67.5), a tanged blade (IN66.62) and a blade fragment (IN73.18)
A triangular tanged arrowhead (IN75.14)
A U-sectioned iron strip with convex sides (IN78.40)
Nine iron strip fragments (IN80.73, 80, 83, 88–90, 92, 97 and 106), a curved strip (IN81.22), three plate fragments (IN82.31, 43 and 44), a bar (IN83.23), a rod (IN84.9), a flat disc (IN88.3) and an unidentified fragment of iron (IN93.90)
A possible lead weight (LD03.4) and a lead spindle whorl (LD03.5)
A lead washer (LD04.2)
A lead nail and a tack (LD06.45 and 53)
Nine pieces of lead waste (LD11.52, 56, 58, 59, 61–3, 65 and 70) and five nodular fragments (LD12.42 and 45)
A flattened bi-convex bone spindle whorl (BA06.4)
A complete headless bone pin (BA08.2) and a bone pin fragment (BA09.6)
A possible bone needle or pin (BA10.4)
Four decorated comb side plates (AR68.2[G] and 4 [G]; AR69.2 [F1]; AR70.5[F3])
Portions of two broken Class F2 comb (AR71.4 and 6)
Two antler pin blanks (AR73.2 and 3)
Four antler handles (AR74.2, 11, 14, 16 and 15), one (14) with elaborate carved spiral ornament
An antler fragment with ring and dot decoration (AR76.2)
A barrel-shaped antler gaming piece (AR75.07)

A faceted and pierced tine tip (AR79.12)
An antler wedge (AR80.2) and a flat antler plate (AR81.12)
A moulded fragment of medium-grained sandstone (SE02.01)
A greywacke chip fragment with incised symbols (SE18.6)
Four possible stone gaming counters (small discoids: SE19.10, 13, 18, 22)
Two stone discoids (SE20.6 and 9)
Six stone spindle whorls (SE24.4 and 17; SE25.12 and 16; SE26.8 and SE28.7)
A stone discoid with multiple perforations (SE30.4)
Three large hones (SE33.3; 34.1 and 3), a small natural hone (SE37.4) and a hone blank (SE71.10)
A fragment of a rotary grindstone (SE39.2) and a granite smoothing stone (SE42.6)
A manufactured, quadrilateral, quartzite burnisher (SE40.5)
A large millstone inner fragment (SE44.3)
A smoothed sandstone slab (SE55.1)
A piece of smoothed porphyry (SE58.26)
A large group of flints comprising:
  Two pebbles (FT01)
  Ten burnt flints (FT22)
  Five waste flakes with retouch (FT04)
  Fifty-five **unretouched** waste flakes (FT04)
  One **retouched** blade flake (FT07)
  A core (FT08)
  Two arrowhead points (FT16) and a graver point (FT15)
  One scraper (FT 17)
  A serrated flake (FT14)
  Thirty-two **retouched** flints (FT24)
A fairly large group of quartz and granite pebbles and vein-quartz fragments (121 individual finds and groups)
A relatively small, but interesting group of metalworking debris including:
  Sixteen crucible fragments (SG15.38–43, 47 and 48) including one with traces of leaded copper (37), one with gold and silver (38), one with leaded brass, bronze and silver (39), one with silver, leaded copper and brass (45) and one with brass and leaded copper (47) one with brass (44), three with bronze and brass (35, 46 and 49).
A fragmented tuyere block (SG28.3)
Numerous scraps of glassy cinder (46; 1028 gm) and a few of crystalline cinder (10: 389gm)
A small group of smithied iron debris (804 gm)
A potentially displaced Group B hearth with bellows protector fragments (SG30, 42)
Three Group B puddling hearths (SG48)
Five fire-cracked stones (18, SE 76)
Four pieces of burnt limestone (SE60)
Scraps of daub and baked clay
Scraps of mortar and clastic lime, and five pieces of rock with lime traces

Three sherd of early medieval vessel glass (GS02.V3 and two unassigned)
Three plough pebbles (SE51)

Table 6.42: Finds from **Period V** graves cutting **Period III** structures and **Period IV** buildings in the south-east part of the *outer zone*.

CHAPTER 7

Period V: Priory and Town
(*c.* 1250 x 1300–1600 AD)

Peter Hill, Dave Pollock, Damien Ronan, Andrew Nicholson

7.1 INTRODUCTION

Period V encompassed a period of about three hundred from the mid- to late-thirteenth to the late-sixteenth century, effectively ending with the Reformation. The archaeological record was dominated for much of this time by the graveyard in the northern part of the **Glebe Field**, and the most important results are the analyses of the skeletal remains (pp 519-92). Structures on the periphery of the graveyard gave valuable insight into the organization of the Priory and the evolution of the town (pp 60-5), while fifteenth and sixteenth century remains overlying the graves record significant changes prior to the Reformation.

Previous excavations. Three of the five previous campaigns of excavation have focused upon the medieval cathedral (pp 8-10), while a fourth (Tabraham 1979) exposed fragments of the northern claustral buildings. These have produced a complementary body of information recording the evolution of the priory, which is summarized in Chapter 2.

Archaeological parameters. The beginning of **Period V** was marked by the abandonment of the last **Period IV** buildings, the drainage of the lowlying ground, the demarcation of a new enclosure system centred upon the cathedral and the development of a graveyard in the northern part of the **Glebe Field** (Figure 2.22). These developments were probably not synchronous and the precise boundary between **Periods IV** and **V** is unclear. Subsequent developments over much of the site were charted by reliable stratigraphic relationships. The end of the period in the late-sixteenth century was marked by the temporary cessation of identifiable activity in the **Glebe Field**, and is intrinsically indistinct.

Stratigraphy and phasing. Most of the **Period V** remains were excavated over four seasons in 1986–89, and the relatively-straightforward sequence presented below only became evident after prolonged post-excavation analysis of a large and complex group of features, and a rich, but intransigent, assemblage of finds. The problem lies in the extensive disturbance caused by the graves, the consequent commingling of finds of different dates, and their re-stratification by worm action (Figure 6.22). These disadvantages were exacerbated by the relative shallowness of the deposits which accumulated in this period, and by extensive damage by subsequent cultivation (e.g. Figure 5.8). The **northern** and **central sectors** revealed five principal phases of activity linked insecurely to a less-satisfactory sequence of five stages in the **southern sector** (Figure 7.1). The stratigraphy of the **northern** and **central sectors** was dominated by the graveyard, but successive burials were interleaved with other features in the western part of the **northern sector**, while there was a single tenuous link with the deposits in the **southern sector**. Subsequent developments in **Phases 4** and **5** were revealed by a sequence of buildings in the eastern part of the **Glebe Field** and by poorly-preserved remains further to the west.

	A	B	C	D
11th C	•			
12th C	•	•		
1200–75	•••	•	•	
1280–1300	•••••	••••	•	
1302–1350		•••••	•	
1350–1406		•	•••	•
1413–1460		•	•	•
1460–1510	••		••••••••	•••••
1542–1588			••••	
1614–1679			•••••	•

Table 7.1: Eleventh-seventeenth century coin finds by area. **A** = Period V graves, **B** = Southern sector, **C** = Graveyard cleaning and overlying surfaces, **D** = Phase 4 and 5 buildings and related deposits.

Chronology. The relative stratigraphic sequence is generally reliable, but its chronology is problematical, despite rich finds of coins and other intrinsically-datable objects. The numismatic

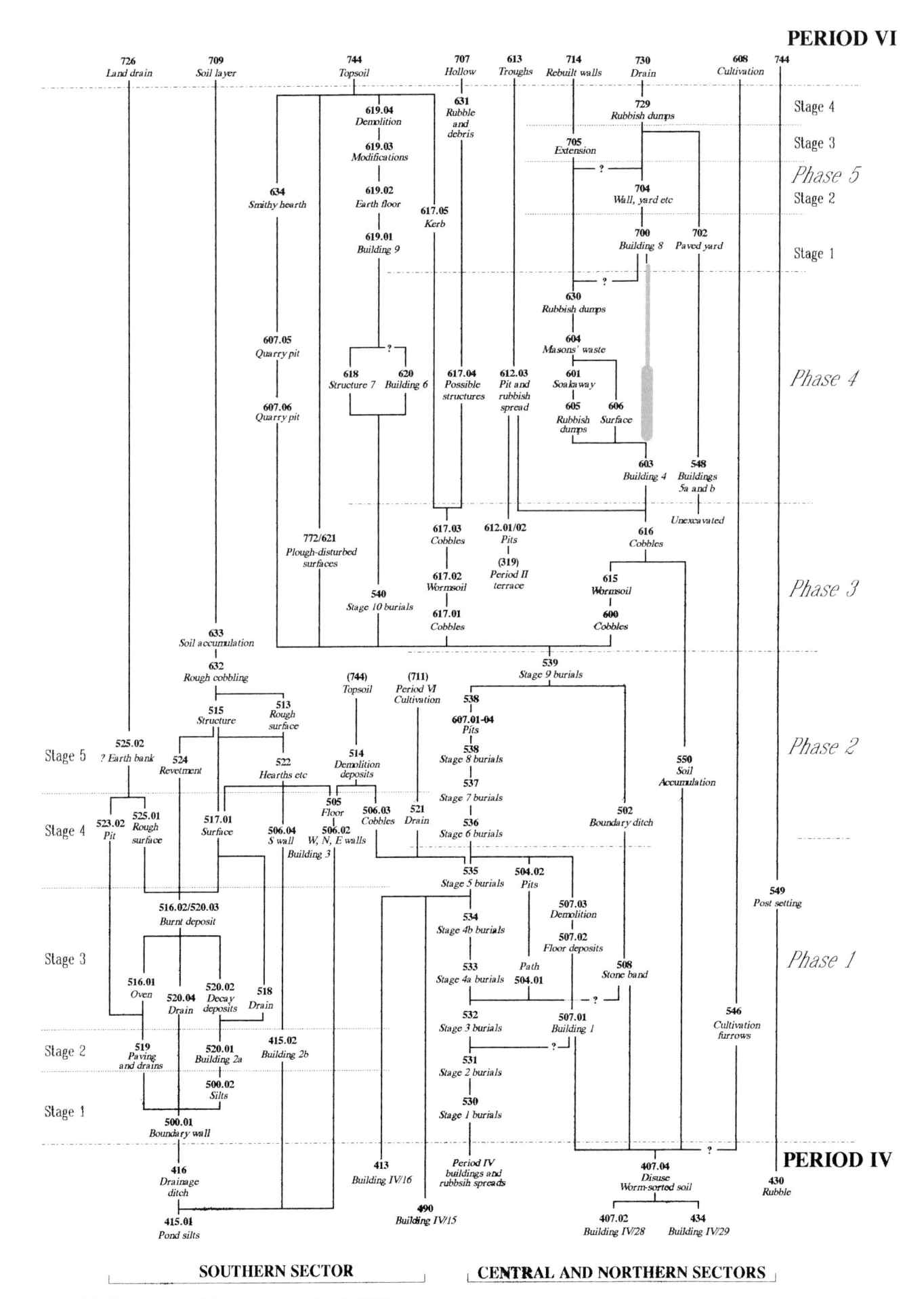

7.1 The stratigraphic sequence in **Period IV**.

evidence is elaborated below (pp 355-7) and summarized in Table 7.1. This shows a relatively clear picture in which eleventh to seventeenth century coins were initially concentrated in the *inner precinct* of the **Period IV** settlement (**A**, Figures 10.44a, 10.45) and shifted in the fourteenth century to the **Period V** deposits in the **southern sector** (**B**, Figures 10.44b, 10.46a). Later issues came from the graveyard surface (**C**, Figures 10.44c, 10.46b) and the **Phase 4** and **5** buildings (**D**, Figures 10.44c, 10.46c and d). It is argued that coins were not deposited in the graveyard while it was in use, and hence that the first burials were no earlier than the later-thirteenth century, while the last large group of graves (539, *Stage 9*) pertained to the late-fourteenth/early-fifteenth century, and the final burials (540, *Stage 10*) to the early- to mid-fifteenth century. This chronology is supported by radiocarbon dates from three skeletons excavated in 1984 (pp 597-8), although a displaced, fragmented cranium with syphilitic lesions (pp 542-4) gave a significantly later date. The coins from the **southern sector** present a relatively coherent sequence from the later-twelfth to the mid-fifteenth centuries (pp 267-8), while coins associated with the **Phase 4** and **5** buildings (Tables 7.3–5) provided an imprecise chronology for developments in the later-fifteenth and earlier-sixteenth centuries. The most surprising aspect of this chronology is the relatively brief span of the evolving graveyard, and the consequent brevity of successive phases of burial.

Finds. A large proportion of the finds from **Period V** contexts came from the graveyard (Tables 6.41 and 42), and most of these have been ascribed to the underlying **Period IV** deposits (pp 237-8). Relatively small groups can be attributed to **Period V** and probably encompass items included in burials and lost on the graveyard surface (Figure 10.49). The clearest examples were copper-alloy pins (BZ03, 4 and 10, pp 360-2), tag-ends (BZ20, p 379) and wire loops (BZ33, p 384), which were concentrated in later burials and may have secured costume or shrouds. Thirteenth to fifteenth century brooches (BZ16) and buckles (BZ18) are also likely to have been included with burials, although potentially displaced by later graves. Other finds (copper-alloy studs, mushroom-headed pins and spur rowels) from peripheral surfaces and graves probably record traffic on the fringes of the graveyard. The large assemblage of later medieval pottery posed complementary problems. Many of these finds came from the graveyard and the overlying re-stratified and disturbed deposits, and most had probably originated in earlier rubbish spreads that had been displaced. Other fabric types were concentrated beyond the graveyard and are likely to have been deposited during its use. The manufacturing debris which characterized **Period IV** was scarce, but the coins probably reflect continuing trading on the fringe of the graveyard (pp 355-7).

The graveyard. The graveyard covered most of the north part of the **Glebe Field**, and the graves in the **Museum Garden** were probably of similar date, although burial seems to have continued here into the sixteenth century. Some 1,651 graves were examined in the two areas, and the remains of 1,605 articulated skeletons were recorded. The original population was undoubtedly considerably larger, and burials probably extended to the south wall of the cathedral. The western boundary of the graveyard lies on the west side of the **Glebe Field** and the southern boundary probably lies slightly to the south of the main trench (Figures 2.22, 2.23 and 6.21). The density of burials diminished in the eastern part of the **central sector**, possibly identifying one side of a contemporary roadway on the line of Bruce Street. There were no burials in the **Fey Field** trench. The centre of the graveyard was densely populated, and successive phases of burial had virtually destroyed some earlier graves, and had probably obliterated others. It was generally difficult to distinguish the edges of individual graves and so to excavate them in stratigraphic order. The confusing picture was exacerbated by changes in the orientation of the graves (Figures 7. 2, 4 and 5) suggesting an anarchic regime of graveyard management.[1] The development of the graveyard was eventually elucidated by identifying stratigraphically-compatible groups of graves with a common orientation. This revealed eleven successive groups (530–540) encompassing ten stages (*1–10*, Figure 7.1), and spanning three phases (**1–3**) in the later-thirteenth to mid-fifteenth centuries. Major shifts in the orientation of the graves at the beginning of *Stages 2, 3, 7, 9* and *10* identify five points when the graveyard was comprehensively reorganized. This probably involved the removal of any previous grave markers, and perhaps the re-levelling of the graveyard surface. The relatively brief span of the graveyard – perhaps *c*. 150 years – implies that these major re-organization occurred at intervals of thirty years or so. Less coherent groups of burials in *Stages 4b* and *8* may, in part, represent attempts to insert extra burials into already populous graveyards.

The graves seem to have been laid out in both rows (e.g. *Stage 2*, Figure 7.2b) and strings (e.g. *Stage 3*, Figure 7.2c), but the archaeological record was generally too dislocated to identify the sequence of burials within specific phases. The evidence was somewhat clearer in the **Museum Garden**, where successive rows of burials could be identified (Figure 9.8). Male and female burials were generally distributed at random, but clusters of burials with genetically-determined traits identified possible

---

[1] One explanation was that the graves were oriented on the position of the rising sun on the day they were dug. The evidence from the 1986–7 excavation seasons was examined by Shana Tarter (1988) who found that 92% of the burials were oriented on 'summer' azimuths (March 15th–October 15th). The disproportionate number of 'summer' burials could not be reconciled with any coherent pattern of seasonal death rates and Tarter speculated that the scarcity of 'winter' burials might have resulted from overcast mornings when graves were aligned with the cathedral.

254 WHITHORN AND ST NINIAN

(a) *Stage 1* (530)

(b) *Stage 2* (531)

(c) *Stage 3* (532)

(d) *Stage 4a* (533)

(e) *Stage 4b* (534)

(f) *Stage 5* (535)

7.2 The development of the **Period V/1** graveyard in the earlier- fourteenth century.

'family plots' within specific late burial phases (p 550). Foetal, perinatal and infant burials were markedly under-represented and most casualties of this age were probably interred elsewhere. Older children were generally scattered among the adult graves, although there were occasional concentrations, most notably in the penultimate group of graves (512) in the **Museum Garden**. The *Stage 9* burials in the **Glebe Field** included a concentration of female and young (perinatal–young juvenile) burials in the north-west part of the graveyard, and there were similar groups at the north-western and south eastern extremities of the *Stage 5* graveyard (535). The large numbers of mature skeletons of indeterminate sex may have obscured other evidence of social organization within successive burial phases.

The graveyard was excavated over a period of seven years (1984, 1986–91) and a number of stratigraphic anomalies accrued. Two blocks were created to accommodate these. Block **541** contains articulated skeletons omitted from the phase scheme, and **542** contains contexts recorded during the excavation, but similarly omitted. The skeletons in **541** are included in the skeletal and dental reports and finds from **542** are treated in the same way as other groups from the graveyard (Tables 6.41 and 42). Block **543** comprised material uncovered while the surface of the graveyard was being removed to identify graves. The finds from these 'cleaning' layers included large quantities of displaced material, but had distinctive components which were either unrepresented in the underlying graves or predominated in the later graves. These included an important group of fifteenth century coins (Figures 10.44c, 10.46) which helped to establish the chronology of the graveyard, and groups of pins and other dress items associated with later graves and subsequent deposits (Figure 10.49).

7.2 THE SEQUENCE

Phase 1

Phase 1 saw the demarcation of a new enclosure system marked by a stone wall at the foot of the slope in the **Glebe Field**. This was probably part of a large oval enclosure, centred upon the cathedral, and still evident in the boundary between the **Glebe Field** and the adjacent burghage plots (Figure 2.22). There was no physical evidence of an inner boundary, but subsequent burials generally respected a limit in the south-west part of the **central sector**, and there may have been an *inner precinct*, perhaps bounded by a hedge, fence or path. The first burials in this putative *inner precinct* were probably broadly contemporary with the new enclosure, while the *outer zone* was occupied by new buildings, though perhaps less densely settled than previously.

These developments can be ascribed to the later-thirteenth century, but their chronology is somewhat ambiguous. The drainage of the low-lying ground seems to have been effected in the mid-thirteenth century (p 267), but the boundary wall oversailed a ditch, which was probably the source of late-thirteenth century shoe fragments (pp 268, 504). A stretch of walling in the **Fey Field** may have been part of this boundary (pp 289-90), but was erected after the deposition of two relatively-unworn pennies of Edward I (CN03.70 and 73) which are likely to have been lost at the close of the thirteenth century. Displaced coins in the *inner precinct* included issues of John and Henry III (Figures 6.38 and 10.45b) which were demonetised in 1279/80, and the area may have continued as a market into the second half of the thirteenth century. A speculative chronology, accommodating the diverse evidence, would date the drainage of the low-lying ground to the mid-thirteenth century, and the demarcation of the boundary and the first burials to the end of the thirteenth century. The intervening period of perhaps thirty or forty years seems to have seen continued trading in the *inner precinct*, although evidence of manufacture in this period is less easy to identify. Coins indicated that commercial activity had moved beyond the graveyard in the fourteenth century, and tenuous stratigraphic evidence from the **southern sector** indicated that **Phase 1** had ended by the mid-fourteenth century (*Stage 3*, pp 268-9).

The graveyard. The new graveyard to the south-west of the cathedral contained some 914 burials. These were generally oriented west/east (true orientation), and revealed five sub-phases (*Stages 1–5*, Figure 7.2). The graveyard did not extend into the south-west part of the **central sector** until *Stage 5*, and may have been constrained by an ephemeral boundary concentric with the outer enclosure.

Stage 1. The first group of burials (530) had been severely disturbed by subsequent graves, but included some 39 burials oriented west-east (Figure 7.2a).

Stage 2. The *Stage 2* graveyard (531) contained 167 burials oriented south-west/north-east (Figure 7.2b). These were probably aligned on the cathedral, but respected the putative southern boundary of the graveyard.

Stage 3. The *Stage 3* graveyard (532) contained 90 burials oriented west/east (Figure 7.2c). A strongly-defined string of graves indicated a boundary or edge, perhaps a path running inside the putative inner boundary. The north-west end of this string comprised six short graves which probably contained infants or children, although no skeletal remains survived in five.

Stage 4. The *Stage 4* graveyard contained 222 burials, sub-divided into two groups (533 and 534). The earlier group (533) contained 176 burials on a slightly different orientation to those of *Stage 3* (Figure 7.2d), but occupying a similar area and respecting the western part of the earlier 'path'.

The later group (534) contained some 46 burials on varying orientations (Figure 7.2e). Some can be seen as relatively late *Stage 4* graves, but others, with aberrant orientations, were perhaps squeezed into the gaps between extant rows of burials.

Stage 5. The *Stage 5* graveyard (535) was the most extensive and populous of the **Phase 1** burial groups with some 338 burials on a regular west/east orientation (Figure 7.2f). The graves extended over the *Stage 3* 'path' and beyond the inferred inner boundary. The most southerly burial underlay a cobbled surface abutting **Building 3**, and so probably predated the loss of early-fourteenth century coins from the overlying demolition deposits (pp 269-70). Two others had been clipped by a poorly-stratified drain (521) ascribed to *Stage 4* (Figure 7.15). These burials provided the only link between the graveyard and the deposits in the **southern sector**, but the relationship must be treated cautiously as they were not linked stratigraphically with the denser graves to the north, and could have pertained to an earlier phase of burial.

Features to the west of the graveyard. Structural features to the west of the graveyard comprised a band of stones, a circular building (**1**) and a shale path (Figure 7.3). Deep spade-dug cultivation furrows further to the west can also be ascribed tentatively to this phase. The band of stones (508) straddled the most westerly *Stage 3* graves, and was probably constructed in *Stage 4* or 5. It survived in a narrow strip of undisturbed ground beneath the modern field wall, but was disturbed by the **Phase 2** ditch, and covered by the **Phase 3** surface. The stones could have been the basal course of a wall, but did not have well-defined faces, and their function is unclear. The north end of this feature was abutted by a shale path (504.01) leading around the south side of **Building 1**. The path sealed the most northerly *Stage 3* graves and was later disturbed by *Stage 6* burials.

Building 1 (507) was built in a deep hollow with dished sides, cut into the northern ridge of bedrock and the flanking deposits of **Periods I–IV**. The construction hollow was abutted by two *Stage 2* graves and the building is likely to have been later. The wall was built of stone bonded with clay, and the inner face survived on the featureless, smoothed rock floor. The outer face probably rested on the rim of the construction cut, but had been completely removed, either when the building was demolished, or by the later graves. Its approximate position was indicated by two inwardly-tapering vents sloping downwards to the sunken floor, and by the shale surface (504.01) to the south of the building. The vents were too narrow to have allowed access and, though similar to the flues of a kiln, showed no evidence of fire. The demolition deposits (507.03) and an a overlying grave produced sherds of black-painted, fourteenth-century window glass which may

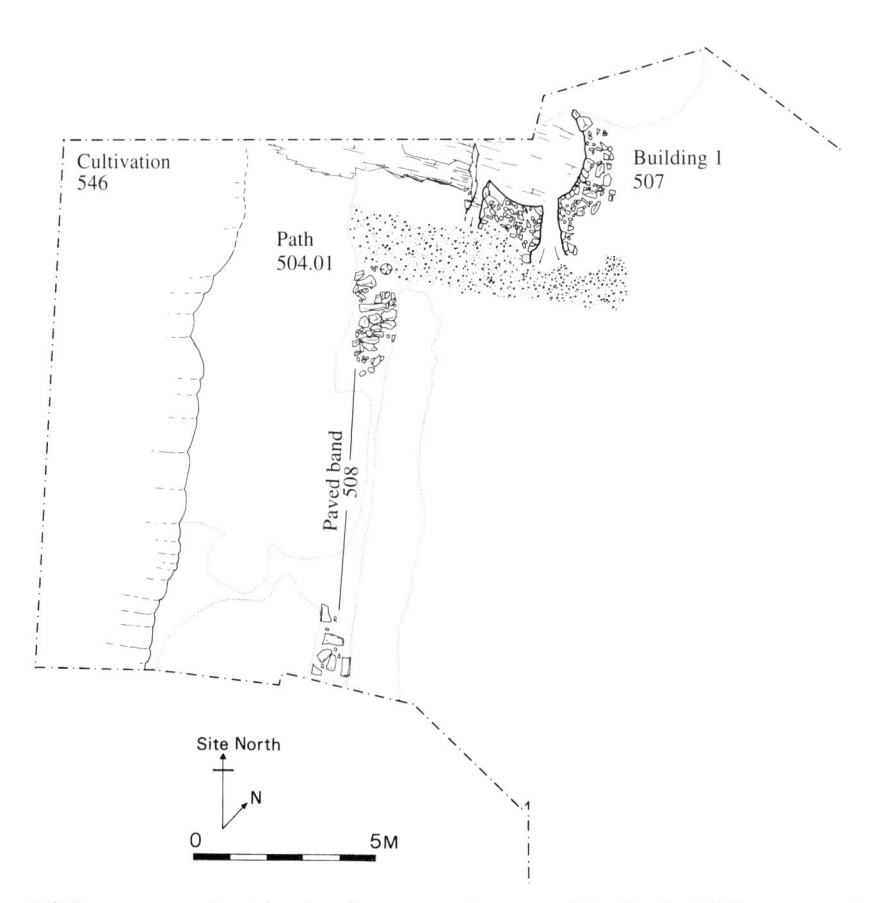

7.3 Structures and cultivation furrows to the west of the **Period V/1** graveyard.

have derived from a window in the building, and two fragments of lead window calmes (LD08.1 and 2) were found on the surface to the south. A late-fourteenth/early-fifteenth century swivel ring (BZ30.10) from the path could have been deposited in **Phase 2**. The few remaining finds from the building and its immediate environs provided no further clues to its function and date. The window glass indicated that it was a relatively prestigious building, while its location on the periphery of the graveyard suggests it could have had a mortuary function. It might have been a well-ventilated, temporary mortuary, analogous to the **Period II** chapel.

The later graves to the east of the building produced large quantities of fragmentary seashells (547) which had neutralized the affects of acid rain and soil, preserving the skeletal remains in this area. The shells are likely to have derived from a thick deposit, possibly imported for the manufacture of mortar, which was subsequently obliterated by the graves dug through it. It cannot be dated precisely, but is likely to have accumulated towards the end of **Phase 1**.

The cultivation. The ends of deep spade-dug furrows (546) some 4 m west of the stone band (Figure 7.3) revealed intensive cultivation of the ground to the west of the Priory, which was also recorded in the **Fey Field** to the north. The ends of the furrows were dug into the **Period II** terrace, disturbing the underlying seventh century rubbish spreads (85.02 etc). There were spade-marks on the floor of the furrows, and the section at the west end of the trench revealed a regular pattern of stony and less stony bands tipping consistently downwards from south to north. These record the gradual progress of a north-facing ridge moving steadily northwards, and destroying the south-facing slope of the adjacent ridge in the process. The **Fey Field** revealed two distinct phases of cultivation; one preceding and one following the erection of the putative boundary wall. The furrows at the west end of the **northern sector** were probably part of the same plot, and are likely to have had a similar history commencing in **Phase 1**, or possibly before, and continuing into **Phase 2**.

The large assemblage of finds included much displaced early material (metalworking debris, B ware pottery) as well as intrusive nineteenth/twentieth century objects deriving from the adjacent greenhouse (p 276). Two thirteenth century coins (CN03.68 and 71) were poorly-stratified, and both could have been lost on the cultivated surface or displaced from an earlier deposit (Table 7.2). The pottery included a range of fabric types, and possibly encompassed displaced material from an earlier rubbish spread and later sherds introduced with manure.

HENRY III, cut halfpenny of London, longcross, c5g–i 1251–72 (CN03.68)
EDWARD I, penny of London, cIIIg 1280–1, moderate wear (CN03.71)

Table 7.2: Coins from cultivated ground to the west of the graveyard (546)

Phase 2

Phase 2 saw the continuing evolution of the graveyard with a further four phases of burial (Figure 7.4). The transition from **Phase 1** to **Phase 2** was marked by changes on the west side of the graveyard. The round building (**1**) was demolished and the next group of burials (*Stage 6*, 536) included a cluster of graves cut into its remains. The western boundary of the graveyard was now marked by a ditch (502, Figure 7.5), and the earlier **Phase 2** burials respected a line to the east which probably marked the position of a bank. A large new building (**3**) in the **southern sector** (*Stage 4*, pp 269-70) was probably built at roughly the same time, and a new earthwork boundary between the town and the ecclesiastical precinct (*Stage 5*, p 270) was built during this phase. Coins indicated that **Phase 2** had ended by the early-fifteenth century (pp 356-7) and may have begun in the mid-fourteenth century.

Stage 6. The *Stage 6* graveyard (536) contained 68 burials with a fairly consistent south-west/north-east orientation (Figure 7.4a). They were concentrated in the northern part of the trench and possibly respected the southern boundary of **Phase 1**. An unusual gap in the north part of the site may be explained by the high density of later graves which may have obliterated further *Stage 5* burials here.

Stage 7. The *Stage 7* graveyard (537) contained 91 burials with a consistent west/east orientation concentrated in the north-east part of the field (Figure 7.4b).

Stage 8. A group of burials (538) sandwiched between the coherently-organised graveyards of *Stages 7* and *9* contained 121 burials (Figure 7.4c). These displayed a range of unusual orientations and included a small group of anomalous, crouched burials. Four distinct elements probably represent successive episodes in this confusing phase of burials:

a – Strings of burials oriented south/north separated by a gap possibly representing a path leading towards the door in the south transept of the cathedral

b – Scattered burials oriented north-west/south-east

c – Scattered west/east burials sometimes post-dating the graves in **group a**

d – Regular south-west/north-east graves which were probably relatively early *Stage 9* burials

Stage 9. The *Stage 9* graveyard (539) contained 275 burials oriented south-west/north-east, and extending into the south-west part of the **central sector** (Figure 7.4d). It was the most extensive and

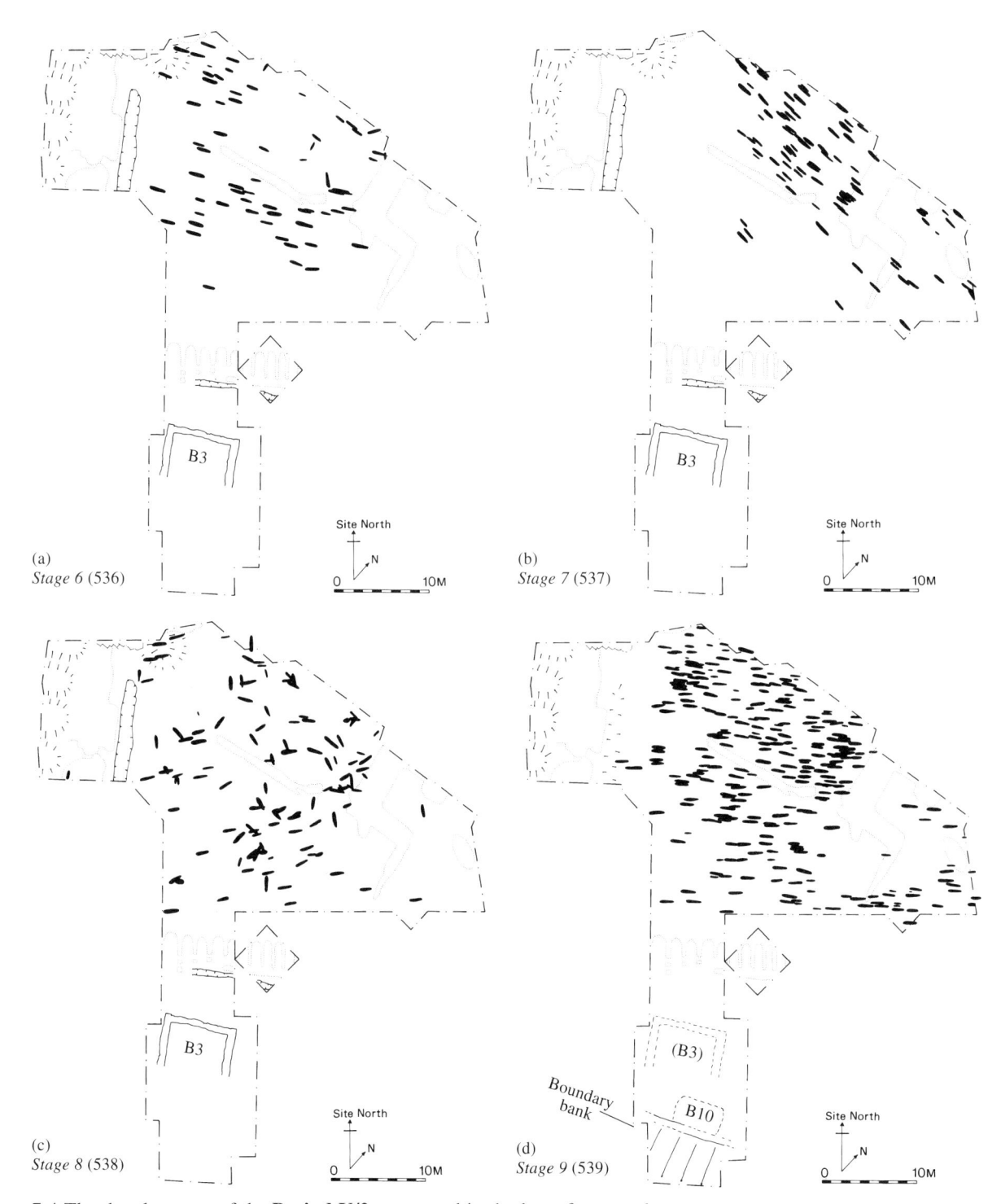

7.4 The development of the **Period V/2** graveyard in the later-fourteenth century.

populous of the **Phase 2** graveyard phases, and was probably contemporary with the later group in the **Museum Garden** (512). The graves were relatively undisturbed, and included a concentration of female and immature burials in the north-west part of the trench, and possible family plots elsewhere (p 550).

The ditch (502, Figure 7.5) was dug to the east of the earlier stone band, clipping the **Phase 1** path. The edges were poorly-defined, and three wide shallow pits on its west side could have been planting pits for hedgerow trees. The eastern side of the ditch was cut by one of the *Stage 9* graves. The soil filling the ditch produced a group of finds including displaced pottery, flints and nails. A worn penny of James I (CN03.12) belongs with a group of fifteenth century coins apparently post-dating the *Stage 9* graves (p

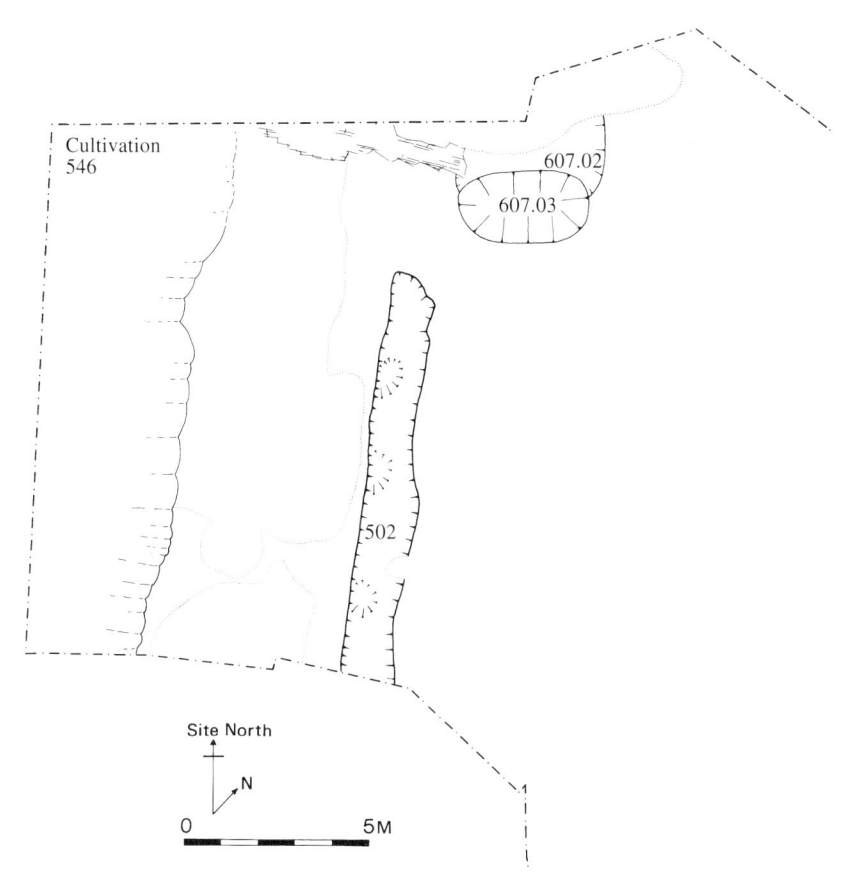

7.5 The **Period V/3** ditch and related features to the west of the graveyard.

356-7, Figure 10.46b). Successive pits cutting the remains of **Building 1**, seem to have been dug during *Stage 8*. They produced a small group of finds including nodules of copper-alloy (BZ39.21 and 22) and a droplet of silver (SR17) pointing to metalworking in the vicinity.

A regular setting of five post-holes in the western part of the **central sector** was cut into the **Period IV** levelling deposits (430). These were aligned with the *Stage 9* graves and produced later medieval pottery (MP07), but cannot be tied more closely to the sequence.

Phase 3

Phase 3 records a period of gradual change in the fifteenth century, during which the graveyard contracted to the north-east part of the **Glebe Field** (Figure 7.6). The ground beyond the graveyard revealed a sequence of surfaces and silt deposits, which apparently comprised a worm-sorted horizon covering the graves, and an overlying road surface. The latter probably formed part of a processional route leading to the west door of the cathedral. The graveyard seems to have fallen into disuse in the mid- to late-fifteenth century, but the roadway continued in use until the seventeenth or eighteenth century (pp 272, 357).

The *Stage 10* graveyard (540) contained fifty-nine burials. Most were oriented west-south-west/east-south-east and these were confined to the north-east part of the **Glebe Field** (Figure 7.12). Other graves to the south lay at right-angles to the Stage 9 burials and may record a final episode in the evolution of the **Phase 2** graveyard.

The 'roadway' covered a large part of the **central** and **northern sectors**, but had suffered extensive damage from later cultivation and other disturbances, and its full extent is uncertain. It is encompassed by three inter-related groups of contexts (Blocks 600/615/616, 617.01–03 and 772/621). The first two comprised similar sequences of stone and silt deposits in different parts of the trench. The third (772/621) were stony layers disturbed by later cultivation and contaminated with anachronous finds. One (772) lay in the western part of the **central sector**, the other (621) beside the field wall in the **northern sector**. These deposits produced a large and confusing group of finds comprising contemporary objects, displaced **Period IV** debris, and intrusive recent material. The earlier material was apparently derived from the disturbed soil filling graves, which had been restratified on the graveyard surface by worms (pp 238-9, Figure 6.22). Diagnostic finds included stick pins, comb fragments, beads and red gritty ware, and many other less diagnostic objects are also likely to have been

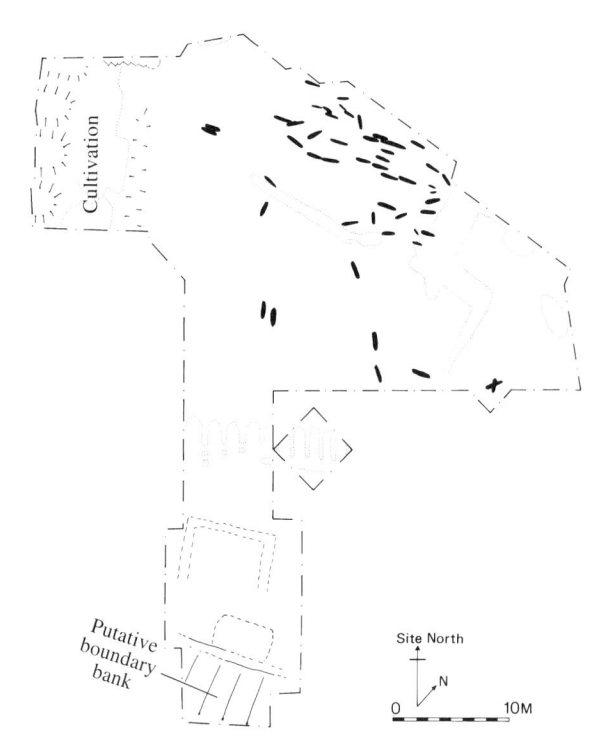

7.6 **Period V/3** graves and broadly contemporary features to the south and west.

displaced. Broadly contemporary finds included coins, spur rowels, tag-ends, wire loops and belt fittings. Some of these, notably tag-ends and wire loops, also occurred in graves, and while some could have been displaced from graves, others seem to have been debris which accumulated on the graveyard surface and the overlying road (Figure 10.49).

The stratigraphy was clearest in the eastern part of the **central sector**, where the **Phase 3** deposits were sealed by mason's debris in **Phase 4**. The **Phase 3** deposits here comprised two stony 'surfaces' (600.01 and 616.01) separated by a layer of silt (615.01). The lower 'surface' and silt produced numerous finds, including much material derived from underlying **Period IV** deposits. The upper 'surface' was virtually barren of finds, which may reflect its relatively brief exposure before it was sealed in **Phase 4**. The two lower layers probably resulted from worm-sorting of the graveyard soil (Figure 6.22), while the overlying stones were the first true surface.

The north-west sector of the roadway (616.06) oversailed the western edge of the graveyard, covering the boundary ditch (502) and an adjacent soil (550) which had accumulated in the earlier phases of **Period V**. The finds from these layers included two domed studs (BZ29.7 and 8) and two hexafoil studs (BZ21.3 and 5). These were probably belt fittings; the former dating to the fourteenth century and the latter to the fifteenth. This area also produced a large group of later medieval pottery, two spatulate-headed stick pins (BZ14.16 and 17), a coin of James I (CN03.10) and a plated fourteenth century prick spur (IN46.5). The assemblage thus ranges in date from the twelfth to the fifteenth century reflecting the shallowness of the deposit, the displacement of earlier material by the graves, and re-stratification by worms.

Phase 4

Phase 4 (Figure 7.7) dates to the later-fifteenth/early-sixteenth century, and records a relatively brief period of construction activity probably associated with the remodelling of the east end of the cathedral (p 63). The principal feature was a new building (**4**, 603) overlying the **Phase 3** roadway in the south-east corner of the trench. Its original function is unknown, as it seems to have been taken over as a mason's workshop before the debris from its construction had been cleared away. It produced a large group of builder's waste, and similar finds accumulated in other parts of the **Glebe Field**. Insubstantial buildings on the north-east side of the trench may have been temporary accommodation for the workforce.

Building 4 had clay-bonded stone walls built directly over the **Phase 3** cobbles (Figure 7.8). The northern and western parts of the building were destroyed in **Phase 5**, but the lower courses of the west wall, a short stretch of the south wall (603), and the west part of the floor had survived. A doorway in the west wall was crossed by the cast of a timber sill and had rebated sockets for the vertical timbers of the door frame. The interior was covered with layers of crushed sandstone, mortar and sand (606), which were probably trampled waste from cleaning and dressing architectural masonry. Rubbish dumps and trampled surfaces (605) beyond the west wall included spreads of builder's and mason's waste. The earliest deposits were probably derived from the construction of **Building 4**, indicating that the site had not been cleared before the masons moved in. These included a dump of clay, which was probably debris from the construction of the walls, and an overlying spread of greywacke tiles and fragments which was, perhaps, waste from roofing the building. A group of architectural fragments does not seem to have any place in this simple building and may have been removed from the Priory. Successive 'surfaces' of trampled, crushed red, pink and beige sandstone probably comprised mason's waste, and indicated sustained use as a mason's yard, though possibly over a relatively short period. The accumulation of debris seems to have affected the drainage adversely and a deep soakaway pit (601) was dug outside the north half of the west wall. The pit was filled with rubble and soil, and produced antler-working debris and a glass *tessera* displaced from the underlying **Period IV** deposits, and decaying dark amber window glass and greywacke tiles deriving from the surrounding builder's waste. Subsequent layers of crushed sandstone (604) covered the door sill and extended from the interior of the building to the yard outside.

Later rubbish dumps beyond the building (630) had been severely disturbed by subsequent features.

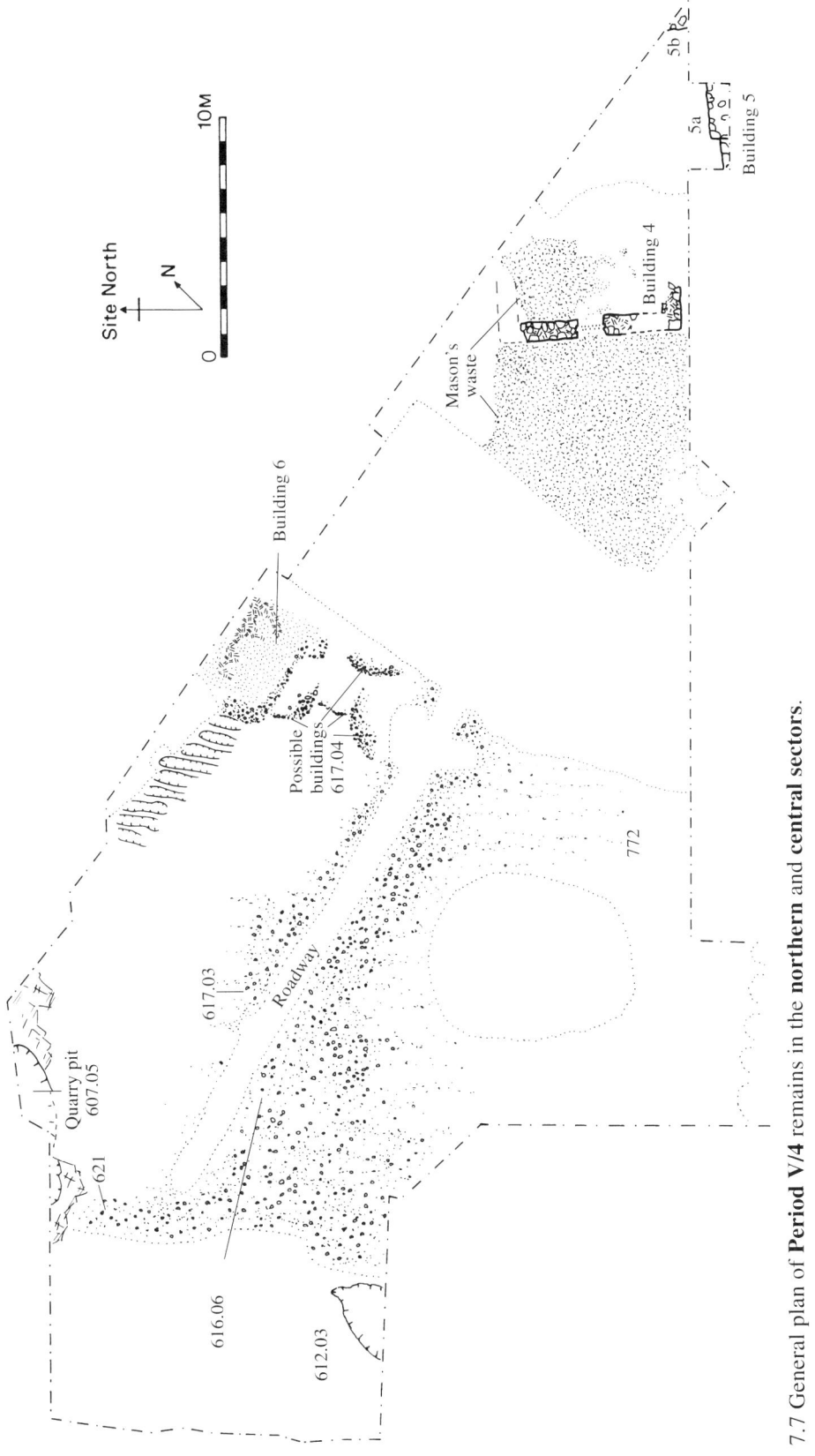

7.7 General plan of **Period V/4** remains in the **northern** and **central** sectors.

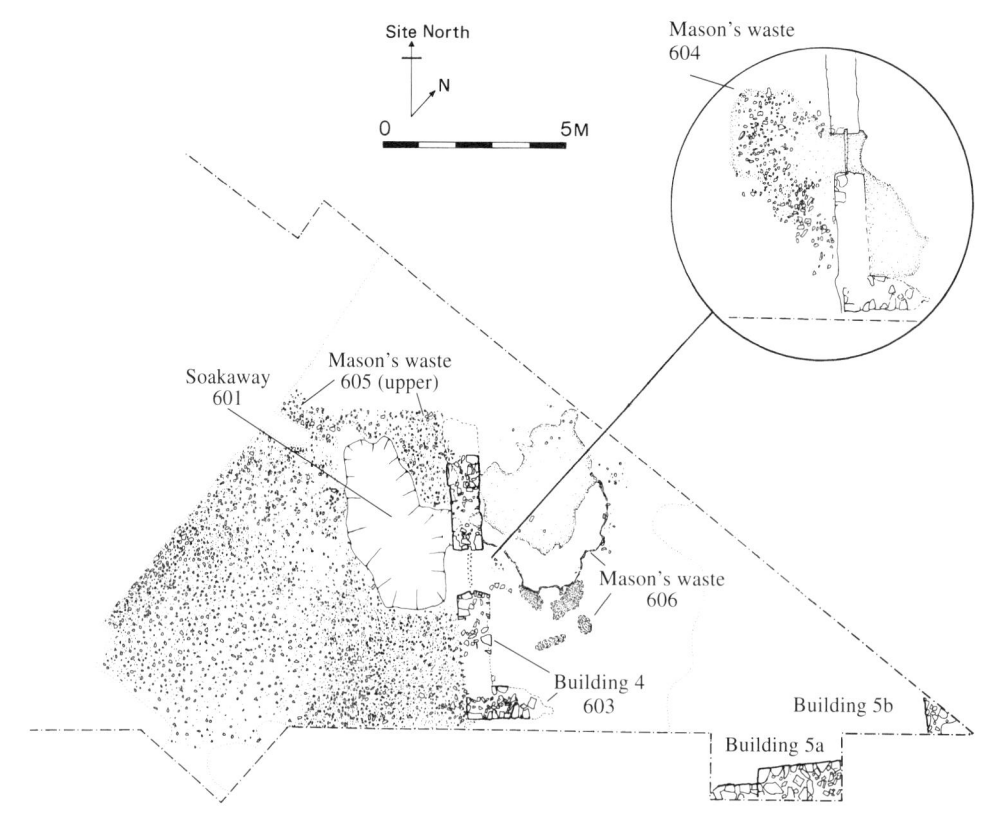

7.8 **Period V/4. Building 4** and associated deposits of mason's waste. Inset shows late deposit of mason's waste spreading to either side of the doorway.

Relatively early deposits produced a last group of architectural fragments, but there were no further layers of sandstone, which indicated that the mason's work was over. The overlying layers included spreads of broken greywacke, siltstone, meta-sediment and phyllite tiles, encompassing the full range of stone tiles used at Whithorn before the introduction of slate in the nineteenth century (pp 445-7). As **Building 4** seems to have been tiled with greywacke and siltstone, the tiles in this later deposit probably came from other buildings, and hint that tilers moved in after the masons. Numerous crumbs of decaying dark amber window glass (GS07) and two lead window-calme fragments (LD08.4 and 5) indicated temporary occupation by glaziers, who may have left a stone calme mould (SE47.2) recovered from a **Phase 5** context in the vicinity. Tools comprised three awls (IN50.29, 30 and 77) and a wedge (IN53.7), while seventeen rolled tag-ends (BZ20.73–89) might have been part of a tradesman's stock.

JAMES III, copper farthing, 1st issue 1465–6, very worn (603, CN03.27)
ENRIQUE III, billon blanca of Burgos 1390–1406, fairly worn (605, CN03.92)
JAMES II, penny of Edinburgh, 1st coinage 1437–51, gD (630, CN03.14)

Table 7.3: Coins from **Building 4** and related deposits.

The deposits associated with **Building 4** produced three coins (Table 7.3), of which the latest (CN03.27) came from the clay bonding of the west wall, while the earlier issues came from later contexts. Two slightly later coins (CN03.17 and 32), associated with the construction of the overlying 'Commendator's house' (Table 7.5), probably originated in the debris surrounding **Building 4**, and were paralleled in the mud-floored building (**6**) to the north-west (Table 7.4). These finds argue that **Building 4** must have been later than the worn farthing of James III (CN03.27), and that it was probably in use during the currency of the Crvx Pellit pennies, and possibly the plack of James IV. **Phase 4** may thus be ascribed to a relatively brief period in the closing decades of the fifteenth century and opening years of the sixteenth (p 357).

Truncated stone walls to the south-east of **Building 4** (Figure 7.8) mark another building or buildings (**5a** and **b**, 548) demolished in **Phase 5**, which may have been erected in **Phase 4**. These unexcavated buildings were aligned with the cathedral and lay within the ecclesiastical precinct, but their function is unclear. The burials of **Phases 1** and **2** were less dense on the east margin of the trench, and **Buildings 5a** and **b** could have been built while the graveyard was still in use. The north-east corner of **Building 5a** was exposed in 1972 (Tabraham 1976, Trench A), and re-examined when the adjacent paved courtyard was excavated in 1988. This revealed the corner of a mortared stone building, abutted by a wide clay-bonded stone wall. The building seems to have been demolished in the early-sixteenth century when **Building 6** was erected, but the inferred sequence may be incorrect - and this could have been the

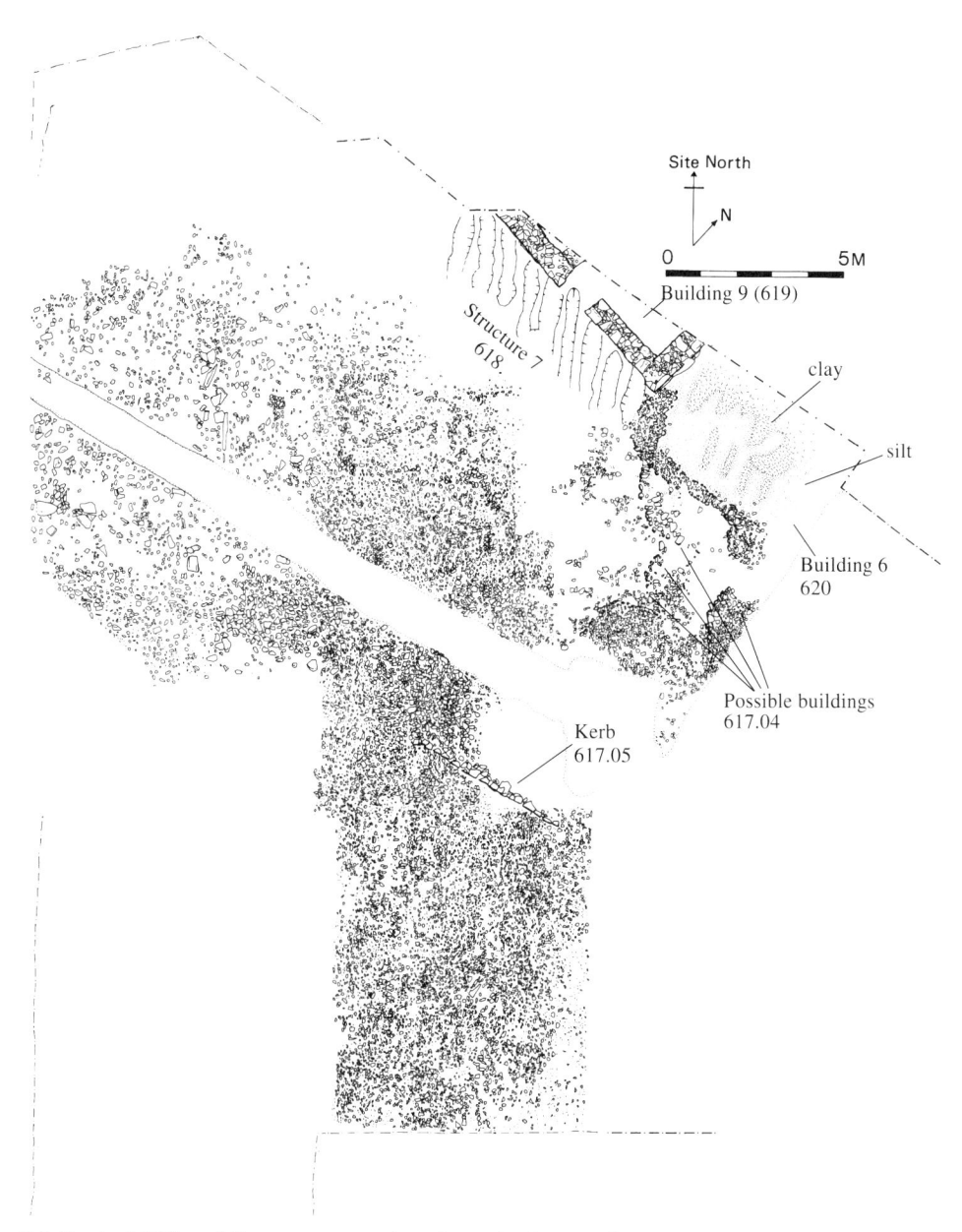

7.9 **Period V/4** and **5** structures and surfaces in the **northern** and **central sectors**.

building depicted in an early nineteenth century water-colour of the priory (Figure 8.2). **Building 5b** was represented by a truncated wall incorporated in the paved courtyard to the east of **Building 8** (Figure 7.11).

Temporary buildings and other construction features. The **Phase 3** graves were oversailed by a complex group of fragmentary structural remains which may represent the temporary accommodation of the workforce and other site buildings (Figure 7.9). Large quarry pits on the north edge of the trench probably pertained to this phase.

Building 6 (620) lay on the north-east side of the trench, and seems to have been a sub-rectilinear, earth-floored, wattle-walled structure. It was represented by layers of silt, capped by a spread of clay, and bounded to the south-west and north-west by shallow gullies, which were overlain by rough cobbling. The silt layers probably comprised successive earth floors, while the overlying clay was perhaps a collapsed daubed wall. The gullies may have been foundation trenches for wattle walls which were abutted by the cobbles. The numerous finds from the building included human bones, antler fragments, quartz pebbles and red gritty ware deriving from the graveyard and underlying rubbish spreads, and occasional intrusive finds of later date (eighteenth century bottle fragments). Two coins of (Table 7.4) indicated a date in the late fifteenth/early sixteenth century, while scraps of mortar, nails, tag-ends (BZ22.69–72) and sherds of iridescent and blue-tinged window glass may also have been contemporary debris.

CRVX PELLIT issue, tIIa later 15th C, moderate wear (CN03.18)
JAMES IV, plack, uncertain type 1488–1513, folded in half (CN03.30)

Table 7.4: Coins from **Building 6** (620)

Structure 7 (618) lay to the north-west of **Building 6**, and comprised nine closely-set narrow trenches packed with rubble and clay. The trenches had been truncated by the foundations of **Building 9** and tailed out to the south. A small group of finds was probably displaced from the underlying graves and gave no clues to the function of this unusual structure.

The ground to the south-west of **Building 6** revealed discrete areas of rough cobbling and arcs of angled stones (617.04), which were probably the remains of other wattle-walled, earth-floored buildings. The cobbles may have been the foundations of earth floors, while the arcs of stones indicated the rounded corners of stake-walled buildings. These fragmentary features were overlain by a spread of rubble (631) which produced a small group of mid-sixteenth century coins (Figure 10.46d).

Two large intersecting pits (607.5–6) were cut into the bedrock ridge on the north edge of the trench (Figure 7.7), disturbing the earlier graves and the northern side of the **Building 1**. The pits were probably dug to quarry the outcropping greywacke, and were filled with layers of rubble, animal bones and seashells. These produced numerous finds including architectural fragments, a possible sculptural fragment (SE14:10), mortar, nails and tiles of greywacke and phyllite. The assemblage is similar to the builder's debris associated with **Building 4**. Sheep bones predominated among the faunal remains (pp 605-7), and the workers were perhaps fed mutton. Large numbers of oyster, periwinkle and cockle shells may also represent food waste, but might have been gathered for shell mortar, or as a metal-working flux. A few heat-glazed fragments of sandstone were probably linked to a spread of similar stones to the south. A small group of metal-working debris included fragments of the dense smithying hearths which become common at this time, and a chunk of glassy cinder containing partly-fused shell fragments. The only dating evidence was a sherd of post-medieval oxidised pottery (MP10).

A shallow hollow to the south (612.03) was dug through the **Phase 3** surface, truncating two earlier pits (612.01 and 02). It was covered by a layer of stony soil which produced a large group of finds including a Crvx Pellit coin (CN03.19), a fourteenth or fifteenth century tripod foot (BZ30.27), pottery, nails and metalworking debris. The coin indicated that this material pertained to **Phase 3** or **4**, and the metalworking debris points to a smithy in the vicinity. The underlying pits may have been dug to rob facing stones from the **Period II** terrace. One (612.02) contained a few sherds of later medieval pottery and can be ascribed safely to the earlier part of **Period V**.

Phase 5

Phase 5 saw the construction of a large stone building (**8**) immediately to the north of the now derelict mason's workshop. It later became the manse, and the Hearth Tax returns of 1692 indicated that, with five hearths, it was the largest building in the Burgh. This may reflect its sixteenth century status, and it can be identified tentatively as the Commendator's house. An early-nineteenth century water-colour (Figure 8.2) depicts the building, much modified, with a main block of two stories, two extensions to the south-west, and a large two-story extension to the north-west. The **Phase 5** remains were highly fragmentary, but probably comprised the western part of the main block and the adjoining extension to the south-west. A fragment of a mortared stone wall under the north-west wall of the west wing of the eighteenth century manse could have been part of the original building. Features in and around the building revealed four principal phases of activity (*Stages 1–4*). The first probably pertained to the first half of the sixteenth century, and the fourth may have extended beyond **Period V** into the seventeenth century. Debris in a sunken courtyard included a small group of fine wares, pointing to the prosperity and status of the inhabitants. The ground to the west produced scattered sixteenth century coins (Figure 10.46d), and was probably still used as a roadway to the cathedral. A stone building (**9**) to the north may have pertained to this phase (Figure 7.10).

Stage 1 saw the construction of the main block of **Building 8** (Figure 7.11). Only the south-east wall (700) survived, but subsequent structural modifications indicated the positions of the south-west and north-west walls. The surviving wall (*c.* 1.0 m wide) was built of unmortared stone resting on foundations some 1.7 m wide. A door was indicated by a probable step on an external 'kerb', and was abutted by a pebbled path leading to the south-east. Two post-sockets rebated into the outer wall are unexplained. The floor of the building had been dug away when a new floor (703) was laid in the eighteenth century. A Crvx Pellit coin (CN03.17) from the foundations may have originated in the debris surrounding **Building 4**. The new building incorporated the north part of the east wall of **Building 4**, and the rest of this wall seems to have survived as a boundary, the doorway now serving as a gate. The sunken courtyard to the east of the building (702) probably dates to this time, although it could have been constructed in *Stage 2*.

Stage 2 saw modifications to the south-east wall and the ground to the east (704, Figure 7.12). An addition to the south-east wall of the original building may have been the base of an external stair, and stones curving to the south-east indicated the line of a new boundary around an extended yard surfaced with cobbles. This boundary was subsequently robbed out, but a stony spread, and an overlying layer of ash and

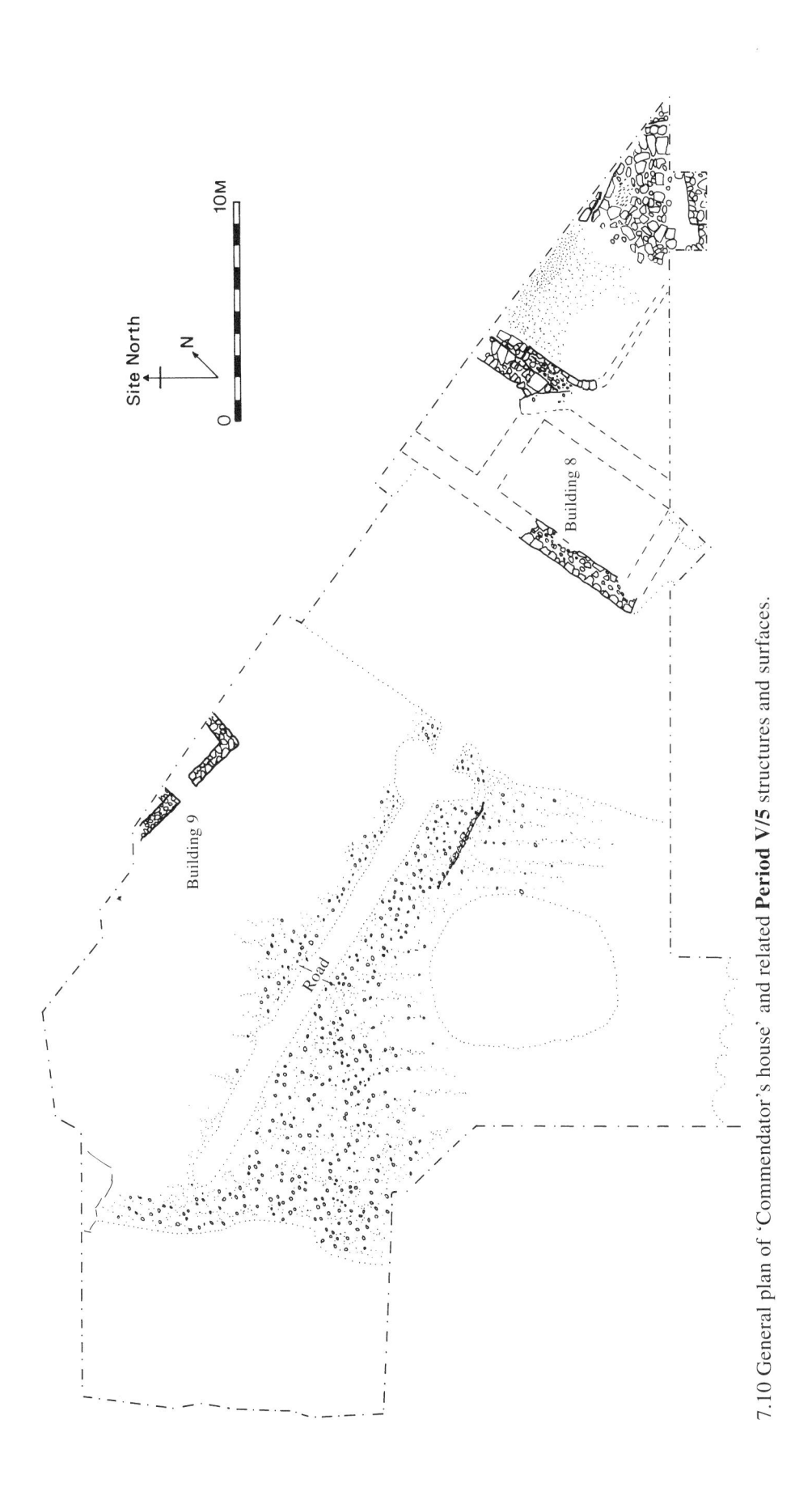

CHAPTER 7

7.10 General plan of 'Commendator's house' and related **Period V/5** structures and surfaces.

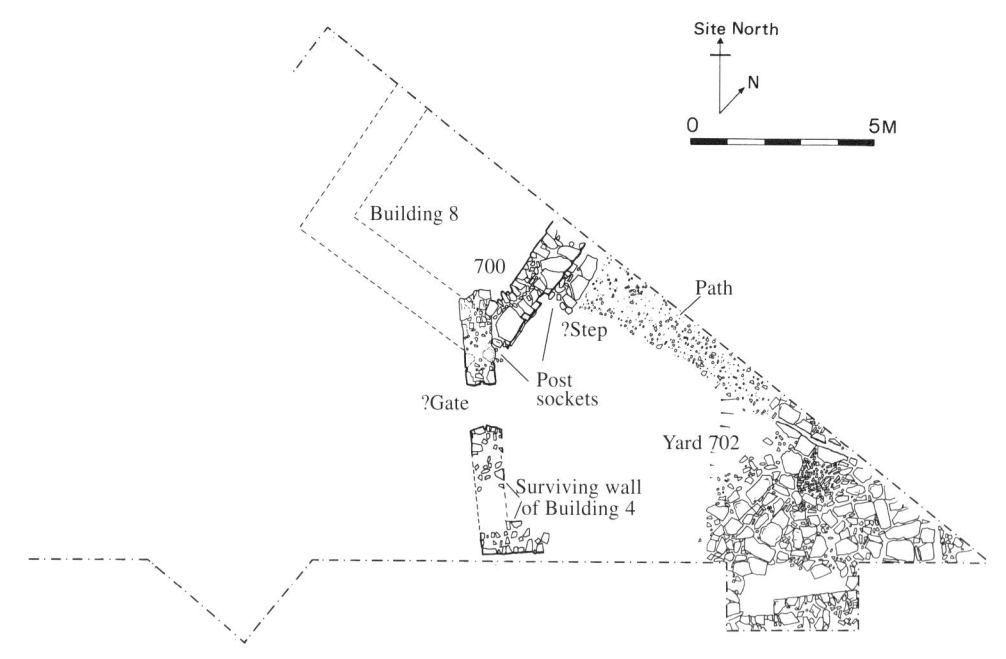

7.11 Fragmentary remains of original **Period V/5** building (*Stage 1*) and adjacent path and yard.

debris, had survived. The ash extended to both sides of the robber trench, and produced a large group of pottery, including parts of five vessels of hard post-medieval oxidised ware (MP10), scattered sherds of the equivalent reduced ware (MP09), pieces of two Beauvais ware platters (MP13, Vs 1 and 2), and fragments of a possible Jordan or urinal (MP35). These were the earliest well-stratified examples of these wares, which may thus have been introduced in the early- to mid-sixteenth century. Fragments of blue and green-tinged window glass mark another new technology, which rapidly replaced the earlier window glass, still seemingly current in **Phase 4**. Other finds included four wire loops (BZ33.10–13), and a stone calm mould (SE 47.2), possibly displaced from a **Phase 4** context. The west wall of **Building 4** seems to have been demolished at the start of this phase, and the robber trench produced more sherds of reduced ware (MP09) and two wire loops (BZ33.14 and 15). An isolated patch of debris underlying the *Stage 3* wall (705) included other sherds from the vessels represented in the ash, and hence giving

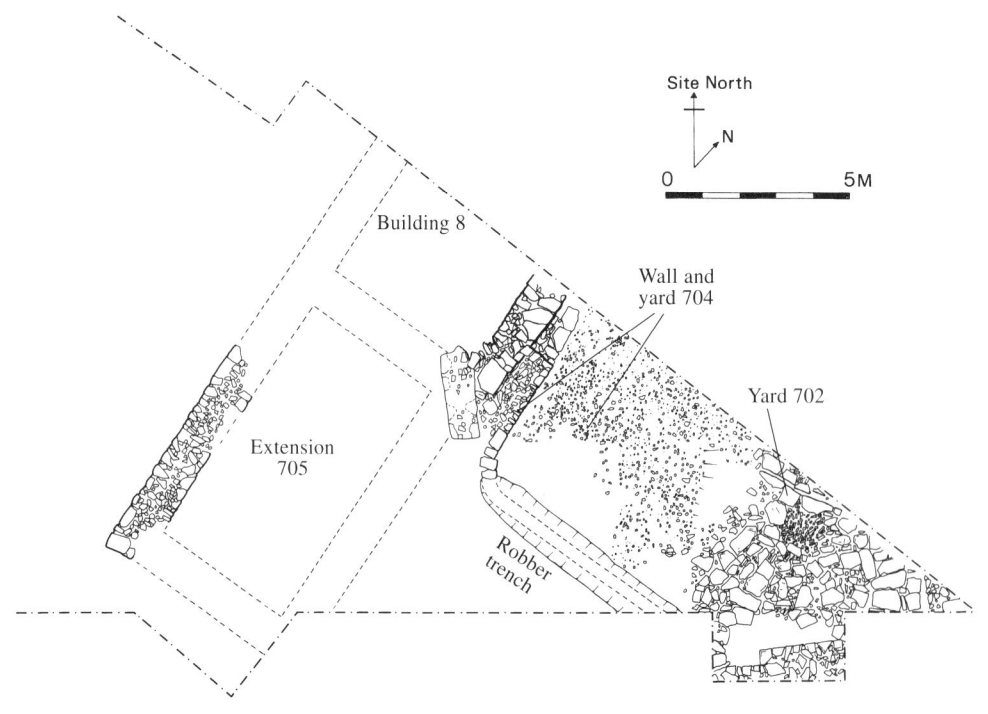

7.12 **Period V/5**. The 'Commendator's house' after modifications in *Stage 2* and the building of an extension in *Stage 3*.

reliable evidence of the construction sequence. The most surprising find was a horse's skull placed in the foundations of the external stair.

Stage 3 saw the construction of an extension (705) at the south-west end of the **Building 8** (Figure 7.12). The basal courses of the unmortared north-west wall survived, with a probable return at the south-east end. A late-fifteenth century penny (CN03.32, possibly 1489–90), found close to the north-west wall of the extension, probably originated in the debris surrounding **Building 4**.

Stage 4 records a period of disuse, and possibly repair, represented by rubbish deposits (729) filling the sunken courtyard to the east of **Building 8**. These had been disturbed by eighteenth/nineteenth century features, and truncated by twentieth century cultivation, but they produced a valuable assemblage of sixteenth/seventeenth century pottery, intermingled with broken stone tiles. The latter may have derived from the adjacent building, and suggest a phase of decrepitude or repair, possibly in the late-sixteenth or earlier-seventeenth century. The pottery included a range of imported wares (MP18, 19, 21and 25), and sherds of post-medieval oxidised (MP10) and reduced wares (MP09) potentially displaced from underlying *Stage 2* contexts.

CRVX PELLIT issue, tIb later 15th C, slight-moderate wear (**700**, CN03.17)
Late 15th C billon penny, probably of James IV, tIa *c.* 1489–90 (**916**, CN03.32)
JAMES VI, post-Union twopence, 2nd issue 1623 (**729**, CN03.44)

Table 7.5: Coins from **Building 8** and related contexts

Outbuildings and surfaces. The ground to the north-west of **Building 8** revealed vestigial evidence of a rectangular compound containing a second stone building (**9**) on a similar alignment. The most tangible evidence for the compound was an insubstantial stone kerb aligned with **Building 8**. The ground beyond it produced a large group of seventeenth century coins (Figure 10.46d), suggesting that it remained in use as a public thoroughfare and informal market, whereas the putatively enclosed ground produced only one coin of this date. Extensive spreads of rubble and silt (631) produced a large group of finds, including displaced eleventh-thirteenth century debris, sixteenth century coins and pottery, and sherds of seventeenth and eighteenth century bottle glass. A large group of metalworking debris was characterised by dense smithying 'hearth bottoms'; an undated smithying hearth (635) to the north-west is the most likely source of this debris, and might account for a large group of nails and other iron objects recovered.

Building 9 (619, Figure 7.9) had clay-bonded stone walls set in shallow stone-filled foundations trenches which were cut into the **Phase 4** structures and the underlying graves. Layers of clayey silt on a rubble substratum marked successive earth floors (619.02).

In a second phase of use the door was blocked and an internal stone partition was erected (619.03). The demolition of the building was marked by a deep, internal deposit of rubble and clay (619.04). The sparse finds gave no evidence of the date or function of the building.

A stone structure (635) overlying the **Phase 4** pits on the northern edge of the trench was probably part of a smithy hearth extending northwards into unexcavated ground. A large group of metalworking debris included concreted smithy waste and 3.5 kg of glassy cinder. Two pieces of non-ferrous 'slag', and fragments of lead (LD11.109) and bronze (BZ41.45) hinted that metals other than iron were being worked.

7.3 THE SOUTHERN SECTOR

The **southern sector** revealed a sequence of thirteenth and fourteenth century structures which were effectively unlinked to the remains in the northern part of the site. The earliest feature was a wall crossing the southern part of the area, which was probably part of a new curvilinear enclosure system (pp 60-1), and subsequently evolved into a earthwork boundary between the ecclesiastical precinct and the town. The other structures in the area were aligned with this boundary, and included successive buildings, apparently continuing the earlier pattern of an outer residential zone surrounding an *inner precinct*. The ground beyond the boundary revealed a distinct sequence of features, but the area examined was too small to identify their function.

The stratigraphy of this area (Figure 7.1) was somewhat fragmented, and recent cultivation and land drains had disrupted the upper layers. The record was, moreover, compromised by over-hasty excavation of the waterlogged deposits at the south end of the trench, which displaced and confused a group of shoe fragments and other datable artefacts. There were separate sequences to either side of the wall, and the features in the north part of the area were not linked with those to in the south. The proposed sequence of five stages (*1–5*, Figure 7.1) is potentially flawed, and the building (**3**) ascribed to *Stage 4* could have been built in *Stage 3*. Disturbance is probably less severe in the ground to the east, which may well preserve a more detailed picture of developments in the later-thirteenth and fourteenth centuries.

The area produced a useful assemblage of coins including more than half of the issues of Edward I. The earliest coins were a worn sterling of David I (CN03.1) from the **Period IV** silts (pp 225-6), and a relatively unworn Henry III penny (CN03.65) from an isolated patch of ash adjacent to **Building 2**. The latter was poorly linked into the **Period V** sequence, but provides an approximate *terminus* for **Period IV** in the mid-thirteenth century. Four coins of Edward I (CN03.72, 75, 76 and 80) were secreted in a *Stage 3* oven (516.01) to the south of the wall. The latest of these (CN03:80) is the most worn, indicating that the hoard was deposited in the early- to mid-fourteenth

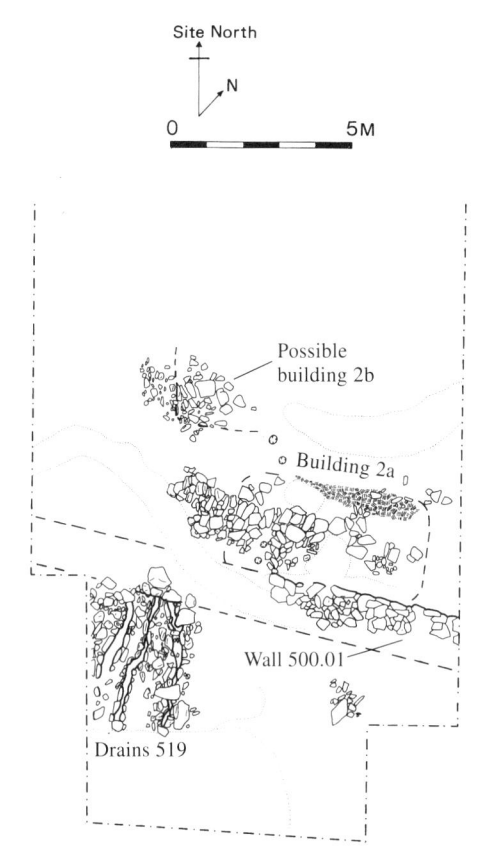

7.13 **Period V**. The *Stage 1* wall and *Stage 2* buildings in the **southern sector**.

century. The relatively unworn earlier coins had probably been withdrawn from circulation as savings at an earlier date. Three further coins of Edward I came from the demolition deposits in **Building 3** (514, CN03.77 and 78) and the overlying topsoil (744, CN03.82). These were probably broadly contemporary with the coin hoard, and indicated that the *Stage 4* structures had been replaced by the mid-fourteenth century. Coins of Edward III (CN03.84), David II (CN03.5) and James I (CN03.11) came from *Stage 5* contexts. These probably post-dated the construction of the new earthwork enclosure which can thus be dated to the mid- to late-fourteenth century. The scarcity of later issues, which were relatively numerous to the north (Figures 10.44c and 10.46b-d), points to a prolonged period of disuse in the fifteenth to seventeenth centuries.

Other finds are detailed in the excavation archive. These included a large group of later medieval pottery consisting largely of local oxidized (MP02) and reduced wares (MP07). The latter predominated in later deposits, but there was too much contamination to elucidate a detailed sequence of fabric types. There were large groups of nails from several deposits, but the tools and manufacturing waste which characterized the underlying **Period IV** structures were absent. The function of this area thus seems to have changed, although its new role is not clear.

Stage 1 followed the drainage of the low-lying ground (p 227), and saw the construction of a dry stone wall some 1.0 m wide (500.01), apparently marking a new outer boundary (Figure 7.13). The east end of the wall was abutted to the north by a rough stone surface, which was in turn overlain by waterborne silt (500.02). Sparse finds included a limited range of oxidised and reduced green-glazed pottery. The wall oversailed a ditch (416) which cut the **Period IV** pond silts, but was not recognised until most of the silt filling it had been removed. A large group of finds, recovered while the silt deposits were being removed, included an Hiberno-Norse stick-pin (BZ14.26), comb-making debris, twelfth and thirteenth century shoe fragments, and sherds of later medieval reduced ware (MP07). The range of dates indicates that this material included finds from the **Period IV** ditch (417.02) as well as more recent objects. The later ditch (416) was probably the source of a group of leatherworking debris, including a range of stitched strap fragments (LR24), a late-thirteenth century shoe upper (LR17.6) and a mid-thirteenth to mid-fourteenth century turnshoe sole (LR19.3).

Stage 2 saw the construction of a small sub-rectilinear building (**2a**, 520.01) immediately to the north of the boundary (Figure 7.13). A second patch of paving (415.02) to the north may have been part of the floor of another building (**2b**), which had been damaged by a later structure (**3**). The south side of the wall was abutted by an area of paving oversailing three closely-set, stone-lined drains (519).

Building 2a (520.01) probably occupied a shallow, sub-rectilinear hollow cutting the *Stage 1* silts, and presumably had wattle walls, although little evidence survived. A primary pebbled floor was overlain by paving, and was bounded to the north by a low ridge of clay, which probably marked the base of a daubed wall. Paving at the west end of the building seems to have been a secondary addition. The sub-rectilinear plan was similar to the latest **Period IV** building (IV/16), but **Building 2a** did not have the distinctive opposed doorways and central hearth (Figure 6.12).

The finds from these features included a limited range of oxidised and reduced local green-glazed pottery, and sherds of thirteenth century Saintonge ware (MP12/02). The paving in **Building 2a** included a broken rotary-quern stone (SE 43:14), crudely made from a block of dressed architectural sandstone which may have originated in the twelfth century cathedral. An underlying layer of ash produced a second rotary quern-stone segment (SE 43:3), an iron taper holder (IN76.2) and three worked flints. **Building 2b** produced a silver ring (SR3), a possible crushed barrel padlock (IN33.12) and a key or bolt fragment (IN34.12).

Stage 3 saw extensive damage to the boundary wall, which was cut by a sinuous stone-lined drain (520.04), while a small, stone-floored, clay-walled oven (516.01) was built to the south of the wall, cutting into the earlier paving (Figure 7.14). Spreads of clay on the floor of **Building 2** indicated the decay

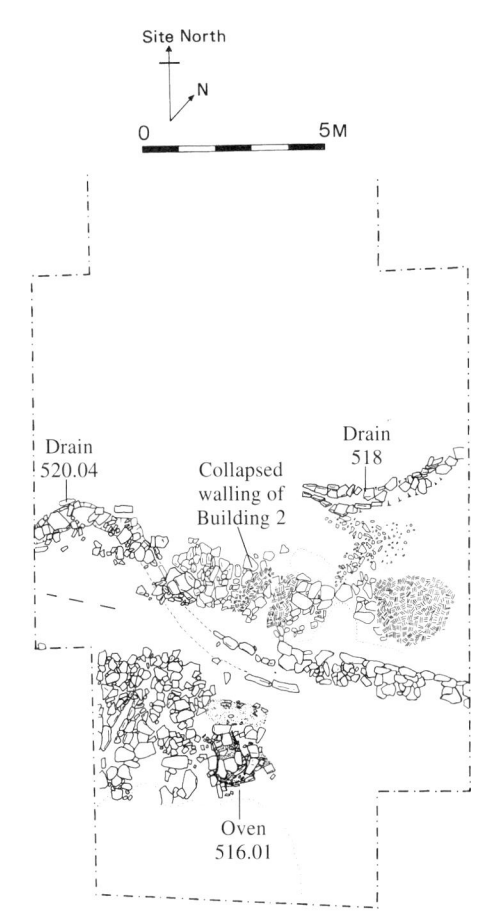

CHAPTER 7 269

remains had been disturbed by recent cultivation and land drains.

Building 3 was defined by three clay-bonded walls (506.02) which occupied shallow foundations (506.01) cutting the **Period IV** rubbish deposits and the buildings to the north. A fragmentary south wall (506.04) was indicated by patches of clay and a line of large stones. The north wall was abutted by a cobbled surface (506.03). A spread of orange ash on the east part of the floor (505) may have been fire debris associated with the destruction of the building. The abandoned building was covered with rubble and soil (514), which produced two worn pennies of Edward I (CN03.77 and 78) and a large group of pottery. The coins are likely to have been deposited in the mid- to late-fourteenth century and, as the building seems to have been later than the coin hoard, it is likely to have had a relatively short life in the mid-fourteenth century. A moderately worn silver half groat of David II (CN03.5) from shale on the

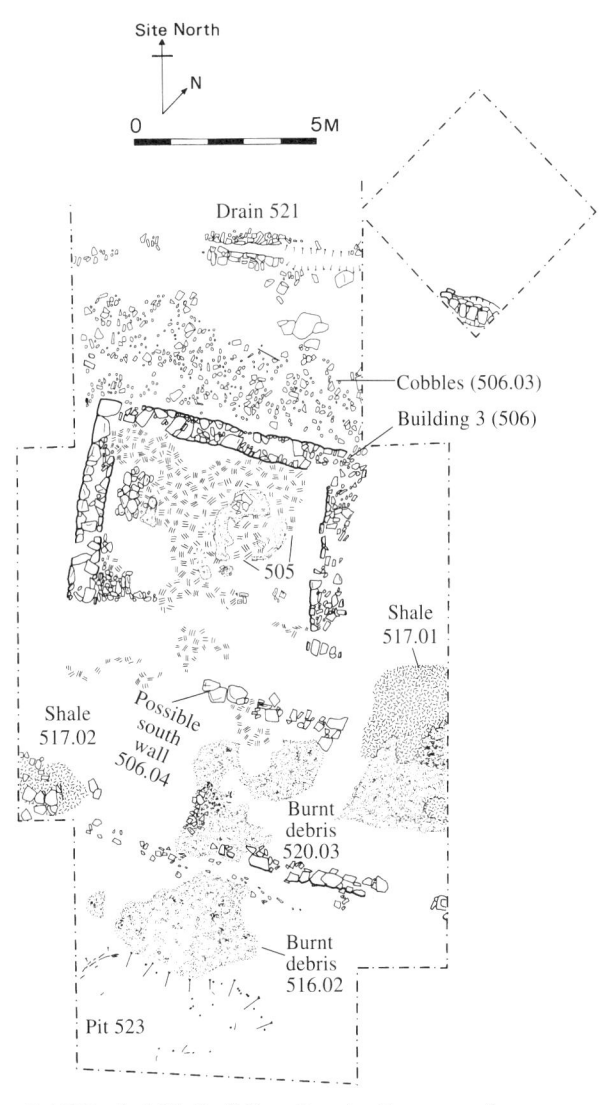

7.14 **Period V**. Debris overlying **Building 2** and related *Stage 3* features in the **southern sector**.

of daubed walls, and a cobbled surface to the north was cut by a second, curving drain (518). The end of *Stage 3* was marked by a spread of orange ash and burnt debris (516.02/520.03) covering the oven, the drain and **Building 2a** (Figure 7.15).

The finds from these features were dominated by sherds of local green-glazed pottery with a marked increase in the proportion of reduced wares. The collapsed walling in **Building 2** produced a round-headed stick pin (BZ14.12), presumably displaced from an earlier context. The hoard of four pennies from the oven dated this stage to the early- to mid-fourteenth century (pp 267-8).

Stage 4 (Figure 7.15) saw the construction of a large, stone-founded building (3, 506) to the north of **Building 2**. It was aligned with the boundary, although the adjacent stretch of walling seems to have been dismantled at this time. A cobbled surface and stone-lined drain (521) to the north postdated the most southerly **Phase 1** burials (535), and the building was probably contemporary with the earlier stages of the **Phase 2** graveyard. Spreads of shale on the east (517.01 and .03) and west (517.02) sides of the trench may have been the remains of a path to the south of the building. The ground beyond the boundary revealed a stony spread (525.01) and a large stake-lined pit (523). There were few stratigraphic links between these features, and the

7.15 **Period V**. **Building 3** and adjacent surfaces (*Stage 4*), and underlying burnt debris from the end of *Stage 3*.

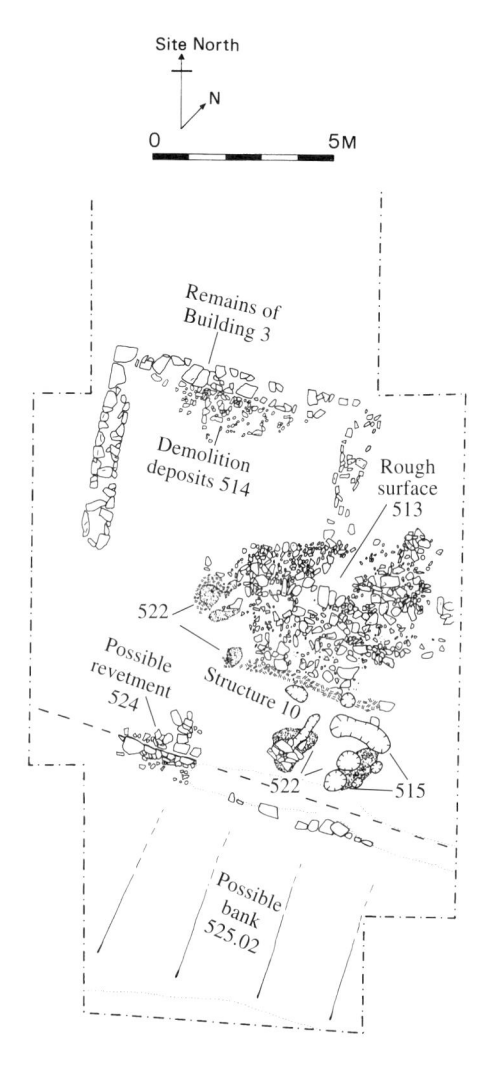

7.16 **Period V**. Fragmentary *Stage 5* remains in the **southern sector**.

east side of the trench (517.03) indicated a slightly later date, but could have been deposited in *Stage 5*.

The *Stage 4* deposits produced numerous finds including large groups of pottery, nails and other iron artefacts. The finds from the foundations of **Building 3** (506.01) were extensively contaminated with **Period IV** material. The other groups have greater integrity.

Stage 5 saw the construction of a new boundary, which was indicated by the tail of an earthen bank extending into the south part of the trench (Figure 7.16). Features cutting the remains of **Building 2** revealed continuing activity in the south part of the area, followed by a long period of disuse which was marked by spreads of rubble (632, 560) overlain by a worm-sorted soil (633). The *Stage 5* remains had been severely disturbed by recent cultivation and field drains (Figure 8.7).

The earthwork bank probably underlies the stone wall separating the town from the **Glebe Field**. The tail of the bank (525.02) extended into the trench, and was contained by a new stone revetment (524) on the line of the original boundary. This suggests that the earlier wall survived elsewhere, and demarcated the north side of the bank, while the new revetment represents a repair in the breach to the south of **Building 3**. The new wall produced a relatively unworn penny of Edward III (CN03.84) indicating that the bank was built in the mid- to late-fourteenth century. An insubstantial and amorphous structure (**10**) overlying **Building 2**, was indicated by a group of pits and post-holes (515) cutting earlier hearths and ash spreads (522). A band of clay indicated a possible daubed wall to the north, and was abutted by a rough stone surface (513) which oversailed the remains of **Building 3**. This fragmentary structure occupied the same stance as **Building 2**, and may have been of similar size. It may thus represent the reconstruction of the *Stage 2* building after the fire at the end of *Stage 3*. A worn billon penny of James I (CN03.11) from the overlying rubble (560) was probably deposited in the later-fifteenth century, and marked the end of the series of later medieval coins from this area.

The groups of finds from the *Stage 5* deposits were generally small, and the later layers (632) were contaminated with recent material. Early post-medieval material was sparse, and the coins and pottery suggested that activity here had virtually ceased by the mid- to late-fifteenth century. The collection included a fourteenth century sword pommel (BZ 30.29) and an early plated barrel-padlock (IN33.11). The latter indicates that **Period IV** finds were still being displaced and redeposited, and the earth bank may have been the source of some of this material.

CHAPTER 8

After the Reformation

Peter Hill, Andrew Nicholson, Damien Ronan

Introduction

The quality of the archaeological record changed after the Reformation and the pace of activity slowed down until the **Glebe Field** finally reverted to pasture in the 1960s. The 'Commendator's house' served as the parish manse until 1813 and remained standing until the late-nineteenth century. Most of the archaeological features recorded related to the development of this building and the cultivation of the adjacent ground. The stratigraphy was straightforward (Figure 8.1) and there were three principal phases of archaeological activity. The manse revealed a long structural history and there was a relatively complex sequence of cultivation remains in the **southern sector**. There was little archaeological activity in other parts of the site, although ploughing and other disturbances had displaced numerous earlier objects. The large assemblage of finds is generally unexceptional, and is documented in the excavation archive.

Phase 1: *c.* 1600–1750

The 'Commendator's house' had become the parish manse by the late seventeenth century, but there seem to be no records of it in the preceding century; the archaeological story peters out in a poorly-dated period of neglect in the late-sixteenth or early-seventeenth century (**Period V/6.3**). The central and western parts of the **Glebe Field** produced a scatter of seventeenth century coins of low denomination (Figure 10.46d), suggesting that the earlier roadway continued in use, apparently skirting the old 'Commendator's house', and leading to a new doorway at the west end of the church. Three coins from soil banked against the west wall of the **Glebe Field** (Table 8.1) span the late-sixteenth/later-seventeenth century, and suggest that the wall was built in the early-seventeenth century.

JAMES VI, hardhead, 1st issue August 1588, very little wear (CN03.40)
CHARLES II, turner 1663, very worn (CN03.59)
ORANGE: FREDERIC HENRI DE NASSAU, copper double tournois 1625–47 (CN03.90)

Table 8.1: Coins from soil abutting field wall (610.03)

This period of relative inactivity lasted until the mid- to late-eighteenth century, and the principal evidence of occupation was a scatter of late-seventeenth and eighteenth century bottle glass in the general vicinity of the manse. There were no complementary finds of clay pipes, and this doubtless reflects the low social status of tobacco smoking, and the acceptability of wine among the higher classes.

Phase 2: *c.* 1750–1900

Renewed activity in the mid- to late-eighteenth century saw the construction of a new wing on the north-west side of the manse, and extensive rebuilding of the original building (Figure 8.3). This probably took place during the long ministry (1743–94) of Andrew Adair, a wealthy landowner, who is buried in the parish kirkyard, and is represented in the archaeological record by a bottle stamp marked:

And
Adair
1777

A new manse was built to the north of the church in 1813, and the church was itself replaced in 1822, leaving the truncated nave of the cathedral as a roofless shell. The original manse was next used as a schoolmaster's house; subsequently as girls' school and soup kitchen, and eventually as the dower house for a minister's widow. Cultivation remains in the western part of the **Glebe Field** probably spanned **Phase 2**.

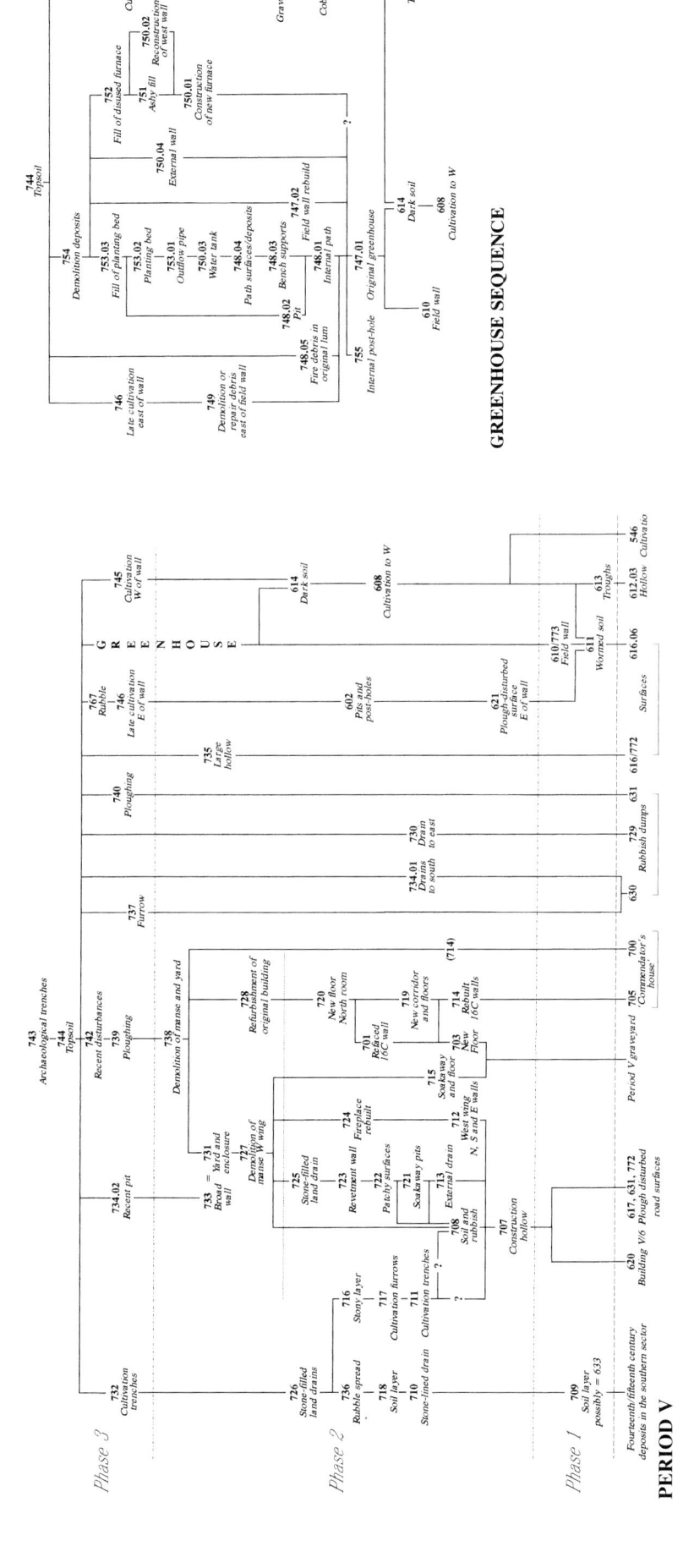

8.1 The stratigraphic sequence in **Period VI**.

8.2 Detail from an undated nineteenth century water-colour showing the Old Manse after the erection of the west wing.

Stage 1. The new wing of the manse was built in a deep hollow (707) which had removed most of the underlying **Period V** graves, and was flanked by a deep rubble-filled drain (713) cutting the underlying subsoil. Drainage was a persistent problem, and a cluster of pits (721) post-dating the drain were probably intended as soakaways. The walls of the new wing lay in shallow foundation trenches which disturbed the upper layers of the **Period I/2** 'shrine'. A rectangular, rubble-filled pit in the east corner of the building was probably a soakaway, and caused further damage to the underlying deposits (Figure 8.4).

An early-nineteenth century water-colour (Figure 8.2) depicts the west wing as a two storey building. The ground-floor room had a fireplace and recessed cupboard in the north-west wall, and two window alcoves in the south-west wall (Figure 8.5). The impressions of timber joists overlying builder's debris attest a wooden floor (715). A doorway in the south-east wall led into the original sixteenth century building, and a second doorway in the south corner opened onto a roughly-surfaced path (722) flanking the north-west wall of the sixteenth century extension. The original building was comprehensively remodelled, and probably largely rebuilt, at the same time. A new north-west wall (714) was built beside the west wing, and the south-east wall may also have been renewed. Successive floors of rough cobbling and beaten clay in the north-east part of the building (703) seem appropriate to a scullery or kitchen, and hint that the original building now housed the domestic offices, while the public rooms were in the new western wing. A corridor leading from the door into the west wing represented a subsequent redesign of the internal arrangements of the old building (719). A layer of pea grit may have been the bedding for a flagged floor. The room to the north was resurfaced with clay, indicating that its former function was maintained, and overlying mortar floors (720), flanked by a wooden partition in the north-east part of the room, recorded subsequent refurbishments. Vestigial joist impressions show that the room to the south-east now had a wooden floor. Minor modifications to the west wing saw the rebuilding of the fireplace on two occasions (724).

Stage 2 (Figure 8.6) saw major structural changes in which the west wing was demolished (727) and replaced by a walled yard (731), while the main part of the building was once again remodelled[1] (728). This involved blocking the former door to the west wing, and subsequently rebuilding the central and north-east parts of the north-west wall of the main block. A possible flagged floor in the north-east room was marked by a mortar screed on foundations of crushed red sandstone. The remains of the west wing were covered with levelling deposits of crushed red sandstone and broken slates which were trampled to form a yard. This was surrounded by a stone wall with mortared foundations. The function of three large post-holes was unclear.

Cultivation remains in the **southern sector** produced large groups of eighteenth and nineteenth century pottery and glass, mixed with displaced earlier material, and probably mark the vegetable garden of the manse. The earliest features were narrow spade-dug trenches running west/east. These were cut by broad furrows running north/south (717), later covered by a spread of stones (716), and subsequently cut by deep rubble-filled land drains (726). A stone-lined and, presumably, flag-capped drain to the south (710) lay close to the surface, and was probably of similar date, although it produced no post-medieval finds, and might have been as early as the fifteenth century. A stone-filled land drain to the north (725) ran into the yard outside the manse. A large shallow pit (735) at the west end of the **central sector** had disturbed the **Period V** graves and underlying **Period IV** deposits. It was filled with layers of rubble and silt, and produced eighteenth and nineteenth century material, as well as displaced finds of earlier date. Its purpose is unclear. The **Market Garden** was also cultivated during this phase, and revealed possible furrows (613) disturbed by ploughing (608).

[1] These changes were not dated closely, but might have coincided with the tenancy of the relict of Reverend Jardine, which commenced in 1878 (Anon n.d., 83). A fragment of an Anglian cross shaft (Whithorn 2; Radford and Donaldson No. 5) was recovered when the Old Manse was demolished some time prior to 1891 (Craig 1992 III, 292). This is likely to have been the partial demolition which initiated *Stage 2*, rather than the final demolition which seems to have been rather later.

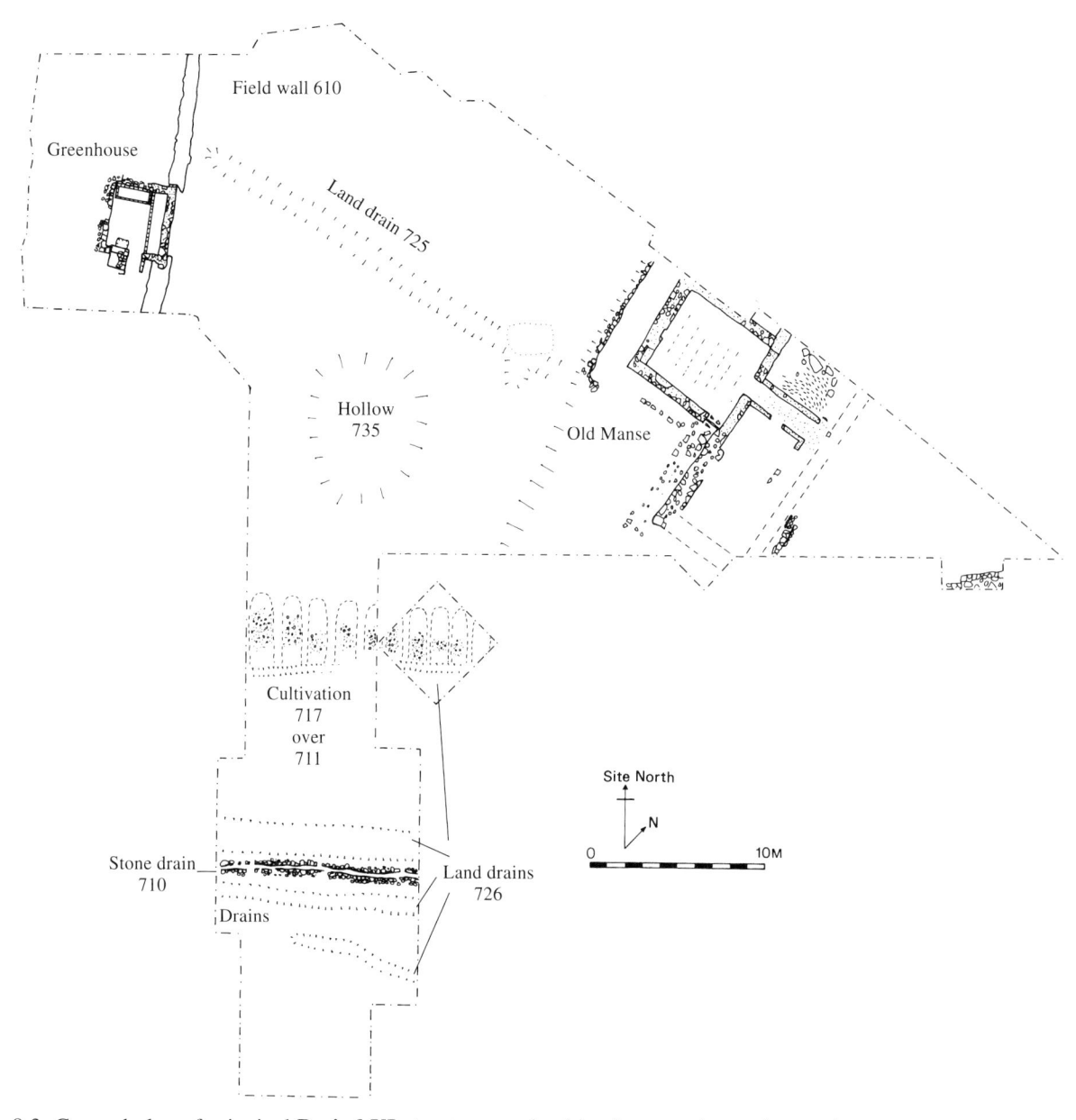

8.3. General plan of principal **Period VI** structures and cultivation remains to the south.

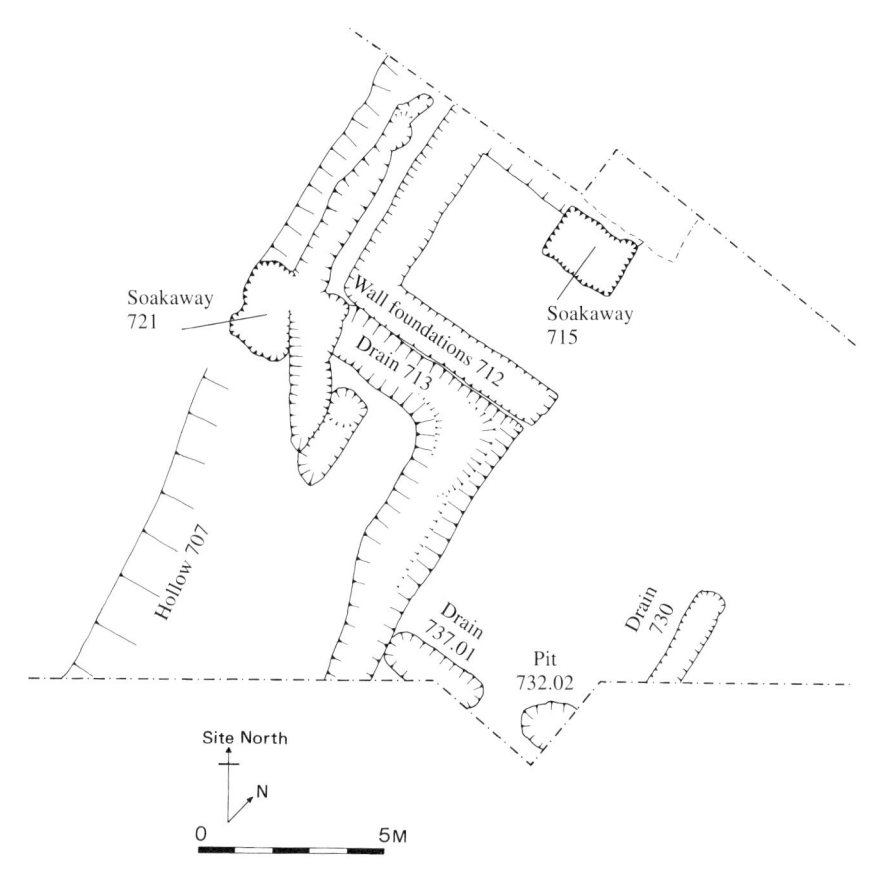

8.4. **Period VI** features disturbing earlier deposits in the eastern part of the **central sector**.

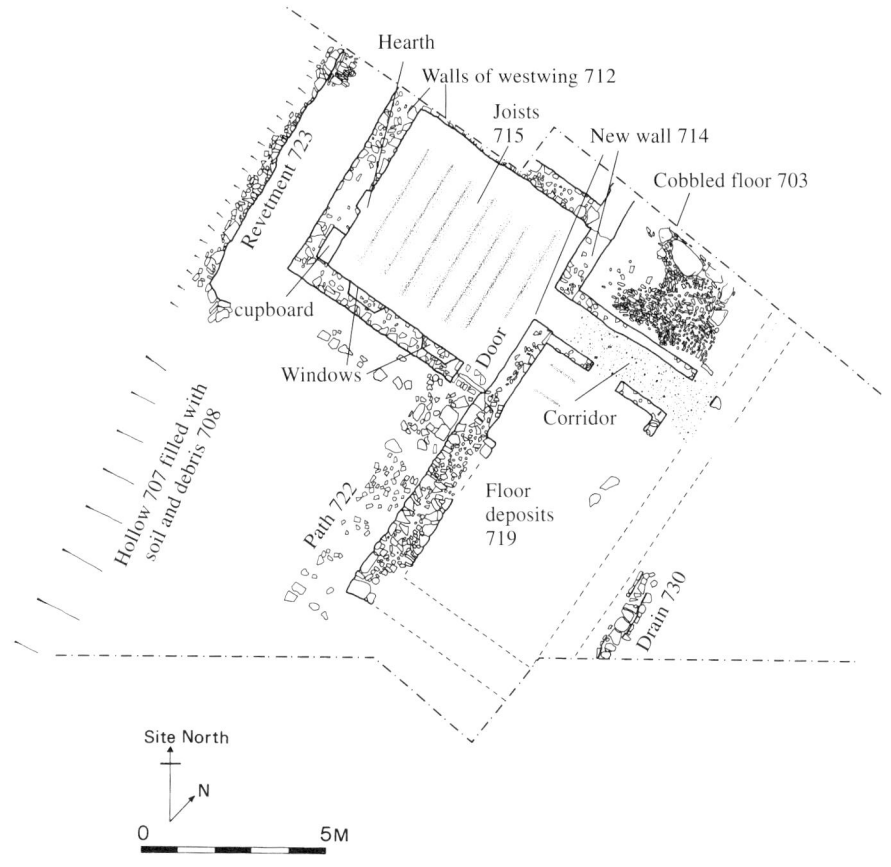

8.5. The manse after the erection of the west wing in the eighteenth century (**Period VI/2.1**).

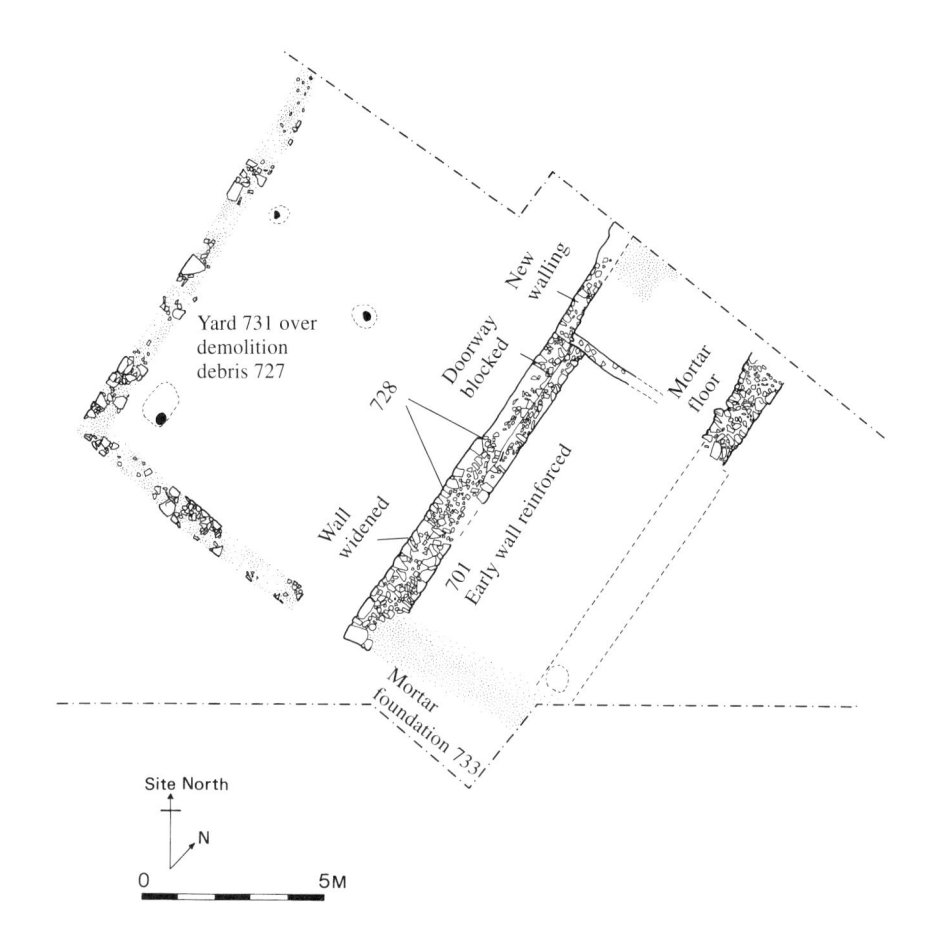

8.6. The Old Manse after reconstruction in **Period VI/2.2**.

Phase 3

Phase 3 carries the story into the present century. A market garden was established in the late-nineteenth century in the **Market Garden** field, and cultivation extended to the **Glebe Field** after the old manse was demolished. One of the greenhouses in the **Market Garden** was excavated in 1989, and revealed a detailed structural history. It had been built into the field wall (610), and had a sunken floor dug down to the level of the Northumbrian terrace. It contained a planting bed and water tank, and was equipped at an unknown date with a coal-fired heating system. Abundant finds included broken window and bottle glass, sherds of terracotta flower pots, iron heel protectors, lamp chimney fragments, the roots of a vine and the bowl of a briar pipe. Cultivation in the **Glebe Field** was marked by plough scores recorded in most parts of the trench (739, 740, 746), and by medieval and post-medieval finds displaced into the topsoil. An equivalent ploughsoil in the **Market Garden** (745) respected the greenhouse, and produced *inter alia* a sixteenth century silver-mounted cabochon of smoky quartz (SR4).

CHAPTER 9

The Museum Garden and Fey Field Trenches

Peter Hill, Jo Moran, Andrew Nicholson

THE MUSEUM GARDEN
Peter Hill and Andrew Nicholson

A small trench was excavated in the winter of 1989–90 to allow the construction of a courtyard linking the back of the Historic Scotland museum with the south doorway of the crypts (Figure 9.1). This involved the removal of the kirkyard wall which overlay builders' debris from the late-nineteenth century renovations of the crypt by William Galloway (pp 8-9). This exposed an earlier kirkyard wall, a flanking track, and a gateway leading to Bruce Street. These features overlay a burial ground which was probably broadly coeval with the **Period V** burials in the **Glebe Field**. The graves had penetrated the bedrock over a large part of the area, and earlier medieval deposits had only survived in the southern part of the trench, and in a narrow strip to the north. These early layers produced relatively few finds, but larger groups of material from the graves and subsequent deposits seem to have been displaced from them. The results would have seemed disappointing without the organisational evidence from the **Glebe Field,** and the contrasting range of finds that it produced. These indicated that the **Museum Garden** trench had lain within the *inner precinct* in **Period I** (Figures 2.2, 4–6), and that it may have been on the periphery of the settled area in the latter part of **Period III**, and throughout **Period IV** (Figures 2.14, 16, 19 and 20).

Stratigraphy and phasing. The stratigraphic sequence is illustrated in Figure 9.2. Most of the relationships were clear despite the relative shallowness of the strata and the extensive disturbance by graves. The sequence is divided into three phases. **Phase 1** encompassed the fragmentary remains preceding the later medieval graveyard, and corresponds with **Periods I–IV** in the **Glebe Field. Phase 2** equates with **Period V,** and saw the development of a graveyard, the construction of a new crypt in *c.* 1500, and continuing burials in the sixteenth century. **Phase 3** corresponds with **Period VI,** and was marked by a period of disuse in the sixteenth-eighteenth centuries, followed by the construction of the cottage now housing the museum, the erection of a new kirkyard wall, and latterly the reconstruction of the crypts.

Chronology. The **Museum Garden** produced few closely-datable objects from secure contexts, but a tentative chronological framework can be erected on the bases of these and other evidence. The principal elements are:

1 Part of a timber building aligned with the **Period II** structures in the **Glebe Field,** and probably part of the middle range of halls (Figures 2.9).
2 A spread of debris (408.01) producing two mid-ninth century coins, and possibly dating to the first reign of Aethelred II at the close of **Period II**.
3 A later-twelfth/thirteenth century deposit underlying the **Phase 2** graves, and contributing pottery and other finds to these and later features.
4 The construction of a new barrel-vaulted crypt towards the end of **Phase 2**, which can be ascribed to the building operations recorded during the reign of James IV, and equated with **Period V/4** in the **Glebe Field**.
5 The reconstruction of the crypt by William Galloway in the late 1880s.

The other stages in the sequence can be related to these horizons, although independent dating evidence was frequently missing.

Finds. The excavation produced a valuable group of finds, but most of the earlier material had been displaced by graves, cultivation and construction. The absence of specific types of objects found in the **Glebe Field** is of particular interest, and has significant implications for the evolving organisation of the site. Such gaps include the earlier types of early medieval pottery and glass (A and B ware, Group A and B glass vessels), and twelfth–sixteenth century coins. The finds included a relatively large group of later medieval pottery, but the tools and manufacturing debris which characterised the **Period IV** deposits in the **Glebe Field** (pp 235-50) were scarce.

THE SEQUENCE

Phase 1

Developments in the early medieval period were represented by a limited area of stratified material in

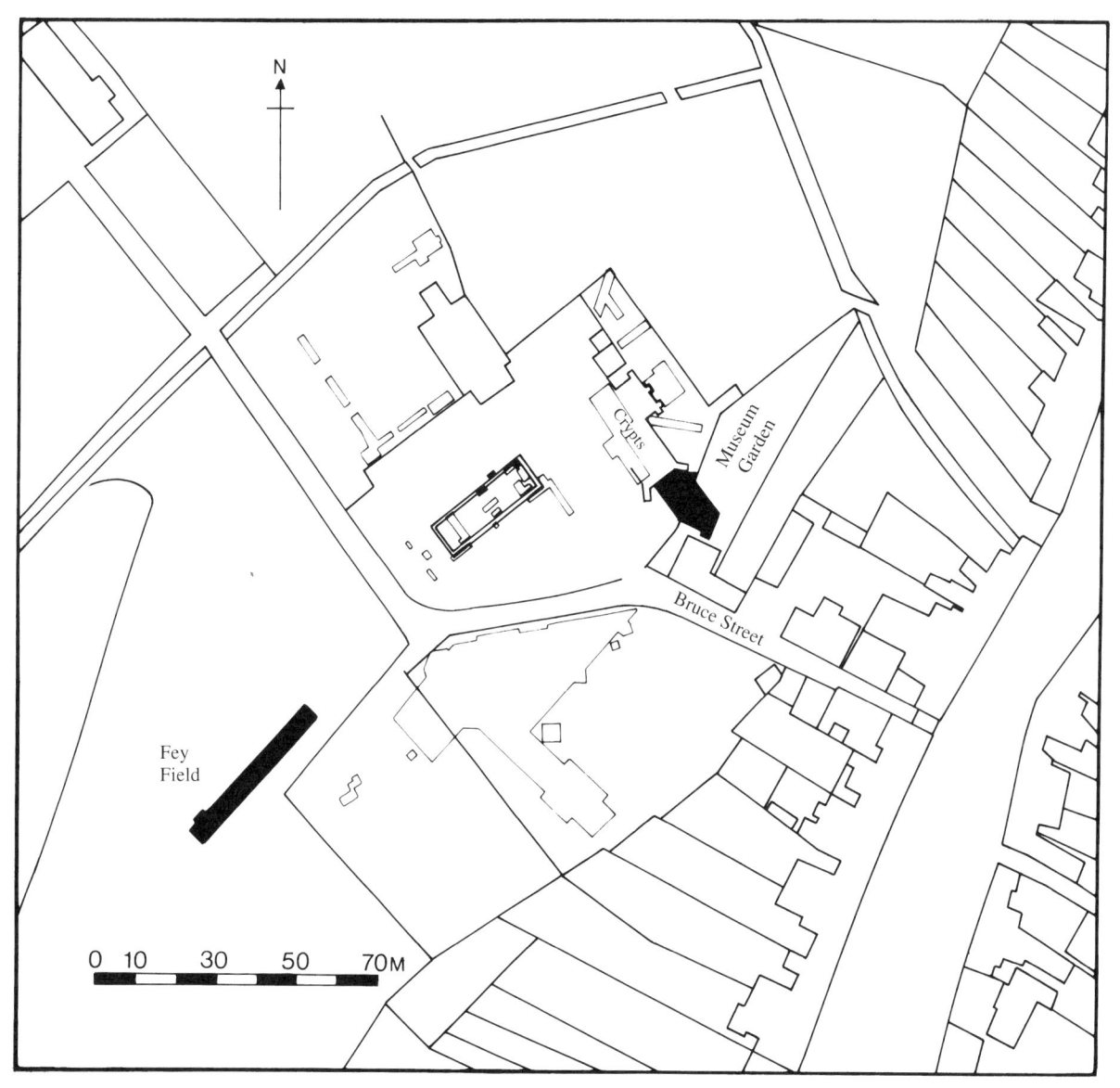

9.1 The locations of the **Museum Garden** and **Fey Field** trenches.

the south part of the trench and a narrow strip to the north (Figures 9.3–5). These deposits probably corresponded with the **Period I–IV** remains in the **Glebe Field**, but can only be correlated tentatively with them.

The southern part of the area

Stage 1. The construction trenches of the *Stage 2* building were cut through a cobbled surface (321) overlying smoothed bedrock, and sealed by a layer of dark soil (Figure 9.3b). This was similar to the **Period I/0** surface (102) in the **Glebe Field** (Figure 3.5), and could have been part of the same roadway, though lying slightly to the south of its projected line (Figure 2.1). The only finds were lumps of glassy cinder from the layer of dark soil which may have been the original source of other metalworking debris displaced into later deposits. These were the only layers ascribable to **Period I**, but later deposits produced scraps of vessel glass (408.01, Table 9.2), a bramble-headed pin (625, Table 9.5), and a sherd of an Ei jar (760, V13) which were probably displaced from seventh century deposits. The paucity of these finds supports the inference that this area lay within the *inner precinct* throughout **Period I,** and so avoided the accumulation of debris characterising the *outer zone*.

Stage 2. The principal early medieval feature was part of the north wall of a building (322) aligned with the middle range of **Period II** buildings in the **Glebe Field** (Figure 2.9). It is likely to have been a similar hall, although it produced no dating evidence, and its original size is unknown. The structural remains

THE MUSEUM GARDEN AND FEY FIELD TRENCHES

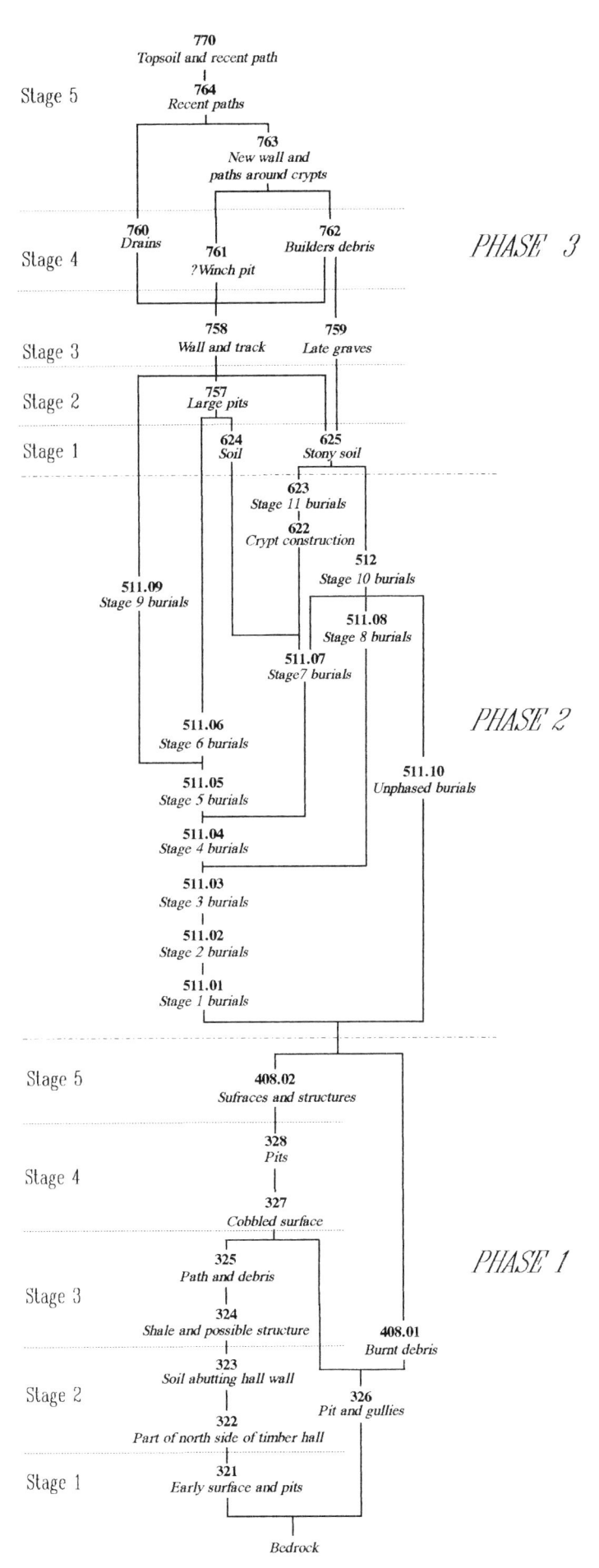

9.2 The stratigraphic sequence in the **Museum Garden**.

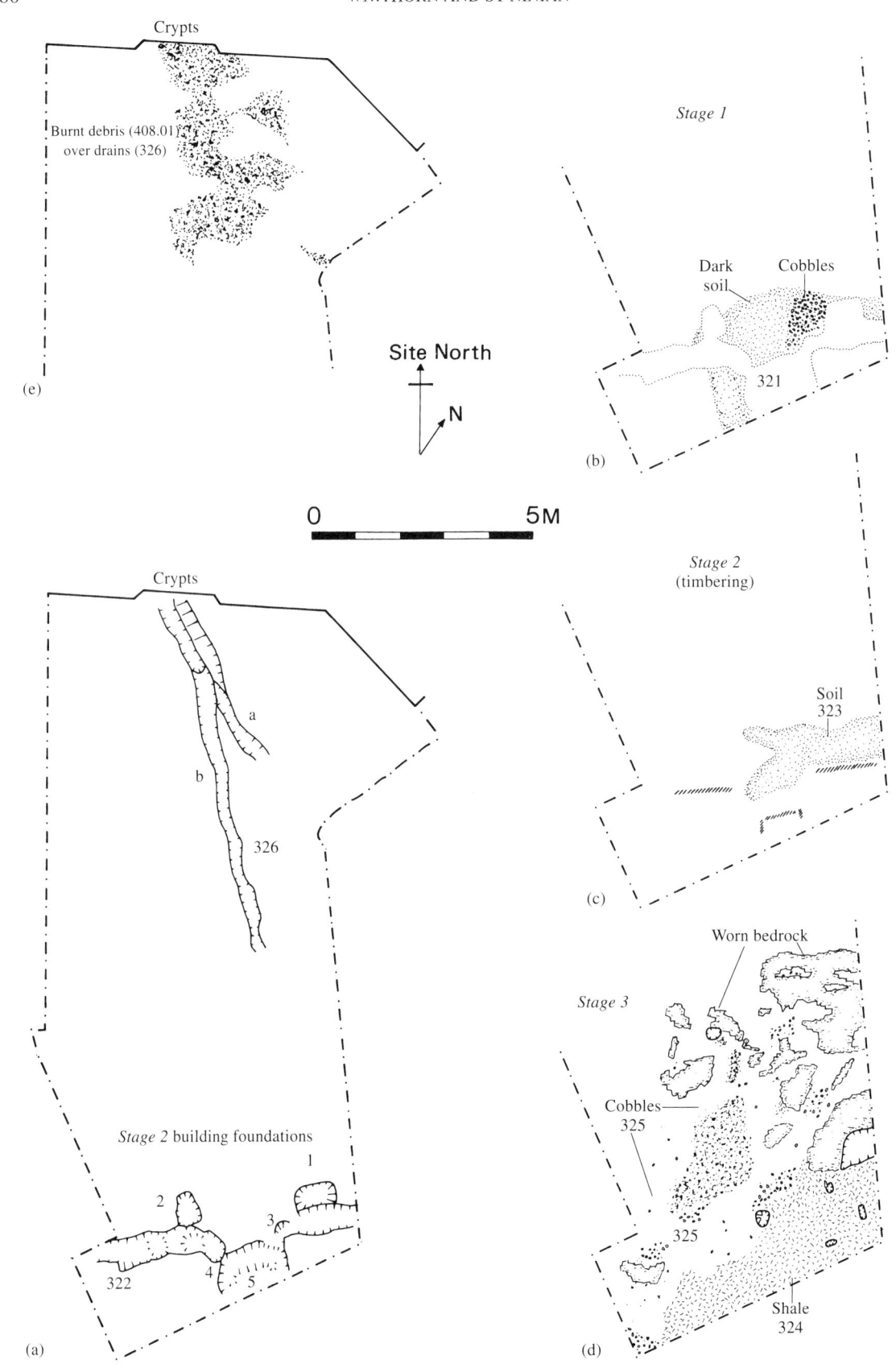

280   WHITHORN AND ST NINIAN

9.3 The earlier structures and deposits in the **Museum Garden**.

comprised the rock-cut foundation trenches of the north wall, and a symmetrical cluster of features forming a wide doorway (Figure 9.3a and c). The building was not recognised until the western part of the foundation trench had been emptied, but sufficient survived to characterise the wall timbers, and to identify the sequence of the construction of the walls and door. The earliest features were two pits (1 and 2) straddling the doorway, and the sockets for two inset doorposts (3 and 4). The foundation trench for the wall was dug after the latter timbers were erected. The eastern part of the trench contained the impressions of continuous planking, which contrasted with the spaced wall timbers of all the larger buildings in the **Glebe Field**. Two deeper sockets in the western part of the trench could have held larger timbers. A secondary doorway was contained by a large rock-cut hollow (5) cutting into the sockets of the original door-frame. Casts of the door timbers, preserved on the south side of the hollow, comprised a deep timber sill jointed into a plank frame (Figure 9.3c). The hollow may have served as a ramp to facilitate the erection of a prefabricated framework which was too heavy to be lifted and dropped into place. No artefacts were recovered from the building.

There was a trampled area outside the door, and two ledges in the bedrock could have been cut to make a path leading to the north. A layer of soil (323) outside the building produced two rounded quartz pebbles, and a small group of metalworking debris (glassy and crystalline cinder, and a lump of smithied iron debris) which was probably displaced from the *Stage 1* surface.

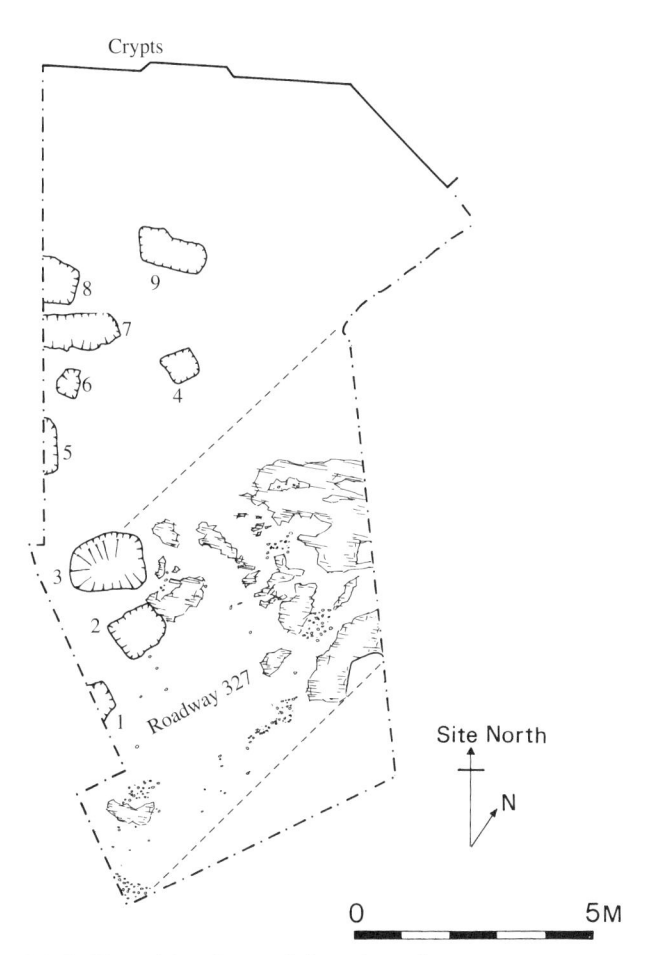

9.4 The **Phase 1.4** roadway and pits to the north-west.

Stage 3. The remains of the hall were overlain by a shale surface associated with a group of post-holes (324), and both could have been part of a new building of unreconstructible form (Figure 9.3d). The shale was abutted by a cobbled surface (325) associated with patches of worn bedrock, and overlain by patches of charcoal. The cobbles and worn rock seem to have been part of a sunken roadway which had removed earlier deposits and subsoil from the central part of the trench. There were no finds.

Stage 4. The continued use of the *Stage 3* roadway was represented by a new surface of cobbles (327) overlying the earlier surfaces (324), and oversailing the south end of the drain to the north (Figure 9.4). The surface and edges of the roadway had been disturbed by graves and other later features, but it is likely to have occupied a hollow dug into the bedrock. The only finds were a tanged iron chisel (IN52.1) and a fragment of a tuyere plate. A group of rock-cut pits on the western side of the trench (328) can be ascribed tentatively to this phase. The most southerly pit clipped the edge of the *Stage 4* surface, but it and the others in this area were sealed by the *Stage 5* deposits. The pits to the north were cut into bedrock and disturbed by *Phase 2* graves, but cannot otherwise be dated. The pits were filled with soil and, sometimes, stones, but did not reveal evidence of timber sockets, and do not seem to have been used for the disposal of rubbish as the only finds was a buckle (IN44.4) from Pit 4. They might have been latrines, and deposits of silty soil in Pits 1, 2, 3 and 9 may have been the remains of faecal waste.

The roadway can be ascribed an unknown period between the mid-ninth and mid-twelfth centuries, but seems inappropriate to **Period III** when the low-lying ground was flooded (Figures 2.15 and 16). It might thus have pertained to the earlier part of **Period IV,** and could have skirted the settlement after the flooded area had been drained. The concentration of pits to the north-west of the road might thus identify a latrine area in the **Period IV** settlement.

Stage 5. Stage 5 was represented by a deep (*c.* 0.65 m) accumulation of soil in the southern part of the trench, and an overlying layer of stones and fragmentary structural remains (408.02, Figure 9.5). These deposits had been extensively disturbed by **Phase 2** graves and other later features, but produced a small group of artefacts which allowed them to be ascribed to the latter part of **Period IV** (Table 9.1). The deep soil layer covered the *Stage 4* roadway and might have been deposited when the low-lying ground flooded in the latter part of **Period IV**. The sparse finds (Table 9.1a) included an iron stick-pin of

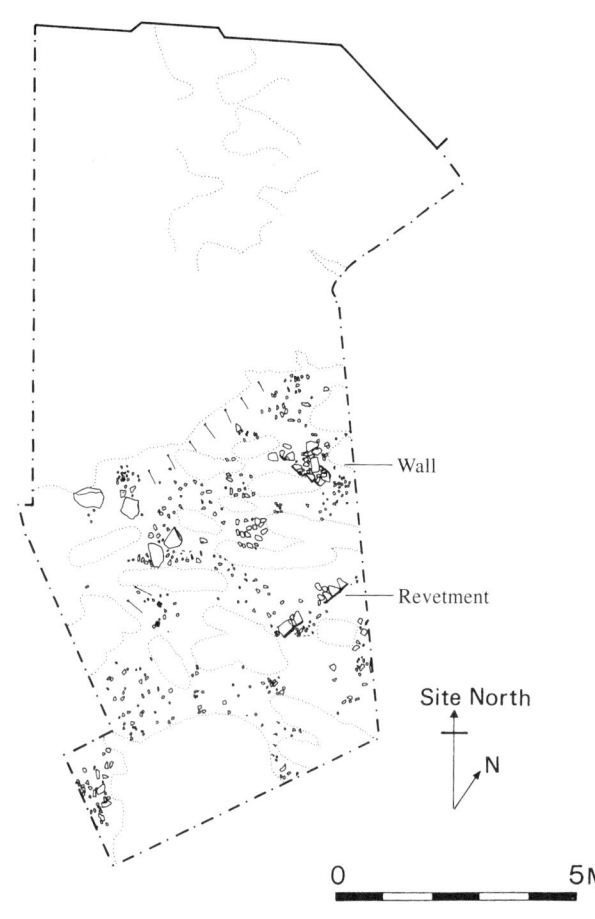

9.5 **Phase 1.5** cobbling and structural remains (408.02).

The northern part of the area

The bedrock lay close to the surface in the northern part of the trench, and the **Phase 1** deposits had been severely damaged by **Phase 2** graves. The principal features were successive rock-cut drains (**a** and **b**, 326, Figure 9.3a) which were overlain by a spread of burnt debris (408.01, Figure 9.3e). The latter produced two mid-ninth century coins, and is likely to have pertained to the end of **Period II**, while the drains could have flanked a **Period II** building underlying the south-east part of the crypt. The south-east part of the later drain (**b**) was sealed by the *Stage 4* cobbles (327), and may have been truncated by the putative hollowed roadway in *Stage 3* or *4*. The only finds from the drain were scraps of bone and charcoal, and an iron needle with a punched eye (IN39.7). The overlying debris was concentrated over the partly-infilled ditches, and included burnt clay, sand and charcoal. The finds included hammerscale and a large hone indicating there was a smithy nearby, which might also account for a broken drawknife and an iron strap (Table 9.2). The three scraps of glass are likely to have been displaced from a **Period I** deposit, and were the only pieces of early medieval vessel glass from this area. The two coins are part of a specialized group from this area, which was probably deposited in the closing years of **Period II** (pp 354-5). The burnt deposit might thus be correlated with the destruction of the church and chapel at the end of **Period II/7** (p 162). The coins, tools and manufacturing debris in this group were matched by the atypical **Period II/7** and **III/1.1** deposits in the Glebe Field (Tables 4.7, 5.3- 5), and may similarly reflect the crisis affecting the **Period II** *minster*. This deposit was almost certainly more extensive, and is likely to have been the source of other finds displaced into the **Phase 2** graves and overlying deposits (Tables 9.3 and 5).

A Phase II styca of Aethelred II: 1st reign, *c*. 841–3 (CN02.55)
A Phase II styca of Eanred, *c*. 837–841 (CN02.58)
Three sherds of Group C vessel glass (C3z, aa and bb)
A wool comb tooth (IN62:8)
A fragment of a drawknife with a looped end (IN69:05)
A strap-like piece of iron (IN80.70)
Four nails, two shanks and a nail head
A miscast lead nail or rivet (LD10.4)
A large, manufactured, greywacke hone (SE33.1)
Hammerscale, scraps of glassy cinder (26.5 gm) and four tuyere fragments (15.8 gm)

Table 9.2: Finds from burnt debris (408.01) in north part of the Museum Garden trench

Displaced finds. As in the **Glebe Field**, most of the finds from the **Phase 2** graves (Table 9.3) are likely to have originated in **Phase 1** deposits. These are also likely to have been the principal source of the finds from two layers of soil oversailing the graves (624 and 625, Tables 9.4 and 5), which were relatively uncontaminated with post-medieval objects. These three assemblages are larger than those from the stratified deposits, but were nevertheless both smaller and less varied than equivalent groups from the **Glebe Field** (Tables 6.41 and 42). The ironworking debris and lead may have originated in the mid-ninth century rubbish in the northern part of the trench (408.01), but other pieces probably came from the

appropriate date. The absence of pottery hints that the deposit is earlier than the thirteenth century. The stone surface oversailed a fragmentary wall and stone revetment, which may have been part of a rectilinear building or platform. The finds (Table 9.1b) included pottery appropriate to the later-twelfth/early-thirteenth century, and a piece of dressed sandstone that could have originated in the twelfth century cathedral, and might have been discarded when the original crypts were built, or when the nave was extended (p 56).

A possible club-headed iron stick-pin lacking its tip (IN41.6)
A fragment of mortar (15.4 gm)
A glazed, sandstone pebble (SE77)
Scraps of glassy cinder (39 gm) and crystalline cinder (6.1 gm)

Table 9.1a: Finds from *Stage 5* soil underlying stone surface

Two tiny fragments of copper alloy (BZ41 29–30)
Two sherds of red gritty ware (MP01) and two of local green glazed pottery (MP2/12)
A tanged punch or awl (IN50.80)
Two nails and a lump of iron (IN93.79)
A chamfered dressed sandstone corner fragment (SE01.4)
A lump of mortar (6.2 gm)
An unretouched flint
Scraps of glassy cinder (44 gm) and two possible tuyere fragments (6.8 gm)

Table 9.1b: Finds from stone surface and related deposits (408.02)

Stage 5 deposits. Two offcuts from antler tines (and a single tooth-plate blank from a later deposit) indicated that the antler-working area in the eastern part of the **Glebe Field** did not extend this far. The pottery included later-twelfth and thirteenth century fabrics, and is likely to have been among debris scattered on the surface cut by the **Phase 2** graves. The quartz and granite pebbles were probably talismanic inclusions in the graves. The penannular brooch and ring could also have been contemporary losses. This area was close to the cathedral in the twelfth and thirteenth centuries, but seems to have been peripheral to the manufacturing and trading activities recorded in the **Glebe Field**.

An antler tine tip, sawn at the base (AR47)
A small tin-plated penannular brooch (BZ16.1)
A round wire loop, possibly a finger ring (BZ23.5)
A copper-alloy offcut fragment with a circular impression at one end (BZ38.78)
A tapering iron ferrule with a rivet (IN65.32)
A complete Class C3 tanged knife (IN66.31), a short, broad tanged chopping knife
(IN66.64) and a knife blade fragment (IN67.4)
An iron strip (IN80.144) and disc fragment (IN88.4)
Eleven nails, six shanks and a nail head*
A lead rivet (LD06.17) and a bent or hooked lead nail (LD06.49)
A molten piece of lead waste (LD13.14) Twenty-five sherds of pottery (MP1 x 3, 2/2 x 2, 2/5, 2/6 x 2, 2/7 x 2, 2/8, 2/11 x 8, 06, 7/1, 12/1 x 3, 14)
A small, greywacke discoid, possible a gaming counter (SE19.23)
A perforated metasediment roofing stone fragment (SE09.61)
A natural flint pebble and four **unretouched** waste flakes
Seven rounded quartz pebbles, two abraded angular, quartz pebbles, three small granite pebbles, and five vein quartz fragments.
Five glazed sandstone and quartzite pebbles.
Scraps of glassy cinder (207 gm) and crystalline cinder (146 gm)
A possible tuyere plate inner fragment (80.8 gm) and three unassigned scraps
A large group C hearth fragment (466.5gm, SG43)
Two symmetrical Group 2 puddling hearths (443 and 599 gm, SG48)

Table 9.3: Finds from graves in Museum Garden trench.
* Two groups of possible coffin nails are omitted.

A body sherd of 19thC green bottle glass.
A sherd of Saintonge ware (MP12/1)
A fractured iron ring, possibly penannular (IN30.19)
An iron bar, one end flattened, one pointed (IN65.33)
A nail
A molten droplet of lead (LD13.15)
Scraps of glassy cinder (93.2 gm)
A tuyere plate inner fragment (19.8 gm) and a saucer-shaped hearth (444.5 gm, SG57)

Table 9.4: Finds from soil overlying graves in south part of area (624)

An antler tine sawn at base (AR26)
A tin plated bramble-headed stick pin (BZ14.2)
A club or bead-headed stick pin (BZ14.42)
An iron needle with a punched eye (IN39.37)
A complete tanged Class D knife (IN66.55)
A tanged pruning hook blade (IN67.06)
A T-shaped fragment of wire or rod (IN78.48) and a flat strip (IN80.145)
Seven nails and a shank
Three sherds of pottery (MP01, 2/11, 6)
A fine-grained, sandstone hone blank (SE71.39)
An **unretouched** flint flake
Three pebbles
A medium-sized glazed sandstone pebble (SE77)
Scraps of glassy cinder (39 gm) and crystalline cinder (101 gm)
A lump of smithied iron debris (48.5 gm SG12)
A large Group 2 puddling hearth (1414 gm, SG50)

Table 9.5: Finds from soil over graveyard in north part of area (625)

Phase 2

Phase 2 was represented by a populous graveyard extending over the entire area (Figures 9.6–8). This is likely to have been broadly coterminous with **Period V**, although the area probably continued to be used as a graveyard after burials had ceased in the **Glebe Field**. Displaced pottery suggests that the first burials were unlikely to be earlier than the later-thirteenth century, while the construction of the crypt on the north side of the trench probably dates to c. 1500, and subsequent burials (623) to the sixteenth century.

The graveyard posed similar problems to those encountered in the **Glebe Field** (pp 253-5), with frequent changes in orientation, and the disturbance of earlier graves. It was analysed in a similar way and revealed twelve successive stages of burials (511.01–09, 512, 623, 758/9) and a small group of unphased graves (511.10). The last stage (758/9, Figure 9.9) pertained to **Phase 3**. The development of the graveyard in *Stages 1–11* is illustrated in Figure 9.8 which reveals the essential coherence of its evolution. Rows of burials were generally clear and may still be inferred among the more disturbed remains (Figure 9.8a). The changes in orientation are similar to those in the **Glebe Field** (Figures 7.2 and 4), although developments in the two areas cannot be correlated precisely. The distribution of aged

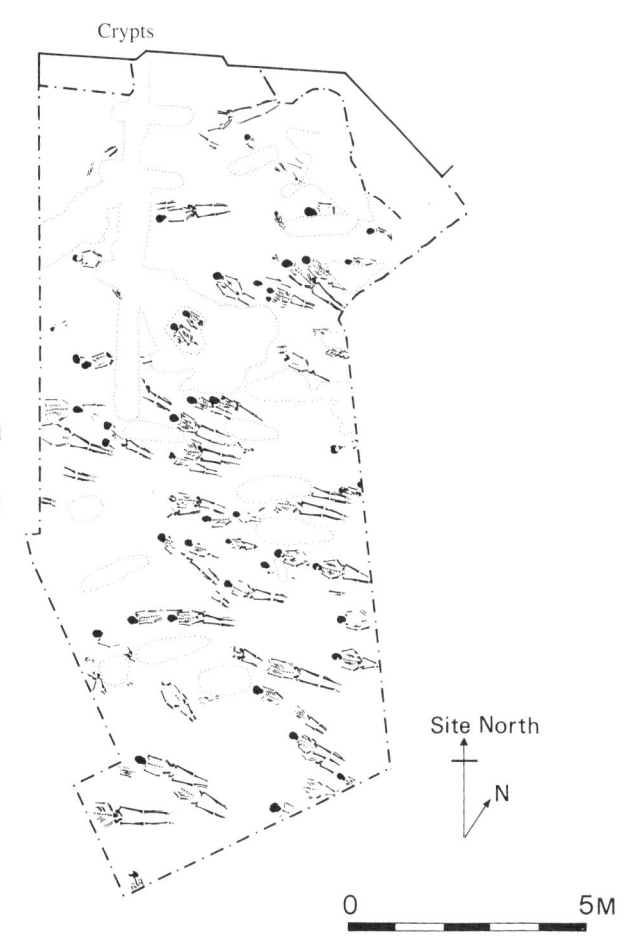

9.6 The earlier **Phase 2** burials (*Stages 1-6*).

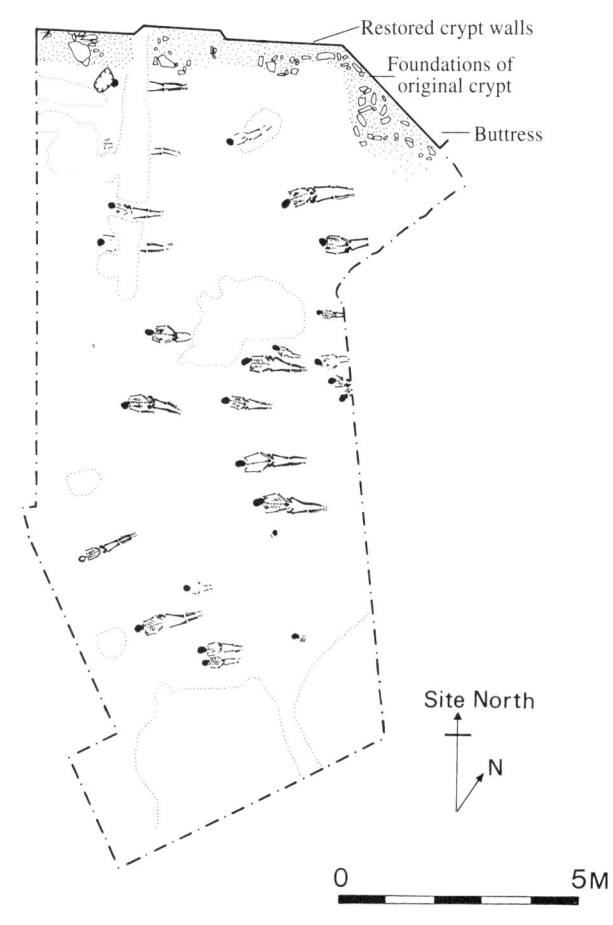

9.7 The later **Phase 2** burials (*Stages 7-11*) and foundations of the south crypt.

Museum Garden trench could thus have lain on the edge of the burial ground in *Stages 6–10*. This area might alternatively have been designated for the burial of a specific group, perhaps young novices or scholars.

Most of the finds from the graves (Table 9.3) are likely to have been displaced from earlier deposits apart from a small penannular brooch and finger ring which could have been personal items, and an iron ferrule that could have come from a pilgrim's staff. A *Stage 10* grave (512/11) produced nineteen nails and nineteen nail shanks. Most preserved traces of mineralized wood, suggesting that they came from a coffin. The nails displayed a wide range of head types (02, 03, 04 x 2, 05 x 2, 06 x 9, 12 x 2, pp 405-8), and the scattered pieces did not reveal a regular nailing pattern. The putative coffin may thus have been made from recycled timbers retaining nails and broken shanks from their primary use, and perhaps secured by the nine nails with rectangular heads (IN06). An iron strip folded into a loop at one end (IN80.44) could have been a simple fastening. Another grave in the unphased group (511.10/77) contained four nails and five shanks, two with mineralized wood, which could have come from a second coffin.

The construction of the south crypt (622) was represented by mortared stone footings in a shallow trench cutting into the bedrock (Figure 9.7).These foundations extended some 0.7 m beyond the walls restored by William Galloway, and were respected by subsequent burials. The restored wall is thus probably in a slightly different position from the original one. The buttress at the south-east angle of the crypt revealed greatest deviation between the original footings and the restoration. The original buttress seems to have been considerably larger than the restored structure and lay at a different angle to the corner of the crypt. This would have been an essential structural support for the crypt and chapel above. The foundations had disturbed a *Stage 7* grave, and the construction of the crypt had probably removed most of the early deposits, although rock-cut features may have survived. The only find was a rolled tag end (BZ20.3) from a post hole beyond the entrance to the crypt, which may have been the socket for a scaffolding pole.

skeletons is of particular interest (Table 9.6, Figures 11.2 and 3). The first five phases of burial (511.01–5) comprised a mature population among which children were rare. The pattern changed in the ensuing phases (511.06–09, 512), revealing a population dominated by children and young juveniles. The subsequent graves (623) reverted to an older population, and the unphased burials (511.10), with a spread of ages, probably included members from both sub-groups. There were similar concentrations of young burials on the extremities of the **Glebe Field** in *Stages V/5* and *V/10*, and the

Stage	1	2	3	4	5	6	7	8	9	10	11	Unphased	Recent	TOT
FO													•	1
PE	•						••			••		••		7
IN	•			•	•							•		4
CH			•			•	•••	•	••	••••••		•		15
YJ		•		•		•••				•••••		••••	•	15
OJ		•	•••						•			••	•	9
SA	•	••	•••							•		•		8
YA	•	•	••								•	••		7
EMA	•••	•	•••							•		•		9
MA		••••	•••	••	•	••	•	•	•		•••••	•		21
LMA	•	•				•				•	•			5
OA														
AD	••	•				•				•		•••••		10
IM												•		1

Table 9.6: Age distribution in successive graves in the **Museum Garden** (ages follow Table 11.1)

a *Stage 1* b Stage 2 c *Stage 3* d *Stage 4*

e *Stage 5* f *Stage 6* g *Stage 7* h *Stage 8*

Site North

0   5M

i *Stage 9* j *Stage 10* k *Stage 11* l Unphased burials

9.8 The development of the **Phase 2** graveyard in the **Museum Garden.**

The final group of burials (623) comprised an unusually regular row of four graves aligned with the doorway of the new crypt. The grave beside the doorway contained three successive burials, and so seems to have been a favoured spot, or was perhaps a family lair.

Phase 3

Phase 3 saw a succession of recent and modern developments corresponding with the **Period VI** sequence in the **Glebe Field**. The restoration of the crypts and subsequent improvements had severely truncated the early deposits in the northern part of the area, and the southern part of the trench had been disturbed by pits and cultivation trenches. Earlier objects had been displaced by these activities, and recent deposits produced several significant finds.

Stage 1 recorded the disuse of the **Phase 2** graveyard, and was represented by layers of soil and stones overlying the graves (Figure 9.9). Stony soil in the northern part of the site (625) probably included the upper parts of the **Phase 2** graves, and produced a relatively large group of finds. Siltier deposits to the south (624) probably comprised a worm-sorted horizon. The finds (Tables 9.4 and 5) are likely to have been displaced from **Phase 1** deposits, and this seems to have been a period of inactivity, perhaps spanning the later-sixteenth and mid-eighteenth centuries.

Stage 2 saw renewed activity in the southern part of the trench, represented by three large pits (757, Figure 9.9) cutting the *Stage 1* soil and underlying **Phase 2** graves. Sparse finds included displaced medieval pottery and sherds of eighteenth century bottle glass. The pits may have been associated with the cottage subsequently converted into the museum.

Stage 3 saw the construction of a new wall associated with a possible gateway and a rough cobbled surface (758, Figure 9.9). These features appear on the Ordnance Survey map of 1850, and can be identified as a fragment of the kirkyard wall, and a gate leading into a field to the north-east. The surface lay directly over the *Stage 1* soil and **Phase 2** graves, and the finds included displaced human bones, later medieval pottery, and a styca of the first reign Aethelred II (CN02.41). The cobbles had been disturbed by two interments. One contained disarticulated remains, presumably reburied after they had been disturbed. The second contained a foetal skeleton, and is likely to have been a clandestine burial outside the kirkyard. The southern side of the surface was bordered by a dry stone revetment in a shallow hollow (578.04) cutting one of the *Stage 2* pits. A group of oriented burials to the north-west (759) would have lain on the edge of the kirkyard, and had been disturbed by William Galloway's excavations.

Stage 4 (Figure 9.10) saw the restoration of the crypts (761, 762) and the cultivation of the garden beyond (760). The renovations were preceded by a survey dated July 1886, sketching the former position of the curving kirkyard wall which had been dismantled to give access to the crypts. Evidence of the restorations included three pits (2–4) containing displaced human bones, a spread of debris including chips of the red sandstone used for the restored walls, and a large pit (1) containing the H-shaped timber sub-frame of a machine, perhaps a winch. Stone-filled trenches in the garden beyond (760) produced scraps of red sandstone, and hence probably post-dated the reconstruction of the crypts. These were dug through the *Stage 2* pits, penetrating the underlying deposits, and produced a number of displaced objects, including later medieval pottery, a stud-headed copper-alloy stick pin (BZ14.27), and the only piece of E ware (V13) from this area. Two pieces of dressed masonry are likely to have originated in the debris cleared from the crypts, as are others from the overlying deposits (764).

Stage 5 commenced with the erection of a new kirkyard wall (763 *pars*) and the laying of new paths leading into and around the restored crypt (Figure 9.10). Continuing developments in the recent past (764) included new paths and surfaces to either side of the wall, and a rock-cut trench for an electricity

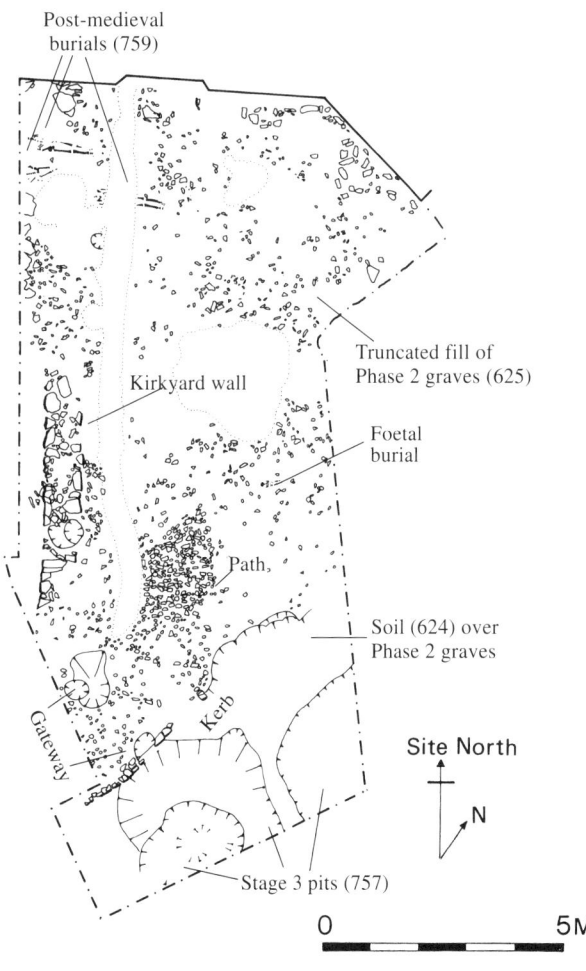

9.9 Eighteenth and nineteenth century features (**Phase 3.1-3**)

cable linking the Museum and crypt. A large group of finds, mostly from the Museum garden, was dominated by recent objects, but included earlier material still being displaced from the **Phase 2** graves and underlying deposits. Two turners of Charles I (CN02.52 and 53) had presumably originated in the *Stage 1* soil, and were the only second millennium issues from the trench.

Conclusions

The excavation demonstrated that the **Phase 2** graves, sixteenth century crypt and nineteenth century restorations had severely damaged the earlier medieval deposits over most of the area, but the cumulative record of stratified and displaced finds provided a useful index of past activity. Similar circumstances probably obtain in the area surrounding the early building to the south-east of the crypts, and access to the ground beyond is precluded by recent graves. The bedrock slopes gradually to the south-west of the crypts, and early medieval deposits are probably less severely disturbed on the south side of the museum garden, and in the adjacent properties. Excavation here might reveal the continuation of the **Period I/1** boundary (Figure 2.2), the remainder of the **Phase 1.2** hall and any adjacent buildings, and probably a series of waterlogged deposits matching those in the southern part of the **Glebe Field** trench. There is a rock outcrop further to the east in the **Museum Garden**, but this remains the only area in the eastern part of the site that is potentially available for future excavation.

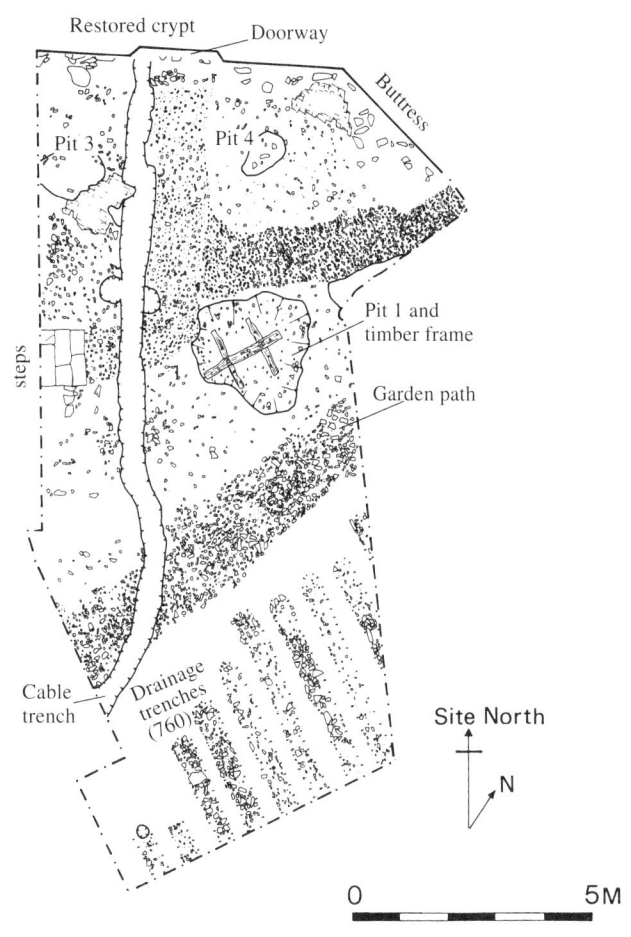

9.10 Later-nineteenth and twentieth century features (**Phases 3.4–5**).

The Fey Field

Peter Hill and Jo Moran

A long exploratory trench opened in the **Fey Field** in 1987 was intended to provide a west-east radial transect of the hill, complementing the south-north transect in the **Glebe Field**. The trench ran from the central plateau of the hill to the flank of a rock outcrop to the west, crossing an area of lower ground (Figures 1.5 and 1.6). The eastern part of this area revealed a relatively deep sequence of deposits, but rock was close to the surface at the west end of the trench, and only shallow stratified remains had survived. The lower ground was not examined fully and no stratigraphic links were established between the two parts of the trench, which are described separately. The excavation was not completed and the trench was backfilled at the close of the 1987 season.

The eastern part of the trench

The eastern part of the trench revealed a deep (*c.* 0.7 m) deposit of cultivated soil, interleaved with the foundations of a demolished wall, and overlying a complex group of structural remain. The wall was excavated by hand, but the soil to either side was removed by machine. The structural remains were relatively undamaged, and most of the overlying soil must therefore have been introduced from elsewhere. The name of the **Fey Field** provides a valuable clue. Fey is an old Galloway word for the intensively-manured infield of infield/outfield cultivation, and derives from Middle English (*fezen*) and Old Norse (*faegja*). These verbs relate to cultivation by removing the surface soil and spreading manure (Grant and Murison 1956), and are appropriate to the introduced soils recorded. A similar process has been noted at Iona and Fearns Abbey, and may have been a feature of monastic agriculture (Barber 1981, 359). Bedrock and boulder clay were exposed at the east end of the trench, but shallow unexcavated deposits probably underlie the buildings further to the west.

The chronology of the structural features was clear. The buildings and associated deposits produced a large group of pottery including a range of fabrics, but not the red gritty ware with which the sequence of later medieval pottery commenced, and these finds are unlikely to be earlier than the early-thirteenth century. The remains of the buildings were later at the close of the thirteenth century. The buildings and earlier cultivation remains can thus be ascribed to the thirteenth century with considerable confidence. The date of the wall is uncertain. It may have been constructed shortly after the deposition of the coins, and if so can be identified as part of the **Period V** enclosure (Figure 2.22). It nevertheless lay relatively close to the surface (Figure 9.12) and, in the absence of firm dating evidence, could have been more recent.

EDWARD I, penny of Lincoln, cIIId 1280–1, slight wear (CN03.70)
EDWARD I, forgery of a penny of London, as cIII 1280–1, slight–moderate wear (CN03.73)

Table 9.7: Coins from turf overlying Phase 2 cultivation

The finds record was compromised by the cultivation and by the mechanical excavation of the upper deposits, but most of the collection is likely to have originated in the thirteenth century deposits, and there was little evidence that earlier material had been displaced nor later finds intruded.

THE SEQUENCE

Phase 1

Phase 1 saw dense settlement represented by at least four buildings (**1–4**) with surfaces and a fence to the east (Figure 9.11). There are likely to have been several sub-phases, but the finds indicated that all pertained to the thirteenth century. A final sub-phase of disuse (**Phase 1b**) was followed by cultivation in **Phase 2**.

Building 1 lay on the north side of the trench and was represented by two patches of burnt daub associated with the casts of stakes, and oversailed by a spread of ash. These were initially interpreted as 'ovens', but with hindsight can be seen as part of the north-east wall of a building occupying a shallow hollow with traces of an earth floor on a rubble substrate. Patches of stones to the west probably pertained to this layer and indicated the position of the south-west wall. There were two internal post-holes, and paving to the east may have been a path leading from a doorway in the north-east wall. Finds from the silt floor and burnt deposits are listed in Table 9.8. The pottery is appropriate to the inferred thirteenth century date, as are the lead nails (p 393) and fiddle-key-headed nail (pp 407-8). A sherd of Group E vessel glass was presumably displaced from an earlier deposit, and was the only object from this trench that could be ascribed to **Period I**.

A sherd of Group E vessel glass (V76)
Eight sherds of pottery (MP2/1, 2/6, 2/11 x 3, 2/12, 06, 07/1)
A piece of folded copper-alloy sheet (BZ38.38)
A lead nail (LD06.40) and a discoid lead nail head (LD06.41)
A decorated stone spindle whorl (SE28.2)
Three nails, two with fiddle key heads, and a bent shank
An abraded, angular quartz pebble and a small granite pebble
An **unretouched** flint
A scrap of glassy cinder (2.2 gm)

Table 9.8: Finds from Building 1 (419)

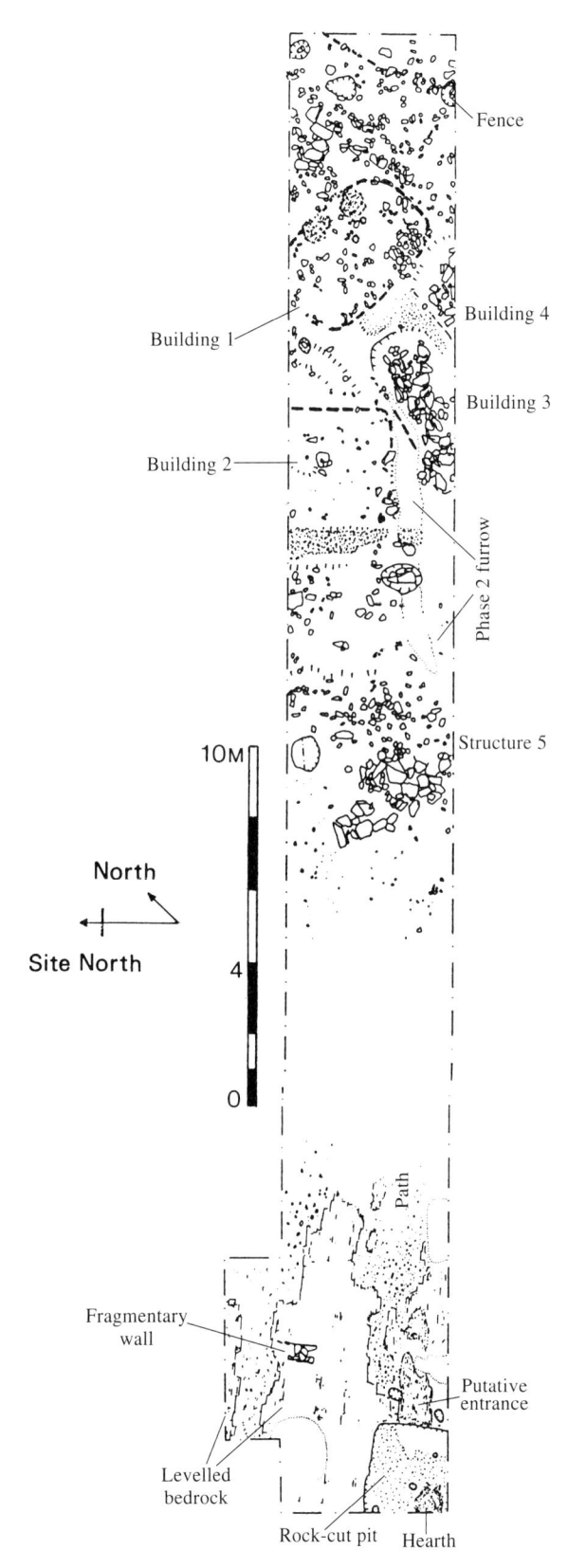

9.11 The **Fey Field** trench. **Phase 1** buildings and associated deposits, and fragmentary structural remains in western part of trench.

disturbed by cultivation and, after a period of fallow, a stone wall was built. The surface beneath the wall produced two coins of Edward I (Table 9.7), both relatively unworn, and hence likely to have been lost

Building 2 lay to the west of **Building 1**, and was represented by an angled trench filled with silty clay which could have been the decayed base of a daubed wall. The southern part of the trench had been truncated by the **Phase 2** cultivation furrow. The 'wall' produced three sherds of pottery (MP2/1, 2/8 and 2/12). A stone-packed pit to the west of the south-west corner could have contained a structural member, and produced two sherds of pottery (MP7/1).

Buildings 3 and 4 were indicated by two shallow hollows on the east side of the trench. Both contained paving overlain by silty soil, and with the rounded corners characteristic of wattle buildings. The hollows are likely to have contained successive sub-rectilinear buildings on a similar orientation to **Building 1**. The silt included a tapering strip of copper-alloy (BZ37.15), a nail, three sherds of pottery (MP2/8, 2/11 and 07/1) and a slag-cake segment. An area of paving to the west oversailed by stony soil, could have been the floor of a fifth building (**5**).

Phase 1b. A thin deposit of clayey silt with patches of pale green and yellow clay overlay the **Phase 1a** buildings in the east part of the trench. This probably comprised the remains of earth floors and decayed daub from the walls, and indicated a period of decay and disuse. It was covered by a irregular paving which was disturbed by later cultivation. The finds (Table 9.9a) probably originated in the underlying buildings and surfaces, and included a similar, though wider, range of objects.

a
An open-looped iron buckle tongue (IN44.30)
A very corroded tanged Class A2 knife blade (IN66.13)
A tanged Class D knife blade (IN66.48)
A boss-like iron plate with a raised ridge (IN82.34)
Eleven sherds of pottery (MP2/4, 2/5, 2/8 x 3, 2/12 x 2, 6 x 2, 7/1 x 2)
Three nails, two with fiddle key heads, and two shanks
An **unretouched** flint waste flake
A rounded quartz pebble.
Eight fragments of glassy cinder (138 gm), a lump of smithied iron debris (79.9 gm) and a slag cake segment (167.7 gm, SG45)

b
A tapering iron ferrule welded on one side (IN87.1)
Six sherds of pottery (MP2/5, 2/9, 2/11 x 2, 6, 9)

Table 9.9: Finds from silty layer (**a**) and overlying surface (**b**, 528)

Phase 2

Phase 2 saw the cultivation of the eastern part of the area, and was represented by a furrow running down the centre of the trench, and by upcast forming ridges to either side. The upcast included bands of small stones and shale, which were probably derived from **Phase 1** surfaces. The **Phase 1** deposits were undisturbed to either side of the furrow and the cultivated soil probably included upcast from adjacent furrows, and additional soil brought in from elsewhere The furrow ran under the **Phase 3** wall and most of the finds (Table 9.10) came from this area, which was excavated by hand. The pottery, nails and cinder were matched in underlying layers, and were probably displaced from earlier deposits. The coins were not, and may have been deposited during or after this phase of cultivation (above).

Two coins of Edward I (CN03.70 and 73)
Two nails, one with a fiddle key head
Twenty-one sherds of pottery (MP2/1 x 3, 2/5 x 2, 2/8 x 5, 2/9 x 5, 2/11, 2/12, 6, 7/1 x 3)
One lump of crystalline cinder (68.1 gm)

Table 9.10: Finds from early ploughsoil (526)

Phase 3

Phase 3 saw the erection of a dry-stone wall running north-south across the trench (Figure 9.12). The wall was $c.$ 0.9 m wide and, though aligned with the west wall of the **Market Garden**, may been part of the **Period V** enclosure.

Phase 4

Phase 4 saw renewed cultivation to either side of the wall. Cultivation to the west had cut into the earlier ploughsoil, truncating the furrow and disturbing the underlying **Phase 1** deposits. This seems to have led to soil erosion, deepening the hollow straddled by the western part of the trench. Cultivation to the east was indicated by a a thick deposit of relatively stone-free soil ($c.$ 0.3 m deep) abutting the wall. This deep soil cannot have originated in the underlying deposits and was probably brought in, perhaps as turves, to improve fertility and provide a deeper tilth. The **Phase 2** ground surface had not survived, suggesting that the turf had been stripped before the new soil was introduced.

Phase 5

Phase 5a saw the demolition of the wall which was reduced to its basal courses, while smaller stones from the core were scattered over the sloping ground to the west. This debris included fragments of meta-sediment and phyllite tiles, and was covered by a thick deposit of dark stony soil (in **Phase 5b**) with traces of cultivation furrows running across the trench. This soil, which was both darker and stonier than the **Phase 4** soil, must have been imported. It nearly filled the hollow to the west of the **Phase 3** wall, but did not extend to the east of it.

Phase 6

Phase 6 saw a final episode of cultivation

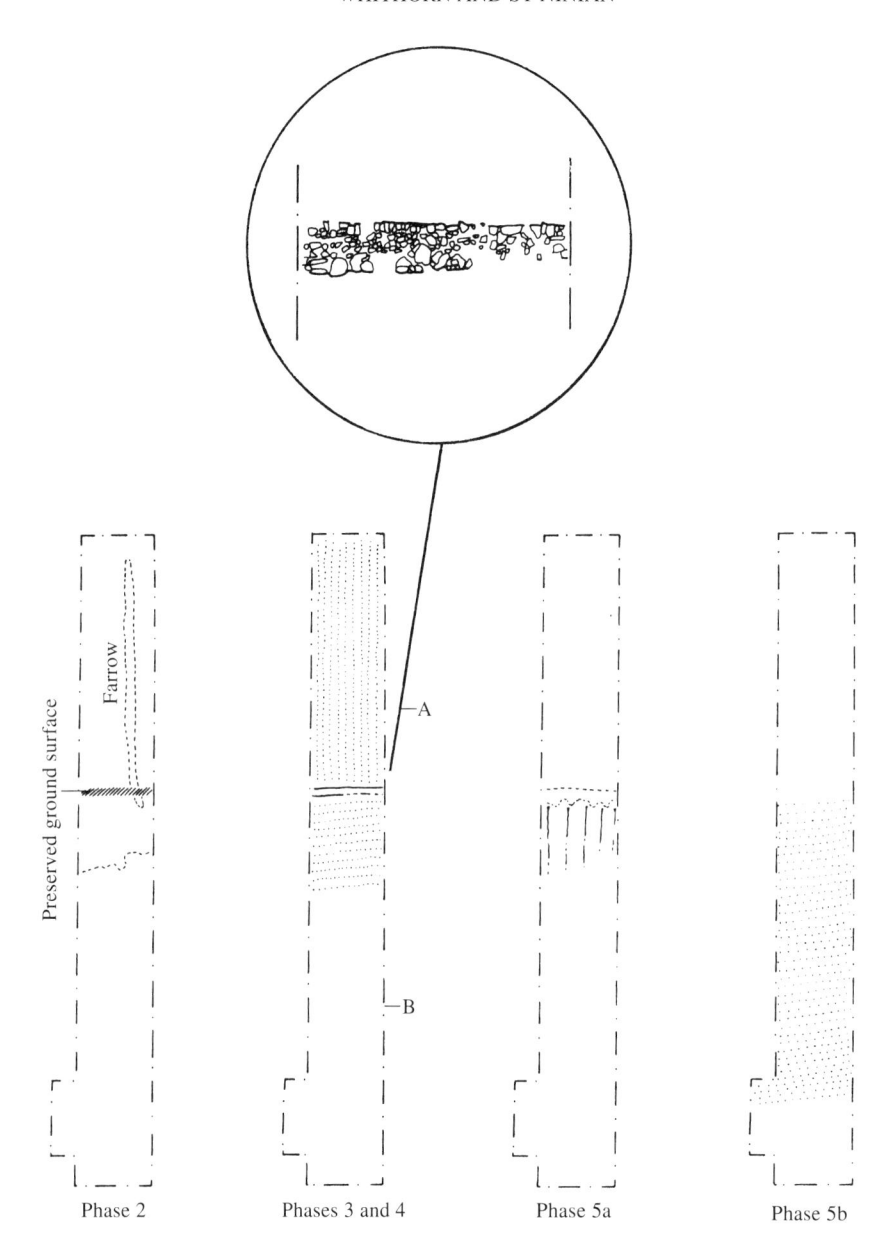

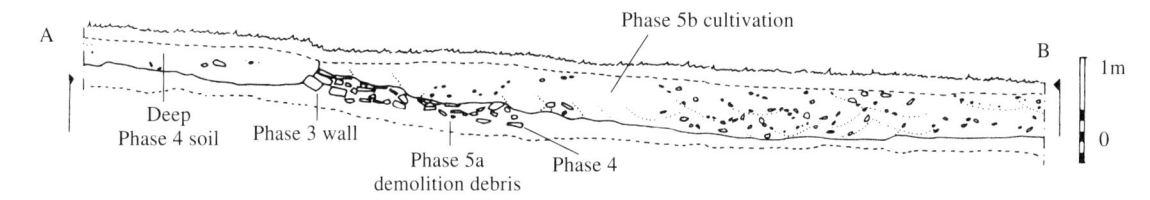

9.12 The **Fey Field** trench. The **Phase 3** wall (inset), and preceding and subsequent phases of cultivation.

represented by the shallow furrows running west-east and still visible in the **Fey Field** (Figure 2.26). Subsequent excavation (Pollock 1993) has established that these pertain to the nineteenth century.

Two copper alloy strips (BZ38.93 and 94)
A sherd of 18thC green bottle glass
A silver brooch pin with a transverse bar (SR07)

Table 9.11: Finds from later cultivated soil and topsoil (766)

Displaced finds. A small group of finds (Table 9.12), recovered when the trench was being cleaned after the mechanical excavation of the cultivated soil, probably originated in **Phase 1** or **2** deposits.

Two iron strips (IN80.71 and 72)
Nine sherds of pottery MP2/3, MP2/4, MP2/6, MP2/8, MP2.11, MP2.12 x 3, 17
A fine-grained sandstone spindle whorl (SE25.7)
A broken Kaolinite spindle whorl (SE28.4)

Table 9.12: Displaced finds (529)

The western end of the trench

The western end of the trench encroached upon a shelf of bedrock, and revealed shallow stratified deposits disturbed by nineteenth century ploughing. The principal feature was the corner of a large rectilinear rock-cut pit. The surrounding area comprised irregular shattered bedrock with bands of boulder clay in the deeper fissures. The fresh fractures of the rock and absence of a developed soil over the clay demonstrated that the area had been levelled, presumably when the pit was dug.

The rock-cut pit was straight-sided, and its base was covered with crushed red greywacke. This surface was cut by two post holes and a hearth, the latter comprising an area of blackened bedrock surrounded by patches of ash and yellow and orange clay. These features suggest that the pit was part of a building with a sunken floor, which would have been some 4.0 • 4.0 m in extent if the hearth lay at the centre. Pebbles pressed into the boulder clay, flanked by an area of worn rock marked a path leading eastwards, which was straddled by two post-holes close to the edge of the pit. These could have supported the frame of a door in the east wall of the putative building. The pit was filled with large stones and dark silt, and covered by a layer of cobbles which lapped against a fragmentary stone wall. This surface produced a fourteenth century buckle (BZ18.12), a flint pebble and five retouched flints. There were no finds from the pit.

The trench clips the north-east corner of a level platform extending westwards to the outcropping rock. This is likely to have been levelled artificially, perhaps to accommodate buildings of which no superficial trace remains. The date of this major operation is uncertain, but it is likely to have preceded the loss of two fourteenth century objects, and could have been broadly contemporary with the thirteenth century buildings to the east.

The final deposit in the west end of the trench comprised a layer of rough rubble which had been disturbed by nineteenth century cultivation, and may have been linked with the stony **Phase 5** ploughsoil to the east. An early-fourteenth century silver brooch pin (SR7) from the topsoil, is likely to have been displaced from the underlying surface.

Conclusions

The interpretation of the **Fey Field** trench is circumscribed by the lack of secure dating evidence from the more recent deposits, and the fact that the excavation was not completed. Despite these problems, the sequence of thirteenth century deposits (**Phases 1, 2** and possibly **3**) seems reliable, and points to a relatively brief period when settlement extended over the western part of the hill. The rock-cut structure may date to this time and seems to have been preceded by extensive landscaping of the outcrop to the west. These remains can be ascribed to the latter stages of **Period IV**, and there are marked similarities between the pottery from this area and from the southern part of the **Glebe Field** (415.01). White gritty ware provides a tenuous artefactual link with the fragmentary **Period IV.5** structures in the **northern sector** (Figure 6.19), and the buildings in the **Fey Field** are similarly located within the inferred *inner precinct* of the **Period IV** settlement (Figure 2.20). The finds are of particular interest. The pottery and nail types were matched in equivalent deposits in the **Glebe Field**, but there was scant evidence of the implements and manufacturing debris so abundant there, and still evident in the **Museum Garden**. The buildings are thus likely to have accommodated a distinct element in the population which was not involved in manufacture. The abandonment of these buildings and subsequent cultivation (**Phase 2**) can be ascribed tentatively to the ambiguous horizon between **Periods IV** and **V** in the later-thirteenth century The overlying wall may have been part of the **Period V** enclosure (Figure 2.22), and this can be tested by exploring its stratigraphic relationship with the boundary of the **Market Garden**, and plotting its course by excavation or geophysical survey. **Phase 4** is effectively undated, but records intensive cultivation within the enclosure and a different regime beyond. The demolition of the wall and subsequent cultivation in **Phase 5** may correspond with the mid- to late-fourteenth century changes in the **southern sector,** which saw the replacement of the ecclesiastical boundary with an earthwork surrounding the town.

The recorded features all seem to be more recent than *c*. 1200 AD, and earlier activity is represented by a single sherd of vessel glass. Early deposits could have been removed when the west end of the trench was landscaped, but the absence of displaced finds further to the east suggests that there is little earlier medieval debris here. This conforms reasonably well with the organizational model proposed in Chapter 2, which argues for a settlement focused on the east end of the hill. The inferred outer boundary of the **Period I/2–4** *monasterium* should cross the eastern part of the trench, and insubstantial features matching those in the **southern sector** (Figure 3.42) may underlie the thirteenth century buildings. The **Period II** *minster* seems have been enclosed by the same boundary, and the absence of large timber buildings is thus unsurprising. The model predicts that the **Fey Field** trench lay within the *inner precinct* during the final phase of **Period III** and throughout **Period IV**. There was no evidence of occupation in the earlier part of this period, but stratified deposits may survive beneath the thirteenth century buildings.

CHAPTER 10

The Finds

Ewan Campbell, Ray Chadburn, Jane Clarke, Derek Craig, Rosemary Cramp, Brenda Dickinson, Peter Hill, Nicholas Holmes, Fraser Hunter, Martin Millett, Andrew Nicholson, Elizabeth E J Pirie, Jennifer Price

Introduction

Peter Hill

Archive catalogues. Full publication of the large assemblage of finds is beyond the scope of this volume. The finds are held by the Wigtownshire Museum Service and detailed archive catalogues of most groups have been deposited in the National Monuments Record (Scotland) and Stranraer Museum, and copies are available on request from the Whithorn Trust.[1]

Measurements etc. Unless otherwise stated, all measurements are in millimetres and grams. The following standard abbreviations have been used: Dims = dimensions, C = circumference, BC = basal circumference, D = diameter, BD = basal diameter, ED = external diameter, ID = internal diameter, RD = rim diameter, PD = perforation diameter, H = height, PH = present height, T = thickness, W = width, Wt = weight.

Contextual information and distribution plots. Finds are generally ascribed to the blocks which are indexed below (pp 639-43). The distribution plots (e.g. Figures 10.46 and 86) frequently disregard the stratigraphic evidence, and for example combine finds from secure **Period IV** features, intrusive **Period V** graves, and overlying deposits (Figure 6.22). This is an indisputably subjective treatment, but the spatial coherence of objects which were stratigraphically dispersed suggests that real patterns of deposition have been identified (e.g. Figure 10.136e). Stratigraphic notes have been appended to some reports by Peter Hill, and equivalent comments have been integrated in those written by Andrew Nicholson.

Outstanding reports. Full reports on the flint and other struck stone, ferrous metalworking debris, and glass beads were incomplete at the time of publication. Summary descriptions are included in the lists of finds in Chapters 3–9.

1984 Finds reports. The catalogues of finds from the 1984 excavations have been integrated with those recovered in 1986–91, and I am grateful to Andrew Barlow, Ian Cox, Hilary Cool, Robin Murdoch, Olwen Owen, and Mike Spearman who submitted reports on these objects.

The Roman Finds

Brenda Dickinson, Peter Hill, Nicholas Holmes, Martin Millett, Jennifer Price

The excavation produced a small group of Roman artefacts and other objects which may have been of similar date. Some of these came from early features and could have been displaced from second-third century deposits. Others came from more recent layers, and the means of their displacement from a notional primary horizon are obscure. The distribution of the finds is illustrated in Figure 10.2 and discussed below.

Charles Thomas has consistently argued (1971, 1981a, 1992a) that Nynia was appointed as the bishop of an extant Christian community occupying a major settlement centre originating in the Roman period, and has placed considerable interpretative

---

[1] The Whithorn Trust, 45/7 George St, Whithorn, Dumfries and Galloway, DG8 8PB

weight upon cremations observed during Ritchie's excavations at the east end of the cathedral (Figure 1.6, p 10), and on wheel-turned pottery which has since disappeared from view. This inferred protohistory of Whithorn is pivotal to his interpretation of the evangelisation of northern Britain, and the Roman finds thus carry a weighty historiographical burden, irrespective of their small number and fragmentary condition. The meaning of this material is, however, far from clear. The contributing specialists present differing assessments. Brenda Dickinson and Martin Millett infer a settlement of appropriate date at Whithorn or in the immediate vicinity, while Jennifer Price speculates that glass fragments were gathered from abandoned military sites in the Scottish lowlands. Ewan Campbell (Pers. Comm.) has compared the pottery with the assemblage from Dinas Powis, where no occupation in the Roman period is acknowledged, and views it as a collection of talismans or souvenirs that is paralleled in early medieval contexts in Ireland (Bradley 1982). Similar problems have been encountered on other early medieval sites. The Roman finds from Alt Clut were initially viewed as early medieval introductions, but specialists have again argued for occupation in the Roman period (Alcock *et al.* 1992).

A small number of potentially-Roman finds are described in other sections of this chapter. A rim sherd from a flanged bowl (PY07.2, p 322), may have been Roman or post-Roman, as may a fragment of a stemmed glass cup or flask (GS02.82, p 315). A copper alloy 'nail cleaner' (BZ24.11, p 377) may be late Roman, but has parallels in early medieval Ireland and came from a secure **Period I** context, while two lead objects (LD03.1 and 09.12) from early contexts may both be of Roman origin (pp 391-2, 395). The most problematical finds are fragments of two large millstones (SE44.3 and 4), one identified as of Roman type, and both appropriate to the mill of a small town or large military establishment (Adam Welfare Pers. Comm.). One can be ascribed to the earlier part of **Period I**, and it has been argued that both record the sophisticated technology of the **Period I** *monasterium* (pp 28–9). It is equally valid to interpret them as debris from the major Roman settlement postulated by Charles Thomas, while the builders' debris ascribed to **Period I/1.2** (p 81) might also be seen as evidence for construction in the Roman period.

The Samian Ware

Brenda Dickinson

All the samian comes from the **Central Gaulish** factory of Lezoux, which was active from the first to the fourth century AD, though its main export to Britain was confined to the Hadrianic and Antonine periods.

Not all the pieces are closely datable, but it is likely that they are all Antonine. It is interesting that the decorated bowl is by a potter whose wares, with the exception of a stamped dish from Rough Castle (Hartley & Dickinson 1980, 247, 75), do not occur on Antonine military sites in Scotland. However, his work would not be remarkable at native settlements in the Lowlands, several of which have produced a number of late second century vessels by contemporary potters (Hartley 1972, 54–5).

The presence of seven different samian vessels strongly suggests the existence of a second century romanised, or part-romanised, settlement in the vicinity. Long-term survival in use is unlikely, since the sherds, though slightly weathered, show no undue signs of wear.

PY01
1 Form 30, in the style of Doeccus i. The ovolo (Stanfield and Simpson 1958, Fig. 44, 2) has a border of his characteristic large beads below it (Rogers A3 1974). The decoration is divided into panels, with one containing a double-bordered festoon; the preceding panel may have a medallion. *C.f.* Stanfield and Simpson (1958), Pl. 149, 1 for a stamped bowl from London which has the ovolo and festoon. Doeccus was one of the latest Lezoux potters to export to Britain, after *c.* AD 160, and his manufacture of decorated bowls probably began slightly later than that of his plain wares. *c.* AD 165–200 (**80.03**, Grave I/25).

2 Dish or bowl. Hadrianic or Antonine (**56.02**).

3 Form 30 or 37 rim. Hadrianic or Antonine (**81.02**, Grave I/66).

4 Two joining sherds of form 18/31R. Early-Antonine (**89**).

5 Form 30 or 37 rim. Antonine (**315.02**).

6 Dish or bowl. Hadrianic or Antonine (**333**).

7 Form 37 base, burnt. Hadrianic or Antonine (**64.02**).

Two sherds (2 and 7) came from early contexts in the **southern sector** (Table 3.38) and could have been displaced from appropriate second century deposits. Three other sherds (1, 3 and 6) came from the eastern part of the **central sector**, where two (1 and 3) were recovered from graves and the third (6) from mid-ninth century ploughsoil. All three could have originated in a scatter of second century debris although the finds from graves may have been talismans, and this might account for the somewhat unusual sherd made by Doeccus. The remaining two pieces (4 and 5) came from the western part of the **northern sector**. The earlier (4) came from the main **Period I/2** midden (89) and was associated with fragments of Group E glass vessels and other late sixth century finds. The others came from debris adjacent to the demolished altar of the ninth century church, which also produced a fourth century coin (Figure 4.21). Both finds were stratigraphically insulated from the original ground surface and are likely to reflect some form of eighth/ninth century antiquarianism (pp 45, 164).

The Roman coarse wares

Martin Millett

The datable material is middle Roman and falls within the normal range of material expected on a site in northern Britain. Nothing need be later than the third century and there is no characteristically fourth century material. I would guess that it derived from a settlement site somewhere in the vicinity of Whithorn, but there is nothing to confirm or deny the presence of a Roman period settlement on the site. I would doubt that sherds like these would have been brought to the site during the early medieval period. I can offer no origins or dates for the last three items although they fall within the normal range of Romano-British fabrics and are almost certainly not imports to Britain.

PY02

1 South Spanish (Baetican) amphora sherd, probably from Dressel 20 (olive oil amphora). Most likely second–third century (**546**).

2 Sherd from a Nene valley beaker with rouletted decoration. Late second–early-fourth century (**96**).

3 Wheel-thrown body sherd in fine oxidised fabric (**222.02**).

4 Wheel-thrown body sherd in fine, slightly micaceous fabric (**309.02**).

5 Counter in wheel thrown fine oxidized fabric (**903**).

Both of the identifiable sherds came from the western part of the **northern sector**. The beaker sherd (2) was securely stratified in a **Period I/2** context ascribed to the third quarter of the sixth century. The large amphora sherd came from fourteenth century cultivation (546) penetrating the original ground surface, which might thus have been deposited at any time previously. It is a somewhat unlikely medieval souvenir or talisman. The other stratified pieces came from the terrace flanking the **Period II/3** church (3) and waterborne silts covering the **Period II** buildings in the **southern sector** (4). Both could have been displaced from earlier deposits elsewhere.

The Roman glass

Jennifer Price

A total of twenty-five pieces of glass have been studied and at least fifteen pieces (GS01.1–12, GS04.1–4, GS03.1) belong to the period of Roman occupation in Britain. Several of the vessel fragments (1–6) represent vessels in use in the first and second centuries; the matt-glossy, cast window fragment (7) comes from a pane made in the first to third centuries, and the conical lump (12) is almost certainly of glass made in the same period. Among the objects, the bangle fragments (GS04.1–4) were produced in the later first or early-second century AD, and the biconical bead (GS03.1) is a Roman type. Other pieces are not easy to date precisely; the flat fragments (8–11) may come from first to second century prismatic bottles, or from late Roman blown window panes, or from post-Roman window panes.

Two early medieval vessel fragments examined have been distorted by heat, and the crazing visible on Nos 1, 9 and 10 may also have been caused by exposure to heat, though other explanations are possible. *Prima facie*, none of these pieces (or the lump, 12) should be regarded as cullet, or as waste products from any glassforming process, unless there is compelling evidence for an interpretation of this kind, such as close association with recognisable glassforming equipment or material. Deliberate reshaping for a secondary purpose, perhaps for reuse as a gaming piece or counter, is discernible on No. 3, and No. 9 and one of the bangle fragments (GS04.1) also have one or more broken edges with heavy wear, indicating that they were reused for some kind of smoothing process.

The rim fragment (1) is difficult to identify. Bluish green glass was very widely used during the first to third centuries, and fire-rounded rims are found on cups, bowls, jars and other vessels. Fragments from small cylindrical cups are known from Flavian sites, such as Elginhaugh (unpublished), but they are commoner in the later second and early-third century as a variant of the colourless cylindrical cups found throughout the North-West provinces (Isings 1957, Form 85), and exemplified in Scotland by the Airlie bowl (Curle 1932, 291, Fig. 3). Nos 3–6 come from well known types of glass containers, Nos 3 and 4 being from square or other prismatic vessel forms, and Nos 5–6 from cylindrical bottles. Cylindrical and square bottles were in use in large numbers on virtually every late first century site in Britain (see Price 1990, 164, 175–7, Fig. 163 for recent discussion in connection with finds from Blackfriars St, Carlisle). Cylindrical bottles disappeared early in the second century, but square bottles, and some hexagonal and rectangular bottles and square jars continued in production after that time, square bottles being found until the beginning of the third century. Thus it would not have been difficult to find fragments of these bottles on abandoned Roman military sites in Lowland Scotland, and this is presumably the origin of the small pieces found at Whithorn.

Fragments of cast, matt-glossy window glass are also likely to have been found on abandoned military sites, as glazed windows were often fitted in the bath-house and in the commandant's accommodation. The panes, which were produced in the first to third centuries, were formed by pouring hot glass into a mould (Boon 1966), and have one dull, flat surface and one shiny, rather uneven surface. The edges are usually thick and rounded though some also have one or more carefully grozed edges (Harden 1974).

In addition, Roman military sites may have provided some of the four bangle fragments, though these are also known from a wide variety of native sites in northern Britain (Kilbride-Jones 1938; Stevenson 1956 & 1976; Price 1988a). The very weathered fragment (GS04.1) appears to come from a Type 1 bangle, though it has a D-shaped section and is less massive than many other pieces, and the opaque red and yellow glass is mixed together to form the bangle, rather than being laid as a capping over a core of another colour. The distribution of Type 1 bangles is concentrated in lowland Scotland, and the fragments are rarely associated with Roman military sites (Stevenson 1976, 51–3).

The fragment of a Type 2 bangle (GS04.2) is very worn, and it may have served as a talisman or keepsake long after the bangle itself had been broken. Re-used bangle fragments have been noted occasionally in Anglo-Saxon burials, as in grave 44 in the Anglo-Saxon cemetery at Norton, Cleveland, where a similar-sized piece from a Type 2 bangle had been set in a silver binding (Sherlock & Welsh 1992, 152, Fig. 47, 44.4), and an Anglian burial at West

Heslerton contained a piece of a dark brown bangle with opaque white trails which may have been part of the contents of a purse (Price 1988a, 354). Type 2 bangles are known in Claudian or Neronian contexts on several sites in southern Britain and one has come from Valkenburg on the lower Rhine frontier (Price 1988a, 342; van Lith 1977). Many more, however, have come from military sites with late first or early-second century occupation in Yorkshire, northern England and southern Scotland.

Two fragments are from Type 3A bangles (GS04.3–4). These opaque white, undecorated bangles have rarely been noted south of Yorkshire and Lancashire, and they are widely spread in northern England and lowland Scotland (Price 1988a, 349–51). All three types of bangles were probably in circulation in northern Britain in the late first and early-second century, though their precise dates are not significant in the present context, as they are likely to have been carried to Whithorn as fragments, long after their production had ceased. Long biconical beads similar to GS03.1 are not a closely dated type. They are mostly found on Romano-British sites in southern Britain, though a few have been noted in Northumberland (Guido 1978, 93, Fig. 37.14).

GS01 VESSEL AND WINDOW FRAGMENTS

1 Rim fragment, cup or small bowl (?). Bluish green. Vertical rim, edge fire-rounded, straight upper body. Crazed, especially on outside surface.
PH 10.5; RD approx 60; T 2.5 **85.01**

2 Body fragment. Bluish green, convex side.
Dims 12.5 × 11; T 4.0 **109**

3 Approximately D-shaped body fragment, prismatic vessel. Bluish green. straight side. broken edges reworked and carefully smoothed for secondary use. Surfaces heavily worn.
Dims 26 × 23.5; T 4.5–6.5 **83**

4 Flat fragment, prismatic vessel. Bluish green. Dull.
Dims 11.5 × 12.5; T 6.0 **109**

5 Small, thick body fragment. Bluish green. Slight evidence for convex curve, possibly cylindrical side.
Dims 5 × 7 **412**

6 Base fragment, cylindrical bottle?. Bluish green. Edge of concave base. Ring of heavy wear on base edge, surfaces worn.
Dims 22 × 20.5 **902**

7 Fragment, matt-glossy window pane. Bluish green. Flat, one surface matt and slightly pockmarked, the other glossy and slightly uneven. Two edges worn, two new breaks.
Dims 21 × 14.5; T 3.5–4.5 **114**

8 Flat fragment, prismatic vessel? or window pane?. Pale bluish green. Dull, surfaces worn.
Dims 27.5 × 6.5; T 5 **238**

9 Two joining flat fragments, prismatic vessel? or window pane?. Pale bluish green. Crazed; surfaces dull, two edges heavily worn.
Dims 26 × 13.5; T 5.5 **55** and **901**

10 Flat fragment, prismatic vessel? or window pane?. Pale bluish green. Dull.
Dims 13 × 7; T 4 **230.01**

11 Flat fragment, prismatic vessel? or window pane?. Pale bluish green. Dull.
Dims 8.5 × 6.5; T 4 **421.01**

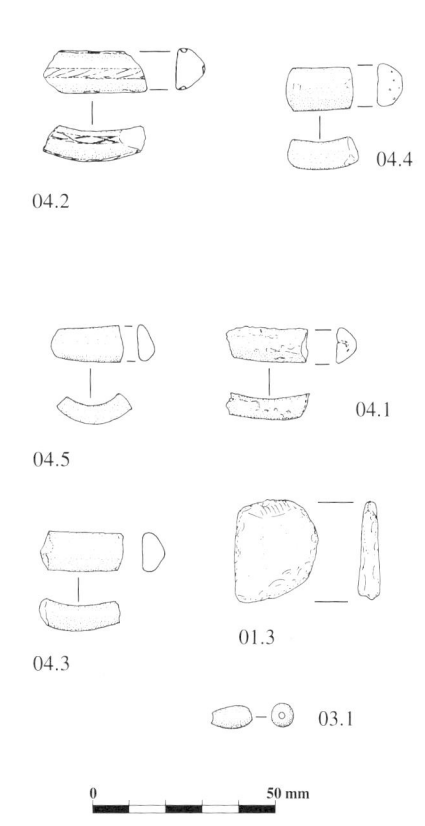

10.1 Roman bangle (GS04), bead (GS03) and glass fragments (GS01).

B MELTED LUMP

12 Small conical lump. Bluish green. Five surfaces, four newly broken, one heavily distorted by heat.
Dims 17 × 13 **82.04 Grave I/115**

Addendum

Peter Hill

An additional piece of window glass (13) from the **southern sector** may also be Roman.

13 Dark green window glass chunk, possibly Roman.
5 × 3 × 3 **64.02**

Six pieces (5, 7, 9a and b, 10 and 13) came from the **southern sector**, five from sixth-seventh century contexts and the sixth (5) from the hearth of a **Period IV** building (IV/4). All could have derived from *in situ* second-third century debris. Six of the remaining pieces came from the western part of the **northern sector**. The bowl or cup fragment came from the deposit immediately over the layers producing the Group E vessel sherds and may have been associated with other unusual vessel fragments in this area (p 325, Figure 10.23). The other pieces came from contexts ascribed to the seventh century. Two fragments (2 and 4) from the **Period I/3** hollow (109) are likely to have been deposited at roughly the same time as a third piece (9) from the **southern sector**. The conical lump (12) came from a **Period I/4** grave cutting the deposits producing the Group E vessel sherds, but a few metres from the concentrations of burnt vessel fragments (FA, p 313) and fused and folded vessel glass (FB, p 314, Figure 10.23). One of the remaining pieces (11) came from a secure **Period III** deposit (421.01) of the later ninth century, and the last (6), though unstratified, could have belonged with the group from the **northern sector**.

GS04.1–4 BANGLE FRAGMENTS

1 Fragment D-shaped section. Opaque red ground, mixed with opaque yellow. All surfaces very weathered, especially in opaque yellow areas.

H 9.5; T 6; ID 72; L 24 **543**

2 Fragment D-shaped section. Bluish green ground, unmarvered dark blue and opaque white cord (clockwise twist, two thin white rods) applied horizontally to apex, two pale yellowish brown and opaque white cords (loose anti-clockwise twist, two thin white rods) applied horizontally close to edges. Surfaces and broken edges very worn.

H 11–11.5; T 8; ID 64; L 27.2 **81.01, Grave I/52**

3 Fragment, triangular section. Opaque white with greenish tinge. Some wear on broken edges.

H 10.5; T6.5; ID 44; L 23 **457**

4 Fragment, triangular section. Opaque white with bluish tinge.

H11.4; T 7.5; ID 44; L 19 **82.03, Grave I/108**

Two bangle fragments (2 and 4) came from **Period I** graves. These may have been talismans, but coincided spatially with a heterogeneous group of glass fragments (Figure 10.23), and could have been associated with glass working (p 325). The two other fragments (1 and 3) are ascribed to the **Period IV** workshop debris in the inner precinct (Figure 6.34), and both could have been commodities of a twelfth-thirteenth century enameller (pp 240, 244).

GS03 BEAD

1 Complete biconical or drop-shaped wound bead. Bluish green, many small bubbles.

L 11.4; max D 6.6; PD 1.5 **75.02**

The bead came from wormed soil over the **Period I/4.5** roadway and is likely to have been deposited in the early-eighth century.

The Tesserae

Peter Hill

A small group of glass tesserae (GS05.1–13) probably belong with the Roman finds, although all but one are likely to have been imported in twelfth-thirteenth century. The sole early example (1), in dark blue glass, came from a **Period I/4** grave and coincided with a concentration of unusual glass fragments (Figure 10.23) including sherds of blue Group C vessels (Vs 18 and 21) and a Group D vessel with a blue rim. The tessera may thus have been a fragment of a vessel, though rather too thick, or a commodity of glass production. The remaining twelve tesserae (ten blue, one yellow and one red), came from a range of **Period V** and **VI** contexts, but are likely to have originated in a **Period IV** workshop (p. 244, Figure 6.24). The tesserae await detailed analysis.

The Roman Coin

Nicholas Holmes

The only Roman coin (CN01.1) from the excavation is a fourth century nummus, and this would be an unsurprising find on a Romano-British site. It comes from a western mint and so conforms with other coins from North British sites. It was however found among mid-ninth century debris on the floor of the **Period II** church, and cannot in itself establish fourth century occupation at Whithorn.

CN01.1 CONSTANTIUS II or CONSTANS, bronze ÆIV of Trier (AD347–8); as RIC VIII, Trier 180
 obv.: legend illegible; diademed bust right
 rev.: [VICTORIAE DD AVGG Q NN]: two Victories standing face to face, each holding wreath and palm; mint mark M/ [TR] P 1.43g; die axis 7.0
both sides off centre; much surface corrosion; worn

Discussion

Peter Hill

The Roman finds were not randomly dispersed and a convoluted stratigraphic argument would be required to ascribe them to a single original horizon. There were three distinct groups of finds (Figure 10.2). Glass predominated among the finds from the **southern sector**, and there were marked concentrations of finds in the northern and southern parts of the area. These were dispersed stratigraphically (Table 3.38), but seem more coherent spatially, and could have been displaced from a second-third century deposit scattered to the south of the **Period I/0** roadway (Figure 2.1), and possibly surrounding Structure I/11. The finds from the **central sector** were more widely dispersed, and included samian sherds from graves, which may have been talismans. The other finds comprised the three

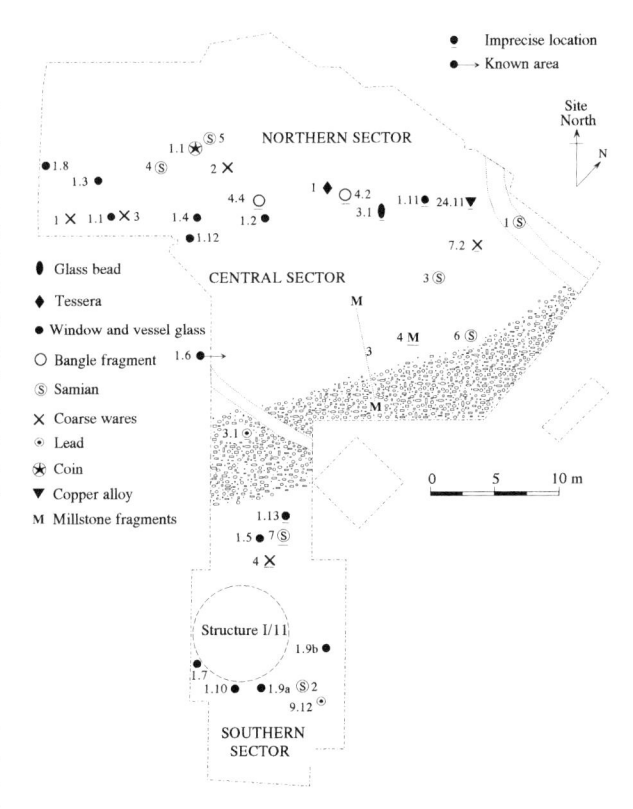

10.2 The distribution of Roman finds.

millstone fragments, a sherd of a flanged bowl (PY07.2), a copper alloy nail cleaner (BZ24.11) and a lead spindle whorl (LD3.1). The date of these pieces is uncertain, but they hint at Roman occupation. The relatively dense finds from the western part of the **northern sector** were absent from the earlier deposits, and included the coin and samian sherd from the floor of the eighth-ninth century church (p 45). The glass sherds were associated with workshop debris of the later sixth and seventh centuries - and are likely to have been imported, albeit perhaps from some other part of the site. The sherds of coarseware are however unlikely talismans and may derive from Roman debris in the vicinity, if not immediately *in situ*.

The datable finds generally pertain to the second or third centuries and there is no clear evidence of occupation in the fourth century appropriate to the late Roman settlement postulated by Charles Thomas. The only finds which might fill this gap are the coin from the ninth century church and a glass vessel fragment of fourth to sixth century date (GS02.82, pp 314-5). Some of the earlier finds do seem to have originated in debris from a second-third century settlement. The undated **Period I/0** features provide a possible context, and are depicted in Figure 10.2. Future excavations in the **Glebe Field** and elsewhere may reveal stratified evidence which will give greater substance to this debate.

The Early Medieval Imports

Ewan Campbell, Peter Hill and Jennifer Price

Introduction

Peter Hill

The **Glebe Field** has produced one of the largest groups of imported early medieval pottery and glass vessels from any western British site and presents a stratified sequence which allows a detailed analysis of evolving trade contacts in the sixth and seventh centuries. The implications are considerable and the evidence, while not unduly complex, requires detailed exposure if the argument is to be sustained. This section comprises separate reports on the pottery and glass by Ewan Campbell and a stratigraphic synthesis by Peter Hill.

The Early Medieval vessel glass

Ewan Campbell

A total of 431 listed sherds of glass were submitted to me in 1992. All of these are from vessels, except for 9 lumps of fused glass. The minimum number of vessels can be estimated at about 80, making this the largest assemblage of glass known from an early medieval western site. The nearest comparable assemblage is from Cadbury Congresbury, which has 333 sherds from a minimum of 60 vessels (Price 1992). The only larger assemblage in Britain at this period comes from the Middle Saxon trading site of *Hamwic*, modern Southampton (Hunter 1980, and more recent finds). The Whithorn assemblage is of great interest, both in terms of the glass itself which has several unique vessels and a group of vessels not found elsewhere in Britain, and in terms of the cultural and chronological light which it sheds on the occupation of the site. Taken along with the imported pottery from the site, this is undoubtedly the most important assemblage to have been recovered from any early medieval site in western Britain or Ireland.

The glass can be divided into a number of broad groups of similar provenance on the basis of form, decoration, colour and technology. **Group A**, engraved vessels of Mediterranean or Late Roman origin, is a small element, but one which has now been recognized from two other Dark Age western sites. These vessels can be seen as valuable space-fillers in the cargoes of the Mediterranean ships which traded amphorae and tableware (Classes A and B ware) to Britain in the late fifth and sixth centuries (Fulford 1989, Campbell forthcoming a). A few of the sherds, especially those from Northumbrian contexts, may represent Roman sherds kept as souvenirs or talismans, but Whithorn is the first site where at least some of these vessels can be securely linked in the same contexts as Mediterranean pottery of the sixth century. **Group B**, vessels of types found in Anglo-Saxon contexts, is also a small element, but is also known from two other important Dark Age sites, Dinas Powys and Cadbury Congresbury. These can be seen as evidence of overland contact with Anglo-Saxon areas (*c.f.* Campbell 1989), or as evidence of complex patterns of trade and re-export from the Continent. These types were produced in England and the adjacent parts of the Continent and can be dated to the sixth/seventh centuries on the basis of associations in pagan graves. Professor Evison has kindly commented on this group and given advice on other vessels. **Groups C** and **D**, respectively decorated and undecorated, form the largest group and one to which most of the glass from other western sites belongs (Campbell 1991, 1995, forthcoming b). These are from an unknown continental source, but can be dated mainly to the later sixth and seventh centuries on the basis of associations with imported continental pottery (Classes D and E ware). They were probably part of the same trading system that brought the pottery, but are not necessarily from exactly the same source area. **Group E** is unique to Whithorn, with similarities to Group C/D, but is possibly manufactured at Whithorn, though this cannot be proved. These vessels have both a distinctive method of vessel formation and unique decorative patterns. On stratigraphic grounds these appear to belong mainly to the later sixth century at Whithorn. **Group F** is the fused glass.

General comments on the nature of the most abundant types (Groups C–E) are given below, with detailed discussion of all the groups under the individual headings in the catalogue.

Vessel types

As with other western assemblages, the commonest vessel type is the cone beaker, with bowls a minor element, and a few other unusual forms occurring. This relative lack of vessel variety contrasts strongly with Late Roman assemblages, and seems to reflect an emphasis on drinking vessels. The bowls could have been used as finger-bowls, but bowls were also used as drinking vessels. Table 10.1 illustrates that the proportions and numbers of vessels of recognisable form are virtually identical for Whithorn and the rest of western sites, but differ from the proportions at Cadbury Congresbury, whose assemblage has a higher Anglo-Saxon and Roman content.

	Whithorn	Cadbury Congresbury	All other sites
Cone beakers	54–55	18	48
Bowls	11–12	10	9
Claw beakers	2	–	2
Cup	1	1–6	1–4
Goblet	1?	–	1?
Flasklet	1	–	3
Jar	1?	–	1–2
Bottle	–	4	–

Table 10.1: Vessel types on western sites.
Cadbury Congresbury: Rahtz *et al.* 1992, 137. Other sites: Campbell 1991, Table 20

A similar situation applies for vessel colour, with the same range and proportion of colours at Whithorn and other western sites. Most of the vessels are not deliberately coloured, the commonest shades being a very pale yellow which can vary to green-yellow, honey or pale amber, or almost colourless. Although the exact shade in this range is useful in distinguishing individual vessels, the range is probably the effect of differing melt and firing conditions rather than compositional differences. The majority of the vessels, therefore, seem to share a similar general metal colour and appearance. This is different from the majority of vessels found in Anglo-Saxon contexts which tend to be greener or browner and more bubbly. Pale greens are much less common, and pale blue-green rare. Deep colours account for a small number of the 80 vessels and a very small proportion (4%) of the sherds: there is one dark brown vessel, three blue (one opaque), two deep green, one pink and one bichrome green/blue vessel. An unusual colour found at Whithorn is a pale amber or honey colour with pink streaks, and it may be that the one pink vessel is a stronger variety of this colour. These vessels are of a rare dichroic type, displaying different colours in reflected and transmitted light, which may indicate they are of 'copper ruby' composition.

Technology

The metal quality is generally very good, with few bubbles or impurities, and shows no sign of devitrification or iridescence. A few vessels are particularly bubbly, making them distinctive. The surfaces are often shiny, even brilliant, though a small proportion of sherds have a matt cloudy surface. That this effect is due to burial conditions is shown by joining sherds which can be matt or shiny. This is not simply a matter of burial context, as sherds of the same vessel from the same context also exhibit this difference, but must be due to micro-environmental differences. Some sherds show signs of wear on the exterior of rims or bases which indicate prolonged usage.

Unlike contemporary vessels in Anglo-Saxon England, a large proportion (at least 60%) of the vessels are decorated with opaque white trails. Again, this proportion is almost identical with that of other western sites, at 59% (Campbell 1991, Table 21), but differs from that of Cadbury Congresbury which is much lower at 23%.

The opaque white decoration which is found on a large proportion of the sherds is due to an opacifier, probably tin oxide, small crushed particles of which can be seen in the trails (Henderson 1993). The use of tin oxide is characteristic of Celtic enamels (Dark Age and earlier), and represents a quite different technology from the Roman derived use of antimony compounds as opacifiers. All Roman continental, Anglo-Saxon and Scandinavian opacifiers so far analysed used antimony based compounds (Henderson Pers. Comm.). This raises the possibility that these vessels were made in Insular contexts, unlikely as it might seem as the vessel forms are typically Continental. The white glass is also full of bubbles which contribute to the opacity, though whether this is deliberate or due to the mixing process is not clear. When the trails are combed into festoons the opacifier can become very diffused, leaving only faint trails of bubbles to indicate the original trail. There is no sign of decay of the white trails at Whithorn, though this is often a feature of the glass from other western sites due to acid burial conditions. Occasionally the white trails have black impurities which have the effect of imparting a green tinge to the white, but this appears to be accidental (see Vessel 73). The trails can be unmarvered, but most are fully marvered as with other western glass. The exception is the vessels of Group E, where the trails near the rim are usually only part-marvered. This may be partly due to different technique of rim formation in this group, which does not involve substantial reheating and reforming of the rim. Marvered and unmarvered trails can be found on the same vessel. Traces of the pontil scar are seen on a number of cone bases and usually appears to have an irregular or sinuous form, except on Vessel 79 where it is discoidal. The scar always overlies marvered trails, showing that marvering of the base was carried out before the vessel was attached to the pontil. All rims are fire-rounded, and all except those of Group E are also thickened. There are no examples of hollow folded rims of the type characteristic of eighth century and later glass from sites such as *Hamwic*, or cut rims typical of Late Roman vessels.

Comparison with other sites

It has already been pointed out that Whithorn has produced the largest assemblage of glass in the Celtic west, in terms of numbers of both minimum vessels and of sherds, but what this tells us about the function of the site is by no means clear. Table 10.2 gives comparative numbers of glass vessels from other important glass sites in the west, along with a summary of certain characteristics of these sites which have been identified as key features from a study of all sites with imported material (Campbell 1991). At least five types of site have produced glass imports: high status fortified sites (forts or crannogs); a newly defined class of possibly high status undefended settlements (Campbell & Lane 1993); possible trading places; monastic or church sites; and small undefended intermediate status settlements. Significant numbers of glass imports are found only on the first three of these types.

It is noticeable that all of these sites, with the exception of Longbury Bank, are fortified hilltops which share a set of characteristics indicative of high status, possibly royal, occupation (Campbell 1991, forthcoming a). Whithorn lacks most of these high status characteristics: fortification, production of personal jewellery especially brooches, weapons, and literary references to royalty, but does share the association between imported glass and pottery and evidence for precious-metalworking, albeit relatively late (pp 117, 403). No certain monastic site of the period has produced large quantities of imported glass and pottery, though it must be said that no major monastic site of the period, except Iona, has been extensively excavated in modern times. Sites in Ireland such as Reask, Clonmacnoise, Derrynaflan, Armagh and Randalstown have produced only a few sherds or vessels. Possible trading sites, such as Dalkey Island, Caldey Island and sites in the Scilly Isles have produced intermediate numbers of vessels. Whithorn differs from these in not having a coastal or island location, and in the scale of the occupation. Incidentally, the Isle of Whithorn shares many of the same physical characteristics as Dalkey Island, and by analogy would be a prime candidate for a trading site in the Whithorn area. The only undefended site in the table which might be related to Whithorn is Longbury Bank in South Wales, but this type of site has all the other characteristics of a high status settlement which Whithorn lacks. In terms of the imports, then, Whithorn is unparalleled in the Celtic West, but it does have similarities to Mid-Saxon

Site	glass vessels	Mediterranean pottery vessels	continental pottery vessels	fortified	gold/silver	brooches	weapons	royal references
Whithorn	80	14	17	No	Yes	No	No	No
High status								
Cadbury Congresbury	60	17	?1	Yes	Yes	Yes	Yes	No
Dinas Powys	38	14	21	Yes	Yes	Yes	Yes	No
Mote of Mark	13+	–	13	Yes	Yes	Yes	No	No
Hen Gastell	10	2	6	Yes	No	Yes	No	No
Dunadd	7	–	30	Yes	Yes	Yes	Yes	Yes
Dumbarton rock	5	2	2	Yes	Yes	No	Yes	Yes
South Cadbury	5	14	1	Yes	Yes	Yes	No	No
Clogher	2	2–8	5	Yes	Yes	Yes	No	Yes
Lagore	2	–	5	Yes	Yes	Yes	Yes	Yes
High status undefended								
Longbury Bank	15	5–7	7	No	Yes	Yes	No	No
Trading Sites								
Dalkey Island	6	3	8	No	No	No	No	No
Samson, Scilly	–	1	12	No	No	No	No	No
Caldey	–	1	1	No	No	No	No	No
Monastic								
Armagh	1	1?	1	No	No	Yes	No	No
Iona	–	1	1	No	No	No	No	No
Reask	1?	2	1?	No	No	No	No	No
Clonmacnoise	–	–	1	No	Yes	No	No	Yes?
Randalstown	1	1	3	No	No	No	No	No
Derrynaflan	–	1	1	No	Yes	No	No	No

Table 10.2: Imports and other characteristics of major sites in the Celtic West in the 6/7th centuries.
Data from Campbell 1991, Tables 1–7, Campbell & Lane 1993, Campbell forthcoming a.

settlement sites such as *Hamwic*, where large quantities of imported glass and pottery are scattered throughout the settlement amongst timber buildings (Brisbane 1988). However the exact function of sites such as *Hamwic* are currently a matter of debate, and may not be directly relevant to the earlier situation at Whithorn.

Catalogue

Approximately 286 sherds are described here and many are ascribed to particular numbered vessels. Sherds or vessels marked with an asterisk are illustrated. In addition, there are 130 sherds which are too small and featureless to be usefully catalogued. These are all undecorated and in the paler colours. A full list is included in the excavation archive.

A. Bowls of Roman or Mediterranean origin

There is a minimum of eight vessels, five certainly with wheel-cut abraded decoration. At least one of these, Vessel 3, is probably of Mediterranean origin and fifth or sixth century date (Price 1992, 134; 1995). Price records only five other examples of these vessels in Britain: in a fifth century Anglo-Saxon grave at High Down, Sussex; in late levels at Silchester; from a Saxon cemetery at Holme Pierrepont, Notts.; from a Late to post-Roman settlement at Trethurgy, Cornwall; and at Cadbury Congresbury. These vessels could have been made in the eastern Mediterranean or in Spain; either source would be plausible if the vessels were imported with the Mediterranean pottery found at Whithorn. The other vessels are not distinct enough for us to be sure whether they are from the same area, or are residual vessels of Roman period manufacture. However, Vessel 1 comes from a good sixth century context which also produced a quantity of Mediterranean pottery, and also should be of Mediterranean origin. The other vessels are found in Northumbrian contexts which also produced Roman glass sherds, making it impossible to rule out a Roman origin, but only Vessels 6–8 have colours similar to Roman engraved glass.

Fragments with wheel-cut abraded decoration

1* **a** & **b**. Rim of bowl, thickened internally and inturned, with wheel-cut engraved design, possibly part of a letter. Metal fine, colourless with pale green tinge, surfaces shiny, some horizontal bubbles, some wear on rim exterior. D. 18 cm, 27°, T. 0.5–2 mm. **a** (**69.02**) joining **b** (**70**).
a comes from **Period I/1.3** debris to the north of Building I/1 (69.02); **b**, probably displaced, from immediately adjacent **Period I/1.6** hollow (70, Figure 3.12).

2* **a–c**. Bodysherds from vessel of unknown form. Two sherds have parts of wheel-cut decoration. Colour distinctive aquamarine, brilliant surfaces, few bubbles. **a** (**237**) **b** (**85.02**) **c** (**247.01**).
All three sherds came from the **northern sector**. **a** and **b** perhaps originate in **Period I/3** rubbish spread (85.02), **c** comes from displaced **Period I** workshop debris (110).

3* Deep bowl or cup with three rows of wheel-cut decoration, including scrolls and a possible inscription.
a. Bodysherd from basal part of large bowl. Wheel-cut decoration of row of running S-scrolls with ?inscription above and a further row of decoration below. Metal thick, pale yellow, matt surfaces. Exterior with unusual fine surface pattern, perhaps indicating the vessel was formed in a mould. D 10–14 cm, T. 1–2 mm (**213.02**).
b. Another tiny sherd with part of wheel-cut ?letter (**537**).
c. Sherd with part of wheel-cut letter (**55**).
Two sherds (**a** and **c**) from relatively late **Period I** contexts in the **southern sector**, the third (**b**) from a **Period V** grave to the south of Building I/1 (Figure 3.8).

4 Tiny sherd with part of wheel-cut decoration on inner surface, perhaps just below rim. Sherd oddly curved. Pale green, shiny surfaces.
From mid-ninth century ploughsoil to the south-east of Building I/1 (399.03), perhaps among associated **Period I/1** domestic debris (Figure 3.8).

5* Bodysherd with part of wheel-cut letter, a cursive *g* or perhaps *b*. Very pale green, not same as Vessel 4. T. 1 mm.
From fill of **Period I/3** grave (81.02, Grave I/68) immediately to west of Building I/1 (Figure 3.8).

Fragments of four vessels can be ascribed to the debris surrounding Building I/1 (Figures 3.8, 10.21), and hence to the earlier part of **Period I/1**. Sherds of the fifth vessel (2) may have originated in the **Period I/3** rubbish spread and are likely to have been deposited at a later date.

Colourless with opaque white trails

These three bowls are obviously related, and share the features of a decolourised, fine metal with a narrow band of horizontal trails just below the rim. Although bowls are found in the western

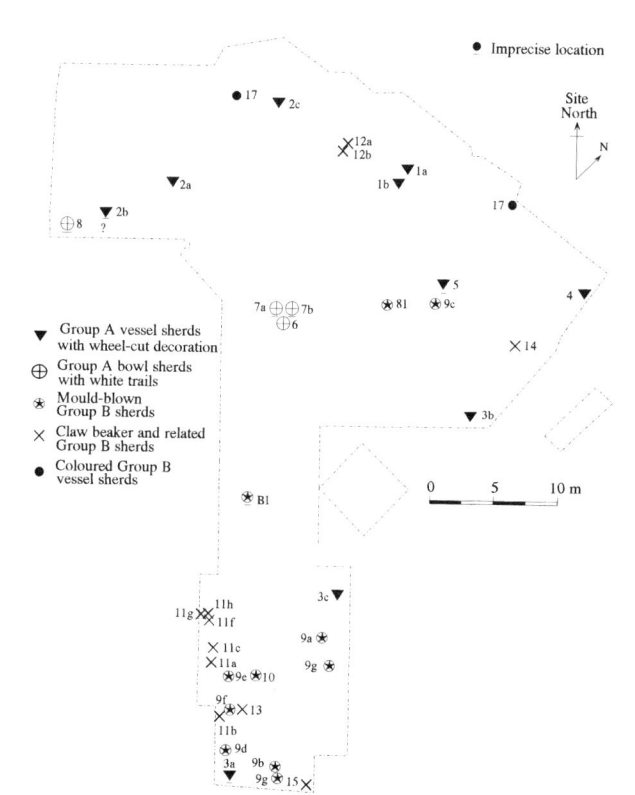

10.3 The distribution of Group A and B glass sherds.

assemblages (see Vessels 48–50 below), Vessels 6–8 appear to be from a different source. They may belong to the same source as the engraved bowls above, though none of the colours match and they are all from different vessels. Alternatively they may be of Roman origin.

6* Rim of bowl, slightly inturned and thickened. Horizontal band of fine marvered trails 2 mm wide immediately below rim. Metal fine, colourless, no bubbles. Exterior scratched and abraded. 21 × 15 × 1 mm. RD c. 18 cm, 10° (**118**).
Among concentration of vessel sherds immediately to the east of Building I/5, probably associated domestic debris (Figures 3.10 and 10.21).

7* Rim of shallow bowl, slightly thickened and inturned. Horizontal band of fine marvered trails 2 mm wide below rim. Metal fine, colourless. Two joining sherds (**a** and **b**), badly chipped. 27 × 14 × 2 mm. RD c. 20 cm, 17° (**399.01**).
From mid-ninth century ploughsoil in western part of **central sector**, but from concentration of vessel sherds immediately to the east of Building I/5.

8* Rim of bowl, strongly inturned. Narrow band of horizontal marvered white trails 2.5 mm wide just below rim. Metal fine colourless/pale green-yellow, shiny. 18 × 9 × 0.8 mm. RD ? (**93.01**).
From **Period I/1.1** ploughsoil at west end of **northern sector**. Imprecisely located but perhaps from domestic debris associated with Building I/3.

The sherds form part of a tight group of bowl fragments in the western part of the trench, which can be identified as debris associated with Buildings I/3 and I/5, and ascribed to **Period I/1.3**.

There are a few bodysherds with accidental abraded lines.

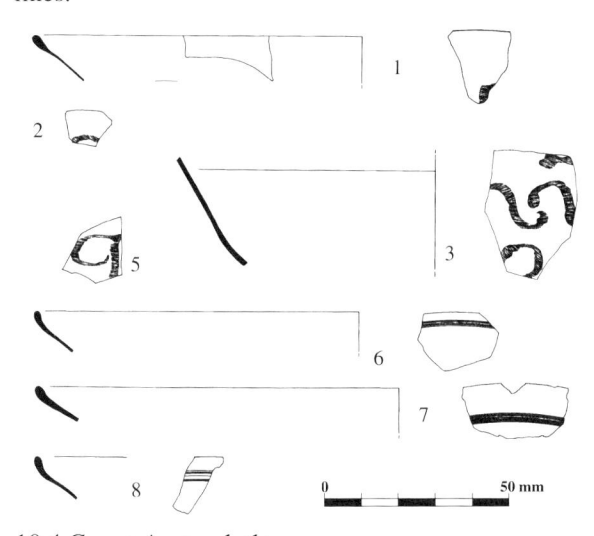

10.4 Group A vessel glass.

A/a. Part of abraded line, not wheel-cut, perhaps accidental. Colourless (**57**).
A/b. Another (**64.04**).

B. Germanic or Anglo-Saxon

There is a minimum of nine vessels in this group, but at least three others in Group D (Vessels 53, 64 & 65) may also belong here.

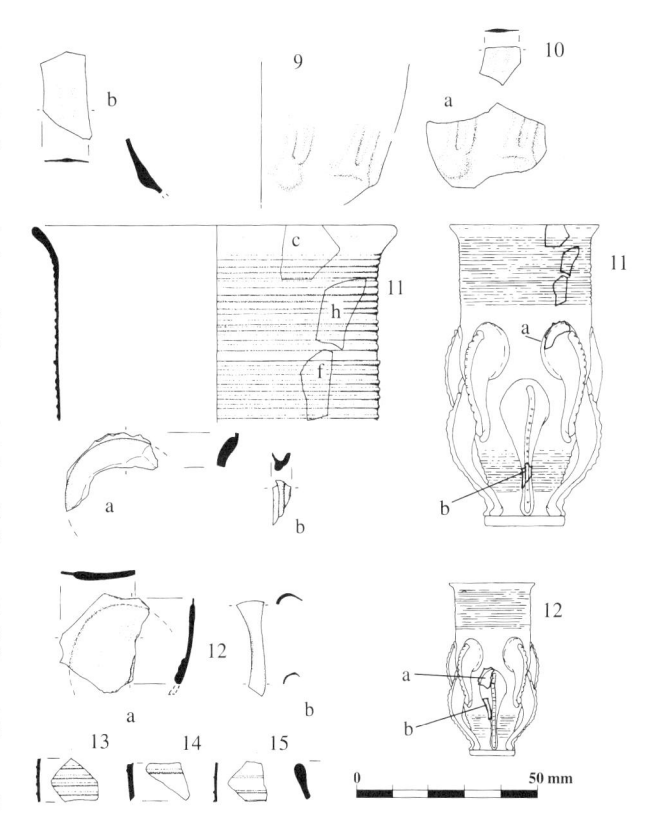

10.5 Group B vessel glass.

Mould-blown

Vessel 9 is a palm cup, a form of vessel otherwise not recorded in the West, though it is a characteristic find in sixth and seventh century pagan Anglo-Saxon graves. The form is similar to Harden's Type Xai (1956a, Fig. 25). The possible horizontal rib below the rim is a feature not noted in English examples of palm cups, but the sherd (**c**) is not certainly from this vessel. Harden follows Rademacher in dating this type to the sixth century (*ibid.*, 142), but the group has not been studied recently. In northern France the type has been dated from the mid-sixth to late seventh century (Perin 1991, 131, form 321). Professor Evison suggests a late sixth/seventh century date. Vessel 10 may also be from a palm cup, but the sherd is too small to be sure of this. A number of sherds from the lower parts of cone beakers with combed decoration have variations in wall thickness which in some small sherds resembles mould-blown ribbing, but is apparently due to the combing effect. Vessel 81 is probably part of a similar vessel in opaque blue glass.

9* Palm cup, pale yellow-green, with pairs of vertical mould-blown ribs ending in bosses or toes. Metal good quality, few bubbles, surfaces shiny.
  a. Basal sherd with two pairs of ribs and their terminals. BD c. 7 cm, T 2 mm, 31 × 18 mm (**104**).
  b. Vertical rib. 10 × 9 mm (**58**).
  c. ?Horizontal rib, W 4 mm, with central groove. One edge is nibbled or grozed. 15 × 12 mm (**399.02**).
The following are probably from the same vessel:
  d. Vertical rib and toe. Surfaces crazed and discoloured, but probably same vessel. 16 × 10 × 2 mm (**58**).

e. Vertical rib, tiny fragment. 9 × 9 mm (**114**).
f. Top of vertical rib dying out. 28 × 18 × 0.5 mm. 23 × 12 mm (**53.11**).
g. Vertical rib, tiny fragment. 15 × 3 mm (**218**).
h. Double vertical rib. 15 × 14 mm (**52.05**).

Seven of the eight sherds came from scattered contexts in the **southern sector**. The earliest are **f** from a **Period I.5** pit and **e** from a **Period I.6** rubbish spread, both ascribed to the mid- to late-sixth century. The last sherd (**c**), imprecisely located, came from mid-ninth century ploughsoil in the **central sector**.

10* Unidentifiable vessel with vertical mould-blown rib, very pale amber. 11 × 9 × 0.5 mm (**52.04**).
From **Period I.9** gully in the **southern sector**, but may have been displaced from an earlier deposit.

Most of the sherds of mould-blown vessels were displaced, but those of V9 may have originated in the **Period I.6** rubbish spread in the **southern sector**, and all three may have been components of the **Stage 3** assemblage (Figure 10.23).

Claw beakers

Claw beakers are abundant in English and Continental contexts, but only two others, both from Dinas Powys (Campbell 1991), are recorded from the West. Unfortunately the vessels are very fragmentary making it difficult to assign them to Evison's types (1982a). Vessel 12 is a dark brown colour similar to one of the Dinas Powys vessels (Harden 1963, Fig. 40, 9), which Evison (1982a, 64) has ascribed to her Type 3c of the mid-sixth century, and probably had the typical snicked trails on the claws. Vessel 11 is a more unusual colour, but still common in Type 3c, and is probably of the sixth century. The everted rim and wide band of trailing below are characteristic of this group (*c.f.* Evison 1982a, Fig. 10k).

11* Pale green/colourless claw beaker. Metal fine, surfaces shiny. Band of at least 20 partially fused self-coloured regular horizontal trails below rim.
a. Base of claw, rather flat profile. No attached trail visible, but dimpling of profile in centre suggests a central trail may have been applied, though this would not have reached the top of the claw. Surface has bands of hair-thin bubble trails, with large elongated bubbles in the metal. The vessel wall around the claw has been deliberately snipped away or grozed. Vessel wall T 1 mm; claw D 3–3.5 cm, claw T 2.5 mm (**56.02**).
b. Small fragment from near tip of claw. Profile asymmetric and slightly twisted, no signs of attached trail. Metal with matt form lines on surface giving appearance of white trail (**56.02**).
c. Rim, strongly everted and thickened on exterior. Five horizontal trails, part fused. Elongated horizontal bubbles. D *c*. 10 cm, 12° (**56.02**).
d. From just below rim, with five trails (**219**).
e. Five trails (**55**).
f. Seven trails (**56.02**).
g. Six trails (**414.02**).
h. Nine trails (**309.02**).

All the sherds came from the **southern sector**, three (**e, g** and **h**) displaced, but five (**a–d, f**) from early contexts. Four of the latter were stratified in the **Period I.3** ploughsoil (56.02) and the fifth (**d**) came from a **Period I.5** building (I/13). These deposits probably date to the earlier-sixth century (p 69).

12* Dark yellow-brown claw beaker. Metal fine, surfaces glossy. As there are only two sherds of this colour in the assemblage it is assumed they belong to one vessel.
a. Base of claw with traces of central applied trail. Profile flat, not expanded, with central dimple around trail, which does not reach top of claw. Vessel wall thin T 0.5 mm, many elongated bubbles in claw. Claw D 3.5 cm, T 1.5 mm (**76**).
b. Part of hollow tube from near end of claw. Oval asymmetric section, approx. 8 mm D (**69.01**).

b is the earliest stratified glass sherd from the *inner precinct*, and **a** was probably displaced from the same deposit. Vessel 12 is thus ascribed to **Period I/1.2**. It preceded the deposition of B**i** and B**ii** amphora sherds, and should thus date to the earlier-sixth century or perhaps before (p 69).

Vessels with self-coloured trails

There are four small sherds with self-coloured trails which cannot be ascribed to vessel forms with any certainty, though they do not belong to any other described vessels. Vessel 13 may be from a claw beaker similar to Vessel 11 but this is not certain. Vessel 14 may be from a cone beaker of the Kempston type, but the colour would be unusual and matched only by a few vessels from the Meuse region (Evison 1972, 63–5). The only other occurrence of this type of cone (and indeed of vertical self-coloured trails) in the West is at Cadbury Congresbury (Price 1992, 135, Nos 14–18) and some possible sherds from South Cadbury (Price and Cottam forthcoming). The type is dated from the fifth to mid-sixth century. Vessel 15 cannot be ascribed to any particular form. The colour is more akin to Roman glass, but does occur in post-Roman examples.

13* Neck sherd with four horizontal trails partially fused. Colourless, surface cloudy. The trailing and form, though not the colour, is similar to Vessel 11. D *c*. 10 cm; T 0.5 mm (**53.11**).

14* Vertical trail, partially marvered, from lower part of thick-walled vessel. Metal pale green-yellow, with small vertically elongated bubbles, exterior scratched. T 1.5 mm (**258**).

15* Sherd with three unmarvered widely-spaced trails. Sherd curved in two directions, trails possibly horizontal. Metal pale blue-green, exterior surface cloudy. 10 × 9 × 1 mm (**50.03**).

Group B1. A tiny sherd with one self-coloured trail. Colourless. Too small to be sure it is not one of the other vessels. (**218**).

Sherds of two vessels (13 and 15) came from early features at the south end of the **southern sector** (**Period I.5** and **7**) and may have been deposited at a slightly later date than the claw beaker (V11). The sherd of the third vessel (V14) came from disturbed soil to the south of Building I/1 and was perhaps part of the associated putative **Period I/1** domestic debris (Figure 3.8).

Deep yellow-green vessel

Vessel 16 is the only sherd in this colour, which otherwise is not found in western assemblages. The colour is more common in Anglo-Saxon vessels and it may therefore belong to the Germanic group. A base sherd of a Kempston-type cone beaker in this colour comes from Cadbury Congresbury (Price 1992, 135, No. 14), but the colour is also found in later Middle Saxon vessels.

16* Rim, thickened on interior. Metal good, with bubble trail showing where rim was folded in, shiny. 9 × 9 mm, T 1.5–3 mm (**220**).

The sherd came from the north wall trench of the **Period II/1** oratory (220) and might have originated in the displaced metalworking debris (110) or the underlying **Period I** deposits.

Olive green vessel

Again this is the only sherd from the site of this colour, which is rare in western assemblages. The sherd is not certainly ancient, but may belong to the Germanic group of vessels.

17 Tiny body sherd, form unidentifiable. Dark olive green, shiny surfaces, no bubbles. 12 × 9 × 2 mm (**73.04**).

The sherd came from the worm soil which accumulated over the **Period I/3** road during **Period I/4** (p 114).

C. Continental: Thin vessels with thickened rims and opaque white trails

This group of vessels is characteristic of western Dark Age sites, being recorded from at least 40 sites in Britain and Ireland (Campbell 1991; forthcoming b). The general characteristics of the continental vessels have already been outlined in the introduction. Group C vessels are mainly cone beakers, tapering with slight concavity towards a narrow rounded base, the rims thickened and often slightly inturned, and with very thin walls, usually around 0.5 mm. The opaque white trailed decoration of this group is almost always fully marvered in. The provenance of the vessels is unknown, as there are no known continental parallels for the running vertical chevron type of decoration on cone beakers. The strong association with E and D ware pottery suggests a source in a similar general area, probably western, but the lack of examples from Merovingian cemeteries has been a problem. Until recently production centres at this period were known only from north-east France, Belgium and the Rhineland – the centres which provided some of the glass found in Anglo-Saxon contexts – but production in the Bordeaux area is now known throughout the fifth to seventh century period (Hochuli-Gysel 1995). The vessels can be subdivided on the basis of colour, form and decoration.

Blue

There are at least two vessels in a pale French Blue colour. Single vessels of this colour, always with horizontal white trails, are found on a number of sites in Western areas: at Ballinderry No. 2 crannog, Co Offaly; Ballycatteen, Co Cork; the Mote of Mark; and Dinas Powys (Campbell 1991, Appendix 15; Campbell forthcoming b). The contexts of these finds suggests a date in the very late sixth or seventh centuries. This colour is exactly the same as the blue rim of Vessel 51. Note also the opaque blue Vessel 52 which is a similar tone.

18* Pale French Blue ?cone with a band of trails at least 15 mm wide below rim.
 a. & b. Rim, thickened internally and externally. Decoration of horizontal white trails of varying widths, some crossing, in bands. Part-marvered. Metal fine, bubbly near rim, shiny surfaces. RD 8 cm, 120° (**96** and **904**)
 c. Sherd from below rim with part-marvered trails (**96**).
 d. Another sherd from slightly lower down. Lowest trails marvered (**90**).

19* Bodysherd from similar vessel to 18, trails less marvered, colour darker, spacing of trails more regular. Metal bubbly with large white inclusion. 14 × 9 × 0.5 mm (**229**).

Additional sherd (C1) probably from Vessel 18 or 19, but the position suggests it could be from another vessel: **a.** Tiny sherd of this colour, with traces of internal self-coloured ?trail or thickening. 9 × 5 × 0.5 mm (**399.02**).

Vessel 18 seems to have originated in the organic soil (96) associated with Building I/6 at the start of **Period I/2** and so perhaps dates to the third quarter of the sixth century (pp 69, 90). The sherd of V19 from the **southern sector** was displaced into a late eighth/early-ninth century context. The associated sherd (C1a) came from the mid-ninth century ploughsoil and, though distant from the others, fits the distribution of other finds ascribed to **Stage 3** (Figure 10.23)

Pink

There are one or two vessels in this distinctive pink/amber dichroic colour. Vessel 20 is an unique vessel, difficult to parallel. The pink colour is not otherwise found in fifth to seventh century glass in the West, except for a single sherd from the Mote of Mark (Harden 1956a, 150, No. 19). Deeper red glass is characteristic of the eighth/ninth centuries (Evison

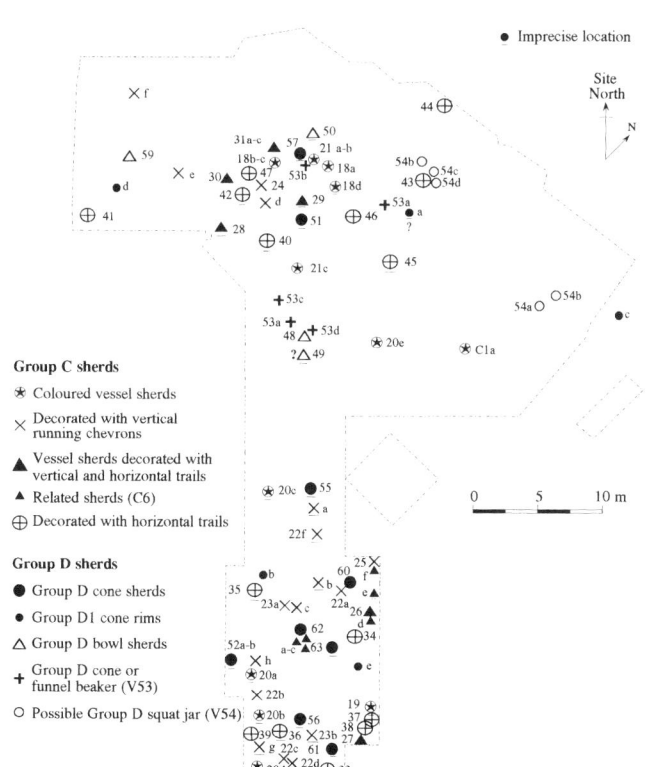

10.6 The distribution of Group C and D glass sherds.

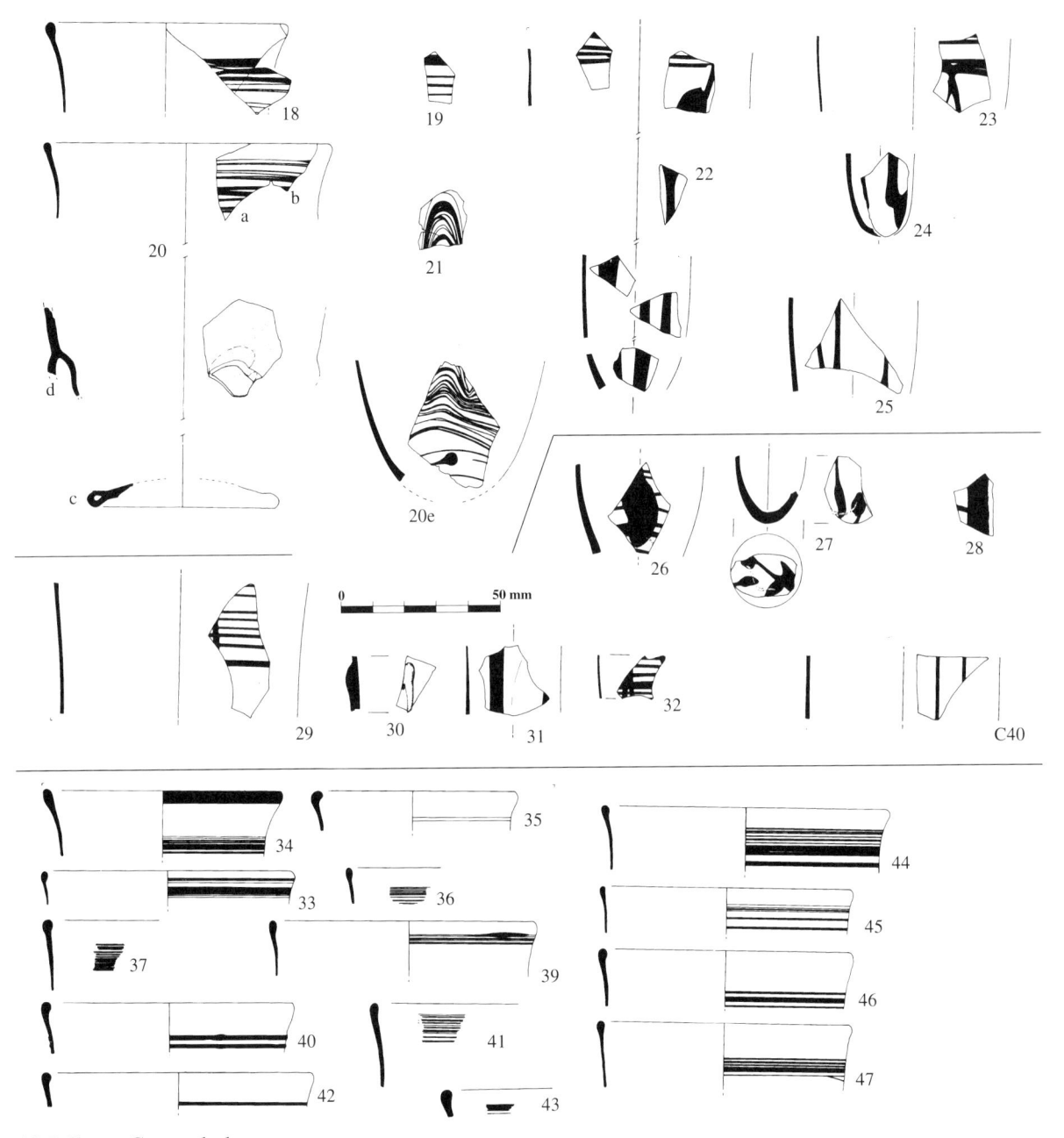

10.7 Group C vessel glass.

1982b, 8), but Vessel 20 may be a late variety of the Roman period technology of copper ruby glass (Henderson, Pers. Comm.). Analysis may resolve this problem. A much paler version of dichroic pink/amber is also found in Group E vessels 66–70, Group D vessels 55–57 and Vessel 22. The form of the vessel is also difficult to parallel. Although the stemmed beaker form persists from the Roman period into the fifth century, and is the basic form of later claw beakers, in these vessels the foot is formed in a different manner, by pushing in the tip of the blown vessel. In Vessel 20 the footring appears to have been made separately, with a properly rounded rim, before being attached to the vessel. Beakers with this type of foot are known from Italy in the seventh century (Evison 1982b, Fig. 3c). The hollow blown boss (or claw?) decoration is also very unusual, though a few such bosses are found on late (seventh century) claw beakers (Evison 1982a, 50–1). Taken together these characteristics suggest a possible seventh century date for Vessel 20, which is not incompatible with the stratigraphic position of the sherds.

20* Footed vessel, perhaps a stemmed beaker or goblet, in a distinctive colour, pale streaky wine-red in transmitted light and pale reddish amber in reflected light, decorated with a band of horizontal marvered white trails and hollow-blown? bosses. Although the sherds are not certainly all from the same vessel, these are the only sherds in this very unusual colour.

a & b. Two joining sherds of rim, thickened internally, with band of horizontal marvered white trails of varying widths below. RD *c.* 9 cm, 30°. **a** (**235.02**), **b** (**61.01**).

c. Basal footring with hollow folded-over rim. The top surface of the rim shows flaws where it has been put down while hot, suggesting it was separately made. Surfaces abraded and cloudy. 22 × 15 × 3 mm. D 6 cm, 40° (**215**).

d. Sherd from lower part of vessel with irregular hollow-blown boss (or failed claw) which has been pulled sideways with a hook. Surfaces abraded. 23 × 28 × 2–3 mm (**213.03**).

The following sherd may belong to this vessel, but the colour is less pink and the stratigraphic position suggests otherwise. The use of an unmarvered spiral trail on the base is paralleled on a green cup? from Longbury Bank (Campbell and Lane 1993, Fig. 7, vessel 2). The festoons have been pulled down with a point which has deeply indented the surface of the glass.

***e**. Basal part of wide cone, cup or deep bowl. Decorated with a wide band of regularly spaced marvered white trails, many bifurcating, pulled down into wide arcs. Below this is a spiral anticlockwise trail of unmarvered white, starting from a large blob. Sherd smashed on excavation. 30 × 40 mm. T 1–3 mm (**106**).

Most of the sherds came from late contexts in the **southern sector** which are compatible with the proposed seventh century date. One came from the upper fill of a relatively late ditch (61.01) which was sealed by the **Period I.11** boundary path, and the vessel can reasonably be ascribed to **Period I.11**. The smashed sherd came from a spread of charcoal on the surface of the **Period I/1.5** graveyard, which may have been contemporary with similar material in the **Phase 1.6** hollow. The sherd might thus pertain to the mid-sixth century.

Vessels in pale colours

Decorated with combed festoons

This is the largest group of decorated vessels at Whithorn, but almost all of the examples seem to belong to the thicker vessels of Group E. Only two small sherds of one vessel appear to belong to Group C, both in terms of their colour and thickness.

21* Bowl?, pale blue-green, with opaque white trails combed down? into neat arcades.
   a. Two small sherds. Metal good, no bubbles. T 0.3–0.8 mm. **a** and **b** joining (**82.03**, Grave I/105).
   c. Tiny sherd of variable thickness (**85.05**).

The sherds came from relatively late contexts (**Period I/4**), but from the same area as the Group E vessel sherds with which they may originally have been associated (Figure 10.23).

Decorated with vertical running chevrons

This type of decoration is a characteristic of vessels in the west, but has remained unrecognized until recently as the full scheme of decoration was not apparent. Reconstruction of a vessel from Dinas Powys has shown that the vessels have a pattern of vertical running chevrons, about six to a vessel, beneath a band of horizontal trails (Campbell 1991, Illust. 66). The asymmetric form of the top of the chevron is distinctive, described as wishbone-shaped by Thorpe (1935, 69), while the bases of the loops tend to merge around the base of the cone. Other certain examples are known from Dinas Powys, Hen Gastell and Longbury Bank in South Wales; Armagh in Ireland; and Mote of Mark in Scotland. There is a strong association with E ware pottery on these sites, suggesting an early-seventh century *floruit*.

Unfortunately all the Whithorn vessels are extremely fragmentary, and none can be associated with any of the rim sherds, but there can be no doubt that some of the rims with horizontal white trails belong to these vessels. There is a minimum of six or seven vessels.

22* Pale pink/amber cone with chevrons and horizontal trails, part-marvered.
   a. Top of wide chevron, with trail taken up from top to form horizontal spiral trails below rim. Trails part-marvered. Metal surfaces cloudy. 17 × 15 mm, T. 0.5 mm. D *c.* 7 cm (**53.07**).
   b. Basal sherd, with parts of two wide vertical trails, marvered. Exterior scratched. BD 3 cm, T. 1.5–2.5 mm. (**236.01**).
   c. Sherd from near base with three wide vertical trails, marvered. 15 × 13 mm, T. 0.7 mm (**901**).
   d. Sherd with base of chevron, marvered. 14 × 9 mm, T 0.8 mm (**54**).
   e. Sherd from below rim with four part-marvered horizontal trails. Not certainly the same vessel. 17 × 11 mm, T. 0.6 mm (**904**).
   f. Part of wide vertical trail, just beginning to turn, possibly top of chevron. Exterior badly burnt, but this seems to be of pink glass (**64.02**).

23* Cone, pale green/colourless, with very narrow vertical chevrons, part-marvered.
   a. Sherd from below rim with five thick horizontal trails, the lower three overlapping. Beneath these is the top of a narrow chevron which pulls down the lower horizontal trails. Trails part-marvered. Metal bubbly, surfaces glossy. D *c.* 6 cm. 22 × 18 mm, T. 0.7 mm (**55**).
   b. Tiny sherd with top of narrow asymmetric chevron similar to **a**. 9 × 9 mm (**58**).

24* Basal sherd of narrow cone with bases of three wide marvered vertical trails, probably chevrons. Metal pale yellow, no bubbles, exterior scratched. 25 × 15 mm, T. 1–2 mm, BD 2 cm (**109**).

25* Sherd of thick pale green vessel with three faint vertical diverging trails, probably the middle parts of chevrons. Metal fine, no bubbles, glossy surfaces. 31 × 22 mm, T. 1.1–1.5 mm. D 4 cm (**901, southern sector**).

Group C2. The following sherds are from vessels different from those above, but the total number of vessels represented is unclear, perhaps another two or three.

   a. Part of top of chevron, part-marvered. Pale honey colour (**64.02**).
   b.* Top of chevron, part-marvered with dark streak. Colourless?, cloudy outer surface (**55**).
   c. Two vertical trails, part of chevron. Colourless (**901, southern sector**).
   d. Tiny sherd with decoration similar to Vessel 23. Pale yellow-green (**109**).
   e. Another similar sherd (**83**).
   f. Sherd from near base with two wide vertical trails not parallel, marvered. Metal pale honey, many bubbles (**85.06**).
   g. Similar sherd, but pale green, bubbly (**232**).
   h. Tiny basal sherd with base of chevron. Exterior badly abraded. Pale ?yellow (**114**).

This group of vessels and associated sherds was widely scattered through the **Period I** deposits generally occurring in later layers such as the **Period I.10** silts (55, 58) in the **southern sector** and the late **Period I/3** rubbish spread (109) in the *inner precinct*. A marked concentration in the **southern sector** was matched by the distribution of E ware (Figures 10.6, 18 and 24). Three sherds (22f, C2a and C2h) are ascribed to earlier contexts in the **southern sector**, but could have been intrusive. This seems to be a relatively late group concentrated in the deposits (55, 58, 109) producing E ware, and so matching the associations recorded on other sites.

Decorated with vertical and horizontal trails

Several sherds come from vessels with a decorative scheme that belongs to neither of the two previous groups. The overall scheme cannot yet be reconstructed, but appears to consist of a number of simple vertical trails, with a band of horizontal trails below the rim, and, in at least one case, a band of spiral trails around the base. The fragments found here may not all be from the same decorative scheme, and at least one (Vessel 28) appears to have been added to a vessel with combed festoons. This type of decoration is a simpler form of the running chevron scheme. There are at least seven vessels represented. No parallels can be cited for the decoration.

26* Basal sherd with eight spiral horizontal trails which overlap a wide irregular vertical streak, both marvered. An irregular pontil scar overlies both sets of trail. Metal pale yellow. BD 3–4 cm. 19 × 27 mm, T. 1–3 mm (**55**).

27* Base of narrow cone. Decoration of at least four vertical trails ending in 'tadpoles' under base, some crossing, marvered. Covered by S-shaped pontil scar. Pale green-yellow, exterior scratched. BD 2 cm. 24 × 20 mm T. 1.5–3.5 mm (**57**).

28* Wide (7 mm) vertical trail apparently applied over two horizontal trails that have been pulled downwards. Part-marvered, many black impurities. Pale yellow (**82.04**, Grave I/115).

29* Band of regular, widely-spaced horizontal trails, part-marvered, overlain by a vertical unmarvered trail. Pale honey, bubbles, surfaces slightly cloudy. D 8 cm, 40 × 15 mm, T. 1 mm (**82.03**, Grave I/107).

30* Top of thick vertical trail, unmarvered, with blob of attachment. Line of black impurities in trail. Pale green (**89**).

31* Lower part of vessel with two wide part-marvered trails. Metal pale green-yellow, bubbly. D 3 cm, **a–b** joining **c** (**89**).

32* Band of horizontal spaced trails over three diverging vertical trails. Colourless (**926**).

Group C6. Miscellaneous body sherds probably from vessels with vertical and horizontal trails.

> **a.** and **b.** Two sherds with single trail, part-marvered. Pale yellow (**53.10**).
> **c.** One trail, part-marvered, with black impurities. Pale yellow (**53.10**).
> **d.** Two faint trails crossing at right angles, orientation unclear. Colourless (**55**).
> **e.** One trail, part-marvered, black impurities. Pale yellow (**55**).
> **f.** Tip of vertical tapering blob, part-marvered. Pale green, bubbly (**901**, **southern sector**).

This group of vessels and sherds generally came from earlier deposits than those with vertical running chevrons, the earliest secure examples being the two vessel sherds from the **Period I/2** rubbish spread (89) in the *inner precinct* from which two further fragments (Vs 28 and 29) from **Period I/4** graves may have been displaced. A group of pale yellow sherds (**a–c**) came from the fill of a pit (53.10) in the **southern sector** ascribed to **Period I.4** although the fill may have been somewhat later. This group probably overlapped with the Group E vessels although it was unrepresented in the earlier of the deposits (100, 96) producing Group E sherds.

Decorated with horizontal trails only

These fifteen rim sherds are all from different vessels, and not from any of the other rims of vessels in this group. As most only preserve the area near the rim, it is impossible to say whether the lower parts of the vessels would have been decorated with chevrons, combing or other trails. However, vessels decorated only with horizontal bands near the rim do occur in western assemblages. All the trails are opaque white, horizontal and fully marvered unless otherwise stated.

Vessel 34 stands out from the rest of this group in having the rim decorated with a wide white trail. The only other example in the west is from the Mote of Mark (Harden 1956a, Fig. 27d, Pl. 17B, 5) which is so similar that it must be from the same workshop. This type of rim decoration, but in blue rather than white, is also found on Vessel 51, which is here ascribed to the seventh century. A rim in contrasting colour is characteristic of eighth century and later vessels, though this is sometimes of bichrome twisted rods. At *Hamwic* there is a funnel beaker with opaque yellow trails on the rim (Hunter 1980, Fig. 11, 5, 10). As Vessel 34 comes from a good pre-Northumbrian context, and is associated with other seventh century pottery and glass, a seventh century date is likely, possibly late in the century.

33* Rim, thickened externally and internally. Fine hair trails start on rim. Metal green-yellow, exterior scratched. RD 8 cm, 30°. 20 × 10 mm, T. 1–2.5 mm (**58**).

34* Rim, thickened externally. Decorated with a wide white trail around the rim, fully marvered in, and a band of fine horizontal white marvered trails lower down the vessel. RD 7–8 cm, 30°. 20 × 20 mm, T. 1–3 mm (**55**).

35* Rim, thickened internally, sharply inturned. Two fine hair trails below rim. Metal pale green-yellow, exterior scratched. RD 6–7 cm, 30°. 15 × 13 mm, T. 0.5–2 mm (**216**).

36* Rim, thickened externally and internally. Band of trails becoming hair thin towards rim. Pale yellow. 9 × 11 mm, T. 1–2.3 mm (**58**).

37* Rim, thickened externally and internally, slight inturn. Band of trails 9 mm wide, crossing and becoming finer towards rim. Pale yellow. RD 7–8 cm, 25°. 22 × 16 mm, T. 0.5–3 mm (**55**).

38 Rim, partially burnt. Band of trails. 17 × 6 mm (**104**).

39* Rim, thickened internally. Narrow band of fine hair trails just below rim, 3 mm wide. Blob for start of trail at top. Pale green-yellow, exterior scratched. RD 8–9 cm, 30°. 24 × 18 mm, T. 1–3 mm (**50.02**).

40* Rim, thickened externally and internally. Two thick trails, only part-marvered. Metal thick, pale green-yellow, exterior slight scratching. RD 8 cm, 45°. 29 × 16 mm, T. 1.8–3.6 mm (**82.03**, Grave I/110).

41* Rim, thickened internally. Band of trails 8.5 mm wide. Metal pale yellow/colourless, many bubbles. 26 × 18 mm, T. 1–2.8 mm (**94.01**).

42* Rim, thickened internally and inturned. One trail survives below rim. Pale green-yellow. RD 8–9 cm, 30°. 10 × 21 mm, T. 2–3 mm (**82.04**, Grave I/111).

43* Rim, thickened internally and externally. Band of trails just below rim. Pale green-yellow. 12 × 8 mm, T. 2–4 mm (**70**).

44* Rim, thickened externally. Band of thick trails with thinner ones above. Metal pale yellow, surfaces crazed, burnt?. RD 7–8 cm, 20°, 13 × 15 mm, T. 0.7–2 mm (**94.02**).

45* Rim, thickened internally and externally. Band of trails, thicker below, hair fine above, at least 11 mm wide. Pale yellow. RD *c.* 9 cm, 15°. 13 × 19 mm, T. 1–3 mm (**81.01**, Grave I/50).

46* Rim, thickened internally. Band of thick trails well below rim. Pale yellow. RD *c.* 8 cm, 20°. 18 × 23 mm, T. 0.7–3 mm (**70**).

47* Rim, thickened internally and externally. Band of trails 6 mm wide, well below rim. Pale yellow, exterior scratched. RD *c.* 8 cm, 22°. 20 × 15 mm, T. 1–2.5 mm (**96**).

Five of the eight vessel sherds with horizontal trails from the *inner precinct* (Vs 40–47) came from secure early context, and the remaining three (Vs 40, 42 and 45) from graves, may have been displaced from equally early deposits. The earliest were two sherds (41 and 44) from dumped material (94.01 and 94.02) originating in **Period I/1.3** (pp 83–5). Sherds of two vessels (43, 46) came from **Period I/1.6** deposits (70) and a third (47) from debris (96) which accumulated at the beginning of **Period I/2**. The seven vessel sherds (33–39) from the **southern sector** generally came from later deposits (notably the **Period I.10** waterborne silts, 55 and 58) and thus support the proposed date for V34, but one (39) from 50.02 was probably contemporary with vessels from the *inner precinct*.

Miscellaneous bodysherds with trails

These small sherds have trails but cannot be assigned to any of the particular groups of vessel discussed above. They are classed in three groups: horizontal, vertical, and other (which includes unassignable trails). Unless otherwise stated, the trails are marvered, the glass is of normal thickness (0.5–1 mm) and horizontal trails are from the area below the rim.

Group C3 Horizontal

a. One broad trail from lower part of vessel, D 4 cm. Pale green (**118**).
b. Part of one broad trail. Pale blue-green (**118**).
c. Two spaced trails. Pale yellow (**74**).
d. Six trails, marvered. Yellow (**94.01**).
e. Part of one broad trail. Pale blue-green (**97**).
f. Two wide trails. Pale green (**119.01**).
g. Two trails, part-marvered. Pale amber/pink (73.01).
h. Two thin trails, spaced. Pale yellow (**109**).
i. Badly burnt. Thick trails, part-marvered (**82.03**, Grave I/107).
j. Five trails, part-marvered. Pale green-yellow (**82.04**, Grave I/113).
k. One trail. T. 1.5 mm. Pale honey (**82.04**, Grave I/116).
l. Two trails. Pale yellow (**64.02**).
m. Nine trails, spaced apart. Pale yellow (**55**).
n. Three trails. Pale yellow (**55**).
o. Three trails. Pale green-yellow, glossy. T. 1–2 mm (**55**).
p. Wide band of regularly spaced trails. Pale amber (**53.09**).
q. Part of one broad trail. Pale blue-green (**216**).
r. Four broad trails, decayed. Pale yellow (**230.01**).
s. Four trails, part-marvered. Pale amber (**246**, Grave II/6).
y. Three trails. Pale honey. T. 1.8–2.5 mm (**246**, Grave II/6).
u. Two trails. Pale yellow (**247.01**).
v. Two thin trails. T. 1.5 mm. Pale yellow (**203.03**).
w. One trail. Large bubble flaws, glossy surfaces. Pale yellow (**255**).
x. Four trails, part-marvered. T. 1.5–2 mm. Pale yellow (**333**).
y. Four spaced trails, shakily applied, part-marvered. Pale honey, glossy surfaces (**399.02**).
z. Wide band of trails, spaced. Burnt (**408**).
aa. Wide band of trails. Burnt (**408**).
bb. Tiny. Two wide trails. Colourless (**408**).
cc. Five trails, part-marvered. Pale green-yellow (**901**, **southern sector**).
dd. Four widely spaced trails, part-marvered. Pale green-yellow (**901**, **central sector**).
ee. Four spaced out trails. Pale honey (**904**, **northern sector**).

Group C4 Vertical

Most of these are probably small sections from the vertical parts of chevrons or combed decoration, but there also appear to be a few sherds from vessels with true vertical trails, often unmarvered or part-marvered. Not enough survives to be sure of the complete decorative scheme.

a. Two widely spaced faint trails on lower part of vessel. Pale honey (**70**).
b. Two trails, faint. Pale green-yellow (**70**).
c. One trail. Pale amber (**73.04**).
d. One trail, unmarvered. Pale honey (**85.02**).
e. One vertical trail. Pale green, bubbly (**82.03**, Grave I/108).
f. Vertical comb(?) marks. Green-yellow (**85.05**).
g. One trail, part-marvered. Pale yellow, glossy surfaces (**64.04**).
h. Sherd with two vertical trails of different widths, part-marvered. Colourless (**64.02**).
i. One wide trail, part-marvered. Pale pink (**114**).
j. and **k**. One vertical trail. Pale yellow/colourless (**52.03**).
l. Part of one vertical trail. Green-yellow (**55**).
m. One vertical trail. Green-yellow (**55**).
n. Two faint trails. Pale yellow (**55**).
o.* Two thin vertical trails, possibly combed. Metal pale yellow-green. Traces of grozing at upper edge giving the appearance of cut rim. D 6 cm (**212.02**).
p. One trail. Pale yellow (**238**).
q. One trail. Pale yellow, glossy surfaces (**901**, **southern sector**).

Group C5 Other

a. Two unmarvered trails, orientation unclear. Pale yellow (**91**).
b. Irregular, widely spaced spiral trail above trail ?pulled downwards. Discoloured (**70**).
c. Sherd with one diagonal (?spiral) trail, marvered. Green-yellow (**89**).
d. One trail, part-marvered, orientation unclear. Colourless, glossy surfaces (**109**).
e. Splinter of thick yellow glass with part of wide trail (**56.02**).
f. Two trails diverging and widening, part-marvered. Pale yellow (**51**).
g. Band of vertical trails pulled down then sideways? Pale amber (**52.02**).
h. Two thin spiral? trails. Pale honey (**399.02**).

D. Continental: thin plain vessels

This group shares the characteristics of Group C, but the vessels are undecorated. Some of the smaller rim fragments may come from vessels which are decorated lower down the vessel, but there is no means of establishing this. In all there is a minimum of 16 vessels.

Bowls

Vessels 48 and 49 are of shades not common in the other continental imports, and they may belong with Mediterranean bowls of Group A. Vessel 50 is quite thick and might belong in Group E or B, but the form of the vessel is indeterminate.

48* Rim of bowl, inturned and thickened. Metal pale blue-green, shiny surfaces, large horizontal bubbles. RD *c.* 16 cm, 15°. 22 × 16 mm, T. 1–3 mm (**118**).

49* Rim of shallow bowl or plate. Metal fine, horizontal bubbles, apple-green. RD 16–18 cm, 10°. 12 × 14 mm, T. 1–3 mm (**904**).

50* Basal angle of flat-based bowl? Metal good, thick, scratched and abraded. Pale yellow. T 2 mm (**82.03**, Grave I/104).

10.8 Group D vessel glass.

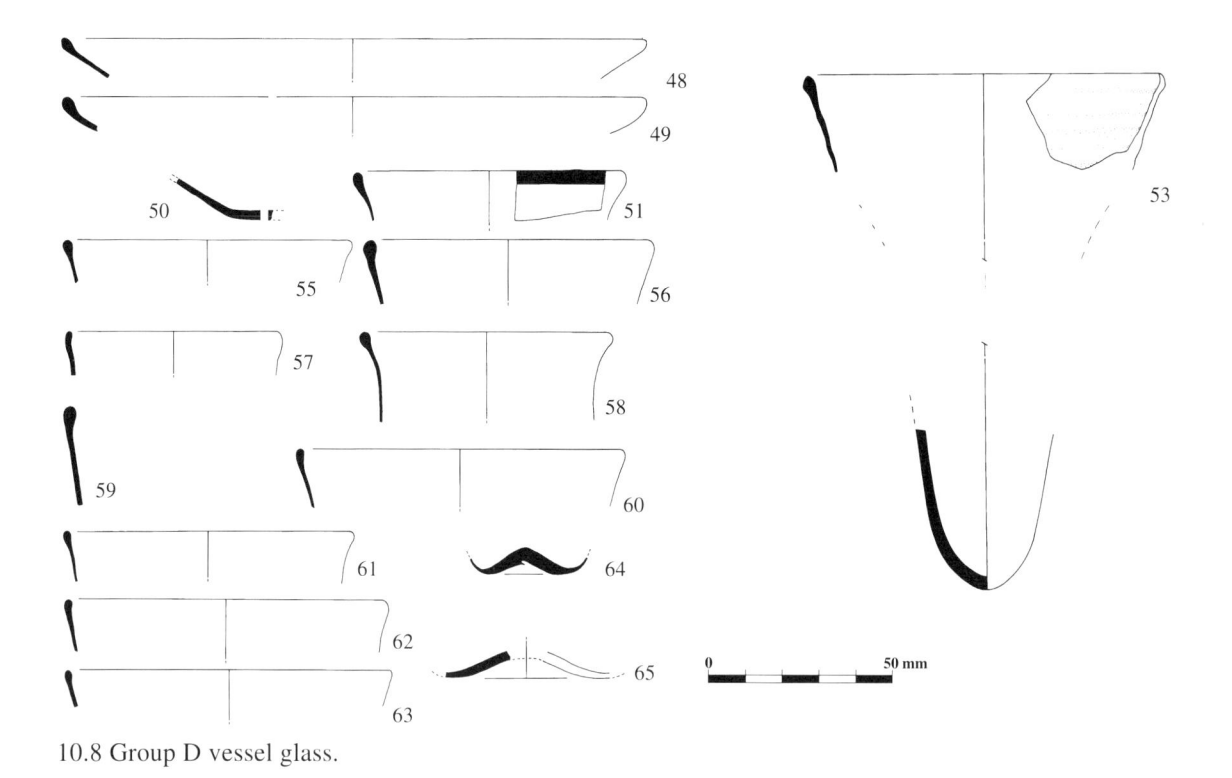

V48 came from the concentration of sherds to the east of Building I/5 (Figures 3.10 and 10.21) in association with two Group A bowls (V6 and 7) and the putative cone or funnel beaker (V53). V49 came from a group of finds disorganised during processing, and either came from this area or from the **southern sector**. V50 came from a **Period I/4** grave cutting into the northern part of the concentration of Group E sherds (Figure 10.23), which argues for its assignation to Group E.

Bichrome

Vessel 51 has a unique decoration, with a band of blue around the rim which has been melted into the body metal before the rim was formed. The colour of the blue is identical to Vessels 18 and 19, and is possibly from the same source. This is the only vessel in the Celtic west with a trail which is other than self-coloured or opaque white. The use of a contrasting colour around the rim is characteristic of eighth century and later vessels from Scandinavia (Evison 1982b, 12) and the Continent (Evison 1991, 139), though this is often in the form of a rod marvered into the rim. A green vessel with a blue rim is recorded from Saint-Denis, Paris, in a Carolingian context (*ibid.*, 144, No. 60a). Vessel 51, and Vessel 34, which has a similar contrasting rim but in white, can be seen as early examples of this later bichrome tradition (Evison 1982b; 1983). Recent work in the south of France has shown that vessels with blue rims were common there in the seventh century (Foy 1995 b). Given the proximity to Bordeaux, it is possible that Vessel 51 is a unique stray find from this area, but this requires further comparison of the vessels to be sure.

51* Rim of cone, thickened. Pale yellow-green, with thick band of French Blue fully fused into rim. Metal bubbly, shiny surfaces. RD 7 cm, 40°. 25 × 13 mm, T. 1.7–3.8 mm (**82.03**, Grave I/109).

V51 came from a late grave (**Period I/4.3**), but coincided spatially with a cluster of blue vessel sherds, and may have originated in a **Period I/2** deposit (Figure 10.23).

Opaque blue

The colour of this vessel is similar to that of Vessels 18 and 19, but differs in being opaque. The opacity may be caused by tiny bubbles, in which case it may not be deliberate. As the form cannot be determined little more can be said about the vessel. In Anglo-Saxon contexts the colour is characteristic of the seventh century.

52 Two tiny sherds of vessel. Colour opaque French Blue. Metal shiny, surfaces with pimples caused by bubbles. 9 × 9 mm, T. 1.2 mm, **a** and **b** joining (**235.02**).

The sherds came from the waterborne silts (235.02) on the west side of the southern sector and were broadly contemporary with the features producing sherds of V20.

Pale green

Vessel 53 seems to be intermediate between Groups D and E. The rim is thickened on the exterior only and the glass is fairly thick, but the interior does not show marks of the pincers, and the rim is flaring rather than upright as in Group E. The colour and metal of Vessels 53 and 54 are more reminiscent of

Anglo-Saxon vessels, and they may belong in Group B. This is supported by their relatively early position in the stratigraphic sequence.

53* Cone or ?funnel beaker with wide expanding mouth and narrow base. Metal pale green, bubbly and distinctive, surfaces shiny.
    a. Rim, thickened externally, with bevelled top. Below the rim the wall is corrugated, possibly fused applied trails. RD 10 cm, 35°. 27 × 36 mm, T. 1.5–4 mm (**248**).
    b–e. Base of cone. BD 3 cm. T. 2–4 mm. Four joining sherds: **b** (**82.03**, Grave I/ 105); **c** (**904, northern sector**); **d** (**118**) & **e** (**399.02**).

54 Vessel of indeterminate form, with a narrow neck so possibly a squat jar, in a similar colour, also bubbly, but not the same vessel.
    a. Tiny neck sherd, strongly everted. (**80.01**, Grave I/15).
    b–e. Body sherds, some quite thin. T. 0.5–2 mm. **b** (**70**); **c** and **d** (**69.02**); **e** (**80.01**, Grave I/14).

Both vessels can be ascribed to the early group of glass associated with the **Period I/1** buildings in the **central sector**. The rim of V53 came from a **Period II** context adjacent to the chapel and was perhaps displaced from an unknown position, together with the industrial debris in 110 (Table 3.35). Two of the base sherds (**d** and **e**) came from the concentration of vessel glass to the east of Building I/5 and a third (**c**), recovered after the excavation finished, probably came from the gully immediately to the north of the building. The fourth sherd (**b**) came from a **Period I/4** grave some way to the north. The distribution of the finds argues that V53 was deposited to the east of Building I/5 in the middle stages of **Period I/1**. Two sherds of V54 came from the early rubbish deposits (69.02, **Period I/1.3**) to the north of Building I/1; a third (**b**) was displaced into slightly later, but immediately adjacent debris of **Period I/1.6**. Two other sherds came from **Period 1.2** graves to the south east of Building I/1 (Figures 3.8 and 10.21). The fragments of the vessel are thus likely to have been among domestic debris scattered around this building and deposited in the earlier-sixth century (pp 79, 323-4).

Amber

These three vessels are all pale amber with pink streaks, no bubbles. They are probably cones.

55* Rim, thickened internally and externally. RD *c*. 8 cm, 25°. 24 × 11 mm. T. 1.2–3.5 mm (**236.01**).

56* Rim, thickened internally and externally. Exterior worn. RD *c*. 8 cm, 25°. 17 × 17 mm, T. 1–4 mm (**61.01**).

57* Rim, thickened internally. Top of rim abraded. RD *c*. 6 cm, 40°. 22 × 12 mm, T. 2 mm (**82.03**, Grave I/105).

Pale yellow/green-yellow/colourless cones

There are at least six vessels in these pale colours which cannot be matched to any of the rims which have white trails.

58* Rim, thickened internally and everted. Metal green-yellow, many bubbles. RD 7 cm, 25°. 24 × 20 mm, T. 1–3 mm (**235.01**).

59* Rim, thickened internally and inturned, possibly a deep bowl. Metal thick with bubbles and black impurities. Outer lip worn. Pale yellow. 20 × 22 mm, T. 2–4 mm (**94.01**).

60* Rim, thickened internally. Metal fine, exterior matt, pale green-yellow. RD 9 cm, 35°. 24 × 15 mm, T. 1–2 mm (**64.04**).

61* Rim, thickened internally and externally. Pale yellow/colourless, no bubbles. RD 7–8 cm, 25°. 13 × 15 mm, T. 0.5–2 mm (**58**).

62* Rim, thickened internally. Pale green-yellow. RD 8–10 cm, 15°. 12 × 13 mm, T. 1–2.5 mm (**53.10**).

63* Rim, thickened internally. Metal pale blue-green, few bubbles, shiny surfaces. RD 9 cm, 30°. 22 × 10 mm, T. 1–2 mm (**212.02**).

The following rim sherds (**Group D1**) are all too small, too fragmentary or too discoloured to be sure they belong to different vessels from those above.

a. Rim, pale yellow, bubbly, cloudy surface (**70**).
b. Rim, pale green-yellow, very scratched (**216**).
c. Rim, pale green, abraded (**439**).
d. Rim, pale yellow (**220**).
e. Rim, colourless (**55**).

The sherds of Vessels 55–63 and the Group D1 sherds were widely scattered, but there was a marked concentration (nine pieces) in the **southern sector** and only five from the *inner precinct* of which three (V57, D1**c** and **d**) came from late or disturbed contexts. The assemblage can be divided into two groups. An early group comprised two vessels (59 and 62) and a pale yellow rim sherd (D1**a**) from **Period I/1** contexts. V59 was one of the earliest pieces of glass from the site and probably belongs with the concentration of bowl fragments from the north-west part of the **Glebe Field** (Figure 10.21). A second, larger group comprised sherds of five vessels (55, 56, 58, 61 and 63) and two linked sherds (D1**b** and **e**) from relatively late contexts in the **southern sector** and including three pieces (Vs 55, 63 and D2**b**) from the final stages (*11–13*) of **Period I**. There thus seem to be two distinct phases when these undecorated vessels were used. The first dates to the early- to mid-sixth century overlapping with the horizontally-trailed vessels of Group C and perhaps some of the Group A and B vessels. The second phase probably pertains to the later-seventh and early-eighth century coinciding with the more exotic Vs 20 and 52, and apparently post-dating the fashion for trailed vessels.

Flask?

Vessels 64 and 65 have kicked bases, the only such bases in the assemblage. Vessel 64 has a small diameter base and very thin walls, suggesting a vessel form such as a cone, flask or small bottle. Kicked bases on cones are an early feature, found on Roman beakers and early Anglo-Saxon types such as a few Kempston-type cones (Evison 1972, 56–7, Fig. 14). The walls of Vessel 64 are exceptionally thin for any early vessel, and it may be that this belongs to a small flask or other closed form. The spiral bubble trails and the irregular strands on the interior might support this view. The only parallels for this type of vessel in the west are two small flasklets, decorated with opaque white trails, from western Ireland, at Mullaroe, Sligo (Harden 1956a, Pl. 19h) and from a nearby crannog on Loch Gara (unpublished). It is possible these are of seventh century date (Bourke, Pers. Comm.). A similar base has been found at Llanelen, West Glamorgan (Campbell forthcoming c).

64* Base of narrow vessel, flattened and pushed in with point to produce kick. Irregular pontil scar in centre. Interior has several irregular strands of glass on surface. Wall very thin. Metal bubbly, with spiral bubble trails, honey colour, exterior cloudy. BD 2.5 cm, T. 0.3–3 mm (**89**)

Jar?

This base sherd is from a vessel with a kicked base, but it is a much thicker vessel, with a wider base. The base is too wide for a cone. Possible forms are squat jars or palm cups, neither of which would not be out of place in a sixth/seventh century context. The vessel may therefore belong to Group B, but there is not sufficient to be sure of this. It is not part of Vessel 9, the only palm cup in the assemblage.

65* Basal sherd, pushed in, with edge of pontil scar. Pale yellow, bubbles only on inner surface. BD 4–5 cm, T. 2–3 mm. 20 × 17 mm (**89**).

Both vessels came from the early **Period I/2** rubbish spread (89) producing the Group E vessels, and perhaps dating to the third quarter of the sixth century (pp 69, 90).

E. Thick vessels with simple rims

This group of vessels is distinguished from the previous two groups by a distinctive method of forming the rim, and by thicker walls and different decorative schemes. They appear to form a coherent group of vessels which has a different production source from the majority of the western vessels, and they occur in a restricted stratigraphic horizon (Figure 10.9). Unlike all the other vessels from Whithorn, the rims are fire-rounded, but not thickened. The interior surface of the rims retain marks of the pincers or other tool, used to fashion the rim, which normally are lost when the rim is reheated and thickened by folding inwards. The rims are all similar: simple, upright, unthickened internally, and with the wall at least 1.5 mm thick. Horizontal trails are unmarvered around the rim, and feathered in a variety of patterns by pulling with a point or comb. These do not form true festoons; the glass of the trails was fairly viscous when tooled, as the vessel had not been reheated to marver the trails. The lower parts of some vessels are plain, but others probably had bands of marvered trails combed down in regular festoons. The vessel forms all appear to be cones, but the form of some of these differs from those in the previous groups. The rim diameter is almost constant at 7 cm, while the bases are wider (3–4 cm) and more rounded than in Groups C and D, giving a more bag-shaped form. The base of Vessel 79 has a discoidal pontil mark similar to some vessels from *Hamwic* (Hunter 1980, Fig. 11,2 Nos 1 & 7). There is a minimum of fifteen vessels, as opposed to fifty in Groups C and D, but the sherds are often large and numerous, giving the misleading impression that this is the largest group of vessels from the site.

No external source can be suggested for these vessels. The rounded bases and unmarvered trails might be seen as early features, but the stratigraphic context of most is in the late sixth century midden. In general these vessels have a cruder appearance, both in form and decorative technique, than Groups C and D, but this may be due to a different workshop tradition rather than being a chronological indicator. No other examples of this group are known from western assemblages. It should be noted that the unusual metal colour of pale amber with pink streaks found in several of these vessels is also found in some of the Whithorn Group C and D vessels, suggesting some connection between the Groups.

The fused glass, Group F, appears to be mainly formed from vessels of this group, and is found in the same stratigraphic contexts as the majority of the Group E sherds (Figures 3.25, 10.9 and .23). The detail of the fused glass (see below) lends considerable weight to the hypothesis that it represents glass vessel-making debris, and that this was taking place at Whithorn.

Pale amber/pink

66* Cone, pale amber with pink streaks, decorated with horizontal trails dragged alternately up and down.
    Rim, simple upright, slightly thickened on exterior. Band of horizontal trails of varying widths, slightly marvered, dragged alternately up and down almost vertically. Metal good, surfaces cloudy, some bubble trails. RD c. 7 cm, 30°. 43 × 18 mm. T 2–3 mm (**82.04**, Grave I/113).

67* Cone, pale amber with pink streaks, decorated with band of horizontal white trails. Not enough of decoration survives to be sure that the trails were not combed.
    a & **b**. Rim, simple upright. Decoration, thin band of unmarvered horizontal white trails, not dragged in 25 mm of circumference. Metal good, surfaces cloudy (14074) or shiny (13628), bubble trails at rim, pale amber with pink streaks. RD 7 cm, 50°. 33 × 40 mm, T. 2–2.4 mm, **a** (**82.03**, Grave I/106) joining **b** (**83**).
    c. Rim, probably joining **a**. As **a**, but surfaces shiny, no decoration. RD 7 cm, 25° (**82.03**, Grave I/105).

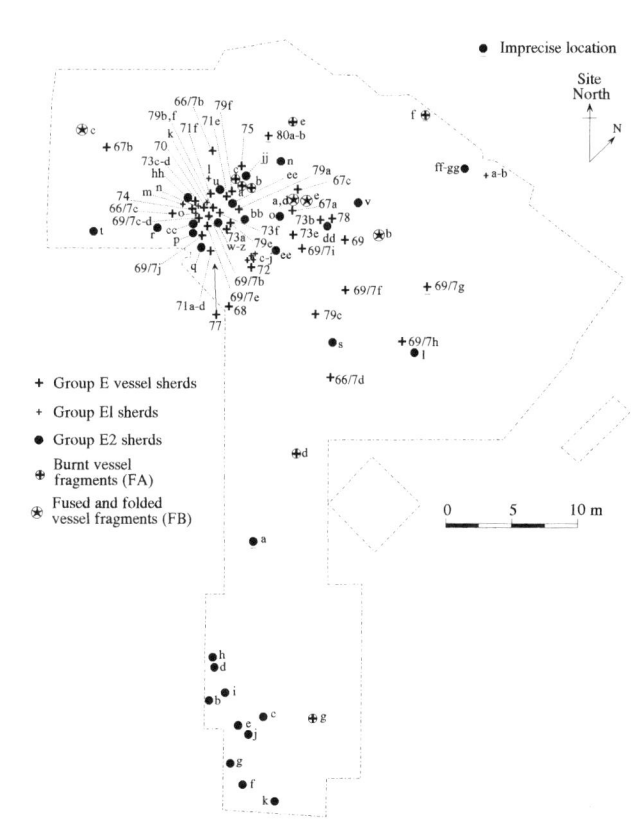

10.9 The distribution of Group E and F glass sherds.

THE FINDS 311

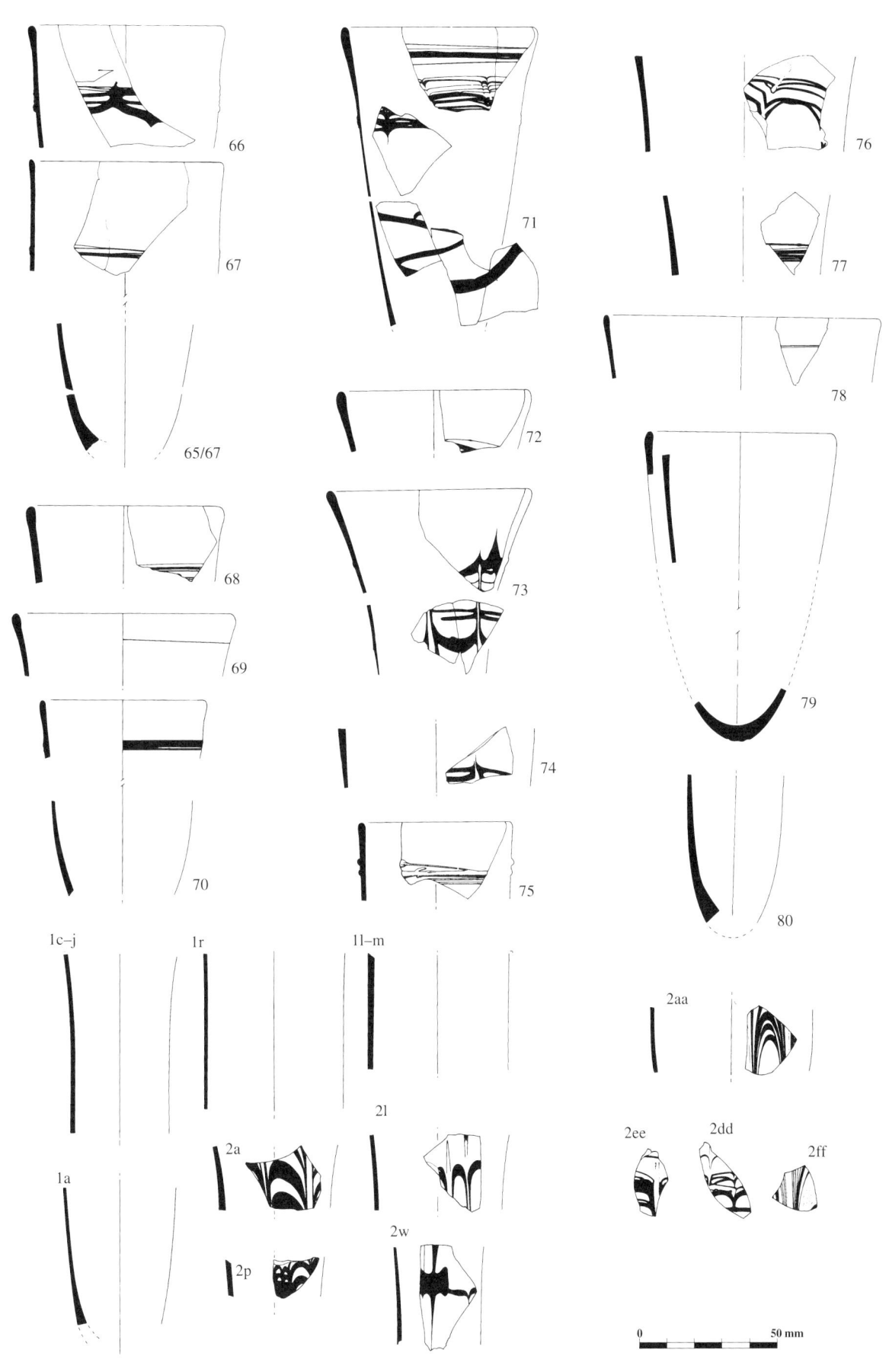

10.10 Group E vessel glass

V66/7 There is a number of sherds of this distinctive colour and thickness which probably belong to Vessels 66 or 67 (listed as **a–d**):
a*. Base of thick cone with rounded base. Shiny surfaces. T. 3.6–5.6 mm. BD 4 cm (**89**).
b*. Just above base. Scratched, abraded, with cloudy surfaces. D 4 cm. T. 3.0 mm (**89**).
c. Thick sherd with signs of pulling with hook. Abraded. 24 × 9 mm, T. 4.4 mm (**85.02**).
d. Sherd with vertical combed trail (**118**).

68* Cone, light pale amber decorated with band of horizontal white trails
Rim, simple upright, thickened externally. RD 7cm. 32 × 26 mm. T 1.6–3.0 mm (Trench 4, **89**?)

69* Cone, pale honey/pink, with one horizontal white trail.
Rim, simple upright, thickened externally. Single thin white horizontal marvered trail. Metal fine, pale honey with pink streaks in transmitted light. Surfaces shiny, rim exterior lip abraded. RD 8 cm, 60°. 40 × 23 mm, T. 2–3.1 mm (**119.01**).

70* Cone, same colour as vessel 69, with band of horizontal white trails.
Rim, simple upright, not thickened. Band of white horizontal trails, partly marvered. Metal as above. RD 6 cm, 45°. 21 × 20 mm., T. 2.7 mm (**89**).

V69/70 There is a number of sherds which could belong to Vessels 69 or 70 (listed as **a–j**):
a. Sherd from near rim. With large white inclusion (**85.02**).
b*. Sherd from near base. BD 4 cm. T. 1.5–2.5 mm (**82.04**, Grave I/113).
c and **d**. Sherds from near base of cone. Pink streak. D 4–5 cm, T. 1.8–2 mm. 1 and 2 joining (**89**).
e–j. Bodysherds. **e** (**82.04**, Grave I/114); **f** (**99**); **g** (**82.01**, Grave I/81); **h** (**79.02**); **i** (**99**); **j** (**203.03**).

Pale yellow/green yellow
71* Cone, pale green-yellow, decoration of horizontal white trails of mixed thickness, irregularly applied in a 3 cm wide zone. The trails have been dragged with a point diagonally downwards at wide intervals.
a & **b**. Rim, simple, unthickened, mouth slightly expanding. Metal good, no bubbles, exterior matt. RD 7 cm, 82°. T 1.5–3 mm. Two joining sherds (**82.04**, Grave I/116).
c. Sherd from lower part of decoration. Trails thicker and more irregular. T. 1 mm (**82.04**, Grave I/116).
Also probably part of this vessel:
d–f. Three joining sherds from lower part of vessel. Decoration of wide marvered white trails in irregular ?spiral pattern. D 3.5 cm. T 1–2 mm. **d** and **e** (**82.04**, Graves I/116 and 111); **f** (**89**)

72* Cone, yellow-green, with band of horizontal white trails.
Rim, simple upright, slight external thickening. RD 6.5 cm. 32 × 22mm. 1.5–3.1 mm (**81.02**, Grave I/72).

73* Cone, pale yellow, with band of horizontal trails 3 cm wide, dragged vertically upwards at wide intervals. The trails have abundant black impurities which give a greenish tinge to the opaque white, but this is unintentional. Metal good, with slightly matt exterior and bubble trails near rim.
a. Rim, simple, unthickened, mouth expanding. Decoration of partially marvered trails dragged up at irregular intervals. RD 7 cm, 70°. T 1.5–3 mm (**109**).
b. Rim splinter (**100**).
c & **d**. Joining sherds from below a, with wide trails dragged upwards. T 1–1.5 mm (**89**).
e. Sherd with dragged trails, many impurities (**247.01**).
f & **g**. Two similar non-joining sherds but with shiny surfaces. f (**82.04**, Grave I/113); **g** (**58**).

74* Vessel similar in decoration to Vessel 71 above, pale yellow, metal thicker, no bubbles.
Sherd from just below rim. Thick partly-marvered white trails dragged up with a point. RD 7 cm. 25 × 17 mm T 2–2.5 mm. (**89**).

75* Cone with narrow mouth, pale yellow-green, with horizontal white trails.
Rim, upright, slightly thickened on exterior. Decoration of thick unmarvered trails, irregularly applied, in horizontal band. Metal good, some large bubbles and bubble trails at rim, surfaces cloudy and discoloured. RD 5.5 cm, 85°. 41 × 27 mm. T. 2.0–3.4 mm (**91**).

76* Cone, pale yellow, with white trails dragged downwards.
Sherd from just below rim decorated with irregular horizontal white marvered trails dragged down diagonally at wide intervals. Metal thick, abraded and scratched. RD *c*. 8 cm, 33 × 30 mm, T. 1–3 mm (**330**).

77* Cone?, pale yellow, with band of horizontal white trails.
Sherd from just below rim, with irregular partly-marvered trails containing black impurities. Metal with few large bubbles, shiny surfaces. D *c*. 6 cm, 28 × 21 mm, T 2 mm (**743.04**).

78* Cone, pale yellow, with a few horizontal white trails.
Rim, simple upright, slight external thickening. Two very fine horizontal trails below rim. RD *c*. 10cm, 20°. 23 × 19 mm, T. 2–2.8 mm (**100**).

79* Cone with rounded base, pale honey-yellow, no decoration
a. Rim, simple upright, slight external thickening. No trails. Metal good, some bubble trails, surfaces shiny. RD 7 cm, 90°. 53 × 15 mm, T. 2.7–4 mm (**89**).
b. Rim as a., but abraded exterior. RD 7 cm, 45° (**82.04**, Grave I/113).

There are other body sherds in this shade which are probably the same vessel:

c & **d**. Base of cone, rounded, with disc-shaped pontil scar. Scratched exterior. BD 4 cm. T. 5 mm. **c** (**82.02**, Grave I/92) joining **d** (**82.04**, Grave I/111).
e & **f**. Two sherds from just below rim. T. 2 mm. **e** (**89**); **f** (**82.04**, Grave I/113).

80* Another cone of this colour with less rounded base.
a & **b**. Base of cone. Metal good, thick, no bubbles, surfaces cloudy. BD 3 cm, T. 2–7.5 mm. **a** and **b** joining (**88.02**).

Group E1. There are several sherds of this general colour and thickness which cannot be attributed to particular vessels in this group. The following are large sections of vessels, undecorated, which show the form of the lower parts of the cones.

a. & **b***. joining. Towards base. Pale green-yellow. D 3–4 cm. T. 1.1–2.6 mm (**71.02**).
c–j*. Lower part of cone expanding upwards with concave sides. Pale green-yellow. Large section smashed into several sherds, some which join. D 3.5–4 cm, T. 1.8 mm (**89**).
k*. Upper body of cone, ?same vessel. D 5 cm, T. 1.2 mm (**89**).
l. & **m***. Just below rim of undecorated pale yellow-green vessel. T. 2.4–2.7 mm. l joining m, both (**89**).
n. Sherd near base. Pale yellow-green. D 5 cm, T. 2.6 mm (**89**).
o. Body sherd. D 5 cm, T. 2.0 mm (**89**).

The Group E vessel and related Group E1 fragments were virtually confined to the **Period I/2** rubbish deposits in the **northern sector**, and related intrusive features (Figure 10.9). The main rubbish spread (89, Figures 3.37, 10.9) produced four (70, 73, 74, 79) of the fifteen vessels; three others (66, 67 and 71) came from graves cutting the deposit; another (69) from the hollow to the east (119.01), two (68 and 72) from an equivalent features in the adjacent 1984 trench (4); one (77) from the backfill of this trench; one (80) from the **Period I/2.3** platform to the north (88.02), and two (75 and 78) from the peaty deposits of **Period I/2.1** and **I/2.2** (91 and 100) in the vicinity. The remaining Group E vessel sherd (76) came from the floor of a thirteenth century building at the east end of the **Fey Field** trench (330). Scattered vessel sherds to the south-east, mostly came from vessels 69 or 70 and may have been displaced and dispersed by later gravediggers. The sherds in Group E1 show a similar pattern with an even stronger concentration in the main rubbish spread (89).

Group E2. There are also a number of sherds, mainly from the lower parts of vessels, which differ in that the trails are usually fully marvered and the combing more pronounced and regular. In some cases the trails are so displaced that they are very faint and consist almost entirely of bubbles rather than white opacifier. Some of these sherds are no doubt from some of the vessels described above, but none can be confidently assigned to any particular vessel and some may belong to Group C (*c.f.* V21).

a*. Sherd with asymmetric festoons combed down. Pale yellow. D 4 cm, T. 1.5–2 mm (**218**).
b. Similar sherd (**114**).
c. Similar sherd (**55**).
d. Similar sherd, trails very faint (**56.02**).
e. Sherd with wide festoon combed down. Pale pink/amber (**53.09**).
f. Sherd with wide festoons, combed down. Pale amber (**901, southern sector**).
g. Sherd from towards base, one unmarvered trail combed down. pale amber (**53.12**).
h. Sherd with traces of vertical combed trail. Green-yellow (**114**).
i. Sherd with traces of combed trails (**114**).
j. Splinter with widely spaced trails, part-marvered, pulled down for short distance. Pale green-yellow (**56.02**).
k. Sherd with five trails combed down. Pale green-yellow (**50.01**).
l*. Sherd with band of trails combed down into three narrow festoons. Pale amber (**253**).
m. Sherd with very pale trails, single trail combed into wide festoon. Pale green-yellow. T. 1 mm (**82.06**).
n. Sherd from just below rim, with two trails combed down. Pale green-yellow. Exterior very scratched. T. 1.5–2 mm (**85.05**).
o. Sherd with base of vertical comb mark. Yellow-green (**99**).
p*. Sherd from towards base. Wide trails combed down into four festoons at irregular intervals. Pale yellow. D 3.5 cm, T. 2 mm (**82.04, Grave I/114**).
q. Sherd with trace of horizontal unmarvered trail combed down. Pale amber (**82.04, Grave I/115**).
r. Sherd with two wide trails combed into festoon. Pale yellow-green (**82.05, Grave I/117**).
s. Tiny sherd with unmarvered trail pulled down. Pale green (**902, northern sector**).
t. Sherd with three faint irregular trails in arc. Pale pink/amber (**85.01**).
u. Sherd with wide trails combed down. Pale yellow (**82.04, Grave I/111**).
v. Tiny sherd with four part-marvered trails pulled down (**82.02, Grave I/86**).
w*. Sherd from near base with very wide trail combed down in three places. The horizontal trail is of variable width. Pale green-yellow. D 3 cm, T. 1–2 mm (**82.04, Grave I/113**).
x. Sherd with irregular wide horizontal trails combed down into two festoons. Pale yellow-green. T. 1 mm (**82.04, Grave I/113**).
y. Sherd with widely-spaced part-marvered trails combed down. Pale amber (**82.04, Grave I/113**).
z. Sherd with two wide trails pulled down and up? alternately. Pale green (**82.04, Grave I/113**).
aa*. Sherd with combed festoons. Many bubbles. D *c.* 6 cm (**82.03, Grave I/110**).
bb. Sherd with combed faint festoons. Yellow (**109**).
cc. Sherd from near base, with faint, wide irregular trails combed down. Pale green, cloudy surfaces (**89**).
dd*. Sherd with irregular trails, part-marvered, combed down. Pale yellow (**100**).
ee*. Sherd with wide and narrow trails, part-marvered, pulled down. Pale amber, exterior very scratched. T. 2 mm (**100**).
ff*. Sherd with numerous fine trails combed down into festoons. Pale yellow (**70**).
gg. Sherd with two trails pulled down. Pale green-yellow (**70**).
hh. Sherd with faint traces of vertical combing. green-yellow (**89**).
ii. Sherd with part of pulled down faint trail. Pale yellow, bubbles (**88.02**).
jj. Sherd near base with traces of combing. Yellow (**89**).

The sherds in Group E2 were more widely scattered than the Group E vessel fragments and related E1 sherds. Most of the twenty-three sherds from the *inner precinct* came from contexts contemporary or later than those producing the Group E vessels, with a concentration in the **Period I/4** graves cutting the primary deposits (89 etc). Two sherds (**ff–gg**) from the east end of the **Period I/1.6** hollow may have been intrusive. The eleven sherds from the **southern sector** are of particular interest as Group E 'vessels' were absent from this part of the site. Seven of these came from relatively early contexts (56.02, *Stage 3*; 50.01, *Stage 5*; 114, *Stage 6* and 53.12 *Stage 7*) indicating that they had a briefer and generally earlier currency than the Group C vessel sherds which were concentrated in the later waterborne silts of *Stage 10*. These sherds might thus have derived from finished Group E vessels, as distinct from the putative workshop debris in the *inner precinct*.

F. Fused glass

There are 9 sherds of fused glass, though a number of other sherds show signs of burning to varying degrees. The fused glass is of two types: thick flat pieces with bubbly surfaces, and a mass of folded vessel with clean surfaces. The first group, of four sherds, is probably all from the same piece and may be the result of intensive burning of a single vessel, though the sherd is noticeably thicker than most vessels from the site.

A. Burnt vessel?

Green/yellow with no trails. Thick glass 3–5 mm, perhaps from base of cone, but distorted and melted. Surfaces bubbly but clean. Fragments are listed as FAa–d.

a. and **b**. joining 60 × 33 mm, T 3–5 mm (**96**).
c. 7 × 6 mm (**109**).
d. 18 × 10 mm (**911**).

Three of the sherds (**a–c**) came from roughly the same spot on the northern edge of the concentration of Group E vessels (Figures 3.25, 10.9 and 10.23). The fourth (**d**) came from a surface abutting the **Period I/2** boundary ditch (120).

(*Addenda PH*). Three similar sherds (FAe–g), initially identified as Roman vessels or Northumbrian window glass, may be appended tentatively to this list

e. Melted pale-yellowish vessel fragment (**88.02**)
f. Pale yellow glass, possibly melted vessel, 25 × 4mm diameter (**305.06**)
g. Light brownish amber glass, 20 × 10 × 4 mm (**55**)

a came from the same area as the other sherds, **b** from the **Period II** children's graveyard in the eastern part of the **northern sector** and **c** from the *Stage 10* waterborne deposits in the **southern sector**.

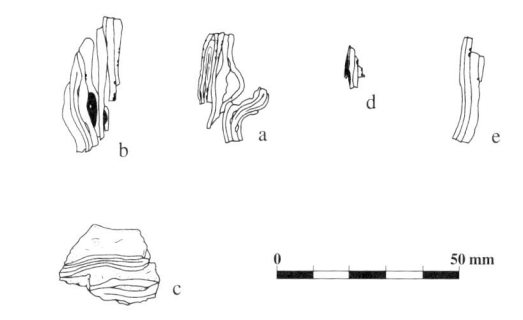

10.11 Group FB glass fragments.

B. Folded vessels (FBa–e)

The pieces comprise layers of vessel glass repeatedly folded over to form thick masses. They do not appear to be formed from disparate sherds fused together, but from single vessels heated and squashed into a large mass. All are yellow/green and retain traces of decoration of opaque white trails, both horizontal and vertical. These masses do not give the impression of being vessels or sherds accidentally fused, but neither do they appear to be a collection of broken sherds melted down in crucibles. There are no molten droplets such as those from Dinas Powys and other sites. In FBa the vessel walls are *c.* 1.5 mm thick with what appears to be a rim *c.* 4 mm thick. FBb shows the same thickness and rim type, making it likely that the original vessels belonged to Group E. However, though it is difficult to be sure, there appears to be chevron decoration within some of the fused masses. This decoration has not been observed on the surviving Group E vessels. The material appears to consist of failed complete vessels from the glass workshop, heated and squashed into convenient lumps for use as cullet. These lumps may have been imported along with the complete vessels (though it is difficult to see why), or they may represent glass vessel manufacture *in situ*. If the latter was the case it would be of unique importance, probably indicating the presence of continental glassworkers at Whithorn. Conclusive proof could only be provided by the evidence of glass-making residues in crucibles. The situation with regard to fused glass on western sites is complex, and each assemblage has to be evaluated on its own merits rather than trying to ascribe all fused glass to the same process (*c.f.* Campbell forthcoming b and Price 1992, 136). Rather similar pieces are known from Hen Gastell, W. Glamorgan (Campbell forthcoming a).

a. Mass of at least 5 layers from vessel with horizontal and vertical (?chevron) white trails. 43 × 34 × 18 mm (**91**).
b. Part of same mass, with thickened rim visible. 47 × 25 × 14 mm (**73.02**).
c. Much paler mass with shiny surfaces. 27 × 20 × 12 mm (**238**).
d. Small piece with wide trail (?chevron). 17 × 12 × 5 mm (**89**).
e. Piece with four layers. 27 × 17 × 7 mm (**90**).

Three of the fragments (FBa, d and e) came from roughly the same spot on the eastern side of the concentration of Group E vessel sherds (89 etc Figures 3.25, 10.9 and 23). The other two came from later contexts (238 and 73), and may have been displaced and scattered from the same original source by later grave digging.

Additional Early Medieval vessels

Jennifer Price and Peter Hill

Fragments of three other vessels were submitted to other specialists, who have ascribed them to this group. The first (81) was originally identified as Northumbrian window glass, a second (82) was identified as Roman and the third (83) pertains to a different tradition of glassmaking, though overlapping with the later vessels described above.

Vessel 81 is a moulded rib from a palm cup or squat jar in opaque blue metal. It is unlikely to be earlier than the seventh century, and probably belongs to Group B. It came from a **Period V** grave cutting the **Period I/1** graveyard (Figure 10.23).

The small fragment of Vessel 82 has not been identified precisely, though the colour and bubbly quality of the glass indicate that it comes from a late Roman or early post-Roman vessel. This might be either a globular flask/unguent bottle with a very short, narrow neck, or perhaps more probably, a small drinking cup with hollow stem and foot. These have not often been recorded in Britain, but they are known in the Mediterranean region in the late fourth or early-fifth century and in Frankish burials (Isings 1957, Form 111). The sherd came from the floor of the hollow (119) dug to the north of the **Period I/1.5** graveyard in the opening stages of **Period I/2**. Its deposition was thus broadly contemporary with that of the anomalous flask (64) and jar (65) from the adjacent rubbish spread (89)

The dark green, appearing black, body fragment with applied, prominent, dark green and opaque yellow twisted rods (Vessel 83) came from the fill of a doorpost socket in the **Period II/3** church (237, p 150). It may thus have been used in the opening phases of **Period II**, or could have been displaced from the underlying **Period I/4** deposits (Figure 10.24). Several vessel forms with bichrome twisted rods occur on sites in northern Europe and Scandinavia in the late seventh, eighth and ninth centuries, including small bowls, squat jars and beakers (see Evison 1988b, 240–44, and Baumgartner & Krueger 1988, 69–76, for recent discussion). Fragments of bowls and other forms have been noted at several sites in England, as at Southampton, London, Barking, Ipswich, Brandon, Whitby and elsewhere (Evison 1988, 240–1), but these generally have a light green or bluish green ground, rather than the very dark green of the Whithorn fragment. There are however a few comparable pieces, including a small body fragment from *Haithabu* with white rods, which is thought to be dark red, though appearing black (Baumgartner & Kreuger 1988, 76, No. 23b). In Britain, a body fragment from a bowl or cup described as dark (probably wine-coloured) with self-coloured and opaque yellow rods was found at Portchester (Harden 1976, 232–4, No. 3, Fig. 145.3), and a dark convex body fragment with very similar self-coloured and opaque yellow rods has come from the General Accident site in York, but the ground colour has not

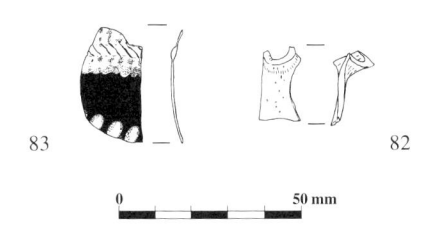

10.12 Vessels 82 and 83.

been established (unpublished). The form of the opaque yellow part of the bichrome rods on the three dark fragments in Britain is noteworthy, as they spread on to the surface of the vessel at either side of the rods. This effect may have been achieved by winding the yellow round a thicker rod of dark green glass which was not sufficiently hot for the yellow to become flush with the surface of the rod (Evison 1988b, 243, Fig. 12.5). The Whithorn fragment has been pressed hard with a pointed tool at intervals along both sides of the surviving rod, and the glass has become sufficiently thin at these points for the colour of the vessel to be established.

81 A moulded rib from a palm cup or squat jar in opaque blue metal. This vessel is unlikely to be earlier than the seventh century, and probably belongs to Group B.

531

82* Fragment of pale green ?flask/stemmed cup, possibly fourth-sixth century. Fragment, lower body and open stem(?), or upper body and neck? Pale greenish, very bubbly. Convex side, short narrow cylindrical stem (or neck), slight evidence for outsplayed foot (or rim). Tooling marks on stem/neck.

PH approx 15; T 1.0 **119.01**

83* Fragment of seventh-ninth century dark-green vessel with bichrome rod ornament. Body fragment. Very dark green ground, appearing black, opaque yellow trails. No visible weathering. Thin convex side, prominent vertical rib crossed by diagonal opaque yellow trails which extend onto body on either side; edges of trails from a second vertical rib (now missing).

Dims 29 × 17; T 0.5 **237**

The Dark Age ceramics

Ewan Campbell

The Dark Age imported ceramics from Whithorn can lay claim to be the most important assemblage of these wares to have been excavated in Britain using modern scientific excavation methods. This is partly due to the variety and quantity of the wares recovered, but mainly to the long and detailed stratigraphic sequence which gives scope for refining the relative and absolute chronology of the wares in Britain. The variety of wares is unmatched outside south-west England/South Wales, with all classes and sub-groups of imports represented except Phocaean Red Slipware (PRS). The catalogue and discussion which follows is based on the author's Ph.D. research on these imports, and information not otherwise referenced, as well as full fabric descriptions, can be found in this work (Campbell 1991).

African Red Slipware

African Red Slipware (ARS) was produced in the Carthage region of Tunisia from the second to seventh centuries AD. A wide variety of red wares were produced, but only the fine red-slipped tablewares were exported. These forms were sometimes decorated with stamped designs. ARS is the rarest of the import wares, found on only six or seven Insular sites, and only in quantity at Tintagel, Cornwall (Thomas 1981b, 8–9) and Dinas Powys, Glamorgan (Campbell 1988, Fig. 27). The forms found in Insular Dark Age contexts can be closely dated on the basis of excavations in Carthage using Fulford's forms (in Fulford & Peacock 1984), and as a group can be shown to belong to the second third of the sixth century (Campbell 1991, 188; forthcoming a). The North African wares are thus probably slightly later in date than the Eastern Mediterranean wares (PRS, B*i*, B*ii* and B*iv*) though there may be overlap.

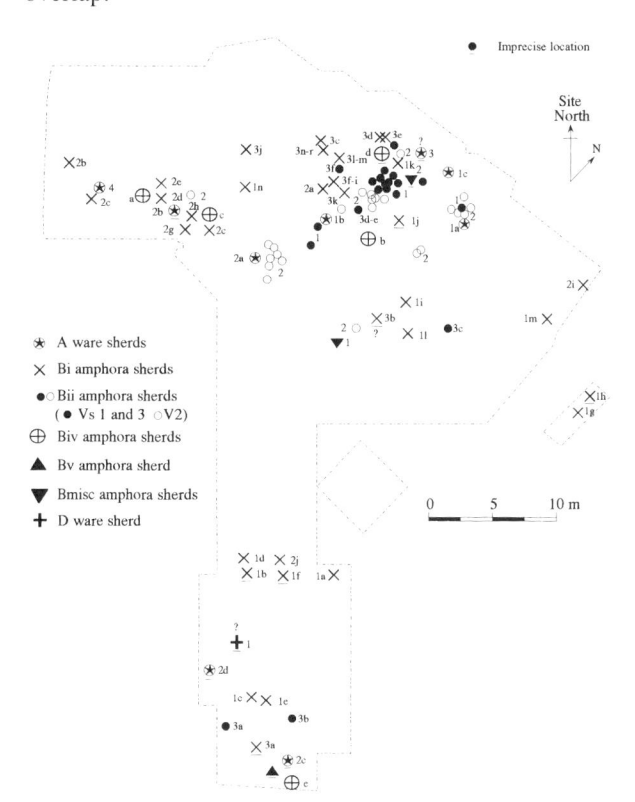

10.13 The distribution of A and B ware.

The nine sherds from Whithorn belong to four different vessels, only two of which, A1 and A2, can be specifically identified. The forms found at Whithorn, Fulford's Forms 50 and 65, were produced through much of the sixth century, but were only common together from c 525 to 575. Although Form 65 was long-lived, the rim form of A2 has several exact parallels in a pit group (B 3.17) of the mid-sixth century at Carthage (Fulford & Peacock 1984, Forms 65.4, 65.6, 65.8). The pottery in this pit group is dated by Fulford to *c.* 525 (*ibid.*, 93) though it has coins of 540–550 (*ibid.* 33). If A4 is from the neck of a closed form such as a flagon, it would be the only such form from an Insular context, and would be also of fifth or sixth century date (*ibid.*, 84–5, Fig. 25, Closed Form 1). If closed forms were being imported, an unusual tubular sherd from the site of the major monastic cemetery at Armagh may also be of this type (Brown & Harper 1984, Fig. 18, 100). The only other ARS from Scotland is a single sherd of Form 65 from the important early Christian monastery on Iona (Reece 1981, 15).

One sherd, A3, has been ground down in an unfinished attempt to make a disc or spindle whorl, and two others have been partially rubbed down on one edge. This re-use of imported sherds is found at other sites and probably reflects a talismanic value placed on these exotic items. The collection and deliberate deposition of a hoard of sherds, comprising a variety of import types, in foundation deposits of hearths and structures interpreted as shrines is recorded at Trethurgy, Cornwall; Dalkey Island near Dublin; and at Cadbury Congresbury, Somerset.

Vessel 1

a*. Rim, of small bowl, Fulford Form 50, with flanged rim. Fabric hard, gritty, with common quartz, rounded to well-rounded, up to 0.5 mm, and occasional yellow limestone fragments. Orange, with similar coloured slip interior and exterior, burnished. RD 16 cm, T. 4 mm. Date *floruit c.* 525–575 (**78.07**).

There are also a base (**b**) and body sherd (**c**) of this vessel. **b** (**82.03**, Grave I/98); **c** (**82.01**, Grave I/76).

All three sherds came from the eastern part of the *inner precinct*, **a** from the soil build-up within the paved ring of the **Period I/2** shrine (Figure 3.12), **c** from a nearby grave and **b** from a grave to the west.

Vessel 2

a*. Rim of large plate, Fulford Form 65, with hammer-head rim. Fabric as A1, slip oranger than body. Abraded on one surface. The rim sherd has been rubbed flat on one edge. RD *c.* 32 cm, T. 7 mm. Date *floruit c.* 525–600+ (**97**)

There are also three body sherds (**b–d**) of this vessel, all abraded on one surface. **b** (**85.01**); **c** (**53.13**); **d** (**52.03**).

a was closely associated with the western concentration of B*ii* amphora sherds in the **Period I/.6** hollow, arguing for a date of *c.* 550 (p 69), and **b** came from a **Period I/2** rubbish spread in the same area. **c** and **d** came from a **Period I.7** pit (53.13) and adjacent rubble surface in the **southern sector**.

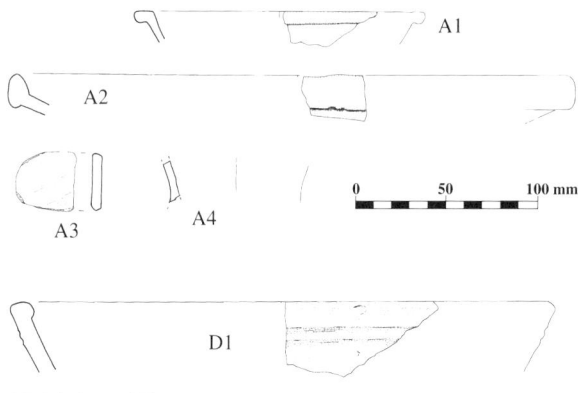

10.14 A and D ware.

Vessel 3*
Half-finished disc or counter rubbed down from body sherd from just below rim. Fabric as A1. T. 6 mm, size 3 × 3 cm (**73.01**).

This sherd came from a **Period I/3** mud layer to the north of the road, but was perhaps displaced from the underlying **Period I/1** deposits (Figure 10.22)

Vessel 4*
Small body sherd from neck(?) of closed form. One edge has been ground flat. Fabric as A1, but no slip on interior which is rilled, not smoothed as in open forms. Unabraded. Neck D 8 cm, T. 4mm, size 3 × 2 cm (**237**).

The sherd came from one of the arcade post-sockets of the **Period II/ 3** church and was probably displaced from underlying **Period I** deposits.

Most of the A ware sherds had been displaced, but their distribution corresponds with the **Stage 2** assemblage (Figure 10.22) to which they may be ascribed. The earliest find (2a) indicates that A ware was introduced with B*ii* amphorae in **Period I/1.6**, but after the B*i* amphorae.

B Ware amphorae

The 211 sherds of Mediterranean amphorae are a large and significant collection. The sherds belong to ten different vessels: three B*i*, three B*ii*, one B*iv*, one B*v* and two B*misc.*, making this the largest collection outside south-west England, where most of the examples are concentrated. Although the vessels cannot be dated in themselves as the types had long production histories, they belong to phases of direct trade, either with the eastern Mediterranean (B*i*, B*ii*, B*iv*) which can be dated by the associated fine wares (Phocaean Red Slipware) to the period AD *c.* 475–550, or with North Africa (B*v*) which can similarly be dated by the associated African Red Slipware to the period AD *c.* 525–550 (Campbell 1991).

Several of the vessels have scratched or painted marks which may have served a variety of purposes. Unfortunately none is complete. Red painted *dipinti* have otherwise been recorded from Insular sites only at Tintagel (Thomas 1981b, 14).

The major concentration of Mediterranean amphora is at Tintagel, which has 93 vessels. Other sites with significant quantities are Cadbury Congresbury (7), Clogher (7) and South Cadbury (11). None of the northern import sites have produced any Phocaean Red Slipware, suggesting that these sites were supplied by redistribution from the south-west, where almost all sites also have PRS. However Whithorn does have ARS, making it possible that there was some direct contact between Whithorn and the Mediterranean world in the middle of the sixth century.

B*i*

B*i* amphorae are characterised by combed ribbing in a band on the shoulder region of a vessel of globular form. Production sites are known in the Argolid region of the Peloponnese, but other areas may have produced similar forms. A wine content has been suggested.

The 46 sherds can be assigned to three vessels on the basis of minor colour and fabric differences. One

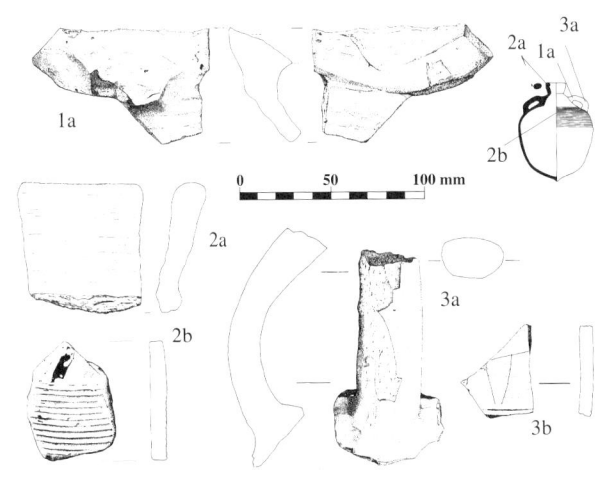

10.15 B*i* amphora sherds.

sherd shows part of a painted *dipinto*, a mark used by traders to identify contents or their property. Another sherd has a scratched graffito, possibly a maker's mark or counting tally.

Vessel 1: uniform orange fabric
a*. Neck/shoulder junction with base of handle attachment. The neck was thrown separately and luted to the body. Abraded. Neck D 16 cm., size 9 × 7 cm (**53.01**).

There are five sherds of this vessel with combed ribbing (**b–d, g** and **h**) and eight others plain (**e, f, i–n**). **b** (**64.02**); **c** abraded (**52.04**); **d** abraded (**214**); **e** abraded (**55**); **f** (**64.04**); **g** (**103.01**); **h** abraded (**427.01**); **i** (**67.02**); **j** (**70**); **k** (**73.01**); **l** (**399.02**); **m** abraded (**399.03**); **n** (**222.01**).

The sherds came from two different areas. Six (**a–f**) came from the **southern sector** where they were concentrated to the north, but mostly came from disturbed contexts. The second group (**g–m**) came from the eastern half of the *inner precinct* where they were widely scattered on the ground surrounding Building I/1 (Figures 3.8, 10.21). A last sherd (**n**) came from a **Period II** context further to the west. Both groups can be identified as domestic debris scattered around **Period I/1** buildings (Figure 10.21).

Vessel 2: uniform buff fabric
a*. Neck and rim, broken at shoulder junction. Exterior pale buff. RD 11 cm, T. 10–17 mm, size 7 × 7 cm (**94.02**).

b*. Bodysherd from upper part of vessel, partly with combed decoration. Part of one stroke of a red-painted *dipinto* survives, 6 mm wide and at least 40 mm long, crossing onto the ribbed decoration. Very abraded (**546**).

There are eight other sherds of Vessel 2 (**c–j**), all with combed ribbing. **c** (**94.01**); **d** (**100**); **e** edge of handle attachment (**91**); **f** (**109**); **g** abraded (**82.04**, Grave I/115); **h** (**82.04**, Grave I/114); **i** (**81.02**, Grave I/61); **j** abraded (**64.02**)

Eight of the sherds (**a–h**) came from the western part of the **northern sector** where original deposits of **Period I/1.3** (94.01) had been disturbed by subsequent hollows (91, 109), graves (82.04), and thirteenth/fourteenth century cultivation (546). All these sherds could have originated in **Period I/1.3** debris and would thus have been broadly contemporary with Vessel 3. The two remaining sherds (**i** and **j**) came from a **Period I/3** grave in the south east corner of the central sector (**i**), and the **Period I/1.3** ploughsoil in the northern part of the **southern sector** (**j**).

Vessel 3: orange with buff/white exterior
a*. Handle and attachment luted to upper body over combed ribbing. Elliptical handle section, 35 × 18 mm. Length 10 cm (**58**).

b*. Body sherd with graffito of three scratched lines just above band of combing. Sherd has very white outer skin, and is possibly from another vessel. Size 4 × 4 cm, T. 7 mm (**399.02**).

There are 18 other sherds of Vessel 3 (**c–s**), three (**c, j** and **m**) with combed decoration. All are fresh and closely associated, suggesting that most are *in situ* where originally deposited. **c–e** (**69.02**); **f–i** joining (**94.02**); **j** (**91**); **k** (**81.01**, Grave I/52); **l** and **m** (**81.02**, GraveI/69); **n–r** joining (**76**); **s** (**249.01**).

The sherds were clustered in the eastern part of the **northern sector** and revealed a coherent pattern of displacement from an original deposit of **Period I/1.3** (69.02), into redeposited spoil and the floor of Building I/6 (94.02), **Period I/3** graves (81.02), the **Period I/4** platform (76), and the **Period II** chapel (249.01). The vessel can thus be assigned to **Period I/1.3** with confidence (Figures 3.11, 10.21). The handle (**a**) and graffiti-marked sherd (**b**) were not linked to this cluster. **a** came from relatively late debris (**Period I.10**) in the **southern sector**, and **b**, unlocated, from mid-ninth century ploughsoil in the centre of the **central sector**.

B*ii*

B*ii* amphorae are characterised by tegulated ribbing which covers much of the body, and twisted asymmetrical handles. As the pattern of ribbing varies greatly in different parts of the body, sherds from a single vessel can appear to the unwary to be from several vessels. The fabric, colour and size of these vessels is very variable, probably indicating a number of sources in the same region. The source is probably somewhere in southern Turkey and they may have held olive oil.

The 167 sherds come from a minimum of three vessels. One sherd of Vessel 3 has an incised cross infilled with red paint. Any Christian significance to this mark can only be speculative, as such marks are normally indicative of contents or other secular meanings.

Vessel 1: pale greenish buff
There are forty-seven sherds from this vessel, but no rim or handle sherds were found. Forty came from the main cluster (Group A) in the eastern part of the **Period I/1.6** hollow (**70**, Figures 3.12, 10.13 and 10.21), three (in 97) lying some way to the west, two displaced into **Period I/3** graves and two from earlier contexts (69.02 and 94.02). There is a full catalogue in the excavation archive.

Vessel 2: pinkish buff
There are a hundred and fourteen sherds from this vessel, found in the three main concentrations in the **Period I/1.6** hollow (Figures 3.12, 10.13 and 10.21), but no rim or handle sherds were found. Groups A and C consisted mainly of the middle part of the vessel, while Group B was mainly of the upper part. Three sherds came from the fill of the gully to the north of the **Period I/1.5** graveyard, four had been displaced into later graves, five into later mud deposits (73.01, 04) and one into a **Period I/2** rubbish spread

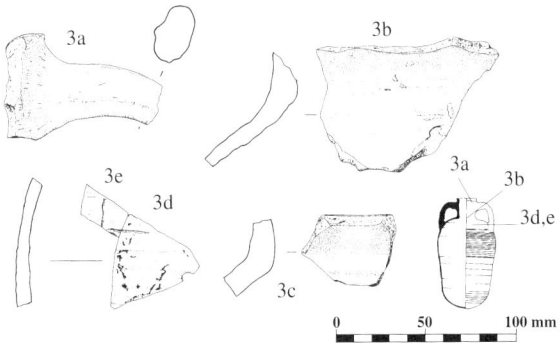

10.16 B*ii* amphora sherds.

(89). Three sherds from earlier contexts (66 and 92) were presumably contaminations. There is a full catalogue in the excavation archive.

Vessel 3
This is a miscellaneous group of six sherds, not certainly all from the same vessel. The body sherds have a distinctive white outer skin which differentiates them from Vessels 1 and 2, but the neck sherds were found in a waterlogged environment and their colour has been affected by the burial conditions. Nonetheless, from their thickness they seem most likely to be from the same vessel.

a*. Rim with handle attached to neck just below rim. Handle pulled, with ribbed asymmetrical section typical of B*ii*. Size 8 × 6 cm. Sherd cracked, possibly burnt, abraded (**53.12**).

b*. Neck and upper body junction, neck separately thrown and luted to body. Abraded. Neck D 11 cm., size 10 × 7 cm (**50.03**).

c*. Neck/shoulder junction. Abraded (**67.01**).

d* and **e***. Joining bodysherds from upper shoulder near neck with incised Latin cross graffito infilled with red paint (both **70**).

There is one other sherd from this vessel – **f** (**94.02**).

Two sherds (**a** and **b**) came from **Period I.7** contexts at the south end of the **southern sector**, the others include two (**c** and **f**) from relatively early contexts in the *inner precinct*. **f** came from the surface flanking Building I/6 and could have been contemporary with the sherds (**d** and **e**) from the adjacent hollow. **c** came from a shallow deposit in the **Period I/1.5** graveyard and may have been deposited at an earlier date.

The B*ii* amphora sherds were concentrated in the **Period I/1.6** hollow and, despite five sherds from earlier contexts, can be ascribed to this phase with confidence. Two sherds of V3 came from slightly earlier contexts in the *inner precinct* and this vessel may have been imported before the others.

B*iv*

B*iv* amphorae or lagaenae are small carrot-shaped vessels with tegulated ribbing and a distinctive highly micaceous fabric. The type has a long production history, but the forms produced after c. AD 400 have two handles, unlike the earlier one-handled forms. A few of the early-form vessels are known from Late Roman contexts in Britain, but most examples are of the later type and found on western Dark Age sites. B*iv* is almost invariably found in association with B*i* and B*ii* amphorae and was part of a package of wares. The production area was probably in the Sardis region of western Turkey. It is not known what products these vessels contained though sesame oil has been reported in scientific analysis. Thomas (1981b, 27) has suggested they were water jars used by merchants and not traded *per se*, but the quantities found suggest otherwise, and this is not a typical water-jar fabric. The small size and narrow neck suggest a costly liquid such as unguents or rare oils.

The Whithorn B*iv* are the furthest north of the distribution, other examples being confined to eight sites in Wales and south-west England. Tintagel is the only site with more than one vessel. Four of these sites are forts (Dinas Emrys, Cadbury Congresbury, South Cadbury, Tintagel), the others being settlement sites (Tean, Grambla, Trethurgy, Longbury Bank). The five sherds are not certainly from more than one vessel. There are a variety of fabrics known of B*iv*

type, with at least two different fabrics occurring in British contexts.

Vessel 1
a*. Bodysherd from lower part of vessel with tegulated ribbing. Fabric medium hard, highly micaceous, slightly gritty feel. Inclusions abundant mica and tiny rounded quartz, scattered dark rock fragments, larger white limestone(?) and mafic minerals. Orange-brown with browner exterior. Unabraded. Vessel D c. 36 cm, T. 8 mm (**85.02**).

b*. Bodysherd from shoulder and beginning of neck, no ribbing. Unabraded. Size 7 × 8 cm, T. 6–7 mm (**67.02**).

c*. Neck sherd with traces of handle luting on exterior. Neck D 8 cm, T. 5 mm, size 3 × 2 cm (**82.04**, Grave I/113).

There are two other sherds: an abraded neck sherd (**d**, **207**) and an unabraded body sherd (**e**, **50.03**)

Four sherds were scattered in the **northern sector** (Figure 10.13), the earliest (**b**) coming from the gully bounding the **Period I/1.5** graveyard. A fifth unabraded sherd (**e**) came from a relatively early deposit in the southern part of the **southern sector**. The sherds coincide spatially with the **Stage 2** assemblage, and the B*iv* vessel or vessels may have been imported with the B*ii* amphorae and associated pottery and glass (Figure 10.22).

B*v*

One sherd is probably from a B*v* amphora, a large cylindrical amphora made in the area of modern Tunisia, ancient Byzacena. As with B*iv*, these amphorae had a long production period and are also found in Late Roman contexts in Britain. Bodysherds cannot be accurately dated in themselves, though where they are found with other Mediterranean imports a post-Roman date can be assumed. B*v* is known from only four or five Dark Age contexts, most being found at Tintagel. The presence of African Red Slipware (produced in the same area) at Whithorn supports the post-Roman dating of this amphora sherd, and it should therefore date to the sixth century like the ARS. These amphorae are known to have been used to transport olive oil.

Vessel 1
* Bodysherd of large amphora. Fabric medium hard, gritty, common quartz, poorly sorted up to 2 mm. Orange with buff outer surface. Abraded. D c. 40 cm, T. 17 mm, size 9 × 7 cm (**50.06**).

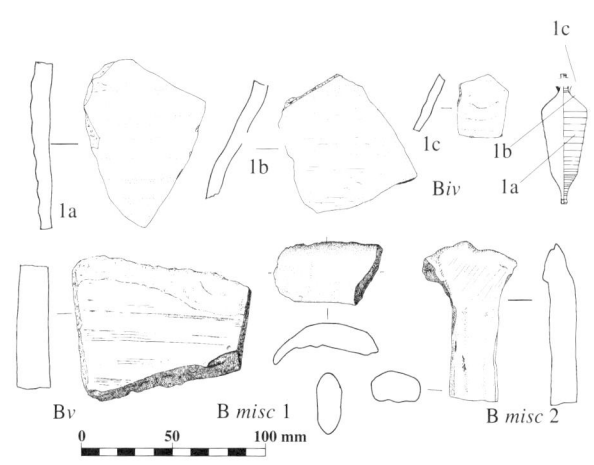

10.17 B*iv*, B*v* and *Bmisc* amphora sherds.

This abraded sherd came from a relatively late context at the south end of the **southern sector** and was presumably displaced.

B*misc.*

The two sherds in this group are both handles from different vessels, but neither is in a fabric found elsewhere amongst the imported amphorae. Vessel 1 has similarities in fabric to B*v*, but is quite different in overall appearance. The form of the handles is not like those on B*i* or B*ii*.

Vessel 1
* Handle of amphora, strongly curved ring form. Elliptical section. Fabric soft, with common quartz, poorly sorted up to 1 mm., well-rounded to sub-angular, occasional rock fragments. Pale pinkish buff. Abraded. Width 33 mm, T. 13 mm (**79.02**, Grave I/1).

Vessel 2
* Handle of amphora and attachment to body. Straight vertical strap handle with faint ribbing on outer surface. Fabric soft, yellow-buff, with rare sedimentary rock inclusions. Section 25 × 14 mm, Length 75 mm. **a–c** joining (**69.03**).

Both handles came from the **central sector** (Figure 10.13) and are likely to have been relatively early. The handle of Vessel 2 came from a rubbish spread overlying one of the layers producing B*i* sherds (V3), but preceding the deposition of the B*ii* amphorae. The handle of Vessel 1 came from a log coffin burial in the **Period I/1.5** graveyard, and is likely to have been deposited at an earlier stage of **Period I/1** when this area was not maintained carefully.

D Ware

D ware is now known to have been produced in western France, probably at a number of centres, and is the latest derivative of the Late Roman stamped fine tablewares of the region. It belongs to the Rigoir's Atlantic Group of the *sigillées paléochrétiennes grises* (Rigoir 1968; Rigoir *et al.* 1973). The plate form found at Whithorn was typically decorated on the basal interior with rouletting and stamps in a variety of motifs, including palmettes, animals and chi-rho crosses. Some of these stamps have been found in Insular contexts, at Dinas Powys, Glamorgan (Alcock 1963, Fig. 28, 6), and at Dinas Emrys, Gwynedd (Savory 1960, Pl. 8b; Campbell 1988, 126–7, Fig. 29, 12). The ware was being produced and used in the first half of the sixth century, for example at Tours (Randoin 1981, 105), but it is not known how far into the sixth century production continued. The Insular evidence supports a sixth century date (Campbell 1991, 29–30).

D ware is a fairly rare import, with most of the ten known sites only producing a few sherds (*ibid.*, 380–3). The only sites with substantial numbers of sherds are Dinas Powys and Briton Ferry, West Glamorgan (Campbell forthcoming b). Most of these sites are fortified high status settlements, some with royal associations. The only two other sites in Scotland are Dunadd, Argyll (Craw 1930, Fig. 10, 12 & 21) and the Mote of Mark, Kirkcudbrightshire (Curle 1914). The only undefended site, like Whithorn, to have produced D ware is Longbury Bank, Pembrokeshire, a site of enigmatic function but possibly a trading settlement (Campbell & Lane 1993).

Vessel 1*
Rim of plate or shallow bowl, Rigoir Form 4. Rim beaded internally, two shallow grooves on exterior below rim. Fabric fine, soft, few inclusions except occasional weathered-out limestone cavities. Dark grey with black slip on interior and exterior, mostly worn off. RD 30 cm, size 9 × 4 cm, T. 1 cm, relatively unabraded (**235.02**).

The sherd came from a relatively late **Period I** deposit in the **southern sector**, but coincided spatially with concentrations of other early finds (Figures 10.21–23), and may have been displaced from an earlier deposit in the vicinity.

E Ware

E ware consists of a variety of forms, mainly jars and beakers with rarer bowls, pitchers, lids and bottles, produced in a hard, gritty, whitish fabric. The source is unknown but probably in western France. Dating evidence is confined to associations in Insular contexts which show a *floruit* in the first half of the seventh century. The earliest vessels may be late sixth century, and some later forms may carry on into the eighth century. Although formerly described as kitchen ware, a detailed study of all occurrences has shown that many were probably used as containers for the importation of rare commodities (Campbell 1991; forthcoming a). However at a few sites they do appear to have been used as cooking vessels, and it is postulated that these occurrences represent the vessels used by merchants for their own cooking purposes and tableware. As is discussed below, Whithorn appears to belong to the latter category. The sites with this type of occurrence include Dalkey Island, and Samson, Scilly, both sites best regarded as trading places or merchant's stop-over points.

There are seventy-four sherds from at least sixteen vessels, making this the second largest concentration of E ware vessels known after that from Dunadd, Argyll. The forms present include an E_2 beaker, four E_3 bowls, an E_4 jug, and ten E_1 jars. These figures are minimum numbers, and as many of the thirty unassigned sherds are in fabrics which cannot be attributed to the numbered vessels, the true figure can be suspected to be higher. As a whole the collection does not give the impression of being primary refuse, as no vessel is represented by more than a few sherds, but most sherds are fresh, showing they have not undergone much disturbance since their original deposition.

The forms of vessel found is of interest in the number of bowls present, only Dunadd and Samson having as many E_3 vessels. There is also a jug, Vessel 6, which is unusual in its small size. The only other possible small E ware jug in Insular contexts is from the Mote of Mark, though the form is found in sixth century Frankish graves, for example at Herpes, Charente and Pitres, Eure (Campbell 1991, Illust. 57). As Vessel 6 comes from an early context, possibly in association with B ware, a date in the second half of the sixth century is possible for this vessel. One tiny sherd has combed ribbing, a rare feature on E ware as most vessels are undecorated. The only other occurrences are at Dalkey Island (Liversage 1968, Fig. 32, ec14) and Samson (Campbell 1991, Illust. 51, E181), reinforcing the suggestion that these three sites are linked in function as places where traders resided. Vessel 1, the E_2 beaker, is also unusual in not being sharply carinated at the shoulder. The only other insular examples are from Dalkey Island (Liversage 1968, Pl. 10, ec6), and Samson (Campbell 1991, Illust. 51), but the form is found widely in Frankish cemeteries (Campbell 1991, Illust. 55–7). Again this points to a connection with Dalkey Island and a possible early date, though the lack of a rim makes it difficult to be sure of this. One E_3 bowl has two incised lines on the carinated shoulder. Although this is common on E_1 jars and E_2 beakers, the only other example is on a bowl from Samson (*ibid.*, Illust. 51).

The forms of most of the E_1 jars are found elsewhere on many sites, but it is of interest that Vessels 7, 9 and 15 are matched at the Mote of Mark. Vessel 16 is more unusual in being very white and thin-walled, with a rim form only paralleled at Dunadd. This vessel has certain similarities to a group of thin-walled imports of later date than E ware, though in a generally similar fabric. These are found at sites around the Firth of Clyde and may be eighth to tenth century in date (Laing 1974b, Fig. 3). Vessel 16 may therefore be late in the E ware date-range.

Many of the E_1 jars from Whithorn show signs of use as cooking vessels, with black deposits on the exterior, spalling, and internal carbon deposits. This is an unusual occurrence but is matched by the assemblages from Dalkey Island and Samson. The tablewares, the bowls, beaker and jug are in contrast free of these signs of burning. It is noticeable that these two groups of ware are spatially distinct, with the cooking wares being found mainly in the **southern sector**, and the tablewares in the *inner precinct* (Figure 10.18). One of the E_3 bowls (Vessel 4) is very worn in the interior, suggesting that food was ground in it as in a mortarium. The taphonomy of the sherds is of interest. Few vessels have produced more than a couple of sherds, this low vessel to sherd ratio suggesting that the E ware is not primary refuse. However there is a lack of abrasion on most sherds, except those from later contexts, showing that the sherds have not suffered any major disturbance. This suggests the broken vessels were thrown on middens which were then spread out, perhaps on gardens or to level up wet areas. A few of the vessels are more complete (Vessels 1 & 2) but large parts of these vessels are missing. This postulated redeposition of the E ware, and also the B ware, makes discussion of the stratigraphy more complex than might be thought initially.

1. Beaker
Vessel 1: E_2 beaker
Base of E_2 beaker*. String cut-off, fingerprints on body exterior. Fabric very hard, proto-stoneware, buff/grey/buff. Basal D 6 cm. Three joining sherds, **a** and **b** (**95**); **c** (**99**). Shoulder of beaker. Maximum D 10 cm. Two joining sherds, **d** (**109**) and **e** (**82.03**, Grave I/104).

All five sherds came from the same area in the western part of the site (Figures 3.12, 10.18 and 22) and are likely to have been deposited in the **Period I/1.6** hollow before the B*ii* amphora and A ware sherds. Two sherds (**a** and **b**) were probably *in situ*, the remainder had been displaced into later contexts

2. Bowls
Vessel 2: E_3 bowl
Complete profile of E_3 bowl with sharply carinated shoulder*. Base with string cut-off and slight pedestal form. Fabric uniform dark buff-grey. Basal D 9 cm, RD 20 cm, height 6.5 cm. Seven joining sherds, **a–e** (**236.01**); **f** and **g** (**53.11**).

Vessel 3: E_3 bowl
Rim of E_3 bowl, profile similar to Vessel 2*. Fabric distinctive pink, coarse, with white surfaces. RD 21 cm. Three sherds. **a** (**109**); **b** (**82.04**; Grave I/114), **c** (**82.04**, Grave I/113).

Vessel 4: E_3 bowl
Rim and profile of E_3 bowl with sharply carinated shoulder and beaded rim*. Interior heavily worn, with carbon deposits near rim. Base sherd with slight pedestal. Fabric dark grey with lighter patches. RD 20 cm, Basal D *c*. 8 cm, estimated height 6.5 cm. **a** (**109**); **b** (**81.01**, Grave I/51).

Vessel 5: E_3 bowl
Rim of E_3 bowl with carinated shoulder decorated with two incised grooves*. The profile is less carinated than the other bowls. Fabric buff, with minute sparkly quartz. RD 20 cm (**58**).

Two of the bowls (Vs 3 and 4) came from the *inner precinct* and two (2 and 5) from the *outer zone* (Figure 10.18 and .24). Both of the former originated in the rubbish spread (109) ascribed to the latter part of **Period I/3**. One of the bowls from the *outer*

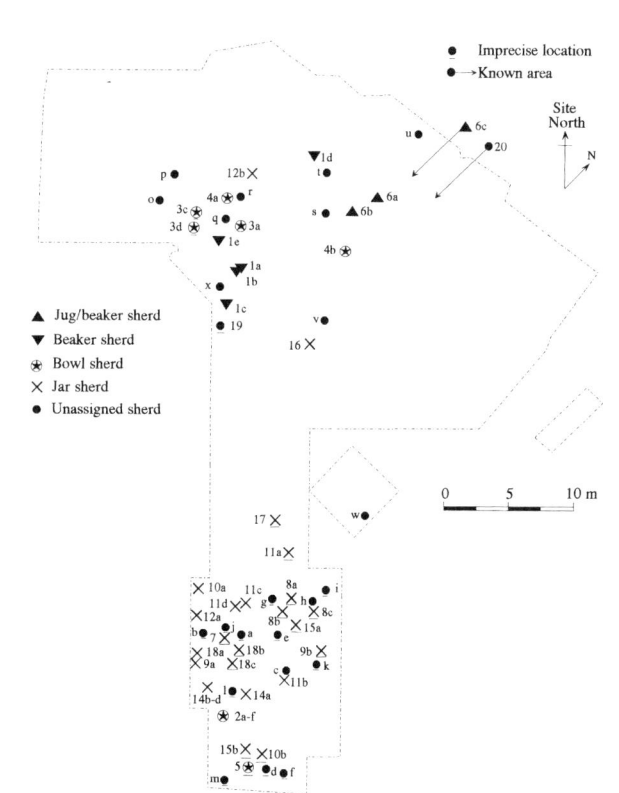

10.18 The distribution of E ware sherds.

zone came from the **Period I.10** waterborne deposits which produced the largest group of E ware sherds. The other (Vessel 2) came from a **Period I.12** post-hole cutting a **Period I.5** pit (53.11). Two sherds were ascribed to the earlier context, but the vessel was almost certainly deposited in **Period I.12**, and would have been broadly contemporary with the construction of Building I/24, perhaps dating to the second or third decade of the eighth century (p 130).

3. Jug
Vessel 6: E4 jug
a*. Strap handle fragment, wheel-thrown. Fabric distinctive, pink with white surfaces, like Vessel 3. **a (70)**.
b and **c***. Base, with string cut-off. Large E$_2$ beaker or small E$_4$ jug. Basal D 6 cm. Same fabric as **a**, but not certainly the same vessel. Two joining sherds **b (70)** and **c (904)**.

The handle of V6 was securely stratified among the B*ii* amphora sherds in the **Period I/1.6** hollow, a second sherd (**c**) found at the same time probably came from the same deposit, and a third (**b**) had been displaced into an adjacent **Period I/3** silt deposit. The vessel can be ascribed to **Period I/1.6** with confidence.

4. Jars
Vessel 7: E$_1$ jar
Rim of E$_1$ jar, with internal lid-seat and tall vertical neck*. RD 17 cm. Fabric mottled black, grey, buff and pink. No signs of sooting. There are traces of a green waxy deposit on the interior (**53.09**).

Vessel 8: E$_1$ jar
a–c*. Rim and shoulder sherds of E$_1$ jar. Strongly everted rim with two grooves on upper surface. Fabric variable, grey, white and pink. Exterior spalled and sooted, interior clean. RD 16 cm, **a** and **b** joining **c** (all **55**).

Vessel 9: E$_1$ jar
a–d*. Rim and bodysherds of E$_1$ jar. Rim everted with strong groove on upper surface. Fabric pale grey, occasionally with pinkish core, black exterior surface with spalling and some sooting. RD 18 cm. **a (117)** joining **b (115)**; **c (903)** and **d (406)**.

Vessel 10: E$_1$ jar
a*. Rim of E$_1$ jar with strong lid-seat. Fabric grey to black, very hard. RD 18 cm, **a (117)**.
b*. Basal angle of E$_1$ jar, almost certainly the same vessel. Exterior sooted, interior not. Base D 11 cm, **b (58)**.

Vessel 11: E$_1$ jar
Rim and bodysherds of E$_1$ jar*. Rim everted, of sub-square section, with strong lid-seat groove and groove on outer face. Fabric brick-red to grey. Interior blackened deposits, exterior spalled. RD 16 cm, **a (64.04)** joining **b (55)**; **c** joining **d**, both (**55**).

Vessel 12: E$_1$ jar
a and **b***. Rim and bodysherd of E$_1$ jar. Rim everted. Fabric pinkish buff to grey. Interior fresh, but inner edge of rim badly spalled, possibly in use. RD 16 cm, **a (235.01)**; **b (220)**.

Vessel 13: E$_1$ jar
Rim of small E$_1$ jar*, weakly everted, with faint groove on inner surface. Rim form almost identical to Vessel 14, made by same hand. Fabric whitish buff with brown outer skin. RD *c*. 14 cm (**760**).

Vessel 14: E$_1$ jar
a–d*. Rim and bodysherd of E$_1$ jar. Rim weakly everted, with faint groove on inner surface. Rim form almost identical to Vessel 13. Fabric black with grey outer skin. Exterior sooted, interior with thick carbon deposits. RD 18 cm, **a** (52.04); **b–d** (**230.01**).

Vessel 15: E$_1$ jar
a and **b***. Rim sherds of E$_1$ jar. Rim everted, rolled and beaded. Fabric buff to grey, flaking. Exterior sooted. RD 16 cm. **a (55)**; **b** (**58**).

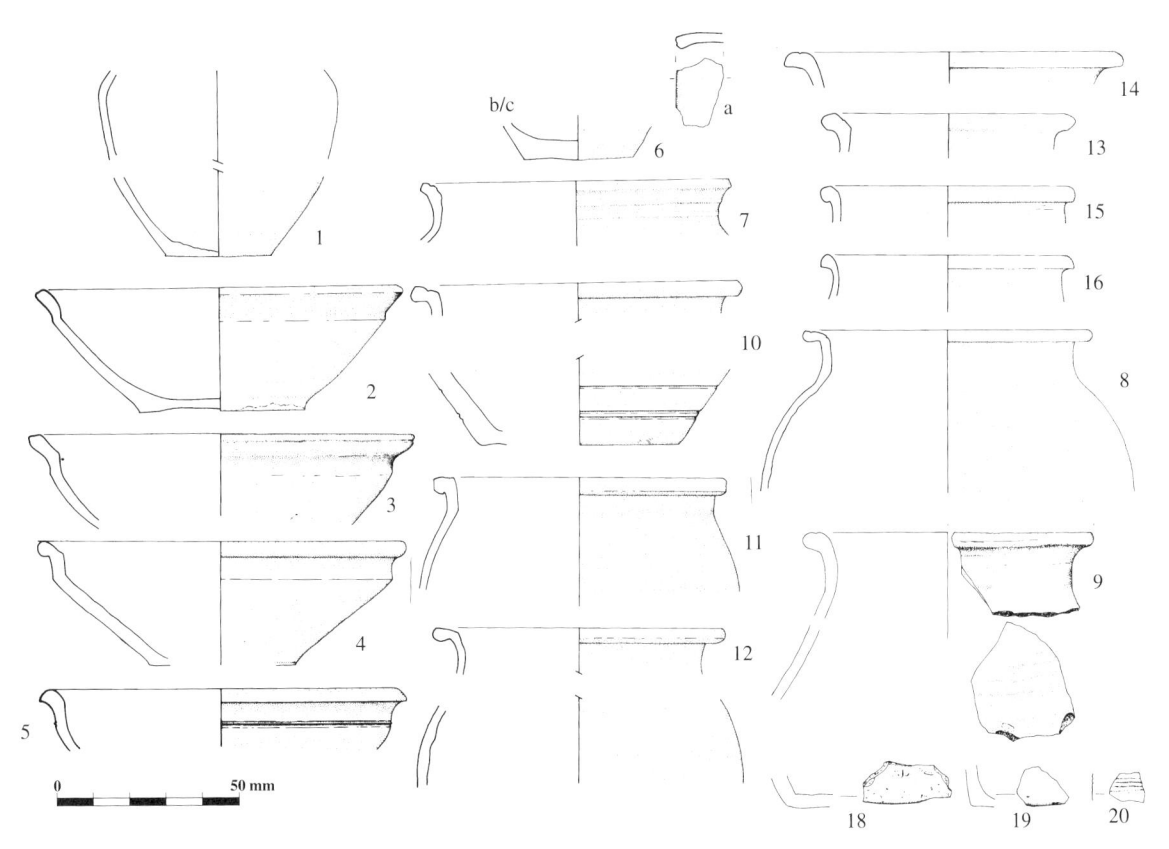

10.19 E ware.

Vessel 16: E₁ jar
Rim of small E₁ jar*. Rim weakly everted, sub-triangular section. Fabric creamy white, with tiny sparkling quartz. RD *c*. 14 cm (**118**).

Eight of the ten jars came from relatively late deposits in the *outer zone*, most originating in the waterborne deposits of **Period I.10**. Vessels 7 and 14 originated in **Period I.8** contexts and may have been slightly earlier, while Vessel 9, ascribed to **Period I.11**, may have been rather later. One of the two sherds of Vessel 12 came from the displaced industrial debris used in the construction of the **Period II/1** oratory (220). The only sherd of Vessel 16 came from the shallow deposits flanking Building I/5, but cannot be dated closely. The last vessel (13) was represented by a single sherd from recent garden soil (760) in the **Museum Garden**, and is one of the rare **Period I** finds from this part of the site.

5. Unassigned sherds
17 Base of E₁ jar. Fabric orange inner, black outer. Exterior sooted and heavily spalled, interior no deposits. Base D 10 cm (**64.04**).

18* Base and body sherds of small E₁ jar. Fabric brown, black exterior, sooted and spalled. **a** (117); **b** and **c** (**235.02**).

19* Base sherd (**902**, **central sector**).

20* Decorated bodysherd, with combed rilling, five grooves. Probably from jar. Fabric grey, exterior sooted (**901**, **northern sector**).

21 Miscellaneous sherds. **a** and **b** (**235.02**), **c** (**55**), **d** (**58**), **e** (**55**), **f** (**58**), **g** (**55**), **h** (**55**), **i** (**55**), **j** (**53.09**), **k** (**115**), **l**, abraded (**236.01**), **m** (**232**), **n** (**70**), **o**, perhaps Vessel 6 (**89**), **p** (**88.01**), **q** (**109**), **r** (**109**), **s** (**73.02**), **t** (**73.02**), **u** (**82.02**, Grave I/82), **v** (**399.02**), **w** Bodysherd, rilled interior, very abraded. Possibly same vessel as 18 (**535**), × (**98**).

Fifteen of the unassigned sherds came from relatively late **Period I** contexts in the *outer zone* and do not conflict with the chronological picture evinced by the vessel fragments. The remaining thirteen from the *inner precinct* include three (**n–p**) from **Period I/1** or **1/2** contexts, one (**o**) potentially a piece of Vessel 6. The others came from 109 and related late deposits, or had been displaced.

Possible imports

Two anomalous vessels (PY07.1–2), both fairly abraded, are potentially Dark Age imports. Vessel 2 is a Roman form which continued to be produced on the Continent and Mediterranean region in the fifth to seventh centuries. If it is not Roman-British, and the fabric suggests it is not, it could be an import. Forms like this were produced in African Red Slipware in the sixth century (Fulford's Form 47), but it is not ARS unless it is an aberrant fabric.

Vessel 1.
Gritty, oxidised cooking pot fabric, wheel-thrown. Inclusions mainly micaceous, coarse, occasional quartz and rock fragments. **a** and **b** (both **89**).

The sherds came from a **Period I/2** rubbish deposit (89) and seem to pertain to an otherwise aceramic horizon (p 325).

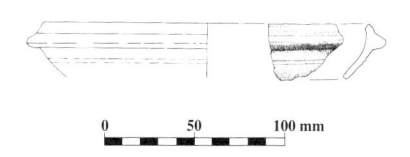

10.20 Flanged bowl (PY07.2).

Vessel 2*.
Rim of small bowl with flange on exterior. Fabric medium hard, gritty. Inclusions mainly quartz, poorly sorted up to 1 mm, rounded to sub-angular. Variable colour, grey to orange-buff, possible traces of orange slip on exterior. Very abraded. RD 18 cm, T. 4 mm (**901**).

The sherd came from the drain surrounding the eighteenth century extension to the manse, and probably originated in the **Period I/0** or **I/1** deposits in the eastern part of the **central sector**.

The Early Medieval imports: distribution and chronology

Peter Hill

The **Period I** features revealed a detailed stratified sequence of early medieval pottery and glass, which can be enhanced by spatial analysis encompassing both stratified and displaced finds (Figures 10.21–24). The most reliable evidence came from the stratified deposits in the **northern sector**. These had been extensively disturbed by graves, but a critical path can be traced through the matrix (Figure 3.4) linking early rubbish spreads (69.02, 94.01 etc.) with the **Period I/1.6** hollow (97/70), and the successive overlying rubbish deposits (100, 96, 89, 85.02, 109 etc.). The shallow deposits in the **central sector** had been damaged by graves in **Periods I** and **V**, and by buildings and cultivation in **Periods II–IV**. These disturbances had displaced important groups of pottery and glass, which can nevertheless be ascribed to the earlier stages of **Period I/1** on the basis of the distributions plotted in Figures 3.8, 3.10 and 10.21. The argument is necessarily weaker than for the stratified finds to the north, but was maintained when sherds of individual vessels occurred in both areas. The problems of the **southern sector** are discussed above (pp 118–9). These were so severe that the provenance of many finds is imprecise, but general trends reflecting the deposition of various sherds from single vessels and groups of vessels are probably admissible.

Intra-site variability. A large proportion of the pottery and glass from the **northern** and **central sectors** seems to have originated in **Period I/1** deposits (Figures 10.21 and 22), when this area lay beyond the *inner precinct*, and most of the later finds came from the *outer zone* (Figure 10.24). The principal exceptions were the large assemblage of glass from the **Period I/2** rubbish spreads (Figure 10.23), and a smaller group of E ware and glass from a **Period I/3** hollow (109, Figure 10.24). Both groups are likely to have included workshop debris, possibly deriving from an artisanal area in the adjacent sector of the *outer zone*. The scarcity of contemporary debris from the **Period I/1.5** graveyard (Figure 10.22) and **Period I/2** shrine (Figure 10.23) indicates that ritual areas were well maintained. The deposition of pottery and glass may thus be seen to characterise domestic, and possibly artisanal, areas usually located in the *outer zone*.

The concentrations of early medieval finds in the

THE FINDS

Glebe Field are not matched in other excavated parts of Whithorn, and previous excavations have produced neither pottery nor glass. The absence of finds from the earlier trenches at the east end of the hill[2] (Figure 1.6) is supported by the evidence from the **Museum Garden** trench (pp 277-87), where only three sherds of vessel glass (all C3) and one of E ware (V13) were found. This area probably lay within the *inner precinct* from the beginning of **Period I** and may thus have been kept clean of debris. The incompletely-excavated **Fey Field** trench spanned the inferred outer boundary of the **Period I** *monasterium*, but only produced one sherd of glass (V76) and no early pottery. The scarcity of early finds from the ground to the east of this boundary contrasts with the large numbers from the **southern sector**, and points to a long-lived functional difference between these two parts of the *outer zone*.

Supply, deposition and sequence

The detailed contextual evidence appended to the catalogues helps to distinguish four principal stages (**1–4**) in the supply of pottery and glass. These stages were of unequal duration, and three (**1, 3** and **4**) can be sub-divided. The finds from the four sub-divisions of **Stage 1** and the undivided **Stage 2** assemblage may represent successive cargoes of trade goods (Alcock 1987b, 68–92; Thomas 1982, 1988b, 1990, Wooding 1987), but the hypothesis that the early Christian communities in Galloway included settlers – perhaps monastic missionaries (Thomas 1992b) – from Gaul, implies that some early vessels could have been brought in by individual immigrants, or as communal property. The three sub-divisions of **Stage 3** may record the transition from imported wares to local products, and so requires an elastic economic model. **Stage 4** was considerably longer than **Stages 1–3**, and its two sub-divisions probably mark changing tastes and trading contacts, but are too broad to correspond with individual cargoes.

Stage 1 was represented by a first batch of Group A vessels with wheel-cut decoration (Vs 1, 4, 5 and perhaps 3); the Group A bowls with opaque white trails (Vs 6–8); the Group B claw beakers (Vs 11, 12) and vessels with self-coloured trails (Vs 13–15); two Group C cones with horizontally-trailed rims (Vs 41 and 44); two Group D bowls (V 48 and 59) and probably a third (V49); a Group D cone or funnel beaker (V53); the putative squat jar (54); three B*i* amphorae and two B*misc* amphorae. Sherds were scattered widely over much of the trench and may be seen as debris surrounding the earlier **Period I/1** buildings (Figure 10.21). Gaps in the distribution of finds generally corresponded with later disturbances which included building platforms in the **northern sector**, the **Period I/1.6** hollow to the south and the **Period I.7–11** buildings in the **southern sector**.

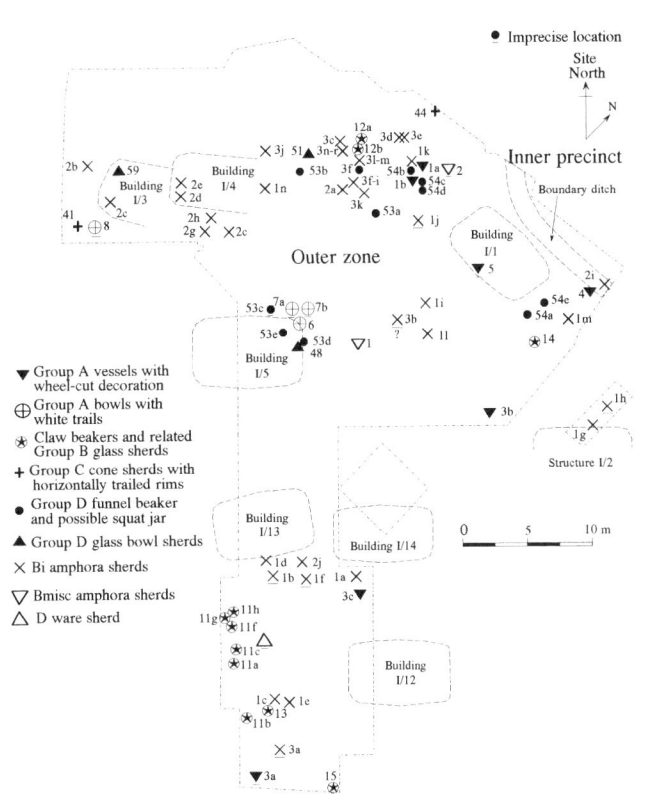

[2] Reports of early wheel-thrown pottery from P R Ritchie's excavations are unconfirmed.

10.21 Early medieval imports: **Stage 1**.

There was no equivalent disturbance on the north-eastern margin of the trench, and the absence of finds here may reflect the different functions of the *inner precinct* and less-tidy *outer zone*.

Spatial and stratigraphic evidence identifies a plausible depositional sequence for the **Stage 1** finds. The earliest finds from the **northern** and **southern sector**s were sherds of claw beakers which are likely to have been the first post-Roman vessels to reach the site (**Stage 1a**). A second sub-group comprised the B*i* amphorae, Group A vessels, and Group D bowls (48, 59 and probably 49), funnel beaker and squat jar. The two sub-groups of Group A sherds had differing distributions with trailed bowl fragments confined to the western part of the site and sherds with wheel-cut decoration scattered to the east and in the **southern sector**. B*i* amphora sherds were associated with scraps of two glass vessels (Vs 1 and 54) in the eastern part of the site (69.02), but overlay a trailed bowl fragment (V8) at the west end of the **northern sector**. This suggests that the white-trailed bowls pertained to an earlier stage of supply, and a similar sequence may obtain at Clogher where a rim sherd from a glass bowl was deposited before a large group of B*i* sherds (Warner 1979 and Pers. Comm.). The Group A bowls (Vs 6–8) were associated spatially with two Group D bowls (Vs 48 and 59), and probably a third (V49), and the Group D cone or funnel beaker (V53). These form a coherent group characterized by colourless and green metal, and the prevalence of shallow bowls. The identification of these vessels as a group relies heavily on spatial factors, but they do seem to record a distinct phase in the supply of glass (**Stage 1b**), which preceded the first cargoes of pottery. The third sub-group (**Stage 1c**) comprises the B*i* amphorae, Group A vessels with wheel-cut decoration, two Group C cones with horizontally-trailed rims (Vs 41 and 44), and the putative squat jar (V54). The association of these diverse wares was demonstrated by stratified finds from the **northern sector**, and the widely scattered sherds make sense as debris surrounding the earlier buildings (I/1, I/2, I/12–14) of the **Period I/1** *monasterium*. The glass includes pale green, colourless and pale yellow sherds, the last (Vs 41 and 44) absent from the **Stage 1b** assemblage. The remaining **Stage 1** vessels comprise a fourth, less sharply-defined sub-group (**Stage 1d**) possibly including the two B*misc.* handles and the earliest B*ii* amphora (V3). The Group B vessels with self-coloured trails were probably deposited after the claw beakers, but cannot be ascribed to a specific sub-group, although the sherd of Vessel 14 fits the spatial pattern of the **Stage 1c** finds.

The chronology of this group is imprecise, but it is effectively bracketed by the claw beakers, purportedly of sixth century date, and the **Stage 2** assemblage ascribed to *c*. 550 AD. It can thus be attributed to the period *c*. 500–550 AD or, with greater latitude in the dating of the claw beakers, *c*. 475–550 AD. It may comprise a mixture of imports and possessions; the former probably including the amphorae, and the latter some of the glass vessels. Associated finds of Haematite and lime from **Period I/1.2** and **I/1.3** contexts attest a regional trade network complementing the more distant contacts revealed by the pottery and glass.

Stage 2 is represented by the finds from the **Period I/1.6** hollow (Table 3.14a and b) and adjacent contexts (Figure 3.12), augmented by related finds from other parts of the site. This group comprised the B*ii* and, probably, B*iv* amphorae; the African Red Slipware; two early E ware vessels (1 and 6); a second batch of Group C cones with horizontal trails (Vs 39, 43, 46 and possibly 40, 42 and 45); and pale-green Group D cones (Vs 60, 62 and a rim, D1a). These finds were restricted to two parts of the trench (Figure 10.22). The larger group was scattered over the **Period I/1.6** hollow and the ground to the north, and may have been debris surrounding Buildings I/6 and I/7, but excluded from the fenced graveyard to the south. A smaller group of finds from the **southern sector** was confined to the southern part of the trench, and might be seen as debris surrounding Buildings I/12 or I/15.

Stage 2 reveals a new pattern of trade continuing extant Mediterranean links, but now including wares from Gaul. This stage is ascribed to *c*. 550 AD (p 69) and is likely to have been of brief duration, perhaps spanning twenty years or so. The **Stage 1** vessel types were generally unrepresented in this assemblage, indicating that tastes or trading contacts had changed. The most striking changes are the replacement of Group A and B glass with Group C and D vessels; the substitution of cones for bowls as

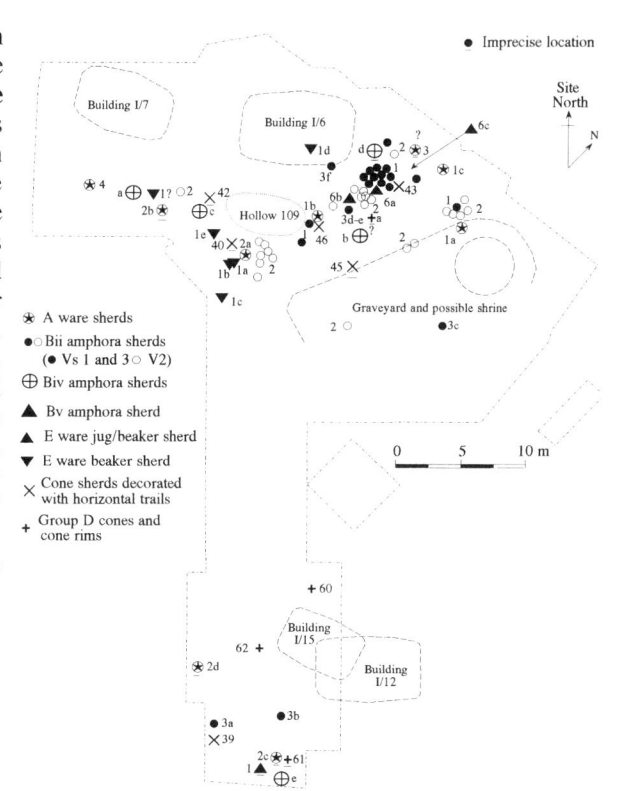

10.22 Early medieval imports: **Stage 2**.

the preferred vessel form; and perhaps a move from wine to oil imports.

Stage 3 followed shortly after the deposition of the **Stage 2** material, and was represented by the rich finds from the **Period I/2** rubbish spreads in the western part of the *inner precinct*, and related sherds from the *outer zone* (Figure 10.23). The assemblage was dominated by Group E vessel fragments and related E1 and E2 sherds, but also included most of the burnt and fused folded fragments (FA and FB), and securely-stratified sherds of Group C and D vessels. The latter comprised fragments of a blue cone (V18); a Group C cone decorated with horizontal trails (47); Group C sherds decorated with vertical and horizontal trails; two Group D vessels with kicked bases (64 and 65, possibly a jar and flask), a flask or stemmed cup (V82) and possibly a Roman bowl (GS01.1). Displaced finds from the same area included fragments of the Group C bowl with combed festoons (V21); three more Group C cones decorated with horizontal trails (40, 42 and 45); a Group D bowl (50); and the bichrome Group D cone (V51). The Group E2 fragments from the main rubbish spread (89) confirm their ascription to this stage, and their wider distribution provides a valuable link with the *outer zone*. The Group E2 fragments there came from a range of **Period I.5–7** contexts, but might originally have been scattered on the **Period I.6** rubbish spread (114). The Group B palm-cup fragments (Vs 9 and 10), mostly from the same area, may also have originated in this deposit, and are ascribed to this stage.

The distribution of **Stage 3** finds differs significantly

THE FINDS 325

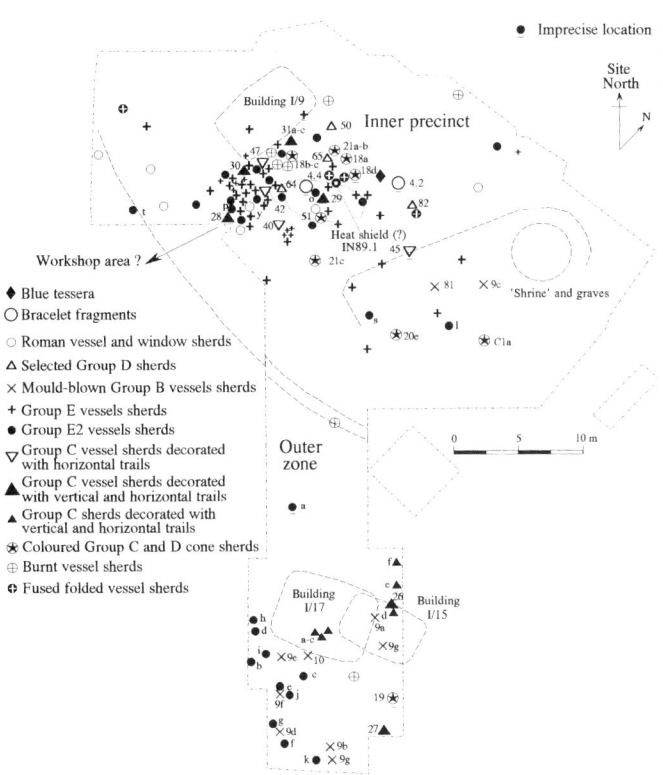

10.23 Early medieval imports: **Stage 3**.

from those of **Stages 1** and **2**. Finds from the **southern sector** were again concentrated in the southern part of the area, and may have been successive spreads of debris surrounding Buildings I/15 and I/17. The finds from the *inner precinct* comprised scattered sherds in the outer part of the zone, and the concentration in the **Period I/2** deposits flanking Building I/9. The scattered sherds extended over the **Period I/1.5** graveyard, but not the **Period I/2** 'shrine' to the east. The concentration of sherds might be interpreted as successive deposits of domestic debris flanking Buildings I/6 and I/9, but the quantity of broken glass, and the associated finds (Tables 3.17–20), suggest otherwise. A closer examination reveals three overlapping sub-groups. The first (**Stage 3a**), and possibly earliest, comprises Group C, D and F sherds (Vs 18, 21, 40, 42, 45, 47, 50, 51, 64, 65, 82, FA and FB) from the north-east part of the deposit; the second (**Stage 3b**) includes the Group E vessel fragments and E1 sherds concentrated to the south-west; and the third (**Stage 3c**), and possibly latest, contains sherds of Group C vessels with vertical and horizontal trails, scattered among both the other groups. The burnt vessel sherds and fused folded fragments from the first sub-group attest the reworking of discarded, vessels and some or all of the associated finds could have been cullet. A perforated iron disc (IN89.1) found beside two of the fused folded fragments, could have been a heat-guard from a tool (p 432). Adjacent graves produced two Roman bangle fragments of opaque white (GS4.4) and bluish green glass (GS4.2); a dark blue tessera (GS5.1) and a fractured molten lump of bluish-green glass (GS01.12). The bangle fragments

may have been burial talismans (p 294), but all four pieces could have been commodities for experimental glass-working. The Group E vessels could have been the product of this experimentation, and might have been discarded because the trails would have muddied the metal on remelting. The E2 sherds were more widely scattered in the *inner precinct* and *outer zone*, and could have come from finished vessels produced by this workshop, broken and discarded after normal use, and concentrated in the residential area. The vessels decorated with vertical and horizontal trails may have been slightly later than the Group E cones, but could also have been local products as this decorative scheme has not been found elsewhere.

The most striking features of the **Stage 3** assemblage are the prevalence of rare and unique vessel types, the heterogeneous concentration of sherds in the **northern sector**, and the strong hints of glass-working. Rare finds include the coloured Group C fragments, the Group D vessels, and the Group B palm-cup and related sherds. These pieces may have been deposited in the earlier part of this stage, and have links with the Mote of Mark (V18), Ireland (Vs 18, 64 and 65), northern France (V9), and perhaps Bordeaux (V51). The Group C cone, or cones, with horizontal trails (V47 and perhaps 40, 42 and 45) offer the only typological link with the preceding stages. The unique material includes the Group E vessels and Group C sherds with vertical and horizontal trails. These seem to have been slightly later than the 'rare' vessels and may mark a phase when external contacts were broken. This later **Stage 3** assemblage thus either records a hitherto unrecognized stage in the trade system reflected at other sites (Table 10.2), or comprises local variants that failed to penetrate the wider market. The deposits producing the **Stage 3** finds contained two sherds of Roman pottery (1.4 and 2.2) and scraps of an unidentified wheel-thrown vessel (PY7.1), but were otherwise aceramic. This stage post-dated the horizon ascribed to *c.* 550 AD, may have been relatively brief, and probably lies within the later-sixth century.

Stage 4 probably spanned the seventh century and the first two or three decades of the eighth. The **Stage 4** finds came from **Period I/3** and **I/4** contexts in the *inner precinct* and **Period I.7–.12** deposits in the *outer zone*, and comprised the E ware jars and bowls; the Group C cones with vertical running chevrons; a late group of pale-coloured (Vs 58, 61, 63, D1**b–e**) and amber Group D cones (Vs 55–7); the olive green (V17) and perhaps the deep yellow-green (V16) Group B vessels; the pale wine-red stemmed beaker or goblet (V20); and perhaps the dark-green vessel ornamented with bichrome rods (V83). The group may include a second batch of Group A vessels with wheel-cut abraded decoration (Vs 2 and perhaps 3), and some of the Group C cones with horizontally-trailed rims from the **southern sector**.

The **Stage 4** finds were concentrated in the *outer zone*, and the *inner precinct* would have been relatively 'clean' without the pottery and glass from the **Period I/3** hollow (109) and related contexts (Figure 10.24). The scattered finds in the *inner precinct* were largely

C cones with vertical running chevrons. The sherds of these vessels are likely to have been scattered around Buildings I/18 and I/20, and sealed by waterborne deposits in **Period I.10**. The Group C cones with horizontally trailed rims (Vs 33–38) from these deposits may have come from vessels decorated with vertical running chevrons further down. Most of the finds from the *inner precinct* are likely to have pertained to this sub group, and include securely stratified sherds of pottery and glass from the **Period I/3** hollow (109) and sherds of a Group A vessel (V2) from adjacent deposits. The **Stage 4a** finds were probably deposited over a relatively long period in the early- to mid-seventh century. The later finds from the *outer zone* (**Stage 4b**) included an E ware bowl (V2) and at least one jar (V9); the stemmed beaker or goblet (V20); and sherds of four Group D vessels (52, 55, 56, 63) and two unassigned rims (D**1b** and **e**). Sparse finds from the *inner precinct* included scraps of two strongly-coloured Group B vessels (16 and 17), two unassigned Group D rim sherds (D**c** and **d**), and perhaps Vessel 57, and possibly the dark green vessel with bichrome rod ornament (V83). Group D sherds from the floor of Building I/24 (V63) and the shale path to the north (V55) were probably deposited in the earlier-eighth century, and the **Stage 4b** assemblage probably spanned the later-seventh and earlier-eighth centuries.

New stronger colours appear in the later sub-group and there is a lower proportion of trailed vessels. The **Stage 4a** assemblage conforms closely with finds from other sites, and it is thus likely that Whithorn was participating in the trade network linking western Britain with Gaul, after the phase of isolation and possibly local production in **Stage 3**. The quality of this participation remains uncertain. The similarities between Whithorn and the putative trading sites at Samson and Dalkey Island, may imply that traders had used the E ware vessels concentrated in the *outer zone*, and the postulated *monasterium* could easily have included a traders' quarter. The **southern sector** faces towards the Isle of Whithorn, and would have been an appropriate area for the accommodation of traders. The change to undecorated Group D cones in **Stage 4b** may correspond with an Anglian presence in the later-seventh and earlier-eighth centuries (p 37), and a shift in trading partners in this period might account for the sherds of two Group B vessels (Vs 16 and 17) from late contexts in the *inner precinct*.

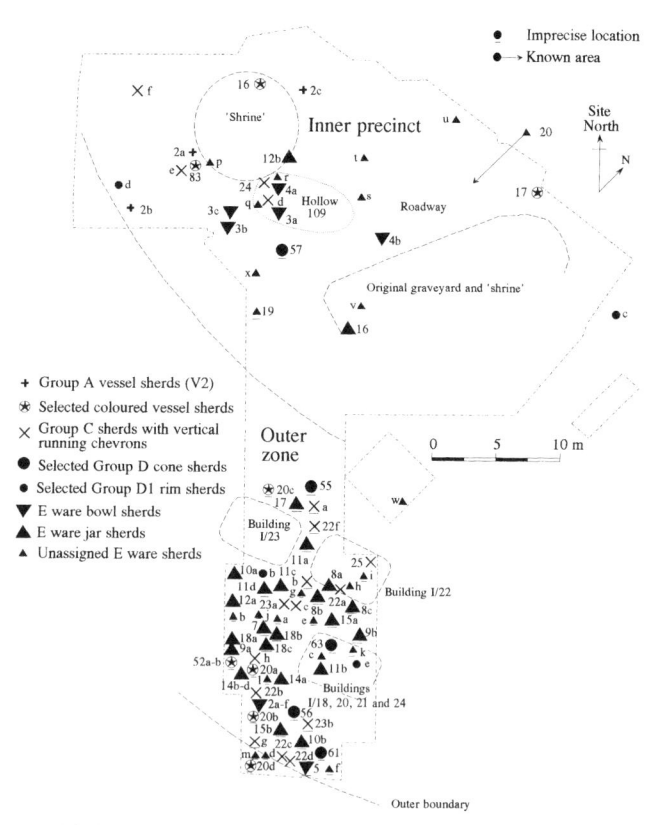

10.24 Early medieval imports: **Stage 4**.

confined to the north-west part of the area, though apparently respecting the **Period I/3** 'shrine', and the **Period I/1** graveyard remained pristine. The dense finds in the **southern sector** were concentrated in the **Period I.10** deposits (55, 58 and 235), but are likely to have been debris surrounding the **Period I.8 and 9** buildings, and either sealed by, or spread on, this layer of waterborne silt. Gaps in the distribution correspond with the sunken floors of Buildings I/22 and I/23, and later drains (230 and 417) cutting the silt deposit. Finds were relatively sparse beyond the outer boundary, but the area exposed was too small too confirm that debris did not extend beyond it. Despite the stratigraphic problems, early and late groups (**Stages 4a** and **b**) can be identified with some confidence. The early group (**Stage 4a**) included most of the E ware jars and Group

The Early Medieval Window Glass

Rosemary Cramp

The site catalogue of this glass was compiled by Jean Comrie and this has been modified with respect to some measurements and to accommodate the terminology to other catalogues of Northumbrian window-glass notably that of Wearmouth/Jarrow, with which this collection is closely comparable. The glass was also the subject of a dissertation from Bradford University (Hold 1991). Some difficulty was experienced with the equipment and resulting output during this work, but I am grateful to the

THE FINDS 327

Department of Archaeological Science for permission to quote some of the firm conclusions.

Quantity

132 sherds of Early Medieval window glass were individually recorded from the site, but some were mere splinters and others small fragments which could be tentatively joined, so that it cannot be said that the sherd count is a significant statistic, and the area which the glass could have covered has not been technically measured. Nevertheless the quantity of sherds and the range of colours is significant when compared with what has been discovered in other ecclesiastical sites of a comparable date, for example at Beverley (Henderson 1991, 124–127) where about twenty fragments of pale turquoise, pale green, olive green, brown, blue, and red streaked have been found; Escomb (Cramp 1971, 26–28) eight fragments of pale turquoise, pale green, light and dark blue; Brixworth, nine fragments, of pale green, emerald green and blue (Hunter 1977, 104–6). Some strongly coloured window glass has also been found at the sites of Barking (Webster and Backhouse 1991, 88), Brandon (Webster and Backhouse 1991, No. 66y), Dacre (Newman forthcoming), Flixborough fourteen pieces (Pers. Comm.), Repton (Hunter forthcoming), as well as Glastonbury (Radford 1958). Even the important later monastic and episcopal site of Winchester has not yielded a greater quantity of glass, or as wide a range of colour (Biddle and Hunter 1990, 350–356; 368–9, Pl. XXVI). Of course it is only valid to compare quantities of glass when they are found in similar contexts such as on the ground surfaces around buildings, rather than in secondary deposits. In relation to the north only Escomb, Wearmouth and Jarrow has produced glass in association with buildings thus being comparable with the Burial Chapel group, (see below), from Whithorn. By far the largest quantity of Northumbrian window-glass so far discovered is from the twin monastic sites of Wearmouth and Jarrow, where 302 and 1,827 respectively sherds are recorded (Cramp 1970a 1970b, 1975, and forthcoming), but the colour range and the physical appearance of the glass from Whithorn is closely comparable. The Whithorn material is moreover extremely important in that it extends the distribution of Early Medieval window glass for the first time to Scotland.

The distribution of the glass

At Whithorn there is, as at Jarrow and Escomb, some correlation between buildings and window glass (Figure 10.25), the most noteworthy of which is a restricted area alongside the south and east walls of the burial chapel (Figures 4.21 and 26). A particularly important group of thirty sherds derives from an intact ground surface covered with burnt debris (318). The range of colours found in this

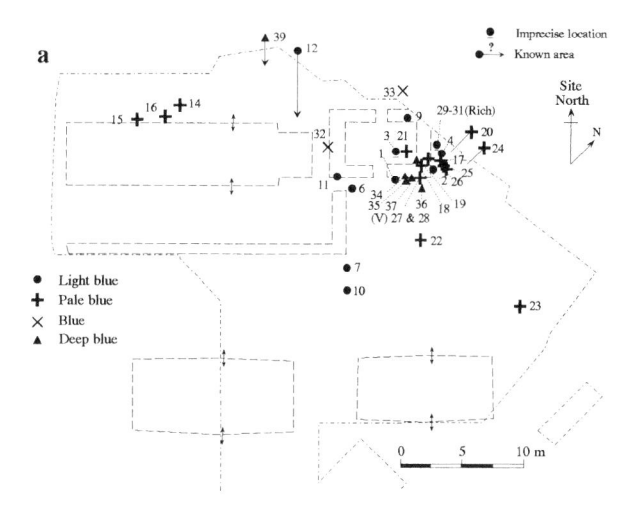

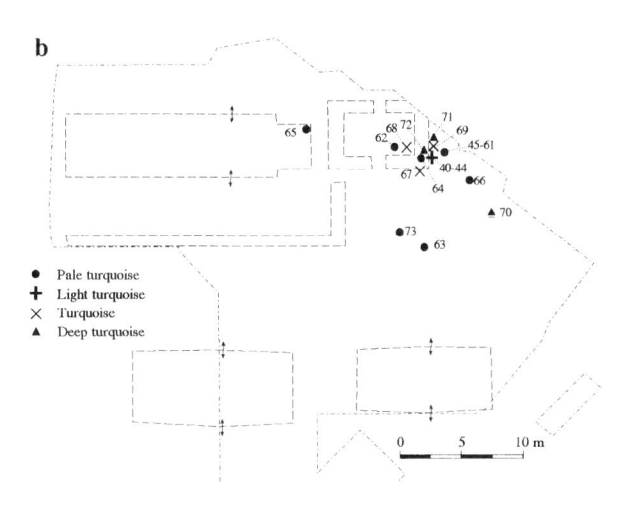

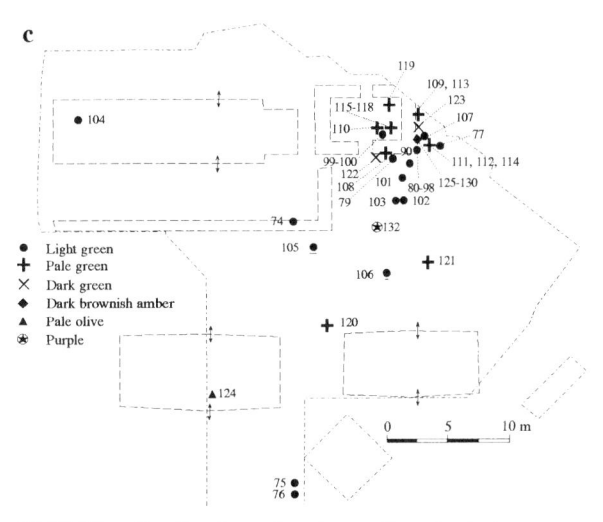

10.25 The distribution of early medieval window glass.

group is particularly rich and could indicate that the south and the east windows of the burial chapel were specially enhanced. The five sherds (nos 14–16, 65 and 104) which came from eighth/mid-ninth century contexts around the church, also represented a good colour range and should perhaps be considered as only a random survival of a larger quantity. There was also a scatter around the 'Northumbrian' buildings in the **southern**[3] and the **central sectors**.

The almost certain relationship of window glass with these timber buildings is interesting, but it is even more interesting – and difficult to envisage – that windows with strongly-coloured glass were fitted to a clay-walled building. It has been, in the past, assumed that Early Medieval window glass was a concomitant of stone buildings, which in the seventh and eighth centuries in north west Europe were invariably ecclesiastical, although from the eighth century onwards high status halls were also built of stone. (There is for example window glass from the Confessor's palace at Old Windsor, Harden 1959, Pl. VIII, 15–16, and see Evison 1988a, 215, for continental glass.) However the topsoil over the timber buildings at Thirlings has produced one piece of clear durable window glass, and the timber buildings site, tentatively identified as ecclesiastical, at Brandon, Suffolk has also produced plain and coloured glass, so that there does not seem to be a firm correlation between architectural forms and window glass although the use of coloured glass must have defined a special status for a building. The site of Whitby, where the excavated buildings had stone footings for timber superstructures, also produced two light blue fragments of window glass, although these may have derived from a stone church on the site (see Cramp 1993, Fig. 7.1 and p 68).

The physical characteristics of the glass

The glass is durable, and Hold's analyses (Hold 1991, 68), demonstrated beyond doubt that the glass was of the high soda-lime-silicate type which might be expected for this period (Harden 1961). His analyses showed that there were compositional differences in the glasses which distinguish not only all of the window from the vessel glasses but some of the window glass from the Roman traditional composition (Hold 1991, table 24 and p. 65). This phenomenon was noted some time ago (Turner 1956) and has been more recently reconsidered in relation to eighth/ninth century glass elsewhere (Sanderson, Hunter and Warren 1984; Heyworth 1991; Brill 1992). It would seem then that as pure soda became more difficult to acquire in north-west Europe, glass workshops attempted a partial adulteration, possibly with marine plant ash.

[3] (*PH comments*) Two sherds (75 and 76) – both light green – from the **southern sector** came from relatively secure **Period I** deposits (64.03), and a third (74) of similar colour was pressed into the surface of the **Period I/4** roadway (75.01). They are too thin to have been fragments of Roman window glass. All three are thus likely to predate the beginning of **Period II**, but could pertain to the later-seventh/earlier-eighth century when there are hints of Northumbrian occupation (p 37).

The Whithorn glass varied in thickness between 1.0 mm and 3.2 mm, with, as is normal elsewhere, the more strongly coloured glass being the thickest (Cramp 1975, 90). It is apparently cylinder blown and many pieces exhibit the diagnostic characteristics of elongated bubbles, matt/glossy surfaces and flame-rounded cylinder edges, see e.g. No. 123. A few, such as No. 85, exhibit the cut edge where the cylinder has been opened up. Sometimes the cut or rounded edge had been left, but most unbroken edges are finely grozed into shape. The grozing of the glass into shape sometimes differs in fineness, and it has been supposed that fine and coarse grozing at Winchester is a chronological indicator, but here, as at Wearmouth/Jarrow, the difference seems to be related to thickness.

The forms of the quarries

Many quarries are severely warped or cracked by heat, and some had reached a molten state (see for example No. 43) so that it is difficult to reconstruct the original shapes. Indeed no quarry was completely reconstructible, but there were clearly rectangular and triangular and curving quarries which could have been set into mosaics of geometric compositions. See Nos 112, 77, 103, and Plate IX.

Colour

The basic metal colour was pale bluish green, of which some fragments in transmitted light, were practically completely colourless, and others were strongly bluish. This is typical of Anglo-Saxon window glass (see Cramp 1975, and Biddle and Hunter 1990, Pl. XXVI) as opposed to Roman window glass which is usually a dark green. The 'Colour' in this basic metal from both periods can derive from the prime ingredients, such as the sand, used in the production, and Hold has noted that the window glass had a markedly lower Fe content than the site vessel glass. There are however some strongly coloured fragments at Whithorn which have been without doubt made for decorative purposes in the windows, whether by manipulating the furnace temperature or by adding metallic oxides. Hold concluded ' The use of both cobalt and copper to achieve blue window glass can be demonstrated and that these elements were also used for the colouring of the light blue/green and light green, pale green, and green or manipulation of furnace conditions and the Fe:Mn ratio' (Hold 1991, 68). The range of light green, pale green, and green or brownish amber may have partly derived from furnace temperature and partly from a higher Fe content.

The Whithorn colour range includes many of the strong colours found at Wearmouth/Jarrow, although the range within the blues, turquoise/blue or green and the yellow-olive greens is less. There is also no red, as opposed to red streaked glass. Red

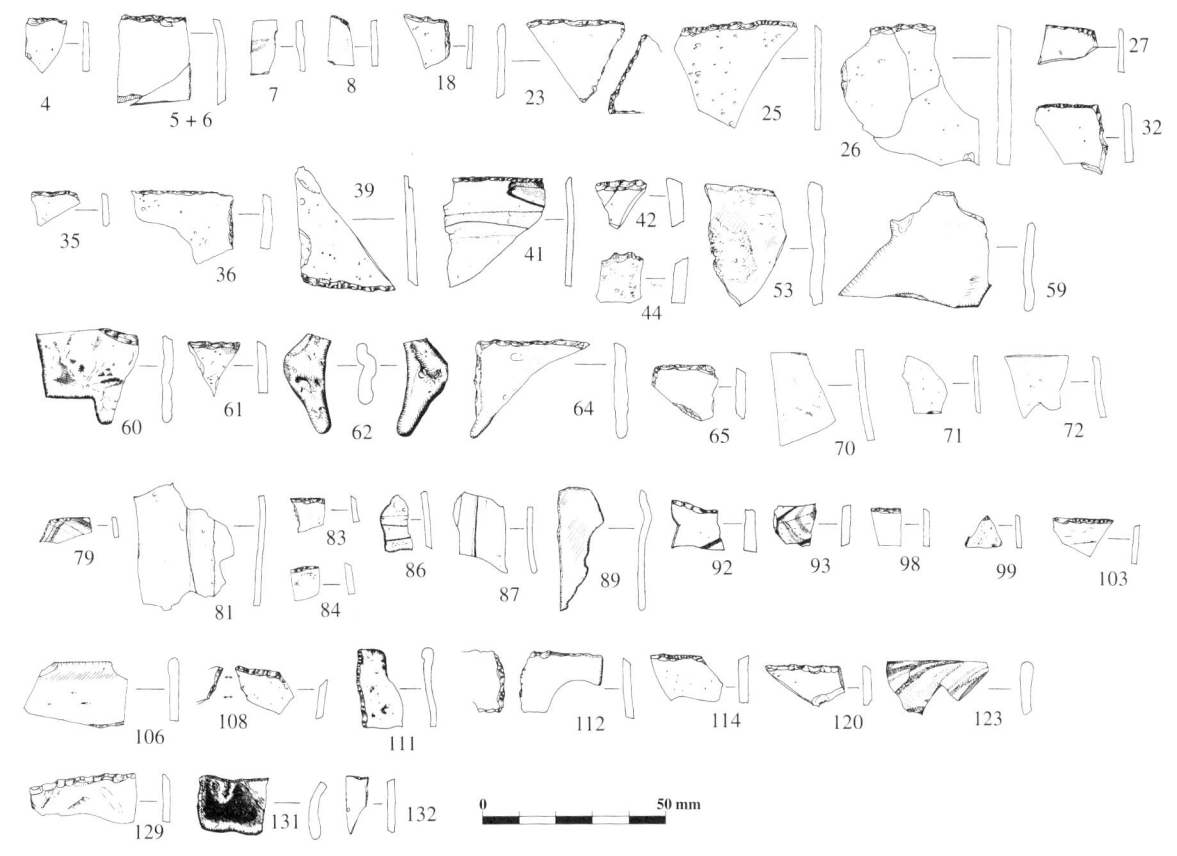

10.26 The early medieval window glass.

is anyway the rarest colour in Early Medieval glass and is not found on other English sites of this period (Cramp 1975, Fig. 4). There are, however, two fragments, one of purple/amethyst (132), and one pinkish (17), which are unusual and not paralleled in other collections which I know. The last mentioned fragment has been visibly created by mixing blue and red but the amethyst is a pure colour.

Red streaked glass is found on many of the English sites and is of two types. In th first type a marbled effect is produced when metallic copper has been stirred into the basic mix (e.g. Nos 82; 109), and in the second trails of red glass have been marvered into the surface of the bubble during the blowing process (e.g. Nos 87: 93). The same phenomena have been noted at Wearmouth/Jarrow and Beverley and sometimes both processes are clearly visible on the same piece, or the fine thread-like red trails cross one another at different depths in the metal. The origins and development of marbled glass have recently been discussed by Vera Evison (Evison 1990). This type of two coloured and streaked glass was clearly popular in the Early Medieval west, and glass here (No. 92), as at Wearmouth/Jarrow, can have self coloured streaks, which may have occurred accidentally in the production process but which could have been used decoratively.

Fixing and composition

The glass in 318 was found with a quantity of charred wood, but with no melted lead, and there are no lead calmes from the site at this time (p 394). This, like some of the Jarrow evidence, could mean that the main frame and even the calmes were of wood (Cramp 1975, 94–5). The glass may have been fitted into the main frame with small spigots or tacks, and occasionally (see No. 67), the melted glass has retained deep indentations which could have been caused by such fixing. One fragment (122) has a wide mark for what could have been a lead or wood frame along the edge, but this is in several ways an odd fragment since it is very thick, a deeper green than the others and very coarsely grozed. Wooden framed windows could have been easily fitted into wooden shuttered openings. Indeed portable windows which could have been made up in major glass workshops and transported to distant sites are a possibility (Cramp, forthcoming). It has often been considered that glass sheets or blocks could have been transported across distances, but then there would have to have been skilled glaziers either located at the site or who would travel with the glass to cut and compose the glass on the site. It is unfortunate that one cannot see from the surviving evidence what type of patterns were composed at Whithorn, and also that there has not been an opportunity to analyse comparatively the glass from Whithorn and Wearmouth/Jarrow – the site which superficially provides the closest comparison.

Catalogue

Light blue
1. Many fine rounded bubbles
   (c.f. 13 and 29–31) 20 × 12 × 2 (**305.02**)
2. Many small elongated bubbles.
   20 × 12 × 1.5 (**305.04**)
3. 8 × 6 × 1 (**207**)
4*. 15 × 11 × 2 (**318**)
5*. One grozed edge, joins **6**.
   20 × 20 × 0.5 (**307**)
6*. One grozed edge, joins **5**.
   15 × 5 × 0.5 (**307**)
7*. One finely-grozed edge.
   12 × 6 × 1 (**479**)
8*. One finely-grozed edge.
   12 × 6 × 1 (**436.01**)
9. It has round bubbles and matt/glossy surfaces.
   18 × 4 × 2.5. (**533**)
10. 15 × 10 × 1 (**538**)
11. 12 × 4 × 1.5 (**539**)
12. Very clear metal.
    12 × 8 × 1 (**904**)
13. Many round bubbles in metal.
    20 × 8 × 1.7 (**903**)
14. 4 × 1. (**313**)
15. 4 × 5 × 1. (**315.01**)
16. Elongated bubbles.
    9 × 12 × 1 (**315.02**)
17. Pale blue, pink-tinged window glass with many small bubbles. Very distorted by heat. The basic colour is a pale blue, but a pale red has been stirred into the melt which gives a pinkish colour.
    21 × 15 × 1–3. (**305.04**)
18*. One surface is matt and the other gloss.
    14 × 10 by 2 (**305.04**)
19. Heat-distorted and crazed but may have been a triangular quarry.
    27 × 25 × 2. (**305.04**)
20. Two abraded, grozed edges.
    10 × 12 × 1.5 (**305.06**)
21. Red streaks (appears mauve), tool or fixing mark on the edge.
    12 × 10 × 1 (**207**)
22. Scrap.
    1 × 2 (**203.05**)
23*. Triangular with two edges grozed, one matt and one glossy surface. The three edges are each 25 mm long × 1.5 mm thick.
    25 × 25 × 25 × 1.5 (**399.02**)
24. Molten, tapering to a point.
    18.7 × 5.9 wide (**904**)

Pale blue/colourless
25*. One grozed edge.
    40 × 24 × 1 (**305.04**)
26*. Over one third of the surface the bubbles within the glass have a crazed appearance. Joins **49** and **50**.
    30 × 20 × 3.5 (**318**)

Very pale blue/colourless
27*. Many small elongated bubbles, joins **28**.
    15 × 10 × 1.5. (**206.01**)
28. Many small elongated bubbles, joins **27**.
    5 × 10 × 1.5. (**206.01**)

Rich light blue
29. Many fine rounded bubbles in metal. Heat cracked and displays surface striations. Same as **30**.
    21.0 × 20.4 × 2.5. (**305.04**)
30. One grozed edge. Same as **00**.
    11.8 × 13.7 × 2.3 (**305.04**)
31. Same as **32**.
    18.1 × 8.5 × 2.1 (**305.04**)

Blue
32*. (**540**)
33. 20.3 × 7.0 (**904**)

Deep blue
34. Many small rounded bubbles.
    20 × 8 × 1 (**206.01**)
35*. One finely grozed edge, matt surfaces.
    6 × 7.5 × 2 (**305.04**)
36*. Two grozed edges. One matt and one glossy surface, elongated bubbles.
    28 × 18 × 2. (**305.04**)
37. One matt and one glossy surface.
    17 × 5 × 2 – (**305.04**)
38. It has elongated bubbles and an uneven, pitted surface. Also a black intrusive spot within the fabric. One corner is slightly upturned. Matt/glossy surfaces.
    20 × 14 × 2.5 (**535**)
39*. One coarsely-grozed edge. One matt and one glossy surface with many bubbles in the metal.
    31.7 × 25.3 × 3.0 (**904**)

Light turquoise
40. Heat-distorted and with pitted surface.
    42 × 35 × 5–2 (**318**)
41*. One fine-grozed edge. This piece is decorated with two fine, dark red lines which are embedded in the metal and a thicker line and swathe which have been marvered into the surface. Many small and some large rounded bubbles.
    25 × 30 × 2 (**318**)
42*. One grozed edge, has many elongated bubbles and thin trail of red glass marvered into one surface.
    9 × 9 × 3.5 (**318**)
43. Distorted and with pitted surface, evidence of grozing on one curving edge.
    40 × 32 × 5–2. (**318**)
44*. One coarsely-grozed edge.
    12 × 11 × 4 (**305.04**)

Pale turquoise
45. 22 × 10 × 2 (**305.02**)
46. Heat-distorted and with a pitted surface.
    22 × 12 × 4–1.5 (**318**)
47. Heat-distorted.
    14 × 12 × 3 – 1 (**318**)
48. Many small elongated bubbles. Slightly melted in one corner. Similar glass to **26**, **49** and **50** but does not join.
    25 × 23 × 3.5 (**318**)
49. One grozed edge, joins **26/50**.
    20 × 10 × 3.5. (**318**)
50. Joins **26** and **49**.
    35 × 20 × 3.5. (**318**)
51. One grozed edge; joins **52**.
    29 × 13 × 2 (**318**)
52. Joins **51**.
    25 × 20 × 2 (**318**)
53*. One partly grozed edge. Heat-distorted and with a pitted surface.
    32 × 25 × 2. (**318**)
54. Many elongated bubbles.
    30 × 10 × 2.5 (**305.04**)
55. Melted, has pitted and rough surfaces with earth picked up from where it fell.
    25 × 21 × 4. (**305.04**)
56. One flame-rounded edge. One matt and one glossy surface.
    11 × 5 × 3 – (**305.04**)
57. Heat-cracked, with many small, rounded bubbles.
    30 × 15 × 1 (**305.04**)
58. 10 × 10 × 1.5 (**305.04**)
59*. Heat cracked with one rough side.
    45 × 30 by 2 (**305.04**)
60*. Heat-cracked with one rough side. There are tiny dark red spots in the metal.
    26 × 20 × 2.5 (**305.04**)
61*. One grozed edge and red splash.
    14 × 14 × 3. (**305.06**)
62*. Heat-distorted with a pitted surface. A row of small indentations may be evidence of fixing.
    25 × 12 × 4 (**207**)
63. Slightly molten, and with one rounded edge.
    11 × 15 × 1.5 (**203.05**)

THE FINDS

64*. With many small bubbles and 2 large ones – 6 × 4mm. Two of the edges are grozed and the grozing appears to be abraded on one side. One point of the triangular piece is rounded by heat.
40 × 15 × 3.2 (**307**)

65*. One grozed edge.
16 × 12 × 3 (**320**)

66. 18 × 10 × 1.2 (**478**)

Turquoise

67. Blob with two indentations on one face.
25 × 15 × 8. (**318**)

68. One grozed edge. One matt and one glossy surface.
35 × 15 × 1.5. (**225.01**)

69. (**411.02**)

Deep turquoise blue

70*. 2 × 14 × 2 (**250.03**)

71*. One matt and one glossy surface, many small bubbles.
17 × 8 × 1 (**305.04**)

72*. Melted corner.
16 × 15 × 3. (**318**)

73. It seems to have fallen molten to the ground and picked up earth in the melted metal.
35 × 10 × ?. (**307**)

Light green

74. One grozed edge. Many bubbles in the fabric. One matt and one glossy surface.
17.9 × 15.1 × 2.9 (**75.01**)

75. 15 × 5 × 2 (**64.03**)

76. Both surfaces dulled.
32 × 7 × 2.5 (**64.03**)

77. Tip of a triangular quarry with two finely grozed edges. One matt and one glossy surface, with many small elongated bubbles. Displays deeper blue-green streaks.
(**226.03**)

78. 23 × 5 × 1.5 (**206.03**)

79*. One grozed edge. With a diagonal self-coloured streak and red trails. One matt and one glossy surface.
20 × 7 × 1.5. (**206.03**)

80. Heat-distorted and with a pitted surface, evidence of grozing on one surface.
15 × 14 × 3–1 (**318**)

81*. With three parallel thin red lines extending from edge to edge within the glass.
35 × 25 × 2. (**318**)

82. Splashes of red and traces of grozing.
10 × 7 × 1.5 (**318**)

83*. One grozed edge.
8 × 8 × 1.2 (**318**)

84*. Traces of red along edge of quarry.
8 × 7 × 1.5. (**318**)

85. Heat-distorted with one grozed edge.
40 × 18 × 4–2 (**318**)

86*. Three thin red lines extending from edge to edge within the body of the metal. One edge grozed. Slightly melted on one edge.
15 × 7 × 2. (**318**)

87*. Two fine red marvered lines.
16 × 13 × 2 (**318**)

88. Melted with pitted surface.
22 × 7 (**305.04**)

89*. Melted probably a corner fragment. It has picked up fragments of soil when it fell molten to the ground.
34 × 12 × 1.5 (tapering to 1 mm) (**305.04**)

90. Melted tapering to 3 mm.
2 × 9 × 6 (**305.04**)

91. Melted.
23 × 20 × 7 (**305.04**)

92*. With a smoky green trail. It has a red trail across one corner.
11 × 11 × 2.5 (**305.04**)

93*. Three scalloped red trails.
10 × 10. (**305.04**)

94. 15 × 8 × 3.5 (**305.04**)

95. Joins **96**. (**305.04**)

96. Joins **95**. (**305.04**)

97. Melted window glass with one probable grozed edge. Both sides are rough. Has a whitish bubbly encrustation on one surface.
19 × 10 × 3 (**305.04**)

98*. One grozed edge. One matt and one glossy surface.
22 × 8 × 1.5 (**305.04**)

99*. 10 × 8 × 1.2 (**207**)

100. 5 × 5 × 1.5 (**207**)

101. 8 × 7 × 2.5. (**339.01**)

102. One grozed edge. One matt and one glossy surface. Similar to **103**.
20 × 10 (**339.01**)

103*. Triangular with one grozed edge. One matt and one glossy surface. Similar to **102**.
13 × 10 × 1 (**339.01**)

104. Elongated bubbles.
15 × 9 × 3 (**315.02**)

105. Flame-rounded edge.
(**476**)

106*. Flame-rounded cylinder edge. Both surfaces dull.
27 × 17 × 2 (**540**)

107. It is twisted form and one rounded edge.
10 × 9 by 1 (**305.03**)

Pale green

108*. Tip of triangle with one certain and one possible grozed edges. Shiny with some strain cracks.
16 × 10 by 2.5 (**206.03**)

109. Melted, surfaces pitted, with red splashes in the metal.
28 × 16 × 3 (**305.02**)

110. Strain-cracked, with many small bubbles.
20 × 6.5 × 3 (**233.02**)

111*. Red trailed, melted window glass with one fine-grozed edge.
21 × 10 × 2 (**318**)

112*. Angle with two grozed edges one slightly curved. Many elongated bubbles.
22 × 15 by 2 (**318**)

113. Melted, very distorted and pitted.
38 × 20 × 4. – (**305.04**)

114*. One grozed edge. One matt and one glossy surface.
14 × 11 × 3. (**305.04**)

115. Melted, distorted with a pitted surface. Tapering to a point with red splashes.
15 × 8 × ?. (**207**)

116. Melted, distorted with a pitted surface with red splashes. Tapering to a point.
27 × 9 × ?. (**207**)

117. Melted joins **118**.
4 × 6 × 2 (**207**)

118. Melted joins **117**.
10 × 10 × 2 (**207**)

119. Melted.
25 × 22 × ? (**207**)

120*. One grozed edge.
20 × 10 × 1.2 (**399.02**)

121. 3 mm thick.
(**422.04**)

Deep green

122. One coarsely grozed, curving edge tapering to a point. One surface matt and pitted and one glossy with an indentation of what may be a calme or wood strip, 7 mm wide, and warped by heat.
25 × 15 × 3 (**206.01**)

Dark green

123*. With a moulded edge and deep red embedded trails. Heat-cracked and pitted. The deep red streaks are embedded in the centre of the glass indicating that the bubble was dipped again after the trail was applied.
28 × 13 × 3. (**305.04**)

Pale olive green

124. One matt and one glossy surface.
15.5 × 7.6 × 2.6 (**902**)

Dark brownish amber

125. The bubbles within the glass are crazed. Possibly joins **126**.
16 × 17 × 2 (**318**)
126. Possibly joins **125**.
5 × 4 × 2 (**318**)
127. Melted and with a pitted surface.
15 × 9 × 1.5. (**318**)
128. Slightly curved.
20 × 10 × 2.5 (**318**)
129*. Heat-warped and with one grozed edge. Two diagonal indentations on one face.
28 × 13 × 2.5. (**305.04**)
130. Heat-cracked.
30 × 15 × 1.5. (**305.04**)
131*. Melted with pitted surface.
17 × 14 × 2 (**305.06**)

Purple

132*. One edge possibly grozed. One matt and one glossy surface. Very clear and free from bubbles.
15 × 5 × 2 (**203.05**)

The Coins

Peter Hill, Nicholas Holmes, Elizabeth J.E. Pirie

Introduction

Peter Hill

The excavation produced a hundred and ninety coins spanning the fourth to the twentieth centuries, and including a wide range of Anglo-Saxon and high-late medieval issues. The coins have made a vital contribution to the chronology of the site, and their distributions (Figures 10.41–46) offer insights into the evolving organisation of economic activities within the settlement. The quality of the stratigraphic record varied from the precise to the profoundly obscure. The deposits producing mid-ninth century coins contained a series of coin groups, recording changes over periods as brief as two or three years. At the other extreme a group of eleventh-thirteenth century coins displaced by the **Period V** graves, had intermingled with fourteenth and fifteenth century issues lost as the graveyard passed out of use. Other coins, particularly the small Northumbrian issues, were recovered by the metal detection of spoil from designated contexts or areas, and thus a more general distribution of the finds is sometimes known when their precise position is unrecorded.

The Early Medieval coins

Elizabeth J E Pirie

Now that excavations on a portion of the site at Whithorn have drawn to a close, it must be considered timely to offer an assessment of the coin-finds, especially since the present total of sixty-five specimens clearly identifies the settlement as a major source of numismatic evidence for the eighth and ninth centuries.

The range and condition of the coins

The range of the material is principally that of the sceattas and stycas issued in Northumbria. The earliest specimen (No. 61) is a sceat of series J, emanating from the Midlands of England early in the eighth century, when the widespread complex of sceattas was entering its secondary phase of development. The Northumbrian sceattas (series Y) belong to the later secondary period and are quite distinct in detail. There is some evidence (as yet unpublished) from Fishergate in York which suggests that, once the northern coinage was established, alien issues were normally excluded from Northumbria. Whithorn, however, attests the presence of a contemporary issue from East Anglia (No. 62). The idiosyncratic coinage of stycas developed during the period c. 790–855 at which time other issues, with the possible exception of Carolingian coins, are rarely found on northern sites. The most modern coin in the present register is the penny (No. 65) struck at Dublin about the middle of the eleventh century.

It is appropriate at this juncture to make some comment on the condition of the specimens. A considerable degree of variation obtains, from the pristine (as Nos 18 and 23) to the poor – the latter state the result either of circulation-wear (as on No. 42) or of corrosion (as on No. 54). Some of the sceattas (see Nos 1 and 61) have suffered in part from oxidization, although the effect is perhaps more noticeable on the Northumbrian than on the Southumbrian example. None of the specimens has been analysed for data relative to the fineness of the silver or the exact composition of the later alloy. On the basis of studies made elsewhere, it is known that even specimens described as being of copper-alloy contain a small amount of silver. Finds made during the 1987 season of excavations at Thwing, in East Yorkshire (report forthcoming), were examined, for some of those coins, struck from dies known to have been used for issues in copper-alloy, *appeared* to be of silver. Analysis confirmed the presence of only the normal low percentage of precious metal; inspection under a microscope was enough to determine that the present surface of the basic copper was only studded with silver. M.R. Cowell, of the British Museum Research Laboratory, has explained this, not as the result of chemical changes which can cause the leeching of innate silver to form a surface enrichment, but as the effect of corrosion having removed only copper from the original surface, leaving behind the silver element of its alloy. In the instance of Whithorn, the same phenomenon can surely be observed on coins 33 and 35, whose appearance matches that of the Thwing material, and, to a lesser extent, on the styca of Monne (No. 52).

Sequence of issue in Northumbria

The complete sequence of Northumbrian coinages must be summarized briefly. At some point in the seventh century there was an issue of gold thrymsas; I have argued elsewhere (Pirie 1992) that these could appropriately be attributed to the reign of Ecgfrith, *c.* 670–685. Aldfrith, *c.* 685–705, certainly had silver sceattas (Pirie, 1984, 209), which were contemporary with the first primary issues long recognized in the south (Rigold 1977). After a lapse during the first decades of the eighth century, Eadberht resumed the practice of coin-production and extended it from sole issues to joint issues for himself and his brother Ecgberht, the archbishop of York. Rigold (1977: series Y) did not detail the complete range of work and even Booth (1984) omitted from the register of accepted issues for Eadberht, Ecgberht and their successors, those specimens which name Aethelred on one die and Eanbald on the other (see Pirie 1984, 212 and Booth 1987: the latter paper accepts such coins as those of Aethelred I by a moneyer Eanbald, during his second reign). The Whithorn specimen (No. 8), by its inclusion of the initial A on the second die, clarifies the identification of Eanbald as archbishop and therefore supports, even if it does not wholly confirm, attribution of another joint regal-episcopal issue to the series of sceattas (see Appendix).

Booth's paper (1984) has done much to sort out the varieties of issue for the sceattas struck in Northumbria. The question of sequence within a reign may still be debatable. Metcalf (1984, 116) has suggested that the coins for Eadberht and Ecgberht, jointly, were concurrent with many of those for the king alone. The alternative classification of Eadberht's sole issues, recently proposed (Pirie, 1996), identifies two concurrent streams, A and B; the main division depends on the stag of the reverse facing to right or left. Although there is a growing number of finds to be recorded, no conclusion has yet been reached on the question of whether or not distribution of each class has a regional bias. Within each class, some developments of sequential import may be noted in that (apart from variations in the spelling of the king's name) the stag appears alone or with additional ornaments in the field. The *triquetra* on the Whithorn specimens (Nos 2–5) would seem to indicate that the coins were marginally later than that with the plainer reverse (No. 1).

There is still no evidence from the period to suggest that the issue of a new variety within a reign resulted in the demonetization of its predecessor or even that the coinage of a new reign entailed the calling in of old coins which were still in circulation. In theory, at least, all the Northumbrian sceattas could have remained current until the point at which a new system of coinage was introduced, *c.* 790.

The styca series as a whole is identified and separated from the earlier sceattas by the practice of naming the moneyer on coins struck for the kings of Northumbria and independently for the archbishops of York. It is now seen to have developed in two main phases (Pirie 1987a). The first, opening during the second reign of Aethelred I (*c.* 790–796) consisted initially of a number of intermittent issues in silver, of increasing baseness, throughout the years until *c.* 830; a second stage of this first phase saw the last of the earlier moneyers striking in copper-alloy, until *c.* 835. The second phase, beginning towards the end of Eanred's reign under the *aegis* of a new team of officials, saw production on a more constant basis and probably on a far larger scale, using the medium of copper-alloy. Such official output continued until about 855. At that point, early in Osberht's reign, production seems to have ceased. From about the time of Reduulf's short-lived usurpation, *c.* 843–844, large numbers of irregular issues were made, as reflections of Aethelred II's authorised coinage. One can argue that it was their unchallenged circulation which eventually forced the collapse of official minting. Irrefutable evidence for the point at which all such issues ceased to be used is lacking. There is a hint from Coppergate, York (AY18/1, 1986, 17), that stycas remained in circulation until the coming of the Vikings. The events of 866–867, indeed, would seem to offer the most cogent reason for concealment of the major hoards.

The stycas of Phase I

Adoption of copper-alloy as the most convenient medium for a practical coinage may have brought to an end the earlier use of silver. At present, the Hexham find of 1832 (Pirie 1987b) is the only one known which attests the deliberate saving of old coins at a time when copper issues were current. The number of silver coins surviving from *c.* 790–830 is therefore still comparatively small but it has so far been impossible to compile a *corpus* of the evidence for the complete period (see Booth 1987) which would form the basis of detailed die-analysis. It is disappointing, therefore, that, with so many specimens of the period now recovered from Whithorn, one is still not in a position to be more precise about the attribution of each within its general span of issue.

Some moneyers are absent from the Whithorn register. There are no coins for Aethelred I by Hnifula or Cudcils. Cudheard, whose work spanned several reigns, is absent for Aelfuald II and for Eanred; presumably, he struck for the latter at the beginning of the reign. Herred, who operated towards the end of the period, is also missing. Eaduulf, who is identified as one of the moneyers for Archbishop Eanbald II, is unrepresented. Some comments can be made about those whose work *is* present. The quality of silver used by Huaetred and Cynuulf (Metcalf *et al.* 1968) suggests that they at least were working soon after Eanred's accession. There is, however, no real evidence yet for the placing of Tiduini (No. 18) and Uilheah (Nos 19–22). One assumes that since Daegberct, Eaduini and Hearduulf (together with Herred) are known to strike in copper-alloy, they were first active not very long before *c.* 830, when the use of silver, as a main ingredient of the fabric, ceased.

Few die-links between coins are known for the sceattas. The Whithorn evidence affords an example: the coin for Eadberht and Ecgberht (No. 6) is struck from a known episcopal die and a hitherto unrecorded regal one. For the issues of Phase I of the styca coinage, the formation of die-links, caused by the repeated use of dies in different combinations, may have been limited – in marked contrast to the extraordinary degree of linking which occurred during the second phase, both within the work of one man and between that of two or more. Evidence of such ties during the years before 830 is still comparatively meagre, and it may be judged remarkable that the twenty-seven early stycas from Whithorn attest nine instances of linking which have not been recorded before, in coins by Ceolbald (Nos 9 and 10), Tiduini (No. 18), Uilheah (No. 19), Daegberct (Nos 23 and 31), Eaduini (where Nos 24 and 25 share the same obverse) and by the episcopal official, Edilueard (Nos 29 and 30). Really extensive linking among the early stycas is hardly to be expected, however, if one is right in identifying the nature of the coinage as intermittent.

The stycas of Phase II

With the issues of Phase II, the situation is very different. Recent research has concentrated particularly on these later stycas in copper-alloy, since they have survived in considerable numbers. Major analysis of the dies and their use has resulted in identification of concurrent groups of regular issues, and their related reflectives, and – in part – recognition of sequence (based on the use of motif), although there is not yet any distinct separation of types. Whithorn affords two examples of additional die-combinations, with coins 45 (Eanred/Aldates) and 52 (Aethelred/Monne). It has been possible to relate the latter and all the other specimens to examples in the Yorkshire Collections (Pirie 1996).

Finds from the first few seasons' work seemed to indicate two remarkable gaps in the evidence: firstly, that there were then no coins representing the years of Aethelred II's first reign, c. 841–843/4; secondly, there were no coins representing the issues, regular or irregular, of Group A. The latter circumstance was somewhat disturbing for, although Group A is comparatively small in relation to Group C, other evidence would suggest that it was Bernician in origin. One would therefore expect its coins to be found in the northern regions of Northumbria. In 1989, I was prepared to say that if it was correct to attribute all of the coins of Aethelred, by then recovered, to the king's second reign, one might suppose there had been a lapse in activity at the site for a year or two. This would account for the lack of an unbroken sequence of evidence. Yet, since late in 1989, four coins (Nos 41, 47 and 48, and 55) in Groups B and C have been recovered which may be assigned, on the evidence of motif-use, to the years 841–843/4. Further, five specimens (Nos 36–40) which represent Group A have also been discovered. The group is not, after all, entirely absent; yet, proportionally (20% of the present tally for the period), it is still not as strong on the site as one might have anticipated. Perhaps, however, this is not to be accounted unusual at Whithorn, where coins from well beyond the immediate locality are seen to occur.

The individuality of the Whithorn coin-evidence

Consideration of the Whithorn coin-finds in relation to those known from other northern sites brings out a number of contrasts which would suggest that Whithorn was markedly individual in the region.

Recent work at nearby Mochrum (Barhobble) has recovered one sceat of Eadberht (Cormack 1990, 8). Yet, at Luce Sands, also in Wigtownshire, no sceattas have been found; only twelve identifiable stycas have been recorded, having been discovered as strays (Pirie 1986, No. 108): four from Phase I, eight from Phase II. Of the latter, only one (Uigmund/Coenred) may have a Bernician rather than a Deiran source. Finds from excavations at Bamburgh (Pirie 1986, No. 87) have not yet been completely recorded. The present, unfinished, register is of stycas from Phase II only; it includes a few specimens capable of relation to Group A, but most of the coins belong to Groups C and D. The Carlisle record begins with the discovery, in the nineteenth century, of a sceat of series Z (Rigold and Metcalf 1984, 249); this is a minor group compared with series J in all its varieties but, like J, Z belongs to the early secondary phase. Blackburn (1984, 71) places the striking of series Z within the years c. 715–720; Stewart (1984, 18) suggests that it is not a southern coinage. More recently, several separate sites in Carlisle have failed to produce specimens of Northumbrian sceattas other than one of Aethelred I and Archbishop Eanbald (from the Cathedral excavations, 1988). The principal record is still only of stycas (see Pirie 1986, Nos 102–06 for finds made before 1983); these, chiefly of Phase II, certainly include examples of work attributable to Group A.

According to the present evidence from Whithorn, the place is clearly unlike these other northern sites in that it not only has a much longer span of Northumbrian issues – from those of c. 737 to those of c. 855 – but also, the number of stycas from Phase I of that coinage is marginally greater than those of Phase II. Certainly, too, since there is as yet no clear evidence of regional production in Northumbria, either for the sceattas or for the stycas of Phase I (and we should still recognize York itself as the mint from which they all came), Whithorn seems to attest a significant degree of coin-use at periods when even the available northern coinage came from a source at some distance. The matter of distance also is reflected in the identity of the four other coins (Nos 61–64), three of which, at least, originated beyond

Northumbria. It need not, therefore, be a matter of surprise that for the years c. 837–55, stycas from the prolific Group C (of Deiran origin) and the related Group D should so far outnumber the more local issues.

Issues other than the Northumbrian

The Whithorn coin-list does bear some similarity to that of Carlisle, for its earliest specimen is a coin from another region, struck at a time when Northumbria had no coinage of its own: the sceat of series J (No. 61), which Stewart (1984, 11) identifies as having emanated from the Midlands. Known distribution (see Rigold and Metcalf 1984) has a certain density in East Anglia; there are outlets along the coast, both to south and to north. Concerning the relevant inland provenances, Repton in Derbyshire is a monastic site. One wonders if there is any real significance in the fact that, of the other known outliers, Reculver/Thanet and Selsey in the south, Whitby and even York (on the Ouse) in the northeast, are all monastic sites of the period? If this association of the series together with its principal iconography, the bird-on-cross (*BMC* type 27), were to identify some part of the J issues as ecclesiastical rather than regal in their authority, it need occasion no surprise that such a coin should be found at another monastic site: Whithorn, in the north-west. Seven of the later coins from Whithorn (Nos 6, 8 and 29–30; 40, 46 and 48) also have ecclesiastical connotations.

Struck slightly later than the sceattas of Eadberht, the coin of Beonna (No. 62) is, however, very much a freak as far as known distribution of the issues is concerned. With the possible exception of a specimen from Dorestadt in the Netherlands, distribution recorded so far, for this East Anglian coinage, is markedly local (Archibald 1985, 28–29). That it is there at Whithorn at all is perhaps extraordinary on two counts: as an outlier, from the East Anglian viewpoint; as a 'foreign' issue in the contemporary Northumbrian context. The find at Whithorn seems to represent the short period, c. 758–765, for which there is no certain evidence of regal coins for Northumbria itself. Miss Archibald (1985, 31) has noted certain affinities of quality and design between the issues of Eadberht in Northumbria and of Beonna in East Anglia. It may be that, in spite of other evidence from Fishergate, York (which suggests very strongly the refusal of Northumbria, after 737, to tolerate most issues from elsewhere), the East Anglian coinage was like enough to the Northumbrian to be acceptable currency, if necessary, at least in the remoter areas.

The pennies of Eadgar by the moneyer Macus and of Cnut by Leofwine of Chester (Nos 63–64) stand apart from all the others since they represent the English coinage of later periods, but they are not without their own numismatic interest. Identification of the first has led to recognition of an instance of die-linking between Macus and Harcer. One may be permitted to remark gently that these ties (recorded in the entry for 63) should already have been noted, from the evidence of the Machrie specimen together with that of the coins in the British Museum. The British Museum *Sylloge* volume (1986) does record further examples of die-linking in the same type, *Horizontal Trefoil* 1, which among others, include dies of Harcer and Macus. A recent survey (Blunt *et al*. 1989, 157–59) comments on the relationship of these links to minting at York, for among the officials involved, Heriger, Æsculf and Durand are known to be York moneyers, and the question of Harcer, Macus and others having also worked there must remain an open one. That the issue occurred early in Eadgar's reign is seen in the date given to the deposition of the Tetney hoard, c. 965 (*BMS*, xxvii). The eleventh century coin struck by Leofwine also attests die-linking; in this instance, the link occurs within the moneyer's own work, for he can be shown to have combined his obverse die with another reverse.

That an English penny of Eadgar is not to be accounted an unusual find in the Whithorn area, lies in the fact that hoards containing such issues have been recovered from Machrie in Islay (already cited) as well as from Iona, in 1950, and from Tiree in 1782 (Stevenson 1966, xx–xxiii, and plates). It may be coincidence that the die-duplicate from Machrie is chipped, as is the Whithorn specimen; the Iona hoard contains many fragmentary coins. One begins to wonder if the coins were broken before they reached the area and were therefore regarded as bullion rather than as negotiable currency. It is recognized that the Machrie and Tiree hoards were deposited c. 975, and the Iona *cache* a decade later. It has been suggested (Blunt *et al*. 1989, 254) that, in areas outside the control of the English king, Eadgar's pre-reform issues circulated for ten years or more after they had been superseded in the south by the reformed coinage, c. 873.

Tenth century coins of the Chester mint are known to have occurred in hoards from Ireland and the Isle of Man (see Pirie 1964, 42); they appeared, too, in the Iona hoard, in 1950. The eleventh century issues from Chester are recorded in continental hoards, not just in Germany but in Russia as well (*ibid*., 43). One may note, further, that Stevenson (1966, xvi) cites the Caldale hoard recovered in Orkney in 1774; this consisted of some three hundred coins, *all* of the one **Short Cross** issue for Cnut. Coins of the mint and coins of the type, then, are already known elsewhere north of the Border.

The little Hiberno-Norse penny (No. 65, below) attests yet another element in the complete picture. Coinage was struck for the Norse kings of Dublin during the years between c. 995 and c. 1150; its initiator was Sihtric III Anlafsson, known as Sihtric Silkbeard. The coins, whose production developed in seven distinct phases, are essentially imitations of English pence; the principal prototypes are the *Crux* and *Long Cross* issues of Æthelræd II (978–1016) which were struck from 991 to 997 and from 997 to 1003, respectively. The *Crux* coins of Phase I (c. 995–c. 1020) from Dublin were virtually contemporary with the originals from the English mints, as were the earliest *Long Cross* imitations, also of Phase I. By the beginning of Phase III (c. 1035–55), the Dublin versions of the *Long Cross* type were stylistically poor, and merit identification as imitations. Such Hiberno-Norse material is known from coin-hoards recovered: not in England, for the English were strict about the exclusion of foreign coin, but in Ireland itself, in the Isle of Man and, in Scotland, at Inchkenneth off the coast of Mull (see Stevenson 1966, xix), in 1830. These Irish pennies have occurred only rarely as single finds. Yet the specimen found recently is not the first one known from Whithorn. Dolley and Cormack (1967) discuss the *Crux* coin of Phase I recovered there at some unrecorded date before 1911, and which is now in the Glasgow Museum and Art Gallery. The *Long Cross* imitation, excavated in 1986, is considerably later in date of issue. The association of both these coins with the site serves to suggest, even if not to confirm, that, during the first half of the eleventh century, Whithorn lay within the sphere of Hiberno-Norse trading interests.

Royal control apart, one has to recognize that it undoubtedly took time for *all* the coins to reach Whithorn in the first place, even if their circulation *en route* was limited. In assessing the date of loss for each, one would do well to allow for a time lag following the suggested periods of issue.

Acknowledgements

Thanks are due to my colleagues, Adrian Norris and Jim Nunney, for their observations on the identity of the surface droplets which were found on the coin of Leofdegn (No. 47, below).

Appendix

Attribution and dating of Whithorn 8: the coin for Aethelred and Eanbald

Stewart (1991) has recently re-instated the identification of a sceat issued jointly by Aetheluald (Eadberht's successor) and Archbishop Ecgberht; this attribution, for a single surviving specimen with no recorded provenance, had come to be overruled in favour of its being a coin of Alchred and Ecgberht (see Booth 1984, Alchred/Ecgberht 6). That Ecgberht, whose tenure of office overlapped several reigns, should have shared the rights of coinage with Eadberht, Aetheluald and Alchred serves to demonstrate that such joint issues were not merely a feature of Eadberht's reign which was later copied, as a whim, by Alchred but were, rather, an orthodox practice in late eighth century Northumbria. With such precedents, the context of such coinage in the time of Aethelred I becomes even more secure, so that one need hardly hesitate longer over recognizing the coins, which name both Aethelred and Eanbald, as having been struck for the king and Archbishop Eanbald I jointly, during the series of sceattas.

In view of the fact that the styca coinage, which names the moneyers, superseded the Northumbrian sceattas during Aethelred I's second reign, c. 790–96, one's instinct was to assign all known specimens of this joint coinage to the king's first reign, c. 774–78/9. Admittedly, to do so might imply the need to reconsider the minutiae of chronology, for Eanbald I is still not recognized as having become archbishop until 779/80. As it stands, the possible overlap of king and cleric might have lasted only a matter of weeks. Yet, in discovery, the Whithorn specimen is associated with certain ninth century stycas of Eanred. The site-stratigraphy does not allow the thesis that ground-disturbance in the ninth century brought the sceat from its primary position into a secondary context. Since it may be thought unlikely (rather than impossible) that a specimen from an earlier coinage should appear as a residual item among issues of a period some thirty-five to forty years later, one should consider alternative dating, for the Whithorn example at least.

Placing the introduction of the stycas in Aethelred's second reign need not imply (as one might have inferred – see Pirie 1987a) that there were no sceattas issued in, or after, 790. The first stycas seem to have been regal issues only; Archbishop Eanbald II did not begin to issue coins independently until the time of Eanred. The initial practice, then, of Eanred's moneyers striking stycas for the archbishop as well serves to attest two points: first, that Eanbald II was still in office much later than 808 (about which year tradition supposes his tenure of the Archbishopric to have ceased); secondly, that Eaduulf, now identified as a moneyer for Eanbald II, cannot convincingly be recognized instead as an official working solely for Eanbald I, during the inaugural period for the stycas. It remains possible, however, that Aethelred I and Eanbald I revived or continued the practice of joint issues, at the beginning of the reign at least, before the launching of the new coinage. Such coins, even if recognized as sceattas, could have remained current throughout the reign and would not necessarily have been withdrawn until the privilege of separate coining-rights (if not at first, the service of separate moneyers) was accorded to Eanbald II, some time after 810.

This does not mean that *all* the coins naming Aethelred and Eanbald should now be assigned to the years 790–96. No example has yet been recorded in any hoard of stycas. One should perhaps distinguish those without any vestige of designation, even for the king, from this single specimen from Whithorn which includes, for Eanbald, the initial *A* of his title. There could well have been issues in both reigns: that with title at the beginning of the second; that without title at the end of the first.

Whether or not this was so, Aelfuald I (*c*. 778/9–88) begins to be conspicuous by his absence from the list of monarchs who, having sole coinage, also issued jointly with their archbishop, during the lifetime of the sceatta series in Northumbria. Judging by the number and variety of new records made in recent years, one may perhaps hope that an appropriate specimen might some day be recovered.

THE FINDS

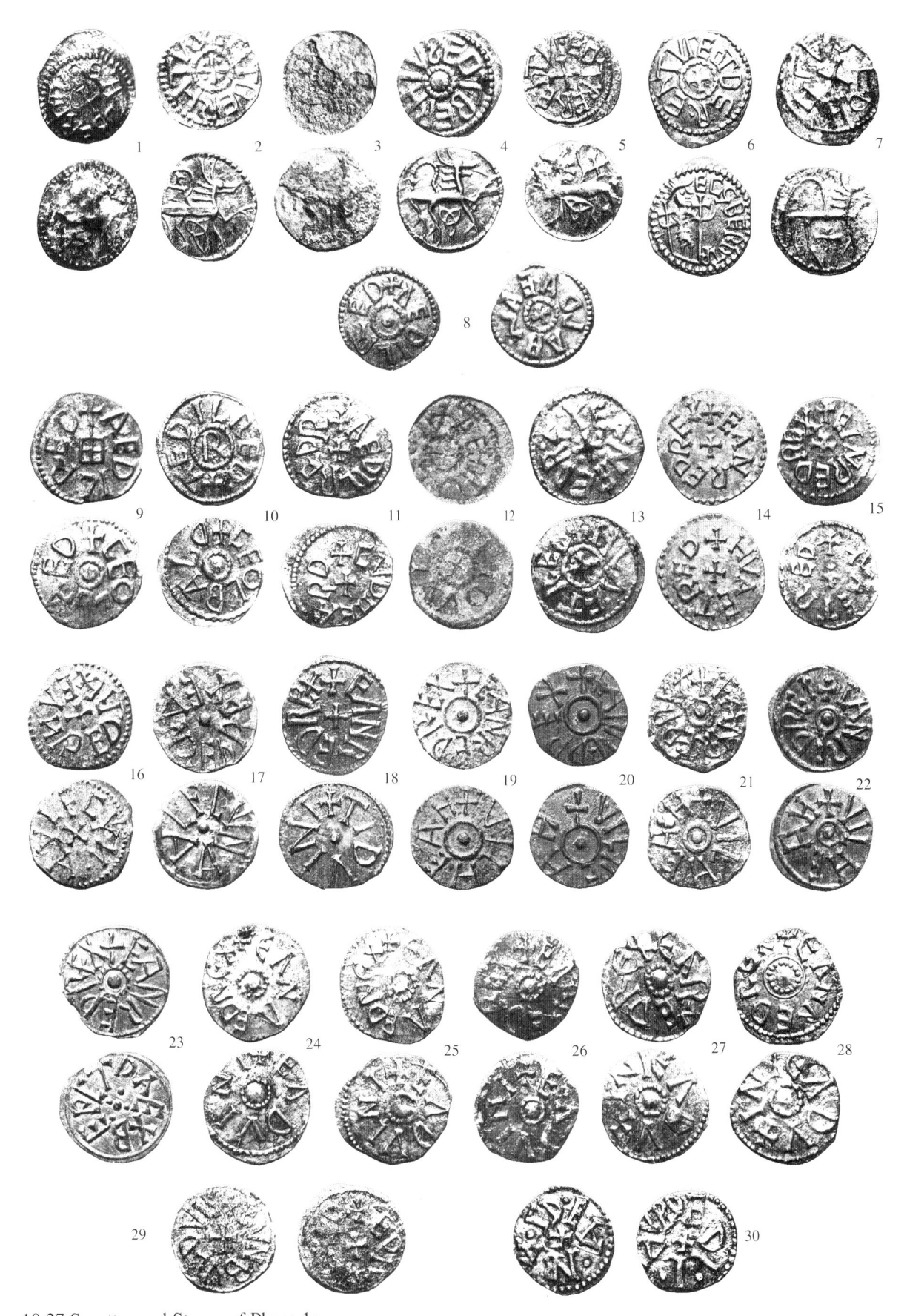

10.27 Sceattas and Stycas of Phase 1a.

Catalogue[4]

I. Northumbrian issues

A. Sceattas (Rigold, 1977: Series Y): struck in silver

EADBERHT, c. 737–758

1. Booth (1984), Class A; Pirie Class Ai
   Obv.: •EADBERhTV{L inverted}, round central cross
   Rev.: Stylized stag, facing right
   Wt.: 0.70gm (10.85gr.); oxidized and rev. worn;
   die-axis: 135°.

The coin is struck certainly from the same obverse and probably from the same reverse, as a specimen (a detector find, as yet unpublished) recovered in 1989 from South Newbald in East Yorkshire [North Humberside]. **250.03**

2. Booth (1984), Class F; Pirie, Class Aii
   Obv.: EOTBERHTVS, round central *Evangelistic cross* within a circle of pellets
   Rev.: Stylized stag, facing right; cross below tail and *triquetra* below body
   Wt.: 1.11gm (17.2gr.); die-axis: 90°.

The coin which shows little sign of wear, is from the same dies as a specimen recovered at Hayton, North Humberside, in 1982 (Booth 1984, F9 and ref. cited; that coin was acquired for the Feather collection, Leeds). **303**

3. Booth (1984), Class F; Pirie, Class Aii
   Obv.: [E]O[TBERHTVS]; central circle of pellets, probably enclosing an *Evangelistic cross*
   Rev.: Stylized stag, facing right; *triquetra* below body
   Wt.: 0.71gm (11.00gr.); die-axis: 270° (?).

The coin's condition is one of considerable oxidization which accounts for its very low weight. It is not possible to match the dies with those of any other recorded specimen. **316**

4. Booth (1984), Class F; Pirie, Class Aii
   Obv.: EOTBERHTVS, round central boss within a circle of pellets
   Rev.: Stylized stag, facing right : tail formed of pellets; *triquetra* under body
   Wt.: 1.09gm (16.85gr.); die-axis: 270°.
   Found in 1984; not in Pirie (1986).

The coin, which shows little sign of wear, is struck from dies very similar to those of a specimen recovered at Malham, North Yorkshire, before 1980 (Booth 1984, F11). **303**

5. Booth (1984), Class D; Pirie, Class Bii
   Obv.: •EOTBEREhTV{L inverted}, round central cross
   Rev.: Stylized stag, facing left; cross below tail and *triquetra* below body
   Wt.: 0.84gm (12.9gr.); die-axis: 135°.

The coin, which shows little sign of wear, appears to have been struck from the same obverse die as a specimen recovered in York in 1881 (Booth 1984, D2). That coin (now YC 15, awaiting publication) has a reverse so damaged by accretion that it is not possible to claim its identity with the Whithorn reverse. **511.11**

EADBERHT AND ARCHBISHOP ECGBERHT, jointly:
c. 737–758

6. 1st die: •EOTBERT •EhTV{L inverted}, round central cross in a circle
   of pellets
   2nd die: ECGBERhTR, to left of figure of the archbishop who holds two crosses
   Wt.: 1.05gm (16.25gr.); die-axis: 165°.

---
[4] Abbreviations used in the catalogue are listed below (p 624).

The coin shows slight traces of wear only on the obverse (the regal die). It is the regal die which appears to be unrecorded. The episcopal die, which has the peculiarity of the *R*, for *Rex*, rather than the *A*, as initial of the archbishop's title, must be the same as that of *BMC* Northumbria 4, *ex* Cotton collection (Booth 1984, Pl 1:20) : the latter is a worn example. **743**

ALCHRED, 765–774

7. The issue has no specific classification.
   Obv.: ALCH, anti-clockwise / RED, clockwise; the letters (*LC*, reversed) all inward-pointing; central cross
   Rev.: Stylized stag, facing right; cross below body and, possibly, a small pellet under tail
   Wt.: 1.10gm (16.9gr.); die-axis: 135°.

The coin is worn by some oxidization. It has been struck from the same dies as a specimen (Booth 1984, No.10) once in the Mack collection (which has now been dispersed in the sale-rooms). **303**

AETHELRED I AND ARCHBISHOP EANBALD I, jointly:
c. 778–780.

8. 1st die: +AEDILRED, round central pellet in a circle of pellets
   2nd die: EANBALDA (the *NB*, as reversed letters), retrograde, round central cross in annulet of pellets
   Wt.: 1.01gm (15.65gr.); die-axis: 30°.

The coin shows only slight traces of wear. Neither die has so far been recorded elsewhere. The inclusion of the final *A*, as the initial of a title for Eanbald, is the first real evidence of the individual's identity as archbishop, and does much to support the attribution of this issue to the sceattas series. At a time when titles were normally omitted from the regal dies, an issue by Aethelred I, at the end of his first reign, or at the beginning of his second, jointly with the new archbishop, Eanbald, would not have been without precedent. **303**

B. Stycas

Phase I: issues of c. 790–c. 835
Phase Ia: intermittent issues in silver, c. 790–830

AETHELRED I: second reign, c. 790–796

9. *Ceolbald*
   Obv.: +AEDILRED, round central cross within a square
   Rev.: +CEOLBAED, round central boss in a circle of pellets
   Wt.: 0.90gm (13.9gr.); die-axis: 180°.

The coin shows some degree of wear. The obverse die is the same as that of a specimen recovered in excavations at Jarrow (Booth 1987, No. 24); the reverse of that example has the same error in the moneyer's name, but is not the same die. **901**

10. *Ceolbald*
    Obv.: +AEDILRED, round *R* within a circle of pellets [note position of initial cross]
    Rev.: +CEOLBALD (the *D*, reversed), round central boss within a circle of pellets
    Wt.: 0.95gm (14.6gr.); die-axis: 0° (as illustrated).

The coin exhibits only a small degree of circulation-wear. It has been struck from the same obverse die as a specimen recovered at York Minster in 1970 (Booth 1987, No. 27; Pirie and Archibald 1995, No. 3); the reverse die is otherwise unrecorded. **903**

11. *Cudheard*
    Obv.: +AEDILREDR, round central cross
    Rev.: +CVDHEARD, round central cross
    Wt.: 0.91gm (14.1gr.); die-axis: 180°.

The coin shows little sign of wear. No die-duplicates have been recorded elsewhere. **303**

12. *Tiduulf*
    Obv.: +AEDIL[RED]R, round central cross in circle of pellets
    Rev,: +TIDVVLF, round central cross in circle of pellets
    Wt.: 0.89gm (13.8gr.), oxidized; die-axis: 150°.

Although the specimen has suffered from oxidization, the detail of letters and central motifs seems to be still crisp, which suggests that loss occurred while the coin was still quite new. Neither die has been traced elsewhere. **250.03**

EANRED, c. 810–830

13. *Huaetred*
    Obv.: .E•A•NREDR•E•X, round *Evangelistic cross*
    Rev.: +HVA.ETRED, round cross in annulet of pellets
    Wt.: 0.82gm (12.6gr.); die-axis: 190°.

The coin shows some signs of wear. No die-duplicates have been recorded elsewhere. **303**

14. *Huaetred*
    Obv.: +EANREDREX, round central cross
    Rev.: +HVAETRED, round central cross
    Wt.: 1.00gm (15.5gr.); die-axis: 270°.

The coin shows little sign of wear. A die-duplicate (as yet unpublished) has been found, in 1991, near Market Weighton, in East Yorkshire. **303**

15. *Huaetred*
    Obv.: +EANREDREX, round central cross
    Rev.: +HVAETRED, round central cross
    Wt.: 0.84gm (13.0gr); die-axis: 0°.

The coin shows little sign of wear. No die-duplicates have been traced. **303**

16. *Cynuulf*
    Obv.: EANREDREx, (the *A*, unbarred; the *N*, reversed), anti-clockwise and inward-pointing, round central cross
    Rev.: CyN•VVLF (the *Y*, runic; the *N*, reversed; each *V*, barred), round central cross
    Wt.: 1.08gm (16.6gr.); die-axis: 60°.

The coin shows little sign of wear; its dies have not been traced on any other specimen. **303**

17. *Cynuulf*
    Obv.: EANREDREX, round central pellet; the legend is anti-clockwise, with inward-pointing letters
    Rev.: CyNVVLF, round central pellet; runic *Y*, and cross-bar to each *V*; wire-line border
    Wt.: 0.84gm (13.0gr.); die-axis: 0°.
    Found in 1984; not in Pirie (1986)

The coin shows little sign of wear. The same dies are known on an unpublished specimen in the Stewart collection. **303**

18. *Tiduini*
    Obv.: +EANREDREX, round central cross
    Rev.: +TIDVINI, round central pellet
    Wt.: 0.86gm. (13.3gr.); die-axis: 240°.

The coin is virtually in pristine condition. It is struck from the same obverse as *BMC* Northumbria 230 (*ex* Hexham, 1832) in combination with a different reverse. **303**

19. *Uilheah*
    Obv.: +EANREDREX (the *N*, reversed), round central pellet-in-annulet
    Rev.: +VILHEAH, round central pellet-in-annulet
    Wt.: 0.93gm (14.3gr.), slight accretion; die-axis: 270°.

The coin shows little sign of wear. It is struck from the same obverse die as specimens in Copenhagen (*SCBI Cop.* I, No.257) and in Liverpool (*SCBI Merseyside*, No.54); the reverse die is otherwise unrecorded. **901**

20. *Uilheah*
    Obv.: +EANREDREX, round central pellet-in-annulet
    Rev.: +VILHEAH, round central pellet-in-annulet
    Wt.: 0.77gm (11.8gr.); die-axis: 90°.

The coin shows little sign of wear. It is struck from the same dies as a specimen in Manchester (*ex* Hexham, 1832: Sugden and Warhurst 1979, No.41). **303**

21. *Uilheah*
    Obv.: +EANREDREX, round central pellet-in-annulet
    Rev.: +VILHEAH, round central pellet-in-annulet
    Wt.: 1.00gm (15.4gr.); die-axis: 90°.

The coin shows signs of moderate wear compounded, perhaps, by corrosion. No die-duplicates have been recognized. **743**

22. *Uilheah*
    Obv.: +EANREDREX, round central pellet-in-annulet
    Rev.: +VILHEAH, round central pellet-in-annulet
    Wt.: 0.96gm (14.8gr.); die-axis: 180°.

The coin shows little sign of wear. No die-duplicates have been recognized. The style of obverse may be judged unusual on Uilheah's work; it appears, rather, to resemble some of the work known for Daegberct. **743**

23. *Daegberct*
    Obv.: +EANREDREX, round central boss in a circle of pellets; wire-line border
    Rev.: DAEXBERCT (the *X*, a runic *G*), round central *Passion cross*; wire-line border
    Wt.: 0.81gm (12.5gr.); die-axis: 170°.

The coin is virtually in pristine condition. The reverse is that which is common to *BMC* Northumbria 86–87 (both *ex* Hexham, 1832). **303**

Nos 24–28, and 33 (for Eaduini) are from dies whose legends normally show the *A* unbarred; those which do have the barred *A* are marked with an asterisk.

24. *Eaduini*
    Obv.: +EANREDREX, round central boss in a circle of pellets; same die as obv. of 25
    Rev.: +EADVINI, round central boss in a circle of pellets
    Wt.: 0.90gm (14.0gr.); die-axis: 170°.
    Found in 1984; not in Pirie (1986)

The coin shows only very slight signs of wear. The style of die is comparatively common for this moneyer, but no full die-duplicates have been recognized elsewhere. **303**

25. *Eaduini*
    Obv.: +EANREDREX, round central boss in a circle of pellets; same die as obv. of 24
    Rev.: +EADVINI, round central boss in a circle of pellets
    Wt.: 1.02gm (15.8gr.); die-axis: 340°.

The coin shows some degree of wear. The style of die is comparatively common for this moneyer, but no full die-duplicates have been recognized elsewhere. **743**

26. *Eaduini*
    Obv.: +EANREDREX, round central boss in a circle of pellets
    Rev.: +EADVINI, round central boss-in-annulet
    Wt.: 0.89gm (13.8gr.); die-axis: 340°.

The coin shows signs of moderate wear. Although dies of similar style are known, no die-duplicates have been recognized elsewhere. **303**

27. *Eaduini*
    Obv.: *EARNEDREX, round central boss in a circle of pellets
    Rev.: EADV+INI, round central boss in a circle of pellets
    Wt.: 1.06gm (16.3gr.); die-axis: 180°.

The reverse of the coin shows rather more wear than does the obverse. The coin is struck from the same aberrant dies as an unpublished specimen in the Lyon collection. **743**

28. *Eaduini*
　　Obv.: *+EANREDREX, round central boss in a circle of pellets, enclosed in a further annulet
　　Rev.: EADV+INI, round central boss in a circle of pellets
　　Wt.: 0.62gm (9.5gr.); die-axis: 45°.

The reverse of the coin shows some degree of wear caused, perhaps, by corrosion rather than by circulation. The low weight now recorded may be exceptional. The specimen is struck from the same dies as *BMC* Northumbria 98 (*ex* Hexham, 1832). **303**

EANBALD II, ARCHBISHOP OF YORK, 796–*c*. 835.

29. *Edilueard*
　　Obv.: +EANBALDAR (1st and 2nd *A*, unbarred; the *L*, inverted), inward-pointing, round central cross
　　Rev.: +EDILVARD (the V, barred), round central cross
　　Wt.: 0.58gm (9.0gr.); die-axis: 90°.

The coin, of low weight, is worn and has suffered some degree of oxidization. It is struck from the same obverse die as a specimen in Copenhagen (*SCBI Cop.* I, No.405); its reverse is very similar to, but not the same as, that of the Copenhagen coin. **303**

30. *Edilueard*
　　Obv.: .EA•NBA•LD (the *NB*, ligatured), round central cross; the legend, clockwise with inward-pointing letters
　　Rev.: EDI•L•AVBD (the A, inverted), round central cross
　　Wt.: 0.77gm (11.8gr.); die-axis: 170°.

The reverse shows some signs of wear. The obverse die is known on another specimen (seen [1980] in stock at Messrs. Baldwin, London) which has a different, less crude reverse. **315.02**

Phase 1b: first issue in copper-alloy, *c*. 830–835

EANRED

31. *Daegberct*
　　Obv.: +EANREDREX, round central cross
　　Rev.: +DAEGBERCT, round central cross
　　Wt.: 0.77gm (11.8gr.); die-axis: 260°.

The coin shows little sign of wear. The obverse die has not been recognized elsewhere; the reverse is the same as that of YC 66. **303**

32. *Daegberct*
　　Obv.: EANREDREX, round central cross
　　Rev.: +DAEGBERCT, round central cross
　　Wt.: 1.11gm (17.1gr.); die-axis: 100°.

The coin shows little sign of circulation-wear, although the effect of surface corrosion has left an artificial, granulated, silver appearance (see discussion above). No die-duplicates have been recognized elsewhere. **743**

33. *Eaduini*
　　Obv.: *+EANREDREX, round central cross
　　Rev.: +EADVINI, round central cross
　　Wt.: 0.66gm (10.2gr.); die-axis: 350°.

The reverse of the coin shows some degree of wear caused, perhaps, by corrosion rather than by circulation. The low weight now recorded may be exceptional. The style of die is known for the moneyer but no matching dies have been recognized with certainty, elsewhere. The reverse of YC 72 is, however, so very similar to that of the present example (it differs only in the detail of the *D*) that one wonders if this factor should be cited as an undoubted instance in which the one tool was altered by minor re-cutting. **303**

34. *Hearduulf*
　　Obv.: EAHREDREX, round central cross
　　Rev.: HEARDVVLF (the *A*, unbarred; the *D*, reversed, round central cross
　　Wt.: 0.56gm (8.7gr.); die-axis: 175°.

The coin shows little sign of circulation-wear, although the full effect of corrosion accounts not only for the abnormally low weight but also for the artificial, granulated, silver surface (see discussion above). The style of dies is common enough for this moneyer (hitherto identified as Uulfheard); no die-duplicates have been recognized elsewhere, but the reverse is the same as that of a specimen (as yet unpublished) discovered near Malton, in North Yorkshire, *c*. 1988. **454**

35. IRREGULAR: reflecting the early coinage of Archbishop Eanbald II This specimen had become bloated with oxidization. When first seen, only two letters (*EN*, the *N* reversed) could be determined, at the upper right-hand side of what was then thought to be a reverse of the later moneyer Monne. Initially, therefore, all relevant retrograde dies, ending in *NE* (with both letters reversed), for that official, were checked, yet without confirming the die-identity. Alternatively, the small number of known irregulars which essay the names of Eanbald and his moneyer Eaduulf were considered. A near, if not exact, match of dies was found on a specimen in the British Museum (*ex BMC* Northumbria 819–868, from Hexham, 1832) which has the readings:
　　Obv.: •ENAB+•A (the *N*, reversed), round central cross
　　Rev.: +EVDV+FE, retrograde, round central asterisk

Most unfortunately, preliminary brushing of the Whithorn specimen on the one side (the obverse, as above), before photography, confirmed the cross in the middle of the legend yet proved the visible *EN* to be fugitive. In the absence of a photograph taken before brushing, there can be no published illustration of the piece as it was when found.
　　The coin now weighs 0.43gm (6.7gr.); the die-axis may be 90°, but in the total absence of clarity had better be considered uncertain. **320**

Phase II: later issues in copper-alloy, *c*. 837–855

The material is arranged according to the main groups and their sub-sections (see Pirie 1987a).

IIA
AETHELRED II, *c*. 841–849

First- and second-reign issues are not yet distinguished for this group; spelling of the king's name determines attribution of specimens to section Ai or to section Aii.

Ai
36. *Monne*
　　Obv.: [+]EDEL[REDRE]X (the *D*, barred in front), round central cross
　　Rev.: [+]MO[NNE] (the first *N*, reversed), round central cross
　　Wt.: 0.69gm (10.6gr.), heavily corroded; die-axis: 270°.

In spite of the coin's very poor condition, it is just possible to distinguish enough of each die to determine its identity as the duplicate of a specimen in the York collection (YC 267). Its obverse (with a very distinctive *X*) is the same as that of No.37. **315.01**

37. *Monne*
　　Obv.: +EDELREDREX (the *D*, barred in front), round central cross
　　Rev.: +MONNE (the first *N*, reversed), retrograde, round central *Passion cross*
　　Wt.: 0.93gm (14.4gr.); die-axis: 190°.

The coin has acquired a thin skin of accretion, but the underlying letters are crisp, which denotes little or no circulation-wear. The dies are those of YC 270; the obverse is the same as that of No.36. **316**

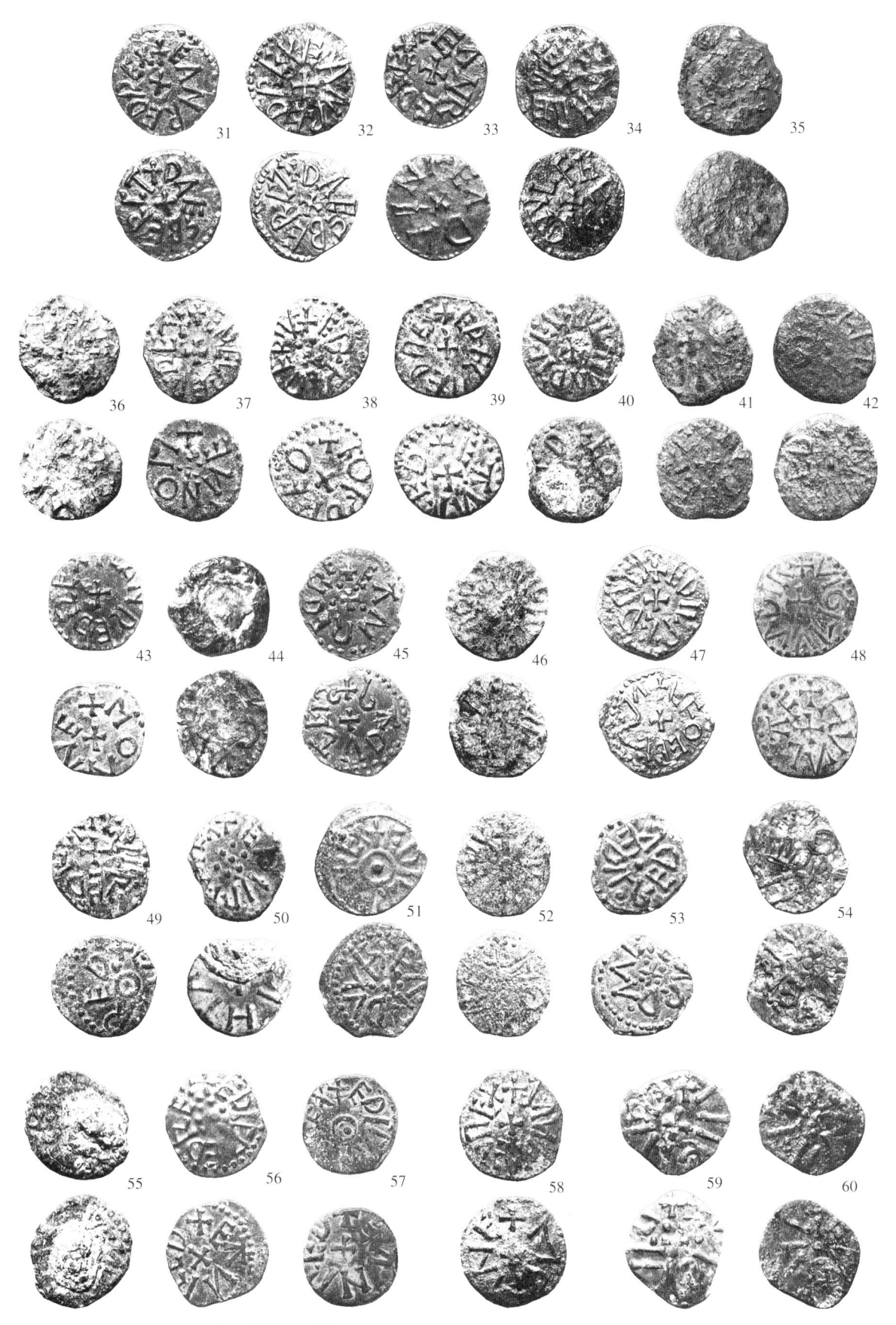

10.28 Stycas of Phase 1b and Phase II.

Aii

38. *Fordred*
> Obv.: +EDFLREDRE (the first *D*, barred in front), round central *Passion cross*
> Rev.: +FORDRED•, round central cross
> Wt.: 1.14gm (17.6gr.); die-axis: 0°.

The coin has slight surface corrosion, but the crisp letters denote little circulation before loss. The dies are those of YC 307. **904**

39. *Eanred*
> Obv.: +EDFLREDRE (the first *D*, barred in front), round central cross
> Rev.: +EANRED (the *A*, unbarred; the *N*, reversed), round central cross
> Wt.: 0.80gm (12.4gr.); die-axis: 180°.

The coin, with some surface corrosion, shows some smoothness of detail as a result of wear. The dies are those of YC 348. **320**

UIGMUND, ARCHBISHOP OF YORK, c. 837–850

40. *Coenred*
> Obv.: +VIGMVNDI•REP, round central cross
> Rev.: +COE[NR]ED, round central cross
> Wt.: 0.54gm (8.3gr.), oxidized; die-axis: 135°.

The coin appears to have suffered far more from corrosion than from circulation. The dies are those of YC 413. Coenred produced regal issues for Aethelred II and for Reduulf; in the former instance, the moneyer shared with Leofdegn an obverse whose legend is attributable to Group Ai. His coins for Uigmund may be assigned to the years c. 841–849. **315.01**

IIB
AETHELRED II: first reign, c. 841–843

41. *Alghere*
> Obv.: +AEDILRED ᴾx, round central cross
> Rev.: +ALGHERE, round central cross
> Wt.: 0.29gm (4.5gr.). heavily oxidized; die-axis: 45°.

The coin is now extremely worn, yet it is still possible to identify the dies as those of YC 509. **758.03**

Aethelred II: second reign, c. 843–849

42. *Eanred*
> Obv.: +AEIL[RE]DR, round central pellet
> Rev.: +EANRED, round central pellet
> Wt.: 0.71gm (10.9gr.); die-axis: 0°.

The coin is now extremely worn. The dies are the same as those of YC 535. **901**

II C: Ci
EANRED, c. 837–841

43. *Monne*
> Obv.: +EANREDREX, round central cross
> Rev.: +MONNE, round central cross
> Wt.: 1.03gm (16.0gr.); die-axis: 180°.

The coin shows little sign of wear. The dies are the same as those of YC 580 (within style *a*). **303**

44. *Monne*
> Obv.: [+EANREDREX (the *A*, unbarred), round central cross]
> Rev.: +MONNE (the first *N*, reversed), round central cross
> Wt.: 0.43gm (6.7gr.), completely oxidized; broken and mended; die-axis uncertain.

As found, the specimen was entirely covered with a thick coat of corrosion. Half of this came away cleanly, to expose detail of the reverse die, which is that of YC 622; another specimen, in better condition, is known from the York hoard of 1842 (Pirie 1981, Winn 21). Unfortunately, it has not been possible to recover any part of the obverse legend, which would confirm this attribution to the reign of Eanred. Nevertheless, even in a series particularly noted for its extraordinary degree of die-linking within reigns – and even between reigns – there is, as yet, no unequivocal instance of this reverse used in combination with any other obverse. **320**

45. *Aldates*
> Obv.: +EANREDRE (the *A*, unbarred; the *D*, reversed), round central *Evangelistic cross*
> Rev.: +LADVTEIS (the *D* and *S*, reversed), round central cross
> Wt.: 0.62gm (9.6gr.); die-axis: 315°.
> Found in 1984; not in Pirie (1986).

The coin shows little wear, but is somewhat chipped at the edge. Similar dies (of style *b*) are known for the moneyer whose name appears in the aberrant version hitherto interpreted as Gadutes, rather than the present Ladutes. No duplicates have been recognized. **303**

UIGMUND, ARCHBISHOP OF YORK, c. 837–841

46. *Edilueard*
> Obv.: +VIGN[VND]ARE[P] (each *N*, reversed; the *A*, unbarred), round central cross
> Rev.: +EDILVEARD (the *A*, unbarred), round central cross
> Wt.: 0.82gm (12.6gr.); die-axis: 0°.

The coin is worn and corroded but its dies can be identified as those of YC 691. Of all the official moneyers, regal and episcopal, Edilueard is the only one who is known also in Phase I. This coin for Uigmund is deemed contemporary with the last coins of Eanred, for the archbishop's title – AREP – is in the form used earlier for Eanbald II. **478**

AETHELRED II: first reign, c. 841–843/4

47. *Leofdegn*
> Obv.: +EDILREDRE, round central cross
> Rev.: +LEOEDEGN (aberrant: the *G*, cursive and ligatured to reversed *N*), round central cross
> Wt.: 1.08gm (176.7gr.), after first brushing; 0.95gm (14.6gr.), after cleaning. Die-axis: 0°.

The dies are those of YC 779. The obverse die is known to have been shared with the moneyer Eanred (YC 716–719). The reverse is one of two, in this style, known with this obverse for Leofdegn. A third reverse, whose retrograde legend has the same peculiar cursive G, is used twice: first, with an obverse known only for Leofdegn; then, with one shared with Brother and his so-called descendants. A die-link, through specimens naming the moneyer Odilo, occurs between other such coins for Aethelred and those of Reduulf. One has argued elsewhere that such poor-quality issues were probably struck for Aethelred during the months of Reduulf's usurpation. One may suggest now, on stylistic grounds, that this particular issue for Aethelred was struck just before Reduulf's bid for power, which could well have occurred as early as 843. The coin, when found unstratified, was almost entirely coated in corrosion on which were embedded fragments of some buff-coloured substance. Although the obverse was recognizable from the portion visible, and preliminary brushing revealed enough of the reverse for die-identity to be established, cleaning was continued until both dies were cleared. This operation has

10.29 No. 47 prior to conservation.

demonstrated two factors: first, an edge-chip confirms that the metallic fabric of the coin has undergone a chemical change; in the second place, though some of the letters have been bloated by re-deposited metal, the underlying detail is still crisp. Again, one judges loss to have occurred fairly soon after striking.

During cleaning, one of the surface-fragments was detached and submitted to a conchologist for his views on its possible identity as shell. Microscopic examination has revealed that the substance is metallic, and very probably lead. It would seem that, on site, the coin was lying where it could be spattered with droplets of molten metal; it could have been wedged at an angle, so that while part of the obverse was wholly protected, the rest of the surface provided a landing-ground for such a spray. One cannot avoid the inference that the coin was on the floor of the church during the building's destruction by fire (pp 162–4). It is worth remarking, finally, that the melting-point of lead is far lower than that of copper, so there need be no surprise that the coin survived the holocaust. **904**

UIGMUND, ARCHBISHOP OF YORK, *c.* 841–843/44

48. *Hunlaf*
   Obv.: +VIGMVNDIR (the *N*, reversed), round central cross
   Rev.: +HVNLAF (the *N*, reversed), round central cross
   Wt.: 0.87gm (13.4gr.); die-axis: 0°.

This episcopal issue, with its use of the *cross* motif on both dies, is deemed to be contemporary with coins of Aethelred II's first reign. The dies have been matched with those of YC 922. That there is little sign of circulation-wear serves to indicate a fairly early loss. **339.02**

AETHELRED II: second reign, *c.* 843–849

49. *Eanred*
   Obv.: +EDILREDREX, round central cross
   Rev.: +EA[N∵]RED (the A, unbarred; the N – off-flan – is reversed), round central pellet-in-annulet
   Wt.: 0.98gm (15.1gr.); die-axis: 270°.

The coin, struck from old obverse die (with the first *D* blurred), has some slight surface corrosion but the detail is still fairly crisp, which denotes a relatively short period of circulation before loss. The dies are the same as those of YC 965. **315.01**

50. *Wihtred*
   Obv.: +EDILRE[DR]EX (the second *R*, reversed), round central rosette of pellets
   Rev.: [+D]IHTRD, round central cross
   Wt.: 0.86gm (13.3gr.); die-axis: 100°.

The coin is chipped and, in part, corroded; the remaining detail shows slight wear. The dies are the same as those of YC 991. **903**

51. *Earduulf*
   Obv.: +EDILR[ED]REX, round central pellet-in-annulet
   Rev.: +EA•RDVVF (the *A*, unbarred), round central *Passion cross*
   Wt.: 0.71gm (11.0gr.); die-axis: 160°.

The coin is chipped and the obverse is worn. The obverse is known, so far, in combination with thirteen reverses of three styles: YC 1020–22 (matching the obverse); YC 1023–28 (intermediate; 1028 is the die-duplicate of this Whithorn specimen); YC 1029–32 (crude and similar to those of the so-called fringe issues, of which 53 is an example). **424**

52. *Monne*
   Obv.: +E[DILR]EDX, round central pellet
   Rev.: +MONNE (first *N*, reversed); central motif uncertain
   Wt.: 0.82gm (12.7gr.); die-axis: 0°.

The coin is extremely worn with traces of granulate silver on the surface. It is possible, however, to identify the obverse with certainty as that common to YC 1160–64. Yet the ghost of reverse-legend visible on the Whithorn specimen corresponds to none of the relevant dies in this small cluster. It is possible that the die is one still unrecorded, although another, very similar, is already known in section Cii (see YC 1499, *ex* first reign); that could have been used again for the present combination. **423.02**

53. *Earduulf*
   Obv.: EDIL•REDR, retrograde, round central cross
   Rev.: EVDDVVL•F (each V, inverted), round central *Evangelistic cross*
   Wt.: 0.73gm (11.3gr.); die-axis: 90°.

The coin is somewhat chipped but in remarkably good condition for a piece struck from somewhat crude dies. These represent a small, and tightly die-linked cluster of coins which cannot be regarded as normal authorized issues. The Whithorn dies are the same as those of YC 1204. **250.03**

OSBERHT, *c.* 849–855 the early years of his reign

54. *Uiniberht*
   Obv.: XO[S]B[RE]HE, round central cross in a circle of pellets
   Rev.: [V]INI[B]ERHT, round central *Passion cross*
   Wt.: 0.97gm (15.0gr.); die-axis: 270°.

The coin, whose clockwise legends are both inward-pointing, is worn by corrosion rather than by circulation, for the surviving detail is as crisp as one might expect on such a late issue. The dies are those of YC 1253. **422.04**

IIC: Cii
AETHELRED II: first reign, *c.* 841–843.

55. Uendelberht
   Obv.: +[EDILRED]REX (the *L*, inverted) [round central cross]
   Rev.: +VEND[ELBERHT] (the *N*, reversed; the *L*, inverted; *HT*, ligatured) [round central cross]
   Wt.: 0.86gm (13.2gr.); die-axis: 0°.

The coin is corroded and worn, but the dies can be identified as those of YC 1445. **408.01**

AETHELRED II: second reign, *c.* 843–849

56. *Eanred*
   Obv.: +EDILREDRE: (the *L*, inverted) round central pellet in a circle of pellets
   Rev.: +EANRED (the *A*, unbarred; the *N*, reversed), round central cross
   Wt.: 1.04gm (16.1gr.); die-axis: 160°.

The coin shows only a slight degree of wear. The dies are those of YC 1512. **404**

57. *Eanred*
   Obv.: +EDILR[EDR]EX (the *L*, inverted) round pellet-in-annulet
   Rev.: +EANRED (the *A*, unbarred), round central cross
   Wt.: 1.00gm (15.1gr.); die-axis: 90°.

The coin, which is struck from the same dies as YC 1536, shows some degree of wear – particularly on the obverse. **399.02**

IIC: Ciii
EANRED, *c.* 837–841

58. *Monne*
   Obv.: +EANREDREX (the first *E* and the *N*, reversed; the *A*, unbarred), round central cross
   Rev.: +MONNE (the first *N*, reversed), round central cross
   Wt.: 0.60gm (9.2gr.); die-axis: 90°.

The coin shows slight surface corrosion, but its exceptionally low weight may indicate that it is almost entirely oxidized. The dies, whose detail is still clear, are the same as those of YC 1602. **408.01**

IID. Irregular issues (related to IIC, c. 843 and later): Di

59. *Nonsense*
    1st die: +ERIIOIIII, retrograde, round central cross
    2nd die: +DIVDVAE (2nd *D*, reversed; *A*, unbarred), retrograde, round central cross; pellets in field
    Wt.: *c*. 0.48gm (7.4gr.); die-axis: 270°.

The coin is slightly worn, but its original low weight is much diminished. The group as a whole includes the principal complex (Dii) of die-linked irregulars which reflect the issues of IIC. The first section (Di) is of small clusters which do not yet join the main chain. The Whithorn dies are those of YC 1821. **399.03**

60. *Nonsense*
    1st die: +VEIIRV, retrograde, round central rosette of pellets
    2nd die: +EVDIII, round central pellet
    Wt.: 0.84gm (13.0gr.); die-axis: 135°.

The coin, which cannot have been very well struck in the first place, is now worn enough for its initial appearance to resemble the style of irregular dies known in the Hexham hoard of 1832 and now attributed to Group A. It is, however, one of a small cluster of issues which have in common the first die. These are, at present, registered within the first section of Group D for they do not, as yet, form part of the main complex of die-linked issues (IIDii) which reflect the official coinage of Group C. The Whithorn specimen is from the same dies as YC 1842; the use of motifs seems to indicate production during Aethelred II's second reign. **315.01**

II. Other issues in silver
A. Southumbrian

10.30 Series J sceat (No. 61).

61. *Sceat*. Rigold, Series J: *BMC* type 85; early secondary phase, *c*. 715–730.
    Obv.: Head, facing right, within a border of pellets
    Rev.: Bird on cross, flanked by annulets; four pellets in front of bird, trefoil of pellets at either side of cross-shaft
    Wt.: 0.85gm (13.15gr.); die-axis: 270°.

As found, the coin had a surface of compacted oxidization which has caused some degree of wear to the dies; the reverse still seems to be somewhat bloated by under-lying oxidization. Coins of the same series have been recovered in the recent excavations (as yet unpublished) at Fishergate, York, and a specimen is known from Whitby (R. and M., 1984, 265), but die-duplicates have not been recognized. **249.01**

10.31 Penny of Beonna (No. 62).

B. East Anglian

BEONNA, *c*. 757-early 760's

62. *Penny of the moneyer, Efe*
    Obv.: BEOXXaREX' (runic NNA), round central pellet in a circle of pellets
    Rev.: EFE, within compartments, round square enclosing central *Passion cross*; the letters flanked by trefoils of pellets
    Wt.: 0.99gm (15.3gr.); die-axis: 75°.
    See Metcalf (1987), 362

The coin shows a slight degree of wear. Although recovered in 1984, it was not reported in time for inclusion in Miss Archibald's *corpus* (1985); the dies are those of two specimens recovered in the dispersed hoard at Middle Harling, Norfolk (1978–81): C41 and C42. The first is now in the British Museum; the second, in the Fitzwilliam Museum, Cambridge (Grierson and Blackburn 1986, Plate 52:1121B). **303**

C. English

10.32 Penny of Eadgar (No. 63).

EADGAR, *c*. 959–975

63. Penny: BMS type HT 1, struck before 973; no mint-signature; moneyer: *Macus*
    Obv.: +EADG[A]RREo, around small cross in inner circle
    Rev.: /MACV/+ + +/ [S]MOT/ ⋮
    Wt.: 0.84gm (13.05gr.); die-axis: 350°.

The coin, which is chipped and crumpled, shows slight wear. Besides the element at the end of the obverse legend, the dies are notable for the idiosyncratic *O* of the reverse. Struck from the same dies is a specimen in Edinburgh (Stevenson 1966: 475, *ex* Machrie hoard, 1850). The reverse is known also in combination with another obverse (*BMS* 953, *ex* Tetney hoard, 1945). The obverse affords evidence of an inter-moneyer link for it is that used for coins by Harcer (*BMS* 929–30: 929, *ex* Ballaquayle hoard, 1894; 930, *ex* Tetney hoard, 1945). **542**

CNUT, 1016–1035

64. *Penny: Short cross issue*, *c*. 1029–1035
Chester mint; moneyer: *Leofwine*.
    Obv.: +CNV / TREXA (the *A*, unbarred), around helmeted bust, facing left, with sceptre in front
    Rev.: +LEOFPINEONLEI, around voided cross within inner circle
    Wt.: 1.04gm (16.1gr.); die-axis: 0°.

The coin, slightly crumpled and with some surface oxidization, shows signs of a little circulation-wear. The specimen is a die-duplicate of a coin, recovered in the Lübeck hoard of 1875 (Dannenberg and Cohn, 1877, No. 446), which is now in

10.33 Penny of Cnut (No. 64).

Copenhagen (*SCBI Cop.* IIIA, No. 1444). One should note, too, that the reverse is used also in combination with another obverse (see *SCBI Chester* I, No. 266). **407.07**

D. Hiberno-Norse

10.34 Hiberno-Norse penny of Phase III (No. 65).

65. *Penny; Phase III, c.* 1035–55: reduced-weight imitation of *Long Cross* issue for Æthelræd II, struck at Dublin; *c.f.* Dolley (1966), no 133 (obverse from same die)
  Obv.: illiterate legend; head to left; pellet before face; cross on neck; triangle of pellets behind head
  Rev.: illiterate legend; long cross, with stylized hand in alternate angles
  Wt.: 0.83 gm (12.8 gr.); die-axis: 175° (as illustrated)
The coin shows signs of very slight wear; it has been broken and mended. **536**

The later Medieval and post-Medieval coins

Nicholas Holmes

A total of 111 coins was recovered, ranging in date from the tenth to the twentieth century. The assemblage as a whole was consistent with continuous human occupation of the excavated area throughout the mediaeval and modern periods, but within this overall picture there were notable concentrations of coins of particular periods within specific archaeological areas and contexts. There were a number of individual finds and groups which are of considerable numismatic interest.

Numismatic significance

Full descriptions of all the coins are to be found in the catalogue. Here it is proposed to draw attention to a number of individual pieces of particular interest and/or rarity and to some groups of coins belonging to types which are generally considered to be rare.

Within the series of Scottish coins, the most notable is undoubtedly the sterling of the reign of David I (No.1, Figure 10.35). It is of a type which was at one time tentatively attributed to the reign of Malcolm IV, but more recent finds have helped to place it in its correct context. The coin was shown to Lord Stewartby, and he has kindly provided the following comments.

> 'This coin belongs to a group, mostly in the name of David I, with an annulet or crescent enclosing a pellet in each quarter of the reverse cross, which was of great rarity before the discovery of the Civil War hoard at Prestwich, Lancashire, in 1972. This group was not represented in the 1818 Watford hoard (early 1140s?), nor in hoards buried towards or after 1150, such as Bute (*c.* 1150 +) or Outchester (*c.* 1170), both of which contained later issues of David I in some numbers. It therefore seems likely to belong to the early or middle years of the 1140s.
>
> Four examples are known of this group with an enigmatic inscription +NERTIVC+ on the most legible specimen (no 2). They are: **1** Burns Fig. 28B; **2** Prestwich hoard; **3** Stewartby collection; **4** the Whithorn coin. Nos 1 and 2 are from the same reverse die by the moneyer Fobalt, with a mint reading that could represent Newcastle (Stewart 1971, 189). The reverse reading of number 3 is unclear, but it may also be of the same moneyer, with a mint name [_]R, perhaps [BE]R for Berwick. No 3 is from the same obverse die as no 1, and no 4 may be from the same obverse die as no 2 (the sceptre head is higher than the bottom of the crown on these).[5] On no 4 the moneyer's name is again unclear, but perhaps the same. The mint name, RO for Roxburgh, is fully legible, however, and geographically consistent with the other issues of this versatile moneyer under David I. He struck coins of David's cross moline (Stephen derivative) type at Roxburgh (Burns 1887, Fig. 24D),and the cross fleury type at Berwick (Burns Figs 1, 2, 4, 4A and 21B) and possibly Roxburgh (Burns 1887, Fig. 21A), while under William the Lion he appears in the early fleur-de-lis type at Roxburgh (Burns 1887, Figs 25B and C) and in the crescent and pellet type at Perth (Burns 1887, Figs 30 and 31).'

Also of note for its rarity is the Dundee halfpenny of Robert II (No. 6, Figure 10.36). There seems to be no published example of a coin from this obverse die, but the reverse is from the same die as Burns 333B, a second specimen in the collections of the National Museums of Scotland, and the Ashmolean specimen (Bateson and Mayhew 1987, no 506).

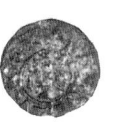

10.36 Robert II halfpenny of Dundee (No. 6). © The Trustees of the National Museums of Scotland 1996.

10.35 David I sterling of Roxburgh (No. 1). © The Trustees of the National Museums of Scotland 1996.

[5] This has been confirmed by Miss M M Archibald and Mrs J E L Murray, after comparison with the Prestwich hoard coin in the British Museum – N H.

A contemporary forgery of a James III 'black farthing' (No. 28, Figure 10.37) is notable for its astonishing crudity. It is surprising that forgers were prepared to risk extremely harsh punishment to produce counterfeits of coins that were in any case of low value and very unpopular among the people of Scotland, but several examples have now been identified. Presumably it was relatively easy to introduce counterfeits into circulation, since many of the official issues were themselves poorly struck.

The forgery of a James IV plack, by contrast, is a

10.37 James III counterfeit farthing (No. 28). © The Trustees of the National Museums of Scotland 1996.

relatively faithful reproduction of a genuine piece in terms of design, although the legends comprise only meaningless sequences of letters (No. 31, Figure 10.38). Counterfeits of coins of this type in the early-sixteenth century are known to have been made in Flanders and to have been introduced into circulation in Scotland in large numbers. Working abroad would clearly have been a safer option for a counterfeiter, but some were prepared to take the risk of carrying on their trade in Scotland itself. One William White is mentioned in various official documents in 1515–6 as having been convicted of striking false placks and pennies (Mrs J E L Murray, Pers. Comm.).

The Whithorn finds are notable for a strong representation of low-denomination coins of the fifteenth century, including two categories which have generally been regarded as rare. Copper CRVX PELLIT coins and 'black farthings', dating from the

10.38 James IV counterfeit plack (No.31). © The Trustees of the National Museums of Scotland 1996.

second half of the century, are still described frequently as rare in catalogues and sales lists, although finds from numerous Scottish excavations since the 1970s have demonstrated that they must have circulated in large numbers, despite their reputed unpopularity. From Whithorn came four CRVX PELLITs and seven or possibly eight farthings. These numbers are not surprising in an assemblage of 111 coins.

Much less to be anticipated were eight billon pennies of James I and II, dating from the period c. 1424–60. Surviving examples of James I pennies are still few, and although they have been classified by Stewart (1967, now Lord Stewartby) into Groups A–D, mostly on the basis of comparison with known issues of groats, it is clear that there are many minor variations within these groups. Unfortunately many of the known specimens are in poor condition, making detailed research and die-linking difficult, but the presence of six coins of Stewart's Groups A and B at Whithorn is of considerable value (Nos 8–13, Figure 10.39). The early James II penny (James I Group D; No. 14, Figure 10.40) is of extreme rarity, and even the later pennies of James II are rare as individual finds. Most of the known specimens at present come from hoards, notably that from Leith (Holmes 1983).

10.39 James I pennies. © The Trustees of the National Museums of Scotland 1996.

10.40 James II penny (James I Group D; No. 14). © The Trustees of the National Museums of Scotland 1996.

In contrast, Whithorn has yielded only two billon pennies of James III (one of these not being a definite attribution). These coins are certainly more common than those of the two earlier Jameses, and it may be that their near-absence from this assemblage, in contrast to the larger numbers of copper farthings of the same period, is of some significance. Certainly the coin record for the 15th century, apart from one groat of James I, is made up of the most debased issues available at any given time – first billon, then copper. Caution must be exercised, however, in view of the expected wider circulation of low-value coins and the natural tendency for people to search more diligently for lost coins of higher face values. The overall picture for the later mediaeval and post-mediaeval periods generally reflects the expected pattern of coin in circulation, i.e. with much low-value coinage of types which would have been used for everyday transactions, and very few higher-value pieces.

Among the English coins, it is notable that there are five cut halfpennies and only three complete pennies from the period prior to 1279, when round halfpennies and farthings were first issued. Again a bias towards smaller denominations is apparent, but the same caveats must be applied as for the later period, with the added factor of the greater difficulty to be encountered in locating cut fragments of coins, once they have been dropped.

Catalogue

Stewart references given in descriptions of Scottish coins refer to I.H. Stewart, *The Scottish Coinage*, 2nd edition (1967). Most of the Edwardian coins were identified and catalogued prior to the publication of J.J. North's sylloge volume on this series (North 1989), and references are therefore to the old (Fox) classification. Refinement of the catalogue by altering the typological references of the coins would not have added to the archaeological information provided by the coin series.

SCOTLAND
1 DAVID I, silver sterling of Roxburgh (c. 1140–50)
obv.:[ ]RTIV[ ]: crowned bust right with sceptre
rev.:[ ]:ON:RO[ ]: plain cross, with ends slightly potent; crescent and pellet and single pellet in each quarter
20.0mm; 0.655g; die axis 4.0
very worn, especially obverse, and somewhat corroded
cf. Burns (1887) 28B, Stewart 15
415.01

2 WILLIAM THE LION, silver penny of Raul at Roxburgh, 2nd coinage, class 2 (c. 1180–95)
obv.: [+L]Є RЄIW[ ]: sceptre head is cross of 4 pellets
rev.: [+]RAVL[ ]BVR : cross potent; crescent and pellet in each angle; stalks on all four pellets; extra pellet in each inner angle
20.0 × 20.5mm; 1.16g; die axis 7.5
obverse poorly struck; some flattening; moderate wear
533

3 ALEXANDER III; silver penny; 2nd coinage; Stewart and North (1991) class B (1280–86+)
obv.: +ALЄXANDЄRDЄIGR'A : cross probably potent; No ligature; 1st A barred, 2nd unbarred, 3rd ?unbarred; hair punch e
rev.: RЄX/SCO/TOR/VM+ : cross potent; reverse B2; 3 type 2
1.035g; die axis 6.0
badly bent; fairly worn
538

4 DAVID II, silver half-groat of Edinburgh, 2nd coinage, type B1 (1357–67)
obv.: +D[ ]+DЄI+GRA+RЄX+SCOTORV : small cross stops
rev.: +D[ ]/PROS/ЄCTOR/mЄOS‡
VILL/ĀЄD/InBV/RGh : nothing extra in angles of cross
2.030g; die axis 8.0
fairly worn; slightly bent
772

5 DAVID II, silver half-groat of Edinburgh, 3rd coinage (1367–71)
obv.: +DĀVID+DЄIGRA+RЄ [ ]COTORVM : star on sceptre handle; 6-arc tressure with trefoils in spandrels; small cross stops
rev.: +DnS/[P]ROT/ЄCTOR/mЄVS‡
VILL/ĀЄD/Inev/RGh : double cross stop;
1.752g; die axis 1.5
slightly clipped; moderate wear with a few areas of flattening
517.03

6 ROBERT II, silver halfpenny of Dundee (1371–90)
obv.: +ROBЄRTVSRЄX
rev.: VIL/LA/DVn/DЄ
14.0 × 13.0mm; 0.43g; die axis 3.0
obverse slightly off-centre; slight to moderate wear
903

7 JAMES I, silver groat of Edinburgh, initial or first variety (1424–37)
obv.:+IACOBVS_DЄ[ ]ACIA*RЄX*[S]COTOR : sceptre to left, 8-arc tressure; lis on cusps; lis stops; no extra marks
rev.: +Dn[S]P/TЄCOT[ ]/[ ]/BATORm[ ]
VILLˣ/A[ ]Є[ ]/Inev/RGhˣ ; lis in first and third angles; pellets in second and fourth; saltire stops; no extra marks
2.07g; die axis 1.0
fairly worn
903

8 JAMES I, billon penny of Edinburgh, Group A (probably c. 1424)
obv.: +IACOBVS[ ]RĀCIAR
rev.: VILL/[ ]/[ ]InB/VRGh
0.782g; die axis 1.5
very worn
742

9 JAMES I, billon penny of Inverness, Group A (probably c. 1424)
obv.: +IĀCOBVS[ ]GRĀ[ ]ЄXS
rev.: VILL/ĀIn/VЄR/nIS
0.582g; die axis 6.0
edge ragged to left of bust; obverse appears extremely worn, but reverse shows only moderate wear
772

10 JAMES I, billon penny of Inverness, Group A (probably c 1424)
obv.: [+IAC]OBVSDЄIGRA_RЄX[ ]:uncertain stop after GRA
rev.: VILL/AIn/nЄ R/nIS
0.50g; die axis 4.5
part of edge disintegrating; some flattening, especially on portrait; fairly worn
550

11 JAMES I, billon penny of Edinburgh, Group B (1424–37)
obv.: IĀCOBVS_DЄITRA[ ] : saltires to left and right of neck

rev.: +[ ]/LLĀ_/Є[ ]nˣ/BVRGh : points between pellets; saltire stop
0.960g; die axis 7.0
obverse probably poorly struck; fairly worn
560

12 JAMES I, billon penny of Edinburgh, Group B (1424–37)
obv.: +IĀCOBVS[ ]ACIAˣR : saltire stop
rev.: [ ]/[ ]D/InBV/RGh
0.83g; die axis 11.0
very slightly bent; fairly worn
502

13 JAMES I, billon penny of Edinburgh, Group B (1424–37)
obv.: [ ]IACTBVS˚DЄ[I]*TRACI[ ] : pellets flanking crown (left one not visible) and neck; lis stops
rev.: +VIL/L_*D/[ ]/[ ]Gh :lis stop; point between pellets in each quarter
0.75g; die axis 4.0
both sides slightly off-centre; fairly worn
903

14 JAMES II, billon penny of Edinburgh, 1st coinage (1437–51)(=James I, Group D)
obv.: +IĀC[OBVS] : DЄI : GRĀCIĀ : RЄX : double annulet stops
rev.: +VIL/-LĀ : Є /[DI]nB/VRGh : single and double annulet stops
0.945g; die axis 2.5
much flattening, but some parts show only slight or moderate wear
630

15 JAMES II, billon penny of Edinburgh, crown groat coinage (1451–c. 1460), Stewart 94, Holmes (1983) type B
obv.: [ ]RARЄ [ ] : saltire on either side of bust
rev.: VIL/[ ]Є /[ ]/[ ] : ? saltire within each group of pellets
0.575g; die axis 1.5
both sides struck considerably off-centre; very worn
542

16 Copper CRVX PELLIT issue, type Ia (later 15th century), as Stewart 95
1.44g
not cleaned; much corroded
535

17 Copper CRVX PELLIT issue, type Ib (later 15th century), as Stewart 96
obv.: +IĀCOBVS * DЄI * GR[ ]ЄX * double and single saltire stops
rev.: +CRVX * P[ ]LIT*OIЄ * CRIII : double saltire stops; large open Cs; pellets on cusps; nothing in spandrels
2.233g; die axis 12.0
obverse mis-struck and appears very worn; reverse slightly off-centre, showing slight to moderate wear
700

18 Copper CRVX PELLIT issue, type IIa (later 15th century), as Stewart 97
obv.: [+]IACOBVS : DЄ I : GRA[ ] :double annulet stops
rev.: CRVXPЄLLITOIЄ[ ]: annulets on cusps; nothing in spandrels
1.527g; die axis 6.0
slightly off-centre; moderate wear
620.02

19 Copper CRVX PELLIT issue, type IIIa (later 15th century), cf. Stewart 99
obv.: +IACOBVS * DЄI * [ ]Є : orb tilted upwards and to left, with rosette in middle; double saltire stops
rev.: +ˣCRVX[ ]CRIII : saltire stop; ?stars on cusps; nothing in spandrels
1.52g; die axis 9.5
angular flan; much surface accretion on reverse; moderate wear
612.03

20 JAMES III, billon penny, class A (c. 1465–75), Holmes (1983) class Ab2 or Ab3
obv.: legend illegible, with initial mark cross; unclothed bust
rev.: [ ]/L[ ]/DIn/[ ] : traces of points or saltires between pellets
0.335g; die axis 9.0
very poorly struck; fairly worn
725

21 Billon penny, almost certainly of JAMES III (1460–88)
obv.: +[ ]S : D[ ]ЄX : double saltire stop
rev.: [ ]/[ ]/D[ ]/[ ]R
0.27g; die axis uncertain
badly chipped; bent; pierced in centre, with lumps of corrosion and textile around hole; probably fairly worn
543

22 JAMES III, copper 'black farthing', 1st issue (1465–6), as Stewart 113
obv.: [ ]ЄXˣSCOT[ ]: crown; saltire stop
rev.: crown V[ ]Є ˣDIRV_ˣ : saltire flanked by small saltires; saltire stops
0.348g; die axis 9.0
edge rather ragged; slight to moderate wear
430

23 JAMES III, copper 'black farthing', 1st issue (1465–6), as Stewart 113
obv.: [ ]COTO[ ] : crown
rev.: crown VI[ ] : saltire flanked by small saltires
0.190g; die axis 6.5
much corroded; probable moderate wear
772

24 JAMES III, copper 'black farthing', 1st issue (1465–6), as Stewart 113
obv.: [ ]XVI_I[ ]: crown
rev.: legend illegible, but includes Є _IV : saltire flanked by small saltires
0.325g; die axis 6.0 or 12.0
much of legends missing; probable moderate wear overall
style of coin appears official, but blundered legends suggest a forgery
772

25 JAMES III, copper 'black farthing', 1st issue (1465–6), as Stewart 113
obv.: legend illegible; crown
rev.: legend illegible; saltire flanked by small saltires
0.240g; die axis 1.0 or 7.0
much of outer ring, with legends, missing; bent; probably moderate wear
772

26 JAMES III, copper 'black farthing', 1st issue (1465–6), as Stewart 113
obv.: IRЄXˣS[ ] : saltire stop; crown
rev.: legend illegible; saltire flanked by small, crude, saltires
0.517g; die axis 2.0 or 8.0
moderate wear
543

27 JAMES III, copper 'black farthing', 1st issue (1465–6), as Stewart 113
obv.: legend illegible; crown
rev.: legend illegible; saltire flanked by small saltires
0.29g; die axis uncertain
some corrosion; very worn
603

28 JAMES III, copper forgery of a 'black farthing', as 1st issue (1465–6)
obv.: very crude design, probably intended to be a crown, with part of an irregular ring of small rectangular marks outside
rev.: very crude design, comprising incomplete saltire, flanked by two diamond-shaped marks, within inner circle; part of 'legend' of rectangular marks outside
1.188g
much of surface flat, probably resulting from poor striking; flan squarish, with corners cut off; probably only slight to moderate wear
543

29 Rectangular piece of copper sheeting, *possibly* a JAMES III 'black farthing'
One face featureless, the other covered with corrosion products
0.236g
254.02

30 JAMES IV, billon plack, uncertain type (1488–1513)
obv.: illegible
rev.: [ ]VRG⁑: double star stop; plain saltire in centre of cross
1.564g
coin folded almost in half, and fairly corroded; moderate wear on reverse
620.02

31 JAMES IV, forgery of a billon plack (1488–1513)
obv.: nonsensical and partly illegible legend, including repetition of XREI
rev.: nonsensical and mostly unreadable legend
obverse and reverse designs are as those on James IV placks
1.662g
some flattening; fairly worn
531

32 Late 15th century billon penny, probably of JAMES IV, 1st issue, type Ia (c. 1489–90)
obv.: illegible, and mostly covered with corrosion products; crown appears to have five lis
rev.: +VIL/[ ]/[ ]/[ ] : annulet between pellets in 1st and 3rd quarters
0.304g; die axis 6.0
cf. Glenluce Hoard 84 and 85 (Stewart 1959)
very worn; obverse much corroded
916

33 JAMES IV, billon penny, 2nd issue, type II (c. 1500–10); as Stewart 132
obv.: [crown I]ACOBVS⁑DЄ I]⁑GRACIA⁑REX: double star stops
rev.: crown V[IL]/[L]A⁑ЄD/[In]BR/VGh⁑ : double star stops; lis in 1st and 3rd angles; crown in 2nd and 4th
0.56g; die axis 5.0
pierced near middle, with lumps of corrosion and textile around hole; some flattening; mostly slight wear
543

34 JAMES IV, billon penny, 2nd issue, type III (c. 1500–10); as Stewart 133
obv.: [ ]IACOBVSDЄIGRA[ ]
rev.: +VIL/LAЄ /DI[ ]/[ ]
0.653g; die axis 4.5
some flattening, due to poor striking; generally slight to moderate wear
926

35 JAMES IV, billon penny, 2nd issue, type IV (c. 1500–10); as Stewart 134
obv.: _IĀCO[ ]GRĀRЄXSCOT
rev.: _VILL/ĀDЄ /ЄD[ ]/[ ]
obverse and reverse initial marks are little more than blobs, and could be either crosses or lis; since there appear to be no stops in the legends, the coin may be of type IVd
0.741g; die axis 10.5
small or clipped flan; some flattening; generally slight to moderate wear
744

36 JAMES IV, billon penny, 2nd issue, type IV (c. 1500–10); as Stewart 134
obv.: [ ]COBVSЄ[ ]GRA[ ]SC[ ]
rev.: _VIL/L[ ]/Є DIn/BVRG : initial mark small and uncertain, no stops apparent in legends, and coin may therefore be of type IVd
0.915g; die axis 7.0
moderate wear, but parts of legends flat; good silvering surviving
731

37 MARY, billon bawbee, 1st period, later type (1542–54); as Stewart 155
obv.: +MARIAR[ ]TORVM
rev.: lis OPPIDVMEDI[ ] : fluted saltire
1.543g; die axis 8.5
moderate wear
631

38 MARY, billon half-bawbee (1542–8); Stevenson (1990) type Cai
obv.: +MARIA•DG[RS]COTORVM
rev.; lis OPPIDVMEDI⁒BVRGI : reverse N; fluted cross
0.94g; die axis 6.0
moderate wear
903

39 MARY AND FRANCIS, billon lion/hardhead, type 2 (1559–60); as Stewart 161
obv.: [ ]COTORDVIEN : dolphins to left
rev.: VICIT[ ]
0.586g; die axis 12.0
worn
615.02

40 JAMES VI, billon hardhead, 1st issue (August 1588); as Stewart 199
0.94g
badly chipped; slight flattening; very little wear
610.03

41 JAMES VI, billon hardhead, 2nd issue (November 1588); as Stewart 200
1.069g; die axis 1.0
very worn
744

42 JAMES VI, billon hardhead, 2nd issue (November 1588); as Stewart 200
1.108g; die axis 11.0
large flan; obverse shows moderate wear, but reverse appears extremely worn, possibly owing to weak striking
631

43 JAMES VI, copper post-Union twopence, 1st issue (1614); as Stewart 216
2.17g
not conserved; fairly worn
904

44 JAMES VI, copper post-Union twopence, 2nd issue (1623); as Stewart 217
1.573g; die axis 1.5
not conserved; probably fairly worn
729

45 Copper turner/twopence of JAMES VI (1614 or 1623) or CHARLES I (1629); as Stewart 216, 217 or 235
1.72g; die axis uncertain
surfaces much corroded
903

46 CHARLES I, silver forgery of a 20-pence piece of 2nd or 3rd issue (1637–42)
obv.: [ ]OTAN[ ]FEHIBR• : bust not fully enclosed; no lozenges above and below XX
rev.: [ ]AIHTOVMFI[ ]
slightly bent; c. 90% of coin survives, in two fragments; extremely worn
903

47 and 48 CHARLES I, copper turners (1632–9); as Stewart 238
two coins found corroded together, obverse to reverse; of the two non-corroded faces, the obverse shows only very slight wear, the reverse a little more
772

49 CHARLES I, copper turner (1632–9); as Stewart 238
only slight wear; slightly corroded
631

50 CHARLES I, copper turner (1632–9); as Stewart 238
slightly bent; surfaces corroded; degree of wear uncertain
744

51 CHARLES I, copper turner (1632–9); as Stewart 238
reverse corroded; moderate wear
615.02

52 CHARLES I, copper turner (1632–9); as Stewart 238
0.61g
corroded; moderate wear
764

53 CHARLES I, copper turner (1632–9); as Stewart 238
0.60g
some corrosion; moderate wear
764

54 CHARLES I, copper turner (1642–50); as Stewart 243 (re-attributed to Charles I)
highly corroded; degree of wear uncertain
744

55 CHARLES I, copper turner (1642–50); as Stewart 243 (re-attributed to Charles I)
very worn and somewhat corroded
772

56 CHARLES I or II, copper turner (1642–50 or 1663); as Stewart 239 or 243
extremely worn
708

57 CHARLES II, copper turner (1663); as Stewart 239 (re-attributed to Charles II)
highly corroded; degree of wear uncertain
744

58 CHARLES II, copper turner (1663); as Stewart 239 (re-attributed to Charles II)
fairly worn; slightly corroded
741

59 CHARLES II, copper turner (1663); as Stewart 239 (re-attributed to Charles II)
1.87g
very worn
610.03

60 CHARLES II, copper bawbee (1679); as Stewart 244
very worn, especially obverse
725

ENGLAND
61 ? JOHN, silver cut halfpenny of London, short cross, probably class 5b(i) (1205–10)
obv.: [hE NRIC]VS•R-EX
rev.: [   ]R•ON•LVN
0.63g; die axis 8.0
obverse corroded; slight to moderate wear on reverse
903

62 HENRY III, silver cut halfpenny of Durham, short cross, class 7 (1217–42)
obv.: [hENRI]CVSR-EX
rev.: [   ]ONDVR
the moneyer is probably Pieres, the only one listed by North (1991) for class 7 at this mint
0.68g; die axis 9.0
moderate wear
611

63 Silver cut halfpenny, probably short cross.
coin enclosed within corrosion of an iron draw-plate, and visible only on X-ray plate
535

64 HENRY III, silver penny of Ion at Bury St Edmunds, long cross, class 2 (1248)
obv.: ✱hENRICVS•REX•TERCI'
rev.: ION/ONS/EIN/TED
1.445g; die axis 8.0
slight wear
538

65 HENRY III, silver penny of Nicole at London, long cross, class 3c (1248–50)

obv.: ✱hENRICVSREX:III' : pellet on each side of head
rev.: NIC/OLE/ONL/VND
1.270g; die axis 2.0
badly bent; only slight wear
520.05

66 HENRY III, silver cut halfpenny of Exeter, long cross, class 3 (1248–50)
obv.: ✱hE N[RICVSRE X]III'
rev.: [   ]/[   ]/ONE /CCE
0.66g; die axis 1.5
some flattening in legends; moderate wear
904

67 HENRY III, silver penny of Walter at Canterbury, long cross, class 5g (1251–72)
obv.: hENRICVSREX . III : X is of the form normal on class 5d–f
rev.: WAL/TER/ONC/A̅N̅T
1.374g; die axis 12.0
double-struck; much of design and lettering indistinct; apparently only slight wear
538

68 HENRY III, silver cut halfpenny of Renaud at London, long cross, class 5g–i (probably 5g) (1251–72)
obv.: [   ]CVSR[   ]
rev.: REN/[   ]/[   ]/[   ]ND
0.23g; die axis c. 5.0
chipped; fairly worn
902

69 EDWARD I, silver penny of London, class IIa (1280)
1.188g; die axis 7.5
worn; some corrosion pitting
539

70 EDWARD I, silver penny of Lincoln, class IIId (1280–1)
1.166g; die axis 8.5
slight wear
526

71 EDWARD I, silver penny of London, class IIIg (North 1989, type 3gi(?)) (1280–1)
much corrosion and surface damage; moderate wear
546

72 EDWARD I, silver penny of Durham, class IIIg (1280–1)
Late S on both sides
1.244g; die axis 12.0
fairly worn; corrosion pitting on both sides
516.02

73 EDWARD I, silvered base metal forgery of a penny of London, class III
obv.: bust and crown as class IIIg, but S of unusual form
rev.: S approximates to early type
1.202g; die axis 11.0
slight to moderate wear, but more on portrait; silvering is flaking off core on both sides
526

74 EDWARD I, silver penny of London, class IVc (1282–9)
1.257g; die axis 10.0
bent; reverse slightly off-centre; worn
430

75 EDWARD I, silver penny of London, class IVd (1282–9)
1.245g; die axis 11.0
slightly bent; struck slightly low on flan; patches of pitting and corrosion; moderate wear
516.02

76 EDWARD I, silver penny of London, class VIIIa (c. 1294–c. 1300)
1.010g; die axis 2.0
only fairly slight wear, but obverse much corroded; reverse corroded only in part of legend
516.02

77 EDWARD I, silver penny of Canterbury, class Xc–e (crown 1) (1302–10)
1.268g; die axis 9.0
worn
514

78 EDWARD I, silver penny of Canterbury, class Xc–e (crown 1?) (1302–10)
1.267g; die axis 12.0
very worn
514

79 EDWARD I, silver penny of London, class Xc–e (crown 2?) (1302–10)
1.273g; die axis 3.0
both sides off-centre; obverse very worn, reverse rather less
616.04

80 EDWARD I, silver penny of London, class Xc–e (crown 3?) (1302–10)
1.147g; die axis 12.0
very worn, especially on obverse; some pitting
516.02

81 EDWARD I, silver penny of Bury St Edmunds, class Xc–e (uncertain crown type) (1302–10)
1.242g; die axis 2.0
mostly coated with a black substance; apparently moderate wear
515.01

82 EDWARD I, Irish silver penny of Waterford, Dolley (1968) 2nd coinage (1281–2)
1.336g; die axis 1.0
portrait weakly struck; otherwise little wear
744

83 EDWARD III, silver halfpenny of London, 2nd coinage (1335–43)
obv.: [ ]DVSR∈XĀHG star
rev.: CIVI/[ ]/[ ]LOII/DOH
0.377g; die axis 6.0
very worn, especially obverse; large piece missing above and to right of bust
543

84 EDWARD III, silver penny of London, 3rd (Florin) coinage, normal type 1 (1344–51)
obv.: +∈ DWR'·ĀnGL·DnS·hYB' : S sideways; annulet stops
rev.: CIVI/TĀS/LOn/DOn : = reverse I
1.244g; die axis 7.0
generally fairly slight wear, but some flattened areas
524

85 EDWARD III, silver penny of Durham, probably pre-Treaty series F or G (1356–61)
obv.: [VS]R∈X[GLI] : normal X ?
rev.: CIVI/[ ]/DVR/[ ]
0.802g; die axis 11.5
worn; much flattening and surface corrosion
543

86 HENRY V, silver penny of York, class G (1413–22)
obv.: +h∈nRICVS×R∈X×Ān[G]LI×∈ : saltire stops; mullet to left of crown, trefoil to right
rev.: CIVI/TĀS ˣ /∈BO/RĀCI : double saltire stop
0.757g; die axis 5.0
slightly bent; some of the lettering shows very little wear, but much of middle of coin is flattened; possibly poorly struck
708

87 Half of a silver penny of York (late 13th–15th century)
obv.: illegible
rev.: CIVI/[ ]/[ ]/[ ]CI
0.64g
very worn; not broken along arms of cross, therefore not a genuine 'cut halfpenny'
621

88 ELIZABETH I, silver sixpence, 2nd coinage (1574); initial mark eglantine
2.84g; die axis 6.0
moderate wear
772

89 CHARLES I, copper 'Richmond' farthing, uncertain type (1625–44)
much corroded
617.04

FRANCE
90 ORANGE:FREDERIC HENRI DE NASSAU, copper double tournois (1625–47); as Boudeau 1006
2.98g; die axis 6.0
some surface corrosion; fairly worn on obverse; moderate wear on reverse
610.03

91 ORANGE:FREDERIC HENRI DE NASSAU, copper double tournois (1625–47); as Boudeau 1006
0.89g; die axis uncertain
surfaces much corroded; probably fairly worn
744

SPAIN
92 ENRIQUE III, billon blanca of Burgos (1390–1406); as Cayon and Castan 1444
obv.: +∈nRICVS:D∈I:GRĀCIA:R∈ : 3-towered castle within 6-arc tressure; annulets in spandrels; B below castle
rev.: +∈nRICVSS:D∈ [ ] : lion rampant to left, within 6-arc tressure
1.73g; die axis 5.0
some flattening; mostly fairly worn
605

Distribution and economic implications

Peter Hill

The coins provide a vital index of economic activity, simultaneously reflecting the evolving relationship of Whithorn with the world beyond, and the organization of activities within the settlement. The latter quality is revealed by distribution plots (Figures 10.41–46) which disregard the stratigraphic havoc wrought by the **Period V** graveyard and other disturbances. No coins have been recovered from previous excavations and, although standards of recovery and reporting have varied, this may identify areas where coin deposition was rare.

The coins can be sub-divided into two large and two small groups. The earliest 'group' is the single Roman coin from the site (pp 164, 296). The first large group comprises sixty-two Northumbrian and Southumbrian coins. These were restricted to a narrow band on the south side of the hill (Figure 10.41), which probably reflects the organization of the *minster*. The second large group comprises a single tenth century coin of Eadgar and the subsequent issues of the eleventh to seventeenth centuries. These were more widely scattered than the Northumbrian coins, but detailed examination (Figures 10.44–46) reveals a peripatetic area of trading activity, initially focused in the *inner precinct* of the **Period III/3** settlement, moving to the *outer zone* in the earlier part of **Period V**, retreating inwards as the graveyard contracted in the fifteenth century, and persisting until the later-seventeenth

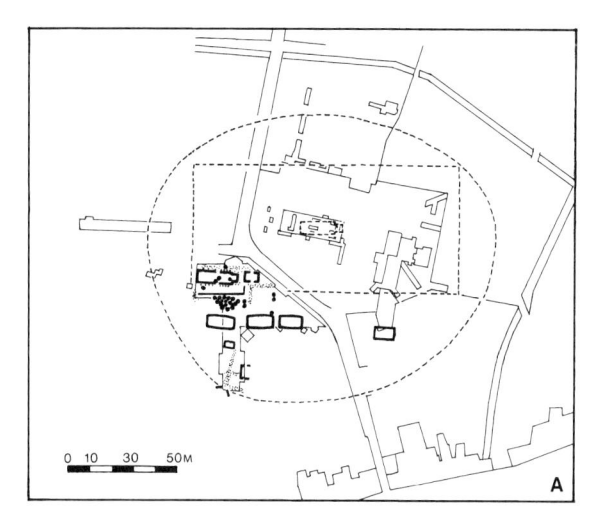

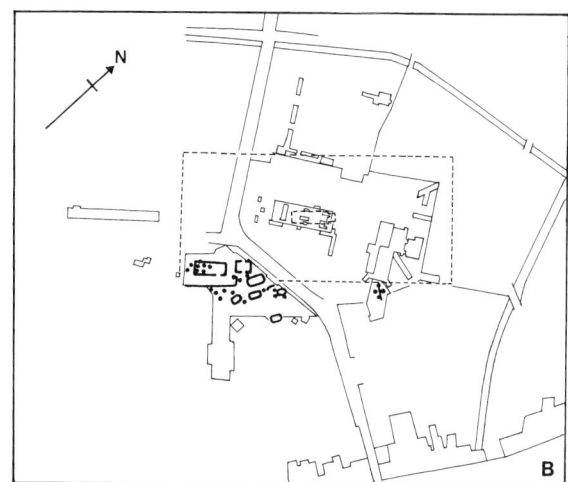

10.41 The general distribution of Northumbrian coins. **A** The *minster* in the earlier-ninth century and the distribution of sceattas and Phase 1 stycas. **B** The restored *minster* in the later-ninth century (**Period III/1**) and the distribution of Phase II stycas.

century on the roadway skirting the Commendator's house. The final group comprises a small collection of eighteenth to twentieth century coins of low value. These were scattered around the manse and market garden, and would be appropriate as stray losses by servants and gardeners. The contrast with the two earlier groups indicates that economic activity had shifted elsewhere by this time.

The eighth and ninth century coins

Sixty-two eighth and ninth century coins have been recovered from the **Glebe Field** and **Museum Garden** trenches, and there are no recorded finds from earlier excavations, nor from the trench in the **Fey Field**. The assemblage can be divided into six groups on spatial and stratigraphic grounds (**1–6**, Figure 10.42), while a seventh (**7**) comprises two unstratified coins from the western part of the **central sector**. The earlier issues were concentrated in the unoccupied area between the halls and the ecclesiastical buildings (Figures 10.43a and b), which may have been a contact zone between the individual wealth of guests and pilgrims, and the corporate wealth of the *minster*. The pattern of deposition changed in the mid-ninth century (Figures 10.41–43) and distinct groups of coins pertained respectively to the crisis at the end of **Period II** (**Group 4**), and the subsequent restoration of the *minster* in **Period III** (**Group 5**). The evolving patterns of coin deposition correspond closely with the phases and groups identified by Pirie (1987a and above), supporting their validity despite the reservations of other scholars in the field (Metcalf 1987a, *passim*). Metcalf has commented:

> '...we need to be able to compare at least three or four large samples of coins from widely separated regions within the Northumbrian kingdom, in order to see whether any of Miss Pirie's groups show signs of being localized in their occurrence,

or different from each other in their behaviour' (Metcalf 1987b, 132).

The coins from **Groups 4–6** display clear evidence of such differences and seem to offer the first of the three or four samples he hopes to see.

Group 1 contains the Series J sceat (61) from the floor of the **Period II/1** burial enclosure (Figures 4.7 and 10.42). This has important chronological implications (pp 40, 136) and its deposition in an otherwise clean environment is surprising. It might have been a stray loss, or a votive deposit associated with the construction of the burial enclosure.

Group 2 comprises some twenty-nine coins (2, 4, 6–9, 11, 13–18, 20–29, 31–33, 43, 45 and 62) from the rubbish spread (303) abutting the **Period II/4** terrace (Figures 4.16, 10.42, 43a and b) and spoil from Trench 4 (743.04 and 903). The earlier coins (2, 4, 6, 7 and 62) were concentrated in the western part of the deposit (Figure 10.42a) and may mark an initial phase of deposition. A second sub-group (**b**) containing the latest sceat (8) and two early stycas (9 and 11), was more widely scattered to the east, although the two sub-groups could not be distinguished stratigraphically. The third sub-group (**c**, Figures 10.43b and c) comprises fifteen Phase Ia stycas of Eanred (13–18, 20–28) and one of Archbishop Eanbald II (29), three Phase Ib stycas of Eanred (31–33), and two Phase II stycas of Eanred, both Ci (43, 45). The later coins (31–33, 43 and 45) are unaffected by circulation wear, and deposition here thus seems to have ceased shortly after the introduction of the Phase II stycas, and before the first issues of Aethelred II, and possibly of Archbishop Uigmund.

It is unlikely that the coins in this large group would have been in circulation at the same time, and it may be viewed as an accumulation of stray losses over a period of seventy or eighty years. It can be explained in various ways. The coins could have been dropped on the floor of the adjacent hall (II/6a–c) and incorporated in debris discarded beyond

THE FINDS 353

its northern doorway; they could have been votive offerings thrown over the parapet around the church; or might have been lost in the course of commercial transactions in the unoccupied ground. They are unlikely to have derived from a hoard as no means of dispersal was evident.

Group 3 comprises three coins (1, 12 and 53) from the clay-mixing pit (250.03) to the south of the burial chapel (Figures 4.16, 10.42 and 43a). Two coins, a worn sceat of Eadberht (1) and a relatively unworn styca of the second reign of Aethelred I (12), came from a layer of silty soil marking an episode of disuse (Figure 4.24), and their respective wear allows

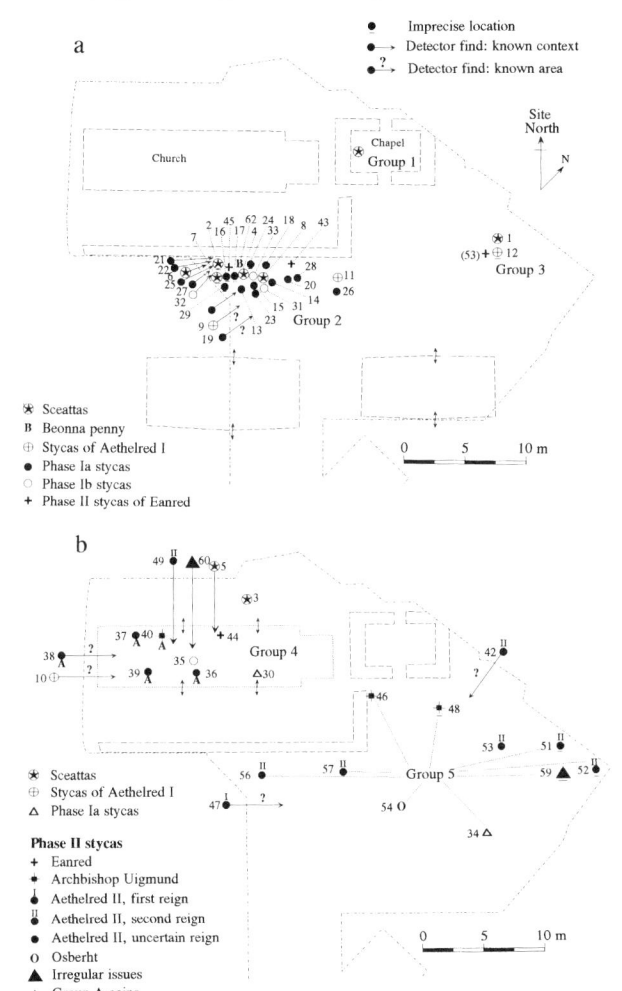

and this coin probably pertains to an equivalent horizon.

Group 4 comprises thirteen coins from the church (3, 5, 10, 30, 35–40, 44, 49 and 60), of which two (10 and 38) were imprecisely-located metal detector finds. One (10) of the three eighth century coins was unstratified, another (3) lay under the paving flanking the **Period III** church, and the third – an unworn sceat of Eadberht (5) – came from the **Period III/2** demolition deposits or overlying floor of **Building III/13**. The last two coins were stratified over the deposits producing mid-ninth century issues, and hence may have been bullion lost in the earlier part

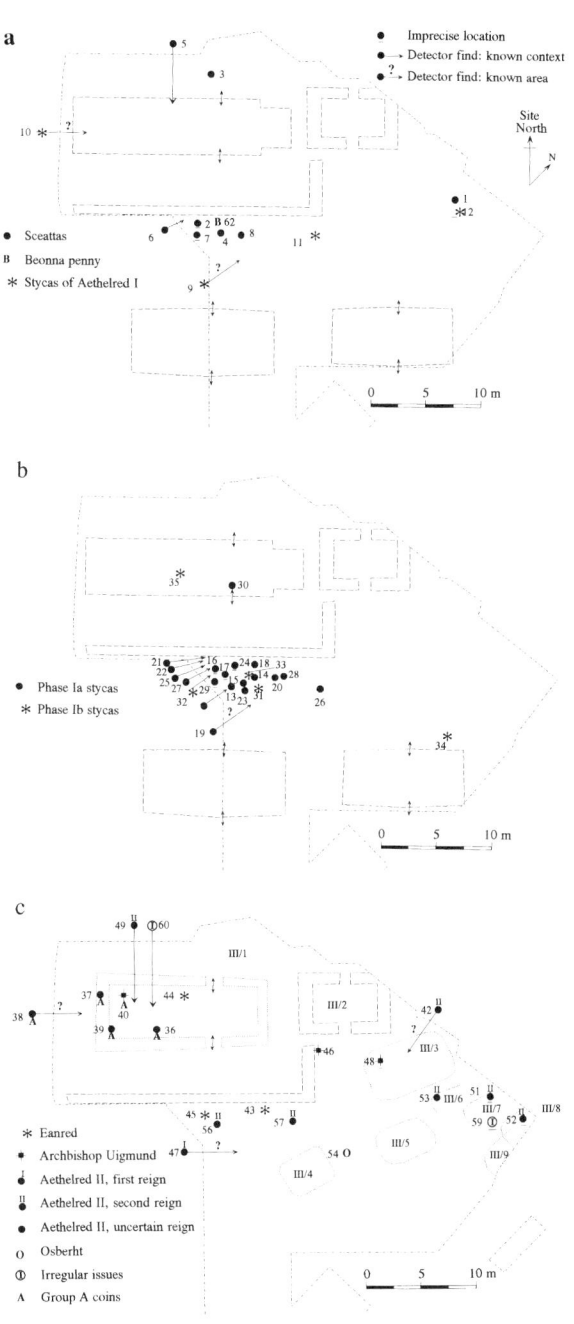

10.42 **Groups** of Northumbrian coins and related issues.

that they could have circulated at the same time. They are likely to have been deposited for similar reasons to the larger groups of contemporary coins from the ground to the west (Figure 10.43). The third coin (53), a styca of the second reign of Aethelred II, came from the upper fill of the pit, and was recovered while the mid-ninth century ploughsoil (399) was being removed. All the other coins of this type were deposited after this episode of cultivation,

10.43 The distribution of eighth and ninth century coins. **a** Eighth century coins. **b** Stycas of Phases I a and b (c. 800-835AD). **c** Stycas of Phase II (c. 837-855AD).

of **Period III**, or votive deposits. The remaining ten coins probably record a brief episode of deposition on the floor of the **Period II/7** building (Figure 4.21b), though recovered from late 'unphased' features (320, pp 157-9), burnt debris from the end of **Period II** (315), and the overlying demolition debris (300.01) in the **Period III** building. They include all the Group A issues (36-40), together with a Group C styca of Monne for King Eanred (44), and two Phase I coins (30 and 35). Two stycas are ascribed to the second reign of Aethelred II. One (49) is a relatively unworn Group Ci coin, the other is a worn irregular issue (60), possibly of Group A, though listed as Di. Stratigraphic *minutiae* (pp 157–9) hint at sub-division within this group, and stycas of Eanred (44), Archbishop Eanbald (35) and Aethelred II (Group Aii, 39) may have been deposited slightly before the irregular issue (60), and coins of Uigmund (40) and the second reign of Aethelred II (49). This thus seems to be a highly specialized assemblage in terms of money supply and date, which probably comprises coinage circulating at Whithorn during a relatively brief period in the reign of Aethelred II. Other stratigraphic groups (**5** and **6**) contained distinct assemblages of his coins. The prevalence of Group A coins and their absence from other parts of the site supports Pirie's contention that these were the product of a distinct moneyers' workshop.

The reason for the deposition of these coins is not immediately clear. They were scattered over the interior of a large and possibly untidy building, and could easily have been lost among the rubbish on the floor (Figure 4.21b, Table 4.7). A burnt gaming piece (BA15) provides a possible explanation, and coins were also associated with gaming pieces and food debris in the slightly earlier rubbish accumulation (303) to the south (Table 4.4).

Group 5 comprises nine coins from **Period III** contexts in the **central sector**, and includes a Phase Ib styca of Eanred (34); two Phase II stycas of Archbishop Uigmund, both Group Ci (46 and 48); four of the second reign of Aethelred II, two Ci (51 and 52) and two Cii (56 and 57); a nonsense issue of Group Di (59) and a Group Ci styca of Osberht (54). Two coins (34 and 56) came from **Period III/2** contexts, but both could have been displaced from earlier layers, or may have been votive deposits associated with domestic hearths (p 200). The remaining seven coins came from **Period III/1** contexts and revealed a coherent stratified progression, commencing with the two coins of Archbishop Uigmund (46 and 48) ascribed to *Stage 1*, and closing with the styca of Osberht (54) deposited at the end of *Stage 4*. The intervening cultivation of *Stage 2* and buildings of *Stages 3* and *4* produced the nonsense coin of Group Di and three coins ascribed to the second reign of Aethelred II (51, 52 and 57). Two other Phase II stycas ascribed to the second reign of Aethelred II, can be assigned to this group. The first (53, Ci) is likely to have been displaced by ploughing in *Stage 2*. The second (42), the only Group B coin from the **Glebe Field**, came from the surface of the **Period V** graveyard in the vicinity of the burial chapel. These coins were concentrated in the northern part of the **central sector** (Figures 10.42c and 43c), continuing the earlier pattern of deposition, but were more widely scattered. Most came from the eastern part of the trench and associated finds show that this area was used by comb-makers (Figure 10.136). The coins could thus have been stray losses in a market area.

Group 6 comprises four coins (41, 50, 55 and 58) from the **Museum Garden** (Figure 10.41) and includes Phase II stycas of Monne for Eanred (Group Ciii, 58), and the first (Group B, 41 and Group Cii, 55) and second reigns of Aethelred II (Group Ci, 50). Only two coins (55 and 58) were well-stratified, but a third (41) may derive from the same horizon. These coins are likely to have been broadly coeval with the group (**4**) from the church, but there were no Group A coins, nor archiepiscopal issues. This hints that the two assemblages are separated by a brief period (perhaps a year or two), but reflect a rapidly changing money supply. The appearance of coins in this area for a brief period in the mid-ninth century (probably in the first reign of Aethelred II) is probably related to the crisis and subsequent reorganisation of the *minster* recorded in the **Glebe Field**.

Group 7 comprises two unstratified coins (19 and 47) from the western part of the **central sector**, of which the earlier (19) probably pertained to **Group 2c** and the later (47) to **Group 5**.

The chronological and spatial distributions of the eighth and ninth century coins are summarized in Table 10.3. There is a clear difference between the early issues in **Groups 1–3** and the later coins in **Groups 4–6**. The earlier coins cannot be seriated stratigraphically although their distributions indicate evolving depositional patterns over a relatively long period. The later assemblages of coins in **Groups 4** and **5** can however be put into sequence, and related stratigraphically to those in the earlier group. The mid-ninth century sequence begins with the later coins of Eanred from the rubbish flanking the terrace (**Group 3**), where deposition seems to have ceased before the first issues of Aethelred II and Archbishop Uigmund. The sequence is continued by the coins from the floor of the church where Group A issues predominated. Phase I and II stycas of Eanred continued to circulate, although now with issues of Aethelred II and Uigmund. Deposition in **Period III** was initiated by two archiepiscopal stycas of Uigmund, continued with Group C coins of the second reign of Aethelred II, and culminated with a single coin of his successor Osberht. The coins from the **Museum Garden** cannot be related stratigraphically with this sequence, but two are ascribed to the first reign of Aethelred II, and they may have accumulated between the deposition of **Groups 3** and **4**. The two irregular issues (59 and 60) came respectively from the floor of the church and the **Period III/1.2** cultivation, and are thus likely to have coincided with the coins of Uigmund and the Group A stycas of Aethelred II.

THE FINDS

	1	2	3	4	5	6	7
Osberht *c.* 849–855					•		
Phase II stycas Aethelred II 2nd reign *c.* 843–849				•	•••••••[2]	•	
Irregular issues *c.* 843 and later				•	•		
Phase II stycas of Uigmund *c.* 837–850				•[1]	••		
Phase II Group A stycas *c.* 841–849				•••••[1]			
Phase II stycas Aethelred II 1st reign *c.* 841–843						••	•
Phase II stycas of Eanred *c.* 837–841		••		•		•	
Phase Ib stycas *c.* 830–835		•••		•	•		
Phase Ia stycas *c.* 810–830		••••••••••••••••		•			•
Phase Ia stycas of Aethelred I *c.* 778–780		•••	•	•			
Sceat of Alchred 765–774		•					
Beonna penny *c.* 757		•					
Sceattas of Eadberht and Ecgberht *c.* 737–58		•••	•	••[3]			
Southumbrian sceat	•						

Table 10.3: Spatial and chronological distribution of Northumbrian and Southumbrian coins.
1 = **Period II/1** burial enclosure, **2** = Rubbish spread between **Period II/4** terrace and halls, **3** = Clay preparation pit (250.03), **4** = Church (all contexts), **5** = **Period III**, mostly central sector, **6** = **Museum Garden**, **7** = Unstratified
•[1] = Group A *styca* of Uigmund entered twice, •[2] = Coin from **Group 3** reassigned to **Group 5**, •[3] = Both from anachronous late contexts.

The tenth–seventeenth century coins

The orderly sequence of eighth-ninth century coins was not matched in subsequent centuries, although the **southern sector** and **Fey Field** produced small groups of stratified coins. Many of the remaining coins from the **northern** and **central sectors** had been displaced by **Period V** graves or other more recent disturbances, and sometimes 're-stratified' by worm action. Despite these unaccommodating stratigraphic circumstances, distribution plots (Figures 10.44–46) present a coherent picture, identifying areas of economic activity and providing an insecure chronological framework for **Periods**

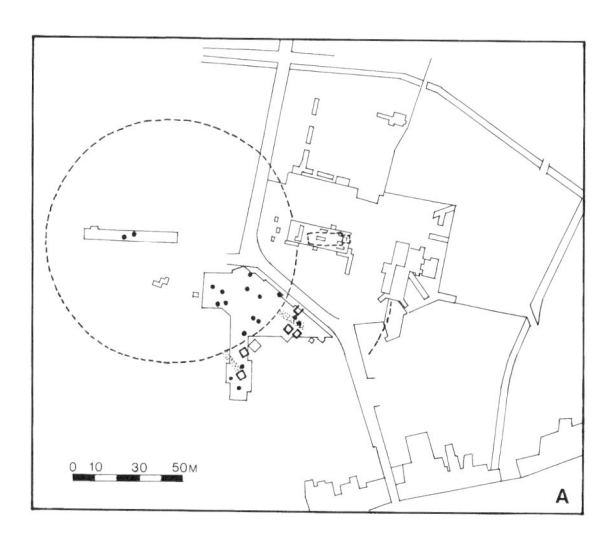

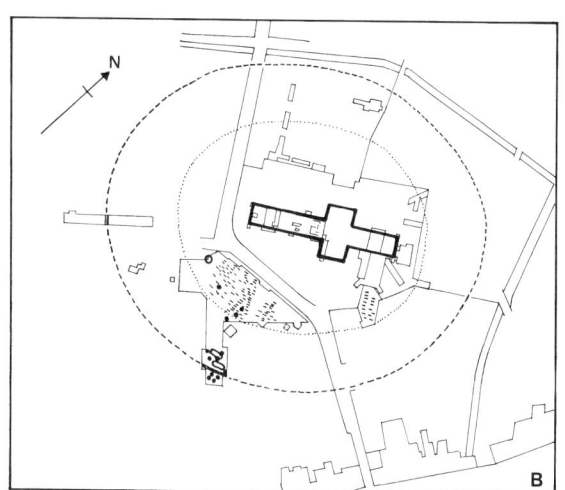

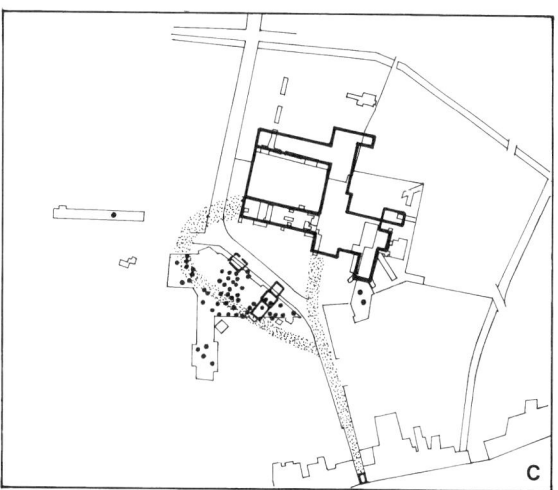

10.44 The general distributions of twelfth to seventeenth century coins. **A** Twelfth and thirteenth century coins. **B** Fourteenth century coins. **C** Fifteenth-seventeenth century coins.

IV–VI. This discussion is based on information provided by Nicholas Holmes on the probable periods of circulation, and dates of loss of the various coins.

The three tenth and eleventh century coins (CN02.63–65) came from the north-west part of the trench. They lay within the band of buildings on the perimeter of the **Period III/3** settlement (Figure 10.45a), and could have been deposited then, or in the early years of **Period IV**. They may have been harbingers of the market evident in the *inner precinct* in **Period IV**, and could have been bullion or circulating currency. The twelfth and thirteenth century coins are mostly ascribed to the latter part of **Period IV** and were scattered widely in the *inner precinct* and *outer zone* (Figure 10.45b). The two or three twelfth century coins (1, 2 and, possibly, 63) came from the *outer zone*, and related finds indicated that all could have been bullion associated with fine metalworking (Figures 6.24 and 6.38, p 246). The thirteenth century coins were concentrated in the *inner precinct*. Four cut halfpennies (61, 62, 66 and 68) came from a restricted area at the west end of the **northern sector**. The large number of cut halfpennies and farthings recorded by metal detectors in recent years, indicates that they played a significant role in the circulating currency of thirteenth century Scotland. Pennies of Henry III and Alexander III and the earlier issues of Edward I were scattered over a wider area. Two relatively unworn pennies of Henry III (64 and 67) from a **Period V/2.8** grave, are likely to been deposited c. 1260 AD, and were probably stray losses preceding the first burials. Two other coins (3 and 69) from graves are more worn and may have been deposited in the early- to mid-fourteenth century, and are thus likely to have been lost in the graveyard and displaced into later graves. The two coins (70 and 73) from the **Fey Field** (Figure 10.44a) complement this picture. Both were deposited within the *inner precinct* of the **Period IV** settlement. They are relatively unworn, are likely to have been lost by the close of the thirteenth century, and may provide a *terminus post quem* for the erection of the **Period V** enclosure (pp 255, 287-8).

The later coins of Edward I (75–82) and subsequent fourteenth century issues (4, 5, 83–85) were concentrated in the *outer zone* of the **Period V** settlement (Figure 10.46a), indicating that economic activity had now shifted from the *inner precinct*. A hoard of coins (72, 75, 76 and 80) came from a small oven immediately beyond the outer boundary and adjacent deposits produced four other coins of Edward I. Wear suggests that all are likely to have been deposited in the early- to mid-fourteenth century. Displaced finds from the **southern sector** included two pilgrims badges (LD09.1 and 2) of approximately similar date, and this area could have accommodated a market selling trinkets and food, while manufacture had moved to the new town. Three of the later-fourteenth century coins (4, 83 and 85) came from the outer margin of the graveyard. Two (83 and 85), both worn, were recovered from the graveyard surface, and the third (4) came from the overlying stony layer (772). These may have been lost in the early-fifteenth century after burials had ceased in this area. The two coins (5 and 84) from the **southern sector** came from late contexts, the relatively unworn penny of Edward III (84) suggesting a mid-fourteenth century date for the **Period V.5** bank, and marking the close of economic activity in this area.

The pattern of coin deposition had shifted again by the fifteenth century (Figure 10.46b). There was only one find from the **southern sector**, and coins of James I, II and III were concentrated in the central part of the trench. None of these coins had been displaced into graves and most were recovered from the graveyard surface (543) and the overlying

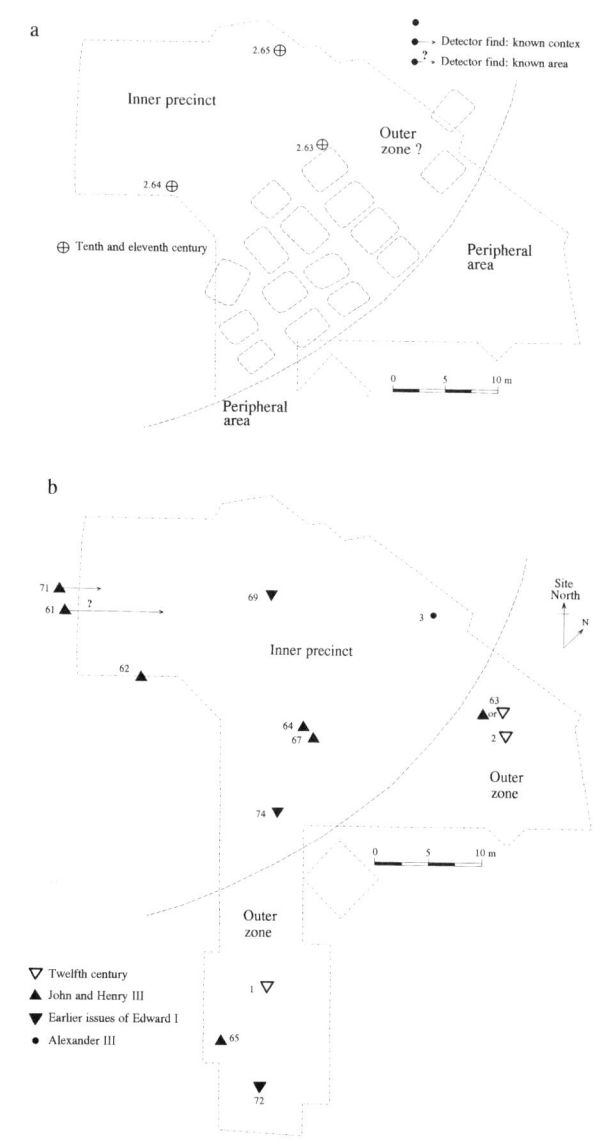

10.45 The distributions of tenth-thirteenth century coins. **a** Tenth and eleventh century coins. **b** Thirteenth century coins.

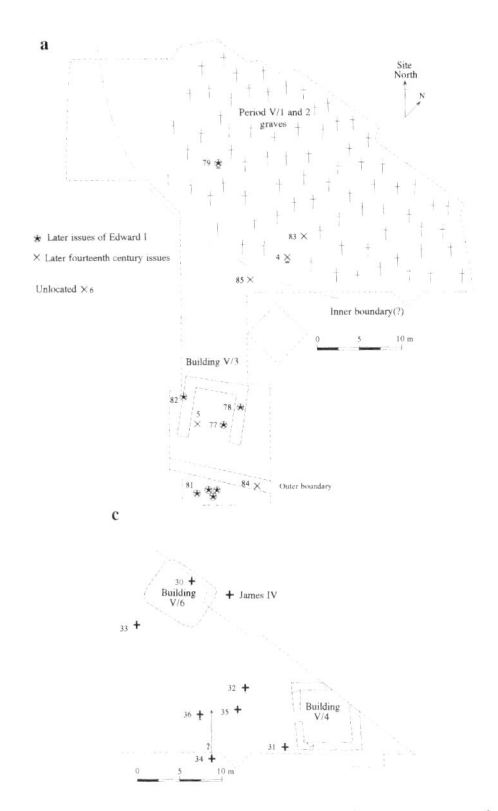

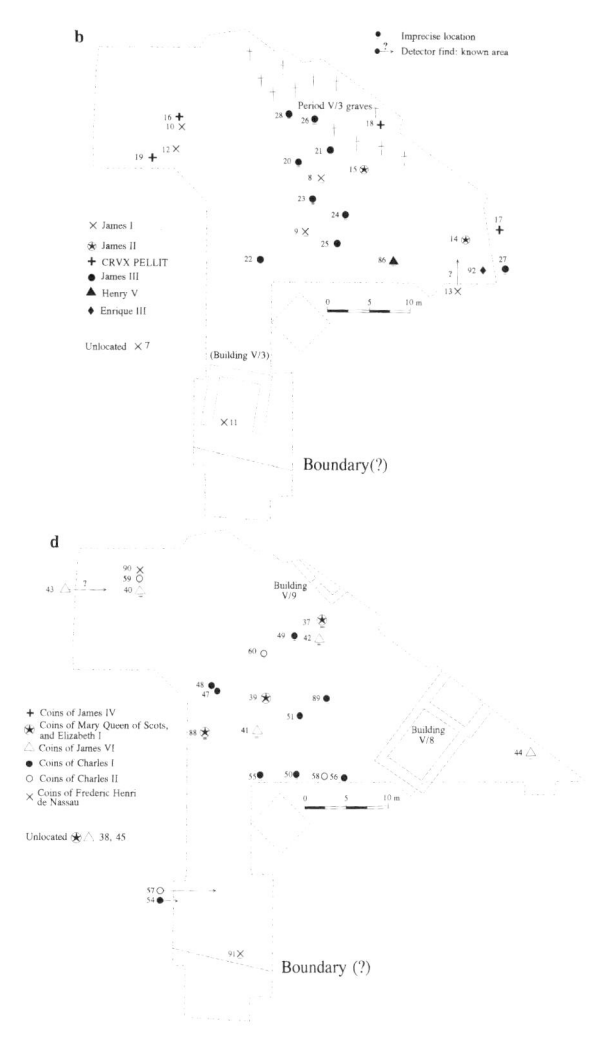

10.46 The distributions of fourteenth-seventeenth century coins. **a** Fourteenth century coins. **b** Fifteenth century coins. **c** Coins of James IV. **d** Sixteenth and seventeenth century coins.

disturbed roadway (772). There were few finds from the area of the **Period V/3** graveyard (540) and the coins may be seen as scattered losses on the roadway skirting the graves and leading to the west door of the cathedral (Figures 2.24 and 25). The more heavily worn fourteenth century coins (83 and 84) came from the same area (Figure 10.46a) and the group may thus have accumulated over a relatively long period in the fifteenth century. The underlying **Period V/2** graves (*Stage 9*, 539) are thus unlikely to be much later than the early-fifteenth century, while the final burials of **Period V/3** (*Stage 10*, 540) may have been broadly contemporary with the deposition of the coins in the middle decades of the fifteenth century. The concentration of copper billon and copper low-denomination coins in this area strongly suggests the presence of a centre of small-scale economic activity, probably a market, during much of the fifteenth century. A tendency for low value coins to predominate on such a site is only to be expected. Broadly contemporary scatters of late-fourteenth and fifteenth century dress items (Figure 10.49), may include items lost by market traders, and complement the picture of bustling activity on the broad roadway leading to the cathedral (Figure 2.25).

The activities leading to coin deposition had moved eastwards by the early-sixteenth century (Figure 10.46c and d). Coins of James IV were concentrated to the east of Building V/8 and include a billon plack (30) from the floor of a wattle building (IV/6). These may have been lost during the renovation of the cathedral in **Period V/4** (p 260). Scattered coins of Elizabeth, and Mary and Francis lay further to the west and may have been lost on the road skirting the Commendator's house. No sixteenth century coins were recovered from the **southern sector**. Continuing activity in **Period VI** was recorded by coins of James VI, Charles I and II, and two double tournois of Frederic Henri de Nassau (90 and 91), the latter belonging to one of a number of types of French provincial copper coins, which seem to have been accepted into circulation in seventeenth century Scotland.. These were concentrated in the western part of the **central sector** (Figure 10.46d), but were scarce in the area to the north-west of the Commendator's house. These indicate continuing traffic on the **Period V** roadway in the seventeenth century, while wear indicates they may have continued to accumulate until the eighteenth century. Scattered coins from the **southern sector**, field wall (610), **Fey Field** (46) and **Museum Garden** (51 and 62) extend the distribution into what seems to have been open ground surrounding the seventeenth century church.

The Hand-Built Dark Age Pottery

Ewan Campbell

There are four different fabrics of these hand-built wares. The most interesting sherd is 4a, which has a grass-marked base. This technique of production is characteristic of Souterrain Ware of north-eastern Ireland, a coarse cooking ware found mainly on settlement sites in Antrim and Down (Ryan 1973). It dates from the eighth century (Baillie 1986) perhaps to the twelfth century. The form and fabric of 4a is similar to Souterrain Ware though this needs confirmation by thin section. Souterrain Ware is confined to Ireland except for a few sherds from Iona, where there was also local production of the type (Campbell & Lane 1988). Grass-marked bases are also found on Viking period vessels from the Outer Hebrides (Lane 1990), but the geology of the inclusions is very different. The same technique is found on Cornish pottery of the eighth century and later (Preston-Jones & Rose 1986). In the Irish and Cornish areas, the production of grass-marked pottery post-dates the period of importation of E ware, as shown by stratigraphic separation at sites where both wares occur (Campbell 1991, 39).

Vessel 2 has a rim form similar to that of Souterrain Ware, and Vessel 5 is also similar, though these are all in quite different fabrics. The two sherds of Vessel 3 are in yet another coarse fabric which could be Souterrain Ware. Given the evidence for the local production of copies of Souterrain Ware at Iona, a similar process could have taken place at Whithorn. These wares should date within the eighth to twelfth century period.

1* Body sherd from shoulder region, starting to turn outwards towards rim. Fabric grass-tempered, soft, silty with no grits. Black with orange surfaces. Exterior sooted. T 5–7 mm (**549**).

2* Rim of bucket-shaped vessel, simple flattened top, slightly inturned. Fabric soft, silty, occasional large organic inclusion cavities, rock fragments and tiny quartz grains. Black, carbon-rich clay. Size 3 × 3 cm, T 9 mm (**431**).

3a and b Two small bodysherds from same vessel. Fabric coarse, gritty, with abundant angular to rounded sandstone fragments, poorly sorted, up to 6 mm., and occasional quartz and mica. Grey-brown with lighter margins. **a**) (**539**), **b**) (**533**).

4a* Basal angle of cooking pot, bucket-shaped form. Base and basal angle grass-marked. Thick internal carbon deposits. Fabric medium hard, coarse, with common large inclusions, poorly sorted rock fragments up to 5 mm, occasional quartz. Black with orange oxidised patches. Size 3 × 3 cm, T 8 mm (**252.06**).

4b Body sherd, probably from same vessel as **a**. Size 5 × 4 cm, T 7 mm (**532**).

5 Basal angle of thick-walled cooking pot. Fabric medium hard, coarse blocky texture, orange to dark grey. Inclusions abundant large quartz, feldspar and golden mica, poorly sorted, sub-angular to angular, up to 2 mm. Sherd disintegrating. Internal carbon deposits (**535**).

Context (PH). Four sherds (3a and b, 4b and 5) came from **Period V** graves, a fifth (1) from a pebble surface (549) over the **Period IV** rubble deposit (430), and the last two (2 and 4a) from contexts ascribed to **Period III**. The distribution of the sherds is illustrated in Figure 10.47. There is a marked concentration around Building III/35 and, as there is only one sherd (5) from the **Period IV** *outer zone*, the **Period III/3** settlement is an appropriate context for these poorly-stratified finds which may therefore date to the later-tenth or earlier-eleventh century. A small group of coarse oxidised sherds (MP03) may be of similar, or earlier date.

10.47 The hand-built pottery (PY07) and the distribution of sherds possibly originating in the **Period III/3** settlement.

The Glass Rings

Jennifer Price

Two possible ring fragments (GS04.5–6) belong to a tradition of glass manufacture current in Britain in the late first millennium AD. The glass is much heavier than equivalent fragments of soda glass would be, and there is little doubt that the composition includes a high proportion of lead. High-lead glassworking is known from tenth century contexts at Lincoln and Gloucester, and has also been

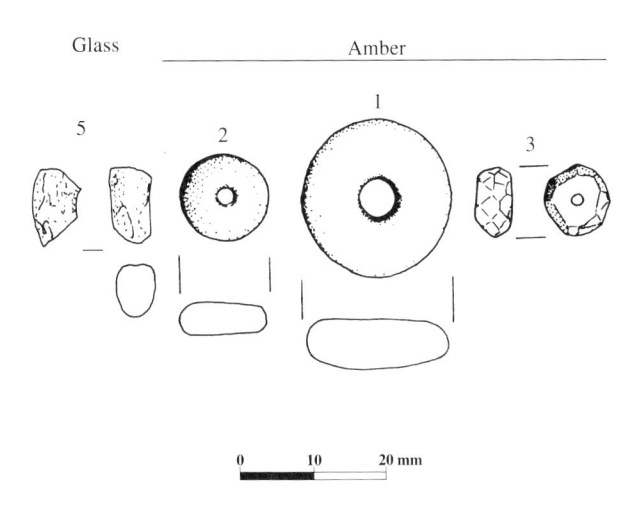

10.48 The amber beads and fragment of glass ring.

recognized at York and probably Jarrow (Bayley 1987, 251–3). At this date high lead glassworking appears to be confined to the production of small objects such as rings, and these have been found at York, Lincoln, Gloucester, Winchester and elsewhere.

GS04.5–6 Finger Rings (?)
5* Fragment, asymmetrical plano-convex section. Pale yellow. Smooth layer of pale weathering over all surfaces. Part of hoop expanding towards bezel?. Very heavy.
H 8–10; max T 4.8; ID approx 24 **411.04**

6 Curved fragment, oval section. Pale yellow. weathering on most surfaces. Part of hoop, very heavy.
Section 5.8 × 6.4; L 10 **533**

Context (PH). The fragments came from debris surrounding Building IV/7 (No. 5) and a **Period V** grave in the eastern part of the **central sector** (No. 6). No. 5 was probably deposited in the mid-twelfth century, but both pieces could have originated in **Period III** deposits of the tenth and earlier-eleventh centuries.

The Amber

Andrew Nicholson

A small collection of amber comprised three beads (01), a lump (02) and two groups of tiny fragments (03). The earliest pieces (1.1, 1.2 and 2.1) came from **Period III** contexts, and probably reflect increased Viking activity in the Irish Sea in the second half of the ninth century. It is probable that the material, if not the items themselves, is of Scandinavian origin, though finds from Armagh record amber working in the Irish Sea province before the Viking Age (Briggs 1985, 102).

Beads (AM01.1–3)

Two annular beads (1 and 2) came from a **Period III/2** building (III/13, 1) and a broadly contemporary grave (III/55, 2), and are similar to beads from Viking burials on Colonsay and Islay (Ritchie 1993, 85 & 89, Fig. 75), and tenth century examples from Lloyds Bank, York (MacGregor 1982, 89, Fig. 47). A third faceted bead (3) from demolition deposits (727) in the west wing of the manse is probably nineteenth century.

1* Golden-brown translucent annular amber bead.
ED 20 T.5 PD 5 **300.02**

2* Honey-coloured translucent annular amber bead. Outer surface has golden coloured degradation or weathering, forming sugar-like crystallisation.
ED 12 T.5 PD 2.5 **305.04**

3* Golden-brown faceted amber bead. Flattened annular shape with circumferential edge cut in irregular facets.
ED 9 T.5 PD 1.4 **727**

Lump (AM02)

A small faceted lump from the waterborne silts in the **southern sector** (309.02) also pertains to **Period III**. It showed evidence of working, but cannot be related with contemporary manufacturing debris.

1 Small amber lump with conchoidal fractures Fractured surfaces suggest deliberate flaking in some places rather than wear or abrasion.
L 8 W 5 T.4 **309.02**

Fragments (AM03.1–2).

A small quantity of powdered fragments was displaced into a **Period V** grave in the north-western part of the graveyard and may have originated in **Period III** deposits. A second group of fragments, including a small faceted lump, came from a fourteenth century hearth in the **southern sector**.

1 Crushed fragments of amber.
540

2 Small quantity of crushed amber including lump with conchoidal fracture lines.
L 5 W 5 T 3.5 **522**

The Non-Ferrous Metals

Andrew Nicholson and Peter Hill

The excavation produced large groups of copper-alloy and leads objects and a small assemblage of silver and gold. There are few links between the finished artefacts in these various materials, but concentrations of metalworking debris and scrap metal record reveal intermittent evidence of an evolving non-ferrous metalworking tradition. There are thus both spatial and straigraphic links between silver objects and crucibles with traces of silver at the close of **Period I** and in **Period II** (Figure 10.87), and there is a similar, if more complex pattern among the debris ascribed to **Period IV** (Figures 6.24 and 10.88). EDXRF analysis of most crucible and mould fragments, and a small proportion of the metal objects has identified some of the links between artefacts, waste and industrial ceramics, and a more comprehensive survey would probably reveal a long sequence of evolving practices from the earlier-sixth century.

The Copper Alloy

Andrew Nicholson

1,236 pieces of copper alloy were split into forty-one morphological groups. The finds were cleaned and stabilised by the National Museum of Scotland and the York Archaeological Trust Laboratories. Most of the objects were well preserved with clear surface detail, and only required light cleaning. Several pieces underwent further laboratory examination for tooling marks, traces of gilding or plating. Energy Dispersive X-Ray Fluorescence (EDXRF) analysis of a small number of pieces was undertaken by the University of Bradford. The most significant groups of objects were dress accoutrements – long pins, belt buckles and strap ends – whose use and style reflect the varying cultural traditions influencing Whithorn in **Periods I–IV**. Later finds of the thirteenth-sixteenth centuries are matched closely by objects from London and other sites, and reflect an apparent cultural uniformity in later medieval Britain. A small, but important group of objects lacks close parallels in the British Isles. This includes a crescent-headed stick pin (BZ14.7) and a plated chape (BZ30.1) from **Period I** deposits, and a speculum handle (BZ30.4) from the **Period II** burial chapel. These and other items are likely to reflect the high status of Whithorn as an ecclesiastical centre and its widespread contacts in continental Europe. A large group of scrap metal and other waste reveals a wide range of industrial activities spanning the early medieval evolution of the site.

The earlier deposits (**Periods I-III**), produced relatively small numbers of finished objects, but included significant stratified finds. Manufacturing waste was more abundant, and successive groups of workshop debris record casting in the earlier-sixth

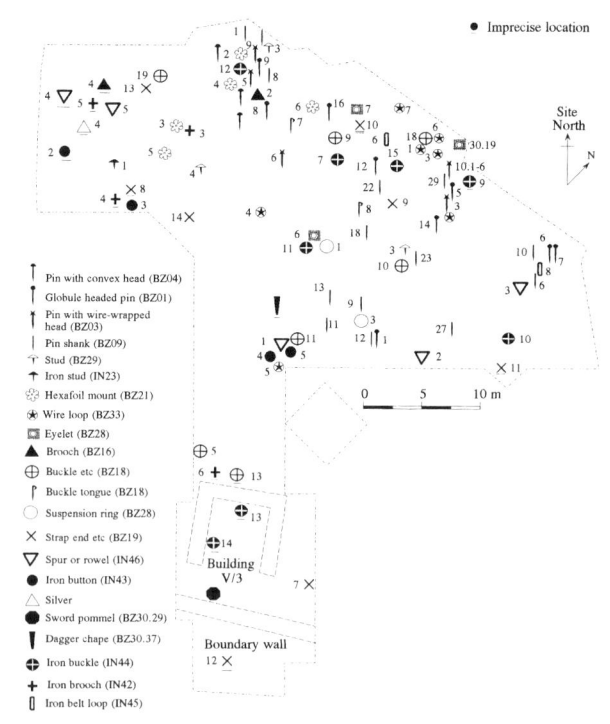

10.49 Dress items and related objects from **Period V** graves, overlying layers, and adjacent deposits.

century, and sheet-working in the seventh. A large group of finds ascribed to **Period IV** included an important series of stick pins (Figure 6.35), and further groups of casting and manufacturing debris. A large proportion of these finds had been displaced by **Period V** graves, and, although spatial analysis has revealed workshop areas (Figures 6.24, 31, 34, 10.71 and 88), the stratigraphic record was too compromised to provide a coherent sequence of diagnostic artefact types. A third large group of finds recovered from the **Period V** graveyard and the overlying deposits was dominated by dress-fittings (Figure 10.49). Many of these are datable to the fourteenth and fifteenth centuries, and the group probably encompasses a relatively small number of objects accompanying burials, and a larger number lost on its surface. Pins predominated in a last large group of finds from the manse and related deposits, while the most recent features produced a range of machine-made objects.

Wire pins (BZ01–10)

The excavation produced three hundred and eighty-four wire pins and pin shanks which are subdivided into ten morphological groups. The series of wire pins seems to have begun during **Period V**, reflecting changing costume styles with an increased use of pins to attach head-dresses and veils (Egan and

Pritchard 1991, 297). The first large group came from the later graves of **Period V/2** dated to the late fourteenth or earlier-fifteenth century. Most of the pins came from the **Period VI** manse, with concentrations in the floor deposits, external surfaces and late-nineteenth century demolition deposits. The floors produced lines of pins which had presumably lodged between the floorboards and had retained their positions as these decayed. These groups include a range of pin types. Some may have been contemporaneous, but the mixture probably reflects the long life of the flooring. Full details of the pins are recorded in the excavation archive.

Pins with globular heads (BZ01)

A hundred and seventeen pins had globular heads (BZ01), with a preferential length range of 21mm to 35mm. Many of the pin heads were wire-wrapped as in BZ03, but were subsequently moulded in a clamp to produce a globular form. Sixteen examples came from the **Period V** graveyard (Figure 10.49) and eight from the overlying buildings and surfaces of **Period V/3–5**. Most of the globular-headed pins came from the **Period VI** manse with concentrations in the floor deposits in the west wing (715), external surfaces (722) and late-nineteenth century demolition deposits. Several had a silvery plating on the shank, and three of these (29, 37 and 111) were analysed by EDXRF. Two pins (29 and 111) were made of copper and plated with leaded zinc, and the third (23) of leaded brass, was plated with zinc. A fourth pin shank (9.61) was of copper or copper alloy, again with leaded zinc plate. Most of these pins can be attributed to the eighteenth or nineteenth century, and scattered earlier finds from the **Period V** graveyard and overlying surfaces were probably intrusive.

Pins with flat round heads (BZ02)

Forty pins with flat round heads (BZ02) ranged in length from 20mm to 39mm. Twenty-four pins came from late-nineteenth century contexts in the former manse and most of the others need not be earlier than the mid-nineteenth century.

Pins with wire-wrapped heads (BZ03)

The second largest group comprised eighty-eight pins with wire-wrapped heads (BZ03.1–88). These are commonly found in fourteenth to seventeenth century contexts on other sites (Oakley 1979a, 260–1; A.R.Goodall 1991, 152; Egan and Pritchard 1991, 299–301). Analysis of complete lengths shows a peak around 29–30mm within a range of 17mm to 45mm. Oakley indicates that pins less than 30mm tend to be later (sixteenth/seventeenth century). Eleven pins came from **Period V** contexts including five (3, 5–8) from the graveyard and four from the overlying surfaces and buildings (**Period V/3** and **4**, Figure 10.49) indicating that they were current from the early-fifteenth century (p 361). Most examples came from the **Period VI** manse with concentrations (19–30) in the floor deposits of the west wing (715), and overlying demolition deposits (738, 53–76). These finds indicate that the pins remained in use until the late-eighteenth century and possibly beyond.

Pins with convex heads (BZ04)

Eight pins had convex heads (BZ04), apparently soldered on, with varying degrees of curvature. Four examples (1–4) came from the **Period V** graveyard, three from the penultimate graves (539) of the end of **Period V/2** (Figure 10.49). An example from Northampton is dated to the late-fifteenth century (Oakley 1979a, Fig. 113 No.161), and was contemporary there with the long pins with wire-wrapped heads (BZ10 below). The Whithorn pins seem to be slightly earlier probably dating to the late-fourteenth century or start of the fifteenth (p 357), a pattern matched in London (Egan and Pritchard 1991, 299). The remaining four pins came from the **Period VI** manse and topsoil and were probably displaced from earlier deposits.

Miscellaneous pins and pin shanks (BZ05–9)

The excavation produced a safety pin (BZ05), a pin with a wedge-shaped head (BZ08), three pins with plated flat heads (BZ06), one pin with a plated round head (BZ07), and a hundred and seventeen pin shanks without heads (BZ09). The pin with a wedge-shaped head came from the debris (630) flanking Building V/4 and so probably dates to *c*. 1500 AD (p 260). The plated pins came from the **Period VI** manse and belong with the related larger groups recorded above. The pin shanks ranged in length from 3mm to 59mm and are of interest due to their number. Four (1–4) came from **Period III** and **IV** contexts, but were probably intrusions from later deposits. A relatively large group (5–21) from the **Period V** graveyard (Figure 10.49) was concentrated in the later graves (**Period V/2**) and cleaning contexts (543), indicating that wire pins were introduced in the later-fourteenth century.

Long pins with wire-wrapped heads (BZ10)

Thirteen very long pins with wire-wrapped heads (BZ10.1–13) ranged in length from 45 to 60mm. Six pins thrust through a snippet of leather (1–6) came from a late **Period V/2** grave (539, Figure 10.49), two others came from graveyard cleaning contexts (543), another from an overlying surface (617.01), a seventh from a land-drain cutting the graveyard and an eighth from the rubbish (630) abutting Building V/4. These contexts indicate that long wire-wrapped pins had a relatively brief currency perhaps beginning at the close of the fourteenth century, and

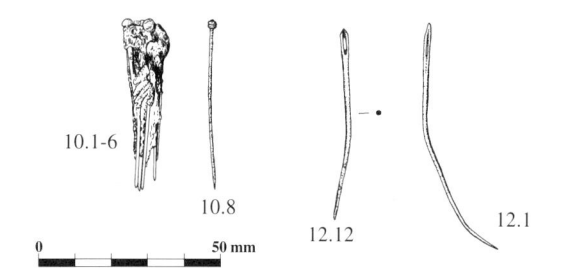

10.50 Pins and needles (BZ10 and 12).

not lasting beyond the end of the fifteenth. They are matched by fifteenth century examples from Northampton (Oakley 1979a, 262–3) and Waltham Abbey (Huggins 1976, 115), and even longer (up to 113mm) fourteenth century examples from London (Egan and Pritchard 1991, Fig. 204).

Thimbles (BZ11)

Twelve thimbles were recovered, mainly from modern and recent contexts in and around the manse. Ten of these are datable to 1900–1920. The other two are nineteenth century types (A. Penman Pers. Comm.).

Needles (BZ12)

Only three of the twenty-three needles (BZ12.1–23) were complete, two were broken at the top of the eye and five broken at the base of the eye. In all these cases some evidence for the method of eye manufacture could be ascertained, and an approximation of complete length determined. The remaining 'needles' comprised shanks with greater diameters than pins (<1mm) and less than stick pins (c. >3mm). The presence of a tapering point differentiated needle shanks from wire, which was usually of a similar diameter. Two main forms of needle eye have been identified (Rollins 1981, 7), those with punched eyes, usually through a flattened head, and those where the shank is split and welded back together at the top, referred to as Y-eyed. The head of a Y-eyed needle is usually lentoid, and may also have been flattened slightly. At Coppergate the identifiable heads occurred in a ratio of 65% punched to 35% Y-eyed, with slightly shifting ratios throughout the Anglo-Scandinavian period (Ottoway 1992, 544–7). Two early needles from the **Period I/3** graveyard (1, 81.01, Grave I/56) and a **Period II** hall (3, II/6, 254) were Y-eyed, as indeed were all the identifiable heads except one, a part-finished needle (11) with a flattened head from the **Period V** graveyard surface (543). The lengths of complete or near-complete examples ranged from 35mm to 73mm with a noticeable difference between those broken at the base of the eye (35mm–46mm), and those with intact eyes (60mm to 73mm). One needle (14) had been formed from a strip which had been folded longitudinally below the head and worked up into a round-sectioned tapering point. The needles were subdivided into fine, standard and coarse sub-groups, and most of the copper-alloy examples were of standard size. An anomalous coarse example (2) came from a secure **Period I** deposit (55) in the **southern sector**.

Almost all the needles came from a restricted area in the southern part of the **central sector** and, though widely scattered stratigraphically, most had probably originated in **Period IV** workshops in the *inner precinct* and south east part of the *outer zone* (Figures 6.26a and b, p 242). The distributions of iron and copper alloy needles differed, indicating that each had specific uses and had been deposited in areas of specialised craft activity. An earlier group from the same area coincided with a concentration of iron needles in the open ground between the halls and ecclesiastical buildings (Figure 10.98).

1* Complete long, fine needle. Shank split and reformed to create eye.
L 72, D below eye 1.4. Eye slot L 6.5, W 0.7 **81.01**

12* Almost complete standard needle – missing point. Flattened head, eye cut or punched.
L 52, D below head 1.8. Eye L 3.5 W 1.4 **543**

BZ13–15 Long pins

The copper-alloy long pins formed one of the largest coherent groups of artefacts, with chronological and typological links with brooches, bone (pp 496-7) and iron pins (pp 418-9), and moulds (p 400). The primary function of these long pins was to secure a cloak around the neck, as seen in burials where the deceased is interred fully clothed. Viking burials at Ballateare and Cronk Moor, Isle of Man have pins at the shoulder and chest respectively (Fanning 1983b, 27, 30). The Anglo-Saxons preferred to use brooches (Owen-Crocker 1986, 52, 68, 117–8, 133, 151), with the notable exceptions of a discrete group of linked pins in the seventh century, and the use of smaller pins associated with female headgear in the seventh and eighth centuries (Owen-Crocker 1986, 102; Webster 1991, 83 and 89).

The pin series at Whithorn commences in the earlier-sixth century with the manufacture and use of nail-headed pins (p 403). These pins have Romano-British antecedents (Stevenson 1955, 283, 286), and moulds for similar pins have been recovered from Dunadd and the Mote of Mark (Laing 1976, 67). These only have the matrices for two pins, but the moulds from Whithorn have five or more, indicating a greater production volume, and mitigating against the suggestion that these pins were '... less popular among the Southern Picts or the British south of the Forth-Clyde line..' (Laing 1976, 60). The stick pins continue into the seventh, and even into the eighth centuries, later than has previously been supposed (Laing 1976, 60). The hipped lower shank of the early pins distinguishes them from the later forms where the tapering shank is smooth, and the lower shank either rounded or square in section. This allows them to be distinguished despite the similarity of their heads (c.f. Laing's comments on 'mushroom'-headed pins; Laing 1976, 65). The longer pins virtually disappear in the eighth and ninth centuries probably due to the Anglian preference for brooches. Examples in silver (SR6) and iron (IN40.52) suggest continued insular contacts. A group of shorter pins (BZ13.1–3, IN40.51, 53–56) may have been used with female dress. Long pins returned to Whithorn in the late-ninth century, indicating increased Hiberno-Norse activity, either through trading or settlement. The continuation of this class into the thirteenth century follows the Irish model, whereas in the rest of Scotland they were being replaced by the medieval annular brooch (Fanning 1983a, 329).

Ornamental pins (BZ13)

This small group of seven pieces (BZ13.1–7) accommodated those pins which did not fall into the distinct morphological group of stick pins, though they have been included with them in other publications (e.g. Laing 1975) as they do form part of a typological sequence.

Three of the pins (1–3) are ball- or club-headed, 41mm to 60mm long, with a pronounced medial swelling to the shank, in the middle of which a transverse groove passed around the pin. The markings around the groove of the best preserved example (1) indicated that the groove had been cut into the pin, and later worn by a cord or light thong. This method of securing a garment with a loop from the head to mid-shank has been postulated for ringed pins (Fanning 1990), and would appear to have been more widespread than first considered. It may also account for the hipping noticeable on other classes of 'Early Christian' pins (Laing 1975, 1976, Stevenson 1955, see BZ14 below). Two pins (1 and 2) came from the **Period II** rubbish dump (303) and the third from the adjacent spread of burnt debris (339.01) to the south of the chapel (Figure 10.98). All three probably date to the early- to mid-ninth century, while a plated ball-headed pin head (7) from **Period III** pond silts (309.02) is of similar type and may have been lost at roughly the same time. The shank scar is too small for it to have been a true stick pin. These pins were probably of Anglo-Saxon origin and closely comparable examples have been found in seventh-eighth century contexts at Barking Abbey (Webster and Backhouse 1991, 92). There are similar bone pins with transverse grooves from the Broch of Burrian dated to the eighth century (MacGregor 1974, 70), whilst others from Buiston Crannog probably date to shortly after 630 AD (A Crone, Pers. Comm.).

A spiral-headed pin (4), from a sump (721) abutting the eighteenth century manse, probably originated in an underlying deposit of **Period I** or **II**.

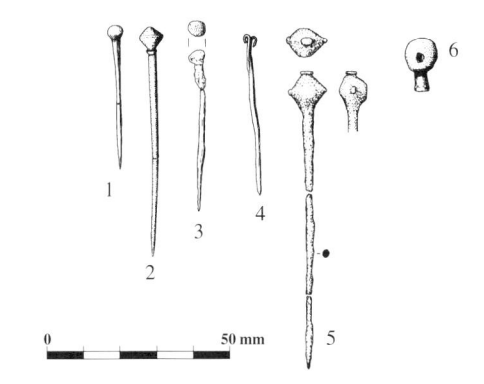

10.51 Ornamental pins (BZ13).

It is directly paralleled by an example from Culbin Sands, Moray and another from 'Western Scotland' in the Mann collection in Glasgow (Laing 1976, 71), and perhaps dates to the eighth century. A knobbed ball-headed pin (5) came from a fourteenth century surface in the **southern sector** (517.01), but appears to be an undecorated example of the late-tenth/early-eleventh century semi-bramble headed pins from St Audoen's Dublin (Armstrong 1922, Fig. 4 No.8). A probable pin head (6) with its shank cut off came from a **Period V** grave, but was close to a concentration of nodular copper-alloy waste in the **northern sector** (Figure 10.71) and may have been scrap awaiting recycling.

1* Club headed pin, ovoid-sectioned shank with shallow transverse groove (functional?) in mid-portion.
L 39 Shank MD 2 Head W 4.5. **303**

2* Club-headed pin, transverse groove round shank. Bi-convex head with faint transverse line above middle. Collared neck, shank tapers to a point, with transverse groove below mid-point.
L 60 Head D 6.8 Shank D2.2 **303**

3* Club headed, tin plated pin with hipped shank, in two pieces. Ovoid-sectioned shank, corrosion obscures features, slight transverse groove midway down. Tin-plated leaded bronze
L 42.5 M dia shank. 2 W of head. 5. **339.01**

4* Pin with bifurcated head, round shank. The shank has been split at the upper portion for 15 mm and the ends flattened and out-turned to form a head, the lower 10mm being re-joined to form the upper portion of the shank.
L 43.5 Shank MD 1.7 Head W 3.5. **721**

5* Ball-headed pin with projecting lugs. Shank broken into three pieces. The head has two opposed lugs at the sides, on the circumference of the sphere, and another at the top. At ninety degrees to the opposed lugs one side has a vestigial lug, whilst the opposed face is slightly flattened.
L 78 Head D 11 Shank D 2.8 **517.01**

6* Ornamental globular pin head cut off from shank directly below collar. Two small hemispherical indentations to one side of the head. The item may not be a pin head, but the truncated fragment of another, unrecognisable, object.
L 14.5 Head D 9 Shank D 2.7 **536**

7* Tin-plated ball-head from pin. Scar evidences location of shank.
D 5.5 Shank dia 2.3 **309.02**

Stick pins (BZ14)

Fifty-two stick pins (BZ14.1–52), were mostly Hiberno-Norse types, though seven (1–7) are earlier. Two of the early group (1 and 2) had distinctive bramble heads. One (1) came from workshop debris (85.04) abutting the **Period I/4** 'shrine', which perhaps dates to the early-eighth century. The other (2) had tin plating around the head, and came from a post-medieval deposit (625) in the **Museum Garden**. Three nail-headed stick pins (3–5) are similar to examples from Broch of Burrian (MacGregor 1974, 70), Buiston Crannog, Ayrshire and Culbin Sands, Moray (Stevenson 1955, 285). One (3) came from the gully around Building I/17 (52.03) in the **southern sector** perhaps dating to the later-sixth or early-seventh century. The other two (4 and 5) came from adjacent anachronous contexts (334 and 715) on the south side of the **Period I/2** shrine. One (4) is an unfinished casting and was probably associated with crucible and mould fragments from this area (Figure 10.86). The most likely origin for both is the debris surrounding Building I/1 (pp 79, 403), and probably dating to the first half of the sixth century. A fragment of a hipped shank (6) with scorped zigzag ornament matches the form of other early pins with pronounced hips, rather than the later pins with flattened lower shanks where the flattened section tends to continue the tapering line of the rest of the shank. It came from the debris scattered among waterborne silts (55) in the **southern sector (Period I.10)** and perhaps dates to mid- to late-seventh century. The last of the early pins (7) is a pristine example of an inverse crescent headed pin, with a square upper shank and octagonal lower shank. It came from a **Period 1/3** rubbish deposit (109) and does not have close parallels, although there are related iron pins from the site (IN41.1 and 2, pp 418-9), and a cruder form of crescentic head can be seen in several of the bone pins from the Broch of Burrian (MacGregor 1974, Fig. 5 Nos 33–6).

1* Bramble-headed stick pin. Flat-topped head brambled round the sides by fine cross-hatching. Two transverse collars at neck. Upper shank expands to mid-portion, where it is again double-collared. The lower portion of the shank is octagonal in section, and is broken above the point.
L 51 Head D 6.5 Shank D 3.4 **85.04**

2* Tin-plated bramble-headed stick pin. Brambled with five rings of cast stubby projecting lugs (*c.f.* 1). Upper portion of shank expands, contracting in mid-portion with distinct hipping above flattened lower portion. Broken at point. Leaded gun metal with tin plate.
L 55 Head D 5.3 Shank D 3.2 **625**

3* Nail-headed stick pin. Flat head with faint traces of ?hammer marks on upper surface. Straight round shank.
L 68 Head D 6 Shank D 2.5 **52.03**

4* Unfinished nail-headed pin, plain head with collared neck. Shank squared at neck, becoming rounded as it expands towards mid point, tapers to broken tip. Casting flash on either side of head and shank
L 47.2 Head D 5.5 Shank D 3.1 **334**

5* Nail-headed stick pin, shank broken.
L 30 Head D 6 Shank D 2.8 **715**

6* Hipped lower shank of stick pin. Shank sub-rectangular at hip where it is broken. Decoration down central axis on larger flat surfaces of point, consisting of incised vertical line overstamped by vertical row of punched stabs with a flat-diamond shape.
L 57 W 5.5 **55**

7* Inverted crescent-headed stick pin. Massive pin, crescentic or axe-headed above two transverse lines. Squared projections above grooved neck. Square-section shank expands below neck, continuing straight to the mid-point, where two transverse grooves define a cube. The edges of the cube have been cut back from the lower end, creating small triangular facets, giving a ballustered effect. Below the mid-point the shank is octagonal in section, rounding off at the point. Thin vertical scratch marks run down all sides of the shank. Horizontal wear marks visible on octagonal portion.
L 175 Head W 17 Shank W 4.5 **109**

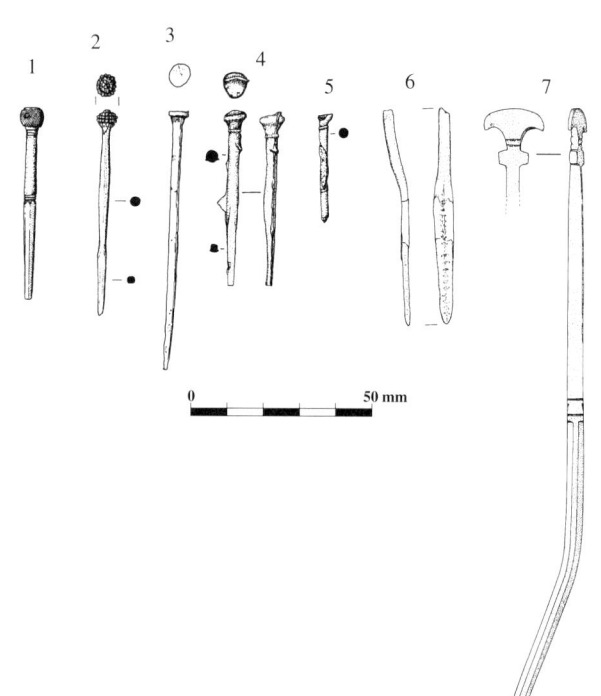

10.52 Early stick pins (BZ14.1–7).

The main group of forty-five stick pins is closely paralleled by finds from Dublin, and is accordingly termed *Hiberno-Norse*. The group probably comprises a series of successive and overlapping types, though the stratigraphic circumstances did not allow its chronological potential to be realised (pp 209–11, 237–9). Eleven pins (8, 9, 10, 14, 16, 20, 25, 28, 40, 46 and 47) came from undisturbed deposits, but four of these were long-lived and poorly stratified, and another was poorly stratified leaving only six pins from securely-stratified chronologically-sensitive contexts. Only three of these (8, 12 and 14) were diagnostic types. Thirteen pins came from **Period V** graves and related contexts and the remainder had been displaced into later deposits, or were recovered from spoil (903). These were scattered widely in the *inner precinct* and *outer zone* of the **Period IV** settlement (Figure 6.35) and no clear patterns can be discerned. The group is

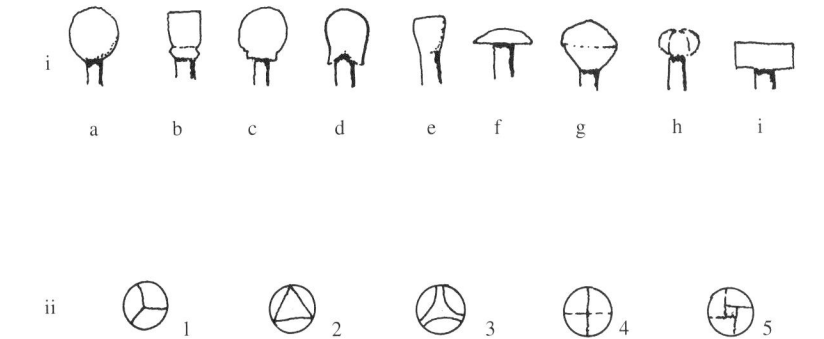

10.53 Hiberno-Norse stick-pins (after O'Rahilly 1973).
i. Head forms: a Round, b Squared spatulate, c Disc spatulate, d Rounded spatulate, e Undifferentiated, f Stud, g Club, h Lobed, i Crutch.
ii. Head decoration types (seen from above).

however likely to have included stray losses of personal possessions, and perhaps stock lost by market traders. There was no evidence that copper-alloy stick-pins were made at Whithorn in this period, although iron examples may have been made and plated on site (pp 245–6).

Thirty-nine of these stick pins (8–46) had recognisable head types, and generally conformed to the classifications of stick pins from Dublin (O'Rahilly 1973). These were categorised by head type and sub-divided in some cases by the top decorative order (Figure 10.53). Even those pins not exactly corresponding to Dublin types could be seen as derived from, or associated with such types, with the exception of a pin with a small cubic head (45) which lacks parallels. Due to the stratigraphic problems, the Dublin classification has been used as a guide in assessing the date and relative sequence of the pins.

The earliest of this group of stick pins (8) is a failed casting (complete with flash 8b) of a round-headed pin. It was found in the mid-ninth century ploughsoil (399), but could have originated in a later, unrecognized earth-floored building. As a ninth century piece this is two centuries earlier than Irish examples, and may indicate a continuation from the ball-headed pins of the seventh century such as those deriving from the moulds from Mote of Mark (Laing 1976, 67). It is broadly contemporary with a similar bone pin from Freswick Links, Caithness (Curle 1939, Pl.XLVIII No.8). Three other round-headed pins were found (9–11), one badly corroded (11) and two (9 and 10) with Type 3 head decoration, the slightly lobed zones containing ring-and-dot ornament. No. 9 came from the rubble (400) banked against the Northumbrian terrace in **Period III/2** and may have been relatively early, although this deposit was contaminated with later finds. The other two pins come from a relatively late (**Period IV.7**) ash deposit in Building IV/10 and a **Period V** building (V/2a) in the **southern sector**. A similar pin from Dublin (Armstrong 1922, 73) had an amber chip in a round setting laid out in this pattern, and may be a precursor of the Whithorn find. All the round-headed pins had plain shanks.

The next group comprises twelve pins with spatulate heads (12–23). The earliest (12 and 13) with collared rectangular heads, were not fully developed, and may also be seen as forerunners of the crutch-headed pins (pp 369-70). No. 12 had been displaced into a **Period V** grave and No. 13 was unstratified. The vertical hatching between horizontal lines on No. 12 also appears on a pin with a more obvious crutch head from the Hebrides (Close-Brooks and Maxwell 1974, Fig. 2 GT974). Five pins (14–18) had squared spatulate heads, generally collared, though only one (16) had a decorated face, a square of four punched dots. One of these (14) was securely stratified in a relatively late (*Stage 7*) **Period IV** building (IV/9) in the **southern sector**, and a second (15) might have been displaced from a broadly contemporary context. Two others (16 and 17) came from adjacent **Period V** surfaces in the western part of the **northern sector**, and the last (18) from a **Period V/4** deposit (630) abutting Building V/4. Three pins (19–21) have disc-shaped spatulate heads. Two (20 and 21) were undecorated, the third (19) displays a cross of five punched dots on both faces. One (20) came from a pit in the **northern sector** (434.02) truncated by **Period V** graves. The others were effectively unstratified. Two nearly identical rounded spatulate pins (22 and 23) have heads which appear to be an intermediate stage between rounded and disc spatulate, with two projecting lugs beginning to form a collar. One (23) came from the graveyard surface; the other (22), from a fourteenth century building (V/3) in the **southern sector**, may have been displaced from underlying debris (415.01) of the later stages of **Period IV**. All the spatulate pins had plain shanks.

The third group comprised three pins (24–26) with undifferentiated heads and a range of decorative designs. One (24) was unstratified, a second (25) came from the poorly stratified **Period IV** rubble band (430) on the west side of the **central sector**, and the third (26) may have originated in the **Period IV.7–9** debris (415.01) in the **southern sector**.

A group of five stud headed pins (27–31) comprises one with a plain head (27) and four (28–31) with radiating grooves on top. These are sometimes described as 'mushroom' headed pins (Laing 1976, 65). The plain-headed pin (27) has long pendant triangles around the neck, whilst the others have plain shanks. Similar pins from Dublin have been dated to the mid-eleventh to mid-thirteenth centuries, and the Whithorn examples possibly pertained to the latter part of this period, although none was securely stratified. Earlier discussions have shown the Romano-British origins of this style (Fowler 1963, 132), and it has been argued that they were a fifth/sixth century form contemporaneous with nail-headed pins (Laing 1976, 65), and with a local example from Luce Sands. The shank morphology (pp 362-3) is, however, sufficiently clear to distinguish the early and late forms with similar heads.

The largest group comprised eight club-headed pins (32–39) with a variety of type divisions. No two pins are quite alike in their decoration. Two pins (32–33) have Type 1 heads. The neck of one (32) is decorated with vertical rows of diagonal stabs between vertical grooves while the other (33) has vertical rows of dots between diagonal grooves. A similar pin (34) with three chips in the top arranged like a Type 1 head also has vertical rows of diagonal stabs on the neck, while another (35) with a Type 2 head has vertical rows of dots between vertical grooves. The grooves on the head of the Type 3 pin (36) continue down the neck, going beyond an interupture zone of dots between transverse grooves. A similar pin (37) has a Type 3 top becoming a sub-triskele pattern around the head and vertical grooves on the neck extending beyond an interupture zone of transverse dots. One (39) of the two pins with Type 5 heads (38–39) has vertical rows of dots between vertical grooves continuing up the neck and onto the head, and is almost exactly matched by a pin from the Hebrides (Close-Brooks and Maxwell 1974, Fig. 3 GT979). The vertical dot arrangement can also be seen on an Irish pin with a Type 3 head (Armstrong 1922, Fig. 1 No.12), probably from Dublin, whilst the other Whithorn pin (38) has them confined to the neck. Four of these pins (32, 33, 36 and 38) came from the **Period V** graveyard and three (34, 35 and 37) from later contexts in the same area. Their absence from earlier, stratified deposits indicates that they may be a relatively late type – as in Dublin – perhaps dating to the later-twelfth/earlier-thirteenth century. There is a closely related series of plated and unplated iron club-headed pins (IN41.3–7), though from rather earlier contexts (p 419).

A small group of anomalous pins (40–44) is similar to the club-headed series, but does not necessarily belong with it. One pin (40) has a flattened club-head, which appears to fall between the stud- and club-headed groups. It has a pendant triangle motif around the neck similar to those on stud-headed pins, but its top bears a triangular design of four ring-and-dots, similar in execution to those on the crutch-headed ring pins (BZ15.6–9). It came from a cobble surface (438) ascribed to **Period III/3** and should, perhaps, be disassociated from the superficially similar, but rather later, club-headed pins. The remaining four pins (41–44) came from the **Period V** graveyard. A plain pin (41) with a rounded head also falls between the club- and stud-headed groups, but lacks the characteristic neck decoration. It is more corroded than most, but appears to lack any markings. An undecorated pin (42) is also similar to the club-headed pins, but has a very small head closer in size to a bead-headed pin. A three-lobed pin (43) has a Type 3 style head with pendant triangles round the neck, and is closer in form to the club-headed series than to the true lobed pins found in Dublin, which are absent from Whithorn. The fifth stick pin (44) has a well-defined triskele pattern around the head, and pendant triangles above two transverse grooves around the neck, confirming its kinship with the club-headed pins. Other Irish triskele pins have a range of neck motifs similar to those on the club-headed series. These are now known to date to around the twelfth century, and it is no longer safe to interpret the triskele motif as a survival from pre-Christian La Tene art.

The last stick pin (45), also from the **Period V** graveyard, is cube-headed, and lacks immediate parallels in copper alloy. This simple pin may be a fourteenth century form which is unrepresented in the Irish series. A crutch-headed stick pin (46), possibly a ring pin (see BZ15 below), was stolen from an early finds display and was thus not available for detailed examination.

Five stick-pin shanks (47–51) include one which was securely stratified, while the remainder had been displaced into **Period V** graves and other anachronous contexts.

8a* Miscast ball-headed stick pin. Head and neck of undecorated ball-headed pin, with casting flash on vertical planar axis. Leaded bronze. 8b Flat and globular casting debris associated with 8a.
L 13 Head D 6 **399.02**

9* Round-headed stick pin (Type 3 head). Ball/round-head with Type 3 trilobate decoration. Tripartite Small head in relation to shank, with undecorated neck.
L 78 Head D 4.3 Shank D 3.5 **400**

10* Round-headed stick pin (Type 3 head) with ring-and-dot in each division. Plain neck, straight shank broken at tip.
L 76 Head D 4.7 Shank D 3 **456.03**

11* Round-headed stick pin (Type 3 head) with trilobate head decoration and plain neck.
L 77 Head D 4.4 Shank D 3 **520.02**

12* Rectangular spatulate-headed stick pin, head divided by two transverse lines, between which is a field of parallel vertical lines. Two faint lines on top. Squared projection above neck, straight shank.
L 99.3 Head W 7 Shank D 3 **535**

13* Squared spatulate-headed stick pin. Possible sub-class, the head being between a square-spatulate and a crutch, with an angled taper to the plain neck. Shank expands in upper portion, continuing as a straight shank to the point. Bent at mid-point and lower portion.
L 109 Head W 5 Shank D 3 **903**

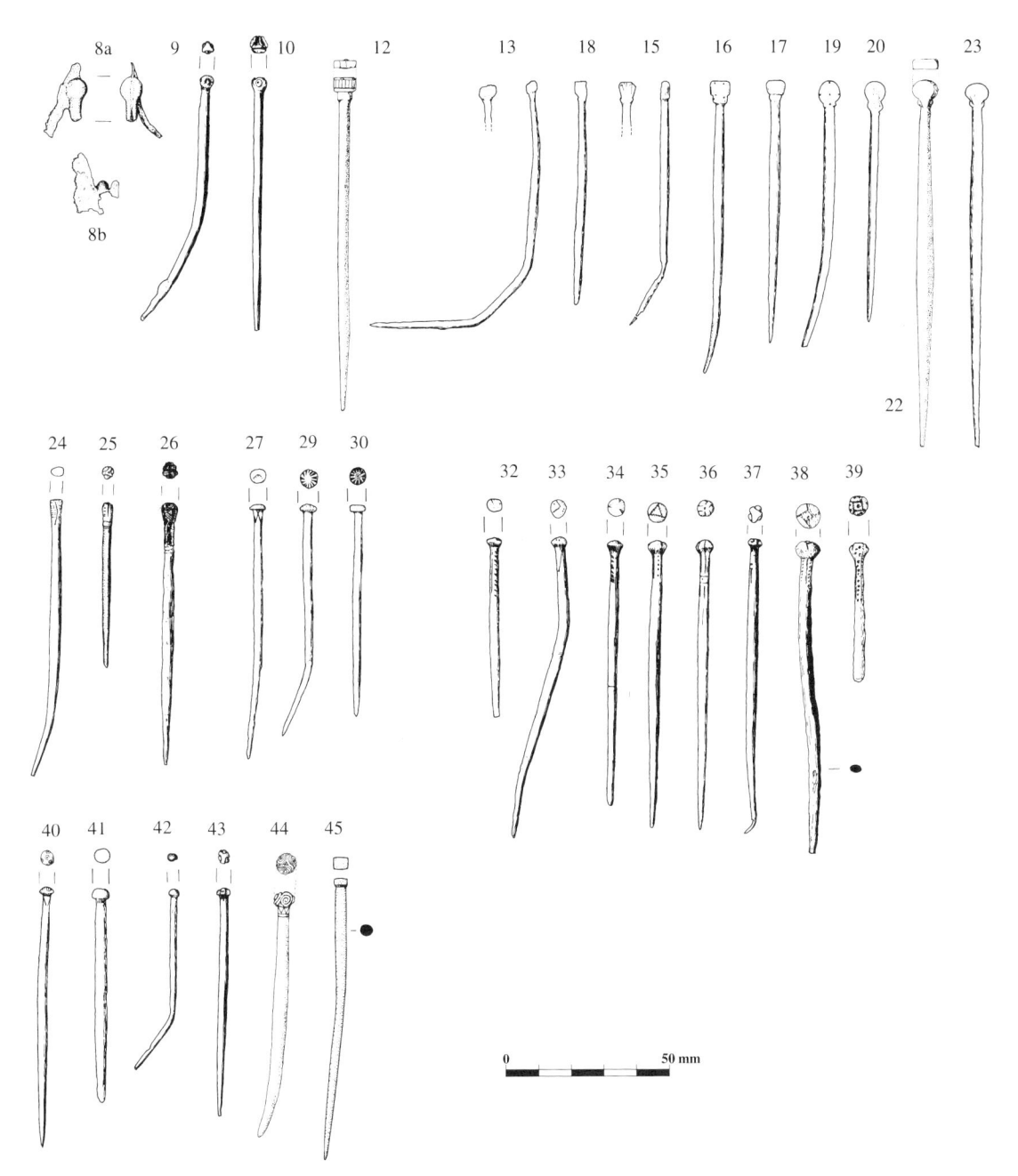

10.54 Hiberno-Norse stick pins (BZ14.7).

14* Squared spatulate-headed stick pin. Plain head with squared projections above plain neck.

L 58 Head W 4 Shank D 3 **414.03**

15* Squared spatulate-headed stick pin. Head tapers down to projecting lugs above plain neck. Shank expands to mid-point then tapers to tip. Bent in lower portion, below which it is badly corroded. Tip broken off (but retained).

L 74 Head W 5 Shank D 3 **506.01**

16* Squared spatulate stick pin. Four dots on both faces. Squared projections above plain neck. Shank expands to mid-point then tapers to tip. Lower portion slightly bent.

L 87 Head W 6 Shank D 3.4 **550**

17* Squared spatulate-headed stick pin. Plain head tapers down slightly to squared-projection/collared neck. Shank expands to mid-point then tapers to tip. Horizontal scratches on upper portion of shank possibly wear marks, but fairly regular so may well be file marks.

L 78 Head W 6 Shank D 3.3 **616.06**

18* Squared spatulate-headed stick pin. Badly corroded, shank expands to midpoint then tapers to tip.

L 66.2 Head W 3.8 Shank D 3 **630**

19* Disc spatulate-headed stick pin. Five dots in cruciform pattern on one face, above pointed projecting lugs. Shank expands slightly from plain neck to mid-point before tapering to broken tip.

L 79 Head W 6.7 Shank D 3.6 **926**

20* Disc spatulate-headed stick pin. Plain head above pointed projections. Straight shank tapering in lower portion to tip.

L 71.2 Head W 6.5 Shank D 2.9 **434.02**

21* Disc spatulate-headed stick pin. Plain head and neck. Straight shank tapering in lower portion.
L 65 Head W 6 Shank D 3 **741**

22* Rounded spatulate-headed stick pin. Plain head above pointed projecting lugs. Shank expands to mid-point then tapers to broken tip.
L 109 Head W 8 Shank D 3.8 **506.01**

23* Rounded or disc spatulate-headed stick pin. Identical to 22, and probably from same mould. Plain head above pointed projecting lugs. Shank expands to mid-point then tapers to broken tip.
L 108 Head W 8 Shank D 3.8 **543**

24* Undifferentiated stick pin, Side of head divided by three vertical lines, between which are six horizontal grooves. Plain top. Shank expands slightly to mid-point before tapering to broken tip. Lower portion of shank bent.
L 83 Head D 3.8 Shank D 3.5 **903**

25* Undifferentiated stick pin with Type 3 head. Tripartite Type 3 divisions on top continue down side of head in vertical grooves, between which are four horizontal stabbed grooves in each field. Three transverse lines form a slight collar round the neck. Shank is relatively straight and broken in lower portion.
L 49 Head D 3.2 Shank D 2.5 **430**

26* Undifferentiated stick pin (Type 4 head?). Complex design – grooved branches form four vertical fields around the sides, with a short horizontal grooved bar between the branch forks. The design is continued onto the top, creating a Type 4 head. Three transverse incised lines create a double collar round the neck. Below this the shank expands to the mid-point before tapering to the tip.
L 78 Head D 5 Shank D 3.7 **523.01**

27* Stud-headed stick pin. Plain slightly domed head with shallow dent to one side. Overlapping pendant triangles round neck. Shank expands slightly to the mid-point before tapering to the broken tip.
L 75.5 Head D 5 Shank D 2.9 **760**

28* Stud-headed stick pin with radiating grooves on head. Slightly domed head. Shank expands slightly to the mid-point before tapering to tip.
L 73 Head D 6.8 Shank D 3 **430**

29* Stud-headed stick pin with radiating grooves on head. Slightly domed head, straight shank bent in lower portion. Scratch marks on shank near bend, probably wear marks.
L 69 Head D 5.3 Shank D 2.9 **504.01**

30* Stud-headed stick pin with radiating grooves on head. Flat head, ring and dot in centre of top. Straight shank.
L 62.7 Head Dia 5 Shank D 2.8 **537**

31* Stud-headed stick pin with radiating grooves Domed head, shank expands to mid-point before tapering to tip.
L 79 Head D 5.3 Shank D 3.1 **540**

32* Club-headed stick pin. Faint lines on top indicate a probable Type 1 head, otherwise a plain head. Neck/upper shank divided into three fields by vertical grooves, between which are diagonal stabbed decoration. Shank expands to mid-point before tapering, lower portion broken.
L 53 Head D 4.6 Shank D 3 **531**

33* Club-headed stick pin. Faint lines on top indicate a probable Type 1 head, otherwise a plain head. Neck has three fine diagonally vertical incised lines. Straight shank bent at upper/mid portion.
L 90 Head D 5.2 Shank D 3.2 **543**

34* Club-headed stick pin. Three small triangular incisions form pseudo-Type 1 head. Neck has three vertical rows of horizontal stabs. Shank expands to mid-point, where it was fractured.
L 79 Head D 5.1 Shank D 2.9 **612.03**

35* Club-headed stick pin with Type 2 head. Lines from head continue down neck, between each is a vertical row of five punched dots. Shank expands to mid-point before tapering to tip.
L 85.7 Head D 6 Shank D 3.6 **708**

36* Club-headed stick pin with Type 3 head. Lines on top terminate before centre, which contains a single punched dot. The lines continue down the neck and upper portion of shank, interrupted by two parallel transverse grooves 2 mm apart, between which are three evenly spaced punched dots. Shank expands to mid-point before tapering to tip.
L 86.3 Head D 5.1 Shank D 3.4 **535**

37* Club-headed triskele stick pin. Top motif continues down sides to form sub-triskele motif. Vertical incised grooves on neck continue beyond interupture zone of horizontal dots aligned with the grooves. Shank expands to mid-point before tapering to bent corroded tip.
L 89 Head D 5.3 Shank D 4.6 **744**

38* Club-headed stick pin with Type 5 head. Central square on head has a single punched dot. Grooves continue down neck, creating four fields filled with irregular vertical rows of punched dots. Shank expands towards mid point where it is broken.
L 41.3 Head D 6 Shank D 3.8 **539**

39* Corroded club-headed stick pin with Type 5 head. Grooves from top do not continue to underside of head, but then continue down the neck. The fields between are filled with vertical rows of punched dots. Central diamond on top contains off-centre punched dot. Straight-sided slightly bent shank tapers in lower portion to broken tip.
L 92.3 Head D 7.7 Shank D 4.2 **903**

40* Flattened club-headed stick pin. Four ring and dot motifs on top, one central, the others evenly spaced round the edge. Pendant triangles at neck. Shank expands to mid point then tapers to tip.
L 77.3 Head D 4.2 Shank D 2.9 **438**

41* Round or club-headed stick pin. Domed head with flat underside. Shank expands slightly below plain neck with some evidence of file marks. Broken at lower portion.
L 63 Head D 5 Shank D 3.7 **543**

42* Club or bead-headed stick pin. Straight shank bent at lower portion below which it is corroded, with broken tip.
L 57.3 Head D 3.3 Shank D 2 **625**

43* Semi-lobe-headed stick pin. Distinctly lobate Type 3 head with pendant triangles round neck. Shank expands slightly to mid point before tapering to corroded broken tip.
L 67.6 Head D 4 Shank D 2.9 **537**

44* Triskele-headed stick pin. Well defined triskele pattern round head. Pendant triangles round neck above pair of transverse grooves. Shank expands to mid point before tapering to tip.
L 73.1 Head D 5 Shank D 3 **531**

45* Cube-headed stick pin. Small plain head, narrowed neck, straight shank tapering in lower portion to tip.
L 84.2 Head W 4.5 Shank D 3.3 **536**

46 Probable crutch-headed pin (missing), with indentations at either side of head. May thus be another ring-pin [see BZ15].
L 83 Head W 6 **413**

47 Probable stick pin shank, tapering to slightly faceted point.
L 110 Shank Dia 3 **411.02**

48 Slightly bent straight stick pin shank, indented 4mm from top.
L 91 Shank D 2.9 **743**

49 Stick pin shank. Broken corroded lower portion of shank.
L 40 Shank D 2.6 **531**

50 Stick pin shank. Straight shank bent in lower portion.
L 63 Shank D 3.8 **615.02**

51 Stick pin shank. Bent shank with slightly flattened neck.
L 59.6 Shank D 3 **535**

Ring pins (BZ15)

The assemblage of nine ring pins (1–9), including two detached rings and two ringless pins, is small when compared to the stick pins, but nevertheless forms the largest single group among the seventy or so ring-pins known from Scotland. Ring pins are predominantly an Irish and Norse phenomenon and their typology and dating has been well covered by the late Dr. Fanning (1983a, 1994). The Whithorn examples generally fit well into his sequence.

The earliest example is an isolated spiral ring (1) from a seventh century grave (82.02, I/91) contemporary with the Irish *floruit* of this style which commenced in the fifth or sixth century (Fanning 1983a, 325). A cube-headed fully-perforated pin (2) with a groove around the base of the head and incised saltire crosses on the unperforated faces, came from an adjacent marginally later road surface (99, **Period I/4.5**). It is badly corroded and some detail may have been lost. The ring and pin may belong together (pp 113, 116), although spiral rings are usually associated with plain or baluster-headed pins. A cube-headed ring-pin from Ireland (Armstrong 1922, Fig. 2 No.4) was seen as a precursor of the tenth century polygonal headed pins, containing, as it did, the interlace motif commonly found in the latter. The pieces may well form the link between the early baluster head and later polygonal head.

A fine example of a plain-ringed polyhedral headed pin (3) came from the floor of a **Period III/2** building (III/13) overlying the **Period III/1** church. This is the commonest class of ring pin in Scotland and Ireland, with a distribution confined to the western Norse provinces, and dating to the tenth century. Examples emanate from Dublin and spread through the Irish sea, Western Isles and Orkney, and on to Iceland and Newfoundland (Fanning 1992, 25). The Whithorn pin with a quatrefoil interlace on each face, closely matches tenth century examples from Cronk Mooar, Isle of Man (Bersu and Wilson 1966,) and Buckquoy, Orkney (Ritchie 1977, Fig. 11 No. 120). As with many stick and ring pins, the pin has been bent to prevent slippage during use providing a tying off point for the cord which would have helped secure the cloak (Fanning 1990, 171). This has aggravated a fault in the metal, creating a tear in the fabric of the pin. Close laboratory examination and X-ray analysis revealed the continuation of the fault, but found no evidence that the 'slot' had been used.

Equally fine is a link-ringed pin (4) with a needle head above a collared and faceted baluster neck from a secure mid- to late-ninth century context (421.01). Baluster and needle headed pins are unusual in Scotland (Fanning 1983a, 325), and Irish examples, such as those from Knowth and Lagore, probably date to the seventh century. A silver pin from the Skaill hoard of *c.* 950 AD (Crawford 1987, Fig. 39) is, however, similar. A badly corroded plate-headed pin (5) does not correspond directly to the Dublin examples (Fanning 1990, 162–3) and lacks Scottish parallels. It was unstratified, but came from the south-east part of the **central sector** and may have originated in **Period III** deposits.

The only group of ring pins comprises stirrup-ringed crutch headed pins with two complete examples (6 and 7), a pin lacking its ring (8), a detached ring (9), and a lost pin (BZ14.46). It is remotely possible that the pin (8) and ring (9) go together – they do fit and both were recovered from the **Period V** graveyard, though at opposite ends of the site – but they probably come from two separate pins. One complete pin (6) is decorated with ring-and-dot motif on both ring and head, and the separate shank (8) and ring (9) both have ring-and-dot ornamentation. The other complete pin (7) has a bordered zone with diagonal incised lines on the head and a plain ring. All the pins have plain shanks.

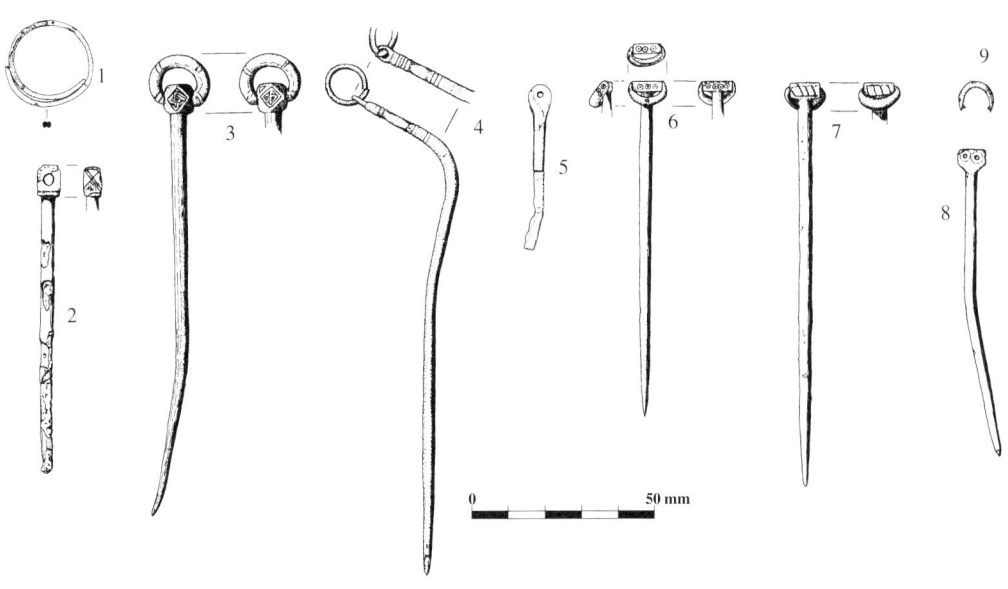

10.55 Ring pins (BZ15).

Scottish distributions tend towards the Western Isles (Fanning 1983a, 329) and a similarly decorated pin was recovered at Jarlshof (Hamilton 1956, 1541), though the ninth century dating has been called into question. An eleventh century date is more appropriate for Irish examples, such as the three from Ballinderry I, or High Street Dublin where the style continued into the twelfth century (Fanning 1969, 10). The Whithorn examples all came from the **Period V** graveyard and had probably been displaced from the **Period IV** debris (Figure 6.35). They are likely to date to the twelfth century and may have been contemporary with the club and stud-headed stick pins, post-dating the crutch-headed stick pins from Dublin (O Rahilly 1973, Fig. E).

1* Ovoid sectioned spiral ring, with overlapping terminals probably from pin. Leaded gun metal, alloy includes silver and gold
D 23 T 1.2 **82.02**

2* Cube-headed pin lacking ring. Badly corroded. Head pierced for a ring (probably spiral or link form), broken towards point. Round, tapering shank.
L 83 Head W 6 Shank MD 3.3 **99**

3* Plain ringed pin with polyhedral head. Facets have incised borders, main panels contained quatrefoil interlace. The ring has four pairs of transverse grooves. Circular section shank tapers to point and is bent at the lower section and point.
L 116 Head W 7.2 Shank MD 4 Ring D 12 **300.02**

4* Link-ringed needle-headed pin with needle head above neck decorated with baluster flanked by triple collars. Circular-sectioned shank.
L 145 Ring D 12 **421.01**

5* Plate-headed pin, pierced, but lacking ring, in two pieces. Non-insula. Shank square-sectioned at neck, turning circular lower down. Rounded head on plate. Lower portion of shank missing.
L 45 Head W. 6 Shank MD 4 **901**

6* Stirrup-ringed crutch-headed pin. Head decorated with four ring and dot motifs on one side and three on the other. Neck has incised pendant triangle pattern. Shank expands from neck to mid-portion, tapering to point, and is of circular section. Ring is D-sectioned.
L 90 Head W 7.5 Shank MD 3.4 Ring D 10.5 **538**

7* Stirrup-ringed crutch-headed pin. Poss. undecorated head. Shank expands towards middle portion before tapering to point. Ring is D-sectioned.
L 107 Head W. 8.5 Shank MD 4 Ring D 12 **542**

8* Crutch-headed pin lacking ring. Two circle and bored dot ornament on sides of head, which tapers towards shank. Bored holes on sides worn from swivel of a ring (probably of stirrup form). Shank circular sectioned, expanding slightly to midpoint where it is bent, then tapering to point.
L 82 Head W 7.4 Shank MD 3 **539**

9* Stirrup ring lacking pin. D-shaped section with two small conical projections for securing it to pin head (probably of crutch form)
535

Brooches (BZ16)

Five brooches (BZ16.1–3, 6 and 7) and two possible brooches or mounts (4 and 5) include two nineteenth century brooches (6 and 7) from topsoil (excavation archive). Brooches first appear in the **Period V** graves (Figure 10.49), and probably coincide with the end of the use of stick-pins, and perhaps point to a widening cultural milieu towards the end of the thirteenth century. A small fine penannular brooch with flattened terminals (1) from the **Period V** graveyard in the **Museum Garden**, would only have been suitable for light cloths such as linen or silk rather than a heavy wool, and may have been used to secure a wimple or to attach hose to braes. A complete annular brooch (2) from the **Period V** graveyard with a simple looped pin and coarse transverse grooving, probably dates to the thirteenth century when annular brooches replaced pennannular brooches and stick pins. Later brooches of similar type, such as that from the Dumfries hoard of c 1310 (Callander 1924, Fig. 1 No.2), have a transverse bar on the pin (see SR7, pp 398-9). A similar brooch with a cast pin, from N. Uist, is described as a possible buckle (Close-Brooks and Maxwell 1974, 292). The brooch lay on, though not pinned through, a section of 2/2 twill woollen cloth (TX02.1, pp 509-10). A semi-circular fragment of thin sheet (5), also from the graveyard, may have been the backing plate from a brooch, and a third possible brooch (4) from fourteenth/fifteenth century deposits in the **southern sector** (515), comprises two sheet discs with opposed projecting strips, attached to a third thicker strip extending the full width between the discs and opposed strips. A flat annular brooch (3) from a recent hollow (735) disturbing the **Period V** graves, is decorated with zigzag scorped lines dividing the face into six fields which are filled with linear ornamentation. Such brooches developed from the fourteenth to

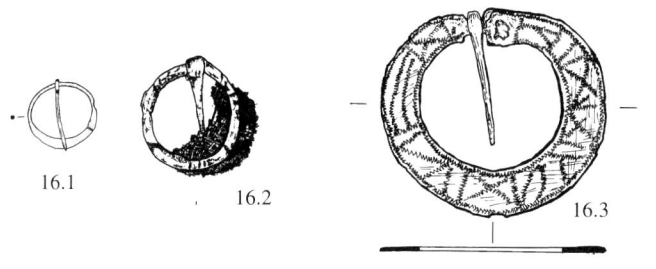

10.56 Brooches (BZ16) and buttons (BZ17).

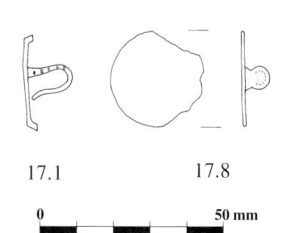

eighteenth centuries and a similar brooch from Urquhart Castle (Samson 1982, Fig. 6 No.90) is probably fifteenth century. Fifteenth century belt fittings and brooches from London have similar zigzag decoration (LMMC 1993, 279).

1* Small tin-plated penannular brooch of square section with flattened expanded terminals, one considerably longer than the other, leaving the opening at one side. Simple flat-section looped ring. Leaded bronze.
ED 19.7 × 17.5 Pin L 18.8 **511.10**

2* Annular brooch with broken pin. Circular section, with incised transverse grooves. The pin is made by longitudinally folding a strip, giving a flat loop and a tapering shank. (see TX02.1, pp 509-10).
ED 28 T 3 Pin L 21 **535**

3* Annular brooch, flat wide facing field decorated with boxes of zigzag incised relief, of a style similar to that found on the shank of late Norse stick pins. Two opposed indents create a narrow strip to allow the simple looped pin to move. The two ends are lapped and riveted together next to the pin. The broken pin is made from a flat sheet, rolled below the loop.
ED 62 × 54 T 1.0 Pin L 37 Rivet head D 4 **735**

4 Possible brooch comprising two circular plates, centrally attached to (broken) rectangular section tapering shaft, and bent to meet each other at the edges. Surviving half of shaft broken into two pieces, tapers to well-defined point. One plate may have been decorated.
Plate D 17.5 T 0.6 Shaft L 25 W 4.6 T 1.2 **515**

5 Possible brooch mount comprising broken fragment of circular disc with central hollow and three concentric circles.
D 15 T 0.3 **535**

Buttons (BZ17)

Twenty-two buttons (BZ17.1–22) mostly came from modern and recent contexts. This group includes two and four hole buttons, flat discs with a rear attachment loop, and a single, spheroid shoe button (13). Eight of the buttons (3–9) were plated with white metal, and one modern example (10) was gilded. Two buttons came from **Period V** contexts. A possible button (1*) of inverted saucer section, was attached by an open hook rather than a closed loop, and came from the **Period V/3** roadway (617.01). A second diamond-shaped button (2) came from the **Period V/4** builders debris (630).

Buckles and belt loops (BZ18)

Twelve buckles, four belt loops and four isolated tongues (BZ18.1–20) spanned the occupation of the site. The two earliest buckles (1 and 2) came from late **Period I** contexts and are very different in form. The first (1) from worm soil (85.05) oversailing the **Period I/4b** shrine, is a flat-sectioned rectangular buckle with a pin loop. The other (2) from a **Period I/4.1** grave (82.01, I/74), has a round-sectioned loop with straight ends and curved short sides, attached to a belt plate of folded sheet with a rounded end and single rivet hole. A similar buckle and plate in iron, from a tenth century deposit at Coppergate, York (Ottaway 1992, Fig. 294 No. 3690), shows the persistence of this basic style. Two buckles (4 and 6) with decorated belt plates can be ascribed to the **Period III**. One was stratified (4, 400) and the other (6) displaced into post-medieval deposits (631). The first buckle (4) is D-shaped with an interlace design on the belt plate, and probably dates from the early-tenth century (p 623). The second buckle (6) is cast with a D-section, the back being the flattened face. The buckle has two raised ridges to receive the pin, and the ends terminate in stylised animal heads on either side of the narrower round-sectioned strap bar. The slot for the pin in the belt plate has rounded ends, and seems to have been made by cutting out a strip between two pre-punched holes. A ring with similar animal-head terminals from Luce Sands was seen as a British copy of a sixth century Pictish object (Laing 1974a, 191), but the upraised snouts and receding chins of the animals on the Whithorn buckle are closer in style to the terminals on the chapes from the ninth century Ninian's Isle hoard (Small *et al.* 1973, Pl. XXIX). The motif and arrangement had a long life, appearing on the rings of plain- and kidney-ringed pins from Ireland (Armstrong 1922, Fig. 5 Nos 2 and 3) datable to the second half of the tenth century. A fragmentary small buckle (5) from the foundations of Building V/3, has a separate strap bar, a feature also found on an iron buckle from Coppergate, York (Ottaway 1992, Fig. 294 No.3692). It may be a small rectangular buckle, of which two similar examples in iron, were recovered from a deposit of *c.* 1280 AD at Swan Lane, London (Egan and Pritchard 1991, 97 Nos 440 and 441).

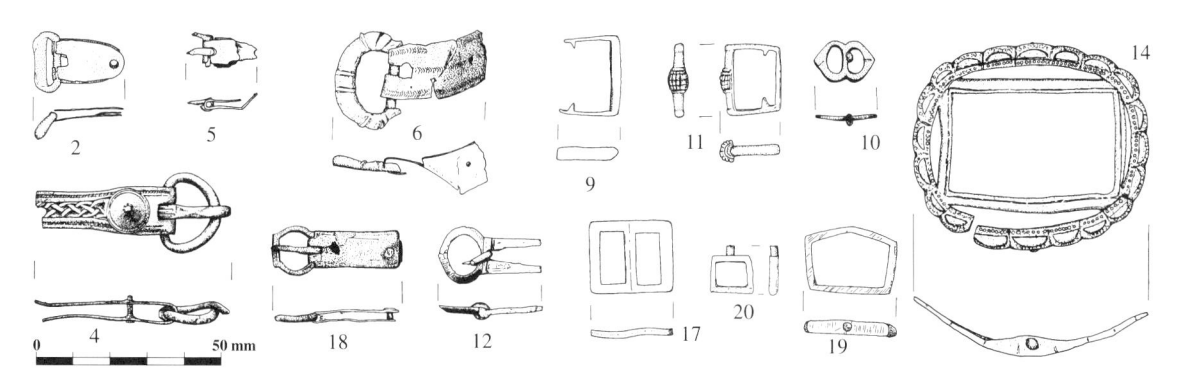

10.57 Buckles and belt loops (BZ18).

Two buckles (10 and 18), two belt loops (9 and 11) and two buckle pins (7 and 8) were recovered from the **Period V** graveyard (Figure 10.49). The belt loops were quadrilateral with projecting internal lugs. The complete example (11) had a hatched bezel on the loop, the other (9) had lost its rear bar. The projecting lugs can be seen on a belt loop from Perth, dated from the early-thirteenth to mid-fourteenth century (Thoms 1982, Fig. 6 No. 59), and on loops from London of the mid-twelfth to mid-fourteenth century (Egan and Pritchard 1991, 231–3). The bezel is a common feature (sometimes degenerating into a knob or projection) from the late-thirteenth century onwards. A similar separately-cast bezel, probably a strap mount, comes from a sixteenth century context in Beverley (A.R. Goodall 1991, Fig. 114 No. 602), and two are recorded from late fourteenth century dumps at Billingsgate London (Egan and Pritchard 1991, 89 Nos 1160 and 1161). The tin-plated buckle with plate (18) is stylistically of the late-thirteenth century, and similar examples are known from Beverley (A.R. Goodall 1991, 148) and Goltho (I.H. Goodall 1975, 91). A small double buckle of pointed figure-of-eight shape (10) from the graveyard surface (543), is probably late-fourteenth or fifteenth century (LMMC 1993, 278; Egan and Pritchard 1991, 213 No. 386). A pentagonal belt loop (19) came from a **Period V/1** surface (504.01). Similar loops from London date from the second half of the fourteenth century (Egan and Pritchard 1991, 231 Nos 1250–1252), and one from Northolt Manor was dated 1370–1425 AD (Hurst 1961, 293). A quadrilateral belt loop with an integral external rivet (20) was probably of similar date. A medieval buckle (12) from the west end of the **Fey Field** trench is of distinctive form comprising an ovoid triangular-sectioned ring with ogival loop, and two prongs projecting rearward to which the belt is attached. A thirteenth century example comes from Riseholme, Lincs (Thompson 1960, 106) and a belt in the Guildhall Museum (L.M.M.C 1993, Fig. 63 No. 7) shows this kind of buckle associated with six-petal decorative studs (see BZ21).

An ornamental buckle with open-work and scalloped edges (14) was among the modern finds from the topsoil. Traces remained of a central iron bar, and one side bore wear marks showing the location of the pin, the buckle had been plated with white metal.

1 Half of a flat rectangular buckle with tongue loop *in situ*.
L 16 W 14 T 1.1 **85.05**

2* Wire loop and attached folded plate with rounded end and single central rivet hole. Slot cut into plate to take tongue which is now missing. A separate related plate, sub-ovoid with central perforation, may have served as a washer for the rivet. Belt width less than 12 mm.
L 25 W 17 **82.01**

3 Flat buckle tongue with angled end, broken off at loop.
L 32 W 4 T 1.7 **399.03**

4* D-ring buckle with interlace-decorated plate. Round section D-ring, butt joint possibly soldered. Rectangular section tongue slightly waisted, with two incised longitudinal grooves at loop. Thin folded sheet belt-plate broken at rivet holes in end furthest from loop. Plates taper away from loop. A single centrally located rivet is enclosed within three scribed concentric circles, whose outer limits disrupt the diagonal hatching which borders the edges of the plate. Between these borders, filling the central field away from the loop, is a simple interlace pattern. The pattern respects the scribed circles, but the apparent rivet hole across which the piece is broken, is cut through the pattern, indicating secondary usage.
L 50.5 Loop W 21 Plate W 13.6 **400**

5* Small broken buckle with separate pin, in situ tongue and folded sheet buckle plate with straight tapering sides, broken off across central single rivet hole. Broken pin is flat with single loop.
L 17 W 8 T 3 **506.01**

6* Decorated D-ring buckle with folded buckle plate decorated with animal heads. Two raised ridges on the ring to accommodate the tongue, with cast pin, the ring terminals are highly stylised animal heads with prominent eyes and well defined snouts. The pin emerges from the mouths. The buckle plate is rectangular with a slot for the tongue and a single small central rivet hole at the open end. Decoration on the front consists of three parallel bands of incised zigzag motifs.
W 27 × 15 T 3.6 **631**

7 Intact buckle pin, one end looped, tapering to point at other.
L 19.5 W 3 T 1.5 Loop ID 3 **530**

8 Large rectangular-sectioned buckle pin, flattened and folded to make complete loop.
L 42 W 7 T 3.5 **539**

9* Broken quadrilateral buckle with two opposed internal protrusions (see No. 11). Flat sides, intact end has slightly convex interior and bevelled exterior section.
L 17 W 22 T 4 **542**

10* Figure-of-eight shape double buckle with pointed ends. Remnants of iron pin on central bar, two slight transverse central indentations at sides of front face to take tongue. Bevelled edges, flat back.
L 17 W 11.3 T 1.2 **543**

11* Quadrilateral buckle with two internal opposed protrusions at narrower end. Thicker D-sectioned side has an external barrel-shaped bezel with a hatched field between two parallel grooves.
L 17 W 19 T 6 × 3 **543**

12* Ovoid ring pronged-buckle, with broken in situ tongue, and two projecting tapering strips – for attachment? Tapering triangular section ring with small raised projection opposite tongue at mid point. Tongue of flat section with simple loop. Two tapered lugs project back along line of belt.
L 32 W 15.5 T 2.0 **527**

13 Ovoid buckle with cast pin and in situ tongue. Tapering D-section with projecting ribbed bezel opposite tongue. Latter is flat section with simple loop and angled point. Leaded bronze.
L 15 W 19 T 3 **744**

14* Tin-plated, ovoid, scalloped, double-sided buckle with central transverse iron pin (now broken) mounted at rear. Open-work scalloped ovoid, with relief lunates surrounded by ribbed work, containing open-work rectangle with central groove on faces. One side of buckle indented from pressure of tongue.
L 68 W 55 T 5 **744**

15 Flat buckle tongue, broken at loop
L 16 W 2 T 1 **704**

16 Sub-rectangular wire buckle with tongue (modern) Fragment of the original leather covering 65 long × 15 wide. Round section wire (3 dia.) loop.
L 19 W 67.5 **747.01**

17* Rectangular buckle, open, with transverse rectangular section bar. Traces of iron staining on the back at one side.
L 23 W 20.2 T 2 **903**

18* Tin-plated buckle with plate. Moulded frame, belt plate is plain parallel-sided folded strip, secured onto sandwiched leather by a single central rivet. The tongue has a simple looped terminal.
Plate L 24 W 9.5 Buckle W 13 T 2 Leather T 2 **539**

19* Pentagonal belt loop. Long side and two adjacent ones rectangular section, other two D-section. Surfaces covered in deep file marks. Remains of iron pin through base.
L 26 W 18 T 3.5 **504.01**

20* Broken quadrilateral belt loop, openwork rectangle with broken projecting cylindrical lug on one. Leaded gunmetal.
L 12 W 12 T 2 **903**

Belt and strap fittings (BZ19a)

A group of fifteen belt and strap fittings (BZ19.1–15) comprises nine strap ends (1–7, 10 and 11), two possible strap ends (8 and 9), three pairs of riveted plates with leather between (12–14) and a hinge (15). Two strap ends (1 and 2) came from **Period I** contexts and both lack immediate parallels. A lobate bronze piece (1) with fine spiral decoration and red enamel inlay came from the western end of the **northern sector** and probably belonged with the fine metalworking workshop debris flanking the **Period I/4.5** platform (Figure 3.34b). It is insular in style and is probably western British, but cannot be categorised more closely. The second object (2) from the **Period I/3** hollow (109), is a delicate two-piece strap end of leaded bronze with incised interlace and a single rivet hole. It would probably not have survived rigorous use at the end of a belt, and may have been part of a book marker or some similar item. EDXRF analysis shows traces of tin from the solder used to join the two plates, a technique mirrored on morphologically-similar sixth century strap ends from Dinas Powys and the cemetery at Herpes, Charente (Alcock 1963, 108).

Three strap ends (3–5) came from the main **Period II** rubbish deposit (303, Figure 10.98) and associated coins provided a *terminus* of c. 840 AD for their deposition. One (3) is a typical example of the Whitby form, with a highly-stylised animal head, split at one end with two rivets to hold the strap. The Whithorn piece lacks these rivets, but there is the stump of an iron stud or rivet in the middle of the main field. As comparable strap-ends are usually highly decorated (D.M. Wilson 1964, 27–9), it is likely that a second decorative plate would have been attached at this point. EDXRF analysis identified tin plating over the animal head, but not on the body of the strap end, supporting the case for an affixed plate. The second strap end (4) is also split, with two rivet holes, but has a sub-triangular form with a long tapering rounded projection, a feature noted on a sub-class of the Whitby group (Wilson 1964, Pl. XL Nos 124–6). A cross has been incised on the front face of the triangular section. The third strap end (5) has an ovoid body, a feature also found on small ninth century strap ends, split with two iron rivets *in situ*.

Three small dot-and-circle motifs are offset in the main field, and the strap end terminates in a long projection ending with a stylised animal head. A final highly-abstracted version of the animal head terminal may be seen in a strap end (6) from the surface to the north of the **Period III** church (316). This is built up from three narrow strips of copper alloy to create the necessary gap for the leather without splitting, and ends in a single rivet still securing a fragment of leather strap.

A later group comprises five objects from fourteenth/fifteenth century contexts (Figure 10.49). A long tapering strap end (7) decorated with zigzag scorped lines, came from late cobbling (513) in the **southern sector**, and is probably fourteenth century. It is constructed from a single sheet folded lengthways, and has a single rivet hole. Such long strap ends are usually associated with female dress, and several examples are known from London (L.M.M.C 1993, 265; Egan and Pritchard 1991, 130). A long tapering fragment, possibly a blank for a strap end (8), was also folded widthways, with a rounded end, though the other end had been cut so no evidence of splitting or rivet holes survived. It came from a pit (612.03) ascribed to **Period V/4**, and probably dating to the later-fifteenth century. A small bevelled decorated piece (9) from the **Period V** graveyard (543) had been pierced centrally and bent at one end. This decorative mount may have been altered to act as a strap end. Bevelled buckle plates from London date from the late-thirteenth to late-fourteenth centuries (Egan and Pritchard 1991, 106–8). The last two strap ends are simple two-plate affairs, one (11) with a small projecting lower lug, and another (10) with a hook. The latter (10) came from the rubble (631) overlying the **Period V/3** road and V/4 buildings, the other (11) from a recent disturbance (734.01) flanking the manse, and matches a group of similar late fourteenth century strap ends from London (Egan and Pritchard 1991, 148).

Three pairs of rectangular plates with rounded corners (12, 13 and 14) were joined by rolled copper alloy rivets in each corner, and lacked decoration. One retained the leather sandwiched between the two plates. All came from contexts ascribed to the fourteenth century (Figure 10.49). An unstratified hinge (15) comprising two interleaved folded sheets around an iron pin, is similar to the plates. Both sheets continue as opposed rectangular plates with rounded corners and were secured by two copper-alloy rivets.

1* Lobate cast ?strap end with separate cast hinge pin and relief spiral design with (red enamel?) inlay. The butt end has two transversely perforated projecting lugs through which a separate 0.7mm diameter pin (broken or worn) is fixed. The decorative field is surrounded by a relief border and consists of a decorated (currently obscured) panel extending into a fine spiral in the lobed section. Traces of an inlay remain. Bronze.
L 25.3 W 11.8 T 2.4 **85.02**

2* Front and back plates of a small ?strap end with a single rivet hole at the butt. Back plate identical to front plate but plain flat sheet. Front plate has a square head, two transverse grooves define

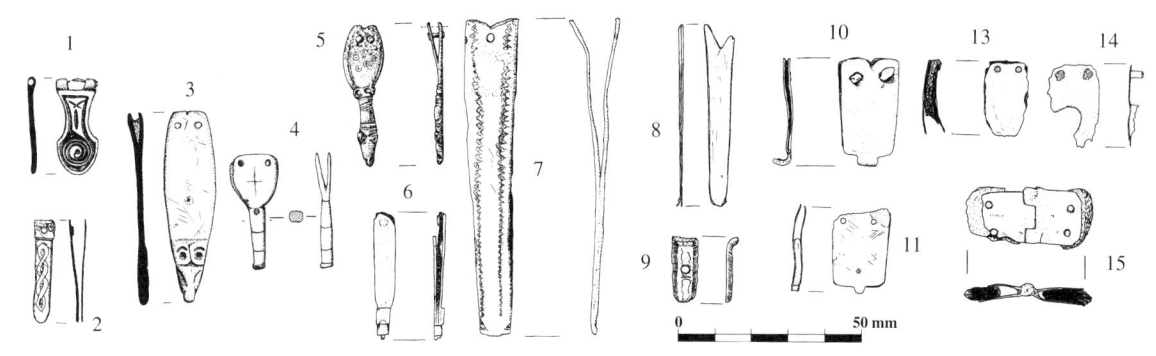

10.58 Belt and strap fittings (BZ19a).

the plain rectangular field for the rivet hole. The shank has straight sides with bevelled edges and tapers at the point. A simple incised interlace fills the field. XRF analysis of grey material on back of each plate indicated tin, possibly used as a solder. Leaded bronze.

L 27.7 Head W 5.5 Shank W 4.0 T 0.5
Hole D 1.4 **109**

3* Pendant strap end terminating in stylised relief animal head. The upper end has been split to receive the belt, and has two small rivet holes. The main field is flat and bare, with a single rivet or peg centrally placed. This may well have secured a separate decorative field to the strap end. The simple chip-carved animal head is raised slightly above the flat field and consists of two ears with lunate openings, two triangular eyes and a well defined snout. Tin plated leaded bronze.

L 50.5 W 14.6 T 2.2 **303**

4* Pendant strap end; two tapering plates with two rivet holes for strap attachment, riveted together with a single rivet at the base, below which the material is rolled to form a sub-ovoid shaft for a further 11mm. Decoration consists of three incised grooves around the shaft, and a roughly incised Latin cross on the front plate.

L 28 W 11 T 3.5 **303**

5* Pendant strap end terminating in stylised animal head. Lobed butt end, curving split upper plates with two iron rivets in situ, below which is a semi-circular section shank, broadening out to the animal head is slight relief. Decoration of the upper plate consists of an incised line following the curve of each side, on the shank three transverse grooves below two punched dots define the upper neck, whilst two more transverse grooves define the lower margin. Two offset punched dots may represent crude eyes on the worn animal head. The back of the piece is plain.

L 37.5 W 10.3 T 3.1 **303**

6* Pendant strap end with possible stylised animal head. Straight sided with single central rivet at top. Tapers at base, where the 'head' is formed by a stepped series of three reducing blocks, the last a tiny 'tongue'. Leather strap maintained within split, back plate plain.

L 33 W 6 T 3 **316**

7 Long tapering straight-sided strap end with convex-V notch and single central rivet hole at butt end. Decoration on front plate consists of two lines, paralleling the sides, of broad incised zigzag design. The clear seam down one side and lack at the other suggest this was made from a single sheet of metal, cut to shape and folded longitudinally.

L 83 W 15 × 9 T 2.5 **513**

8* Possible blank for strap end. V notch at butt end, long tapering straight sides and a rounded end, currently split. The central seam on each edge indicates that the piece was cut with snips.

L 48 W 8.2 T 1.3 **612.03**

9* Possible strap end. Decorated mount, bent and broken off at one end, the rear is flat and plain, the front is flat with bevelled edges. Decoration consists of a central panel of diagonally linked circles, ending in a lobate cross motif. The rivet hole cuts through the design. The bevelled edges have fine diagonal incised hatching.

L 15.8 W 7.5 T 1.6 **543**

10* Two plate sub-rectangular strap end with hooked terminal. Slightly lobed butt end with two in situ copper-alloy rivets sandwiching a layer of material, possibly leather. The plates taper slightly, and the upper plate ends with a flat projecting strip 6mm long turned inwards through ninety degrees.

L 29 W 17 T 1.8 **631**

11* Two plate strap end with small projecting tongue. Slightly tapering rectangle with two small lobes at open end, around the rivet holes (rivets now missing), third centrally placed rivet in situ above tongue. The lower half of the strap end has a thin edging strip attached to the two plates.

L 23.5 W 15 T 2.4 **734.01**

12 Two sub-rectangular plates connected by two rivets at one end, probably sandwiching an organic layer. Badly corroded.

L 19 W 11 **523.01**

13* Two plain sub-rectangular plates of copper alloy riveted together with two copper alloy rivets at one end, sandwiching a leather strap.

L 19 W 12 T 4.6 **504.01**

14* Two opposed sub-rectangular plates, originally attached by four rivets, of which three survive. The large central perforation may well be secondary. In four pieces.

L 22 W 14 **538**

15* Two pairs of sub-rectangular copper alloy hinge plates, with iron pin. Opposed plates are joined at open ends by two rivets, sandwiching leather straps.

L 34.5 W 15 T 3.5 **903**

Binding strips (BZ19b)

Four folded binding strips (BZ19.16–19) are wider and thinner than the strap plates, though also secured by rolled copper-alloy rivets. Three (16–18) came from **Period I** deposits, and the fourth (19) from a **Period V** grave, could have been displaced from a **Period I** deposit in the **northern sector**. Three (16, 18 and 19) preserved fragments of wood between the sheets, and similar objects from Traprain Law also contain traces of wood. There are sixth/seventh century parallels from Buiston Crannog (Munro 1882, 228) and Dinas Powys (Alcock 1963, 110) where they were seen as clamps to attach a rim-binding to a wooden bucket. Two of the strips (17

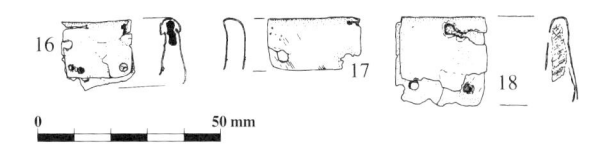

10.59 Binding strips (BZ19b).

and 18) came from secure contexts, both relatively late in **Period I**, and probably dating to the later-seventh/earlier-eighth century.

16* Folded over copper alloy strip with three rivet holes, sandwiching organic material. Two rivet holes at the open end, and two ?secondary holes adjacent to one edge and the open end. A 4mm long 1.5mm diameter hollow-tubed rivet is associated with the piece but now separate.
L 18 W 20 T 0.5 **52**

17* Folded-over copper alloy binding strip with two rivet holes at open end.
L 14 W 25 T 0.5 **73.03**

18* Folded-over copper alloy strip with two rivet holes, sandwiching organic material. One side broken off along rivet holes. Upper plate has a scalloped open end, and the remnants of a second plate riveted to it extending away from the open end. The wood appears to contain a tubular copper alloy rivet.
L 24 W 24 T 0.5 **85.04**

19 Folded-over copper alloy binding strip, now in three pieces, sandwiching wood. Badly corroded – no evidence of rivet holes.
L 35 W 16 Strip T 0.8 **532**

Tag ends (BZ20)

A hundred and forty-four rolled tag ends range in length from 10mm to 47mm, with a preferential range of 17mm to 26mm. Some were rolled tubes, others were tapered towards the end. A group of thirty-one tags from London range from 25 to 40 mm in length, and the limited variety of tags suggests a standardised form (Egan and Pritchard 1991, 281). Almost all the tag ends came from the latest graves of **Period V/1** (535) and subsequent **Period V** deposits. Three examples (4–6) from **Period III** and **IV** contexts were probably intrusive, but a large rolled tag end (1) from a **Period I/4** grave (82.05, I/118) was wider than the later examples, and seems to have been a distinct earlier type. There was a close spatial association between the tag ends and the **Period V** graveyard (Figure 10.60a), and none was found in the **southern sector**. Twenty-seven examples (7–33, 62) came from some twenty-two graves, and these might have been attached to laces securing costume or shrouds. A further nineteen (34–53) came from 'cleaning' contexts (543), and thirteen (54–61, 90, 91, 94–6) from the overlying cobbles and related deposits. The **Period V/4** deposits produced twenty-six examples (63–89), including a concentration of sixteen (73–89) in the builders' waste (630) abutting Building V/4 (Figure 10.60b). Most of the remaining forty-seven tag ends (97–144) came from recent contexts (708, 741, 744 etc) disturbing the **Period V** deposits in the same area. The chronological picture is relatively clear. The **Period V/1** graves are ascribed to the first half of the fourteenth century, and tag ends may thus have been introduced c. 1350 AD. Their currency seems to have ended at the close of **Period V/4**, perhaps in the opening decades of the sixteenth century. A single tag end was found in an early-fourteenth century deposit at Waltham Abbey (Huggins 1970, 144), the rest were fifteenth century or later (Huggins 1976, 115–7). In London two tag ends were dated to the mid-thirteenth century, whilst the others are all from contexts attributable to c. 1330 AD or later (Egan and Pritchard 1991, 281), and reflect the increased use of laces in the tighter, figure-hugging costumes fashionable from the fourteenth century onwards (Egan and Pritchard 1991, 284). By contrast, rivet-less tag ends from Northampton were mainly of mid-sixteenth or seventeenth century date, with lengths between 20mm and 40mm (Oakley 1979a, 262–3, Fig. 114).

Six-petal flower studs (BZ21)

Five hexafoil flower studs of varying size (BZ21.2–6) were concentrated on the north-west side

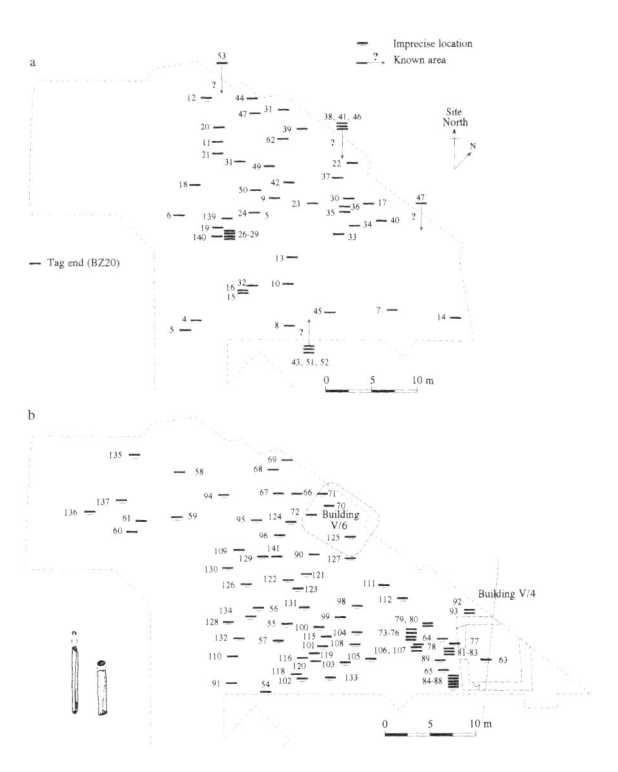

10.60 Tag-ends (BZ20). **a** Finds from graves and related contexts, **b** Finds from **Period V/4** buildings, surfaces and overlying deposits.

of the **Period V** graveyard (Figure 10.49), occurring in a late grave (4, 539), cleaning contexts (6, 542 and 2, 543) and the **Period V/3** surface (3 and 5, 616.06). A thirteenth century belt and buckle in the Guildhall Museum (L.M.M.C 1993, Fig. 63 No.7) is decorated with five similar studs, and a hexafoil stud with a

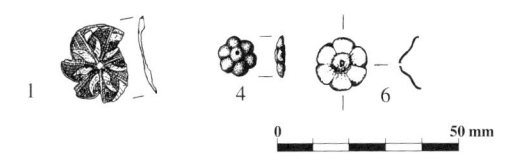

10.61 Hexafoil studs (BZ21).

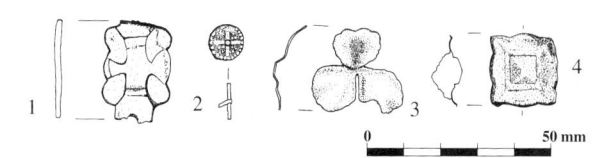

10.62 Decorative mounts (BZ22).

central rivet hole from Northampton is akin to the Whithorn ones, and was dated to the fourteenth century, by which time they were in common use in London (Egan and Pritchard 1991, 186). The studs are thus likely to have come from a belt lost in the late-fourteenth or early-fifteenth century and dispersed over the graveyard surface. A plate with a more complex septafoil motif (1) may have also have been a belt mount, in the same way as a fourteenth century quatrefoil plaque of similar construction from Northampton (Oakley 1979a, 254). It came from relatively late debris (631) overlying the **Period V** graveyard and **V/4** buildings.

1* Broken convex circular plate with complex impressed foliate design in six sections. Small flat central boss but no perforation – it may have been attached to a back plate and may be a brooch, though the layout does suggest an affinity with the earlier stud series.

Original D 23 **631**

2 Six-petal stud, impressed design with inturned rim and central perforation, folded in half.

D 15 **543**

3 Broken six-petal impressed convex stud with small central perforation. Current diameter 14 mm, no surviving edge or rim, and original diameter probably c. 18mm. In two pieces.

616.06

4* Convex six-petal flower impressed stud with small central perforated dome.

D 11 **539**

5 Six-petal impressed convex stud with shallow convex central dome and flat collar around small central perforation.

D 21 **616.06**

6* Convex six-petal flower impressed stud, with small central perforated dome.

D 11 **542**

Decorative mounts (BZ22)

Four other decorative mounts (BZ22.1–4) for belts or clothing include a broken lobed fragment (1) with an incised design about a central cross. It came from a **Period III** soil layer (407.01) overlying the Northumbrian church, and perhaps originated in the destruction deposits (315) marking the end of **Period II**. A round medieval stud (2) with cross and pellets is similar in design to Long Cross coins, suggesting a late-twelfth century date. It came from the cultivation furrows (546) at the west end of the **northern sector**. Unstratified finds included a thin shamrock mount (3), probably stitched on at the centre, and a squared quatrefoil plate with a pyramidal central stud (4), and an iron shank or rivet at the rear.

1* Lobed mount, broken at both ends, one of which has a rivet hole. Central motif is a possible cross, with projecting lobes between the arms.

L 27 W 18.5 T 1.8 **407.01**

2* Circular disc with cast crux and pellet design. Short cross centred on rivet or stalk, within beaded border. Three pellets between each arm of the cross.

D 10 T 0.8 Shank L 3.6 Shank D 1.1 **546**

3* Decorative mount in the form of a shamrock. Thin sheet three-petal design, individual petals convex, with broken edges. Between two of the petals is a narrow slit penetrating to the centre, perhaps for attachment.

L 25.5 W 22.5 T 0.5 **743**

4* Squared quatrefoil mount with pyramidal centre. Iron shank centrally located at rear.

L 19.4 W 18.3 T 1 **903**

Finger rings (BZ23)

Fourteen undecorated rings (BZ23.1–14) are interpreted as finger rings, although three open rings with tapered terminals (6, 8 and 10) could have been earrings, as suggested by a silver ring (SR02) found on the skull in a **Period V** grave, and postulated for two open rings from Beverley (A.R. Goodall 1991, 148). EDXRF analysis showed two of the later rings to be tin plated, and revealed traces of a lead/tin solder at the join on the earliest ring (1). Two rings (1 and 2) came from **Period II** deposits and a third from an insecure **Period III** context (3, 429). Three (4, 5 and 7) came from **Period V** graves, and a fourth from a possible **Period V/1** boundary (6, 502). The remaining seven rings came from more recent contexts although several could have been displaced from earlier deposits.

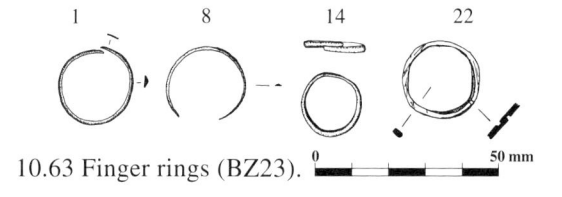

10.63 Finger rings (BZ23).

1* Triangular-sectioned ring with overlapping flattened terminals. EXRDF analysis suggests originally joined by lead/tin solder. Leaded copper and silver.

ED 21 ID 18.2 **224.01**

2* Square-sectioned gunmetal ring with overlapping terminals.

ED 22 ID 19 **303**

3 Three fragile fragments of wrap-around convex strip, almost certainly from a ring.

ID c 18 **429**

4 D-sectioned ring – no terminals, but does thin down to a fine plate in one section.

ED 20 ID 16.5 **531**

5 Round wire loop, possibly a finger ring.
ED 20 ID 18 **511.07**

6 Flat-sectioned band tapering towards (broken) terminals, badly corroded.
ED 20 ID 17.8 **502**

7 Ovoid sectioned ring tapering to flat overlapping terminals. Ring very worn opposite terminals.
ED 19.6 ID 18 **542**

8* Triangular sectioned ring tapering to pointed terminals – one broken – currently opened though possibly originally closed together.
ED 21 ID 19.5 **616.07**

9 Bent strip of copper alloy of triangular section, bevelled exterior, corroded. Rounded terminals. Tin-plated leaded brass.
L 49 Probable original D 16 **617.04**

10 Fragment of D-sectioned ring with tin plating tapering towards (now missing) terminals. Tin-plated leaded speculum.
L 24 Probable original D 20 **611**

11 Bent strip ring of shallow D-section, one terminal flattened and broadened – possibly from hammering terminals together as it serves no decorative purpose.
L 64 Probable original D 20 **631**

12 Flat strip ring with tin or silver plating. Flat band wrap-around with flat terminals, some small spots of silvering externally evident near join. Speculum.
ED 17 ID 15.5 **726**

13 D-sectioned ring with large flattened bezel to fore (9mm × 12mm) and tapering to join at rear.
ED 23 ID 21 **754**

14* Ovoid sectioned ring tapering to flattened overlapping terminals.
ED 17 ID 15 **901**

Toilet implements (BZ24)

A small group of toilet implements (BZ24.1–11) comprises five pairs of tweezers (1–5), three razor fragments (6–8), an ear scoop (9), a small file (10) and a probable nail cleaner (11). Four pairs of tweezers (1–4) came from **Period II–IV** deposits, and the fifth (5) may have been displaced from a similar context. Three came from buildings (II/14, III/12 and III/41) and the fourth (2) from debris surrounding Building IV/7. The Whithorn group of tweezers is unusual. Most tweezers are associated with early Anglo-Saxon burials (Smith 1993, 46; Hills 1977, 25 and Figs. 111–118), though a pair of flat undecorated tweezers does occur in a late Saxon layer at Northampton (Oakley 1979a, 256). Three pairs of tweezers (1–3) were made by folding a simple flat strip of metal around a rod, as are three iron tweezers (IN74.1–3), although two of these come from rather later contexts. One (1) of these pairs has the remnant of a wire ring, probably a suspension loop, and another (2) showed traces of gilding. The other two tweezers are both shaped and decorated. The set (4) from a small **Period II** building (II/14, 215) has been folded straight over, and had snapped on excavation. The more elaborate pair (5) has a loop decorated with herringbone grooves, below which is a narrower handle where the two strips meet. The edges and flat blades below the collared neck are decorated with zigzag scorping.

Three fragments of thin blades with fine triangular sections worn at the leading edge are interpreted as razor blades. One (6) came from seventh century pond silts in the **southern sector** (55), the others from the **Period V** graveyard surface (7, 543), and the debris flanking Building V/4 (8, 630). The small ear scoop (9) came from a marginally earlier context (601) in the same area as the third razor, and may be of Roman origin, as could the small file (10) from the **Period V** graveyard, although EDXRF revealed it as a complex alloy of pewter-plated leaded gunmetal inappropriate to this period.

The ring-headed two-pronged item (11), possibly a nail cleaner, was found beside an early-sixth century building (I/1, Figure 10.2) and may also be of late Roman origin. The forked bevelled lower end is similar to a strap end from Tartworth, Gloucestershire (Hawkes and Dunning 1961,24), and forked nail cleaners are known from other early Saxon sites (Smith 1993, 46; Hattatt 1993, 447). A similar object with three prongs turned through 90° from Flixborough, was tentatively identified as a latch-lifter and dated to the eighth/ninth century (Webster 1991, 100). Two-pronged toilet implements from Clogher and Stoneyford in Ireland have been identified as Roman (Bateson 1973, Fig. 3, 1 and 3), although this has been questioned (Laing 1985, 266).

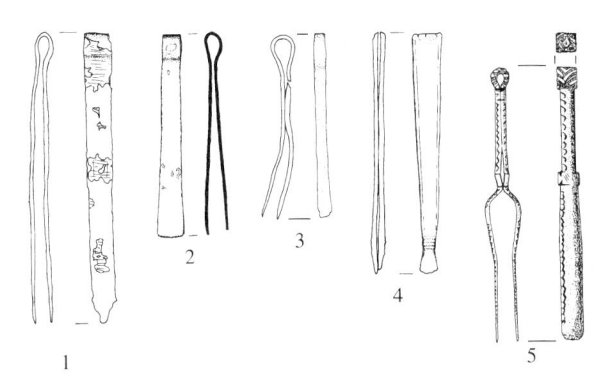

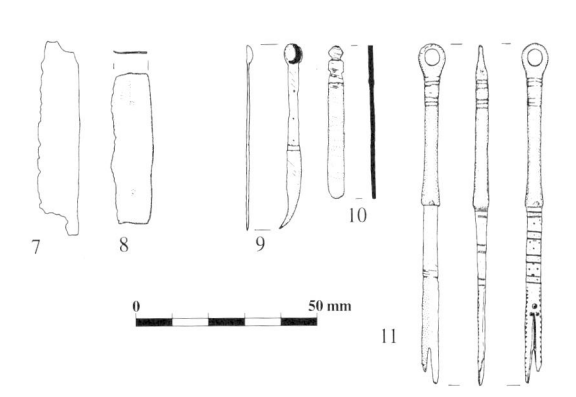

10.64 Toilet implements (BZ24).

1* Simple flat tweezers made from strip, pinched below looped head to provide tension. Small wire suspension loop partly surviving. Blades tapered at point; in two pieces.
L 77 W 7 T 1.0 Wire L 12 D 1.0. **300.01**

2* Gilded flat tweezers made from strip, pinched below looped head to provide tension, expanding towards the ends. Gilded bronze.
L 53.7 W 4 × 8.5 T 1.1. **411.04**

3* Flat tweezers made from strip, pinched below looped head to provide tension, expanding to flattened ends. One blade corroded and broken below neck.
L 48.5 W 4.0 T 1.0. **466**

4* Decorated tweezers made from folded strip. The blades taper to a collared neck before splaying into wedge-sectioned ends. Fine incised line borders both faces, four raised collars at neck.
L 63 W 88 T 1.6. **215**

5* Fine decorated tweezers of bent strip, pinched together below looped head, extending to flat collared neck, where the blades are separated again for tension before expanding slightly to flattened ends. Incised zigzag decoration borders the blades and handle, but is absent at the collar. The head is decorated with a herringbone pattern of deeper grooves containing fully round the loop.
L 73 W 6 **772**

6 Fragment of thin section razor blade, tapering slightly towards one end, transversely fractured at both ends.
L 31.3 W 11.5 × 10 T 0.5 **55**

7* Fragment of thin section razor blade, cutting edge chipped, tapering slightly towards one end. Transversely fractured at both ends, slightly bent.
L 51 W 11.2 × 10.4 T 0.7 **543**

8* Fragment of thin section razor blade, cutting edge damaged, slightly tapering to one end, transversely fractured at both ends.
L 39 W 11 T 0.7. **630**

9* Shaped flat strip with blunted curving point at one end, and small shallow circular bowl at the other. Two transverse grooves near mid shaft – the implement has broken into two pieces along the upper one. Nail cleaner or ear scoop.
L 50 W 4.2 × 2.7 T 0.8 Bowl D 5.5. **601**

10* Flat bar with decorative head. Markings on blade – transverse lines on faces, diagonal lines on sides – indicate use as a file. Rounded end, thickens at neck where it tapers, with a flat square 'collar' and a flat hexagonal head. Pewter-plated leaded gun metal.
L 40 W 4.3 T 1.0. **536**

11* Ring headed fork implement. Round sectioned handle expands at both ends, baluster-effect motif, at neck below loop, created by two sets of three incised grooves around entire handle. At the lower end of the handle expands to a sub-rectangular section with a triangular indent on each broad face. The mid portion of the implement is of flat rectangular section. The front broad face has four pairs of transverse incised lines each with a horizontally convex face between, and the three fields between the bands are decorated with punch dot motifs – two in the upper field, three in a triangle in the middle field, and four in a diamond in the lower field – a single central dot occurs in the second convex band. One side has three sets of transverse incised lines with convex bands between, whilst the opposing side has three matching convex bands without the flanking incised bands. The lower portion of the implement has a flat front face and a bevelled rear face. The front edges have small diagonal chip marks along the entire length, and the end of the implement splits into two prongs (one broken) with a well defined central groove extending up the face and ending in a three dot triangular deep punched motif. The rear face of the middle and lower portions are plain, but transverse lines probably indicate the use of a file in the final shaping process.
L 90 W 5.4 T 4.5 **74.01**

Tools (BZ25)

Six items classified as tools (BZ25.1–6) comprise a stylus (1), two styli/scribers (2 and 3), and three tapering squared-section bars (4–6) which may have been awls. The stylus (1) is round to the mid-shank where a baluster marks the change to a finely tapering octagonal point. Styli are known from seventh and eighth century contexts at the monastic sites of Jarrow and Barking (Webster and Backhouse 1991, 90), a century later from Whitby (D M Wilson 1964, 200), and from deposits of similar date at Flixborough (Webster and Backhouse 1991, 100–101) and Brandon (Webster and Backhouse 1991, 86–7), where the octagonal section above or below a moulding is reproduced. Two similar objects (2 and 3) may be styli, or perhaps scribers or prickers used in laying out of illuminated manuscripts (Backshouse 1981, 28–31). One (2) is of tapered copper alloy tube, with solid tapering silver points inset at each end. The other (3) has a single point, a baluster at mid shank, and a tapering tang for a handle. The stylus (1) came from waterborne silts (415.01) which accumulated in the **southern sector** towards the end of **Period IV**. It could have been displaced from an eighth or ninth century context in this area, but was perhaps related to other styli and prickers in iron and copper alloy from the **Period V** graveyard, which originated in **Period IV** workshop debris (Figure 6.30, p 245). The stylus/scribers both come from late contexts (600.01 and 746), but could have been displaced from **Period IV** deposits.

The three bars (4–6) are hammered and taper at both ends. They resemble some of the iron awls, but may be just lengths of partly worked material as at Coppergate, York (Bayley 1992, 783–4). Two (5 and 6) came from the **Period V** graveyard, but probably originate in workshop debris of **Period IV**. The third came (4) from a later deposit (631) overlying the graveyard, but may have had a similar origin.

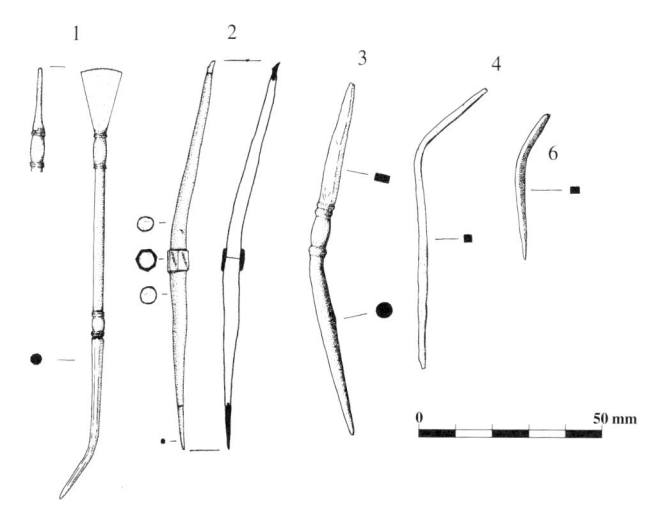

10.65 Tools (BZ25).

1* Stylus with baluster decoration at neck and mid-shank. The shank is of circular section between the two balusters, becoming octagonal from the lower baluster to the point. The stylus is bent 17mm above the point in a manner similar to the stick pins, and may therefore have been re-used as one.

L 119 Shank MD 2.5 Head W 11.4 **415.01**

2* Stylus or scriber with central heptagonal 'collar' and circular-section tapering points. The collar has a line of V-shaped incisions running diagonally across each face, creating a motif akin to a fish-spine. Traces of silvering remain at each point, and in the incisions on the collar. One point is broader than the other and may be broken. Leaded gun metal with silver/gold.

L 102.5 W 5.3 Shank MD 4.4 **746**

3* Circular-section tapering stylus or scriber with baluster at mid-point and rectangular-sectioned tapering tang. Possible handle remnants in corrosion products on tang.

L 94 Shank MD 4.3 Tang L 33 **600.01**

4* Square section rod tapering towards the ends, both of which are broken. Hammer marks create a scalloped effect on the surfaces. This piece may have been intended as a scriber, or may be an unfinished piece.

L 86 W 3 T 2.3 **631**

5 Square-sectioned tapering point, flattened at current end of shank. Possible scriber, or maybe unfinished rod. Badly corroded.

L 40 W 2.2 T 2.3 **538**

6* Bent rectangular section tapering bar, possible awl. Bent just above widest point. Lower end tapers to a point, upper tapered end more blunted.

L 42 W 2.6 T 1.7 **531**

Drawer handles (BZ26)

Two bulbous headed objects (BZ26.1* and 2) with square shanks, one leading to a hand cut screw thread, are post-medieval drawer handles, as may be a bulbous loop lacking its shank (3). One (2) came from debris abutting Building V/4 (605), and so perhaps dates to the late-fifteenth century. The other two came from more recent contexts (744 and 614), but may originate in similar late medieval contexts. No. 1 was made of arsenical leaded copper.

Fish hooks (BZ27)

A group of four fish-hooks (BZ27.1–4) includes two (1 and 3) from early contexts, and a third (2) from the chest of a **Period V** burial (536), which may have been used as an *ad hoc* shroud pin. The last is the smaller of the two definite fish-hooks, though still larger than most modern hooks. It was probably used for sea fishing and is the right size for salmon or bass. An unusually large hook (1) from a mid-sixth century rubbish spread (100), was almost certainly used for sea fishing and would have been suitable for catching for tope, large cod or conger eels. A possible fish-hook (3) lacking a barbed point, came from one of the small Northumbrian buildings (II/15, 218). Iron fish hooks (IN56.1–3, p 424), lead line weights (LD09.4–10, p 394) and fish bones (pp 602-3) provide further evidence of sea-fishing.

1* Large rectangular section fish-hook with single barbed point and expanded flattened head. Almost certainly for sea fishing, it could have been used for tope, large cod or conger eels.

L 97 Shank W 4.3 Shank T 3.0 **100**

2 Fine circular wire fish-hook with single barb point and flattened head. The head appears to have been split to form a hole, and has broken across the lower end of this.

L 63 Head W 4.2 **536**

3 Bent sub-circular section hook broken across splayed head and below point.

L 47 Head W 3.7 **218**

4 Probable broken wire fish hook with thread in corrosion layers.

L 28 T 1.0 **722**

Functional rings (BZ28)

A group of twenty rings and fragments (BZ28.1–20) comprises objects which through size or form, are unlikely to have been finger rings. Eight pieces (13–20, excavation archive) came from modern or recent contexts: several were evidently machined and included curtain rings, nuts and washers. Five of the earlier objects (1–5) are butted wire rings and were probably simple suspension loops (Figure 10.49). Two small wire rings (6 and 7) from late burials (539 and 540) in the **Period V** graveyard had fragments of cloth adhering to them, and may have acted as reinforcing eyelets (Figure 10.49). The other objects are of uncertain function. A fragment (8) of a ring from a **Period I/4** grave (82.04, I/114), was possibly part of a small buckle and may derive from the adjacent metalworking debris (85.02 or 04). A hollow gilded ring of leaded brass (10) from mid-ninth century fire debris (339.01), can perhaps be associated with finds from the Northumbrian church. A round D-section ring (12) from the **Period V** graveyard is of unknown function, but may have originated in the scattered **Period IV** debris in the inner precinct.

1 Squashed butted wire suspension ring.

D 10.5 × 8 T 1.3 **543**

2 Small butted wire suspension ring.

D 9 T 1.0 **543**

3 Small butted wire ring.

D 6 T 1.0 **600.02**

4 Butted suspension ring of round section wire.

D 10 Wire D 1.6 **744**

5 Small butted ring of round section wire.

D 6.4 Wire D 1.3 **600.04**

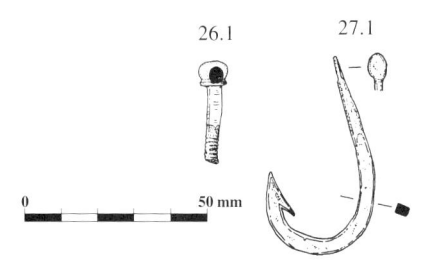

10.66 Drawer handle and fishhook (BZ26 and 27).

6 Small ring with associated textile, eyelet.
539

7 Wire ring with attached textile, eyelet.
540

8 Possible ring or buckle loop fragment, tapering round section.
L 18 T 2.8 × 1.2 **82.04**

9* Ovoid section link, probably riveted.
D 14 T 2.0 **319**

10* Gilded ring of rolled sheet, edges meet at centre of inner face. Mercury gilded leaded brass.
D 14 T 1.7 **339.01**

11 Fragment of ring,
T 0.8 **534**

12 Fully circular D-sectioned ring,
D 34 T 2.0 **543**

19 Rolled ring, flat on one side, groove round other.
D 12.4 T 2 **903**

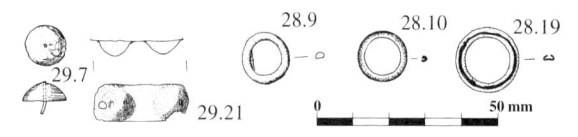

10.67 Rings and studs (BZ28 and 29).

Domed studs (BZ29)

A group of twenty domed studs (BZ29.1–20) included fourteen hammered sheet studs (3–16) usually with a stalk or a hole to receive one. Stalked domes are widespread on medieval sites over a wide time range and two belts from London (L.M.M.C 1993, Fig. 63 Nos 4 and 9) retain such studs, while examples have been found locally in a late-fifteenth century context at Threave Castle (Caldwell 1981, 109). Six of the Whithorn studs (7–11, 16) came from mid- to late-fifteenth century contexts (Figure 10.49). Three studs (12–14) from recent layers may have been displaced from similar deposits, but three others (4–6) from **Period V** deposits (534, 546, 550) in the western part of the **northern sector**, are likely to have been earlier. A strip with two embossed domes (21) may also be a belt fitting of similar date. The remaining five objects include two plated domed studs (17 and 18) with squared shanks from the manse, which are probably items of furniture decoration; a Wigtownshire Constabulary button (19) which has been bossed into a low dome; and a low dome (20) with incised decoration possibly representing a phallus and a face. A solid stud (1) with thick shank from **Period I/4** wormed soil (75.02) may have come from a furnishing or an object such as a book cover, as might a similar stud with an iron content (2) from a contemporary grave (82.04, I/116).

1 Solid domed stud with short thick shank. In two pieces. Leaded bronze.
D 12 Shank D 4.3 Shank L 9 **75.02**

2 Squashed domed stud with central stalk. Some iron content, may be plated. In two fragments.
D 9 **82.04**

7* Hemispherical domed stud with central wire stalk fixed through it.
D 9.3 Stalk D 1.4 **616.04**

21* Sub-rectangular plate with two embossed domes, and a central rivet hole at either end. Probable belt fitting.
L 26 W 10 T 0.3 **615.01**

Miscellaneous objects (BZ30)

A group of seventy-three miscellaneous objects (BZ30.1–9, 11–69, 71–75) includes doorknobs, washers, eyelets, an oil lamp wick-holder, a Verey light cartridge, a compass arm, a clock hand, a harness swivel loop and a keyhole plate from modern and recent deposits (archive). Thirty objects (1–9, 11–29, 72 and 74) came from secure medieval layers (pre c. 1500 AD), but other medieval and possibly-medieval finds had been displaced into more recent deposits or were recovered from spoil or other unstratified contexts. The decorated strips in BZ35 and fragmentary objects in BZ37 have been classified as possible scrap, but might otherwise have been included in this group.

Stratified **Period I** deposits produced three unusual objects (1–3), and two others (16 and 63) from displaced material were potentially contemporary (63) or earlier (16). A tin-plated chape (1) from the main **Period I/3** rubbish spread (85.02) in the west part of the **northern sector** lacks comparanda in Western Britain, and is smaller than contemporary U-shaped sword chapes from Anglo-Saxon burials. It could have been associated with the fine metalworking waste which accumulated in **Period I/4.5** (Figure 3.34b). Two other objects, a fragment of cut or cast strip (2) from a **Period I/4** grave (82.03, I/107) and a cased iron blade (3) from silts to the east (73.02), were broadly contemporary. The latter comprises two parallel separated iron strips held together by three round flat-headed plated copper alloy rivets. Possible mineralised organic remains appear to exist at the core between the iron strips. Traces of a possible rounded terminal could be seen on the X-ray. Only one displaced object appears to have earlier parallels. A figure-of-eight shaped plate with possible perforations and iron rivets (63), is similar to an object from Dunadd (Craw 1930, Fig. 3 No.10), and possibly to two iron objects (IN78.2 and 4) from early contexts. It fell from a section in the **southern sector**, but cannot be located more precisely.

There were only two unusual objects (4 and 5) from **Period II** contexts, both associated with the burial chapel. The mid-ninth century fire debris (207) inside the building produced a fine piece of interlace knot braid (5) in a simple Stafford knot pattern. This open-work design could consist of metal threads wrapped round a fibre core, and would have been couched onto the underlying garment. A corroded handle of tin-plated speculum (4) was recovered during the demolition of a baulk to the south of the chapel and could have derived from early **Period II** deposits or from the displaced **Period I** metalworking debris re-used at the beginning of

Period II. Scraps of wood and bark in the socket were secured by two copper alloy pins. Considerable work has been invested in this handle, yet the presence of bark on the wooden core suggests that it was also present on the original wand to which the handle was fitted.

The largest group of medieval material came from stratified deposits of **Period III** and **IV**, and the confusing stratigraphic environment of the **Period V** graves and associated surfaces (Figure 6.22, pp 237–50). A tubular needle case of folded sheet (62) came from the eastern part of the **central sector**, and probably originated in the **Period III** deposits. It is recessed to take end plates which are now lost, and has a centrally pierced upper plate for suspension. Similar objects occur in ninth and tenth century contexts at *Haithabu*, the central suspension hole differentiating them from early Saxon examples which tend to be suspended from one end. Objects of less certain function include a possible buckle pin encased in iron concretion (9), from the debris surrounding Building IV/7; a fragment of a possible handle (74) from Building IV/13, comprising a tapering bar decorated with herringbone grooves on its bevelled upper sides, and ending in a sub-rectangular terminal with two iron rivets; and an irregularly grooved rod (8) from the rubble bank in the *inner precinct* (430). An enigmatic fragment of flat curved sheet (6) from Building III/24, has toothed external projections and two perforations. Toothed edges are seen in two ninth century Saxon brooches (Hattatt 1993, 218), but they were cast as opposed to sheet. An unusual object resembling a modern bath plug (72) came from the **Period IV/3** rubble bank (430) in the *inner precinct*. The hollowed lower section is pierced by four evenly spaced holes, and the upper faceted hexagonal projection appears solid. It could have been the cap or butt of a staff, and has similarities with a bone and iron cap of Middle Saxon date from *Hamwic*, Southampton (Holdsworth 1975, 47). The silver-plated bangle (7) came from shallow deposits (424) in a disturbed area in the eastern part of the site and might pertain to **Period III** or **IV**. EXRDF analysis indicated that it was made of leaded brass with a silver component deriving either from plating or from the use of a lead/silver ore. The detached spiral ring from a ring-pin (BZ15.2) has a similar composition. A flat bar with a polyhedral head (18), possibly relating to ninth century pins with similar heads, came from a **Period V** grave in Trench 5 and could have been displaced from the **Period III** debris beyond the settlement. Three broken objects (12, 15 and 24) among a concentration of scrap in the north part of the *inner precinct* (Figure 10.71), include a tapering rod with a hooked end (12), similar to an eyeless needle; a trilobate terminal (15); and a keyhole from a barrel padlock (24). A cast ewer foot with three lobed projections (17) came from an area producing crucible sherds (Figures 6.24, 31 and 10.88). Other objects more widely scattered include a cast open-work fragment with roughly-filed surfaces (16); small, flat horseshoe-shaped strip with pierced terminals (21) may have been part of an unfinished object, but could not be linked with other groups of metalworking debris. A possible tripod leg (71) came from spoil deriving from the **Period IV** or **V** deposits in the south part of the **southern sector**. This seems to have been a failed casting in leaded bronze, and may have been associated with other scraps of metalworking debris from this area (Figures 6.24, 31, 10.71 and 88).

Several objects can be attributed to **Period V**. A cast leg from a tripod pitcher (27) has a typical fourteenth-fifteenth century tapered plain foot (27) paralleled by a ewer from Battersea (L.M.M.C 1993, Pl.LIII). It came from a pit (612.03) to the west of the **Period V** graveyard and was probably scrap awaiting recycling (pp 264, 385, 389). A small liquid measure (11) from the cultivation in the western part of the **northern sector** (546) shows evidence of turning and is stamped with a fleur-de-lis within a diamond. A three-arched, bevelled belt-hanger (23) from the graveyard (543) is comparable to a fourteenth century example from Beverley (A.R. Goodall 1991, 148). A tin-plated dagger chape (37) is of the plain pointed form common in the late-fourteenth and early-fifteenth centuries (LMMC 1993, 288). It came from a recent hollow (735) cutting the graveyard, but may originally have been deposited with coins, spur rowels and other objects on the **Period V/3** roadway (Figure 10.49). A shaped piece (26) with three rivet holes and a slot, from debris abutting Building V/4 (605) may be a lock plate. An early post-medieval wire loop (31) from a late pit in the **northern sector** (602) is probably a dress fastener, and an unstratified pierced handle (68) may come from a copper pan or skillet. More enigmatic finds include a long thin, square-sectioned rod (40), forked (but broken) at one end, and pierced at both ends; and a a small round wire loop attached to a small socket with an opposed corroded area (69). Two objects came from the **Period V** deposits in the *outer zone*. The wheel pommel of a sword of fourteenth century form (29, London Museum Type VIII) came from rubble overlying Building V/3 (Figure 10.49), and was associated with coins of similar date (Figure 10.46a). The clay packing survives, preserving the shape of the tapering rectangular tang. A fragment of decorative open-work (28) from the foundations of this building may have been displaced from the underlying **Period IV** debris (415.01).

1* Corroded tin plated U-shaped chape with horizontal grooves on upper front surface, a single groove follows the line of the inside edge. No grooves at the rear. Below the grooves is a single iron rivet, the upper part of the other side is broken. A domed knob projects from the bottom of the chape. Tin-plated bronze.

L 32 W 19 T 8.3 **85.02**

2* Cut and shaped fragment of sheet. Possible failed casting.
L 16 W 10 T 1.1 **82.03**

3 Possible iron blade, cased in copper alloy with three plated rivets.
73.02

4* Corroded and damaged cylindrical handle with concave sides and closed slightly domed butt end. Three incised transverse lines

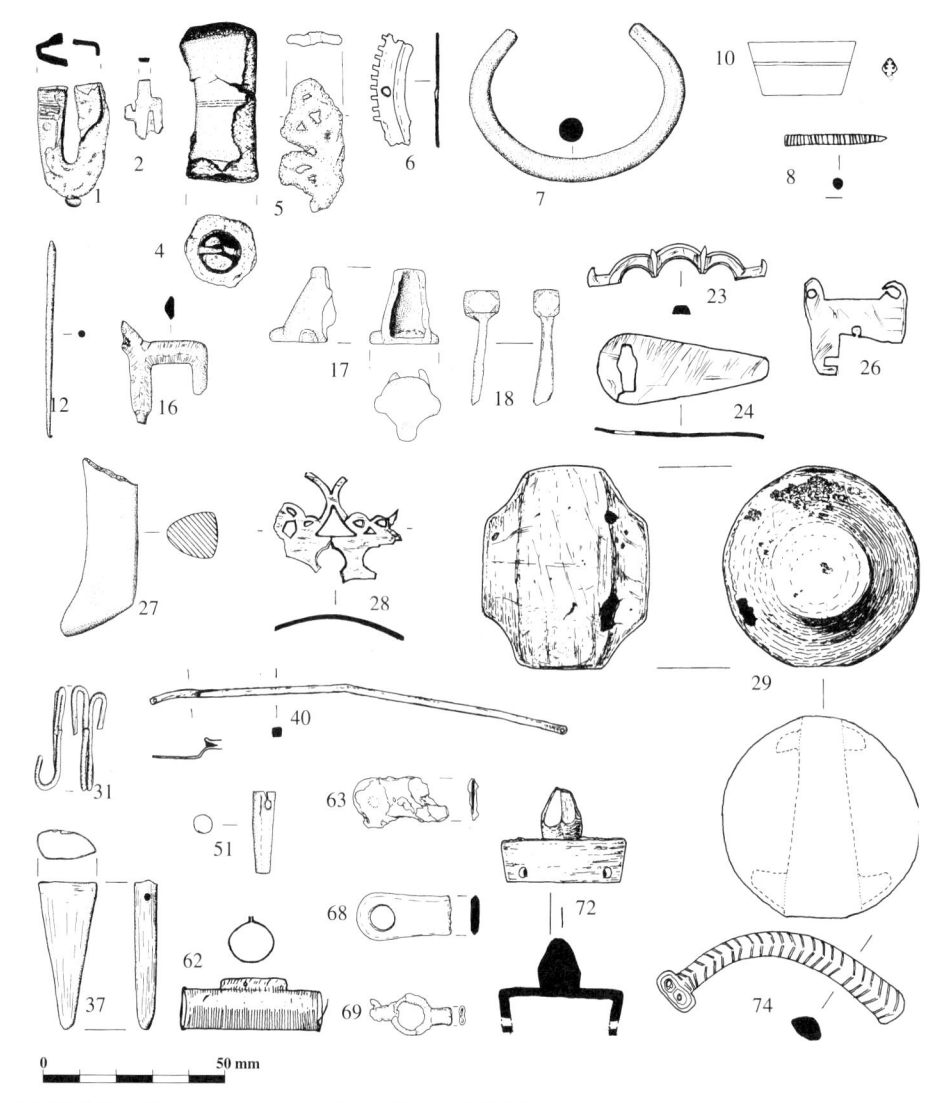

10.68 Miscellaneous copper-alloy objects (BZ30).

round middle. Single iron rivet at lower end, part of wooden core survives. Tin-plated speculum.

L 42.8 ED 16.8 × 21.5 ID 11.4 **0**

5* Piece of filigree with one and a half 'Stafford Knot' patterns attached to a lower border. Badly corroded, possibly an embroidery piece for attachment to a garment.

L 35.4 W 18.3 T 3 **207**

6* Spoked, pierced curved strip fragment. Flat sheet with central rivet hole, one end fractured across another rivet hole. Nine roughly equally sized and spaced projecting square spokes round outer edge. Incised groove runs parallel to inner edge, inside rivet holes. Possibly part of a mount.

Projected ED 80 L 30 W 9.6 T 0.8 **427.02**

7* Circular-sectioned tapering bar or bangle with rounded terminals. Traces of silver plating near one terminal. Leaded brass with silver plate or lead/silver ore.

ED 58 × 43 ID 47 × 33 T 6.2 × 4.2 **424**

8* Round pointed shank, broken at one end. Irregular spiral groove around whole length.

L 27.7 D 2.9 **430**

9 Shank or buckle pin in iron matrix.

W 2.3 T 1.5 **411.04**

11* Liquid measure with internal and external pairs of transverse grooves. Base shows internal evidence of turning, and has a fleur-de-lis proof stamp.

D 29 × 21.5 T 2.5 **546**

12* Tapering needle or pin. No eye, just a rounded end, and with a distinct small hook to the point.

L 53 D 2.3 **535**

13 Disc with central ferrous stud or rivet.

D 11 T 3.2 **535**

14 Length of rolled wire with an obvious seam, folded and doubled back to create a loop, perhaps as a dress fastening.

L 21 W 16 D 1.2 **538**

15 Trilobate terminal with broken shank.

D 15 T 6 Shank D 6 **539**

16* Cast(?) fragment of triangular section tracery – perhaps a casting sprue, though it does appear to have been filed.

L 27 W 24 T 3 **539**

17* Cast hollow foot with three projecting lobes, and a raised collar at the broken upper end. Probably from a tripod skillet.

L 22 W 17 T 2.3 **539**

18* Flat tapered bar, broken, ending in polyhedral head with faceted corners.
L 30, Bar W 5 × 2.5 T 1.3, Head W 7 T 5 **539**

19 Hexagonal plate with a central perforation, eyelet.
D 8 T 1.0 **542**

20 Stamped disc with embossed motif. Pelleted circular border around a capital B, the lower loop pierced by a transverse feather, above a scroll with the upper case inscription.
D 23 T 0.5 **542**

21 Flat horseshoe-shaped strip with pierced terminals.
543

22 Small rough disc with central perforation.
ED 8 ID 2 T 0.4 **543**

23* Three arched belt hanger. Vertical ridges between arches, upper and lower edges of arches bevelled. Side projections turn up through 90° at end.
L 49 W 5 T 3 **543**

24* Pear-shaped key hole plate from barrel padlock pierced at lower end by a rectangular slot. Slot has off-centre concavity on opposed sides, possibly for allowing passage of key shank. Extensive scratch or file marks on one face.
L 47 W 19 T 1 **547**

25 Eyelet.
D 7 T 0.4 **601**

26* Pierced plate, poss. from lock, basically quadrilateral with rounded corners, two rounded pierced projection on one side at corners. Another perforation in centre. Rectangular slot cut parallel to shorter edge.
L 28 W 26 T 1 **605**

27* Broken convex triangle-shaped leg with tapering ovoid foot, from tripod skillet or ewer.
L 47 W 14 T 15 **612.03**

28* Broken convex openwork fragment. Curved sheet with symmetrical design, central perforation below concave-sided triangle, knotwork to either side. All edges broken.
L 36 W 29 T 1.2 **506.01**

29* Wheel pommel, filled with clay. Rectangular perforations at both ends for tapering tang. Clay filling has deteriorated on both sides at top and bottom adjacent to tang slot. Many worn scratch marks on surfaces.
D 53 W 45 T 1.3 **633**

30 Thick corroded curved plate (a), possibly the wall of a vessel and a detached fragment (b) cemented to a stone.
a) L 29 W 19 T 3.5 b) L 17 W 15 T 4 **631**

31* Wire bent into a hook, for a garment or curtain (in two pieces).
L 26 W 9 D 1.2 **602**

37* Tin-plated triangular chape, terminal or ferrule, single rivet hole near top of one edge. Single sheet with seam down one edge, soldered with lead/tin solder.
L 39 W 16 **735**

40* Thin pierced and forked bar, possibly a balance arm. Square section bar bent (probably deliberately) in centre. One end transversely perforated, the other splits into two thinner arms, one broken. Intact arm also transversely perforated.
L 115 T 2 **731**

51* Hollow tapering point, unlike tag ends.
L 33 D 2 **746**

62* Cylindrical needle case with incised decoration, lacking ends. Made from single sheet, butted upper seam, with projecting central plate, perforated off-centre. Incised transverse lines round lower portion.
L 39 Ht 13.8 ED 12.7 T 0.8 **901**

63* Figure of eight shaped plate, much corroded. X-ray reveals two perforations, one in either end swelling, with traces of ferrous material.
L 28 W 12 **902**

68* Flat handle, perforated rounded terminal, broken.
L 25 W 11 T 3 Hole D 6 **903**

69* Round section wire ring with two opposed rectangular lugs, one of which appears to attach to another, broken ring.
L 24 D 10.5 Wire T 1.3 **903**

71 Triangular casting in leaded bronze, possibly a failed casting from a vessel with tripod legs.
L32 W 26 T18.4 **903**

72* Perforated hollow plug (?) with octagonal boss. Sides taper in slightly towards bottom. Pierced by four evenly spaced holes of 2.5 dia. Upper projection has rounded lower portion, with eight facets tapering towards the top. An area of corrosion near the projection's base suggest the possibility of an iron rivet or bar.
ED 31 × 34 ID 26 × 28 Ht 25 **430**

74* Possible handle (riveted to vessel) or mount. Tapering curved bar ending in sub-rectangular terminal. Convex triangle section. Upper surfaces have paired incised grooves along length. Terminal has smaller plate and two iron rivets. Other end probably broken.
L 74 W 9 T 5.8 **488**

Chains (BZ31)

Five lengths of chain and a single link (BZ31.1–6) were made of distinctive figure-of-eight links, and were probably parts of three separate chains. One (1) came from shale overlying the mid-ninth century ploughing and was probably deposited in or around one of the **Period III** buildings. A second fragment (2) from Building IV/3 could have been a contemporary loss or might have originated in the underlying **Period III** debris. The third chain was represented by a relatively long piece (3) displaced into a **Period V** grave, and smaller fragments (5, 6 and, perhaps, 4) from adjacent later contexts. The chains can thus be ascribed tentatively to **Period III** and perhaps the earlier years of **Period IV**, although the link forms are not characteristic of the

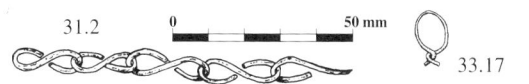

10.69 Chains and wire loop (BZ31 and 33).

period, and are closer to later medieval links (Egan and Pritchard 1991, 318–20). They may have been used in hanging vessels or on balance scales, as opposed to the more elaborate forms used in jewellery.

1* Eight extended-S links. Links butted closed except for last loops. Smaller links to one end.
Wire T 1.3 Link L 17–24 Total L 149 **399.02**

2* Four and a half figure-of-eight links, butted closed.
Wire T 1.5 Link L 18–23 Total L 93 **411.02**

3 Chain in six fragments totalling twenty-four small figure-of-eight links.
Wire T 0.8 Link L 4–7 Total L 90 **535**

4 Single figure-of-eight link.
Wire T 2 L 15 **631**

5 Three fine figure-of-eight links.
Wire T 1.0 Link L 15–16 Total L 40 **708**

6 Extended-S link joined with figure-of-eight link.
Wire T 1.5 Total L 42 **715**

Wire loops (BZ33)

Seventeen small loops of twisted wire (BZ33.1–17*) are paralleled by examples from a late-fourteenth to early-fifteenth century context at Threave Castle (Caldwell 1981, 108), and a fifteenth century layer at Northampton (Oakley 1979a, 260). They seem to have been introduced to Whithorn at a similar date, and there are four examples (2–5) from the later burials in the **Period V/2** graveyard (538, 539, Figure 10.49). Four others (7–9, 17) from the graveyard (542) and overlying surfaces (615 and 772) may also have originated in graves. A single example from an earlier grave (533) was probably intrusive. Others (10–15) associated with the 'Commendator's House' (V/8), and probably date to the early-sixteenth century. Two pieces of twisted wire (BZ32.11 and 18) may be fragments of similar objects. Their function is uncertain although their presence in graves and rubbish spreads argues that they were used in both costume and shrouds.

	Loop diameter	Wire diameter	
1 Small wire loop twisted at base	7	0.8	**533**
2 Small wire loop twisted at base	7.6	1.0	**538**
3 Squashed wire loop twisted at base	16 estimated	1.4	**539**
4 Broken small wire loop twisted at base	6	0.7	**539**
5 Broken, corroded wire loop twisted at base	10	0.8	**539**
6 Wire loop twisted at base	12.8	1.5	**540**
7 Small wire loop twisted at base	6	0.9	**542**
8 Wire loop twisted at base	8	0.9	**542**
9 Wire loop twisted at base	14	1.2	**615.03**
10 Broken wire loop twisted at base	11	1.2	**704**
11 Squashed wire loop twisted at base	10 estimated	0.8	**704**
12 Wire loop twisted at base	9	0.8	**704**
13 Wire loop twisted at base	11	1.3	**704**
14 Looped wire terminal twisted at base	8.3	1.2	**705**
15 Looped wire terminal twisted at base	7.9	1.2	**705**
16 Broken wire loop twisted at base	13	1.1	**741**
17 Wire loop twisted at base	10	0.8	**772**

LD = loop diameter, WD = wire diameter, e = estimated

Commodities and waste (BZ32, 34–40)

Peter Hill and Andrew Nicholson

Roughly 22% of the assemblage comprises finds identifiable as craftsmen's commodities and waste, and what may have been scrap metal awaiting recycling. The chronological and spatial distributions of the main groups are summarised in Table 10.4 and detailed descriptions are included in the excavation archive. The group comprises fragments of wire (BZ32), rod, bar and tube (BZ36), which were probably craftsmen's supplies; decorated strips (BZ35), utilised strips and sheet fragments (BZ37), which may have been scrap; nodular waste (BZ39) and pellets (BZ40), indicating remelting and casting; and fragments of sheet and strip (BZ38), and rivets and tacks (BZ34), which probably include craftsmen's waste and scrap. There are a number of interesting groupings and concentrations. The largest assemblage came from **Period I** deposits in the *inner precinct* where there were concentrations of strip and sheet in the rubbish spreads (94.01, 85.02, 85.04) in the western part of the **northern sector** (Figure 10.70). There was no associated evidence of casting, and these could derive from the manufacture and repair of vessels similar to the heavily-repaired Early Medieval bowl from Dowalton Loch (Hunter 1994, 57–62). Decorated fragments (BZ35) came from a distinct suite of contexts further to the east (69.02, 67.01, 70, 75, 109), and probably include scrap associated with casting in the earlier part of **Period I/1** (Figure 10.86). These differences, and the relative abundance of scrap, suggest careful sorting to keep the alloys pure and avoid producing quaternary alloys (Bayley 1992, 806). Further analyses would be required to confirm this hypothesis. Finds were sparse in the contemporary deposits in the *outer zone* (Figure 10.70), and were equally scarce in **Period II** contexts. The **Period III** finds offered slender evidence of copper-alloy working in the south-eastern part of the site in **Phase 1**. Most of the stratified **Period IV** finds came from the *inner precinct* and the uppermost layers in the south-east part of the *outer zone*

THE FINDS

(Table 6.28). These finds generally coincided with concentrations of displaced material from the **Period V** graves, which reveal distinct workshop areas associated with remelting (Figures 6.31 and 10.71), wire-working (Figure 6.34), and possibly enamelling (Figures 6.31 and 24, pp 240, 244). A more detailed examination (Figure 10.71) emphasises the spatial distinction between strip fragments which were concentrated in the south-east part of the **central sector**; sheet, sparser and more widely-scattered to the west; and a concentration of nodular waste and scrap metal to the north. The last included utilised waste (BZ37.16, 17, 20 and 21) and broken artefacts – a pin head (BZ13.6), a pin or needle (BZ30.12), a trilobate terminal (BZ30.15), and a barrel padlock lock-plate (BZ30.24). These can be identified as scrap awaiting recycling, and remelting suggested by nodular waste and possible scrap, may have continued on the western fringe of the graveyard during **Period V**. A small group of strip fragments (BZ38.70–76) can be attributed to the construction work in *c*. 1500 AD, but there was little subsequent evidence of copper-alloy working, and the relatively small group of finds from topsoil and related recent contexts is likely to have derived from medieval deposits.

Wire (BZ32)

Twenty-four sections of wire or fine circular section rod were concentrated in the **Period V** graveyard,

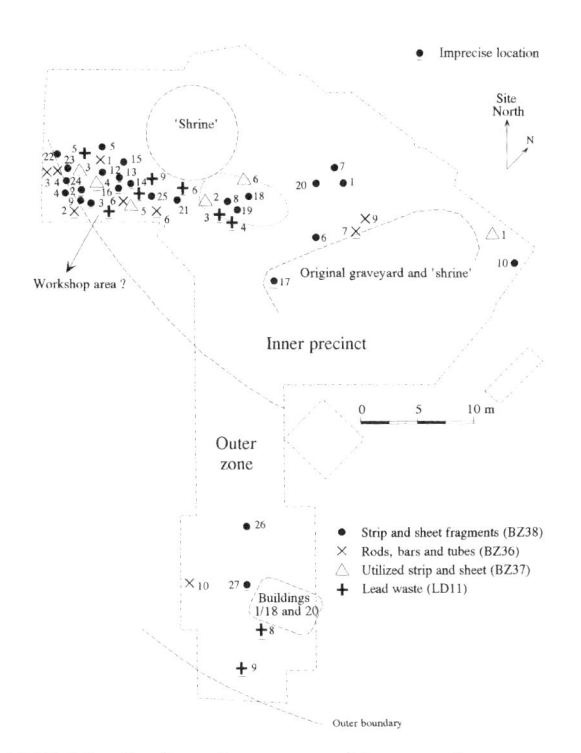

10.70 Distribution of scrap metal in seventh century deposits.

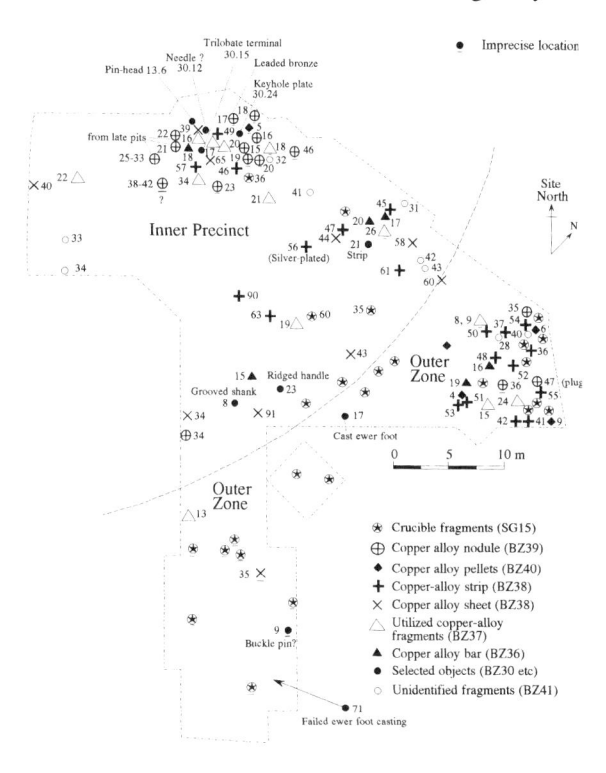

10.71 Distribution of scrap metal ascribed to **Period IV** (probably twelfth/thirteenth centuries).

	a	b	c	d	e	f	g	h	i	Total
Spoil and other unstratified		4			5	6	5	5	5	30
Topsoil		3	1	1	4	4	1	1	5	20
Period VI	1	1	2			3	4	4	3	18
Period V: Museum Garden								1		1
Period V: *outer zone*			1	1				1		3
Period V: *inner precinct* non grave	1	4	2		6	6	4	1	14	38
Period V: graves		7	1		6	20	5	1	6	46
Period IV	1	2	2		2	5	1	1	1	15
Period III		2	1	1	1				5	10
Period II/7–III/1 (315, 339 etc.)	2		2		1	2	2			9
Period II		1			4				2	7
Period I: *outer zone*			1			2			1	4
Period I: *inner precinct*	6		8	1	5	13	10	2	12*	57
Total	**11**	**24**	**21**	**4**	**34**	**61**	**32**	**17**	**54**	**258**

Table 10.4: Chronological and spatial distribution of copper alloy waste etc.
a Decorated strips, **b** Wire, **c** Rod, **d** Tube, **e** Utilised scrap, **f** Strip (38), **g** Sheet (38), **h** Sheet or strip fragments (38), **i** Lumps and nodules.
* In two groups, probably **Period I**.

indicating a specialised workshop in the *inner precinct* of the **Period IV** settlement (Figure 6.34). A small group of wire drawn from flat strips was associated with Building V/4 and probably dates c. 1500 AD. As at Coppergate, York (Bayley 1992, 782) most were in short lengths and may have been part of metalworkers' stock rather than finished items. Two pieces (1 and 12) were drawn or hammered between two swages, while another two (3 and 4) were hammered, as was another piece (10) from the graveyard. Two pieces of inter-twisted wire (11 and 18) may have been fragments of wire loops (BZ33), and came from contexts of appropriate date.

1* Round section wire, drawn or swaged.
L 96 D 1.4 **247.02**

4* Round section wire, not drawn.
L 53 D 2.0 **430**

Rivets and tacks (BZ34)

Five tubular rivets (BZ34.1–5) were probably detached from other objects such as belt plates and binding strips. Two single-sheet tacks (BZ34.6–7) from modern layers were made of a folded single elongated diamonds of sheet and would have been used for patching vessels, where they were slotted through a fine slit and the ends folded back. A similar tack was found in a fifteenth century context at Luce Sands (Jope *et al.* 1959, 270), and a seventh century patch (BZ37.4) retains three smaller tacks.

5* Rivet with single hammered end and attached small rectangular plate.
L 13 D 2 **531**

6* Tack made from a single sheet of copper alloy folded to give a rectangular head and tapering split shank.
L 14 W 9.5 **772**

7* Tack made from a single sheet of copper alloy folded to give a rectangular head and tapering split shank, one side of which is bent over.
L 19 W 12 **764**

Decorated strips (BZ35)

Ten decorated pieces (BZ35.1–10) seem, with one exception (9), to have been waste or discarded fragments, and a concentration of finds in **Period I** deposits can be linked tentatively with crucible and mould fragments (Figure 10.86). A fragment of sheet (2) from a **Period I/1.3** context (69.02) has a simple punched dot border, and a fine decorative band of zigzag pattern with red enamel (1) filling the fields is paralleled at Dinas Powys (Alcock 1963, Fig. 19 No.7), although its ultimate origin is unclear. A thin tube with transverse grooves (4) may be a binding, or the handle of a fine cosmetic brush, as with similar larger tubes on early Anglo-Saxon burial sites (Brown 1974, 151). It came from debris (85.06) under the **Period II/1** enclosure wall, but another fragment (3) from an earlier context (70) could have

been part of the same object. A possible miscast piece (6) appears to be of an animal head, and came from the **Period I/4.5** roadway (75.01) which also produced a grooved gunmetal bar (12) and other evidence of copper-alloy working (Tables 3.30 and 31, Figure 10.87a). A broken piece of a tin-plated mount made of leaded speculum (7) from the mid-ninth century ploughing (399) is too small to give any clear idea of its original form or function. A broken fragment of leaded brass (8) with an incised circled cross with smaller crosses in the intervals, is equally enigmatic. It is inlaid with a black substance which may be silver or niello. It came from the burnt debris in the **Period II/7** church (315.01), and may have formed part of an ecclesiastical ornament, or was perhaps the arm of a simple pectoral cross. A finely-incised folded strip secured with three rivets (9), from the **Period IV** wall in the *inner precinct* (486), exhibits long tendrils with three looped interlaces. The area between the tendrils is cross-hatched and the use of engraved ornamentation is seen as a Scandinavian rather than Insular tradition (Michelli 1993, 183).The axiality, symmetry and unified composition of the design are suggestive of the Ringerike ornamental style. The straight outlines are atypical of Scandinavian workmanship, but are seen on a mount from Jarlshof (Hamilton 1956, Pl. XXIX No. 1) It probably dates to the mid- or later-eleventh century when the style became prevalent in Britain and Ireland (Fuglesang 1980, 47–51).

1* Cast(?) strip with relief borders and zigzag pattern. Possible enamel inlay in recessed fields. Both ends broken. Bronze with tin plate.
L 42.5 W 3.6 T 1.3 **67.01**

2* Cut and broken plate. Two edges decorated with punched dots, two rivet holes at one end.
L 30 W 11.5 T 0.3 Hole D 2.5 **69.02**

3 Fragment of rolled tube with groups of transverse incised lines (see 4).
L 17 D 2.6 T 0.3 **70**

4* Tube fragment, longitudinally fractured and rolled. Four bands of two or three transverse incised grooves (see 3).
L 31 D 2.4 T 0.5 **85.06**

5 Small fragment of thin plated, sheet, with two associated small lumps. Bronze with tin plate.
L 13 W 9 **109**

6* Corroded piece, possibly a mis-casting, the lentoid ear and pronounced snout of a stylised animal are visible.
L 22 W 7.2 T 2.3 **75.02**

7* Broken fragment of possible mount with stud on rear and traces of tin plating on the front. Leaded speculum with tin plate.
L 22 W 7 T 1.3 **399.02**

8* Broken strip end with cross motif and silver/niello inlay. Tapering plate with rounded end. Faint incised decoration on one face. Terminal cross in circle motif, decoration continues up towards transverse fracture at tapered end. Possibly plated. Could be end of mount or arm of pectoral cross. Leaded brass.
L 19 W 17 × 8.3 T 1.2 **315.01**

9* Decorated strip, folded in half and connected by three copper alloy rivets. The back is plain, the front has a repeated design of ribbon-like interlaced animals, with cross-hatching in the central band between the interlaced knots. In two pieces.
L 71 W 7 T 0.5 **486**

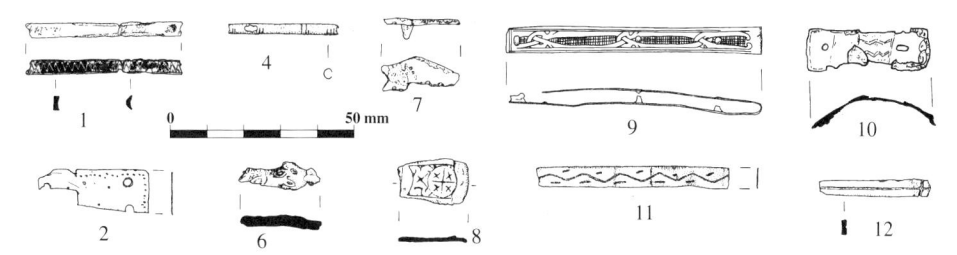

10.72 Decorated strips (BZ35).

10* Heavily corroded strip, perforated at both ends. An uncorroded section in the middle evidences two parallel incised, zig-zag lines. The strip is bent, and this may be original.
L 34 W 10.8 T 1.2 **417.02**

11* Strip, broken at both ends, back plain, front has engraved central wavy line with short horizontals in the bends. Leaded gun metal Possible lead-tin solder on rear.
L 52 W 5 T 0.4 **725**

12* Rectangular section tapering bar, one surface possibly hammered. A 0.5mm deep groove runs medially down one face, and is crossed by a transverse groove 2.3 mm from the broader end. Traces of a whitish material exist at the bottom of both grooves. Tin-plated leaded gun metal.
L 32 W 5 × 4 T 2 **75.01**

Rods, bars and tubes (BZ36)

Seventeen fragments of rods, one bar fragment, four fragments of tubes and two pieces of indeterminate form (BZ36.1–24) include ten pieces (1–10) from **Period I** deposits, concentrated in the western part of the **northern sector** (94.01, 85.01 and 02, Figure 10.70). A smaller group ascribed to **Period IV** (15–20) was more widely scattered (Figure 10.71) though coinciding with other groups of copper-alloy debris. None of the rods showed evidence of having been drawn, though a couple may have been rolled or swaged (BZ36.9). The squarer-section rods all evinced traces of hammering, again matching the rather later waste from Coppergate, York (Bayley 1992, 781–2), where a cross-pein hammer was used to reduce bars and rods to the required thickness prior to use.

1* Rolled rod or wire, broken at one end.
L 12.2 D 1.8 **94.01**

2 Fragment of rod or wire.
L 18 D 1.8 **94.01**

3 Fragment of rod or wire (unused rivet?).
L 14.2 D 2 **85.01**

4 Fragment of square section rod.
L 24 W 3 **85.01**

5 Fragmentary point of tapering rolled tube.
L 11 D 2 **85.02**

6 Rolled rod or wire, broken at both ends.
L 21.5 D 2 **85.02**

7 Broken rounded rod or shank, pointed at one end.
L 26 D 2.4 **82.01**

9* Sub-square section rod, pinched at one end, traces of hammering on upper surface.
L 71 W 2.9 T 1.3 **75.01**

10* Broken sub-rectangular section rod, tapered at one end.
L 45 W 4.3 T 3.7 **56.02**

11* Broken fragment of curved sub-rectangular section rod or bar.
L 16 W 7 T 4 **494**

22* Square section (?)hammered rod.
L 83 W 2 T 1.7 **621**

Utilised strip and sheet (BZ37)

Thirty-five pieces of strip, sheet and plate (BZ37.1–35) revealed evidence of use usually comprising one or more perforations for fastenings or rivets, or deliberate shaping. A relatively small group (1–5) from **Period I** contexts was concentrated in the main **Period I/3** rubbish spread (85.02, Figure 10.70). There was no associated remelting waste, and these may be debris from the manufacture and repair of vessels. The group included a broken patch (4) with three single-sheet tacks (see BZ34). The sheet is broken along two slots to take further tacks, and has subsequently been cut. The tacks have only one surviving arm, and were probably broken when the patch was removed. **Period II** finds (6, 7 and 10) include a possible back-plate of a strap end in leaded gunmetal (10) from the **Period II/7** church (315.01). Four slightly later pieces (8, 9, 11 and 12) from **Period III/1** buildings include two thin scraps of tin-plated leaded speculum sheet (8 and 9), and are part of a small group of later-ninth century copper-alloy debris from the eastern part of the **central sector**. Most of the fragments ascribed to **Period IV** (15–22) came from the concentration of scrap and nodular waste in the north part of the *inner precinct* (Figures 6.31 and 10.71).

1 Two fragmentary plates with rivet holes and folded edge.
a) L 27 W 11 T 0.5, **b)** L 11 W 8 T 0.3 **80.01 Gr I/9**

2 Curved strip of convex binding or edging with rivet hole and transverse groove at one end, the other end is broken.
L 37 W 44 T 0.2 Hole D 1.2 **89**

3 Broken plate fragment with square perforation, possibly for nail.
L 18 W 14 T 0.5 **85.02**

4* Curved patching sheet (**a**) with three folded sheet 'paper-clip' type fasteners. Also separate sheet fragment (**b**).
a) L 33 W 28 T 0.5, **b)** L 27 W 22 T 0.3 **85.02**

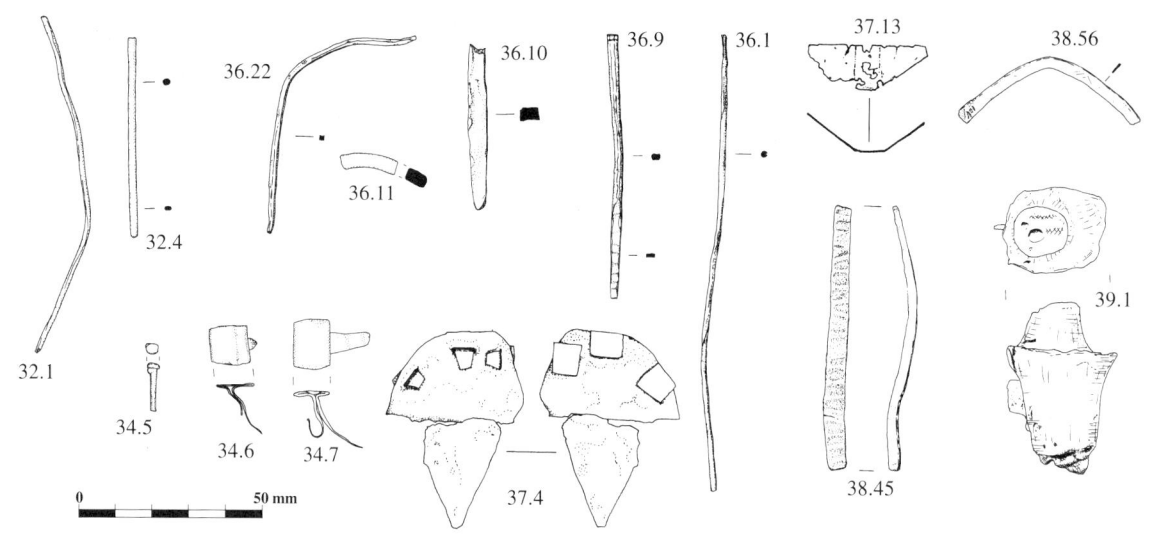

10.73 Copper-alloy wire, tacks, rods, sheet, strips, patch and casting plug (BZ32–39).

5 Rectangular plate with square perforation in one corner. The adjacent corner was probably perforated, but is broken off. Traces of a central ridge suggest it may have been bent around something, or used as a retaining plate.
L 28 W 20.5 T 0.2 **85.02**

6 Broken fragment of curved strip, possibly decorated, and five associated fragments. Leaded bronze.
L 22 W 6.5 T 1.4 **220**

7 Tapering strip with rounded end and single central rivet hole at other.
L 23 W 6.5 T 0.5 **203.05**

8–9 Two thin tapering strip fragments with traces of tin plating. Tin-plated leaded speculum.
a) L 14 W 5 T 0.1 **b)** L 21 W 6 T 0.1 **423.02**

10 Tapering thin strip with rounded end, ragged edges and a single central perforation at the flat end. Possibly a back plate for a strap or tag end. Leaded gun metal.
L 21 W 7 T 0.3 **315.01**

11–12 Two fragments of sheet with rivet holes.
a) L 12 W 7 T 0.2, **b)** L 6.5 W 4 T 0.2 **423.01**

13* Fragile sheet with cut angled sides and many perforations and holes which could be functional or corrosion.
L 38 W 13 T 0.2 **415.01**

14 Tapering strip, fractured across rivet holes at each end.
L 16 W 7 × 4.3 T 0.2 **418**

Strip and sheet waste (BZ38)

A hundred and fifteen fragments of sheet and strip (BZ38.1–115) comprise almost half of the assemblage of commodities and waste (Table 10.4). Most had cut edges and a quarter of the pieces had been folded. There were two main concentrations. The earlier pertains to **Period I** and came from the rich rubbish deposits on the western side of the *inner precinct* (Figure 10.70). Sheet fragments predominated and the associated patch (BZ37.4) and other worked pieces indicate these may have been debris from the repair, and possibly manufacture of vessels. These finds were spatially distinct from an earlier group of casting debris (Figure 10.86), and probably date to the earlier seventh century. Strip fragments predominated in a later group of finds ascribed to **Period IV** (Figure 10.71), and were concentrated in an area of the *outer zone* producing crucibles.

1 Curved strip with (?)beaten surface.
L 35 W 14 T 1.0 **69.02**

2 Fragment of sheet.
L 12 W 7 T 0.4 **94.01**

3 Fragment of sheet.
L 9 W 8.5 T 0.4 **94.01**

4 Three fragments – possibly decorated. XRF analysis: Cu, Sn, Pb, trace Zn. Leaded bronze.
94.01

5 Broken strip of waste.
L 45 W 4 T 0.7 **94.06**

6 Concave fragment – wall of tube(?)
L 23 W 18 T 2.4 **79.02 Gr 1/7**

7 Rolled and folded strip.
L 32 W 13 T 6 **70**

8 Strip folded at both ends.
L 23 W 6 T 0.3 **89**

9 Fragment of sheet or strip.
L 12 W 5 T 0.5 **85.01**

10 Broken sheet fragment.
L 34 W 21 T 0.3 **81.02 Gr I/61**

11 Broken strip folded in half.
L 35 (×2) W 9 T 0.3 **85.02**

12 Sheet fragment.
L 19 W 13 T 0.3 **85.02**

13 Sheet fragment, possibly plated.
L 17 W 14.5 T 0.3 **85.02**

14 Strip fragment.
L 12 W 7 T 0.3 **85.02**

15 T-sectioned strip, broken along one edge.
L 43 W 4 T 2.5 **85.02**

16 Slightly tapering strip with central ridge.
L 29 W 11 T 0.8 **85.02**

17 Strip with faintly scratched surface.
L 28 W 7 T 1 **82.02 Gr I/93**

18 Large piece of folded over sheet.
L 77 W 55 **82.03 Gr I/107**

19 Thin sheet fragment.
L 19.5 W 13 T 0.3 **82.03 Gr I/108**

20 Tapering strip.
L 31 W 12.5 T 0.8 **73.02**

21 Disintegrating sheet fragments.
T 0.2 **82.04 Gr I/113**

22 Folded over strip, possibly more than one piece.
Strip T 0.3 **85.04**

23 Strip fragment.
L 23 W 9 T 0.9 **85.04**

24 Sheet fragment.
L 9 W 7 T 0.3 **85.04**

25 Thin sheet fragment.
L 17.5 W 15 T 0.2 **82.05 Gr I/117**

45* Thick strip or bar with hammer marks. XRF analysis: Cu, Pb, Sn, v. low Zn, Ag present. Unusual alloy which may indicate composition from re-used fragments. Leaded bronze.
L 73 W 5.5 T 2.8 **532**

56* Fragment curved strip of silver-plated leaded gun metal.
L 58 W 4 T 1 **539**

Nodules and casting waste (BZ39)

Fifty-three nodules of melted alloy (BZ1–46) from twenty-two distinct contexts point to remelting and possibly casting. Two groups from **Period I** include eight nodules from a **Period I/2** grave (I/50) and four rivulets from a poorly-stratified rubbish spread in the western part of the **central sector** (118). Three pieces from **Period II** contexts perhaps originated in the displaced **Period I** metalworking debris. There were two main concentrations of nodular waste, both from the north-west part of the site. The first comprises nodules displaced into **Period V** graves and associated with a cluster of scrap metal (Figures 6.31 and 10.71). The other came from **Period V** pits in the same general area and could have derived from the same primary source or from continuing activity on the fringe of the graveyard in the fourteenth or fifteenth century. Associated finds, notably a fourteenth/fifteenth century ewer foot (BZ30.27) from one of the pits, commend the latter view. A late deposit in this area (746) produced a group of nodules (38–42) preserving the shape of a crucible. The only piece of definite casting waste (47) is a plug of speculum from the gate of a mould, recovered from the late fifteenth century soakaway (601) outside Building V/4. It coincided spatially with a concentration of crucible fragments ascribed to a **Period IV** workshop (Figures 6.31, 10.88), but these did not reveal traces of speculum and it could have been earlier. A mass of fused folded sheet (34) from a recent deposit (735) was probably medieval, but cannot be linked with other concentrations of debris (Figure 10.88).

17 Drop of molten waste. Leaded bronze.
542

34 Large flat nodular mass of (?)melted copper alloy. Would appear to be folded sheet waste subjected to a high temperature. Leaded bronze.
L 48 W 37 T 8 **735**

47* Plug of copper alloy, traces of flash show it to be casting waste, from the pouring hole of a mould. Speculum.
L 44 D 25 × 32 **601**

Pellets (BZ40)

Ten droplets or pellets were scattered among **Period I** to **V** deposits. There was a group in the south-east part of the **central sector**, which coincided with a concentration of crucible fragments and pieces of strip ascribed to **Period IV9** (Figure 10.71).

Non-attributable fragments (BZ41)

Sixty fragments were so small as to enable no information to be drawn from them.

The Lead

Andrew Nicholson

The excavation produced four hundred and eighty pieces of lead or lead alloy (Table 10.5). Most had been utilised, but the majority are best regarded as waste material awaiting recycling. Lead artefacts occurred in some of the earliest deposits (**Period I/0**, 102; **Period 1/2**, 51, Figure 10.2) and there was evidence of lead working among the **Period I/3** industrial debris (85.02 etc, Table 3.22, Figure 10.70); in a suite of mid-ninth century deposits within and adjacent to the **Period II** church; in the debris ascribed to **Period IV** (Figure 6.31); and in features of c. 1500 AD associated with building work on the cathedral. Leadworking waste predominated in the first of these groups and could have derived from building repairs, although no specific structural context can be identified. The second group included a wider range of finds indicating various crafts using lead implements and lead scrap or fabricating lead objects. Although perhaps commoner in later contexts, most categories spanned **Period IV,** and so reveal an evolving pattern of lead utilisation in the eleventh to thirteenth centuries. Roughly 20% of the collection was recovered by the metal detection of spoil (903) which produced two pilgrim's tokens (LD09.1 and 2) and other important finds. The most significant objects were two complete crushed lead vessels (LD01.1 and 2), apparently associated with Building IV/7 (p 223), and possibly used in the preparation of furs.

	01	02	03	04	05	06	07	08	09	10	11	12	13	Total
a: Topsoil/unstratified		1	2	3	2	11	2	9	16	2	38	87	7	180
b: **Period VI**				1		3	1	1	1		8	3		18
c: **Period V: Museum Garden**						2							2	4
d: **Period V:** *outer zone*		4	1								5	3		13
e: **Period V:** *inner precinct* non grave	1	1	2		1	4	2	5	1		37	3	2	59
f: **Period V:** graves		2	5	2	5	18				2	24	6	5	69
g: **Period IV**	2	2	1		5	7			2	2	8		2	32
h: **Period III**					1	2			1		4	7		15
i: **Period II/7–III/1** (315, 339, etc.)					1	1				2	12	17*	1	33
j: **Period II**			1		1	3					18	11	1	35
k: **Period I:** *outer zone*						1			1		2		2	6
l: **Period I:** *inner precinct*			1	1		1			3		6	4		16
Total	3	10	13	7	16	53	5	15	25	8	162	141	22	480

Table 10.5: Chronological distribution of lead finds.
01 Vessels, **02** Perforated discs, **03** Spindle whorls, **04** Washers, **05** Weights, **06** Rivets, nails and tacks **07** Tags, **08** Calmes etc, **09** Miscellaneous, **10** Casting waste, **11** Leadworking debris, **12** Nodular waste, **13** Droplets
* includes group of *c.* 700 pieces from the floor of the church counted as one.

Lead vessels (LD01)

A group of three 'vessels' (LD1.1–3) comprises two complete basins and a post-medieval pot lid with an attached leather thong. The two basins came from mid- to late-twelfth century deposits, and are part of a small, but expanding corpus of such objects. The earliest British group are fourth century Roman tanks decorated with Christian symbols, and identified as baptismal vessels (Thomas 1981a, 220–5). A three-piece lead vessel of Middle Saxon date was found at Riby Crossroads, Lincs. (Cowgill 1994), and there are two more vessels of similar date from Flixborough in the same area (Leahy 1995, 352). Three others from Garton, Yorks are Anglo-Scandinavian, and an undated, but potentially contemporaneous vessel, containing a hoard of iron tools, was recovered from Stidriggs, Dumfriesshire (M.L. Haynes, Pers. Comm.).

One vessel (1) retains an inward-turned lip over a wooden frame, to which it is secured by irregularly-spaced clenched lead nails. The other (2) has no surviving woodwork, but has similar nail holes – some well-formed and primary, and others just punched through and probably secondary – and was made the same way. Closely-spaced paired holes in the rims may have been for suspension loops, a feature noted on other vessels. If the vessels were suspended, the timber frame would have prevented the lead tearing under the strain, as well as giving shape and rigidity to vessels which were thin-walled in relation to their size and volume. Both vessels are undecorated. They were found in the **Period IV/7–11** silts (415.01) in the **southern sector**, but perhaps lay in the shallow gullies around Building IV/7 (p 223), and were probably lost accidentally when the area flooded. Lead is, of course, unsuitable for work with open heat, though the Garton vessels had sooted bases and patched holes in the base where the lead had melted. Lead vessels were often used for dyeing in the later-medieval period, as both copper alloy and iron react with the dyestuffs and effect the resulting colours, and in tawing which also requires an inert container for soaking skins. The evidence from the adjacent ditch (417.02, Table 6.10, pp 223, 616-7) for the skinning of cats thus provides a plausible explanation for these two vessels which could have been used for the preparation of cat skins.

1 *Squashed complete vessel. A clear change of angle marks the junction between side and base, suggesting a flattened base, though it appears to be of one piece, lacking any visible seams. The rim is inturned over a hoop of wood. Surviving fragments of wood indicate that it was a branch or wand, utilised with the bark still in place. Where perforated by nails or rivets, the shank diameter is greater than half the wood diameter. Six roughly equidistant circular holes are spread around two-thirds of the rim, with another irregular (possibly secondary) hole, and a single circular hole is visible in the other third. Despite the folding, there is no obvious sign of any other perforations in the last third. Three of the holes still have rivets *in situ*, and debris from within the vessel included another circular-shanked rivet, and a square-shanked nail with a clenched tip (possibly from the irregular perforation).
Rim C 1132 Rim-Base H 165 BD 435 Rivet Head D 11–12 Rivet Shank D 7 Rivet/Nail L 24–36 **415.01**

2 *Large squashed complete vessel with sides folded inwards. No clear change of angle between sides and base, suggesting a rounded base and slightly globular form. The rim is inturned, though there are no traces of wood remnants from this vessel. However there are round and squared perforations round the rim. These tend to occur in pairs, spaced roughly equidistantly around the circumference. In some cases these pairs consist of one round and one squared perforation (perhaps suggesting a refurbishment), in others two squared holes. One pair of holes is marked by a cruciform pattern of impressed closely spaced parallel lines 5–6mm long (this pattern was also seen on an isolated rivet head in LD06), probably from a tool. No nails or rivets were found associated with this vessel.
Rim C 1280 Body Max C 1603 Rim-Base-Rim 980 **415.01**

3 *Knobbed circular disc with, central raised circular knob with leather thong, wrapped around edge (a pot lid). Upper surface scratched and with a 3mm diameter and 2mm deep puncture hole.
D 62 T 7 Knob D 19 T 6 **617.03**

Perforated discs (LD02)

Ten perforated discs (LD02.1–10) lack the characteristic wear patterns found on the surfaces and edges of spindle whorls (LD03) and washers (LD04). The objects are relatively uniform in size, ranging

10.74 Lead vessels (LD01).

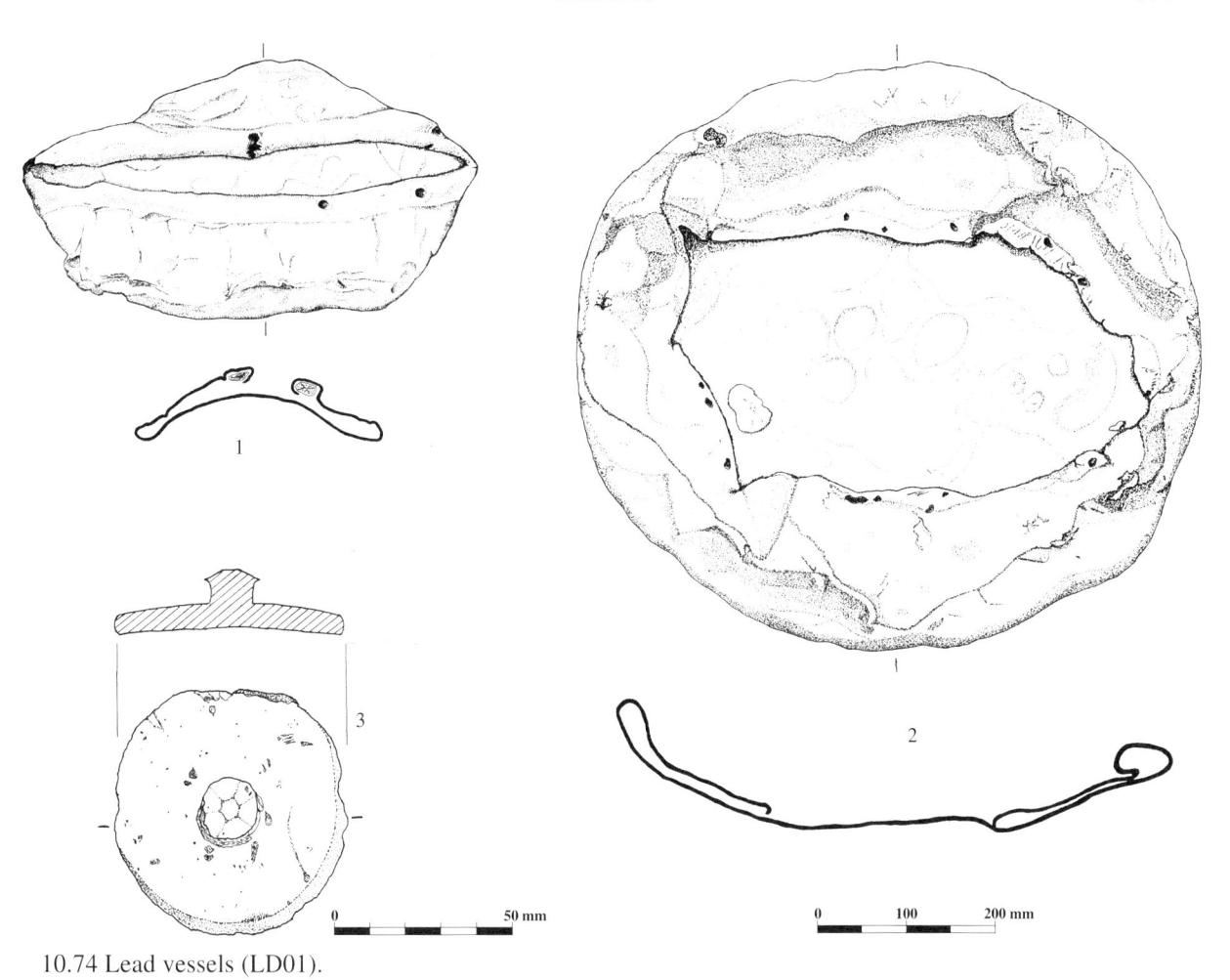

from 18 to 27mm in diameter, and from 1.5 to 3mm thick. Seven of the ten pieces (1–7) came from the **southern sector** and, though widely dispersed stratigraphically, may have originated in the debris scattered in the waterborne silts of **Period IV.7–9** (1, 415.01) and the buildings to the north (2, 456.02, IV/5). This suggest that they had a specific function and may even have been part of a set. The remaining three (8–10) came from **Period V** contexts, two (8 and 9) in the graveyard and one (10, 550) on its western edge, but probably originated in the **Period IV** debris, and may have been contemporary with the larger group to the south.

Spindle Whorls (LD03)

Thirteen perforated discs (LD03.1–13) were interpreted as spindle whorls on the basis of circumferential wear patterns. Five (4, 5, 7, 9 and 13) were plano-convex and six were flat discs of varying size (19.5–28mm in diameter) and thickness (2–6mm). Most of the whorls would have been suitable for spinning heavy tightly-spun woollen fibres, although two small examples (4 and 7) would only have been suited to finer thread. Seven (4–11) of the eleven stratified whorls came from the **Period V** graveyard and related contexts (600.01, 550), but were probably displaced from the **Period IV** debris (Figure 6.29). An eighth (3) came from an undisturbed **Period IV** deposit (430) in the same area, and a ninth (11) from an early **Period V** context (520.05) in the **southern sector**. These whorls thus seem to have had a limited currency in the eleventh/twelfth to thirteenth centuries, and their distribution indicates they had a specialised function, perhaps associated with the manufacture of warp thread for weaving (p 243). There are comparable examples from Irish sites such as Carraig Aille II (Proudfoot 1961, 116) and a decorated lead whorl of eleventh-thirteenth century date is known from Northampton (Oakley 1979b, 287 Fig. 126). An example from Threave Castle (Caldwell 1981, 111 Fig. 10) indicates that the type persists locally into the fifteenth century.

There are two anomalous early finds, an irregular ovoid disc (1) sealed by the **Period I/0** road (102), and a domed example (2) from an early **Period II** surface (203.05). Comparable early lead whorls are known from Mucking (Webster & Cherry 1973, 142) and Dinas Powys (Alcock 1963, 122 Fig. 23).

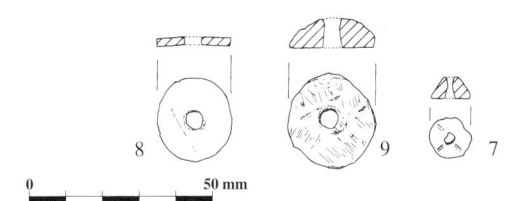

10.75 Lead whorls (LD03).

1 Irregular ovoid perforated disc. Upper surface plano-convex. Spindle whorl?
L 28 W 25 T 7 PD 5.5 **102**

2 Dome-shaped object with bi-conical perforation on base.
H 18 W (base) 17 W (top) 15 Base PD 9 Top PD 3 **203.05**

3 Slightly bent, ovoid disc with circular central perforation and chipped edges.
L 19.5 W 21 T 3. **430**

4 Circular perforated plano-convex disc.
D 7.5 T 4.5 PD 5 **533**

5 Slightly irregular, round perforated disc with one flat and one plano-convex side, and central perforation.
D 19 T 4 PD 8.5 **533**

6 Transversely-folded circular disc with a round central perforation.
D 22.5 T 1.5 PD 5 **535**

7* Circular-based, plano-convex perforated dome.
D 10 T 6.5 PD 2. **539**

8* Circular disc with round, central perforation.
D 19.5 T 2 PD 5.5 **550**

9* Plano-convex perforated disc with flat base. Base has knife scores from working.
D 25 T 7 PD 7 **542**

10 Circular disc with round central perforation, slightly dented.
D 21 T 1.5 PD 5 **600.01**

11 Circular disc with round central perforation.
D 28 T 2.5 PD 6 **520.05**

12 Bent circular disc with round, central perforation.
D 26 T 3 PD 9 **903**

13 Irregular ovoid disc, one flat, one plano-convex side with central perforation.
L 28 W 22 T 6 PD 9 **904**

Washers (LD04)

Seven perforated discs (LD04.1–7) with diameters ranging from 17mm to 22.5mm, and thicknesses from 1mm to 2.5m, had surface marks indicating use as washers for nails or bolts. One (1) came from the **Period I/3** rubbish spread (85.02), and two (2 and 3) from the **Period V** graveyard. The remainder (4–7, archive) came from spoil or other recent contexts.

1 Ovoid disc with sub square perforation with striations on both sides.
L 17.5 W 14 T 1.0 PD 6.0 **85.02**

2 Circular disc with round central perforation and rim on the outer edges where they appear to have been squared in. Underside of perforation also shows rim from punch.
D 21 T 2.5 PD 8 **537**

3 Irregular circular disc w/ round central perforation.
D 21.5 T 2.5 PD 5 **543**

Weights (LD05)

Fifteen objects (LD05.1–15), mostly discoid, have been identified as possible weights, and a last (16) is a definite weight. A group of scaled weights is based around a unit of c. 22.6g (8), with examples representing × 2 (13), 2/3 (10), 1/2 (1), 1/3 (11), 1/5 (2 and 3) and 1/10 (7) of this unit. Contemporary Norse weights appear to have been based around the 24 g øre and 8 g ertog (± 0.8 g), used in arm rings and bar money (Warner 1976), and the Whithorn group, though on the light side, may also relate to this standard.

One weight of 58gm (16) has a triangular, gilded, copper-alloy, decorative insert mount divided into four fields with relief borders. A central triangle links to the points of the outer, and the resulting three bays each have an incised crouching animal with prominently-spiralled hips, round eyes and a long snout, all in an insular style of the late-ninth century. The use of decorative inserts in lead weights is characteristically Norse (Alcock *et al.* 1992, 292; Graham-Campbell 1980, 88–9). Triangular mounts are unusual, and the Whithorn example may originally have come from an openwork circular piece, as occurring on some Irish ring-pins (Armstrong 1922, Pl.XIII Fig. 3 No.3; Mahr 1932 Pl.18 No.2).

Three of the weights (1–3) pertained to the later-ninth century. The earliest (1, 11.3 gm) came from a post-hole in the **Period II/6** church (310), and a similar, truncated cone weight (13.9 gm) was recovered from Alt Clut (Alcock *et al.* 1992, 292). A second (2, 4.62 gm) came from the burnt debris to the south of the chapel (339.01), while a third (3, 4.1gm) from **Period III** debris (494) in the eastern part of the **central sector** may have been broadly contemporary. Ten of the remaining thirteen weights came from the *inner precinct* and were probably among the scattered **Period IV** material (Figure 6.38). Three (4–6) came from stratified contexts, five (7–11) had been displaced into **Period V** graves, and the last two (13 and 16) came from disturbed layers (772) in the west part of the area. Two (14 and 15) of the remaining three came from spoil (903) and the last (12) came from a secure early-sixteenth century deposit in the eastern part of the site (704, **Period V/5**). The absence of weights from the **Period IV** buildings in the *outer zone* argues that, while these may have been used as workshops, trading took place in the *inner precinct* (pp 246–7).

1 Dome-shaped object, possibly weight.
Lower D 13.5 H 11.3 Wt 11.3 **310**

2 Ovoid-based weight.
Base 8 × 10 H 10 Wt 4.62 **339.01**

THE FINDS

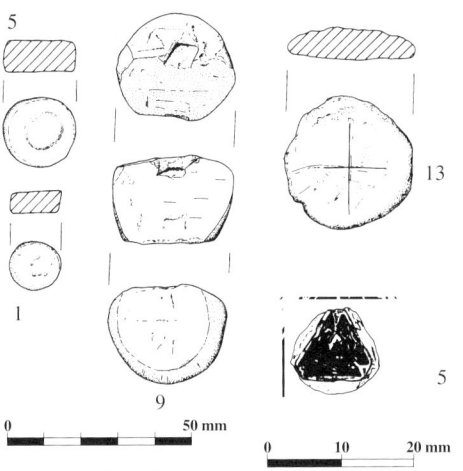

10.76 Lead weights (LD05).

3 Irregular ovoid disc.
D 17 T 2. Wt 4.1 **494**

4 Circular disc with incised cross on one surface. Counter or /weight.
D 12 T 1 Wt 1.8 **457**

5* Small, thick disc.
D 18.2 T 9 Wt 26.13 **457**

6 Smooth flattened conical piece with flat base.
L 21 Base L 14.5 Base W 7. Wt 9.31 **432**

7 Disc with clipped edge.
D 14 T 1.3 Wt 2.29 **530**

8 Irregular ovoid-shaped disc with circular punch mark on one side.
L 35 W 30 T 3 Punch mark D 2.5. Wt 22.6 **534**

9* A once barrel-shaped weight, cut smoothly on the perpendicular, and roughly on the longitudinal planes. The curved outer side shows score marks from the cutting process. Square indentation on upper surface.
L 28 D 25. Wt 122 **539**

10 Thick flat disc, probable weight.
D 17 T 4.8 Wt 15.2 **542**

11 Circular disc with two gouges on one side, counter or weight.
D 6.5 T 5 Wt 7.71 **543**

12 Circular disc with one rough, one smooth side, possibly weight.
D 11 T 0.5. Wt 0.41 **704**

13* Flat-based plano-convex- sectioned disc. Upper surface very flat, base has cross incised on it.
D 24 T 4.5. Wt 44.8 **772**

14* Circular disc, possibly weight.
D 13.5 T 6. Wt 9.62 **903**

15 Small ovoid disc with round hole tapering to a rectangular incision on base.
D 9.5 T 3.5 Hole D 2. Wt 2.02 **903**

16* Lead weight with inset triangular bronze decorative mount. The mount is divided into four fields with relief borders, a triangle centrally, with divisions from the points to the points of the external triangle. Within the three outer fields are the incised motif of a crouching animal, with prominently spiralled hips, round eyes and a long snout, all in an insular style. These have been gilded. The central triangle has a rilled rim with small punched dots on the upper surface. A triangular insert in the centre is badly damaged.
L 26.2 W 25.3 T 15.5 Wt 58 **772**

Nails, rivets and tacks (LD06)

Fifty-three nails, rivets and tacks (LD06.1–53), with shanks ranging from 13 to 55mm in length, are listed in the archive. Rivets (1–28) were generally distinguished by their round shanks, whereas the nails conformed to their iron equivalents with square, hammered shanks and round flat (=IN01), flat expanded (=IN04), inverse pyramid (=IN05), angled (=IN09) and flat offset heads (=IN12). No specific uses for lead nails have been recorded previously and it has been thought impractical for such long shanks to be associated with vessels (Foreman 1991b, 157). The clenched nails and rivets securing the rims of the sheet vessels (LD01.1–2) reveal one possible function and a construction technique which could have been used for other objects. Most of the nails and rivets came from stratified **Period IV** deposits or the **Period V** graveyard (Table 10.5), and so probably reflect artisanal activity in the *inner precinct* (Figure 6.32, pp 244–5), and specifically the manufacture and repair of vessels. One rivet (1) came from a secure **Period I** context (**Period 1.3/4**, 94.01), one (2) from **Period II** and two (3 and 4) from **Period III**. Nails and tacks show similar patterns with a broken nail (34) from **Period II** (220) and a tack (48) from the mid-ninth century plough-soil (399.02). There were no rivets or nails in two early concentrations of sheet waste (85.02; 303, 315, 339), which might thus have been derived from roofing. Two failed castings (LD10.3 and .4), one from the **Museum Garden** (4, 408) and one unstratified (3), show that rivets and nails were manufactured at Whithorn, although the workshop is unlocated.

Tags (LD07)

Five possible tags (LD07.1–5) are all different in form. One (1) is a simple disc with a pair of central perforations, and may simply be the core of a covered button, although copper alloys are generally preferred for this. Another (3) is a rimmed disc with two central slits, while a third cast disc (2) has a raised rim containing a pattern of raised pellets and has been broken at a protrusion on one edge. A fourth (4), also broken, is a plain sheet with a relief border and inscribed W.R.N. in relief. All are probable tags. The only definite tag (5) is a more complex object of two circular sheets, joined at three points around a common circumference, creating two small slots on the rim opposing a single larger one. When the cords are passed through and tightened, the tag is then sealed with a stamp. Similar items continued in use in Customs work until the 1960's. Two of the tags (1 and 2) came from fifteenth century contexts, a third (3) may have been seventeenth century, and the other two (4 and 5) were recovered from spoil.

1 Circular disc with two equally-spaced perforations.
D 18. T 0.7 **600.01**

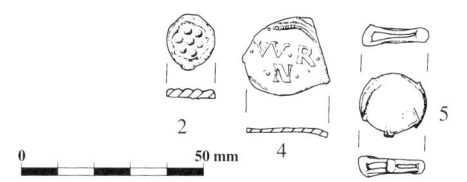

10.77 Lead tags (LD07).

2* Circular disc with raised rim and flower dot pattern on one side. The other side plain, but with nodule possibly for a shank.
D 12 T 1.5 **615.01**

3 Circular disc with two equally spaced central slits and small rim round outer edge on one side. Possible tag.
D 17. T 0.8 **610.03**

4* Ovoid-shaped piece with one cut or broken edge. One side has the letters W.R.N. and part of a border in relief. Possibly part of a seal.
L 21.5 W 18 T 1.2 **903**

5* Circular hollow tag formed from two thin plates, joined in three places to form two small openings opposing a large one.
D 17.5. **903**

Window calmes (LD08)

A small group of window calmes and ventilators (LD08.1–16, archive) included five calmes (1–5) from **Period V** deposits, and eight (6–13) from more recent contexts, topsoil and spoil. Two came from the path outside Building V/1 and were presumably associated with the painted fourteenth century glass from the same area. The other three pieces came from debris (605, 630) associated with Building V/4 and so probably date to c. 1500 AD. These may reveal the presence of glaziers working on the cathedral although the associated finds of plain glass indicate they derive from a less important building. The absence of lead calmes from the deposits producing Northumbrian window glass is discussed above (p 329). Three cross-shaped fragments (14–16) from late contexts can be identified as ventilators for leaded windows (Foreman 1991b, 158 Fig. 119 No. 118).

Miscellaneous objects (LD09)

Pilgrim Tokens (1 and 2). Two pilgrim's tokens were recovered from spoil. The first (1) is a rectangular plate with a full length portrait of a bishop with lombardic script down both long edges, and four perforations for attachment. It is nearly complete save for the upper part, including the head. The bishop wears a long full chasuble of thirteenth-fifteenth century form, with a superhumerale. He holds a crozier with a foliate crook in his left hand and his right hand is raised in blessing. At his right foot is a pascal lamb in front of a foliate motif probably representing the tree of life. A pair of possible shackles in the lower left has been taken to associate the figure with St. Ninian, although images of St. Leonard use the same motif. The second token (2) is more fragmentary, again rectangular, but this time 'landscape' as opposed to 'portrait', with a lettered border and central decorated panel. Two bearded, haloed figures are shown, though only the head of the left figure survives. The figure on the right holds a cross-headed staff in his extended right hand, and a key resting over his shoulder in his left. He wears a pleated garment. The composition and design are very similar to an unprovenanced token of SS. Peter and Paul in the British Museum (Spencer 1968, Pl. IV No.7). English pilgrims badges tend to be attached to the garment by pins, and stitching as indicated by the perforations on the Whithorn pieces, is a Continental practice. Similarly English, Scandinavian and German badges tend to openwork designs, with solid medallions prevalent in France, the Low Countries, Spain and Italy (Spencer 1968, 139). The identification of the first token with Ninian (Hill 1988a, 24) is thus likely to be incorrect, and both were perhaps casual losses by visitors to the shrine.

Pendant (3). A looped pewter pendant came from the **Period V/3** roadway (600.01), but could have been displaced from earlier deposits. Two projecting squared lugs above a flat triangle lead to a tapered rounded shank with a transverse perforation. The eye of faith may see it as cruciform, but it lacks any direct parallel. Triangular pendants of bone and limestone, the latter from a thirteenth century context, were recovered from Flaxengate, Lincoln (Mann 1982, 11–2).

Line Weights (4–10). Five pieces of carefully-rolled lead sheet (4–8) with a central, transverse channel may have been used as line weights and contrast with the relatively common pieces of folded sheet saved for reuse (LD11). Three were stratified, two (4 and 5) coming from **Period I** graves, and the third (7) from a **Period IV** structure (IV/26). One of these (5) came from the same area as a large copper-alloy fish hook (BZ27.1). A more definite fishing weight (9), with morphological parallels continuing in use locally to recent times, is a 'hogback' shaped piece with a perforation at each end. Similar objects of stone from late Norse phases at Jarlshof were compared with contemporary Shetland line blocks (Hamilton 1956, 183), also recovered at Birsay (Ritchie 1993, Fig. 47), where a slightly flatter example in lead was also recovered (Hunter 1986, 183). An ovoid perforated disc (10) from topsoil matches an object from Dinas Powys which was interpreted as a line weight or sinker (Alcock 1963, 122, Fig. 23 No.4).

Pin (11). A lead-alloy pin, possibly of leaded bronze, with an angled cuboid head and a tapering shank came from a hollow (85.07) adjacent to the **Period I/4.5** 'shrine', and was associated spatially with a group of fine metalworking debris (p 117, Figure 3.34b). It may have been a failed casting, but seems to have been filed and finished, and so could have been a former for a mould. The type of head is unknown in Scotland (Laing 1975, 1976).

Miscellaneous (12–25). Several objects were recovered whose function has not been determined. Foremost is a large perforated disc with three transverse grooves around the outer edge (12). It could be a stacking weight with a value ascribed to the visible external grooves, but lacks parallels. The perforation is nearly central, and the object may have functioned as a flywheel in a similar fashion to a whorl. It comes from one of the earliest deposits in the **southern sector** (51), and may relate to an undefined late Roman industrial practice.

A small flat circle with opposed splayed 'wings' (13) from the 'roadway' (438) surrounding the **Period III/3** settlement, lacks parallels or any suggestion of function. **Period IV** deposits produced a small wire-like fragment (14), and Period VI layers a double disc with a projecting sprue (15), similar to the knob on the contemporary lid (LD01.03). A tongueless buckle (16) from topsoil in the **southern sector** possibly dates to the fifteenth century (c.f. Oakley 1979b Fig. 108 No.24). The remaining finds from recent features, topsoil and spoil (archive) comprised a broken spoon handle (17), two lead shots (18 and 19), two fragments of plumbing pipe (20 and 21), a thick-walled cylinder (22), a ring (23), a pierced cast fragment (24), and a patching sheet with circumferential perforations (25).

1* Damaged Pilgrim's Token. Frontal full portrait of (?)saint, now lacking head. Figure wears clerical dress – a full chasuble, a hooded robe and a stole. The right hand is raised as in blessing whilst the left holds a crozier with foliate head. Below the right arm is a tree with spreading branches, with a semi-seated quadruped at its foot looking up at the human figure. These may represent the Paschal Lamb and Tree of Life. A damaged motif in the other lower corner appears to be a foliate design, but might represent a pair of shackles. Lombardic script, badly damaged, occupies the left and right borders: Left – B (or R) AT I – ; Right – INII –. Four holes perforate from the front to enable the token to be fixed to a garment.

903

2* Two conjoined fragments of broken Pilgrim's token. Pictorial image in 'landscape' format of two bearded, haloed figures. Only the head, and possibly the left hand, of the left figure survives. The right figure holds a cross-headed staff in his extended right hand, and a rod or key over his left shoulder in the other. A pleated garment drapes over his arms. Only fragments of the relief lettered border survive, the piece being broken across both corners:
Top – LI+ ; Right – AP(O) ; Lower – OL (O)

L 28 W 32 T 1.5 **903**

3* Pendant, upper shaft pierced for attachment. Square projecting arms or lugs above flat triangle. Rounded shank transversely perforated at top. XRF identifies as pewter.

L 24.5 W 7.5 T 4.8 **600.01**

4 Tube of rolled sheet, possible line weight.

L 29.4 D 8.7 **80.03 Gr I/27**

5 Tube of rolled sheet, possible line weight.

L 27.3 D 9.0 **82.03 Gr I/110**

6 Rolled sheet, possible line weight.

L 26 D 7 **903**

7 Tapering tube of rolled sheet, possible line weight.

L 47.5. W 8 **407.02**

8 Rounded piece of rolled strip, possibly plumb bob or line weight.

L 25 D 12 **903**

9* Smooth elongated hogback dome pierced at both ends. Possible counter balance from winch etc. or sea fishing weight.

L 83 H 28 PD 5 **903**

10* Perforated lump of lead, possible fishing weight?

ED 23 × 20 ID 7.2 **744**

11 Pin with cuboid head at 45° to shank. Shank broken and casting lines smoothed out.

L 23 Head W 5 T 5 Shank D 2.3 **85.07**

12* Perforated disc with three-grooved edge, possibly a flywheel or weight(?) Slightly uneven in thickness. Central perforation worn on one side.

D 56 T 13 PD 12 **51**

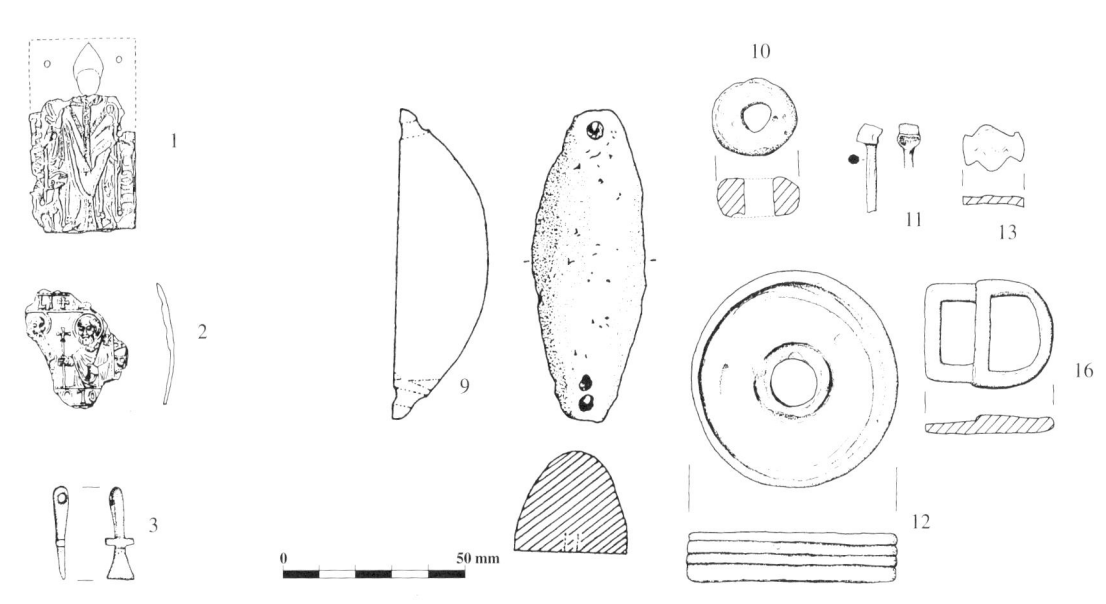

10.78 Miscellaneous lead objects (LD09).

13* A shaped piece in a crude thistle form. Central circle with opposed expanding 'wings'.

L 16.5 W 12 T 2.3 **438**

14 Tapering wire-like piece of lead. With sub-triangular nodule on one end.

L 19 W 4.2 **430**

15 Possible miscast lid handle (*c.f.* LD1.3). Two tier disc with a projecting sprue.

D 17 and 10 H 10.5 **611**

16* Tongueless buckle. D loop with rectangular loop of half thickness projecting to rear. D-loop is rounded section, the rest is square or flat. Pronounced wear marks on one corner of the D loop.

L36 W 29 T 4 **744**

LD10–13 Leadworking debris

Lead-working debris occurred in all levels of the excavation, though the few stratigraphic associations between casting debris (LD10), folded or cut waste retained for re-use (LD11) spillage (LD12) and droplets (LD13) suggested that most leadworking took place outwith the excavated areas. The last two groups do not necessarily associate directly with lead working, as they could occur anywhere where lead had come into close contact with heat i.e. the burning of the burial chapel.

Lead-casting debris (LD10)

Eight pieces (LD10.1–8) are attributable to on-site lead-working in the mid-ninth to later twelfth/thirteenth centuries. These include two plug fragments from moulds (1–2), both displaced by **Period V** graves (Figure 6.31 a and b), and two miscast nails or rivets (3 and 4) with lead flashing from seepage between the mould halves. A large plano-convex ingot (5) from the **Period IV.6** ditch (417.02) was formed by melting lead in a shallow container, possibly of fired clay. After partial cooling the object was extracted, probably by some form of tongs to judge by the distinctive circular impressions on one edge, and the still molten centre slipped outwards in the opposing direction. It is closely paralleled at Beverley (Foreman 1991b, Fig. 119 No. 820), and a fragment of lead sheet waste (7) from a mid-ninth century deposit (339.01) producing other lead-working waste (Table 10.5), bears a similar circular impression with localised discoloration. A smaller plano-convex ingot (6) came from a **Period III** or **IV** deposit (424) in the eastern part of the **central sector** (Figure 6.31 c). A lump of possible ore (8) was recovered from spoil (903). Two objects (7 and 4) can be ascribed to the mid-ninth century with confidence, and a third (5) was probably deposited in the later twelfth century. The remainder are likely to have been displaced from **Period III** or **IV** deposits.

1* Waste bar or casting plug, cut at both ends.

L 20 D 13 **533**

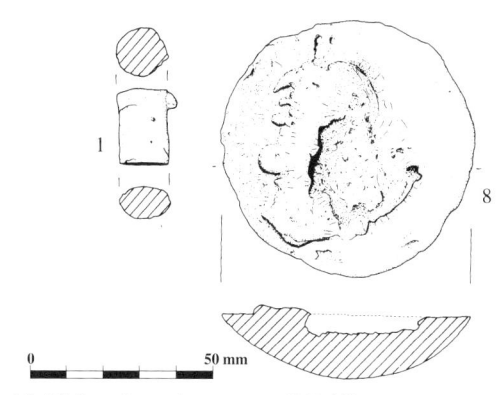

10.79 Lead casting waste (LD10).

2 Ovoid plug, one end cut.

D 12 T 9.5 **538**

3 A rivet-shaped piece with an elongated nodule halfway down shank. The other side appears to have been cut. Possible miscast rivet or waste.

Ht 14.3 W 20.5 **903**

4. Miscast nail or rivet.

16 × 15 **408.01**

5* Convex disc with rough underside.

D 70 T 18.7 **417.02**

6 Discoid, plano-convex piece of lead.

L 25.5 W 22 T 5 **424**

7 Waste piece with a circular indentation on one side and scratches on the reverse.

L 32 W 21 **339.01**

8 Domed lump of lead waste with one flat edge showing cutting marks, probably ore.

45 × 29 Ht 30 **903**

Lead Waste (LD11)

A hundred and sixty-two pieces of lead waste (LD11.1–162) include a partly used ingot, strips, bars, sheet fragments, parings, rough lumps, and spillage or casting waste. Most of the parings, strips and sheet fragments have at least one cut edge, presumably with shears on the thinner pieces, and evidently by a chisel or blade on the thicker pieces, particularly the bars and rods. A large piece of folded sheet (115) from 525.01 has nail or rivet holes along one edge similar to those on the rims of the vessels recovered from earlier deposits in the same area. A large ingot (112) from the foundations of Building V/3 (506.01) had several tooling marks, including a large cut into one side indicating the use of an axe or similar tool. One side had incised parallel grooves, apparently dividing the piece into convenient strips prior to cutting. Parallel scratch lines on the upper surface testify to axing or adzing of material, leading to the curled raised lip of displaced material. Lead waste was recovered from a wide range of deposits (Table 10.6), and there were notable concentrations in later **Period II** deposits, and in the debris ascribed to **Period IV** (Figure 6.31).

	a	b	c	d	e	f	g	h	Total
Spoil and other unstratified	12	3	19		1				32
Topsoil		1	3						4
Period VI	5	1	1						7
Period V: Museum Garden									
Period V: *outer zone*	1	1		1			1	1	5
Period V: *inner precinct* non grave	1	8	3			24*		1	37
Period V: graves	13	4	3	1	1	1			23
Period IV	2		6	1					9
Period III		3	1						4
Period II/7–III/1 (315, 339 etc)		3	8	1					12
Period II	4	3	9			2			18
Period I: *outer zone*			1	1					2
Period I: *inner precinct*	3	2	1						5
Total	42	29	55	5	1	27	1	2	164

Table 10.6: Chronological distribution of lead waste (LD11).
a Sheet/folded sheet, **b** Strip, **c** 'Waste', **d** Rod, **e** Bar, **f** Paring, **g** Ingot, **h** spillage. *23 from one context.

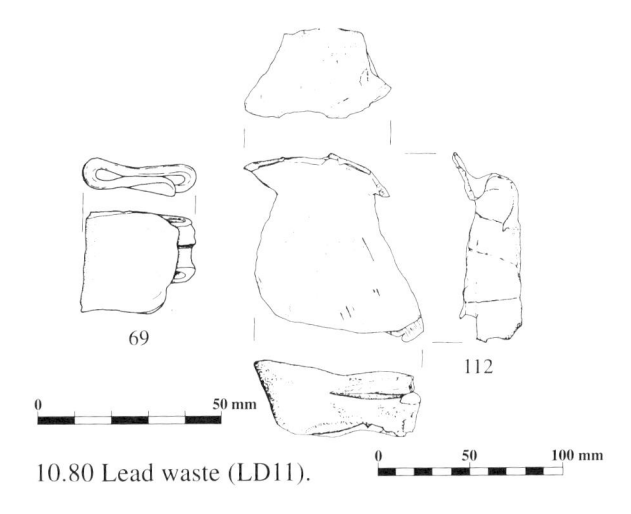

10.80 Lead waste (LD11).

69* Folded piece of waste sheet with wide score mark on one side.
L 30 W 25 **540**

112* Part of lead ingot showing gouging and cutting marks.
88 × 71 × 31 **506.01**

115 Folded piece of waste with nail or rivet holes along one edge.
59 × 55 **525.01**

Nodular waste (LD12)

One hundred and forty-one nodular pieces (LD12.1–141) represented cooled un-formed molten lead. Such pieces are sometimes classified as spillage associated with lead-working (e.g. Foreman 1991b, 158–9; Bayley 1992, 779), but many were attributable to the fire which engulfed the Northumbrian church in the mid-ninth century (Table 10.5i). A small group of nodules ascribed to **Period IV** coincided with crucible fragments with traces of lead and copper alloys (Figures 6.24 and 10.88), and includes one with a notably high copper content. These were probably casting or alloying waste, and others (7–15, 303) associated with crucible fragments in **Period II** (Figure 10.87b) invite a similar interpretation. Most of the remaining pieces came from spoil or disturbed deposits and no other working areas can be identified.

Droplet and driblets (LD13)

Twenty-two droplets and driblets of lead (LD13.1–22) were widely dispersed (Table 10.5). Some may have derived from the destruction of the church or similar accidents, but others may have been associated with the casting debris in LD10 and nodular waste in LD12.

The Gold and Silver

Andrew Nicholson

Seventeen silver finds (SR1–17) and four gold objects (AU.1–4) include decorative artefacts, manufacturing waste and bullion. Groups of finds from **Periods I**, **II** and **IV** can be ascribed to fine metalworking shops indicated by crucibles, tools and other debris. The remaining objects can generally be identified as stray losses of rings and other personal possessions.

The first group of finds pertains to the closing years of **Period I** (perhaps *c*. 700 AD) and seems to have derived from a workshop immediately to the west of the excavated area. The debris ascribed to this hypothetical workshop (Figures 3.34 and 10.87a) included a small gold ingot (1) and a piece of gold rod (2), which may have been secreted beneath a stone beside the **Period I/4.5** platform. A small group of stone moulds, silver objects, crucibles with traces of silver and fragments of putative heating trays can be ascribed to the same general period (Figure 10.87). The gold ingot (AU1) displays shallow concave tooling marks on the upper surface, but no striations, indicating that they were caused by hammering rather than a knife. The associated length of gold rod (AU2) was partly cut and then broken at both ends. There are no parallels for the ingot and, though ingot moulds are known from several sites of similar date in Scotland and Ireland, most appear to have been associated with copper alloy working (Edwards 1990, 92). There is a similar fragment of gold rod from the later-tenth century hoard from Iona

(Stevenson 1951, 171), and fragments of gold wire occur in several Norse hoards, but are unusual at earlier dates. A fragment of silver foil (SR16) and a gilded silver strip formed into an ovoid mount (SR10) came from **Period II** contexts, but probably originated in the **Period I** workshop debris. The strip may have been a throat mount from a sheath, if the ovoid shape is original, though similar scabbard mounts are considerably larger (Evison 1967, Figs 9 and 10), and no mounts associated with the smaller scramasaxes are known. The Whithorn mount may originally have been round, and so similar to the gilded cup mounts from Sutton Hoo (Bruce-Mitford 1979, 63), which were attached to the wooden cups by strips folded over the mount and rim, and riveted in place. This would account for the lack of any visible mounting attachments or rivet holes on the Whithorn piece. The decoration on the mount is probably cast, and takes the form of a simple interlace with lentoid loops between raised borders. The join is carefully placed at the junction of two loops and is secured by a lead-tin solder. The interlace is paralleled by the border on the leather binding of the late-seventh century Stoneyhurst Gospels (De Hammel 1994, Fig. 2.7). A silver hinge (SR11) from a shallow deposit (118) on the west side of the **central sector**, could have been deposited at any point between **Period I/1.3** and **1/4.4**. The hinge is flat with the loop for the pin projecting to the rear, and may originally have come from a box or casket, but lacks immediate parallels.

A smaller group of finds from **Period II** contexts (Figure 10.87b) comprised a ball-headed pin (SR06) from Building II/15 (Figure 10.98), and a simple closed loop silver ring (SR01) from the main rubbish deposit (303). Related finds indicate continuing silver smithing in the vicinity, and include two small pieces of silver spillage (SR14 and 15). The top of the pin had six radiating grooves, and, whilst not directly paralleled, is similar to an iron pin (IN41.52) from the **Period II** rubbish spread (303), and to copper alloy or bone pins from contemporary sites such as Lagore or the Broch of Burrian (Stevenson 1955, 283–4). This seems to indicate insular contacts continuing into the period of Anglian dominance. The **Period III** debris accumulation in the **southern sector** (309) produced a plain gold finger ring (AU3), lacking any diagnostic features, but indicative of material wealth not evident in the sparse collection of finds from the contemporary buildings.

The third group of gold and silver probably originated in a craftsman's workshop in the latter part of **Period IV**, although most of the objects had been displaced into **Period V** graves (Figure 6.24). These finds comprised six fine strands of silver wire (SR8), a fragment of ring money (SR13), a folded piece of a thirteenth century gold fillet (AU3) and an open silver ring (SR2). the ring money and fillet fragment were probably bullion awaiting recycling, and the wire was probably a silversmith's commodity. The ring could have been part of the craftsman's stock or an ear ring associated with a **Period V** burial. The ring money (SR13) is a cut end fragment from an undecorated diamond-section armring, a characteristic Norse form dating to the late-tenth or eleventh century (Graham-Campbell 1976, 123). At 6.26 grams it is outside the usual range for the standard Norse *ertog* of 8 grams (Warner 1976, 141), although the broadly contemporary lead weights also vary from the accepted standards (pp 392-3). The cut and folded gold fragment (AU3) is the end of a fillet for securing a wimple, and is closely paralleled by a thirteenth century fillet found during repair work in the nunnery of St. Ronan's Chapel, Iona (Curle 1924, 109). Bulk sieving of the contents of the main **Period IV** drainage ditch (417.02) produced a small Obsidian cabochon mounted on a silver base plate (SR5). It was found untarnished, raising suspicions that it had been planted, but it is matched in form by contemporary objects, and could have been debris from the postulated jeweller's shop (p 240).

A decorated silver ring with a small pyrimidical bezel (SR3) from **Period V/1** paving in the **southern sector** (415.02), was perhaps lost in the mid- to late-thirteenth century. A somewhat later robbing pit in the **northern sector** (607.02) turned up a silver waste droplet (SR17), but its original location is uncertain. The remaining three silver finds came from modern and recent deposits. A brooch pin with transverse bar (SR7) from topsoil at the western end of the **Fey Field** trench (766), is from a type of brooch which was common in Scotland and the North of England in the fourteenth century. These brooches are annular, circular or octagonal in form, and sometimes have talismanic inscriptions. A complete example in a hoard from Dumfries could be reliably dated by numismatics to *c*. 1310 (Callander 1924, 161–3). A plain silver mount with a smoky quartz cabuchon (SR4) is also Scottish and dates to the sixteenth century. It came from recent cultivation (745) in the western part of the **northern sector**, but might have been lost beside the processional route to the cathedral (Figures 2.24 and 10.49). A plated teaspoon (SR12) from the Manse was probably *in situ*.

The Gold (AU)

1* Small ingot with hammer marks on upper surface. The lack of striations on upper surface point to hammering rather than trimming by knife. The ends of the ingot are slightly rounded, and the bar tapers slightly along its length. No evidence of casting marks.

L 24.6 W 7 T 3.4 Wt 6.87 **85.02**

2* Slightly curved, circular section rod fragment with a transverse groove round one end. Both ends are cut through by a blade to ⅔ of their width, then broken.

L 18.5 D 2.4 Wt 2.87 **85.02**

3* Cut terminal of decorated strip with perforation. Slightly tapering strip with rounded end, in which is a centrally located perforation. The border is of repousse dots. The other end is cut.

L 16 W 7.7 T 0.4 **539**

4* Plain round circular-section finger ring.

ED 22 ID 19.7 **309.02**

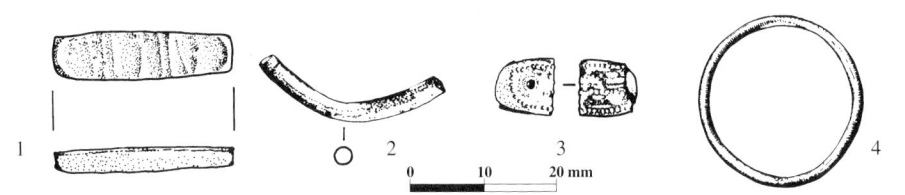

THE FINDS 399

10.81 Gold objects (AU).

The Silver (SR)

1* Closed plain circular finger ring of ovoid section.
ED 22 ID 19.7 **303**

2* Simple ring of tapering circular-section.
ED 15.8 ID 14 T (max) 1.4 **542**

3* Finger ring with decorated triangular bezel & shoulder flattened-pyramidical bezel. Both broad sides of bezel and shoulders are decorated with low relief design. One side of the bezel is a good triquetra, the other a more debased design. The shoulders have a quatrefoil motif. The band of the ring is of ovoid section.
ED 22 ID 19.3 **415.02**

4 Smoky quartz cabuchon in plain silver mount. The mount encircles the stone lengthways, exposing two thirds if its surface and has a scalloped edge. The back of the stone, of which one third of the surface is exposed by the mount, is flattish in profile. A loop at one of the narrower ends of the mount shows little sign of wear. The stone is now cracked and the silver mount strip is broken at one point, near to the loop.
L 20 W 11 T 10 **745**

5 Obsidian cabuchon on ovoid silver sheet base plate with raised edges in 'rope-chain' effect silver wire. Mounted within is a polished obsidian cabuchon. A small folded stem centrally located on the rear of the base plate may be for securing the setting as part of a larger object.
L5.5 W 4.2 T 3.4 **417.02**

6* Ball-headed pin with six radial grooves on upper part of head. Filing marks extend around the shank for 6mm below the head.
L 77 Head D 6.7 **218**

7* Early-fourteenth century round section brooch pin with transverse, rectangular section bar at upper end. Above the bar is a flat-sectioned loop. Extensive filing around the crossbar and a transverse fracture through the loop suggests that the original loop may have worn thin and been replaced.
L 44.6 Shank D 2.2 W 7 **766**

8 Strands of fine wire (poss. embroidery) Small fragments of wire, of less than 0.5mm diameter.
425.02

9 Small perforated bead.
D 6 **82.02**

10a* Strip with relief borders and interlace design, rectangular in section, folded into an ovoid ring and soldered at the rear. The design occurs only on the front face. Probably a throat mount from a knife scabbard. 10b, detached fragments from 10a.
Total length of strip (if unfolded) 87 W 4.8 T 1.8
Internal dimensions of ring L 33.5 W 8.5 **222.01**

11* Hinge with perforated expanded terminal. Strip with projections at neck below rounded terminal, lacking signs of wear. The strip thickens in two steps at the opposed end. The socket to take the hinge pin is vertically aligned at 90° to the plane of the strip. Its external surface has two equally-spaced longitudinal

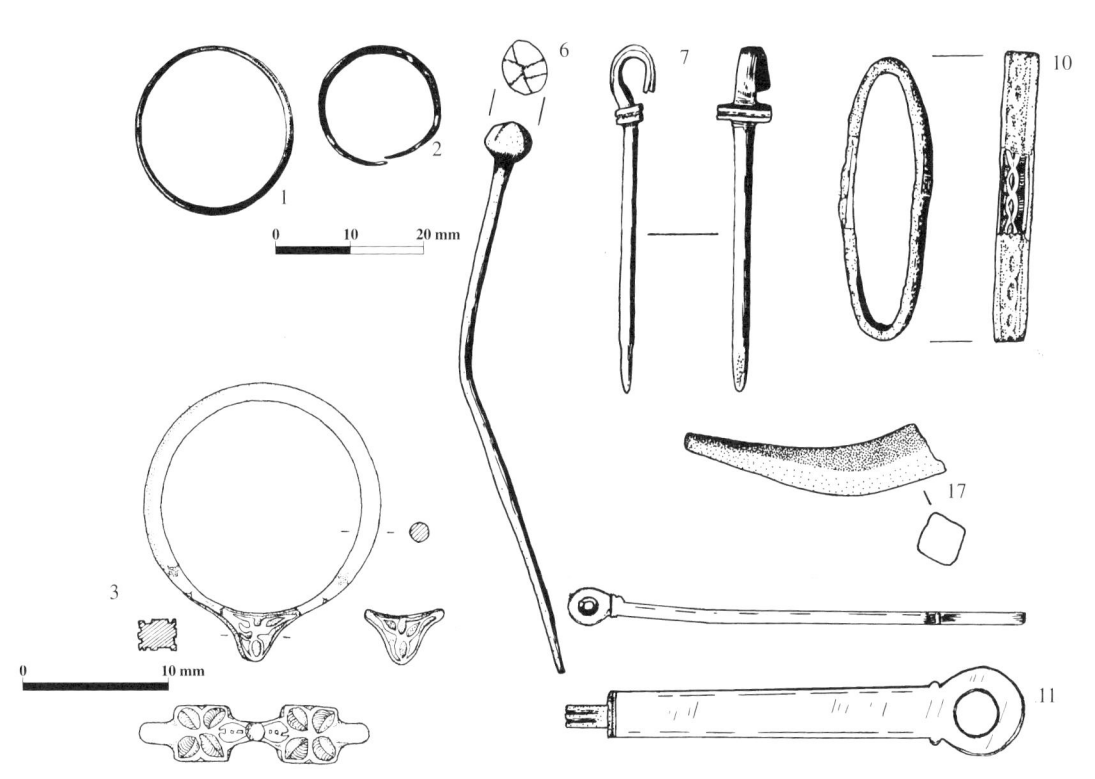

10.82 Silver objects (SR).

grooves. The hole is biconical. Filing marks evident on several surfaces.

L 63.4 W 13 T 0.5 × 1.5 **118**

12 Teaspoon, probably silver plating over base alloy. Ovoid bowl with plain tapering handle expanding towards rounded upper end.
738

13* Cut end of tapering diamond-section ring-money, cleanly cut, probably by a knife or chisel.

L 36 W 8 T 7.5 Wt 6.26 **534**

14 Thin fragment of silver spillage.

L 12 W 8 T 0.3 **303**

15 Thin fragment of silver spillage.

L 8 W 4 T 0.3 **303**

16 Fragment of silver foil/sheet.

L 12.5 W 4 T 0.1 **86**

17 Droplet of silver waste

L 18 W 6 **607.02**

Moulds, Crucibles and Related Metalworking Debris

Peter Hill and Andrew Nicholson

The excavation produced scraps of roughly sixty four crucibles (SG15.1–64); fragments of ten ceramic object moulds (SG17.1–10) and one of stone (SE46); six putative stone ingot moulds (SE45.1–5, 44.4); and a small group of possible heating tray fragments (SG26.1–12). Related finds in other categories include a small group of non-ferrous 'slags' (SG14); one piece of lead ore (LD10.8); ingots, mould plugs and failed castings in copper-alloy and lead; and spillage and nodular waste of silver, copper-alloy and lead. The distributions of finds ascribed to the **Period IV** workshops (Figures 6.23–39, particularly 6.24, 27, 30, 31 and 34, 10.88) identify further possible links with coins, gold and silver bullion, burnt limestone, glass *tesserae* and bangle fragments, Haematite polishers, iron punches, and other artefacts and commodities (p 241–2). The picture is simpler in earlier periods, but spatial analyses (Figures 10.86–88) again identify coherent concentrations of crucible and mould fragments, scrap metal and casting waste.

Crucibles (SG15)

One complete crucible (31), fragments of two crucible lids (10 and 42) and sixty-six sherds (a few joining) of varying size were all from small 'thumb crucibles'. Forty-seven fragments were analysed by Energy Dispersive X-ray Fluorescence (EDXRF; Gilmour 1993, Gooder 1993) revealing traces of a range of copper alloys, silver, gold and lead (Figures 10.86–88). Crucible fragments were concentrated in **Period I** and **IV** deposits, and revealed an interesting, though manifestly incomplete, picture of evolving high temperature metal working.

Ceramic moulds (SG17)

Ten fragments of ceramic moulds (SG17.1–10) include eight from **Period I** and two from **Period IV** or **V**. Most of the **Period I** moulds appear to be for the multiple casting of stick pins. Three (2, 4 and 8) have several channels converging towards the tip, two others (5 and 7) have parallel grooves, and two (1 and 6) have single grooves. One fragment (2) displays the matrices for five or six nail-headed stick-pins similar to the three copper alloy pins from the site (BZ14.3–5). The large number of pins from a single mould suggests a considerable volume of production. EDXRF analysis identified traces of leaded brass in two moulds (5 and 6) and an unspecified copper alloy in two others (2 and 7). The remaining **Period I** mould fragment (3) had been used for an atypical lead alloy, and preserves the matrix of a curved object with a raised central ridge conforming in size to contemporary penannular brooches. The **Period IV** mould (9) has two converging deep U-section curved grooves, noticeably different from the **Period I** moulds, but the original form of the casting is uncertain. A second fragment (10) from a **Period V** context (521) may have been the gate of a mould, and revealed traces of brass and leaded brass, matching adjacent crucible fragments (SG15.53a–c, Figure 10.88).

Possible heating-tray fragments (SG26)

A small group of industrial ceramics was characterised by a hard, though not vitrified surface, coarse fabric and off white/pale pink colour. Although none have been analysed, these can be identified tentatively as fragments of heating trays. The twelve fragments (or groups of fragments, SG26.1–12) were concentrated in the **Period I** deposits in the **southern sector**, and in the displaced **Period I** debris (110) used in the construction of the ecclesiastical buildings at the beginning of **Period II**.

Stone ingot-moulds (SE45)

A small group of ingot moulds (SE45.1–5) is matched by several from early medieval settlement sites in Britain and Ireland (Craddock 1989, 174; Edwards 1990, 90–1). Ingots of gold, silver and copper alloy provided a convenient mode for carrying surplus metal, and were the raw material from which the specialist craftsmen worked. EDXRF analysis of the stone ingot moulds was relatively inconclusive, but suggested lead working in some cases.

Three of the ingot moulds (1, 55; 2, 80.02 and 5, 58) came from **Period I** contexts, and two others (3 and SE44.4) from **Period II** deposits may have been displaced. Their spatial distribution is interesting. The earliest (2), from a **Period I/2** grave, was perhaps associated with crucibles, a pin mould and other metalworking waste ascribed to **Period I/1** (Figure 10.86). Two others (1 and 6) came from the relatively late waterborne silts (55, 58; **Period I.10**) in the **southern sector** and were loosely associated with a small group of tuyere, mould and crucible fragments. One displaced mould (3) came from the Northumbrian church (237), but may have originated in the specialised metalworking debris (85.04) which accumulated at the end of **Period I/4**. The fine compass-drawn design perhaps echoes the arciform crosses from this area (pp 102, 437-41) and could even mark it as ecclesiastical property. The displaced, reused millstone fragment (SE44.4) might have originated in the **Period I/1** activity linked with No.2 (Figure 10.86). One (4) of the two remaining moulds came from a **Period IV** context (430) in the *inner precinct*, and the other (5) from topsoil in the **southern sector**. Both could have been displaced from earlier contexts. The ingot moulds were generally disassociated from the larger groups of metalworking debris, but given that comparable workshop sites (e.g. Moynagh Lough, Bradley 1993) often lack ingot moulds, it suggests that the ingot production was viewed as a separate craft from fine metalworking and ironworking.

Stone object mould (SE46)

The bivalve rosette mould (1) was among the specialised metalworking debris abutting the **Period I/4.4** platform and perhaps dates to c. 700 AD. EXRDF analysis was inconclusive, but associated finds include gold, copper alloy and lead (Table 3.33).

Crucibles (SG15)

9* Crucible rim body sherd (Bronze?).

82.02

10* Crucible lid. (Silver, Copper alloy) Three analyses on the exterior and one on the cross-sectional area indicated the presence of copper, zinc, lead and silver.

30 × 28 × 35 **73.02**

Ceramic Moulds (SG17)

1* Fragment of mould, probably bi-partite, used to manufacture at least one stick pin. Only a section of the shank remains. Interior analysis revealed copper with some zinc and lead. Exterior analysis showed some lead and very small zinc, but no copper. The proportionally low copper may indicate a brass, or may be the remains of bronze.

88.02

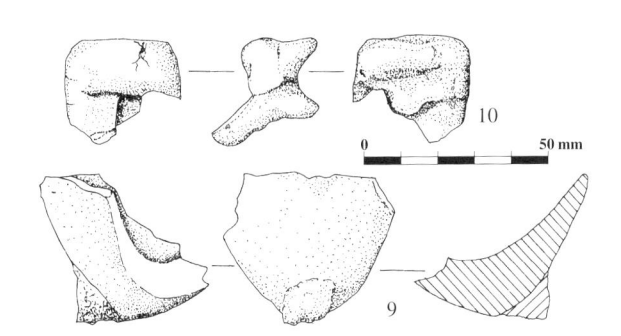

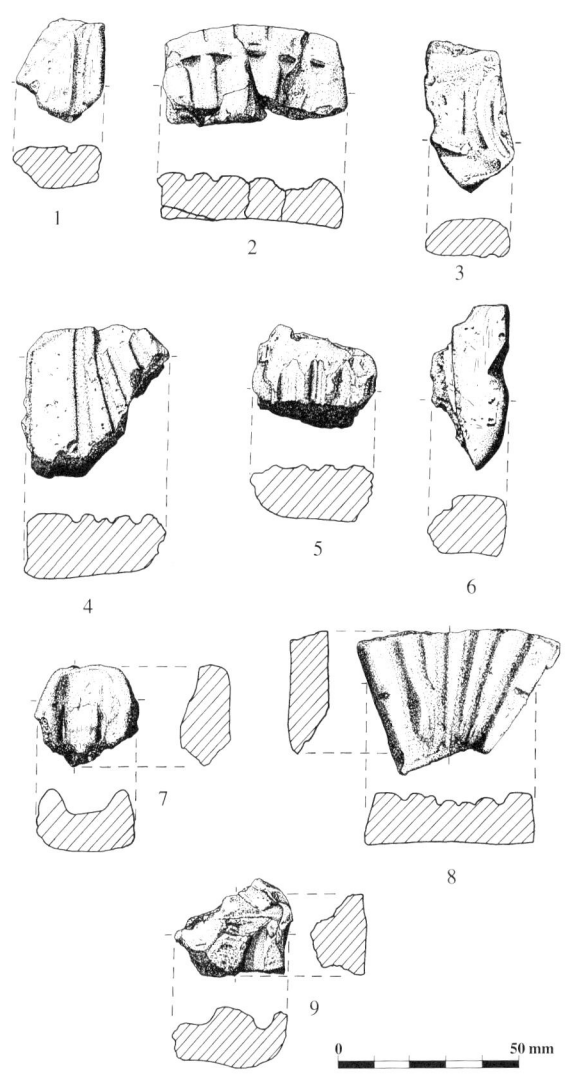

10.84 Ceramic moulds (SG17).

2* Half of bi-partite mould for casting of at least five (probably six) nail-headed pins. Head and upper shank portions survive. The pins are aligned tapering towards each other at the point, possibly to allow for a single pouring mouth. Transverse grooves cut in the upper edge of the mould do not penetrate, and are probably alignment marks for keying in the upper half of the mould. Examination of the interior resulted in a zinc peak with a trace of lead. analysis of a smaller triangular piece detected a possible copper trace, definite zinc and some lead. Rear, external face sterile. A different internal area analysed resulted in a definite copper peak and good zinc and lead results. Definite copper alloy.

80.03

3* Possible mould fragment. One surface has part of a curved groove, of shallow U-section. Two even more shallow broad grooves converge to one side of the curved groove. Interior analysis revealed zinc and lead, exterior sterile. Difficult to classify, possibly a lead alloy.

81.01

4* Fragment of bi-partite mould for at least four stick pins. The four shanks taper towards each other. Interior analysis resulted in zinc and lead, exterior only showed a trace of zinc. Probably a copper alloy with enhanced zinc and lead remaining.

82.03

5* Fragment of (?)bi-partite mould, with three parallel grooves. This contrasts with the moulds for stick pins, where the grooves

10.83 Crucibles (SG15).

converge. Analysis of the middle of the interior detected high copper, zinc and lead concentrations. Exterior sterile. A definite copper alloy, possibly leaded brass.

73.02

6* Fragment of mould with a single narrow groove nearly parallel with the outer edge. Possibly for the manufacture of stick pins. Analysis of the interior detected copper, lead and zinc. Exterior proved almost completely sterile of significant elements. A copper alloy, possibly leaded brass.

90

7* Fragment of bi-partite mould for at least two stick(?) pins, evidencing pouring mouth and terminal points of shanks. two perpendicular grooves in the broken upper edge are of unknown purpose, appearing too deep for keying points, but not functioning as vents as they do not penetrate the fabric. Analysis of the interior resulted in zinc and a small lead peak. exterior sterile. Probably a copper alloy with enhanced zinc and lead.

76

8* Fragment of bi-partite mould for six stick pins. The six shanks taper towards each other and emerge into a single pouring mouth. The transverse grooves on each outer edge do not penetrate the fabric, and are therefore alignment marks for the other half of the mould (NA).

55

9* Fragment of mould, two U-sectioned converging grooves, much larger than those associated with stick pin moulds (Bronze/Brass).

901

10 Possible gate fragment (Brass/Leaded Brass).

521

Stone Ingot Moulds (SE45)

1 Trapezoidal-section sandstone fragment, broken across slightly curving, deep U-section bar mould (120mm × 10mm × 10mm). Analysis halfway along channel resulted in small zinc and good lead results. Further towards the intact end of the channel tests resulted in more zinc and lots of lead. Rear face showed only a trace of zinc and no lead. Probably indicative of lead working.

L 165 W 110 T 70 **55**

2 Fractured sub-rectangular greywacke slab. Smooth upper surface includes the right-angled corner of a pecked, flat-bottomed depression (145mm × 98mm × 3mm), and a roughly chipped bar mould (70mm × 12mm × 3.5mm). Two analyses of the depression showed only a slight trace of zinc, as did tests on the chipped mould and the rear face, thus no indications of use.

L 315 W 190 T 43 **80.02**

3* Sandstone slab with six ovoid ingot moulds with sloping sides. Four of the moulds are in a rough line along one edge, a fifth is set at 90° to the line and the last at an angle. Moulds 35 × 15 × 6mm; 45 × 14 × 5mm; 40 × 12 × 5mm; 45 × 13 × 5mm; 47 × 17 × 3mm; 45 × 17 × 4mm. Incised design of at least five small overlapping compass-drawn circles (10mm diameter) on surface between moulds. Examination of four of the moulds gave small or trace zinc results and trace or no lead. One mould produced trace zinc and a small amount of lead, the other gave no zinc but a large lead peak. Rear face had trace zinc and no lead. Indicative of lead working.

L 145 W 120 T 22 **237**

4* Broken greywacke slab with three parallel channels, possibly bar moulds (W 6 T 4). Moulds have convex-sloped sides and flat base. One channel had a small copper peak and some zinc. Another had zinc but no copper, and the last contained a possible trace of copper, a trace of lead and zinc. the rear had only zinc. Possibly for copper alloy, but levels are very low.

L 69 W 39 T 23.2 **430**

5 Ingot mould, two rectilinear bar moulds (45 × 15 × 10mm; 35 × 10 × 5mm), flat-bottomed with inwardly sloping sides. Pecked lentoid mark on upper surface is not a mould.

L 145 W 85 T 50 **58**

Stone Object Mould (SE46)

1* Flat sandstone pebble with roughly incised X on one face. Opposed face smoothed, with carved rosette mould centrally placed. The design consists of a conical centre enclosed by a circle, from which eighteen grooves radiate. The sides of the mould slope in slightly to facilitate removal of the cast object. At the upper edge of the mould two opposed channels are cut into the surface, becoming deeper as they progress away from the centre. These grooves terminate prior to reaching the edge of the mould, and are thus not necessarily to allow the egress of air. If the mould were an open mould these two projecting elements of the finished object could have been bent at their narrow point, adjacent to the rosette, to form a mount or ring. Adjacent to the terminus of one groove is a shallow depression, and it could be that this is a keying point, indicating that the original mould was bi-partite – an unusual feature in this medium, more commonly found on ceramic moulds.

L 77 W 55.6 T 6 **85.02**

Chronology, distribution and associations

Moulds and crucibles were concentrated in two stratigraphically distinct horizons. The earlier comprises finds from **Period I** and **II** contexts. Many of these came from graves and other disturbed contexts, and none can be linked securely to working

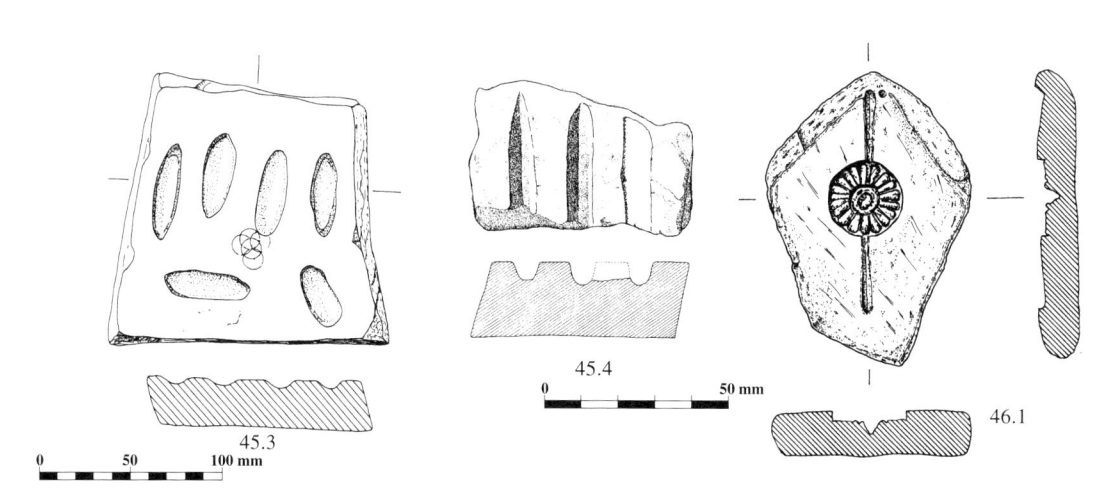

10.85 Stone bar and object moulds (SE45 and 46).

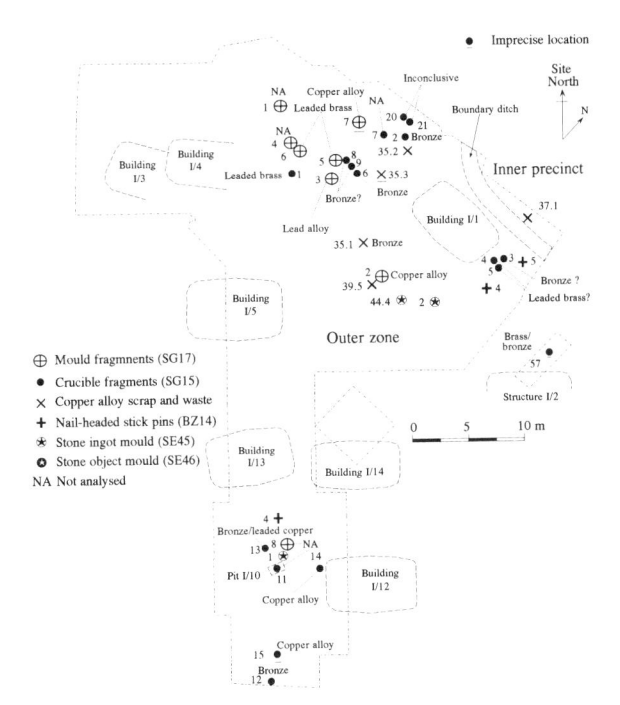

10.86 Casting debris and related finds ascribed to the earlier-sixth century.

areas within the trench. Five groups may nevertheless be identified (Figures 10.86 and 87). The first (Figure 10.86) comprised scattered fragments from the eastern part of the **northern sector**, and included scraps of six crucibles (1, 2, 6–9) with traces of either bronze (2, 6, 8 and 9) or leaded brass (1). These coincided broadly with six mould fragments (1, 3–7) for casting stick-pins and perhaps a penannular brooch, including two (5 and 6) with traces of leaded brass, and two with unspecified copper (7) and lead (3) alloys. Adjacent finds include two pieces of copper-alloy scrap (BZ35.2 and 3). The earliest crucible fragment (1) came from a **Period I/1.4** deposit (94.02), and the earliest mould (1) from displaced debris (88.02) used to extend the platform of Building I/9 in **Period I/2**. The group is nevertheless likely to have had a common origin, and was probably deposited in **Period I/1** before the erection of Building I/6. The second group was more widely dispersed in the central and eastern parts of the **central sector**, and comprised three crucible fragments (3–5), the mould for nail-headed pins (2), and two stone ingot moulds (SE44.4 and 45.2). Scattered copper alloy finds from the same general area included two nail-headed stick-pins (BZ14.4 and 5), one (4) an unfinished failed casting, eight nodules (BZ39.5), a broken ornamental strip of tin-plated bronze (BZ35.1), and possible scrap (BZ37.1). The crucible fragments again revealed traces of bronze (3) and leaded brass (4 and 5). Most of these finds had been displaced, but all are likely to have originated in debris scattered around Building I/1, and earlier than the **Period I/5** graveyard. The third group comprised six crucible sherds (11–16), a mould fragment (8), and two stone ingot moulds (1

and 5) from the **southern sector**. These were dispersed stratigraphically, but concentrated spatially, and are likely to have had a common origin, perhaps in association with the **Period I.4** pit (10) which produced one crucible sherd (11). The crucible fragments revealed traces of bronze (12 and 13), leaded copper (13), and unspecified copper alloys (14 and 16). There was only one ceramic mould fragment (8) from the area, although heating tray fragments (1–3) came from broadly contemporary, though different, contexts. A nail-headed stick pin (BZ14.4) from the gully flanking Building I/17 could have been associated with these finds. Pieces of copper alloy and lead waste were sparse in this part of the *outer zone* (Figure 10.70, Tables 10.4–6), and the metalworking finds may all have originated in the brief episode of industrial activity in the opening years of **Period I/1** (pp 27–8, 81, 122–3).

These three groups make sense spatially as debris scattered around the earlier **Period I/1** buildings, and their distribution matches that of the first group of Early Medieval pottery and glass (Figure 10.21). The finds are all likely to have originated in deposits pertaining to the early years of **Period I** in the earlier-sixth century. They mainly indicate work in bronze and leaded brass, and so contrast with the wider range of copper alloys worked subsequently (Figures 10.87 and 88). This fits the pattern of a gradual move away from well-defined alloys in the post-Roman period (Bayley 1988, 205).

The fourth group can be ascribed tentatively to the closing years of **Period I**, but includes finds from **Period II** contexts in the **northern sector** (Figure 10.87a). It comprised seven crucible fragments (10, 17–22) including a lid (10) and a body sherd (17) with traces of silver, the stone rosette-mould (SE46.1), a multiple ingot mould with traces of lead (SE45.3), and seven heating tray fragments (5–10, 12) from the displaced **Period I** debris (110). The analyses of the remaining crucible fragments (18–22) were mostly inconclusive, although one (19) revealed possible traces of brass. The group coincided broadly with the concentration of fine metalworking waste abutting the **Period I/4.5** platform (Figure 3.34b), and with scattered silver finds further to the east. Lidded crucibles from Dinas Powys were used to melt gold and copper alloys (Alcock 1963), while crucibles of similar date from Hartlepool were used for silver. At Dunadd different forms of crucibles tended to be used for different metals, and the lidded forms were again used for silver (Bayley 1988, 199). Together these point to a relatively brief phase of prosperity and fine metalworking, possibly pertaining to the closing years of the seventh century and opening decades of the eighth.

A small group of crucible fragments provides rare evidence of industrial activity in **Period II** (Figure 10.87b). Two fragments (23 and 24) from the main rubbish spread (303, pp 160–1) were associated with nodular lead (LD12.7–15) and silver spillage (SR14 and 15). A third (25) from the wall trench of Hall II/7 revealed traces of complex alloys and probably pertains to this period. A fourth fragment (26) from

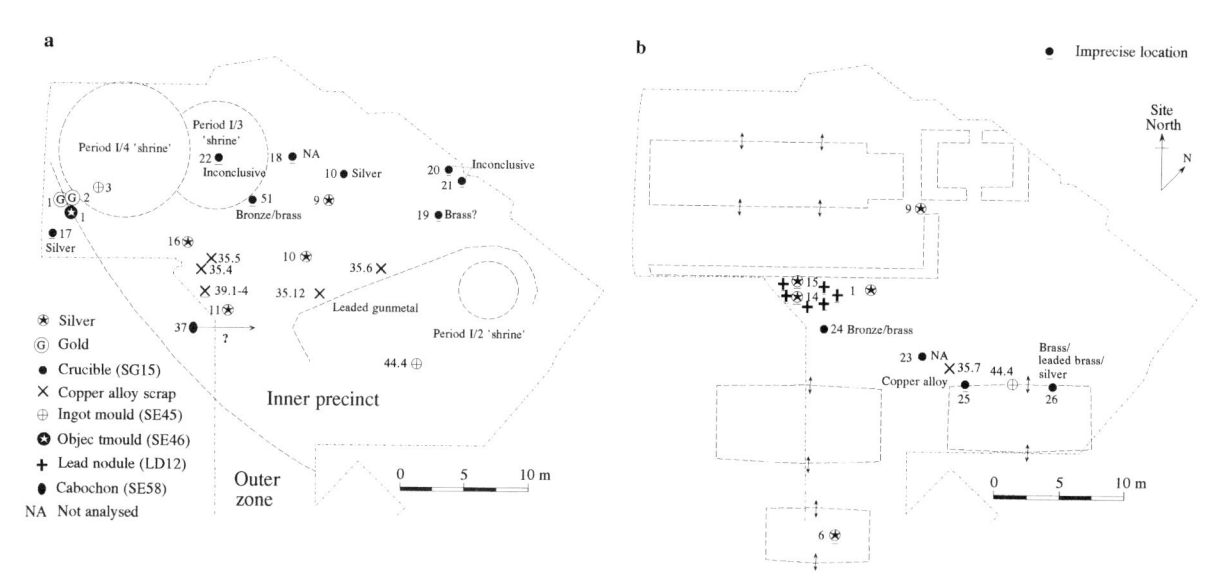

10.87 The evidence for precious metal-working in the later-seventh to earlier-ninth. **a** Finds ascribed to the later-seventh/earlier-eighth centuries. **b** Finds from **Period II** rubbish spread (303) and related deposits.

the mid-ninth century ploughsoil (399.02) revealed traces of brass, leaded brass and silver, but may have been misattributed, as later fragments from this area revealed a similar range of metals (Figure 10.88).

The largest group of crucible fragments comprised six (27–32) from **Period IV** deposits, twenty-one (33–52) displaced into **Period V** graves and related contexts (Figure 6.24), and three more (53–55) from **Period V** deposits in the **southern sector** (Figures 10.71 and 88). These were concentrated in the *outer zone*, and can be ascribed to the latter part of **Period IV**, probably dating to the later-twelfth and earlier-thirteenth centuries. Analysis revealed traces of a wide range of metals and alloys, including gold, silver, lead, brass, leaded brass, bronze and leaded copper. A concentration of fragments with traces of lead and leaded alloys in the **southern sector**, is appropriate to a casting workshop. This might have produced the failed ewer foot of leaded bronze (BZ30.71) from this area, and could explain the presence of a partly-used lead ingot (LD1.112) and lead spillage (LD12.113). Some of the fragments came from the foundations and floor of Building V/3 (506.01 etc), but are likely to have originated in the uppermost **Period IV** deposits. The fragments from the south-east part of the **central sector**, had traces of gold, silver and more unleaded alloys, and suggest the casting of ingots for wrought work. Most of these fragments came from areas with shallow stratification, and some could have been displaced from **Period I** deposits. The fragments ascribed to **Period IV** nevertheless make a valuable contribution to the picture of specialized workshop areas, with heavier industrial activities concentrated in the *outer zone* (pp 247–9).

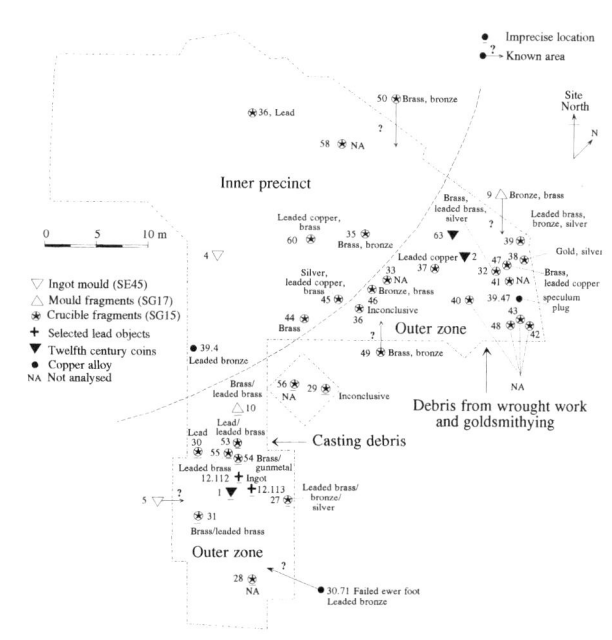

10.88 Crucibles and related finds ascribed to **Period IV**.

The Iron

Andrew Nicholson

The 6791 iron finds were categorised by form, and grouped by function, covering areas such as nails, structural ironwork, tools, knives, locks and keys, dress fittings and horse fittings. A distinct group of eighth-ninth century chest/coffins (IN32) is treated separately (pp 412-5), though sharing features (nails,

THE FINDS

	Nails etc	Fittings	Dress items	Tools	Knives	Waste
Period I/3 workshop debris (85.02)	36	6	5	7	1	12
Displaced **Period I** debris (110)	54			6		22
Period V graves: *inner precinct*	481	13	22	44	26	59
Period V graves: *outer zone*	188	7	8	14	4	17
Graveyard surface	213	3	7	4		9
Period V cultivation (546)	31	8	1	1	1	16
Total	**1003**	**37**	**43**	**67**	**32**	**135**

Table 10.7: The distribution of iron finds in selected larger groups.

locks, keys and chest fittings) with other categories. Finds from spoil (903) and from modern and recent contexts (700–770) were dealt with in a more summary fashion.

All of the iron finds from the 1984 trial excavations were examined by X-radiography (SDD743–756; SDD949–954), and some of the 1986–7 material was also dealt with (NMS 127–133). Some of these finds were conserved. A sample of the 'more interesting' finds was sent to the laboratories of the York Archaeological Trust in 1992 (YAT 2773–2829), and the results of the X-radiographs led to the bulk of the iron (excepting items from modern and recent deposits, though including potentially redeposited material from these contexts) also being examined by X-radiography (YAT2848–2898, 2907–2932). As with their examination of the Coppergate material (O'Connor 1992), it was discovered that about 10% of the finds initially identified as nails, and thus given a relatively low priority, were objects such as awls, blades, stick pins, styli, and even half of a spur rowel. X-radiographs also greatly facilitated the identification and clarification of shape, features and non-ferrous plating for other classes.

The line illustrations are based on the X-radiographs which give the clearest picture of the objects, but as most objects were only X-rayed from one direction, these and the measurements are necessarily two dimensional. Some objects are identifiable though X-rayed from unfavourable directions, and these are generally not illustrated. On items such as knife blades the corrosion can form up to 30% of the thickness of the blade, rendering pointless any attempt to measure this value on uncleaned finds. This report is therefore, in some respects, a summary guide to the rich archaeological resource excavated, with the hope that time and funds will allow further analysis in the future.

Concentrations of iron objects (Table 10.7) in various medieval deposits, show a wide range of types, and probably reflect differing depositional circumstances. Two groups from **Period I** (85.02 and 110) were characterized by large numbers of nails and metal waste, and were associated with cinder, tuyere fragments, and other ironworking debris (Tables 3.22 and 35). Both are thus likely to include debris from smithying, and the iron objects may have been waste awaiting reuse. Most of the finds from the **Period V** graves can be ascribed with confidence to the **Period IV** debris in the *inner precinct* and *outer zone*, and spatial patterns indicate specific workshop areas (Figures 6.26, 27, 28, 33 and 36). The large numbers of nails are less easy to explain, but these could have been included in a levelling deposit introduced in **Period IV** (Figures 6.3 and 5). A concentration of nails from the graveyard surface and the overlying deposits is equally enigmatic, as this seems to have been open ground, although spurs and dress fittings fit happily with other debris (Figure 10.49). A last assemblage from the cultivation (546) to the west of the graveyard includes a concentration of nails and waste, and an interesting group of chains and fittings.. There were no comparable finds from equivalent layers in the **Fey Field**, and these finds could have been displaced from the underlying **Period I** deposits (85.02, 110), or the mid-ninth century debris in the church (315, Figure 4.21).

Nails

Some 3,857 nails and nail fragments represent 56.8% of the iron finds. 1,504 of these came from recent contexts, and 2,318 are discussed below. The remaining 35 are accounted for by pieces still attached to coffin fittings. Twelve sub-groups (IN01–12) were identified by head type (Figure 10.90), and a thirteenth (IN13) comprises small nails or tacks. The remaining pieces comprise unclassified nails (IN14), nail shanks (IN15) and detached heads (IN16). The distributions of these various groups are summarized in Table 10.8. A significant proportion of the nails categorised by head type were either complete, or were merely lacking their tips – giving a shortfall of some 1–5mm in their total length. This generally affects determination of preferential lengths within the category as opposed to affecting the range of lengths covered by the category as a whole. Detached nails associated with the chest/coffin burials fittings are included in the general data on nails; those still attached to brackets and locks are described with the fittings (IN32). Most of these nails had flat round heads (IN01 and IN02), and several were plated, on the shank as well as the head. The corrosion on most of these nails preserved mineralised wood, and the general absence of similar evidence on the nails from the **Period V** graves, shows that the latter did not come from coffins. The nails pose an interpretative problem as they were concentrated in deposits of scrap metal,

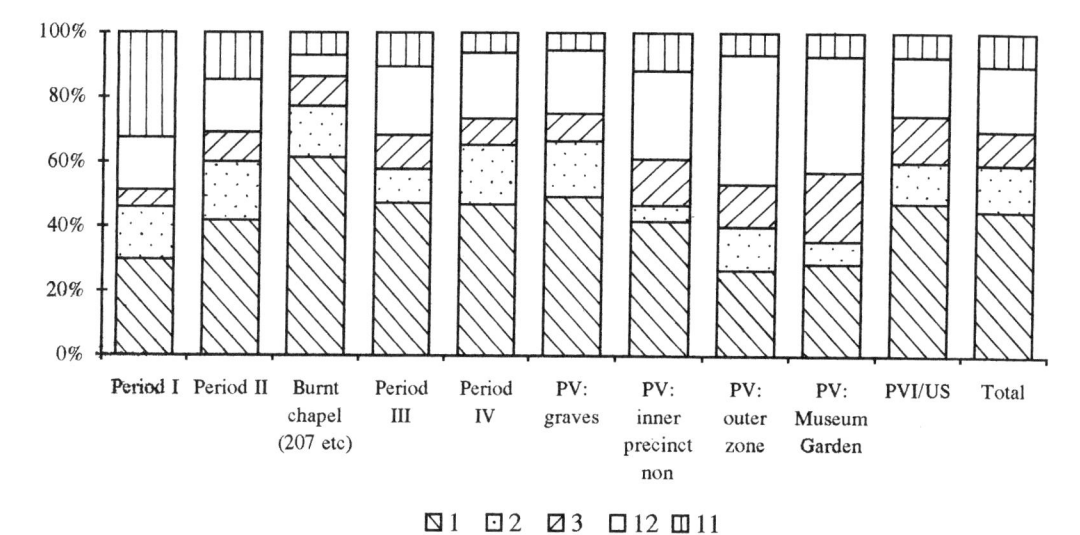

10.89 Chronological distribution of structural nails.

and scarce or absent from most of the timber and wattle buildings.

A large group of 'structural' nails is divided into five sub-groups (IN01–3, 12, 11) on the bases of their head shapes and the relationship of the shank to the head. These are likely to have fulfilled a common range of purposes. All would have had their heads formed by having the square shank held in a nailing iron or hole in an anvil, and the projecting end of the shank struck by a hammer. The differences in head form may simply relate to the degree of care taken in finishing the nail, as opposed to a deliberate distinction. There were minor fluctuations in the proportions of the different nail types over time (Figure 10.90), but the larger samples show a broadly consistent pattern. The main exception is the specialised group from the burial chapel (pp 166-7), in which nails with flat round heads (IN01) predominated. A distinct group of nails with small heads (IN11) matches the other 'structural' nails in terms of length and chronological distribution, but may have had a special role as 'hidden' nails in finely-finished work. A concentration of these nails in a **Period I/1.3** rubbish deposit is thus of particular interest, as are later groups from the **Period II** church and burial chapel.

Nails with round flat heads (IN01)

Two hundred and twenty four nails had flat round heads generally with the shank located centrally. 87% were complete or lacked only their tip, and these ranged in length from 15mm (lacking tip) to 130mm (complete), with a concentration around 25–53mm, and a significant number (22%) of 60+mm.

Nails with offset flat round heads (IN02)

Seventy-one nails had flat round heads with the shank either very off-centre or, more usually, at one

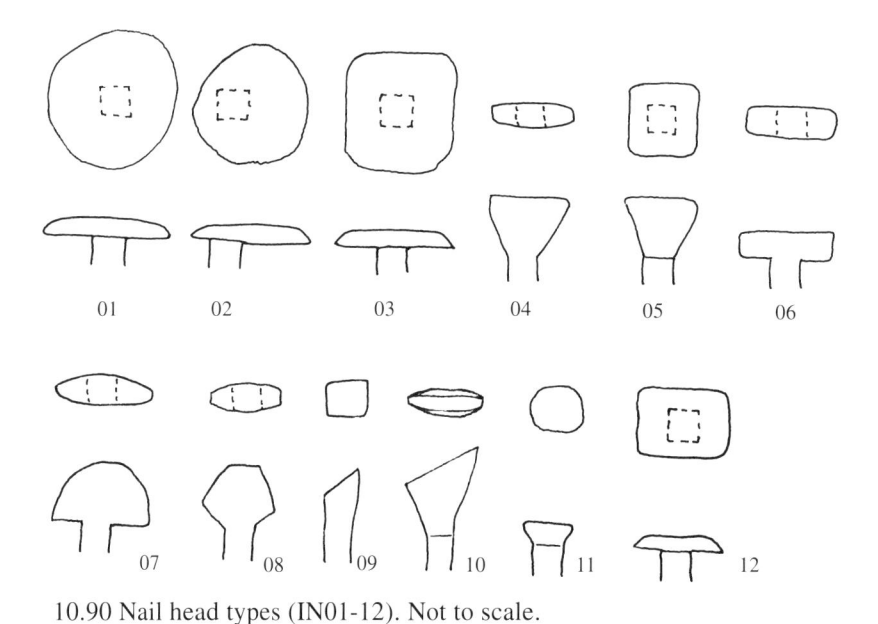

10.90 Nail head types (IN01-12). Not to scale.

	01	02	03	12	11	04	05	06	07	08	09	10	13	14	15	16	Total
PVI/topsoil/US	26	7	8	10	4	12		26	4		4	3	3	71	115	8	**301**
PV: Museum Garden	4	1	3	5	1	2	2	13	1		5	1	1	5	35	1	**80**
PV: *outer zone*	4	2	2	6	1	2		9	1		2	1		39	40	9	**118**
PV: *inner precinct* non grave	32	4	11	21	9	31	3	32	2	1	7	8	4	151	123	13	**452**
PV: *graves*	65	23	11	26	7	35	3	46	20	1	11	3	3	110	160	15	**539**
Period IV	23	9	4	10	3	5	3	18	10	3	3		2	30	70	8	**201**
Period III	9	2	2	4	2	3	1	2	2	1	2			16	31	3	**80**
Burnt church (315)	6		2	2	1			1					1	8	19	2	**42**
Burnt chapel (207 etc)	27	7	4	3	3								1	40	59	12	**156**
Period II	17	10	3	7	7		1	3	1	1	1		1	30	87	24	**193**
Period I: *outer zone*	4		1												7	1	**13**
Period I: *inner precinct*	7	6	1	6	12	1					5		1	20	69	15	**143**
Total	**224**	**71**	**52**	**100**	**50**	**91**	**13**	**150**	**41**	**7**	**40**	**18**	**15**	**520**	**815**	**111**	**2318**

Table 10.8: Chronological and spatial distribution of nails.

edge. They range in length from 20mm (lacking tip) to 113mm (complete), with 22% of 60+mm.

Nails with flat square/sub-square heads (IN03)

Fifty-two nails with flat square or sub-square heads were very similar to the preceding categories, in form, length range (20mm–101mm) and the proportion of nails of 60+mm (23%).

Nails with flat rectangular heads (IN12)

A hundred and one nails with flat rectangular heads should be considered as a variant form of the flat square-headed nails (IN03). They range in size from 21mm (lacking tip) to 95mm (complete), with 15% being 60+mm long.

Nails with small heads (IN11)

Fifty nails (IN11) had distinctly small heads, some a mere swelling, others slightly flattened. They ranged in lengths from 19mm (lacking tip) to 132mm (complete), with a sizeable portion (34%) of 60+mm, and so matched the 'structural' nails (IN01–3, 12). There was a marked concentration in early deposits (69.02, 94.01, 85.02), but their distribution otherwise matches that of other 'structural' nails.

Nails with flattened expanded heads (IN04)

Ninety-one nails with flattened expanded heads (IN04) had heads flattened in the same plane as the shank. These were probably made by being held flat on an anvil and having the end of the shank hammered, creating a slight splaying away from the shank as the material spreads on flattening. 82% of the nails were complete or lacked only their tips, and these show a more restricted length range than the 'structural' nails, from 20mm–65mm, with the majority (58%) between 25mm and 40mm and only two just over 60mm. Examples were concentrated in contexts ascribed to **Period IV** and they are thus likely to have been introduced in the tenth or eleventh century.

Nails with inverse pyramid heads (IN05)

Thirteen nails (IN05) have well formed heads with equal splaying sides. Eleven were complete or lacking tips, and ranged in length from 25mm (lacking tip) to 67mm (complete), with seven between 30mm–40mm. They were concentrated in contexts ascribed to **Period IV**. Their distribution gave no clue as to their use.

Nails with rectangular (hammer) heads (IN06)

A hundred and fifty nails have a T-shaped head of the same thickness as the shank. With a single exception at 90mm, the nails fall into a length range of 20mm–70mm. This form of nail head occurs in small numbers at Coppergate (Ottaway 1992, 707–9) from the eleventh century, and is found in twelfth-seventeenth century deposits in Northampton (Oakley 1979d, 275–7), and in a variant downwards-angled form at Beverley (Foreman 1991a, 133–4) from the twelfth century onwards. At Northampton it was suggested that they were horseshoe nails, the successor to the 'fiddle-key' headed nails (IN07 and IN08), but at York the two types appear to be contemporary, and the longer nails from Whithorn would have been unsuitable for shoeing. The two types seem to have coexisted at Whithorn during **Period IV**, but hammer-headed nails probably continued in production long after the fiddle key nails. The York nails are mainly 35mm–45mm long, matched to some extent by Whithorn and Northampton. The relatively long length of several of the pieces from Northampton, Beverley and Whithorn would seem to suggest that some were used as building nails too.

Nails with 'fiddle-key' heads (IN07)

Forty-one nails with fiddle key heads (IN07) were concentrated in deposits ascribed to **Period IV**. The limited range of lengths (23mm to 47mm) is shared by the sub-fiddle key nails (IN08 below), and by similar nails from York. They are frequently associated with horseshoes on other sites like King's Lynn (Clarke and Carter 1977, Fig. 134), Coppergate, York (Ottaway 1992, 707–9) and Beverley (Foreman

1991a, Fig. 111). Examples were concentrated in specific areas of the *inner precinct* in **Period IV**, and loosely associated with horseshoe fragments (Figure 6.33), identifying possible farrier's workshops.

Nails with sub-fiddle key heads (IN08)

Seven nails (IN08) similar to the fiddle key group, but with less-rounded triangular or polygonal heads, may be seen as forerunners or variants of the D-shaped 'fiddle key' nails.

Nails with angled/clipped/pinched heads (IN09)

A small group of forty nails (IN09) had a slight thickening at the head, whose upper surface would be at an angle of around 45°. In some cases it was possible to determine how the head had been formed. Clipped nails had been struck by a sharp tool, such as a chisel held at an angle, whilst resting on a flat surface. In some cases penetration was not complete and the edges show signs of being broken off. Pinched heads are very similar, but have traces of a second sharp edge cutting opposite the side from which the main cut had been made. Only 55% of the nails were complete or lacking tips, and these ranged in length from 27mm–65mm. Examples were widely dispersed, with five from scattered **Period I** deposits, and other in deposits ascribed to **Period IV** and subsequent periods.

Nails with a tapering heads (IN10)

Eighteen nails with tapering heads ranged in length from 23mm–51mm. There were two examples from **Period II** deposits, but the remainder came from the later **Period V** graves and overlying deposits. This suggests they were in common use from the later-fourteenth century.

Tacks or small nails (IN13)

Fifteen nails, twelve complete and two lacking tips, were less than 20mm long. Most had slightly swollen heads, though one was expanded, one domed, and two flat. A group of four were recovered from the soil overlying the **Period V** graveyard (615.01), and three more from the **Period V** graveyard itself.

Nails with a head (IN14)

This extensive category with five hundred and twenty finds encompasses all those nails whose head form could not be determined by physical examination, or from the unidirectional X-radiograph. Of these some three hundred and sixty were complete or lacking tip. Their comparative lengths reflect that for nails as a whole, with a concentration around 20mm to 50mm (73% of measurable nails), and with 17% of 60+mm.

Nail shanks (IN15)

Eight hundred and fifteen pieces identified as broken nail shanks were usually distinguished by their square, or nearly-square, cross-section. They range in length from 10mm to 92mm, and show a concentration between 20mm and 50mm. Some are a result of fractures occurring during excavation, but most show ancient breakages. There does appear to be some correlation between concentrations of nails with long shanks (e.g. 69 and 207) and the longer broken shank fragments, which probably represent additional nails, rather than simply the missing pieces of broken nails present. The proportion of nail shanks (and detached heads) diminished gradually, peaking at nearly 60% in **Periods I** and **II**.

Nail heads (IN16)

A hundred and eleven nail heads were identified, several of them tentatively from X-radiographs of unpromising lumps. Only fifteen had visible shank stubs *in situ*, confirming that most nails broke directly below the head (see above). Most of the nail heads are of the flat circular/square/sub-rectangular form (IN01, 02, 03, 12), and their distribution is similar. A preferential width or diameter of 17mm to 25mm is indicated.

Staples (IN17)

Thirty-five detached staples were found, in addition to those used in the chest-coffin burials (IN32), those still attached to hasps or hinges (IN24), and the sub-group of long staples (IN18). Of these nineteen were U-shaped, fourteen squared, one looped, and one rounded. Most of the staples had rectangular or sub-rectangular sections, with slightly tapering arms. The rectangular staples varied in head width (i.e. the distance between the arms) from 14mm to 60mm (with corresponding arm lengths of 12mm to 83mm), whilst the U-shaped ones had a much more limited head width range of 8mm to 28mm, with a closely-matched group of width 14mm–18mm and length 40mm–55mm. These are similar to the staples used as hasp or hinge fittings, and most of the U-shaped staples as well as the single looped staple, were probably part of similar fittings. Six of the staples (four U-shaped, two angular) had arms whose terminals were bent through 90° away from the plane of the staple, a form of clenching for added security after they had passed through the timber. As with the York material a thickness of 10mm to 25mm is indicated for the wood.

Long staples (IN18)

This group of twenty staples (IN18.1–20) shared very similar characteristics, distinguishing them from the other staples. Starting out as a strip *c.* 70mm long by

Unclassified nails (IN14)

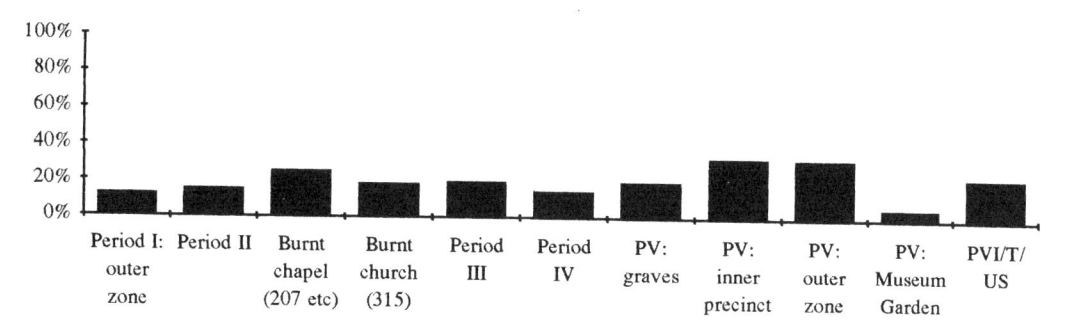

Nail shanks (IN15) and nail heads (IN16)

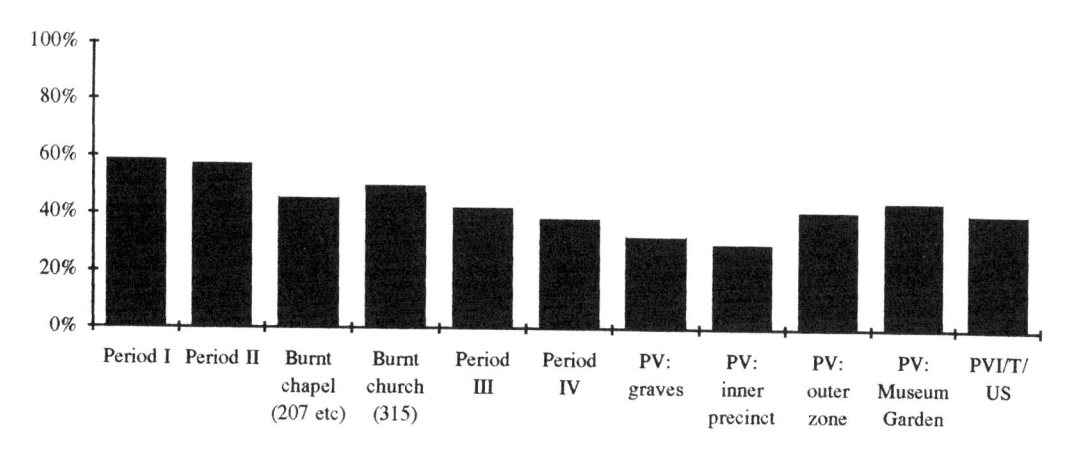

Classified nails (IN01-13)

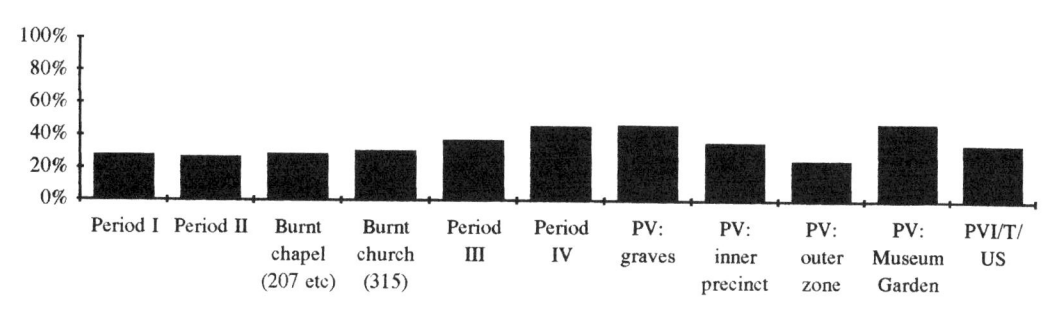

10.91 Chronological distribution of classified, unclassified and broken nails.

c. 15mm wide tapering towards the ends, the last 8–12mm of each end is bent through 90° to form a rectangular staple. The ends are too short to have penetrated through a timber, and they may have been used to secure two adjacent timbers in place while other activities, such as gluing, took place. They were concentrated in **Period III** deposits with a group of four concreted together (2–5) from the **Period III/1.4** platform (465) and three (6–8) from the **Period III/2.1** boundary ditch. Later examples were concentrated in deposits ascribed to **Period IV**, and they thus seem to have limited currency between the later-ninth and thirteenth centuries, although there is one earlier example from a **Period I.2** building (I/9, 88.01). Two similar items, unfortunately unstratified, were found at Goltho (Beresford 1975, Fig. 40).

Clench nails (IN19)

Eighteen nails, mainly with flat round heads (as per IN01), had been hammered through timbers and then had a small plate, the rove, placed over their tips which were clenched over to secure the nail in position. Two main forms of rove were noted, a square or quadrilateral one and an elongated diamond-shaped form. The nails were generally of 31mm to 45mm long, the squared roves around 21mm square, and the diamond-shaped roves 35mm by

	17U	17	18	19	20	21	22
PVI/topsoil/US		••	•	•	•••		•••
PV: Museum Garden							
PV: *outer zone*	•••				•••		•
PV: *inner precinct* non grave	•••	•	••	••••	••		•••
PV: graves	•••••	••	••••••	••••••	•••••	•	
Period IV	••	••••	••	••	•••••		
Period III		••	••••••••	•••	••	•	••••
Period II	••••			••	••	••	••••
Period I: *outer zone*							
Period I: *inner precinct*	••	•••	•		••	••••	•
Total	19	14	20	18	24	8	15

Table 10.9: Distribution of staples, clench-nails, rivets and bolts.

18mm. The gap between nail head and plate indicates the thickness of the overlapped planks they secured. This usually lay between 19mm and 34mm, but in one instance was only 12mm. Two clench nails from secure **Period II** deposits can be dated to the earlier-ninth century, but most can be ascribed to **Period IV**.

Clench plates (IN20)

Twenty-four detached clench plates or roves (IN20.1–24) include three with surviving clenched nail tips. Four were distinctly diamond-shaped, the rest square or quadrilateral. A strip of three roves (IN20.17) is of particular interest. The holes are cut or drilled and the line along which it would be cut is marked by incised grooves. This indicates that square and quadrilateral roves were pre-formed by perforating a strip at regular intervals and preparing the cut lines for the individual pieces, allowing them to be carried in quantity and cut when needed. Two roves (1 and 2) came from **Period I** deposits (89 and 118) and three (3–5) from **Period II**. Most however can be ascribed to **Period IV**. These include a group of three from a building (IV/18) in the east part of the **central sector**, and four more (including the strip of three) from **Period V** graves in the same area. Associated finds hint at the presence of a smithy (pp 229–30), and these may have been part of the blacksmith's stock.

Rivets (IN21)

Eight small iron rivets from 10mm to 20mm in length, were usually distinguishable from nails by their small size and round section. These were concentrated in earlier deposits and include two (3 and 4) from a **Period I/4** grave (I/113). Riveted plates and strips (IN78.2, 4, 6, 12, 23 and 29) have a similar chronological distribution, identifying this as a construction technique common in the sixth and seventh centuries, and relatively rare thereafter.

Bolts (IN22)

Sixteen bolts (IN22.1–16) were similar to the larger nails, but tended to have round sections and lacked pointed tips. Nine appear intact and range in length from 50mm to 140mm. The bolts had a restricted distribution. Four (2, 4–6) came from deposits to the east of the **Period II** burial chapel, and four (3, 7–9) from related deposits (251, 339) in the central part of the **central sector**. Three others from late deposits in the same area could have been displaced from contemporary layers by **Period IV** graves. These are thus likely to have been used in the structure of the chapel, perhaps in its inferred shingled roof (pp 166-7), and possibly in the large hall (II/7, II/9) to the south. Their specific function, however, is unclear.

Studs (IN23)

Two studs (IN23.1–2) include a stud with a domed head plated with tin (2), from the surface (550) to the west of the **Period V** graveyard, which produced related studs in copper alloy (Figure 10.49).

Structural Ironwork

A broad group of objects (Figure 10.92) relating to the furnishing and fabric of buildings is referred to as structural ironwork. The stratigraphy sometimes allows association with specific buildings, such as a chain complex and wall-hook from Building II/12, and hinges, locks and latches from the **Period II** church. These complement sparse literary descriptions for contemporary buildings (Karkov 1991). Chests, indicated by fittings and locks, or in their re-use as coffins, had a long currency in **Periods I–IV** as befits such utilitarian objects.

Hinge and hasps (IN24)

A group of hinges and hasps (IN24.1–12) probably includes chest, door, and shutter fittings. The first complement the evidence from the chest/coffins (IN32), and some of the staples (IN17) may have been part of similar fittings. Three pieces from the **Period I/3** rubbish spread (85.02) comprise a U-eyed hinge with rivets connecting the parallel strips (2); a linked looped staple, ring and riveted plate (1); and a broken looped hasp (3, York Type 2). These could have come from the upper part of a chest secured by a sliding bolt lock (IN33.1), which is likely to date to the earlier-seventh century. The main **Period II** rubbish spread (303) produced an articulated chest hinge (4) comprising a looped bracket secured by a U-shaped staple, and preserving mineralised wood. The burnt debris in the **Period II** church (315) produced two looped brackets (7 and 8), and two simple hinges in the form of interlinked U-shaped staples (5 and 6). These may have come from a simple window shutter located on the north side of the building (Figure 4.21). A figure-of-eight shaped hasp (9) from a **Period III** deposit (400), may have come from a chest and a looped staple with an attached ring (10) from a **Period III/3** building (III/35, 476) could have been a tether. A swivel hasp (11) from a **Period IV** building (IV/18) may have come from the door. The only fitting from the **Period V** graveyard (542) comprised two broken tapering strips connected by a pin hinge (12).

Lynch pins (IN25)

Two of the three lynch-pins (IN25.1–3) were tapering square-sectioned shanks with a looped terminal. The earliest pin (1) from a **Period I/2.1** deposit (100) probably dates c. 550 AD, and a second (2) from worm-sorted soil (251) probably pertains to the first half of the ninth century. A hollow(?) plated bar with a looped terminal (3) from Building IV/8, was different and its identification as a lynch pin is less certain.

Hinge pivots (IN26)

Four hinge pivots (IN26.1–4) were recovered. Two (1 and 2) had square-sectioned tapered shanks for insertion into a wall, and round-sectioned spindles. The larger (1) came from the main **Period II** rubbish spread (303). The smaller of the two (2) is too small for a door, but could have possibly served for a shutter. It came from mid-ninth century ploughsoil (333) to the east of Hall II/7, and could have originated in a window in the east gable. Another from debris (617.05) over the **Period V** graveyard (3) had a more ovoid section spindle, while the fourth (4, unstratified) was of circular section throughout – a bent rod forming a crude pivot.

Latches (IN27)

Three slightly curved strips with a bent or hooked end, and two rods of similar shape, may have been latches (IN27.1–5). In all cases the hooked end is intact, whilst the other end of the bar or rod is broken, so there is no evidence of possible pivot points. One of the pieces (1) from the floor of the **Period II** church (315.02), is plated, probably with tin. Two (3 and 4) were found in a **Period IV** rubble bank (430), another (2) came from the floor of Structure II/11 (259), and the last (5) from the **Period V** cultivation (546).

Handle (IN28)

Half of a curved drop-handle (IN28.1) was found in a late **Period V/2** grave (539). The end of the handle is bent against the line of the curve into a short (9mm) tapering projecting stub which would have inserted into some form of socket to enable the handle to swivel. The handle, of ovoid section, is 12mm thick at its widest point at the apex of the curve, tapering to 7mm where it is bent to form the stub. It may be plated. Viking period handles from York (MacGregor 1982, 84; Ottaway 1992, 646–7) are more rectangular, and this convex form may be later.

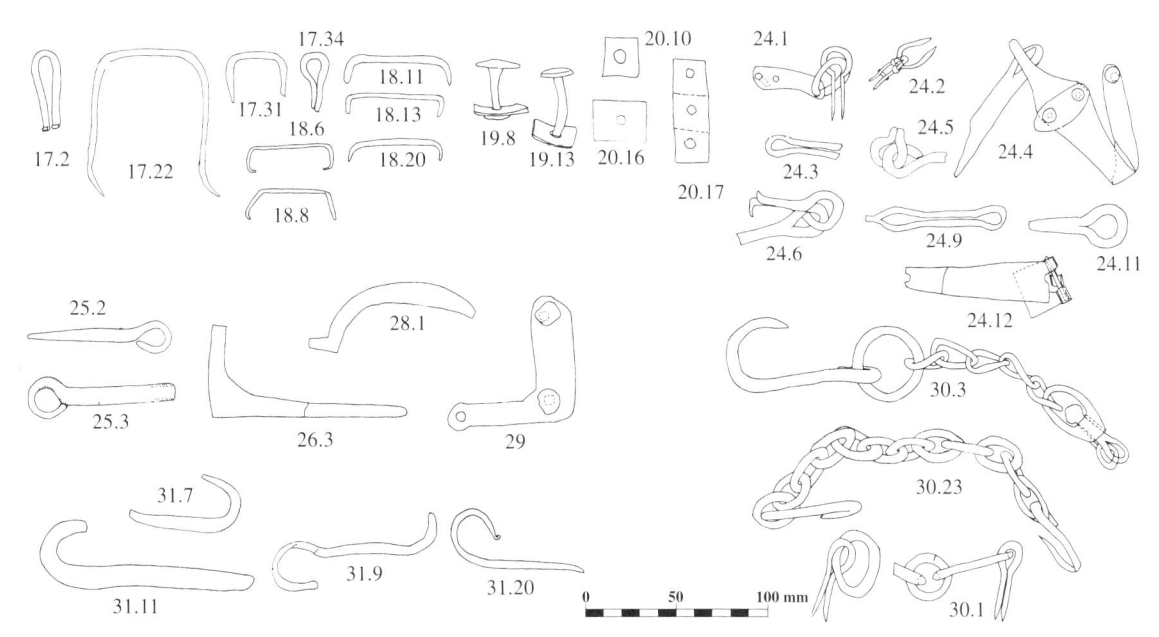

10.92 Iron structural fittings (IN17-31).

Other structural ironwork (IN29)

Four other pieces (IN29.1–4) may also have been structural. A right-angled bracket (1) with an affixing nail at each end, came from a **Period I/2** grave (80.03, Grave I/32), and may have been a coffin fitting (see IN32 below). A rectangular loop with mineralised wood on the arms (2), from a **Period I/3** rubbish deposit (109) could be a staple with inturned arms, but none of the other staples were finished in this fashion. A bar (3) from a **Period III** building (III/38), was flattened and perforated at each end and could have been the central element of a hasp. A simple looped swivel ring (4) from a **Period V** grave, may have originated in the putative **Period IV** smithy in the east part of the **central sector**.

Chains, links and rings (IN30)

A group of chains, links and rings (IN30.1–32) was treated together as it was not possible to tell whether individual rings were part of a chain or other linkage, or objects in their own right. It was not possible from examination of the X-radiographs to discern significant wear patterns which could have elucidated this. Five sections of chain (1–4, 22) include a length of three alternate round and ovoid links (1) linked to a looped staple, and an associated circular link from a small **Period II** buildings (II/12, 214). These two pieces were probably joined and are likely to have been an internal fitting. The looped staples would have secured it strongly, whilst the chain would ensure limited movement, perhaps to an aperture. Three sections from medieval deposits in the western part of the site comprise a badly corroded piece with at least three sub-rectangular links (2) from a fourteenth/fifteenth century ditch (502), and two lengths (3 and 4) from the adjacent cultivation (546). One of the latter (4) comprises a slightly corroded group of ten connected links (4) and some wire of similar diameter. The other (3) was a well preserved arrangement of a swivel ring attached by a chain of five links to a large ring and hook. The spindle appears to bifurcate below the ring with each arm ending in an elongated loop, and traces of a strip or ring fitting between them are visible on the X-radiograph. The chain links are ovoid with a 90° twist in the middle. The final chain (22) comprising two looped hooks joined by a length of twelve ovoid links, came from the eastern part of the **central sector** (904) and may have originated in the **Period IV** deposits there.

Seventeen individual links or rings (5–21, 23) included closed circular and penannular forms, with diameters ranging from 15mm to 83mm. Within both forms some were of constant diameter whilst others tapered at both ends. Two of the penannular rings were ovoid rather than circular. Most were of relatively circular section, though the largest example (from 546) is of rectangular section. The links range in date from the later-sixth century (89) through to modern and recent, though there is a noticeable absence in the **Period IV** material, and none of the distinctive waisted links found on contemporary sites (Ottaway 1992, Fig. 273; Arwidsson and Berg 1983, Pl.16).

Hooks (IN31)

Thirty hooks (IN30.1–30) vary in size and form, reflecting their usage. Four were S-shaped, of which one may be a fish-hook (3, 85.02), whilst the other three (5, 15 and 19) were more certainly suspension hooks. One (5) came from a **Period I** grave (I/118) cutting the same early seventh century deposit (85.02), the other two are ascribed to **Period IV** (15, 430 and 19, 543). Two hooks (1 and 4) had flattened shanks, creating small rectangular plates, one of which was perforated, and could have been part of a hinge or catch mechanism. Both came from **Period I** deposits (83 and 94.01). A hook (21) from the **Period V** graveyard (543) ended in a small triangular plate, and another (25) from the ploughing (546) was probably a wall hook as it terminated in a larger perforated rectangular plate with a nail *in situ*. Three others (7, 11 and 12) had straight square or rectangular shanks with blunted ends, for fixing into a wall. All three came from **Period II** contexts and they are appropriate to a period of timber rather than wattle buildings. One (7) came from the main rubbish spread (303), a second (11) from Building II/12, and the third (12) from the burnt debris (339.02) to the south of the burial chapel. The remaining hooks lacked diagnostic functional features.

Chest/coffin fittings (IN32)

The **Period II** burial chapel enclosed four graves (II/1–4) containing timber coffins, and a fifth (II/4b) had probably been obliterated (p 170). Three of these coffins (1, 2 and 4) had iron fittings, and a rounded plate from the fourth (II/3) could have been one also. Two of the graves to the east (II/10 and II/54) also produced iron fittings. One of these (II/54) preserved the lower part of a small iron-bound chest (Chest/coffin 5), the other (Chest/coffin 6) is less certain. Three of the Chest/coffin burials (II/2, II/3, and II/10) can be ascribed to the opening years of **Period II** possibly dating *c*. 710–730 AD. The other three are less closely dated, but precede the fire of *c*. 845 AD, and are likely to pertain to the eighth century. The fittings were examined by Richard Heawood (Heawood 1990), and his report has been summarized and updated to accommodate additional information from X-radiographs taken by the YAT laboratories (Heawood and Nicholson, in prep.).

Two of the chests (4 and 5) had sliding bolt locks, and the key for one (4) was found inside the coffin. A second key for a sliding bolt lock was found in a similar position in Grave II/2, and the remains of a possible lock survive in a sample of carbonised wood from Chest/coffin 1. There was no evidence to suggest that either of the keys had accompanied the bodies. Traces of mineralised textile from both the keys may then relate to a covering over the coffin, rather than a shroud or costume. Coffins with locks have been noted elsewhere (Evison 1987, Riddler 1980), and suggests that they may originally have been chests, and they are accordingly termed 'Chest/coffins'. This hypothesis is supported by the fact that fittings seem to have been missing from two of the coffins (1 and 4) and these could have been lost during earlier use as chests.

The four Chest/coffins (1, 2, 4 and 5) with well-preserved fittings all followed a similar design (Figure 10.93). The fittings fell into three main categories: angle-irons, hinges and locks, with a small number of pieces whose original form or function was uncertain. Angle-irons had two unequal arms tapering away from a 90° bend, and ending in rounded or expanded circular ends. Hinges took two forms: a) a tapering strap with a looped terminal (*c.f.* Ottaway 1992, 3307 and 3386), as found in Graves *II/1* and II/54, or **b**) a figure-of-eight shaped hasp secured at either end by U-shaped staples, as found in graves *II/1* and II/4. This difference may relate to the different depositional dates of the two pairs of chest/coffins. Several of the heads on nails fixing the brackets and hinges to the chest/coffins were plated with tin, as were some of the shanks and staples. This plating was probably achieved by a dipping process.

Chest/coffin 1 (32.101–106). Grave II/1 contained an incomplete set of fittings comprising a single angle iron (103), two figure-of-eight-shaped hasps (101 and 102), and two unidentified fragments (103 and 104), one probably a U-shaped staple (104). The angle-iron came from the NW corner and the hinges are probably the western and central ones from a set of three on the north side of the grave. Further unidentified pieces preserved within a block of carbonised wood may have been part of a lock on the south side of the grave.

Chest/coffin 2 (32.201–225). The Chest/coffin in Grave II/2 had one of the most complete sets of fittings. Two angle-irons (201–208) support each vertical edge, and three (209–214) support each lower edge. In most cases where the arms of the angle-iron are of unequal length, the longer arm corresponds to the longer face, which could relate to practical or aesthetic considerations. Three loop-ended straps (215–217) sat above the brackets on the northern side panel, their heads just above the level of the upper corner brackets. No direct evidence existed for U-staples associated with the loop-ended strips, but a badly corroded bracket fragment (223) was located at a similar height on the northern side, between the eastern and central strips. Two round-ended straps (218 and 219) on the southern side were positioned opposite the hinges, and may relate to lid fastenings. A small fragment (221) was centrally located, and could have come from a lock mechanism. A two-pronged key (220) was found directly below this, resting on the base of the coffin where it had presumably fallen when the lid decayed. Mineralised wood remains on the fittings show that the long sides and base of the chest/coffin were made of planks set lengthways along the long axis, whilst the ends were of planks with the grain running vertically. Evidence from Chest/coffins 2 and 4 suggests the planks were 20–24mm thick.

Chest/coffin 3 (32.301). A single broken fragment of a rounded plate from Grave II/3 may be a fitting, but its form does not correspond to any of the pieces from the other graves.

Chest/coffin 4 (32.401–421). The Chest/coffin in Grave II/4 was tilted, with the lower northern edge resting on the bottom of the cut, and the southern edge some 20cm higher. It had a nearly complete set of fittings. There were seven angle-irons at the corners (401–407), but the lower bracket from the south-east corner was missing. Three more angle-irons (408–413) supported each of the lower long edges. Two hinges (414, 415) above the northern angle-irons comprised bent figure-of-eight shaped hasps secured at either end by U-staples. The western hinge was missing, supporting the view that this was a re-used chest, which had already lost a hinge and a bracket. Two additional stapled hasps (416, 417) lay at the top on the south side opposite the hinges, and a probable western one was again missing. Centrally located on the southern side was a draw-bolt lock mechanism (419) with an exterior lock plate (420). The plate has a central slot to accommodate the key shank (Figures 10.93 and 94), and four holes to take the prongs. The X-radiograph shows that the bolt is in the locked position between its retaining staples. The key (418) found some 30cm to the west, fits the lock, and was probably placed on top of the chest/coffin, subsiding to the base when the lid decayed. A broken spiral terminal (421) located 15cm below the uptilted SE corner of the coffin may be a fitting, but does not match any of the other pieces.

Chest/coffin 5 (32.501–513). Grave II/54 lay beyond the chapel, and its upper fill had been disturbed in **Period III/1**, removing the fittings from the upper part of the Chest/coffin (5) that it contained. This would explain the lack of corner brackets, which occur *in situ* at a higher level in the other graves, though the full set of six angle-irons (501–507) from the lower edges survived. Broken looped strips (509 and 510) lying between the end pairs of brackets, which may have been lid fixtures connected with the hinge system. A single loop-ended strap (508) secured by a U-shaped staple, was probably part of the western hinge which had slumped down the side of the grave. It is comparable with the three *hinges* from Chest/coffin 2. Two other U-shaped staples (512, 513) from

10.93 Chest coffins and iron fittings (IN32).

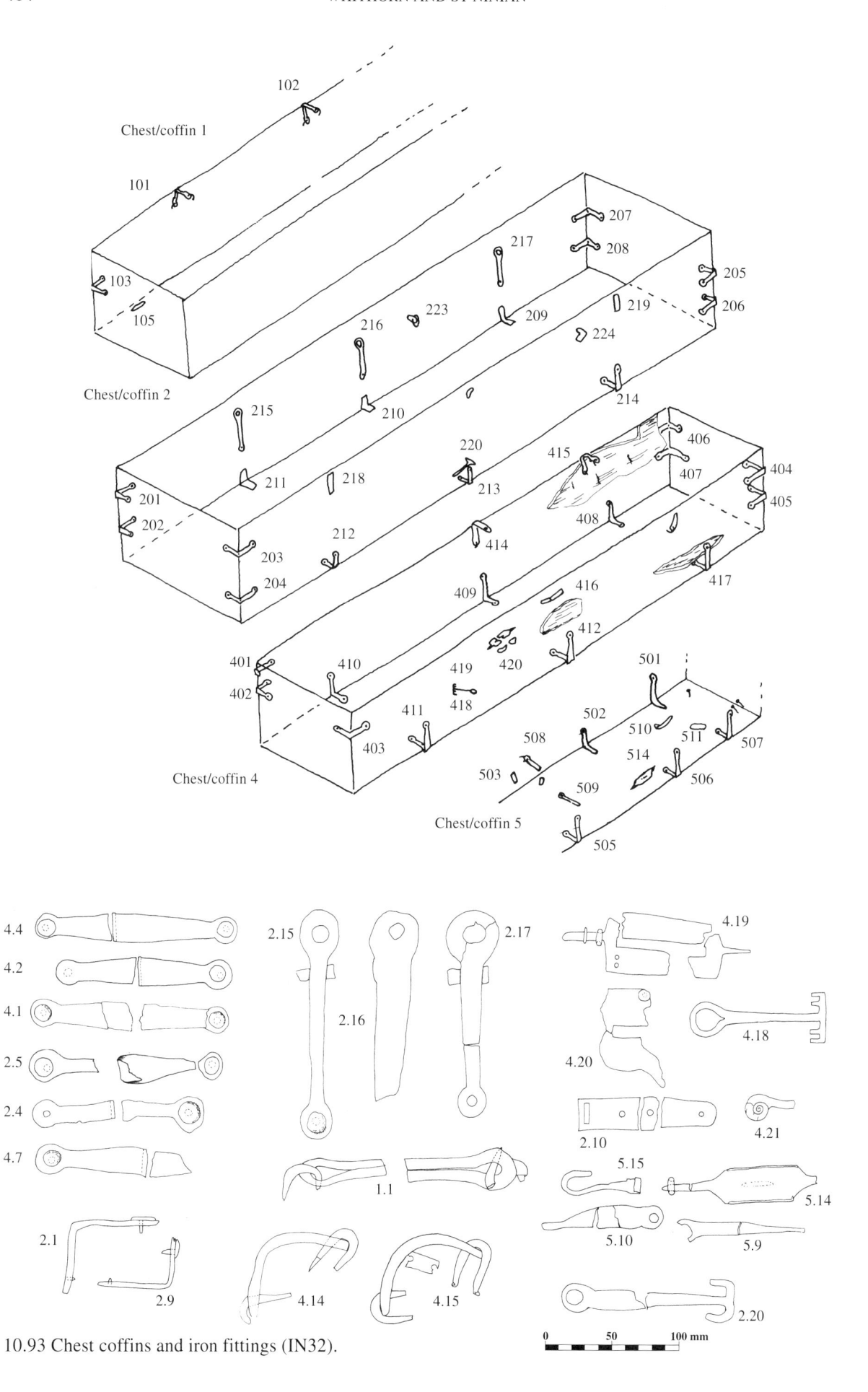

displaced material above the grave, can be reasonably ascribed to the Chest/coffin, and probably relate to the lid hinges. A sliding bolt lock (514) was centrally located adjacent to the southern edge. The X-radiograph is not clear, but there appears to be no central slot to take a key (*c.f.* No.4

above), and it has an additional looped object with a flattened end (515), which may be a spring mechanism to keep the plate under tension. One end of the sliding bolt is broken, but the other passes through a retaining staple, indicating that this coffin may also have been locked, though no key was found. A bent object (516), perhaps two U-staples, came from 15cm north of the chest/coffin, and may be part of the fastening for the lid.

Chest/coffin 6 (32.601–2). Two convex-sided staples may be intended as fittings, or may be dog-joiners to secure butted planks (see IN18).

The distinctive Whithorn angle-iron, with arms narrowing towards rounded terminals, are matched in an eighth/ninth century context at Garton Slack, E. Yorkshire (Mortimer 1905, Fig. 717), and at Dacre, Cumbria (Ottaway, forthcoming). Straight-sided angle-irons and straps appear at Monkwearmouth (Clogg, forthcoming) and Ripon (Hall and Wyman 1986). The loop-headed hinge plates are likewise paralleled at Dacre, Garton Slack and Ripon, as were the draw-bolt locks, which also occur at Thwing (Yorkshire Archaeological Society 1986) and York Minster (Ottaway, Pers. Comm.). Whilst there is an apparent association of coffin fittings with Middle Saxon monastic houses, it is not possible to demonstrate that the burials are those of ecclesiastics or specifically monks, rather than of secular persons. Garton Slack, Thwing and Ripon seem to indicate that laymen could also be buried with in coffins with fittings, and the correlation between monasteries and coffin fittings could perhaps be explained in terms of the attraction of monastic houses as prestige burial places.

Locks (IN33)

Twelve locks, or parts thereof (IN33.1–12), were found in addition to those on the chest/coffins (above) and fragments of a lock from the **Period II** church (IN90.4). The only earlier example (1) is a sliding bolt with an oval perforated plate from **Period I/3** workshop debris (85.02) probably dating to the earlier-seventh century. Until now the earliest Post-Roman example of this form is a complete lock from the cemetery at Ailcey Hill, Ripon (Ottaway 1992, 660). Another sliding bolt (2) from the surface (617.01) over the **Period V** graves was probably displaced. A complex object (IN78.41) may be another lock of uncertain design.

The earliest (3) of nine barrel padlock fragments (3–12) came from a mid-ninth century deposit (302), although there was a barrel padlock key (IN34.3) from the underlying rubbish deposit (303), and decorative fragments (IN90.4) from the adjacent church. The only complete example (11) came from a late medieval layer in the **southern sector** (633). It appears on the X-radiograph to be internally similar to the complete lock from Coppergate, York (Ottaway 1992, 3610

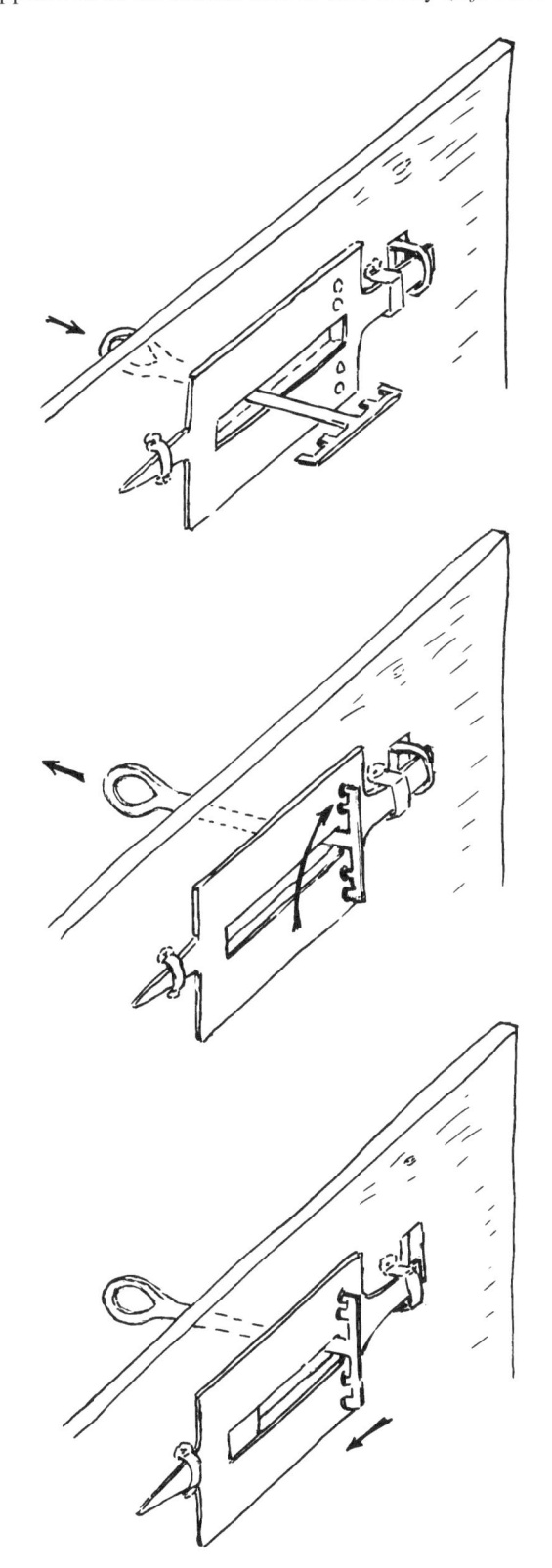

10.94 Reconstruction of sliding bolt lock from chest/coffin 4.

Pl.XXXVa–c), with some evidence of non-ferrous plating and applied decoration in the form of wavy line strips. The pear-shaped end-plates and attached free arm tube indicate a similar pre-twelfth century date. Plated iron sheets (12) from Building V/2b (415.02) are probably part of padlock case deposited in the later-thirteenth century. The remaining seven pieces (4–10) are the U-shaped sliding bolts from barrel padlocks with twin-bladed leaf-springs. Five of them (4, 5, 6, 9 and 10) have the end-plate from the padlock attached, indicating that the lock had been broken deliberately. Four of the eight padlocks ascribable to **Periods IV** and **V** came from the *outer zone*, three (10–12) from **Period V** contexts in the **southern sector**, and one from the graveyard surface in the east part of the **central sector**. Two fragments (7 and 8) from the northern part of the site could have been associated with a copper alloy lock-plate (BZ30.24, Figure 10.71).

Keys (IN34)

Nineteen keys of various forms (IN34.1–19) were found in addition to the two from the chest coffins. The earliest (1) from a **Period I/4.4** deposit (73) is possibly a key for a sliding bolt or a latch mechanism. The main **Period II** rubbish spread (303) produced another sliding bolt key (2), as well as two keys for barrel padlocks (3 and 4), with circular bits at right-angles to the stem. There were two more barrel padlock keys (5 and 6) from **Period IV** deposits (425.01 and 445, Building IV/21), and a third (13) from the foundation of Building V/3 (506.01), was probably of similar date. Four others (10, 14, 17 and 18), from the **Period V** graveyard (10), post-medieval cultivation (14, 608), **Museum Garden** (18, 770), and spoil (17) may also have been displaced from **Period III** or **IV** deposits. The earliest (9) of five keys (7, 8, 9, 15, and 19) with loop-terminals, hollow stems and bits came from the **Period V** graveyard (532) and dates to the twelfth/thirteenth century (LMMC Type III; LMMC 1993, 136). Four of these keys were tin plated, in contrast to only one (6) of the barrel padlock keys.

The best preserved key (16), from a box-padlock, came from the topsoil in the northern part of the **southern sector**, but could easily have been displaced from **Period IV** deposits by cultivation in **Period VI**. It has an elaborately-shaped bit and conjoined T-shaped wards. The stem tapers equally towards the bit and the perforated plate at the end, on the same plane as the bit. Through this is a suspension loop, a wire ring with butted terminals. Similar keys from the late twelfth century occur at Castle Acre (Goodall 1982, Fig. 40)

Weights (IN35)

A triangular piece, unusual in its shape, could be a weight (IN35.01). It came from the **Period V** graveyard (538) and was unfortunately badly corroded, thus rendering attempts to determine its original weight as futile. A 2lb steelyard weight (2) among demolition material in the greenhouse (754) could have been displaced from a medieval context.

Vessels

A small group of fragments from vessel fragments and fittings (IN36–38) includes pieces of iron vessels, a handle and a possible lid. These can mostly be ascribed to the prolonged aceramic period in the eighth to twelfth centuries, and complement vessels of wood indicated by copper-alloy fittings, copper-alloy indicated by sheet waste and patches, and lead. The iron vessels probably had a specialised form, but their specific function is unclear.

Vessel body fragments (IN36)

Nine plate fragments (IN36.1–5) may have come from straight-sided vessels, perhaps plates or trays. Four of pieces (1a–d) from a **Period II** hall (II/9, 253), include one fragment with an upturned curved edge 3mm high. Two plate fragments (2a and b) came from a **Period IV/I** cobble surface (432), one of which was pierced by a shank, possibly from a repair. A rim sherd (4) came from a soil accumulation in the southern part of the trench (525.01), another (3) from cleaning layers within the **Period V** graveyard (543), and a third (5) from the overlying disturbed surface (772). The last three are likely to have originated in **Period IV** deposits.

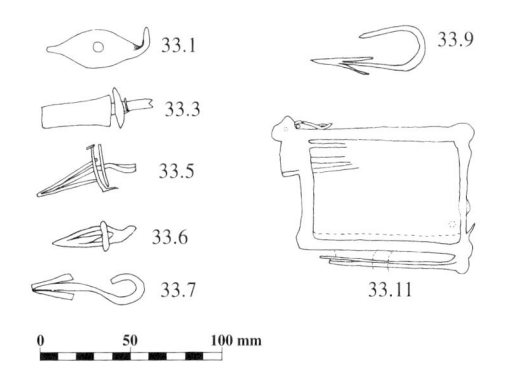

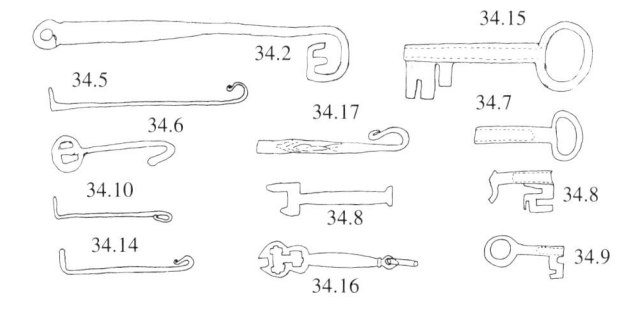

10.95 Locks and keys (IN33 and 34).

Lid (IN37)

A concave disc in six fragments, from the medieval ploughing layers in the western part of the **northern sector** (546) may have been a lid. Its original diameter was *c*. 135 mm and its pronounced curvature distinguished it from the other vessel fragments. It may nevertheless have been some other form of plate or tray.

Possible vessel handle (IN38)

A curved rod broken at both ends, but with remnants of one flattened terminal with a central perforation, may have been the handle from a small vessel. It came from an unphased **Period I** feature between Graves I/49 and I/66.

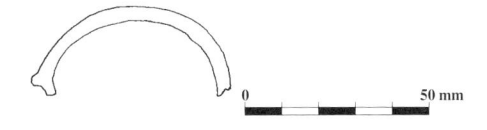

10.96 Vessel handle (IN38).

Needles (IN39)

Eighty-four needles (IN39.1–84) include fifty-two with a distinguishable eye form, the generally diagnostic feature. Thirty-nine (1–39) have punched eyes, and four others (40–43) have a flattened head preparatory to punching. Only ten (44–53) had Y-eyes, where the shank is split, and rejoined above the eye. Thirty-two of the needles were complete, and a further thirty-two were broken at the eye or tip. Intact needles ranged in length from 28 to 71mm, with half between 42 and 52mm.

The needles display unusually clear patterns of deposition. There is a significant difference in the chronological distributions of Y-eyed and punched-eyed needles (Table 10.10), the former first occurring in the **Period V** graveyard, though ascribed to the eleventh-thirteenth century **Period IV** debris in the *inner precinct*. This contrasts with Coppergate, York where they occur from the ninth century (Ottaway 1992, 547). A large proportion of the assemblage came from the **Period V** graveyard, but spatial analysis indicates that these had been displaced from **Period IV** deposits in the outer part of the *inner precinct* (Figure 6.26a). There were concentrations of fine and coarse needles (Figure 6.26b), but the different eye types were mixed. There was an equally clear pattern in **Period II** (Figure 10.98). The seven relatively complete needles (1–7) all had punched eyes and, together with two broken needles (56 and 74), were confined to the ground surrounding and to the north of the halls, with concentrations around Hall II/6 and in the open area to the south of the burial chapel. Most were of standard size, but one was coarse (3) and one fine (5). Needle work is likely to have been a female occupation at this time, and copper-alloy and iron dress pins which are specifically female dress items (p 362), were confined to the same general area. Eight needles (8–15), again all with punched eyes, came from **Period III** contexts, but some are likely to have been displaced from the underlying **Period II** deposits, and they are included in Figure 10.98.

Dress Fittings and Riding Equipment

Personal accoutrements and riding fittings occurred at all levels (Table 10.11), and can generally be ascribed to stray losses, although a concentration of iron stick-pins may identify a booth or workshop in the **Period IV** settlement (Figure 6.35), and horse shoe and harness fittings associated with Building V/3 suggest a smithy in the vicinity. The iron finds were often stylistically complementary too non-ferrous objects, and some (i.e. buckles and pins) can be incorporated in recognized typological series. The comprehensive X-radiography programme identified an important group of iron stick pins, sometimes with traces of tin and copper alloy plating, and similar items may remain unrecognized in collections from other sites.

	IN39P	IN39Y	BZ12	IN39	IN39+BZ12	40a
PVI/topsoil/unstratified		•	•••••••	9	16	9
PV: Museum Garden	•			1	1	
PV: *outer zone*		•	•	1	2	2
PV: *inner precinct* non grave	••••	•	•••	9	12	3
PV: graves	•••••••••••••••	•••••••	•••••••	36	43	11
Period IV	•••		••	8	10	10
Period III	••••••••		•	9	10	6
Period II	•••••••		•	9	10	3
Period I: *outer zone*			•		1	1
Period I: *inner precinct*			•	2	3	4
Total				84		49

Table 10.10: Needles, pins and pin fragments (not plated pins).
P = needle with punched eye, Y = needle with Y eye.

	'Dress' pin	Pin	Stick pin	Ring pin ?	'Brooch'	'Buckle'	'Buckle' tongue
PVI/topsoil/unstratified	•	•••••••••••••*	•		••	••••	
PV: Museum Garden							
PV: *outer zone*		••			•	••	
PV: *inner precinct* non grave		•••	•		•	•	••••
PV: graves	•	•••••••••••••	••••••	•••••	•	•••••••	•••••
Period IV		••••••••••		••		•	••••
Period III		••••••	•••			•	•
Period II	•••••	•••			•	••	•••
Period I/3–4		•••			•	•••	•
Period I/1–2		••	•••				
Total	7	53	14	7	7	21	18

Table 10.11: Chronological and spatial distribution of dress fittings.
*Includes five wire-wrapped pins concreted together.

Pins (IN40)

Sixty-two objects (IN40.1–61) were identified as pins, and others from modern and recent deposits in and around the manse, matched their copper alloy counterparts (BZ01–10), in head form and length. Most of the 'pins' were fragmentary and of small diameter, and some may be broken needles or fine wire. There were examples from most periods, and they clearly predate the copper alloy pins which were scarce before **Period V**. The pins are seldom longer than 40mm, but a single broken example (29) some 84 mm long from the **Period V** graveyard, may correspond with fourteenth century pins from London (Egan and Pritchard 1991, Fig. 204).

Several pins with thicker shanks and bulbous heads (IN40.51–57), correspond to the copper-alloy ornamental pins (BZ13.1–3). EDXRF analysis identified tin-plating on two examples, and X-radiographs revealed plating on the others. A small ball-headed pin (51) from the clay mixing pit (250.03), probably dates *c.* 800 AD, and three club-headed pins (52–4) from the main **Period II** rubbish spread (303) may be contemporary or slightly later. Two (53 and 54) are very similar to the associated copper alloy pins (BZ13.1 and 2), although without the medial swelling on the shank, although this is present on an unstratified pin (55). The third (52) is similar to the large silver pin (SR6) from Building II/15 (pp 398-9). The last two (56 and 57) have larger heads and unusually thick tapering shanks, appearing more akin to nails than pins, though their head form is not found amongst the recognized types. One (56) was securely stratified in the **Period II/7** church (315.01) and was probably deposited in the mid-ninth century. The second (57), though displaced by

Period V graves, could have originated in a similar deposit further to the east. The related iron and copper alloy pins were concentrated in the northern part of the **central sector** (Figure 10.97), and may have been among debris originating in the halls to the south. They were probably used in female head dress (p 362), and their distribution supports the hypothesis that the halls were used by guests.

Stick pins (IN41)

A group of longer pins (IN41.1–26) comprises fourteen stick pins (1–14), seven loop-headed pins (15–21), and four shanks lacking heads (22–26). Three stick pins (1–3) and a shank (2) came from **Period I** contexts. The earliest (1) with a distinct T-shaped head, came from the **Period I.3** ploughsoil (56.02) in the **southern sector** and so precedes the casting of nail-headed copper alloy pins (p 403) and is likely to date *c.* 500 AD if not before. A shorter pin with a perforated crescentic head (2) from a **Period I/2** grave (I/32) is likely to date to the later-sixth century if it accompanied the burial. Both have distinct collars, and may be grouped with the early crescentic copper alloy pin (BZ14.7), although this was deposited at a rather later date in **Period I/3**. A third object (IN64.1) from the same deposit as No. 1, has a similar collar, but has been identified as a stylus, though it too could be the head of a pin. Another crescentic headed pin (14) came from spoil, but the date of its recovery indicates that it was also from early material. An unusually early club-headed pin (3) from a **Period I/2** deposit (89) has a medial swelling on the shank, but lacks the distinct hipping characteristic of early copper alloy pins.

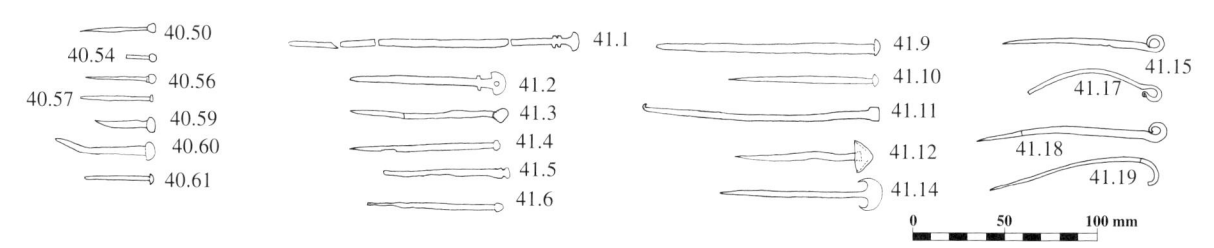

10.97 Pins, stick pins and possible ring pins (IN40 and 41).

THE FINDS   419

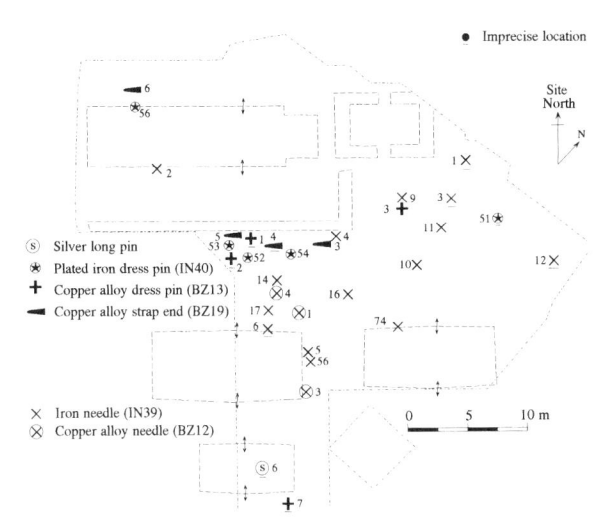

10.98 The distribution of dress pins and needles from **Period II** and **III** contexts.

There were no stick pins from **Period II** contexts apart from a possible broken shank fragment (23) from the burnt deposits in the church (315.01). **Period III** deposits produced two pins (4 and 5) and two shanks (24 and 25). One pin (4), possibly trilobate or club-headed, came from a building (III/18), whilst the other (5) with a plated faceted head, and the two headless shanks, came from the waterborne silts (309.02) in the **southern sector**. A club-headed pin (6) from the **Museum Garden**, came from an equivalent deposit (408.02, pp 281-2). These three pins are all earlier than their equivalents in copper alloy, but a larger sample would perhaps be needed to establish their precedence. The only stratified iron stick pin from **Period IV** was a headless shank from Building IV/21, but displaced finds from the **Period V** graveyard included another club-headed pin (7), three stud-headed stick pins (8–10), a squared spatulate pin (11), and a pin with a flattened, rounded triangular head (12). The stud-headed and squared spatulate pins are similar to copper-alloy examples, but were concentrated on the border of the **Period IV** *inner precinct*, and might have been produced in an adjacent workshop. The last pin (12) is similar in shape to a thirteenth century pin from Perth (Bogdan and Wordsworth 1978, 21), although also akin to the early crescentic pins. An unusual stick pin with a small rectangular head (13), came from mid-fourteenth century demolition deposits in Building V/1.

Seven loop-headed pins (15–21) are similar in many ways to the loop-headed copper alloy pins from Irish sites. These however tend to be early in the ring-pin series (see BZ15), and as all the iron pins came from **Period IV** and **V** contexts, they are more likely to come from brooches (e.g. the pin on No. 1, Figure 10.99). Four pins (17–20) came from the **Period V** graveyard, a fifth (15) from the **Period IV.1** antler-working debris (425.01), a sixth (16) from Building IV/4, and the last (21) from an unphased hollow in the **central sector**.

Brooches (IN42)

Six possible brooches (IN42.1–6) and a brooch pin (7) were recovered. Two brooches (2 and 5) were simple penannular rings of constant diameter with plain butted terminals, and loop-headed pins (one broken) *in situ*. One (2) from the **Period II/1** oratory (220) could have been lost during the construction of the building in the earlier-eight century. The other (5) came from the foot of the post-medieval field boundary wall (610.03). A third penannular brooch (1) tapered from the centre to out-turned spiral terminals. It was recovered during the removal of a baulk in the western part of the **northern sector**, but is likely to have originated in the **Period I/3** rubbish spread (85.02), and so probably dates to the earlier seventh century. A fragmentary section of a circular loop with a pin (3) from a **Period V/1** grave (532), may be part of another penannular brooch or buckle. An annular ring with outurned terminals (6) from the foundations of Building V/3 (506.01) may be a brooch lacking its pin, or a harness fitting (Figure 10.49). A plated circular brooch or shoe buckle with a pin (4) came from a fifteenth century hollow (612.03), and an isolated brooch pin (7) from spoil.

Buttons (IN43)

Four buttons (IN43.2–5) from pre-modern contexts, were scattered to the south and west of the **Period V** graveyard, and may have been among the dress items lost as it passed out of use (Figure 10.49). A small (9mm diameter) disc with a central perforation (IN43.1) from a **Period IV** ditch (416) may also have been a button or fastener.

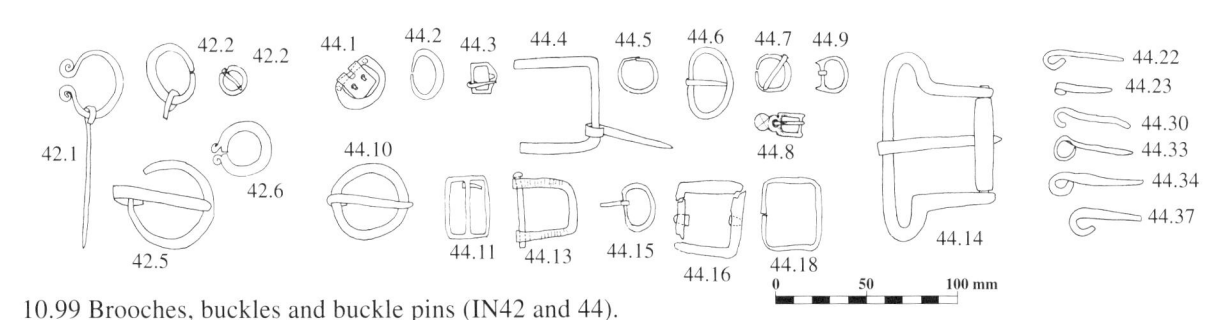

10.99 Brooches, buckles and buckle pins (IN42 and 44).

Buckles (IN44)

Twenty-one buckles (IN44.01–44.21), eighteen detached buckle tongues (IN44.22–44.39), and two possible buckle fragments (IN44.40 and 41) spanned the occupation of the site. The three earliest buckles (1, 2 and 20) came from a **Period I/3** rubbish spread (85.02) ascribed to the earlier-seventh century. All are D-ringed, and one (1) has an attached buckle-plate. New buckle forms appeared in **Period II**, with a quadrilateral buckle (3) from a layer (250.03) in a puddling pit of c. 800 AD, and a square buckle (4) from a pit (328) in the **Museum Garden**, which is earlier than the mid-ninth century. A single D-ringed buckle (5) came from a **Period III** building (459, III/40), and a sub-ovoid buckle (6) from **Period IV** rubble (430).

A sub-square buckle (13) from the foundations of Building V/3 (506.01, Figure 10.49) has incised transverse grooves on the arms adjacent to the pin, in which traces of a non-ferrous material are evident on the X-radiograph. It is unclear whether these are inlaid, or the remnants of a more comprehensive plating. This, and another large buckle (14) from the same area (506.02), have separate rollers, and so may have been used with horse harness (Egan and Pritchard 1991, 53). Three other buckles (8, 14 and 15) and one of the isolated tongues (36), also showed traces of plating. Tin plating helps to reduce rusting on iron objects frequently exposed to the weather. Seven buckles (7–12, 21) came from **Period V** graves (Figure 10.49), four D-ringed (9, 10, 12 and 21), two square (7 and 8), and one a double rectangle (11). One of the square buckles (8) had an integral rivet-plate, a feature noted on copper-alloy buckles from London dated 1200–1350 AD. They are thought to have a specialised function, possibly for securing spurs (Egan and Pritchard 1991, 108). A D-shaped buckle (9) from a **Period V** grave (534) has small backwards-projecting spurs, a feature of limited currency in the second half of the fourteenth century (Egan and Pritchard 1991, 72; Fig. 43). Two buckles (10 and 11) were found with skeletons, one (10) lying on the right femur and beneath the right hand. The others are likely to include objects displaced from **Period IV** deposits and lost during **Period V**.

Buckle tongues were scattered through the stratigraphy, the earliest (22) coming from a **Period I/4** deposit (73.02).

Finger rings (IN45a)

Three small rings (45.1–3) were interpreted as finger rings rather than structural ironwork due to their small size. Two small tapering penannular rings came from early contexts, one from a **Period I/1** grave (I/4), and the other (2) from a **Period I/3** hollow (109). A hexagonal ring (3) from the **Period V** graveyard (543) cannot be dated closely.

Strap retainers (IN45b)

Seven strap retainers and belt guides (IN45.4–10) are paralleled in ninth to twelfth century deposits at Coppergate (Ottoway 1992, 688–9), and twelfth to fifteenth century ones at London (Egan and Pritchard 1991, 229–235). An incompletely finished guide (4) came from the mid-ninth century ploughing (399.01), and a plated strap retainer (5) came from a **Period IV** building (IV/10). The remaining five (6–10) came from the **Period V** graveyard (Figure 10.49) and overlying fifteenth/sixteenth century deposits. These include two more unfinished pieces, one broken. A rectangular loop with a hook at 90° to the loop (13), also from the **Period V** graveyard, is probably another belt fitting or fastener.

Dress fittings (IN45c)

A broken spiral terminal (45.11) from a **Period III** structure (III/9, 420.01) and an intact fastening with spiral terminals (45.12) from a fourteenth/fifteenth century ditch (502) are akin to a complete eye fitting found at Coppergate (Ottaway 1992, 698).

Spurs and rowels (IN46)

A small group of spurs and rowels (IN46.1–5) comprises a single prick spur (5) with deeply curved arms broken at the terminals, dating to the fourteenth century (LMMC 1993, 94ff); a broken rowel spur (4) with a mid length shank of fourteenth/fifteenth century type (LMMC 1993), and three rowels (1–3). Two of the rowels (1 and 3) have eight points, the other (2) has six. The diamond-shaped points on the six point rowel (2)

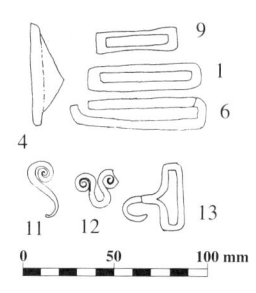

10.100 Strap retainers and dress fittings (IN45).

suggest a date in the early fifteenth century. Both spurs and rowels had evidence of non-ferrous plating, probably tin, and the rowel spur appeared to have incised lines highlighting the interfaces of the surfaces, as much clearer lines of plating were visible on the X-radiograph. Rowels from the **Period IV** rubble bank (1, 430) and a **Period V/1** grave (2, 535) are likely to have been intrusive, and the others came from more recent deposits (3, 615.01; 4, 614; 5, 616.06). All are likely to have been part of the scatter of dress items lost on the roadway in the later phases of **Period V** (Figure 10.49).

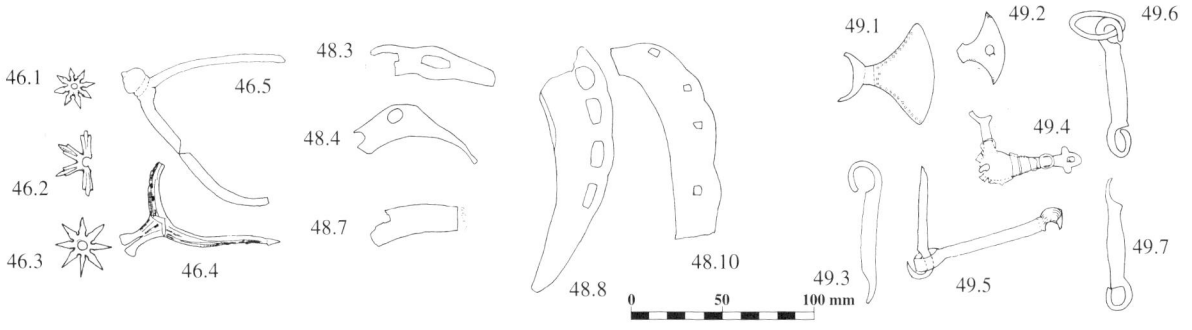

10.101 Spur (IN46), horseshoe (IN48) and bridle (IN49) fragments.

Boot plates (IN47)

Three heel protectors (IN47.4a and b, 5) and three shaped strips (IN47.1–3) conforming to the forepart of a shoe were found. The heel protectors are often found on recent boots with stacked heels, and came from relatively recent deposits. The strips are highly unusual, the more so as one (1) occurs in a **Period IV** structure (IV/10, 414.04) and the others (2 and 3) from **Period V** features (518 and 525.01) in the same general area. A date range in the later-twelfth to late thirteenth century is likely. No parallels are known, and the turnshoes in use at this time would not have been able to accommodate such items, nor have any of the soles excavated evidence of such additions. They could have been used on some form of wooden clog or overshoe, and it may be significant that all were recovered around the waterlogged area.

Horseshoe fragments (IN48)

The earliest (1) of the thirteen horseshoe fragments (IN48.1–13) came from east gable of the **Period II/1** oratory (220), but was probably part of the displaced **Period I** metal-working debris (110), and its deposition should therefore be dated to the early eighth century or before. It has a wavy outline caused by the displacement of material as the countersunk holes for the nails were driven in, and relatively thin branches, as do all the earlier pieces. From the late thirteenth century onwards the holes were not countersunk, and thus their outlines remained plain. The first examples of this form (5–7) came from later **Period V** graves. Horse shoe fragments generally coincided with groups of fiddle key nails (Figure 6.33), possibly revealing farriers' shops. The fragments produced a consistent maximum width in the range 18mm to 24mm, with the average being 20mm.

Horse harness (IN49)

The only readily identifiable items of horse harness were parts of seven snaffle bits (IN49.1–6/5), four of them broken cheek-plates. Half of an axe-headed cheek-plate (1) was redeposited into a **Period I/4** grave (82.02, I/89), and is thus likely to be earlier than the later-seventh century. It had a non-ferrous plating, and the X-radiograph indicated a border decorated with circle motifs on the axehead-shaped portion. An undecorated example (2) from the main **Period II** rubbish spread (303), probably dates to the later-eighth or earlier-ninth century. This unusual form is paralleled by seventh century objects from Lagore (Laing 1975, 291) and Sutton Hoo (Martin Carver Pers. Comm.). The remaining pieces (3–7) came from the **Period V** graveyard and more recent contexts. Two linked fragments (4) from the **Period V** graveyard (539) are decorated with a non-ferrous foil applied over a diagonally-hatched surface prepared to receive them, rather than being plated. A mouthpiece consisting of two links connected by a central ring (5), all with traces of non-ferrous plating, is a later medieval development (LMMC 1993), and came from a late **Period V** cobble surface (617.02). Two similar pieces (6 and 7), both from debris over Building V/3, show a later development of this form, and could have been part of the same bit.

Tools

A large collection of tools (IN50–65, 69, 72) spanned the occupation of the site, though concentrated in deposits ascribed to **Period IV** (Table 10.12). The examination of these finds was hampered by the lack of investigative cleaning, and many identifications are accordingly imprecise.

Awls and punches (IN50)

Eighty-one objects (IN50.1–88) can be identified as awls or punches on the basis of the X-radiographs. This imposes certain limitations. The difference between a punch with a tapering square-section, and a nail shank or headless nail, is very hard to detect, and was primarily deduced from the structure of the metal within the object. Nails have an uneven mottled structure, which is constant from head to tip. Tools generally have a more even composition with clear longitudinal striation. The points sometimes show indications of tempering, whilst the butts may have fine cracks as a result of repeated striking. It can still be difficult to differentiate between a fine punch and

	50	52	53	54	62	63	65	69	72
PVI/topsoil/unstratified	4	1	1				2	2	
PV: Museum Garden							1		
PV: *outer zone*	2	2		1	1		7		
PV: *inner precinct* non grave	6	1	1		1		8	1	1
PV: graves	26	4		1	7	3	7	3	
Period IV	9	2	2		1	3	5	2	3
Period III	4	1	1		1		5		
Period II	11	1	1	2	3	1		1	
Period I/3–4	7	4			3		3		
Period I/1–2	3	1	2				1	1	
Total	72	17	8	4	17	7	39	10	4

Table 10.12: Chronological distribution of selected tool types and specialised knives.
50 = Awls and punches, **52** = Chisels and gouges, **53** = Wedges, **54** = Files, **62** = Wool comb teeth, **63** = Weaving tensioners, **65** = Miscellaneous tools, **67** = Hooked knives, **69** = Drawknives, **72** = Shears.

an awl, and of the eighty-one objects, thirty-four (1–34) are identified as awls, thirty-three (35–67) as punches, and the remainder (68–88) are indeterminate.

Fifteen of the awls were tanged (1–15), as opposed to only five of the punches (50–54), reflecting the nature of the materials on which they were used (six of the indeterminate tools were also tanged). All of the awls have a square cross-section on the working end, whilst some of the tangs are rectangular, and in one case hexagonal. The tang of one awl (8) is bent over, to secure it at the butt end of the handle. Most of the punches are also of square-section, though four (42, 55, 59 and 64) are round. Awls are multi-purpose tools and so cannot be used to identify specific activities, though sometimes pointing to workshop areas (Figures 6.27 and 28). Examples were widely scattered in space and time (Table 10.13), although tanged awls were virtually confined to **Period II** deposits (2–5), and the **Period V** graveyard. The latter group was concentrated in a restricted area (Figure 6.28), pointing to an unknown specialised activity in the *inner precinct* of the **Period IV** settlement. Untanged awls were widely dispersed, though still concentrated in **Period V** graves. Four examples from **Period I** graves (16, I/8; 17, I/91; 18, I/75; and 33, I/109) could have been personal possessions. Punches, by contrast, have more specialised uses usually relating to metalworking. The group probably includes punches, gravers, and scorpers, but this cannot be determined without investigative cleaning. They were nevertheless absent from the richest group of metalworking debris (85.02) in **Period I** (Figure 10.70). Punches were commoner than awls in **Periods III** and **IV**, and the combination of stratified and displaced finds (Figure 6.27) reveals concentrations in the *outer zone* and in specific areas of the *inner precinct* of the **Period IV** settlement. These coincided with groups of metalworking debris (Figure 6.24).

Point (IN51)

A small square-sectioned point (IN51.1) from the **Period III** church (316), tapered at the top to a squared-off butt end, which had a fine crack, possibly caused by percussion. At 36mm long it seems too short to have been a practical punch and no other function can be suggested.

Chisels and gouges (IN52)

Sixteen objects (IN52.1–16) can be identified as chisels or gouges, and other possible examples are listed as files (IN54) and miscellaneous tools (IN65). Eight objects (1, 2, 4, 8, 10–12, 16) with wide flat rectangular-sectioned blades, pronounced shoulders and tangs, are likely to have been woodworking chisels or gouges. Three (4, 10, 11) from **Period I** deposits in the western part of the **northern sector**, can be ascribed to the seventh century, and include two probable gouges (10 and 11). Related woodworking tools include a probable drill bit (IN65.5) from a broadly contemporary deposit (55) in the **southern sector**. A fourth chisel (1) from a road surface (327) in the **Museum Garden** is poorly dated. A long chisel from the **Period IV.7** rubble

	Tanged awl	Awl	Punch	Tanged punch	Punch?	All awl	All punches
PVI/topsoil/unstratified	••		•		•	••	••
PV: Museum Garden							
PV: *outer zone*			••				••
PV: *inner precinct* non grave		••	•		••	••	•••
PV: graves	••••••••	••••••	••••	••	••	•••••••••••••	••••••••
Period IV		••	••		••••	••	••••••
Period III		•	••	•		•	•••
Period II	••••	••	•	•	•••	•••••	•••••
Period I/3–4		•••	•	•		•••	••
Period I/1–2	•	•	•			••	•
Total	15	17	15	5	12	30	32

Table 10.13: Chronological distribution of awls and punches.

square shank splaying out at the blade, which displayed evidence of tempering. The butt has many fine longitudinal cracks, and a slight bearding around the edges, showing considerable use. It was probably a mason's chisel and came from a mid- to late-sixth century layer (114) in the **southern sector**. A second small cold chisel from a **Period I/4** grave (I/114) was probably displaced from the underlying seventh century rubbish deposits (85.02 etc). The main group of cold chisels (6, 7, 9, 13–15) came from **Period IV** and **V** contexts and included four (6, 7, 9, 13 and 14) from the western part of the *inner precinct* of the **Period IV** settlement (Figure 6.28). These may indicate an area used for stone-working. A fifth example (15) from debris over the graveyard (631) is undatable, but a sixth (9) from the floor (505) of Building V/3 probably dates to the mid-fourteenth century.

Wedges (IN53)

Eight tapering wedges (53.1–8) are all small, with lengths ranging from 39mm to 53mm, and widths from 7mm to 15mm, and thus are more suited to splitting material such as antler or wood, rather than stone or logs. Two (1 and 2) came from an early **Period I** rubbish deposit (94.01), two from mid-ninth century deposits (3, 315.01 and 4, 339.01), and two from **Period IV** contexts (5, 407.02, Building IV/28, and 6, 415.01). They were conspicuously absent from areas with concentrations of comb-making waste, and are thus likely to have been used for some other purpose. Two of the objects identified as small cold chisels (IN52.13 and 15) may also have been wedges. One (13) came from the **Period V** graveyard (542) and the other (15) from an overlying layer of debris (631).

Possible files (IN54)

Four objects (IN54.1–4) were more probably files than tanged chisels, although the blade shape is the same. The tangs of these pieces are bent above the shoulders so as to be offset above the plane of the blade. One (2) has a tapering square blade, and the X-radiograph shows regularly spaced deposits of non-ferrous material along one side of the blade, indicating its use in metalworking. It came from Building III/19 (479), and a second (1) came from the mid-ninth century cultivation (339.01) in the vicinity. Both may have originated in mid-ninth century debris flanking the **Period II** terrace (302, 339; Tables 5.3–5). A third (3) from the **Period V** graveyard (543) may have come from a **Period IV** workshop, and the fourth (4) from the foundations of Building V/3 (506.01), was loosely associated with horseshoe fragments, harness buckles and other tools.

Sickles (IN55)

A fragment of a sickle blade (IN55.1) from a **Period I/3** midden (85.02) probably dates to the earlier-

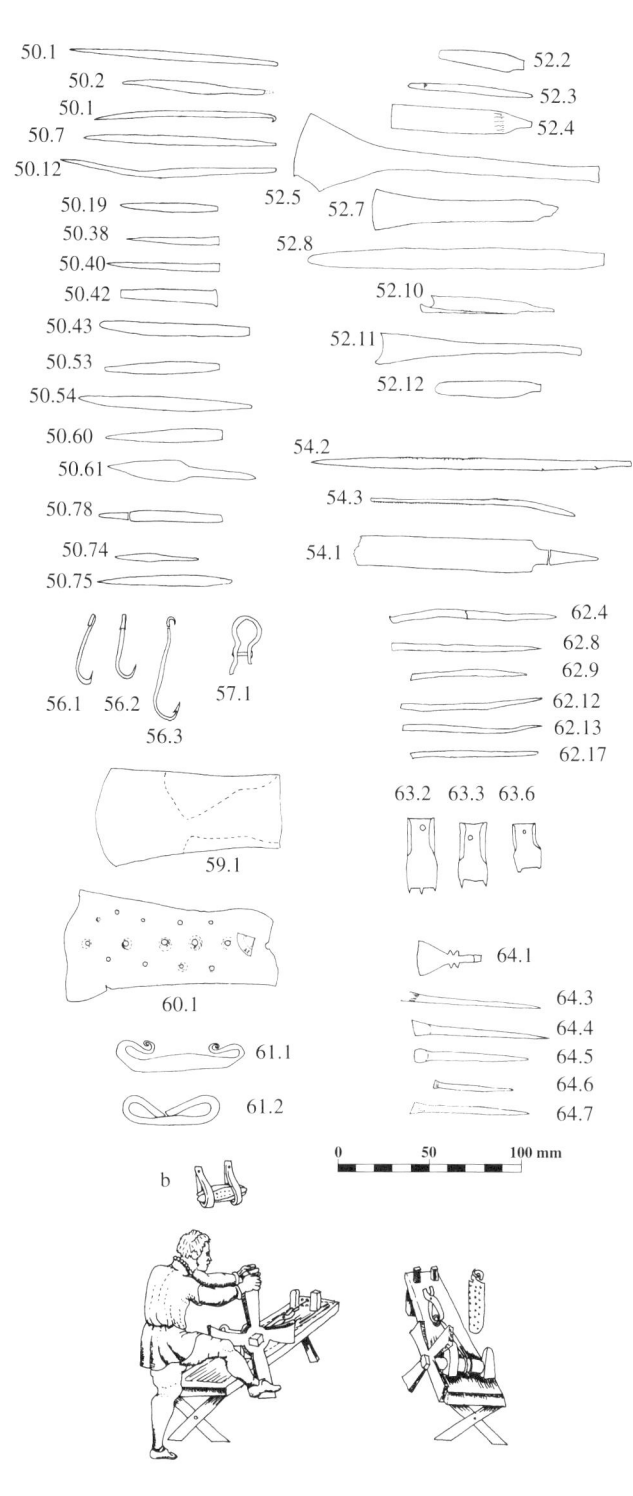

10.102 Tools (IN50–64); **b** Drawplates in a sixteenth century workshop (after Cherry 1992, Figs 23 and 24).

bank (414.01) in the **southern sector**, and two smaller examples (2 and 12) from the **Period V** graveyard, can be ascribed to **Period IV**, although not associable with other woodworking tools. The last possible chisel (16) came from a fourteenth century deposit (517.02) in the **southern sector**. Eight untanged tools (3, 5–7, 9, 13–15) are probably bar or cold chisels. The best specimen (5) has a thick seventh century. It was broken across the blade at both ends and at the base of the tang, and had a maximum surviving width of 20mm. Three other sickle fragments, mostly more intact, came from the modern and recent deposits.

Fish hooks (IN56)

Four fish hooks (IN56.1–4) were identified. The two smaller ones (1 and 2) lacked barbs, and the tops of their shanks were flattened and splayed to enable the line to be tied on. This was also seen in the copper alloy fish hooks (BZ27, p 379). The larger fish hook (3) was barbed, and the top of the shank looped. The smaller ones are suitable for local fish such as salmon, and the larger could be for sea fishing, not only for salmon but bass or tope. The smaller hooks came from the **Period II/7** church (1, 315.02) and Building III/35 (2, 476), and the larger one from later-twelfth century deposits (415.01) in the **southern sector**. A fourth small hook (4) came from spoil (903), and an S-shaped hook (IN31.3) from the **Period I/3** rubbish deposit (85.02) may also have been a fish hook.

Bucket fitting (IN57)

A loop with opposed riveted strips 8mm apart (IN57.1), is likely to have been a bucket fitting (IN36 above), and would have taken a rope or drop handle. It was found on the **Period I/4.5** roadway (99) and was thus broadly contemporary with copper-allow binding strips from bucket rims (BZ19b, pp 374-5).

Spade (IN58)

A damaged spade blade with a central socket containing wood fragments was found at the base of the seventeenth century field boundary wall (610.03).

Adze (IN59)

A complete small socketed adze was found among the **Period I/1.6** debris (70). The blade only tapers slightly towards the socket, whose wings are wrapped round but do not meet.

Drawplate (IN60)

The drawplate (IN60) from the **Period V** graveyard is unique in Britain, although paralleled in Scandinavian material from *Haithabu*, Mästermyr and Tjele (Graham-Campbell 1980, note 72, Nos 414–5; Roesdahl 1982, 106, Fig. 27 AA). It was found at the base of the throat in an east–west burial (535), but is likely to have been displaced from the underlying **Period IV** deposits, and was associated spatially with other fine-metalworking debris (Figure 6.24). A cut short-cross silver halfpenny (CN03.63) trapped in the corrosion may be an issue of Henry II or III, and could have been bullion used by the silversmith. The object seems to be a flat plate with slightly concave long sides, and broken at one end. The X-radiograph revealed three lines of holes on the long axis of the plate, most with traces of a non-ferrous residue around them, which EDXRF analysis identified as silver. The central line contained five large holes and a possible sixth, all evenly spaced. The two outer rows had their holes placed at the intervals between the central row, thus reducing the weakening effect of perforation on an object which would have been subjected to stress in its use. An additional hole is offset from the right hand row to reduce stress. The holes range from 3.5 to 1.2 mm in diameter (Table 10.14) with a graded sequence at 0.2 mm intervals from 1.8 to 3.5 mm, although three gauges (2.2, 2.6 and 2.8 mm) are duplicated. Drawplates are described in the contemporaneous twelfth century work of Theophilus:

'Two iron [plates] three fingers wide, narrow at the top and bottom, thin throughout and pierced with three or four rows of holes [of diminishing size] through which wires may be drawn'
(Hawthorne and Smith 1979, 87).

though it should be noted that the Whithorn plate is a different shape. Later medieval illustrations (Figure 10.102) show how the plate was clamped securely in place and wire attached by pincers to a windlass, was drawn through a succession of holes until the required thickness was obtained.

Left	Centre	Right	*
	2.2		
2.4		1.2	
	3.3		2.2
2.6		1.8	
	2.7		
2.8		2.6	
	3.5		
3.1		2.0	
	2.8		

Table 10.14: Draw-plate hole sizes (in mm).
* = Extra hole on right side

Strike-a-lights (IN61)

Two bow-shaped rectangular-sectioned strips with recurved ends are strike-a-lights (IN61.1–2). One (2) came from post-medieval deposits (631). The other (1), though unstratified, is likely to have been deposited in the seventh or eight century.

Wool comb teeth (IN62)

Seventeen pieces (IN62.1–17) were identified as teeth from wool combs rather than long nail shanks or stick pins. Complete examples range in length from 62mm to 84mm, and from 3.5mm to 5mm in width. They are generally square in section, and thinner than nail shanks of similar length, which average 7–8mm in width. The earliest examples (1–3) came from **Period I/4** graves (1, I/107; 2, I/83; 3, I/111), and one (1) is only identified tentatively as a wool comb tooth. The scarcity of other artefacts used for wool processing and low numbers of sheep at this time, suggest that these may have had a different unknown function. The earliest well-dated example (8) came from a mid-ninth century layer (408.01) in the **Museum Garden**, and a second (16) from an overlying grave (512) may have originated in this deposit. Two others from poorly-stratified **Period II** deposits (4, 320, Table 4.3; 5, 258) are likely to have been contemporary or slightly earlier, and a third (6) from Building III/27 (405) is rather later. A group of six teeth (9–14) from the **Period V** graveyard, and one (17) from an overlying deposit (631) coincided with other artefacts relating to wool-processing in the south-east parts of the *inner precinct* and *outer zone* of the **Period IV** settlement (Figure 6.29). The last tooth (15) from the **Period V.2** paving (519) beyond the boundary wall is probably slightly later.

Weaving tensioners (IN63)

Seven distinctive objects (IN63.1–7) of flat sheet, have slight wings bent to form an open socket with a flat base. Away from the socket they splay out slightly before ending in a straight flat edge, at the outer edges of which are two small triangular prongs. In at least one case there is a centrally located prong as well. Parallels are known from Wood Quay, Dublin and from Raunds, Northampton. It has been suggested that they were fixed to wooden battens at the socket, and that the prongs are pushed between the threads on the edge of a piece of material during weaving.[6] The battens are secured, enabling the cloth to maintain a constant width by keeping an evenly-spread horizontal tension to both edges. The earliest (1) came from mid-ninth century deposits (315.01) in the **Period II** church. The remainder came from a restricted area in the eastern part of the **Period IV** settlement (Figures 6.29, 10.134), and were associated spatially with other wool-processing equipment. Two of these (2 and 3) were stratified in buildings (IV/21 and IV/22) in the south-east part of the *outer zone*, three (4–6) had been displaced by **Period V** graves, and the seventh (7) came from residual **Period IV** debris (457) in the *inner precinct*.

Styli, scribers or prickers (IN64)

Twelve objects can be identified tentatively as styli, scribers or prickers (IN64.1–12). A single head with a broken shank (1) came from early ploughsoil (56.02) in the **southern sector**. Displaying the classic splayed triangular head of a stylus, it has a double collar, or more probably lugs, at the neck. This feature is not seen on similar later styli, such as those from Whitby, Brandon or Flixborough (Webster and Backhouse 1991), but does occur on two contemporary iron stick pins (IN41.1 and 2, pp 418-9), and this could also be the head of a pin.

Ten of the remaining eleven implements came from the **Period V** graveyard, and the last (11) from the **Period IV** rubble bank (430) was probably of similar date. Most (2–9) took the form of a tapering shank, sometimes expanded medially, with a point at one end, and a slightly splayed flattened head, sometimes angled at the top edge, at the other. They differ from the broadly contemporary nails with angled heads (IN09) which show no evidence of flattening at the head, and have thicker less-tapered shanks. A similar object with a flat diamond section to the angled head was recovered from Coppergate, York (Ottaway 1992, 606–7). The objects were concentrated on the eastern side of the site, spanning the *inner precinct* and *outer zone* of the **Period IV** settlement (Figure 6.30). Despite their resemblance to styli, these could have been used for marking masonry, or they could have been associated with the copper-alloy sheet and strip (Figure 6.31), either as gravers for marking out, or as scorpers for decoration as seen on a later brooch (BZ16.3) and strap end (BZ19.7). A rod pointed at both ends (10) may be a crude pricker or scriber, as may a tapering rectangular-sectioned rod (11).

Unclassified tools (IN65)

Forty objects (IN65.1–40) may be tools. In most cases the structure of the iron visible on the X-radiograph showed strong longitudinal lines, and sometimes a fine graining at one end indicative of hardening. This suggested that the items had been manufactured with some care in a similar fashion to more certain tools, even when a specific use could not be determined. Five objects (1–5), mostly unidentifiable, from **Period I** contexts included a possible bit for a drill or auger (5) from a seventh century deposit (55) in the **southern sector**, and a perforated implement (3) from a **Period I/3** grave (I/62). There were none from **Period II** contexts, in which identifiable tools were anyway sparse. A socketed gouge (9) and a possible cosmetic scoop (10) were among five objects (6–10) from **Period III** deposits. The largest group comprises sixteen objects (11–22, 24, 25, 38 and 42) ascribed to **Period IV**, although most had been displaced by **Period V** graves. Concentrations of finds in the south-east part of the *outer zone* (15, 19, 21, 22) and west part of the *inner precinct* (11–13, 24, 25 and 37) identify possible workshop areas. The first group included a possible hammer (19) and coincided

---

[6] This identification arose from a discussion session at the Medieval Europe 1992 conference, and is believed to be unpublished.

spatially with smithy debris (hammerscale), partly-finished roves (IN20) and other iron-working waste (Figures 6.32 and 33). The second group included a tanged boring bit (24), the other pieces are of uncertain function. An isolated object (16) from the eastern end of the **northern sector** may have been a bit or a chisel. Two similar objects (1 and 11) are straight bars, one slightly waisted perhaps by wear (11), with opposed projections at either end. They came from **Period I** (1, 118) and **IV** deposits (11, 430), but are likely to have met the same unknown function. A bevelled strip with a plated head (29) from disturbed material (523.01) at the south end of the **southern sector** may have been a toilet implement rather than a fine tool. Two tanged object from debris (631) overlying the **Period V** graveyard are morphologically similar to knives. One (34) has a riveted scale tang, but the tapering blade has a U-section similar to a shoehorn. The other object (35) appears to be edged, but the tip, if not broken, is unlike any of the usual knife forms. A square-shanked tool with a hooked end (40) from the **central sector** may have originated in **Period IV** debris.

Select catalogue

1* Square section bar terminating in small hook at one end, broken at other.
L 50 W 5.8 **118**

2 Tapering flat pointed object.
L 38.9 **118**

3* Square sectioned tapering bar with sub-rectangular flat expanded head pierced below centre, shank broken.
L 45 W 10 T 3 Hole D 3 **81.02**

4 Square section rod with two 90° bends in the centre, giving opposed tapering shanks lacking tips.
L 65 max W 6 **109**

5* Square section bar, one end flattened and pointed, the other a blunt rounded point. Possibly a small bit for a twist drill or auger.
L 71 Bit W 5 Shank W 3 **55**

9 Socketed object with U-shaped blade (?) with broken edge, tapering to a square shank. Possibly a gouge
L 75 Blade W 16 Shank W 7 **300**

10 Very fine square-sectioned bar with one end flattened and splayed. The other end appears to be flattened and splaying at the break. Could possibly be a cosmetic scoop.
L 35 W 2.4 × 1.2 **472 (III/30)**

11 Waisted bar (?) with opposed hook ends.
L 70 **430**

16* Square section bar flattened and broadening at one end, where the rounded edge shows increased wear on one side. The butt end is also slightly swollen with small longitudinal cracks suggesting impact or stress damage. Probably a chisel or bit
L 144 Shank W 10 Bit W 18 Butt W 17 **542**

19 Large square section bar, one end flat the other tapering to a blunt point. Probably a hammer head, although its density prevents the X-ray from determining if a handle socket exists for certain, though one is hinted at.
L 134 W 40 T 41 **533**

20 Broken rod with one end flattened and pierced. Rod with concave sides, expanding around perforation.
L 93 W 17 × 8 Hole D 4.6 **535**

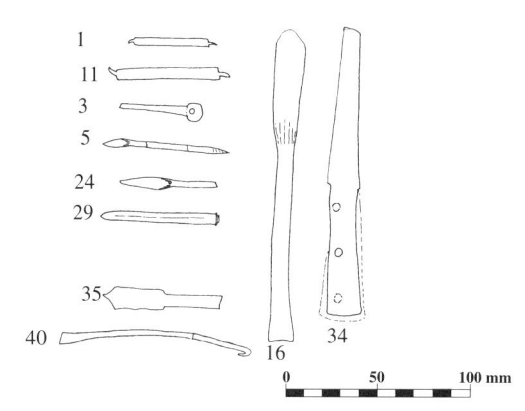

10.103 Miscellaneous tools (IN65).

22 Tanged object, possible tool. Tang occupies about half of total length, and is thicker than the flat, spatulate half. This latter does not have the characteristic X-ray signature of a blade. its initial appearance is similar however to a fragmentary folding knife from Coppergate, York. (Ottaway 1992, No. 2981.)
L 71 W 14 **539**

23 Triangular section rod with 90° hook at one end. The other end tapers to a blunt point and is slightly upturned in the same direction as the hook.
L 186 W 8 T 7 **546**

24* Boring bit with tang. Sub-square shank with flattened tapering head. X-ray indicate hammer marks.
Total L 53 Head L 27 W 7 **600.02**

29* Bevelled strip with plated head, possibly a toilet file.
523.01

32 Square section bar, one end flattened, one with blunt point.
L 90.5 W 5 **624**

34* Scale tanged tool with U-sectioned tapering blade. The tang broadens towards the hilt, and was affixed to the handle by three rivets.
Total L 156 Blade L 85 Blade max. W 26 Tang max W 25 **631**

35* Badly corroded tanged spatulate (?)tool, apparently broken at both ends, the blade expands away from the tang.
L 64 Blade L 33 Blade W 15 Tang W 7.2 **631**

36 Rod or bar, one end shows fine gradation on X-ray indicative of hardening (as is evidence on the cutting edge of knife blades for instance) and appears slightly splayed. The other end shows a much more fragmented structure, possibly the result of continued blows or stress.
L 231 W 9 **744**

38 Composite wood handle, iron tang, alloy butt; broken. Concave round handle broken at one end with centrally located square tang, the latter capped at the butt with a non-ferrous material.
L 62 D 20 × 15 Tang W 5 Cap W 10.5 **903**

40* Square-shanked pin(?) with one end flattened, one hooked. End splayed and flattened, the pointed end hooked through 180°.
L 102.4 **915**

Knives (IN66)

Seventy-two knives (IN66.1–72) and eleven fragments (IN66.73–83) were positively identified, in addition to hooked knives (IN67), swivel knives (IN68), drawknives (IN69), and unattributable blade fragments (IN72). Comparable studies have generally failed to associate blade forms with specific activities, and the Whithorn collection is no exception. The blade length and shape may be one determinant of function, another is the length of the handle. Longer handles allow more pressure to be applied, the blade being used horizontally or at a slight angle, whilst short handles would be held almost vertically and emphasise the use of the tip of the blade.

Following the practice established by Patrick Ottaway at York (1992, 559), the Whithorn knives were divided into classes based on the form of the blade back. The back forms are determined by placing a straight edge against the back to see if it comprises two straight parts meeting at an angle (Class A), a straight rear and concave curved front part (Class B), a straight rear and convex curved front part (Class C), a wholly curved convex back (Class D) or a wholly straight back (Class E). In addition the line of the rear part of the back in relation to a line drawn from the blade tip to the mid-point of the tip of the tang was used to subdivide those blades with a straight rear. Whilst in some cases it was possible to reasonably estimate the positions of tips in incomplete knives, in thirteen cases it was not possible to even determine the back form, and at least two blades fell outside the classes altogether.

Class A
Fifteen (1–3, 5–16) knives were of back form A, and another (4) with straight front and rear parts meeting at a distinct angle is either A or D. Three sub-divisions were recognized: the rear of the back was horizontal, and therefore roughly parallel to the cutting edge (Class A1, four examples, 7–10), upward sloping (Class A2, four examples, 11–14), or with a slightly downward sloping rear part (Class A3, 3 examples, 15, 16 and possibly 4). The others are too corroded or lack tangs, thus rendering assignation impossible.

One of the blades (5) from the **Period V** graveyard (543), has a very short blade in relation to the length of its tang (1:4), and is paralleled by a knife from Lurk Lane, Beverley (Goodall 1991, 132) identified as a possible surgical knife, based on contemporary illustrations. The earliest Class A knife (11) came from the **Period I/4.5** roadway (99), and this seems to have been the dominant form in **Periods II** and **III** although the sample is small. An A3 knife (15) of fourteenth century form from a **Period V/2** grave (539) could have been a contemporary deposit, though recovered from the grave fill.

Class B
Only one knife (17) had a straight rear part and concave front, a form found to be unusual at York and Thetford (Ottaway 1992, 565). It was one of only three knives from the **Period V** *outer zone*.

Class C
The most common class, with twenty-one examples (18–38), and a further one (39) which may be form C

or D. As with Class A this group can be subdivided by the relative position of the rear part of the blade back: horizontal (Class C1, five examples, 18–22), upward sloping (Class C2, one example, 23), or downward sloping (Class C3, ten examples, 24–33). Five pieces (34–38) were too corroded or lacked sufficient tang to enable clear categorisation. Ottaway comments that differential wear on the blade can cause the relative position of the blade tip to move, and thus possibly alter the attribution to a particular sub-group. It is noticeable in the Whithorn blades too that Class C blades appear to be extensively worn, more so than other categories, and

	A	B	C	D
PVI/topsoil/unstratified	••		•••	••
PV: Museum Garden			•	•
PV: *outer zone*		•	•	•
PV: *inner precinct* non grave	•		•	
PV: graves	•••••		•••••	•••••
Period IV	••		••	•••••••
Period III	••		•	•
Period II	•••		•	•
Period I/3–4	•		••••	
Period I/1–2			••	

Table 10.15: Chronological distribution of classifiable knives.

this may reflect on their original use. Class C knives were the dominant form in **Period I**, through apparently replaced by Class A in **Periods II** and **III**. The large C2 blade (23) came from one of the earliest deposits (69.01) in the **northern sector**. The other early knives were mostly C1 (18–20) or unclassified (36 and 37). There was only one C3 knife (24) from a late **Period I** deposit (73.02), the remainder coming from a late **Period IV** deposit (25, 407.04), **Period V** graves (26–28, 30), a **Period V** ditch (521, 30) and hollow (612.02, 29).

Class D
The next most common class with sixteen clear examples (40–42, 44, 46–54, 56–58), and three (43, 45 and 54) which are probably class D, but may be broken blades from shears. Class D blades are not present in **Period I**, and single examples (40 and 41) occur in **Periods II** and **III**. However it is clearly the most common form of blade back in **Period IV**, and twelve of the Whithorn pieces came from the twelfth century or later.

Unclassified
Three (59–61) of the unclassified knives (59–72) came from **Period II** contexts. A small knife blade (60) with a highly convex cutting edge is similar to a blade from Beverley identified tentatively as a surgical knife (Armstrong *et al*. 1991 No.327). A single example of a scale-tanged knife (71) came from the **Period V** graveyard (542), and two further examples from modern and recent deposits. Two unusual tanged blades (64, 511.1 and 65, 722) had squared off tips and may have been small chopping knives. An unstratified knife (67) with a broken tang has a straight back with highly convex dip at blade

10.104 Knives (IN66–69).

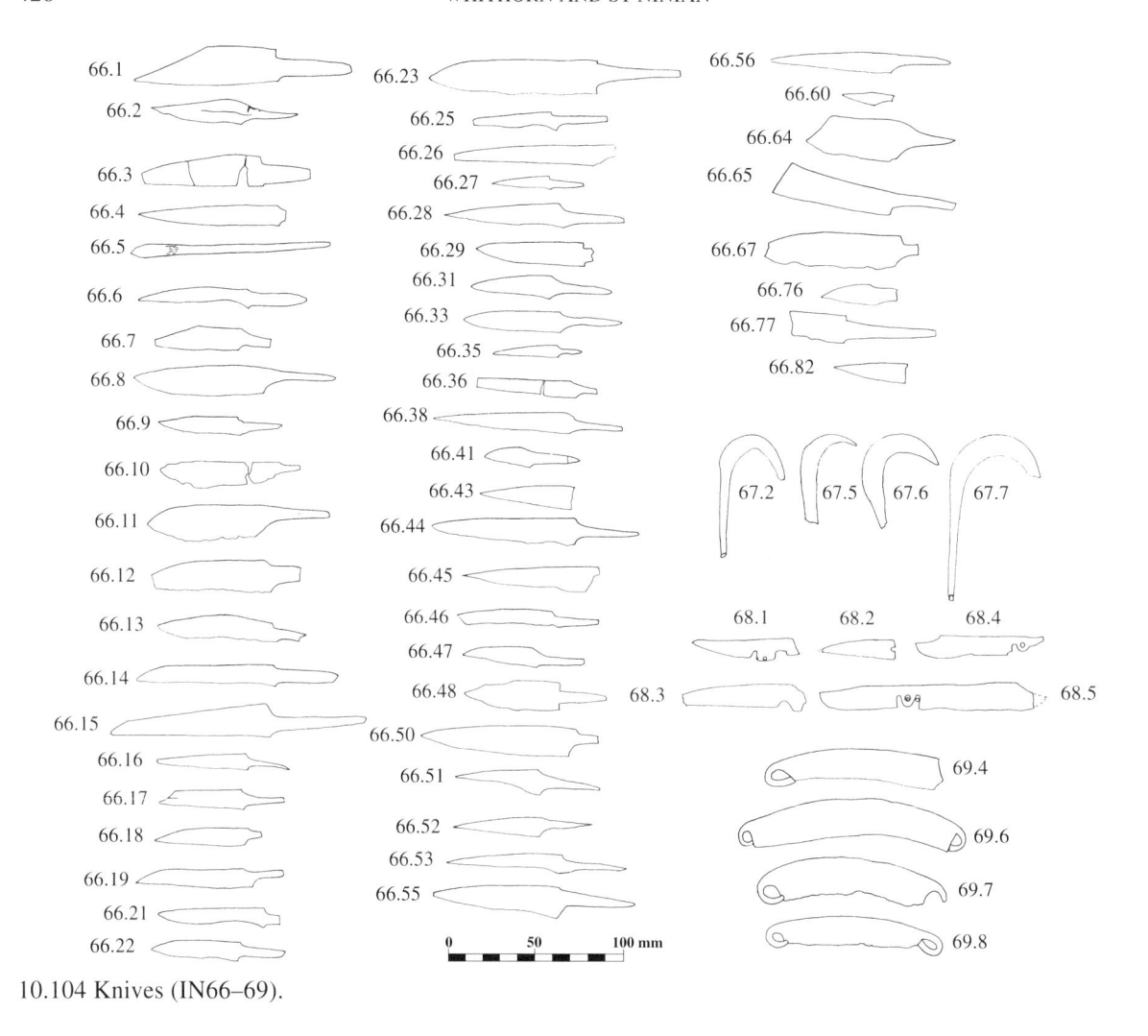

tip, and is paralleled by a late-twelfth century example in the Museum of London (Cowgill *et al.* 1987, 78 No. 4).

Hooked knives (IN67)

Seven whittle-tanged knives (IN67.1–7) with curved short blades, are morphologically identical to pruning knives, although their distribution argues for some different function. They are of a consistent size, with blades 50mm long and 10mm wide, and a tang of 50mm. The earliest (1) came from the **Period IV** rubble bank (430), two others (2, 3,) from adjacent graves (Figure 6.28), and a fourth (7) from a recent hollow in the same area (542). These are all likely to have originated in the **Period IV** deposits in the *inner precinct*, and they may mark the position of a workshop, or possibly market stall. A fifth example (5) from a grave in the east part of the **central sector** extends the distribution into the *outer zone*, and remaining two (4 and 6) from the **Museum Garden** were probably contemporary, though recovered from a medieval grave (4, 511.03) and the overlying soil (6, 624).

Swivel knives (IN68)

Five swivel knife blades (IN68.1–5) were identified. Swivel knives have two blades, often of differing form, one on either side of a central pivot. U-shaped notches beside the pivot lock the blade against a stop-bar when downwards pressure is applied (Figure 10.105), while the hand grip helps to retain the other blade slotted in the handle. These are clearly specialised tools and finds are concentrated on urban sites and earlier emporia, including York, *Hamwic*, Dorestadt and *Haithabu* (Ottoway 1992, 588). Biddle (1990, 738–41) suggests these knives were used by scribes, and Ottaway adds wood- and bone-working as possible alternatives (1992, 587). Antler-working is a fourth possibility, but the finds associated with the Whithorn knives point, if anything, to wood-working.

Only one of the Whithorn knives (5) had two fully identifiable blade forms (B1 and A1). This piece was remarkably intact, the X-radiograph showing the hinge rivet still in position, as well as the small non-ferrous stop-bar to hold the blade in use tight against the handle. Two blades (1 and 2) came from **Period I** deposits. One (1) came from soil flanking the

Period I/3 roadway (73.01), which may have accumulated in the earlier-seventh century, but included displaced finds of mid-sixth century date. The second (2) from the **Period I.10** silts (55) in the **southern sector** was probably deposited in the midseventh century. Both thus predate the earliest other example from Britain, found in an eighth century context in Southampton (Ottaway 1992, 588). A third blade (3) from later waterborne deposits (309.02) in the same area was probably deposited in the later-ninth or tenth century, and two others (4 and 5) from **Period V** graves (Figure 6.36), probably originated in the **Period IV** debris in the *inner precinct*, although one (5) could have originated in **Period I–III** deposits.

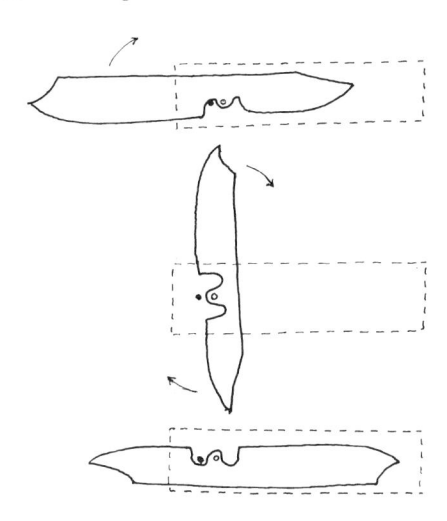

10.105 Reconstruction of swivel knife No.5.

1* Part of a swivel knife. One blade broken. Both U-shaped notches and traces of the pivotal pin survive. Blade back is straight or very slightly concave, and the convex edge rises to meet it at the point. This is an unusual form similar to the lone Class E blade from Coppergate, York (Tweddle 1992, No. 2939).

Total L 60 Blade L 34 Blade W 12 **73.01**

2* Probable swivel knife blade lacking its tip, and transversely fractured across a central perforation. A similar blade appeared at Coppergate, York (Tweddle 1992, No. 2975), where the rivet around which the blade swivels was *in situ*.

L 43 W 10 **55***

3* Swivel knife blade broken at point and around pivotal rivet. One of the U-shaped notches for locating the blade within the handle survives. The back form is slightly convex, tapering down towards the point (Class D).

L 74 W 12 **309.02**

4* Swivel knife with one blade broken. The surviving blade, probably the longer of the two, has a blade back rear which is parallel to the tip-pivot line, with a deeply concave front part (Class B1). One U-notch for the locking pin and the central pivot are extant, and the second blade has fractured off along the other U-notch.

Blade L 55 Total L 73 W 12.5 **539**

5* Almost complete swivel knife. The longer blade lacks its tip, but can be recognized as a Class B1 blade. A non-ferrous rivet is present in the U-shaped locking notch, showing that the long blade was within the handle at the time of deposition, possibly because of its broken tip. The shorter blade has a much straighter front portion of the blade back, falling into Class A1. The iron pivoting rivet is also *in situ*

Overall L 123; B1 blade L 66 W 14; A1 blade L 44 W 13; Iron rivet D 2.5; Non-ferrous rivet D 2

539

Drawknives (IN69)

A distinctive group of eleven drawknife blades with looped terminals (IN69.1–11) was concentrated in the *inner precinct* of the **Period IV** settlement (Figures 6.28, 10.136d), although there are earlier examples from a later-sixth century rubbish spread (1, 89), and a mid-ninth century deposit (5, 408.01) in the **Museum Garden**. Three of the knives (6, 7 and 8) are intact, with lengths of 100mm (8), 130mm (6) and 132mm (7). The use of looped terminals rather than tanged handles is unusual, and there is only one fragmentary example from York (Ottaway 1992, 589). The three complete drawknives came from **Period V** graves cutting into a spread of comb making debris (425.01) ascribed to the early years of **Period IV**. Roughed out comb tooth- and side-plates have shallow scalloped working marks indicating the use of a drawknife (pp 479-80), and these blades could have been used, although the association is imperfect. Another broken drawknife (4) was associated with comb-making debris in Building IV/4 (pp 224-5). The earliest fragment (1) was also associated with comb-making debris (Table 3.18; Figure 10.136a). The other broken drawknives were more widely scattered and less clearly linked with comb-making debris.

Cutlery (IN70)

Six pieces of cutlery (IN70.1–6) comprise four forks (1–4), a knife (5), and a decorated, plated spoon handle (6). All came from recent contexts.

Razors (IN71)

Two narrow thin blades (IN71.1 and 2) with straight backs were probably razors. One had a worn curved edge, the other a perforated end which may have held a rivet allowing the blade to be folded onto a handle. One (1) came from the **Period V** graveyard and the other from the overlying surface (772), but both could have originated in the **Period IV** debris.

Shears (IN72)

A complete pair of shears (3), three blades and fragments (1, 2 and 4) came from a restricted area in the northern part of the **southern sector** (Figure 6.36). Three Class D 'knife' fragments (66.43, 45 and 54) could also have come from shears, and two (45 and 54) came from the same area. Three pieces (1, 2 and 45) were securely stratified in **Period IV.7** buildings (IV/9 and IV/12), which may thus have been used for cloth processing. The complete pair of shears came from the surface overlying the **Period V** graveyard (617.03) a short distance to the north. The blades have slightly sloping backs indicating an early-mid thirteenth century date (Cowgill *et al*. 1987, Fig. 70).

Non-attributable blades (IN73)

Thirty objects (IN73.1–30) are probably blades, or fragments thereof, although this is sometimes uncertain without cleaning to identify an edge. In other cases it was possible to identify a fragment as a blade, but not possible to assign it to any particular class. The fragments were widely scattered in space and time.

Tweezers (IN74)

Three pairs of iron tweezers (IN74.1–3) of simple flat strip, closely matched their copper alloy counterparts in form (BZ24.1–5, pp 377-8), although none was decorated or gilded. One pair (1) came from the **Period IV.6** ditch (417.02), a second (2) from an overlying surface (525.01), and the third (3) from the surface (616.04) overlying the **Period V** graveyard. A fourth possible pair (IN78.34), apparently contained in an iron case, came from the **Period V** graveyard (542). The copper-alloy tweezers mostly came from **Period II** or **III** deposits, and the use of iron thus seems a later practice.

'Arrowheads' (IN75)

Fourteen 'arrowheads' (IN75.1–14) were concentrated in the **Period V** graveyard, but most are likely to have originated in the underlying **Period IV** debris. The earliest (1), by no means a positive identification, came from a **Period I/2** grave (80.03, I/25), and was barbed and tanged. Eleven (2–12) are simple socketed points and their identification as arrowheads is problematical as similar objects were also used to sheath the tips of bow staves, which would account for the plating observed on several examples. The earliest (2) from a layer of wormed soil (251) flanking the **Period II** chapel, is plated with copper-alloy, and the socket retains mineralised wood. Two (3 and 4) came from the **Period IV** rubble bank (430), and others from the **Period V** graves (5–7) and overlying surfaces (8) may have originated in similar deposits. The **Period V** graveyard also produced a socketed triangular head (13), and a long triangular head with a long shouldered tang (14). The latter (14, and possibly 13) would been suitable for hunting such as deer, the socketed-points would have been more suitable for small game and birds. Two other possible arrowheads (IN78.37 and 46) came from broadly contemporary contexts (37, 532 and 46, 506.01).

Candle holders etc. (IN76)

A group of lighting accessories (IN76.1–4) was concentrated in the **southern sector** and may have originated in the later buildings of **Period IV** and their **Period V** successors. A Y-shaped taper holder (2) with curled terminals came from Building V/2a (520.01), and a three-pronged pricket (3) from topsoil (744) in the northern part of the area, has twelfth century parallels (Ottaway 1992, No. 3678), and may have originated in the underlying **Period IV** buildings. A second bifurcated taper holder (1) from the **Period V** graveyard in the **northern sector** could have been displaced from **Period IV** debris, or from the underlying **Period III/2** buildings (perhaps III/16). These lacked any base or other support, but could have been inserted easily into the wattle walls of the small **Period IV** and **V** buildings, or driven into solid timber members. There are similar objects, though lacking a central spike, from other medieval sites such as York and Tamworth (Ottaway 1992, 679 Fig. 293). A candle snuffer (4) from topsoil over Building V/3 is likely to have been deposited in the later-fourteenth century.

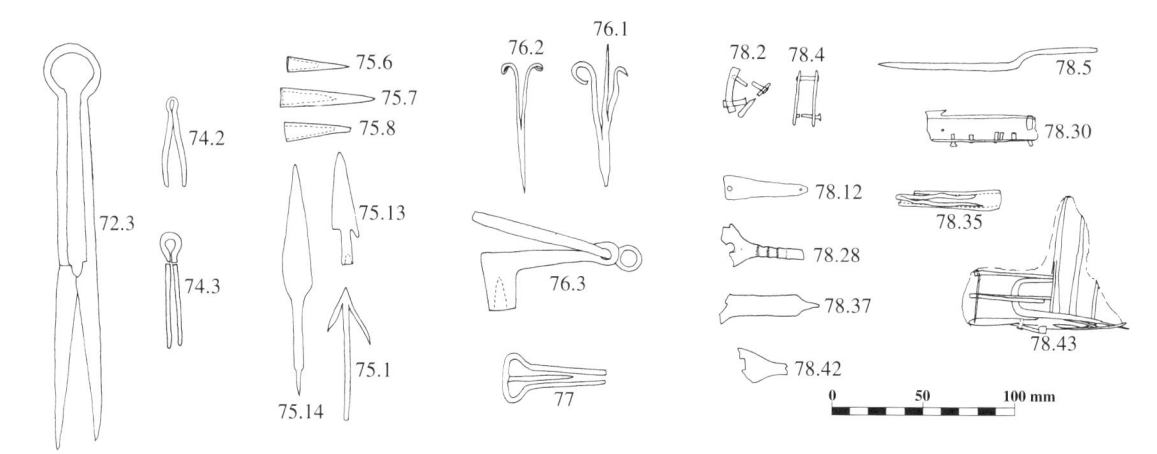

10.106 Shears (IN72), tweezers (IN74), arrowheads (IN75), lighting accessories (IN76), Jews harp (IN77) and miscellaneous objects (IN78).

Jew's Harp (IN77)

An intact Jew's Harp from the **southern sector** (517.03) was probably deposited in the mid- to late-fourteenth century.

Miscellaneous artefacts and fragments (IN78)

Fifty-two objects (IN78.1–52) whilst clearly parts of manufactured objects, were either too corroded or fragmentary to be identified, or of uncertain purpose and not obviously paralleled elsewhere. A large proportion of these items came from earlier contexts, though in general their distribution was fairly even throughout the stratigraphy. The pieces range from unintelligible corroded lumps to complex, but perplexing objects such as a possible lock (41). Ten broad sub-groups can be defined:

a) Two complex artefacts (28 and 41) comprised a broken object surrounded by pieces of bent wire (28) from the **Period IV** flood deposits (415.01) in the **southern sector**, and a possible lock of uncertain type from the **Period V** cultivation (546).
b) Eight possible implements and tools (1, 5, 26, 27, 30, 34, 36 and 39) include two early objects: an implement with a curved tip (1) from an earlier-sixth century deposit (69.03), and a tanged tool of unusual shape (2) from a **Period I/4** grave (I/88). The remainder can be ascribed to the **Period IV** debris in the *inner precinct*, and include an object like a split pin (26), and a shanked implement with a perforated head, from the **Period IV** rubble bank (430). Speckling around the perforation suggests it was in contact with a non-ferrous metal. Finds from graves comprise a possible pair of tweezers in a case (34), a plated bifurcated strip with a possible tang (39), and a tapering rod (30).
c) Six 'shaped' objects (8, 10, 11, 14, 42, 48) were concentrated in early deposits. A bent object with a possible ball terminal from a **Period I/4** grave (I/114), may have been displaced from the underlying rubbish layers, a knobbed lump (10) came from the early cultivated soil (56.02) in the **southern sector**, and a fragmented object (11) with a spiral terminal came from the overlying waterborne silts (55). A fragment of a plated fitting with baluster decoration (14) came from the foundations of the **Period II/1** path (247.01). Two later finds comprise a plated trilobate object (42) from the worm soil over the **Period V** graveyard (615.02), and a T-shaped fragment of wire or rod (48) from an equivalent deposit (625) in the **Museum Garden**.
d) Seven riveted plates and strips (2, 4, 6, 12, 23, 29 and 38) were concentrated in earlier contexts, as were detached rivets (IN21). Two similar pairs of riveted plates (2 and 4) came from sixth (97) and seventh century (109) deposits in the same part of the trench. These interesting objects may have been mounts and can be compared with an undated copper-alloy plate (BZ30.63). A possible strap-end (12) came from the surface abutting the **Period II/1** boundary wall (86.01), and a riveted loop (23) from the mid-ninth century debris to the south of the chapel (339.01). Two more complex pieces (29 and 38) are ascribed to **Period IV**.
e) A possible pin (17) with a plated globular head and unusual square shank, came from an earlier-ninth century deposit (251) and was probably contemporary with other plated pins (IN40.51–55). Its shank however is short (18 mm), and it is more likely to have been an ornamental fitting.
f) Five sockets (16, 37, 46, 50 and 51) include a probable tool socket with a rivet hole (16) from the displaced debris (110) used in the construction of the **Period II/1** buildings; two possible arrowheads (37 and 46) from the foundations of Building V/3 (46, 506.01) and the **Period V** graveyard (37, 532); a flat-based ferrule or cap (50) from debris over the **Period V** graves (631); and a large curved sheet (51), which could be part of the socket of an agricultural implement (904).
g) Six fragmentary objects (3, 7, 18, 21, 43 and 44) are too incomplete for interpretation.
h) Six objects (20, 24, 31, 35, 47 and 49) are akin to nail shanks, but have distinctive radiographic signatures and could include tools and pins.
i) Three unusual strip fragments (19, 22 and 40) include a thick strip (22) sandwiched between two thinner ones, from the **Period III** church (316).
j) Two bars (13 and 45).
k) Five unidentifiable corroded objects (9, 15, 25, 32, 33 and 52).

Strap end (IN79)

A tapering strip with a rounded end, secured at the basal end by a single centrally placed non-ferrous rivet, is possibly a strap or belt end. It came from the **Period I/1.6** hollow (70) and was probably deposited in the mid-sixth century. A second object (78.12) from the foundations of the **Period II/1** boundary wall (86.01) may also be a strap end.

Strip and strip waste (IN80)

A hundred and forty-nine pieces classed as strips were differentiated from plates (IN82) by virtue of having a length measurement usually at least twice that of the width. Most of the pieces are broken, either discarded fragments, unfinished pieces or material retained for recycling. As such their importance is related to their stratigraphic distribution rather than any intrinsic value.

The group from the early graves is probably displaced material from the early midden (85). Two of the pieces were perforated, indicating that they had seen use prior to breaking. This may well be workshop waste, in contrast to the spread of material around the earliest terrace structures (220), where the pieces may well be related to the buildings, with at least one piece having an *in situ* nail, and another pierced to receive two nails. There are none from the later church until its destruction by fire (315), and the paucity (four pieces) is in contrast to the large number of nails from the same deposit. Similarly the four fragments from the medieval stone building in the **southern sector** (506, V/3) contrast to a much larger group of nails. The largest number of strips occur in the **Period V** graveyard, principally from the later graves (538 and 539), and the contemporary ploughsoil to the west (546).

Curved strips (IN81)

Twenty-five strips (IN81.1–25) were noticeably curved along the plane of their width. In general this smaller sample's distribution matched that for straight strips. A piece from a **Period II** building (II/13, 217) had hammer marks on its upper surface.

Plates (IN82)

Seventy-two fragments were classed as plates. In general their width was greater than half of the length measurement (see IN80 above). Unlike the strips, plates are not well represented in the midden and waste deposits (85, 109, 303), though they do occur in the buildings (220 and 315). Again there is a good showing in the **Period V** graveyard and ploughsoil, with another grouping in the post-medieval layers (614 and 615) overlying the same area.

Bars (IN83)

Thirty-five pieces were classed as bars, differing from strips in their greater thickness – in several cases the bars were sectionally square. Some of these can be seen as blanks of semi-finished material awaiting further working. This is reflected in a distribution more inclined to 'occupation' deposits rather than the large buildings and middens where other waste material occurs. Similarly they are scarce in the **Period V** graveyard and ploughing.

Rods (IN84)

Seventeen rods were found (IN84.1–17), though some may be more properly defined as bars. Generally rods are longer than bars in relation to their width, and many are rounded in section as opposed to the usual rectangular form of the bars. Also by contrast to bars their distribution is primarily from grave and midden deposits, both Early Christian and Medieval.

Tubes (IN85)

Three tubes (IN85.1–3) identified from X-radiographs all came from seventh century layers (55, 82.04 and 85.03). The fragment (3) from the **southern sector** is some form of socket containing traces of mineralised wood.

Cylinders (IN86)

Two fragments of cylindrical objects (IN86.1 and 2) also came from early deposits. A cylinder (1) from an early pit in the **southern sector** (53.01), is 27 mm long and 16mm in diameter, and surround a second broken iron object. The second (2) came from the collapse of the **Period II** enclosure wall (248), and is rather larger (43.5mm long and 32 mm in diameter). It has a rimmed base enclosing sides made from a separate tube.

Ferrules (IN87)

Three ferrules (IN87.1–3) from high medieval contexts could have come from the tips of staffs. A tapering ferrule with a welded seam up one side (IN87.1), came from the **Fey Field** (528), and is probably thirteenth century. Two smaller ferrules (2 and 3) came from a grave in the **Museum Garden** (2, 511.03), and the graveyard surface (3, 772). The latter could have been among the objects lost on the roadway leading to the late medieval cathedral (Figure 10.49)

Discs (IN88)

Four discs (IN88.1–4), include two with possible stalks (1 and 2), which may be flat-headed studs. Both came from flood deposits in the **southern sector**, one (1) ascribed to **Period III** (309.2) and the other (2) to **Period IV** (417.02). The other two lack stalks, and came from **Period V** graves.

Perforated discs (IN89)

Six perforated discs (IN89.1–6) include two (1 and 3) with square central perforations, which could either be washers or protective plates. The earlier (1) came from a later-sixth century rubbish spread (89) producing fused glass, and the later (3) from a **Period IV** structure (IV/20) producing hammerscale. They could thus have been handle guards for tanged tools used in association with a high-temperature hearth or furnace. Three others (2, 4 and 6) with circular central perforations are probably washers. One (2) came from the main **Period II** rubbish spread (303), the others from **Period V** deposits (4, 550 and 6, 546) to the west of the graveyard. The last disc (5) from the **Period V** graveyard (542) has a central circular perforation, with four smaller circular ones spaced evenly around it. These could be mounting points, or the item may be similar to the stone discs with multiple perforations (SE30), which are linked tentatively with cord-making, and are also ascribed to the **Period IV** debris (Figure 6.37).

Wire (IN90)

Twenty-four pieces of iron wire (IN90.1–24) include three lengths (1–3) from seventh century rubbish deposits (85, 109). A larger group from the **Period V** graveyard (9–14, 18) was concentrated in the *inner precinct* of the **Period IV** settlement (Figure 6.34), and two others came from late structures in the *outer zone* (7, IV/13 and 8, IV/26). A section of looped plated wire (4) from the east end of the **Period II** church (313) is closely matched by wire decorating the tenth century barrel padlock case from Coppergate, York (Ottaway 1992, Plate XXXVa–d), and a possible lock fitting (IN80.57) was found nearby. A piece of twisted wire (14) from the **Period V** graveyard (539) may have been part of a handle. Four pieces of wire (5, 13, 15 and 20) are pinched at regular intervals. The earliest piece (5) from a mid-ninth deposit (339.02), is pinched in one plane only, at 6.5mm intervals. The other three (13, 15 and 20) are pinched alternately in two planes at right angles to one another. One (13) came from the concentration of wire in the **Period V** graveyard, the others from the western part of the **northern sector**.

Cast or machined objects (IN91)

A large group of modern objects included three pieces contaminating earlier contexts.

Pellets (IN92)

A single example, probably a pin head, but too small to easily identify, came from the burial chapel (249.01).

Unattributable lumps and fragment (IN93)

A hundred and thirty pieces were so fragmentary or badly corroded that attribution to a category was not possible. Originally this category was quite numerous, but X-radiographic analysis identified many of the lumps as nail heads or shanks, as well as dress loops, buckles and rings. Not unexpectedly a sizeable proportion of unidentifiable pieces came from the earliest deposits, as well as a large group from the displaced debris (110) used in the construction of the **Period II/1** buildings in the **northern sector**.

The Sculptured Stones

Derek Craig

The stones have been divided into three groups: incised, relief, and compass-drawn, which includes arciform, marigold and circle designs. The Whithorn Museum numbering system has not been adopted here, as this includes other sculpture from Brighouse, Boghouse, Craiglemine, Elrig, Gleniron Several, Longcastle, and Monreith, but omits three cross-heads from Whithorn now in the Royal Museum of Scotland (Radford and Donaldson 1984, 27–30). Thirty-six early medieval sculptured stones have previously been discovered in excavations at Whithorn priory or from buildings within the town (Craig 1992, III, 281–369, Pls 170–89), and thirty-two later medieval stones have been recorded by Historic Scotland.

Overall dimensions are given as length, width and depth.

A. Incised

1 Irregular slab with one broken edge, the reverse damaged. The surface is flat except around the borders of the stone. Within this almost circular area is an incised linear cross, possibly originally symmetrical, but now measuring 28cm × 22cm. The arms of the cross are slightly uneven.

This type of simple incised linear cross has not previously been found at Whithorn, and examples are only known locally at St Ninian's Cave (RMS IB 207: Craig 1992, III, 265, Pl. 167c) and Ardwall Isle (Thomas 1967, 158–9, Fig. 32, Pl. XIX b). Thomas identifies these as the earliest form of grave marker (1971, 116, Pl. III; 1987, 10), but Hamlin has emphasised that the type is not closely datable (1982, 286). See also Henderson 1987, 49. However, this example was found stratified in late seventh/early eighth-century paving, and is therefore one of the earliest crosses from the site.

Greywacke, L 42cm, W 40cm, D 3.5cm, **236.01**

2 Irregular slab in three fragments, the surface uneven, the reverse damaged. On the surviving face is a faintly incised cross within a circle. The circle is unfinished, and comprises about half the arc, with a radius of 10cm. Both cross-arms are 20cm long. One is bisected symmetrically but composed of multi-outline scratches, the other is asymmetrical and runs from the damaged surface to the slope.

This type of cross is similar to No 1, but was found stratified in twelfth century paving adjoining Building IV/17. As noted above the type is not closely datable, but this stone is likely to have been reused from an earlier phase.

Greywacke, L 57.5cm, W 37cm, D 7cm, **439**

3 Slab with incised outline cross and other graffiti on one face, the back and edges irregular.

The cross is set at an oblique angle across the width of the face, near its centre. The head has four scratched, wedge-shaped arms, only partly joined in the middle, and is set on a linear stem which terminates in a triangular base. This stem is bisected at an angle by an incised line running the length of the stone, abutted to the left of the cross by two adjacent triangles, both decorated with incised parallel lines. There are two pocked depressions, one at the left end of the transverse line, the other on the stem of the cross.

The cross is 13cm long, its head measuring 7cm high by 5cm wide. The two triangles are 4cm high by 3cm wide.

This appears to be a convenient flat surface used for graffiti, as with the simplest compass-drawn circles discussed below. But it was found in a late sixth-century grave (I/45), and is therefore the earliest stratified sculpture from the site.

Thomas has noted simple grave-markers at Ardwall Isle, which also appeared to be inhumed with the skeleton (Thomas 1967, 158). There is a comparable slab from St Ninian's Cave, with an asymmetrical linear cross with barred terminals, now in the Royal Museum of Scotland (IB 300. Donations 1969–70, 296, No. 13).

Greywacke, L 31cm, W 18.5cm, D 2.5cm, **81.02** (Gr I/45)

4 Flake with incised cross potent on one face, pocked and grooved circle on the reverse.

A. Near the centre of the stone but abutting one long side is a deeply incised linear cross with transverse terminals and an extended foot. The terminals of the longer arm are equidistant

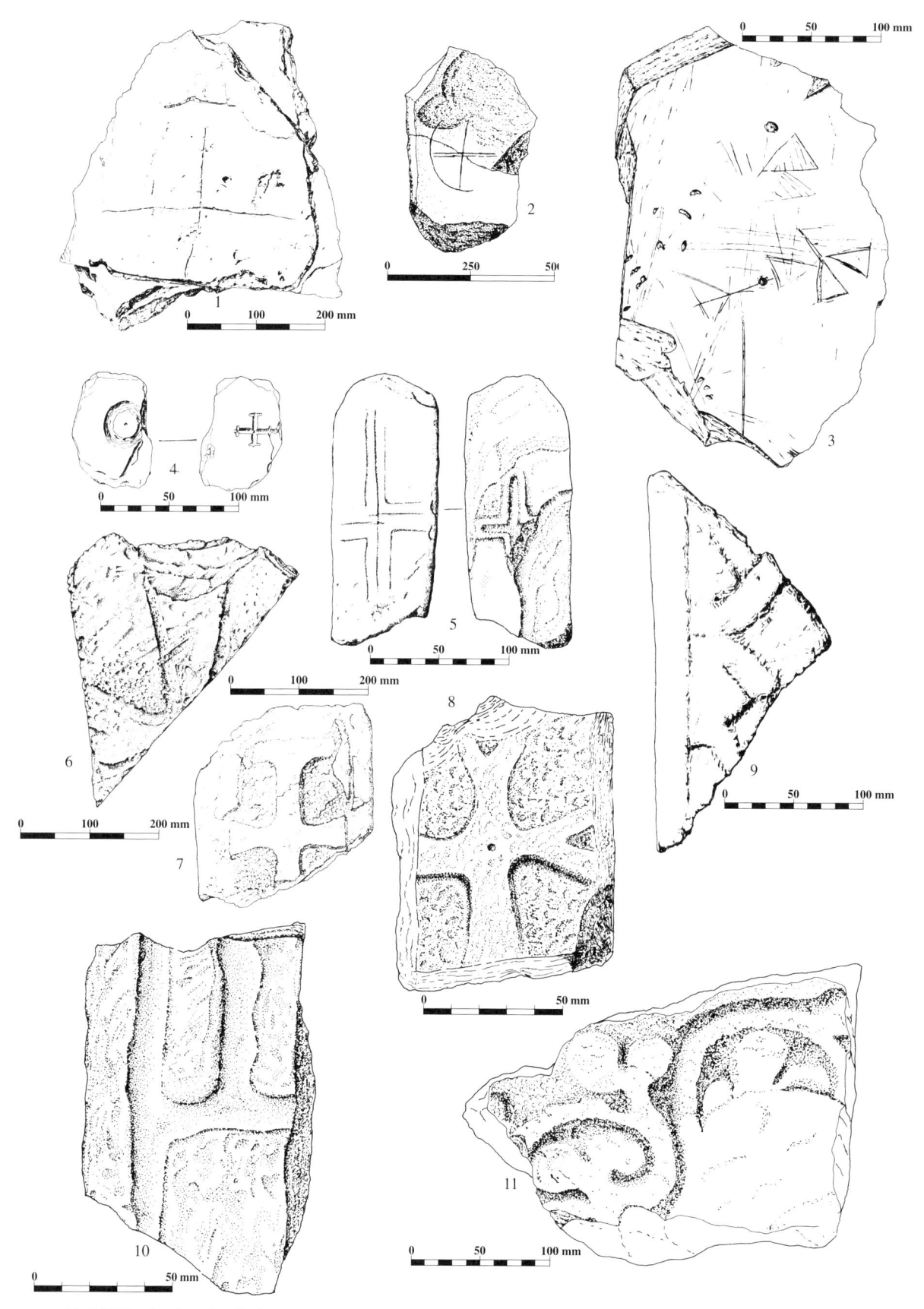

10.107 Incised and relief sculptures (SE14).

from the centre, but there is a bulbous foot beneath the transverse bar. The cross is formed by straight V-shaped grooves 3mm wide by 1mm deep, with deeper, possibly drilled, depressions at the crossing of the terminals, except the lower arm, which is deepest at the bulbous foot. The arms taper off beyond the terminals. The cross is 2.3cm wide and 3.2cm high, including the foot. The two side terminals are 9mm long, the upper and lower terminals 8mm long. The terminal grooves are 2mm wide.

At an oblique angle to the upper arm, on the broken edge of the stone, is a depression formed by a dotted half circle 1.1cm in diameter, with six incised dots, an inner ring and a central dot.

B. On the reverse face of the stone, but not opposite the cross, is a deeply cut ring, with a broad U-shaped channel showing evidence of rough pocking and grooving, and a small central depression. The channel is about 6mm wide by 2mm deep, and the inner diameter of the ring is 2cm, the outer 3.3cm.

The cross seems too deeply and neatly cut for a motif piece. It may have been made for burial within a grave, or as an amulet for private devotion, as with its closest parallel, the *Duibhin Deagláin*, Co Waterford, Ireland, which was found in a grave at St Declan's oratory in Ardmore. This measured 5.5 by 4.4cm with a deeply cut cross with lobed terminals on one face and a circle on the other (Rynne 1980, 83, Fig. 3b). The edges of the stone are broken, damaging the dotted circle on Face A, but the border around the ring on Face B is of roughly equal width, suggesting that this face may represent a secondary use of the stone. The difference in technique used on either side is comparable to No 5, but on that slab the two sides appear to be contemporary.

The significance of the small dotted circle on Face A is unclear, though it is similar to a mould found at Nendrum monastery, Co Down (ASNI 1966, Pl. 80). But the Whithorn example appears too shallow to have been used for metalworking. This function would be more appropriate for the deeply cut ring, or even the cross, which has a channel leading from the bulbous foot to the edge of the stone.

Unstratified, from level of thirteenth/fifteenth century graves.

L 8cm, W 6cm, D 1cm, **904**
Hill 1988a, 18

B. Relief

5 Small slab with incised and relief crosses on opposite faces. The edges of the slab are rounded, and the broad faces narrow slightly towards the foot of the stone. The summit is curved, and the base irregular and probably broken.

A. The incised cross is asymmetrical, measuring 10cm high by 6.5cm wide, with the side arms at different levels, and the upper arm narrower and displaced. The upper terminal is 4cm from the top, with the side arms running up to the edge of the slab. Each arm consists of three parallel grooves. The outer grooves meet at right angles in the armpits. The central groove of the upper and lower arm is continuous, but those of the side arms separately cross the vertical line. The channels are smoothly incised and U-shaped, 2mm wide by 1mm deep, but a number of the grooves show signs of multiple scratches. The terminals of the cross are left open, but there are two tangential grooves by the upper terminal. Beneath the lower arm of the cross the surface of the stone is roughly dressed with short vertical grooves. These would have been hidden if the cross stood upright in the ground.

B. The relief cross is 6cm from the top, and the remaining side arm on the left runs up to the damaged edge of the slab. The arms are 2.5cm wide, with the upper arm 4.5cm long (from the centre) and the side arm 3.5cm. Adjacent to the upper arm and above the side arm the surface has been pocked back, but the lower armpit of the side arm is defined by a broad shallow groove, and the area beneath this has been left in relief. The lower and right arms, and the area between the upper arm and the summit, have been defaced. Both the two remaining arms have a shallow central groove, 4mm wide by 1mm deep, but that in the upper arm stops short of the terminal, which is rounded. The broad grooves on this face are pocked, in contrast to the incised technique used on Face A. There is no evidence of pocking in the lower part of the stone, but most of the equivalent area to Face A is missing.

The contrast in technique used on the opposed faces is striking, but the central groove on both crosses, and their placing on each face, with a gap at the top and the side arms reaching to the edge of the stone, show that the two crosses are almost certainly contemporary, and therefore that the two techniques could be used together at will. This suggests that the chronological significance of incised or pocked ornament in this area, as proposed by Thomas for Ardwall Isle (Thomas 1967, 152–3), may be less clear-cut than previously thought; but carving on both sides of the stone appears to be a fairly late feature, and incised and relief ornament on opposite faces is also found on the disk-headed cross-slabs (see Collingwood 1922–23, Figs 23, 25), which include median grooves in the 'stopped-plait' interlace (*op. cit.*, 217–8). The cutting of crosses on both faces, and the rough dressing at the foot of Face A, show that this slab was intended to stand upright in the ground. It was found displaced in a fourteenth century context.

Greywacke, L 19cm, W 7.5 > 7cm at base, D 1.8 > 1.75cm, **744**

6 Upper left hand corner of a cross slab, with two surviving edges, and part of a grooved outline cross on the remaining face. The reverse face is split and uneven. The left edge is straight, and chamfered at the back. The upper edge is curved but partly damaged. Two incomplete arms of the cross remain, with expanded terminals and narrow curved armpit. The upper terminal is damaged, but the left terminal appears to be divided, as on No 8. The surface of the cross is uneven, with the outline formed by shallow pocking which has partly extended into the adjacent ground. The angle of the surviving edge in relation to the cross suggests that the slab tapered towards the foot of the stone, and was therefore probably an upright grave marker. It overlay a group of earlier burials (Hill 1984, Illust. 6).

This stone and Nos 7 and 12 were found reused in twelfth century structures and may represent a phase of site clearance associated with the revival of the bishopric and the establishment of the Premonstratensian priory. A comparable iconoclastic reuse of earlier sculpture may be seen in the case of the cross-heads discovered in the foundations of the chapter house at Durham cathedral (Brown 1937, 216–20; Coatsworth 1978, 85), or the similarly displaced slabs and cross-shafts at St Andrews (Allen and Anderson 1903, 350–1, Fig. 376; Fleming 1931, ix, Fig. 30), again associated with the twelfth century Norman reforms.

Greywacke, L 38cm, W 33cm at top, D 5.5cm, **428.02**.
Hill 1984, 22, 36, 44, 46, No. 19, Illust.17.19; Hill 1987a, 18

7 Incomplete slab, with a hammer-headed cross carved in relief on one face. The summit and one edge of the stone are flat, the other is slightly convex. The back is split and uneven, and the lower part of the slab is missing.

The cross is carved in relief against a pocked ground between the arms, which extends into the borders beyond the terminals of the side arms. Above these, on the right side an edge moulding and part of the ground have been left in relief, though separated by a groove, but on the left side an isolated fragment of moulding links the terminals of the side arm and the hammer-head. Beyond this the surface has been cut back, and there is no edge moulding adjacent to the curved left side of the slab. The surface is also cut back at the top of the slab above the hammer-head. The upper corner on the right side is squared, but the opposite corner has been damaged. The cross is placed within these irregular borders. The side arms are wedge shaped with expanded terminals and curved armpits. The upper arm is straight but expands into a bar terminal, giving the cross a hammer-headed form. Part of the surface of this terminal has split off, and the relief is deepest between the arms of the cross.

The irregular and asymmetrical nature of the border decoration suggests that this slab may be unfinished, and it may have been abandoned when the surface of the bar terminal sheared off.

This is the only hammer-headed cross-slab known from Whithorn, but another has recently been found at Barhobble, 10 miles (16 km) to the north-west (Cormack 1989b, 5–6, No. 5, Fig. 4), and a slab very similar to this was found at Shallochwreck in southern Ayrshire (Foster 1958–60, 9–11, Fig. 1). There is also a cross of this type on one of two pillars found at Boghouse farm, Mochrum, near Barhobble (Anderson 1926–27, 116–18, Fig. 3), and larger examples are known from the area at Glenluce (Anderson 1935–36, 141–3, Fig. 3) and Kilmorie (Collingwood 1922–23, 216, Fig. 13). The type is a characteristic Viking age form (Bailey 1980, 182–3), datable to the tenth or eleventh century.

This stone and Nos 6 and 12 were found reused in twelfth century structures and may represent a phase of site clearance associated with the revival of the bishopric and the establishment of the Premonstratensian priory. See above.

Medium-grained sandstone, L 29cm, W 26cm, D 4.5cm, **414.01**.
Hill 1987a, 8; Hill 1988a, 18, Fig.14; Hill 1987b, 10

8 Upper right hand fragment of a miniature cross-slab, with a cross with divided terminals carved in relief on one face. The reverse face is smooth and flat, and the surviving edges are slightly rounded.

The surface of the cross is smooth, and set in relief against a pocked background. The two surviving arms of the cross are wedge-shaped, and the shaft is swollen, but the curved armpits are asymmetrical, and outlined by shallow grooves. The terminals of the expanded arms are split by V-shaped hollows, slightly deeper and rounded in the angles. There is a small round depression near the centre of the cross head.

The upper terminal of the cross is damaged, but the other is separated from the right edge of the slab by a pocked groove outlining a plain border moulding. The edge also survives on the upper right side, curving upwards towards the summit. Therefore this corner of the slab is complete, despite damage to the upper border, and the concave upper edge implies that the summit of the slab was formed by an S-shaped curve, like the top of a shield or a modern gravestone. The angle of the adjacent edge in relation to the cross shows that the slab tapered towards the foot of the stone.

The divided terminals and the form of this cross-slab suggest that it may date to the twelfth century refoundation of the site. It was reused in a path associated with a thirteenth/fourteenth century building adjacent to the boundary of the graveyard. A similar dressed slab, though without the divided terminals, was found at Craiglemine, 3 miles (5km) to the south-west (Anderson 1925–26, 266–7, Fig.1; Radford and Donaldson 1984, 29, No. 20).

Medium-grained sandstone, L 10cm, W 8cm, D 2.1 > 1.4cm, **504.01**.

9 Irregular fragment, probably from a cross shaft or slab, with one surviving edge, and part of an interlace pattern on the remaining face. The reverse face is damaged. The edge is straight and flanked by a curved moulding. Within the remaining part of the panel are two registers of plain interlace with unfinished triangular bar-terminals butted against the side. Not enough survives for the pattern to be reconstructed. The strands are 2cm in width, and carved in a flat-topped technique, with pecked ground between.

This piece does not follow the stopped-plait technique common on most sculpture decorated with interlace known previously from Whithorn (Collingwood 1922–23, 217–8), but plain strands are also found on Whithorn Museum 3, 7, and 38 (*op. cit*., Figs 12, 16; Craig 1992, Pls 176b, 180a, 180c). The plain interlace and the unpinned loops may link this piece with 3, but no other Whithorn stone has triangular knots on the edge of the panel. This type of unfinished terminal is rare, and not found on any other sculpture in Galloway. Bar terminals are usually found on closed-circuit patterns, as on Monreith (Collingwood 1922–23, Fig. 21), though there is a series of such loops on the side of Boghouse 1 (Anderson 1926–27, Fig. 3), but these do not form part of a panel. The unfinished appearance of the terminals relates this piece to Whithorn Museum 13 and 19 (Collingwood 1922–23, Figs 23, 29). The straight edge is unusual, as the edges of all cross-shafts from Whithorn except 5, 7, 17, and 38 are convex (*op. cit*., Figs 11, 16, 25). These four also have plain interlace on one face, and this piece appears to belong to the same group, of tenth or eleventh century date. It was found in the thirteenth/fifteenth century graveyard.

Medium-grained sandstone, L 26cm, W 12cm, D 5.5cm, **543**.
Hill 1988a, 18, Fig. 14

10 Irregular edge fragment with a number of broad, roughly pocked grooves on the surviving face. The reverse face is damaged, and daubed with mortar.

The grooves are 1cm wide and 0.3cm deep. Two grooves lie parallel to the surviving edge, the one nearest the edge is abutted by a third, slightly curved channel, which is joined at right angles by the second. There is a depression at the edge of the adjacent area.

These grooves do not appear to form interlace, but resemble the decoration on cross-slabs recently found at Barhobble (Cormack 1990, 9, Nos 8 and 9, Fig. 7). From the backfill of a late fifteenth century quarry pit probably dug when the west end of the cathedral was reconstructed.

Medium-grained sandstone, L 12cm, W 8cm, D 2.5cm, **607.05**.

11 Irregular fragment, probably from a cross shaft or slab, with the remains of plant scroll ornament on one face. Part of one narrow edge survives next to the broad, recut end of the stone. The reverse face is partly damaged, but with a smooth surface on one half. The plant scroll appears to include two tendrils which form volutes enclosing triple leaf terminals, and from one volute sprout two paired leaves adjacent to the border. The pattern is too damaged to reconstruct, but the leaves are of a broad cloverleaf form. Adjacent to the surviving edge is a fragment of moulding. The leaves and stems are not modelled, but are carved in flat relief with pocked ground between. The leaves vary between 3 and 4cm in diameter, the stem is 1.5cm wide.

This is the only carving with plant scroll found at Whithorn, and the only piece of plant scroll found west of Kirkcudbright, with the exception of the cross slab at Kilmorie in the Rhins (Craig 1991, 49–52, Fig. 4.5). But the volutes do not seem to be symmetrical, as on the classic Anglian sculpture found at Hoddom in Dumfriesshire (Radford 1952–53, Pls VIII, IX; Craig 1992, Pls 50–54) or Rascarrel to the east of Kirkcudbright (Craig 1992, Pls 93, 94), and the leaf form suggests that this piece is late, possibly dating to the twelfth century (*c.f*. Collingwood 1927, 175, Figs 214, 215). It was found in a fourteenth century context.

It is however possible, though less likely, that this is due to the use of greywacke rather than the sandstone found to the east, which has made it difficult to produce the usual rounded strands and modelled leaves, and that the piece represents a failed attempt in the Northumbrian period to introduce a style unsuited to the local geology.

Greywacke, L 28cm, W 21cm, D 5cm, **525.02**.
Craig 1991, 51

12 Irregular fragment, possibly from a cross-head, with one surviving edge, and a contoured ring boss carved in relief on the remaining face. The reverse face is damaged. The edge is straight and chamfered. The decoration consists of a domed boss 5cm in diameter surrounded by two raised rings divided by grooved channels. These channels have a curved profile. Beyond the outer ring the surface has been cut back, leaving the central area in relief. The carving has been done in a pocked technique, without being smoothed. The rings are about 2.5cm wide.

Ring bosses are found both at the centre of the head and within the keyhole armpits (unless hollowed) of all the disk-headed 'Whithorn School' crosses, as on Whithorn Museum 8, 14, and the two heads now in the Royal Museum of Scotland (Collingwood 1922–23, 224 (a), (c), Figs 22, 33; Craig 1992, Pls 177a, 177c, 187a, 187c). But all these have deeply incised, V-shaped channels, without the contoured U-shaped profile seen on this piece. Most of the surviving bosses carved in relief at the centre of disk-heads are surrounded by a single narrow groove. The armpit bosses are surrounded by a broad ring, but in most cases this is single. See also the examples from Craiglemine (Craig 1992, Pl. 110c), Glenluce (Anderson 1935–36, Fig. 2), and Monreith (Allen and Anderson 1903, Fig. 517). The only example of a double ring is Whithorn Museum 14, but this has a narrow inner and a broad outer groove, both with V-shaped channels as noted above (Collingwood 1922–23, Fig. 33).

However, if the chamfered edge is original, this cannot be the centre of a cross-head, as the outer ring would be too near the edge, nor can it be part of a keyhole armpit as the edge is at the wrong angle to form the circumference. It therefore follows that the edge is a later recutting, or else this ring boss was not part of a cross-head.

This stone and Nos 6 and 7 were found reused in twelfth century structures and may represent a phase of site clearance associated with the revival of the bishopric and the establishment of the Premonstratensian priory. See above.

Greywacke, L 18cm, W 15cm, D 2.5cm, **410**.
Hill 1988a, 17, 18, Fig. 14; Hill 1987a, 10.

13 Incomplete stone vessel carved in relief with a hollow in the top, surrounded by a zig-zag border above two arched panels surviving on adjacent faces, one of which shows a cross, the other possibly the defaced head of a figure. The grain of the stone is so coarse that it is difficult to distinguish details of the carving.

The stone is 11.5cm wide at the top, tapering to 8cm at the base. The right side is sheared off below the rim, and the back and base are completely broken off. In profile, the stone is now wider at base than top, varying from 8 to 6cm in depth. Originally the object seems to have been almost straight sided, tapering slightly from top to bottom. The lower part is square in section (though the corners are chamfered), the upper part including the rim is circular. The rim is not indented except at the corners.

The circular hollow in the top of the stone is 7cm in diameter, and 3.5cm deep. Approximately half of the hollow remains, and the base is rounded rather than flat or pointed. There is minimal evidence for vertical tooling in the hollow, and no evidence of residues or pounding. The rim is about 2cm wide.

Below the circular rim is a zig-zag border of incised pendant triangles 2.5cm high in the centre, expanding to 3.5cm in the corners. There are five (or ten) surviving triangles, three across the front, each 2.5cm wide at base. The top of the stone is roughly level, so the triangles, otherwise equilateral, are longer in the corner angles between the arched panels below. The curved borders of these panels form roll mouldings about 2cm wide and appear to be undecorated. There is a vertical groove between the moulding around the cross and the moulding round the 'figure', and the corner angle is chamfered.

The cross, which is carved in relief against a pocked background, is approximately 7cm high and 6cm wide, with narrow curved armpits and widely splayed arms, but the right arm and shaft are damaged. The broad upper arm terminal is bowed, following the curve of the arch, and the surviving side arm is also slightly convex. The upper terminal is 5.5cm in width, as opposed to 4cm on the side arm. There are parabolic hollows to the upper armpits of the cross, but the lower remaining hollow is wider. There was therefore probably a narrow tapering shaft rather than a lower arm.

In the adjacent panel to the left, the relief carving has been defaced, but appears to represent the head and shoulders of a figure. The 'head' stands slightly proud of the background, but the hollow between the 'head' and the 'shoulder' is deeper than the adjacent ground. The ground between 'head' and border is 2cm wide. The staff mentioned in Hill 1988a, 5, and Hill 1990, 17, appears to be a ridge of stone related to the defaced figure. The left half of the panel is missing.

The hollows of the armpits on the cross resemble those on a fragment found previously at Whithorn (Radford and Donaldson 1984, No. 4; Collingwood 1922–23, 215, Fig. 8), which also has parabolic upper, and wider lower angles; but the cross is circular, and there is a central depression. A similar cross can also be seen on York Minster 29 (Lang 1991, Illust. 121), though without the convex terminals.

As a piece of church furniture, this object seems to be unique, though it partly resembles a vessel from York, recorded without context but assumed to be pre-Conquest (Collingwood 1909, 203, fig; RCHM(E) 1975, xliv, Pl. 25a; Lang 1991, 114, Illusts. 397, 398). This vessel is hollow on top and also has pendant triangles below the rim, but is waisted and circular in profile. Plain stone vessels are known from Jarrow and Monkwearmouth (Wessels 1986, 26–8, No. 11, Fig. 10), but the type of pendant triangles on the Whithorn and York vessels appear to be a skeuomorph of the metal vandykes attached to Anglo-Saxon buckets, such as that from Hexham, of probable eighth century date (Bailey 1974, 147–9, Pl. XXV a; see Bailey 1980, 79; Lang, *loc. cit.*). These triangles are lengthy on the buckets found in pagan Saxon graves, but the ninth century horn mount from Burghead has similar zig-zag triangles to this piece (Graham-Campbell 1973a, 44, 47–8, Pl. XV). This type of ornament is also known from stone sculpture discovered at Jarrow, Northallerton and Ripon, acting as a border on cross-arms and church furniture (Cramp 1974, 136, Pls XXII b, c, f; XII a, b). It is therefore likely that this object belongs to a similar context, and can be dated to the late eighth century, a period when figures under arches were a common sculptural motif (Collingwood 1927, Figs 87–92; Cramp 1971, 59–61, Pls 47–8).

It was found wedged into the top of a post-hole in a small Northumbrian building (II/14), and may have been reused as a socket stone. The building almost certainly dated to the mid- to late-eighth century, so the object may have been broken at an early stage in its use. The lack of residues or burning, and the extremely gritty nature of the stone, make it difficult to identify its original function, which was certainly ecclesiastical, though perhaps a cresset lamp or candle holder[7] would be more appropriate than a holy water stoup (Hill 1990, 17), since the sandstone is permeable, but it is coarse enough for the vessel to have acted as a mortarium. The hollow would have held enough flour to make the host for a small number of communicants, and special ovens solely for baking the host are known from later medieval contexts. The decoration of this object and the chalice-like shape of the York vessel would also be appropriate to this function.

The geology of the stone is striking, since the western part of Galloway is dominated by greywackes and shales (Greig 1971, 34–41), and this is the material used for most of the early medieval sculpture from Whithorn and its area (Craig 1992, I, 38–9).

D.L. Schofield of the Department of Geology, Durham University, has kindly identified the stone type of this vessel as: 'Coarse grained, pale-buff coloured sandstone, average grain size 1–2mm diameter. The clarts (mainly quartz with some fresh and weathered feldspar) are angular sub-rounded. Very sparse mica, yellow-brown cement, some dark staining on part of specimen'.[8] This type of carboniferous material is unusual in Dumfries and Galloway, with very small coastal exposures 17 miles (27km) to the east of Whithorn, at Abbeyhead, Kirkbean, and Southerness (Greig 1971, 73), described on the 1:50,000 map as coarse-grained sandstones and conglomerates, but is commonly found in the areas of Northumberland and Cumbria which belong to the Lower Carboniferous Calciferous Sandstone Measures.[9]

It is unusual in studies of early medieval sculpture to be able to recognize pieces made out of non-local stone (*c.f.* RCAHMS 1982, 17; Cramp 1984, 184), but it is clear from the maps that this type of coarse sandstone is not found within the Whithorn peninsula. A liturgical function may therefore have made its import essential, possibly from the area of Northumbria to the east. The unusual form of the vessel itself suggests that it is perhaps more likely to have been brought in as a finished object than as raw sandstone. Its artistic links and its geology both emphasise the Northumbrian connection with Whithorn at this period.

Coarse-grained sandstone, H 13cm, W 11.5 > 8cm, D 8 > 6cm,
215.
Hill 1988a, 5, 6; Hill 1988b, 11; Hill 1988–90, 16–17, Fig. 15;
Gaimster, Margeson and Barry 1989, 229

C. Compass Drawn

(i) Arciform Crosses

14 Lower part of a flat tapering slab, one side straight, the other curved in at the base, with partly squared edges, decorated on one face with the remains of an incised cross-of-arcs, carved throughout in double outline. Part of the circumference including one complete terminal and one corner of another survives. Linking the corners of each terminal but not abutting them is one complete and one incomplete concave arc. The compass point for the complete arc can be identified on the lower part of the slab as a small depression. Measured from this, the radii of the two concentric incised lines are 10 and 10.5cm.

These arcs are not concentric with the side of the incomplete arm, as indicated in the drawing in Hill 1987a, 4. This has the same radius, but the compass point is placed on the

---

[7] Stone lamps have been found in medieval contexts in London and Winchester (London Museum 1954, 175, Fig. 54; Barclay & Biddle 1990, 985, 991, Fig. 308a), and in Ireland (Moore 1984, Figs 37–9), but with the exception of a few reused architectural pieces from London, none of these are decorated.

[8] This staining occurs on the broken part of the stone adjacent to the figure panel, and on the defaced 'head' of the figure. It therefore cannot be contemporary with its use.

[9] I am grateful to David Schofield for his comments on the geology of this piece. Other geological identifications are by Ray Chadburn.

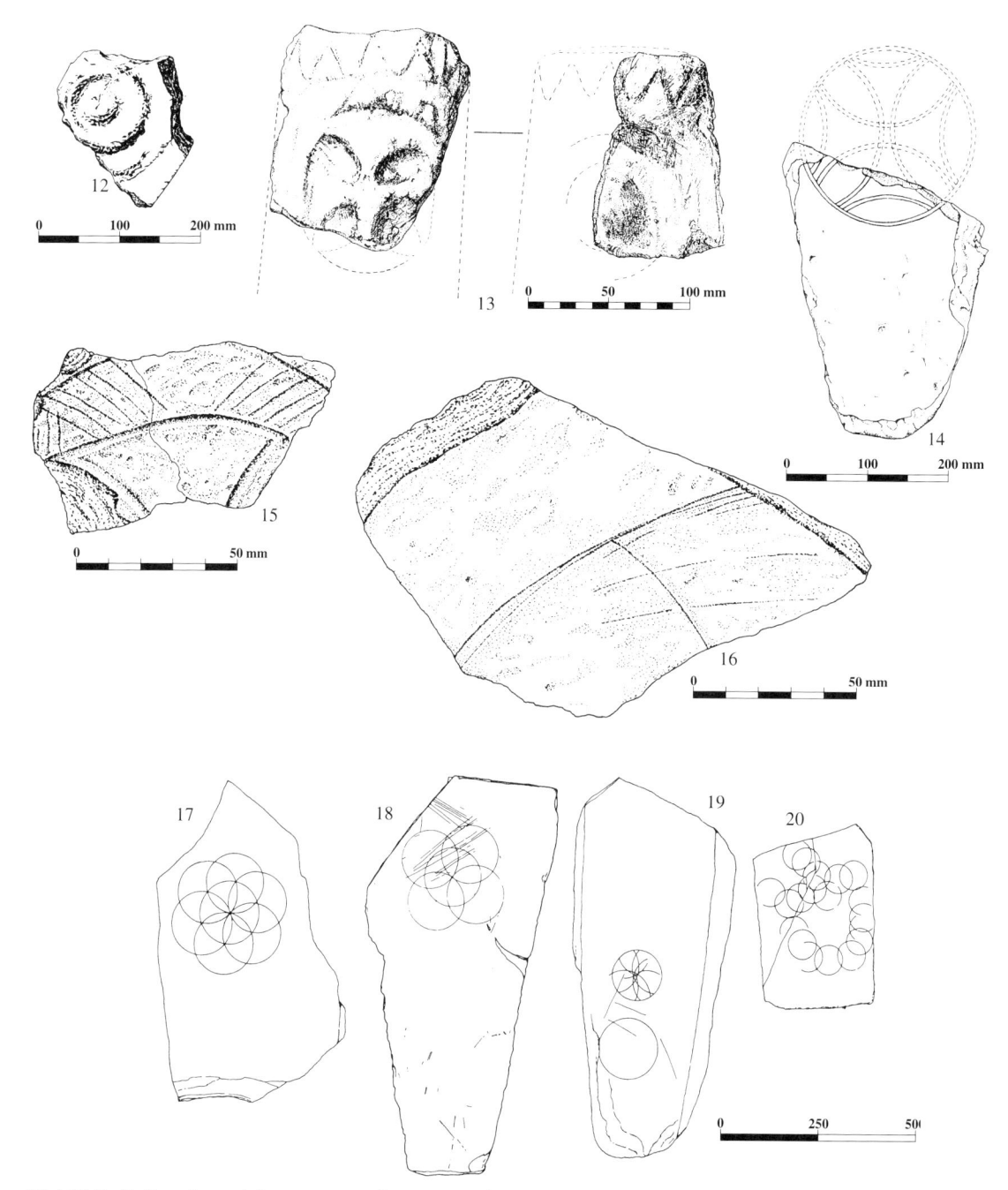

10.108 Relief sculptural fragments and compass-drawn crosses and designs (SE14).

circumference at the centre of the terminal. The radius is the same length as the width of the terminal arc. Consequently, the cross can be reconstructed with the arcs intersecting close to the central point.

This type of arciform cross with linked terminals has not previous been found at Whithorn or elsewhere in Galloway, but examples can be seen at Maughold and Ronaldsway in the Isle of Man, 24 miles (39km) to the south (Kermode 1907, 111–12, Nos 26 and 27, Pl. X; Megaw 1939, Pl. 173.5). But this Whithorn cross-of-arcs is unusual in that both circumference and cross-arms are double outlined. The circumference lines are positioned closely together on Maughold 46 (26) but the cross-arms are single. Double-encircled arciform crosses of the Maughold type are also found in Ireland, at Ballyvourney (Henry 1965, Pl. 50) and Clonmacnois (Lionard 1961, Fig. 9.11).

This slab probably dates to the seventh century, but was reused in a tenth century building (III/16) overlying the east end of the defunct church.

Medium-grained sandstone, L 39cm, W 22cm, D 6cm, **464**.
Hill 1987a, 4; Youngs, Clark and Barry 1987, 184.

15 Part of an incised cross-of-arcs with decorated border, in two fragments. The reverse face is uneven.

The outer part of one cross-arm remains, 6cm wide at the terminal, with the converging arcs of the stem surviving on both sides. The reconstructed radius for this arm is also 6cm. Beyond the terminal is a border area varying between 1.9 and 2.2cm in width, enclosed by an incised outer margin. This is not parallel to the circumference of the inner arc forming the terminal, so the two circles cannot have been concentric.

Within the outer border are three groups of parallel incised lines. Two of these are divergent, the other is partly cross-hatched on the left side. The divergent groups extend beyond the circumference into the remains of an outer decorative area, where they are also cross-hatched. The complete group on the left consists of six parallel lines, the other has five. These decorative grooves are V-shaped, and 1mm in width. The grooves round cross and border are U-shaped, varying in width between 2 and 3mm. All the channels are smoothly incised.

The variation in width of the outer border makes it difficult to reconstruct this cross, but it was clearly closer to the decorated arciform crosses found at Maughold in the Isle of Man, 24 miles (39km) to the south, than any other cross-of-arcs found at Whithorn (*c.f.* Kermode 1907, Pl. X; Megaw 1950b, 177). The parallel lines are reminiscent of the runes on Maughold 42 (25), but the cross-hatching is too regular to form lettering.

One fragment came from a bank of rubble to the south of the church, probably dating to the eleventh century, but with later contamination. The other was unstratified.

Greywacke, L 9.5cm, W 5.5cm, D 1.5cm, **430, 903**.

16 Outer fragment of a cross-of-arcs, showing the incised circumference and part of one arm. The surviving edge is chamfered and lies roughly parallel to the circumference at a distance of 4.5 to 5cm. The reverse face has split off. Both circumference and arm have an estimated radius of 11cm. The circumference is formed by intercutting multiple grooves, varying in width. The outer two grooves are 1mm wide, with a flat bottom, and there are two narrower inner scratches. The grooved arc of the cross-arm is about halfway between in width. The intercutting arcs of the circumference are evidence for the use of a compass from a slightly varying central point, rather than the compass having opened up during use. The use of compasses in the early medieval period is discussed below.

This piece was found in a mid- to late-seventh century grave (I/106), and is therefore one of the earliest stratified crosses from the site.

Greywacke, L 16cm, W 8.5cm, D 1.3cm, **82.03**.

(ii) Marigold Designs

17 Irregular slab with an incised hexafoil design, carefully executed and relatively unworn. Six interlocking circles of the same diameter, equidistant around a central point and forming a 'marigold' cross, which is surrounded by a seventh circle of the same diameter, linking the inner crossing points.

Diameter of circles 15.2cm, overall dimensions of figure 30.4cm.
Incorporated in the paved floor at the west end of the interior of the later-ninth century church.

Greywacke, L 81cm, W 46cm, D 6cm, **316**.
Hill 1990, 9, Fig. 8a; Hill 1991b, 11; Hill 1992a, 23.

18 Worn paving slab with cross of five circles at one end, faintly incised and crossed by several transverse lines.

Four interlocking circles of the same diameter, equidistant around a central point and linked by a fifth circle of the same diameter, forming a cross-of-arcs

Diameter of circles 14.6cm, overall dimensions of figure 29.2cm.
This slab was reused in a tenth century building overlying the east end of the defunct eighth/ninth century church.

Greywacke, L 97cm, W 43cm, D 9cm, **463**.
Hill 1990, 22, Fig. 8b

19 Narrow tapering slab, with imperfect compass-drawn 'marigold' design at the centre of one face, and adjacent larger circle.

Diameter of marigold 12.3 cm, larger circle diameter 14.5 cm.
This appears to derive from a prototype such as No 17. It was found on the path S.E. of the entrance to the burial chapel, probably in use between the later-eighth and late-tenth centuries. See also Nos 22, 23 and 24.

Greywacke, L 93cm, W 34cm, D 13.5 cm, **206.02**.
Hill 1988a, 10; Hill 1990, 14.

(iii) Circle Designs

20 Thin rectilinear slab in two fragments, with three straight edges. The face of the slab is covered by a series of intersecting compass-drawn circles of the same diameter, irregularly spaced but in places forming a chain. There are at least nineteen circles, faintly incised, though not all are complete.

Diameter of circles 7.2cm.
Used as a paving slab in a late eighth century surface outside the burial chapel.

Greywacke, L 44.5cm, W 28.5cm, D 5cm, **227.01**.

21 Large paving stone with a chain of three overlapping compass-drawn circles set diagonally on one face.

Diameter of circles 16.2 cm
Graffiti on paving flanking the late ninth century church.

Greywacke, L 96 cm, W 76 cm, D 9.5 cm, **316**.

22 Worn paving stone with three compass-drawn circles.
Diameters 12 cm
Graffiti on paving S.E. of the entrance to the burial chapel, which was probably laid in the later eighth century and continued in use till the late tenth century. See also Nos 19, 23, and 24.

Greywacke, L41 cm, W29 cm, D 6 cm, **206.02**.

23 Worn paving stone with two concentric compass-drawn circles.
Diameters 6.7 cm and 16 cm.
Graffiti on paving S.E. of the entrance to the burial chapel. See above.

Greywacke, L 88cm, W 52cm, D 11cm, **206.02**.

24 Massive slab with worn, compass-drawn designs. Incomplete three-quarter circle, with part of a divergent outer circle, possibly due to the compass having slipped.

Diameter of inner circle 1.5cm.
Graffiti on paving S.E. of the entrance to the burial chapel. See above.

Greywacke, L 89cm, W 53cm, D 11cm, **206.02**.

Discussion of compass drawn designs

Small compass-drawn circles, both on their own and intersecting to form arciform crosses, have only recently been recognized from the early medieval period on large irregular stone slabs. Previously, examples were only known from carving in wood, bone or on small stone flakes, in the form of motif-pieces (O'Meadhra 1979, Nos 46, 75, 116, 118, 144), and usually in a palimpsest with other forms of decoration.

In the early 1980s, a slab was discovered in the churchyard of the former monastic site at Maughold, Isle of Man, apparently through grave digging, with two plain circles and a cross-of-arcs (Trench-Jellicoe 1985, II, 256–7). In 1992 a recumbent stone lying outside a cottage at Ladywell in Perthshire was found to have three circles in a line, with a cross-of-arcs at the centre and six compass-drawn arcs forming a pattern in both the outer circles (King 1992, 78–9). Compass-drawn circles and lightly incised arciform crosses have also been found on a recumbent grave marker with dressed and chamfered edges found at The Hirsel, Berwickshire, apparently of post-Conquest date (Cramp and Douglas-Home 1978, 227–8, 230, No. 3, Pl. 14a). In the recent excavations at Tintagel churchyard, Cornwall, two slabs with compass-drawn circles were found, one with three plain circles, the other with circles intersecting in two groups of four to form cruciform motifs (Nowakowski and Thomas 1990, Figs 12b, 13). Neither of these appears to have been discovered *in situ*, but they were interpreted as having been covering slabs over cist graves (*op. cit.*, 17–22), like another slab with a crude single circle which was found in this position (Nowakowski and Thomas 1992, 10, Fig. 9).

In addition, since the discovery of the Whithorn slabs in 1987, other examples have been found in the immediate area. In 1993 a stone built into a wall at Kirkmadrine church near Penkiln, 5¼ miles (8.5km) north of Whithorn was recognized as having one row of four interlocked circles and another row of four separate circles, some with radial lines (Cormack 1993b, 26). At the same time, a stone-lined grave discovered in the excavations at Barhobble, 10 miles (16km) to the north-west of Whithorn, was found to include two decorated slabs, one with two overlapping circles and a third interlocked, and the other with eight overlapping circles (Cormack 1993, 26). The Whithorn discoveries suggest that slabs of this type found with the cist burials at Barhobble and Tintagel may be reused paving rather than funerary decoration.

The compass-drawn graffiti at Whithorn appear to post-date the slabs with arciform crosses, discussed below, which seem to be of seventh or eighth century date. Most of the circle decoration is associated with worn paving slabs outside the entrance to the burial chapel, laid in the late-eighth century, but possibly exposed till the late-tenth century, which appear to have been used as a convenient smooth surface for geometrical experiment or graffiti. The exceptions to this appear to be the 'marigold' crosses Nos 17 and 18, one of which was embedded in paving in the interior of the later-ninth century church, and the other reused in a tenth century building overlying it. These carefully laid out and sharply incised slabs appear to be finished designs rather than experiments, and form a sub-group related to the other arciform crosses, Nos 14–16.

The compass-drawn slabs also provide indirect evidence for the structural background to early medieval decoration, particularly in a monastic context.[10] Apart from the evidence of motif-pieces noted above, compass-drawn decoration has been identified in the early medieval period from the pricked vellum of manuscript pages, in particular the Lindisfarne Gospels (Bruce-Mitford 1960, 174, 221–3, 226–7). This has provided evidence for compasses with a minimum radius of 0.75mm (*op. cit.*, 226). Attempts to identify the remains of compass or divider arms from early medieval contexts have been made in Ireland, at Nendrum, Co Down (Lawlor 1925, 146), Garryduff, Co Cork (O'Kelly 1962, 47–8), and Gransha, Co Down (Lynn 1985, 88; see O'Meadhra 1987, 58, 59, 73). None of these examples is certain, since as O'Kelly showed, the minimum radius of the circles would have been limited by the arms lying adjacent rather than opposed (*op. cit.*, 47), and the example from Nendrum, which has now disintegrated, would have been loosely jointed (Philips 1960, cited in O'Meadhra 1987, 73). Only Nendrum is clearly an ecclesiastical site (ASNI 1966, 292–5), but all three sites produced compass-drawn graffiti (O'Meadhra 1979), and Nendrum has also produced arciform cross sculpture (ASNI 1966, Pls 78, 81).

Prior to the 1986 excavations, no cross-of-arcs had been found at Whithorn, with the exception of Whithorn Museum 36, which has three intersecting, roughly drawn arciform crosses on the face now hidden from display (Craig 1992, III, 300–1, Pl. 174b). The only other example known from the area is on the inscribed pillar Whithorn Museum 2, which was first recorded on Mains farm, about 0.75km to the south of Whithorn, before being removed first to the side of the road and later to the museum (M'Kerlie 1877, 418; Craig 1992, III, 191–7).[11] In consequence, Trench-Jellicoe (1980, 203; 1985, I, 244) has seen the link between the Rho-incised crosses-of-arcs at Whithorn and Maughold as deriving from the Manx site, where five arciform crosses have been found (Kermode 1907, Nos 21, 25, 26, 27, 117; Trench-Jellicoe 1985, I, 238–45). The new discoveries at Whithorn alter this balance, and point to a closer link between the two sites than has previously been apparent.

Apart from the crosses-of-arcs, grooved circles are known on a number of pieces of sculpture from the Whithorn area, particularly Whithorn Museum 4, which has an equal-armed cross within a circle on one face and two adjacent incised circles on the reverse, with an incised spiral in part of the complete circle (Collingwood 1922–23, Fig. 8). This form of equal-armed cross within a circle is also seen on the other face of Whithorn Museum 36, which has two such crosslets between the cross and the runic inscription (Craig 1992, Pl. 174a). The same type, but at a larger scale, is also found on a pillar from St Ninian's Cave, No. C.5, which has three equal-armed crosses within circles, one above the other (Maxwell 1885, Pl. VII, Fig. 1).

The interest in geometric circle ornament demonstrated on the newly discovered pieces, the Whithorn incised crosses and the sculpture from St Ninian's Cave suggests that earlier views that saw the disk-headed crosses as originating in the cross-of-arcs were probably correct (Simpson 1935, 50, 93–4; Thomas 1971, 108), and that this was a development of a long-lived regional motif, possibly stimulated by the veneration of a single monument with this motif. The present excavations have shown that pillars may have acted as foci for burial at Whithorn in the early period (pp 91–2), and it is likely that a mechanism of this sort was behind the continued use of this motif in this area (*c.f.* Thomas 1992a, 10, 19).

The present group of sculpture differs from most previous finds from the site in that it has expanded the range of types known from Whithorn, rather than providing variations on a locally known form. It also

---

[10] Cramp has also noted the use of compasses in laying out the curved terminals of several crosses from Lindisfarne and Hartlepool (Cramp 1984, 13).

[11] See Appendix 1.

provides sculptural evidence from the period of the Anglian occupation of the site in the eighth and early ninth centuries, a period that has previously been largely absent from the known sculptural record at Whithorn (Collingwood 1922–23, 215–16; Radford 1948–49, 96). Yet cross-of-arcs sculpture has not been found in the area of Anglo-Saxon England, except one example in relief at Lindisfarne (Cramp 1984, Pl. 200.1122), and only two examples are known from Wales (Nash-Williams 1950, No. 302, Fig. 194, Pl. XX; No. 308, Fig. 201, Pl. IV). The predominant quantity of this type has come from sites in Ireland, particularly on the west coast (Henry 1937, Pls XXIX–XXXIII; Henry 1945, Pl. XXVIII; Lionard 1961, Fig. 9), but also from Gallen priory, Co Offaly (Kendrick 1939, 18–19, Fig. 11, Pl. VI). It may therefore be remarked that at a period when the historical record shows links with Anglo-Saxon England, the predominant type of sculpture shows connections with Ireland. It should however be noted that none of the arciform sculpture was clearly *in situ*, but appears to have been reused in later flooring. It is therefore likely that this sculpture reflects the contacts of the site prior to the establishment of the Northumbrian bishopric.

It should be emphasised that the predominant type of sculpture previously known from Whithorn, the disk-headed cross-slabs with 'stopped-plait' interlace on the shaft (Collingwood 1922–23, 217–24, Figs 14–37; Craig 1991, 153), have not been found in the area south of the priory church excavated between 1984 and 1991. The piece with concentric rings carved in relief, No 12, and the fragment of plain twist pattern, No 9, have been shown above to differ in important respects from other sculpture previously known from the site. Because most of the sculpture of this type were found in the nineteenth century in cuttings made by William Galloway at the crossing and east end of the priory church (Figures 1.6 and 12.2, Hill 1984, 1–2, Illust. 1; Craig 1992, I, 73–4), it may be suggested that either the focus of sculptural activity shifted north in the later period, possibly through the opening of a new burial ground, or that the site was zoned in some way (*c.f.* Alcock 1988b, 332; Mytum 1992, 83), with stone-carving taking place in specific areas.

The Jet, Shale and Cannel Coal

Fraser Hunter and Andrew Nicholson

The bulk of the twenty-two 'shale' artefacts are beads, spindle whorls and fragments of bangles and rings. All were finished or part-finished objects, the latter in varying stages of completion suggesting on-site working, but apart from a trimmed lump of bitumen (SH6), there was no specific working debris to indicate the precise manufacturing site, such as that from Flaxengate, Lincoln (Mann 1982, 45).

The objects were analysed by X-radiography and X-ray fluorescence [XRF], combined with physical characteristics (Hunter *et al.* 1993, Davis 1993, Hunter 1994). This identified a single example of jet (SH05) almost certainly from Whitby; two shales (SH01.07; 04.02), and a lump of bitumen (SH06). The bulk of the assemblage was not as elementally distinctive, but eight pieces (SH01.1, 6, 10, 11, SH02.1–3, SH03.2) were a coherent material type interpreted as cannel coal in view of their conchoidal fracture, smooth fracture surface and general lack of laminar structure. No secure identification can be suggested for the remaining objects. One piece (SH01.12) with a conchoidal fracture was distinguished by a highly lustrous fracture surface, and was clearly distinct from other materials in the assemblage. Three others (SH01.2, .5, SH04.1) show more shale-like characteristics, best seen as a canneloid shale variant or highly organic oil shales. A further four objects could be separated analytically, three more organic pieces (SH01.03; 03.01; 03.03), and one (SH01.01) with a high lead and yttrium content. Two final two objects (SH01.9, SH02.4) did not display clear enough attributes to allow them to be classified.

The results show that a wide range of raw materials was in use, with cannel coals and their variants being dominant. The question of how much is local, and how much imported is harder to answer. The jet is an import: the rest are less clear-cut. Cannel coals are typically found in Carboniferous deposits, and are for instance well known in the Ayrshire Coal measures (e.g. Richey *et al.* 1925). There are no suitable Coal Measure deposits recorded in Wigtownshire, the nearest being around Thornhill (Greig 1971, Fig. 13; Barnes 1989). which would suggest most of the material was imported. It is possible however that there were small local deposits, now unknown or worked out, while material could also be present in drift deposits or washed up on beaches.

Half of the artefacts were fragments of armlets (SH01.1–11), usually of D-shaped section. Four pieces (3, 4, 10 and 11) with bevelled external faces come from unfinished bangles, and two others (1 and 9) have been reworked after breakage. Tooling marks on some pieces indicated working, possibly with a knife, the faces being filed smooth. Similar armlets are a common feature of late prehistoric and early historic sites, occurring in duns and crannogs along the western seaboard (Peltenburg 1982, 205; RCAHMS 1971), and locally at Portpatrick (Duns 1894, 127–9; Callander 1916, 237), Dowalton Loch crannog and Luce Sands. Examples from the Mote of Mark, Kirkcudbrightshire (Laing 1973, 123) show that shale continued to be worked locally into the later-sixth to seventh century, and there are later pieces from ninth and tenth century contexts at

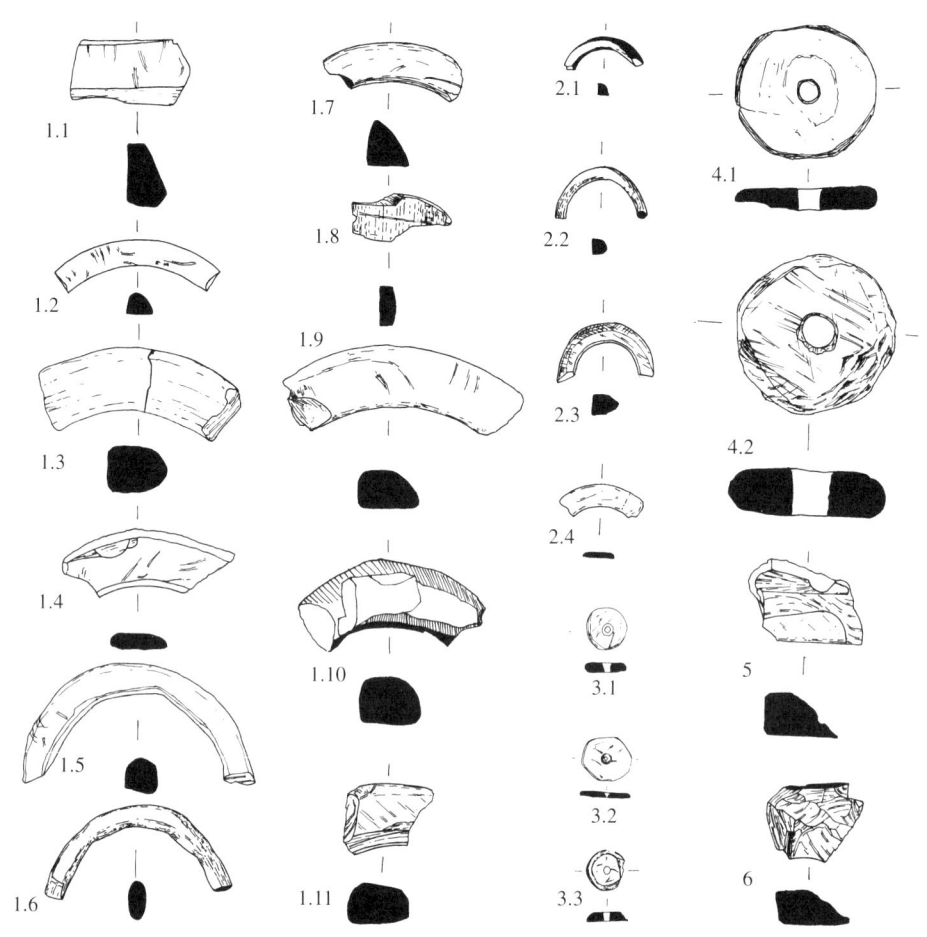

10.109 Objects of shale, jet and cannel coal (SH1-6).

Jarlshof (Hamilton 1956, Fig. 56, No.7) and Winetavern Street, Dublin (O'Riordain 1971, 77). The earliest armlet fragments (1.1 and 2) from Whithorn came from early eighth century contexts (232, 236.01) in the **southern sector**, while a later group extends from **Period III** into the earlier part of **Period V**. One of the unfinished fragments (3) came from the debris (309.02) surrounding the **Period III** settlement, and a second (4) from the foundations of Building IV/18 may have been of similar date. A third (10) from Building V/8, was probably displaced, and the last (11) was unstratified. Four ring fragments (2.1–4) revealed a similar distribution, with one (1) from the **Period II/4** terrace (319), a second (2) from **Period III/1** cobbling (421.02), and two others (3 and 4) from **Period V** graves probably displaced from **Period III** or **IV** deposits. Other excavated shale rings tend to be earlier (Peltenburg 1982, 188; Webster and Cherry 1975, 231) or later (MacGregor 1982, 89). The three beads (SH03.1–3) were all discoid, two (1 and 2) with bi-conical perforations, and the thickest (3) with a straight-sided drilled perforation. One (1) was securely stratified with a **Period III/1** burial (305.04) Although similar beads range widely in date – an almost identical one was found in a late medieval context at Threave Castle (Good and Tabraham 1981, Fig. 20 No.204) – a close parallel was found in an eighth century context at Kiondroghad, Isle of Man (Gelling 1969, 75). The last two artefacts were thick discoid spindle whorls (SH04.1–2), similar to other stone whorls from the site (pp 00), and coming from unremarkable **Period IV** and **V** contexts (Table 10.18). The only piece of working debris – a possible object blank of bitumen (SH6) – came from a **Period I/2** rubbish spread (89) which was roughly a century earlier than the earliest artefacts. Unfortunately the one piece of jet (SH5) was a fragment of a squared perforated object which cannot be identified.

The restricted currency of these ornaments is of some interest, and perhaps reflects the status of the inhabitants. They first appear at the end of **Period I**, when the introduction of timber-framed buildings points to cultural change, maybe settlement by Northumbrians (pp 37–8). They recur from the beginning of **Period III**, but are absent from the slightly earlier Northumbrian rubbish spreads (303 etc) which produced a different range of ornaments

(Tables 4.4–6). The significance of their introduction and reintroduction is difficult to evaluate as we do not know if they were appropriate to male or female dress, and, while common on secular sites, they may not have been out of place in an ecclesiastical community.

Bangles (01)

1 Fragment of well finished bangle, reworked after breakage. Polygonal section, fractured laterally and transversely. The bevelled external faces are slightly concave. Tooling marks are evident on the interior face. Possibly cannel coal.
L 32 W 17 T 10 **232**

2 Fragment of well finished bangle, fractured laterally and transversely. Convex inner and outer surfaces. Possibly canneloid shale.
L 45 W 5 T 7 **236.01**

3 Fragment of unfinished bangle, broken in two on excavation, possibly along an antique fracture. One end displays a possible perforation, though it may be a fracture along the bedding planes. Flattened convex upper, lower and inner faces, outer face D-shape sharply convex. All surfaces roughly smoothed. Unclassified 'organic'.
L 55 W 12 T 16 **309.02**

4 Fragment of unfinished bangle, laterally and transversely fractured, with roughly finished surfaces.
L 47 W 4 T 14.5 **440**

5 Broken quadrilateral bangle with flattened convex faces. Irregular width and thickness, surface polish may be through wear. Possibly canneloid shale.
L 99 ED 65 ID 49 W 8 T 7 **417.02**

6 Broken ovoid-section bangle with about half remaining (165 degrees): lenticular section, outer surface slightly ridged, inner surface flatter: outer circumference smoothly circular, inner circumference appears slightly and regularly segmented in convex sections approximately 11 to 12mm long. Highly polished and worn. Possibly cannel coal.
ED 52 ID 41 T 5.4 W 9. **456.03**

7 Fragment of well finished bangle, laterally and transversely fractured. Flattened inner surface, convex outer surface, tooling marks on inner face. Shale.
L 37 W 12 T 10 **464**

8 Fragment, probably from bangle, quadrilateral section, with flat upper and lower faces and slightly convex inner and sloping outer faces. Unclassified.
L 27 W 13 T 4.5 **546**

9 Fragment of well-finished bangle, reworked after breakage. Flattened lower and inner surfaces, convex upper/outer surface. Tooling marks on lower surface across the grain. Possibly cannel coal.
L 65 W 10.5 T 16 **533**

10 Fragment of unfinished bangle, flattened convex upper, lower and inner surfaces, sloping convex outer surface. Possibly cannel coal.
L 51 W 14 T 18 **700**

11 Fragment of unfinished bangle, flat lower surface, flattened upper surface with bevelled edges onto convex outer and inner faces.
L 23 W 10.5 T 17 **902**

Rings (02)

1 Fragment of finger ring, triangular section with flat lower and inner faces and a convex outer face. Possibly cannel coal.
ED 25.5 ID 19.5 T 3 **319**

2 Broken finger ring, sub ovoid section with convex well finished faces. Possibly cannel coal.
ED 26 ID 19.5 T 4.2 **421.02**

3 Fragment of ring, possibly a finger ring, with flat well-finished inner and lower faces, and roughly (?)finished upper and bi-conical outer faces. Possibly cannel coal.
ED 26 ID 18 T 5.3 **535**

4 Fragment of ring or bangle, with well finished inner face. Flat rectangular section. Unclassified.
L 26 W 2 T 9 **540**

Beads (03)

1 Roughly finished bead with bi-conical central perforation.
D 11 W 2 T 9 **305.04**

2 Discoid bead with bi-conical central perforation. Possibly cannel coal.
D 16 × 13 Hole D 4 × 1.2 T 2 **903**

3 Broken tapered disc bead. Tapered disc with convex splayed outer edge, of jet or jet-substitute. Very regular, perforation completely cylindrical, probably drilled. Fractured along natural planes, and broken at edge. Highly polished remaining surfaces.
D 12 × 9.5 Hole D 2.4 T 4 **616.07**

Spindle Whorls (04)

1 Laminating discoid spindle whorl with straight-sided central perforation. Finished outer edge and smooth upper and lower surfaces. Possibly canneloid shale.
D 38 × 34 Hole D 6 T 6 **415.01**

2 Discoid shale spindle whorl with straight-sided central perforation. Roughly finished outer edge with scratched and worn upper and lower surfaces. Shale.
D 42 Hole D 9.5 T 12.4 **525.01**

Object (05)

1 Fragment of squared perforated object of Whitby jet. Opposed faces and outer perpendicular face with bevelled edges. Slight tooling marks on outer face, upper and lower faces highly polished.
L 34 W 20 T 11.5 **506.01**

Working Debris (06)

1 Lump of bitumen, possible object blank, edges formed by natural planes, upper and lower surfaces flaked.
L 25 W 21 T 9 **89**

The Stone

Ray Chadburn, Peter Hill, Andrew Nicholson

A large collection of stone objects comprises architectural fragments (SE01–06), tiles (SE07–13), graffiti (SE17) and gravestones (SE18), artefacts (SE19–50), utilised stone (SE51–57), imported stone (SE58–71) and miscellaneous stone finds (SE72–77).

The architectural stone

Andrew Nicholson

The excavation produced eighty-nine pieces of architectural stone including thirteen fragments of sandstone waste. Most of these came from fifteenth century or later contexts, and comparatively little worked building stone was recovered, given the size of the medieval priory and its proximity to the excavated areas. A large number of fragments and complete blocks was recovered from the soakaway and yard surfaces around the late medieval building (V/4) in the south-east part of the **Glebe Field**, reflecting building work at the close of the fifteenth century. Further finds from overlying **Period V/5** contexts and the later manse may have been displaced from this original deposit and subsequently reused. Other pieces had been built into the present field wall and were recovered during repairs. The **Museum Garden** trench produced a relatively large group of finds, generally from late contexts. This included medieval fragments originating in the Priory, and masons' waste (SE06) from the late nineteenth century renovations by the Marquis of Bute (pp 8–9).

The architectural building stone was divided into six categories (SE01–06) by form and function. Full details of individual pieces are recorded in the excavation archive.

Dressed masonry (SE01)

Thirty-five fragmentary pieces of sandstone (SE01.1–35) with one or more dressed faces represent just over a third of all the building stone. A chamfered stone (4) from the **Period IV** deposits (408) underlying the **Period V** graves in the **Museum Garden** could derive from the construction of the original twelfth century church or even modifications in the thirteenth century (p 62). A second chamfered stone (2) recovered from a **Period III/1** grave (305.04) was more problematical, and is the only evidence for a stone building in the ninth century. A third dressed stone (SE43.2) reused as a quern came from a fourteenth century context (517.01) in the **southern sector**. Fine-grained red sandstone flags came from relatively recent contexts, although fragments of red sandstone (SE06) from the masons' workshop (Building V/4) and two late graves indicate that it was used in the late fifteenth century. Other pieces of red sandstone from the **Museum Garden** were associated with the Marquis of Bute's restoration of the crypts. Fragments of sandstone flags from the area of the Manse appear to relate to the west extension and later rebuilds in the eighteenth and nineteenth centuries.

Moulded and decorated fragments (SE02)

Fourteen stones (SE02.1–14) were decorative. The most common form was a vertical concave (10 and 11) or convex (2, 6 and 13) moulding from an arcade or pier. All of the decorative stone appeared to be medieval except for two halves of an ornamental stone ball (14) associated with the late eighteenth century Manse. The largest group of fragments (1–4 and 7) was associated with the late fifteenth century mason's workshop (Building V/4), and included a fragment of window tracery (1), and one with a high-relief leaf-shaped moulding (4). The simple forms of the mouldings indicate a date prior to the second half of the fourteenth century, which is consistent with the inference that many of the fragments were discarded during the renovations of c. 1500.

Pivot stones (SE03)

Four stones (SE03.1–4) with distinctive hemispherical sockets usually worn by rotational wear, were presumably used to cap or contain a moving shaft. Their most probable use is for taking a wooden pin from a door pivot, akin to timber examples found in Hiberno-Norse dwellings in Dublin (Murray 1983). None was found *in situ*. One was found in a **Period 1/4** drain (230.01) in the **southern sector**, another from rough cobbling (513) over a medieval building (V/3) in the **southern sector**. The others had been redeposited in late contexts.

Functional pieces (SE04)

Eight pieces (SE04.1–8) had specific structural functions, such as door jambs, although none was found *in situ*. One door jamb (4) had a simple rebate, whilst the other three jambs (1–3) were chamfered (two flat, one concave) and rebated. Only one of these jambs (3) was weathered to a degree which would suggest external use. A fragment of a window sill or lintel (5) has a rectangular socket for a bar and a vertically sided channel into which the glass would have been set. The sixth piece (6) was a weathered, roughly-finished stone trough or drain with a shallow U-sectioned hollow terminating in a squared off end.

Column sections and fragments (SE05)

Fourteen sections of columns or fragments thereof (SE05.1–14) included seven (2–8) from debris associated with the late fifteenth century mason's workshop (V/4) and related contexts, which had probably been discarded as unsuitable for reuse. Despite the small size of the sample it was possible to detect three groups of conformities in diameters (90–96mm, 140mm and 160mm). Most of the columns were attached to piers, except for the two smallest (6 and 10) which may have been from window tracery.

Masons waste (SE06)

Most of the waste material (SE06) came from the dumps around the mason's workshop (Building V/4) and debris associated with the rebuilding of the crypt in the late nineteenth century. Most of the waste is of red sandstone, but this may be due to selection by excavators rather than reflecting a true distribution of builders' waste, most of which was discarded.

The stone tiles

Andrew Nicholson and Ray Chadburn

Large quantities of stone tiles were recorded from fifteenth century and later deposits. A range of stone types was used defining six categories of tiles (SE7–12). A seventh category (SE13) encompasses tiles which were accessed, but not retained for detailed study. In many cases only a sample of the tiles (usually complete tiles and perforated fragments) was retained, but the relative proportions of the various geological types are probably reliable as the selection process was effectively random.

Five size-groups were identified spanning four of the six geological categories (Figure 10.110). Group 1 comprised tiles of varying length (200mm to 340mm) and width (78mm to 114mm), but with a consistent length/width ratio of 3:1. These would have been used to even up the ends of rows to form straight edges to the roof. Groups 2 and 3 shared a length/width ratio of 2:1, but displayed two size clusters. Group 2 tiles were relatively small (c. 240mm–270mm long and 112mm–127mm wide) and the Group 3 tiles were slightly larger (290mm–330mm long and 146mm–162mm wide). The Group 4 and 5 tiles shared a common length/width ratio of 3:2, but can be split into two overlapping groups by size. Group 4 tiles were about 250mm–280mm long and 170mm–190mm wide, whilst those in Group 5 were 270mm–300mm long and 180mm–220mm wide.

Examples of most tile types were recovered from **Period V** graves (Tables 6.41 and 42), but these were probably intrusive and the earliest secure finds were associated with Building V/4, and so date to the end of the fifteenth century. The sequence of deposits in this area suggests that the earliest tiles were of greywacke (SE07) and were perhaps tilers' waste from the roof of the building. Subsequent deposits identified as builders debris (630) produced siltstone (SE08), meta-sediment (SE09), and phyllite tiles (SE10). These may have derived from the repair of the cathedral, and could either be discarded old roofing or tilers' waste from the later stages of repair. The overlying Commendator's House (V/8) may have been roofed with meta-sediment tiles, while the eighteenth-nineteenth century manse was roofed with siltstone, and latterly grey and blue slate (SE11 and 12).

Greywacke tiles (SE07)

Ninety-nine greywacke tiles (SE07.1–99) comprise the second commonest type of tile and were represented in all size groups (Table 10.16). Greywacke tiles were present in the construction debris abutting Building V/4 (605) and were perhaps waste from its roof. This was the earliest securely-stratified group of tiles and a few examples from **Period V** graves were probably intrusive. Although greywacke is available locally, it is less suitable for tiles than the other types of stone due to it poor cleavage, and was perhaps superseded after they were introduced.

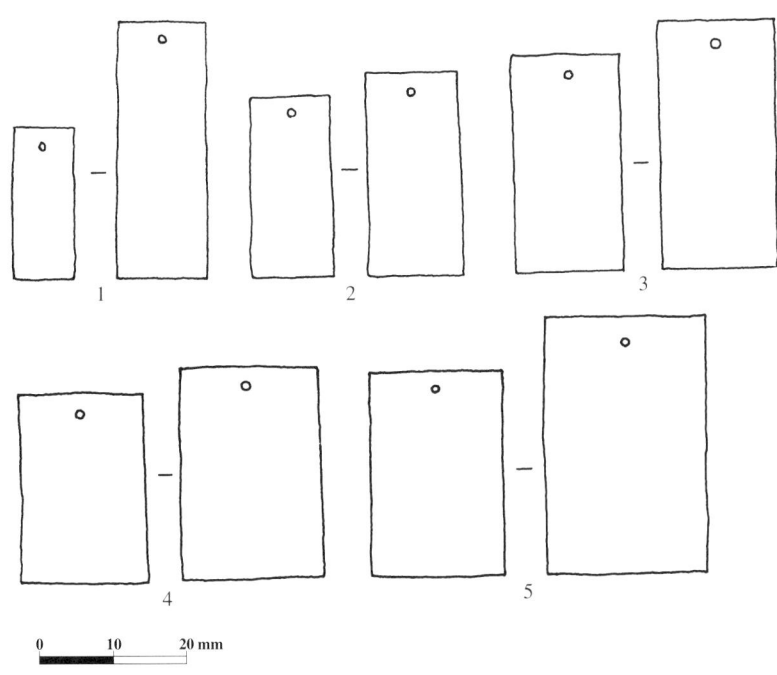

10.110 Roof tile size groups.

Siltstone tiles (SE08)

The largest category comprises a hundred and twenty-six siltstone tiles, represented in all the size groups, but with a substantial number (30.4%) of non-standard sizes. There were four examples in deposits (605, 630) associated with Building V/4, but most came from contexts (713, 721, 722) directly related to the western extension of the Manse, and can be ascribed to its construction and periodic repair in the eighteenth and nineteenth centuries. Large numbers of siltstone tiles from topsoil contexts probably derive from the demolition of this building, while scattered finds from the west part of the Glebe Field were associated with eighteenth-nineteenth century pottery originating in the manse. Siltstone beds are interleaved with the greywacke deposits and are thus readily accessible locally. Siltstone has better cleavage than the greywacke, but has little strength, and it is surprising to find it used so freely when better stones (SE09–11) were available.

Meta-sediment tiles (SE09)

Some eighty meta-sediment tiles (SE09.1–80) were represented in size groups 1, 2, 3 and 5 (Table 10.16). Apart from occasional intrusive finds from **Period V** graves, they first occurred in the builders' waste (630) abutting Building V/4. A subsequent group came from debris (729) on the courtyard of the Commendator's House (Building V/8) which may thus have been roofed, in part, with meta-sediment tiles. They were scarce in deposits linked to the eighteenth-nineteenth century manse, and may thus have been a relatively short-lived type, possibly confined to the sixteenth century. The meta-sediment is a greywacke-type rock with fine to coarse grains of angular and sub-angular rock fragments. The argillaceous cementing material shows low grade metamorphism with slight schistocity of the intergrain matrix producing slatey cleavage by the partial recrystallisation and reorientation of the mineral particles. The lithology of this rock shows a close similarity to a coarse-grained sandstone occurring to the west of the Loch Ryan Fault, and a concealed intrusion at Sandhead (Kimbell and Stone 1992) may account for the metamorphism. The quarry site – or sites – have not been identified.

Phyllite Tiles (SE10)

Fifty-eight phyllite tiles (SE10.1–58) were represented in all five size groups (Table 10.16). This was the smallest group of pre-Modern roofing tiles and examples were widely scattered. The earliest secure group came from the builders' waste (630) abutting Building V/4. There were no subsequent concentrations indicating that phyllite tiles were not used in the roofs of the Commendator's house and later manse. Phyllite is a coarser-grained and less-perfectly cleaved rock than slate, but finer-grained and better cleaved than greywacke and stronger than siltstone. It is formed by low temperature regional metamorphism and though not available in the immediate vicinity, is widespread to the north-west of Whithorn.

Grey slate tiles (SE11)

Nine tiles of grey slate (SE11.1–9), represented in the first three size groups (Table 10.16), were concentrated in the area of the eighteenth-nineteenth century Manse. Their conformity with the sizes of earlier tiles indicates they were used for roof repairs. The grey slate is a fine-grained argillaceous rock with good cleavage, but no recrystallisation, formed by low grade regional metamorphism. It does not occur in the immediate vicinity of the site, but quarries are recorded at Cairnryan, Kirkmaiden, Kells and Castlewigg, the last only two miles from Whithorn. This is the most suitable of the rocks available in the district, and its scarcity and late introduction suggest that its potential was not recognized until a relatively late date.

Blue Slate Tiles (SE12)

Ten pieces of blue slate (SE12.1–10) were associated with repairs to the Manse, apart from a single example from the **Museum Garden**. Blue slate is only found in the first three size groups (Table 10.16), and the slates were probably imported from Wales.

	Group 1 n	Group 1 %	Group 2 n	Group 2 %	Group 3 n	Group 3 %	Group 4 n	Group 4 %	Group 5 n	Group 5 %	Ungrouped n	Ungrouped %	Total
Greywacke (**07**)	8	20	9	22.5	8	20	12	30	3	7.5			40
Siltstone (**08**)	1	2.2	1	2.2	10	21.7	11	23.9	9	19.6	14	30.4	46
Meta-sediment (**09**)	15	30.6	6	12.2	13	26.5			15	30.6			49
Phyllite (**10**)	4	13.3	7	23.3	5	16.7	6	20	8	26.7			30
Grey slate (**11**)	1	25	1	25	2	50							4
Blue slate (**12**)	1	25	1	25	2	50							4

Table 10.16: Roof tile: size groups and geological categories. Fragments not assigned to groups are omitted.

The graffiti and gravestone

Peter Hill

Gravestones (SE17)

Fragments of one or two gravestones (SE17.1–2) were recovered from the manse and adjacent, more recent contexts. One fragment (1a) built into a refaced internal wall (714) of the original building displays the date 1725 which – though it is unclear whether this was a *valete* or a *salvete* – provides a valuable *terminus post quem*.

Graffiti (SE18)

The small group of graffiti (SE18.1–8), mostly from late contexts, is disappointing in light of Whithorn's claim to an unusually long history of literacy and the abundant slatey rocks inviting scratched messages and pictures. The only truly pictorial piece (3, Figure 10.111), portraying a possible multi-legged insect, came from a late context in the **Fey Field** (765) compatible with the inscribed date of 1664. The message is unclear. Two other graffiti (2, 722 and 4, 703) came from the manse, a third (7) from relatively recent cultivation (621) in the west part of the Glebe Field, and a fourth (1) from topsoil. A fragmentary piece (6) from the **Period V** graveyard bears three small circles (o's or 0's). The last (8) bearing the number '18' came from the fire debris (207) in the Northumbrian burial chapel. It is similar in size to stone gaming pieces (SE19), but the numerals are unparalleled and irrelevant to contemporary games. It could thus have been a token, possibly relating to the inferred role of the chapel as an entry point to the ecclesiastical precinct for the living and the dead (pp 42, 45). The only graffiti stone from **Period I** (SE14.3) is included among the sculptural fragments on the basis of an incised cross (pp 433-5), but the other markings argue that it belongs in this category.

The stone artefacts

Andrew Nicholson

The stone artefacts (SE19–50) were grouped according to function or activity association, with the miscellaneous artefacts (SE50) listed as a separate category. Stones which were utilised rather than manufactured were classed separately (SE51–57). It is a large, unspectacular and essentially functional collection which has, nevertheless, important implications for the evolving organisation of the *monasterium* and its economy.

Stone Discoids (SE19–22)

Some fifty stone discs or discoids was divided into four size groups (small, medium, large and very

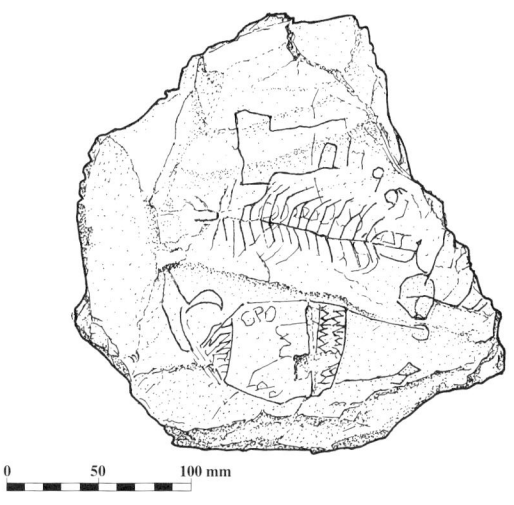

10.111 Graffiti stone (SE18.3)

large; SE19–22). A comparable collection of discoids from the broch and souterrain site at Hurly Hawkin, Angus (Henshall 1982, 233–5) was divided into four types (a–d) dependent on the relative proportions of grinding and flaking applied to the piece. Whithorn has produced none of the more polished types identified in this scheme, most of the objects being roughly chipped discs without the evidence of grinding characterising Henshall's Type d. The only pieces from Whithorn with evidence of grinding or wear round the outer edge (Type c) fall within groups SE19 and SE20, and the only piece with a ground face (SE19.22) is also marked centrally on each face, perhaps drilling guide points in the manufacture of a spindle whorl.

Small discoids (SE19)

The smallest size category comprised twenty-four discoids (SE19.1–24) with diameters ranging from 12.1mm to 31.5mm, of which a third fell into the 22–24mm range. The thicknesses ranged from 1.4mm to 8.0mm, though both these were exceptional pieces, the rest falling into two distinct groups with half the discoids being between 2mm and 3mm thick and another third between 6mm and 7mm. There was no correlation between diameter and thickness, with some smaller discs being up to 6mm thick, and some of the larger ones as thin as 2mm. All the discoids were weighed to assess if they could have been used as weights, but there was little conformity even within the groups of fairly uniform size. Three of the discoids were marked; one (12) with a rough cross on each face, one (5) with scored lines on each face, and a third (22) with a small hole in the centre of each face and a faceted upper surface. This last was the heaviest discoid within the category, and was perhaps an unfinished spindle whorl.

Eight of the discoids had ground edges and may have been used for 'an as yet unidentified rubbing process' (Henshall 1982, 235). The most reasonable interpretation is that the pieces were used as gaming counters, and those with diameters of 22–30mm would fit the gaming boards recovered from the site. The cross-marked discoid (12) might thus have been marked to identify it as different from the rest – *hnefatafl*, for instance, requires one piece to represent a 'king'. However, at Dunadd a stone disc was recovered inscribed with the Christian evocation '*i[n] nomine*' (Christison and Anderson 1905, 311), so a religious connotation is possible.

The chronological distribution of the small discoids is illustrated in Table 10.17 and their spatial distribution in Figure 6.37. Two examples (9 and 16) came from secure **Period IV** contexts, both relatively late, and many of the remainder had been displaced into **Period V** graves presumably from **Period IV** deposits in the *inner precinct* and *outer zone*. A concentration from **Period V** and **VI** contexts in the western part of the northern sector comprised the seven smallest pieces (1–7) which could have been part of a set of playing pieces lost in the inner part of the *inner precinct* in **Period IV** or **V**. A cross-marked discoid (12) came from the builders' waste (630) abutting Building V/4 and a related **Period V/4** context (605) produced a second (19). The gaming pieces seem to have been introduced during the later stages of **Period IV** and Merels boards appeared at roughly the same time, perhaps due to the increasing secularisation of the community.

Medium-sized discoids (SE20)

Sixteen discoids (SE20.1–16) were of intermediate size with diameters from 34mm to 52.6mm, and thicknesses from 3mm to 11.4mm. Although the pieces were spread across this range without any grouping, the category as a whole was distinct from the ones above and below it. Again, weighing the discs gave no areas of conformity. Seven of the discoids had ground edges (see above). Discoids of similar size have been found at Jarlshof (Hamilton 1956, 84; Fig. 55), Kildonan (Fairhurst 1939, 214) and Hurly Hawkin (Henshall 1982, 235; Fig. 9) in contexts dated from the fourth to the tenth century, and some may have been used as rubbers. They may have been used for an outdoor game in which they were thrown or tossed either on the ground or on ice (Foreman 1991d, 108). They seem to be too small for pot lids, the usual interpretation of the larger discoids.

The distribution of the medium-sized discoids contrasts with that of small ones (Table 10.17) arguing that they were not related functionally. Three (3, 8 and 13) came from secure **Period I** contexts, but there were none from **Periods II** and **III**. Most came from the **Period V** graveyard (1, 6, 9, 14) and underlying **Period IV** deposits (2 and 4), and are likely to have originated in the **Period IV** debris which accumulated in the *inner precinct* in the eleventh-thirteenth centuries (Figure 6.37).

Large discoids (SE21)

Eight (1, 3–9) of the nine large discoids (SE21.1–9) had averaged diameters of 75–82mm, the last (2) being slightly smaller at 65mm. The discoids ranged in thickness from 5–22mm, mostly lying between 11mm and 15mm. Similar discoids from the Wheelhouse and Norse phases at Jarlshof (Hamilton 1956, 114) frequently occurred in middens, and were interpreted as pot lids, as were three from Freswick, Caithness (Curle 1939, 107), and one from Kildonan Phase III (Fairhurst 1939, 212). A coarser piece of similar size from Beverley was interpreted as a gaming piece (Foreman 1991d, 108).

The large discoids were widely dispersed in space and time, but were generally relatively late, and there were none from **Periods I** and **II**. One (4) possibly pertained to **Period III** and a second (3) to a relatively late stage in **Period IV**. Two (7 and 8) came from the **Period V** graveyard and were potentially displaced from **Period IV** debris. Two of the remainder (1 and 5) came from builders' waste (605) abutting Building V/4, and a third (9) from a relatively late **Period V** deposit (513) in the **southern sector**. With the possible exception of No.4, they coincide with the currency of pottery, supporting an interpretation as pot lids, although they were too small to have covered any of the excavated vessels with the possible exception of flagons. They could have been used as weights to prevent a lighter covering from being easily dislodged.

	Small discoids		Gaming boards	Medium-sized discoids	
	Well-stratified	Potentially displaced		Well-stratified	Potentially displaced
Topsoil/unstratified		••			••
Period VI		•••		•	
Period V/4–5	•••				
Period V/1–3	••	•••••••••••	#		•••••
Period IV	••		# #	••	
Period III	•				
Period II					
Period 1				•••	

Table 10.17: Incidence of small discoids, medium discoids and gaming boards.

Very large discoid (SE22)

A single broken example of a very large discoid (SE22.1) with an estimated diameter of 150mm was recovered from the **Period V** graveyard. It was also unusually thin (3.1mm) and can reasonably be interpreted as a pot lid subject to the reservations above.

Gaming boards (SE23)

Three stones (SE23.1–3) were recovered with gaming boards incised on one or more faces, and two other stones (SE23.4–5) had incised lines which may be the fragmentary remains of gaming boards. One stone (2) had two merels boards, one incised on each side, whilst another (1) had a single merels board incised on one side. The third piece (3) had a *tafl* board of seven by seven squares, the smallest possible for this range of games which require a central point or space. It is of similar size to the well known wooden board from Ballinderry, and the three incised stone boards from ninth century Norse deposits at Buckquoy, Orkney (Ritchie 1977, 187). It was probably used for playing *Brandubh*, an Irish version of the *tafl* game with a king, or *branan*, in the central spot surrounded by four defenders being beset by eight attacking pieces, or its Norse equivalent *Kotungatafl* (Pennick 1984, 20). The two merels boards came from relatively late **Period IV** contexts in the **southern sector**, one (1) from the rubble bank (414.01) abutting the *Stage 7* buildings, and the other (2) from the drain in Building IV/13. Both were thus probably deposited in the later-twelfth century. The *tafl* board came from the **Period V** graveyard, and may have been displaced from a context of similar date. The two possible board fragments came from earlier contexts, but neither is convincing. Gaming pieces of stone (SE19 and SE 50.1) and antler (AR75) occur from the early stages of **Period III**, but there are two smaller bone pieces (BA15.2 and 15.3) from the **Period II** midden (303). The combined evidence suggests that board games with playing men were rare until the later part of **Period IV**, but continued until the end of the fifteenth century.

Spindle Whorls (SE24–28)

Seventy-two of the ninety-stet spindle whorls from the site were made of stone (Table 10.18), reflecting the abundance of stone in relation to other mediums in the vicinity. The other whorls were made of bone, shale, lead and one possible example in copper alloy. Representative and distinctive whorls are illustrated in Figure 10.113.

The size of a whorl is directly proportional to the length of the spindle, and is of direct bearing upon the type of material and nature of the thread to be spun, with heavier whorls being used for heavier threads, or even twine. The stone spindle whorls (SE24–26) range in weight from 4.1 to 29.0 grams,

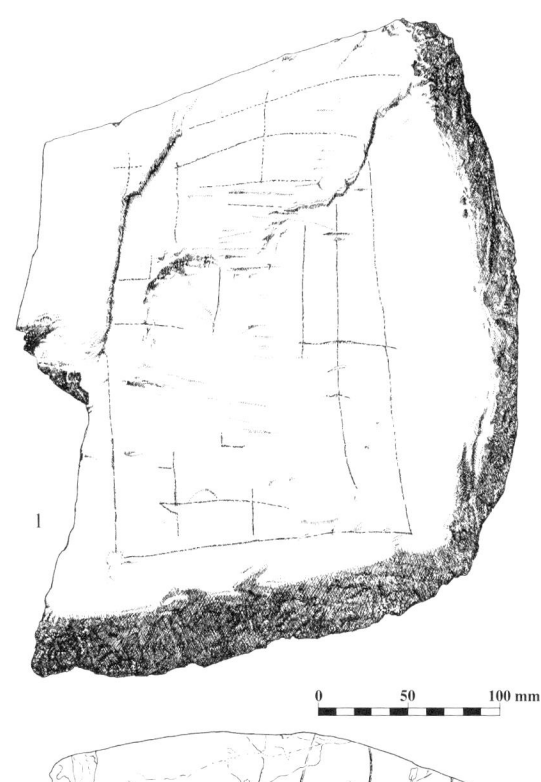

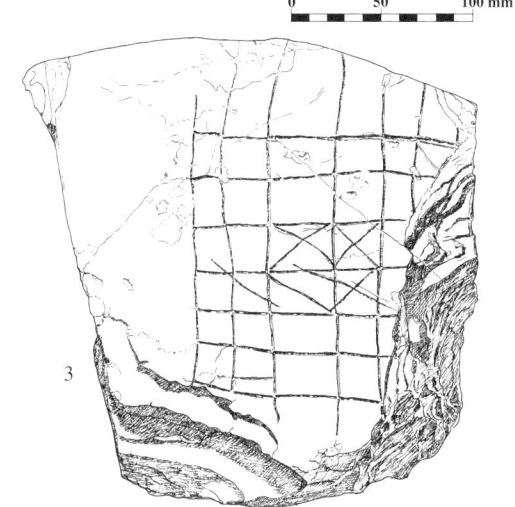

10.112 Gaming boards (SE23).

and are significantly lighter than comparable groups from Beverley (Foreman 1991d, 107), Flaxengate, Lincoln (Mann 1982, 25), and St. Peter's Street, Northampton (Oakley and Hall 1979, 289), suggesting the spinning of finer threads.

Twenty-three whorls (SE24.1–23) had averaged diameters of 36–40mm, though their thicknesses varied, giving weights between 6.35 grams and 29.00 grams for complete whorls. Most were made of sandstone or greywacke, with two examples of mudstone, and a single example of phyllite. A second group of sixteen uniformly-sized (31–35mm diameter) whorls (SE25.1–16) range in weight from 6.8 grams to 14.8 grams, and conforms with the size of the smallest whorls generally found on urban medieval sites. All were made of fine-grained sandstone or greywacke. A third group of fourteen fine-grained sandstone or greywacke whorls (SE26.1–14) was perceptibly smaller, ranging in weight from 4.1 grams to 11.05 grams. Six exceptionally small perforated discs (SE27.1–6) weighed between 1.25 grams and 1.9 grams. These may have been stone button cores, but they generally display wear patterns consistent with use as whorls. All but one are made of very fine-grained greywacke, the other being fine-grained sandstone. Twelve atypical whorls (SE28.1–12) comprised six decorated whorls (1–3, 5, 11 and 12), two (4 and 9) made of kaolinite, three unfinished (6, 7 and 10) and one (8) of unusual form, though made of the normal fine-grained greywacke. Several of the whorls which were included in this category on other criteria were also of unusual form. Decoration took a variety of forms, mostly involving incised lines on the upper surface. In most cases this was fairly crude, with only one example (SE28.5) of well-cut concentric circles, three in number, about the central perforation (although this pattern was repeated on the possible bronze whorl). This whorl has an atypical plano-convex profile, and the other decorated whorls were flat discs, as were the vast majority of the undecorated pieces. The two kaolinite whorls were asymmetrically bi-conical and there was a single example of a symmetrically biconical whorl (SE28.8).

The distributions of the various groups of whorls display clear trends despite the considerable problems of displacement (Table 10.18). Examples were rare from **Periods I** and **II**, and relatively few came from secure contexts after the start of **Period V**. The whorls in SE24 were concentrated in **Period IV** contexts, but had already appeared in **Period III** and a single example pertains to the end of **Period I**. The six examples from the **Period V** graveyard were probably displaced from **Period IV** debris which may have been the ultimate origin of three later examples. The small whorls (SE26) show a similar pattern to those in SE24. The intermediate whorls (SE25) show a significantly different distribution with no examples from **Period IV** contexts, and three from potentially secure **Period V** deposits. These could thus be contemporary with the graveyard. The unusually small whorls (SE27) were concentrated in a restricted part of the **Period V** graveyard, indicating a specialised craft involving fine spinning practised in the *inner precinct* in **Period IV** (Figure 6.28). The distribution of the anomalous whorls (SE28) does not conform closely with those of the other types. Two of the decorated whorls came from early deposits (2, 330 and 5, 399.02) and two others (3, 631 and 1, 704) came from potentially-secure **Period V/4–5** contexts from which plain whorls were absent. Decoration may thus characterise periods when spinning was a rare activity. The three most complex decorated pieces (5, 11 and 12) are all of fine-grained sandstone, and although generally smaller, may fit into a group of decorated whorls from ecclesiastical sites in Dumfriesshire (Williams 1966), and provide a possible date range for these unstratified finds. Two of the unfinished whorls came from a late **Period IV** context in the *inner precinct* (6, 407.04) and a **Period V** grave (7, 539), and so indicate one of the many activities in this area during **Period IV**. The third (10) came from Building II/6 (254), and is one of a small group of unusual whorls from **Period II** contexts. The two finely-finished kaolinite whorls are of particular interest. The Kaolinite derives from fireclays in Upper Carboniferous strata to the west of Loch Ryan, and there is an exposure at Low Knockglass to the south-west of Stranraer. Other objects and object blanks from this source have been recovered from Hoddom, Barhobble and Torrs Warren,[12] and there are thus no good grounds for linking the Whithorn whorls to Romano-British objects of Lithomarge or Kaolinite reported by Stevenson (1976). One (4) came from a poorly stratified context (529) in the **Fey Field**, but is likely to have been among the thirteenth century material predominating there. The other (9) came from the topsoil in the northern part of the **southern sector**, but could easily have been originated in a deposit of similar date.

SE24

15* Fine-grained, greywacke, spindle whorl with no wear on centre perforation

D 38 Hole D 8 Wt 12.8 **719**

SE25

11* Conically perforated disc of fine-grained greywacke, larger flat faces formed along natural bedding planes, circumference chipped

[12] We are grateful to W.F. Cormack for this information in advance of publication.

	SE24	SE25	SE26	SE27	SE28	SH04	BA06	LD03	Total
Topsoil/unstratified	•	•••	•••		K			••	10
Period VI	••			•					3
Period V/4–5	••	••		•	DD			•	8
Period V/1–3	••••••••	••••••••	••••	•••	KU	•	•••	••••••••	35
Period IV	••••••••		•••••	•	DDU	•	••	•	20
Period III	•••	••	••		D		•		9
Period II					D•U			•	4
Period I	•	•			•			•	4
Total	23	16	14	6	13	2	6	13	93

Table 10.18: Distributions of spindle whorls
SE = Stone; **SH** = Shale; **BA** = Bone; **LD** = Lead
D = decorated, **U** = unfinished, **K** = Kaoilinite.

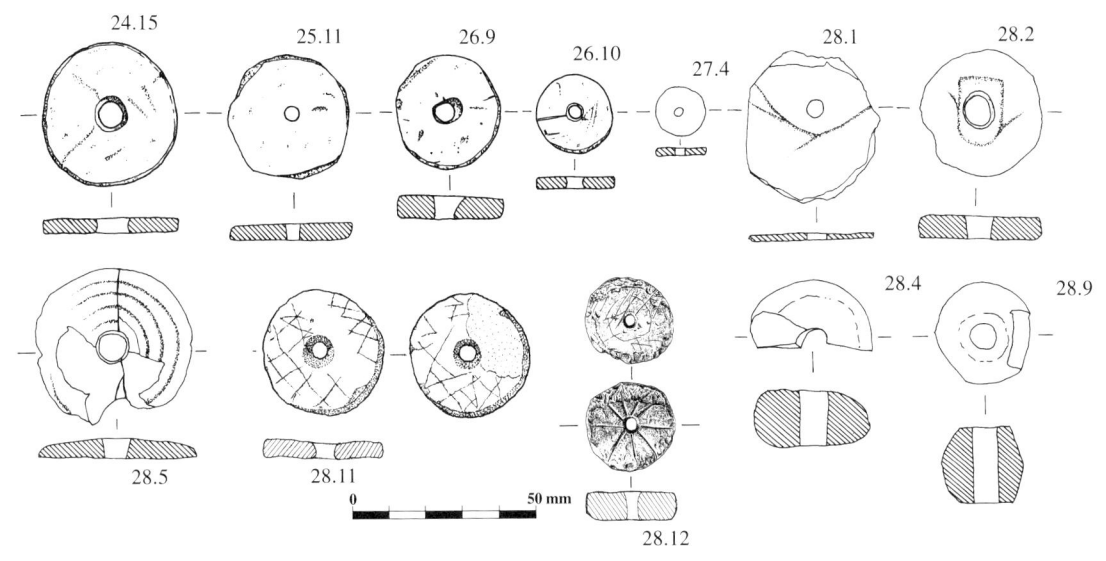

10.113 Stone spindle whorls (SE24–28).

and partly ground in short facets to produce approximately octagonal plan; central perforation asymmetrically placed.
L 33 W 5 T 4 **427.01**

SE26

9* Biconically perforated disc of fine-grained light reddish brown micaceous sandstone. Approximately circular, with 2 flat facets more or less diametrically opposite on circumference, which is completely ground. Both faces are on natural, bedding, planes, parallel. Perforation more or less central. Abraded and scratched.
ED 30 ID 8 T 6. Wt 6.9 **400**

10 Biconically perforated disc of yellow-brown, fine-grained micaceous sandstone, very nearly circular, edges and faces ground.
ED 20 ID 5 T 3.7. Wt 5.7 **923**

SE27

4* Flat circular very fine-grained greywacke disc with vertical central hole.
ED 13.4 ID 2.7 T 2.2. Wt 1.25 **539**

SE28

1* Flat rough disc of fine-grained greywacke with vertical off-centre hole. Three connecting incised grooves on one face.
ED 40.9 × 37.7 ID 5.3 T 2.0. Wt 8.75 **704**

2* Flat thick sub-circular fine-grained sandstone disc with conical central hole surrounded by incised lines on one face.
ED 34.0 × 32.5 ID 8.4 × 6.1 T 6.0 Wt 11.0 **330**

3 Fragment of large flat sub-circular medium-grained sandstone disc with biconical central hole ringed at 3mm by an incised groove.
ED 54.9 ID 11.5 × 7.3 T 10.1. Wt 22.95 **631**

4* Fragment of Kaolinite whorl with convex upper and lower surfaces. Vertical central hole.
ED 19.5 × 32.4 × 18.1 ID 7.9 T 15.2 Wt 15.6 **529**

5* Two conjoined fragments of a decorated, fine-grained sandstone whorl. The lower face is flat and undecorated, whilst the upper surface is convex, more so at the edge and flattening towards the centre. The conical central hole is ringed by four concentric, evenly-spaced incised grooves, possibly created by turning the whorl on a lathe.
ED 43.3 ID 8.2 × 5.2 T 5.0 × 2.8 Wt 8.0 **399.02, 911**

6 Flat sub-circular disc of fine-grained sandstone with central conical hole (incomplete biconical perforation?). Probably unfinished whorl.
ED 40.5 × 36.3 ID 5.6 T 4.9. Wt 16.0 **407.04**

7 Flat roughly elliptical disc of very fine-grained greywacke with two off-centre conical holes (incomplete biconical perforations?). Unfinished whorl.
ED 36.1 × 31.0 ID 5.2 and 2.4 T 4.7 × 3.5 Wt 9.75 **539**

8 Large flat sub-circular very fine-grained greywacke disc with large biconical central hole.
ED 53.0 × 44.5 ID 18.1 × 15.6 T 5.0 Wt 23.0 **303**

9* Chipped biconical Kaolinite whorl with vertical central hole.
ED 14.2 × 22.7 × 14.5 ID 7.0 T 19.9 Wt 19.95 **744**

10 Flat, sub-circular disc, with a blind perforation on each face. The holes are misaligned for a true perforation. One perforation is 11.3mm wide by 4mm deep, the other 12.1mm wide by 7mm deep.
ED 43.7 Th 17.8 Wt 44.4 **254**

11* Very regular disc of fine-grained micaceous grey sandstone with conical perforation, edges ground perpendicular to faces, slightly convex, faces ground flat and parallel. Each face is decorated with a complex design of incised lines, 0.5 wide, V-sectioned.
ED 30 ID 8 T 6 Wt 10.15 **490**

12* Biconically-perforated discoid of fine-grained brown/grey micaceous sandstone. Both faces almost completely ground flat. The circumference has been chipped and flaked to an approximately circular outline, then ground in 7 short facets, angles also rounded. Both faces bear incised markings as decoration, one having 9 nearly regularly disposed radial grooves from perforation to circumference, one of which continues over the edge to meet a single radial groove on the other side. This groove cuts a more or less concentric, approximately circular scratch which surrounds the perforation at 5–11mm from its edge. The nine obverse radial grooves are V-sectioned, c 2mm and 1mm deep, the single one on the reverse being less than 1mm wide and deep, and consisting of a single cut, rather than the repeated scorings of the others.
ED 52 ID 15 T 5. Wt 48.1 **428.02**

'Loom weights' (SE29)

Twelve objects (SE29.1–12) were classified as loom weights by the analogy with discoveries elsewhere, although this identification does not accord well with the circumstantial evidence. Most were thick, roughly-shaped discs of greywacke or sandstone, with central biconical drilled holes (7mm to 21mm diameter). Two (5 and 10) were rounded water-worn pebbles of fine-grained greywacke with central biconical holes, and two others (2 and 9) were carefully fashioned toroids, one (9) of fine-grained greywacke, and the other (2) of coarse-grained sandstone. The latter shape is paralleled by a tenth century baked clay example from Coppergate, York (Hall 1984, 98).

Five 'loom weights' (1, 4, 5, 9 and 11) came from **Period I** contexts, another (10) from construction (247.01) at the start of **Period II**, probably originated in **Period I** debris, and a seventh (3) came from a **Period II** building. The three examples (2, 12 and 13) from the **Period V** graveyard came from areas in the **northern sector** where the graves were dug into the displaced metalworking debris used in the construction of the Northumbrian church, and may have originated in it. The two remaining examples (6 and 7) came from the **Period V/3** surface (7, 616.07) and the debris abutting Building V/4 (6, 605). Ten of the 'loom weights' can thus be ascribed to **Period I**, but evidence of spinning (Table 10.18) and woolworking (IN62) at this time was sparse, while the faunal remains indicate that sheep were scarce (pp 605-7). There were no stratified 'loom weights' from **Period III** and **IV** contexts in which spindle whorls and wool heckles (IN62) were relatively abundant and sheep more common. The weights were moreover widely scattered (Figure 10.116a), and so contrast with the clusters or lines of weights identifying stored looms or weaving sheds at Jarlshof (Hamilton 1956, 113), West Stow 3 and Mucking 84 (Arnold 1988 Fig 2.3). The toroid stones (2 and 9) are similar to bellows protectors, but there is no single convincing interpretation for these pieces.

9* Transversely and horizontally fractured fragment of ovoid, fine-grained greywacke 'loom weight' with biconical central hole.
D 64 × c. 70 Hole D 6 Wt 70.5 **247.01**

Discs with multiple perforations (SE30)

Five stone discs with multiple perforations (SE30.1–5) include two complete objects (2 and 3), one broken (1), and two fragments (4 and 5). Two (1 and 2) had central biconical drilled holes of a larger size than the peripheral holes, and may originally have been spindle whorls, though the central holes reveal rotational wear, which may have been integral to their later function. The broken piece (1) has evidence of three peripheral biconical holes (c. 2.5mm diameter), and the spacing indicates a missing fourth. One intact disc (2) has two opposing trimmed sides, with three peripheral holes of 2.0mm to 2.5mm diameter around one curve, and two peripheral holes opposite. The other intact disc (3) has three off-centre holes (2.5mm diameter) set in a triangular pattern. While these pieces may have been used for tablet weaving, the use of stone is unusual, and

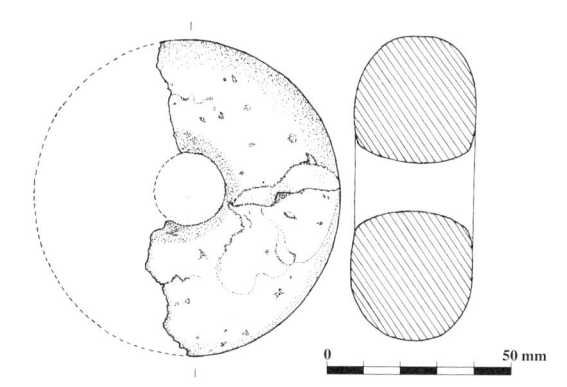

10.114 'Loom weight' (SE 29.9).

examples from other sites are made of leather, wood or bone (Collingwood 1982, 24–7, Pl. 2–7). A more probable use would have been for plying thread or cord, with the ends of the strands secured, a strand through each small hole, and the disc being turned to impart the necessary twist to the yarn/cord. This twisted cord could then be tightened using a heavy whorl. Three of the discs (1, 4 and 5) came from the **Period V** graveyard, and presumably originated in the underlying **Period IV** debris, pointing to a specialised craft practised in the *inner precinct* and *outer zone* at this time (Figure 6.37). A fourth (2) was unstratified, and the last (3) came from the path (236.01) around the **Period I.12** buildings in the **southern sector**.

1* Fragment of perforated fine-grained sandstone disc. Central hole, two complete outer and one partially complete outer hole survive. Central hole 4.5mm diameter, outer holes 2.5mm. A fourth outer hole may be conjectured for the missing portion. All the holes are biconical and show signs of wear, as does the outer edge. Whether the central hole is contemporary with the outer ones is uncertain; the item may be a re-used spindle whorl with the central hole being the original. If the item were used for plying or tablet weaving, the central hole would have been used for securing the tablets together, if the operation was to be interrupted.
D 23.9 T 6.0 **541**

2* Very fine-grained greywacke disc with two opposing sides trimmed to straight edges. Ovoid central hole, with three small outer holes near one curved edge, and two holes near the other. Central hole biconical, 8mm × 6.2mm with high degree of wear. Outer holes biconical, dia. 1.8–2.6mm, with little sign of wear. No indication if the central and outer holes are contemporary. The piece may be a re-used spindle whorl. Length measurement may have been original diameter.
L 41.5 W 36.0 T 5.3. Wt 12.8 **903**

3* Ovoid very fine-grained greywacke disc with three perforations in a triangle. Biconical holes 2.5mm diameter, offset from centre. Distance between hole centres 11.3–13.1mm. Upper surface has partially fractured off on both faces; the surviving portion on one face shows a series of small parallel striations, which may be wear marks. Probably used for plying wool or twine.
D 51.5 × 45.4 T 4.1. Wt 17.2 **236.01**

4 Fragment of very fine-grained sandstone disc with three perforations. All three perforations are biconical, but only partially survive. Two diameters can be estimated, at 6mm and 4.5mm, but too little of the third survives. A V-section groove is roughly cut round one of the perforations.
D 13.8 T 6.2. Wt 6.9 **537**

5 Fragment of very fine-grained greywacke disc with three possible perforations. Only a small portion of the outer edge

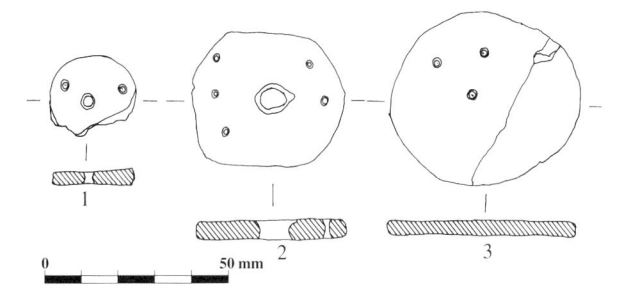

10.115 Discs with multiple perforations (SE30).

survives, but it is slightly curved; a curved inner edge may be part of a perforation. One of the other perforations is biconical, with a diameter of 2.8mm, while the third is straight, with one slightly conical end, and a diameter of 3.4mm.

L 24.6 W 23.7 T 8.7. Wt 4.2 **535**

Perforated stones (SE31)

Five stones, each with a single perforation (SE31.1–5), did not conform to any of the above types and were grouped separately. Two (1 and 2) may have been intended for use as spindle whorls, but were too irregular in shape to attribute to any of the whorl categories. Two (3 and 4) were small rectilinear plates, fractured transversely across the perforation. The last (5) from a **Period I/3** rubbish deposit (109) was originally interpreted as a fragment of a loom weight. It is of comparable thickness, but unlike the others the hole has only been drilled from one side, and there are indications of a fair degree of rotational wear. It may have been used in a furnace to shield the bellows from the heat, the tuyere fitting through the central perforation.

1 Broken, thin, rectilinear, phyllite flake with ovoid perforation – 6.9mm long. Curved edge indicates it may be an unfinished whorl or disc.

L 35.0 W 21.1 T 2.6. Wt 3.6 **212.02**

2 Broken, rectilinear, fine-grained sandstone fragment with biconical perforation – 5.3mm diameter. Possible unfinished whorl.

L 41.0 W 31.8 T 8.4. Wt 9.5 **506.01**

3 Broken, triangular, fine-grained greywacke flake with conical perforation – 3.6mm diameter.

L 54.6 W 34.0 T 5.8. Wt 14.2 **615.02**

4 Broken, flat, angular phyllite flake with small hole.

L 14 W 11 T 1.8 Hole D 2.7 Wt 0.4 **246**

5 Medium-grained greywacke fragment with concave quarter circle wear pattern which could be a central perforation of a 'loom weight'.

Width/radius c 40 T 15 Wt 35.4 **109**

Hones (SE32–38)

The local availability of sandstones and greywackes of varying degrees of coarseness obviated the need to import hones, although exotic hard very-fine-grained stones (quartzites and porphyry) were still required for burnishers and fine polishers (pp 456-8). The hones were thus classified by morphology rather than geology, unlike the assemblages from most comparable sites of the period. Indeed only one manufactured hone of phyllite, two hones of mudstone (still probably local), and one modern carborundum hone, contrasted with twenty-seven hones of sandstone and sixty-four of greywacke. Forty of the hones (SE35.1–14 and SE38.1–26) utilised natural rounded elongated beach cobbles of sandstone and greywacke, and sixty-five similar stones (SE71.1–65) with little or no evidence of use were presumably gathered from the local beaches for use as hones, and are classified as 'hone blanks' (SE71). These manifest a similar geological range with thirty-four of sandstone, thirty of greywacke and one of siltstone. The remaining hones are quadrilateral, and encompass carefully shaped artefacts (SE33 and 36) and utilized natural pieces of rock (SE32, 34 and 37). Comparanda for these hones can be found on most similar sites, both rural and urban (e.g. York, Beverley, Northampton, Winchester, Jarlshof, Hurly Hawkin). In most cases suitable local stones are used as well as imported hones, thus whilst there are few hones directly comparable to the naturally-rounded elongated cobbles, their local equivalents are present. The notable exceptions are the bar hones (SE32), which are only recorded on the urban sites, and may therefore relate to a degree of urban craft and industrial specialisation.

The chronological distributions of hones (Table 10.19) reveal clear patterns, and spatial analysis helps to identify workshop areas within the evolving **monasterium** (Figure 10.116). There was a concentration of hones in **Period I**, and they were sparse in **Period II**, **V** and **VI** deposits. Large hones (SE32–35) were particularly abundant in **Period I**, and these were concentrated in the western part of the **northern sector** (Figure 10.116a) where they were associated with metalworking debris and other implements. There was a smaller cluster in the outer part of the *outer zone*. There was a significant concentration of large and small hones in the debris scattered around the **Period III** *minster* (309.02, 438), while the contemporary buildings only produced small hones. Hones – and large hones in particular- were strikingly under-represented in the **Period V** graveyard, pointing to a range of activities (smithying, tool repair) which were not pursued in the *inner precinct* in **Period IV** (Figures 6.23, 10.116b).

Bar hones (SE32)

Twelve hones (SE32.1–12) were so large as to be practically non-portable. Seven were greywacke and five sandstone; all were of medium- or fine-grained stone. Another greywacke bar hone (SE50.11) re-used a pecked shaft. Because of their size only two of these hones utilised beach cobbles, and the remainder

	Bar hones		Large hones			Small hones	
	SE32	SE33	SE34	SE35	SE36	SE37	SE38
Topsoil/unstratified	•••	•		••	••		••••
Period VI					•		••
Period V/4–5					•		•
Period V/1–3		•	••		••••	••	
Period IV	•	•		•••	••••		•••••
Period III	••	•	•	•••	••••		••
Period II		•		••	••		•
Period I	••••••	••	••••	••••	••••••	•••	••••••••••••

Table 10.19: Chronological distribution of hones.

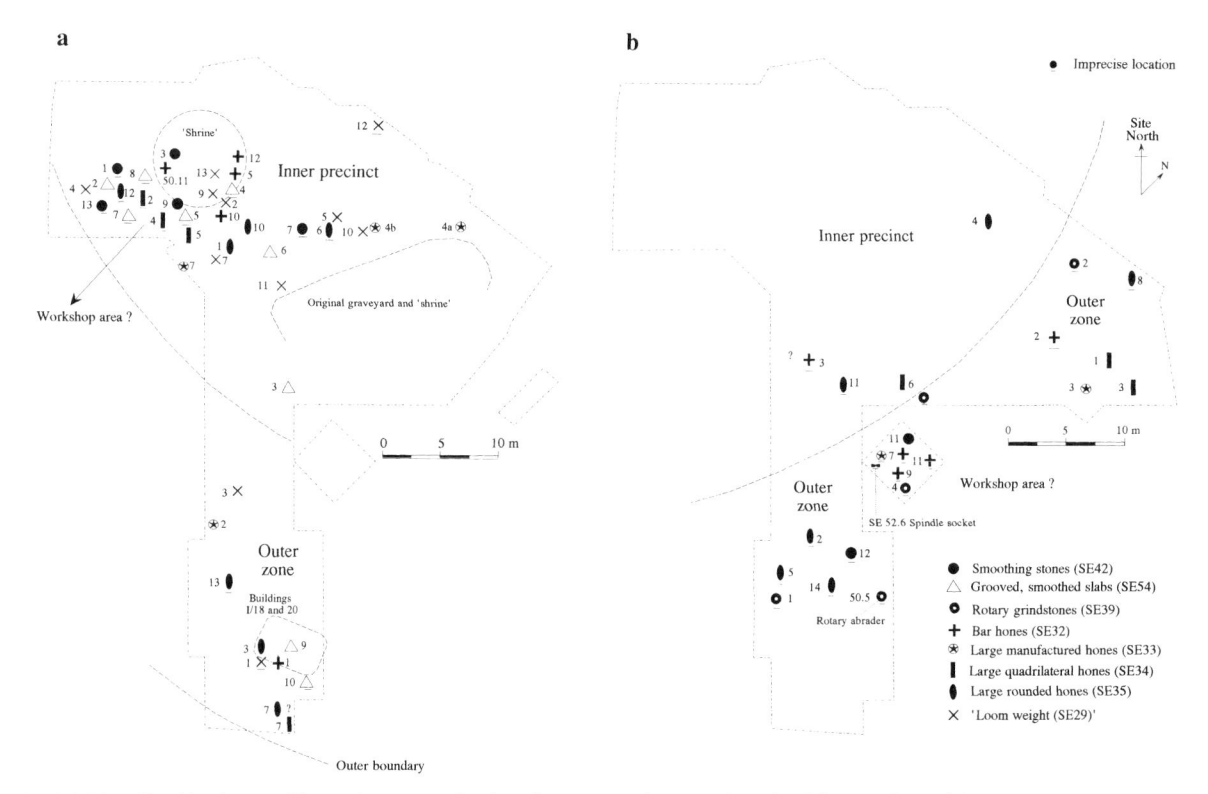

10.116 The distributions of large hones and related stone tools associated with metal working.
a Finds ascribed to **Period I**. **b** Finds ascribed to **Periods III** and **IV**.

were natural quadrilateral sections of stone. They were mostly unworked, though three had been trimmed with their ends rounded off, and could thus be defined as manufactured. A sandstone hone (12) possibly reused a fragment of architectural stone. The bar hones can be interpreted as workshop equipment. Four (5, 10, 12 and 50.11) came from **Period I** deposits in the western part of the **northern sector** (Figure 10.116a), and two others (6 and 8) were recovered from this area after the excavation ceased. These probably originated in the workshops believed to lie beyond the trench. A second group (7, 9 and 11) from the **southern sector** included two from the **Period III** pond silts (309.02), and all probably originated in the debris surrounding the **Period III** *minster* (Figure 10.116b). A ninth (1) came from Building I/24 and the remaining three (2–4) were unstratified.

Large manufactured hones (SE33)

Seven large deliberately shaped hones (SE33.1–7) generally had quadrilateral cross-sections, and squared or rounded ends. Though cumbersome, these would have been portable, and this was confirmed by a biconical-conical hole for a suspension loop on one (1). Four of these hones were of sandstone and two of greywacke. The seventh (4) has one end of fine-grained greywacke and the other of fine-grained sandstone, and was perhaps selected intentionally from a geological interface to exploit the different abrasive qualities of the two rock types. These hones were generally more worn than the other large hones (SE34 and 35) indicating that the manufactured hones were used in preference to the unshaped natural rocks. Most of the hones had been used on both of the broader faces, and sometimes the edges as well. Three of the hones (5, 6 and 7) had V-section longitudinal grooves down the centre of a broad face. These used to be interpreted as point sharpeners, but experimental attempts have failed to do anything other than round off a point. The hones were again concentrated in early contexts (Table 10.19) with two (4 and 7) from **Period I** deposits and a third (2), possibly displaced from a **Period I** context (Figure 10.116a). One of the others (6) came from the **Period III** debris surrounding the *minster*, and a second (3) from a **Period V** grave, may have been displaced from a contemporary deposit to the east (Figures 6.23, 10.116b). A last hone (1) from mid-ninth century debris (408.01) in the **Museum Garden** conforms with this pattern of deposition in the *outer zone*.

Large natural quadrilateral hones (SE34)

Seven rough blocks of split rock (SE34.1–7), five of greywacke and two of sandstone, had been utilised as hones. In most cases only a single face was worn, and this suggests the casual use of locally available material. The hones were again concentrated in seventh century contexts with four (2, 4, 5 and 7) from **Period I** (Figure 10.116a), of which two (4 and 5) came from industrial debris of **Period I/3** (85.02), a third (2) from late rubble (90) in the same area, and the fourth (7) from the waterborne silts (58) in the **southern sector**. Two later finds (1 and 3) from the south east corner of the **Period V** graveyard, were probably displaced from **Period III** or **IV** deposits (Figures 6.23, 10.116b). The other (6) came from paving in a **Period III** building (III/41).

Large natural rounded hones (SE35)

Fourteen large naturally-rounded hones (SE35.1–14) utilised beach cobbles of which eleven were greywacke and three sandstone. Nine were of fine-grained stone which was probably selected intentionally. As with the natural quadrilaterals, only one broad face of the stone tended to have been utilised for sharpening. These hones were again concentrated in early contexts (Figure 10.116a), but show a wider chronological spread than the other large hones (Table 10.19) with more examples (Figure 10.116b) from **Periods III** (2, 4 and 11) and **IV** (5, 8 and 14). The latter group included two (3 and 14) from the *Stage 7* buildings in the **southern sector**, which also produced a concentration of 'hone blanks'

Small manufactured hones (SE36)

The second largest category of hones comprised twenty-four small manufactured hones (SE36.1–24), including five of sandstone, sixteen of greywacke, one of phyllite, one of mudstone, and a modern carborundum stone (24). Eighteen were of fine-grained stone, and one (13) of very-fine-grained phyllite. These small portable stones would have been used to put a finished edge on blades such as knives and razors. Three of the hones (1, 2, and 8) were pierced for suspension loops, whilst two others (3 and 5) had incomplete perforations. As with the larger manufactured hones (SE33), these showed signs of use on more than one face and at the edges. This relatively intensive use was reflected in the fact that seventeen of the hones were broken, a rate three times that of the equivalent naturally-rounded hones (SE38). The chronological distribution (Table 10.19) shows a wider spread than for the large hones, but most (save the carborundum stone) were probably earlier than **Period V**. Eight (33.3%) of the hones came from buildings, suggesting that they were personal equipment rather than workshop tools. Three (5, 13, and 14) of the five examples from **Period V** contexts came from the western end of the **northern sector** (Figure 6.23), and could have been displaced from the underlying **Period III** buildings.

Small, quadrilateral hones (SE37)

A small group of five hones (SE37.1–5), four of which were broken, utilised small flakes cleft from larger blocks. In most cases only one surface, usually a broad face, was used. Three of the pieces were fine-grained greywacke, and two medium-grained sandstone. Two (4 and 5) came from the **Period V** graveyard, the remaining three (1–3) from **Period I/3** industrial debris (3, 85.04) and adjacent graves (82.04; 1, Grave I/113 and 2, Grave I/115).

Small natural rounded hones (SE38)

The largest group of hones (SE38.1–26) comprised twenty-six small naturally-rounded beach cobbles. They displayed a similar geological range to the manufactured hones, with nineteen of greywacke, six of sandstone, and one of mudstone, seventeen of which were fine-grained. These pieces were rather more worn than the larger rounded hones (SE35), although generally with less wear than the small manufactured hones (SE36). They were again concentrated in early deposits (**Periods I–IV**) with a large group (2, 3, 13, 16, 18, 23) from the **Period I/3** industrial debris (85.02) and intrusive graves (82.04). Only three (11%) examples (6, 17 and 20) came from buildings, and these utilised cobbles were perhaps not treated as personal equipment, unlike the small manufactured hones. There were none from the **Period V** graveyard, and they were less widely distributed than the 'hone blanks'.

SE32

8* Transversely fractured fine-grained, greywacke bar hone (now in 2 pieces) of sub-rectangular section with tapering rounded ends. One broad face shows clear evidence of use as a hone, the others less so. Concave indentations at one end indicate secondary use as a hammerstone.

L 271 W 63 T 32 **904**

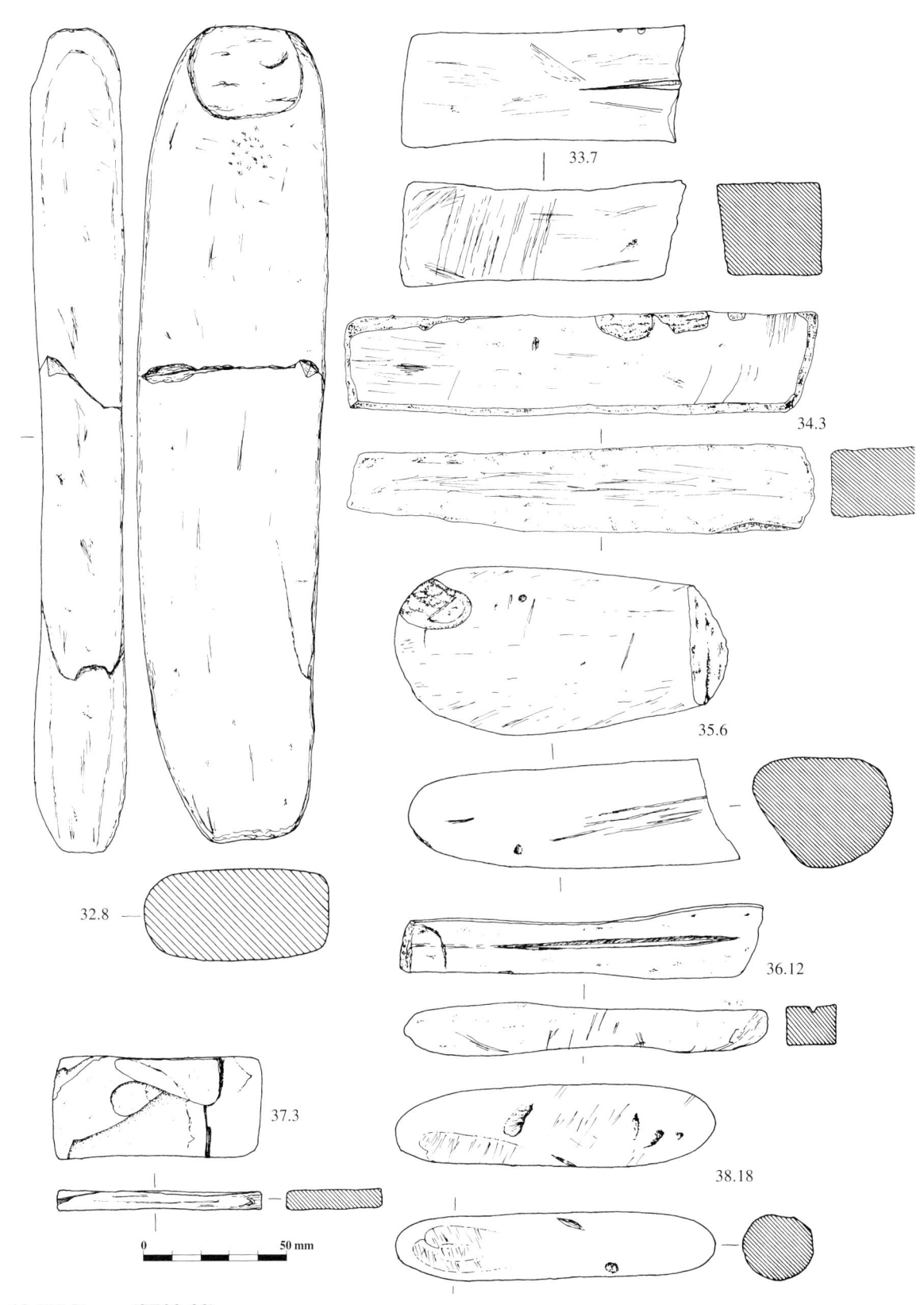

10.117 Hones (SE32–38).

SE33

7* Large manufactured sandstone hone. Part (approximately two-thirds) of a square-sectioned hone, three of the long faces worn very smooth and slightly concave longitudinally, the remaining one partly ground, and scratched subsequent to this. The surviving end has been squared off along a natural fracture plane by pecking; on the face opposite the partly ground one. Two parallel, V-sectioned grooves extend from the fractured edge longitudinally down the face, the larger groove being approximately central 32mm long, 2mm wide × 1mm deep, tapering to a fine score, towards the squared-off end. The other groove is fainter 22mm long, 1mm wide, 0.5mm deep, also tapering in the same direction and finishing 6mm nearer the edge. One of the vertices of the squared-off end is bevelled off, mainly on the partly grooved face. The two long edges joining the 3 main faces are quite sharp and right-angled, the two joining the partly ground face to the others being bevelled off.

L 94 W 38 T 30 **82.05**

SE34

3* Broken large natural quadrilateral, greywacke hone. Rectangular section hone. Two faces and both ends roughly dressed, the other two faces show degrees of wear, the broad face being worn slightly concave. The narrow worn face has a pair of small (9mm and 13mm) longitudinal grooves.

L 161 W 34 T 25 **535**

SE35

6* Large natural rounded fine-grained greywacke hone. Transversely fractured stone with rounded end. Flattish face evidences slight wear, one side has a series of longitudinal grooves associated with sharpening.

L 111 W 57 T 38 **73.02**

SE36

12* Small manufactured sandstone hone. Rectangular section. Narrow longitudinal groove in the centre of one of the broad faces, extending three quarters of the length.

L 125 W 30 T 19 **414.02**

SE37

3* Broken small natural quadrilateral fine-grained greywacke hone. Small stone with squared ends, horizontally fractured (possibly deliberately) on one face. Both faces and sides slightly concave with wear. The chipped face shows a degree of polish in its undamaged areas.

L 72 W 33 T 10 **85.04**

SE38

18* Small natural rounded fine-grained greywacke hone. Elongated rounded pebble with one artificially flattened face. Flattened face evidences longitudinal wear, whilst adjacent edge shows small transverse grooves.

L 110 W 28 T 22 **85.02**

Rotary grindstones (SE39)

Four fragments of rotary grindstones (SE39.1–4) were all made of sandstone of a slightly coarser grain than was generally chosen for hones. They may have been used to put the initial edge on a blade, with the hones used in gradually finer grades to produce a clean edge. Anglo-Scandinavian parallels are known from Coppergate (Roesdahl et al. 1981, YDL 4–6), Lloyds Bank (MacGregor 1982, 76) and Parliament Street (Tweddle 1986, 184) in York. All four came from areas producing large hones (Figure 10.116b). Two came from rubbish mixed with pond silts in the **southern sector**, one (4) from **Period III** (309.02) and the other (1) from the latter part of **Period IV** (415.01). A third (2) from the **Period V** graveyard, probably originated in **Period IV** debris in the south-east part of the *outer zone*, and the fourth (3) fell from the side of the trench in the same area.

1 Fragment of large pink/brown sandstone rotary grindstone. Circumference worn uniformly more to one edge than the other. Fire damage occurred after breakage.

ED 392. ID 62 T 63 **415.01**

2 Fragment of medium-grained sandstone, rotary grindstone. Circumference worn smooth, internal hole biconical roughly dressed, off centre.

ED 204 ID 74 T 27.5 **543**

3* Fragment of sandstone, rotary grindstone. 93.0 × 60.0mm by 54.0mm deep. Distance from grinding surface to centre hole – 50–60mm. Projected diameter – 165.0mm.

L 93 W 60 T51 **902**

4* Fragment of red sandstone rotary grindstone. Segment of a perforated disc of old red sandstone, flat faces formed along

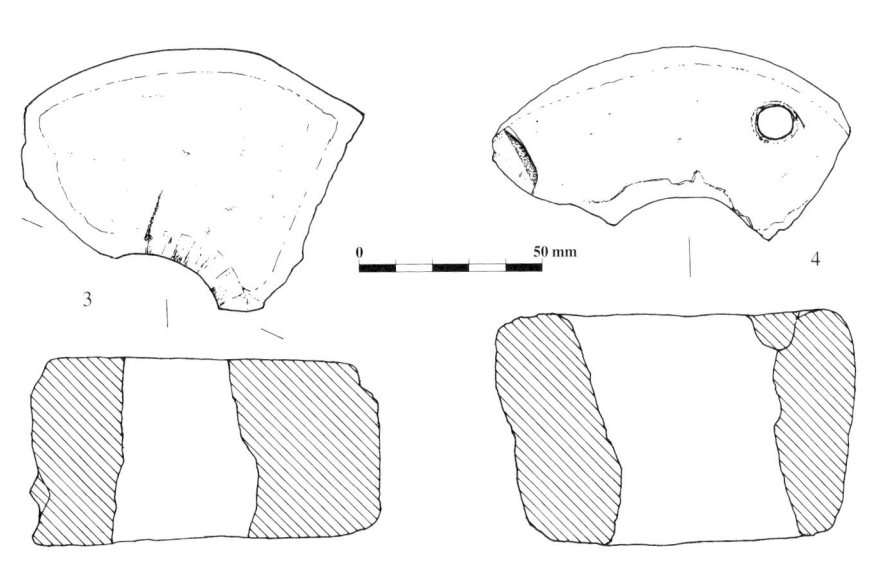

10.118 Rotary grindstones (SE39)

natural laminations, one original to piece, one a fracture plane. Two radial breaks, transverse, define *c.* 50 degrees of circumference, the profile of which is very slightly convex. The central perforation is irregular, presumably to key in with drive shaft, possibly 60–70mm in diameter, inner surface retains pockmarks of original cutting out, and tapers slightly inwards from surviving original face.

Proj. D150 T 24 **309.02**

Quadrilateral burnishers (SE40)

Six small, quadrilateral burnishers (SE40.1–6) were all finished to a high degree, with evenly cambered sides tapering towards each end, and with carefully bevelled edges at each end. Five quartzite ones (2–6) are sub-rectangular, whilst a sixth of porphyry (1) is of evenly diminishing square section. Slight wear on the longitudinal edges and on opposed corners at the ends indicates use for rubbing or polishing. Unlike the hones there were no significant striations on the faces, suggesting that they were not fine hones for use on blades. The hardness of the rock and its smooth texture means that these small well-finished implements would have been ideally suited as burnishers, and could, for example, have been used to polish enamel or gems, or to burnish gold, silver, or pattern welding. They are comparable in form to one from the Norse levels at Jarlshof, Shetland (Curle 1935, 300, Fig. 33, No. 7), and can also be compared with a more elongated example from early-fourteenth century levels at Canal Street, Perth (Blanchard 1984, 510, 511 Fig. 14, No. 3). Parallels for the quartzite are found on wheelhouse sites in north-western Scotland. A single porphyritic example of similar form and date was found at Freswick (C. Batey, Pers. Comm.). The quartzite probably originates to the north of the Highland fault, but the burnishers could have been produced locally from glacial erratics or beach deposits. Their manufacture would have involved considerable work and the intelligent use of abrasives starting with varying grades of sand, and finishing with a rock of equal hardness.

The three securely-stratified burnishers (3, 4, and 6) came from late **Period IV** contexts, two (3 and 4) from the mixed debris and pond silts (415.01) in the **southern sector**, and one (6) from the uppermost surviving deposits (450, Table 6.28) in the east corner of the trench. A fourth (5) from insecurely-stratified **Period IV** deposits (427.03) in Trench 2 was relatively close to the find-spot of No. 6, and the remaining two (1 and 2) came from the **Period V** graveyard. This was, thus, a relatively tight group, perhaps dating to the mid- to late-twelfth century, and indicating a specialised craft spanning the *inner precinct* and *outer zone* (Figure 6.30, pp 240, 243). The burnishers coincided broadly with scattered debris pointing to fine metalwork and enamelling (Figures 6.24 and 31), and could have been associated with either craft.

1* Manufactured quadrilateral porphyry (possibly quartzite) burnisher. Polished stone of sub-square section. The faces are convex in longitudinal and transverse planes, creating an even taper towards both, well finished, ends. The surfaces are all highly polished and smooth. Faint striations on all four main faces are longitudinal. Two opposing corners at the ends show more wear than the others, and would conform to a use as a fine rubbing stone.
L 59 W 13.6 T 13.5. Wt 23.0 **539**

2* Manufactured quadrilateral quartzite, burnisher. Smooth ovoid stone with two parallel straight longitudinal sides. The broad faces are convex in longitudinal and transverse planes, while the narrow faces are convex in the longitudinal plane only. The surfaces are all polished and smooth. Faint striations on the two broad faces are transverse, whilst the narrow faces evince no discernible markings.
L 64.5 W 28 T 14. Wt 56.1 **532**

3* Manufactured quadrilateral quartzite burnisher. Smooth ovoid stone with two parallel straight, longitudinal sides. The faces are convex in longitudinal and transverse planes. The surfaces are all polished and smooth. Faint striations on all four faces are transverse. One of the ends also shows faint signs of wear.
L 48.5 W 22 T 11.5. Wt 25.1 **415.01**

4* Manufactured quadrilateral quartzite burnisher. Smooth ovoid stone with two parallel straight longitudinal sides. The faces are convex in longitudinal and transverse planes. The surfaces are all polished and smooth. Faint striations on the two broad faces are transverse, whilst on the narrow faces they are longitudinal over transverse.
L 44 W 19.5 T 12. Wt 20.0 **415.01**

5 Manufactured quadrilateral quartzite burnisher in form of rectangular prism, all faces convex along both length and breadth, pale yellow-brown, very highly ground and polished.
L 45.6 W 19.9 T 10.5 Wt 15.5g **427.03**

6* Manufactured quadrilateral quartzite burnisher. Smooth ovoid stone with two parallel straight longitudinal sides. The faces are convex in longitudinal and transverse planes. The surfaces are all polished and smooth.
L 64 W 25 T 19 **450**

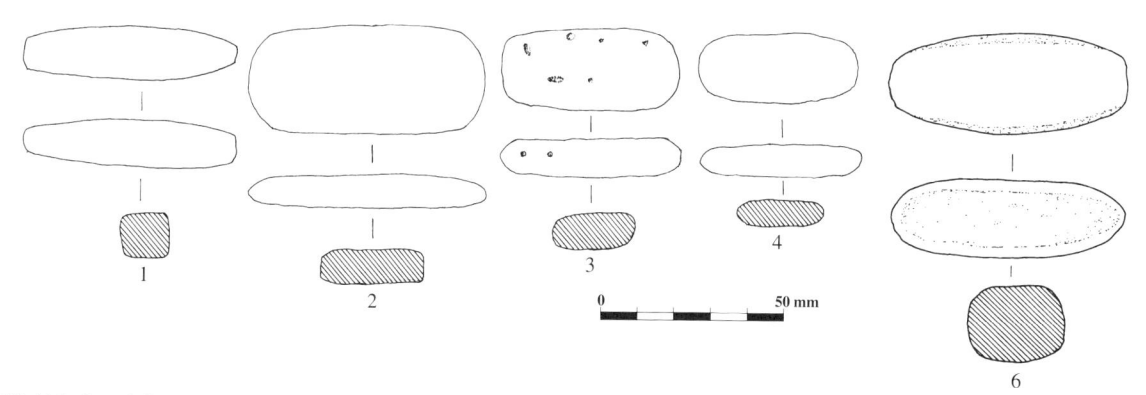

10.119 Quadrilateral burnishers (SE40).

Polishing/rubbing stones (SE41)

Three polishing or rubbing stones (SE41.1–3) are all fine-grained with polished surfaces, and may have been used in the same way as the burnishers (SE40), but do not conform to any specific form. A striking spheroid black basalt cobble (1) with at least sixteen small worn facets rounding it off, was found with a granite cobble on the floor of a **Period I** pit (53.05) in the **southern sector**.

1 Black basalt (?) polishing/rubbing stone. Sub-spherical stone with smooth, polished surface. At least sixteen facets, presumably to enhance spherical appearance.
Diameter varies between 38 and 44. Wt 97.5 **53.05**

2 Porphyry polishing/rubbing stone. Smooth flat stone, of tapering ovoid shape, with smooth, highly polished surface.
L 59.5 W 36.5 T 13. Wt 52.45 **743**

3 Possible polishing/rubbing stone of quartzite. Smooth ovoid pebble. One broad face convex, the other flat. The flat face has faint off-transverse wear marks, and faint silver coloured markings which may be associated.
L 35.5 W 22.5 T 13. Wt 16.5 **430**

Smoothing stones (SE42)

A group of thirteen smoothing stones (SE42.1–13) comprised cobbles of granite, sandstone, diorite and quartzite, with a single worn surface. These are interpreted as rubbing or smoothing stones. They were of much coarser texture than the burnishers and polishing stones (SE40 and 41), but the smooth surface was worn to a high degree of polish, particularly on the granite examples. These water-worn stones were larger than the polishing stones (SE41), and appear to have been selected by size to allow a comfortable grip around the rim when held in the palm of the hand. They generally came from relatively early deposits, with five (1, 3, 7, 9 and 13) from **Period I**, and two others (5 and 8) from the displaced metalworking debris (110) used in the construction of the original **Period II** oratory (220). Six of these (1, 3, 5, 8, 9, 13) came from the western part of the **northern sector**, and five were from deposits associated with metalworking debris and hones (Figure 10.116a). Two others (11, 456.03 and 12, 415.01) from late **Period IV** contexts had similar associations (Figure 10.116b), and a role in metalworking seems likely, although other functions are possible. The sandstone pieces would have been used as a abrasives, while the granites would have been more suitable for polishing, but could also have been used for descaling iron objects during forging.

Quernstones (SE43)

A group of twenty rotary-quern stones (SE43.1–20) comprised fifteen broken or incomplete upper stones, two lower stones and three unascribed fragments. Some of the fragments with insufficient diagnostic features could come from millstones (SE44). Ten of the pieces were sandstone, five granite, three conglomerate, one greywacke, and one of metasedimentary rock. The fine-grained local rocks used for hones are unsuitable for milling, and the greywacke and metasediment querns would probably have crushed the grain rather than grinding it. The granite querns were probably made from local glacial erratics, but the conglomerates and coarser sandstones would have been imported, the former perhaps from the Isle of Man. One upper stone (2) was roughly made from dressed ashlar, perhaps removed from the cathedral in the twelfth or thirteenth century.

The chronological and spatial distributions of the querns are interesting. A small group from **Period I** includes the unsuitably fine-grained greywacke upper stone (13) from the paved surround (78.04) of the **Period I/2** shrine. This may have been a relic of late Iron Age or Romano-British settlement in the area. Two others (5 and 18), both made of granite and fragmentary, came from the western part of the **northern sector**, and perhaps originated in the industrial debris in this area of the *inner precinct*. There were no querns from the buildings in the *outer zone*, and none from **Period II** contexts, despite the extensive use of stone in the successive terraces around the church and other features. Querns appeared – or reappeared – in the later stages of **Period III** with two fragments of muscovite granite (16 and 17), perhaps pieces of the upper and lower stones of the same quern, and one (9) of medium-grained sandstone. All three had been reused in buildings (16, III/36, 17, III/27 and 9, probably III/30), and a fourth of medium-grained sandstone (4) from a **Period V** grave (539) could have originated in a contemporary structure (perhaps III/30). Three more querns came from **Period IV** contexts all in the *outer zone* (8, 445, IV/21; 10, 488, IV/13 and 12, 417.02). These comprised one of granite (8), perhaps part of the broken quern from the same area in **Period III**, and two of sandstone, respectively medium- (10) and coarse-grained (12). **Period V** contexts in the *outer zone* (**southern sector**) produced five more querns, two (3 and 14) from the floor of Building V/2 (520.01), and three from later, fourteenth century contexts (2, 517.01; 19, 524 and 20, 523.02). Three of these were sandstone (2, 3 and 14), and two (19 and 20) of an exotic conglomerate similar to that used for two large nineteenth century millstones recovered from the town in 1992. Two of the remaining five querns came from fifteenth-seventeenth century contexts (1, 631 and 7, 616.01), of which one (7) was a conglomerate. The last three were unstratified; two (11 and 15) from the *inner precinct*, and one (6) from the *outer zone*. The assemblage thus indicates that querns were used within the *monasterium* from the tenth till the fourteenth century, but rarely, if ever, before. Despite displacement and reuse, their concentration in the *outer zone* was probably significant, and points to a long period when individual households were responsible for the preparation of their own cereals, and were thus unlikely to have eaten communally. The absence of querns in **Period II** and their relative scarcity in **Period I** indicates that a different regime obtained in which resources were controlled centrally, and meals were perhaps communal. This was supported by the distribution of millstones which were confined to **Period I** and **II** contexts. The most surprising implication of the distribution of querns was that they seem to have continued in use in the thirteenth and fourteenth centuries when the Priory might have been expected to have its own mill, and so to have exercised control over the food supply.

2* Broken, sandstone, rotary quern upper stone. 2 pieces representing approximately half of an upper rotary quern stone, broken radially and transversely, of light yellow-brown Carboniferous sandstone. Pick-dressed, apparently from a section of a dressed, squared ashlar block, of which two sides remain, the corner having been rounded off and a handle socket sunk into the upper surface, 30mm, Base = 10mm, depth = 24mm. The original dressing of the block took the form of oblique broaching, which survives in patches. After some time this socket became useless due to part of the circumference shearing off, and another L 30mm W 12mm T 22mm was placed in a less mechanically advantageous position (120mm as opposed to 160mm from centred). The feed hole of the hopper is c 78mm in diameter. The under surface is smooth, concave, with no dressing marks, and carbon-stained all over in patches, with adhesions. Part of one of the mortises for the tenons of the central spindle survives at the edge of the feed hole on this face, rounded, 26mm deep L 310mm W 350 Th 45–70. Although superficially resembling the 'Western' Iron Age broch and wheelhouse querns (Mackie, 1074, 138) (from 1st century BC onwards), it is from a secure medieval level and may well be a bit of reused priory masonry, dating from the 12th Century AD onwards.

517.01

10* Large segment of decorated, medium-grained sandstone, rotary quern upper stone with offset handle socket. Socket 27mm diameter, 26mm depth, well worn, set 37mm in from edge of offset, 114mm from central hole. Grinding surface shows greater wear around central hole and around perimeter.

ED 337 ID 85 T 38.5 **488**

13* Broken, damaged, fine-grained greywacke rotary-quern upper stone The ovoid hole (66 × 53mm) is off-centre, and assuming that initially it would have been in the centre of the stone, the quern would therefore have been at least 380mm in diameter. Only a small patch survives of the original worn surface on the underside of the stone, as much of it has flaked off. The quernstone is now broken, and in two pieces.

L 329 W 331 T 72.0 **78.04**

16* Damaged, granite, rotary quern (?) upper stone. Convex upper surface, two opposing edges broken off, no trace of handle socket. Worn sub-circular central hole. Grinding surface worn more towards edges, and slightly concave. Granite (muscovite).

ED 426 ID 68 × 63 T 65 **470**

20* Segment of conglomerate, rotary quern upper stone, with handle socket set 36mm in from rim. Socket 28mm diameter, 24mm depth. Convex upper surface with low raised lip 34mm wide round inner hole. Flat lower surface shows no sign of wear.

ED 333 ID 85 T 54 **523.02**

Millstones (SE44)

A small group of millstones (SE44.1–4) comprises complete lower (1) and upper stones (2) from a late pit in the Northumbrian church (320, Figure 4.18), and fragments of two larger stones (3 and 4), one certainly, and both possibly, pertaining to **Period I** (Figure 10.2). The complete upper and lower stone are of similar size and fit together reasonably well, but would not perhaps have been effective due to the differing hardnesses and other qualities of the granite upper stone and sandstone lower stone. They are of similar size to the slightly later rotary querns, but the topstone has sockets for a metal rynd identifying it as a mill stone. The symmetrical opposed sockets on the top of the stone are closer to the hopper than the handle sockets on rotary querns and perhaps supported a brace. The stone is both small and heavy, and was not necessarily intended for cereal as it would have been capable of crushing and milling more robust commodities. The two earlier stones were probably larger. The outer fragment (4) came from a stone about 1.0 m in diameter, while the inner fragments (3) reveal a large hopper and part of a large rynd appropriate to a substantial stone. Neither would be out of place in a Roman context, and they would be appropriate to a mill serving a fort or other major settlement (Adam Welfare Pers. Comm.). One of the inner fragments (3a) came from paving in the **Period I/1.5** graveyard (67.02), and the joining piece (3b), from a **Period V** grave nearby, was probably displaced from the same surface. The outer fragment (4) found nearby, had been re-used as a packing stone for the northern wall of a Northumbrian hall (II/7), but had already been reused for an ingot mould. It cannot thus be closely dated, but is likely to have pertained to **Period I**, and could have been contemporary with the other stone. Both were made of medium-grained Carboniferous or Triassic sandstone, but probably came from different quarries. These rocks are widely distributed, though not occurring locally, and the millstones could have come from Antrim, the Isle of Man, Cumbria, the NE Solway coast, or the Midland valley. They have

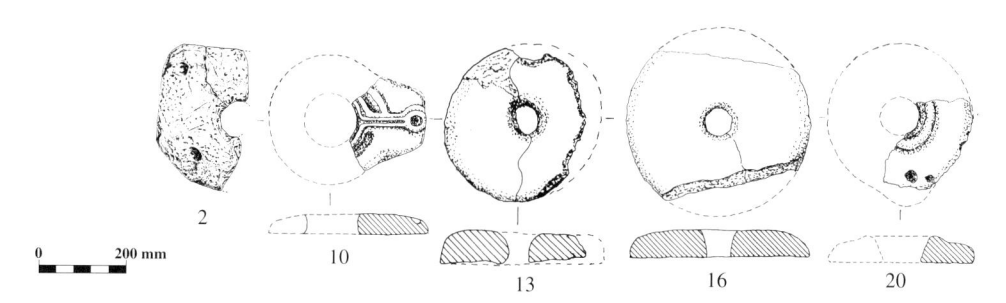

10.120 Querns (SE43).

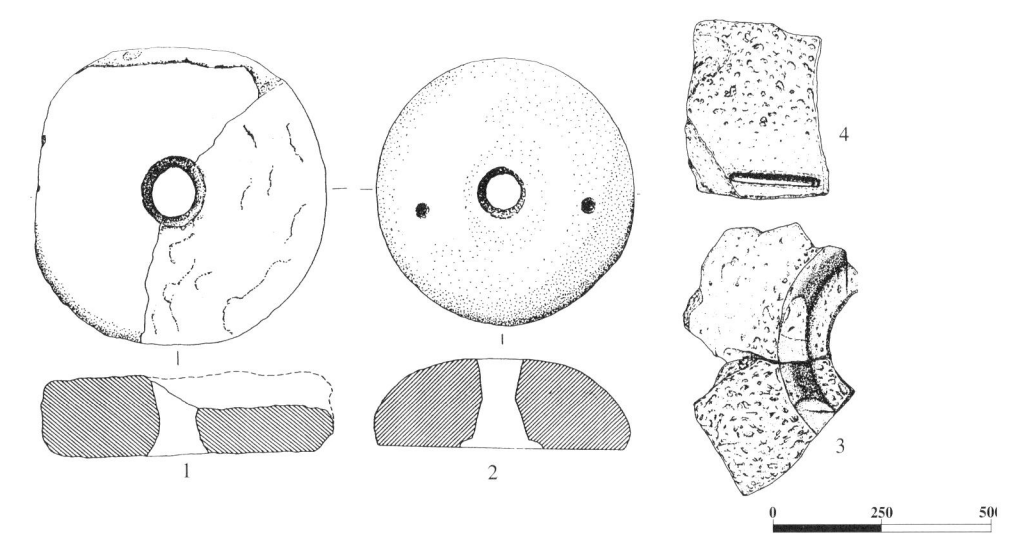

10.121 Millstones (SE44).

important implications for the early history of the site (pp 29, 460).

1* Complete sandstone, mechanical mill lower stone. Roughly circular with slightly ovoid central hole. Grinding surface slightly concave, with more wear indicated towards the centre, where the hole is surrounded by a slight lip. Biconical central hole.
ED 458 ID 68 max /27min T 116 **320**

2* Complete granite (muscovite) mechanical mill upper-stone with two opposed handle sockets, set 54mm and 59mm in from rim. First socket diameter 25mm, 22mm depth; second socket 19mm diameter, 12mm depth. Biconical centre hole, with two smaller, opposed sockets on the edge of the grinding surface, diameter 22mm, depth 18mm. Grinding surface flat, showing signs of wear. Upper surface convex.
ED 406 ID 98 max/56min T 114 **320**

3* Two conjoining inner fragments (a and b) of medium-grained, sandstone upper millstone.
  a) block of red sandstone with rounded ridge extending for 160mm across one surface of the stone. The band is 40mm wide and 25mm thick at one end tapering to nothing at the other. It runs parallel to a curved edge on the stone which displays tooling. There are deep tooling scars on the underside.
L 200 W 200 T 100 **67.02**

  b) block of red sandstone with rounded ridge – 36.0mm wide by 17.5mm deep extending across the upper surface of the stone for 85.0mm, and located c. 44.0mm from the curved edge and parallel to it. There is rough tooling on both flat surfaces, but neither display signs of wear. On the lower surface, a wedge – 37.0mm × 65mm wide by 25.0mm deep is cut into the stone, close by the curved edge. Presumably to accommodate the rynd.
L 210 W 135 T 110 **542**

4* Outer fragment of medium-grained, pinkish sandstone millstone, re-used as a bar mould. One surface has regular flecking grooves. The opposed surface is smooth, and has seen secondary use with the pecking of a deep U-section bar mould (95 × 12 × 7) with slightly sloping sides and rounded ends. Analysis showed a trace of zinc in the mould, and on the adjacent surface, indicating that the mould may not have seen use. Original diameter of millstone c. 1m.
L 235 W 170 T 105 **253**

Ingot and object moulds (SE45 and 46)

Stone ingot and object moulds are discussed above (pp 401-2).

Calme moulds (SE 47)

Two fragments of moulds, used for the production of strips of H-section lead window calmes to retain the glass panels, probably relate to late medieval refurbishment of the cathedral. All of the lead calmes recovered (p 394) had a similar profile. The moulds would have been simple two-piece affairs, and the low melting temperature of lead meant that stone moulds could be used time and time again. One (2) came from debris abutting the Commendator's house, and was probably deposited c. 1500 AD. The other came from a fourteenth century surface in the southern sector.

1 Fragment of bi-partite mould for the manufacture of H-section window calmes. Two parallel sets of paired grooves.
L 101 W 51 T 2 **517.01**

2 Half of bi-partite mould for the manufacture of H-section window calmes. A deep hole adjacent to one edge provided the keying point for the other half. The external surfaces are chamfered and well finished, and the piece may possibly have been re-used. Two parallel sets of paired grooves, grooves 5mm apart, 3mm deep.
L 125 W 50 T 25 **704**

Slate pencils (SE48)

Recent contexts produced some forty-four round and polygonal slate pencils (SE48.1–44, archive). The earliest examples came from the deposits (728) associated with the demolition of the west wing of the manse in the later-nineteenth century, with further concentrations in the subsequent demolition deposits (738), and the recent paths (770) behind the Priory Museum. Previous reports (e.g. Hill and Pollock 1992, 34) have associated the slate pencils with the use of the former manse as a school in the nineteenth century, but the association is weak and they should more properly be seen as part of a general scatter of nineteenth to early-twentieth century debris with wider functional implications. The small, relatively-well stratified group indicates that polygonal pencils were earlier than round ones.

Stones with artificial hollows (SE49)

Five stones with artificial hollows (SE49.1–5) include four (2, 90; 1, 238, 3, 222.02 and 4, 229) from broadly contemporary later-seventh and eighth century contexts, of which three (1–3) came from the vicinity of the Northumbrian church. They could have had a common function, perhaps as containers for oil or water used for ritual ablutions. One of the stones (1) lay beside the steps leading to the **Period II/3** church (238) with its uneven base firmly supported, and the hollow on the upper face. A second (2) came from the debris (90) associated with the collapse of the **Period I/3** shrine towards the end of **Period I/4**, and the third (3) from the rubble (222.02) banked against the **Period II/3** terrace. A large granite dome (4) with a large hollow in its apex, and insubstantial pecked channels on its flanks, was perhaps an incompletely manufactured object on which considerable labour had already been expended. It came from the foundation trench of Building II/18. The fifth (5) was built into the modern field wall (773) and could be of any date.

1 Irregular sandstone boulder with shallow sub-circular pecked hollow (155mm × 130mm × 18mm deep) with level base (100mm × 100mm). Hollow shows little sign of wear. The base of the boulder is uneven.
L 400 W 350 T 170 **238**

2 Worn sandstone slab with fractured edges and worn, pecked, oblong hollow with sloping sides (150mm long by 20.0mm wide by 20.0mm deep) on the flatter of two surfaces.
L 370 W 230 T 64 **90**

3 Thick greywacke slab with pecked surface (150.0mm × 170.0mm) around a shallow, worn, pecked, oval hollow (6.0mm × 6.0mm × 2.0mm deep) subsequently worn smooth on one surface.
L 340 W 265 T60 **222.02**

4 Large fractured granite dome with flat base and slightly worn large concavity in upper surface (80mm diameter and 45mm deep). Some evidence of pecked channels down exterior sides.
L 254 W 208 H 149 **229**

5 Broken worn sandstone block with two pecked hollows, pecks and scores.
773

Miscellaneous artefacts (SE50)

Sixteen 'miscellaneous stone artefacts' (SE50.1–16) had been shaped or manufactured in order to perform a specific function. An equivalent group of miscellaneous utilised rocks (SE57) is described below (pp 468–9).

1* A triangular pendant, the motif incised on a water-worn sandstone pebble which was then pierced for suspension. The reverse has a simple incised cross, whilst the cross on the obverse is contained within three concentric triangles. This may be representative of the Trinity, though three concentric triangles appear on some gaming boards, and the use of three triangles was also associated with the cult of Odin (Pennick 1984, 13). It came from Building IV/7 and so probably dates to the later-twelfth century.

2* A faceted coarse-grained sandstone gaming piece with a domed top, probably from the **Period IV.8–9** deposits in the **southern sector** (525.01), may have been used as a king piece in association with the gaming discs (SE19).

3* A finger ring of fine-grained sandstone with wear on the inside. This small ring may have been for a child and came from **Period III** deposits in the south-east corner of the **central sector** (494).

4* A piece of slate, certainly used as a roofing tile, it has three radiating lines incised on one side and may have originally been part of a sundial. It came from the debris over the **Period V/4** roadway (631).

5* A fragment of a circular piece with a roughly-hollowed biconical interior, a small socket for a handle in the upper rim, and evidencing slight wear on the underside and considerable wear to a high degree of polish on the exterior. The interior may have fitted to some form of spindle or shaft, and the device appears to be a form of rotary abrader, though not a grindstone as these have a pronounced camber on their outer surfaces whilst this one is consistently flat. It came from the debris (414.04) surrounding Building IV/7 (Figure 10.116).

6 A well-finished fragment of fine-grained sandstone from the **Period I.10** deposits (55) in the **southern sector** has smoothed faces and a smooth outer edge. It may fall into the Class A discs defined by Henshall at Hurly Hawkin, though it is considerably larger than other examples. An alternative suggestion is that it formed part of an early grave marker, though no parallels are known.

7* A fragment of a polygonal sandstone stone vessel with a deeply curved interior basin. The interior is highly polished and smooth. A square hole has been pecked through the side and may well be a secondary feature, as the workmanship is well below the standard of the rest of the vessel. A similar octagonal sandstone vessel with polished interior and a secondary hole cut into the bottom of the basin was found at Luss, by Loch Lomond (Lacaille 1944, 46). This was interpreted as a mortar later re-used as a basin, and was not dated. Octagonal fonts are known in Scottish churches from the late twelfth century, and Whithorn Priory has an example of an early thirteenth century bucket-shaped font which also utilises a side drain. The vessel fragment was found in one of the graves in the **Period II** burial chapel at the start of the 1991 excavation season and, though it had probably fallen from the side of the grave its provenance is uncertain.

8* A sandstone pebble with a hollow in one of the broader faces came from a **Period I/2** grave (I/17). The hollow evidences rotational wear and is lined with patches of a red material, perhaps a pigment. It is likely to have been a small mortar for grinding pigment.

9* This piece was originally classified as a bar hone, and it was certainly used in a secondary context for sharpening blades, with a worn concave area on one of the faces. However it appears to have been pecked out as a quadrilateral shaft, with neatly squared edges and a ridge, badly damaged, down the centre of each face. The original shaft tapered slightly. It came from the displaced debris (110) used in the construction of the **Period II** buildings. There are no contemporary parallels known for this item.

10* Although re-used as a pounder, this piece was originally a fishing weight, paralleled by a similar object in lead (LD09.9).

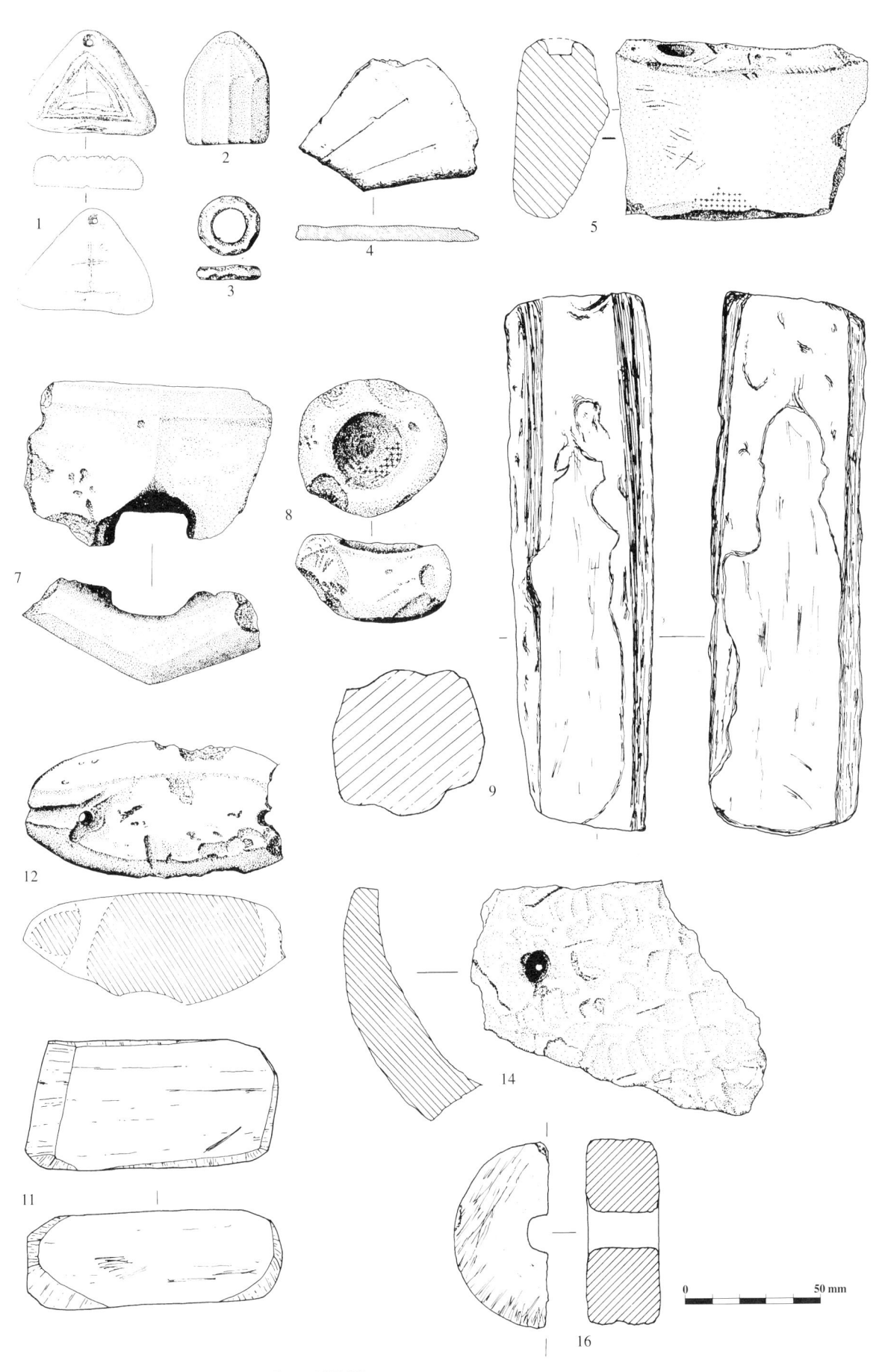

10.122 Miscellaneous stone artefacts (SE50).

These match Norse examples from Jarlshof, where their morphological similarity to halter blocks is considered (Hamilton 1956, 183), and Underhoull, Unst, Shetland (Small 1966, Fig. 12). The schist is not found locally, and it may derive from the Northern Isles or Norway. It came from topsoil in the **central sector**, but could have originated in a **Period III** or **IV** deposit disturbed by graves.

11* A faceted hand-sized greywacke block with some evidence of wear on the broad faces and at the ends, this piece may have served as a rubbing block. It came from the early debris (94.01) at the west end of the **northern sector**.

12 and 13 Two small quartzite stone balls, probably for recreational use.

14* A fragment of the rim and wall of a steatite bowl, is pierced by a conical hole for suspension. The rounded form and rim suggest a Class II bowl of ninth/tenth century date, again paralleled by many examples from Jarlshof. No trace of burning exists on the interior or exterior to determine use as a lamp or cooking pot. It came from a patch of ash overlying the **Period II** terrace, and was probably deposited in the latter stages of **Period III**.

15 A flat slab with deep U-section grooves on opposed faces, causing a fracture. It came from Building III/40 and was identified as a possible bar mould. EDXRF analysis indicated that it had not been used in metalworking.

16* A medium-grained sandstone disc with a squared biconical perforation may have been a flywheel for a bow drill or similar implement. The wear patterns around the circumference were similar to those on whorls, rather than grindstones, but still clearly indicative of rotary action. The two pieces came from a **Period I/4** grave (82.03, Gr I/109) and a **Period II** building (215, II/14), and the object could have originated in the **Period I/3** industrial debris (85.02, 109 etc) in the north-west part of the *inner precinct*.

The utilised stones

Peter Hill and Andrew Nicholson

Plough-pebbles (SE51)

The **Glebe Field** produced three hundred and twenty-nine plough pebbles (SE51.2-330) and a possible plough fragment (SE51.1) which has been stabilised, but awaits detailed examination. The assemblage is of great importance due to its considerable size, the stratigraphic details of deposition and, most significantly, the chronological evidence. Plough pebbles were inserted into the wooden parts of mouldboard ploughs which came into contact with the soil to preserve them from erosion. Pebble-studded plough soles have been discovered in Danish bogs (Fenton 1963), and similar pebbles in a range of hard rocks have been recorded from central and northern England (Phillips 1938), Scotland (Clarke 1972, Fenton 1963, Hamilton 1956), Ireland (O'Kelly 1976, 1978, Brady 1988), Denmark (Lerche 1970a and b), and the Auvergne and Loire regions in France (Dauzatt 1934, Patte 1952). Secure dating evidence has hitherto proved elusive. The Danish ploughs have been dated to the high to late middle ages, and the stratified Scottish examples come from thirteenth to fourteenth century contexts. Brady has argued (1988, 55–6) that plough pebbles originated in eastern Ireland in the thirteenth century, and were diffused thence. The Whithorn assemblage begins with securely-stratified examples from the late-fifth/early-sixth century (**Period I/1**), and continued to accumulate until the seventh century. An apparent hiatus in the eighth century probably reflects the organisation of the site, rather than a change in plough technology. A final large well-stratified and closely-dated group was associated with the cultivation (399) of the **central sector** in the mid-ninth century. The stratigraphic details and chronological arguments are rehearsed in Chapters 3 and 5, and the implications of the technology and its chronology are discussed above (pp 28–9, 191).

Some two hundred and thirty-three pebbles were quartz and eighty-six granite. All are local beach or river pebbles, and no clear chronological patterns in the use of quartz or granite can be distinguished (Table 10.20). Nine sandstone pebbles with similar facets are included in this category, but were probably not used in ploughs, and may be of natural origin. The pebbles were sub-divided into four morphological groups dictated by the form of the worn facet. One hundred and twenty-five with relatively flat facets may have been used to protect the axles of wheeled ploughs (Lerche 1970a, 144) or, more probably, wheeled vehicles (A. Fenton, Pers. Comm.). There was a concentration of quartz pebbles with flat facets in **Period I/1** deposits (Table 10.21). One hundred and twenty pebbles with gently-rounded facets, sixty-five with asymmetrical (unilateral) facets, and nine with symmetrical (bilateral) facets are all classic 'plough pebbles'. The eight symmetrical pebbles may have been dislodged and replaced, resulting in double wear facets.

The chronological distribution of plough pebbles is illustrated in Table 10.20. Two hundred and twenty-

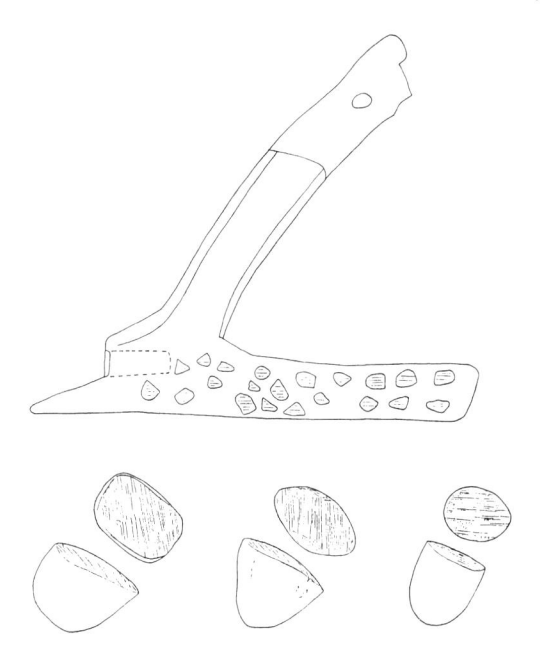

10.123 Plough-pebbles (SE51) and examples surviving in a Danish ploughsole (after Fenton 1963).

THE FINDS

	Quartz		Granite		Total
	n	%	n	%	
Topsoil/unstratified	17	7.3	4	4.7	21
Displaced	14	6.0	3	3.5	17
Mid-9C ploughing	37	15.9	17	19.8	54
Sub total	**51**		**20**		**71**
S Sector Displaced	6	2.6	1	1.2	7
S Sector **Period I**	17	7.3	8	9.3	25
Sub total	**23**		**9**		**32**
?Displaced **Period I**	21	9.1	11	12.8	33
Period I/2–4	73	31.3	29	33.7	102
Period I/1	48	20.6	13	15.1	61
Sub total	**142**		**53**		**195**
Total	**233**		**86**		**319**

Table 10.20: Chronological and spatial distribution of plough pebbles.

eight examples can be ascribed to **Period I** of which a hundred and ninety-five came from the *inner precinct* and thirty-two from the *outer zone*. Both groups include examples displaced into later contexts, but generally not attributable to the mid-ninth century cultivation. The *inner precinct* finds are sub-divided into three groups. The first comprises sixty-one examples ascribed to **Period I/1** (Figure 10.124a), including assemblages from the **Period I/1.1** plough soil (p 80) and intrusive graves and the early rubbish spreads (94.01) in the north-west part of the area. The second group comprises a hundred and two pebbles (Figure 10.124b) from later **Period I** contexts (Phases 2–4), and was dominated by finds from rubbish spreads (89, 85.01 and 02, 109, 73.01 and 02) in the north-west part of the area. There was no evidence of contemporary cultivation in the vicinity, and the most plausible interpretation is that these pebbles were discarded during the repair of ploughs (pp 99–100). The presence of the putative plough fragment in this suite of deposits, and the recurrent evidence for smithying gives some weight to this hypothesis. Attention was perhaps focused on the plough irons, and the pebbles may come from discarded plough soles, or were perhaps pried loose and replaced with less worn stones. A third group of displaced finds included pebbles from the construction trenches of the halls, which were dug into the **Period I/1.1** ploughsoil, and a large group from the metalworking debris (110) used in the construction of the **Period II/1** oratory (220), which perhaps originated in another area where ploughs were repaired. The smaller assemblage from the *outer zone* (Figure 10.124a) includes finds from the **Period I.3** ploughsoil, material possibly displaced from it, and perhaps a relatively small group of pebbles reflecting plough repair. The stratigaphic evidence thus suggests that plough pebbles were introduced at the start of **Phase 1** in the late-fifth/early-sixth century when much of the site was ploughed, and continued in use into the seventh century, when the archaeological evidence suggests plough repair, rather than *in situ* cultivation.

The second group (Table 10.20, Figure 10.124c) is ascribed to a brief phase of cultivation in the middle

10.124 The distributions of plough-pebbles (see text).

	Flat				Shallow				Unilateral				Bilateral			
	Q n	G n	Tot	%	Q n	G n	Tot	%	Q n	G n	Tot	%	Q n	G n	Tot	%
Topsoil/unstratified	3	3	6	4.8	7	–	7	5.8	6	1	7	10.8	1		1	11.1
Displaced	6	2	8	6.4	3	–	3	2.5	5	1	6	9.2				
Mid-9 C ploughing	6	11	17	13.6	21	3	24	20	9	2	11	16.9	1	1	2	22.2
S Sector displaced	3	1	4	3.2	2	–	2	1.7	1		1	1.5				
S Sector PI	6	4	10	8	8	4	12	10	2		2	3.1	1		1	11.1
?Displaced PI	7	8	15	12	11	–	11	9.2	2	3	5	7.7	1		1	11.1
Period I/2–4	17	16	33	26.4	35	10	45	37.5	19	3	22	33.8	2		2	22.2
Period I/1	24	8	32	25.6	14	2	16	13.3	9	2	11	16.9	1	1	2	22.2
Total	**72**	**53**	**125**		**101**	**19**	**120**		**53**	**12**	**65**		**7**	**2**	**9**	

Table 10.21: Chronological distribution of plough pebbles by geology and facet shape. Q = Quartz, G = Granite

years of the ninth century (pp 190-2). This group includes fifty-four pebbles from the cultivated soil, and a further seventeen from later contexts which can reasonably be ascribed to it. There were no subsequent concentrations of plough pebbles and the use of pebble-studded mouldboard ploughs, perhaps with wheeled fore-carriages, may have ceased by the later-ninth century. There was a surprising correspondence with the evidence of the mill- and quern-stones. The heavy plough would have represented a major investment in materials and draught animals, and is appropriate, as is milling, to an organised community with strong central control. A technological change in **Period III** indicated *inter alia* by the disappearance of large ploughs and milling, and the re-emergence of querns, was perhaps a reflection of a major shift in the organisation of the *minster* and its communal aspirations.

Spindle sockets (SE52)

Two socketed quartzite cobbles (SE52.1–2) are identified as spindle sockets as distinct from the door pivots in SE03. These would have been the bearings for rotating metal shafts, and could have been used in a horizontal mill (e.g. Edwards 1990, Fig. 23) or, set vertically, as bearings for a large grindstone. One of the stones (1) was unstratified, the second (2) came from a **Period IV** building (IV/5). Underlying and adjacent deposits produced hones and small rotary grindstones (Figure 10.116): a large grindstone would have been an appropriate piece of equipment in this area.

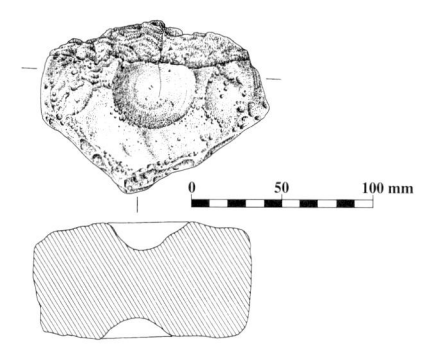

10.125 Stone bearing (SE52.2).

1 Fractured exotic quartzite cobble spindle socket or bearing with a highly polished socket (26mm diameter by 17mm deep) on one slightly convex surface

903

2 Natural block of white quartzite. Sub-angular with two opposed parallel flattish faces, into each of which a ground and polished, nearly hemispherical hollow has been sunk. Half the block is stained from a 'tidemark', on the plane of the major axis, by a dark carbonaceous material up over the side and one of the hollowed faces. The hollow in the stained face is more pointed or sub-conical in section than the other, L 32mm T 20mm; over this is superimposed a secondary hollow up to 38mm wide occurring 13mm above the base of the primary hollow, apparently due to the grinding agent, which at this time had a larger radius of basal curvature (i.e. flatter and more rounded) being reinserted at a slightly different angle, possibly by shifting of the block in the ground, assuming it had been buried up to the 'tide-mark'; the other hollow is 15mm deep and up to 43mm in diameter, remnant pecking being intermittently visible round the outer edge, although most of the circumference is broken away. The interior of this hollow is more highly polished, being absolutely glassy with many fine parallel striations; the stained face hollow has striations, but presents a more matt appearance. They can be explained as being bearings for a rounded spike presumably metal or metal-shod, which rotated frequently and with great force through at least 360 degrees, a central point and ring scratch covering a complete and perfect circle being present in the base of each hollow Both flat surfaces also have discontinuous patches of polish in one plane where the high spots have been reduced, as though by a large flat disc rotating over these surfaces, or else the block itself grinding against an underlying stone slab when the pivot was bearing on the opposite face. Broken on the non-stained side, presumably leading to its inversion and the use of the other face, which was stained by soot or smoke, and finally abandoned when the whole block sheared through under the force of the pivot. Millstone base, grindstone or potter's wheel bearing etc. Not a door (unless revolving!) pivot.

L 120 W 91 T 65 **456.02**

Flakes with serrated edges (SE53)

Six sandstone or greywacke flakes with serrated edges (SE53.1–6) possibly include natural and manufactured objects. The most convincing piece is a semicircular greywacke flake (6) with eleven notches on the chord forming thirteen teeth (Figure 10.126). Five other unshaped flakes (1–5) have similar serrations and could have been used for the same unknown purpose. Three of these (3–5) came from the **Period V** graveyard (Figure 6.37), and a fourth (2) from an overlying layer of silt (615.05). All four are likely to have originated in **Period IV** debris. The semi-circular artefact (6) came from a relatively late

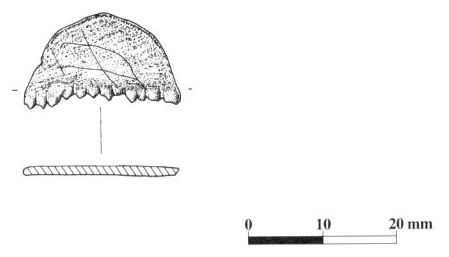

10.126 Flake with serrated edge (SE53.6).

context (522, perhaps fourteenth/fifteenth century) in the **southern sector**. This could have been used for combing swags on pottery although there was no evidence that pottery was made here or elsewhere on the site. The last piece (1) came from the eastern platform (76) built towards the end of **Period I/4**.

6* Shaped, fine-grained greywacke semi-circle snapped diametrically and notched, or toothed along the nearly straight edges so formed. Both larger flatter faces formed along natural bedding-planes, edges ground, apart from toothed one. Eleven V-shaped transverse cuts, intersecting with the sloping face of the diametric fracture, produced thirteen more or less sharp, saw-tooth like points. These cuts appear to have been made with a metal blade. Slight polish on very tips of teeth. Possibly a comb for making swags on pottery. If originally discoid, then c. 3g.
L 22 W 2 T 1.5 **522**

Grooved and incised slabs (SE54)

Thirty stones (SE54.1–30), generally slabs and sometimes with a smoothed surface, display various combinations of scratches, U-shaped grooves, incised V-shaped scores, and pock-marks. There were three distinct stratigraphic groups. The earliest comprises fifteen stones (1–14, 24) from **Period I** and **II** contexts, all of which probably pertain to **Period I** (Figure 10.116a). Thirteen examples from the *inner precinct* include five (2, 5, 7, 8 and possibly 4) from industrial rubbish spreads (94.01, 88.01, 85.02), and four (11, 12, 13 and 24) from **Period II** contexts, but potentially associated with displaced metalworking debris (110, pp 117–8). The only example (9) from a building (I/18) is atypically scratched rather than scored or incised. The second group comprises nine examples (15–23) from **Period III** and **IV** contexts of which eight came from buildings, six of **Period III** (16, III/10; 17, III/22; 18, III/22; 19, III/27; 20, III/28 and 21, III/44), and two of **Period IV** (22, IV/4; 23, IV/23). The last group comprises two stones (25–26) from fifteenth-sixteenth century contexts. There is a marked contextual contrast between the first and second groups. The **Period I** finds were generally associated with workshop debris, occurring in similar contexts to hones and polishing stones (Figure 10.116a). The stones in the second group were almost certainly domestic equipment, serving combined functions as whetstones, point-sharpeners, cutting-boards and 'anvils'. They were relatively scarce from the well-preserved **Period IV** buildings and were thus perhaps no longer standard equipment. The absence of examples from the *in situ* and displaced **Period IV** deposits in the *inner precinct* is striking, particularly in light of the numerous metal blades and points which would have needed sharpening (Tables 6.41 and 42).

2* Greywacke fragment with deep incisions and grooves, with at least seventeen narrow grooves (2.0mm or less wide by 2.0mm or less deep), extending diagonally in a haphazard fashion across one surface of the stone from a broken edge. These grooves are cut at one end by two right angle grooves. The wider and deeper grooves are the result of persistent re-use of the channel.
L 220 W 80 T 19–27 **94.01**

7* Smoothed greywacke slab with deep incisions and scratches. Has one artificially smooth surface extending over one edge. A discreet area some 20mm wide of 6 thin grooves – 170mm long × 1.0mm wide on the long axis of the stone, run from about the middle to the edge. Two similar grooves extend across and down the edge at right angles to the main group (91/13855/0).
L 313 W 15 T 44 **85.02**

9* Oval greywacke slab with shallow scratches
L 410 W 290 T 40 **52.04** (I/18)

14* Broken, greywacke boulder with numerous pocks and incised grooves. Two of the four surfaces are weathered. Extending to the edge of the stone, are many narrow grooves, basically running in the same direction across the stone. They measure from 55.0mm long by 1.0mm deep to c. 160.0mm long by 2.0mm wide and deep. Cutting across these grooves are a number of short stab-like cuts c. 10.0mm long. Beyond this area is a series of peck marks.
L 305 W 165 T 105 **253** (II/9)

19* Smoothed triangular greywacke slab with scratches, grooves and pocks. with two smooth flat surfaces, and three fractured edges including one with wear. Three groups of shallow grooves, all extending the same direction, and comprising of lines 1.5mm wide and 1.0mm deep or less by 85mm long maximum, are located on one of the smooth surfaces. Also three pecked out hollows – 10.0 × 10.0mm : 5.0 × 10.0mm : and 5.0mm × 15.0mm by 1.0 to 2.0mm deep are close to one of the groups, but do not impinge.
L 385.0 W 220.0 T 27.0 **427.02** (III/27)

20* Smoothed, greywacke slab with two smooth flat surfaces, one smooth side, and three fractured sides including one with wear. A deep, 4.0mm groove 215.0mm long and 2.0mm wide with a flattish base, extends parallel from 43.0mm to 50.0mm from the smooth edge, and terminates just short of the fractured edge with wear, where it bifurcates. The other end is truncated by a fractured edge. A cluster – 20.0mm wide by 160mm long of shallow grooves, are located c 40.0mm from the 'deep' groove and extend in the same direction.
L 270.0 W 160.0 T 48.0 **482** (III/28)

22* Smoothed greywacke slab with incised grooves and pocks. One smooth surface bears a shallow incised groove extending across the stone and four pecked indentations one of which cuts the groove near to the centre of the stone.
160 × 110 × 25 **412** (IV/4)

30* Smoothed fine-grained greywacke slab with numerous aligned incisions. A restricted worn area on one surface – 340 × 210mm, extends to an edge. Cutting into this worn surface are many thin incised grooves, all of which extend in the same direction, some intersecting and most parallel to each other. The stone is laminating and the scored surface is now loose and in eight pieces.
L 445 W 310 T 40 **904**

Smoothed slabs (SE55)

Three smoothed slabs (SE55.1–3) of greywacke (1 and 3) and sandstone (2) were distinguished from the stones in SE54 by the absence of grooves and

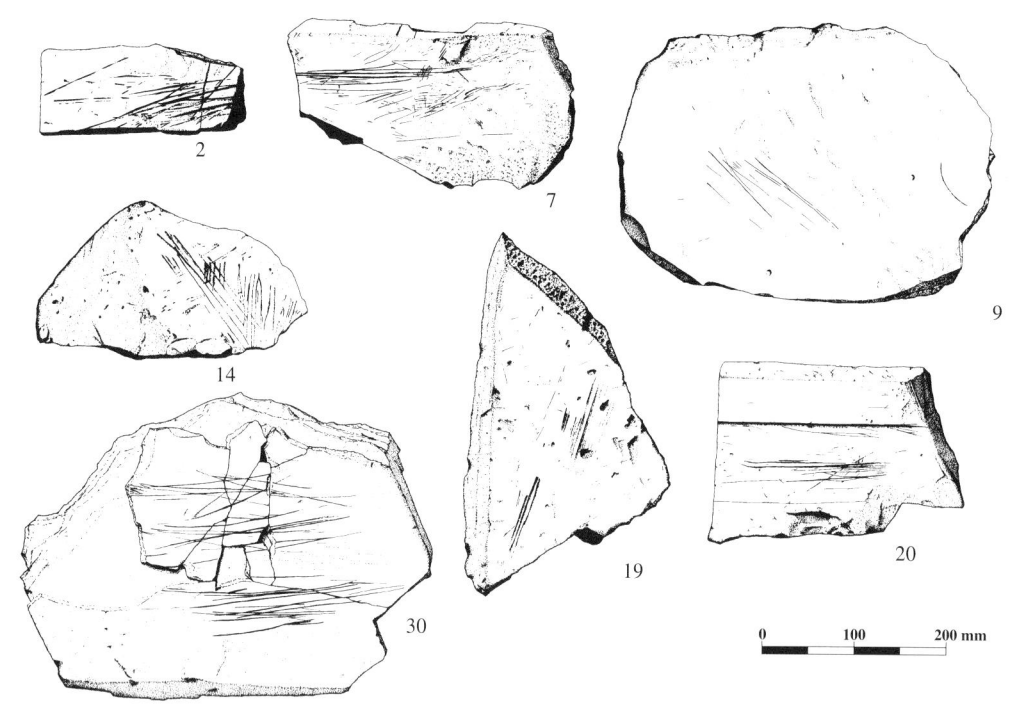

10.127 Grooved and incised stones (SE54).

incisions. Two (1 and 2) were merely smoothed, the third (3) displays pock marks and pecked hollows. The two smoothed slabs (1 and 2) came from the **Period V** graveyard and were probably displaced from the underlying **Period IV** debris (Figure 6.24). The third came from debris associated with the construction of the Commendator's house in **Period V/5**. The two slabs from the **Period V** graveyard coincided with concentrations of fine metalworking debris, and could have been associated equipment, perhaps being used for further attenuation of the silver wire pulled through the draw-plate (p 424).

'Anvil' stones (SE56)

Two grewacke slabs (SE56.1–2) display concentrations of pock marks. One came from the paving in Structure IV/28, the other (2), a much larger stone was unstratified.

Miscellaneous utilised stones (SE57)

Some twenty-two, widely-varying stones (SE57.1–22) show evidence of utilisation, but do not fall into coherent categories. A few of these objects are of considerable interest, though perplexing purpose. The remainder (excavation archive) reflect the occasional utilisation of local stones for unknown purposes.

A massive greywacke slab (1) broken across a large regular circular perforation (c. 0.09 m diameter) was included in a paved surface on the north side of the **Period I/1.6** hollow (97). The 'Early Christian' context invites comparison with the slab shrines of western Ireland (and a possible example from Ardwall isle, Kirkcudbrightshire) described, *inter alia*, by Charles Thomas (1971, 141–3). These sometimes incorporated perforated slabs allowing the relics to be touched. The Whithorn slab seems more massive than those illustrated by Thomas (1971, Fig. 63), but might come from a similar structure, though perhaps rectangular rather than tent-shaped. There was however no appropriate earlier ritual focus within the excavated area and this interpretation is speculative. A perforated rhomboid block of sandstone (3) from the debris surrounding the **Period III** *minster* (456.01/309.02) was perhaps a weight, similar to the 'loom weights', but of unspecific function. A fragment of a sandstone slab (4) bears a vestigial compass-drawn arc and incised V-grooves on three faces. It came form the **Period V** graveyard (543), and was perhaps a fragment of a seventh sculpture (*c.f.* SE14.14–16), reused as a 'pin-sharpener' (*c.f.* SE54). A greywacke fragment (5) from Building IV/15 (490) has a burnished blackened surface possibly stained with pitch. The group includes the threshold stone (6) from the **Period III** chapel (306) and an unstratified stone (7) with similar wear patterns. The remaining pieces (8–22) came from contexts spanning the occupation of the site, but have little to add to its interpretation.

Exotic, imported and transformed stones

Ray Chadburn and Peter Hill

A large assemblage of unworked stones includes pieces imported from near and far, and shows the early exploitation of distant mineral resources. The most important groups are Haematite, used both as ore and for polishing; limestone and lime, imported from the start of **Period I**, and 'white stones', mostly gathered from local beaches and perhaps fulfilling a range of ritual and functional ends. Other categories have specific contributions to the interpretation of the site. Heated and fire-cracked stones possibly reflecting cooking or steam baths, were concentrated in **Period IV** contexts. Hone blanks (SE71, pp 453-4) show the exploitation of a local resource throughout the early development of the site, while 'exotic stones' (SE58) include possible charms or amulets from further afield

Exotic stones and gems (SE58)

A group of thirty-five 'exotic stones' (SE58.1–35) and three gems (SE58.36–38) includes keepsakes, jewellers commodities, gems and other exotic anomalies. The most obvious 'keepsake' is a highly-polished belemnite (21, Phraemocone, possible *cylindroleuthis*) from Building V/2 (520.02), which definitely comes from the East coast, and may derive from Whitby shale. Pebbles of rose quartz (8), granite (22), banded quartzite (34) and sandstone (29 and 30) display a similar enhanced polish, and are similarly likely to have been keepsakes or talismans collected from beaches in the vicinity. A pebble of ferruginous quartz (6) from a **Period I/4** grave (I/107) is similar, but displays wear suggesting use as a burnisher. A flake of mica garnet schist (1) originates in the Highlands and might have come from a glacial erratic, or from an imported hone. The most surprising find is a small piece of mica (10) from the fill of a post-hole in the **Period II/3** church. The flakes of muscovite are too large to come from exposures on the Isle of Man, and it may derive from alpine strata in Europe. It is likely to have been displaced from a **Period I** deposit in the western part of the **northern sector**. A second stone (27) from the **Period II/1** church (220) may have a similar exotic origin.

Seven pieces of rock or quartz crystal (11–13, 15, 18–20) are all exotic, and are likely to have been imported as charms or relics, or for the manufacture of jewellery. Two crystals, both thin unmodified pieces broken from larger crystal beds, came from early contexts. One (13) came from a **Period I/2** building (1/9, 88.01), and has a blood-red Haematite-stained tip. The other (11) from the burnt deposits (315.02) on the floor of the **Period II** church, could have been part of a votive collection of anomalous objects (pp 45, 162-4). A banded quartz crystal (15) from the floor of a **Period III** building (III/3) was isolated from other relevant finds, but the remaining five pieces of crystal can be linked with the postulated jewellery manufacture in the latter part of **Period IV**. The finest piece (12) is the tip of a clear rock crystal, probably detached for use as a gem. One side has perfect facets, but the other is flawed by the blow which removed it, and it may have been discarded for this reason. It came from the fill of a **Period II** drain (230.03), but associated finds suggest this was contaminated with material from the main **Period IV** ditch (417.02). A second crystal (18) came from this later ditch, and two others (19 and 20) came from the same part of the site. The distribution of the crystals is included in Figure 6.24, and all are likely to have been associated with the fine metalworking, jewellery-making and enamelling evident in the latter phases of **Period IV**.

A piece of green porphyry (26) from the **Period V** graveyard (539) has been the subject of a separate study by W.F.Cormack (1989a). It probably derives from quarries in Southern Laconia in Greece, and is one of a large – and growing – number of fragments derived from classical architectural veneers and decorative panels, dispersed to ecclesiastical and urban sites in northern and western Europe. Cormack cites nine examples from Scotland, fifteen from Ireland (*op. cit.*, 44, 47) and fifty from Denmark. Subsequent research (Cormack forthcoming) has extended the distribution to Iceland and the Pharoes. The finds-spots vary but they were common in contexts of the eleventh-thirteenth centuries. Cormack offers a range of interpretations for the two Wigtownshire finds, but speculates that these – and finds from Movilla, Co Down and St Ninian's Isle – originated in a dilapidated Anglian shrine at Whithorn, dismantled and distributed as relics in the eleventh/twelfth centuries. The Whithorn fragment was found among a group of displaced crucible fragments (Figures 6.24, 10.88) supporting an alternative suggestion that the porphyry was commodity used in the manufacture of jewellery (*op. cit.*, 47), or was perhaps one of the items traded in this putative market area (pp 247-8) as seems likely at Dublin (Wallace 1985, 135). This is supported by the contemporary authority of Alexander Neckam (1157–1217) who lists amber, adamant, serpentine (*ophelta*) and marble among the stones carved by goldsmiths and requiring sharp chisels (Campbell M 1991, 121).

Three gem stones comprise a smoky quartz cabochon (38) in a plain silver mount (SR4), and two unmounted cabochons of quartz (36) and smoky quartz (37). One of these (36) came from the **Period I.10** flood deposits (58) in the southern part of the **southern sector**, and probably dates to the seventh century. The other (37) came from the shallow **Period I–III** deposits in the western part of the **central sector**. The date of its discovery suggests it is relatively early, and it might have been associated with the rich finds from this part of the site ascribed to *c*. 700 AD (Figure 10.87a).

1 Mica garnet schist, a Highland rock, probably a glacial erratic, but could be a flake from a hone.

415.01

6 Ferruginous quartz pebble, used as polisher, probably for polishing silver or copper alloy.

82.03

8 Rose quartz pebble, local(?) beach pebble with handling polish.

411.04

10 Mica flakes (muscovite), possibly from Spain. Flakes too large to have come from Isle of Man, condition indicates object been looked after carefully.

237

11 Undamaged, exotic rock crystal.
315.02

12 Top of rock crystal, probably broken off intentionally for use as jewel. Perfect facets on one side, flawed on the other where struck.
230.03

13 Exotic quartz crystal with Haematite, possibly collected due to blood-red Haematite tip for use as charm or jewel.
88.01

15 Banded quartz crystal with damaged tip reminiscent of strike-a-light. Definitely not local, it is like agate, but a crystal, possibly jewellery-related.
478

18 Vein quartz with Haematite. Bad colour, but otherwise similar to 12–15, 19 and 20.
417.02

19 Badly damaged large rock crystal, similar to 20.
632

20 Large exotic quartz crystal, probably from hydrothermal vein, one end battered unequally could have been mounted.
451

21 Polished, east coast belemnite (Phraemocone, possible cylindroleuthis) jurassic – cretaceous.
520.02

22 Granite beach pebble with enhanced handling polish. Origin uncertain.
249.01

26 Exotic stone (porphyry, medium quartz or labrodite?). Medium pyroxene crystals, groundmass dark. Saw cut marks one flat side/possibly one edge. Cross abrasions one side only. Opposite side saw cuts i.e. saw cuts protected since initial cuts or larger block cut down. Large green penocrysts central ethedral with pale green inclusions (lathe shaped).
539

27 Exotic sandstone with quartz vein, Highland(?) or Alpine.
220

29 Broken polished fine-grained sandstone pebble (16.4gm).
456.01

30 Chipped polished fine-grained, sandstone pebble. (13.45gm).
456.01

34 Small banded polished quartzite pebble. Possibly local beach pebble (Sandhead area), but with characteristic handling polish.
533

36 Unmounted plano-convex quartz cabuchon.
D10 H 4 **58**

37 Unmounted plano-convex smoky quartz cabuchon.
D 5 H 3 **901**

38 Smoky quartz cabuchon in plain silver mount (sixteenth century Scottish).
745

Limestone, calcareous sandstone and 'plastered pebbles'

The traditions of the 'White House' and the discovery of the lime-based builders' waste which supports them (pp 27–8, 81) underline the potential significance of a small group of calcareous rocks which are exotic to the area.

Unburnt limestone (SE59) and burnt limestone (SE60)

Nine pieces of unburnt calcareous rock (SE59.1–9) include six of limestone (1–3, 5, 6 and 8) and three of hard chalk (4, 7 and 9). The former include three pieces with fossil corals and bivalves similar to those in the Kirkbean outcrop of Carboniferous (Dicentian) strata including the Arbigland Group. The limestone may thus have been imported from the Solway Coast between Dumfries and Dalbeattie. The hard chalk may derive from the Cretaceous chalks in Northern Ireland. The distributions of burnt and unburnt limestone, and a range of lime products and waste are illustrated in a simplified form in Table 10.22. Single pieces of burnt and unburnt limestone from early contexts (**Period I/1**) were greatly outnumbered by fragments of clastic lime with which they were not associated closely. It is impossible to determine whether these pieces were associated with lime burning at Whithorn or had been imported for some other reason, perhaps from the same place as prepared lime. A second group of finds from **Period I** contexts came from the industrial rubbish spreads (85.02, 109) of **Period I/3**, and includes burnt limestone, clastic lime, and scraps of plaster and mortar. A larger and more varied group from the beginning of **Period II** was concentrated at the east end of the enclosure wall (247) which had probably been coated in limewashed sand plaster (p 143). This included burnt and unburnt limestone, clastic lime, plaster and mortar. This may have been debris from the construction or repair of the principal *Northumbrian* church, and the association – albeit on a small scale - of raw limestone, waste lime and lime coatings, argues that the builders may have imported and burnt lime for this operation. A group of ten 'limed' stones from the same area bear driblets of $CaCO_3$, or have deposits in cracks and interstices. Similar deposits can be seen at the foot of limewashed stone walls which may explain these unusual and geologically-unlikely stones. There were relatively few finds from the later part of **Period II**, **Periods III** and **IV** which may have seen the temporary demise of lime technology. Scraps of burnt limestone displaced into **Period V** graves (Figure 6.31) coincided with *tesserae* and fine metalworking debris (Figure 6.24), and could have been used as a glaze modifier in the production of enamel (p 244).

Calcareous sandstone (SE61)

A small group of fragments of calcareous sandstone (SE61.1–14) weighing less than half a kilogram (359.4 gm), includes crumbs from early contexts (1 (9.3gm), 109; 2 (16.9gm), 226.03; 3 (11.5gm), 463, III/17), but mostly came from the **Period V**

THE FINDS   471

	Limestone Unburnt n	Limestone Burnt n	Clastic lime gm	Chalk plaster gm	Plaster gm	Mortar (a) gm	Mortar (b) gm	Limed Stones n
Topsoil/us/recent	•••	•••••••••	428	285	28	2740	7739	••
Period VI	–	–	–	–	–	1225	474	–
Period V/4–6	•	–	15	–	7	1249	1184	–
Period V/1–4	–	•••••••••	248	169	94	523	163	•••••
Period IV	–	••	13	–	–	17	15	–
Period III	–	•	393	–	–	13	20	–
Period II late	••	•	–	–	–	–	64	••
Period II early	••	••••••	1283	70	341	74	–	•••••••••
Period I/3	–	•••	521	–	19	14	–	••••
Period I/1	•	•	8700	10	63	–	–	–

Table 10.22: Distribution of burnt and unburnt limestone and lime products

graveyard and later deposits. The calcareous sandstone is exotic to Whithorn, and may derives from the Triassic, Kirklinton sandstones and marls from the Isle of Man. It could have been introduced accidentally with the associated saliferous marls which could have been exploited for their salt content. The finds from the graveyard were concentrated in a small area and were probably associated with the manufacturing or trading activities in the *inner precinct* in **Period IV**.

Haematite polishers and ore (SE62)

A collection of Haematite (SE63.1–49) comprises two main groups, probably with completely different functions. A large assemblage of chunks of massive Haematite (25–41, 115 lumps weighing 9,730 gm) can be traced to a spread of ore (69.01) deposited to the north of Building I/1 in **Period I/1.2** (p 81). Two further chunks from later **Period I** contexts (42, 83 and 43, 85.05) might have been displaced from this group, but probably derive from a different deposit. Two lumps of heated massive Haematite (44) from early industrial features (51) in the **southern sector** were broadly contemporary with the main unheated group from 69.01, and an immediately overlying deposit (55) produced a lump of heated botryoidal Haematite (45). These may have derived from an area where ore was roasted preparatory to smelting, perhaps with a pond for washing further to the east. Two other pieces of heated Haematite (222.01, 46; 206.01, 47) from early **Period II** contexts, were perhaps similarly linked to the two unheated pieces (42 and 43) from later **Period I** contexts, and two scraps of botryoidal Haematite fused to slag (23, 73.02 and 24, 203.01) can also be ascribed to this group.

A second group comprises twenty-one lumps of botryoidal Haematite with the characteristic 'bunch of grapes/kidneystone' surface, of which eighteen are artificially smoothed. These were probably used as fine polishing or burnishing stones, probably for fine metalwork. Examples were more widely scattered in space and time than the massive Haematite. There was a concentration in **Period I** contexts in the *inner precinct* (1, 93.01; 2, 94.01; 3, 80.03; 4, 109; 5 and 6, 82.03; 7, 75.02), and three finds from **Period II** and **III** contexts (8, 220; 9, 227.02 and 10, 333) probably originated in **Period I** deposits. There were three concentrations. Two pieces (1 and 2) came from **Period I/1** contexts in the western part of the **northern sector**, and a second cluster (3, 10 and 48) from the eastern part of the **central sector**, is likely to have been of similar date, though displaced by later buildings, graves and cultivation. A third cluster (4–9) from the centre of the **northern sector** could have originated in the **Period I/3** debris associated with a hollow (109). Later finds (11 and 12, 495; 13, 430; 14, 417.02; 15, 533; 16, 543; 17, 506.01; 18, 729 and 19, 767) from a range of **Period IV** and **V** contexts (Figure 6.24) coincided with one concentration of crucible fragments, and were perhaps associated with a fine metalworking shop in the later part of **Period IV**. One lump of massive Haematite (48, 258) had been smoothed, and two others (21, 52.01 and 22, 415.01) which had been both heated *and* smoothed, may have been roasted for smelting, and subsequently reused as polishers. One of these came from a **Period I.5** building (12, 52.01) overlying the **Period I.4** industrial debris (51) in the **southern sector**.

Quartzite bead stone (SE63)

A large chunk of exotic red quartzite with white veins bore four hollow-drill scars presumably where slugs of stone had been removed, perhaps to make beads (Figure 10.128). The stone had broken across the drill holes either by accident or to facilitate the removal of the stone slugs. The other surfaces of the stone had been roughly-dressed, perhaps to identify the most suitable points for drilling. The rock probably originates to the north of the Highland Boundary Fault, and though possibly a glacial erratic, could have been imported. It came from a **Period III** building (479, III/21), but there was no associated working debris, and it may have been worked elsewhere on the site, perhaps at an earlier time. A similar, though unworked, cobble (2) from the original **Period II** burial chapel (249.01) may have been selected for the same purpose.

1 Exotic quartzite cobble with four hollow drill holes exposed on the face of the fractured edge. 80% of the pebble surface is roughly trimmed to a rounded form with a flattish base. The walls of the holes are polished and the base convex with a well defined cut edge. Two holes are drilled from the top and two from the bottom, but are not aligned and do not join up. The holes are 15mm diameter tapering slightly at the base and are **A**–30; **B**–16; **C**–8; **D**–19mm deep.

85 × 50 × 50 **479**

White stones (SE64–68, 70 and 72)

'To him who conquers I will give some of the hidden manna, and I will give him a white stone, with a new name written on the stone, which no one knows except him who receives it.'

Apocalypse II:17

'. . . although you may write the name of the devil on a white stone, nevertheless he [the devil] signifies the uttermost darkness.'

Bede

During the trial excavation in 1984 it was observed that many of the **Period V** graves contained white pebbles (usually quartz or granite) and cattle teeth. These were interpreted as ritual deposits, and a study of finds from the 1987 excavation (Baker 1988) supported this inference, and explored the archaeological antecedents and symbolic meaning of such deposits. In this and the ensuing years of excavation 'white stones' were collected with assiduity, and some 13,657 specimens were accumulated of which roughly 13,000 came from stratified contexts (Table 10.23). The group is sub-divided into seven categories:

Rounded quartz pebbles (SE64) are probably beach pebbles, deriving from the numerous quartz veins in the local greywackes.

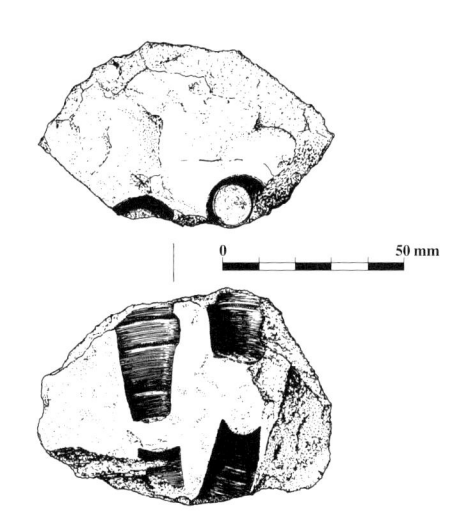

10.128 Drilled quartzite (SE63.1).

Abraded angular quartz pebbles (SE65) are less eroded than the pebbles in SE64, and perhaps derive from stream beds.
Granite pebbles (SE66) are rounded beach pebbles of pale granite, mostly local Granodiorites.
Granite cobbles (SE67) are larger beach stones, again mostly local Granodiorites.
Miscellaneous pebbles (SE 68) are similar in size to SE64–66, generally of pale colours, and mostly sandstone, though including a few examples of greywacke and basalt.
Pebbles and other stones stained or encrusted with Calcium Carbonate (SE70). This is a relatively large and entirely enigmatic group of small rounded sub-angular and angular pieces of quartz or greywacke with veins of quartz. In some the interstices of the quartz crystals, and sometimes other cracks, are filled with white calcium carbonate, others are encrusted with a similar basic material. The calcium carbonate was dissolved with acid from two rounded specimens, revealing smoothed quartz on the exterior, but unworn quartz crystals in the interstices. This is incompatible with any natural weathering process, but could result from angular fragments of vein quartz being tumbled together with calcareous rock, perhaps to pulverise lime, or more probably hard chalk. This explanation accommodates the physical and chemical evidence, and accounts for a geological phenomenon which cannot have occurred naturally. It may however strain archaeological credulity by inventing a piece of lime-processing plant, for which there seems to be no parallels.
SE72 Unabraded vein quartz fragments were probably derived from the underlying bedrock, and were the only members of the group which need not have been brought to the site.

The distributions of the several categories of 'white stones' are illustrated in Table 10.23. Examples were widely scattered in space and time, but there were significant concentrations from the **Period I** *inner precinct*, **Period II** deposits and the **Period V** graveyard. A fourth concentration in the **Period I** deposits in the *outer zone* reflects the large number of vein quartz fragments (SE72), which were probably displaced from the underlying rock and are of no significance. The concentration from the *inner precinct* in **Period I** is accounted for by the four graves capped by pebbles and cobbles, which produced 3919 specimens (Table 3.3). The remaining 546 'white stones' were widely dispersed, and included some from graves, and others from 'industrial' rubbish. The large group from **Period II** contexts included a cluster of 362 pebbles surrounding a doorpost in Building II/15, but most came from the displaced metalworking debris (110, Table 3.35) used in the initial construction of the buildings in the northern range (pp 117–8). Many of these came from the area in and around the chapel, and may have been displaced from the pebbled cover of Grave I/82, but others

THE FINDS

	64	65	66	67	68	70	72	Total	%
Recent/Topsoil/US	288	101	75	7	3	44	208	**726**	*5.3*
Period VI	167	36	31		17	26	76	**319**	*2.3*
Period V (non grave)	199	69	76	37	2	38	146	**567**	*4.2*
Period V graves	726	267	224	10	10	161	396	**1794**	*13.1*
Period IV	91	17	32	1	19	11	565	**736**	*5.4*
Period III	324	55	76	3	14	30	115	**617**	*4.5*
Period II	931	326	423	14	98	142	285	**2219**	*16.2*
Period I: *outer zone*	86	71	220		19	6	1778	**2142**	*15.7*
Period I: *inner precinct*	855	1471	1594	18	43	382	102	**4465**	*32.7*
Total	**3667**	**2413**	**2751**	**90**	**225**	**840**	**3671**	**13657**	

Table 10.23: Chronological distribution of 'white stones'.

from more westerly contexts cannot be linked to **Period I** graves.

The overall impression is that, while large numbers of 'white stones' can be accounted for by grave covers, many can not, and for whatever reason, they were regularly included in accumulations of rubbish. The group from the **Period V** graves is somewhat problematical. The original observation that pebbles were placed by the knees of burials was not confirmed by subsequent excavation, and the numbers of pebbles from graves varied considerably. The significance of these finds is supported by the relative scarcity of examples in the underlying deposits of **Periods III** and **IV** through which the graves were dug. The pebbles could have been displaced along with other debris (Tables 6.41 and 42), but on balance, it is likely that most were introduced during the life of the graveyard. They were too few and too scattered to have been disturbed grave covers, and may thus, with due caution, be treated as burial talismans spanning the use of the graveyard in the later-thirteenth to mid-fifteenth century. Baker's suggestion that white stones were an 'an admission ticket to the "other world"' (1988, 25) offer a plausible explanation for their role in burial rites. The incidence of 'white stones' in the successive **Period I** burials may be significant. Pebbles were found in two of the eight graves in the **Phase 1.5** graveyard (4 and 7); in three of the thirty-one **Phase 2** graves (12, 14 and 34); in five of the thirty-three **Phase 3** graves (43, 51, 54, 59 and 61) and in twenty-two of the forty-seven **Phase 4** graves (74–80, 83, 84, 86, 87, 90, 91, 101, 104–8, 111, 113–116, 118). This pattern corresponds with the use of pebble covers, of which one pertains to the latter part of **Phase 3**, and three to **Phase 4**. The ritual uses of 'white stones' were thus concentrated in the latter part of **Period I**, perhaps dating to the second half of the seventh century and opening decades of the eighth. Continuing ritual use in the eighth to late-ninth centuries is indicated by pebbles from the **Period II** children's graveyard and overlying **Period III** burials. The ritual use of white stones in Christian graveyards has been extensively studied (e.g. Crowe 1982) with occurrences in Scotland, Ireland, Wales and the Isle of Man (Nowakowski and Thomas 1992, 9). Whithorn has provided what is perhaps the largest sample yet available, but 'white stones' were not confined to burials, and seem to have been collected and deposited somewhat promiscuously.

Hone blanks (SE71)

Hone blanks are discussed above pp 453-4.

Scored and scratched stones (SE73, 74 and 75)

A large collection of scored, scratched and marked stones includes forty-eight with glacial or plough scars (SE73), ten with potentially-fortuitous cross marks (SE74), and three with miscellaneous 'chisel' marks (SE75).

Heat-glazed (SE76) and fire-cracked stones (SE77)

Fire-cracked stones (SE76) and glazed pebbles (SE77) were recovered from every period (Table 10.24). A concentration of fire-cracked stones from the **Period V** graveyard probably originated in the bank of fire-reddened greywacke (430) spread over the **central sector** in **Period IV.3**. The source of this stone is uncertain, but it may represent 'burnt mound' material used to heat water for cooking, or to generate steam for bathing. 'Burnt mounds' are generally of Bronze Age date, but a group in the East Rhins produced eleventh to thirteenth century AD dates (Russell-White 1990, Barber 1990b, 102), and were thus broadly contemporary with the Whithorn deposit. Similar fire-reddened greywacke fragments were used for the hard core underlying the earth floors of the **Period III/3** buildings in the **central sector**, which perhaps date to the tenth/early eleventh

	76	77
Recent/Topsoil/US	10	33
Period VI	16	5
Period V (non grave)	6	25
Period V graves	24	25
Period V total	30	50
Period IV	13	12
Period III	8	1
Period II	12	11
Period I: *outer zone*	8	4
Period I: *inner precinct*	23	6
Total	**120**	**122**

Table 10.24: Chronological distributions of fire-cracked (SE76) and glazed (SE77) stones.

century. Fragments of local sandstones and greywackes predominate among the fire-damaged stones, but they include cracked igneous rocks (Diorite, Granite, Porphyry, Gabbro and Basalt) which would have been more effective as water heaters, and less-prone to splitting (Buckley 1990b, 171–2).

Most of the heat-glazed pebbles (SE77) are local sandstones, and the glazing is an unsurprising consequence of their exposure to high temperatures. The only notable concentration came from the surface (600.04) overlying the **Period V** graves in the north part of the site, which may have derived from the **Period V/5** smithy (635) to the north.

The Antler

Andrew Nicholson

'Some say that this was how Cerball was killed: he was going into Cell Dara (Kildare) eastward along the street of the stone steps, with a proud horse under him, when he came opposite a comb-maker's workshop; at that moment the comb-maker set out his antlers, when the horse was opposite him outside, and the proud horse shied backwards, and he [Cerball] struck his own spear, in the hands of his own servant, who was behind him (and Uille was the name of that boy, or the name of the comb-maker). Cerball died of that wound at the end of a year, and he was buried among his forefathers in the graveyard of Nas.'

(Fragmentary Annals of Ireland, Radner 1978, 166–7)

Some two thousand and fifty pieces of antler, most with evidence of working, comprise one of the largest assemblages from Britain, comparable with groups from Dublin, York and *Hamwic* in the British Isles, and *Haithabu* (Ulbrich 1978), Lund (Christopherson 1980), Ribe and Birka (Ambrosiani 1981) on the continent. These and other sites show that antler-working, and specifically comb-production, were urban crafts, and the Whithorn material should be seen as part of the same ninth to twelfth century North European pattern. Studies of the distributions of comb types and decorative motifs have identified the activities and markets of itinerant craftsmen, and the finds from Whithorn display recurrent links with Irish craft schools. The excavation has revealed a detailed picture of the organisation of this craft in different workshops, identifying a comb-makers 'quarter' established in the third quarter of the ninth century, and enduring until the later phases of **Period IV** in perhaps *c.* 1200 AD (Figure 10.136).

A series of well-stratified groups of antler allowed the identification of differing attributes of workshop and discarded dump deposits (Table 10.25), as well as preferential methods of composite comb production. A quarter of the pieces were parings or shavings from antler working, and another quarter could be directly related to the construction of composite combs – more than seven times the amount of material specifically attributable to production of other objects, such as gaming pieces, pins and handles. Almost all the material derives from red deer, and only five pieces of roe deer antler were recorded, although roe deer bones were more frequent than red (p 613). Although most of the collection pertains to **Periods III** and **IV**, there is a small, but interesting group from **Period I** indicating limited comb production in the sixth/seventh century.

There is no standard terminology for describing antler waste and the system used here has been evolved by the author, whilst the classification of combs follows MacGregor (1985) and Dunlevy (1988). The construction of composite combs and the process of their manufacture, has been discussed elsewhere (Galloway and Newcomer 1981, MacGregor 1985, 74–6) and a summary will suffice here. Two elongated side-plates were cut and smoothed, and carefully-shaped rectangular tooth-plates were sandwiched between them (Figure 10.129). Rivets, usually of iron in the Norse period, though more frequently of copper alloy in the later medieval period, were used to secure the side-plates and clamp the tooth-plates in place. When the tooth-plates were secured the teeth were cut with a saw, and the individual teeth shaped and polished. The back of the comb would be trimmed to remove the projecting remnants of the tooth-plates, creating distinctive trapezoidal offcuts. Decoration was usually only applied to the side-plates, and consisted of incised lines – criss-cross, parallel or diagonally hatched – and ring-and-dot motifs. Combinations of motifs could be used on the same comb. The design of these combs seems simple, but their manufacture required precise measurements of the various components and a high quality of finishing. The combs from Whithorn display close morphological and decorative links with Ireland, and the Irish typological sequence (Dunlevy 1988) has been used to classify them. Dunlevys's typology identifies ten classes of which three (B, F and G) are present at Whithorn. Class B comprises double-edged composite combs. These were introduced into Ireland in the third century (Dunleavy 1988, 354), and are closely paralleled on Western Scottish sites of the seventh to ninth centuries (e.g. Dun Cuier, Barra Young 1956, 318; Dunadd, Christison and Anderson 1905, 316 and Broch of Burrian, Stevenson 1955, 287). Class F is a single-edged Viking type with sub-divisions based on the cross-sectional appearance of the side-plate. F1 combs have relatively deep, flat or thin C-shaped side-plates (e.g. Figure 10.131, No. 71.2), whereas Class

F2 combs have a more rounded thicker C-shaped plate (e.g. Figure 10.131, No. 71.4), and Class F3 have bevelled or trapezoidal section side-plates (e.g. Figure 10.131, Nos 70.9 and 10). Class F1 combs are generally dated to the mid-ninth to tenth century, although Irish examples continue into the eleventh century, and a similar late date is possible for some of the Whithorn finds. Class F 2 combs have been found from the late-ninth century to the early-twelfth, and overlap with Class F3 combs which were current from the tenth to later-twelfth centuries. Class G comprises single-edged, straight-backed composite combs with an almost semi-circular profile, and have a long currency in the ninth to thirteenth centuries. Most of the comb fragments from Whithorn had been displaced by **Period V** graves, but a combination of stratigraphic and spatial evidence allows a tentative sequence of types to be advanced (Figure 10.136).

Catalogue

The classification of the material was based around the utilisation of the various parts of an antler, sub-divided on the bases of tool and fracture marks to determine if preferred working practices could be identified (Figure 10.129). This system means that some categories were identified of which there were no examples in the collection. This classification helped to clarify the procedures of comb production (Table 10.25) and some categories have been grouped in production clusters rather than numerical order in this report.

A: Waste

Basal Antler (AR01–11)

One hundred and twenty-four pieces of basal antler had been discarded after the removal of the beam and brow tine. They are of value as they record the minimum number of antlers processed at Whithorn, and displayed a range of working techniques complementing that from other parts of the antler. As with other collections (e.g. York, Macgregor 1978, 46; Lincoln, Mann 1982, 44; Dublin, O'Roirdain 1971, 75), the vast majority of antler was collected after it had been shed (116 out of 127 examples), and only eleven pieces retained skull fragments with butchery marks (AR5). The latter can be sub-divided by their later treatment: one piece is sawn through the pedicle, one through the burr, four are sawn through the beam below the brow tine, and the remaining five are sawn above the brow tine. Three of these last have sawn brow tines, and two have cut brow tines.

Only twenty-one pieces had the burr removed below the brow tine (AR1–4) mostly by sawing (Figure 10.129). The sawn beams had usually been rotated at least once, often twice, to prevent the blade catching, leaving saw marks some 1.4mm to 2.6mm wide. The thickness and density of basal antler precludes breaking as a method of truncation and there was only one broken piece (AR3). Most of the burrs were truncated above the brow tine. Seven pieces (AR6), although so

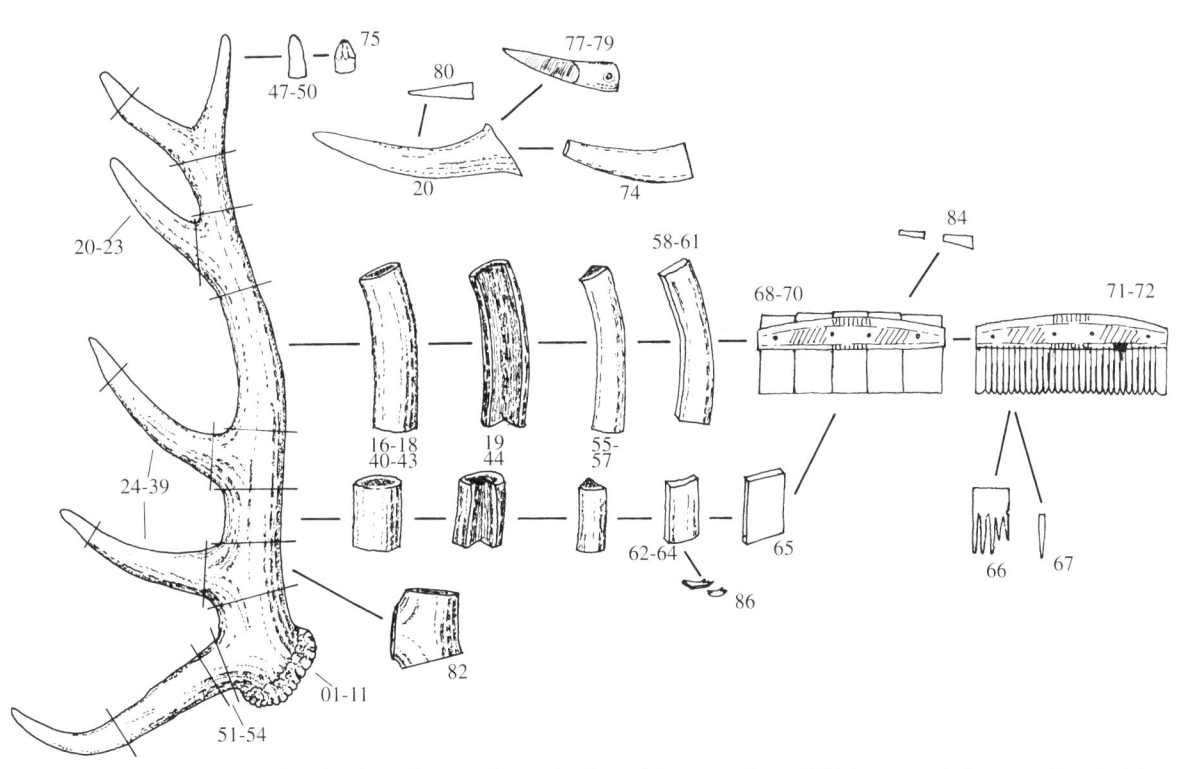

10.129 The conversion of antler into the combs and other objects made at Whithorn, and the associated object blanks and waste.

Preparatory	Early comb production	Early tine adaptation	Mid-stage comb production	Late-stage comb production	Comb repair
01–11 (W)	16–18 (R)	20–31 (R)	19 (R/W)	61 (R)	
12–14 (R)	40–43 (R)	32–39 (R/W)	44 (R/W)	65 (R)	
90 (R)	82 (W)	47–54 (W)	55–60 (R)		
		62–64 (W)			
		83 (W)			66–67 (W)
					68–71 (R/W)
			82 (W)		

Table 10.25: Antler categories and comb-production stages.
R = primarily exploitable resource, W = primarily waste.

abraded that the treatment of the beam was uncertain, still had saw-marks on the junction of the brow tine. As with most of the sawn tines, these were sawn completely across at the base, usually from the bottom upwards. The commonest method of treating basal antler (55.6%) was to saw the beam above the brow tine, and saw the brow tine as well (AR8). This leaves a quantity of usable material above the burr and coronet and is one of several indications that usable antler was discarded. The beam was generally sawn around – i.e. turned at intervals – whilst the tine was sawn across. It was sometimes possible to break the beam when all the denser tissue had been sawn through. This would not be possible on tines cut from below (see AR06) and in several cases knife marks were found in the acute angle of the junction, cutting down towards the beam, in order to complete the removal of the tine. Where it was possible to distinguish, the tines appear to have been removed before the beam was sawn up. Only two pieces had cut brow tines (AR09), reflecting the difficulty of this working method (MacGregor 1985, 63–4). These could be easily distinguished by the 'dogtooth' edge around the denser tissue, suggesting cutting with a chopping tool – perhaps an axe or cleaver, rather than the finer marks characterising knife work. The marks cut in towards the beam. On eleven pieces (AR10) the beam had been sawn, and the brow tine had been broken in antiquity. No evidence of working was found around the tine base, though most examples had been displaced into **Period V** graves so the fractures may be post-depositional.

Beams (AR12–19)

The beam, with its thick layer of compact tissue and general lack of curvature, provides the most useful portions for comb-making, being suitable for tooth-plates and side-plates. After the burr and tines had been removed the beams were divided into cylindrical sections (AR16–19) of appropriate length for making combs. These could also have been used as handles for larger tools and implements, but none of the Whithorn handles appear to come from beams, and deposits containing beam debris are likely to indicate comb manufacture. These sections are described below (pp 478-9), the remaining beam fragments are generally offcuts from their production or pieces discarded as unsuitable.

Five beams, though sawn off from their burrs, still retained their tines (AR12). In three cases only the upper part of the beam, with tines and crown, remained, indicating that the lower section of beam had been utilised. Again this seems to indicate a surplus of antler with only the best parts seeing use. Twelve beams had broken tines (AR13). As with the broken brow tines there was no evidence of working, but in this case more pieces came from contexts which would mitigate against post-depositional damage. Half the beams (AR14) had at least one sawn tine and in many cases the bez and tres tines were sawn, whilst the crown and upper tines remained intact. As the circumferential curvature of a tine affects its suitability for comb manufacture, it is significant that only the larger tines have been removed. The remaining tines on these examples would have been suitable for small handles, but had not been utilised. Three beams with sawn tines also

	A		**B**		**C**		**D**		**E**		**F**	
	Cat	nos	Cat	nos	Cat	nos	Cat	nos	Cat	nos	Cat	nos
Beam sawn	01	7	07	6	08	69	09	2	10	11	11	0
Beam cut	02	0										
Beam broken	03	1										
Removal uncertain	04	13			06	7						

Table 10.26: Basal antler categories.
A = removed below brow tine, **B** = brow tine intact, **C** = brow tine sawn, **D** = brow tine cut, **E** = brow tine broken in antiquity, **F** = brow tine broken recently.

A		B		C		D		E	
Cat.	nos	Cat.	nos	Cat.	nos	Cat.	nos	Cat.	nos
12	5	13	12	14	19	90	3	15	28

Table 10.27: Categories and numbers of antler beam pieces and fragments.
A = beams with attached tines, B = beams with broken tines, C = beams with sawn tines, D = beams with cut tines, E = beam fragments.

had cut tines, which, as with the cut basal antler, seemed have been cut by a chopping action towards the base of the tine, on both sides and in the acute angle of the junction. It is uncertain why some tines were cut.

Tines (AR20–46)

Tines were used for a variety of purposes. The lower portion could be utilised for comb tooth-plates, providing that the curvature was not too great, and also for the connecting side plates, but is also suitable for handles on small tools such as knives and awls. The upper portions of tines were used for a range of implements exploiting their shape, structure and strength (AR77–80). The tine fragments comprise intact tines, tips, bases and central sections. These display a range of working marks identifying twenty six different categories (AR20–46, Tables 10.28 and 30). Most of these pieces had been discarded as waste during the production of combs and other objects, but some may have been partly-prepared and never used.

Twenty-three whole tines were sawn off at their basal end (AR20), three times as many as those with cut bases (AR21), and about the same amount as those whose bases were broken off from the beams (AR22). When looking at antler tines as a whole, 34.3% of tines were recovered intact, again showing that the total antler resource was under-exploited, and 59.4% of all tines were sawn in some fashion, with saw marks some 1.5mm–2mm wide.

The small number of tines sawn at base and tip (AR24, 13) contrasts with the numerous sawn tine tips (AR47, 88), and shows that most sawn tines were utilised, either for comb-plate blanks or handles. Although only five tines were sawn at the base and cut at the tip (AR25), the use of two different tools on the same tine is noteworthy. Given that cutting antler must have been significantly harder than sawing it, one can only assume that the cutting must relate to some other factor. Thirty-eight tines with sawn bases had their tips broken in antiquity (AR26), and of all the antler tines without tips, breakage accounts for some 54.5%, as opposed to 21.5% sawn, 8.3% cut and 15.7% unknown due to recent damage or abrasion. Although some tines may have been broken prior to shedding, the large number of broken tine tips indicates a common working practice.

Tine tips (AR47–50) and bases (AR51–54)

A large group of tine tips and bases seem to have been discarded when handles or sections were made from the central parts of tines (Table 10.29). The largest groups were sawn (AR47) and broken (AR49) tine tips, and the numerical contrast between the eighty-eight sawn tine tips and twenty-six tines with their tips sawn off demonstrates that over two thirds of the latter had been utilised. Whilst the lengths of the tips varied considerably, the criteria for where to cut appears related to curvature and circumference, with 34mm as the minimum circumference, but mostly falling into two groups between 41mm and 73mm. The sixty-three tine tips with broken bases (AR49) show this was a favoured method of tip removal, though it is unclear how this was done. As with sawn tine tips, the principal range of circumference at the base of the tip is 41mm to 72mm.

In all the tine bases (AR51–54) the tine had originally been sawn off from the beam, and sub-divisions relate to subsequent treatment (Table 10.29). By comparison with total numbers of removed tines, only one in seven had their basal end separately removed. The most likely reason for

	A		B		C		D		E	
	Cat.	nos	Cat.	nos	Cat.	nos	Cat.	nos	Cat.	nos
Sawn at base	20	23	24	13	25	5	26	38	27	5
Cut at base	21	8	28	1	29	0	30	1	31	1
Base broken in antiquity	22	21	32	10	33	7	34	21	35	1
Base broken recently	23	22	36	2	37	0	38	0	39	10

Table 10.28: Tine modification.
A = intact tine, B = sawn at tip, C = cut at tip, D = tip broken in antiquity, E = tip broken recently.

	A		B		C		D	
	Cat.	nos	Cat.	nos	Cat.	nos	Cat.	nos
Tine tips: base treatment	47	88	48	9	49	63	50	1
Tine bases: distal treatment	51	9	52	8	53	6	54	0

Table 10.29: Tine tips and tine bases.
A = sawn, B = cut, C = broken in antiquity, D = broken recently

removing the tine base would be for trimming handles to the right length and circumference. The proportions of saw and knife work reflect differences in working techniques dictated either by the use and function of the finished item or by the availability of tools. The former is more likely given the prevalence of sawing in other categories.

Waste (AR82, 83, 85 and 86)

Antler waste offcuts were divided according to whether they derived from tine junctions (AR82) or not (AR83). At the beam/tine junction the grain of the antler splits and lies in two directions, thus making such areas unsuitable for use in combs, where the strength lies in the uniform direction of the grain (MacGregor and Currey 1983, 73). Over twice as many waste offcuts came from junctions as from other areas (167:77), indicating that the structural properties of the antler were understood, and the junctions discarded accordingly. Many of the seventy-seven pieces in AR83 appeared to be fragments split off during the preparation of tooth-plates, which were too narrow or short to be of further use. Sixty-seven tine offcut/trimmings (AR85) were distinguished from the non-junction fragments by their external circumferential curvature, which precluded their use for flat tooth-plates. A large group of tine fragments (AR45) was too fragmentary to be ascribed to more specific categories. Five hundred and fifteen parings and shavings (AR86) were by far the most numerous category, and helped to distinguish areas of specific workshop activity from dumped waste deposits. The fragments included shavings cut by a knife or drawknife, as well as pieces chopped or hacked by an axe or similar implement.

B: Comb Making Debris

Most of the material described above was debris from the preparatory conversion of antlers, and subsequent preparation of cylindrical sections from beams and tines in the early stages of comb production (Table 10.25). The collection includes a large number of pieces illustrating the later working stages in the production of combs. The survival of this material is somewhat surprising and demonstrates that more antler was prepared for use than was eventually required. The processes are illustrated in Figure 10.129 which shows the sub-division of sections into wedge-shaped segments, and their subsequent working into the tooth and side-plates of composite combs. It was essential that the regularly-spaced teeth sawn at the end of the process should not coincide with the junction of two tooth-plates (Figure 10.130), which were thus prepared to a precise range of widths already evident in the guide marks on the sections. A second series of metrical standards controlled the lengths of the tooth-plates and the sections from which they were produced, indicating that taller plates were prepared for the arched centre of the combs (Figure 10.129). Selected measurements (Figure 10.130) reveal the comb-makers' precision.

Sections (AR16–19, 40–44)

Cylindrical sections from beams (AR16–19) and tines (AR40–44), sawn at both ends, were produced after tines, junctions and burrs had been discarded. Relatively short sections were garnered from the beam between the bez and tres tines and longer ones from between the tres tine and crown. The latter are probably the most useful zone of antler, being equally suitable for comb tooth-plates, comb side-plates, and handles. Some sections show small preparatory saw cuts (1.2mm to 2.3mm wide) which were then not used. Others have small nicks, probably made by a knife, in the outer circumference of their upper or lower ends which were guide marks are for splitting off segments to form rough plates (MacGregor 1985, 57). Nineteen beam sections (AR19) had a segment removed, in all cases by splitting. Two antler wedges (AR80, Figure 10.136d) could have been used for splitting the segments as at *Haithabu* (MacGregor 1985, Fig. 34, after Ulbrich 1978). Although relatively few beam sections were recovered, their length range effectively matches that of the commoner segments (AR55) and tooth-plate blanks (AR62–64, Figure 10.130).

As with beams, the tines were sawn into sections (AR40–44) to be turned into comb tooth-plates. Only six sections were the right size for making tooth-plates, and most were much smaller with lengths ranging from 9mm to 27mm. These may represent trimming waste, possibly from handles, as opposed to an unutilised resource.

Segments (AR55–57)

Segments are triangular blocks of antler split from sections of beams and tines, and subsequently worked into tooth-plates. These have been extensively recorded at *Haithabu* (Ulbrich 1978) and Lund (Christophersen 1980), but less frequently elsewhere. The segments are divided into three categories: one

A	B		C		D		E		Total		
	Cat.	nos	Cat.	nos	Cat.	nos	Cat.	nos	Cat.	nos	
Beam sections	**16**	17	**17**	0	**18**	0			**19**	19	**36**
Tine sections	**40**	23	**41**	0	**42**	3	**43**	1	**44**	2	**29**

Table 10.30: Beam and tine sections.
A = sawn at both ends, **B** = one end cut, **C** = one end broken in antiquity, **D** = one end broken recently, **E** = with segment removed.

THE FINDS 479

A		B		C	
Cat.	nos	Cat.	nos	Cat.	nos
55	44	56	45	57	35

Table 10.31: Segments.
A = segments from beam sections, **B** = segments from tine sections, **C** = segments of uncertain origin.

derived from beam sections (AR55), one from tine sections (AR56), and a third of uncertain origin (AR57) due to the small size of the fragments. The group probably includes a mixture of prepared suitable pieces and discarded segments of inappropriate width or curvature. An analysis of the widths and lengths of the three groups of segments revealed a broad similarity in the range of lengths (Figure 10.130), with distinct peaks between 32mm and 42mm, but noticeable differences in the widths probably due to the surface curvature of the raw material, allowing greater flat segments from the beam than the tine. The segments from beams showed the greatest width range, whilst those from tines logically tended towards the lower values (Figure 10.130). The thirty-five segments of uncertain origin fell into two distinct width groups (Figure 10.130). The wider ones were similar to tine segments, while narrow segments were probably waste discarded when others of requisite width had been struck off.

Side- and tooth-plate blanks (AR58–65)

Side-plates and tooth-plates were made by smoothing and shaping segments of appropriate length, and the assemblage includes large numbers of partly-manufactured plates (Table 10.32). These may have been unused reserves, or could have been discarded as flawed after initial preparation.

Side-plates (AR58–61)

Eighteen partly-manufactured side-plates revealed interesting evidence of working practices, which were generally matched by the more numerous tooth-plates. Seven side-plates roughed out on both sides (AR58) all appear to have been split from pre-sawn sections. These had been shaped by trimming the sides with a knife or a drawknife, but neither the interior cancellous tissue nor the exterior guttering had been removed. Five roughed out side-plates (AR59) had their interior surface smoothed, leaving broad shallow scoop marks across the entire width. These indicate the use of a drawknife, as opposed to the finer 'chatter' marks produced by a knife. In two cases the outer face was roughly smoothed, though the guttering is still evident. This may have been done to aid the holding of the plate in a clamp to facilitate working, or indeed may be the result of such a process. Six side-plates had been fully smoothed on both faces (AR61), but lacked tooth marks, rivet holes, or decoration, and had probably not been used. All belong to the group of single-sided combs with arched spines typical of the Norse period. They come from five different plates, two are flat Class F1 plates, and three are bevelled Class F3 plates.

Tooth-plates (AR62–65)

Tooth-plate blanks were made by trimming the segments split from sections, and displayed similar working practices to the side-plates. Selected measurements reveal similar patterns of length to the sections and segments, while the widths correspond with the requirements of tooth-spacing (Figure 10.130). The plates in the largest group (AR62) still had rough exterior and interior faces with both ends sawn and, in complete examples, both sides split. Thirty-four plates (AR63) have had their inner face trimmed first. The cancellous tissue was removed, possibly by knife, and the surface smoothed with a drawknife, leaving a distinctive slightly scalloped interior. In only two cases (AR64) was the guttered exterior trimmed and smoothed, again by knife, before the cancellous core was entirely removed, showing that it was customary to clean and trim the inner face first. Forty-eight plates trimmed on both faces (AR65) included forty-two sufficiently intact to measure (Figure 10.130). Tempel has observed that tooth-plates must be of even thickness when they are clamped by the side-plates (Tempel 1969), and the range of thicknesses (2mm to 6mm) in this category, and the lack of any filing or polishing marks, suggest that these pieces still required further work. Only one fragment of waste (AR84.21) can be ascribed to a later stage of production. It came from a tooth-plate which had been smoothed on both sides, and had the lower end chamfered on both sides prior to tooth cutting.

	A		B		C		D	
	Cat.	nos	Cat.	nos	Cat.	nos	Cat.	nos
Side-plate blanks	58	7	59	5	60	0	61	6
Tooth-plate blanks	62	118	63	34	64	2	65	48

Table 10.32: Side and tooth-plate blanks.
A = rough on both sides, **B** = rough on outer side, smoothed on inner side, **C** = rough on inner side, smoothed on outer side, **D** = both sides smoothed.

Off-cuts and trimmings (AR84)

Some offcuts (AR84) were obviously the direct product of later stage comb manufacture. The distinctive trapezoidal plate offcuts, formed when the tooth-plates are sawn flush with the back of the comb, formed the majority of this category, though a few pieces could be identified as the sawn off ends of trapezoidal or bevelled comb side-plates from Class F3 combs.

Measurements

Selected measurements of sections, segments and tooth-plates are illustrated in Figure 10.130. The lengths of tooth-plates correlated with those of segments (AR55–7), but their widths varied greatly, with intermittent peaks. This peaking suggests that the plates were trimmed to a width relating to a known interval to contain a whole number of teeth in a plate (Ambrosiani 1981). This is further enhanced when one looks at the entire range of tooth-plates (Figure 10.130) where peaks occur at 2–3mm intervals across the entire range of widths. The lengths of tooth-plates trimmed on both sides (AR65) peak at 33mm, 41mm and 49mm, and their widths show a marked preference for 19–21mm.

C: Combs

There were no intact combs, and the comb fragments have been ascribed to six categories (AR66–71), with a seventh (AR72) reserved for the first complete example. The fragments were concentrated in the south-east part of the **central sector** (Figure 10.136e and d), and many of these are likely to have been debris from the repair of combs in Building IV/18 during the earlier part of **Period IV**. Others can be ascribed tentatively to other phases, although the stratigraphic evidence is generally unhelpful.

Eleven tooth-plates with sawn teeth (AR66), without attached side-plates, all show some degree of wear, but most have lost their teeth. Intact plates with two split sides ranged from 15mm to 24mm in width. Some had been trimmed by knife to conform with the curved back of the comb, or had rivet holes in one edge, indicating that they derived from finished items. Nine separate teeth (AR67), five found together, ranged in length from 21mm to 25mm. Horizontal striations and banding show they had been used before they were broken. Eight of the plates and six of the teeth came from the south-east part of the **central sector**, and, though extensively displaced, were concentrated around the doorway of Building IV/18 (Figure 10.136d and e). These may well have been discarded after being replaced in their combs by new plates.

Four fragments of undecorated side-plates with rivet holes and saw marks on one edge (AR68.1–4) all had deep rounded well-polished D-shaped profiles identifying them as Class G. They are not as deep as examples from Dublin, and are best matched by a group recorded as 'Probably Strokestown, Co. Roscommon' (Dunlevy 1988, 405). Three of the pieces (1–3) have teeth of about 1.5mm basal width with saw marks 0.5mm wide, whilst the fourth (4) has finer teeth of 0.8mm to 1mm wide with saw cuts of 0.2mm to 0.3mm. One (3) came from Building IV/18, two others (2 and 4) from overlying graves (Figure 10.136b), and the fourth (1) may have been displaced from the broadly contemporary spread of waste (425.01) to the north-east (Figure 10.136d). These may have been deposited in the later-eleventh century conforming to the tenth to twelfth century date range of this class.

Six side-plates from four different combs had decoration but no rivet holes (AR69.1–5). Three had traces of tooth cuts, and wear on the other one indicated it too had seen use. Two pieces (2a and b) are bevelled with saw-cut, diagonally-hatched decoration, and are either the ends of the same plate or opposed plates from the same Class F1 comb. A third (1) with ring-and-dot decoration, also appears to be part of an F1 side-plate. The other pieces (3–5) are small fragments, with ring-and-dot or sawn diagonal hatching. The three identifiable F1 comb fragments (1, 2a and 2b) had all been displaced into **Period V** graves, and could have originated in **Period III** or **IV** deposits.

Undecorated Comb Side-plates (AR68)

1 Badly abraded fragment of Class G side-plate, fractured across rivet holes. Undecorated smooth faces, faint evidence for saw marks on lower edge. Traces of iron staining around rivet hole.
L 20 W 11.8 T 3 **631**

2* Fragment of Class G side-plate, broken laterally across rivet holes. Smooth convex section with no decoration on exterior face. Back edge smooth, straight slope. Saw marks from tooth cutting on lower edge.
L 40 W 9.5 T 3.2 Saw marks 25 Spacing 1.5 **535**

3 Fragment of Class G side-plate, broken across one rivet hole. Smooth convex section with no decoration on exterior face. Back edge slightly convex. Saw marks from tooth cutting on lower edge.
L 23.5 W 9 T 2.5 Saw marks 13 Spacing 1.7 – 1.8 **440**

4 Fragment of Class G side-plate, broken across one rivet hole. Smooth convex section with no decoration on exterior face. Back edge straight, slightly sloped. Very fine teeth indicated by saw marks.
L 19.5 W 7 T 2.5 Saw marks 20 Spacing 0.9 **533**

Decorated Comb Side-plates (AR69)

1* Abraded fragment of Class F1 side-plate, broken on all sides. The decoration consists of a rough line of 'dot-and-ring' motifs, bounded by an incised groove, on the lower side of the sloping face.
L 26 W 9.5 T 3.5 **533**

2a* Triangular sectioned Class F1 side-plate, broken at both ends, and longitudinally fractured post excavation. Appears to be from the same comb as 2b; the cuts for the teeth do not match up, suggesting that these two are two ends of the same plate rather than opposing plates from the same end. The incised diagonals are

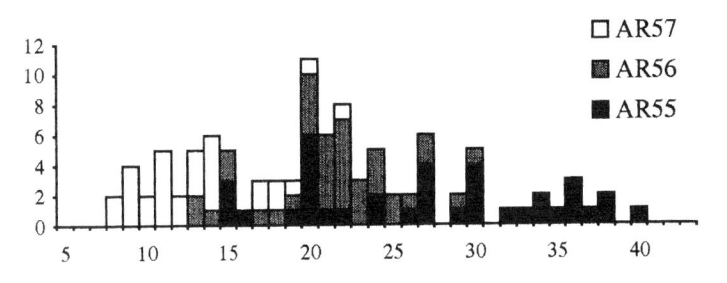

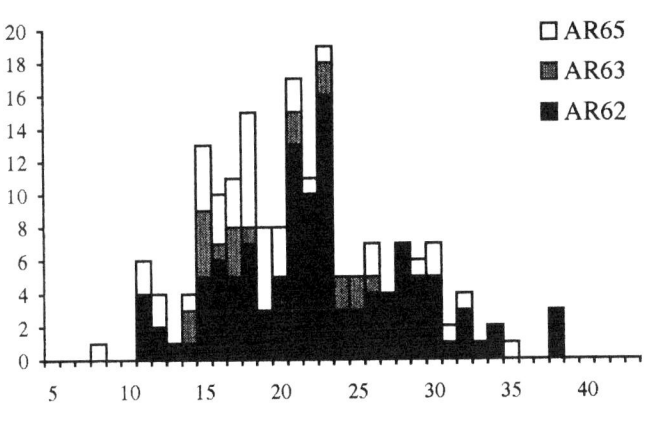

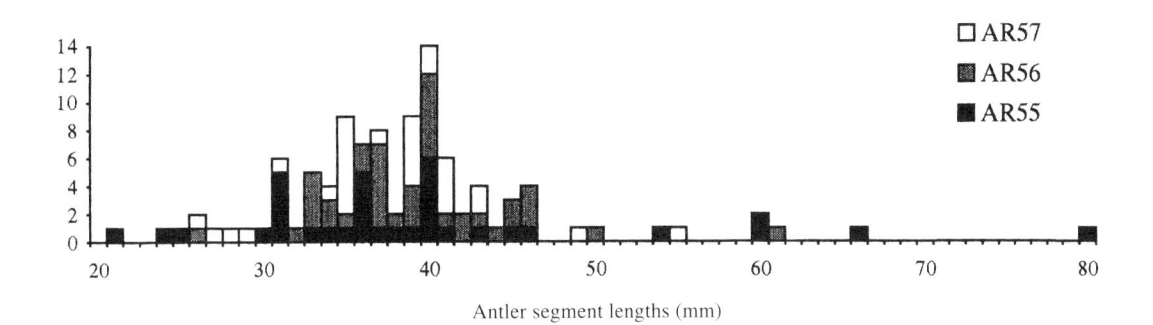

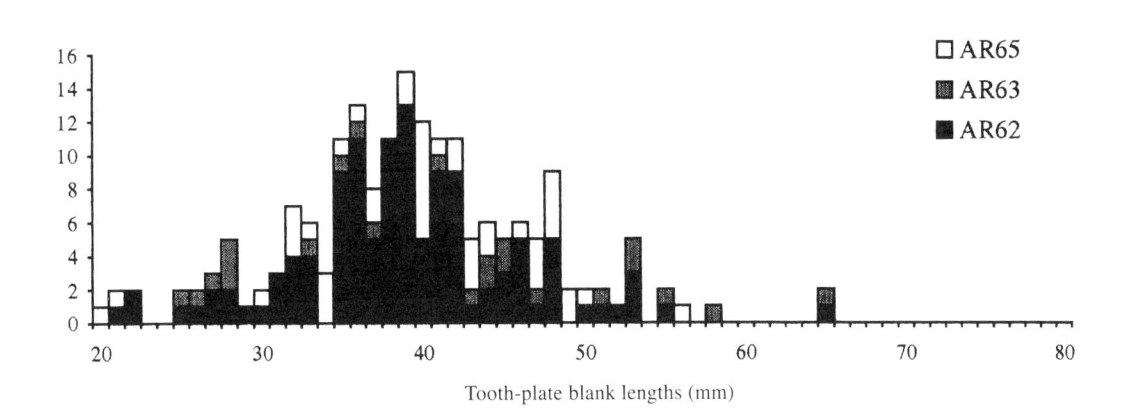

10.130 Comb-making debris measurements.

from upper left to lower right. The saw cuts for the teeth are about 0.3mm wide, and are spaced between 1.2 and 1.6mm apart.

L 40.5 W 16.5 T 3.8 **537**

2b* Triangular sectioned Class F1 side-plate broken at both ends. Both sloping faces are edged with incised longitudinal grooves top and bottom, with the intervening panel filled with diagonal incised hatching, going from upper left to lower right. The teeth were cut after the decoration, as their cut marks intrude into the pattern on the lower, straight edge of the plate. The upper back edge is convex.

L 31.5 W 15 T 4.3 **537**

3 Two tiny burnt fragments of comb side-plate. The first has one complete and one partial 'dot-and-ring' motif, and traces of a horizontal incised line. The second piece, which appears to join the first, has a raised band adjacent to the join, then an incised horizontal line. Perpendicular to this, and cut into the edge of the fragment, are three parallel cuts – possibly caused by the cutting of teeth into the comb – spaced 2.5mm and 2.7mm apart.

L 8.5 W 4 T 2 L 8.5 W 3 T 2 **430**

4 Burnt fragments of decorated side-plate, the surviving decoration consists of parallel diagonal cuts and ridges c. 0.5mm wide, bordered by two fine incised lines cut after the decoration.

L 12 W 5 T 3 **414.03**

5 Class F3 side-plate in two pieces. Central longitudinal zone bordered by double parallel grooves, containing area of diagonally hatching of evenly spaced (?)sawn lines. Outer edges of the plate bordered by a single groove. Teeth cut.

L 36 W 15 × 13 T 3.5 **415.01**

Ten fragments of side-plates (AR70.1–10) had both decoration and rivet holes, or iron staining from lost rivets. The earliest piece (1) is from a double-sided composite comb of Class B with iron rivets and sawn transverse grooved decoration. The parallels are all from Ireland (Lagore, Ballinderry 2, Lough Gara, Dunlevy 1988, 354, 376–382, Fig. 3) or Western Scotland (Dunadd, Christison and Anderson 1905, 316, Fig. 48; Broch of Burrian, MacGregor 1974, 80–4; Buiston Crannog, Munro 1882, Fig. 218), and are dated from the seventh to ninth centuries. The comb came from a burnt deposit abutting the east end of the **Period II** church (Figure 10.136b), probably dating to the mid-ninth century (p 157), although possibly somewhat earlier.

Two plates (2 and 3) came from Class F1 combs. One fragment (2) has a central zone of criss-cross sawn lines bounded by two pairs of transverse lines, which is paralleled at York (Waterman 1959, Pl 18; MacGregor 1982, 93–94), Birka (Ambrosiani 1981, 15–19), London (Pritchard 1989), Winchester (Galloway 1990, Fig. 183, No. 2160), Dublin and other Irish sites (Dunlevy 1988, 395–6). The other larger fragment (3) is unusual, having four deep longitudinal grooves, apparently saw-cut in stages, and then linked by knife work. A parallel from Flaxengate, Lincoln (Mann 1982, 4, Fig. 3) is dated to the ninth century. The fragment is secured by an antler or bone peg, which seems to have been a temporary replacement for the original iron rivet. One side-plate fragment (4) with a thick D-shaped profile, is probably Class F2, but the decoration of sawn diagonal hatching across longitudinal cuts in the longitudinally central zone is more characteristic of Class F3 combs, where the central zone of the trapezoidal face is flat. It was securely stratified in Building III/9 (Figure 10.136b) and so probably dates to the third quarter of the ninth century (p 191). F2 and F3 combs were found together at Dublin Castle (Dunlevy 1988, 366), but the associated material was dated to the late eleventh/ twelfth centuries.

The remaining six fragments (5–10) are all from Class F3 combs, recognisable by their distinctive trapezoidal section, and all have differing combinations of motifs. Two pieces had ring-and-dot motifs in the flat central band, one (7) a straight row with plain sloping faces, the other (8) with the ring-and-dot in a zigzag pattern on the central band, and saltire motifs on the extant sloping face. Both are paralleled by Irish combs from Dublin and Knowth, Co Meath (Dunlevy 1988, 367). Four fragments (5, 8, 9, 10) with blocks of saw-cut parallel lines are paralleled in Ireland (Dunlevy 1988, 366, Fig. 8) and York (MacGregor 1985). Two of the F3 comb fragments (7 and 9) came from secure **Period IV** contexts compatible with the tenth to twelfth century span of their Irish parallels. The others, and both the F1 comb fragments, had been displaced into **Period V** graves and the overlying deposits.

Decorated Comb Side-plates with Rivet Holes (AR70)

1* Plano-convex Class B side-plate, transversely fractured across the rivet holes at each end. Simple decoration covers one rivet hole and consists of two pairs of parallel lines. Tooth spacing is unusually wide, at 2mm to 2.5mm, with the cuts being about 0.5mm wide.

L 33 W 14 T 4 **320**

2* Laterally and transversely fractured fragment of Class F1 side-plate with two rivet holes, one at each end. Convex outer surface, with decoration commencing in the middle of the fragment and continuing over one of the rivet holes. Transverse decoration edged by two pairs of parallel grooves, field decorated by X design using two parallel lines for each arm, each X meeting at the inner and outer edges.

L 40 W 9 T 3 **715**

3* Plano-convex Class F1 side-plate transversely fractured, with a rivet hole at one end and another 14mm in from the other fracture. This rivet hole is filled by a bone/antler rivet or peg. Decoration consists of four well-defined longitudinal grooves, one just in from and parallel to each edge, and a pair down the centre connecting the rivet holes. Tooth cuts are about 0.3mm wide, and spaced from 1.1mm to 1.5mm apart.

L 57 W 14 T 4 **542**

4* Small tapering fragment of plano-convex Class F2 side-plate, transversely fractured at both ends, one of which has a rivet hole. Teeth cuts in lower edge are about 0.3mm wide and evenly spaced 1.7mm apart. Decoration consists of four longitudinal grooves in the centre of the convex face and about 1mm apart, leaving three upstanding sections between. The outer two of three are cut by diagonal grooves about 1mm apart, creating a 'rope' effect, but the inner section is plain.

L 21 W 10 T 4 **420**

5* Trapezoidal-sectioned Class F3 side-plate fractured across rivet hole. The central zone has saw-cut diagonal lines adjacent to the rivet hole, the back outer zone has vertical lines.

L 37 W 17 T 4 **535**

6* Plano-convex Class F1/3 side-plate transversely fractured across rivet holes at both ends. Both edges of outer face have a thin longitudinal groove, cut by the saw marks from the teeth on the lower edge. The central portion of the outer face has two pairs

THE FINDS 483

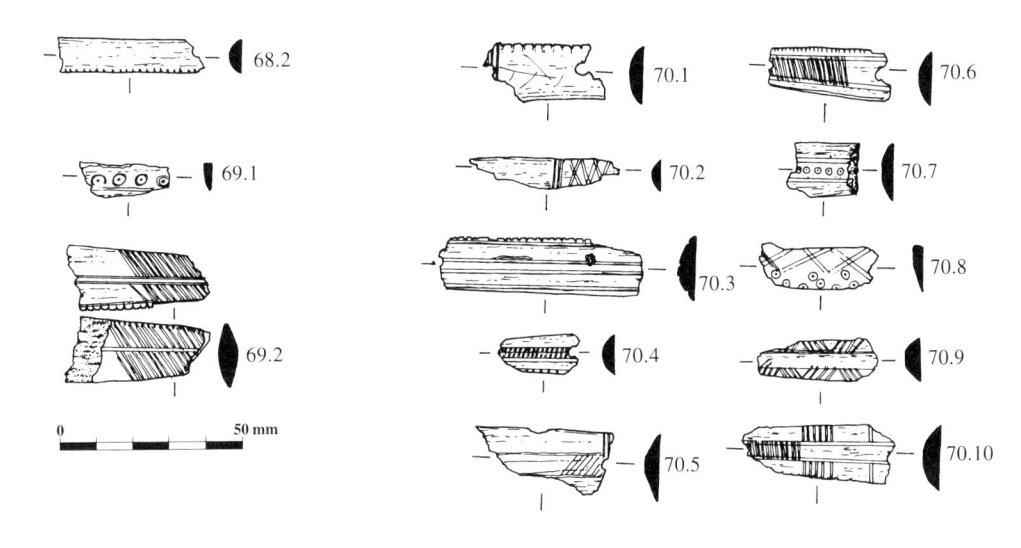

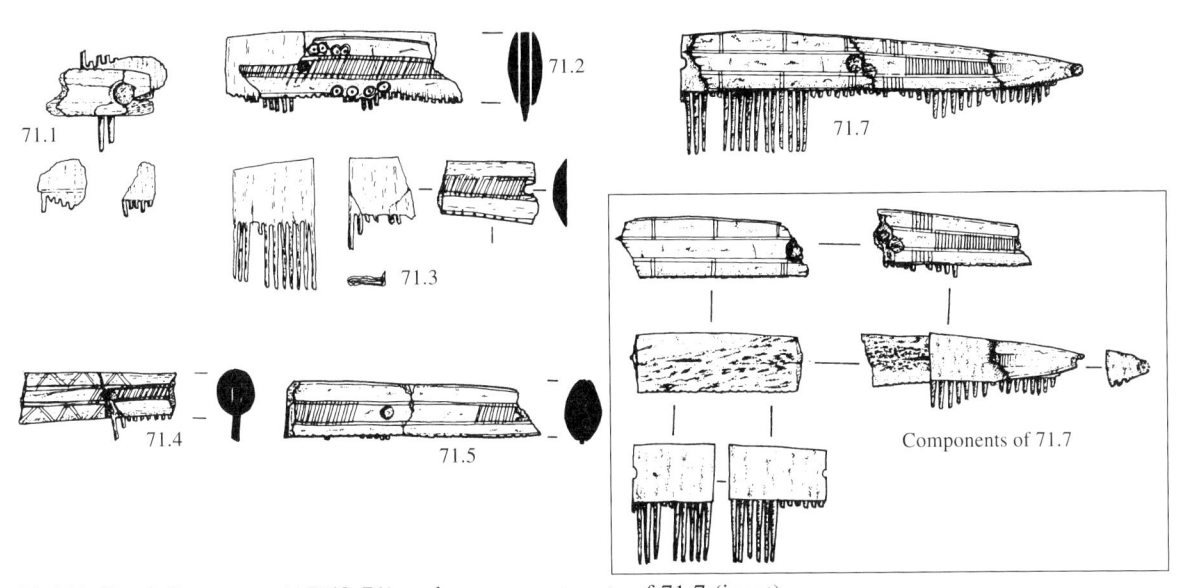

10.131 Comb fragments (AR68-71) and component parts of 71.7 (inset).

of incised lines, between 4mm and 6mm apart and following the line of their respective edges. Between these the field is covered with evenly spaced diagonal hatching, continuing right up to one rivet hole, but stopping 6mm short of the other. The saw cuts for the teeth are about 0.3mm wide, and are spaced between 1.4mm and 1.9mm apart.

L 34 W 12.5 T 3 **539**

7* Class F3 side-plate with flat central band on outer surface and sloping faces to the edges. Transversely fractured, iron staining indicates a rivet hole at one end. Lower edge has faint saw marks from tooth-cutting. Upper face has longitudinal groove parallel to outer edge. Central flat face is bordered by two sets of parallel lines, with a wavy line of circle-and-dot motifs between.

L 19 W 13.5 T 3.5 **432**

8* Longitudinally fractured fragment of Class F3 side-plate. Iron staining at both broken ends indicates the presence of rivets (29mm apart). The flat central face of the outer surface is decorated with a zig-zag pattern of 'dot-and-ring' motifs (2.6mm diameter). The sloping side face has a pattern of incised 'double-line Xs'. It is not possible to say if this is the panel nearer the teeth or not, as the edge is abraded.

L 32.5 W 11 T 3.5 **536**

9* Trapezoidal section of Class F3 side-plate, transversely and longitudinally fractured with possible rivet hole at narrower end. No decoration on central flat field, which is bounded by a thin incised line along each edge. One edge poorly executed with a second line diverging from the first. In the outer sloping fields the decoration consists of a zig-zag pattern form by opposing diagonal blocks of four parallel incised lines. Where each block meets, at inner and outer edges, the first line in each block overlaps the other.

L 34 W 12 T 4 **415.01**

10* Tapering section of plano-convex Class F3 side-plate transversely fractured at both ends across rivet holes. Central longitudinal portion of outer face slightly flattened. Decoration consists of an incised line parallel to each edge, the lower one cut by the tooth-cutting, and a pair of parallel lines at each edge of the flattened central portion. The decoration on each outer field parallels the other, with a block of eight parallel transverse lines, 9mm apart, from the outer single incised line to the inner pair. 11mm towards the centre is a single pair of transverse lines. In the central flattened zone the block of transverse lines commences where the outer blocks cease, and continues for at least 16 lines as far as the outer rivet hole.

L 42 W 14 T 3.5 **600.01**

Seven broken finished combs (AR71.1–7) were recorded. The earliest (1) is a Class B double-sided comb with coarse teeth on one side and finer teeth on the other, iron rivets and a robust undecorated D-shaped side-plate. This is a Western British style current in the seventh to ninth centuries, and the fragment came from a **Period I/4** deposit, probably dating to the later-seventh century (90, Table 3.27, Figure 10.136a). Another (2) is clearly part of a Class F1 comb with deep C-shaped sides decorated with sawn diagonal lines in the central band, overlying paired longitudinal lines, with two groups of ring-and-dot motif. Similar combs, lacking the circle-and-dot motif, are known from Dublin. Three other pieces are harder to define as their central decorative band makes it hard to determine if they are trapezoidal and thus of Class F3. If this is not the case then one (3) is Class F1, one (4) is Class F2 and the third (5) is somewhere between, having the depth of an F1 combined with the robust thickness of an F2. These are decorated with parallel lines, usually sawn, but in one case (4) cut by knife. The parallels are again generally Irish, where sawn lines are associated with F3 combs, although the zigzag motif on No. 4 occurs on fragments from Flaxengate, Lincoln (Mann 1982, 4–6) and York (MacGregor 1982, 93–4). One fragment (6) is clearly from a C-shaped Class F2 comb with cross-hatched decoration that is paralleled at Lloyds Bank, York (MacGregor 1982, Fig. 49, 526) and Dublin (Dunlevy 1988, Fig. 7, 2). The final piece (7), the most complete comb from Whithorn, is similar in section to Class F1 combs, but displays an unusual ending to the side-plate, which tapers at the top and bottom, terminating in an iron rivet at the point. Although the end tooth-plate is missing there is no evidence of a crest. The decoration of chequered bands of parallel saw cuts at the end is, however, matched by Irish examples from Knowth (Eogan 1974, Fig. 42) and Lough-a-Trim (Dunlevy 1988, Fig. 8).

Two fragments with similar decoration (2 and 3) from **Period V** graves cutting Building III/15, and a side-plate fragment (70.6) from an adjacent **Period IV** surface, could have been pieces of a single Class F1 comb, possibly originating in one of the **Period III/2** buildings (Figure 10.136c). This would have been an appropriate companion for the tenth century ringed pin (BZ15.3) from Building III/13, as both are diagnostically Hiberno-Norse. Three other comb fragments (4, 6 and 7) were among the debris associable with Building IV/18 (Figure 10.136d and e), and are likely to have been debris from comb repair.

Broken Combs (AR71)

1* Broken central portion of Class B comb, with two loose, broken tooth-plates. The shallow-C sectioned sideplates are of bone rather than antler, with antler tooth-plates. A single large-headed iron rivet survives 8mm in from the end of the Sideplate, and the comb is broken across another rivet hole centred 20mm away. The rivets pass through the centre of the individual tooth-plates. The teeth are coarse on both sides, 1.5–2mm wide at their base with a 0.7mm gap between teeth.

90

2* Broken central section of Class F1 comb and detached tooth-plate. Two side-plates transversely fractured at rivet holes at either end with an intact central rivet. Loose tooth-plate fits adjacent to rivet, and would appear to have been riveted at both ends, whereas the more central plate was only riveted at one edge. One of the side-plates is slightly offset, hence the saw marks from tooth cutting penetrate more deeply than usual into its lower edge. The surviving tooth-plates have the stumps of nine and eleven teeth respectively, the cuts being about 0.5mm wide and occurring at 2mm intervals, coarser then some examples. The decoration is divided into three longitudinal fields by a well-cut line just in from and parallel to each edge, and two pairs of parallel lines defining a central zone. The central zone is covered by diagonal grooves, right to left in an unbroken sequence. In the outer fields groups of ring-and-dot motifs are used (two groups of four, one of four and one of six remaining).

Tooth-plate (loose) L 21 W 24 T 3.
Comb fragment: L 64 W 18 T 11 (4 & 3 & 4) **543**

3* A fragment of a Class F1/3 comb comprising two tooth plates, one broken, one whole, connected with a shallow convex side-plate secured by an iron rivet. Although currently separate components, these were excavated as a whole *in situ*. The riveting uses the system of connecting the side-plates together at the junction of two teeth plates. The large intact tooth-plate evidences rivets at each end, a feature associated with the outer portions of combs; it has six intact teeth, three chipped ones and two broken off at the base. The teeth shows wear striations along one face but are clean on the other, indicating a uniform direction of use. The intact teeth are about 18mm long and shaped to a taper at the point. The broken plate has the stumps of six teeth left. The rivet is 10mm long and 2.4mm in diameter. The side-plate, whose teeth cuts match the larger tooth-plate, has an incised line just in from the lower edge. Two longitudinal lines in the central zone are connected by diagonal parallel incisions 1mm apart. A second longitudinal line runs outside the band on the inner sloping face. The rivet hole was added after the decoration had been cut.

Tooth-plate: L 32.5 W 23 T 3.
Tooth-plate: L 22 W 17 T 3.
Side-plate: L 22.5 W 16 × 14 T 4.
Rivet: L 10.5 D (shank) 2.7 (head) 3.8 × 2.8 **542**

4* Broken central portion of intact Class F2 comb, currently in four separate conjoining fragments. One rivet survives *in situ*, and the piece is transversely fractured at either end along the line of the two adjacent holes. Two tooth-plates meet at the surviving rivet. Only one tooth is left, and that broken. However no signs of excessive wear or striations were visible. Decoration on the convex side-plates is divided into three longitudinal fields by two pairs of incised lines towards the centre, these parallel their respective edges and thus converge towards the outer end of the comb. Between them on the central field is a block of roughly incised diagonal lines from right to left, cut by the central and outer rivet holes but terminating before the inner one. The two outer fields have a zig-zag motif using paired lines, which do not overlap (*c.f.* AR70.09).

L 41 W 13 T 9.6 (3.7 & 2.1 & 3.8) **535**

5* Broken central portion of Class F comb. Two conjoined sections. Sideplates F1 in style, with three decorative zones as per F3. Central zone decorated with two groups of knife-cut diagonal hatching. one rivet survives, at the junction of two tooth-plates, and the piece is fractured across another rivet hole.

L 69 W 15 T 9 **415.01**

6 Two pieces from the same side-plate, and two associated tooth-plates of Class F2 comb. The side-plate is divided into three decorative fields by lightly incised longitudinal lines, emphasising the trapezoidal section. The central zone is undecorated. The outer zones have a chevron pattern, in double parallel lines, overlapping at each end. Both fragments have broken across rivet holes, where there are traces of iron staining. Both of the tooth-plates lack teeth, and one is broken along one side.

Side-plates: L 32 W 17 T 3.6; L 39 W 16 T 3.8
Tooth-plates: L 18 W 15.6 T 2; L 18 W 11 (broken) T 1.8 **427.03**

7* Two thirds of broken finished comb (Class F1), fractured across rivet hole. If symmetrical, the comb would have had only two central rivets, and one at each end. The side-plate has two paired longitudinal lines, dividing the side-plate into three decorative zones. The central zone has a broad band of vertical hatching towards the outer end and stopping short of the rivet. Vertical hatching in the outer zones commences where the inner zone ceases, forming a small block, with further more widely spaced divisions formed by pairs of vertical lines. Two of the surviving tooth-plates have intact teeth, 17mm long, 1.3mm wide at base with a 6mm gap between teeth.

Overall L 110.5 W 32 T 10 **442**

D: Other Artefacts

Pins (AR73)

By contrast with bone (pp 496-7), which was frequently used in **Period IV** for functional and decorative pins, only one small completed point with wear marks (1), and two possible pin blanks (2 and 3) were recovered.

1* Antler pin, pointed at both ends, evidencing wear. Rectangular-sectioned fragment cut on all sides and tapered at both ends. Possibly intended for use as a pin/awl point.

L 33 W 4 T 4 **466**

2* Square-sectioned antler fragment cut on all sides and possibly intended for use as a pin/needle awl point.

L 36 W 3.5 T 2.5 **531**

3* Broken rectangular-sectioned fragment cut on all sides, possibly intended for use as a pin/needle /awl point.

L 27 W 4 T 2.5 **537**

Handles (AR74)

Fourteen definite handles (AR74.1–14) included both crudely smoothed and elaborately carved examples. Most were probably for knives or similar tools, and all were made from tines, as were two potentially unfinished handles (15 and 16). The commonest and most basic form (1–7) consisted of a sawn tine section with the cancellous material removed (or subsequently lost), and the guttering smoothed off, leaving either a rounded or faceted ovoid-section handle to accommodate a whittle tang. A better finished version (8) from Building IV/6 has a smooth, polished exterior with ring-and-dot ornamentation forming a simple cross. A similar handle, complete with blade, came from a tenth/eleventh century context at York (Waterman 1959, Fig. 7). A second group (9–12) comprises handles slotted at one end to take a scale-tanged knife. Again these range from crude barely-smoothed examples to one with polished ring-and dot ornament and a transverse perforation for a suspension thong (12). Two of these (11 and 12) had been displaced into **Period V** graves, the other two (9 and 10) came from **Period I** deposits.

One handle (13) is a tine cut at both ends, and with the guttering smoothed. Lines of parallel transverse knife cuts may have been added to secure extra grip. The upper end has a triangular socket in the cancellous material suggesting it could have held an awl or point. The final definite handle (14) is an elaborately carved tine with a shallow socket with a single perforation near the mouth. Above the plain perforated collar are two rows of incised herringbone-style ornament. Above this a deeply carved spiralling design works its way up towards the tip, unfortunately broken. The lower terminals of the spirals end in a hooked motif reminiscent of Jelling style metalwork of the late tenth century. The handle came from a **Period V** grave in the eastern part of the **central sector**, and could have been displaced from **Period III** or **IV** deposits. It may have originated in the debris in Building IV/18 (Figure 10.136d and e), and might thus have been an unrepairable object discarded by a craftsman. Two more pieces (15 and 16) may also be handles, but their longitudinal perforations are incomplete.

1 Badly foliated and abraded handle. Socket would appear to be in upper end of tine – no surviving evidence of tool marks, basal end broken. Outer surface survives as 25+ fragments – appears roughly smoothed.

L 61 Socket D 11 × 8.5 Socket depth 38.5 **53.11**

2* Abraded and broken handle for wittle tang, one sawn end. Socket continues entire length of surviving fragments. At sawn end there is a second, tiny hole in the face 1.5mm diameter, set 3mm from the main socket. This hole is c. 2mm deep.

UC 70 L 32 Socket D 10.5 × 8 **531**

4* Fragment of roughly smoothed antler handle longitudinally split with roughly smoothed sides. Worked on sides and ends by knife.

L 83 D 21 **903**

5 Highly abraded tine handle for wittle tang, sawn at base end. Handle is broken at one end; hole transverses entire surviving length of handle, but some of this may be related to post-depositional abrasion. Surviving sections of outer surface indicate a smoothly polished handle.

BC 75 UC 75 L 73 Socket D 7.5 **544**

6* Small abraded handle for wittle tang. Only roughly smoothed, with knife cuts still evident in one location. The diameter of the hole at the base may be exaggerated by abrasion to the core.

BC 85 UC 79 L 54 Socket BD 18 × 15 UD 12 × 11 **423.02**

7* Smoothed handle for wittle tang. Abraded and broken handle, sawn at one end. A few surviving traces of a polished outer surface. The handle tapers towards both ends. The sawn end, though broken, retains a trace of a possible socket of c. 7mm diameter.

BC 71 Middle C 76 UC – L 63 **904**

8* Broken longitudinally-perforated handle, two pieces joined. Basal end sawn, upper end knife-trimmed. Socket continues along entire length. Outer surface trimmed and polished. Decorated with ring and dot motif of 2mm diameter. In some case a flat facet has been cut to facilitate scribing the motif. Part of the design is a cross. The tang appears to have been inserted at the basal end, and 14mm from the end is a small (1.5mm diameter, 13.5mm long)

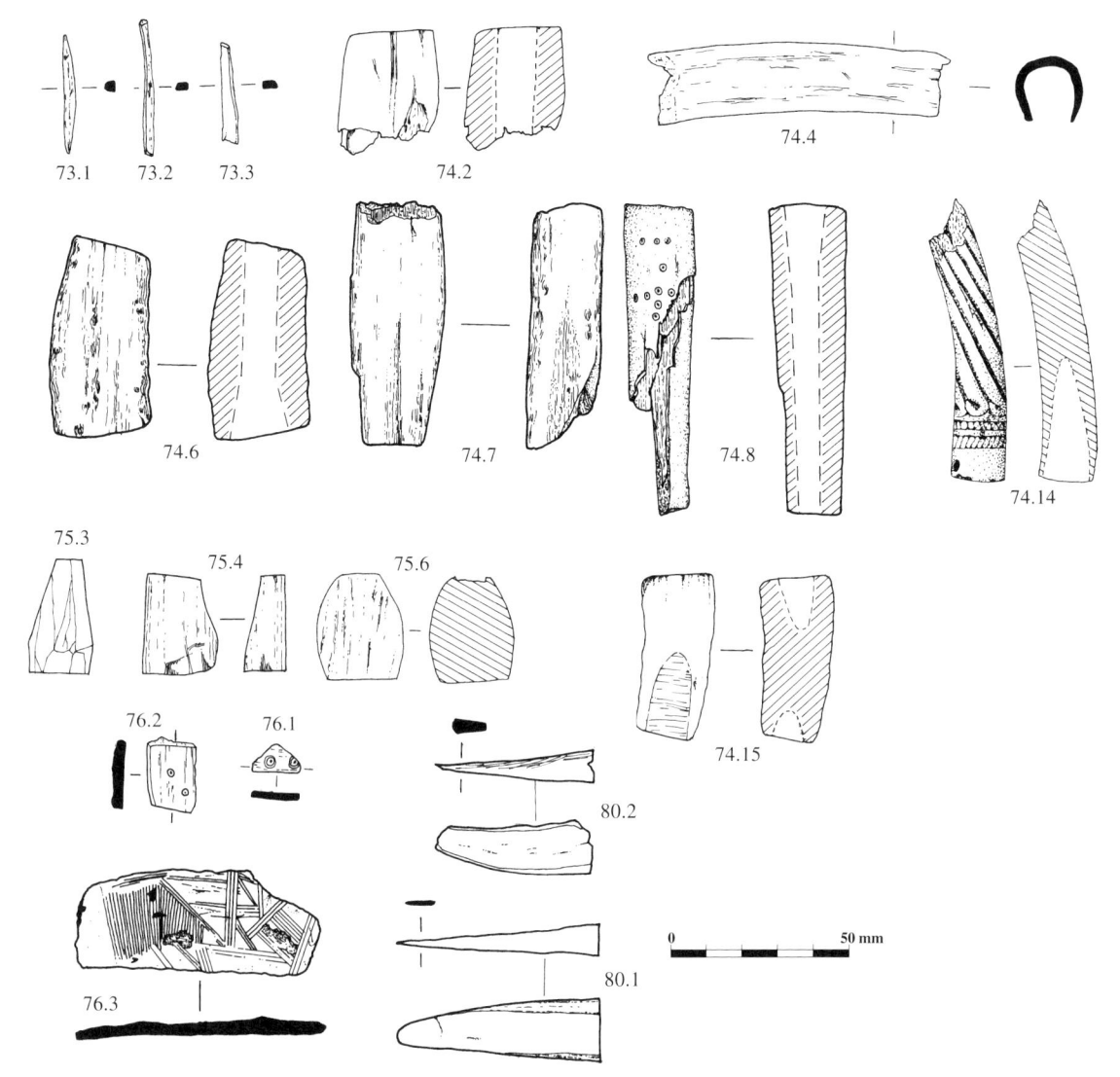

10.132 Antler points (AR73), handles (AR74), gaming pieces (AR75), decorated fragments (AR76), and wedges (AR80).

iron pin, which pierces through one side and transverses the width of the socket, but does not emerge through the other side.

BC 73 UC – L 85 Socket D 9 × 7.5 **410**

9 Rough, slotted tine handle cut at both ends, with slot (28mm long) in (?)upper outer surface. Abraded piece, so uncertain if any pre-depositional smoothing of outer surface. Possibly a crude handle.

L 129 BC 107 UC 96 **83**

10 Small, broken worn, but not smoothed, tine handle, with slot cut at basal end, and broken off towards tine tip. The slot transverses the entire width of the base, where it is 4mm wide, and narrows to a width of 2mm. There is no sign of a central socket, and the curve of the handle is on the same axis as the slot. Two broken fragments are part of one side of the slot. Toolmarks on one indicate that the slot was at least trimmed, and probably cut, by a knife.

BC 71 UC 52 L 69 Slot L 19.5 Slot W 4 × 2.5 **51**

11 Slotted smoothed tine handle, abraded, sawn at base and at tip end. Hole cut/drilled down centre from upper end. Two opposed slots, possibly with sawn sides, and rounded ends, cut through the sides – perhaps to stop wide plate/blade from pivoting about the tang. Wear patterns indicate that the slots were horizontal, and the handle would appear to be for left-handed use, with the forefinger along the top of the handle, the thumb along one side and gripped against the other fingers, with the base seated in the palm of the hand.

BC 86 UC 56 L 93 Hole D 9.5 Slot W 7.5 L 15.5 Hole depth. 29 **539**

12 Antler tine handle with slot cut and split at one end presumably for blade, now in two pieces. Slot 19mm deep and 2mm wide cut through ring-and-dot incised decoration thereby post-dating it. Second ring-and-dot motif 6mm round from the first is highly worn. Sides of tine smooth and faceted, one side badly abraded post-deposition. Basal end of tine evidences transverse perforation, presumably for suspension thong, however it also displays evidence of lateral chopping or cutting. Upper end of tine sawn across.

L 106 Basal D 22 Upper D 19 **542**

13 Improvised tine handle sawn at tip with triangular wedge-shaped socket in middle of end. Basal end roughly cut and broken. Outer surface has been smoothed, with parallel transverse cuts indicating the possible use of a drawknife. The piece would appear to have been roughly shaped for use as a handle, with a triangular-sectioned metal fitting in one end – possibly a tang for an awl.

L 120 BC 61 UC 42 **461.01**

14* Highly decorated handle broken at upper end. Basal end highly abraded, probably initially sawn, then knife trimmed. Socket at

basal end. Hole of 2.8mm diameter 2mm from basal end on inner curve, only penetrates one side; worn, but no evidence of iron staining. Decoration consists at the basal end of two bands of carving in a herring bone pattern about a central band. The rest of the handle as far as the break consists of long tendrils carved in high relief, twisting around the handle, and ending in a hook motif.
BC 51 UC 42 L 79 Socket D 12.5 Socket depth 20.5 **535**

15* Abraded tine, sawn at both ends, with two adjoining facets cut at the upper end. The holes in both ends appear too rounded to be naturally abraded, but only the one at the basal end shows slight evidence of wear around the mouth. Socket depths of 15mm (B) and 7mm (U) do not indicate significant tangs.
BC 66 UC 53 L 45.5 Basal socket D 10.5 Upper socket D 8 **535**

16 Badly abraded and broken handle with rounded longitudinal hole through cancellous material.
L 66 **427.03**

Gaming Pieces (AR75)

A group of seven gaming pieces (AR75.17) comprises five (1–5) made from tine tips, with cylindrical bases and faceted knife-cut tapering tops, and two barrel-shaped pieces (6 and 7) roughly carved from tine sections. They were concentrated in the south-east part of the **central sector**, and though widely dispersed in **Periods III** to **V** contexts, are likely to have originated in the **Period III** antler workshops there (Figure 10.136b), and would thus predate the first certain gaming boards from the site (p 449).

1 Tine sawn at both ends, faceted around basal end then cut in tapering facets towards upper end. Gaming piece.
L 21 BC 55 UC 40 **412**

2 Worn tine segment, sawn at base, upper end too abraded to determine. Faceted around the base and tapering towards the top, the upper part was probably originally faceted (see No. 1), but has been smoothed. A gaming piece.
D 23 × 15 H 26 **420**

3* Tine segment sawn at both ends, with facets cut around all sides and narrowing the piece towards the upper end. A gaming piece.
D 19 × 9 H 32 **438**

4* Faceted tine gaming piece, vertically fractured. Slight knife trimming round base, sawn at both ends.
D 22 H. 27 **535**

5 Tine, broken at one end and abraded, this may be a gaming piece though it is taller than most. It is not faceted unlike the others, and may be an unused section of tine [AR40].
L 30 BC – UC 46 **901**

6 Barrel-shaped tine section, gaming piece (or weight) with both ends flattened. Shaped by knife.
D 25 H. 30 **542**

7 Barrel-shaped tine section, possible gaming piece. Both ends sawn, sides knife-trimmed.
D27 H.32 **427.03**

Decorated fragments (AR76)

Three fragments, obviously not from combs, were decorated. A small burnt fragment (1) from a **Period I** ditch (216), had ring and dot designs on both faces. Another small piece (2) from the **Period III** waterborne deposits (309.02), with untrimmed external guttering also had ring-and-dot ornamentation. A third piece (3), probably redeposited into Building IV/3 from the same waterborne deposits, was extensively covered with blocks of parallel incised lines. No pattern was distinguishable, and this may be a trial piece for later work on comb side-plates.

1* Small fragment of antler plate, one side split. Both faces smoothed and decorated with ring-and-dot motifs, one whole and one partial one on each face. Burnt.
L 14 W 7 T 2 **216**

2* Fragment of beam, outer surface intact, inner surface smoothed, both ends sawn and both sides split. Inner surface has two ring-and-dot motifs, 1.8mm across, one deeper than the other. Perhaps an offcut used as a test piece.
L 19 W 14 T 3.5 **543**

3* Badly deteriorating fragment of beam with smoothed inner and outer surfaces. Outer surface is covered with a pattern of crossing paired lines, with vertical or diagonal hatching in some of the enclosed fields. The flat bases of the lines with a fine ridge up the middle indicate that two adjacent cuts were used to create each one. No coherent pattern is visible in the design, but while one end is sawn and the pattern respects this, the other is broken, so the picture is incomplete. This may be a trial piece, or perhaps the work of an older child.
L 69 W 28 T 6.5 **411.02**

Utilised Tine Tips (AR77–80)

Tine tips were routinely produced during the preparation of tine sections, and many seem to have been discarded as waste (AR47–50). A few were fashioned into gaming pieces (AR75), and others were converted into simple implements, some of which may have been components of more complex devices.

Thirteen tine tips (AR79.1–13) have faceted points and perforations, mostly blind transverse holes midway along their length or towards the basal end. The holes in three (5, 8 and 11) are elongated with evidence of considerable wear, and in one instance (8) a second hole has been cut near the original. Similar implements are known from other sites, but they remain unexplained, although Radley (1971, 51) speculated that examples from York had been used for pegging out hides. The simple working and wear marks on the Whithorn examples are sufficiently clear to establish how they were used, but not what they were used for. The facets convert the tip from smooth rounded points into rectilinear wedges, which would have allowed them to be lodged securely in squared sockets in a timber frame. The blind perforations have generally been smoothed by rotational wear and were presumably the sockets for a thin spindle of a harder material, probably metal. The ovoid hollows indicate that these spindles were subject to uneven lateral tensions, while the secondary replacement holes suggest a tight fit was required. All thirteen came from the eastern part of the **central sector** (Figure 10.134), and can be ascribed to **Period IV**. The stratified finds were loosely associated with weaving tensioners (IN63), and their general distribution coincided with other objects relating to textile production (Figure 6.29). It is thus possible that the tines were components of looms, perhaps serving as bearings for spindles of thread.

Seventeen similar implements (AR77.1–17) are faceted, but unpierced. Fourteen came from **Period IV** deposits or had been displaced into **Period V** graves, and their distribution corresponded broadly with that of faceted and pierced implements (Figure 10.133), though also extending into the **southern sector**. Some have deep transverse notches across their bases, as do other examples from York (MacGregor 1982, 100, Fig. 53), and they probably had a specific function relating to one or more of the craft activities practised in **Period IV**. The faceted tips would have allowed them to be securely fixed in sockets cut into timber, and the basal grooves could have been worn by stout thread or wire.

Four tines (AR78.1–4) were pierced but show no other evidence of working. The perforations are all different. One occurs in the base of a tine tip (4) and may have accepted a peg or dowel; an abraded tip (3) has a blind transverse perforation, whilst a more complete, but badly abraded and broken tine (2) has a complete transverse perforation. A complete tine (1) has a sloping perforation entering on one side and emerging out of the cancellous material in the sawn basal end.

The distributions of these three types of utilized tines are illustrated in Figure 10.134. Almost all can be ascribed to **Period IV**, and four concentrations in the eastern part of the site may be identified tentatively as debris from specific workshops. The densest concentration (A) includes stratified weaving tensioners and pierced faceted tines from relatively late **Period IV** contexts (Structures IV/22 and IV/25), and earlier faceted tines from Building IV/17 and IV/21. A second group (B) to the south, could have been associated with Building IV/18. A second large group (C) on the outer margin of the *inner precinct* also displays the spatial association of weaving tensioners and pierced faceted tines. Most of these objects had been displaced by **Period V** graves, but four (IN63.7, AR77.3, AR79.2 and 3) came from undisturbed deposits, and are likely to have been deposited at an early stage of **Period IV**. It is unclear whether these mark a workshop, or debris originating in the *outer zone*. The fourth group (D) coincided with the main concentration of comb-making debris (Figure 10.136d), and could have been debris from a workshop in the *outer zone*.

Two carefully shaped and trimmed wedges (AR80.1–2) are matched by one from *Haithabu*, which was used for splitting antler (MacGregor 1985, Fig. 34). Both had been displaced **Period V** graves (Figure 10.136d), but one (1) coincided with the concentration of comb-making debris in the *inner precinct* of the **Period IV** settlement (425.01, Figure 6.2), and the other (2) with the scattered antler debris on the path to Building IV/19 (Table 6.24).

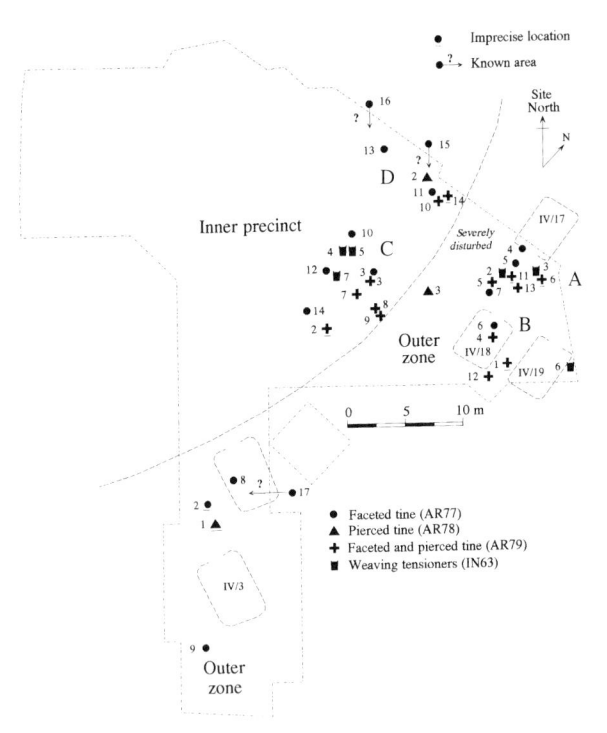

10.133 The distributions of faceted and pierced antler tines (AR77–79), and weaving tensioners (IN63) ascribed to **Period IV**.

Faceted Tine Tips (AR77)

1* Fully faceted tip, square sectioned at basal end, with smoothed knife cut facets. External cut at tip trimmed to form a curved 'blade', evidencing signs of wear. Possibly a 'creaser'.
L 77 BC 55 **52.03**

2 Abraded tine tip sawn at basal end with two opposed facets at tip worn smooth. One continuous in a rougher cut towards the basal end. External curve at tip also worn.
L 94 BC 72 **309.02**

3* Tine tip with sawn basal end, longitudinally split towards basal end to form rough facet.
L 62 BC 50 **425.01**

4* Tine with tip faceted quadrilaterally. Some rougher knife work slightly lower down, but the majority of the tine is not worked or smoothed. Sawn at base, tip broken.
L 101.5 BC 71.5 **439**

5 Tine tip with faceted inner and outer curvature. Sawn basal end. Abraded.
L 56 BD.16.4 **439**

6* Faceted antler tine tip.
440

7 Faceted antler tine tip with basal end and tip broken. One side roughly knife cut smoothly worn facet, cut towards tip. Opposing face has shorter facet also cut towards tip, and also worn.
L 55 BC 60.5 Tip W 13 T 4.5 **445**

8 Faceted antler tine tip.
410

9* Tine with tip faceted quadrilaterally. Sawn at basal end but most of tip broken. Majority of the tine unworked and only one patch worn, near to basal end.
L 107 BC 71 **417.02**

THE FINDS 489

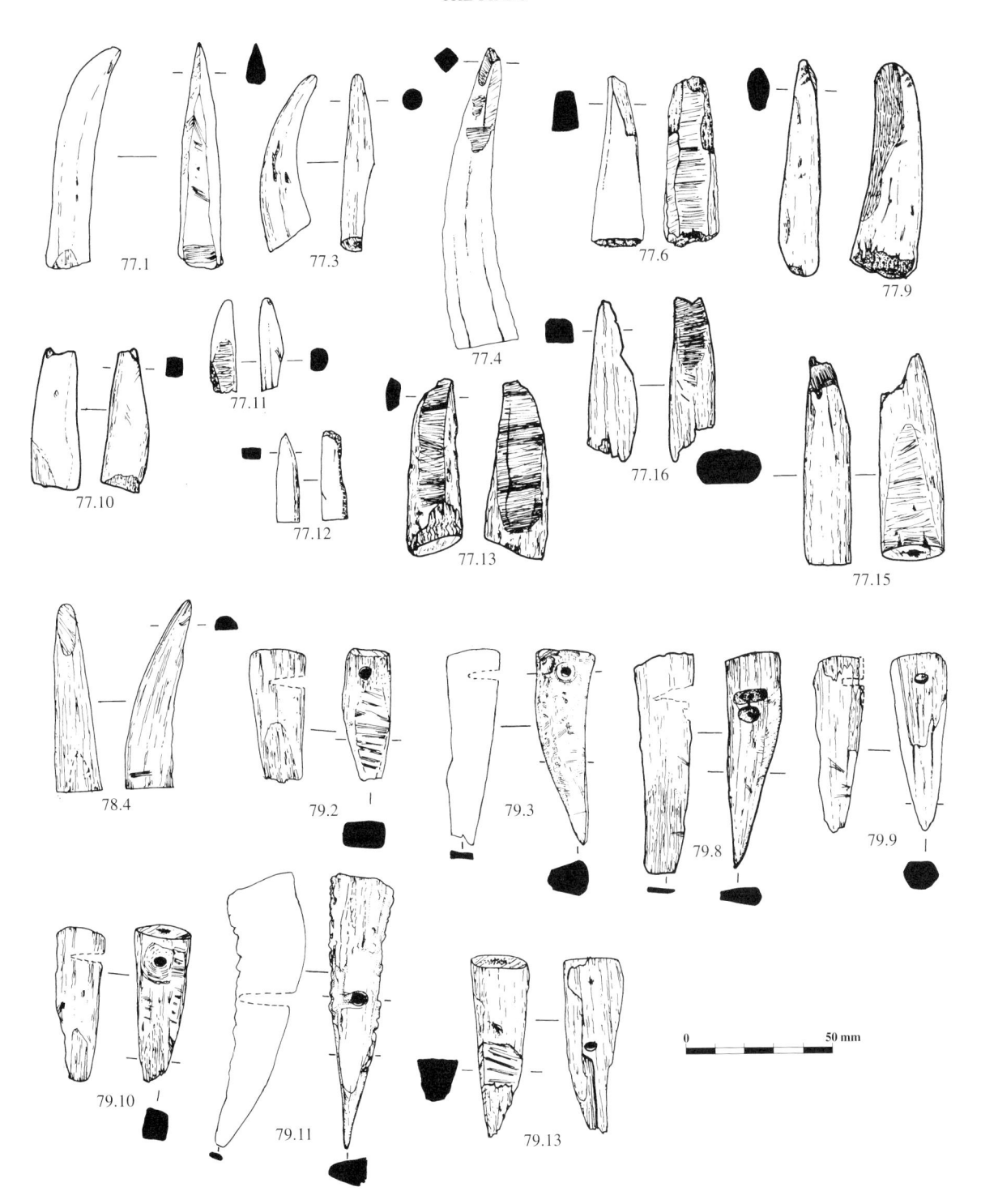

10.134 Utilised tines (AR77–79).

10* Tine tip, broken at both ends. One side roughly faceted towards tip. All surviving exterior worn smooth towards tip. Two rough knife cuts on internal curve.

L 73 BC 67 **531**

11* Tine tip, sawn at basal end, broken at tip. Two opposed facets towards tip worn smooth, as is rest of exterior surface. One facet has longitudinal striations.

L 46 BC 57 **531**

12* Fragmentary tip with single cut facet.

L 31.5 BC 38 **534**

13* Segment of tine with split edges trimmed to opposed facets, sawn at basal end and broken at tip.

L 32 W 7 T 9 **535**

14 Tine tip with sawn basal end. Two opposed faces very roughly cut, and one face with a sawn section.

L 59 Basal D 66 **539**

15* Tine tip sawn at basal end. One side faceted towards tip.

L 59 BC 67 **542**

16* Abraded tine sawn at basal end, broken at tip. One side

faceted towards basal end. Some knife working, badly abraded, on opposite side towards tip.
L 67 BC 78 **543**

17 Faceted antler tine tip.
904

Perforated Tines (AR78)

1 Complete, abraded tine, sawn at base. Hole pierced from one side through to base, with bi-conical wear pattern.
L 197.5 BC 133 Hole D 4 **309.02**

2 Badly abraded tine sawn at basal end. Hole penetrates 11.5mm [tine 14mm diameter at that point] deep, set 12mm from basal end.
L 45 BC 61 Hole D 4 × 3 **531**

3 Badly abraded tine, broken at both ends. Hole pierces through tine from one side face to the other. One face broken (around exit point?).
L 117 BC 94 UC 58 Hole D 6.5 **543**

4* Worn tine tip, sawn at base with parallel saw-mark (L 9mm W 1.5mm) 4.5mm from base. Hole centrally placed in base, 10mm deep.
L 60 BC 61 Hole D 7.5 **743.04**

Faceted and Pierced Tine Tips (AR79)

1 Faceted and pierced antler tine tip. Knife-cut squared point with grooving on inside curvature. Broken across perforation, whose lip evidences wear.
L 51 PD 4.5 **427.02**

2* Faceted and pierced antler tine tip. Sawn basal end, rectangular section cut(?) tip. three sides smooth facets, inner curvature grooved by cutting/chopping marks. Parallel knife marks on outer curvature below facet. Blind perforation with possible rotational wear on inner curvature at basal end.
L 43 PD 4.7 × 3.3 **495**

3* Faceted and pierced antler tine tip. Sawn basal end, rectangular section point faceted on four sides. Small area of cutting/chopping marks on one side. Blind perforation at basal end on opposing side. Elongated hole indicates rotational wear, with additional double groove 1.5mm outside the hole.
L 63.5 PD 3.4 × 2.4 **425.01**

4 Faceted and pierced antler tine tip. Sawn basal end with knife-cut facets around rim. Three sides faceted at point, chopping/cutting marks on inner curvature below facet. Ovoid blind perforation on outer curvature, suggesting rotational wear.
L 62.4 PD 6.2 × 3.7 **440**

5 Faceted and pierced antler tine tip. Sawn base, point faceted on four sides. Cut/chopped zone below facet on interior curved surface. Perforation on outer curvature at basal end; elongated holes extends to edge, sides straight at edge suggesting knife-cut. Flattened, slightly dished area extends up to 9mm around perforation and exhibits smoothed surface patches suggesting wear, probably rotational.
L 63.7 PD 9 × 3.6 **445**

6 Faceted and pierced antler tine tip. Badly abraded basal end, probably sawn. Point faceted on two sides. Ovoid, blind perforation on outer curvature just above the midpoint.
L 67 PD 5.2 × 3.8 **448**

7 Faceted and pierced antler tine tip. Sawn base, point faceted on two sides. highly elongated blind perforation on upper curvature. Smaller hole at base of perforation suggests a point to the item which caused the wear. A second, less elongated perforation lies just above the first.
L 72.6 1st PD 10.6 × 3.7: 2nd PD 5.2 × 3.4 **531**

8* Faceted and pierced antler tine tip, sawn base, point broken recently. Point faceted on four sides. Cut/chopped zone below facet on one side. Ovoid blind perforation in smoothed facet at basal end on opposite side. Second round shallow hole set just above it. Clear evidence of rotational wear on surface around perforation.
L 50.5 PD 5 × 2.9 **533**

9* Friable and badly abraded faceted and pierced antler tine tip, sawn base, point faceted on two sides. Chopped/cut zone below facets on interior curvature, elongated blind perforation near basal end on opposite side.
L 56 PD 4.2 × 2.4 **533**

10* Faceted and pierced antler tine tip. Longest of the tips, sawn base. Point faceted on both sides and upper curvature. Blind perforation at lower end of facetting on upper curvature. As with 79.* it extends to the edge with cut sides. the bottom of the perforation just pierces through the cancellous material to the other side, possibly effected during use.
L 93 PD 9 × 4.3 **542**

11* Badly abraded faceted and pierced antler tine tip, sawn base. Much of surface lost, but point apparently faceted on four sides. Cut/chopped zone below facet on inner curvature. Ovoid blind perforation midway along outer curvature.
L 57 PD 5.1 × 3.2 **719**

12 Badly abraded faceted and pierced antler tine tip, base probably sawn. Point faceted on four sides. Deeply cut/chopped zone on inner curvature below facet. Ovoid blind perforation at basal end on outer curvature. Small hole (D *c.* 1mm) at base of perforation suggests pointed device causing rotational wear.
L 62 PD 6.5 × 4.8 **535**

13* Faceted and pierced antler tine tip. Sawn base, point faceted on four sides. Cut/chopped zone on one side, ovoid blind perforation at basal end on opposite side.
L 56 PD 6.4 × 3.6 **450**

14 Faceted and pierced antler tine tip. Sawn base, point broken recently. Faceted up to base on one side, other side deeply faceted Ovoid perforation through basal end of facets.
L 32 PD 5 × 4.3 **542**

Wedges (AR80)

1* Tine tip, sawn at basal end, two opposing sides split and trimmed to form a wedge.
L 56.5 W 13 T 9 **530**

2* Tine tip, broken at point and basal end, two opposed sides split and trimmed to form a wedge.
L 43 W 15 T 9 **539**

Other worked or utilised antler (AR81)

Fourteen miscellaneous pieces of worked or utilised antler (AR81.1–14) include a small number of identifiable artefacts and other objects of uncertain function. Three pieces from **Period I** contexts (5, 10 and 14) include a possible amulet (5) and a working pad (14). Most of the remaining items came from **Period III** and **IV** deposits or had been displaced into subsequent layers. The small number and limited range of these objects emphasise the virtually exclusive use of prime antler for combs and handles.

A shaped and hollowed beam section (1) appears to have served as a toggle, a tine tip (2) had been sharpened to a point and displayed wear suggesting it was used as an awl, and a tine base (3) was shaped for use as a bung. One burr (4) had been hollowed out leaving just the corona with the inner surface well worn to a polish. Two similar examples, one in the British Museum and another in the Museum of London are unprovenanced, but may have been amulets, perhaps for cattle (Roes 1963, 71), and they are said to pre-date a later-ninth/tenth century cult relating to the use of tines (MacGregor 1985). A flat discoid of basal burr with the corona removed (5) was amongst the earliest antler finds (69.02), and is paralleled by Late Roman and sub-Roman amulets of a similar form (MacGregor 1985).

An abraded mouthpiece for a whistle or flute (6) with an undercut lip and an ovoid hole in the upper surface came from a secure late-ninth century context (422.04, Figure 10.136b), and seems to be without parallel. It would appear to have been separate from the body, a feature not noted in other whistles of this period (Megaw 1961; Roes 1963, 59–61; Mann 1982, 16). Although morphologically similar to modern whistle mouthpieces, the hole lacks the sharp blowing edge characteristic of wind instruments, and, if it is such, would have required a separate reed. Vertical flutes (O.Fr. *Flageol*) were known in France in the eleventh century, but not in Britain before the twelfth century (R. Dawson, Pers. Comm.). No date has been suggested for reed variants of the modern 'tin whistle' due to the perishable nature of the evidence, though utilisation of reeds for whistles continued in the area until quite recently (H. Nicholson, Pers. Comm.).

A screw-threaded object with a raised central collar (7) is another unusual find. One thread is solid whilst the other is hollowed. Although broken, this could have been the end of a 'bobbin', paralleled by examples from Goltho (Beresford 1975, 77) and York, though the latter were completely perforated axially.

Several other pieces were less easy to explain. Two antler tines (8 and 9) had grooves cut completely around their exterior. These showed slight signs of wear, and they may have served as tethering pegs. Another broken fragment (10) had been cut all the way round one end, creating an effect akin to a modern 'dolly peg', whilst a fourth tine (13) had the top crudely cut to form three points. Although similar to a pottery stamp from *Hamwic* (Holdsworth 1980, Fig. 10,2), the piece is much coarser, and no appropriate stamped pottery was found. Two polygonal sheets of compact tissue (11 and 12), apparently cut down from a beam/tine junction to ensure maximum surface area, were considerably larger than those used for tooth-plates, and may have been destined for decorative use, as the split grain would have reduced their integral strength. A large burr (14) with the beam and brow tine sawn off, was punctured over its larger surfaces by several triangular pyramidical indentations, probably from some form of tool, and may have served as a pad. Such pads were found in abundance at Broxmouth, East Lothian in Middle Iron Age contexts (Gibson forthcoming).

1* Sawn base of tine, cut at both ends and hollowed out, creating a thin-walled tube. Both ends worn, the upper one more so. Whole piece is highly abraded.

L 34 BC 118 UC 110 **536**

2* Tine tip, cut and laterally split along most of its length, sharpened to a point at the basal end. Cut and wear would indicate right-handed use as an awl or pricker.

L 159 D 54 **530**

3* Probable bung. Tine offcut sawn at both ends. Lower end is sawn below its joint with the beam, thus one end is considerably more splayed than the other. This has been accentuated by trimming the material on one side of the junction with a knife and smoothing off the ridges on the tine. The result is a piece which would appear to have been used as a bung, perhaps for a small barrel or leather water bottle.

L 50.5 BC 115 UC 78 BD 43.5 × 28.8 Tip D 26.5 × 20.5 **454**

4* Chatelaine or amulet. Burr corona trimmed off along one side and hollowed out on the interior. Interior shows high degree of wear, in some places worn to a smooth polish. The exterior at the trimmed section is also worn, as is the lower surface around the ring. It is possible that the trimmed edge was secured to a strap loop, whilst the rest was used by some kind of rope or thong, such as usage as a tethering ring or chatelaine.

Outer C 194 Inner C 93 Inner D 30 × 26 **722**

5 Antler burr trimmed to rough discoid, one side sawn one side knife trimmed, edges cut, split and trimmed. Similar in size to some stone discoids, it may have been used as a counter.

D 45 × 40 T 11 × 7 **69.02**

6* Probable mouthpiece for whistle, with D-shaped hole in the upper portion, the underpart being cut in an acute concave fashion to accommodate the lower lip. The piece is highly abraded, but the lack of corrosion products or staining would appear to preclude a metal body. Ethnographic parallels exist for reed whistles to which the mouth piece could be attached, with a fipple of clay or beeswax.

L 36 D (outer) 16 D (inner) 11 **422.04**

7* Laterally fractured piece consisting of a screw-thread at either end – one rounded off, the other (?)cut – with a raised collar in the middle. Conical indentation at one end may be fixing point for attachment to a lathe, enabling the piece to be turned and the screw thread engraved. Length of intact thread 13mm. The cut end has a threaded length of 5mm and has its centre hollowed out with a socket of 5mm diameter, 10mm deep ending in a rounded point. Presumably it was part of a mechanism, and used to increase tension or adjust fit. No parallel is known for it, the only vaguely similar items having been used as turning pegs on musical instruments.

L 22.5 D 13 × 11 **543**

8* Sawn tine broken around cut groove. Sawn off at basal end. Shallow-V knife-cut groove encircling (though not properly aligned) 67mm from base. Another circumferential knife cut 11mm beyond coincides with the fracture. three isolated knife marks occur on the outer curve of the tine.

L 94 BC171 **906**

9* Sawn tine with (?)worn groove at upper end. Tine sawn at basal end. Wide shallow groove 70mm from basal end, no evidence of knife marks.

L 105 BC 112 **412**

10 Tine fragment, laterally fractured, one end cut and trimmed. The area 6mm below the cut end has been cut and trimmed to form a narrower neck, leaving a head akin to a 'dolly peg' in modern clothes pegs.

L 30.5 W 12.5 T 7 **85.02**

11 Flat plate of antler. Two sawn ends, part of one side split, other two edges broken. Both faces have a scalloped surface, indicating working by knife.

L 49 W 37.5 T 4.5 **531**

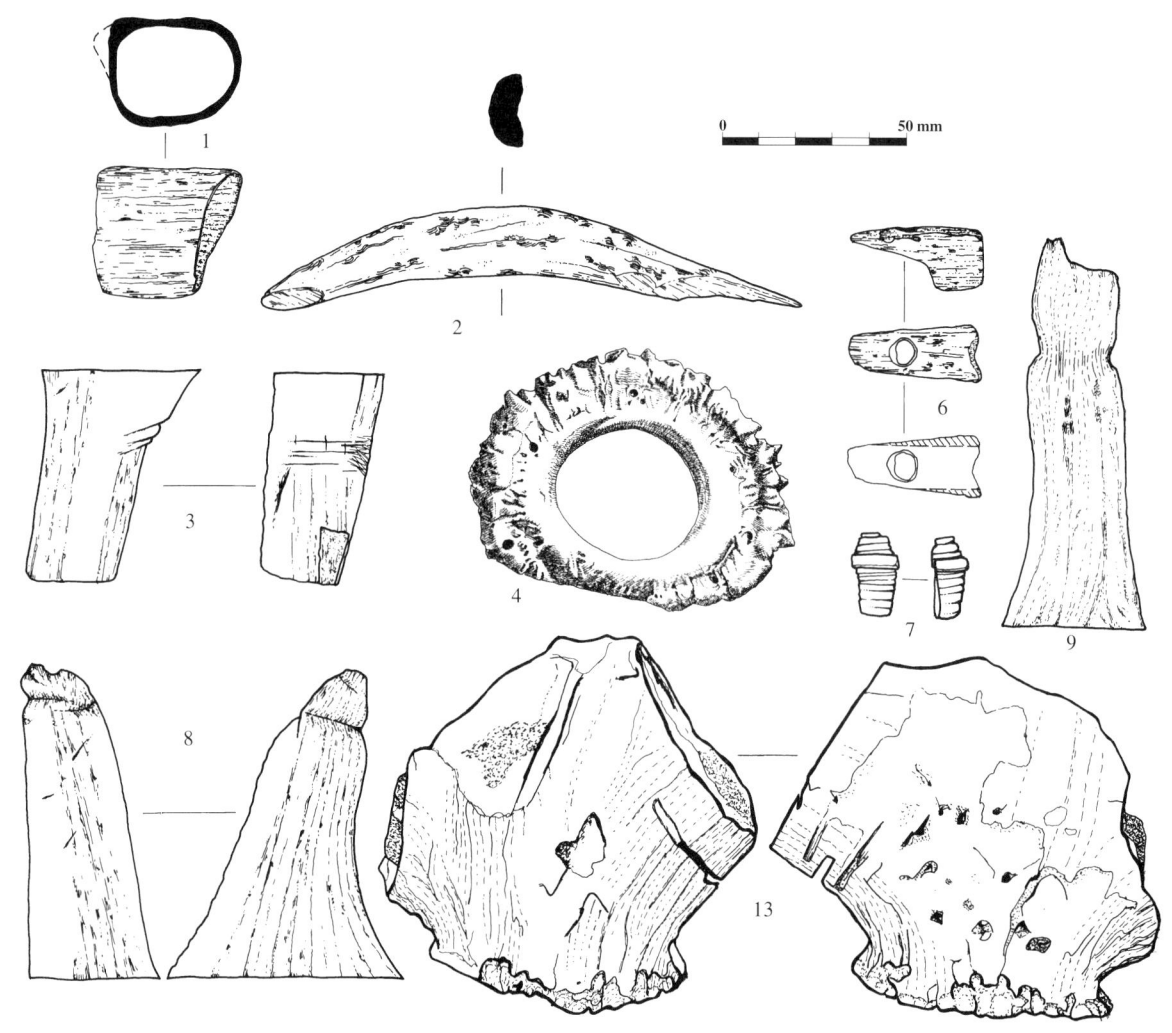

10.135 Miscellaneous antler artefacts (AR81).

12 Flat plate of (?)antler. One edge split, four broken edges. One face smoothed, the other with a scalloped surface, indicating working by knife.

L 43 W 26.5 T 2 **533**

13 Sawn antler tine with tip end cut to three points, all worn. Tine sawn at base, cut at tip. Two parallel saw marks 7mm and 11mm from base. Top has been cut to leave three upstanding points, but this does not appear to be the same as the *Hamwic* pottery stamps (Holdsworth 1980) being much coarser work. Tops of points appear worn and abraded.

L 98 BC 104 UC 68 **425.01**

14* Antler burr, used as pad. Shed burr with beam, bez and brow tine sawn. Several secondary saw marks 2mm wide on underside of beam. The broad area on both sides have several straight-edged, tapering indentations, pyramidical or tetrahedral in shape, and probably formed by punches or awls. These utilised areas have flattened coruscations and a fair amount of surface damage.

Basal D 207 Beam D 153 **88.01**

E: Roe Deer Antler

Five fragments of roe deer antler (AR87.1–5), two of which joined, comprise two intact antlers, one piece with the tines removed at the crown, and a detached crown and tines. Roe deer antler is unsuitable for composite comb manufacture as it is much smaller than red deer antler, and the presence of intact tines suggests that no other uses were recognized.

STRATIGRAPHIC GROUPINGS

The antler finds were concentrated in contexts ascribable to **Periods III** and **IV**, but earlier groups revealed comb-production in the later-sixth/earlier seventh centuries, and possibly before.

Period I

The earliest antler working debris from the *inner precinct* indicates a tine-based industry, probably producing handles. A group of tines and tips from debris (94.01) overlying Building I/3 may have been related to the contemporary ironworking, and may derive from an early off-site workshop. The deposits around and over Building I/9 produced a small amount of displaced tine-based debris, as well as the basal pad (AR81.13), whereas a broadly contemporary rubbish spread (89, Table 3.18), though predominantly tine-based, included some indications of comb manufacture. A tine-based industry, again associated with ironworking debris was evident in the overlying **Period I/3** rubbish deposit (85.02), while a slightly later hollow (109) produced a dissimilar group of antler, with increased amounts of basal antler and diagnostic comb-working debris (Table 3.23a). These linked deposits indicate a workshop or range of workshops in the vicinity, and probably dating to the later-sixth and earlier-seventh centuries.

The finds from the *outer zone* contrast with the groups from the *inner precinct*, and included more basal antler, tines, and beam sections, which are more characteristic of dumped waste material than workshop debris. A badly broken beam (Figure 10.136a **i**) from a poorly stratified, though possibly early context (54) in the *outer zone*, was sawn or marked up into three long sections. These would have been appropriate for making the long tooth-plates of double-sided Class B combs which are generally of third to eighth century date. The earliest stratified material is generally undiagnostic, though, as in the *inner precinct*, some tines and handles were associated with ironworking debris. The earliest stratified comb-making debris (Figure 10.136a ii, 53.13, **Period I.7**, p 126) coincided broadly with its appearance in the *inner precinct*. Antler was scarce in the later deposits (55/58 etc) that produced large groups of other finds.

Period II

The **Period II** deposits produced little antler and this may reflect activity segregation within the reorganised settlement. The small groups of stratified material (303, 215) indicate continued comb production in an off-site workshop.

Period III

Most of the antler derives from comb production during **Periods III** and **IV**, and a long sequence of workshop and dump deposits is documented in Chapters 5 and 6. The **Period III** deposits demonstrate that comb-making was established as an important industry at the beginning of **Period III** (Figure 10.136b) and associated coins date this horizon securely to the reign of Aethelred II in the mid-ninth century (pp 189, 354). The earliest comb-making debris came from the floor of Building III/3 (478) and the adjacent ploughing (399.02). Building III/8 produced comb tooth-plates, some tine debris, and a few parings, indicating that this was a primary working deposit. Building III/9 produced a diagnostic assemblage of workshop deposit with finds concentrated around the doorway representing all stages of comb production, from the initial division of the beams and tines, through the sawing of sections and the removal of segments, to the preparation of tooth-plates and trimming of finished combs. Over four hundred parings and numerous discarded offcuts show this to be a primary working area. The proposed date range of 845–865AD is appropriate to the Type F2 comb (AR70.4) from this building, and accords well with continental examples (Ambrosiani 1981, 23–32), although slightly earlier than the late-ninth to tenth century pieces from High Street, Dublin and Pudding Lane, London (Dunlevy 1988, 364–5). Building III/11 overlay Building III/3, and, if one includes the redeposited material (465), produced the sections, segments, tooth-plates and parings indicative of a workshop dealing with the middle and later stages of comb production. This contrasts with the wider range of activities in Building III/9 and suggests that different stages of comb manufacture may have taken place in adjacent workshops. A concentration of gaming pieces may have originated in these later-ninth century deposits. Continuing comb production in **Period III/2** (Figure 10.136c) was evident in Building III/18 which produced segments and tooth-plates reflecting the middle and later stages of comb-making, and more particularly in Buildings III/22 and 23, the former producing primary debris from the mid and later stages, whilst the latter evidences only the early and middle stages of comb manufacture. Characteristic debris from Building III/27 shows that comb production continued in **Period III/3**, although the relative paucity of material suggests that the industrial focus had moved away from the excavated area. Debris in the **southern sector** (309.02) included antler waste (Table 5.36) complementing the workshop deposits uphill. The waste is characterised by larger proportions of basal antler, beams, tines and offcuts, with fewer comb plates and parings.

Period IV

Comb production continued for most of **Period IV**, but apparently cased before the end of the period. The richest evidence came from the early buildings (IV/17–19, 22) in the south-east part of the *outer zone*, and the adjacent open ground in the *inner precinct* (Figures 6.2, 10.136d and e). These buildings can be identified as workshops, and there was recurrent evidence of comb-making and repair in the relatively well-lit doorways. The assemblages of antler from them again suggest that different stages of comb-production took place in separate buildings, and might perhaps be attributed to apprentices and master craftsmen. A concentration of comb fragments coinciding with Building IV/18 (Figures 6.35, 10.136e) argues that these were debris from the repair of combs, while the promiscuous mix of types suggest the maintenance of obsolete combs. The sustained deposition of material, along with the specialisation shown, suggests a permanent, domestic industry centred around this cluster of buildings. The functional relationship of the workshops with the mass of antler debris (425.01) from the *inner precinct* is difficult to assess as the intervening deposits had

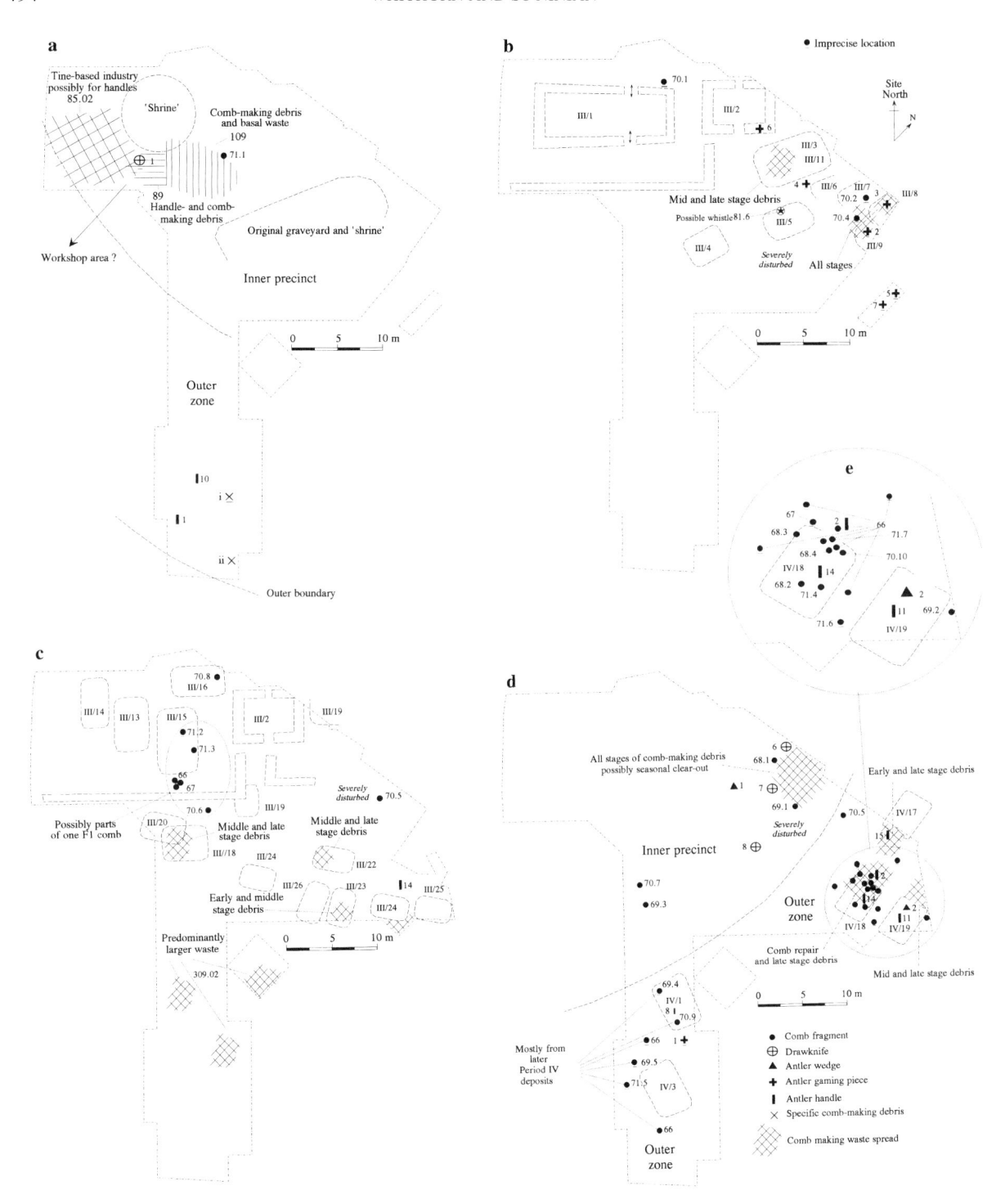

10.136 The distributions of antler-working debris and related objects. **a Period I**, **b Period III/1**, **c Period III/2**, **d Period IV** (including displaced finds).

been truncated by later features (Figure 6.21). Additionally, two thirds of the material which probably derives from this mass of debris, and three-quarters of the material from the workshop complex, had been displaced by **Period V** graves. Taking this displaced material into account, it can be seen that there is a difference between the finds from the buildings, where discrete groups relate to the stages of comb production or repair (Table 10.25), and the more general finds from the mass of debris, which cover the entire spectrum of antler utilisation. While the latter could have been an outdoor working area, as suggested by the presence of drawknives, its composition and distribution suggest one or more dumps of debris, possibly an end of season clear out from the nearby workshops. The earliest material in the **southern sector** was generally displaced from the **Period III** debris (p 200). The first definite contemporary finds from Building IV/6 (410) gave evidence of comb-production and possibly handle manufacture, although the lack of parings suggested that this was not a primary deposit. Continued working in the **southern sector** was revealed by large antler waste, including much viable raw material, from the deteriorating drainage ditch (417.02), and the overlying pond silts (415.01). The latter produced debris from all stages of comb production, including those not represented in the adjacent Buildings IV/9 and 12, which produced a concentration of segments and plates from the mid stages of comb making. The confusing, though relatively undisturbed, stratigraphy of the **southern sector** provided a clear picture of the rapid decline of antler exploitation towards the end of **Period IV**. This is an imprecisely dated horizon, but can be ascribed tentatively to *c.* 1200 AD.

Conclusion

Examination of the antler material from Whithorn has enabled us to determine preferential working procedures during the construction of composite combs. Analysis of the dimensions of comb tooth-plates shows a preferential length of 36–43mm for the optimum use of the raw material, and the spread of widths with distinct 'peaks' attests to the theory that tooth-plates came in a series of standard widths relating to even tooth spacing. Shed antler, presumably collected from the surrounding countryside, was extensively used as it was elsewhere (MacGregor 1989, 107–8), and a sufficiency of the raw material enabled pieces of secondary value to be discarded up to the end of the twelfth century, when the imposition of Forest Laws curtailed its availability.

The decorative patterns on the comb fragments match Irish examples more closely than comparable material from England and the Continent, lending support to Ambrosiani's hypothesis of the trade being carried out by itinerant professionals. An 'Irish Sea circuit' would be an appropriate model for the correlation of such motifs across a variety of contemporary sites. However the distribution of workshop debris, in what were presumably permanent structures, suggests that antler-working at a 'professional' level was conducted on regular basis from the ninth to the twelfth centuries as one of a series of urban trades, associated with the adjacent market.

The Bone and Horn Artefacts

Andrew Nicholson

A relatively small group of bone artefacts and worked bones comprised some eighty objects of which thirty-three (thirty-one buttons and two nit combs) were relatively modern. The earlier material was concentrated in **Period IV** contexts, and mostly seems to have pertained to a relatively brief period in the twelfth/thirteenth centuries. A small group of earlier finds includes playing pieces and a handle, while a Class B comb with bone side-plates (AR71.1) is described above (pp 484).

Buttons (BA01–04)

Thirty-one buttons were divided into categories dependent upon the number of attachment holes. Within the categories most buttons followed a similar form, and categories BA01–BA03 were all morphologically the same, only BA04 which comprised flat discs with no rim were distinctly different.

The fifteen four-hole buttons (BA01.1–15) all had a rounded, raised rim, with some variations of the central zone, and had been turned on a lathe. Seven of the pieces had been stained a brown colour, a feature only found on four-hole buttons. Five buttons had three holes (BA02.1–5), and a single five-hole button (BA03) was found. All of these buttons were from nineteenth century or later deposits. Ten buttons had a single central hole (BA04) and appear to be slightly earlier than the multi-hole forms, occurring in late eighteenth/early nineteenth century deposits in the manse and associated midden and drain deposits.

Nit combs (BA05)

One virtually complete double-sided nit comb (1) and a toothless end fragment of a second (2) were found in late nineteenth century deposits. The complete comb (1) seems to be made from a sheet of pressed horn. The fragment has many worn striations at the base of the teeth.

1* Double-sided nit comb made from a single piece of pressed horn. Two pieces now joined, one side is missing only eleven teeth, whilst the other lacks two thirds of its number. Teeth are cut at ½ inch intervals, sixty-six per side. The end rims are convex.
L 60.7 W 42 T 1.0 Teeth L 12 **738**

2 Fragment of double-sided nit comb. Many wear marks at base of teeth but no teeth surviving, and it is not possible to calculate spacing. comb.
L 31 W 18 T 1.7 **760**

Spindle whorls (BA06)

A group of six bone spindle whorls (BA06.1–6) comprised one (1) from a deposit ascribed to **Period III**, two (2 and 3) from relatively late **Period IV** deposits in the **southern sector** and three from the **Period V** graveyard. Five were made from pierced

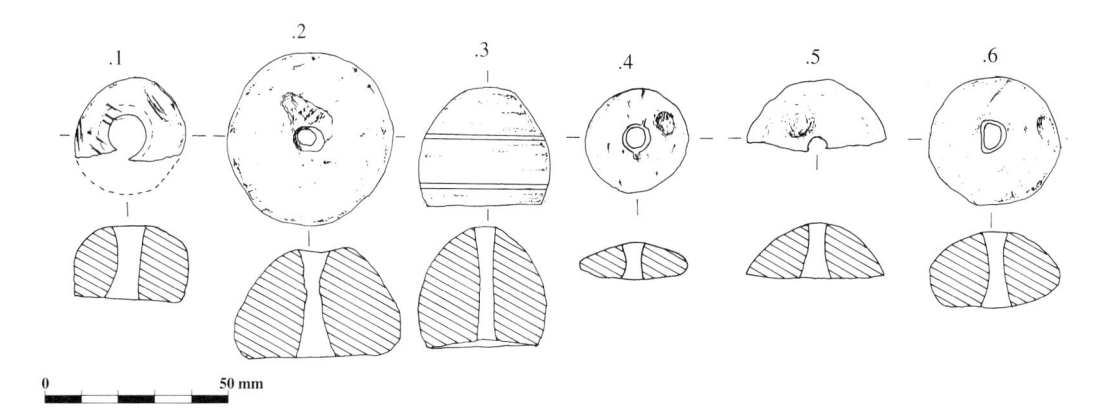

10.137 Bone whorls (BA6).

femur heads and, and the sixth (6) from a possibly human humerus. Several had been trimmed by knife to ensure a smoother and rounder circumference. The only decorated whorl (3) has a pair of parallel incised grooves cut by turning the whorl on a lathe. Although bone whorls predominate on some Anglo-Scandinavian sites, it is very much dependent upon the availability of suitable materials, and bone whorls are greatly outnumbered by stone at Whithorn (Table 10.18). The whorls from the **southern sector** probably pertained to the later-twelfth/earlier-thirteenth century, and a similar date is appropriate to the examples (4–6) displaced by **Period V** graves. Their distribution coincided broadly with that of other whorls (Figure 6.29), and they cannot be linked with specific craft workshops.

1* Broken whorl, flat base and knife-trimmed vertical side with convex upper surface. Bi-conical central perforation.
D 31 T 20 Hole D 13 × 5 **252.06**

2* Head of femur with bi-conical central perforation for use as a spindle whorl. Hole drilled from both ends. Edges trimmed by knife to produce a more rounded form.
D 45 T 25 Hole D 11 × 7 **415.01**

3* Well made conical whorl with concave base, decorated with two pairs of parallel incised grooves, 6 mm and 19 mm from base. The surface is well polished, though one side of the whorl has been damaged by fire. The central hole is drilled and relatively straight sided.
D 34 T 27 Hole D 6 **414.02**

4* Flattened bi-convex whorl with bi-conical perforation.
D 27 T 10 Hole D 6 × 4 **533**

5* Broken plano-convex whorl with bi-conical perforation, burnt.
D 36 T 14 Hole D 8 × 6 **543**

6* Bi-convex whorl with bi-conical perforation, slightly off-centre at top and angled to emerge centrally at the base. Possibly a human humerus.
D 32 T 18 Hole D 8 × 6 **542**

Ornamental pins (BA07)

Seven pins, some broken, with heads of identifiable form (BA07.1–7) comprised one 'nail-headed' (4), three 'nail-headed' with a circle of projecting lugs beneath (1–3), two club-headed (5 and 6), and one with a flat expanded square head (7). Plain 'nail-headed' pins are generally tenth century (Hamilton 1956, 148; Mann 1982, 10), and nail-headed pins with additional decoration somewhat later. The club-headed pin is generally thought to be of seventh/eighth century date (Laing 1973, 67–8; Stevenson 1955, 283), and several examples from the Mote of Mark had been used as formers for moulds in which to cast bronze equivalents, but there are tenth century club-headed pins from the Norse site at Freswick, Caithness (Curle 1939, 98). The square headed pin has a late tenth century parallel from Lloyds Bank, York (MacGregor 1982, 91). Despite the relatively early dates of these *comparanda*, the three well-stratified pins (1, 3 and 7) came from contexts ascribed to the second half of the twelfth century or later. The others came from the **Period V** graveyard, and could easily have been displaced from rather earlier deposits (Figure 6.25).

1* Broken pin with flat round 'nail' head, below which is a ring of six projecting lugs. The shank tapers to a point.
L 32 & 6 Head D 6 Shank D 4 **410**

2* Complete pin with splayed head, possibly a small 'thistle', below which are four projections. Circular shank tapers beyond mid-point. Tip abraded, possibly broken.
L 66 Head D 7 Shank D 3 **531**

3* Broken pin with flattened head, possibly a 'nail' head, below which are eight elongated projections. Straight rounded shank broken around mid point.
L23 Head D 4.6 Shank D 2.5 **414.03**

4* Pin with flat round 'nail' head, shank expands from neck to mid section before tapering to point, well polished surface.
L 98 Head D 7 Shank D 5 **534**

5* Broken pin with flattened club head and tapered neck, two pieces.
L 19.5 Head D 5 Shank D 3.5 **533**

6* Broken pin with club head, shank expands from neck to mid-section, where it is transversely fractured.
L 49 Head D 6 Shank D 4 **615.05**

THE FINDS

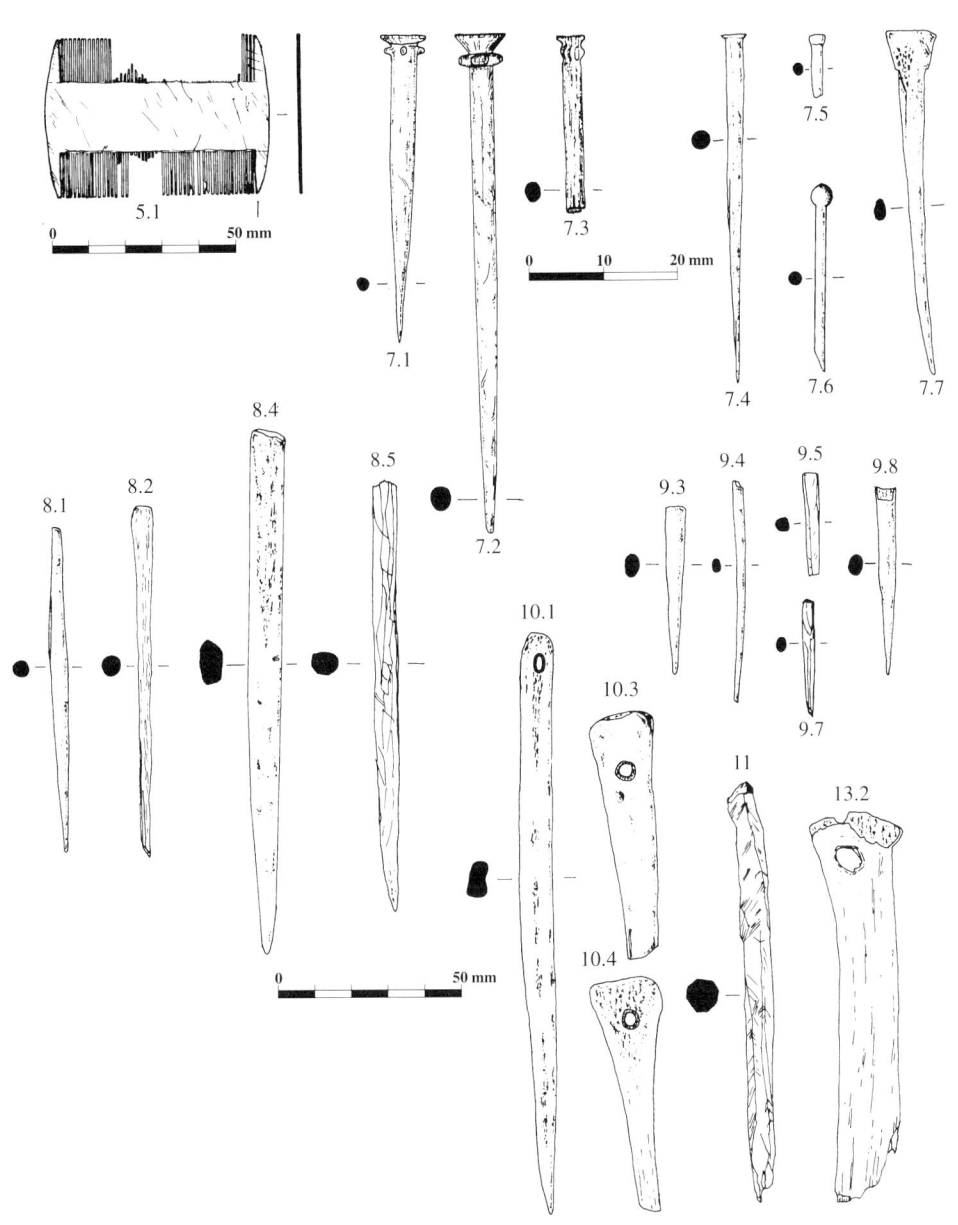

10.138 Bone nit-comb (BA1), ornamental pins (BA7), weaving implements (BA8), points (BA9), perforated bones (BA10), and miscellaneous bone artefacts (BA11–13).

7* Complete pin with flat expanded head; sub round shank, with well-polished surface, tapering to a point.
L 92 Head W 13 Shank D 6 **411.04**

Weaving implements (BA08)

This group comprised three complete double-ended tools (1–3) with carefully-finished rounded shanks, and two single-pointed polished bone splinters (4 and 5). The former have shanks swelling at the mid-point, and tapering towards each end. These are paralleled by examples from ninth to eleventh century midden deposits at Jarlshof (Hamilton 1956, 151), where they were interpreted as pins, and from *Hamwic* (Hinton 1980, 77). The other two pertain to MacGregor's single pointed tool class (MacGregor 1985, 188–9), and have numerous parallels including tenth century examples from Beverley (Foreman 1991c, 186) and Flaxengate, Lincoln (Mann 1982, 25), and twelfth century ones from Gloucester (Heighway 1979, Fig. 24). It has been suggested that these are an English phenomenon, but aside from the Whithorn pieces they also occur on several Scottish sites from the North Atlantic Iron Age onwards (e.g. Freswick, Curle 1939, Pl.XLVIII No.3 and 6; Bac Mhic Connain, Callander 1932, Fig. 13; Broch of Ayre, Graeme 1914, Fig. 11). Two of the double-pointed tools came from the east end of the **central sector** *outer zone* and were associated spatially with other possible weaving tools ascribed to **Period IV** (Figures 6.25 and 10.134). They were probable used for lifting up warp threads and beating down weft threads. The two single-pointed implements came from the southern end of the **southern sector** where there was no other evidence of weaving, and are likely to have had a different function.

1* Complete weaving implement or headless pin, expanding to mid-section and tapering to point, well polished surface.
L 85 Shank D 4.7 **427.02**

2* Complete weaving implement or headless pin, round shank with polished surface tapering to the point. The pin is in two pieces, both showing evidence of post-depositional abrasion.
L 93 D 7 **535**

3 Possible broken butt end of weaving implement.
L 37 D 5.6 **539**

4* Large complete weaving implement or headless pin, sub-square shank tapers to point, with a highly polished surface.
L 136 Shank W 8.5 T 5.4 **523.01**

5* Complete weaving implement or headless pin, expanding to mid-section and tapering to point. Shank sub-rectangular at butt, rounded from mid-section down, well polished surface.
L 104 Shank D 6.5 **523.01**

Point fragments (BA09)

Eight pointed fragments (BA09.1–8) from pins or weaving implements, lack other diagnostic features. One (1) came from the **Period III/1** boundary ditch. The others came from **Period IV** or **V** contexts (Figure 6.25), and include two well-stratified fragments (2 and 3) from later-twelfth century deposits in the **southern sector**.

1 Broken tapering shank in two pieces, broken at both ends.
L 30 D 4.2 **436.01**

2 Fragments of a short tapering point.
415.01

3* Broken tapering point, well polished.
L 43 D 6.2 **414.02**

4* Broken tapering point.
L 32 D 3.6 **542**

5* Broken tapering point, with polished surface.
L 48 D 4.5 **542**

6 Broken shank, tapering to a point.
L 58 D 3.5 **534**

7* Fragment of tapering round shank, broken at both ends.
L 28 D 4.8 **535**

8* Possible broken shank evidencing wear, abraded.
L 37 D 5.6 **539**

Needles and pierced pins (BA10)

Five pierced bone implements (BA10.1–5) probably include coarse needles and pins. A complete highly-polished needle with a rounded head (1) has Frisian parallels (Roes 1963, 70–1 Pl.LIV No.18), and similarities with examples from Flaxengate, Lincoln (Mann 1982, 25–6). Two other polished and pierced pieces are probably needles (2 and 4). The other two pieces (3 and 5) are pig fibulae, and pierced examples are found in a wide variety of North European sites from the prehistoric period until the thirteenth century. Three of the objects (1, 2 and 5) came from secure **Period IV** deposits, a fourth (3) from rubble deposited in **Period III** but contaminated with **Period IV** finds, and the fifth from a **Period V** grave in the eastern part of the **central sector** (Figure 6.25).

1* Large needle, or pierced pin, with sub-triangular shank tapering at the lower end. The surface is well polished to a high gloss.
L 154 W 8 T 5 Hole D 2.6 **417.02**

2 Bone needle or pierced pin, manufactured from small bone. Trimmed to a point at one end, the other end has a bi-conical hole cut through the natural swelling at the end of the bone, across which it has fractured.
L 46 W 5.5 Hole D 3.2 **445**

3* Broken pig fibula with bi-conical perforation at one end.
L 63 Head W 15.5 T 6 Shank W 10 **400**

4* Broken implement, possibly a pin/needle judging by the polished surface, drilled at one end.
L 63 Head W 17 T 6 Shank W 6 **533**

5 Pig fibula drilled at one end, the other end is flat and spatulate.
L 111 Head W 14 T 4.5 Shank W 6.5 **417.02**

Pin blank (BA11)

A single cut and faceted piece of bone from the **Period V** graveyard can be identified tentatively as a pin blank. The absence of other examples indicates that pin-making was not among the numerous crafts practised in the excavated part of the *inner precinct*, and may well have been omitted from the repertoire of the Whithorn craftsmen.

11* Cut and faceted tapering bone, evidencing knife work. Probably an unfinished pin blank.
L 107 D 9 **533**

Bone toggle (BA12)

A single perforated pig phalange (BA12) can be identified as a toggle, and has numerous parallels in Anglo-Scandinavian archaeology. In common with others (Oakley 1979, 313) the grooving on the distal end has been accentuated, though this feature is lacking in finds from Lincoln and Beverley (Foreman 1991c, 184).

12 Phalange with bi-conical transverse perforation, a toggle.
L 48 Hole D 4 **431**

Miscellaneous worked bones (BA13–BA19)

A small group of miscellaneous worked bones is sub-divided into seven categories, some represented by a single example. These included three perforated bones of uncertain function (BA13.1–3); the handle and head plate of two different toothbrushes (BA1 6.1–2) from recent contexts; a double-pronged implement (BA17) fitting the criteria for this controversial class of object (MacGregor 1982, 95–6); and five fragments with slight evidence of working (BA19.1–5), two (3 and 5) shaped to points, one with a cut notch (4), one (1) a cut out section of cattle leg bone, and a trimmed and longitudinally perforated bone (2) which is similar to objects interpreted as tallow holders (Mann 1982, 27) or butchery tools Foreman 1991, 187–8.

A fragment of a handle (BA14) and three gaming pieces (BA15.1–3) are of particular interest as they came from secure **Period II** contexts, and are thus significantly earlier than the other bone artefacts. The handle fragment has a lateral perforation for a suspension thong, and was perhaps the butt end of a small knife or tool handle. Bone is more susceptible to stress fracturing than antler, and is only likely to have been used for delicate items where pressure would not be applied. The three gaming pieces (BA15.1–3) comprise a fire-damaged dome made from a femoral head sawn across the base (1), and two small plano-convex pieces made from turned animal teeth. The first came from the burnt deposits in the **Period II/7** church (315.01), and the others from the adjacent rubbish deposit (303). A lathe-turned bone bead (BA18) from the **Period V** graveyard is paralleled by a fifteenth century bead from Northampton (Oakley 1979c, 318).

Perforated Bones (BA13)

1 Bone fragment with conical perforation.
L 19 Hole D 2.7 **542**

2* Broken bone with opposed holes at one end.
L 104 Hole D 7 **607.05**

3 Astragalus with bi-conical central perforation.
Hole D 5.5 L 59 **635**

Handle (BA14)

1 Fragment of butt end of bone handle with perforation on one side near end, and traces of a possible opposed hole. The butt end has been sawn level.
D 17.5 L 31.5 Hole D 2.5 **315.02**

Gaming Pieces (BA15)

1 Convex dome of burnt bone with sawn flat base, possibly a gaming counter.
D 20 T 9.4 **315.01**

2 Convex dome of animal tooth, probable gaming piece. Lathe turned with saw marks across base.
D 11.4 Ht. 6 **303**

3 Convex dome of animal tooth, probable gaming piece. Lathe turned with saw marks across base.
D 10 Ht. 5 **303**

Two-Pronged Implement (BA17)

1 Bone section, longitudinally split. One end has been worked by a knife to form a small broad point, the other has been trimmed. The shape indicated a possible use as a scriber, with the edges smoothed to ease use in the fingers and palm, or as a broken example of MacGregor's (1982, 1985) two-pronged implement.
L 78 W 17 T 10 **535**

Bead (BA18)

1 Small rounded bead with transverse perforation.
D 6 T 3.8 Hole D 3 **543**

Worked Bone Fragments (BA19)

1 Bone section with cleavage marks and possible knife trimming marks. One end is faceted and possibly worn.
L 88 W 16 T 11.5 **420**

2 Abraded bone with hollowed centre – possibly a worn rough handle or 'socketed point'.
L 66 D 23 **533**

3 Bone sliver shaped into a point – a rough tool (?)
L 38 W 6.5 **543**

4 Bone fragment with an inverse-pyramid notch cut into it, along which it has broken.
L 16 W 9 T 4 **600.04**

5 Bone sliver, possibly utilised for its spatulate or pointed qualities.
L 97 W 13 **909**

The Leather

Andrew Nicholson

The excavations yielded some 3,302 pieces of leather of which 3,030 came from the waterlogged deposits in the **southern sector** (pp 221-4), mostly from the **Period IV.6** deposits in the blocked drainage ditch (417.02). Twenty-six pieces of recent leather were concentrated in the **Museum Garden** (764 and 770) and manse demolition deposits (738), the former group including footwear discarded by the William Galloway's workmen in the late nineteenth century. The remaining pieces were unstratified. The material from the **southern sector** included several pieces and fragments from shoes, ranging in date from the late-twelfth century to the early-fourteenth century. The large number of waste fragments with evidence of working points to the presence of at least one leatherworking workshop in the near vicinity. 4.6% of the medieval leather displayed evidence of manufacture. This contrasts with a figure of 9% for a deposit of similar size and date from Lucy Tower,

Lincoln, where there was matching evidence for leatherworking, but more signs of cobbling in the form of repairs and clump soles (Mould 1986). The Lincoln material may reflect a concentration of similar activities at a single locale, whereas at Whithorn there may be a divergence in specialisation, with leatherworking and cobbling in different workshops.

The assemblage is consistent with similar groups from Scotland and elsewhere. The shoe soles and uppers conform to the general typology for Scottish shoes proposed by Thomas (n.d., 1986, 1987) and are complementary to the only other material from Galloway, the fourteenth century deposits from Threave Castle (M.C. Thomas 1981), where the continued development of styles can be seen. Two edge bindings (LR23), probably from a single object, were the only pieces without identifiable parallels.

Stratigraphy

The finds from the **southern sector** fall into four groups. Five pieces were securely stratified in **Period I** pits (53.01, and .14), but a further 177 pieces from the upper fill of late **Period I** ditches (230.03 and 216) probably belonged with the **Period IV** assemblage. The second group comprised 2,776 securely-stratified pieces from **Period IV.6** deposits, most (2,675) being recovered from the comprehensive sieving of the fill of the main ditch (417.02, Table 6.10). These probably represent a rapid and brief accumulation beginning as the drainage deteriorated and ending when the area flooded (pp 217-9). The finds in this group were thus a reliably associated assemblage of contemporary objects with parallels from more securely dated sites dated to the second half of the twelfth century. The third group comprised seventy-seven pieces recovered from this area before the successive ditches (417 and 416) were recognized. These poorly-stratified finds (assigned to Block 523.01) may have originated in the **Period IV.6** deposits, but some were typologically later and probably came from a later context which may have been the final drainage ditch (416) or an unrecognized pit. This would have been an appropriate context for the pieces ascribed to the mid- to late-thirteenth century (e.g. 17.6, 19.3, 24.2-12). The fourth group was recovered from spoil removed this area (903), and included twelve strap fragments (LR24.2-11, 13 and 14) with distinctive stitching patterns. A single example (24.12) was recovered from a stratified context in the final drainage ditch (416) which was the most likely source of these pieces, but not necessarily of others from 903.

Classification

The leather finds were divided into twenty-eight categories on the criteria of usage, hide type, evidence of working and period. The identification of hide type was

	Thickness mm	Trimmings No.	%	% Total Leather
01 Cattle	0.3–4.0	742	66	22.5
02 Sheep/Goat	0.3–1.5	11	1	0.3
03 Deer	0.5	2	–	
04 Uncertain	0.3–4.0	368	33	11.1
All Trimmings		**1123**	**100**	**34.0**

Table 10.33: Leather trimmings (LR01–04).

provisional as many of the pieces had been cleaned but not conserved, and the identification was undertaken in the field. Furthermore many of the pieces had delaminated, making the assessment of hide type and original thickness difficult to determine. Full catalogues of shoe uppers (LR17), soles (LR19) and fittings (LR22); edge bindings (LR23), belt strap sections (LR24) and discs (LR25, 26) are presented below, other categories are described in the excavation archive.

Trimmings (LR01–04)

Trimmings were distinguished by their linear shape, with the long cut sides usually tapering to a point at one or both ends. They were from 0.3mm to 4.0mm thick, most pieces lying between 1.0mm and 2.0mm. Four sub-divisions (LR01–04) were determined by hide type.

Offcuts (LR05–07)

Leather offcuts were defined as pieces with at least one cut edge, and encompass a wide range of shapes and sizes. The larger size of the offcuts generally enabled more of them to be positively identified by hide type than the trimmings. No pieces of deer hide were identified. The thickness of the hide ranged from 0.3mm to 5.5mm, with most pieces in the 0.5mm to 2.0mm range. Three sub-divisions were determined by hide type.

Discards (LR08)

	Thickness mm	No.	% Offcuts	% Total Leather
05 Cattle	0.3–5.5	809	71.2	24.5
06 Sheep/Goat	0.3–2.0	25	2.2	0.8
07 Uncertain	0.3–3.0	302	26.6	9.1
All Offcuts		**1136**	**100**	**34.4**

Table 10.34: Leather offcuts (LR05–07).

Six pieces of leather appear to have been discarded as completely unusable, five due to a concentration of folds in the skin, while the sixth was apparently a section from around an udder. The five creased pieces had a curved edge cut differently from their other edges, possibly representing the initial skinning of the animal.

Scraps (LR09–12)

Leather 'scraps' were fragments without evidence of working. Their edges were torn or possibly worn though it was hard to distinguish the two. Many scraps were in poor condition, thus it was harder to assess the hide type, by which the class was sub-divided.

Offcuts with linear impressions (LR13)

	Thickness mm	No.	% Scraps	% Total Leather
09 Cattle	0.3–3.0	305	45.8	9.2
10 Sheep/Goat	0.5–1.5	12	1.8	0.4
11 Deer	0.5	2	0.3	–
12 Uncertain	0.5–1.5	347	52.1	10.5
All scraps		**666**	**100**	**20.2**

Table 10.35: Leather scraps (LR09–12).

Forty-three offcuts (LR13.1–43) had creases or scored lines on their grain side. Thirty-five pieces had a single line running parallel to a cut edge, which probably marked a pattern drawn on the leather prior to working. These were explicable in the case of shoes where the leather was stretched over a last after marking out, but before being trimmed to shape. The stretching may have resulted in excess leather so that the offcuts retained the original impressed pattern marks. Two pieces (4 and 14) had twin impressed lines running parallel to a cut edge, probably as a result of a similar process. Two other pieces (1 and 23) had a single short impressed line which was not parallel to any cut edge, and a third (8) had several lines. The lines were often impressed rather than incised, with no cutting of the surface of the grain, indicating the use of a specific tool with a narrow blunted point, rather than a knife or awl.

Offcuts with tool impressions (LR14)

Twenty-three offcuts (LR14.1–23) displayed distinct impressions on the surface, which were probably made by tools, and on one (1) by fingernails as well. Four different marks were distinguished: **a)** an elongated U 6 mm long; **b)** a broad line 5 mm long upturned at both ends; **c)** a similar smaller shape some 3 mm long; and **d)** a 5 mm by 3 mm sub-rectangular mark. The second mark (**b**) may have been produced by the same tool as the last (**d**), but held at an angle leaving a partial impression. Several slightly curved linear impressions varying from 3 mm to 7 mm long may have been created by special tools, or by the application of a knife with a convex-edged blade held at an angle to the surface. Some of the marks were associated with the tooling of specific fragments, coinciding with one of the cut edges. The random distribution of marks on two pieces (7 and 10) suggested that they had been used as pads.

Scraps with a worn surface (LR15)

A hundred and thirty scraps of leather with no evidence of working (LR15.1–130) had markedly worn outer surfaces. These were probably remnants of worn shoe soles discarded by the cobbler when he was replacing the sole. Most of the fragments were quite small, and the number of discarded soles cannot be estimated.

Worked leather (LR16)

Twenty-five pieces of 'worked leather' (LR16.1–25) encompassed offcuts with more evidence of working than cut edges, and others where the nature of the cuts suggested a specific use. There were several sub-groups with similar features. Twelve pieces had cut or pierced holes or slits. The holes had been stretched after cutting in two examples (3 and 10), and the proximity of an unusually cut edge (see LR07 above) suggests that it occurred when the hide was pegged out during tanning. Two other fragments (8 and 9) had pierced holes suitable for nails, and may have been intended for similar use although there was no evidence of stretching. Another six pieces had one edge composed of small ragged slashes or V-shaped nicks at regular intervals of between 5mm and 7mm. These may well be traces of former stitch holes where the piece has been subsequently trimmed, especially if they were edges which had been overstitched. Three pieces (4, 8 and 21) had been folded prior to cutting, but their purpose was unclear. Two further pieces (9 and 14) were cut through the grain side by V-shaped grooves removing some of the material, and so differing from the impressed lines on the other marked pieces (LR13). One piece (20, Figure 10.42) may have come from a garment or object. Two faint lines were incised parallel to one cut edge, with irregular stitch-holes between. The piece was torn along another line of stitch-holes adjacent to a distinct crease which terminated in a larger hole, probably for a rivet or other fastening, and lay at 90° to the cut edge. Two more perforations also lay at 90° to the cut edge. The only decorated piece (1, Figure 10.139) was an offcut, torn across one end, with a 'stopped plait' interlace motif incised on the grain side, and an incomplete interlace pattern incised on the flesh side. One of the central lozenges on the grain side has been shaded with fine incised diagonal lines. The ornament is paralleled on the bridle mounts from the burial at Balladoole, Isle of Man (Bersu and Wilson 1966, Fig. 14–15), even down to the partial pattern on the reverse, and is linked stylistically with the 'Whithorn School' crosses ascribed to the later-tenth and eleventh centuries (pp 621-3). The piece probably dates to the tenth century despite its apparent association with a sequence of shoes commencing two centuries later.

Shoes

The two principal forms of shoe construction, turnshoe and welted, were both represented in the assemblage, but there was no evidence for the intermediate turn-welt stage (Thornton 1973). Turnshoes were made inside-out with the flesh, or inner surface of the leather, facing outwards during construction. They consisted of an upper, possibly composed of one or more sections, and a single sole serving as both outer sole and insole. The lasting margin or lower edge of the upper was pierced with oval grain to flesh holes, usually about 1.5 mm by 3 mm, through which the stitching passed, the thread then entering the edge of the sole, and exiting on the flesh side. The stitch length, or distance between the centres of the stitch-holes, was usually 5 mm to 7 mm. Sections of upper were joined together by butted seams with edge-flesh stitching, invisible on the grain side of the leather. The completed shoe was then turned inside-out; the sole now had the grain side outwards, or downwards, and the flesh side inside, or upwards. Some turnshoes included a *rand*, a strip of leather (usually wedge-shaped but sometimes flat) with a grain-flesh stitching channel. The rand was placed between sole and upper, to strengthen the seam and make it more watertight. Examples from Perth (Thomas n.d.) show this development occurring in the twelfth century. Early in the sixteenth century it was discovered that if the rand was stitched to the outside of the upper and insole, and not placed between them, the finished shoe did not have to be turned as the outer sole could be sewn directly to the outer part of the rand, at which point the rand becomes known as a welt. Welted outer soles are thus distinguished from turnshoe soles as they have grain to flesh stitching channels. Further build-up of soles and heels took place by nailing or pegging additional layers to the outer sole.

Shoe uppers (LR17)

Only seven uppers (LR17.1–7), comprising two vamps, four quarters and a triangular insert (7), could be distinguished definitely. No material remained in any of the holes to give an indication of the type of thread used in stitching. Scottish patterns of turnshoe uppers and soles from the twelfth to fifteenth centuries have been classified by Thomas (n.d., 1986, 1987), and the Whithorn pieces generally conform to this typology.

Two pieces (1 and 2) were from the same shoe of style Type E. This was a simple low-cut shoe, often with no form of fastening. The vamp and quarter were stitched together with a butted edge to flesh seam, with 18 stitch-holes at intervals of 3mm to 4mm. As both pieces were worn away at the heel it was uncertain whether they were a two-piece upper or both part of a single-piece upper. The upper edge of the vamp and quarters also had edge to flesh stitches which were probably used to attach a top-band, a feature paralleled at York (Tweddle 1986, 248) and Perth (Thomas n.d.), rather than additional upper sections, a feature only seen on continental examples (Hald 1972 and Thompson 1967). The quarter also had a V-shaped line of blind stitching on the interior which was probably used to hold the stiffener (5) at the heel.

A third piece (3, also style E) was a quarter cut along its rear edge, where impressions of wear indicated the former presence of stitches. This could well have been one half of a two-piece quarter. There was no evidence for a top-bad on this fragment. Two quarters (4 and 5) were a variation on Style D(i) with inside lacing connects the vamp and quarters. The lower part of the seam between vamp and quarter was butted and edge-flesh stitched, whilst three holes for thongs or laces occupy the upper part of the junction. Edge-flesh stitching on the upper edge of both fragments was probably used for a top-band. The second vamp (6), also of Style D(i), had six thong holes at the seam, although unlike the others, the top hole shows no sign of wear and may not have been used. A reconstruction of the shoe, including the lacing method based on the wear patterns on the grain side of the vamp, is illustrated in Figure 10.140. Edge-flesh stitching at the seam, and parallel tunnel stitching on the far side of the holes in the flesh side, were for the attachment of a facing to reinforce the tie-holes. At Perth this style

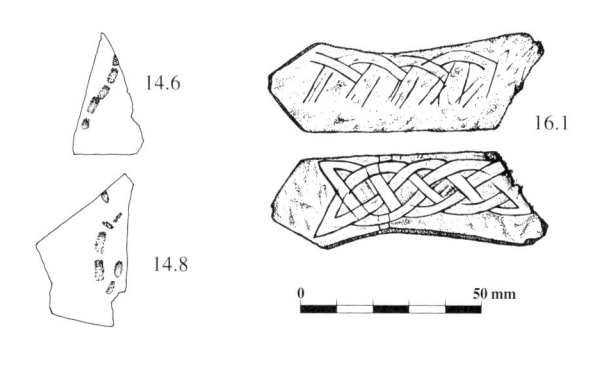

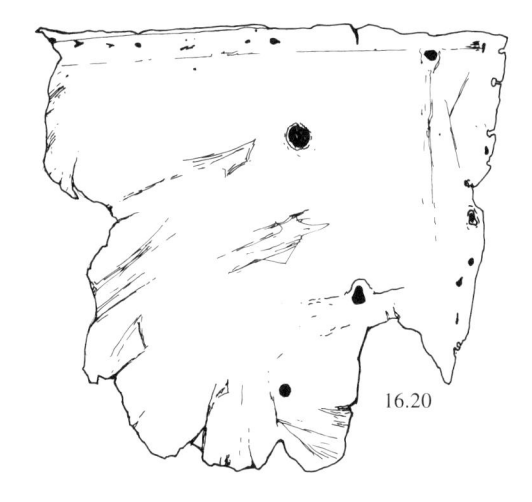

10.139 Tooled and worked leather (LR14 and 16).

was dated to the second half of the thirteenth century. A row of tunnel stitching on the flesh side descended from the upper edge to the lasting margin at a point opposite the seam for attaching the vamp to the quarter. This may have been designed to pull the leather in and reinforce it at a stress point, or to secure a lining. Edge-flesh stitch-holes around the top were probably from the attachment of a topband, which may also have secured a lining had one been fitted. A V-shaped line of tunnel stitching on the flesh side at the heel was used to attach a heel stiffener.

1 Shoe upper (quarter) with two cut sides and four torn sides, probably associated with No. 2. Two cut edges have edge/flesh stitching at 3–4mm. Shorter side was for attaching to vamp, longer side shows evidence of overstitch for the addition of a top band.

73 × 42 × 1.5 **523.01**

2 Shoe upper (vamp) probably associated with No. 1. Edge/flesh stitching on two sides at 3–4mm. Shorter side has 18 holes as per quarter (1), longer side shows evidence of overstitching for top band. A shallow V-shaped line of stitch holes on the interior may be for a reinforcement at the top of the heel. The creasing around the heel and worn edge may indicate a sole rising up at the heel (*c.f.* York; Coppergate 627). The lower edge has six and a half holes at 5–7mm, 2mm diameter holes with no signs of stretch or wear; sole may have been thronged rather than stitched on. If stitched, a rand must have been used.

174 × 114 × 1.5 **523.01**

3* Possible remains of shoe quarters/insert, delaminated. One side has nine edge/flesh holes at 4–5mm. Second side has seven grain/flesh holes at 4–5mm, overstitch. Third side cut leaving wear marks indicating stitching formerly present. Fourth side cut.

59 × 48 × 1.5 **417.02**

4* Complete quarter. Lower edge has nine throng/stitch holes at 6–7mm and three slashes 6mm long to take fastening throngs. Upper edge has edge/flesh overstitching at 4mm intervals. Sides have edge/flesh stitching at 2.5mm–4mm.

60 × 53 × 1.5 **417.02**

5 Quarter (PHS Type Di) with three thong holes on shorter edge, which is cut away below the holes, possibly for a strengthening insert. No evidence for top band or heel stiffener.

130 × 52 × 1.5 **417.02**

6* Vamp worn away at forepart and outside edge lasting margin. Stitch-holes of lasting margin at 4–8 mm intervals. One edge has edge-flesh holes for attachment of a quarter, the other has six holes, the lower five evidencing wear patterns, for thonging (Style Di). Edge-flesh stitch holes around the upper edge may be for affixing a top band or possibly a liner. A triangle of tunnel stitching indicates the former presence of a heel-stiffener, the lower edge of which would have been incorporated at the lasting margin. Edge/flesh stitch-holes by the thong-holes and a parallel line of tunnel stitching show that an internal reinforcing band was located over the thong holes. A line of close tunnel stitching from the upper edge to the lasting margin lies on the forepart opposite the vamp-quarter junction.

L 370 W 161 T2.3 **?523.01**

7 Triangular insert for vamp/quarter interface with edge/flesh holes on two longer sides, grain/flesh on third – possible top band.

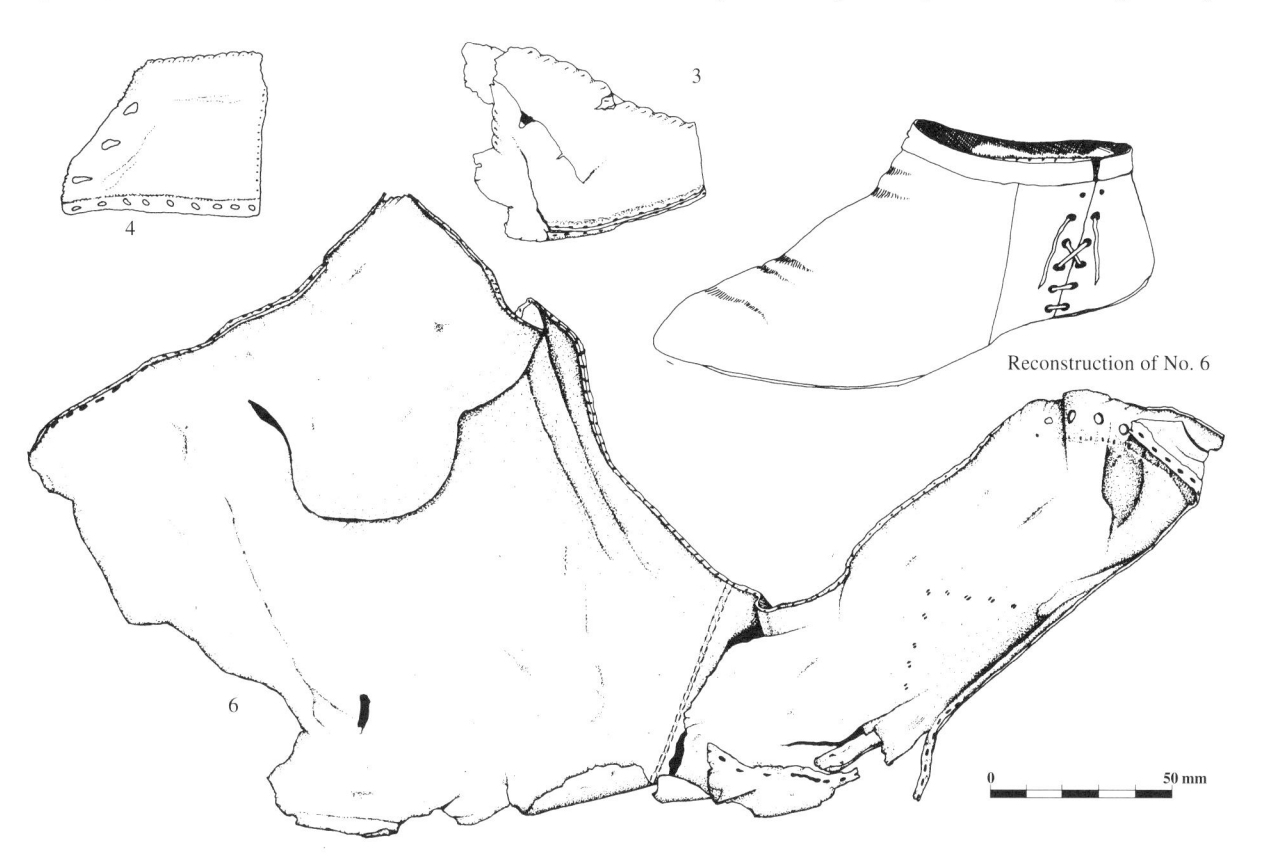

34 × 29 × 1.5 **417.02**

10.140 Shoe-upper fragments (LR17).

10.141 Turnshoe soles (LR19).

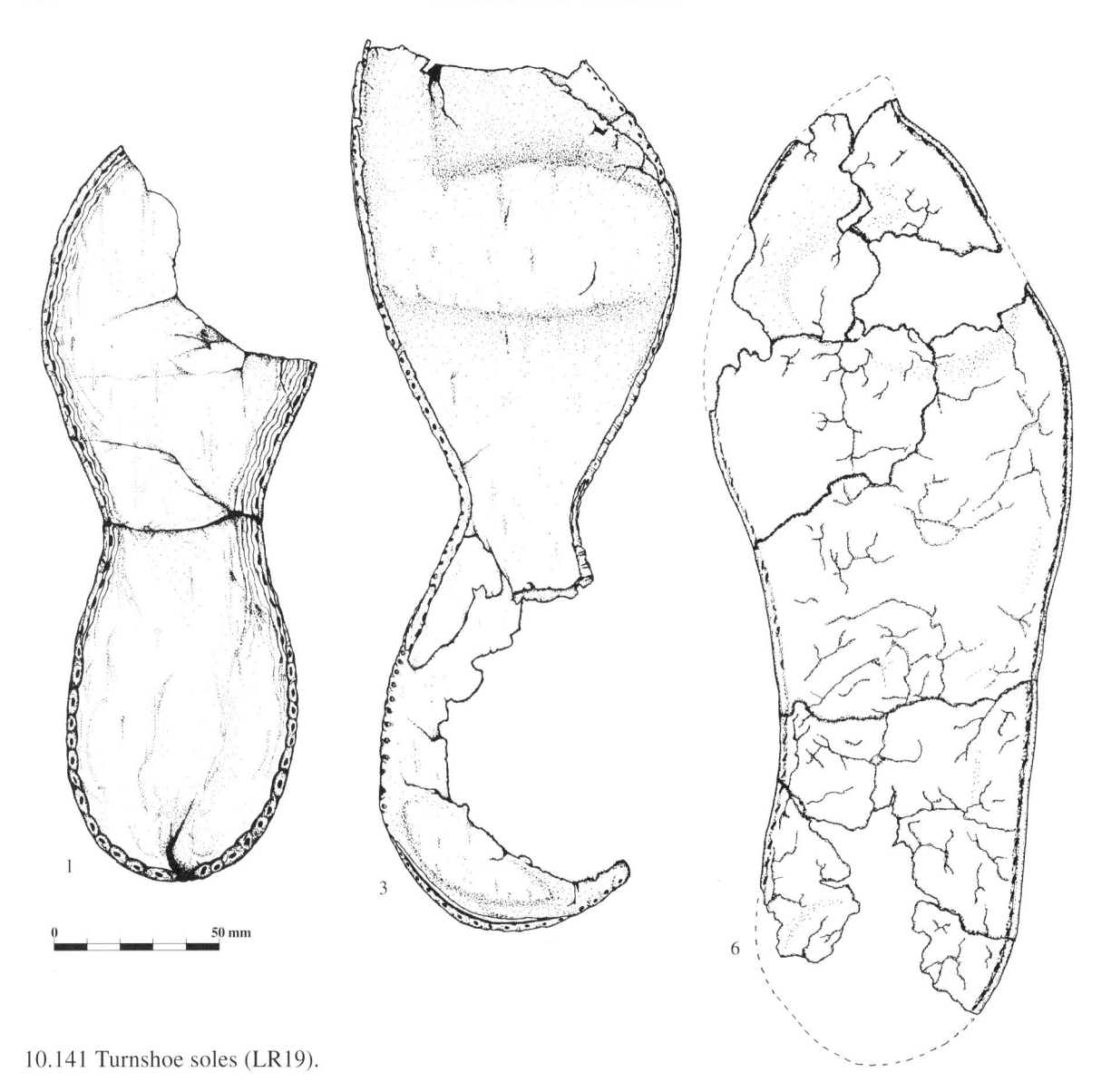

Fragment with grain-flesh stitch-holes (LR18)

Thirty-nine fragments with grain-flesh stitch-holes along one edge (LR18.1–39, archive), many worn or torn, were probably parts of turnshoe uppers.

Shoe soles (LR19)

Thirteen turnshoe soles (LR19.1–12) were mostly single pieces, but four (2, 6, 12 and 13) comprised several related fragments. Only five soles were sufficiently complete for their original shape to be reconstructed and all were worn in the heel and forepart. The classification of sole types and suggested dating follows Thomas (1986, 1987).

The forepart of the first sole (1) was worn completely away, but wear patterns indicated that it was worn on the left foot. It had a definite waist and curved foreparts, and probably ended in a rounded or oval toe. It conforms to PHS Type 2, dated twelfth to thirteenth century. Two other soles (9 and 10) had the more natural foot shape with a pronounced waist and inwardly curving foreparts of the PHS Type 3, dated from the twelfth to fourteenth century, but concentrated in the second half of the thirteenth century. The more complete of the two (10) has a series of grain-flesh stitch-holes to attach a repair or clump sole. Another sole (3) was of similar shape, but had an exaggerated, narrow waist, and whilst it may also be a Type 3, the narrowness of the waist was more characteristic of PHS Type 5, dated from the mid-thirteenth to mid-fourteenth century.

The other identifiable soles were earlier. One (6), comprising seven fragments, was much straighter than the others, with slight waisting and a central point at the toe. This falls into PHS Type 6 and probably dates to the second half of the twelfth century. A complete sole (11) with no pronounced waist, and a broad instep, belongs to Type 1, as does a fragmentary sole in three parts (2). Both probably date to the twelfth century. Three incomplete soles (4, 5 and 13) were also of Types 1 or 6. The other three soles (7, 8 and 12) were fragmentary, but tended to have pronounced waists. The lack of foreparts means they cannot be ascribed to specific classes, but the surviving diagnostic features indicate a date range from the twelfth to late-thirteenth century.

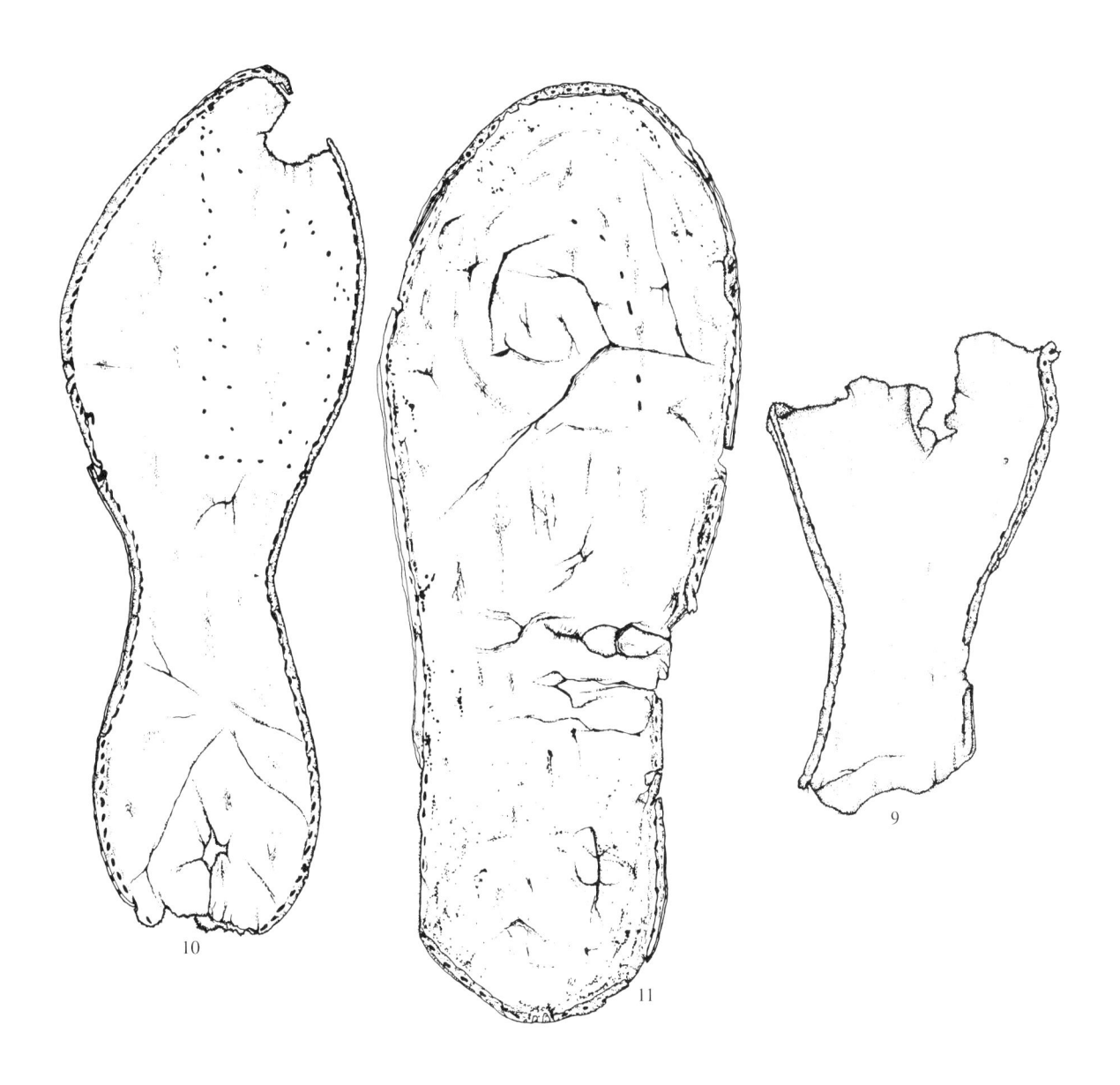

1* Left foot, turnshoe sole worn at forepart (PHS Type 2). Grain/flesh holes at 7–8 mm spacing, torn and worn away at forepart, small amount of wear at heel. Lasting margin stitch-holes at 5–7mm intervals. Associated with inner sole (LR22.01).

216 × 83 × 1.5 **523.01**

2 Badly worn fragmentary sole (PHS Type 1) in three parts, lacking forepart and heel. Broad instep. Lasting margin stitch-holes at 5–9mm intervals.

173 × 86 × 2.0 **417.02**

3* Right shoe inner sole with second inner sole adhering in places, worn at heel and toe (PHS Type 5) Surviving length 267mm (probably original 285mm). Thickness 1.5mm and 1.0mm. Large portion of heel and toe missing. Pronounced waist 37mm wide as opposed to 95mm across forepart. Lower sole grain side is interior, so an external sole must of been used. The sharp profile of the edge of the sole in conjunction with the edge/grain stitching, indicates the use of a rand. Stitch-holes at 5–6mm spacing.

523.01

4 Worn, fragmentary shoe sole (PHS Type 1 or 6) with twelve and a half edge/flesh holes at 5–7mm.

82 × 36 × 1.5 **523.01**

5 Worn, fragmentary shoe sole (PHS Type 1 or 6) with fifteen edge/flesh stitches at 5–6mm.

115 × 72 × 3.0 **417.02**

6* Sole in seven fragments (PHS Type 6). Elongated grain/flesh stitches at 5–7mm. Pointed toe. Probable original length c. 270mm. Heel, forepart and toe badly worn.

417.02

7 Fragmentary shoe sole twenty-two and a half edge/flesh stitches at 5–6.5mm.

112 × 69 × 4.0 **417.02**

8 Worn fragment, probably trimmed piece of shoe sole.

94 × 77 × 3.5 **417.02**

9* Part of sole (PHS Type 3), worn away at forepart and heel,

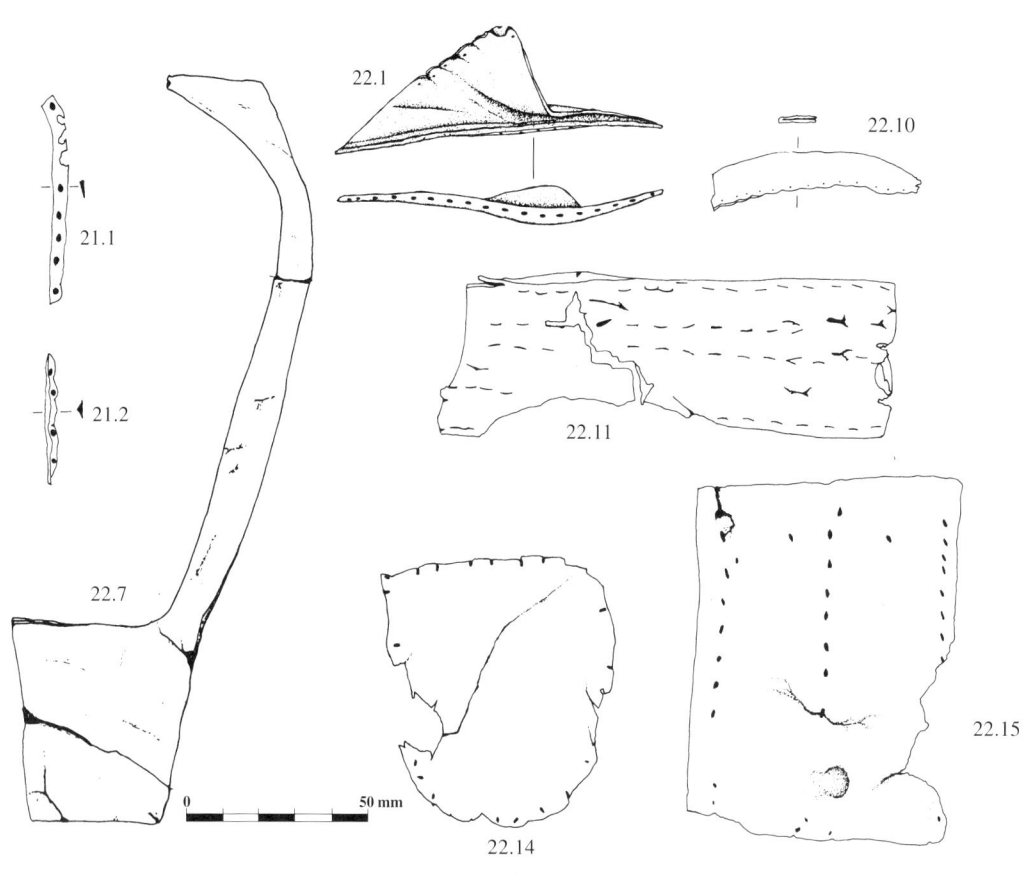

10.142 Rands (LR21) and shoe fittings (LR22).

narrowed waist. Edge/flesh lasting margin stitch-holes at 5–9mm intervals.

147 × 91 × 2.0 **903**

10* Complete worn shoe sole (PHS Type 3) with stitch-holes for clump worn away at toe and heel. Waisted, with slightly pointed toe. Double row of irregularly-spaced stitch-holes on half of forepart shows location of probable repair clump. Lasting margin stitch-holes at 5–7mm intervals

261 × 94 × 2.0 **523.01**

11* Complete, cracked and delaminated shoe sole (PHS Type 1). Natural foot shape with broad instep. Stitch-holes around ball of foot show location of former clump sole. Edge/flesh lasting margin holes at 5–7mm intervals.

283 × 112 × 2.0 **417.02**

12 Seven conjoining fragments of a shoe sole, original form uncertain.

    a 41 × 22 × 1.5mm, worn, four torn sides
    b 26 × 19 × 1.5mm, worn, five torn sides
    c 31 × 11 × 1.5mm, worn, four torn sides
    d 46 × 21 × 1.5mm, heel fragment, six and a half edge/flesh stitch-holes at 5–7mm
    e 32 × 19 × 1.5mm, heel fragment, five and a half edge/flesh stitch-holes at 5–7mm
    f 91 × 27 × 1.5mm, instep fragment, eleven edge/flesh stitch-holes at 6–7mm,
    g 64 × 11 × 1.5mm eight edge/flesh stitch-holes at 5–7mm

417.02

13 Two fragments of left sole (PHS Type 1 or 6)
    a Fragment with six edge/flesh stitch-holes at 6.5mm. 76 × 67 × 2.0.
    b Fragment with twenty-two edge/flesh stitch-holes at 6.5mm. 119 × 40 × 2.0

417.02

Fragments with edge-flesh stitch-holes (LR20)

Seventeen fragments with edge-flesh stitching channels (LR20.1–19, archive), were worn or torn, and sometimes delaminated. All can be reasonably assumed to have come from turnshoe soles

Rands (LR21)

Five strips identified as rands (LR21.1–5) displayed the characteristic triangular section (Figure 10.142; 21.1 and 2), a grain-flesh stitching channel, and both long sides cut. Other pieces with one long side cut and the other worn were assumed to be worn fragments of uppers. Rands were introduced at Perth during the twelfth century, and it is probably significant that only one of the rands came from the earlier group of material (417.02).

Shoe fittings (LR22)

Twenty-two shoe fittings (LR22.1–22) included heel stiffeners, inner soles, top bands and clumps. Two definite heel stiffeners (1 and 2) were triangular, with small stitch-holes on the two edges where they would have been tunnel stitched to the uppers. The lasting margins had much larger holes, matching those on the lasting margins of uppers, and implying that the stiffener was incorporated into the original design, and fastened onto the sole at the same time as the upper. A third possible example is assigned to LR18 (13). A group of inner soles comprised two heels (3 and 4) and three foreparts (5, 6 and 7), all re-cut to provide repair clumps, and a single intact example (8). Inner soles were distinguished by their shape, the absence of stitching channels, and the pattern of wear on the grain side which would have faced upwards on an inner sole, as opposed to downwards on a turnshoe outer sole. The complete inner sole (8) was associated with a Type 2 sole (LR19.1). Another offcut (9) which appeared to have had two clumps removed from it, may have originally been a turnshoe upper. Three top bands (10–12) included a plain folded band (10) whose lower edge had achieved a scalloped appearance through the wear pattern of the overstitching. The others (11 and 12) were folded and stitched along top and bottom, with two lines of parallel cuts at one end, perhaps for securing a toggle or closing device. The four clumps comprised two worn seats or clump heels (13 and 14) with traces of tunnel stitching around all edges, and two pieces which may have been clump soles (15 and 16). One of these (15) was unusually thick (5.5mm) and had three rows of grain-flesh stitch-holes, as well as intermediate ones at each end. Two crescentic pieces (17 and 18) had polygonal exterior edges and smoothly-curved interior edges. These appear to be offcuts from the heel of a turnshoe with a rounded sole, trimmed after sewing and before turning (see below). Two tab-like pieces (19 and 20) may originally have been cut from the vamp of a shoe in order to form a throat. Two other pieces (21 and 22) had raised longitudinal ridges, and may have been fragments of shoe uppers, with the ridge running up the centre of the vamp. These are paralleled at York (Tweddle 1986, Fig. 108) and Winchester (Thornton 1990, Nos 1930 and 1940).

1* Triangular heel stiffener with lasting margin holes at 5mm. Upper edge holes irregular at 4–6mm evidence overstitching. Both upper edges partly cut away (for replacement?).
85 × 38 × 1.0 **523.01**

2 Heel stiffener with three cut sides and one torn. Lower edge has 10½ possible throng holes at 4-7mm; upper edges stitches at 5–7mm, overstitched.
72 × 38 × 1.0 **523.01**

3 Heel from turnshoe inner sole with two cut sides and two torn. No grain side.
77 × 49 × 1.5 **52.03**

4 Heel from turnshoe inner sole with one cut side and one torn. Scored around edge with no trace of stitching.
84 × 47 × 2.0 **417.02**

5 Offcut form re-used inner sole, probably for seat/clump with three cut sides.
71 × 33 × 2.0 **417.02**

6 Offcut from re-used inner sole, probably for seat/clump with three cut sides and one torn.
68 × 44 × 1.5 **417.02**

7* Recut inner sole. Sole shaped piece lacking any peripheral stitch-holes, from which a section resembling a forepart has been cut, probably for a clump sole.
200 × 57 × 3.0 **523.01**

8 Fragment of shoe inner sole (PHS Type 2: late 12c.) with one curving up at edge, worn on grain side.
106 × 18 × 2.0 **523.01**

9 Delaminated re-used upper(?), probably for clumps or seats.
138 × 96 × 1.5 **417.02**

10* Top band from turnshoe. Folded strip with lower edges scalloped in appearance due to overstitch. Worn along folded edge. 12 holes at 5–7mm. Possibly deer hide.
59 × 11 × 2 × 10 **904**

11* Top band from turnshoe with slashes right through raised ridge down middle. No sign of wear on most cuts. May be stiffening band for top of boot or shoe, folded along ridge.
123 × 46 × 2.5 **417.02**

12 Probable top-band from shoe overstitched on one edge. One end cut and one torn.
91 × 20 × 0.5 **417.02**

13 Badly worn seat or clump heel for right foot with stitch-holes at 5–7mm.
73 × 66 × 3.5 **417.02**

14* Very worn seat or clump heel for right foot with holes for tunnel stitching evident round edges.
72 × 63 × 1.0 **417.02**

15* Clump sole with cut edges. Three parallel lines of stitch-holes, one along each edge and one down the central axis. Two intermediate stitch-holes between the rows at the neatly cut end.
96 × 72 × 5.5 **904**

16 Probable clump with irregularly-spaced grain/flesh stitch-holes around outer edges. Badly worn towards ball of foot.
94 × 56 × 2.5 **417.02**

17 Polygonal trimming with cut sides probably from turnshoe heel after stitching.
53 × 5 × 2.0 **417.02**

18 Polygonal trimming (two cut sides) from turnshoe heel after stitching.
67 × 7 × 3.0 **417.02**

19 Folded offcut, possibly from vamp throat
55 × 18 × 2 × 1.5 **417.02**

20 Offcut, possibly from vamp throat, with one cut and two torn sides
68 × 31 × 1.0 **417.02**

21 Ridged offcut, possibly from shoe upper (or last?) with one cut and two torn sides Ridge parallel to edge. Hair still attached.
31 × 24 × 1.0 **417.02**

22 Delaminated, ridged offcut, possibly from shoe upper.
70 × 29 × 1.5 **417.02**

Bindings (LR23)

Two pieces (LR23.1–2), probably from the same object, appeared to have been edge bindings. At 1.5mm thick and only 4mm and 6mm deep they did not seem to have been top-bands, though they were folded longitudinally with opposed stitching channels. Both displayed considerable wear along their folded edge, but none around the stitch-holes, suggesting that the latter were not under a great deal

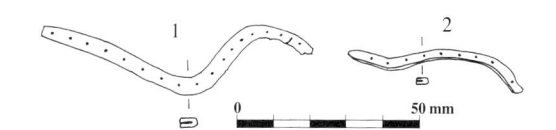

10.143 Bindings (LR23).

of tension. The holes were centred at 4–5mm and much more evenly spaced than those from turnshoes.

1* Folded binding strip with seventeen holes at 4–5mm (round, little wear or stretch) through both sides. Considerable wear on folded edge. Binding (*c.f.* turnshoe trim below).
82 × 6 × 2 × 1.5 **904**

2* Folded binding strip with ten holes at 4–5mm probably same as No. 1.
51 × 4 × 2 × 1.5 **904**

Belt and strap sections (LR24)

Twenty-one sections of straps (LR24.1–19) included a large group (2–12) with rows of pierced stabs parallel to their long edges. Several of these had slightly chamfered long edges, and whilst some were torn at both ends, suggesting breakage during use, most had been cut at the ends. Two pieces (5 and 6) displaying the same pattern of diagonal pierced holes, had been cut at the same points, and the holes were exactly aligned, and so must have been mounted back-to-back when pierced. Parallels from unstratified contexts at York (Tweddle 1986, 225) also survived as cut sections, while actual belt pieces from sites in Perth have been dated to around the end of the thirteenth century (Thomas 1987, 183), as are other examples from English towns (Clarke and Carter 1977, 361–2; Platt and Coleman Smith 1975, Fig. 162–3). It has been suggested that the stitching was used to prevent the leather stretching, and it may have been coloured for decorative effect (Tweddle 1986, 255) The earliest belt form (1) has two parallel horizontal slits, across which it has been torn. This was possibly the end of a tie-belt, the other end would have been cut with two thongs, which passed through the slits and were then secured. A thin strap (20) with stitch-holes at one end, was probably a strap retainer, while a tapering strap (19) had a worn oval hole (8 mm by 12 mm) in the broad end, which was probably used to receive a toggle.

1 Torn end of tie belt with two slits. Three cut sides and one torn.
37 × 20 × 3.0 **411.04**

2 Strap section with double rows of diagonal pierced holes with no signs of wear parallel to the long edges. Both ends cut, long edges chamfered.
56 × 37 × 3.5 **903**

3* Strap section with double rows of diagonal pierced holes with no signs of wear. Both ends cut and long sides chamfered.
39 × 34 × 3.0 **903**

4* Strap section with double rows of diagonal pierced holes with no signs of wear. One side has an additional pair of holes between the rows at one end. Both ends cut and long edges chamfered.
42 × 34 × 3.5 **903**

5* Strap section with two double rows of pierced holes, no sign of wear (by awl), chamfered edges. Secondary(?) transformation into parallelogram.
64 × 35 × 4.0 **904**

6* Strap section with double row of pierced holes. 4 rows of pierced holes (diamond-section awl), pierced and cut at same time as No. 5. No signs of wear.
64 × 35 × 2.0 **904**

7* Strap section with double (and added) rows of pierced holes. Six rows of pierced holes (short rows in middle added after), outer holes paired.
69 × 32 × 2.5 **904**

8* Folded strap end with single and double rows of pierced holes. Cut at one end, torn at other. Cut end has a single row of stitch-holes down one long side and a double row down the other, extending as far as the crease marking the fold. The torn end has a single row of holes down each side.
89 × 29 × 2.8mm **903**

9 Strap section with single rows of stitch-holes parallel to long edges. One end cut, one torn.
85 × 22 × 3.5 **903**

10* Tapering strap section with two single rows of eleven stitch holes at 6.5mm. Worn surface, holes may be well worn.
71 × 34 × 4.0 **904**

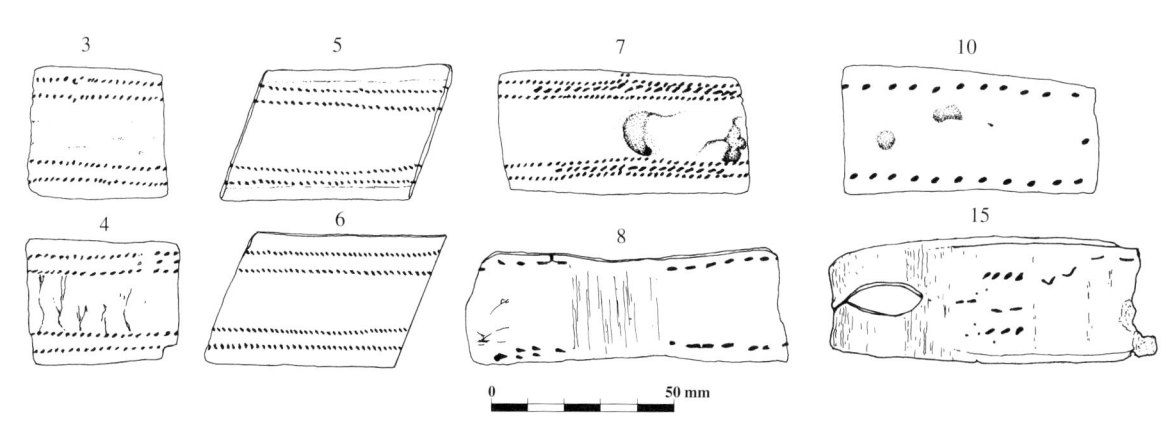

10.144 Belt and strap sections (LR24).

11 Re-used strap section with single rows of pierced holes. One row of stitch-holes cut by possibly- secondary perforation.
44 × 16 × 1.5 **903**

12 Strap with stitch-holes 3mm from the edge and a slashed hole 15mm long, 10mm from one of the two broken ends. The stitching occurs on both edges for 90mm at the end nearest to the slashed hole, and then continues on one edge for the full length of the strap. The holes are slashes 5mm long and 7mm apart..
350 × 25 × 3.5 **416**

13 Torn belt end with single hole (7mm × 4mm) for buckle tongue. Little wear.
114 × 23 × 3.5 **904**

14* Perforated, folded strap fragment cut at one end, torn at other. Cut end is split by stretched ovoid hole. Three longitudinal rows of stitch-holes down part of the centre of the fragment. the outer two rows are diagonal piercings. An irregular line of stitch-holes continues from one of the outer rows as far as the tear. An incised line runs parallel to each edge, set 2mm in, and extending as far as the ovoid hole, beyond which point the edges are chamfered.
88 × 34 × 3.5 **903**

15 Delaminated strap fragment with two cut sides and two torn.
54 × 11 × 3.0 **417.02**

16 Possible strap end with one tapered end
57 × 11 × 1.0 **417.02**

17 Possible belt or strap end with five cut sides and one torn, delaminated
26 × 11 × 1.5 **417.02**

18 Tapered belt or strap end with two cut sides and one torn. Grooved on flesh side parallel to edge.
55 × 14 × 1.0 **417.02**

19 Tapering strap with worn ovoid hole (12mm × 8mm) probably for toggle; three cut sides and one torn.
113 × 23 × 2.0 **417.02**

20 Strap keeper with incised lines and two pierced stitch holes.
59 × 10 × 3.5 **904**

21 Strip with five cut sides, probably offcut of trimmed belt
117 × 16 × 2.0 **417.02**

Discs (LR25)

A group of three small discs (LR25.1–3) includes two flat discs (2 and 3) with the same diameter (21mm) from the same context (417.02). These may have been gaming tokens like the stone discoids (SE19) of similar size (pp 00). The third disc (1), from a planting bed in the greenhouse, is unlikely to be ancient.

1 Small cut disc
D 30–31 T 2 **753.03**

2 Small disc, possible gaming counter.
D 21 × 20 T 1.5 **417.02**

3 Small worn and split disc, possible gaming counter.
D 21 × 20 T 1.0 **417.02**

Perforated discs (LR26)

Two perforated discs (LR26.1–2) include one (1) perforated by an off-centre hole with signs of wear. It may have functioned as some form of washer, or may have been an identifying tag attached to another item. The other disc has a conical perforation with little sign of wear.

1 Perforated disc with off-centre hole (D 4mm) showing slight signs of wear.
D 35 T 1.0 *411.04*

2 Thick disc with conical perforation.
D.33 T 4.5 Hole D 4.5 *903*

The Textiles

Andrew Nicholson

Some fifty-four fragments of textile were recovered from the excavation; a single Z-spun thread survived from Hiberno-Norse waterlogged deposits, six fragments were associated with material from the medieval gravefield and the remaining forty-seven pieces were found in modern deposits, mainly associated with the greenhouse in Area L. In addition to actual fabric two textiles can be identified from mineralised deposits associated with copper alloy artefacts. The medieval textiles associated with a brooch (BZ16.3) and a buckle (BZ15.2) fall into York Class V textiles (Hedges 1982), being coarse textiles, soft to the touch, of loosely spun wool. One (2.1) is of tabby weave, whilst the other (1.1) is of simple 2/2 twill. Neither shows visible evidence of dyeing, but no chemical tests have been done. Spinning was relatively uniform and even, with no traces of gores or uneven weaving visible to preliminary examination. On one of the fragments (1.1) associated with the pin of the brooch, the selvedge incorporated a 3-ply warp thread on the outer edge, to add a degree of strength to the edge of the cloth.

TX01

1 Five fragments of woollen 2/2 twill, grey-brown in good condition. One fragment has a selvedge incorporating a three-ply thread, and is associated with an ?organic accretion and the broken shank of the brooch pin (BZ16.3) with which the textile was found. On the larger pieces one side appears more matted than the other. System 1/9/S/0.8 System 2/14/S/0.7.
L 58 W 32 T 2
L 32 W 21.5 T 2.3
L 24 W 23 T 3.2 (selvedge)
L 20 W 11 T 1.5
L 14 W 8 T 1.5
735

2 Length of Z-spun woollen thread. Mid-brown, loosely spun, good condition.
L 41 T 0.5 **417.02**

TX02

1 Three fragments of woollen tabby; S-spun, combed. Good condition, greenish-brown. Another fragment is still attached to the associated brooch (BZ15.2). Wa/7/Z/1.0 We/6/Z/1.0.
L 22 W 16 T 1.5, L 13 W 7 T 1.5, L 12 W 8 T 1.5 **535**

The Wooden Artefacts

Andrew Nicholson

Amongst the collection of twigs, stakes and structural timbers recovered from the waterlogged deposits of the **southern sector** were four pieces of artefactual woodwork (WD3.1–4), two (1 and 2) associated with vessels and two (3 and 4) with tools, providing a glimpse of how a primary resource was exploited.

A cone-shaped piece of with faceted surfaces (1, 230.03) may be the discard from the hollowing of a vessel, though with none of the characteristic signs of turning (Barber 1981a, 328–9). However, hazel (*Corylus avellana*) is generally unsuitable for vessels, and no examples were found of hazel from the only comparable collection of local material at Threave Castle (Barber 1981b, 116–7). A carved vessel lid (2) of willow (*Salix sp.*) from the main **Period IV** drain (417.02), also utilises a timber not normally associated with vessels, though two turning cones of willow were found in the ditch at Iona (Barber 1981a, 335). Surface marks indicate that the lid was worked with a knife. A pressure indentation survives on the lower surface of the flange and lip.

A longitudinally-fractured handle (3) also from the **Period IV** ditch (417.02), would have been suitable for a knife or similarly-tanged tool. It has a small rounded hole in one end, linked internally with a larger stepped hole in one edge. It is unclear whether the latter was as a result of wear by the tang, or a secondary feature. Again the type of timber (*Pinaceae*) is unusual, as hardwoods such as ash or holly were usually preferred for handles.

A piece of yew (4, *Taxus Baccata*) from the **Period IV** ditch (417.02), has carefully shaped arms with transversely-perforated ends, one bi-conical, the other cylindrical and slightly larger. A square cut slot in the centre has a central cylindrical perforation. The piece was originally identified as a balance arm from a set of scales, but the construction of a facsimile led to a reappraisal appropriate to yew's properties of resilience and resistance to splitting. The piece is now seen as one arm of a small frame saw, which would have had a transverse beam fitting into the central slot, linking it to a second identical arm. The cylindrical hole in one terminal is for the rivet

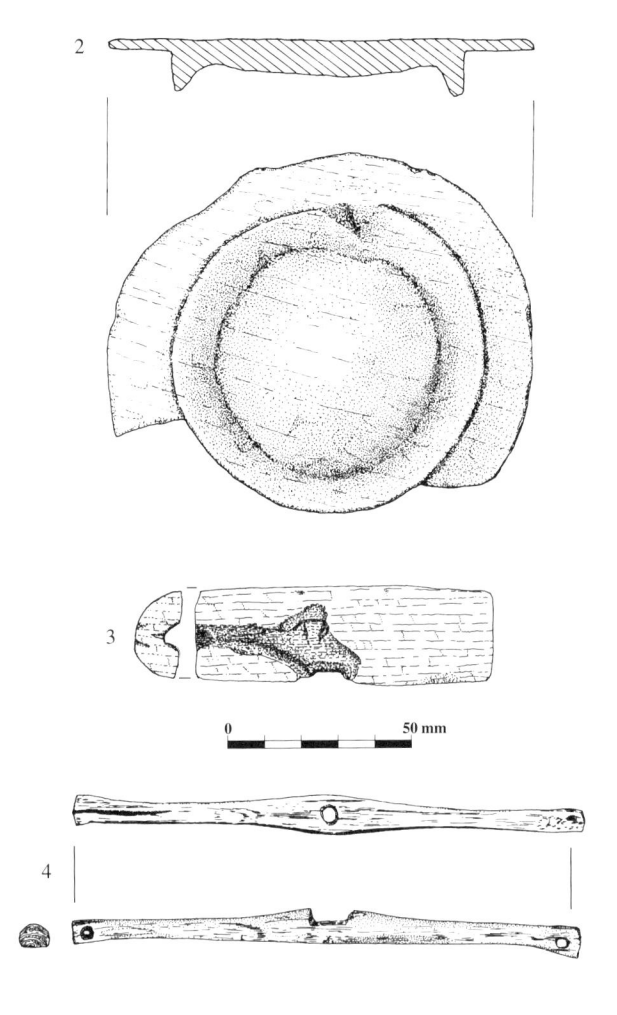

10.145 Wooden artefacts

to locate the blade, whilst the smaller bi-conical hole at the other terminal would have accommodated the twisted cord or gut which applies the necessary tension to provide rigidity to the blade. It can be comfortably held with two fingers to either side of the transverse beam. Whilst it may have been used for woodworking, it would also have been suitable for antler working, and many antler offcuts exhibited saw marks.

The Later Medieval Pottery

Jane Clarke

The later medieval pottery from the 1984, and 1986 to 1991 excavations has been studied as a single collection, incorporating the unpublished work of E. Cox on the 1984 material. A full catalogue is stored with the site archive. The basic quantitative value used in the catalogue is the individual sherd, cross-referenced to fabric type, vessel number (where sherds join), site context and phasing.

The assemblage was sorted into fabric type, examined under binocular microscope (× 20), and worked extensively for joins. The identification of fabric types was made according to characteristics of texture, hardness, inclusion content and sortedness, colour and surface treatment. The type series includes several common and well-recognized Scottish medieval fabrics, together with a range of

European imports. The recognition and definition of local fabrics, which form the bulk of the assemblage, proved more problematic, due to a lack of comparative stratified assemblages and of known kiln sites, both in the Galloway region in general, and in the Machars area in particular.

There has been little regionally-based discussion of the medieval ceramic tradition in SW. Scotland. The identification of local fabrics from historically-dated sites, such as Glenluce Abbey (Cruden 1951), Kirkcudbright Castle (Dunning *et al.* 1958) and Threave Castle (Haggarty 1981), provides some chronological and spatial framework for the Whithorn assemblage, as does Truckell and Williams' review of the medieval Galloway pottery in Dumfries museum (Truckell and Williams 1967), despite their questionable dating for much of the material (Haggarty 1981). It is evident that the integrity of fabric types identified at Whithorn must be subject to further petrological examination, in order to establish the validity of discriminatory characteristics, before patterns of inter-site distributions can be meaningfully discussed. However, despite the fact that much of the Whithorn material comes from redeposited contexts, there is sufficient stratigraphical evidence to confirm some chronological sequence of local fabric types.

The best twelfth to fourteenth century contexts (415.01, 520.01–03, 505, 517.01, and possibly 632) come from the **southern sector**, linked to a poorly stratified series of coins, and a relatively well stratified coin hoard (p 267). A later-twelfth/earlier-thirteenth century date is given for pottery from later **Period IV** contexts, although the number of well-secured finds is low. The finds from the graveyard, and especially from the earlier graves, can be considered as redeposited material from an extensive earlier-twelfth/thirteenth century midden (pp 237–250). This is convincingly demonstrated by the distribution of a red gritty ware (Fabric 1, Figure 6.39), but is also evident with other fabrics (such as fabrics 2/01, 2/05, 2/06 and 6), which tend to cluster in the earlier graves, and in the distribution of Saintonge ware (Fabric 12), which may be ascribed to the thirteenth century. This suggests that the fabrics contemporary with the graveyard (*c.* 1300–1450) will be infrequent finds in graves. Further independent dating is given by the coins from cultivation to the west (546, 526), suggesting a late (last decade) thirteenth century date, and by a later-fifteenth/sixteenth century sequence in the eastern part of the **central sector**, which gives a fairly reliable date for the introduction of post-medieval fabrics 9 and 10.

Fabric 1: Red gritty ware

This is a very homogeneous group in terms of fabric (well sorted crushed quartz tempered) and form (globular cooking pots), and represents the earliest local medieval fabric type found at Whithorn. Globular cooking pots are a well recognized type form in SW. Scotland and N. England (Dunning *et al.* 1958; Hodges and Jope 1956). The fabric has a wide distribution over the site, and is stratigraphically consistent with a date of the mid-to late-twelfth century. It is concentrated in grave fills, but is absent from the earlier **Period IV** contexts and from the relatively uncontaminated fourteenth century deposits (particularly 517.01) in the **southern sector**. Most of the red gritty ware from this area probably originated in the pond silts (415.01), sealing the main ditch (417), and was possibly contemporary with the later **Period IV** buildings in (IV/414 and 413) for a period of about 50 years. The best dating evidence is a worn sterling of David I (*c.* 1140–1150), probably a late-twelfth century loss. The relative abundance of this red gritty ware in post-medieval contexts can be generally explained as secondary redeposition of material already displaced by the **Period V** graveyard. Interestingly, it is absent from the trench in the **Fey Field** which was almost certainly occupied during the currency of the ware.

Sherd count: body: 191; rim: 48; base: 19.
Fabric: red paste, with well sorted, frequent, angular quartz gritting, often breaking through the surface.
Surface: mostly unglazed, with very occasional splattered green, brown and orange glaze on internal and external surfaces; frequent internal/external burning with heavy sooting on external bases; no decoration; frequent pronounced rilling.
Form: only one form represented: i.e. globular, even walled, cooking pots with everted rims and flat bases.

Fabric 2: Local medieval green glazed wares

The bulk of the Whithorn fabrics indicates a widespread use of local carse clays, producing a range of sandy, iron-rich ceramic pastes. These have been grouped together as Fabric 2, a broad group including a wide range of fabric description and vessel form, from coarse, heavy, cooking pots to well-sorted, fine walled, jugs and storage vessels. These variations have been recognized in thirteen sub-groups (fabrics 2/01 to 2/13), with some sub-groups characterised by certain functional forms, such as pinched spouted jugs in fabric 2/05, and sagging-based cooking pots in fabric 2/06.

Fabric 2/01

This is a small, relatively early and short-lived, group, spatially concentrated in the **Fey Field** trench, the western part of the **northern sector** and the **southern sector**. The best dating evidence comes from the **Fey Field** where it was found with **Period IV** structures (418, 419), and then displaced into thirteenth century cultivation (526). It may overlap with red gritty ware (Fabric 1) in the **southern sector**, on the slim evidence of association in the **Period IV** pond silts (415.01), and it is generally absent from more recent uncontaminated deposits.

Sherd count: body: 23; rim: 5; handle: 30; base: 12.
Fabric: heavy coarse fabric with mixed quartz and iron oxide inclusions.
Surface: patchy green glaze; some external burning; occasional applied thumbed strip decoration
Form: thick, unevenly walled vessels with rough surface finishing; proportionally large number of handles present.

Fabric 2/02

This is a small group, generally late, dated to the mid-fourteenth century by one sherd, from the **Period V.3** oven (516, p 268).

Sherd count: body: 32; rim: 7; handle: 1.
Fabric: hard fabric, with frequent, well sorted fine quartz inclusions.
Surface: green glaze, often thickly applied.

Fabric 2/03

Another small group, almost all from the southern part of the **southern sector**, where the contexts are consistently late. A mid- to late-fourteenth century date is suggested stratigraphically for this group.

Sherd count: body: 8; rim: 2; base: 2.
Fabric: orange/red paste, with well sorted, quartz and black iron oxide inclusions.
Surface: mostly unglazed, with occasional external burning.

Fabric 2/04

A small group, dated to the *mid- to late*-fourteenth century in the southern part of the **southern sector**. The general absence from the graveyard is explicable if the fabric and graveyard were contemporary.

Sherd count: body: 33; rim: 9; base: 1.
Fabric: pale orange paste, with fine, well sorted, rounded quartz inclusions.
Surface: occasional splattered green glaze, with some sooting on base.
Form: even walled, wide mouthed jar form, with possible rim seating.

Fabric 2/05

A relatively large group, well distributed over the site, and possibly dating from the later-thirteenth to mid-fourteenth century. The small group of sherds from the graveyard may derive from early thirteenth century debris displaced upwards, a suggestion supported by its presence in earlier graves.

Sherd count: body: 81; spout: 7; rim: 22; handle: 20; base: 11.
Fabric: orange/red paste, with frequent, mixed quartz inclusions.
Surface: partial green/brown glaze and/or red slip, including internal slip; rouletted decoration.
Form: includes jugs, with pinched spouts; thumbed bases; rod and strap handles.

Fabric 2/06

Stratigraphically dated to the later-thirteenth century from its presence in early **Period V** deposits in the **southern sector** (500.01, 520.01 415.02), though also present in the underlying **Period IV** pond silts (415.01) and in the **Fey Field** (419). The small group of finds from the graveyard is compatible with redeposition (as fabric 2/05); there is no concentration in later deposits, which would be expected if it was still current.

Sherd count: body: 35; rim: 5; base: 20.
Fabric: slightly soft and abraded, with mixed, uneven, quartz inclusions.
Surface: frequent external, and occasional internal, burning; occasional splattered glaze.
Form: cooking pots with sagging bases.

Fabric 2/07

Possibly late-thirteenth to fourteenth century, although too small a group to assign with any confidence.

Sherd count: body: 14.
Fabric: pinkish-red, slightly gritty, fabric with well-sorted, angular quartz inclusions.
Surface: dark green or yellow/green glaze.

Fabric 2/08

A coherent group, with a strong presence in thirteenth century contexts (418, 520, 526, 528), and a general absence from uncontaminated *mid- to late-*fourteenth century contexts. It therefore has a suggested currency throughout the thirteenth century and early fourteenth century. Graveyard finds would thus indicate disturbance of earlier midden deposits (as fabric 2/05 etc.).

Sherd count: body: 98; rim: 3.
Fabric: soft and abraded, fine orange paste with mixed quartz and Fe inclusions.
Surface: some abraded green glaze; rouletted decoration.

Fabric 2/09

A relatively small group, from fairly-secure early thirteenth century contexts (413, 528; less secure 415.01), and no certain evidence of later currency. Sherds from late-thirteenth century ploughing (526) in the **Fey Field** may derive from underlying structures (528). Graveyard finds are compatible with this interpretation (as fabric 2/05 etc).

Sherd count: body: 48; rim: 4; handle: 6; base: 1.
Fabric: heavy, coarse, abraded, orange paste, with mixed quartz/organic/Fe inclusions.
Surface: splattered green glaze; some scored decoration; heavy external burning.
Form: heavy, uneven, thick walled vessels; rod and strap handles.

Fabric 2/10

A consistently late-group, dated to the mid- to late-fourteenth century from contexts in the southern part of the **southern sector**. It is absent from early graves, and therefore from the pre-graveyard debris. A group from the furrows (546) at the west end of the **northern sector** is consistent with other evidence for continuing cultivation in the fourteenth century.

Sherd count: body 71; spout: 3; rim: 11; handle: 8; base: 1.
Fabric: fairly soft, abraded, pale orange fabric with frequent, well sorted, fine quartz inclusions.
Surface: abraded glaze; rouletted and applied strip decoration.
Form: jug form, including one vessel from 1984 trench with complete rim and handle (no base).

Fabric 2/11

A large, long lived type, with a good sequence in the thirteenth century (415.01, 414.04, 418, 419, 520.01 etc.), if not before, but is also common in mid-to late-fourteenth century contexts. Sherds were widely scattered in the graveyard and in peripheral **Period IV** deposits (430, 459, 451, 457) and so probably represents a spread of in situ and displaced thirteenth century material. A long currency of c. 1200–1400 is suggested.

Sherd count: body: 272; rim: 12; handle: 5; base: 15.
Fabric: slightly soft red paste, with well sorted small quartz/Fe inclusions.
Surface: green glaze; applied thumbed strips; rouletted decoration and incised lines.
Form: evenly walled jar/jug form with some thumbed bases; rod and strap handles.

Fabric 2/12

This fabric divides stratigraphically into two separate groups, one thirteenth century (430, 451, 415.01, 408.02, 418, 419, 528 and 520) and one from mid-fourteenth/fifteenth century contexts (505, 514, 616.06, 632). It is scarce in intervening contexts.

Sherd count: body: 104; rim: 4; base: 5.
Fabric: very soft and very abraded pale orange/buff fabric, with mixed quartz and Fe oxide inclusions.
Surface: some green glaze or white/red slip; some external sooting.

Fabric 2/13

A small group, restricted to the **southern sector**, and probably fourteenth century in date.

Sherd count: body: 1; base: 5.
Fabric: fairly soft fabric, with large quartz inclusions.
Surface: abraded green glaze.

Fabric 3: coarse oxidised ware

A small group of coarse wares that could be early medieval. One sherd came from Building III/15, two others from later contexts in the vicinity, and three clustered further to the east (Figure 10.47).

Sherd count: body: 2; rim: 4; handle: 1; base: 1.
Fabric: slightly soft, red fabric with large mixed, angular inclusions.
Surface: unglazed.

Fabric 4: Coarse oxidised ware

A small group, with two sherds from later-twelfth century contexts (415.01, 417.02), the remainder of later date.

Sherd count: body: 10; rim: 5.
Fabric: coarse orange/red paste with large, very angular, quartz inclusions; laminated fracture.
Surface: thick crazed yellow/green glaze, and white slip; occasional burning.

Fabric 5: coarse reduced ware

Small group including one sherd from Building IV/25 and another from the **Period IV.3** rubble spread (430). Possibly twelfth century.

Sherd count: body: 3.
Fabric: coarse reduced dark grey fabric, with frequent well sorted, quartz inclusions.
Surface: unglazed.

Fabric 6: Scottish white gritty ware

White gritty wares are well recognized in early medieval (late-twelfth/thirteenth century) contexts from the Scottish east coast, with a kiln site at Colstoun, East Lothian (Thoms 1976), and from the Borders, with a possibly production site in Tweedale (Haggarty 1985; Crowdy 1986). The identification of any source site for the Whithorn white gritty wares requires further petrological analysis. The presence of white gritty wares at the nearby site of Cruggleton (Haggarty 1985; Cormack, Pers. Comm.), where the ceramic assemblage as a whole is much more biased towards non-local fabrics than that of Whithorn, suggests that white gritty wares were coming in to the site by sea with a range of other imports (Haggarty Pers. Comm.).

At Whithorn, white gritty ware is present in **Period IV** (415.01) and **V** (520s, 500.02, 528) contexts, suggesting a later-twelfth/early thirteenth century date for its introduction, with a currency continuing to the mid-fourteenth century (517.01, 506.02), but probably not beyond. The graveyard finds are consistent with a pattern of redeposited thirteenth century debris.

Sherd count: body: 107; spout: 1; rim: 8; handle: 2; base: 8.

Fabric:	white gritty fabric, with frequent, well sorted quartz inclusions.
Surface:	mostly unglazed, with some green glaze; external burning.
Form:	cooking pot and jug/jar forms.

Fabric 7: Reduced green glaze

Reduced fabrics, often in pastes similar to the local oxidised fabrics (fabric 2), have widespread distribution throughout the later medieval period, particularly during the late-fourteenth and fifteenth centuries, before being replaced by the late/post medieval fabrics (fabrics 9 and 10). The bulk of the Whithorn reduced wares are grouped in fabric 7/1. A small portion, with distinctive fabric/surface characteristics, are catalogued separately as fabrics 7/2, 7/3, 7/4.

Fabric 7/1

A large group with a few sherds from **Period IV** contexts probably of thirteenth century date, becoming predominant in the fourteenth century, and probably replaced, rather than supplemented by, fabrics 9 and 10 in the late-fifteenth century.

Sherd count:	body: 349; rim: 5; handle: 6; base: 13.
Fabric:	reduced grey fabric, with mixed, well sorted inclusions
Surface:	partial green glaze on upper part of vessel, with oxidised surfaces where unglazed; occasionally darker green, thicker glaze; rouletted and cordon decoration; occasional external burning.
Form:	large vessels; jug/jar forms.

Fabric 7/2

A small group concentrated in the **southern sector**, and with only one sherd from the graveyard; probably of mid-fourteenth century date.

Sherd count:	body: 12; base: 1.
Fabric:	slightly soft, reduced fabric, with organic temper.
Surface:	thick lustrous yellow/green glaze.

Fabric 7/3

A small group, confined to the **southern sector**, where it is absent from secure early contexts and is probably mid-fourteenth century in date.

Sherd count:	body: 11.
Fabric:	slightly gritty, with small quartz and distinctive red Fe inclusions.
Surface:	dark mossy green glaze.

Fabric 7/4

Another small group, mostly from the southern part of the **southern sector**, generally from fourteenth century contexts, and virtually absent from the graveyard.

Sherd count:	body: 19.
Fabric:	reduced fabric with frequent, well sorted quartz inclusions.
Surface:	distinctive mossy green glaze

Fabric 8

A small group of hard, reduced wares mostly from the eastern part of the **central sector**. One sherd comes from Building IV/17a, possibly twelfth/thirteenth century date.

Sherd count:	body: 5; rim: 1; base: 1.
Fabric:	hard reduced fabric with surface oxidation; frequent fine quartz inclusions.
Surface:	abraded green glaze; internal burning on base; fingernail impressions on internal surfaces.

Fabric 9: Post-medieval reduced ware

Apart from some intrusive finds in thirteenth and fourteenth century contexts, fabric 9 was concentrated in deposits flanking the 'Commendator's house' (V/8, 704, 705, 729), with a fairly-tightly stratified appearance in early sixteenth century contexts. Post-medieval reduced wares become common on Scottish sites from the late-fifteenth century, continuing through to the eighteenth century with little change, with a possible kiln site in the Glasgow area (Haggarty 1980).

Sherd count:	body: 90; rim: 5; handle: 4; base: 3.
Fabric:	hard, dense, reduced, dark grey fabric with fine, well-sorted quartz inclusions
Surface:	dark green lustrous glaze, with incised and applied decoration; knife trimming at base.

Fabric 10: Post-medieval oxidised ware

This group has a particularly tight distribution in the vicinity of the Commendator's house (V/8, 704, 729), and probably represents a small number of vessels, stratigraphical dated to the very late-fifteenth to sixteenth centuries, and contemporary with the post-medieval reduced wares.

Sherd count:	body: 74; rim: 1; handle: 1; base: 8.
Fabric:	hard, dense, red fabric with fine, well sorted, frequent quartz inclusions.
Surface:	even, thick green/purple glaze.

Fabric 11: Mica tempered ware

A small group of body sherds, probably representing a single vessel, all from the debris (630) flanking Building V/4 and probably dated to the end of the fifteenth century or opening decades of the sixteenth. The distinctive large mica inclusions are typical of prehistoric Manx pottery, and may characterise later medieval fabrics up to the sixteenth century, after which time there is no tradition of local ceramic production on the Isle of Man (Garrad 1977; Garrad 1978).

Sherd count: body: 5.
Fabric: very coarse, friable, grey reduced paste, with laminated fracture; very distinctive frequent large mica and frequent angular quartz inclusions.
Surface: abraded green glaze.

Fabric 12: Saintonge

Saintonge green glazed wares have a long lifespan, from the mid-thirteenth century, through to the late-fourteenth century (Watkins 1987, 125–9) and are common finds from medieval sites in SW. Scotland:, such as Ayr (unpublished), Kirkcudbright Castle (Dunning et al.1958), Glenluce Abbey (Cruden 1951) and Cruggleton (Haggarty 1985). The small collection from Whithorn is divided into a finer group (fabric 12/1) and a more typical group (fabric 12/2).

Fabric 12/1

A small group, from graveyard and later contexts, which may be early (*c.* 1300) in the lifespan of Saintonge.

Sherd count: body: 9; handle : 1.
Fabric: off-white paste, with fine mica and red Fe oxide inclusions.
Surface: pale green glaze, speckled with darker green, heavily pitted fabric 12/2.

Fabric 12/2

This group is generally more typical of the Saintonge, with some coarser variations, and decorative thumbed applied strips, common to thirteenth and fourteenth century Saintonge wares (Platt and Coleman-Smith 1975). Sherds were concentrated in the **Period V** graveyard and were probably displaced from the underlying thirteenth century debris, while sherds from later contexts were possibly displaced from earlier burials. Its presence in contexts beyond the graveyard (430, 451, 520.01) suggests a thirteenth century date, with a single intrusion into a later-twelfth century ditch (417).

Sherd count: body: 27.
Fabric: off-white paste with coarser inclusions than 12/1 of flint, and red and black Fe oxides.
Surface: green glaze as 12/1; decorative thumbed applied strips and incised lines.

Fabric 13: Beauvais earthenwares

Beauvais earthenwares are high quality ceramics, possibly dating from the late-fifteenth century, but more likely from the early/mid-sixteenth century (Hurst *et al.* 1986, 106–16).

Fabric 13/1

The green glazed, comb decorated, platters from Whithorn seem to be exceedingly rare in Scotland, the more highly decorated sgraffito types being somewhat more common. At least three, and possibly as many as five, plates are represented at Whithorn: vessel 1 came from worm soil/rubbish (614) in the western part of the **northern sector**; vessel 2 from rubbish (704) flanking the Commendator's house (V/8); and vessel 3 from topsoil in the southern part of the southern sector. Other sherds are from post-medieval contexts or later disturbance.

Sherd count: body: 12; rim: 3; base: 4.
Fabric: good quality, hard fired, off-white to cream, fine paste, with fine mica inclusions.
Surface: bright green glaze; comb decoration
Form: hammer-headed plates; possibly as many as 5 vessels.

Fabric 13/2

A small rim sherd in yellow-glaze Beauvais, from debris (704) flanking the Commendator's house (V/8) and probably dating to the early - to - mid-sixteenth century.

Sherd count: rim: 1.
Fabric: off-white paste, with no prominent inclusions.
Surface: yellow glaze

Fabric 13/3: possible Beauvais

From demolition debris (514) over Building V/3 in the **southern sector**.

Sherd count: body: 1.
Fabric: off-white paste with fine red Fe oxide and mica inclusions.
Surface: unglazed

Fabric 14: Northern French

Northern French fabric, probably thirteenth/fourteenth century. Sherds widely scattered and generally from relatively late contexts.

Sherd count: body: 7; rim: 2; handle: 2.
Fabric: slightly coarse white paste, with mixed quartz and Fe oxide inclusions.
Surface: green glaze.

Fabric 15: French

One sherd, too small to date typologically, from post-medieval century ploughsoil (608) in western part of **northern sector**.

Sherd count: rim: 1.

Fabric: white paste with occasional angular quartz inclusions.
Surface: abraded green glaze
Form: rim from a narrow necked vessel, possibly a flagon, costrel or small jug.

Fabric 16: French

A single sherd from debris (704) flanking Building V/8, probably earlier-sixteenth century.

Sherd count: handle: 1.
Fabric: white fabric with occasional quartz inclusions.
Surface: green glaze,

Fabric 17: possible French

Group with a characteristically thirteenth century distribution (415.01, 500.02, 520.02), probably present in the pre-graveyard rubbish spread, and sufficiently rare in fourteenth/fifteenth century deposits to have little representation in later and topsoil groups.

Sherd count: body:14; handle: 2; base: 4.
Fabric: very abraded, soft, white fabric, with slightly laminated fracture; occasional angular quartz and calcite inclusions.
Surface: abraded green glaze; some external burning.

Fabric 18: probable Loire

Two sherds from sixteenth century debris (729) in yard to south of Building V/8, possibly from narrow necked Loire jugs (Hurst *et al.* 1986, 99–100).

Sherd count: spout: 1; handle: 1.
Fabric: well sorted, fine white paste, with few inclusions.
Surface: mostly unglazed, with occasional splattered yellow-green glaze.
Form: jug

Fabric 19: Martincamp

Martincamp flasks are very common in sixteenth century contexts in Scotland. Two sherds were recovered from sixteenth century debris (729) to the south of Building V/8.

Sherd count: body: 2; base: 1.
Fabric: Type II (Hurst 1966, 54–9); light buff/grey, highly fired fabric, with occasional very fine mineral inclusions.
Surface: unglazed.

Fabric 20: late French

Late French fabric, from a relatively late grave (539), and from recent rubbish deposits (762) in the **Museum Garden**.

Sherd count: body: 2; base: 1.
Fabric: off-white fabric, with slightly laminated fracture; inclusions of fine mica and occasional black Fe oxide.
Surface: abraded bright yellow glaze.

Fabric 21: late French

Small group mostly from debris (729) to south of Building V/8, probably later-sixteenth century.

Sherd count: body: 3; base: 2.
Fabric: fine red paste, with occasional white quartz inclusions.
Surface: internal and external white slip and/or yellow-brown glaze.

Fabric 22: Spanish

The kicked up shape of this handle sherd suggests that it may have come from a Seville costrel, of probable seventeenth century date (Hurst *et al.* 1986, 63–4). The sherd came from a recent disturbance (741) beside the manse, that also produced a sherd of cuerdo seco (fabric 23).

Sherd count: handle: 1.
Fabric: fine, slightly soft, off-white paste with Fe oxide inclusions.
Surface: thin, abraded, white Sn glaze (or slip)
Form: possible costrel handle.

Fabric 23: cuerdo seco

A single handle sherd of *cuerdo seco* ware, possibly from a jar lid (Lewis and Evans 1982, 80–1, Fig. 6b). *Cuerdo seco* wares, from Seville, were decorated with polychrome designs by a lost wax technique, with areas of different coloured glaze separated by unglazed lines (Hurst *et al.* 1986, 60–2). There are no known Scottish parallels for this sherd; finds in southern England and Wales (for example from London, Southampton, Colchester, Canterbury, Exeter, Penhow Castle) have a date range of late-fifteenth to mid-sixteenth century (Lewis and Evans 1982, 80–1; G. Haggarty, Pers. Comm.).

Sherd count: handle: 1.
Fabric: soft, fine, buff fabric.
Surface: white and green Sn/Pb glaze on both surfaces, with *cuerdo seco* decoration on one face.
Form: fragment of small rectangular-sectioned handle.

Fabric 24: possible Spanish

A small group of body sherds, probably from a single vessel, possibly a Seville olive jar of sixteenth/seventeenth century date (Hurst *et al.*

1986, 65–7). Sherds were concentrated in the western part of the **northern sector**, and possibly originated in a **Period V/4** pit (607.02) though scattered beyond.

Sherd count: body: 19; rim: 1; handle: 2; base: 2.
Fabric: coarse, off-white, fabric with mixed, uneven temper and reduced core.
Surface: pronounced rilling, with brown, abraded slip.
Form: probably only one vessel represented; closed form with rounded base.

Fabric 25: Low Countries red wares

Low countries red earthenwares have a widespread British distribution from the early fourteenth century, becoming more common after 1350 (Watkins 1987, 140–1). Five sherds from the **southern sector** came from appropriate **Period V.4** deposits (523, 505 etc), while other finds from the graveyard were probably deposited while it was in use.

Sherd count: body: 15.
Fabric: fine, orange/red paste with well mixed, fine, quartz inclusions.
Surface: glossy red/brown glaze, frequently pitted; applied decorative cordon.

Fabric 26

Unknown fabric concentrated in the graveyard and related more-recent contexts; hence possibly displaced from thirteenth century deposits.

Sherd count: body: 16; rim: 2; base: 2.
Fabric: off-white paste with reduced core and slightly laminated fracture; mixed mineral inclusions.
Surface: abraded (brown) green glaze on both external and internal surfaces.

Fabric 27

Unknown fabric, comprising two sherds of the same vessel, from **Period V** cultivation furrows (546) in western part of **northern sector**.

Sherd count: body: 2.
Fabric: slightly soft, cream coloured paste, with quartz and Fe oxide inclusions.
Surface: pinkish slip and abraded green glaze.

Fabric 28

Unknown fabric, from insecure late context (631) with much later intrusive debris.

Sherd count: body: 1.
Fabric: white fabric with fine quartz inclusions.
Surface: abraded yellow glaze.

Fabric 29

Unknown fabric, probably of late-fourteenth century date.

Sherd count: body: 2; handle: 1; base: 1.
Fabric: gritty pink/white fabric with frequent, well sorted, fine quartz inclusions.
Surface: green glaze.

Fabric 30

Unknown fabric, from rubbish spreads (729) to south of Building V/8; probably sixteenth century.

Sherd count: base: 4 (joining).
Fabric: abraded white gritty fabric, with frequent, well sorted, fine quartz inclusions.
Surface: abraded yellow-green glaze on both surfaces.
Form: base of possible jar or jug.

Fabric 31

Unknown fabric, possibly late-fourteenth/early fifteenth century in date.

Sherd count: body: 3; handle:1; base: 1.
Fabric: very gritty off-white fabric, with frequent, well sorted, quartz inclusions.
Surface: yellow brown glaze, mottled with dark brown.

Fabric 32

Unknown fabric, from topsoil context.

Sherd count: body: 2.
Fabric: hard fired white paste with no prominent inclusions.
Surface: abraded, crazed, turquoise glaze on both surfaces.

Fabric 33

Unknown fabric, possibly Northern English.

Sherd count: rim: 3.
Fabric: reduced grey fabric, with fine quartz inclusions.
Surface: green glaze.

Fabric 34

Unknown fabric

Sherd count: body: 3.
Fabric: fine, soft, pale yellow fabric.
Surface: abraded dark red/black glaze.

Fabric 35

Unknown fabric, from debris (704) flanking

Commendator's house; probably early/mid-sixteenth century.

Sherd count: body: 5; rim: 3.

Fabric: slightly soft, buff fabric, with very fine mica and quartz inclusions.
Surface: green glaze with brown flecks.
Form: from single vessel, possibly a Jordan or urinal.

CHAPTER 11

The Environmental Material

Amanda Cardy, Anne Crone, Donald Davidson, Sheila Hamilton-Dyer, Peter Hill, Jacqui Huntley, Dorothy Lunt, Finbar McCormick, S. Metcalfe, Eileen Murphy and M.E. Watt

The Human Bones
Amanda Cardy

The human skeletal material falls into three main temporal groups: sixth to early-eighth century (**Period I**), eighth–ninth century (**Periods II and III/1**), and *c*. 1300–1450 AD (**Period V/1–3**). Whilst it seems likely that the **Period V** group represents the general population from which it was drawn, both the earlier groups were highly specialised in different ways. The bulk of the material is from **Period V** and this is presented first, and defines the terms and discusses the conditions affecting the earlier samples (pp 552-60). The dental material from the articulated skeletons was examined to provide a full picture of each individual.

Acknowledgements
I would like to thank Drs. M.F. Bruce, J.F. Cross and A. Penmann for valuable advice, criticism and enthusiasm, Dr. D. Jones of Dumfries Royal Infirmary for radiological assistance and interpretation of findings, and Damien Ronan, Peter Hill and the rest of the archaeological team for assistance with archaeological information.

THE LATE MEDIEVAL CEMETERY

1. INTRODUCTION

Data was obtained from 1605 skeletons, 1553 of which were available for post-excavation analysis as some skeletons were in too poor a condition to survive lifting. Many skeletons were truncated by later grave cuts, and just 19% of the material was judged to be of moderately good or better condition. The condition and completeness of the material affected the information obtained from each skeleton and from the group as a whole.

Owing to time and financial constraints the disarticulated material could not be examined although by chance it has provided valuable pathological information (section 4.2.5 below).

The sites used for comparative purposes are listed in Appendix 1.

2. DEMOGRAPHY

2.1. Methods

Age
Standard criteria were used to determine age at death of immature skeletons (Workshop of European Physical Anthropologists, 1980). When dental and/or epiphyseal evidence was unavailable, long bone length was employed using standards developed on the dentally-aged material. Each skeleton was then assigned to a broad age category (Table 11.1) to facilitate analysis and comparison with other groups.

Adult material is much more difficult to 'age' accurately than immature material. None of the currently available macroscopic techniques can be considered reliable in archaeological material where the condition and completeness of the remains is variable. Adult skeletons were therefore assigned to broad age categories which were primarily based on degenerative changes, although other factors such as dental attrition and cranial suture closure were taken into account (Table 11.1). The pubic symphysis was rarely sufficiently well preserved to assist in age estimation.

The category of 'subadult' is included with adults in the following analyses as this group had probably attained adult social and biological status. Some subadults undoubtedly will have been classified as 'young adult' when the latest fusing epiphyses were unavailable. 'Immature' as used in the text refers to all individuals below approximately 18 years of age.

Sex
The sex of adult and near-adult skeletons was assessed using standard morphological criteria (e.g.: Workshop of European Physical Anthropologists 1980; Krogman and Iscan 1986). Sex was assigned to 12% (19/159) of old juveniles and no attempt was made to sex material younger than this as the sexually dimorphic characteristics do not become pronounced until puberty. 90 to 95% of adults may be confidently sexed where the remains are complete,

Foetal	(FO)	0–7 months in utero
Perinatal	(PE)	Birth +/- 2 months
Infant	(IN)	2 months–2 years
Child	(CH)	2–6 years
Young juvenile	(YJ)	6–12 years
Old juvenile	(OJ)	12–18 years
Subadult	(SA)	18–25 years
Young adult	(YA)	No/slight degenerative change
Early middle age	(EMA)	Slight/moderate degenerative change
Middle age	(MA)	Moderate degenerative change
Late middle age	(LMA)	Moderate/severe degenerative change
Old age	(OA)	Severe degenerative change
Adult	(AD)	Dental and/or skeletal development complete. Insufficient information for closer assessment
Immature	(IM)	Dental and/or skeletal development incomplete. Insufficient information for closer assessment

Table 11.1: Age categories employed in this study.

in good condition and of known provenance (Krogman and Iscan 1986), but when preservation is variable and norms are unknown, as in many archaeological samples, the rate is often much lower.

The most confidently sexed individuals ('male', 'female') are treated separately from those with less confident sex assessment ('?male', '?female') throughout this report unless otherwise stated.

2.2. Results

Approximately one third (512/1605) of the skeletons were immature and two thirds (1093/1605) were adult (Figures 11.1 and 11.2).

Figure 11.1 suggests that relatively few immatures died in the first two years of life and that most died as juveniles. When the number of months encompassed by each age category is taken into account, however, there is an even rate of death in children, young juveniles and old juveniles (2.2–2.3 deaths per month), fewer in infants (1.2 deaths per month) with a peak in the perinatal period (7 deaths per month).

The perinatal period is associated with high mortality in groups with low standards of nutrition and hygiene, as probably prevailed in late medieval Britain. Comparison of the infant mortality rate of the present series (29 deaths of those less than one year of age per 1000 live births) with those expected in a society with low standards of nutrition and hygiene (perhaps between 54 and 170/1000 [UNICEF 1993]), suggests that the youngest age groups are severely under-represented, a phenomenon that is generally acknowledged in the archaeological world. Rodwell (1989) proposes various contributory factors that include specific areas for burial of small children, disturbance of shallow children's graves by later activity and loss of fragile bones through normal post-depositional processes. Patterns of mortality may vary greatly, even between groups with similar proportions of immature skeletons and which are closely related both geographically and temporally (e.g. Cardy 1993). Detailed analysis of mortality within the immature group was not undertaken because of the potential influence of these many variables.

More than one quarter (306/1092) of adults could not be more closely aged, usually because of incomplete or poorly preserved remains. Just 10% of 'aged' adults apparently survived to late-middle or

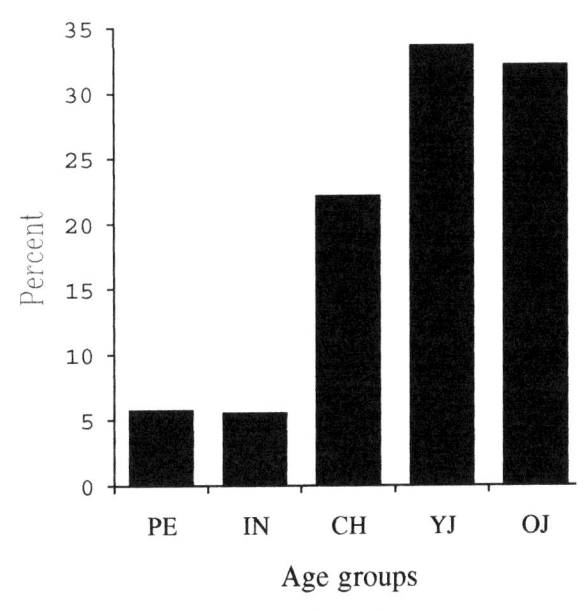

11.1 Age groups of later medieval immature skeletons.

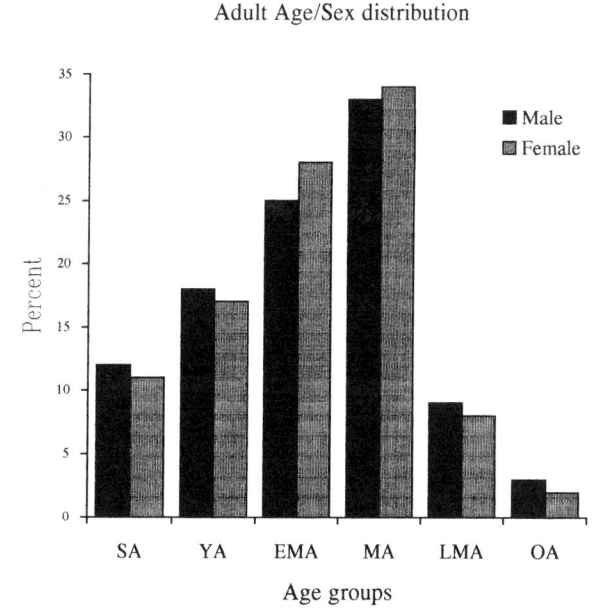

11.2 Age and sex groups of later medieval adults.

THE ENVIRONMENTAL MATERIAL

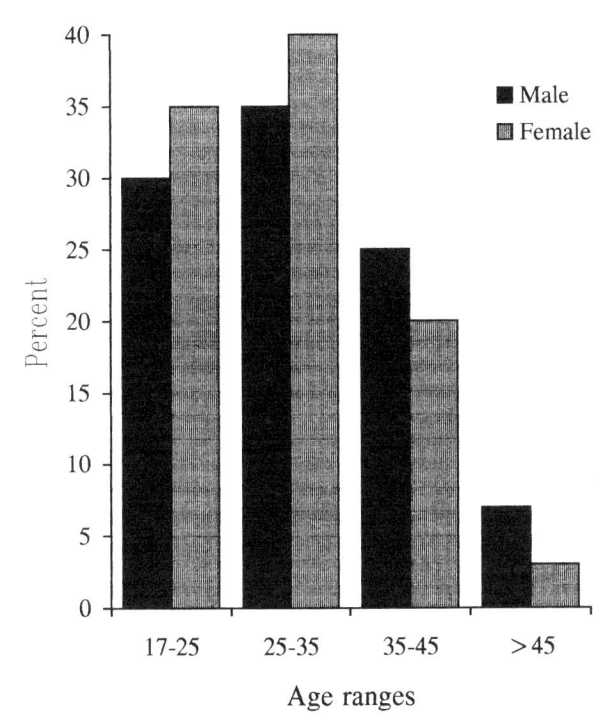

11.3 Age and sex groups of later medieval adults using Brothwell criteria.

old age although it should be noted that a disproportionately large number of old adults may have been 'lost' in the unaged and unrecovered material. Osteoporotic bones, common in the elderly, may be especially susceptible to post-depositional deterioration (Walker, Johnson and Lambert 1988).

The evidence was considered sufficiently reliable to assign sex to two thirds of the adult population. Slightly more females than males were identified (356/670 female/?female, 314/670 male/?male), a difference that is not statistically significant.

The age distribution of the sexed adults is illustrated in Figure 11.2. There is little difference in the pattern of mortality between men and women although the male 'curve' is somewhat smoother, with more female deaths occurring in early middle and middle age. The mortality pattern produced from dental attrition is slightly different and indicates slightly earlier female death (Figure 11.3, Brothwell 1981 standards). The results of the dental study (pp 561-68) also suggest that the age distribution for males and females is broadly similar. The possibility of differential rates of dental attrition and ageing of male and female skeletons is highly problematic and is not considered here.

2.3. Discussion

Immatures formed between 28% and 32% of the population in most phases of graveyard use (range 17%–42.5%, Table 11.2), the extremes of the ranges being seen in groups with small sample sizes in which more bias may be expected (but see the **Museum Garden**, below). Similarly, the overall distribution of adult age and sex throughout the phases was fairly even (Tables 11.2 and 3), females forming between 44% and 62% of sexed material. Whilst there may be some pattern in the spatial distribution of ages and sexes, it seems that a sufficiently large area of the cemetery was excavated for the overall picture to be unaffected. It was therefore assumed that the cemetery was used for the general population during all phases and all material was combined for analysis. The **Museum Garden** (Area M) seems to differ from this general trend, displaying a shift from a mixed, but predominantly adult population, to one composed mainly of children and young juveniles (Table 9.6, Figures 9.6–9). This group also differed from the main part of the site in terms of dental pathology (pp 572, 578, 585).

Despite the probable under-representation of small children, the proportion of immature deaths (one third of individuals dying before 18 years of age) and few adults apparently reaching old age suggests that environmental conditions were far from ideal.

Apparent earlier death of females is a common finding in archaeological samples, differing from today's developed and undeveloped worlds where women tend to outlive men by approximately five years. The possibility of differential rates of ageing of male and female skeletons and dental attrition is highly problematic and is not considered here.

No attempt was made to estimate fertility as available methods of skeletal series are unreliable.

	530	531	532	533	534	535	536	537	538	539	540	MG
(FO)					1					1		
(PE)		3	2	1	1	5		1	2	5	1	7
(IN)	2	2		1		4	1	5		6		4
(CH)	7	13	4	13	4	17	4	4	4	13	2	15
(YJ)	2	13	13	16	6	33	6	5	8	29	5	14
(OJ)	3	14	11	18	2	37	3	8	6	20	8	8
(SA)	1	5	2	7	3	26	3	8	13	19	4	8
(YA)	1	16	7	14	5	27	6	7	14	24	7	9
(EMA)	1	17	8	21	4	29	8	16	17	38	10	9
(MA)	7	23	8	27	5	60	15	10	20	47	13	20
(LMA)		7	2	4	3	14		3	2	16	3	5
(OA)		1	1			7		1	2	6		
(AD)	10	34	18	36	9	56	18	18	25	34	1	10
(IM)	1	2	4			4	1	2		3	1	1
Total	35	150	80	158	43	319	65	88	113	261	55	110

Table 11.2: Numbers of individuals in each age category by phase.

	530	531	532	533	534	535	536	537	538	539	540	541	MG
Male	4	20	5	17	4	35	10	15	23	40	16		18
Possible male	2	7	5	16	4	19	4	7	8	16	3	2	3
Male/?male total	6	27	10	33	8	54	14	22	31	56	19	2	21
Ambiguous adult		4	1	2	2	12	2	1	2	14			4
Female	3	20	10	16	7	50	15	16	20	56	14		18
Possible female	2	11	3	14	2	33	4	6	9	16	4		2
Female/?female total	5	31	13	30	9	83	19	22	29	72	18		20
Indeterminate	9	43	24	47	10	75	17	18	32	46	2	5	23
Adult total	20	105	48	112	29	224	52	63	94	188	39	7	68
Immature	15	45	32	46	14	95	13	25	19	73	16	8	57
Total	35	150	80	158	43	319	65	88	113	261	55	15	125

Table 11.3: Numbers of individuals in each sex category by phase.

3. BODY BUILD

3.1. Stature

Stature was estimated using long bone measurements following Trotter and Gleser (1958). The bone(s) associated with the lowest standard error of estimate were used. Where the right and left bones were present but of unequal length the maximum measurement was used. Measurements from the left and right sides were not mixed.

Figure 11.4 shows the distribution of stature of 103 males and 117 females. The male mean was 170 cm (5'7") with a range from 158 to 183 cm. The female mean was 156 cm (5'1.5") with a range from 139 to 169 cm. When ?males (n = 25) and ?females (n = 23) were included, the male mean was lowered by 1 cm while the female mean remained unchanged.

Table 11.4 lists the mean stature of males and females from various British archaeological and documentary populations. Whithorn fits in well with these groups. The height of modern Britons did not reach modern standards until after the last World War when conditions improved enough for more people to reach their genetic potential for height. Stature can increase significantly in one generation given appropriate stimuli (Stewart 1980), and young adults today are generally 2 to 5 inches taller than their grandparents (Knight 1984).

Stature estimates can contribute to the assessment of the health status of a population. Those from the present group indicate a population which was probably subject to frequent episodes of 'stress' (nutritional and/or disease) during childhood which restricted growth and limited adult stature.

3.2. Head shape

Very few crania were recovered intact and few measurements could be taken. No attempt was made to reconstruct crania for the purposes of obtaining measurements. Of the 18 calvaria from which maximum length and breadth could be measured 39% (7) were doliocranic (long and narrow) and 61% (11) were mesocranic (medium). The range was from 72 to 78.9 with a mean of 75.6. There was no evidence of pathological deformation or other cranial anomaly.

Period	*Region/Site*	*Male Stature*		*Sample Size*	*Female Stature*		*Sample Size*	*Source*
Neolithic	British	172	5'8"	25	–	–	–	Beddoe, in Brothwell and Higgs, 1969
Bronze Age	British	176	5'9"	–	–	–	–	Manchester, 1983
Bronze Age	Scottish	171	5'7"	18	160	5'3"	11	Bruce, 1986
Iron Age	Maiden Castle	168	5'6"	26	–	–	–	Goodman and Morant 1938
Anglo Saxon	London	164	5'4"	–	156	5'1.5"	–	Zivanovich, 1986
C10–C16th	St Helens, York	169	5'6.5"	large	157	5'2"	large	Dawes, 1980
C11–C12th	St Nicholas Shambles	173	5'8"	94*	157	5'2"	94*	White, 1988
C13–C15th	Whithorn	169	5'6.5"	128	155	5'1"	140	This study
C6–C7th	Whithorn	176	5'9"	5	–	–	–	This study
C13–C16th	Aberdeen	168	5'6"	21	160	5'3"	10	Cross and Bruce, 1989
C13–C17th	Linlithgow	170	5'6.5"	15	156	5'1"	21	Cross and Bruce, 1989
C15–C16th	Logies Lane	169	5'6.5"	14	156	5'1"	4	Cardy, 1993
C16–recent	Ensay	166	5'5.5"	86	155	5'1"	100	Miles, 1989
1881	Britain	167	5'6"	–	–	–	–	From Waldron, 1989
1886	Britain	166	5'5.5"	–	–	–	–	From Waldron, 1989
1891	Britain	167	5'6"	–	–	–	–	From Waldron, 1989
1896	Britain	168	5'6"	–	–	–	–	From Waldron, 1989
1901	Britain	169	5'6.5"	–	–	–	–	From Waldron, 1989
1903	Britain	171	5'7.5"	–	–	–	–	From Waldron, 1989
Modern	British	177	5'9"	large	163	5'4"	large	Knight, 1984

Table 11.4: Mean stature of British populations.
*males and females combined

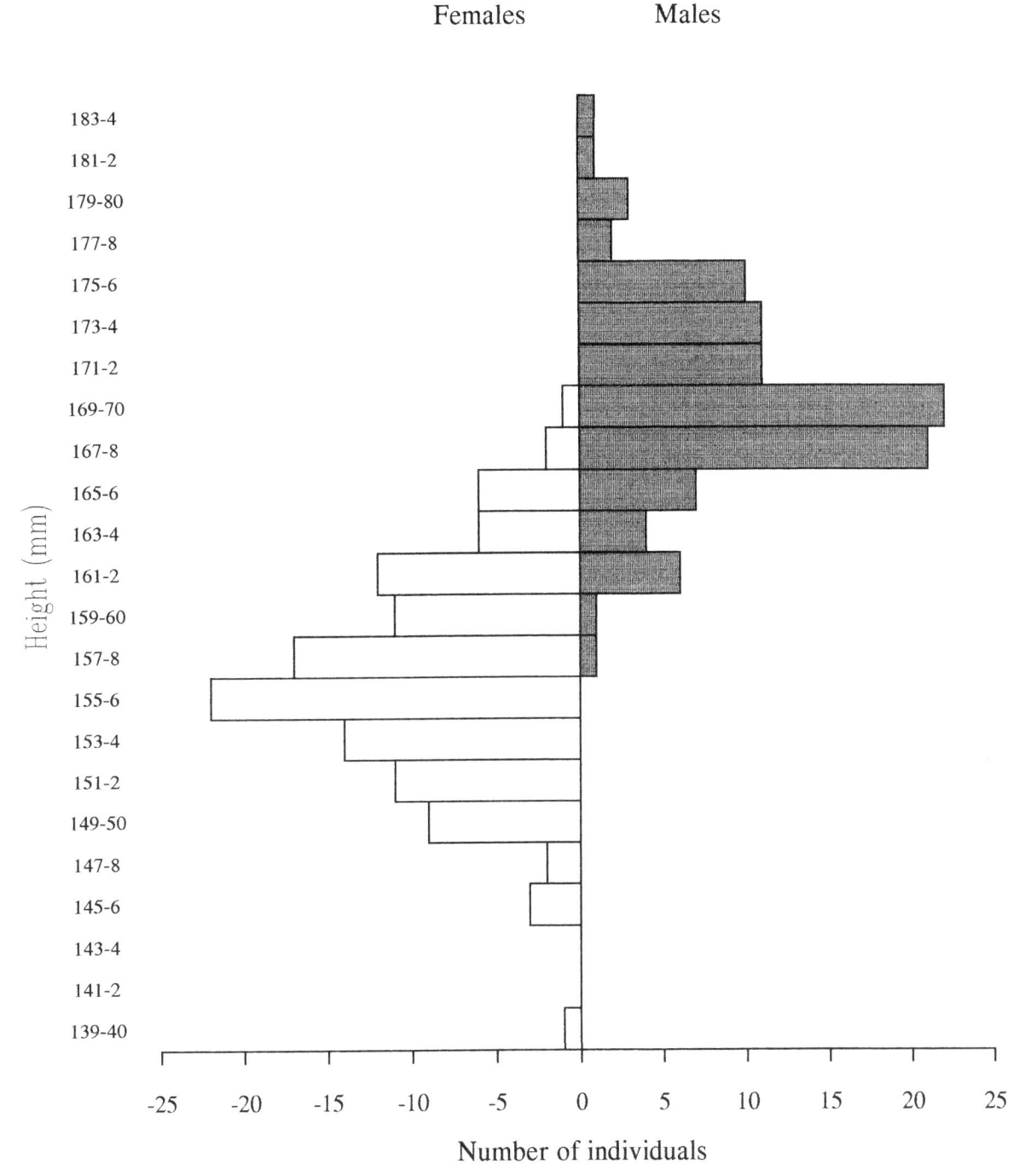

11.4 Male and female stature in later medieval population.

3.3. Lower limb shape

External femoral and tibial shaft shape is commonly described by the meric and cnemic indices respectively, which measure the relative 'flattening' of the upper portion of the bone. The femur tends to be more flat from front to back and the tibia from side to side in archaeological groups compared with modern western populations.

Table 11.5 compares the frequency of flattening of the femur in the present group with frequencies reported from other sites (sides and sexes combined).

Site	Platymeric <84.9		Eurymeric 85–99.9	
Whithorn	90%	(308 B)	10%	(164 B)
St Helen-on-the-Walls	86%	(301 I)	14%	(49 I)
Logies Lane	81%	(39 B)	19%	(9 B)
St Nicholas Shambles	78%	(56 I)	22%	(17 I)
Linlithgow	69%	(68 B)	31%	(30 B)
Aberdeen	64%	(46 B)	36%	(26 B)

Table 11.5: Meric index (adults only).
Sample size in brackets. I = individuals, B = bones.

	Male				Female				All adults			
	Left(n)		Right(n)		Left(n)		Right(n)		Left(n)		Right(n)	
Platymeria	87%	(46)	92%	(55)	89%	(64)	93%	(62)	88%	(160)	91%	(148)
Eurymeria	13%	(8)	8%	(5)	11%	(8)	7%	(5)	12%	(21)	9%	(14)
Total bones		54		60		72		67		181		162

Table 11.6: Meric index by sex: Whithorn.

The present sample tends towards the higher end of reported ranges for platymeria (flattening). The distribution of platymeria in the present sample by side and by sex is shown in Table 11.6. The left femur was slightly more rounded than the right in both sexes although the differences were not statistically significant, and female femora were slightly more flat than male femora.

Table 11.7 compares the frequency of flattening in

Site	Platycnemic <62.9	Mesocnemic 63–69.9	Eurycnemic 70–99.9
Whithorn	15% (61 B)	45% (186 B)	40% (164 B)
Logies Lane	11% (7 B)	21% (14 B)	68% (44 B)
Aberdeen	10% (8 B)	30% (25 B)	60% (50 B)
St Nicholas Shambles	9% (4/46 I)		
St Helen-on-the-Walls	7% (24/360 I)		
Linlithgow	6% (6 B)	33% (32 B)	61% (60 B)

Table 11.7: Cnemic index (adults only). Sample size in brackets. I = individuals, B = bones.

the tibia in the present group with frequencies from other sites (sides and sexes combined). The present sample fits towards the higher end of reported ranges of platycnemia (flattening). The distribution of the cnemic index by side and by sex for the present sample only is given in Table 11.8. The left tibia was

relatively small and gracile immature femur and indicates a need to refine assessment methods. Flange development appeared to be inversely related to femoral size and general robusticity, the largest femora often having no flange development whilst the smallest femora often displayed a strong flange. This appears to be verified by the higher frequency noted in females than males. The flange appears to act as a buttress as most stresses are transmitted down the outer margin of the femur during locomotion (Lee 1984), and it may well contribute to the high frequency of platymeria seen in archaeological groups. The flange is usually absent from modern western femora.

Various explanations have been proposed to account for variation in bone shape. Buxton (1938) suggests that where nutrients are in short supply and bone-building material limited, bone is laid down where it is most needed (i.e. side to side in the femur and front to back in the tibia), whilst other workers suggest that platycnemia is related to 'squatting' (sitting on the haunches). More recent studies suggest that although nutrition may affect bone density, it probably has limited effect on shape which is mainly dependent upon activity (Brock and Ruff 1988). As yet this debate is unresolved but merits further study since it may reflect life-style variations.

	Male				Female				All adults			
	Left(n)		Right(n)		Left(n)		Right(n)		Left(n)		Right(n)	
Platycnemic	14%	(9)	8%	(4)	19%	(16)	9%	(7)	19%	(43)	10%	(18)
Mesocnemic	48%	(32)	54%	(26)	38%	(33)	41%	(31)	43%	(96)	48%	(90)
Eurycnemic	38%	(25)	37%	(18)	43%	(37)	49%	(37)	38%	(85)	42%	(79)
Total Bones		66		48		86		75		224		187

Table 11.8: Cnemic index by sex: Whithorn.

slightly flatter than the right in both sexes. The differences were statistically significant when considering paired tibiae (Students paired 't' test), but were not significant when unpaired tibiae were included.

A lateral flange was frequently noted on the proximal femoral shaft and subjective assessment of its presence or absence was made. A flange was noted in 63% (67/106) of males, 71% (97/137) of females and 71% (96/135) of immatures. Flange development appeared to be age related, none being noted before three years of age, but with 38% in children (6/26), 84% in young juveniles and 88% in old juveniles. The high frequency in juveniles compared with adults is probably attributable to the more prominent appearance of the flange on the

4. HEALTH STATUS/LIFE-STYLE

Skeletal data provide the most direct evidence of the health status and disease burden of past populations when no written records survive, although the evidence is often unclear and imprecise. Few of the diagnostic techniques which are used in the living can be applied to dry bone and only the broadest outline of the individual's life history may be known. The types of response bone can make to a stimulus are limited and different diseases may produce similar bony reactions. Acute diseases from which many of the population may have died (such as cholera, typhus, bubonic plague, influenza, etc.) leave no bony evidence as they kill or are resolved before changes in the bone structure develop. Evidence of non-infective pathology such as degenerative joint disease (osteoarthritis) and that caused by trauma (e.g. fractures and Schmorl's nodes) are easier to diagnose.

Evidence of health status in terms of trauma, infection, childhood morbidity and other conditions is discussed below.

4.1. Trauma

4.1.1. Fractures

Analysis of the type and distribution of fractures within and between populations may elucidate aspects of social organisation and life-style. The number of fractures noted is likely to be an underestimate because those suffered at or close to death are difficult or impossible to distinguish from post-mortem breaks and as some fractures will inevitably be 'lost' from collections in which remains are incomplete and/or fragmentary.

Fractures of the vertebrae associated with osteoporosis are discussed in section 4.3.2 and were not included in the following analysis.

Seventy-three adults and seven immatures suffered at least one fracture or possible fracture sufficiently long before death to show healing. Almost three quarters of the most securely 'sexed' fractures were in males (70%, 31/44), reducing to 65% when ?males are included.

Sex	n	%
Male	31/217	14
Female	13/253	5
?Male	6/97	6
?Female	5/103	5
Ambiguous	3/45	7
Indeterminate	7/211	1

Table 11.9: No. of fractures as a proportion of the number of individuals at risk.

Table 11.9 gives the number of fractures as a percentage of the total number of individuals of each sex. Whilst comparisons of such figures would be inappropriate between skeletal series in which preservation was less than perfect, it was felt that they may be useful within a site. Males were almost three times more likely to suffer a fracture than females. The very low percentage in those of indeterminate sex no doubt reflects the generally poor condition of this group.

A predominance of fractures in males is commonly seen in British archaeological groups (e.g. Aberdeen, Linlithgow [Cross and Bruce 1989], Kirkhill, St Andrews [Bruce, Cross and Kerr 1990], Logies Lane, St Andrews [Cardy 1993], Cirencester [Wells 1982] and St Helen-on-the-Walls, York [Dawes 1980]), no doubt reflecting life-style in the stresses and traumas each sex was subject to.

The number of fractures in each major long bone as a proportion of the number of bones at risk is given for adults in Table 11.10 and for immatures in Table

	Male and ?Male Left	Male and ?Male Right	Female and ?Female Left	Female and ?Female Right	Unknown Left	Unknown Right	Total Left	Total Right
	No. %	No. %	No. %	No. %	No. %	No. %	No. %	No. %
Clavicle								
'Complete'	0/67 (0)	2/57 (3.5)	0/84 (0)	0/83 (0)	0/23 (0)	0/19 (0)	0/174 (0)	1/158 (0.6)
Humerus								
Prox	0/67 (0)	0/67 (0)	0/89 (0)	0/68 (0)	0/15 (0)	0/20 (0)	0/171 (0)	0/155 (0)
Diaph	0/130 (0)	0/118 (0)	0/150 (0)	0/139 (0)	0/44 (0)	0/48 (0)	0/323 (0)	0/306 (0)
Distal	0/140 (0)	0/132 (0)	0/152 (0)	0/140 (0)	0/52 (0)	0/53 (0)	0/343 (0)	0/326 (0)
Complete	0/60 (0)	0/61 (0)	0/75 (0)	0/62 (0)	0/13 (0)	0/18 (0)	0/148 (0)	0/141 (0)
Radius								
Prox	0/86 (0)	0/65 (0)	0/101 (0)	0/93 (0)	0/21 (0)	0/14 (0)	0/208 (0)	0/162 (0)
Mid	1/119 (0.8)	0/96 (0)	0/119 (0)	0/97 (0)	0/25 (0)	0/15 (0)	1/257 (0.4)	0/208 (0)
Distal	0/97 (0)	2/76 (2.6)	2/92 (2.1)	0/79 (0)	0/19 (0)	1/12 (8.3)	2/210 (0.9)	3/167 (1.8)
Complete	0/55 (0)	2/47 (4)	0/55 (0)	0/50 (0)	0/11 (0)	0/6 (0)	0/121 (0)	2/103 (1.9)
Ulna								
Prox	0/134 (0)	0/137 (0)	0/132 (0)	0/141 (0)	0/41 (0)	0/51 (0)	0/308 (0)	0/327 (0)
Mid	0/104 (0)	0/96 (0)	0/100 (0)	0/107 (0)	0/27 (0)	0/28 (0)	1/231 (0.4)	1/229 (0.4)
Parry	1/105 (0.9)	1/92 (1.1)	0/102 (0)	0/110 (0)	0/27 (0)	0/28 (0)	1/234 (0.4)	1/239 (0.4)
Complete	0/54 (0)	0/39 (0)	0/41 (0)	0/36 (0)	0/12 (0)	0/7 (0)	0/107 (0)	0/82 (0)
Femur								
Prox/neck	0/164 (0)	0/156 (0)	0/168 (0)	0/169 (0)	1/57 (1.7)	0/59 (0)	1/389 (0.3)	0/384 (0)
Mid	0/179 (0)	2/173 (1.2)	0/177 (0)	0/189 (0)	0/88 (0)	0/83 (0)	0/444 (0)	2/445 (0.4)
Distal	0/145 (0)	0/139 (0)	0/140 (0)	0/140 (0)	0/54 (0)	0/56 (0)	0/339 (0)	0/335 (0)
Complete	0/120 (0)	2/116 (1.7)	0/117 (0)	0/116 (0)	0/35 (0)	0/31 (0)	0/272 (0)	2/263 (0.8)
Tibia								
Prox	0/112 (0)	1/101 (1)	0/107 (0)	0/116 (0)	0/44 (0)	0/44 (0)	0/263 (0)	1/261 (0.4)
Mid	1/148 (0.7)	0/135 (0)	1/148 (0.7)	0/145 (0)	1/77 (1.2)	1/75 (1.3)	3/373 (0.8)	1/355 (0.3)
Distal	0/119 (0)	1/102 (1)	0/118 (0)	0/126 (0)	0/63 (0)	0/56 (0)	0/300 (0)	1/284 (0.4)
Complete	0/88 (0)	2/73 (2.7)	1/90 (1.1)	0/91 (0)	1/32 (3.1)	0/32 (0)	2/210 (1)	2/196 (1)
Fibula								
Mid	0/85 (0)	1/95 (1)	0/95 (0)	0/100 (0)	0/30 (0)	0/33 (0)	0/210 (0)	1/218 (0.5)
Distal	2/71 (2.8)	1/65 (1.5)	0/86 (0)	0/95 (0)	0/26 (0)	0/27 (0)	2/183 (1.1)	1/187 (0.5)
Complete	2/29 (6.9)	1/28 (3.6)	0/44 (0)	0/36 (0)	0/9 (0)	0/6 (0)	3/82 (3.6)	1/70 (1.4)

Table 11.10: Frequency of fractures in adults.

	Left		Right	
	No.	%	No.	%
Clavicle				
'Complete'	0/54	(0)	0/52	(0)
Humerus				
Proximal	0/59	(0)	0/57	(0)
Mid	1/77	(1.3)	1/74	1.3
Distal	0/69	(0)	0/60	(0)
Complete	1/69	(1.4)	0/71	(0)
Radius				
Proximal	0/63	(0)	0/58	(0)
Mid	0/78	(0)	0/69	(0)
Distal	0/43	(0)	0/49	(0)
Complete	0/26	(0)	0/36	(0)
Ulna				
Proximal	0/90	(0)	0/97	(0)
Mid	0/70	(0)	0/75	(0)
Parry	0/70	(0)	0/75	(0)
Complete	0/25	(0)	0/31	(0)
Femur				
Proximal	0/158	(0)	0/171	(0)
Mid	1/153	(0.7)	0/165	(0)
Distal	0/113	(0)	0/116	(0)
Complete	1/99	(1)	0/98	(0)
Tibia				
Proximal	0/121	(0)	0/109	(0)
Mid	0/141	(0)	0/133	(0)
Distal	0/105	(0)	0/103	(0)
Complete	0/84	(0)	0/82	(0)
Fibula				
Mid	0/77	(0)	0/65	(0)
Distal	1/59	(1.7)	0/51	(0)
Complete	1/38	(2.6)	0/32	(0)

Table 11.11: Frequency of fractures in immatures.

11.11. Because of the fragmentary nature of much of the material each bone was divided into three portions which were recorded as present or absent. The proximal and distal portions were considered present if at least ⅓ was substantially intact, with the exception of the distal radius where only ⅕ had to be present, as fractures of this portion often occur just above the distal articulation (Colles' fracture). The shaft of each bone was considered to be present if at least ⅔ was substantially intact. The clavicle was considered complete even if a small amount from either extreme was missing as fractures rarely occur in these regions.

The fibula and the distal radius were the most frequently fractured bones. Fractures of any type were unusual in children, probably because any breaks were likely to have been greenstick fractures which healed quickly and well. The humerus was notable for its lack of diaphyseal fractures in adults. Two 'possible' diaphyseal greenstick fractures were seen in immatures, one avulsion fracture of the medial epicondyle in an adult male (SK 1005) and a 'possible' fracture of the proximal humerus of a middle-aged female (SK 891).

Fractures were assessed for most probable cause. Spiral fractures and avulsion fractures were considered most likely to have been caused by indirect, accidental violence, whilst transverse fractures including parry fractures (associated with raising the arm to ward off a blow) were considered to result from direct violence, which may or may not have been deliberate.

Most fractures were assessed to have been caused by indirect trauma. Of the six considered to have been caused by direct violence, five were in males (one male and one ?male had 'parry' fractures; two males had transverse fractures of the femoral shaft; one male had a fracture of the blade of the right scapula and one female had a fracture at the base of the spine of the right scapula). The fractures in women were generally of the hands, feet and ribs, with one Colles' fracture and one small 'possible' fracture of the anterior border of the tibia. Fractures in men were more variable and included several examples of fractures in the major long bones. Fractures of more than one 'region' (a 'region' may be the lower leg, the forearm or the ribs) were noted in six males and two females. No individual had more than three fractured regions although this may include ten or more fractured bones when individual ribs were counted. A very violent episode, probably of a compressive nature, caused the 'butterfly' fracture of both pubic bones in one late-middle-aged male (SK 1583), an injury which is sometimes associated with rupture of the urethra and bladder. This individual, however, lived for a considerable time after the injury as the bone was well healed.

Most fractures had healed in good alignment. Exceptions were the clavicle of SK 1183 (Figure 11.5) and the spiral fracture of the left tibia and fibula of SK 637. The distal portion of the tibia of SK 637 was displaced laterally by approximately 10 mm and there was an area of bony union between the two bones in the area of fracture. Despite the poor alignment, the healing was strong and disability was probably minimal in both cases. The deformity of the proximal tibia of SK 625 (Figure 11.6) was probably caused by fracture of the proximal tibia during childhood which, on healing, caused premature and uneven fusion of the growth plate. There was some compensatory growth in the medial condyle of the distal femur. Early arthritic changes had developed as a consequence of the abnormal forces and the individual would have suffered some degree of disability.

Healing may occur without union of the fractured ends if damage is severe or if there is insufficient immobilization of the bone. The femoral neck fracture of an unsexed adult (SK 660), displaying resorption and severe degenerative change, provided the only such example in the present series (but see 6th–7th-century report). Non-union is a common complication of femoral neck fractures as the blood supply to the femoral head is easily disrupted. Such injury is usually associated with osteoporosis (section 4.3.2) and is particularly common today amongst elderly women in whom it may still be associated with significant morbidity and mortality.

Whilst bones may heal well and in good alignment without treatment, as studies of fractures in wild gibbons have shown (Schultz 1939, cited in Merbs 1989), evidence of effective bone setters in late medieval Whithorn is indicated by the two femoral shaft fractures which have healed with minimal deformity and shortening. The muscles around the femur contract strongly when the bone is fractured, pulling the broken ends over one another and the bone must be reduced if severe deformity is not to develop. There was no clear evidence of infection associated

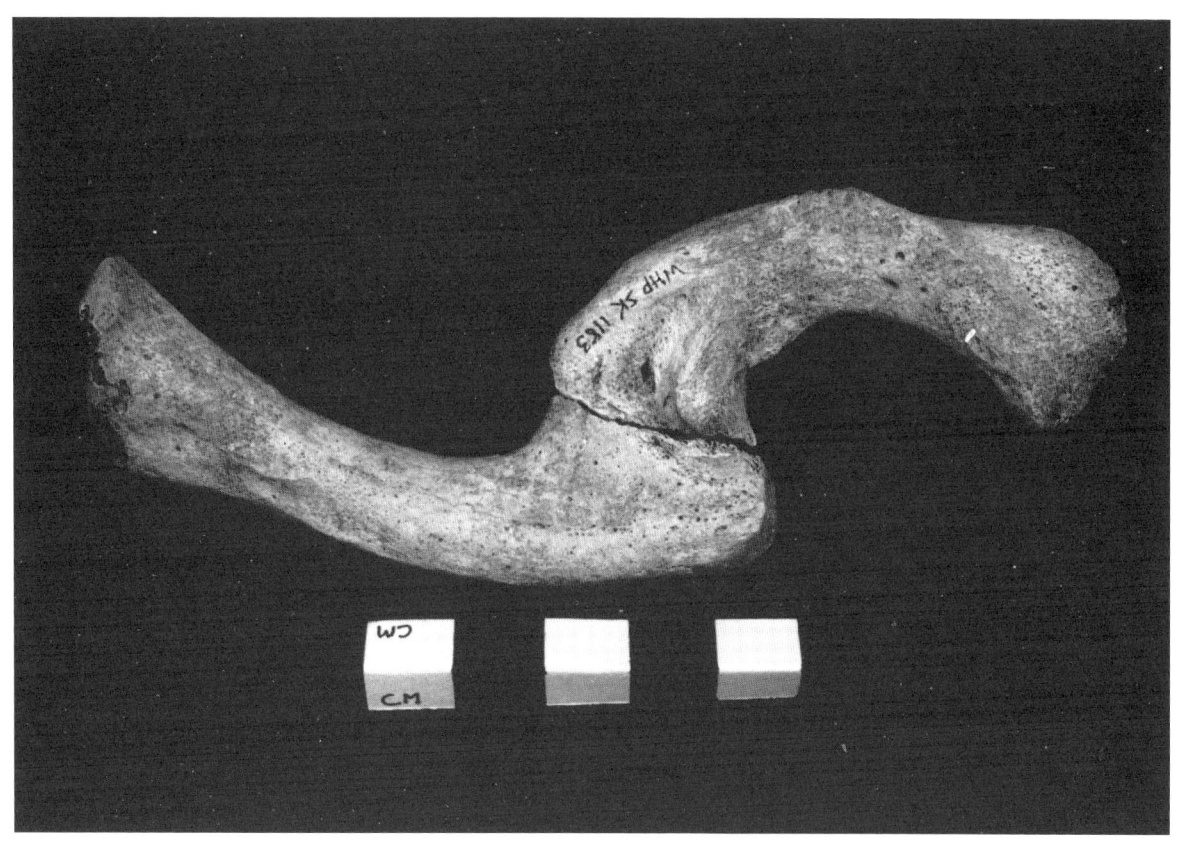

11.5 Inferior view of fractured clavicle (SK 1183).

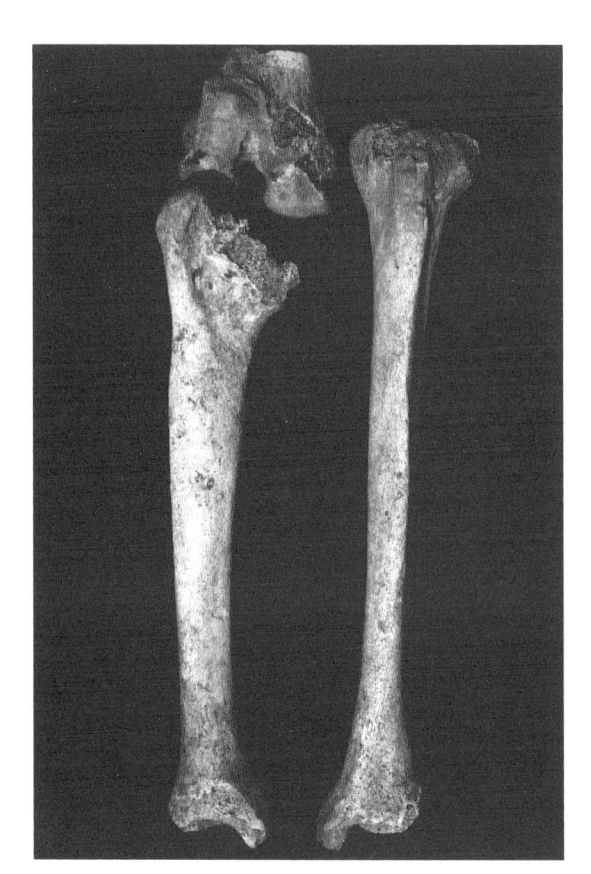

11.6 Probable healed fracture of right proximal tibia (SK625).

with any fracture which suggests that all fractures were closed (i.e. the skin not broken), or that evidence of infection was remodelled and eradicated with time.

Compression fractures which were considered to have been the consequence of a traumatic episode unrelated to osteoporosis were seen in one female, two ?females, one male and one adult of indeterminate sex. The female predominance may indicate either a type of activity that exposed women to such injury, or a failure to recognise the early stages of osteoporosis. The fractures were associated with other evidence of trauma in two individuals (middle-aged male SK 1080: multiple rib fractures, Colles' fracture, avulsion of styloid process of the ulna and fracture of the left fifth metacarpal; early middle-aged female SK 556: intervertebral osteochondrosis). The unusual site of the seventh cervical vertebra was fractured in SK 1004 (middle-aged adult of indeterminate sex), an injury which may be associated with carrying heavy loads on the head. The remaining cases were in poor condition and a close assessment could not be made.

Avulsion fractures with non-union may account for the missing tuberosities of the fifth metatarsals seen in two individuals, and the characteristic flat and pitted navicular tuberosities seen in seven adults/subadults (Figure 11.7). Such injuries are caused by forcible inversion or eversion of the foot respectively (Wiles 1960) and as such may be caused by 'going over on the ankle'. Avulsion of the tuberosity of the navicular is uncommon in modern

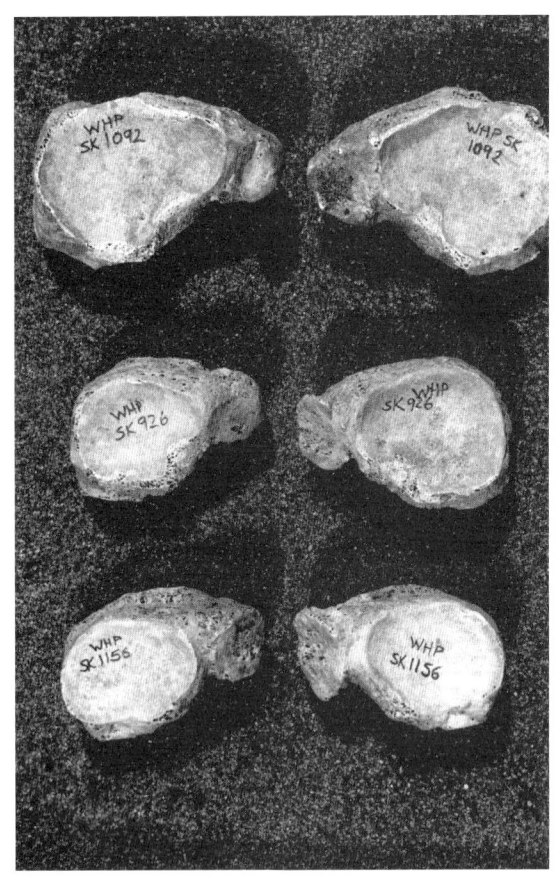

11.7 Naviculars with flat, pitted tuberosities, various skeletons.

practice and there may be an alternative explanation for the unusual and typical appearance of these bones. Wells (1982, 188) reports a similar navicular in the Cirencester group but does not attribute the anomaly to a fracture. These bones have not been included in the present figures as the diagnosis is unclear. Three further examples of avulsion fractures were noted, one of the medial epicondyle of the left humerus of the male SK 1005 (who also had osteochondritis dissicans of the capitulum of that humerus), one of the styloid process of the ulna in the male SK 1080 (associated with other fractures, see above), and the other of the right transverse process of the first thoracic vertebra of SK 19 (?female, old adult, also with osteochondritis dissicans of both distal femora), although differential diagnosis includes non-fusion of the epiphysis. None of these injuries is likely to have had seriously detrimental effects.

The individual examples of fractures are listed in Appendix 2.

4.1.2. Cranial injury

The crania of thirteen adults and subadults had lesions which may have been caused by trauma. Six were male/?male, four were female/?female and three were of ambiguous or indeterminate sex. The left parietal was involved most often (seven individuals,

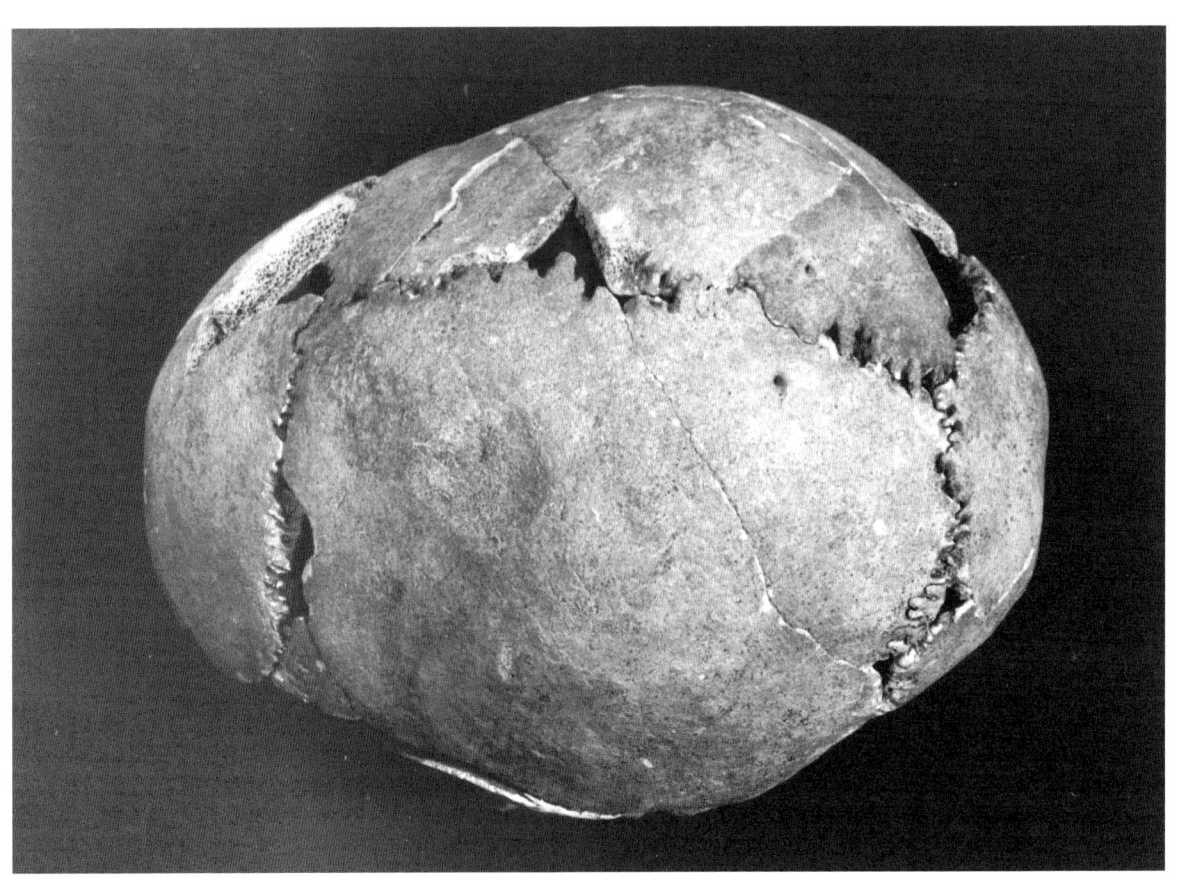

11.8 Type 'A' lesion of left parietal (SK 1150).

seven lesions), followed by the frontal (five individuals, seven lesions) and the occipital (two individuals, three lesions). Detailed frequencies of affected crania are not given because of the fragmentary nature of most cranial material.

The lesions fall into a number of distinct groups:
A. Shallow, flat, circular lesions of the left parietal, as though a thin 'slice' of bone was removed (e.g. SK 1150, Figure 11.8).
B. Lesions with bevelled edges consistent with trepanation by the scraping technique.
C. Small, neat, rounded lesions resembling the 'slingstone' wound described by Wells (1982, 164).
D. Lesions of the frontal bone with sharper profiles, possibly caused by a blade (e.g. SK 1108, Figure 11.9).
E. Shallow lesions with smooth profiles resembling 'thumb prints'.
F. Linear wound which pierced both tables probably caused by a sword blade (Figure 11.10).
G. Lesions evident on both tables, possibly cranial osteomyelitis (one individual with two lesions, parietal lesion similar in terms of size, shape and location to the 'slice' parietal lesions, except that the bone surface is infective, Figure 11.11).

Most wounds were well healed and with no evidence of infection, exceptions being SKs 1081 and 684 (see below). Table 11.12 lists the lesions according to site and type. Some of the more interesting cases are described in more detail below.

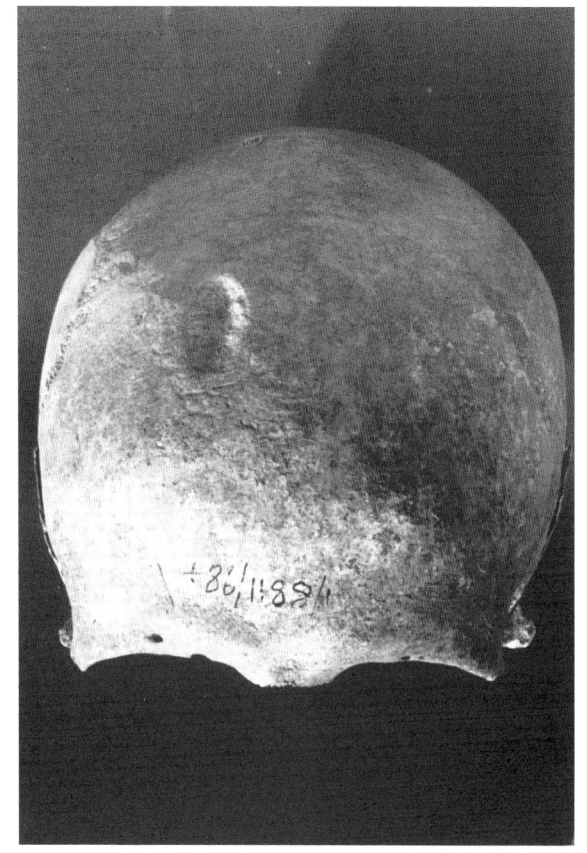

11.9 Type 'D' lesion of frontal (SK 1108).

SK 684 (old adult male, Figure 11.10): a healed wound of the occipital, probably caused by a blade which pierced the inner table. Above this and spanning part of the right parietal and occipital was a well-healed lesion with bevelled edges, consistent with trepanation by scraping. The external diameter of the lesion was 60 mm and the piece of bone removed was approximately 25 mm in diameter. The internal surface of the occipital between the lesions displayed an active infection which may well have

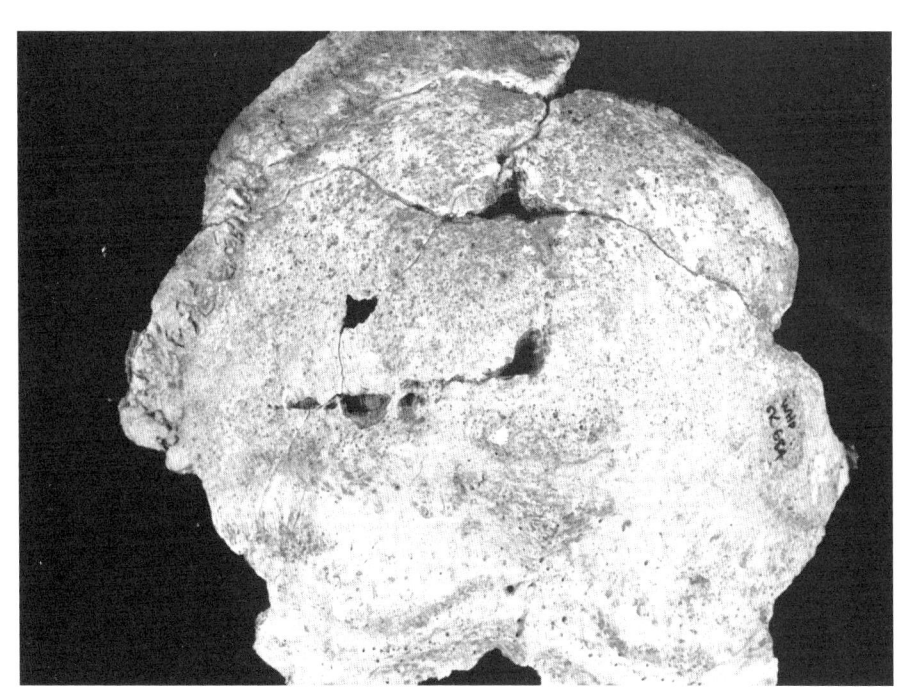

11.10 Probable blade wound of occipital (SK 684).

11.11 Destructive lesions of left parietal and frontal (SK 1081).

caused death. Trepanation is often associated with cranial injury (Wells 1982) and has formed part of the treatment of many disorders, from cranial injury to spirit possession, in various cultures through much of history.

SK 261 (subadult, ?female): a depression with bevelled edges on the left posterior parietal, of normal bone quality. The central region of the depression was missing and the inner table was eroded post-mortem. Differential diagnoses include trepanation, depressed fracture or an unusually deep type 'A' lesion, complicated and obscured by post-mortem damage.

SK 1081 (subadult male, Figure 11.11): one frontal and one parietal lesion. The inner and outer tables were both affected by an infective/destructive process with relatively little new bone development. The aetiology is unclear but may involve cranial osteomyelitis subsequent to failed trepanation, or haemolytic spread of infection from an unknown focus. The parietals were porous as were the proximal ulnae and manubrium. In addition there was

SK	Age	Sex	Bone(s)	Side	Lesion Type	Size (mm)
261	SA	?F	Parietal	Left	B/A?	26 (max D)
622	MA	F	Frontal	Central(2)	E	13×10.5×1
631	LMA	?M	Parietal	Left	E	13×8×1
684	OA	M	Occipital		F	see text
			Occip/Par	Right	B	see text
1033	EMA	F	Parietal	Left	C	6×6×2
1081	SA	M	Parietal	Left	G/A?	24 (max D)
			Frontal	Right	G	16.5×14.5
1082	MA	M	Frontal	Right	D	26×14×1.5
1108	LMA	UK	Frontal	Left	D	10×7×1.5
			Frontal	Right	D	13×7×2
1110	AD	UK	Frontal	Right	D	12×12×2
1143	MA	UK	Parietal	Left	A	29 (max D)
1150	MA	?M	Parietal	Left	A	22 (max D)
1336	SA	M	Occipital	Left	C	8×8×2
1558	YA	?F	Parietal	Left	A	22×25

Table 11.12: Cranial lesions.

disruption of the infero-posterior surface of the shaft of the right humerus, expansion of the spine and acromion process of the scapulae and a 'skirt' of ossification projecting inferiorly for 7 mm from the inferior margin of CV2, representing growth into the anterior longitudinal ligament.

At least eight of the thirteen crania may have been injured by edged weapons and may thus reflect interpersonal violence, although other interpretations such as healed infective lesions or lesions caused by soft tissue conditions (such as sebacious cysts or lipoma) must also be considered. It is noteworthy that women were affected almost as often as men, in contrast to long-bone fractures and other evidence of traumatic stress.

4.1.3. Subluxation

Very few examples of dislocated joints were noted. Many joint dislocations can easily be reduced (put back in place) and only those which are long-standing cause detectable bony changes.

The proximal and middle phalanges of one finger of SK 650 (middle-aged male) were fused with flexion of approximately 30° and lateral angulation of approximately 40°. The finger may have been fractured or laterally dislocated with subsequent fusion.

The left humeral head of SK 1033 (middle-aged female) was under-developed and 'flat', with moderately severe marginal lipping, possibly with slight anterior dislocation of the joint (Figure 11.12). The condition may be a consequence of avascular necrosis (bone 'death' due to a defect in the blood supply) of the humeral head although the reason for this is unclear. This skeleton also displayed multiple Schmorl's nodes, intervertebral osteochondrosis and a cranial lesion (type 'C', above). The right humerus was not recovered.

4.1.4. Schmorl's nodes

Schmorl's nodes are pits or depressions on the surface of the vertebral body caused by herniation of the intervertebral disc material into the bone. They develop in response to trauma, usually thought to be of a sudden, compressive nature such as heavy lifting. A number of studies report no relationship between Schmorl's nodes and age (e.g. Hilton *et al.* 1976; Saluja *et al.* 1986), and Resnick and Niwayama (1978) suggest that nodes are most likely to develop in young adults in whom the pressure within the intervertebral disc is still high. The clinical significance of the nodes is unclear as they are often asymptomatic in the living.

Schmorl's nodes were noted in 196 adults and at least six old juveniles, and involved spinal elements from TV4 to SV1. Frequencies of affected individuals were determined in thoracic spines which were largely complete from TV6 to TV12 and/or those in which at least four of the five lumbar vertebrae were present.

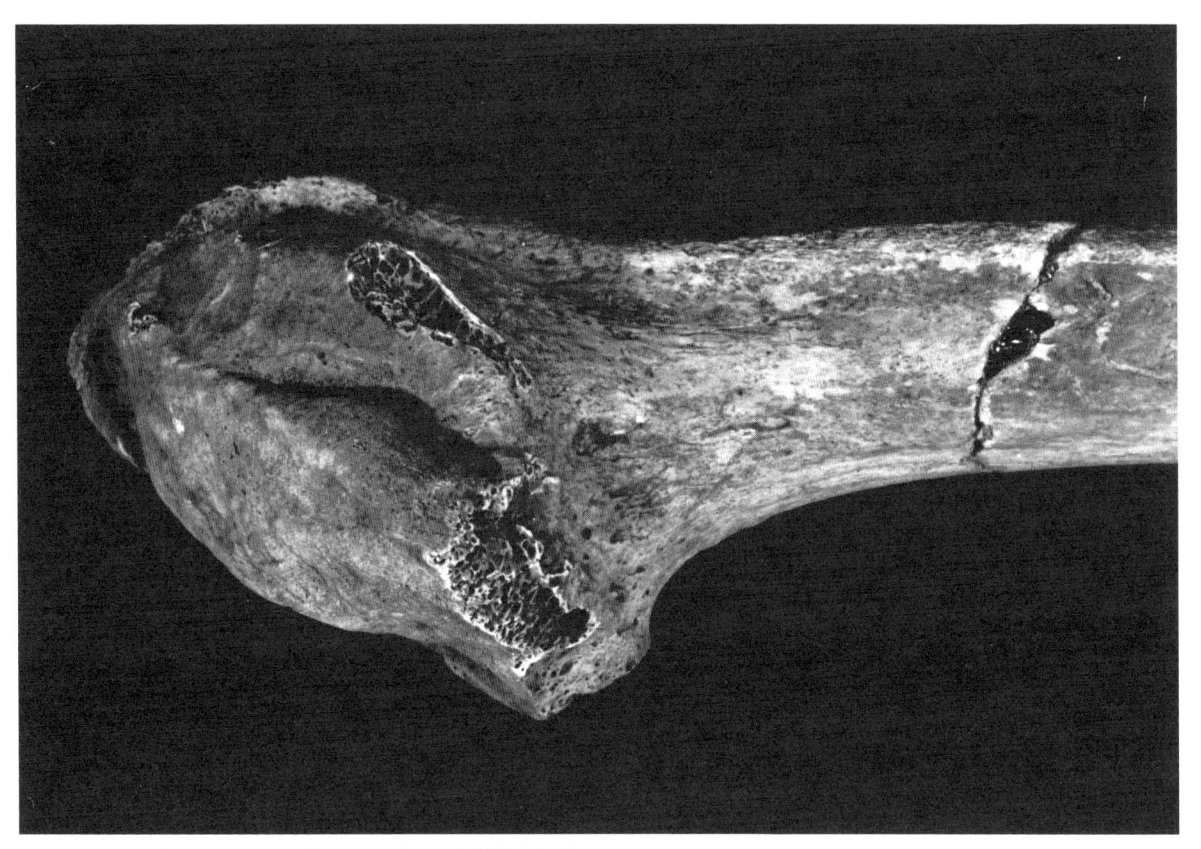

11.12 Avascular necrosis of humeral head (SK 1033).

	Male		Female	
	n	%	n	%
Thoracic	30/41	73	22/50	44
Lumbar	31/61	51	25/56	45

Table 11.13: Frequency of Schmorl's nodes by region and sex.

The thoracic and lumbar spines of females were equally affected by Schmorl's nodes whereas males were affected much more often in the thoracic than in the lumbar region. The frequencies are shown in Table 11.13 below. The difference between males and females was significant at the 0.01% level in the thoracic spine, but was not significant in the lumbar spine. A similar pattern was noted in groups from Aberdeen and St Brides, London (Saluja *et al.* 1986).

Frequencies were much lower in 'old juveniles', 17% (2/12) of thoracic and 4% (1/24) of lumbar spines displaying Schmorl's nodes. The youngest individual affected was aged between 14 and 18 years (SK 494, ?male) although very slight depressions were noted in the spines of a number of younger individuals.

The frequency and sex distribution of Schmorl's nodes varies between populations, with females displaying most variation. Table 11.14 compares the percentage of men and women with Schmorl's nodes from various sites. Four times as many men as women had Schmorl's nodes at St Nicholas Shambles, London, although the frequency quoted for the thoracic spine (8.6: White 1988) is very low by the standards of the Scottish samples quoted, although the St Nicholas figures may contain both adults and immatures.

	Male %	Female %	Source
Ipswich Blackfriars	55	22	Mays 1991
Logies Lane	57	54	Cardy 1993
Whithorn	57	35	This report
Aberdeen	72	67	Cross and Bruce 1989
St Brides, London	75	20	Saluja *et al.* 1986

Table 11.14: Frequency of Schmorl's nodes in various British populations.

Sexual dimorphism in factors causing Schmorl's nodes would appear to be greatest in the eighteenth-century London group and least in the eastern Scottish groups with Whithorn in an intermediate position. Such variation is tantalising, indicating different factors operating between the sexes in different societies – regional and temporal – which may reflect differences in life-style. The development of Schmorl's nodes is incompletely understood and interpretation is difficult, although it seems probable that groups in which Schmorl's nodes are more frequent were more subject to physical stresses. Frequencies of Schmorl's nodes may show correlations with other stress markers, but such a study is unfortunately beyond the scope of the present analysis.

4.1.5. Intervertebral osteochondrosis (IVO)

Osteochondrosis of the spine is manifest as semi-circular lytic lesions of the anterior part of the vertebral body, usually in the lower thoracic and lumbar regions. Resnick and Niwayama (1978) suggest that multiple Schmorl's nodes in early life may lead to this disorder, and Kelley (1982) suggests that IVO is related to physical stress, probably during the second and third decades of life. In older individuals the lesions may become indistinguishable from other degenerative changes.

IVO was noted in eight males/?males, twelve females/?females and three adults of indeterminate sex. Immatures were unaffected. Male and female spines were affected in different regions, males being affected throughout the spine from T4 with a peak at T12 whilst females were predominantly affected in the lumbar spine. Employing the same criteria for 'complete' spines as those outlined above (section 4.1.4) 7.3% (3/41) of male and 4% (2/50) of female thoracic spines, and 3% (2/61) of male and 16% of female lumbar spines had IVO. The much greater frequency in the female lumbar spine is surprising and requires examination. A type of behaviour specific to women may have caused these lesions although, unusually, almost all of the affected women also had 'complete' spines (and were thus included in the computation) which may indicate sample bias.

Four fifths of those with IVO also had Schmorl's nodes, almost always of the affected region (divided broadly into thoracic and lumbar spine). In some, the lesions were multiple and associated with severe degeneration of the surface of the vertebral body, and in others the lesions were isolated. The youngest individual with IVO was an 18–24-year-old male (SK 632) who also displayed a healed fracture of the right femoral shaft.

4.1.6. Spondylolysis

Separation of the vertebral body and superior facet joints from the inferior facet joints is characteristic of a condition known as spondylolysis. The precise aetiology is unknown, but both stress and congenital factors are generally thought to be involved, although the defect was not demonstrated in the studies of foetal or neonatal material reviewed by El-Najar and McWilliams (1978). The separation may be unilateral or bilateral, and reunion of separated elements may occur. Spondylolysis may be asymptomatic or may cause chronic low back pain and spinal stenosis (narrowing) if the defective vertebral body slips forward (Eisenstein 1978). The lower lumbar vertebrae, and LV5 in particular, are most often involved.

Spondylolysis was noted in three adults and three subadults (five males/?males and one female). The fifth lumbar vertebra was affected in four individuals, LV4 in one (in combination with LV5), an unidentified lumbar vertebra in a fifth individual and SV1 in the sixth.

Frequencies were calculated using only largely

complete vertebrae or vertebral arches. Separate neural arches were found in 3.2% (4/124) of adult LV5s and 0.9% (1/115) of adult LV4s. More males than females were affected (LV5 male: 7.1% [3/42]; LV5 female: 2% [1/49]; LV4 male: 2.4% [1/41]; LV4 female: 0%). A frequency for the first sacral vertebra could not be determined as the affected vertebra was not itself complete. Additional evidence of trauma was found in three individuals with spondylolysis (femoral shaft fracture; fracture of the left second and third metacarpals; bony roughening at the distal tibia–fibula articulation).

4.1.7. Enthesopathies/bony roughening

Roughening or bony outgrowths known as enthesopathies may develop in response to stress in areas where the tendons or ligaments are attached to the bone. These markers may record a single, high-level episode or repeated minor episodes. Twenty-nine percent (62/217) of males and 13% (33/253) of females had such markers (62 males, 33 females, 13 ?males, 6 ?females and 28 adults of either ambiguous or indeterminate sex).

Men had more lesions in the lower limb and women had more lesions in the upper limb. Of the lower limb, the linea aspera (to which the muscles which extend the lower leg on the thigh are attached) was affected in 15 males and one female; the insertion of the Achilles tendon into the calcaneus, the distal tibia/fibula articulation and the insertion of the quadriceps into the patella (again indicating strong extension of the lower leg on the thigh) were affected in almost three times as many men as women. Of the upper limb, the insertion of the triceps muscle into the head of the ulna (which extends the forearm) and the attachment of the muscles of the forearm into the epicondyles of the humerus (which flex and rotate the forearm, and extend and flex the wrist and fingers) were affected in more women than men despite the much smaller number of women with enthesopathies overall. Table 11.15 lists the number of individuals affected in each region.

The evidence suggests that men were more involved in levels of activity which caused these lesions, especially of the lower limb, such as in strong bracing of the lower limb in static bending and stretching, powerful pushing with the lower limb, and travel over rough ground. The evidence from females suggests that they were generally more sedentary but involved in tasks requiring strong use of the upper limb, especially those involving strong extension of the forearm (as in chopping motions), and strong movements of the wrist such as would be used in wringing clothes, washing and pounding.

4.1.8. Oestochondritis dissicans (OCD)

Osteochondritis dissicans is a trauma-related condition of the joint which is probably caused by an interruption of the blood supply to an area of bone

	NC	CVO	Cl	Sc	ME	LE	PU	RT	UT	P	LT	GT	LA	PAT	PTF	SL	DTF	ACH	RIB	IC	Isc	Pub
Enthesopathy																						
Male	0	2	2	0	0	2	4	1	0	0	2	0	3	6	3	2	7	19	4	3	3	2
Female	0	3	1	1	3	4	9	0	0	1	0	2	0	2	1	0	0	7	1	0	2	0
?Male	2	2	0	0	0	0	1	0	0	0	0	0	1	0	1	1	0	0	0	0	1	0
?Female	0	0	0	1	0	1	1	1	1	0	0	0	0	0	0	0	0	2	1	0	0	0
UK	0	2	0	0	0	1	6	0	0	0	0	0	0	1	0	0	2	8	1	0	1	0
Roughening																						
Male	0	0	0	0	0	0	1	4	1	0	0	0	12	0	0	1	3	0	0	1	4	0
Female	0	0	0	0	0	0	0	0	2	0	0	0	1	0	0	0	4	0	0	1	2	0
?Male	0	0	0	0	0	0	0	1	0	0	0	0	0	0	0	2	0	0	0	0	0	0
?Female	0	0	0	0	0	0	0	0	0	0	0	0	1	0	0	0	0	0	0	1	0	0
UK	0	0	0	0	0	0	0	1	2	0	0	0	1	0	0	0	0	0	0	0	0	0
Combined																						
Male	0	2	2	0	0	2	5	5	1	0	2	0	15	6	3	3	10	19	4	4	7	2
Female	0	3	1	1	3	4	9	0	2	1	0	2	1	2	1	0	4	7	1	1	4	0
?Male	2	2	0	0	0	0	1	1	0	0	0	0	1	0	1	3	0	0	0	0	1	0
?Female	0	0	0	1	0	1	1	1	1	0	0	0	1	0	0	0	0	2	1	1	0	0
UK	0	2	0	0	0	1	6	1	2	0	0	0	1	1	0	0	2	8	1	0	1	0

Table 11.15: Enthesopathy/bony roughening in adults.

NC – Nuchal crest
CVO – Superior extension of odontoid facet of C2
Cl – Clavicle
Sc – Scapula
ME – Medial epicondyle of humerus
LE – Lateral epicondyle of humerus
PU – Insertion of triceps into head of ulna
RT – Radial tuberosity
UT – Ulna tuberosity
P – Phalanges
LT – Lesser trochanter
GT – Greater trochanter
LA – Linea aspera
PAT – Patella
PTF – Proximal tibia/fibula
SL – Soleal line
DTF – Distal tibia/fibula
ACH – Insertion of Achilles tendon into calcaneus
RIB – Rib tuberosity
IC – Iliac crest
Isc – Ischium
Pub – Pubis

and involving damage to the overlying cartilage. OCD is most common today in the knee in adolescent and young adult. It is manifest in the dry bone as a defect of the joint surface which may be predominantly lytic (destructive) or proliferative, forming a bony 'plug' which fills the defect and rises above the articular plane.

Seventeen males/?males, fourteen females/ ?females (including one old juvenile), nine adults of indeterminate sex and two unsexed old juveniles had lesions attributable to OCD. The youngest individual was a 13–16 year old with a lesion of the capitulum of the right distal humerus (SK 1523). The distribution of lesions in males and females varied slightly, males displaying more large joint lesions than females.

The knee was the site of 60% (12/20) of male and 47% (7/15) of female lesions. Table 11.16 shows their distribution within the knee. The distal femur displayed more lesions overall than the tibia. Most femoral lesions were cited on the medial condyle whereas those of the tiba tended to occur on the lateral condyle. Both tibia and femur were affected in four individuals.

The elbow was affected more often in women than in men (21% [4/19] of male and 33% [5/15] of female affected joints). Other areas affected, in descending order of frequency, were the hip, ankle, toe, shoulder and head of the first metatarsal (but see section 4.1.9 below).

The evidence from OCD tends to confirm that from fractures and enthesopathies, and indicates a tendency for men to be subject to more traumatic

	Medial condyle no.	lesions	Lateral condyle no.	lesions	no. SKs	no. bones
Femur	18/26	(69%)	9/26	(35%)	15	23
Tibia	3/11	(27%)	9/12	(75%)	9	11

Table 11.16: Distribution of lesions within the knee.

stress overall than women. Men tended to be most affected in the lower limb whilst women were more affected in the upper limb.

4.1.9. Defects of the articular surfaces (DAS)

A characteristic defect of unknown aetiology, but possibly related to osteochondritis dissicans, was observed on many joint surfaces. The defect was characteristically single and lytic, and varied from a slight depression or 'pinprick' with intact cortical bone, to a 'crease', to a larger defect involving the cancellous bone, occasionally with a bony nodule within the defect. There was rarely any evidence of the defect on the opposing joint surface and within a particular joint the site affected was characteristic. One individual may have several affected joints. In most cases the defect appears to be distinct from typical OCD although some overlap was noted in examples which did not easily fall into either category. DAS have been noted by many workers (various pers. comm.) but are not commonly reported in the literature. Examples of the defect in the proximal phalanx of the great toe examined by a

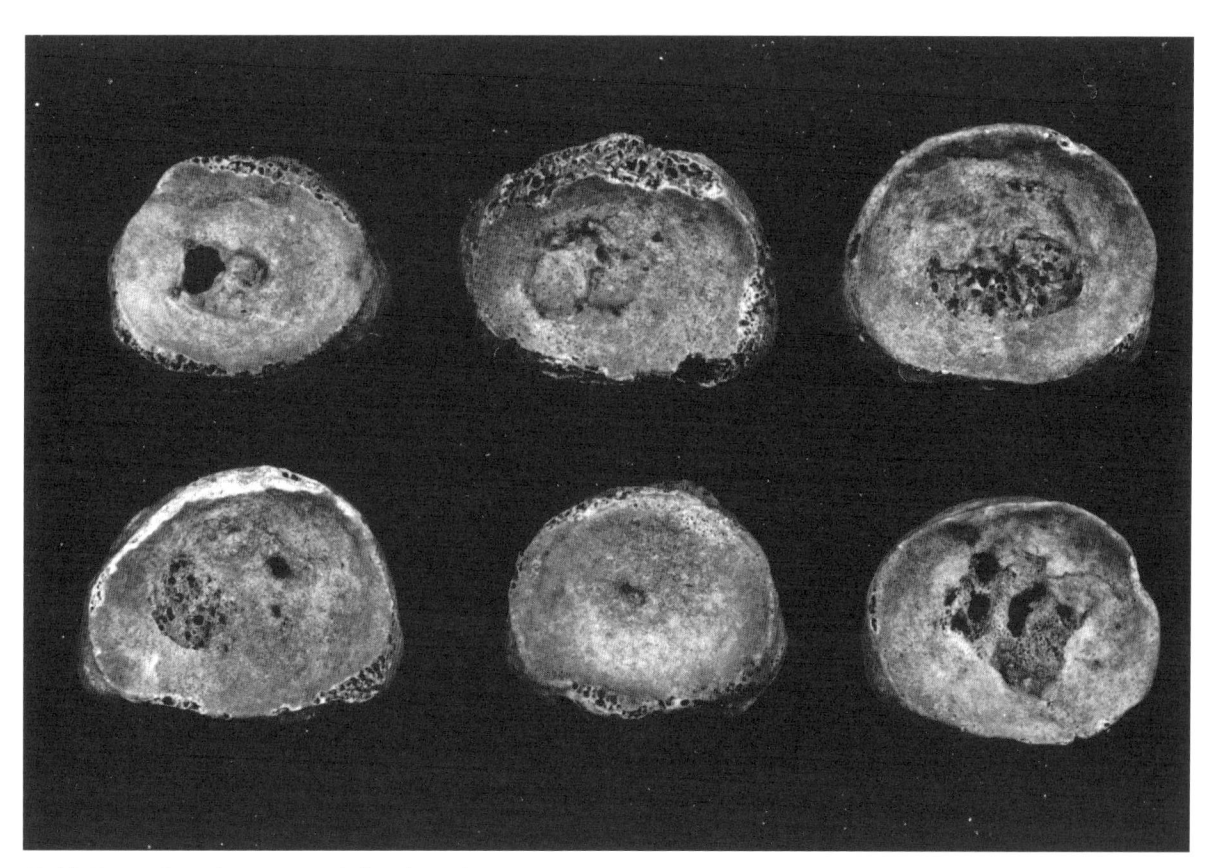

11.13 Examples of 'great toe defects', various skeletons.

radiologist could not be detected on X-ray and were considered to be of no clinical significance (Dr D. Jones, pers. comm.).

Frequencies were recorded for the bones in which the defect was considered to be most common. These were the proximal facet of the first phalanx of the great toe (Figure 11.13), the talus facet of the navicular (Figure 11.14), the base of the first metatarsal (Figure 11.15), the superior facets of the second cervical vertebra (Figure 11.16) and the trochlea of the distal humerus. A frequency for the whole sample was available for the great toe, for SKs 1–444 and 585–1620 for the first metatarsal, second cervical vertebra and navicular, and a random sample of 231 adult distal humeri. The results are summarised in Table 11.17 and are presented with comparative data from other groups. Male and female figures do not include ?males and ?females. None of the differences between the sexes reached statistical significance.

Great toe (GTD)
A more or less central defect of the proximal facet of the first phalanx of the great toe was observed in 36% (122/337) of adult bones and 47% (16/34) of immature bones. Slightly more males than females had defects. The youngest individual affected was aged between five and nine years.

Navicular (ND)
The precise location of this defect was variable, although all were on the concave facet of the bone. The defect was observed in 16% (37/225) of left and 14% (31/216) of right adult naviculars, and in 8% (3/38) of left and 8% (3/38) of right immature bones. The youngest individual affected was aged between 13 and 16 years.

First metatarsal (MTD)
The precise location of defects on the base of the first metatarsal was variable. Defects were noted in adult bones; 7% (13/186) of adult left and 8% (13/168) of adult right first metatarsals being affected. Men had more defects than women, and the left and right sides were almost equally affected in both sexes.

Second cervical vertebra (CVD)
This defect was typically sited just within the postero-lateral margin of the superior facet joints, sometimes extending towards the centre of the facet. Defects were noted on 9% (23/259) of adult left and 7% (18/246) of adult right facets, and in 8% (6/72) of immature left and 10% (7/67) of immature right facets. Males were affected more often than females (male: left 8.6% [6/70], right 6.4% [4/62]; female: left 8.7% [8/92], right 2.2% [2/91]).

Distal humerus (TD)
The location of this defect was constant, sited on the inferior aspect of the trochlea, just medial to its lateral border. Defects were noted on 8.5% (10/117) of adult left and 7% (8/114) of adult right trochlea. Males were affected

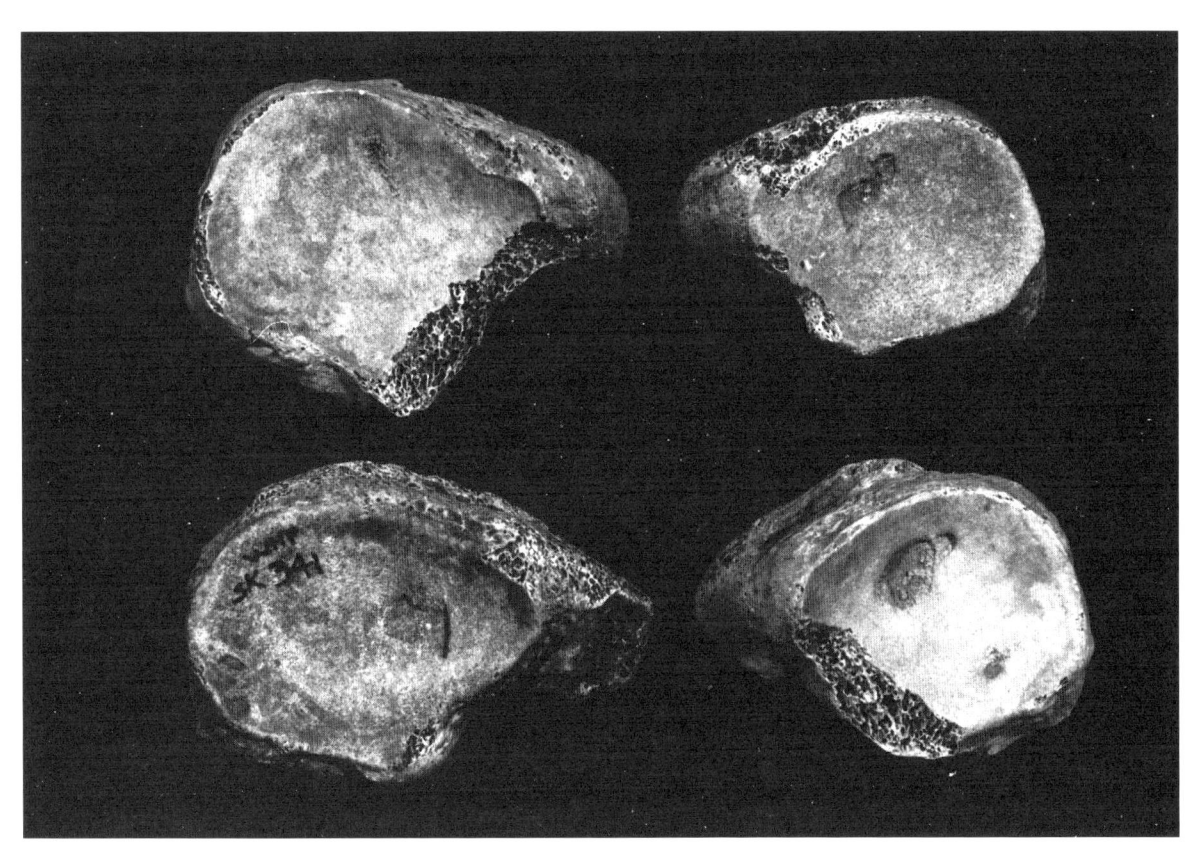

11.14 Examples of 'navicular defects', various skeletons.

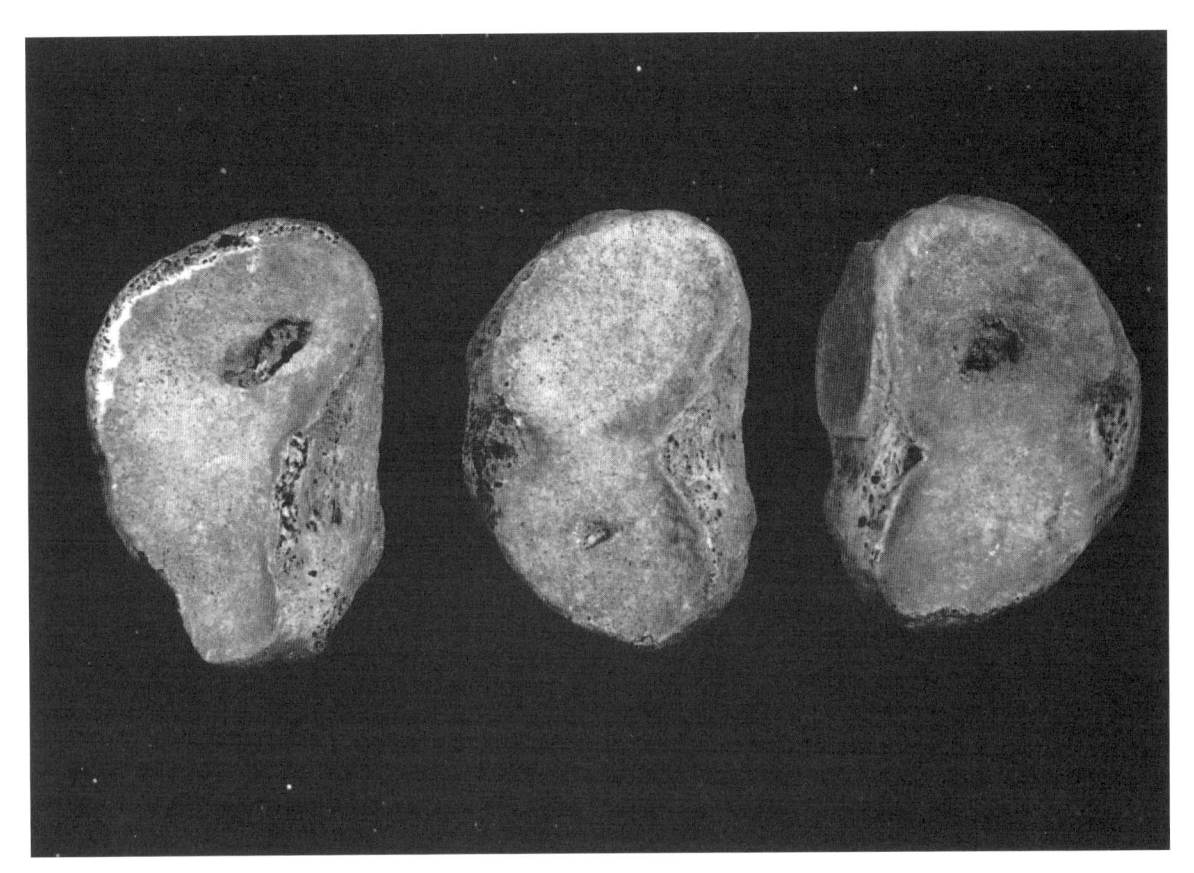

11.15 Examples of defects of MT1, various skeletons.

more often than females (male: left 13.5% [5/37], right 11% [4/36]; female: left 3.7% [2/54], right 8.3% [4/48]).

Other
Other joint surfaces affected by these defects are listed in Table 11.18. Defects were noted more often in males than in females and in the foot more often than in any other region.

If an aetiology involving trauma (cf. OCD?) is invoked for this defect, the frequency observed in each joint may reflect the relative levels of stress that the joint is subject to. Those in the foot may reflect the stresses of locomotion which pass from the heel to the ball of the foot and into the big toe. The sex differences, usually with more defects in males, may support a stress-related aetiology, although the

DAS	Site	Male n	%	Female n	%	Immature n	%	Total sample n	%
GTD	WHLM	35/91	38	42/116	36	16/34	47	138/380	36
	WHEM							6/12	50*
	LL							6/13	46
ND	WHLM	12/99	12	27/157	17	6/76	8	62/428	14
	WHEM							2/8	25*
	LL							1/33	3
MTD	WHLM	13/88	15	9/122	7	0/26	0	24/302	8
	WHEM							1/8	12*
	LL							1/41	2.5
CVD	WHLM	10/132	8	10/183	5	13/139	9	54/644	8
	WHEM							1/11	9*
	LL							0/59	0
TD	WHLM							15/226	

Table 11.17: Frequency of defects in articular surfaces (DAS).

WHLM = present sample
WHEM = C6th–C7th Whithorn sample
LL = Logies Lane, St Andrews
* = adults only

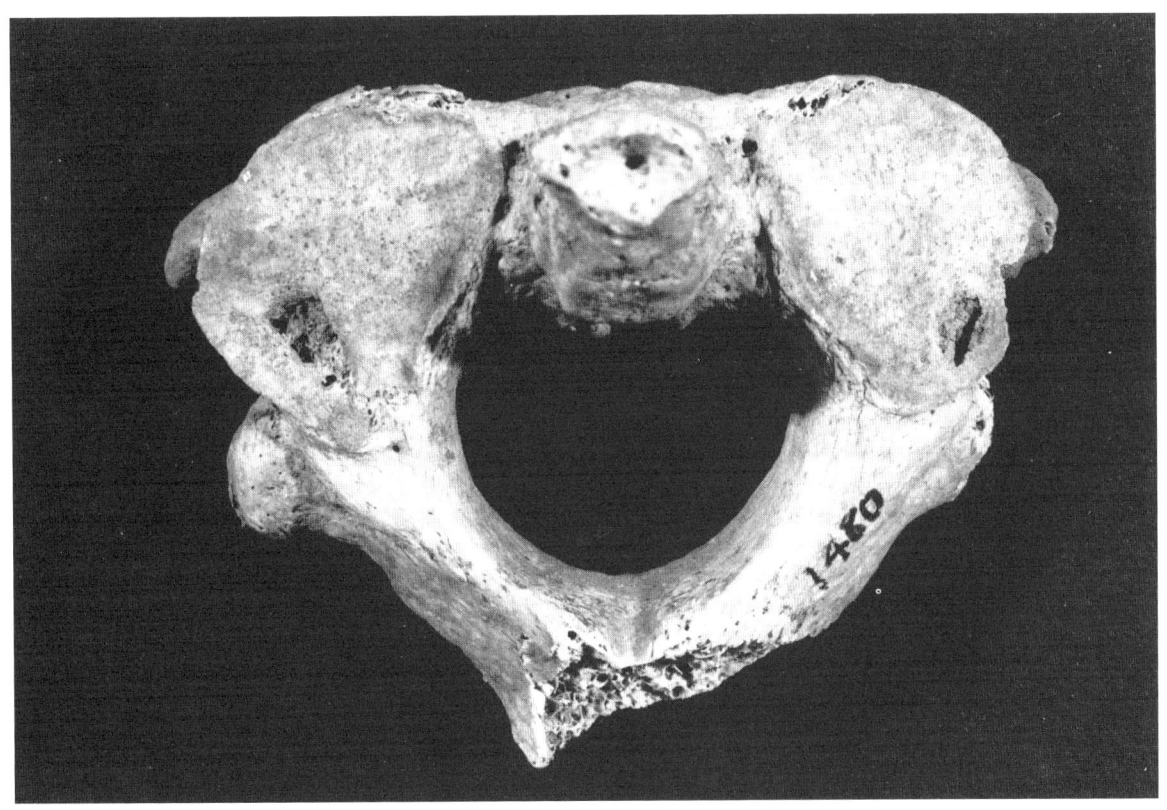

11.16 Example of defect of CV1.

	M/?M	F/?F	UK	IM	Total
	n	n	n	n	n
Joint surface					
Scapula: glenoid	5	1	3	–	9
Humerus: capitulum	1	–	–	1	2
Ulna: olecranon	1	–	–	1	2
Scaphoid	2	–	–	–	2
Finger	2	–	–	–	2
Patella	1	–	–	–	1
Fibula: proximal	1	–	–	–	1
Fibula: distal facet	–	1	–	–	1
Tibia: distal facet	6	4	2	1	13
Talus: tibial facet	2	2	1	–	5
Talus: posterior calcaneus facet	8	1	–	1	10
Talus: mid calcaneus facet	–	–	2	–	2
Talus: navicular facet	1	–	–	–	1
Calcaneus: posterior talus facet	3	1	2	–	6
Calcaneus: mid talus facet	–	–	1	–	1
Calcaneus: anterior talus facet	–	1	–	–	1
MT base (MT2 and 3)	3	–	–	–	3
Toe (other than great toe)	1	–	–	1	2

Table 11.18: Number of examples of defects in articular surfaces.

M = male; ?M = possible male; F = female; ?F = possible female; UK = unsexed; IM = immature.

differences were not statistically significant, and accurate frequencies were not available for many joints. A developmental aetiology cannot be excluded although none of the defects follow lines of fusion. Comparisons between sites showed similar frequencies for the 'big toe' in all sites, but much lower frequencies for other lesions at Logies Lane. The sample sizes were too small for meaningful statistical analysis. Other, larger comparative samples are needed to elucidate these features.

4.1.10. Degenerative joint disease (DJD)

Degenerative change at the joints (osteoarthritis) is the most common pathology seen in most skeletal collections. DJD is incompletely understood but is probably best explained by a multifactorial model in which age, trauma, endocrine agents, heredity, sex and diet all play a role (Jurmain 1977).

Two main types of DJD are usually distinguished: primary osteoarthritis where the changes appear to reflect skeletal ageing, and secondary osteoarthritis when the changes reflect an alteration of the joint mechanics as when a fracture heals out of alignment. Primary DJD is often generalised whereas secondary DJD is usually limited to one joint. Primary DJD was used to 'age' adults in the present sample.

It is difficult to give an accurate account of the frequency of DJD because of the fragmentary nature of much of the material. Frequencies of joints affected as a proportion of the number at risk are therefore not given although the relative amounts of DJD in different areas is examined. The frequency of DJD in fingers and toes will inevitably be under-reported as these small bones are often lost during excavation.

Degenerative changes were most common in the

spine. The thoracic and lumbar facet joints were affected almost equally with less DJD in the cervical region (but see 'eburnation' below). Of the margins and surfaces of the vertebral bodies, the cervical region was most affected followed by the lumbar, thoracic and sacral regions. The articulation of the ribs with the transverse process of the thoracic vertebrae was among the sites of most frequent degenerative change, and appeared to be one of the earliest areas affected.

Of the appendicular joints, the knee was affected most often (149 individuals), followed by the hip (140 individuals), the shoulder (75 individuals), the wrist (67 individuals), the elbow (64 individuals) and the toes (44 individuals). Other joints were affected less frequently.

Degenerative change was judged to be secondary in fifteen individuals although there were probably examples which remain unidentified. In a minority of cases the causal factor could be determined, such as the severe, localised DJD of the wrist consequent upon fracture and slight misalignment of the radial diaphysis in the middle-aged male SK 657.

Eburnation develops when the articular cartilage is completely eroded and bone rubs on bone, affected areas becoming dense and polished. It is diagnostic of severe DJD and was noted on 87 individuals. The distribution of eburnation did not closely match that of less severe DJD. Most was seen in the spine, but the cervical facet joints – which were the least affected by less severe DJD – had more eburnation than any other region (25 individuals; 14 each in the thoracic and lumbar regions). The hip was affected next most often (10 individuals) followed by the wrist (8 individuals), the distal metatarsals (8 individuals) and other joints. Men and women displayed eburnation in different areas. Eight males but no females had eburnation of the hip, but more women had DJD in the cervical region of the spine and in the phalanges of the hands perhaps indicating preferential use of these regions by women.

Unusual small, raised, compact deposits, some of which were eburnated were noted on the articular surfaces of the fingers of SK 1164 (middle-aged female).

Sero-negative arthropathies such as rheumatoid arthritis have a different aetiology and are discussed in section 4.4 below.

4.1.11. Periosteal new bone development (PNBD)

Direct trauma, infection or venous stasis (e.g. varicose veins) may cause inflammation of the periosteal membrane which covers the non-articular surfaces of all bones, stimulating the membrane to produce new bone over the original bone surface. The new bone is largely separate from the old cortex initially – appearing flaky in the dry state – but with time usually becomes remodelled and incorporated into the old cortex.

As with other skeletal collections the tibia and/or the fibula were the most frequent sites of PNBD and 63% (94/150) of all cases involved these bones. The medial surface of the tibia has very little subcutaneous protection making it vulnerable to traumatic injury. The involvement of each tibial surface was recorded for all individuals with tibial periostitis. Slightly more periostitis was noted on the medial surface (71%) than on the lateral (66%) or posterior (37%) surfaces indicating trauma in at least some cases. Some diseases, however (e.g. syphilis), preferentially deposit periosteal new bone on the cooler bone surfaces such as the medial and lateral tibial surfaces. PNBD is discussed in more detail in section 4.2.1 below.

4.2. Infection

4.2.1. Periosteal new bone development (PNBD)

Infection is indicated if the bone(s) displaying PNBD are well protected by subcutaneous tissues, or if the involvement is extensive. Specific infections known to cause PNBD include typhoid fever, tuberculosis, syphilis, leprosy and hypertrophic pulmonary osteoarthropathy (such as bronchial carcinoma, bronchiectasis and metastatic tumours of the lungs) although the lesions themselves are unfortunately rarely diagnostic of a particular condition.

Evidence of PNBD was noted in 150 individuals. The lower limb was affected in 79% (118) of cases, 63% (94) involving the tibia and/or the fibula, 19% (28) the femur, fourteen of these involving both the femur and the lower leg. 11% of adults with at least one complete tibia had PNBD of that bone. The upper limb was involved in 13% (19) of all cases, eleven of these also involving the lower limb.

Frequencies of long-bone PNBD were calculated using bones that were largely complete, and the results are presented for adults and immatures in Tables 11.19 and 11.20 respectively. As expected the highest frequency was seen on the adult tibia. Both sexes had more deposits on the left than the right tibia and males had more deposits overall than females although none of the differences reached statistical significance. The frequencies of tibial periostitis by side and by sex are given in Table 11.21. Immatures were affected less often than adults in all bones.

Similar frequencies of affected tibiae were quoted in the little comparative data available. Mays (1991) reports a frequency of 13.2% in adults with one or both tibiae present, and Wells (1982) estimates that between 10% and 12% of Cirencester tibiae were affected. Other studies also find much less PNBD in the upper than the lower limb.

The visceral surface of the rib (the surface in contact with the internal organs) was affected in 14% (21) of all cases of PNBD, in combination with other bones in two individuals (SK 734, a late-middle-aged

	Left		Right	
Clavicle	0.9%	(1/105)	2.2%	(2/92)
Humerus	0.7%	(1/148)	2.8%	(4/141)
Radius	–	(0/121)	1.9%	(2/103)
Ulna	–	(0/106)	–	(0/82)
Femur	4.0%	(11/272)	3.4%	(9/264)
Tibia	12.4%	(26/210)	10.7%	(21/196)
Fibula	8.5%	(7/82)	4.3%	(3/70)

Table 11.19: Frequency of PNBD in adults.

	Left		Right	
Clavicle	–	(0/36)	–	(0/26)
Humerus	1.5%	(1/68)	–	(0/71)
Radius	–	(0/26)	–	(0/36)
Ulna	–	(0/25)	–	(0/31)
Femur	5.0%	(5/99)	4.1%	(5/98)
Tibia	8.4%	(7/83)	2.5%	(2/81)
Fibula	–	(0/38)	3.1%	(1/32)

Table 11.20: Frequency of PNBD in immatures.

	Left		Right	
	n	%	n	%
Male	11/68	16.1	7/56	12.5
Female	10/74	13.5	7/75	9.3

Table 11.21: Frequency of PNBD in the tibia by side and sex.

female with deposits on the posterior aspect of the shaft of the left femur and SK 450, an old juvenile with deposits on the external surface of the right ilium, porosity of the posterior aspect of the mid thoracic vertebral arches and apparent PNBD at the margins of the vertebral facet joints). Deposits on the visceral surface of the ribs may indicate lung infection such as pneumonia or tuberculosis, although the present evidence is insufficient for such a diagnosis.

Fine periosteal deposits were noted on the internal surface of the calvarium in four individuals, one male (SK 632), one subadult female (SK 244), one adult of unknown sex (SK 1366) and one child aged three to four years (SK 78). The deposits occurred predominantly in and around the Pacchionian depressions of the frontal and parietal bones although the occipital bone was also affected in SK 78. The patchy endocranial deposits of SK 244 were accompanied by greyish, partially healed deposits over most of the external surface of the frontal bone. SK 632 also had periosteal deposits of the humeri, tibiae and fibulae, and a well-healed fracture of the right femur. The aetiology of endocranial deposits is unclear although they are known to occur in meningitis, congenital syphilis and scurvy. They probably also occur in other conditions which are as yet unknown. Healed periosteal deposits were noted on the endocranium of a skeleton thought to be a pituitary dwarf (Roberts 1987).

Four crania had small, compact but prominent endocranial deposits on the frontal bone close to the frontal crest. The aetiology of these deposits is unknown and the pathologists and radiologists consulted considered them to be of no clinical significance. The individuals affected were adult males and females with no common pathological complex (SKs 636, 646, 784, 985). Four individuals had vertebral deposits:

SK 450 (old juvenile) – Deposits at the margins of the thoracic facet joints (described above);

SK 468 (old juvenile) – Deposits of the anterior and anterolateral aspects of LV3 and LV5;

SK 1364 (middle aged ?female) – Unusual deposits on the articular surface of at least three facet joints of the lumbar spine;

SK 1019 (young adult female) – Unusual compact, striated and nodular periosteal deposits on the anterior aspect of CV1 and CV2 (Figure 11.17). The remaining cervical vertebrae show slight bony build-up on the anterior aspect of the bodies. In addition there was PNBD of the proximal fibulae (tibiae unaffected) and there was an unusual degree of dental pathology in an individual of this age (6/18 teeth carious, 7/18 or 10/21 teeth lost ante-mortem [depending on assessment of third molars as congenitally absent or lost ante-mortem]).

The mandible was affected with PNBD in four cases, one of which was associated with dental abscesses from which the infection may have spread, and another with extensive post-cranial periosteal deposits. The ilium was affected in five individuals, in combination with other bones in four of these. The anterior aspect of the sacrum was affected in three individuals, being especially severe and sclerotic in SK 678 (section 4.4.2 below), and in combination with slight, healed PNBD of the lower limb, expansion of the bone of the left patella and nodular, porous, sclerotic bone of the anterior surface of the pubic bones in SK 906 (early middle-aged female). The calcaneus was affected in five individuals, two associated with deposits of the upper and lower limb, and one with deposits of the lower limb only.

Generalised periosteal deposits were noted on 26 skeletons. One of these, a gracile subadult male (SK 1162) also displayed an unusual lesion which perforated the left zygoma (cheek bone). The perforation measured 10 mm in diameter, the external surface being porous and reactive for several millimetres around this. The aetiology of the lesion and its relationship to the post-cranial PNBD remains unclear after consultation with clinicians.

Interpretation of the frequency and distribution of PNBD is difficult. Systemic infection is implicated in those with generalised deposits and probably many other cases. Although some tibial deposits appeared to be of the type seen in syphilis there was insufficient evidence for this diagnosis to be considered reliable. A specific diagnosis could not be made in any case.

4.2.2. Osteomyelitis

Osteomyelitis is an infection of the bone marrow, the bone tissue itself and the periosteum, usually by a pus-producing organism. The organism may be introduced directly into the bone via an

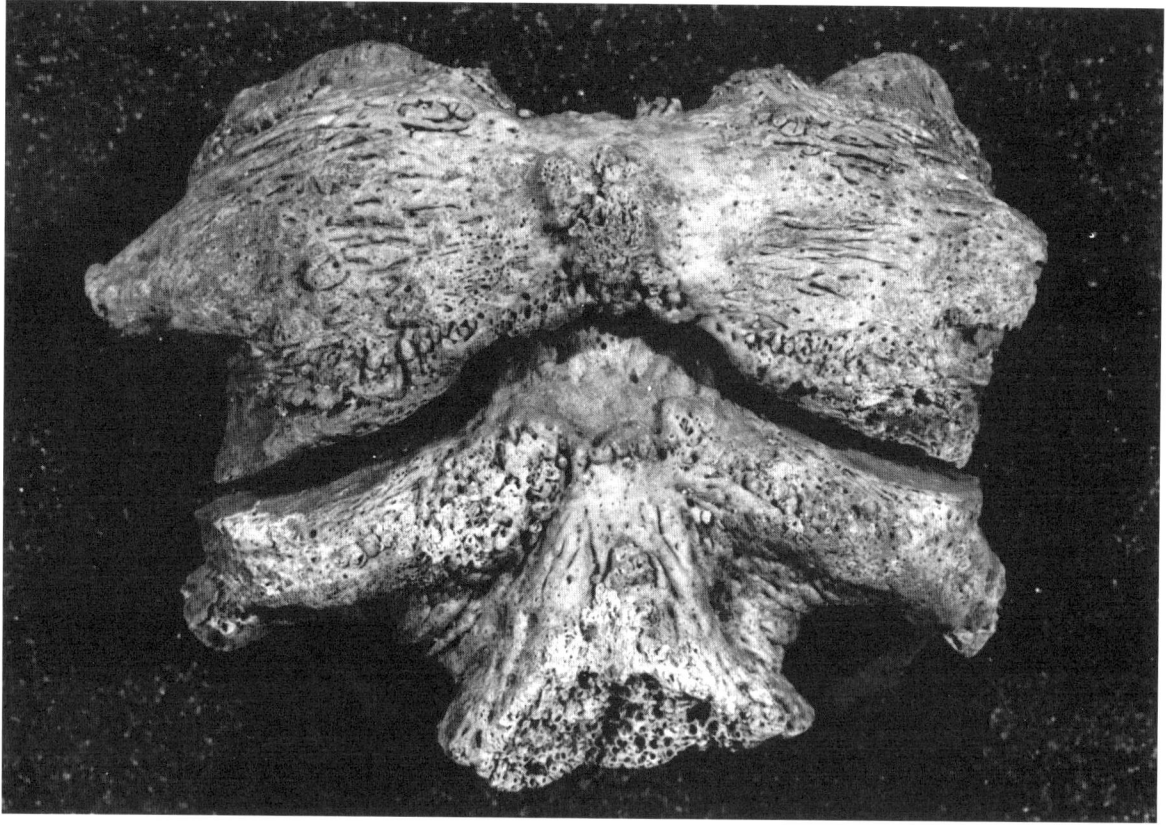

11.17 New bone on anterior aspect of CV1 and CV2 (SK 1019).

overlying wound such as a compound fracture or via the blood stream from a distant focus of infection. The condition may continue for many years with suppurating wound and occasional flare-ups. A 'jacket' of new bone, the involucrum, may form around the old bone, which may be perforated by multiple cloacae (openings) allowing pus to escape from the medula of the bone. If the infection enters the joint (as in pyogenic arthritis) the articular cartilage is destroyed and bony ankylosis (fusion) may occur. Chronic osteomyelitis is unusual in the modern antibiotic era, but once established, is extremely difficult to treat and may lead to amputation of the limb. A possible complication of osteomyelitis (and indeed any infection, including a tooth abscess) is septicaemia which can rapidly lead to death.

There were sixteen individuals with osteomyelitis or possible osteomyelitis in the present sample, eight male/?male, two female/?female, five adults of indeterminate sex and one old juvenile. The lower limb was involved most often (14 cases: the tibia in seven, the femur in six and the fibula in five) with one example in the upper limb and one example in the cranium (Figure 11.11). Pyogenic arthritis with bony ankylosis was indicated in two individuals, the tibia and talus being involved in SK 655 and the tibia, talus and calcaneum in SK 564. The joint appears to have been involved but without bony ankylosis in SK 1494 (humerus and ulna) and in SK 901 and SK 633, both of which have tibiae with large openings in the distal facet.

The present sample differs from the expected pattern in several respects. There were no obvious examples of fractures via which the infective organism may have entered and no evidence of an involucrum. There were no examples in children which is the age group most vulnerable today. It may have been that in the past children succumbed to serious infection rapidly and before overt bony involvement, or that affected bones were especially fragile and subject to severe post-mortem deterioration and therefore not available for analysis.

Individual examples of osteomyelitis with age and sex are listed in Appendix 3.

4.2.3. Disuse atrophy/asymmetry

Bones require appropriate mechanical loading to develop properly and to maintain their shape and strength. Disuse leads to atrophy, deformity and osteoporosis and may be the consequence of many factors including nerve damage through trauma, and infection by agents such as the polio virus. The polio virus type 1 organism causes paralysis in approximately 1% of those infected and has been a major problem throughout history, usually afflicting juveniles.

A number of individuals in this series had evidence of atrophy. These are described below.

SK 661 (young adult female) was interred with the knees flexed upwards, such that the knees were uncovered first on excavation. Her upper body, although gracile (vertical humeral head diameter 40 mm) was normal, whilst her spine showed some scoliosis and the innominates and lower limbs were gracile, distorted and underdeveloped. The ilia were 'flat' with a very wide sciatic notch and shallow acetabulae. The borders and muscle markings of the lower limb were undefined, the right side being somewhat more gracile than the left. The femoral heads were very small (approx. 35 mm) but of normal shape and neck angle, although there was anteversion of the neck and anterior bowing of the diaphyses. The lesser trochanter (which provides attachment for the ilio-psoas muscle which flexes the thigh on the trunk) was very pronounced. The tibial plateaux which are usually slightly concave, were convex and the intercondylar eminences were ill-defined. Whilst the thoracic and lumbar vertebrae were slightly compressed laterally, the main feature of the vertebral bodies was the 'wavy', uneven surface from side to side, and 'tall' lumbar vertebrae. The spine had a double curve allowing the head to be retained in the mid-line. Calculation of stature from the lower limb (left fibula) was 146 cm, 19 cm less than from the upper limb (left radius) indicating onset of disuse before growth was complete. The scoliosis may be a consequence of the paralysis. A possible scenario is of polio infection in childhood, leading to paralysis of the lower limb and scoliosis of the spine.

SK 630 (early middle-aged male) was one of three in the medieval cemetery to be buried face-down. The impression in the ground was of a very robust upper body and especially broad shoulders. As with SK 661 the pathology involved distorted innominates, unequal disuse atrophy of the lower limb and slight spinal scoliosis. The femora displayed an obtuse neck angle, horizontal epiphyses and slightly mushroom-shaped heads (the acetabulae were unfortunately very damaged). The lesser trochanter was very prominent. The femoral shafts were narrow from side to side and wide from front to back and the linea aspera appeared as only one lip through most of its length. The tibiae were less distorted and most of the normal contours and borders were retained. All thoracic vertebrae below TV5 displayed Schmorl's nodes and slight compression of the right side. Estimation of stature from the upper limb (right humerus) was 176 cm, 8 cm greater than from the lower limb (left femur, the longer of the two), indicating onset of disuse before growth was complete. There was unusual, symmetrical build-up of compact bone on the medial aspect of both first metacarpals, a feature not noted on any other skeleton, suggesting a form of behaviour – perhaps locomotion with crutches – causing pressure on this area of the hand. The robusticity of the upper body indicated that this individual was very physically active and strong. A scenario similar to that of SK 661 could be envisaged, although this individual retained more use of the lower limb and developed a very strong upper limb.

The right lower limb of SK 1336 (subadult male) was flexed over the left on excavation. Inequality of size and shape of the lower limb was noted, the right femur being shorter and more platymeric than the left. Unfortunately the skeleton was in poor condition and a more detailed assessment could not be made.

The lower limb of SK 53 (early middle-aged female) was flexed on the right side of the body on excavation. Only one femur was present and this was very small in relation to the rest of the skeleton. The tibia was very eroded but appeared to be cylindrical rather than 'triangular' in shape indicating that the bone was not subject to normal stresses. Again the poor condition precludes further analysis.

The right foot of SK 636 (middle-aged ?female) was distorted. The calcaneus and talus were most severely affected and were approximately 30% smaller than their left counterparts. The navicular facet of the talus was twisted medially and inferiorly. When the foot was articulated the talus was twisted laterally by 90°. The right tibia was gracile with relatively undefined borders, suggesting some disuse of the affected limb. This may be an example of club foot.

SK 622 (middle-aged female) displayed slight asymmetry of the appendicular skeleton. The left upper limb was up to 20% smaller than the right, whilst the difference was less than 10% in the lower limb. A generalised condition was manifest as increased porosity and lumpy, uneven areas which resembled gentle thumb prints in the bone. There were also two depressions of unknown aetiology on the frontal bone (section 4.1.2) and much ante-mortem molar loss.

The mandible of SK 1425 (late-middle-aged female) displayed pronounced asymmetry of the rami, the right ramus being abnormally gracile, and ascending at a more acute angle than the left side. Both rami were damaged post-mortem and both condlyes were missing. The cranium was fragmentary but showed no gross abnormality on reconstruction. The right glenoid fossa (for articulation with the jaw) was damaged but appeared to be flat and roughened.

4.2.4. Tuberculosis

Tuberculosis is one of the few specific diseases which can be identified from the bones. Between 5% and 7% of those contracting the disease develop bony changes, and of those 25% to 50% show the spinal features from which the disease is usually diagnosed (Steinbock 1976). This 'Potts spine' is characterised by destruction and collapse of the anterior part of the bodies leading to kyphotic fusion (angulation giving the appearance of a hunched back), usually in the lower thoracic and/or lumbar region. One quarter of those with vertebral tuberculosis will develop paraplegia (Anderson, 1985, 9.3). Other large joints may be affected although the changes may be indistinguishable from septic arthritis and other severe joint conditions. The pulmonary form of tuberculosis may also cause deposition of new bone on the visceral surface of the ribs (section 4.2.1).

Bony evidence of tuberculosis in the present sample is sparse and unclear, contrasting with the material from **Period I** (pp 588-9). The thoracic and lumbar spine of SK 662 (middle-aged female) displayed severe DJD with bony ankylosis between TV4 and TV5, TV8 and TV9, TV12 to LV3, and between LV4 and LV5 (the vertebral bodies between TV10 and LV5 were missing, and fusion in these regions was seen in the arches). A large, entirely lytic lesion was present in the anterior aspect of the bodies between TV4 and TV5, and there was kyphosis with an angle of approximately 120° between TV12 and LV1. The right ilium displayed a circumscribed lytic lesion on the auricular surface and there was slight periosteal new bone formation on the external iliac blade. A possible explanation is severe spinal DJD superimposed upon tuberculous infection. Degenerative changes of this degree are unusual in an individual of this age.

Other possible examples of tuberculosis include the severe destruction of the elbow in SK 524, the fusion of the patella to the distal femur in SK 1373, the 'scooped' out vertebrae of SK 954 (who may also have leprosy, see below), and the gross destruction of the hip in SK 1459 (Figures 11.18 and 19), in whom differential diagnoses include septic arthritis, and hip dislocation.

4.2.5. Syphilis

Syphilis belongs to a group of infections caused by the treponemal spirachaete. Other diseases in the group are pinta and yaws (prevalent in tropical areas), non-venereal/endemic syphilis (prevalent in warm, arid areas) and venereal syphilis (no geographic boundaries but not found where another form predominates). Bone changes may occur in the latter three conditions, although only endemic and venereal syphilis are of relevance in Britain.

History records an epidemic of a new disease – syphilis – throughout Europe around 1500 AD, shortly after the return of Columbus from the Americas. This has prompted some workers to propose a New World origin for the disease. A growing body of evidence, however, suggests that syphilis was present in Europe prior to 1500 AD but that it had not been recognised as a disease as distinct from leprosy (Steinbock 1976 and an increasing number of British and Irish skeletal examples).

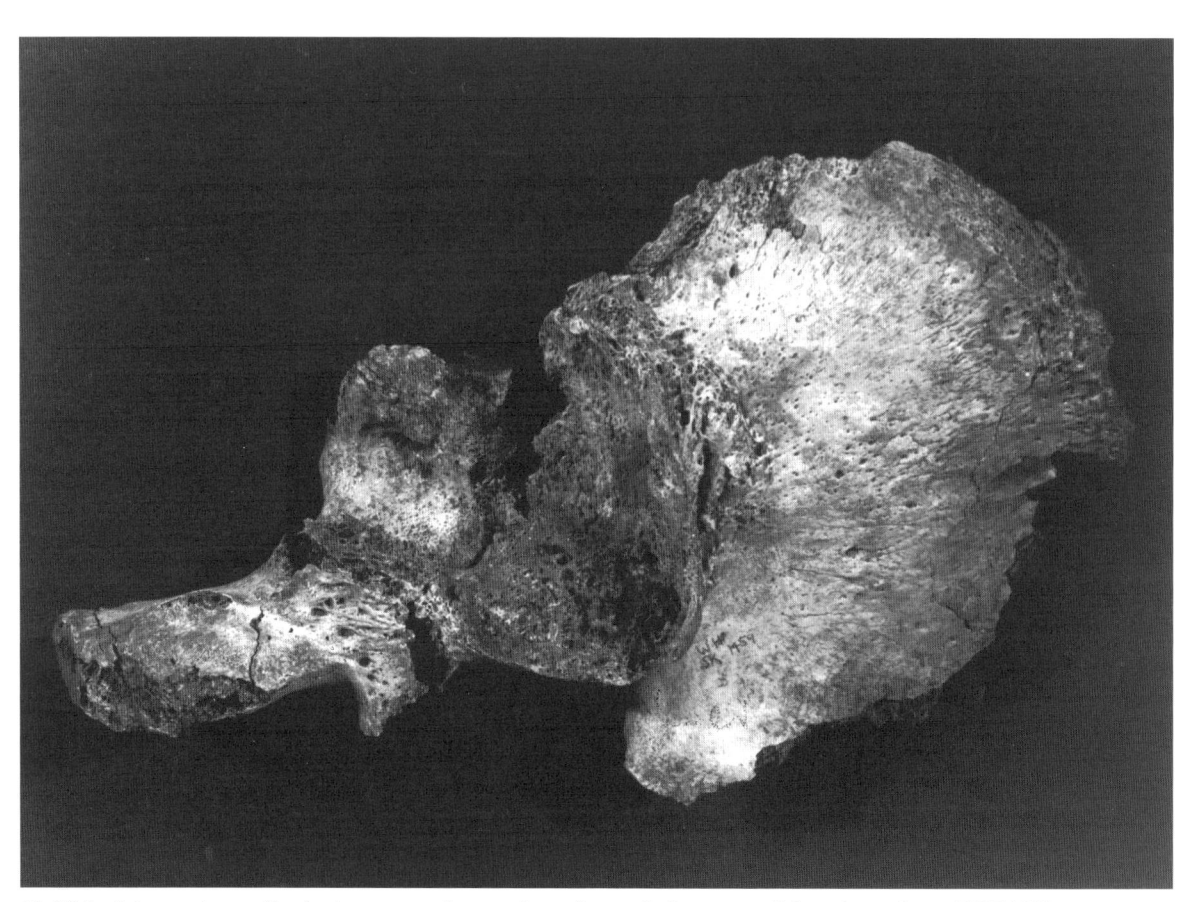

11.18 Left innominate displaying gross destruction of acetabulum, possibly tuberculous (SK1459).

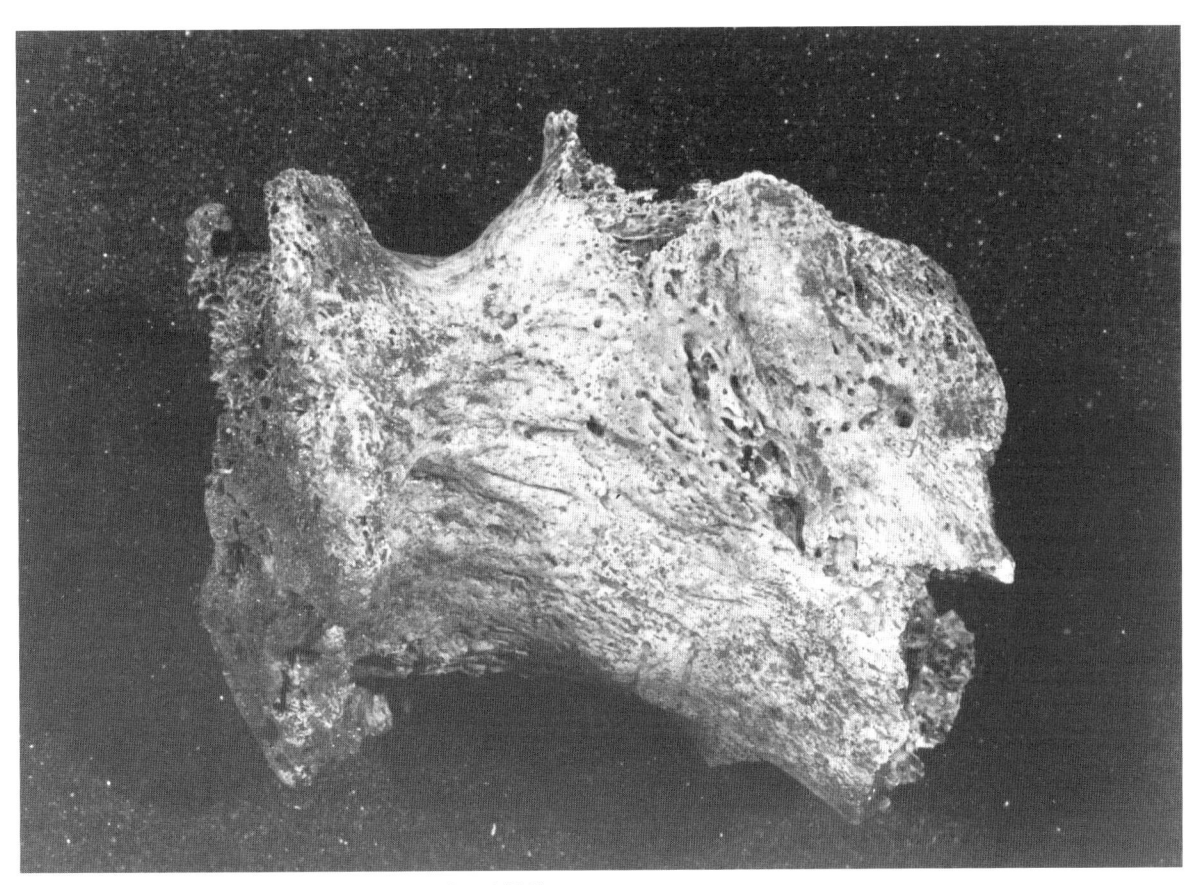

11.19 Left femoral head, anterior view (SK 1459).

The bony changes of the tertiary (third and final) stage of syphilis are often non-specific, including both localised and generalised periostitis (especially of the tibia) and osteomyelitis. More characteristic changes occur on the cranium where a combination of bone destruction and new bone formation create a typical 'worm-eaten' appearance known as caries sicca. Caries sicca is usually regarded as diagnostic of acquired syphilis.

There were many examples of periostitis in the collection (section 4.2.1), some of which could have been caused by treponemal infection, but none of which was diagnostic of the condition. The cranium of a young adult female with typical caries sicca came to light by chance from amongst the disarticulated material indicating the presence of pre-Columbian syphilis at Whithorn (Figure 11.20, p 598). In addition, two 'mulberry molars' generally associated with congenital syphilis were noted in the disarticulated dental material (p 592), providing further evidence for the presence of treponemal infection in the Whithorn population.

4.2.6. Leprosy

Leprosy was very common in Europe around the time of the Crusades (1096–1221) but began to decline at the beginning of the Renaissance, possibly due to improved living conditions. Approximately 1% of a population may be infected with *Mycobacterium leprae* where leprosy is endemic, and of those approximately 15% will show skeletal changes (Steinbock 1976). Unfortunately the bones most often affected (the small bones of the hands and feet and the nasal area) survive relatively poorly in archaeological material, and skeletal evidence of leprosy may therefore be scarce even in populations in which the disease was common.

One possible example of leprosy was noted in the present group. SK 954 (early middle-aged female) displayed a resorbed proximal phalanx of the great toe, typical of the condition. One other foot phalanx was recovered and this displayed slight resorptive changes at the distal end. No metatarsals were recovered and the hands were normal. The inferior surface of the left calcaneum was flat, the tuberosities almost entirely lacking, which may indicate nerve involvement. There was severe PNBD with osteitis (expansion of the bone tissue itself) of the distal tibiae and fibulae which may be associated with leprosy. Two vertebrae displayed 'scooped out' lesions which may be attributable to tuberculosis although it is not certain if the lesions are ante-mortem or post-mortem. If post-mortem, the erosion is unique in the late medieval collection (but see SK 1630, p 554). Tuberculosis and leprosy are closely related, and tuberculosis may develop in the leprous patient whose immune system is compromised. Unfortunately the cranium of this individual was not recovered.

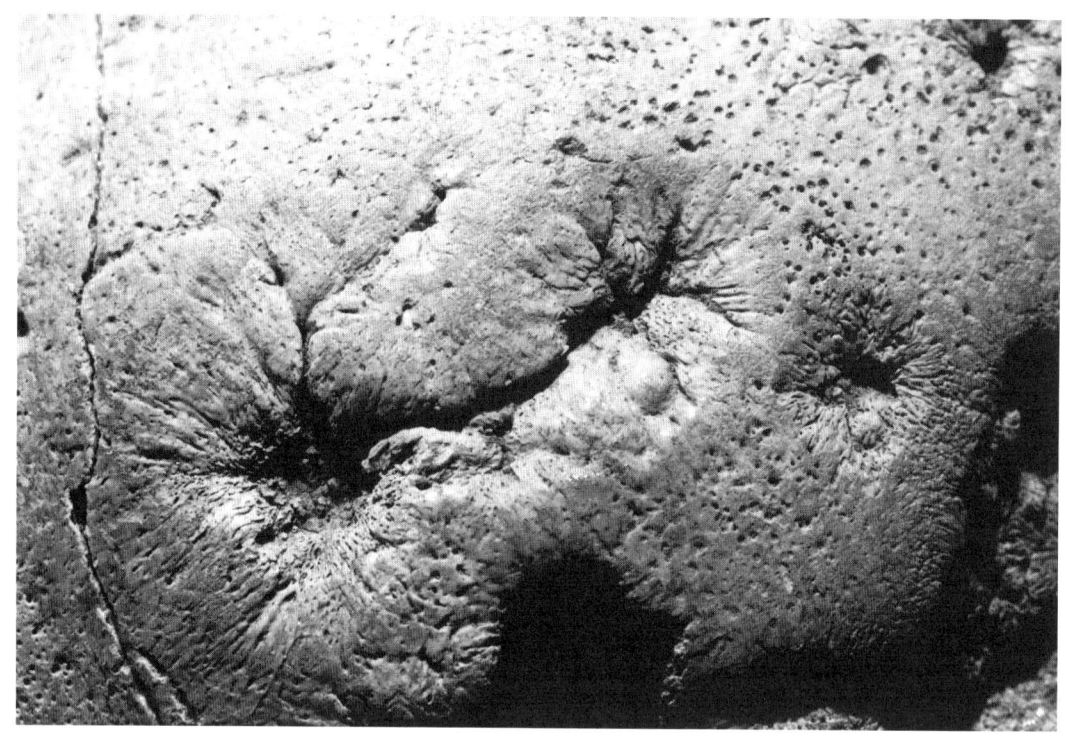

11.20 Disarticulated cranium displaying lesions consistent with treponemal infection.

4.2.7. Miscellaneous

Some individuals displayed conditions which appeared to be of an infectious/inflammatory nature although no specific diagnosis could be made:

SK 523 (middle-aged male): acute inflammatory condition of the articular surfaces of the base of the third, fourth and fifth metacarpals of the right hand. The carpals were not recovered.

SK 906 (early middle-aged female): displayed a pathological complex including a 'stone-like', greenish appearance of the first and second cervical vertebrae, and of the left laminae of CV3 and CV4; ossification of the ligamentum flava of the middle and lower thoracic spine; sclerotic new bone on the anterior surface of the sacrum and slight deposits on the anterior surface of LV5; evidence of inflammation on the anterior aspect of both pubic bones; slight, healed, symmetrical PNBD of the femora, tibiae and fibulae; expansion and porosity of the anterior surface of the left patella; and two healed rib fractures.

SK 1070 (middle-aged female): displayed severe erosion of the base of both second metatarsals. The erosion extended for a short distance onto the shaft. The phalanges were extremely slender, possibly indicating disuse atrophy as a consequence of the inflammatory condition.

SK 1401 (late-middle-aged male): displayed PNBD of the lower limb and mandible, with more subtle changes to the upper limb including slight porous swellings and remodelled areas. The bones were heavy. Three left ribs had healed fractures.

4.2.8. Conclusions

Despite ample evidence of infection in this sample, the causal organism could rarely be identified. There was no unequivocal evidence of tuberculosis although lung infection of some kind is implicated in cases of rib periostitis. Treponemal infection was positively identified in one disarticulated calvarium and may have caused some of the tibial or generalised periostitis, although no evidence of congenital syphilis was found. Typhoid fever, a disease associated with poor hygiene, may cause PNBD by haematogenous spread months or years after infection and may thus account for some examples of PNBD. One probable example of leprosy was identified.

4.3. Metabolic disease

4.3.1. Nutritional deficiency

Few vitamin deficiencies leave evidence on the bones. Those which may do so include deficiencies of Vitamin D and C.

Vitamin D is needed for the adequate mineralisation of bone. Deficiency causes the condition known as rickets in children and osteomalacia in adults. The deficiency may be caused by lack of exposure to sunlight (in the presence of which the body synthesises its own vitamin D), dietary deficiency (not enough meat/green leafy vegetables) and/or malabsorption in the gut. Skeletal manifestations of rickets include bowing of the weight-bearing bones (lower limb if the child is walking, upper limb also if the child is crawling); reduction of the femoral neck angle (coxa vara), enlargement and 'cupping' of the ends of the long bones; thinning and 'bossing' of the cranium; and defects in the tooth enamel. Rickets may be combined with other conditions such as scurvy, and evidence of one may confuse evidence of the other. Severe osteomalacia causes 'softening' and bending of weight-bearing bones sometimes with 'buckling' of the pubic rami (at the front of the pelvis) causing narrowing of the pelvic canal and difficulty at parturition. Pseudo fractures known as Looser's zones may be evident radiographically. The condition is most common today in immigrant women living in purdah in countries with low levels of sunlight, who have a poor diet and frequent pregnancies and lactations.

There was no unequivocal evidence of rickets, and none of osteomalacia in the present sample. Rickets is not commonly encountered in archaeological populations, and is not well documented until the increase in industrialisation in the eighteenth and nineteenth centuries. The most convincing case was seen in a four-year-old child (SK 6) who displayed slight antero-lateral bowing of the tibiae and femora; coxa vara; a femoral shaft which was wide from front–back and narrow from side–side with a generally 'squat' appearance; and ante-mortem loss of the deciduous lower incisors. The 'rosary ribs' and cranial bossing usually associated with rickets were absent. Other possible diagnoses include congenital syphilis, although the dental stigmata which may accompany this condition were absent. A number of other skeletons had slightly bowed lower limbs and these are listed in Appendix 4.

Vitamin C deficiency impairs the synthesis of collagen. This has a number of effects including poor healing of wounds and weakening of the capillaries which may cause sub-periosteal haemorrhage. Skeletal evidence is difficult to interpret and includes ossification of sub-periosteal haemorrhages. No clear evidence of scurvy was found although some examples of patchy, localised periostitis may have been caused by this condition.

Iron deficiency anaemia is discussed in section 4.5.1 below.

4.3.2. Osteoporosis

Osteoporosis is caused by an imbalance of bone resorption and bone production, and results in bones of decreased density which are fragile and liable to fracture with minimal trauma. The condition may be associated with disease (e.g. Cushing's syndrome), medical treatment (e.g. long-term steroid therapy), old age (senile osteoporosis), or other unknown factors (idiopathic osteoporosis). Most osteoporosis in archaeological groups is probably of the senile form when the changes are associated with decreases in particular hormone levels. These changes occur rapidly in women after the menopause, but much more gradually in men. Osteoporosis is seen most often in women after the fifth decade and in men after the age of seventy (Roberts and Wakely 1992). Osteoporotic bones tend to fracture in areas of rapid turnover such as the vertebral bodies and the femoral neck. Vertebrae may also become dished and compressed, causing a decrease in stature and dorsal kyphosis (the 'dowagers hump') sometimes seen in elderly women. Femoral neck fractures tend to occur approximately 15 years later than vertebral fractures (Revell 1986, 186, quoted in Miles 1989, 60), and are difficult to heal. Thirty percent of beds in modern orthopaedic wards are occupied by those with fractures associated with osteoporosis (National Osteoporosis Society 1993).

Evidence of osteoporosis was noted in at least 38 skeletons, usually evidenced in light, fragile bones, especially the vertebrae. Compression fractures, compression without fracture and/or dishing of the vertebral bodies was present in 45 individuals, although not all cases appeared to be the consequence of osteoporosis. Only one femoral neck fracture was noted in the entire collection (0.13% [1/773] of adult femoral necks) reinforcing the impression that few individuals reached advanced age although such fractures would not be identifiable if they were repaidly followed by death.

4.4. Sero-negative arthropathies

4.4.1. Rheumatoid arthritis

It is often suggested that rheumatoid arthritis has a recent origin as it is so common today (affecting approximately 3% of females and 1% of males in temperate climates: Anderson 1985), but is rarely reported in archaeological collections. This apparent difference may be a consequence of the nature of the disease as typical rheumatoid lesions are entirely erosive and may be indistinguishable from post-mortem changes if the bones are in less than perfect condition. Rheumatoid changes may be difficult or impossible to distinguish from artefact even in recently defleshed bones (Rothschild *et al.* 1990). As many rheumatoid individuals also develop osteoporosis; their bony remains are especially fragile and liable to post-mortem disintegration.

Rheumatoid arthritis was not noted in the group. Fused digits were seen in 22 individuals, six in the hand and most of the remainder being the little toe. Fusion of digits may occur in rheumatoid individuals, but it may also be a consequence of severe osteoarthritis or trauma. In no case was there further evidence to suggest rheumatoid arthritis as the causal factor in these individuals.

4.4.2. Other sero-negative arthropathies

Other sero-negative arthropathies such as ankylosing spondylitis, psoriatic arthritis and Reiters syndrome may leave evidence on the bones. Diffuse idiopathic skeletal hyperostosis (DISH) is included here as the

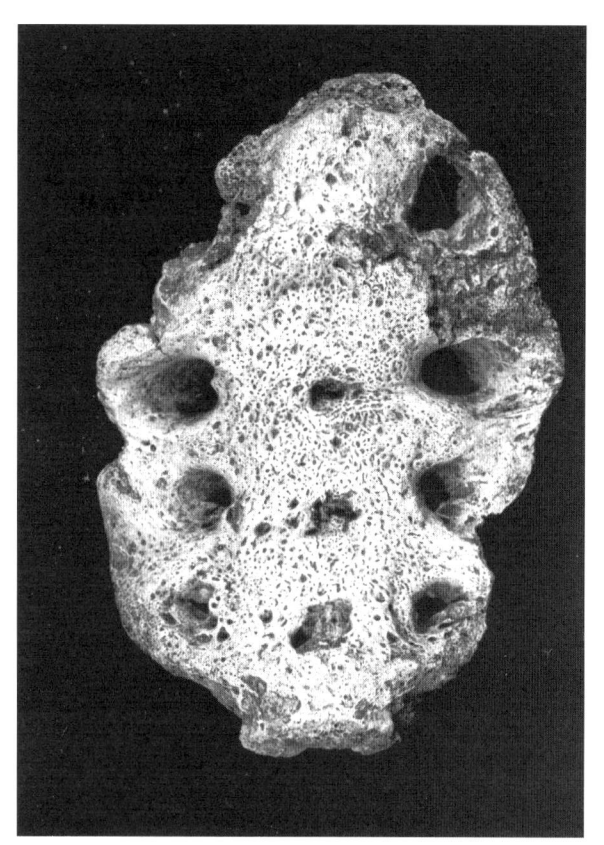

11.21 Anterior aspect of sacrum displaying deposits of sclerotic new bone (SK 678).

syndrome is very similar to ankylosing spondylitis, although the precise aetiology is unknown. The common features of this group of disorders are fusion of the spine, often with involvement of the sacro-iliac joints, development of enthesopathies around the pelvis and the heel, and a tendency for males to be affected more often than women.

Three individuals had fusion of some spinal elements which could be attributable to a sero-negative arthropathy, although all affected spines were incomplete. All were male, one also displaying multiple enthesopathies which may indicate ankylosing spondylitis or DISH. However, this individual also displayed evidence of traumatic stress in the form of a fractured fibula and severe DJD, and strenuous activity may thus be implicated in development of the lesions. The anterior aspect of the sacrum of SK 678 (Figure 11.21) was covered with deposits of thick, woven new bone with a sclerotic appearance which may indicate a sero-negative arthropathy such as Forrestier's spine although the rest of the spine of this individual was normal.

The scant evidence of DISH in the present population contrasts with the high frequency found by Mays in the Ipswich Blackfriars. It has been suggested that DISH may be associated with obesity (Julkunen et al. 1971, in Mays 1991) which may have been a problem for medieval monks, but apparently not for the people of medieval Whithorn.

No unequivocal evidence of sero-negative arthropathy was found in the present group. Detection of these conditions, and of rheumatoid arthritis in particular, was hampered by the condition of the remains.

4.5. Childhood morbidity

High childhood mortality and relatively short stature suggests that childhood was punctuated by periods of nutritional shortage and/or illness. Where the child survives the stress, 'markers' may remain on the teeth and/or bones, and the age at which the upset occurred can be estimated. Horizontal grooves or pits on the teeth are known as enamel hypoplasia and represent 'upsets' which occurred whilst the tooth was developing (pp 586-7). Harris lines in the bones (lines of increased density) represent the recovery phase following the upset and are examined by section or X-ray, and as such are beyond the scope of this study.

4.5.1. Cribra orbitalia

Pitting in the roof of the eye socket known as cribra orbitalia is usually thought to indicate childhood iron deficiency anaemia (IDA, Stuart-Macadam 1985). The deficiency may be of dietary origin but is perhaps more likely to reflect a high disease/pathogen load. Pathogens may cause IDA directly, as in the destruction of the red blood cells in malaria or in the blood loss from the intestines in hookworm infestation, or indirectly as the body may reduce the amount of available iron in the blood serum as a generalised response to stress. In this way IDA may confer some protection against disease as many micro-organisms need iron from their 'host' in order to replicate (Stuart-Macadam 1992). The picture is further complicated by scurvy and eye infection, both of which may produce similar lesions. The three may be impossible to distinguish in the archaeological context.

Almost one third (30%, 128/422) of individuals displayed pitting, half of which was minor and very little of which was severe. Pitting was most common in immatures (42%, 55/132), followed by women (34%, 32/95) and men (15%, 13/86). The difference between men and women is significant at the 0.05% confidence level, but that between immatures and adults was not significant. Moderate or severe pitting was seen in 19 individuals (15% of cribra cases, 4.5% of the total sample). The most severe type of lesion with expansion of the trabecular bone into the orbit was seen in only two individuals, both adults of indeterminate sex. This is in marked contrast to the children buried in **Period II**, 70% of whom had cribra orbitalia, 50% of which was of the trabecular type (pp 558-9).

The evidence indicates that a mild condition was present in a substantial proportion of the late medieval population, which may reflect iron deficiency anaemia, disease load, scurvy or eye infection. The variation with age, which is seen in many other sites, may indicate higher mortality in immatures with pitting, healing and obliteration of pitting with age, or more probably a combination of the two. The higher frequency in women than men is more difficult to explain, especially within a model of childhood IDA. The larger female requirement for iron is not evident until puberty, well after skeletal evidence of IDA is thought to develop (Stuart-Macadam 1985). Preferential feeding of male children would confer greater resistence to IDA, both through better overall nutrition enabling the child to resist/recover from disease more effectively, and specifically by increasing the availability of iron. Sex differences in frequencies of IDA are also reported from other sites, but with no consistent pattern (e.g. White 1988, Hirata 1990, Mays 1992, Wells 1982).

4.5.2. Porotic hyperostosis

Porotic hyperostosis is taken to involve thickening and porosity of the parietals, occipital or frontal, and excluding the orbital plates, for the purposes of this report. The aetiology is thought to be the same as that of cribra orbitalia, and in some studies the two are not distinguished. Porotic hyperostosis was noted in 37 individuals and was slight in most cases. The parietals were involved most often (30/37). A frequency could not be determined because of cranial fragmentation, but males and females appear to have been approximately equally affected (10 males, 13 females). Five immatures were affected. Half of those with porotic hyperostosis did not have cribra orbitalia, one of these being the male SK 1081 who may have been suffering from cranial osteomyelitis (pp 530, 540). In this case, at least, the porosity was probably related to the infection rather than to IDA. As with cribra orbitalia, porotic changes of the cranium were much more severe and common in the immature sample from **Period II**, indicating that different factors were operating in the two populations.

5. TUMOURS

No evidence of malignant disease was encountered. Benign tumours of the cranium known as button osteomata were noted on two adult males and three adult females (left parietal in two cases, right parietal, occipital and frontal in one case each). The osteoma on the right parietal of SK 1087 (middle-aged female) was unusually large and prominent, and had a maximum diameter of 39 mm and a height of approximately 7 mm.

6. DEVELOPMENTAL/CONGENITAL

A number of conditions were noted which were probably of developmental or congenital origin. These include pathological conditions such as Perthes' disease and slipped ephiphysis, and others unlikely to have any clinical significance such as variation in vertebral number/form.

6.1. Joint disorders

Perthes' disease is a self-limiting condition caused by a temporary disruption of the blood supply to the femoral head. It most commonly affects children between 4 and 8 years of age, and boys are four times as likely to be affected as girls. The condition is bilateral in 12% of cases. The femoral head may become enlarged and flattened superiorly, predisposing to secondary osteoarthritis in adult life.

Perthes' disease was considered to have caused the changes seen in four individuals, all male/?male. The condition was unilateral (RHS) in two individuals (SK 1324, early middle-aged male, Figure 11.22, and SK 1193, adult male), and bilateral in two individuals (SK 1325, subadult ?male) and a less certain diagnosis in SK 969, subadult male). All affected individuals died before secondary DJD developed, although the condition itself is not life-threatening.

The epiphysis of the femoral head may slip out of position (usually inferiorly and posteriorly) during adolescence, possibly due to weakness at the growth plate during the adolescent growth spurt. The femoral head may

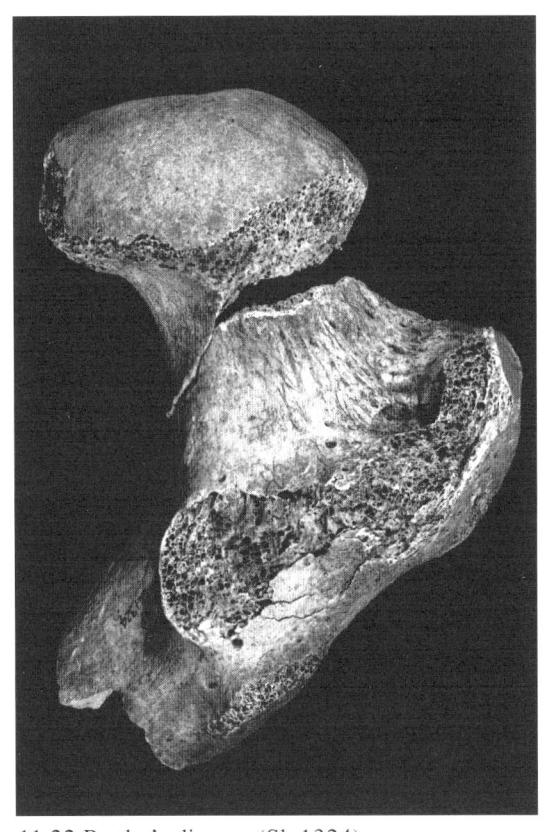

11.22 Perthe's disease (Sk 1324).

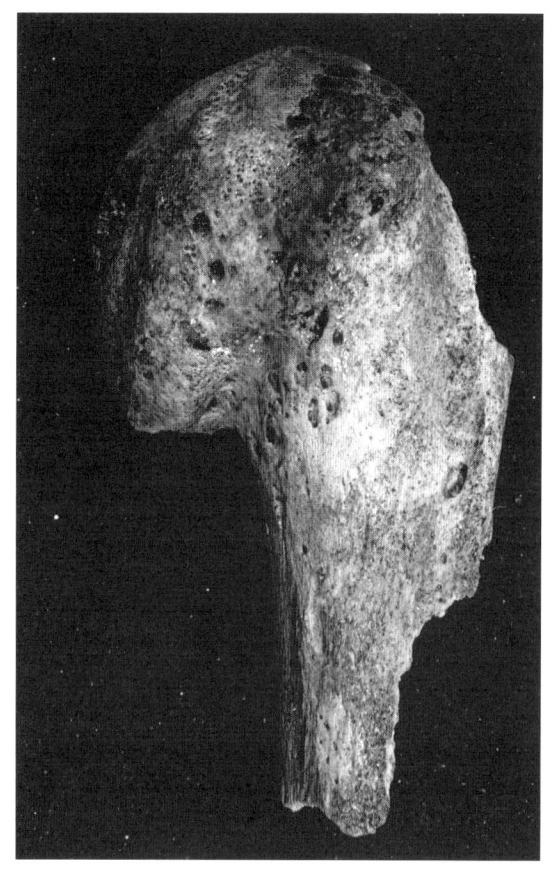

11.23 Slipped proximal epiphysis or healed fracture of the humerus (SK 891).

become necrotic (die) causing collapse and loss of its spherical shape, and predisposing to development of secondary osteoarthritis in early adult life. Boys are affected more often than girls and 20% of cases are bilateral. The condition may be associated with obesity and deficient gonadal development. The condition was not positively identified in the present sample, although it may be difficult to distinguish this condition from Perthes' disease.

The humeral head of SK 891 (middle-aged female) appeared to have a slipped proximal epiphysis, although this is an unlikely diagnosis in a non-weight-bearing joint. An old healed fracture was considered a more likely explanation (Figure 11.23).

Avascular necrosis may have caused the 'flattened' humeral heads seen in SK 1033 (Figure 11.12, middle-aged female) and SK 1306 (late-middle-aged male). The right humerus of SK 1033 was not recovered and the condition was bilateral in SK 1306. Both individuals displayed severe degenerative changes of the shoulder, probably as a consequence of the deformity.

6.2. Spondylolysis

The aetiology of spondylolysis may have a congenital component and is discussed in section 4.1.6 above.

6.3. Variation in vertebral number/form

Variation in the number and form of the thoracic and lumbar vertebrae is common in the region of transition between the two types. Some examples have undoubtedly gone unrecognised as most spines were incomplete and frequencies were not calculated. Variation in the form of the first cervical vertebra was also encountered and this is discussed in section 6.5 below.

Transitional vertebrae (those with characteristics of two adjacent types of vertebrae) were noted at the thoraco-lumbar junction in 11 individuals, and at the lumbo-sacral region in 15 individuals. Three individuals had six lumbar vertebrae and four had six sacral vertebrae. Analysis of burial patterns did not reveal clustering of affected individuals which may have indicated family plots, although one such cluster was noted in the **Period I/4** cemetery (pp 555-6).

6.4. Spina bifida

Spina bifida is characterised by incomplete fusion of the posterior vertebral elements, usually in the lower spine. The severity of the condition varies from the asymptomatic spina bifida occulta to forms which are incompatible with life. It is generally assumed that archaeological examples are of the occult type as those with more severe forms would probably not have survived.

Deficiency in the posterior sacral elements was noted in 16 individuals and in the first cervical vertebra in two individuals. Of the sacra, one was completely open, four were deficient at SV1 only (one individual also being deficient in CV1), one at SV1 and SV2 (the rest not recovered), two at SV2–SV5, and eight of SV3–SV5 or SV4–SV5.

Calculation of frequencies included only complete sacra or sacral elements. Of sacra which were complete from SV1–SV4, 6.4% (3/47) had spina bifida. Taking the elements individually, 4% (5/122) were deficient in the first element, 3.6% (4/110) in the second, 5.4% in the third and 6.9% in the fourth. A frequency for the fifth was not available, as deficiency was not noted unless in combination with other unfused elements, as it was considered a normal variant.

6.5. Deficient fusion of the first cervical vertebra

Deficient fusion of the first cervical vertebra (the atlas) was noted in four individuals. Two were unfused in the posterior arch and as such are a form of spina bifida, and three were unfused anteriorly. The first cervical vertebra is subject to much variation in the number of ossification centres, and the conditions noted here may be a consequence of this. The individual examples are described below.

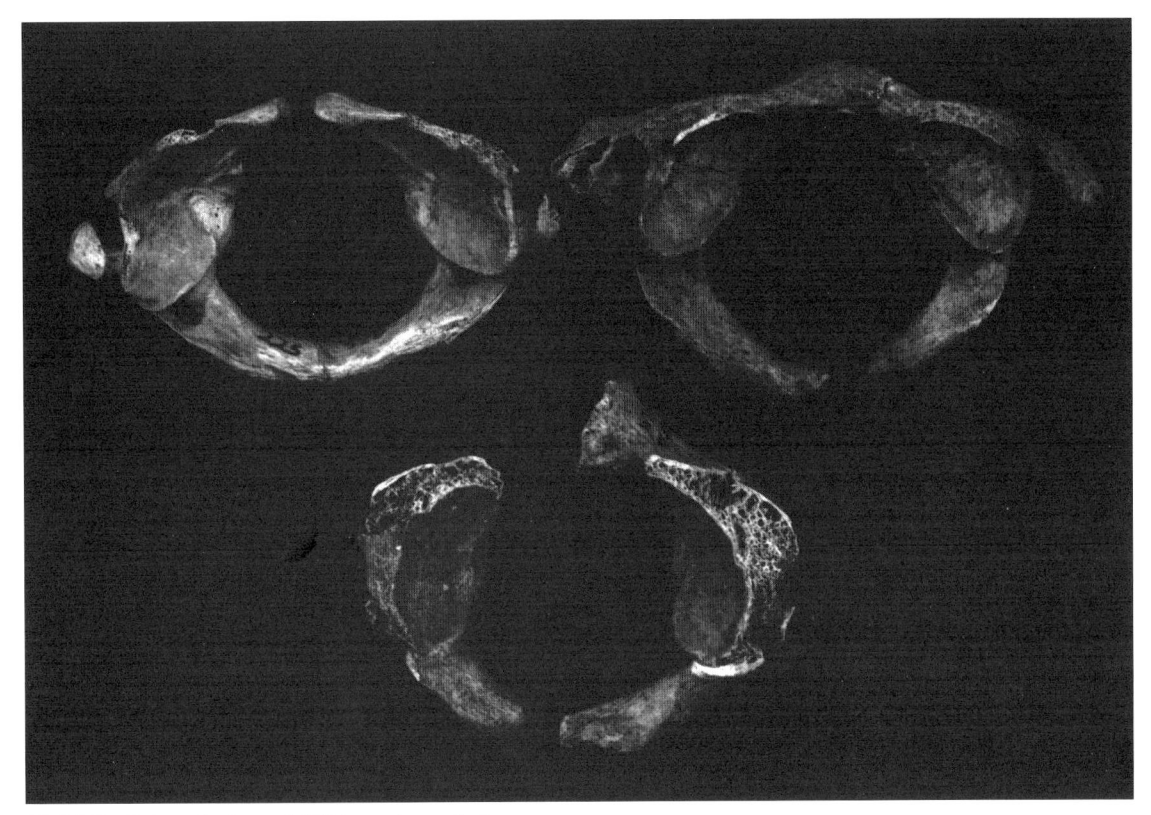

11.24 Deficient fusion of CV1, various skeletons.

The atlas of SK 1254 (subadult female) was unfused anteriorly and posteriorly. Each half of the posterior arch terminated in a blunt point (it is not known if the points met). Each half of the anterior arch was apparently formed from an extension of ossification from the lateral mass, the unfused elements being enlarged, flattened and roughened, and probably in close approximation in life. The odontoid process of the axis was somewhat shorter than normal and the facet for the arch of C1 was small and off-centre (Figure 11.24).

The posterior arches of the atlas of SK 1014 (subadult ?female) were slightly asymmetrically unfused, and may not have met in the mid-line (Figure 11.24). There was also spina bifida of the first sacral element.

The atlas of SK 225 (6–10 years) was unfused in the anterior mid-line, each element forming half of the facet for the odontoid process of the axis, and terminating in a blunt point (Figure 11.24).

The anterior arch of the atlas of SK 475 (12–14 years) was unfused and missing. The arch usually fuses with the lateral masses at approximately seven years of age.

These examples of non-fusion may have been of little or no clinical significance as the ligaments around the first and second cervical vertebrae are very strong and probably effectively held the unfused elements in place. The absence of disuse atrophy in the affected skeletons would support this view, and suggests that there was little or no nerve involvement.

6.6. Vertebral fusion

Fusion of two or more adjacent vertebrae was noted in 13 individuals. Congenital fusion was considered the most probable cause in five cases as there was no extra bony growth, degenerative change, or evidence of trauma or infection. The cervical spine was affected in four individuals (the arches and the bodies in two cases each) and the mid-thoracic spine in the fifth (arches of two mid-thoracic vertebrae). The fusion was limited to two or three vertebrae in each case.

6.7. Other congenital conditions

Both first metatarsals of SK 1057 (early middle-aged male) were disproportionately short. The rest of the skeleton including metatarsals, although not all were present, was normal. Many skeletal dysplasias may affect the first metatarsal, but most also affect other bones. The individual was probably unaffected by the condition.

The sternum – a bone that was poorly represented in the sample – was pierced in SK 721 (young adult male).

The pattern of congenital abnormality noted in this group was not unusual.

7. MISCELLANEOUS CONDITIONS

A number of miscellaneous conditions were noted:
SK 631 (late middle-aged ?male): Very deep groove for the meningeal vein which terminated in a

deep, enlarged Pacchionian depression causing the outer table, which was very thin in this region, to bulge slightly. This individual also had 'thumb prints' on the posterior parietals (section 4.1.2).

SK 651 (middle-aged female): Disturbance and enthesopathies of the muscle insertions around the pelvis including the greater trochanter and ischial tuberosity. The iliac blade displayed a number of broad, shallow depressions on the external surface. There was some DJD of the vertebrae but no bony bridging which may have indicated a sero-negative arthropathy.

8. NON-METRIC TRAITS

A number of non-metric traits are commonly recorded in order to examine population differences and associations. The traits generally have no known biological significance. Some of the conditions noted in section 6 may be regarded as non-metric traits.

At birth the frontal bone of the cranium is divided vertically in the mid-line by the metopic suture. This suture usually fuses in early childhood, but occasionally the two halves remain separate in a condition known as metopism. Metopism occurs in approximately 10% of modern Caucasoids and Mongoloids, and in 2% of Negroids (Krogman and Iscan 1986, 119). Retention of the suture is usually seen as genetically determined (e.g. Torgerson 1951) although alternative explanations have been proposed (see below).

11.4% (64/563) of crania from the present sample were metopic. More females than males displayed the trait (female: 13.7%, 19/139; male: 10.8%, 12/111) although the difference was not statistically significant. There was a concentration of affected females in the latest two phases of graveyard use (539 and 540, Figures 7.4 and 7.6) in which 22% of women (10/45) and 12% of men (4/34) were metopic. There appeared to be some spatial clustering of metopic individuals both within and between phases, perhaps indicating family burial areas. Partial metopism was present in four further individuals (0.7% of frontals, 4/567), the superior third of the suture being unfused in three, and the distal third in the fourth. The total frequency of metopism at Whithorn is compared with those from other areas and periods in Table 11.22.

Evidence from the Isle of Ensay and from Linlithgow may support the genetic argument. One quarter of crania from the earliest three levels at Ensay (approximately 1500 AD to 1800 AD) were metopic, reducing to about 5% thereafter. Miles postulates that the high frequency reflects a period of geographic and genetic isolation which ended in the nineteenth century when the 'metopic gene' of the indigenous population was 'diluted' by genes of incomers (Miles 1989). A high frequency of metopism was observed in the Linlithgow series where 18 of the 21 cases were recovered from the chancel, cloister or nave of the church (Cross and Bruce 1989), perhaps indicating that families carrying the 'metopic gene' were buried in these areas.

Metopism	Mean male stature	Sample size	Mean female stature	Sample size
No	169.1	51	156.2	64
Yes	167.5	6	156.7	12

Table 11.23: Stature in metopic and non-metopic individuals.

Alternative explanations for metopism propose an association between the trait and poor nutrition and health (e.g. Reimann 1978, Zivanovic 1982). This was examined in the present sample by looking at the relationship between cribra orbitalia (taken to represent nutritional deficiency, albeit with caveats, pp 546-7), stature (short stature taken as a gross indicator of nutritional shortage and/or ill health) and metopism, and no clear associations found. Cribra orbitalia was present in 30.6% (15/49) of metopic and 30.8% (96/311) of non-metopic individuals. Metopic males were 1.6 cm shorter than their non-metopic counterparts, whilst metopic females were 0.5 cm taller (Table 11.23). It should be noted that the sample of individuals with data for both metopism and stature is very small.

Site	Date	% Metopic	n	Source
England				
Trentholme, Kent	Romano-British	5	?	Warwick 1968*
St Helen-on-the-Walls, York	C10th–C16th	11	~550	Dawes 1980
St Nicholas Shambles, London	C11th–12th	11.3	106	White 1988
Spittalfields, London	C16th	8.2	488	Morant and Hoadley 1931*
Whitechapel, London	C17th	8.7	275	Macdonnell 1904*
Moorfields, London	C17th prob.	6.7	120	Macdonnell 1906*
Faringdon, London	C17th	9.6	355	Hooke 1926*
Scotland				
Whithorn	C13th–C15th	11.4	563	This report
Aberdeen	C13th–C16th	18	57	Cross and Bruce 1990
Linlithgow	C13th–C17th	22	95	Cross and Bruce 1990
Ensay	C15th–C18th	21	162	Miles 1989
Loggies Lane, St Andrews	C15th–C16th	28	42	Cardy 1993
Kirkhill, St Andrews		17	100	Bruce, Cross and Kerr 1990

Table 11.22: Frequency of Metopism in various British populations (*from Miles 1989).

9. ARCHAEOLOGICAL NOTES

Most burials were typically 'Christian', being single, extended burials with the hands crossed on the pelvis or chest, and roughly oriented with the head to the west and feet to the east. Most were probably simple shroud burials as little evidence of either coffin nails or straight-sided or square-ended graves was found. Those which did not conform to this pattern are described below with other burials of note.

Twenty-four tightly or loosely flexed burials were noted. The position appeared to have been determined by a geographical barrier (a wall) in two cases, and may have been determined by disease in eight of the remainder. Of these, three had evidence of disuse atrophy of the lower limb (SKs 53, 661, 1336) and five had evidence of infection (PNBD – localised and generalised – in three and osteomyelitis of the distal femur in two). The flexed position may therefore reflect deformity during life.

Six individuals were buried in a reversed position (i.e. head to the east). Two of these were in a double grave, a middle-aged male (SK 1113) and a subadult of indeterminate sex (SK 1115). The others were a subadult male (SK 1311), two old juveniles (SKs 151 and 380) and one young juvenile (SK 114). SK 380 had severe calculus deposits around the teeth on one side of the mouth indicating a period of debility or facial palsy before death. There were no other features of particular note in this group. Possible explanations for this mode of burial include accident (e.g. the orientation of the body obscured by a shroud), or the burial of priests or suicides.

Three prone burials were noted. In each case the hands were found in the usual position at the front of the body. Two of the burials (one male and one female) were in poor condition but appeared to be 'normal' in all respects. The third burial (SK 630, early middle-aged male) displayed uneven disuse atrophy of the lower limb, and is described in section 4.2.3 above. Perhaps the burial position reflects his disability, although the skeletal evidence indicates great strength and much use of the upper body.

Five double burials were noted, three on the usual west–east alignment (a pair of perinatal infants, two juveniles and one early middle-aged ?male with a one-year-old infant), one aligned north–south (subadult male and young adult male) and one aligned east–west, i.e.: reversed (middle-aged male and subadult of indeterminate sex).

Two females were recovered with near or full-term foetuses in the pelvic region. In one case the foetal cranium was well down in the pelvic basin indicating that death occurred during childbirth. The pelves of both women appeared to be normal, and the reason for death could not be determined, although possible causes include placenta previa and eclampsia.

Bones that were disturbed when a grave was being dug were generally placed back in the grave in no apparent order, but occasionally were placed in careful patterns around the new burial, usually a child. The most striking example was of a perinatal infant (SK 1604) who was buried on the thoracic region of an earlier burial, a young adult female (SK 1558). The humeri of the female had been removed from the skeleton and placed over the baby in a cross which, with the adult cranium, gave a 'skull and cross bones' effect.

One possible example of decapitation was noted. The articulated cranium, mandible and first two cervical vertebrae were located under the left elbow of a torso and pelvis which included fragmentary lower cervical vertebrae (SK 1396). The second cervical vertebra of the cranium showed no ante-mortem damage and the vertebrae of the torso were too eroded to provide useful information. The age and sex of the torso and cranium are compatible although the association between the two cannot be proved.

10. CAUSE OF DEATH

Cause of death could be suggested for very few individuals. Most of those from 'normal' archaeological populations probably died of infectious diseases which kill quickly and leave no bony evidence. Bone damage from injuries that caused immediate or rapid death cannot usually be distinguished from post-mortem damage in dry bones. Cause of death could be suggested for one male who suffered infection of the inner table of the cranium following cranial injury (SK 684), two females with full-term foetuses in the pelvic region indicating complications of late pregnancy and/or childbirth, and one example of a possible decapitation.

11. SUMMARY

Whithorn appears to have been an important centre of pilgrimage from at least the 700s AD and may have reached its peak during the reign of James IV, although it continues to the present day. The period between 1286 and 1406 – almost exactly that covered by the cemetery – was one of political unrest and upheaval, the 'local' landowners vying with English and Scottish kings for power over the region. We may expect the skeletal population to reflect these factors in a number of ways. For example, we may expect to find a higher proportion of the chronically ill, the elderly and/or the 'better off' from the pilgrimage trade, and perhaps a high proportion of males with evidence of traumatic injury representing the warring population. The pilgrim population, however, was probably a transient one, and the skeletal evidence would support such a view as the skeletal population appears to be 'normal' in all respects with quite low rates of fracture, apparently 'normal' rates of PNBD, relatively few with evidence of chronic illness. For the same reasons we may exclude the possibility of a large proportion of population being composed of soldiers, suggesting that the skeletal sample is largely composed of natives of Whithorn, largely unbiased by the direct effects of pilgrimage and warfare.

The sample was treated as a 'cross section' of the population as both sexes were present in roughly equal proportions and as all ages were represented, although in reality the population probably represents some six generations. Analysis of mortality patterns suggests that the youngest age groups were substantially under-represented, a common feature of archaeological groups. A generally 'harsh' environment was indicated by the high mortality rate in childhood, despite the under-representation, and the short life span and short stature of the adults. Episodes of malnutrition and/or ill health were common as evidenced by the frequency of enamel hypoplasia and cribra orbitalia. The presence of Schmorl's nodes in juveniles indicates that they participated in arduous physical activity from an early age.

Most indicators pointed to greater overall exposure of men than women to physical stress and trauma. Women, however, appeared to suffer more stress in the upper limb than men, whilst men suffered more in the lower limb. Whilst men and women were approximately equally exposed to stresses causing Schmorl's nodes in the lumbar spine, men were much more likely to develop lesions in the thoracic region. The finding at most striking odds with this general pattern is the high frequency of intervertebral osteochondrosis in women which remains unexplained. Women apparently suffered stresses of a different nature, as they appear to have died slightly earlier than men, and twice as many women as men had cribra orbitalia, perhaps indicating preferential feeding of male children.

There was little evidence of specific nutritional deficiency apart from iron deficiency anaemia, although a number of individuals may have suffered from mild vitamin D or C deficiency (evidenced by bowed limbs and patchy periostitis). Stature estimates indicate that the population as a whole was slightly, and probably constantly, undernourished.

There was much evidence of bone inflammation and infection although the specific causal organism could be identified in very few cases. Lung infections which may include tuberculosis and/or pneumonia seem to have been quite common as evidenced by periostitis of the visceral surface of the rib. Syphilis was positively identified in one calvarium, and it is possible that the disease caused some examples of periostitis. Non-specific infections causing periosteal new bone development of the lower limb were very common although, in line with other sites, the upper limb was much less involved. Only one probable example of leprosy was noted although the areas of the skeleton most affected are frequently lost or damaged in archaeological contexts. This individual may have also contracted tuberculosis, probably secondarily to leprosy infection. Tuberculosis was not positively identified, although it may have caused the pathology in a number of individuals, and commonly develops without skeletal involvement. Poor nutrition and disease probably interacted with one another, one exacerbating the effects of the other. The population was probably more vulnerable to infections that are not generally considered serious today under modern western nutritional standards.

There was some evidence of medical intervention. There were two examples of possible, and successful, trepanations, one of which may have been an attempt to treat a blade wound. Most fractures healed in good alignment and without infection, and at least some of these would have needed reduction and splinting.

The differences between the sexes in many respects (disregarding the morphology from which sex was determined) were most pronounced between the most securely sexed material, reducing when those in the 'grey' area were included. This may be because some in the 'possible' categories have been incorrectly sexed, or it may imply that ?males and ?females approach the opposite sex in terms of behaviour as well as 'sexing' morphology.

THE PERIOD I GRAVEYARD
MID-SIXTH TO EARLY-EIGHTH CENTURIES

1. INTRODUCTION

The **Period I** graveyard was much less intensively used than the later Medieval cemetery, and far fewer graves were disturbed by later burials. Unfortunately, however, skeletal remains were less frequently preserved, and of the 118 graves excavated (Figure 3.2), only 59 produced skeletal material. In most cases this was in poor condition, sometimes consisting solely of fragments of dental enamel. Most of the remains, and all of those in reasonable condition (five individuals, four adjacent to one another, Grave nos. 75–78, Figure 3.33), came from the fourth phase of graveyard use (**Period I/4**), and probably date to the later-seventh century.

Whilst most graves contained material from one individual, one – the 'special' grave (I/18, Figure 3.19) – always conspicuous for it's size, arrangement of surrounding paving, mode of construction and apparent focal position for surrounding graves – contained the remains of at least four individuals (Section 8).

2. DEMOGRAPHY

The methods for assessment of age and sex and the age categories employed are described above (pp 519-20). Problems were encountered in ageing 'old juveniles' as evidence from tooth root or epiphyseal development was not available and in these cases the less reliable method of dental wear was used.

Approximately three quarters of the skeletons (40/53) were adult and approximately one quarter (13/53) were immature. None was younger than approximately seven years of age, and age could not be determined in five individuals. The age distribution of the adult material compared with that of the later-

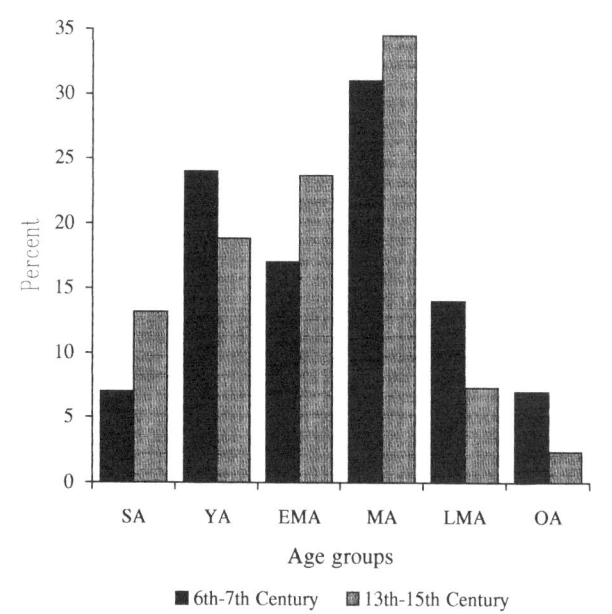

11.25 Comparative distributions of age groups in **Period I** and **V** adult populations.

medieval group is shown in Figure 11.25. Twenty-one percent of adults were judged to be late-middle-aged or old, twice the proportion seen in the later-medieval series.

Sex could be assessed in only 21 skeletons. Fourteen were male or ?male, and seven were female or ?female. Analysis of age by sex was not undertaken because of the small sample size.

The predominence of males and the paucity of those from the younger age categories indicates non-random burial practices.

3. BODY BUILD

Stature could be estimated for five of the males and for one female. The male mean was 176 cm (5'9", range 170–179 cm) and the female stature was 168 cm (5'6"). These means are greater than those of the later-medieval group and approach those of modern Britons (Table 11.4).

No crania were recovered which were both intact and undistorted, and no measurements could be taken.

The meric index could be determined for two males and one female. One male and one female were platymeric and one male was eurymeric.

The cnemic index could be determined in one male and two females. The male was mesocnemic and the females were eurycnemic. Approximate measurements of four further individuals were taken, three of which were eurycnemic and one mesocnemic.

4. HEALTH STATUS/LIFE-STYLE

Surprisingly for such a small group there was evidence of much trauma and disease. Each skeleton that was in reasonable condition presented at least one condition of note.

Fractures

The right clavicle of SK 1643 (middle-aged male, Figure 11.26) was fractured at the junction of the medial two thirds with the lateral third. This common injury may be caused by falling onto an outstretched

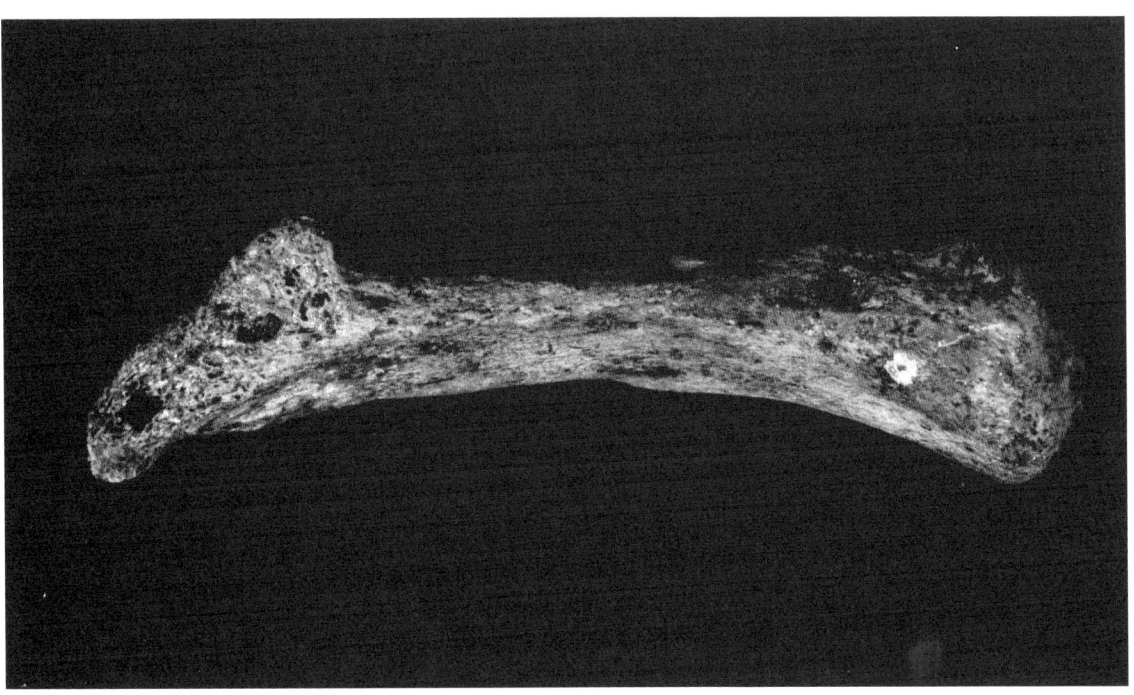

11.26 Fractured clavicle with non-union of fractured ends (SK 1643).

arm. Unusually the medial portion of the bone showed resorption and remodelling, but did not unite with the lateral portion. The lateral portion was not located, even though the deficiency was noted at excavation. Non-union is usually caused by insufficient immobilisation of the bone during healing. Both humeri were normal, suggesting that death occurred before any changes could develop at the shoulder joint.

Schmorl's nodes

Most preserved spines had Schmorl's nodes. Five were male/?male and two were female/?female. All complete thoracic spines (four individuals, all males), and two thirds of complete lumbar spines (one male, one female) displayed Schmorl's nodes. The sample size was too small for more detailed analysis.

Spondylolysis

One example of partial spondylolysis was noted at the unusual site of the first sacral vertebra (SK 1630, ?female). This individual also displayed multiple Schmorl's nodes and possible early spinal tuberculosis (below).

Enthesopathies

One skeleton displayed an enthesopathy at the site of the insertion of the Achilles tendon into the posterior aspect of the calcaneus (heel bone, SK 1646, late-middle-aged ?male). Another had roughening of the medial lip of the linea aspera (SK 1621 adult ?male). Both sites were commonly affected in the later-medieval group.

Defects of the articular surface (DAS)

Small defects on a number of joint surfaces were noted. Frequencies were available for the proximal phalanx of the great toe, the talus facet of the navicular, the base of the first metatarsal and the superior facets of the second cervical vertebra. These frequencies are compared with those from other groups in Table 11.17. The defect was also noted on the articular surface of the olecranon of the ulna (SK 1642) and on the posterior talus facet of the calcaneus (SK 1544), both sites which were occasionally affected in the later-medieval sample.

Degenerative joint disease (DJD)

Degenerative changes were most common in the spine. Most were seen in the facet joints of the thoracic vertebrae, followed by the margins of the cervical vertebral bodies. As with the later-medieval material, eburnation was most common in the facet joints of the cervical vertebrae. Of the large joints, the hip was affected most often, followed by the shoulder, elbow and knee. The hip was the only large joint to show eburnation, probably as a consequence of secondary osteoarthritis (see below).

Secondary osteoarthritis was judged to have caused the changes noted in two individuals. SK 1643 (middle-aged male) displayed severe DJD with new bony development on and around the right femoral head, some of which was eburnated. The diameter of the affected head was 59 mm compared with 52 mm on the unaffected side, possibly indicating a developmental condition such as Perthes' disease, although the shape of the femoral head was not grossly abnormal. This individual also displayed an ununited fracture of the right clavicle. A developmental or congenital condition may also have caused the degenerative changes noted at the right hip of SK 1652 (middle-aged ?female). The femoral neck angle was obtuse, but the shape of the femoral head appeared normal. The acetabulum could not be assessed.

Periosteal new bone development (PNBD)

The inner surface of the frontal bone of the cranium of SK 1657 (old juvenile) displayed fine deposits of new bone. The cause of such deposits is unknown, although meningitis, scurvy and congenital syphilis have been implicated. The right clavicle of SK 1644 (young adult male) displayed substantial healed deposits with bony expansion. The remainder of the skeleton could not be assessed because of post-mortem erosion, although it is probable that other bones were also affected. Systemic infection is indicated. SK 1641 (old adult, indeterminate sex) displayed PNBD of the floor of the nasal cavity indicating nasal infection.

Tuberculosis

Between 6% and 12% of individuals with tuberculosis develop the spinal changes by which the disease is usually identified in skeletal material (Steinbock 1976). Three possible examples of vertebral tuberculosis were noted in the present series, a very high frequency for such a small sample. Each is described below.

The spine of SK 1642 (young adult male) was generally poorly preserved but survived largely intact in the lower thoracic and lumbar region where TV12–LV2 displayed kyphosis of approximately 125°, ankylosis and gross destruction of the anterior aspect of the vertebral bodies. The posterior arches of the vertebrae were fused (Figure 11.27).

SK 1630 (young adult ?female) displayed 'scooped out' areas on opposing surfaces of the thoracic and lumbar body surfaces with resorption of exposed trabeculae and no new bone formation. Examination by a light microscope may indicate post-mortem damage (C. Roberts, Pers. Comm.), although if this is the case, the damage is unique amongst the 1750 skeletons examined.

SK 1637 (late-middle-aged male) displayed severe compression of TV6 and LV3 with some fusion with the adjacent bodies. An infective process such as tuberculosis is indicated by the severe destruction of the inferior body of TV6 (Figure 11.28) and the fusion between the body surfaces of LV3 and LV2. The spine felt light and osteoporotic, and the molars were substantially worn indicating old age, although there was little degenerative joint disease in this individual.

The visceral surface of the ribs which may show PNBD in tuberculous infection were too eroded to examine in SK 1642 and SK 1637, and unaffected in SK 1630.

Cribra orbitalia

Cribra orbitalia was present in one third (3/9) of the sample. The pitting was mild in all cases and the frequency was unremarkable.

5. DEVELOPMENTAL/CONGENITAL

One skeleton (SK 1630 ?female) had partial spondylolysis of the first sacral vertebra.

Four individuals displayed anomalies of vertebral number or form:

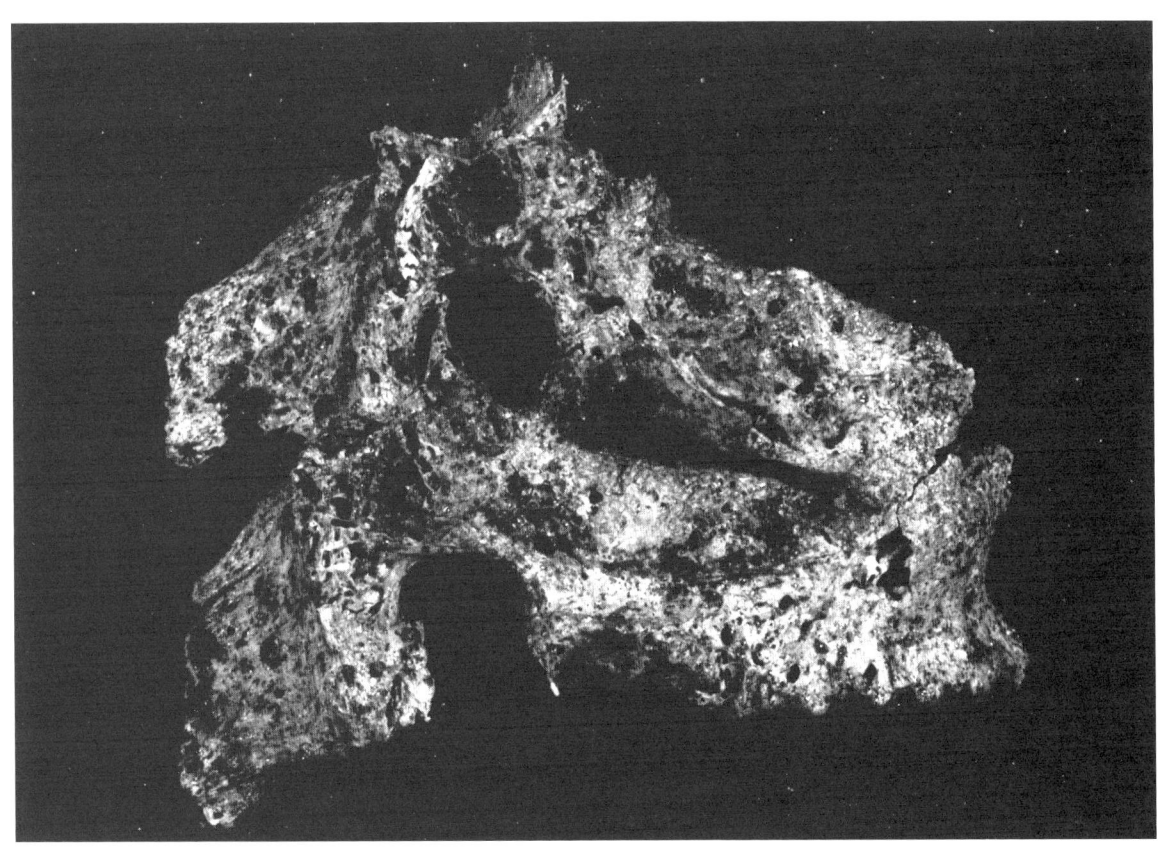

11.27 Kyphosis and fusion of spine indicating tuberculosis (SK 1642).

11.28 Partial fusion of TV6 and (SK 1637) LV3 and LV2.

SK 1637: Sacralisation of L5.
SK 1642: Curved superior facets of TV12.
SK 1643: Curved superior facets of TV12 and sacralisation of LV5.
SK 1644: 13 thoracic vertebrae.

Three of these individuals (SKs 1637, 1642, 1643) were buried side by side in log coffins, perhaps indicating familial relationships.

SK 1654 (very fragmentary ?male) displayed fusion of the laminae of the third and fourth cervical vertebrae which may have been of congenital origin.

Two skeletons displayed DJD of the hip which may have been the consequence of a congenital hip condition such as Perthes' disease or hip dysplasia. These are described in section 4 above.

6. NON-METRIC TRAITS

Ten percent (2/19) of frontal bones were metopic, a 'normal' frequency for a caucasian population and comparable with that of the later-medieval group. A suprascapular foramen was noted in SK 1644.

7. DESCRIPTION OF INDIVIDUAL SKELETONS

The five best preserved skeletons came from adjacent log coffin burials (Figure 3.33) and each is briefly described below. This is followed by descriptions of other skeletons of interest.

SK 1641, grave 74: elderly, robust individual of undetermined sex and in relatively poor condition. Pathology included PNBD on the floor of the nasal cavity and severe DJD of the spine.

SK 1637, grave 75: late-middle-aged male. Stature 176 cm (5'9"). Very robust. Possible spinal tuberculosis. Schmorl's nodes from TV8–LV1. Sacralisation of LV5. The frontal sinuses were filled with cancellous bone.

SK 1642, grave 76: young adult male. Stature 177 cm (5'10"). Interred in a reversed (east–west) orientation. Possible spinal tuberculosis. Lumbarisation of TV12.

SK 1643, grave 77: late-middle-aged male. Stature 179 cm (5'10.5"). Severe, probably secondary, DJD of the right hip, possibly consequent upon a developmental anomaly such as Perthes' disease. Fracture of the left clavicle with non-union of the broken ends. Left humerus was normal. The tuberosities of the naviculars were flattened and pitted (section 4.1 p 535). Slight Schmorl's nodes from TV7–TV11. Lumbarisation of TV12 and sacralisation of LV5.

SK 1645, grave 78: early middle-aged male. Stature 170 cm (5'7"). Relatively incomplete. Although not especially tall this individual was very robust.

Other skeletons showing conditions of note from other areas of the cemetery comprise:

SK 1630, grave 98: young adult ?female. Possible spinal tuberculosis. Schmorl's nodes of thoracic and lumbar vertebrae. The zygoma (cheek bones) were formed from three ossification centres, the fusion lines of which met in the central area of the zygomatic body.

SK 1652, grave 115: middle-aged ?female. Moderate DJD of the right femoral head. Left unaffected. Femoral neck angle was more obtuse on the affected side, possibly indicating a developmental or congenital condition which caused secondary DJD.

SK 1654, grave 101: late-middle-aged ?male. Probable congenital fusion of the laminae of the third and fourth cervical vertebrae with severe DJD of the inferior facet joints of C2, possibly as a consequence of this.

8. THE 'CENTRAL' GRAVE

The fragmentary dental remains of four individuals together with a small amount of disarticulated, severely eroded human bone were recovered from this grave. Two of the three 'skeletons' found on the floor of the grave were apparently undisturbed by successive interments (SKs 1677 young adult/ subadult, 1678 subadult/old juvenile), the third being slightly disturbed (SK 1679 middle-aged adult). The fourth individual (SK 1676 middle-aged adult) was represented by dental fragments and a left zygoma recovered from the upper fill. No attempt was made to sex the remains.

9. SUMMARY

The small and biased sample precludes drawing conclusions about the general population, but displays a surprising number of interesting features. The overall impression is of very 'male' males with a high frequency of unusual pathology and spinal anomaly, which may indicate a specialised population, perhaps of warriors or high-status males. At least four of the row of five skeletons were large males who displayed a high frequency of spinal anomaly and pathology, suggesting non-random burial and perhaps familial relationships. The apparent presence of spinal infection in three of this small sample, two of which were side by side is noteworthy, and may also indicate non-random burial. Perhaps the group includes those who travelled to Whithorn in the hope of benefiting from the healing influence of St Ninian and who died there, perhaps including soldiers of high rank.

PERIOD II
THE 8TH–9TH CENTURY BURIALS

The skeletal material encompassed by this report was excavated from around and within the Northumbrian burial chapel. The material falls into five groups, and each is discussed individually and in broadly chronological order. The methods employed to determine age and sex are discussed above (pp 519-21).

THE INTERNAL BURIALS

Four incomplete but undisturbed burials were recovered from within the chapel (Figure 4.27), at least three of which had been buried in wooden chests, (pp 168, 412-5, Figure 10.93). Two skeletons were probably male, one was a large female and one was of indeterminate sex. Each is briefly described below.

SK 573: fragmentary skeleton in poor condition. Adult of indeterminate sex.

SK 574: middle-aged/old ?male. Stature 177 cm (5'9.5", left femur). Both hips displayed severe degenerative changes with eburnation. The proximal femoral shaft had a low, wide lateral flange (meric index 67.5). The tibiae could not be measured accurately but were in the mesocnemic or eurycnemic range. Age assessment was difficult, the degenerative changes indicating advanced age, but the dental wear indicating middle age.

SK 581: middle-aged female. This skeleton was sexed on the basis of the shape of the pubic bone, but was within the male range for general skeletal robusticity. There were Schmorl's nodes and degenerative changes of the surfaces and margins of the vertebral bodies.

SK 582: early middle-aged ?male. Stature 179 cm (5'10.5", right femur). No pathology or other degenerative change noted but little evidence survived.

The stray fragmentary calvarium of a mature adult of unknown sex was found in the debris of the burial chapel. The endocranial surface of the frontal bone displayed generalised uneven swellings consistent with a diagnosis of hyperostosis frontalis interna. This condition may be non-pathological and associated with ageing, but it is also a central feature of Morgani-Stewart-Morel syndrome which is a generalised metabolic condition associated with virilism and obesity (Armelagos and Chrisman 1988).

In summary all individuals buried within the chapel were robust and tall, two being some 9 cm taller than the late-medieval male mean. Stature may be seen as a gross indicator of childhood health and nutrition, and these individuals may represent those who reached their genetic potential for height. Privileged status is also indicated by burial within an obviously 'special' building. There was also some evidence of strenuous physical activity, the female displaying Schmorl's nodes, and all individuals being robust.

THE EXTERNAL BURIAL

The cranium, dentition and right upper arm of an early middle-aged adult of indeterminate sex was recovered from just south of the burial chapel (SK 716, grave II/5). The dentition was unusual, displaying uneven wear on the left and right sides, ante-mortem loss of the right mandibular second and third molars, and impaction of the third right maxillary molar. There were calculus deposits on the occlusal surfaces of the right molars and the left maxillary molars, and severe caries of both maxillary second premolars.

THE CHILDREN'S CEMETERY

The remains of 56 children were excavated from an area abutting the east wall of the burial chapel (Figures 4.29 and 5.5). The condition of the remains was variable, but generally poor, and only two skeletons were substantially complete. Seven skeletons were too poorly preserved to be lifted. The length of long bones was measured *in-situ* if the bone was 'intact' in the ground but unlikely to survive lifting, facilitating fairly close ageing even when no material was subsequently recovered. A quantity of disarticulated material from pits and from general grave soil was also recovered and examined.

All material was immature except for one cranial fragment. Four infants may have been born up to two months prematurely, and the oldest child was aged between 9 and 12 years. Three skeletons were assigned to the general category of 'immature' and five were given either/or assessments because of poor preservation.

The pattern of mortality shown in Figure 11.29 reveals a large peak of deaths in the perinatal period. Figure 11.30, which compares the present and the late-medieval samples, reveals large differences between the groups. Such variation is unlikely to be

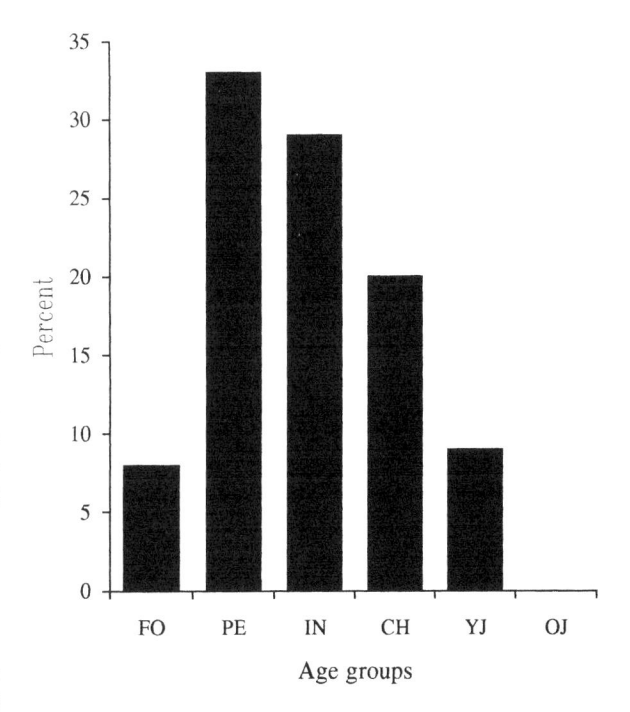

11.29 Distribution of age groups among immature population from **Periods II** and **III**

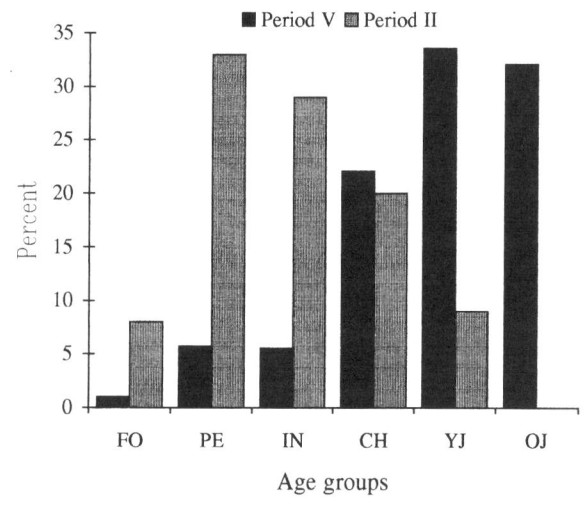

11.30 Comparative distribution of immature age groups in **Period II–III** and **V** populations.

accounted for purely in terms of variation in mortality, and must, to a large extent, reflect selective burial of particular groups. Within the 'Northumbrian' children's cemetery, all burials from the earliest phase of use were perinatal or infant whilst later groups also contained older children (perinatals/infants 55%–67%; children/young juveniles 7%–27%).

One fracture was noted in a child of approximately eight years (SK 83). The injury appeared to be an antero-posterior (front–back) crush fracture of the femur at the mid shaft point. Although healed, the bone felt light and fragile, perhaps indicating that normal use of the limb had not yet been resumed.

The most striking feature of this group was the unusually high frequency of severe cribra orbitalia and porotic, expansive cranial changes. Eight of eleven crania (73%) displayed cribra orbitalia, four having the most severe form with expansion of trabecular bone into the orbit (36% of the total or 50% of those with cribra orbitalia). By contrast, cribra orbitalia was observed in less than half (42%) of the later-medieval immature sample, the severest form being seen in only two individuals, both adults (1.5% of all examples of cribra orbitalia). At least three crania from the Northumbrian group had porous expansion of cranial bones other than the orbits, although only one case conforms to the expected pattern of porotic hyperostosis. Other crania appeared to show porotic changes but were too eroded for unequivocal assessment. Neonates were not included in the present calculation. The most extensively affected individuals are described below.

SK 82 (9–12 months) displayed severe cribra orbitalia, and expansion and porosity of the temporals and of the inferior aspect of the parietals. There was new surface growth at the postero-inferior aspect of the parietal and frontal. Some ribs (right and left) displayed unusual multiple pitted/scooped

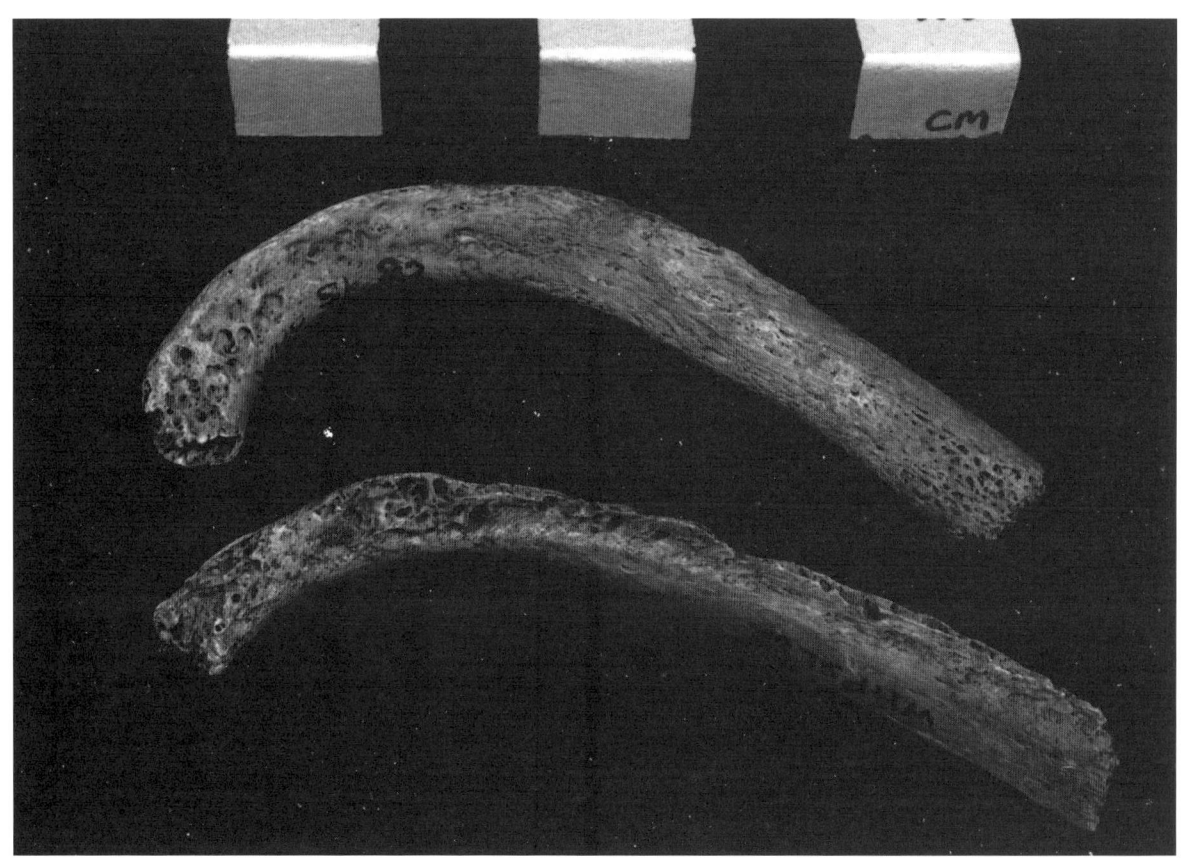

11.31 Unusual pitting and scooping of subcostal groove of left and right ribs (SK 82).

out areas in the subcostal groove (Figure 11.31) and/or thickening and expansion of the costal end of the bone, usually seen as an indicator of IDA. The metopic suture was fused and obliterated through most of its length.

SK 89 (approximately nine months) displayed severe cribra orbitalia and porotic expansion of the cranial bones with loss of the outer table. In section the bones had the appearance of up to six or seven horizontal layers, overlain by a layer with a vertical arrangement of trabeculae – the 'hair on end' appearance characteristic of severe anaemia, the fragments being up to 7 mm thick. Deposits were severe from the lateral aspect of the orbits, extending onto the parietal bones. Other regions were severely affected but could not be closely identified. One fragment (parietal?) had severe deposits which came to an abrupt end 7 mm from the suture, the bone between the deposits and the suture appearing to be normal. The 'normal' bone may represent growth after healing. There were no post-cranial remains.

SK 705 (immature) displayed partial and premature fusion of the sagittal suture (craniosynostosis), with expanded and porous bone extending for approximately 12 mm to either side of the suture. There was a 'worm-eaten' appearance on the internal table in this region. There were no post-cranial remains.

The cranial evidence described above indicates factor(s) operating in Northumbrian Whithorn which, if present in the later-medieval period, were much less significant. The factors may include different feeding practice, greater loads of intestinal parasites (and by implication lower standards of hygiene), different disease patterns, and/or a specialised burial population (e.g. those that were sick and brought to Whithorn because of its reputation as a healing centre, which was at its height during the Northumbrian period). The factor(s) appear to have been in operation throughout the use of the cemetery.

Childhood stress as reflected by enamel hypoplasia is discussed in the dental report.

An antero-posterior (front-back) crush fracture of the femur was noted in a child of approximately eight years (SK 83), the injury being at the mid shaft point. Although healed, the bone felt light and fragile, indicating disuse of the limb.

Non-specific periostitis was noted on one rib of a 2.5 to 3.5 year old (SK 602), and on the disarticulated humerus of a child of approximately 18 months. The ribs of a nine-month-old infant displayed multiple pits and scooped out areas within the costal groove, the aetiology of which could not be determined. No evidence of infection by specific organisms was found.

A further striking feature of the children's cemetery was the non-conformity in burial type. Body position and grave orientation could be determined in 35 burials and these fell into six groups. Only 37% (13/35) were of the typical 'Christian' type, being extended on a west–east alignment.

This variability contrasts strongly with the uniformity apparent in the later-medieval cemetery.

Whilst 12% of the Northumbrian burials could be 'accidental' (i.e. the reversed and prone burials), only 0.6% of the medieval burials could be as interpreted in this way. The apparent lack of systematic burial may reflect the general trends of the time, the way small children were treated, or some feature of this particular group. An alternative explanation may be burial whilst the body was still in rigor mortis, the burial position reflecting the position in which the child died. Analysis shows no clear association between burial position and age, although there may be a tendency for younger children to be flexed. Unfortunately, the adult counterpart of this cemetery has not been discovered. The classes of inhumation are listed below, the number of each being given in brackets.

West–east, extended (13).
West–east, loosely flexed on left side (9).
West–east, loosely flexed on right side (6).
East–west, extended (4).
East–west, loosely flexed on left side (2).
West–east, prone extended (1).

Thirteen skeletons were too fragmentary to determine either body position or orientation.

The present sample provides clear evidence of non-random burial practice, the burial population obviously being very specialised in terms of age and pathology. The presence of premature infants and those who may have died at birth may indicate that the stillborn were considered eligible for burial within consecrated ground.

The cause of the high rate of severe cribra orbitalia and cranial changes is not clear but probably involves differences in social and/or biological factors between Northumbrian and later-medieval populations.

THE BUNDLE OF BONES

Overlying the children's cemetery was a 'bundle' of bones which was probably wrapped in a soft leather or cloth roll. The bundle contained the almost complete skeleton of a young adult female, a few elements of a more robust individual, probably an early middle-aged male, and a few animal bones (Figure 5.5).

The primary burial (SK 1576) was probably partially decomposed when her remains were 'gathered', as some joints appear to have been loosely articulated and two cervical vertebrae were closely articulated. The cranium was placed within the fragmentary cranium of a larger individual at the west end of the bundle. There was gross destruction of the inferior body of the second lumbar vertebra and destruction of the third lumbar vertebra although very little of this survives. There was little or no new bone formation and a diagnosis of vertebral tuberculosis or vertebral osteomyelitis seems probable. There was also spondylolysis of L5 (section 4.1.6 pp 532-3) and a partial fracture/ spondylolysis at the unusual site of the left laminae of the second thoracic vertebra.

Fragments of robust long bones (right humerus, left and right femoral diaphyses) were also present which may be from the same individual as the larger, outer calvarium (SK 1577).

This deposit, which is unique at Whithorn, is open to interpretation. Perhaps the simplest interpretation involves the death of SK 1576 (possibly from tuberculosis) elsewhere, where she was allowed to largely decompose. Some time after her death, but before decomposition was complete, the remains were carefully gathered, wrapped and reinterred beside the chapel. The fragments of SK 1577 may represent an earlier interment that was disturbed by the burial of SK 1576, perhaps deliberately included in the reburial as SK 1576's cranium was carefully placed within that of SK 1577.

THE CREMATION

Overlying the bundle of bones was a spread of burnt human bone with a total weight of approximately 2070 grams (Figure 5.5). The size of the fragments ranged from very small to 45 mm in length, suggesting that the bones were crushed after burning. Fragments of at least four individuals were present (4 × left zygoma) and all appear to be adult or near adult. Most fragments were pale yellow or white, and some cranial fragments had a black inner layer. There was little distortion of the fragments although the long bones show horizontal cracks, indicating burning whilst still 'green' (Stewart 1979, 59–68). There were few completely calcined fragments. No dental enamel survived but ten roots were recovered, from both single rooted teeth and from molars. Two of these displayed hypercementosis, a condition that may be associated with dental disease or advancing age. Little evidence of articular surfaces or of vertebrae was found, most fragments being cranial or diaphyseal.

APPENDIX 1

Sites used for comparative purposes.

Site	Period	Sample size	Reference
Linlithgow (Carmelite)	C13th–C17th	207	Cross and Bruce 1989
Aberdeen (Carmelite)	C13th–C16th	126	Cross and Bruce 1989
Logies Lane, St Andrews	C15th–C16th	121	Cardy 1993
Kirkhill, St Andrews		330	Bruce, Cross and Kerr 1990
Whithorn	C13th–C15th	1605	This volume
Whithorn	C6th–C7th	59	This volume
Whithorn	C8th–C10th	56	This volume
Ipswich Blackfriars	C13th–C16th	250	Mays 1991
St Helen on-the-walls, York	C10th–C16th	1041	Dawes 1980
St Nicholas Shambles, London	C11th–C12th	234	White 1988
Isle of Ensay	C16th–recent	416	Miles 1989
Cirencester	C2nd–C5th	407	Wells 1982

APPENDIX 2

Fractures.

SK no.	Sex	Age	Bone(s)
7	?M	MA	Right third metatarsal, shaft.
19	?F	OA	Pedicle of one upper TV, avulsion?
29		CH	Humeral shaft, possible.
66	?M	MA	Right second metatarsal, shaft.
75	UK	MA	Proximal fibula (or enthesopathy?).
140		OJ	Left inferior fibula.
211		OJ	Left humerus, mid shaft.
233		YJ	Right humerus, at deltoid tuberosity.
259		OJ	Right tibial fragments. Possible, with osteomyelitis.
273		YJ	Fibula fragment.
341	?M	SA	Left and right navicular tuberosities, avulsion?
409		OJ	Left femur, proximal 1/3 point, possible.
514	M	MA	Rib fragment: fibula at proximal 1/3 point.
526	UK	MA	Left first metatarsal, shaft.
528	M	MA	Two hand phalanges fused, possible.
533	M	MA	'Parry' fracture of right ulna. Healing not complete.
561	M	SA	Right femur, mid shaft.
586	M	EMA	Rib fragment.
622	F	MA	Left distal radius, possibly pathological.
625	M	SA	Right tibia, proximal. Fusion of growth plate during childhood; left fibula, distal chip.
626	M	EMA	Right tibia, distal 1/3 point. Spiral.
627	M	EMA	Proximal facet of one foot phalanx; avulsion of tuberosity of right navicular?
632	M	SA	Right femur at proximal 1/3 point.
637	UK	MA	Left tibia and fibula, spiral, bones fused.

SK no.	Sex	Age	Bone(s)
645	M	EMA	Right clavicle at lateral 1/3 point.
656	M	MA	Left first metacarpal, 'crack' in proximal facet.
657	M	MA	Left radius, distal 1/3 point.
660	UK	Ad	Left femoral neck. Non-union.
664	UK	YA	Fibula, unidentified fragment.
670	?M	MA	Tuberosity of left fifth metatarsal, avulsion?
680	UK	Ad	Tuberosity of left and right fifth metatarsals, avulsion?
732	?F	OA	Left distal radius, possible.
734	F	LMA	Rib fragment.
754	F	MA	Rib fragment.
760	?M	SA	Left second and third metacarpals, shaft.
768	UK	MA	Foot phalanx, shaft.
771	M	MA	Rib fragment, possible.
790	F	EMA	Rib (4); right scapula (base of spine).
804	?F	EMA	Foot phalanx, 'crack' in proximal facet.
824	F	EMA	Rib, two fragments.
870	F	MA	Left capitate, avulsion fracture ?
872	M	MA	Right distal radius, possible.
891	F	MA	Left humerus, neck, possible. Rib, fragment.
892	M	EMA	Wedge-shaped piece of bone detached from antero-superior rim of one lumbar vertebra.
982	?M	MA	Left ulna 'parry' fracture; right fifth metacarpal, shaft.
1005	M	EMA	Left humerus – avulsion of medial epicondyle?
1006	?M	MA	Right clavicle, possible.
1013	M	EMA	Rib fragment; one proximal and middle phalanx fused.
1018	?F	YA	Left tibia, anterior border 'pushed' medially. Possible.
1031	?M	Ad	Left distal tibia, distal 1/4 point. Possible.
1051	UK	MA	Right radius, distal.
1060	F	MA	Shaft of one metacarpal.
1064	F	LMA	Right hand, first metacarpal fused with trapezium, second and third metacarpals fused with carpals.
1080	M	MA	Right distal radius with loss of styloid process of ulna; multiple ribs; left fifth metacarpal, shaft.
1081	M	SA	Rib (1).
1116	M	OA	Right distal tibia; rib; foot phalanx, proximal facet.
1139	F	MA	Left third metacarpal, shaft.
1141	M	LMA	Multiple ribs; right scaphoid facet of radius; right fourth metacarpal, shaft.
1145	M	MA	Rib fragment.
1160	M	MA	Multiple ribs.
1166	F	LMA	Right first metatarsal, shaft.
1183	M	EMA	Right clavicle (healed out of alignment); rib fragment.
1201	M	MA	Fibula, unidentified fragment.
1233	F	MA	Left maxilla.
1242	F	MA	Right navicular tuberosity, avulsion?
1284	M	MA	Right fifth metatarsal, shaft.
1298	UK	MA	Right navicular tuberosity, avulsion?
1327	M	YA	Rib fragment.
1377	UK	MA	Hand phalanx, shaft.
1388	M	MA	Right scapula, lateral blade.
1391	M	LMA	Hand phalanx.
1401	M	LMA	Three ribs – pathological?
1434	?F	EMA	Rib fragment, possible.
1496	UK	Ad	Right distal tibia – 'crack' in articular surface.
1550	F	Ad	Right clavicle, medial 1/3 point.
1522		YJ	Rib with possible infection.
1544	M	Ad	Left navicular tuberosity, avulsion?
1563	?F	EMA	Left first metatarsal-phalangeal joint. Medial condyle is 'crushed' and phalanx has a crack in proximal facet.
1573	M	YA	Rib fragment.
1583	M	LMA	Left and right pubic bones, 'butterfly' fracture.

APPENDIX 3

Osteomyelitis.

SK no.	Sex	Age	Bone(s) affected
259	UK	OJ	Right tibia, possible (very poor condition).
520	UK	Ad	Left fibula shaft.
564	UK	Ad	Right tibia, possible, fused with talus and calcaneus.
586	M	EMA	Right fibula shaft, possible (fragment).
628	?M	EMA	Right tibia and fibula.
633	?F	SA	Right tibia swollen and 15 mm longer than LHS. Large opening in distal facet.
648	M	MA	Left distal femur.
652	UK	YA	Right distal femur and fibula.
653	UK	Ad	Right distal femur, possible.

SK no.	Sex	Age	Bone(s) affected
665	UK	Ad	Right tibia, whole shaft swollen. Fused with talus.
901	F	EMA	Left tibia, opening in distal facet. Left and right fibulae.
1031	?M	Ad	Left femur (distal 2/3).
1056	M	EMA	Right femur, mid-shaft.
1081	M	SA	Cranium – frontal and left parietal.
1373	?M	MA	Left femur and patella fused, possible.
1459	M	Ad	Hip, possible (tuberculosis?).
1494	?M	Ad	Left humerus (distal 2/3) and ulna (proximal only present).

APPENDIX 4

Individuals with bowing of the lower limb.

SK no.	Sex	Age	Details
6		CH	Described in text.
32	UK	MA	Some antero-lateral bowing of tibiae.
39	M	SA	Slight antero-laterally bowing of tibiae.
142		CH	Proximal femoral shafts have a bony build-up anteriorly creating a 'border'. Femora are stocky and appear bowed anteriorly.
199		CH	Slight anterior bowing of femora.
201		CH	Anterior bowing of femora. Cortex is porous.
214		IN	Slight anterior bowing of tibiae.
220		PE/IN	Slight bowing of tibiae.
358		YJ	Lateral bowing of tibiae in the distal 1/3.
360		IN	Anterior bowing of femora.
453		CH	Slight medial bowing of tibiae.
527	UK	YA	Slight lateral bowing of femora. Linea aspera is medially placed.
650	M	MA	Slight lateral bowing of femora. Strong medial flange.
809	F	MA	Femora are bowed anteriorly.
1279	M	MA	Slight lateral bowing of femora.
1305	M	SA	Slight anterior bowing of tibiae.
1359	M	YA	Slight lateral bowing of femora.

The Human Dentitions

D. A. Lunt and M. E. Watt
Department of Oral Sciences, University of Glasgow

1. INTRODUCTION

Although the sheer quantity of human remains recovered from the excavation make this a most valuable collection of skeletal material, there are certain problems which render its study difficult.

The material is in an extremely fragmentary state. In over 1700 articulated burials, only one skull survives in an almost intact condition and two more are partially preserved. Parts of the cranial vault are intact in many cases, but the cranial base and bones of the upper face are often missing, and the maxilla has almost always been detached fom the rest of the skull. Very frequently the palate and alveolar process are all that remain of the maxilla, and they are broken into several pieces. Even the mandible, a robust bone which usually survives well in the ground, is in this material often to be found in several pieces and the condyle and coronoid process from one or both sides may be missing. Because of the lack of the cranial base which carries the glenoid fossa of the temporo-mandibular joint, the separation of the maxilla from the skull, and the fragmentation of maxilla and mandible, the occlusal relationship between maxilla and mandible cannot be accurately established in most cases.

In addition to the mechanical fragmentation of the bones, many of the specimens have suffered to varying extents from post-mortem degradation of bone, and of the dentine and cementum of the teeth. This is due to soil action and involves the breakdown of collagen which forms the fibrous matrix of all three tissues (Beeley and Lunt, 1980). The effects of this gradual decomposition of collagen vary from a slight surface erosion of the cervical region of the root to complete loss of parts of the tooth. Major destruction of the tissues usually begins at the apices of the roots and works gradually towards the crown. Eventually the whole of the root will be destroyed and the coronal dentine will then be attacked, ultimately leaving only a shell of enamel. In the Whithorn material there is a complete range from teeth which are totally unaffected by this condition to teeth which are represented only by fragments of enamel shells. Presumably differences in soil conditions across the site have led to the variation in state of preservation of the dentitions.

Of the *c.* 1700 articulated burials, 972 yielded some part of the jaws and/or dentition, though in many instances only a small fragment was present. The proportion of burials with dentitions was lower than that at some other medieval sites. Among the disarticulated material, 693 jaw fragments yielded some useful information concerning the dentition. It has not been possible to make any attempts to match these fragments, often very small, either with the incomplete articulated jaw specimens or with other disarticulated fragments. In addition, 5506 teeth were present loose. No attempts could be made to reunite loose teeth with empty sockets in the jaw fragments.

The articulated skeletal material has been divided by the excavators on archaeological grounds into seventeen groups. **Groups 1–14** come from the main trench in the Glebe Field, while **Groups 15–17** come from the smaller excavation in the Museum Garden. **Group 1** comprises the mid-sixth to early-eighth century material from the **Period I** graveyard, **Group 2** the eighth and ninth century burials associated with the burial chapel in **Periods II** and **III**, and **Group 3** the two burials ascribed to **Period IV**. **Groups 4–9** comprise the earlier **Period V** burials (**Period V/1**, *c* 1300–1350) and **Groups 10–14** the later ones (**Period V/2 and V/3**, c 1350–1450). **Groups 15–17** probably date to a similar period as **Groups 4–14**, but cannot be correlated specifically with them. (We are indebted to the excavation director Mr Peter Hill for information concerning the details of phasing.) Sixty-four specimens (6.6% of the total) were not assigned to any phase. An important aspect of the present investigation has been to ascertain whether discernible differences in the dentition exist between the various phases.

It should be pointed out that data were recorded from all but a handful of specimens before the full details of skeleton phasing were received. The identity of most **Group 1** and **Group 2** specimens was known at the time of examination, but virtually all medieval specimens were examined 'blind'.

In the report which follows, the articulated material has been considered as of prime importance, though some additional information has been obtained from the disarticulated material and loose teeth.

2. AGE

2.1. Age estimation – methods

The age at death of each person represented by a dentition or fragment of a dentition has been estimated. In juveniles, age may be assessed using the stage of development of the dentition. Once the teeth are fully formed, the degree of wear or attrition of the permanent teeth may be used to give an indication of age.

There are several methods for estimating age from the stage of development of the dentition. The detailed plots of development of the permanent mandibular canines, premolars and molars published by Moorrees *et al.* (1963) are generally considered to provide the most accurate chronology of tooth development in caucasoids, since they are based on large longitudinal studies of white children from Boston and Ohio. These plots serve to show the extremely wide variation in the timing of tooth development, but are cumbersome in use. Furthermore, the teeth in an individual dentition seldom show stages of development which correspond to the means for a single age in the Moorrees plot. The tables of values for predicting age calculated by Smith (1991) from the Moorrees data had not been published when the study of the Whithorn material was begun. Another system for estimating age from the development of the dentition was published by Demirjian *et al.* (1973, 1976). In this system, the stages of development of permanent teeth were given weighted values which were summed and the age read off from a table or graph. This system has the disadvantage that either four or seven specific teeth must be present, which was often not the case in the fragmentary Whithorn material.

The quickest method of estimating age from dental development is to use one of the chronological charts in which drawings of the jaws at yearly or shorter intervals show the stage of dental development to be expected at that age. An early version of such a chart was published by Schour and Massler (1941). Very similar charts were produced by Ubelaker (1978) and Hillson (1986). The Schour and Massler chart is the best drawn and easiest to use, but is now considered suspect as the nature and quantity of material on which it was based were not specified. The Hillson chart is based directly on the Schour and Massler chart and gives the same result. In their efforts to 'unify methods in paleo-demography' with respect to 'europids' only, Ferembach *et al.* (1980) recommended the use of the Ubelaker chart. However, reference to Ubelaker's volume shows that the chart which Ferembach *et al.* copy was intended to refer to American Indians and other non-white populations, though the material on which it is said to be based is a mixture of American white, black and Indian. Thus the Ubelaker chart does not seem appropriate for use with European material. In fact it varies relatively little from the Schour and Massler chart, but has the defect that some stages of development of some teeth are inaccurately drawn.

In the initial studies of the very large quantity of juvenile material from Whithorn, the Moorrees and Demirjian methods were considered too time-consuming and often inappropriate. Assessment by use of a chart was selected as the most suitable method, and since the Ubelaker chart was not entirely satisfactory, the Schour and Massler chart was chosen for age assessment in the juveniles. Each dentition was matched to the nearest stage on the chart, though frequently the teeth in a given dentition showed stages of development which could not all be related to a single age on the chart. When teeth were developing within the jaw-bones, radiographs of the specimens were taken in order to provide the maximum information.

The charts mentioned above do not cover the stages of development of the third molars, and age has been assessed in individuals between 15 and 20 from the stage of development of the third molar using the charts published by Johanson (1971). Any individual showing incomplete development of third molar roots has been assigned an age below 20, based on these charts.

Further, more detailed studies of dental development in the Whithorn juveniles are being undertaken.

Once the teeth are fully developed, the method commonly employed to assess age is based on the degree of attrition of the occlusal surfaces of the permanent molars. These three teeth erupt at roughly six-year intervals and show a gradient in attrition which persists throughout adult life. Working from a baseline constructed from the correlation between attrition and developmental age in the juveniles, Miles (1963) published a scale in which age is plotted against the degree of attrition in all three molars. This study was carried out on a group of Anglo-Saxon skeletons and strictly the scale refers only to that population. However, it is found to be suitable for use with many prehistoric and early historic population groups. A more generalised scale, based on the Miles scale, was published by Brothwell (1972).

In theory, a scale of attrition should be established by Miles' method for each population group under examination, though this is seldom possible because of the scarcity of juvenile skeletons of the appropriate ages. In the case of the Whithorn material, there were sufficient juveniles to allow a population-specific scale to be constructed, and it had been hoped that this could have been prepared and consequently more reliable ages could have been derived for the adults. The time-scale for the preparation of this report was unfortunately too short to permit this study to be completed. It has therefore been necessary to estimate the ages of adults using the published scale of Brothwell, though it has been obvious that in many cases this scale is not appropriate, as the molars have not all shown degrees of attrition compatible with a single age group. It is intended to examine the possibility of preparing a more accurate scale for age estimation in the Whithorn adults at a later date.

In the Brothwell scheme, the youngest group is identified as ranging from 17 to 25 years. However, Johanson (1971) showed that in his Swedish material, the roots of third molars were always complete by 20. In the present study, specimens with attrition comparable to Brothwell group 17–25 and with full development of third molar roots were assigned to an age group 20–25. Only if the third molars were not present was a specimen assigned to the group 17–25 which bridges adolescents and adults. The remaining adult dentitions were assigned to the groups 25–35, 35–45 and 45+, following Brothwell's scales. In some instances it proved impossible to place a dentition in one of these categories, usually due to marked discrepancies in attrition between upper and lower jaws, or between right and left sides, and in such cases the dentition was assigned to a broader group 20–35 or 25–45. These groups were also used in specimens whose molars were not present.

It must be emphasised that these techniques are not considered to give a highly accurate estimate of real age at death. Even the estimation of age in children, which is often thought to give an accurate result, may not do so. Reference to the work of Moorrees *et al.* (1963) shows how variable the chronology of tooth development may be: some developmental stages of certain teeth show ranges of variation extending over three or four years. Some permanent teeth show ranges of variation of as much as six years for the later stages of root development. Thus, in attempting to estimate age, the assumption has to be made that the child was not only normal but also average in its development. There may also be some question as to whether the chronology of tooth development in earlier periods was similar to that observed at present.

The age categories applied to adult dentitions may bear even less relation to the real ages of the individuals. However, age estimation allows specimens to be grouped into sets of roughly comparable age and for these sets to be placed in order of ascending age. Age estimates obtained from the dentition have generally been shown to be closer to true chronological age than estimates derived from the skeleton. In the present report, it should be clearly understood that in all cases it is the dental age of the individual which has been assessed.

With the exception of the skeletal material excavated in 1986, only the jaw-bones and dentitions have been studied, and in no instance has the post-cranial skeleton been examined. It is not possible to make a reliable estimate of sex from the jaws or dentition, and we are much indebted to Ms Amanda Cardy for supplying information concerning the sex of the articulated skeletons where this could be ascertained. They were classified as 'male', 'possible male', 'female', 'possible female' and 'indeterminate' or 'ambiguous'.

2.2. Age distribution – results

Using the techniques detailed above, it was possible to assign all dentitions in the articulated material to an age category, except for four specimens from **Period I** which consisted only of small fragments of broken enamel shells. Tables 11.24 and 11.25 show the distribution of the 972 dentitions from the articulated burials, divided by phase, sex and age group. Juveniles and adults have been tabulated separately since the juveniles cannot be sexed. (A few of the oldest juveniles had been

Whithorn All Phases – Juveniles

	Period I	II	IV				Period V Glebe Field							Museum Garden					
Group	1	2	3	4	5	6	7	8	9	10	11	12	13	14	15	16	17	NP	Total
Foetal		4						1					3					1	9
At birth		5			2				1			2			2	1			13
0.1–0.5		1		1	1				2		1					1			7
0.6–0.9		2							3	1			1	1	1			2	11
1		3							1		1		1		1				7
1.5					1								3						4
2		1		1	2		2			2	1		2		1	1		1	14
2.5		1			1			2	1				1					1	7
3							2	4	2				1			1		1	11
3.5					1								1						2
4		1			3				3				1	1	1	1			11
4.5						1		1										1	3
5		2		1	3	1			1			2	2	3		1		1	17
5.5						1								1					2
6		1		1		2	2		2	1			3	3	2	1		1	19
6.5	1													1				1	3
7	1				1	1				1			2	3	3	3			15
7.5								1		1				2				1	5
8		2		1				1	1			1		2	1	2	2	2	15
8.5		1						1		1								1	4
9							1	1	1	8			1		4			1	17
9.5								1											1
10					3			1		2						1		3	10
10.5	1					1					1			1				1	5
11					1	1				4				2	1			1	10
11.5														1				1	2
12		1				2	1			1				1	1		1	1	9
12.5						1				1									2
13								1		2		1	1		1	1	1		8
13.5						1				1									2
14						1	1	2		3		1	2		2	2	1		17
14.5							1							1					2
15	1				2			1	5									1	11
16					3	1	2		1	1	1		2		1				12
17					1		3		3				1	2		2		1	13
18					1		4	1	2	1	1	4	5	2	4	1			26
19					1				2				1		1			1	6
Totals	4	25	0	6	30	13	26	10	53	9	11	17	52	10	26	14	0	26	332

Age Groups of Juveniles

	Period I	II–III	IV				Period V Glebe Field							Museum Garden					
Group	1	2	3	4	5	6	7	8	9	10	11	12	13	14	15	16	17	NP	Total
–9.9–0	0	9	0	0	2	0	0	1	1	0	0	2	3	0	2	1	0	1	22
0.1–5.9	0	11	0	4	12	2	6	5	13	3	5	2	15	2	5	4	0	7	96
6–12.9	3	5	0	2	6	8	8	2	20	4	2	5	20	3	8	7	0	14	117
13–19.9	1	0	0	0	10	3	12	2	19	2	4	8	14	5	11	2	0	4	97
Totals	4	25	0	6	30	13	26	10	53	9	11	17	52	10	26	14	0	26	332

Table 11.24: Distribution of Whithorn Juveniles by Age and Phase. NP = phase unknown.

sexed, but as they represented a very small proportion of all juveniles, sexing in these cases had been ignored.) The use of six-monthly intervals in ageing the juveniles should not be taken as an attempt at hyper-accuracy. It indicates either dentitions which showed a stage of development halfway between two stages on the published scale, or dentitions in which some teeth indicated a specific age and other teeth suggested that the individual was a year older.

When the material is divided in this way, it will be seen that the numerous sub-groups generally contain very small numbers of specimens, and in order to make meaningful comparisons it is necessary to combine groups in one way or another. Most phases have relatively small numbers of individuals, only **Groups 9** and **13** containing reasonably large numbers of specimens.

The juvenile specimens (Table 11.24) are scattered widely over the age range with little evidence of

Withorn All Phases – Adults

	Period I	Periods II–III	Period IV	Period V Glebe Field		
	Group 1	Group 2	Group 3	Group 4	Group 5	Group 6
	MM M FF F U	MM M FF F U	MM M FF F U	MM M FF F U	MM M FF F U	MM M FF F U
20–25	2 1 2			1	1 2 1	1 1
25–35	1 2 1 3	1 1		1 1	1 2 1 4 7	1 1 3 2 1
35–45	3 5 4			1 1 1	7 2 4 3	1 1 1 3
45+					1	1 1
20–35						
25–45	1 3		1		1 1 1	2
Total	6 6 2 2 12	0 1 1 0 0	0 1 0 0 0	2 1 2 0 1	10 6 8 5 10	2 4 4 2 8
MM+M, FF+F	12 4	1 1	1 0	3 2	16 13	6 6

	Period V Glebe Field					
	Group 7	Group 8	Group 9	Group 10	Group 11	Group 12
	MM M FF F U	MM M FF F U	MM M FF F U	MM M FF F U	MM M FF F U	MM M FF F U
20–25	3	1 1	3 7 5 6	2 2	2 1 1 1	1 2 2
25–35	3 2 4 4 4	1 1 1 1 1	8 5 15 4 15	4 8 1	4 1 8 2	10 2 5 3 10
35–45	4 3 3 2 2	1 2	8 2 14 7 14	3 1 1 4	1 1 1 3	2 6 2 1
45+	1 1 1	1 1	2 1 2 6	2	1 1 1	3 1 1
20–35	1					1
25–45	1 1		1 1 2 1		1	1
Total	9 6 8 7 10	1 1 4 1 5	22 9 38 19 41	6 3 11 1 8	8 4 10 1 6	16 4 14 6 13
MM+M, FF+F	15 15	2 5	31 57	9 12	12 11	20 20

	Period V Glebe Field			Museum Garden		
	Group 13	Group 14	Group 15	Group 16	Group 17	Group Unknown
	MM M FF F U	MM M FF F U	MM M FF F U	MM M FF F U	MM M FF F U	MM M FF F U
20–25	2 8 1 2	2 1 1 1	1 1 1			1 1
25–35	12 3 12 3 14	7 8 2 1	4 2 5	2		3 2 2 2 7
35–45	9 6 16 1 13	3 2 1	1 3 2	1		3 2 1 8
45+	4 1 3 1	1	2 1 1 1		2	1 2
20–35	1 1		1			
25–45	1 1 2 1 1	1	2			
Total	29 11 41 7 31	10 2 12 4 3	8 2 9 0 9	1 0 2 0 2	0 0 0 0 0	5 5 4 3 18
MM+M, FF+F	40 48	12 16	10 9	1 2	0 0	10 7

Total 606

Dubious

	Group 1	Group 2	Group 3	Group 4	Group 5	Group 6
	MM M FF F U	MM M FF F U	MM M FF F U	MM M FF F U	MM M FF F U	MM M FF F U
17–25	8					2
Unknown	4					

	Group 7	Group 8	Group 9	Group 10	Group 11	Group 12
	MM M FF F U	MM M FF F U	MM M FF F U	MM M FF F U	MM M FF F U	MM M FF F U
17–25	1 2		4		2 1	
Unknown						

	Group 13	Group 14	Group 15	Group 16	Group 17	Group Unknown
	MM M FF F U	MM M FF F U	MM M FF F U	MM M FF F U	MM M FF F U	MM M FF F U
17–25	1 3	1	1		1	3
Uknown						

Total 34
Overall Total 640

Table 11.25: Distribution of Whithorn Adults by Age, Sex and Phase.
MM = male, M = possible male, FF= female, F = possible female, U = sex undetermined

clusters, the only possible exceptions being the group of foetal and neonatal specimens from **Period II** (**Group 2**), and the 9 year olds in **Group 9**. For further study it is convenient to group the juveniles into four categories as follows:

-0.9 – 0   foetal and neonatal;
0.1 – 5.9   the period of the deciduous dentition;
6 – 12.9   replacement of deciduous by permanent dentition;
13 – 19.9   development of third molars.

The distribution of specimens in these four categories is shown at the bottom of Table 11.24.

Examination of Table 11.25 shows that many of the adults could not be sexed and in most phases the numbers of sexed adults, when subdivided by age group, become very small. For most phases, the total numbers of males and females are reasonably close, except for **Period I (Group 1)** where there are noticeably more males than females, and **Group 9** which has almost twice as many females as males.

When the phases are considered individually

Group 9 (535)

	M	%	F	%	Total	%
20–25	3	9.4	12	21.1	15	16.9
25–35	14	43.7	19	33.3	33	37.1
35–45	10	31.2	21	36.8	31	34.8
45+	3	9.4	2	3.5	5	5.6
17–25						
20–35						
25–45	2	6.2	3	5.3	5	5.6
Totals	32	100	57	100	89	100

Group 13 (539)

	M	%	F	%	Total	%
20–25	2	4.9	9	18.7	11	12.4
25–35	15	36.6	15	31.2	30	33.7
35–45	15	36.6	17	35.4	32	36.0
45+	5	12.2	3	6.2	8	9.0
17–25	1	2.4			1	1.1
20–35	1	2.4	1	2.1	2	2.2
25–45	2	4.9	3	6.2	5	5.6
Totals	41	100	48	100	89	100

All Phases

	M	%	F	%	Total	%
20–25	18	8.8	33	14.3	51	11.7
25–35	81	39.5	101	43.9	182	41.8
35–45	68	33.2	70	30.4	138	31.7
45+	23	11.2	12	5.2	35	8.0
17–25	3	1.5	2	0.9	5	1.1
20–35	2	1.0	3	1.3	5	1.1
25–45	10	4.9	9	3.9	19	4.4
Totals	205	100	230	100	435	100

Table 11.26: Percentage Distribution of Males, Females and Combined Sexes in each Age Group in Groups 9 and 13 and All Phases combined.

(Archive table 1), there are some differences in the percentage distribution of age groups in the males and females, though often the differences are not great and they show no general trend in direction. The small numbers of sexed individuals in many of the phases preclude a full comparison between the sexes on the basis of separate phases. Table 11.26 shows the percentage distribution of age groups in **Groups 9** and **13**, and also in the males and females of all phases combined. Both **Groups 9** and **13** show a larger percentage of females in the 20–25 age group, and **Group 9** has a larger percentage of males in the 25–35 age group. When all phases are combined, the differences between male and female age distributions are reduced. On the available evidence, it would appear that the age distribution is not markedly different for males and for females.

In order to examine possible differences in overall age distribution between the phases, adult males and females have been combined. This allows the relatively large numbers of unsexed adults to be included, and also permits juveniles and adults to be compared at the same time. The overall percentage age distribution in separate phases is shown in Table 11.28. The most striking features are the small proportion of juveniles in **Period I (Group 1)** and the very large proportions of juveniles in **Period II (Group 2)** and in the later burials from the Museum Garden (**Group 16**). **Group 2** consists almost entirely of children and a large proportion of these are from the two youngest age categories. When all four juvenile categories are summed, it will be seen that the proportions of juveniles in **Groups 4–8** and in **Group 15** (from 38% to 50%) are rather higher than the proportions of juveniles in **Groups 9–14** (24% to 30%). The proportions of the categories of adults appear to be fairly constant, some variation being observed in the smaller phases. Most of the adults are to be found in the 25–35 and 35–45 age categories, with much smaller percentages in the other age groups.

The data for all phases have been combined to give the overall percentage age distribution for the entire Whithorn material. It will be seen that the percentage distributions for the largest individual phases, **Groups 9** and **13**, are not only very similar to each other but also similar to the overall percentage age distribution.

The overall percentage age distribution for the articulated material is compared with that for the disarticulated fragments in Table 11.27. There is a reasonable degree of similarity in age distribution between the two groups of material, though there are slightly fewer juveniles in the disarticulated material. The increase in the 25–45 age group in the disarticulated material reflects the fact that many fragments were very small and did not carry the molars essential to a more precise age estimate. The age distribution figures for the Whithorn material may also be compared with those obtained from the Kirkhill site in St Andrews, where the medieval material consisted of 24% juveniles and 76% adults (Lunt 1986).

Age Distribution

	Articulated		Disarticulated	
	n	%	n	%
–0.9–0	22	2.3	1	0.1
0.1–5.9	96	9.9	54	7.8
6–12.9	117	12.0	102	14.7
13–19.9	97	10.0	48	6.9
All Juveniles	332	34.2	205	29.6
20–25	75	7.7	61	8.8
25–35	252	25.9	175	25.3
35–45	197	20.3	98	14.1
45+	49	5.0	27	3.9
17–25	30	3.1	32	4.6
20–35	5	0.5		
25–45	28	2.9	95	13.7
Unknown	4	0.4		
All Adults +Dubious	640	65.8	488	70.4
Totals	972	100	693	100

Table 11.27: Comparison of Percentage Age Distribution in Articulated and Disarticulated Material.
n = number of dentitions in articulated skeletons or disarticulated fragments.

All Individuals in each Age Group in each Group

Group	1	2	3	4	5	6	7	8	9	10	11	12	13	14	15	16	17	NP	Total
–0.9–0	0	9	0	0	2	0	0	1	1	0	0	2	3	0	2	1	0	1	22
0.1–5.9	0	11	0	4	12	2	6	5	13	3	5	2	15	2	5	4	0	7	96
6–12.9	3	5	0	2	6	8	8	2	20	4	2	5	20	3	8	7	0	14	117
13–19.9	1	0	0	0	10	3	12	2	19	2	4	8	14	5	11	2	0	4	97
Total Juvs	4	25	0	6	30	13	26	10	53	9	11	17	52	10	26	14	0	26	332
20–25	5	0	0	1	4	2	3	2	21	4	5	5	13	5	3	0	0	2	75
25–35	7	2	0	2	15	8	17	5	47	13	15	30	44	18	11	2	0	16	252
35–45	12	0	0	3	16	6	14	3	45	9	6	11	45	6	6	1	0	14	197
45+	0	0	0	0	1	2	3	2	11	2	3	5	9	1	5	2	0	3	49
Total Adults	24	2	0	6	36	18	37	12	124	28	29	51	111	30	25	5	0	35	573
17–25	8	0	0	0	0	2	3	0	4	0	3	0	4	1	1	0	1	3	30
20–35	0	0	0	0	0	0	1	0	0	0	0	1	2	0	1	0	0	0	5
25–45	4	0	1	0	3	2	2	0	5	1	0	1	6	1	2	0	0	0	28
Unknown	4	0	0	0	0	0	0	0	0	0	0	0	0	0	0	0	0	0	4
Total Dubious	16	0	1	0	3	4	6	0	9	1	3	2	12	2	4	0	1	3	67
Total Individs	44	27	1	12	69	35	69	22	186	38	43	70	175	42	55	19	1	64	972

All Juveniles and Adults, Percentage of Total in Group

Group	1	2	3	4	5	6	7	8	9	10	11	12	13	14	15	16	17	NP	Total
–0.9–0		33.3			2.9			4.5	0.5			2.9	1.7		3.6	5.3		1.6	2.3
0.1–5.9		40.7	33.3	17.4	5.7	8.7	22.7	7.0	7.9	11.6	2.9	8.6	4.8	9.1	21.1		10.9	9.9	
6–12.9	6.8	18.5	16.7	8.7	22.9	11.6	9.1	10.8	10.5	4.7	7.1	11.4	7.1	14.5	36.8		21.9	12.0	
13–19.9	2.3				14.5	8.6	17.4	9.1	10.2	5.3	9.3	11.4	8.0	11.9	20.0	10.5		6.2	10.0
% Juveniles	9.1	92.6	50.0	43.5	37.1	37.7	45.5	28.5	23.7	25.6	24.3	29.7	23.8	47.3	73.7		40.6	34.2	
20–25	11.4		8.3	5.8	5.7	4.3	9.1	11.3	10.5	11.6	7.1	7.4	11.9	5.5			3.1	7.7	
25–35	15.9	7.4	16.7	21.7	22.9	24.6	22.7	25.3	34.2	34.9	42.9	25.1	42.9	20.0	10.5		25.0	25.9	
35–45	27.3		25.0	23.2	17.1	20.3	13.6	24.2	23.7	14.0	15.7	25.7	14.3	10.9	5.3		21.9	20.3	
45+					1.4	5.7	4.3	9.1	5.9	5.3	7.0	7.1	5.1	2.4	9.1	10.5		4.7	5.0
% Adults	54.5	7.4	50.0	52.2	51.4	53.6	54.5	66.7	73.7	67.4	72.9	63.4	71.4	45.5	26.3		54.7	59.0	
17–25	18.2					5.7	4.3		2.2		7.0		2.3	2.4	1.8		100	4.7	3.1
20–35							1.4					1.4	1.1		1.8				0.5
25–45	9.1		100		4.3	5.7	2.9		2.7	2.6		1.4	3.4	2.4	3.6				2.9
Unknown	9.1																		0.4
% Dubious	36.4		100		4.3	11.4	8.7		4.8	2.6	7.0	2.9	6.9	4.8	7.3		100	4.7	6.9
Totals	100	100	100	100	100	100	100	100	100	100	100	100	100	100	100	100	100	100	100

Table 11.28: Age Distribution and Percentage Age Distribution in each Group.

3. PATHOLOGICAL CONDITIONS

The pathological conditions encountered in the jaws of skeletal specimens may be divided into those of local dental origin and those which are manifestations of general systemic disease. Since the former are much commoner than the latter, they will be more likely to show any differences which may exist betwen archaeological phases and will be considered first.

3.1. Dental pathology – acquired

The conditions which will be considered under this heading include acquired conditions of the teeth such as dental caries, exposure of the pulp due to caries, exposure of the pulp due to severe attrition, and dental calculus; conditions of the supporting tissues and alveolar bone, including periodontal disease, dental abscesses/cysts and *in vivo* loss of teeth; developmental conditions of the teeth such as enamel hypoplasia, malformations of teeth, congenital absence of teeth, supernumerary teeth and embedded teeth.

3.1.1. Dental caries

Previous studies have shown a gradual increase in the prevalence of dental caries in Britain from prehistoric periods to medieval times, and a further increase to the 17th century and later (Moore and Corbett, 1971,

11.32 Early occlusal carious lesion in a mandibular third molar. Adult aged 35–45, **Group 13**.

1973, 1975; Lunt, 1974). The establishment of successive phases in the cemetery at Whithorn presents an opportunity to investigate possible differences in caries prevalence between earlier and later medieval periods at the site.

The condition of dental caries can be diagnosed with reasonable certainty in skeletal material. The larger lesions form obvious cavities within the tooth and may be associated with exposure of the pulp and a chronic dental abscess or cyst in the supporting alveolar bone. Smaller lesions must be differentiated from post-mortem erosion of the tooth surface, which often occurs. However, the shape of a carious lesion and discolouration of the dentine in its base usually suffice to distinguish the true lesion from the ravages of post-mortem erosion. It is important to realise that the location of carious lesions in medieval and earlier periods is rather different from that seen at the present time. While occlusal cavities in the crowns of the teeth and lesions of approximal enamel (the commonest forms in modern times) do occur in the earlier periods (Figure 11.32), many of the lesions in skeletal material are located at the neck of the tooth on either the approximal or the buccal surfaces (Figures 11.33 and 34). Early lesions at the neck on the approximal surfaces may easily be missed.

In the comparison of caries prevalence in skeletal material of different periods or phases, the methods employed in research on caries in modern populations cannot be used. In the latter, indices known as the DMFS and DMFT indices are based on the number of decayed, missing and filled surfaces or teeth in an individual, assuming that missing teeth have been lost as the result of caries. This technique is inappropriate for use with skeletal material, especially when it is very fragmentary, since many teeth and jaw segments will have been lost post-mortem and their status cannot be known. In addition, it would not necessarily be correct to assume that teeth lost *in vivo* have been lost due to caries.

In the study of caries in earlier population groups, the prevalence of the condition may be indicated by expressing the number of teeth observed to have carious lesions as a percentage of the number of teeth erupted into function and therefore at risk.

The articulated burials at Whithorn provided 13,530 erupted permanent teeth and 1572 erupted deciduous teeth. These numbers appear large, but when they are divided among 17 phases, 5 categories

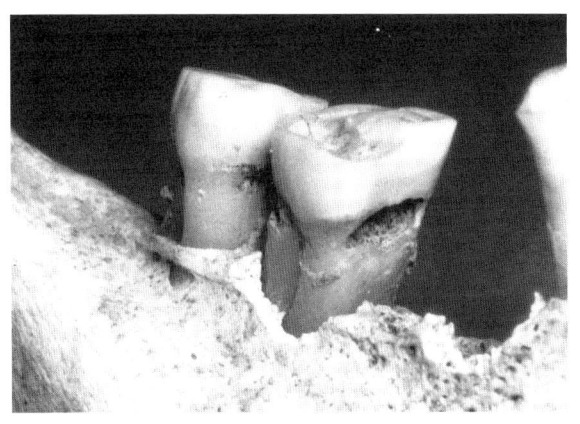

11.33 Approximal cervical carious lesion in a mandibular permanent second molar. The alveolar bone has been damaged post-mortem. Adult aged 35–45, **Group 13**.

of sex and 11 age groups, and may belong to one of 32 permanent or 20 deciduous tooth classes, the numbers in the final sub-groups may be very small indeed. In order to obtain meaningful caries prevalence figures, it is necessary to combine some of these categories.

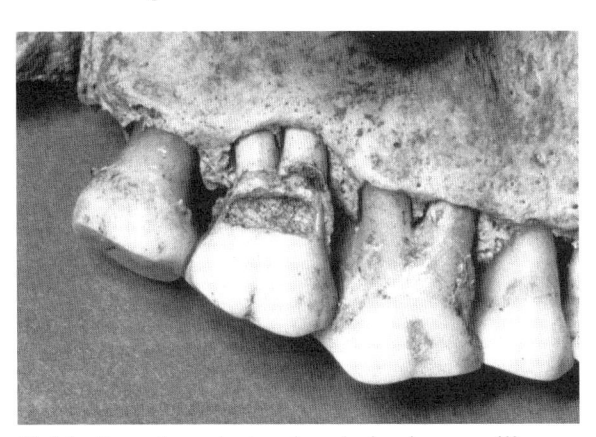

11.34 Buccal cervical carious lesion in a maxillary permanent second molar. Note localised alveolar bone loss in relation to the lesion and line of calculus on the root apical to the lesion. Adult aged 25–35, **Group 13**.

Dental caries prevalence, permanent dentition
In order to facilitate the assessment of caries prevalence in the permanent dentition, we may first consider whether it is possible to combine teeth of the same class from right and left sides of the jaw. Though dental caries may attack one side of the mouth to a greater degree than the other in an individual, there is no reason why caries should favour one side or the other in the population as a whole. When the teeth present and teeth with carious

Permanent Teeth: All Groups

Quadrant	UR Pres	Caries	%	UL Pres	Caries	%	LR Pres	Caries	%	LL Pres	Caries	%
6–12.9	222	2	0.9	213	3	1.4	259	3	1.2	259	3	1.2
13–19.9	497	2	0.4	466	5	1.1	533	6	1.1	530	10	1.9
20–25	425	8	1.9	427	9	2.1	443	10	2.3	445	5	1.1
25–35	1157	91	7.9	1164	108	9.3	1336	88	6.6	1295	90	6.9
35–45	598	71	11.9	583	82	14.1	699	88	12.6	737	82	11.1
45+	118	19	16.1	112	11	9.8	163	25	15.3	157	12	7.6
17–25	96	2	2.1	89	3	3.4	86	1	1.2	71	2	2.8
20–35	28	2	7.1	37		0.0	32		0.0	28	1	3.6
25–45	48	9	18.7	55	12	21.8	63		0.0	58	4	6.9
Unknown										1		0.0
Totals	3189	206	6.5	3146	233	7.4	3614	221	6.1	3581	209	5.8

Table 11.29: Percentage of Carious Permanent Teeth in Right and Left Quadrants. UR = upper right, UL = upper left, LR = lower right, LL = lower left.

lesions were tabulated for separate phases, separate sex categories, separate age groups and individual tooth classes, the final numbers in the sub-groups became so small that for most phases it was impossible to calculate percentages of carious teeth. This procedure was feasible only for **Groups 9** and **13** and all phases combined (Archive tables 2–10). When these figures for separate tooth classes were examined, some discrepancies in caries prevalence between right and left sides were noted, though in many cases the figures were virtually identical. The discrepancies are due to the fragmentary nature of the material and the fact that many articulated burials were represented by only one quadrant of the jaws.

When the material from all tooth classes and all phases was combined (Table 11.29), the percentages of carious teeth in right and left quadrants was similar throughout all the age groups. The only differences greater than 2% were observed in the age groups 45+, 20–35 and 25–45, all of which contained small numbers of individuals. The discrepancies observed were not consistent for side. Thus there does not seem to be any significant side-specific difference in caries prevalence, and the decision was therefore made to combine data from left and right sides. This table also shows in a crude fashion the variation in caries prevalence associated with age and indicates that in further work the age groups should generally be kept separate.

The next question to be considered is whether there are variations in caries prevalence between males and females. In some earlier studies, no difference in caries prevalence was observed between males and females, while in others some sex-related variation in caries prevalence was recorded (Hillson, 1986; Larsen *et al.*, 1991).

The numbers of individuals to whom sex could be assigned were relatively small. Even omitting the juveniles, there remained many of the adults for whom a determination of sex had been impossible. It was also found necessary to combine specimens in which a definite sex diagnosis had been made with those in which sex diagnosis was more doubtful, in order to maximise the number of sexed individuals. As in the study of right–left differences, comparisons on the basis of percentage caries prevalence figures could be made only for **Groups 9** and **13** (Archive tables 11 and 12) and all phases combined (Table 11.30). In the separate **Groups 9** and **13**, there was some variation in caries prevalence, with the higher values found sometimes in males and sometimes in females. When all phases were combined, the differences in caries prevalence between males and females were reduced and in most instances were negligible. Only in the small 45+ age group was there a consistently large difference, with females showing a higher caries prevalence for almost all tooth classes.

Since there did not appear to be consistent sex differences in caries prevalence, all individuals were combined irrespective of sex in order to study possible differences in caries prevalence between phases. Although this procedure increased the numbers of specimens in sub-groups, the numbers in some phases were still too small to give meaningful results. It was therefore decided to combine certain phases in further study. **Groups 1** and **2** remained as representing the archaeologically distinct **Periods I** and **II**. **Group 3** (**Period IV**) contained only one specimen and had to be ignored. The early **Period V** groups (**4–8**) were combined, but the much larger **Group 9** was allowed to stand on its own. **Groups 10–12** of **Period V/2** were combined while the large **Group 13** was combined with the small **Group 14**. The three groups (**15–17**) from the Museum Garden were also combined. This resulted in seven phase groups which could be compared.

The numbers of permanent teeth present and at risk, the numbers of carious teeth and the percentages of carious teeth for the seven phase groups are shown in Archive tables 13–19, in which all maxillary and mandibular teeth are shown separately for nine different age groups, beginning with the group 6–12.9 years. Below the age of 6 years, only a few first permanent molars may be emerging and they will not have been in function for sufficiently long to be considered at risk. In **Period II (Group 2)**, only 35 erupted permanent teeth were present, and none was carious. This phase will not be considered further here. The tables show that in all phases, the

Teeth Present: All Groups

Maxillary	U1 M	U1 F	U2 M	U2 F	U3 M	U3 F	U4 M	U4 F	U5 M	U5 F	U6 M	U6 F	U7 M	U7 F	U8 M	U8 F	Total M	Total F	Total
20–25	28	44	24	46	31	54	31	54	30	54	30	59	34	55	27	40	235	406	641
25–35	82	100	78	103	102	129	111	128	118	134	115	140	116	146	86	109	808	989	1797
35–45	44	53	42	48	56	70	58	65	61	62	56	57	60	53	46	37	423	445	868
45+	11	6	17	5	21	7	18	10	20	8	15	4	17	4	8	6	127	50	177
20–35	4	4	3	4	4	4	1	5	3	6	4	4	4	5	4	6	27	38	65
25–45	5	2	3	6	4	8	6	8	4	6	5	7	5	6	5	4	37	47	84
Totals	174	209	167	212	218	272	225	270	236	270	225	271	236	269	176	202	1657	1975	3632

Mandibular	L1 M	L1 F	L2 M	L2 F	L3 M	L3 F	L4 M	L4 F	L5 M	L5 F	L6 M	L6 F	L7 M	L7 F	L8 M	L8 F	Total M	Total F	Total
20–25	24	40	26	48	25	55	29	53	28	54	32	59	34	58	25	44	223	411	634
25–35	82	92	95	122	116	150	116	161	132	166	120	149	131	161	101	120	893	1121	2014
35–45	51	49	63	54	74	72	80	75	83	75	69	57	82	74	54	55	556	511	1067
45+	17	3	23	5	28	15	26	12	25	8	19	6	20	3	19	4	177	56	233
20–35	2	3	3	3	3	4	3	5	4	5	4	6	4	6	2	3	25	35	60
25–45	5	6	6	7	8	6	6	7	2	8	1	6	4	6	5	4	37	50	87
Totals	181	193	216	239	254	302	260	313	274	316	245	283	275	308	206	230	1911	2184	4095

Carious Teeth: All Groups

Maxillary	U1 M	U1 F	U2 M	U2 F	U3 M	U3 F	U4 M	U4 F	U5 M	U5 F	U6 M	U6 F	U7 M	U7 F	U8 M	U8 F	Total M	Total F	Total
20–25											1	2	1	1		3	2	6	8
25–35	1		1		2	1	3	8	9	10	13	19	24	21	7	17	60	76	136
35–45		2	3	3	9	4	5	5	7	6	9	12	13	18	9	12	55	62	117
45+		2		1			1	1	4	1	3	2	2	3	3		2	7	18	25
20–35									1		1						2	0	2
25–45			1				1			1		2	1	4	1	4		2	3	14	17
Totals	1	4	5	4	11	7	9	18	18	21	27	39	42	47	16	36	129	176	305

Mandibular	L1 M	L1 F	L2 M	L2 F	L3 M	L3 F	L4 M	L4 F	L5 M	L5 F	L6 M	L6 F	L7 M	L7 F	L8 M	L8 F	Total M	Total F	Total
20–25			1									3	4	1		2	5	6	11
25–35							2	1	3	8	16	11	24	13	22	8	14	41	81	122
35–45	2	1		2	4	1	3	2	9	7	16	12	18	22	9	13	61	60	121
45+			1		1	2	2	4	4		4	3	2	2	3	3	17	14	31
20–35														1			0	1	1
25–45													1	1		2	1	3	4
Totals	2	1	2	2	5	5	6	9	21	23	31	42	38	49	20	34	125	165	290

Percentage Teeth with Caries: All Groups

Maxillary	U1 M	U1 F	U2 M	U2 F	U3 M	U3 F	U4 M	U4 F	U5 M	U5 F	U6 M	U6 F	U7 M	U7 F	U8 M	U8 F	Total M	Total F	Total
20–35											3.3	3.4	2.9	1.8		7.5	0.9	1.5	1.2
25–35	1.2		1.3		2.0	0.8	2.7	6.2	7.6	7.5	11.3	13.6	20.7	14.4	8.1	15.6	7.4	7.7	7.6
35–45		3.8	7.1	6.2	16.1	5.7	8.6	7.7	11.5	9.7	16.1	21.1	21.7	34.0	19.6	32.4	13.0	13.9	13.5
45+		33.3		20.0		14.3	5.6	40.0	5.0	37.5	13.3	50.0	17.6	75.0		33.3	5.5	36.0	14.1
20–35									33.3		25.0						7.4		3.1
25–45			33.3				12.5			12.5		33.3	20.0	57.1	20.0	66.7		50.0	8.1	29.8	20.2
Totals	0.6	1.9	3.0	1.9	5.0	2.6	4.0	6.7	7.6	7.8	12.0	14.4	17.8	17.5	9.1	17.8	7.8	8.9	8.4

Mandibular	L1 M	L1 F	L2 M	L2 F	L3 M	L3 F	L4 M	L4 F	L5 M	L5 F	L6 M	L6 F	L7 M	L7 F	L8 M	L8 F	Total M	Total F	Total
20–25			3.8									5.1	11.8	1.7		4.5	2.2	1.5	1.7
25–35					1.3	0.9	1.9	6.1	9.6	9.2	16.1	9.9	13.7	7.9	11.7	4.6	7.2	6.1
35–45	3.9	2.0		3.7	5.4	1.4	3.7	2.7	10.8	9.3	23.2	21.1	22.0	29.7	16.7	23.6	11.0	11.7	11.3
45+			4.3		3.6	13.3	7.7	33.3	16.0		21.1	50.0	10.0	66.7	15.8	75.0	9.6	25.0	13.3
20–35														16.7			2.9	1.7
25–45													25.0	16.7		50.0	2.7	6.0	4.6
Totals	1.1	0.5	0.9	0.8	2.0	1.7	2.3	2.9	7.7	7.3	12.7	14.8	13.8	15.9	9.7	14.8	6.5	7.6	7.1

Table 11.30: Caries Prevalence in Males and Females of All Groups

11.35 Large approximal carious lesions of adjacent maxillary permanent first molar and second premolar. Adult aged 25–35, **Group 9**.

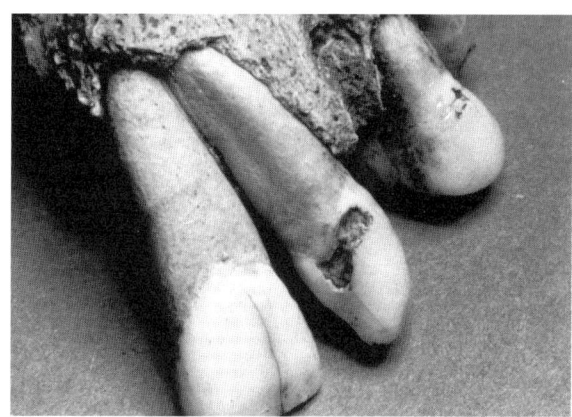

11.36 Carious lesion of labial enamel in a maxillary permanent second incisor. The premolar shows evidence of hypoplasia. Adult aged 25–35, **Group 9**.

teeth chiefly affected by caries were the molars (Figure 11.35). Fewer premolars were involved, and even fewer incisors and canines (Figure 11.36). In all phases and in the case of almost all teeth, there was a continuous increase in the percentage of teeth affected from age group 20–25 to 25–35 to 35–45. In the younger age groups, the numbers of carious teeth were small and thus the percentage figures tended to fluctuate. In the age group 45+ and the indeterminate groups 17–25, 20–35 and 25–45, the numbers of teeth present were small, and this also led to fluctuation in the percentage figures.

With the figures displayed separately for individual teeth, it is not easy to identify variations between the phases. The most obvious differences appear to be between **Period I (Group 1)** and the other phases, though as **Group 1** is small and is distinct from the large Late Medieval sample in a number of ways, it is unwise to place too much emphasis on these differences. However, it may be pointed out that caries does not appear in **Period I** in age groups younger than 25–35, whereas caries is found in the juveniles of the 6–12.9 age group from the early years of **Period V (Group 5** onwards).

In order to clarify any possible differences in caries prevalence between phases, the figures for all teeth within a particular phase and age group have been summed. Table 11.31 shows the results of this procedure. The figures show that in general there are considerable similarities between **Groups 4–8, 9, 10–12** and **13–14**, while **Period I** and the Museum Garden assemblage (Groups **15–17**) show different patterns of caries prevalence.

A more detailed examination of Table 11.31 shows that in juveniles, the percentage of teeth affected by caries was low, ranging generally from zero to 1.7%, though the older juveniles in **Groups 13–14** showed a slightly higher prevalence at 2.8%.

The youngest group of adults showed caries prevalence ranging from zero in **Period I (Group 1)** to 3.3.% in **Groups 10–12**. Each phase showed a consistent increase in caries prevalence from 20–25 to 25–35 to 35–45. This increase was not always maintained in the small group 45+, which showed considerable fluctuation in caries prevalence. In

	Period I			Period V																		All later		
				Glebe Field													Museum Garden			Medieval Groups		
	Group 1			Groups 4–8			Group 9			Groups 10–12			Groups 13–14			Groups 15–17			Groups 4–17		
	P	C	%	P	C	%	P	C	%	P	C	%	P	C	%	P	C	%	P	C	%
6–12.9	17	0	0.0	231	4	1.7	182	1	0.5	59	0	0.0	220	0	0.0	108	3	2.8	800	8	1.0
13–19.9	27	0	0.0	506	6	1.2	418	2	0.5	280	1	0.4	425	12	2.8	286	2	0.7	1915	23	1.2
20–25	111	0	0.0	289	2	0.7	463	7	1.5	307	10	3.3	452	10	2.2	66	1	1.5	1577	30	1.9
25–35	127	5	3.9	9.4	60	6.6	992	78	7.9	1115	91	8.2	1284	109	8.5	298	14	4.7	4593	352	7.7
35–45	177	27	15.3	514	47	9.1	600	78	13.0	271	37	13.7	736	96	13.0	146	8	5.5	2267	266	11.7
45+	0	0	0.0	53	13	24.5	134	10	7.5	133	9	6.8	115	31	27.0	79	4	5.1	514	67	13.0
17–25	66	0	0.0	87	2	2.3	60	4	6.7	21	0	0.0	48	0	0.0	23	0	0.0	239	6	2.5
25–35	0	0	0.0	27	0	0.0	0	0	0.0	20	1	5.0	51	2	3.9	27	0	0.0	125	3	2.4
25–45	18	0	0.0	44	4	9.1	86	15	17.4	1	0	0.0	72	6	8.3	2	0	0.0	205	25	12.2
Totals	543	32	5.9	2655	138	5.2	2935	195	6.6	2207	149	6.8	3403	266	7.8	1035	32	3.1	12235	780	6.4

Table 11.31: Caries Prevalence in All Permanent Teeth in each Group.
P = number of teeth present, C = number of carious teeth.

general, however, the increase in caries prevalence with increasing age is well demonstrated.

The age group 25–35, which in all phases except **Period I (Group 1)** contained by far the largest number of specimens, showed a slight but continuous increase in caries prevalence from the earliest **Period I (Group 1)** to **Period V/3 (Group 13–14)**. This may be evidence of a very slight but consistent increase in caries prevalence generally from the earliest to the later periods. Unfortunately this trend was not repeated throughout in the smaller 35–45 or 45+ age groups, and the question of an increase in caries prevalence with time must remain open.

The pattern of caries prevalence in **Period I (Group 1)** differed from the rest in the absence of caries in juveniles and young adults, and the remarkably high caries prevalence in the age group 35–45. In the Museum Garden assemblage (**Groups 15–17**) there was a high prevalence of caries in the younger juveniles and a markedly lower prevalence in the adults of all age groups. The overall caries prevalence for separate phase groups is shown in the bottom line of Table 11.31 and indicates a consistent increase in caries during **Period 5** (from **Groups 4–8** to **Groups 13–14**). The overall caries prevalence in **Period I (Group 1)** has been affected by the high figure for the 35–45 age group. The Museum Garden assemblage (**Groups 15–17**) shows a comparatively low overall caries prevalence.

Caries prevalence in the entire group of later medieval skeletons was obtained by combining the data from **Groups 4–17**. The results are shown in Table 11.31. The major age groups show a consistent increase in caries prevalence with increasing age and the pattern is repeated in the indeterminate age groups. The final overall caries prevalence figure for all teeth, all age groups and all later medieval groups is 6.4% of permanent teeth at risk.

This figure may be compared with the overall caries prevalence figures for the medieval burials at Kirkhill, St Andrews of 6.8% (Lunt 1986), for medieval burials from Aberdeen of 5.1% (Kerr et al., 1988), and for medieval burials from Linlithgow of 'almost 8%' (Cross and Bruce, 1989). A group of later skeletons from the island of Ensay in the Outer Hebrides, dated c. 1500 to 1600 AD, showed a slightly higher caries prevalence of 10.2% (Miles, 1989).

All caries prevalence figures so far published for Scottish medieval material have been lower than the figure of 11.1% caries prevalence reported by Tattersall (1968) for English medieval skeletons from a 12th–14th century site near Cambridge.

The caries prevalence of 5.9% in **Period I** at Whithorn is higher than the 2.8% prevalence in the broadly contemporary Long Cist population from Hallowhill, St Andrews or the 4.3% prevalence in long cist material from a number of other sites (Lunt, 1986).

Although there may be some evidence for a slight increase in caries prevalence in **Period V**, the pattern of caries prevalence in these groups is reasonably similar and in order to investigate caries prevalence by tooth class, the figures for these phases have been summed. The results represent caries prevalence in

Permanent Teeth Present: Groups 4 to 14

Maxillary	U1	U2	U3	U4	U5	U6	U7	U8	Total
6–12.9	71	56	12	18	15	127	20		319
13–19.9	87	90	101	108	108	127	123	22	766
20–25	80	80	99	99	92	104	106	76	736
25–35	204	200	257	265	289	294	298	217	2024
35–45	101	88	135	135	135	124	126	102	946
45+	19	21	29	30	28	18	20	13	178
17–25	11	15	19	19	21	25	20	5	135
20–35	6	5	6	4	7	7	7	8	50
25–45	6	10	12	14	13	15	14	11	95
Totals	585	565	670	692	708	841	734	454	5249

Mandibular	L1	L2	L3	L4	L5	L6	L7	L8	Total
6–12.9	83	68	21	21	19	138	23		373
13–19.9	95	107	121	125	122	139	133	21	863
20–25	79	89	96	105	104	109	111	82	775
25–35	184	243	305	314	335	309	335	246	2271
35–45	101	119	164	169	173	146	179	124	1175
45+	24	31	46	39	34	29	27	27	257
17–25	1	6	7	9	13	20	22	3	81
20–35	1	6	5	6	8	8	8	3	48
25–45	12	13	15	18	11	10	15	14	108
Totals	583	682	780	806	819	908	853	520	5951

Carious Teeth: Groups 4 to 14

Maxillary	U1	U2	U3	U4	U5	U6	U7	U8	Total
6–12.9						3			3
13–19.9						4	2		6
20–25				1		6	4	3	14
25–35	3	2	4	14	27	47	55	30	182
35–45	2	4	11	9	14	23	34	28	125
45+	2	1	1	6	5	5	6	3	29
17–25						2	2		4
20–35					1	1			2
25–45		2	1	1	2	6	7	2	21
Totals	7	9	17	31	49	97	110	66	386

Mandibular	L1	L2	L3	L4	L5	L6	L7	L8	Total
6–12.9						2			2
13–19.9				2	2	7	3	1	15
20–25		1			1	3	7	3	15
25–35	2	2	4	7	29	43	44	25	156
35–45	3	2	5	5	19	36	41	22	133
45+		1	3	6	4	9	5	6	34
17–25						1	1		2
20–35							1		1
25–45							2	2	4
Totals	5	6	12	20	55	101	104	59	362

Percentage of Teeth with Caries: Groups 4 to 14

Maxillary	U1	U2	U3	U4	U5	U6	U7	U8	Total
6–12.9						2.4			0.9
13–19.9						3.1	1.6		0.8
20–25				1.0		5.8	3.8	3.9	1.9
25–35	1.5	1.0	1.6	5.3	9.3	16.0	18.5	13.8	9.0
35–45	2.0	4.5	8.1	6.7	10.4	18.5	27.0	27.5	13.2
45+	10.5	4.8	3.4	20.0	17.9	27.8	30.0	23.1	16.3
17–25						8.0	10.0		3.0
20–35					14.3	14.3			4.0
25–45		20.0	8.3	7.1	15.4	40.0	50.0	18.2	22.1
Totals	1.2	1.6	2.5	4.5	6.9	11.5	15.0	14.5	7.4

Mandibular	L1	L2	L3	L4	L5	L6	L7	L8	Total
6–12.9						1.4			0.5
13–19.9				1.6	1.6	5.0	2.3	4.8	1.7
20–25		1.1			1.0	2.8	6.3	3.7	1.9
25–35	1.1	0.8	1.3	2.2	8.7	13.9	13.1	10.2	6.9
35–45	3.0	1.7	3.0	3.0	11.0	24.7	22.9	17.7	11.3
45+		3.2	6.5	15.4	11.8	31.0	18.5	22.2	13.2
17–25						5.0	4.5		2.5
20–35							12.5		2.1
25–45							13.3	14.3	3.7
Totals	0.9	0.9	1.5	2.5	6.7	11.1	12.2	11.3	6.1

Table 11.32: Caries Prevalence in grouped Mediaeval Phases from Glebe Field.

all **Period V** groups from the main excavation site, but exclude the medieval material from the Museum Garden excavation, and are shown in Table 11.32 for maxillary and mandibular teeth separately. This shows that caries attacks the incisor and canine teeth much less frequently than the premolars and molars. The increase of caries prevalence with age is also well demonstrated. The table shows that the first permanent molars may be affected as early as age 6–12.9. Other teeth are involved with advancing age, until by age 25–35 all teeth are subject to attack by dental caries. The highest caries prevalence is seen in the molars where up to 31% of a particular tooth class may be affected by the disease. The final overall caries prevalence figures show 7.4% of maxillary teeth were affected by caries, compared with 6.1% of mandibular teeth.

Caries prevalence by tooth class in the main later medieval group at Whithorn (**Groups 4–14**) was compared with the results obtained by Kerr *et al.* (1988) for medieval material from Aberdeen. In order to do this it was necessary to add together the figures for maxillary and mandibular teeth. The combined percentage caries prevalence figures for maxillary plus mandibular teeth are shown in Table 11.33, together with the corresponding figures extrapolated from the table published by Kerr *et al.* (1988). The two sets of figures have been shown separately, since the age groups of juveniles were divided on a slightly different basis in these studies. In the Aberdeen material, no incisors or canines were found to be carious, and the prevalence of caries in the molars was generally somewhat lower than in the Whithorn dentitions. An interesting difference in the Aberdeen study is that the prevalence of caries in the age groups 16–25, 26–35 and 36–45+ was found to be similar, and there did not appear to be the increase in caries prevalence with age which is such a constant feature in the Whithorn material. However, it should be pointed out that the total number of teeth studied in the Aberdeen skeletons was much lower (1088) than at Whithorn (11,200) and this may well account for some of the differences between the two population groups.

A comparison may also be made between the figures for caries prevalence in the entire group of articulated skeletons (Archive table 20) with those recorded from the disarticulated fragments and the loose teeth. The numbers of erupted teeth present, divided by tooth class and age group, the numbers in each category presenting carious lesions, and the percentages of carious teeth are shown separately for maxillary and mandibular teeth of the disarticulated fragments in Archive table 21. Similar figures for the loose teeth are given in Archive table 22, but in this case specific age groups cannot be assigned to the specimens and they have been graded by degree of attrition. (Of 4,946 loose permanent teeth, 273 were unidentifiable, 683 had been unerupted and therefore not at risk of caries, while post-mortem erosion of 415 rendered an assessment of caries impossible.)

The general patterns of caries prevalence in the disarticulated fragments and loose teeth are similar to those observed in the articulated material, and in most instances show an increase in caries prevalence with increasing age or severity of attrition. A few exceptions may be found, especially where numbers of specimens are small. The overall percentage caries prevalence figures by tooth class for the three categories of material are shown in Table 11.34. The caries prevalence for incisors, canines and first premolars is similar in all three groups, though the figures for the disarticulated fragments are slightly lower than the others. In the case of second premolars and molars, the figures for the disarticulated fragments are lower than those for the articulated material, while the figures for the loose teeth are sometimes lower and sometimes higher than for the articulated specimens. The differences are probably due to the fragmentary nature of the material. Many of the disarticulated fragments were very small, and in a situation where the bone is being broken up

Whithorn Groups 4 to 14

Maxillary and Mandibular

	I1	I2	C	PM1	PM2	M1	M2	M3	Total
6–12.9	0.0	0.0	0.0	0.0	0.0	1.9	0.0		0.7
13–19.9	0.0	0.0	0.0	0.9	0.9	4.1	2.0	2.3	1.3
20–25	0.0	0.6	0.0	0.5	0.5	4.2	5.1	3.8	1.9
25–35	1.3	0.9	1.4	3.6	9.0	14.9	15.6	11.9	7.9
35–45	2.5	2.9	5.4	4.6	10.7	21.9	24.6	22.1	12.2
45+	4.7	3.8	5.3	17.4	14.5	29.8	23.4	22.5	14.5
17–25	0.0	0.0	0.0	0.0	0.0	6.7	7.1	0.0	2.8
20–35	0.0	0.0	0.0	0.0	6.7	6.7	6.7	0.0	3.1
25–45	0.0	8.7	3.7	3.1	8.3	24.0	31.0	16.0	12.3
Totals	1.0	1.2	2.0	3.4	6.8	11.3	13.5	12.8	6.7

Aberdeen Skulls, Kerr, et al., 1988

Maxillary and Mandibular

	I1	I2	C	PM1	PM2	M1	M2	M3	Total
6–15							7.1		1.1
16–25						10.0	19.5	11.1	5.4
26–35				2.7	11.1	7.6	9.1	15.8	5.6
36–45+				5.0	8.8	8.6	10.2	7.7	5.3
Totals	0.0	0.0	0.0	2.6	7.3	6.6	11.9	12.2	5.1

Table 11.33: Percentage Caries Prevalence in Permanent Teeth from Whithorn and Aberdeen.

Maxillary

	U1	U2	U3	U4	U5	U6	U7	U8	Total
Articulated	1.0	1.6	2.9	4.2	6.4	10.3	14.1	14.3	6.9
Disarticulated	0.0	1.7	2.2	3.5	6.6	8.8	9.5	8.5	5.7
Loose	0.7	0.9	2.2	4.4	4.2	6.4	14.5	17.1	5.8
Totals	0.8	1.4	2.6	4.1	6.1	9.5	13.5	14.2	6.5

Mandibular

	L1	L2	L3	L4	L5	L6	L7	L8	Total
Articulated	0.7	0.7	1.4	2.2	6.4	10.8	11.8	12.9	6.0
Disarticulated	0.0	0.0	0.5	0.4	2.3	8.9	9.9	9.1	4.8
Loose	0.0	2.1	1.5	2.5	6.2	8.6	14.5	14.4	6.4
Totals	0.5	0.8	1.3	1.9	5.6	10.1	11.8	12.5	5.9

Maxillary and Mandibular

	I1	I2	C	PM1	PM2	M1	M2	M3	Total
Articulated	0.8	1.1	2.1	3.1	6.4	10.6	12.8	13.5	6.4
Disarticulated	0.0	0.7	1.3	1.9	4.2	8.8	9.8	8.9	5.2
Loose	0.4	1.3	1.8	3.5	5.3	7.6	14.5	15.8	6.1
Totals	0.7	1.1	1.9	3.0	5.8	9.8	12.6	13.3	6.2

Table 11.34: Percentage Caries Prevalence in all articulated skeletons, disarticulated fragments and loose teeth from Whithorn.

disintegration is more liable to occur where the bone is already weakened by the presence of disease. The ravages of dental caries and its final effect on the alveolar bone will make severely affected teeth more likely to fall out post-mortem, and this could account for the increased caries prevalence in some of the molars which were found loose.

Combining all categories of material, the final caries prevalence in 20,297 permanent teeth at risk is 6.2%.

Site of carious lesions
Mention has already been made of the fact that dental caries may attack different areas of the tooth surface, and that the areas which are in modern times the commonest site for attack (occlusal surfaces of posterior tooth crowns and approximal enamel of anterior tooth crowns) are not those which were most commonly involved in medieval and earlier times. It is thus of interest to examine the frequency of attack at different sites in the phased material from Whithorn, to establish whether there may be any difference detectable with period at this site.

Carious lesions have been divided into categories which vary between anterior teeth (incisors and canines) and posterior teeth (premolars and molars). For anterior teeth, lesions were classified as: cervical of the approximal surfaces; cervical of the labial or lingual surfaces; enamel caries of the approximal surfaces; enamel caries of the labial surfaces (Figure 11.36); and gross caries where the origin of the lesion was no longer detectable. For posterior teeth the categories were: cervical of the approximal surfaces (Figure 11.33); cervical of the buccal or lingual surfaces (Figure 11.34); occlusal lesions which commence in the enamel (Figure 11.32); enamel caries of the approximal, buccal and lingual surfaces; gross caries (Figure 11.37). Cervical lesions are those which begin at the junction of crown and root, with the primary site of attack in the cementum of the root, though enamel will subsequently be undermined as the lesion spreads through the cementum and dentine. Lesions entirely on the root surface have been classified along with the cervical lesions of the appropriate surface.

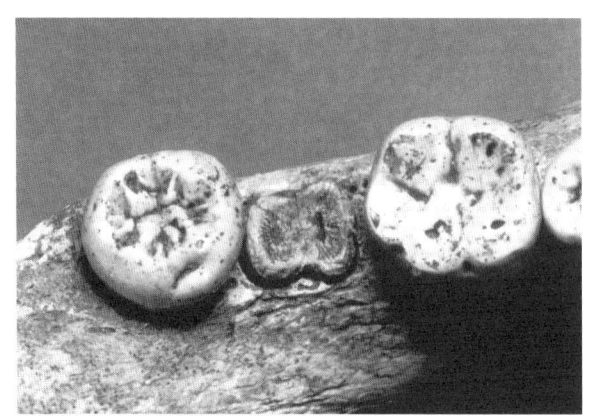

11.37 Gross caries of mandibular permanent second molar, destroying the crown and leaving a carious root stump. Adolescent aged *c.* 18, **Group 13**.

Preliminary examination of the data showed that the distribution of lesions was different in juveniles and in adults, but that age group had no significant effect within these categories. There were no carious lesions of anterior permanent teeth in juveniles. The numbers of carious lesions of posterior permanent teeth in juveniles are shown in Table 11.35. The numbers of lesions are small and it is not appropriate to work percentages. However, it may be noted that almost all the lesions in juveniles have had their origin in an attack on the enamel. It is also of interest to note that a few lesions in juveniles had progressed so rapidly as already to have reached the status of 'gross lesion'.

Table 11.33 also shows the distribution of lesions by site in anterior and in posterior teeth of adults. Numbers of lesions are in some instances higher than the number of teeth with caries, as a tooth may show more than one lesion. The numbers of lesions in anterior teeth were small, but showed that in each phase the majority of lesions were of the approximal cervical type. When **Groups 4–14** were combined, percentage values could be calculated and indicated that 80% of lesions were to be found at the cervical margin, while barely 10% had originated on an enamel surface and 10% were too large to be classified.

The numbers of lesions in posterior teeth allowed percentage distribution of types of lesion to be calculated for grouped phases. There was a general similarity in the pattern of carious sites of attack, with the approximal cervical lesion showing the greatest frequency and accounting for 48%–65% of lesions. Lesions of enamel were the least common in all phases, but there was a slight increase in the proportion of occlusal lesions in **Groups 10–12** and **13–14**, and an increase in lesions of approximal or buccal enamel in **Groups 13–14**. Thus the later medieval phases may give a slight indication of an increase in the 'modern' type of lesion, though the cervical lesions were still by far the commonest type. Large lesions of uncertain origin made up 10%–19% of the total, except in **Period I (Group 1)** where they accounted for 32% of lesions: however, the number of lesions from this phase was small.

Cervical lesions of both approximal and buccal surfaces were often found in conjunction with localised areas of alveolar bone loss (Figure 11.34). Particularly in interdental areas, the alveolar bone loss sometimes appeared to be more advanced than the carious lesion, suggesting that periodontal inflammation had caused loss of septal alveolar bone, thus producing a stagnation area in which the carious lesion subsequently developed.

Number of lesions in individual dentitions
The largest number of carious teeth observed in a single dentition was 21, in an individual from **Group 9** whose age was difficult to assess because of the extent of dental disease, while an adult in the age group 25–35 from **Group 10** showed 18 lesions in 13 teeth.

Juveniles (6–19.9) – Posterior Permanent Teeth

Site of Lesion	Groups 1	4–8	9	10–12	13–14	15–17	All Artic	Disartic	4–14	%4–14
Cervical Approximal	0	3	0	0	0	0	3	0	3	11.1
Cervical buccal/lingual	0	0	0	0	0	0	0	0	0	
Occlusal	0	6	2	1	5	4	19	8	14	51.9
Enamel approx/buccal	0	2	0	0	3	1	8	0	5	18.5
Gross	0	0	1	0	4	0	5	0	5	18.5
Total	0	11	3	1	12	5	35	8	27	

Adults (20–45+) – Anterior Permanent Teeth

Site of Lesion	Groups 1	4–8	9	10–12	13–14	15–17	All Artic	Disartic	4–14	%4–14
Cervical Approximal	4	6	15	5	12	0	43	1	38	62.3
Cervical buccal/lingual	0	2	6	1	2	0	11	0	11	18.0
Occlusal	1	1	0	0	2	0	4	0	3	4.9
Enamel approx/buccal	0	0	2	0	1	0	3	0	3	4.9
Gross	2	2	3	0	1	0	8	0	6	9.8
Total	7	11	26	6	18	0	69	1	61	

Adults (20–45+) – Posterior Permanent Teeth

Site of Lesion	Groups 1	4–8	9	10–12	13–14	15–17	All Artic	Disartic	4–14
Cervical Approximal	12	83	108	74	151	17	475	93	416
Cervical buccal/lingual	4	19	29	36	34	7	140	22	118
Occlusal	1	7	10	13	25	0	65	17	55
Enamel approx/buccal	0	3	6	4	17	2	32	6	30
Gross	8	15	36	23	38	3	132	14	112
Total	25	127	189	150	265	29	844	152	731

Percentage Incidence of each type of Lesion
Adults (20–45+) – Posterior Permanent Teeth

Site of Lesion	Groups 1	4–8	9	10–12	13–14	15–17	All Artic	Disartic	4–14
Cervical Approximal	48.0	65.4	57.1	49.3	57.0	58.6	56.3	61.2	56.9
Cervical buccal/lingual	16.0	15.0	15.3	24.0	12.8	24.1	16.6	14.5	16.1
Occlusal	4.0	5.5	5.3	8.7	9.4	0.0	7.7	11.2	7.5
Enamel approx/buccal	0.0	2.4	3.2	2.7	6.4	6.9	3.8	3.9	4.1
Gross	32.0	11.8	19.0	15.3	14.3	10.3	15.6	9.2	15.3
Total	100	100	100	100	100	100	100	100	100

Table 11.35: Sites of Carious Lesions in Permanent Teeth

Dental caries prevalence, deciduous dentition
The prevalence of dental caries in the deciduous dentition has been studied in the Whithorn material. None of the few deciduous teeth from **Period I (Group 1)** was carious. The numbers of deciduous teeth in the other phases are considerably smaller than those of permanent teeth and it has been necessary to group phases in the same manner employed for the permanent teeth. The **Period II (Group 2)** dentitions include a considerable number of deciduous teeth and this phase appears as a separate entity since it represents the distinct Northumbrian period. The later medieval phases have been grouped as for the permanent teeth: **Groups 4–8, 9, 10–12, 13–14** and **15–17**.

The numbers of deciduous teeth which were erupted and at risk of caries, the number of carious deciduous teeth, and the percentages of carious deciduous teeth for these phase groupings are shown in Archive tables 23–28.

No deciduous incisors displayed carious lesions in any phase. Deciduous canines were also unaffected by caries except for a single carious mandibular canine recorded from **Groups 13–14**. With this sole exception, caries affected only the deciduous molars. Within the phases, the carious molars appear to be scattered randomly among the juvenile age groups, including the children aged 0.1–5.9 years. The percentages of specific teeth affected by caries range from zero to 14% and no clear pattern of differences can be observed between the phases.

An attempt to clarify possible differences between the phases by combining a) all the deciduous molars and b) all the deciduous teeth in each phase is shown in Table 11.36. In all phases, the children aged 6–12.9 show a higher prevalence of dental caries than those aged 0.1–5.9. When the groups are compared, one figure stands out: the very high caries prevalence in the children aged 6–12.9 from the **Period II** graveyard. The variations between other phases for this age group do not show any consistent increase or decrease. The children aged 0.1–5.9 in **Groups 2, 4–8** and **9** show low levels of caries, while the corresponding age group in **Groups 10–12, 13–14** and **15–16** has not been affected by caries.

Deciduous Teeth Present

Groups	1		2		4–8		9		10–12		13–14		15–17		Total	Total
Maxillary	DE	All	DE	All	DE	All	DE	All	DE	All	DE	All	DE	All	DE	All
0.1–5.9			17	49	64	124	21	45	16	43	29	75	20	38	167	374
6–12.9	5	7	12	21	43	68	43	58	26	42	57	79	29	40	215	315
13–19.9						1					1	2		1	1	4
Totals	5	7	29	70	107	193	64	103	42	85	87	156	49	79	383	693
Mandibular																
0.1–5.9			25	50	87	161	23	59	19	48	34	78	20	42	208	438
6–12.9	4	5	12	18	51	70	45	58	22	37	59	71	39	48	232	307
13–19.9					1	1	3	3	2	2	1	2			7	8
Totals	4	5	37	68	139	232	71	120	43	87	94	151	59	90	447	753

Carious Deciduous Teeth

Groups	1		2		4–8		9		10–12		13–14		15–17		Total	Total
Maxillary	DE	All	DE	All	DE	All	DE	All	DE	All	DE	All	DE	All	DE	All
0.1–5.9			1	1	1	1	1	1							3	3
6–12.9					1	1	2	2	1	1	3	3	1	1	8	8
13–19.9																
Totals			1	1	2	2	3	3	1	1	3	3	1	1	11	11
Mandibular																
0.1–5.9					6	6									6	6
6–12.9			5	5	4	4	4	4			2	3	3	3	18	19
13–19.9																
Totals			5	5	10	10	4	4			2	3	3	3	24	25

Percentage of Deciduous Teeth Present with Caries

Groups	1		2		4–8		9		10–12		13–14		15–17		Total	Total
Maxillary	DE	All	DE	All	DE	All	DE	All	DE	All	DE	All	DE	All	DE	All
0.1–5.9			5.9	2.0	1.6	0.8	4.8	2.2							1.8	0.8
6–12.9					2.3	1.5	4.7	3.4	3.8	2.4	5.3	3.8	3.4	2.5	3.7	2.5
13–19.9																
Totals			3.4	1.4	1.9	1.0	4.7	2.9	2.4	1.2	3.4	1.9	2.0	1.3	2.9	1.6
Mandibular																
0.1–5.9					6.9	3.7									2.9	1.4
6–12.9			41.7	27.8	7.8	5.7	8.9	6.9			3.4	4.2	7.7	6.2	7.8	6.2
13–19.9																
Totals			13.5	7.4	7.2	4.3	5.6	3.3			2.1	2.0	5.1	3.3	5.4	3.3
Combined																
0.1–5.9			2.4	1.0	4.6	2.5	2.3	1.0							2.4	1.1
6–12.9			20.8	12.8	5.3	3.6	6.8	5.2	2.1	1.3	4.3	4.0	5.9	4.5	5.8	4.3
13–19.9																
Totals			9.1	4.3	4.9	2.8	5.2	3.1	1.2	0.6	2.8	2.0	3.7	2.4	4.2	2.5

Table 11.36: Caries Prevalence in Deciduous Teeth in all Phase groups.
DE = deciduous molars only

No consistent pattern of change in the prevalence of caries in the deciduous teeth can be observed between the phases at Whithorn.

The caries prevalence in all first deciduous molars irrespective of age group is 3.0% and the corresponding figure for deciduous molars is 4.3%, and in all deciduous teeth, 2.5%. These figures may be compared with that for caries in deciduous teeth in the Kirkhill, St Andrews population, where 4.3% of deciduous teeth displayed carious lesions. There was a greater difference between the younger and the older children from the Kirkhill site, with caries prevalence of 0.7% in children aged 0.1–5.9, and 10.8% in those aged 6–12.9 (Lunt, 1986). It is surprising to see the high deciduous caries prevalence in the **Period II** population from Whithorn, as studies of contemporary skeletal material from long cists had revealed no caries of deciduous teeth (Lunt, 1986).

Among the deciduous teeth from the disarticulated fragments, caries was not observed in deciduous incisors from either jaw, or in mandibular deciduous canines. Caries was noted in a single maxillary deciduous canine. No carious deciduous incisors or canines were found among the loose teeth. The numbers of erupted deciduous molars, the numbers with carious lesions and the percentages of carious deciduous molars in the disarticulated fragments and loose teeth are shown in Archive table 29. The percentage prevalence figures are to some extent erratic, presumably due to the relatively small numbers involved. In most cases, however, the older juveniles or the more heavily worn teeth show a higher prevalence of caries.

The sites of carious lesions in deciduous teeth are similar to those observed in permanent posterior teeth. The lesions in deciduous teeth of different phases are scattered randomly among the possible sites, with rather more approximal cervical lesions (Figure 11.38) in **Groups 13–14** and

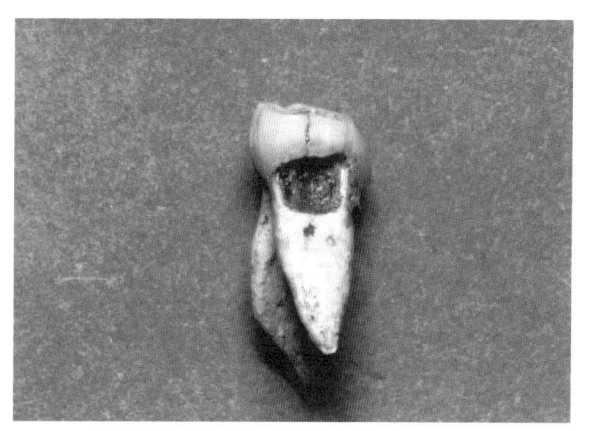

11.38 Approximal cervical carious lesion of a mandibular deciduous first molar. Child aged *c.* 7 years, **Group 13**.

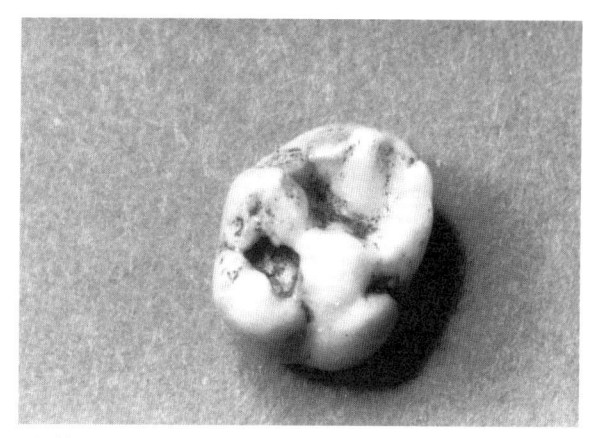

11.39 Occlusal carious lesion of a maxillary deciduous second molar. Child aged *c.* 3 years, **Group 4**.

Groups 15–17, and more occlusal lesions (Figure 11.39) in **Groups 4–8**. The numbers of lesions are too small for differences between phases to be apparent. When the data for all phases are combined, the number of approximal cervical lesions (16) is only a little greater than the number of occlusal lesions (13). There are six lesions of approximal enamel and one example of gross caries.

Of 12 lesions in deciduous teeth from the disarticulated material, eight are approximal cervical lesions, three are occlusal and one is a buccal cervical lesion. Eleven deciduous molars among the loose teeth displayed carious lesions, of which seven were approximal cervical lesions and four were occlusal lesions.

The distribution of sites of carious lesions of deciduous teeth appears to lie between that of carious lesions of permanent teeth in juveniles, where most lesions are of enamel, and the distribution of carious lesions of permanent teeth in adults, where most lesions are of the approximal cervical type.

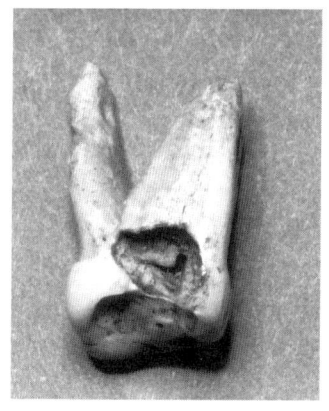

3.1.2. Pulp exposure due to dental caries

If the lesions of dental caries are allowed to progress unchecked or untreated, the stage will eventually be reached when the lesion will break through into the central pulp cavity of the tooth, with resultant infection of the soft pulp tissue. Examples of such pulp exposure were observed in permanent teeth of all grouped phases at Whithorn (Figure 11.40). The numbers of carious permanent teeth, the numbers of carious teeth with pulp exposure, and the percentages of carious teeth with pulp exposure are shown separately for **Groups 1, 4–8, 9, 10–12, 13–14** and **15–17** in Archive tables 30–35.

Pulp exposures are largely but not entirely confined to the premolar and molar teeth. Exceptions are to be found in **Group 1** (a maxillary second incisor and a maxillary canine), **Groups 4–8** (a maxillary second incisor), **Group 9** (a mandibular canine) and **Groups 13–14** (a mandibular canine). Pulp exposures are also mainly found in the older age groups, but there are examples of pulp exposures in a few carious permanent first molars of juveniles in **Groups 4–8, 9** and **13–14**.

The group from the Museum Garden (**Groups 15–17**), which in any case show a low caries prevalence, also shows a markedly lower proportion of lesions which have progressed to pulp exposure than do the other phases. **Group 1 (Period 1)** appears to show a high proportion of carious teeth in which the lesion has progressed to pulp exposure, though this may be misleading as the numbers involved are small. The remaining phase groups (**4** to **14**) show lower porportions of carious teeth with pulp exposure, and while there are variations between the phase groups, the overall patterns are similar.

The data for the later medieval **Groups (4–8, 9, 10–12** and **13–14)** have been combined in order to give a clearer impression of the extent of pulp exposure due to caries, and the resulting figures are shown in Table 11.37. Caries may proceed to pulp exposure at any age and it is interesting to note that of the few first permanent molars which have

11.40 Lateral pulp exposure due to caries in a maxillary permanent first molar. The outline of the pulp chamber is clearly visible. Adult aged 25–35, **Group 13**.

Permanent Teeth with Caries: Groups 4 to 14

Maxillary	U1	U2	U3	U4	U5	U6	U7	U8	Total
6–12.9						3			3
13–19.9						4	2		6
20–25				1		6	4	3	14
25–35	3	2	4	14	27	47	55	30	182
35–45	2	4	11	9	14	23	34	28	125
45+	2	1	1	6	5	5	6	3	29
17–25						2	2		4
20–35				1	1				2
25–45		2	1	1	2	6	7	2	21
Totals	7	9	17	31	49	97	110	66	386

Mandibular	L1	L2	L3	L4	L5	L6	L7	L8	Total
6–12.9						2			2
13–19.9				2	2	7	3	1	15
20–25		1			1	3	7	3	15
25–35	2	2	4	7	29	43	44	25	156
35–45	3	2	5	5	19	36	41	22	133
45+		1	3	6	4	9	5	6	34
17–25						1	1		2
20–35							1		1
25–45							2	2	4
Totals	5	6	12	20	55	101	104	59	362

Pulp Exposure due to Caries: Groups 4 to 14

Maxillary	U1	U2	U3	U4	U5	U6	U7	U8	Total
6–12.9						1			1
13–19.9						2			2
20–25									
25–35				2	8	18	8	10	46
35–45		1		3	5	9	8	8	34
45+				5	1	2	1	3	12
17–25						1			1
20–35						1			1
25–45					2	4	4	2	12
Totals		1		10	16	38	21	23	109

Mandibular	L1	L2	L3	L4	L5	L6	L7	L8	Total
6–12.9						1			1
13–19.9						3	1		4
20–25						1			1
25–35			1	1	4	16	8	6	36
35–45			2	2	6	12	5	3	30
45+				2	1	4	1	3	11
17–25									
20–35									
25–45							1	1	2
Totals			3	5	11	37	16	13	85

Percentage of Carious Teeth with Pulp Exposure: Groups 4 to 14

Maxillary	U1	U2	U3	U4	U5	U6	U7	U8	Total
6–12.9						33.3			33.3
13–19.9						50.0			33.3
20–25									
25–35				14.3	29.6	38.3	14.5	33.3	25.3
35–45		25.0		33.3	35.7	39.1	23.5	28.6	27.2
45+				83.3	20.0	40.0	16.7	100.0	41.4
17–25						50.0			25.0
20–35						100.0			50.0
25–45					100.0	66.7	57.1	100.0	57.1
Totals		11.1		32.3	32.7	39.2	19.1	34.8	28.2

Mandibular	L1	L2	L3	L4	L5	L6	L7	L8	Total
6–12.9						50.0			50.0
13–19.9						42.9	33.3		26.7
20–25						33.3			6.7
25–35			25.0	14.3	13.8	37.2	18.2	24.0	23.1
35–45			40.0	40.0	31.6	33.3	12.2	13.6	22.6
45+				33.3	25.0	44.4	20.0	50.0	32.4
17–25									
20–35									
25–45							50.0	50.0	50.0
Totals			25.0	25.0	20.0	36.6	15.4	22.0	23.5

Table 11.37: Pulp Exposure due to Caries in Groups 4–14 (later medieval).

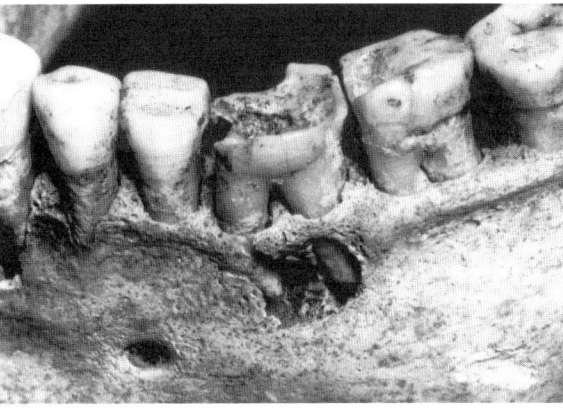

11.41 Dental abscess due to caries in a mandibular permanent first molar. The carious lesion can be seen on the mesial and occlusal aspects of the molar. The opening in the bone below the premolars is a normal anatomical feature, the mental foramen. Adult aged 35–45, **Group 9**.

developed caries in the juveniles, a relatively high proportion showed rapid progression of the lesion to expose the pulp. Most pulp exposures occurred in posterior teeth, and between 15% and 37% of carious lesions in posterior teeth had advanced to the stage of pulp exposure.

In almost all instances where the pulp had been exposed, and the supporting alveolar bone was present, a dental abscess or dental cyst had developed at the apex of the root, due to infection travelling through the pulp tissue into the apical periodontal tissues. Often these lesions were large, perforating the alveolar bone and thus easily visible to the naked eye (Figure 11.41). The smaller lesions which had not yet perforated the bone could be observed on radiographs. In a few cases an abscess could not be detected: in some instances this was due to post-mortem destruction of the internal structure of the bone or its infiltration by soil, and in a very few specimens there may have been a small lesion not yet detectable by radiograph. Abscesses were observed in association with a few carious teeth which did not have a pulp exposure detectable to the naked eye. In these cases, the radiograph showed that the carious cavity had approached very close to the pulp and there was probably a microscopic exposure.

Carious lesions of deciduous teeth may also proceed to pulp exposure. Isolated examples of carious exposure of the pulp in deciduous second molars were observed in specimens from **Groups 4–8** and **Group 9**, and the solitary example of a carious deciduous canine from **Groups 13–14** may also have had a tiny pulp exposure. Abscesses were observable in connection with both second molars.

An unphased juvenile aged 12 showed an interesting sequence of events. A carious lesion of a mandibular second deciduous molar had exposed the pulp and caused the formation of an apical abscess which had enveloped the crown of the developing second premolar, delaying eruption of the latter tooth.

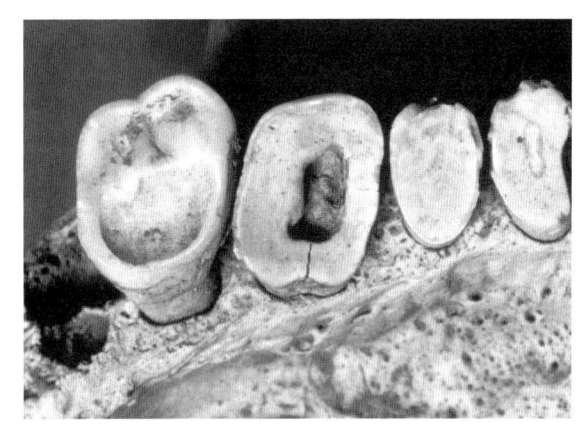

11.42 Occlusal pulp exposure due to severe attrition of a maxillary permanent first molar. The outline of the pulp chamber can be seen in the first premolar. In this tooth the pulp chamber is filled with secondary dentine. Adult aged 35–45, not phased.

3.1.3. Pulp exposure due to attrition

Pulp exposure may also result from the otherwise normal process of attrition of the occlusal or incisal surface of a tooth, and occurs in advanced attrition when the deposition of secondary dentine is inadequate to protect the pulp. This may be due either to an extremely rapid rate of attrition or to a failure in the deposition of secondary dentine. Given the severe attrition seen in many teeth, often revealing the outlines of the original pulp chamber, it is remarkable how often the further formation of dentine in advance of attrition has served to protect the pulp and allow the tooth to remain in a normal functional state. Nevertheless, there are cases in which the protective mechanism has been insufficient and the pulp has become exposed.

Examples of pulp exposure due to attrition were observed in all phase groups at Whithorn (Figure 11.42). The numbers of erupted permanent teeth, the numbers of teeth with exposure of the pulp due to attrition, and the percentages of teeth affected by this type of pulp exposure are shown separately for **Groups 1, 4–8, 9, 10–12, 13–14** and **15–17** in Archive tables 36–41. Since the estimation of dental age in adults is based on the degree of attrition, it is to be expected that the cases of pulp exposure due to attrition will be found in the older age groups. In all phases, most teeth with pulp exposure due to attrition are to be found in individuals in the 35–45 and 45+ age groups. A few examples, chiefly of permanent first molars, were found in individuals attributed to the age group 25–35. Unusually, pulp exposures were observed in a mandibular second incisor and canine of an individual aged 20–25 in **Group 12**, and must be due to some local factor.

The percentages of teeth with pulps exposed due to attrition in the age groups 35–45 and 45+ are shown for separate phase groups in Table 11.38. Any tooth may show the condition, but posterior teeth were more likely to be affected than anterior teeth. In all phases,

Group 1 (**Period 1**)

Maxillary	U1	U2	U3	U4	U5	U6	U7	U8	Total
35–45						22.2			2.5
45+									

Mandibular	L1	L2	L3	L4	L5	L6	L7	L8	Total
35–45									
45+									

Groups 4 to 8 (530–534)

Maxillary	U1	U2	U3	U4	U5	U6	U7	U8	Total
35–45		4.2	3.6	2.9		25.0	6.1		5.7
45+				100	100	100	25.0		38.1

Mandibular	L1	L2	L3	L4	L5	L6	L7	L8	Total
35–45						12.8	2.1		2.1
45+						66.7			12.5

Group 9 (535)

Maxillary	U1	U2	U3	U4	U5	U6	U7	U8	Total
35–45			2.3	2.6		38.9			5.8
45+	42.9		10.0	11.1	22.2	83.3	60.0		27.3

Mandibular	L1	L2	L3	L4	L5	L6	L7	L8	Total
35–45		3.0		2.2		2.6			0.9
45+				9.1	18.2	44.4	11.1		10.1

Groups 10, 11 and 12 (536–538)

Maxillary	U1	U2	U3	U4	U5	U6	U7	U8	Total
35–45							5.9		1.0
45+		25.0	18.2	9.1	25.0	71.4			20.3

Mandibular	L1	L2	L3	L4	L5	L6	L7	L8	Total
35–45						10.0			1.2
45+	16.7		7.7		11.1	12.5	20.0		8.1

Groups 13 and 14 (539 and 540)

Maxillary	U1	U2	U3	U4	U5	U6	U7	U8	Total
35–45		2.9		4.1	4.3	37.2			6.2
45+			16.7				20.0		4.7

Mandibular	L1	L2	L3	L4	L5	L6	L7	L8	Total
35–45		2.6	1.8			6.2	3.1		1.8
45+						50.0	40.0	16.7	8.3

Groups 15, 16 and 17 (**Museum Garden**)

Maxillary	U1	U2	U3	U4	U5	U6	U7	U8	Total
35–45				9.1	28.6	33.3			9.1
45+		20.0			75.0	100	40.0		29.4

Mandibular	L1	L2	L3	L4	L5	L6	L7	L8	Total
35–45									
45+		20.0			14.3	80.0	33.3	50.0	22.2

Table 11.38: Pulp Exposure due to Attrition as Percentage of All Teeth Present in all phase groups.

more maxillary teeth were affected by this type of pulp exposure than mandibular teeth. **Group 1** shows a very low prevalence of the condition, only two maxillary molars being affected. In all other phases, the patterns and proportions of teeth affected are similar, with the maxillary first molar showing the highest prevalence of pulp exposure due to attrition, though in **Groups 15–17** the maxillary second premolar shows an equally high prevalence of the condition.

As in the case of pulp exposure due to caries, the condition of pulp exposure due to attrition is associated with the formation of a dental abscess or dental cyst, and the latter conditions were observed in most of the cases of pulp exposure due to attrition in the Whithorn material (Figure 11.43).

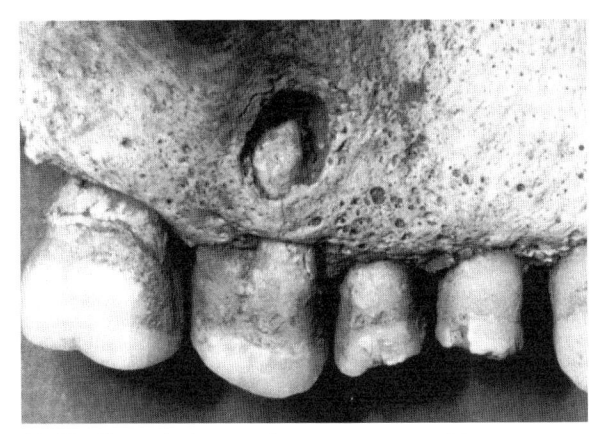

11.43 Dental abscess due to severe attrition, same specimen as Fig. 11.42.

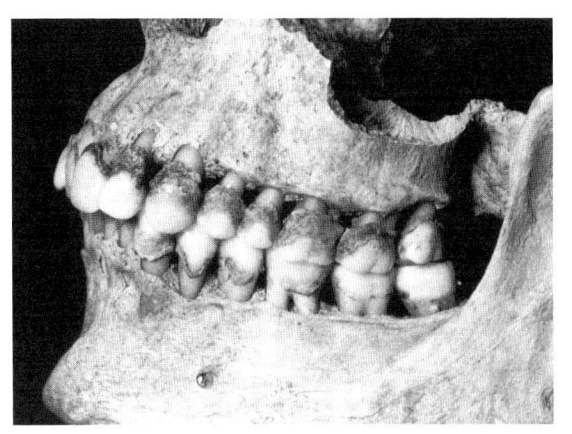

11.44 Deposits of calculus in an adult aged 25–35 from **Group 10**.

Although deciduous teeth often became quite heavily worn in the older children, no examples of pulp exposure due to attrition were observed in the deciduous teeth in any phase.

3.1.4. Severe attrition of anterior teeth

In four dentitions from the articulated material and in five disarticulated fragments, the anterior teeth were observed to be much more heavily worn than would be warranted by the degree of molar attrition, and this may indicate some occupational use of the incisor teeth.

3.1.5. Hypercementosis

The roots of the teeth are covered by a layer of mineralised tissue called cementum, which forms part of the attachment of the tooth to its socket by embedding the ends of the fibres of the periodontal ligament. Throughout adult life, the layer of cementum gradually thickens, especially near the apex, and this is considered a normal age change. In some teeth there is an excessive deposition of cementum, a condition known as hypercementosis.

Teeth with hypercementosis were observed in some thirteen dentitions, though many more teeth still *in situ* in the bone may have been affected by the condition. The specimens which were observed all came from the later phases (**Groups 9–14**) of the main excavation or from the **Museum Garden**. A most unusual overgrowth of cementum was observed in a mandibular second premolar of an adolescent from **Group 10**. This took the form of a 'ruff' or 'collar' of cementum at the neck of the tooth. Part of the buccal cusp had been lost, but the crown of the tooth otherwise seemed normal. The explanation of this condition may be that the buccal cusp had been fractured due to trauma *in vivo*, and the root may also have suffered some damage in the cervical region. The 'ruff' of cementum may have been an attempt to provide a natural splint for the damaged root. A radiograph shows that the root of the premolar is slightly misshapen, but there is no clear evidence of a root fracture.

3.1.6. Dental calculusa

Deposits of dental calculus (tartar) are frequently seen on the teeth in skeletal material. The presence of these mineralised deposits is often considered to be associated with a low level of oral hygiene, though it should be pointed out that in modern times individuals vary markedly in their tendency to accumulate calculus, irrespective of dental hygiene.

The study of calculus in skeletal material is difficult because the deposits are very readily lost post-mortem during even the most careful cleaning, leaving only slight traces behind. It is therefore impossible in many cases to assess the extent of the deposits.

Calculus was observed in most of the adult specimens in the Whithorn material of all phases (Figure 11.44). Even in dentitions which at first appeared to be free of calculus, careful examination of the teeth revealed small fragments of former deposits, often on the protected approximal surfaces. No attempt has been made to assess the extent of calculus formation, since so much of the main deposit has been lost in many cases. In some specimens, the calculus deposits had remained more or less intact, and it was possible to observe all degrees of calculus deposition from very slight amounts through moderate and heavy deposition to extremely large masses almost engulfing the crowns of the teeth. Such gross deposits of calculus were usually observed on only one side of the dentition, suggesting that chewing had been restricted to the opposite side of the mouth as a result of some other painful dental condition.

Calculus was also observed in the juveniles, though some of the youngest children did not appear to show calculus formation. Slight calculus was seen in a child aged 1 year and there were moderate deposits in a child of 4 years. Most of the older children and adolescents showed some evidence of calculus.

The formation of dental calculus was widespread at all ages and at all periods of the Whithorn population, and this may suggest that little attention was paid to oral hygiene.

3.1.7. Periodontal disease

Disease processes of an infectious nature may attack the supporting periodontal ligament of the tooth and this in turn leads to the destruction of the alveolar bone. Considerable amounts of alveolar bone may be lost, leaving the tooth attached only by its apex.

In skeletal material, the infected soft tissue of the periodontium has been lost post-mortem and only the condition of the supporting alveolar bone can be observed. There are, however, difficulties in relating apparent loss of bone to the extent of periodontal disease, since it has been clearly shown that during the functional period, teeth erupt further from the original socket (Whittaker *et al.*, 1985). This movement of teeth during adult life compensates for the amount of tooth substance lost in the course of occlusal attrition and prevents over-closure of the jaws. These eruptive movements of the teeth are slight and occur very gradually, but may result in the exposure of a considerable amount of the root. The difficulty lies in separating such normal exposure of the root from the abnormal exposure of the root due to bone loss in periodontal disease.

Periodontal disease causes one specific lesion of the alveolar bone which can be detected. This is a vertical loss of bone lining the socket, which results in the formation of an obvious gap between the root of the tooth and the bone of the socket. Such a gap is known as an infra-bony pocket.

In skeletal material from medieval and earlier periods, attrition of the occlusal surfaces is a marked feature, due probably to the coarse, tough or gritty nature of many foodstuffs. It would therefore be expected that there will be further eruption of teeth in adult life and exposure of the root is far in excess of the amount which could be assigned to compensatory eruption of the tooth, and it seems reasonable that this should be considered as evidence of periodontal disease, as should the presence of obvious infra-bony pockets (Figure 11.45). Other features such as lipping of the alveolar bone have sometimes been considered as indicating periodontal disease but may be less reliable indicators.

In the present study, periodontal disease has been assessed in a highly subjective manner, taking into account the presence of infra-bony pockets and the degree of excessive exposure of the roots, and has been recorded on a scale of 0 to 3:

grade 0 = no clear evidence of periodontal disease;
grade 1 = evidence of infra-bony pocket formation on one or more teeth, often with moderate loss of alveolar bone, to a greater extent than is consistent with exposure due to eruption;
grade 2 = general severe loss of alveolar bone, to a greater extent than is consistent with exposure due to eruption, with or without the presence of infra-bony pockets;
grade 3 = extreme loss of alveolar bone, many teeth being retained only by the apices.

This method is not very satisfactory since it depends entirely on subjective judgement. However, the more detailed method of examination of individual interdental septa in each individual, introduced by Kerr (1988), was too time-consuming in the circumstances of the present report and, in any case, could not have been applied to many of the specimens, owing to post-mortem damage of the alveolar bone.

The results of this superficial study of periodontal disease are shown in Table 11.39. **Groups 1, 2** and **15–17** have been kept separate for archaeological reasons, and **Groups 4–14** have been combined as representing the main later medieval group from the site. The numbers of specimens from **Periods I** and

11.45 Periodontal disease in the mandible of an adult aged 35–45 from **Group 13**. There is an infra-bony pocket at the root bifurcation of the first permanent molar.

Number of Individuals

	Grade 0	Grade 1	Grade 2	Grade 3	Total
Group 1	4	4	3	1	12
Group 2	6	1	0	0	7
Groups 4–14	285	164	65	15	529
Groups 15–17	37	10	4	0	51
Total	332	179	72	16	599

Percentage Incidence of each Grade

	Grade 0	Grade 1	Grade 2	Grade 3	Total
Group 1	33.3	33.3	25.0	8.3	100
Group 2	85.7	14.3	0.0	0.0	100
Groups 4–14	53.9	31.0	12.3	2.8	100
Groups 15–17	72.5	19.6	7.8	0.0	100
Total	55.4	29.9	12.0	2.7	100

Table 11.39: Prevalence of Periodontal Disease in all phase groups. (Groups 4–14 combined)

II in which the periodontal condition could be assessed were small, and the results are probably unreliable. In slightly more than half of the dentitions from **Period V (Groups 4–14)**, there was no clear evidence of periodontal disease, while one third showed evidence of the earlier stages of the condition. Severe loss of supporting alveolar bone occurred in 12% of dentitions and extreme loss in 3%. The teeth in the final category were close to being lost *in vivo*.

Periodontal disease was also observed to affect the deciduous dentition in a few juveniles. Periodontal pockets were noted in six children ranging in age from 2 to 8 years: there was one child from each of the **Groups 2, 8, 10, 11, 14** and **15**. Most of the pockets affected the embrasures between first and second deciduous molars, but in the youngest child the pocket lay between canine and first deciduous molar.

3.1.8. Dental abscesses and dental cysts

Infection of the pulp of the tooth, tracking through pulp chamber and root canal, and causing infection within the peridontium and bone at the apex of the tooth, in the form of a dental abscess or dental cyst, has already been mentioned under the headings of pulp exposure due to caries, and pulp exposure due to attrition. In many cases of abscess the tooth is still *in situ* and the cause of the abscess can be determined but there are also numerous instances where the tooth has been lost post-mortem and the cause of the abscess cannot be determined. There are also a few cases where the cause of the abscess is not obvious although the tooth is *in situ* and, in addition, a very small number of periodontal abscesses. It therefore seems necessary to examine the prevalence of dental abscesses *per se*. As it is the bone condition and not the tooth which is under consideration, the number of bone lesions must be related, not to the number of teeth present but to the number of 'tooth positions' in the jaw. It should also be stated that it is impossible in bone specimens to differentiate between a chronic dental abscess the centre of which consists of granulation tissue, and a dental cyst which has an epithelial lining and contains fluid. Both lesions develop an enclosing layer of compact bone and thus appear similar in dry specimens. They can be differentiated by histology when the soft tissues are present. Since both lesions have the same aetiology and produce the same destruction of alveolar bone, distinguishing between them is not important in this context. All lesions will be referred to as 'dental abscess', though some of them were probably cysts.

The numbers of permanent tooth positions present in the jaw specimens, the numbers of positions involved in abscess formation, and the percentage of tooth positions affected by abscesses are shown for separate tooth classes and age groups for **Groups 1, 4–8, 9, 10–12, 13–14** and **15–17** in Archive tables 42–47. Most abscesses

Maxillary

	U1	U2	U3	U4	U5	U6	U7	U8	Total
Group 1		4.3	8.7	13.6	4.5	16.0	14.3	15.0	9.7
Groups 4–8	1.8	4.2	2.2	4.1	5.2	8.7	3.6	1.9	4.2
Group 9	1.9	1.8	1.6	3.1	3.6	14.4	5.0	2.7	4.6
Groups 10–12	2.3	1.5	3.7	2.1	4.7	9.3	3.7	1.9	3.8
Groups 13–14	2.5	5.1	2.5	6.1	7.3	14.2	3.3	3.7	5.7
Groups 15–17				1.6	9.2	8.7	4.5		3.2
Total	1.9	3.1	2.4	4.2	5.6	12.0	4.2	2.9	4.8

Mandibular

	L1	L2	L3	L4	L5	L6	L7	L8	Total
Group 1	4.2		4.3		3.6	6.2	9.1	13.8	5.5
Groups 4–8	1.1	0.5	1.0	1.0	2.7	9.0	3.1	1.3	2.7
Group 9	1.4	0.5	0.4	2.7	1.8	9.1	4.2	4.5	3.3
Groups 10–12	0.6	0.6	1.7		0.5	6.2	4.4	2.0	2.2
Groups 13–14	2.0	2.3	1.5	2.1	5.1	7.9	5.6	3.2	3.9
Groups 15–17		1.4			1.4	11.5	4.1	2.6	3.0
Total	1.3	1.1	1.1	1.4	2.7	8.3	4.5	3.1	3.2

Table 11.40: Prevalence of Abscesses (All Causes) as Percentage of Tooth Positions in all phase groups.

were found, as would be expected, in the older groups of adults, though in some cases younger adults and juveniles were affected. There was generally a slightly higher prevalence in the maxilla than in the mandible.

The numbers of specimens in some sub-groups were small and, in order to compare phases, different age groups were combined, as shown in Table 11.40. Maxilla and mandible have been considered separately. The jaw specimens from **Period I (Group 1)** showed a relatively high prevalence of abscess formation, particularly in the maxilla. The group from the Museum Garden (**Groups 14–18**) showed a lower prevalence of abscesses than the others. The remaining groups (**4–14**) showed rather similar patterns of abscess formation. The tooth most commonly involved in abscess development was the maxillary first permanent molar.

The prevalence of abscesses in the deciduous dentition was also examined and the results are shown in Archive tables 48–51. One further abscess associated with a maxillary second deciduous molar, and an abscess of a mandibular first deciduous molar could be added to those abscesses already noted in association with pulp exposure in carious deciduous teeth.

An examination has also been made of the proportion of abscesses in the permanent dentition due to different causes, expressed as a percentage of all abscesses. The results are shown in Archive tables 52–75 and Table 11.41. The numbers of specimens in **Groups 1** and **15–17** were small and the percentage distributions for these groups should be treated with caution.

As far as the main later medieval groups are concerned, there was some variation between phases, and also between maxilla and mandible. In a relatively large proportion of abscesses, the tooth responsible had been lost post-mortem (31%–49% in the maxilla and 29%–47% in the mandible) and this renders a detailed comparison of the distribution of

Numbers of Abscesses

Maxillary

	Caries	Attrition	Cause Unknown	Tooth Missing	Perio.	Total
Group 1 (**Period I**)	9	2	0	6	0	17
Groups 4–8 (530–534)	8	22	1	14	0	45
Group 9 (535)	19	22	4	21	0	66
Groups 10–12 (536–538)	9	11	3	18	0	41
Groups 13–14 (539 and 540)	27	21	2	53	6	109
Groups 15–17 (Museum Garden)	1	13	0	3	0	17
Total	73	91	10	115	6	295

Mandibular

	Caries	Attrition	Cause Unknown	Tooth Missing	Perio.	Total
Group 1 (**Period I**)	4	0	1	7	0	12
Groups 4–8 (530–534)	10	10	5	22	0	47
Group 9	21	12	1	27	0	61
Groups 10–12 (536–538)	13	10	0	10	1	34
Groups 13–14 (539–540)	25	15	6	42	4	92
Groups 15–17 (Museum Garden)	2	10	0	7	0	19
Total	75	57	13	115	5	265

Percentage Prevalence

Maxillary

	Caries	Attrition	Cause Unknown	Tooth Missing	Perio.
Group 1 (**Period I**)	52.9	11.8	0.0	35.3	0.0
Groups 4–8 (530–534)	17.8	48.9	2.2	31.1	0.0
Group 9 (535)	28.8	33.3	6.1	31.8	0.0
Groups 10–12 (536–538)	22.0	26.8	7.3	43.9	0.0
Groups 13–14 (539–540)	24.8	19.3	1.8	48.6	5.5
Groups 15–17 (Museum Garden)	5.9	76.5	0.0	17.6	0.0
Total	24.7	30.8	3.4	39.0	2.0

Mandibular

	Caries	Attrition	Cause Unknown	Tooth Missing	Perio.
Group 1 (**Period I**)	33.3	0.0	8.3	58.3	0.0
Groups 4–8 (530–534)	21.3	21.3	10.6	46.8	0.0
Group 9 (535)	34.4	19.7	1.6	44.3	0.0
Groups 10–12 (536–538)	38.2	29.4	0.0	29.4	2.9
Groups 13–14 (539–540)	27.2	16.3	6.5	45.7	4.3
Groups 15–17 (Museum Garden)	10.5	52.6	0.0	36.8	0.0
Total	28.3	21.5	4.9	43.4	1.9

Table 11.41: Aetiology of Abscesses in all phase groups.

abscesses due to other causes of little value. If all groups are combined, the tooth had been lost post-mortem in 39% of maxillary abscesses and in 43% of mandibular abscesses. Caries accounted for 25% of maxillary abscesses and for 28% of mandibular abscesses, while 31% of maxillary abscesses and 22% of mandibular abscesses could be attributed to excessive attrition. Periodontal abscesses and abscesses whose cause was obscure made up small proportions of the total.

Specimens where the cause of the abscess was obscure showed neither a deep carious lesion approaching the pulp, nor an obvious pulp exposure due to severe attrition. In some cases, it is possible that moderate attrition had caused a microscopic exposure of an unusually high pulp horn.

In other instances, particularly in anterior teeth, trauma to the tooth may have been the cause of an apical abscess. For example, in an adult in **Group 9**, an abscess was observed in connection with a maxillary second incisor the crown of which appeared perfectly healthy. The root of the tooth showed an area of resorption at the apex but otherwise appeared sound. A radiograph revealed an otherwise undetectable fracture of the root, and it seems likely that the tooth had suffered a blow which fractured the root and caused the death of the pulp. Infection of the dead pulp tissue then resulted in the formation of an apical abscess and subsequent resorption of the root.

In another interesting case of an abscess at the apex of an apparently normal mandibular second premolar, the time of the traumatic incident which probably caused the abscess could be determined. The individual, from **Group 8**, was aged 25–35 at the time of death, but the root of the premolar involved in the abscess had not been fully formed. The extent of root formation suggests that the individual was

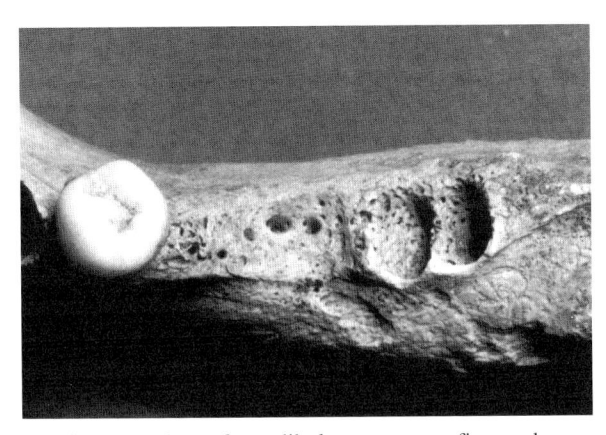

11.46 *In vivo* loss of mandibular permanent first molar. Bone healing has occurred, but pitting of surface suggests slight residual infection. Socket for second molar (lost post-mortem) can be seen. Third molar was congenitally absent. Adult aged 25–35, **Group 13**.

Maxillary

	U1	U2	U3	U4	U5	U6	U7	U8	Total
Group 1	10.5	8.7		13.6	13.6	24.0	9.5	15.0	12.0
Groups 4–14	4.9	5.5	2.0	3.9	5.1	12.3	9.3	8.0	6.4
Groups 15–17		1.5	1.6		3.1	5.0	1.5	3.8	2.1

Mandibular

	L1	L2	L3	L4	L5	L6	L7	L8	Total
Group 1	4.2			12.5	10.7	12.5	6.1	6.9	6.8
Groups 4–14	8.0	3.8	1.8	4.0	6.1	17.5	10.8	7.7	7.8
Groups 15–17	3.8				5.2	5.2	2.6	2.4

Table 11.42: Prevalence of Tooth Losses in vivo as Percentage of Tooth Positions for all Phase groups. (Phases 4–14 combined.)

aged 12–13 at the time of the accident, i.e. trauma to the tooth had occurred shortly after it erupted.

Some abscesses became extremely large, causing considerable loss of bone in the jaw, and in several cases had involved the roots of neighbouring teeth which were otherwise healthy. In five specimens, an abscess of an upper molar had perforated into the maxillary sinus and in one of these specimens the condition was bilateral.

3.1.9. Tooth loss in vivo

A tooth may be lost *in vivo* as the end result of advanced caries, excessive attrition or severe periodontal disease. Once the tooth is lost there is of course no means of knowing the cause, although if one of the conditions mentioned is seen in other parts of the dentition, it may be the most likely option. After the tooth is lost there is, in many cases, some evidence of residual bone infection (Figure 11.46), but this will most often subside and eventually the alveolar process where the tooth was lost will acquire a smooth surface of well-healed compact bone.

It is necessary to differentiate *in vivo* tooth loss from spaces in the dentition where teeth have failed to develop (congenital absence). The tooth most commonly found to be congenitally absent is the permanent third molar, and unless there is evidence of residual bone infection the decision whether a missing third molar was lost *in vivo* or congenitally absent can be difficult. Observation of attrition facets on the distal surface of the second molar, or of considerable loss of height of alveolar bone in the molar areas would confirm or strengthen the diagnosis of *in vivo* loss.

The numbers of permanent tooth positions present, the number of teeth diagnosed as lost *in vivo*, and the percentage lost *in vivo* are shown for separate tooth classes, age and phase groups in Archive tables 76–81. From these tables it seems that teeth were lost *in vivo* with almost equal frequency from the mandible and from the maxilla. The older adults were most often affected by *in vivo* tooth loss, but smaller numbers of teeth were lost *in vivo* in younger adults.

Group 1 differed from others in the high proportion of premolars lost *in vivo*, and in having a higher prevalence of *in vivo* loss in the maxilla than in the mandible. **Groups 15–17** showed low levels of *in vivo* loss. The remaining group (**4–14**) showed similar levels of *in vivo* tooth loss. Table 11.42 shows the overall percentages of *in vivo* tooth loss for the combined age groups of **Group 1, Groups 4–14** and **Groups 15–17**. From this table it can be seen that the molars were the teeth most likely to be lost *in vivo*.

There was no direct evidence as to whether surgical interference was involved in any case of *in vivo* tooth loss. From the appearance of many dentitions in the older adults, it was obvious that teeth were often allowed to remain *in situ* until they fell out. In some jaws, the extent of attachment between tooth and bone was so slight that the tooth could almost have been plucked out between finger and thumb.

A few cases were noted in which deciduous teeth had been lost *in vivo* as a result of disease or trauma, instead of being shed in the normal way. The most extreme example was a child aged 7 from **Group 10**, in whom all four mandibular deciduous molars had been lost. The bone had healed over and there was little to be seen of the successional developing premolars except on a radiograph. Another mandibular first deciduous molar may have been lost due to disease in a child from **Group 9**. A maxillary first deciduous incisor had been lost in a child of 5 from **Group 5**.

The extent of residual bone infection in cases where permanent teeth had been lost *in vivo* is shown by tooth class and age group for **Group 1, Groups 4–14** and **Groups 15–17** in Archive tables 82–84. There is some indication in the figures for the largest phase group, **4–14**, that the proportion of areas showing residual infection was slightly reduced in the older age groups, suggesting that in the older adults some teeth had been lost some time before death, allowing the infection to subside and the bone to heal. This is not shown consistently for all tooth classes.

There appeared to be little difference between phases in the extent to which residual infection was still present in areas where teeth had been lost *in vivo*. Taking all groups together, residual infection was still evident in 46% of cases of *in vivo* tooth loss.

3.1.10. Traumatic damage

There was relatively little direct evidence in the Whithorn material of traumatic injuries to the teeth or jaws, though it is impossible to tell what part trauma may have played in the loss of teeth during life.

Mention has already been made of two cases where abscesses associated with apparently healthy teeth could be shown to be due to trauma and it is probable that other cases of abscess where the cause was obscure were the result of trauma to the tooth.

There were no examples in the Whithorn material of broken incisal corners, frequently seen in the maxillary incisors of modern children. The rapid wear of incisal edges in medieval individuals rendered the teeth less liable to fracture after they had been in function for a time, but even in medieval children the incisors would have been vulnerable for a few years after they had erupted at the age of 7–8.

One maxillary first permanent molar in a mature adult from **Group 11** showed traumatic damage which may have occurred *in vivo* rather than post-mortem. In another very strange case, a maxillary first premolar in an adult of 25–35 years from **Group 12** appeared to have had the buccal root fractured *in vivo*. The apical half of the root had been lost and its socket filled with new bone. The maxillary first premolar often has two long and very slender roots, but it is difficult to imagine what episode could have caused the damage which appears to have been inflicted here.

Trauma may cause severe haemorrhage into the pulp and the decomposed blood products may result in dark staining of the tooth. A dark mandibular first incisor was observed in a 13-year old child from **Group 5**. In this dentition, both mandibular first incisors showed abscess formation, and the obvious interpretation is that trauma to the incisors had caused death of both pulps with severe haemorrhage in the case of one tooth, followed by apical abscess formation.

A maxillary permanent first incisor among the loose teeth showed an unusual bright blue discolouration of a narrow band of enamel near the cervical margin of the crown. It has not been possible to discover any likely cause for this intrinsic staining of the tooth, other than a different manifestation of staining due to haemorrhage in the pulp.

The frequent loss of teeth *in vivo* has already been described. In many cases, a considerable amount of alveolar bone was lost during this process, but the general shape of the jaw was usually maintained. In one adult from **Group 11**, both mandibular left incisors had been lost *in vivo* and the surface of the jaw in this area appeared to be deformed, suggesting that the teeth may have been lost due to trauma together with a piece of the alveolar bone, which in this area is thin and easily fractured. Unfortunately, post-mortem bone damage complicated the situation in this specimen and the diagnosis is not certain.

3.2. Dental Pathology – Developmental

3.2.1. Enamel hypoplasia

The development of the dental tissues is not a smoothly continuous process. There is a diurnal rhythm in the deposition of enamel and dentine with very slight resting phases between the daily increments of tissue matrix. These resting phases produce infinitesimal variations in the structure of the tissues, which can be identified under the microscope even in fully mineralised teeth. Some of the normal resting phases are slightly more pronounced and in the case of the enamel can be observed with the naked eye as fine lines known as perikymata on the surface of the crown. The perikymata are most easily observed on the labial surfaces of anterior teeth and are usually most distinct in the cervical region.

If for any reason the normal development of the tissues is disturbed, and the disturbance occurs over a limited period, the resulting defect in the tissue will adopt a linear configuration following the normal incremental pattern. In the case of enamel, defective formation of enamel matrix leads to a fault in fully formed enamel known as enamel hypoplasia. In its most severe form, enamel hypoplasia appears as a line or band of pits on the enamel surface, following the pattern of the perikymata. In a less severe form, enamel hypoplasia may appear as a continuous groove, sometimes with microscopic pits in its base. In other cases, a slight accentuation of the perikymata may be observed, but this may simply represent a slight variation in the normal incremental rhythm. By reference to the tables or diagrams of tooth development, it is possible to assess the probable age of the child when an upset to tooth formation occurred. Hypoplasia can only occur during the period of development of the crowns of the teeth, and thus must relate to disturbances between birth and 8 years, except in the case of third molars, whose crowns may not complete development until 15 years.

There may be many causes for the occurrence of enamel hypoplasia. Certain congenital conditions, many major systemic illnesses and childhood fevers have been implicated, among others (Pindborg, 1982). In a few cases there may be a local cause. Another possible cause of enamel hypoplasia, and one which has aroused a good deal of interest, is malnutrition and it has been suggested that the extent of hypoplasia may act as an indicator of environmental stress in a population. It is, however, impossible to decide whether hypoplasia in an individual is the result of a general malnutrition affecting the whole population or the result of a major illness in that individual which does not necessarily imply a general epidemic. Goodman and Rose (1991) point out that it is not yet known 'how useful an indicator enamel hypoplasias will prove to be, and exactly what they are most likely to indicate'.

Although the gross variety of pitted hypoplasia is easy to identify, problems may arise in the diagnosis of the linear type. The relatively slight lines which

THE ENVIRONMENTAL MATERIAL

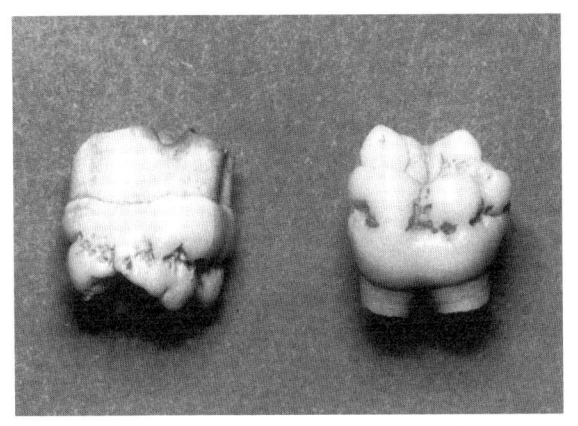

11.47 Gross pitted hypoplasia of permanent first molars in a child aged *c*. 6 years from **Group 5**. The disturbance occurred at approximately 1 year of age.

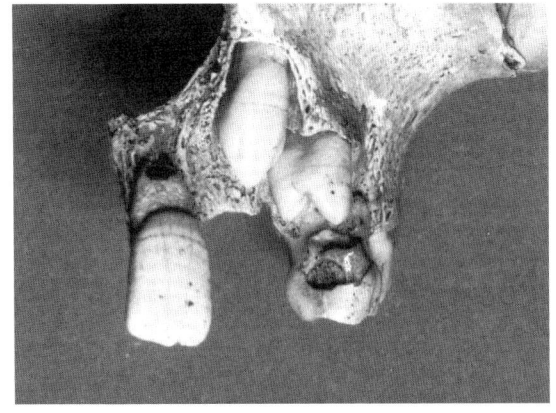

11.48 Linear hypoplasia in a child aged *c*. 8 years from **Group 13**. The heavily marked line in the erupted first incisor indicates an upset between 3 and 4 years. The double lines in the unerupted canine and premolar suggest disturbances between 4 and 6 years.

we have called 'accentuated perikymata' often do not extend on to all surfaces of the crown and are not observed in all teeth which should have been developing at the same time. It therefore does not seem likely that they are due to a general systemic upset, but are more likely to be due to local variations in the normal incremental process within the tooth. Yet there is a gradation between accentuated perikymata and deeper lines which would be classified as linear hypoplasia and it is not always easy to know where the line should be drawn. Even with the more obvious linear hypoplasias, cases are often seen where teeth which should all have been developing at the same time do not all display the linear defects. Only the gross pitted variety of hypoplasia is usually consistent in having defects at the appropriate levels in all teeth developing at the time of the incident.

Hypoplastic defects are caused during development, but remain in the enamel throughout the life of the tooth. However, during adult life the process of attrition of the enamel surface will remove the finest lines. The perikymata certainly disappear, though accentuated perikymata can still be seen in some adult teeth. The deeper grooves of linear hypoplasia are probably not removed, nor the pits of gross hypoplasia.

In studying the Whithorn material, all features from gross pitted hypoplasia (Figure 11.47) and linear hypoplasia (Figure 11.48) to accentuated perikymata were recorded in individuals of all ages, though in many specimens, hypoplasia could not be accurately assessed because of post-mortem loss, or damage to the teeth. The results have been presented only for juveniles and young adults in order to avoid any bais caused by attrition in the older individuals.

The distribution of dentitions with accentuated perikymata, linear hypoplasia and pitted hypoplasia are shown in Table 11.43. Different grades of hypoplasia were observed in the teeth of one specimen, but each individual has been entered only once, by the most advanced grade of hypoplasia observed in that dentition.

No examples of linear hypoplasia or pitted hypoplasia were recorded in the dentitions from

Number of Dentitions

	Normal	Accentuated Perikymata	Linear Hypoplasia	Pitted Hypoplasia	Total
Group 1	5	3	0	0	8
Group 2	2	6	0	0	8
Groups 4–8	33	28	14	5	80
Group 9	18	34	11	2	65
Groups 10–12	13	23	5	2	43
Groups 13–14	16	37	13	3	69
Groups 15–17	10	16	6	1	33
Total 4–17	90	138	49	13	290

Percentage Incidence

	Normal	Accentuated Perikymata	Linear Hypoplasia	Pitted Hypoplasia
Group 1	62.5	37.5	0.0	0.0
Group 2	25.0	75.0	0.0	0.0
Groups 4–8	41.2	35.0	17.5	6.2
Group 9	27.7	52.3	16.9	3.1
Groups 10–12	30.0	53.5	11.6	4.7
Groups 13–14	23.2	53.6	18.8	4.3
Groups 15–17	30.3	48.5	18.2	3.0
Total 4–17	31.0	47.6	16.9	4.5

Table 11.43: Enamel Hypoplasia in Juvenile and Young Adult Dentitions.

Periods **I** and **II**, but the numbers of specimens suitable for study were small. The remaining phase groups showed similar distributions of the grades of hypoplasia. When the material from **Groups 4–17** was combined, a third of dentitions appeared completely normal and slightly less than half showed minor accentuation of the perikymata. The remaining 20% showed evidence of disturbance of enamel formation, mostly in the form of linear defects. Only 4.5% of dentitions showed evidence of gross pitted hypoplasia.

It has not been possible in the time available to carry out a full analysis of enamel hypoplasia by tooth class and further study of this aspect of the material is planned. Any tooth may be affected by each grade of hypoplasia, but the cervical region of the long crown of the mandibular canine is particularly susceptible to linear defects.

It should be noted that a few examples of enamel hypoplasia in deciduous second molars were observed.

3.2.2. Malformations of teeth

Normal variations of tooth morphology and the presence of features such as additional cusps do not form part of the remit of this report. One example of a grossly malformed tooth was found among the loose teeth. This was a maxillary central incisor whose crown had a deep fold on the palatal surface and was also set at a marked angle to the root. There had been some serious injury to the tooth germ while the hard tissues were developing. The enamel of this specimen also showed gross pitted hypoplasia.

3.2.3. Congenital absence of teeth

It occasionally happens that an entire tooth fails to form and the tooth is then said to be congenitallly absent. The deciduous dentition is very rarely affected by this condition.

The permanent teeth most commonly found to be congenitally absent are the third molars and the condition may affect from one to four of the four third molars in an individual, in any permutation. The Whithorn material was too fragmentary to allow an accurate assessment of the number of individuals affected by congenital absence of third molars or an assessment of the numbers of third molars found to be absent in individuals. Instead, the prevalence of congenital absence has been expressed as the proportion of third molar positions in which the tooth was judged to have been congenitally absent. The problem of differentiating in some cases between congenital absence and *in vivo* loss has been discussed in the section on *in vivo* loss of teeth. Care was taken in the case of juveniles that the individual was older than the latest age at which the tooth ought to commence development. In every case, radiographs were examined for evidence of the tooth or its crypt forming in the jaw before a diagnosis of congenital absence was made.

Congenital absence of teeth was not observed in the material from **Period I (Group 1)**. The numbers of tooth positions, numbers of teeth congenitally absent, and percentage of tooth positions in which the tooth was congenitally absent are shown in Archive tables 85–89 for **Groups 4–8, 9, 10–12, 13–14** and **15–17**.

In each phase, the teeth most commonly found to be congenitally absent were the third molars and in each case the prevalence of absent third molars appeared to be higher in the mandible than in the maxilla. This may reflect the true situation or it may be that some maxillary third molars judged to have been lost *in vivo* had in fact been congenitally absent. The figures range between 8% and 16% of maxillary third molars absent, and between 19% and 29% of mandibular third molars absent. In this respect, **Groups 15–17** shows no marked difference from the other phase groups. If all phase groups are combined the final prevalence of congenital absence is 11.4% of maxillary third molars and 23% of mandibular third molars.

Small numbers of other permanent teeth were occasionally observed to be congenitally absent. Next in frequency to third molars were mandibular second premolars, 1.7% of which were absent in the dentitions of all phases combined. In the case of these teeth the diagnosis of congenital absence was more reliable, as in several cases the deciduous second molar was still *in situ* and radiographs showed that the premolar was not developing beneath it. In other cases, although the deciduous tooth had been shed, the space left in the jaw was wider than that occupied by a premolar.

Small numbers of maxillary second incisors, mandibular first incisors, mandibular second molars and maxillary second premolars were also diagnosed as congenitally absent.

In some cases, teeth of more than one class were absent in the same individual. Third molars and mandibular second premolars were congenitally absent in seven specimens from Whithorn, while in three specimens, third molars and maxillary second incisors were absent. Single examples were found of absence of third molars together with a maxillary second premolar, a mandibular first incisor and both mandibular second molars.

In cases of congenital absence of permanent teeth with a deciduous predecessor, the deciduous tooth may remain in function long after the age at which it would normally be shed. Several examples were seen in the Whithorn specimens, where deciduous canines and second molars had remained *in situ*. Usually the strain of mastication in an adult dentition is too heavy for such a deciduous tooth and it will eventually be shed. In some cases, however, the retained deciduous tooth may become fused or ankylosed to the alveolar bone and in this situation the ankylosed tooth often becomes submerged below the level of the adjacent permanent teeth. Two examples of this condition were seen in the Whithorn material. In a 14 year old from **Group 12**, one mandibular second premolar was congenitally absent. The second deciduous molar was retained, had become ankylosed and was submerged well below the permanent first premolar and first molar on either side of it. An 18 year old from **Group 12** also showed congenital absence of a mandibular second premolar with retention of the deciduous second molar, which showed early signs of ankylosis and submergence. In both of these cases, the mandibular second premolar on the opposite side of the jaw had developed and erupted normally.

3.2.4. Supernumerary teeth

Very occasionally, teeth may develop which are additional to the normal dentition. They may be found in any part of the jaw, but are commonest in the incisor and molar areas. In some instances, the supernumerary tooth has a morphology approaching that of the nearest members of the normal dentition and then is known as a supplemental tooth. In other cases, the supernumerary tooth is abnormal in shape and is often a small peg-shaped structure.

A few instances of such supernumerary teeth were found in the Whithorn material, scattered randomly among the phases. In very few specimens was the supernumerary tooth found *in situ*. In some instances, the socket for the small additional tooth was observed but the tooth had been lost post-mortem, while supernumerary teeth found with other dentitions could not be ascribed to the dentition with certainty as the jaws were fragmentary and no socket was present where the supernumerary might be expected to lie.

Two examples of supplemental incisors were found in the Whithorn material. One case from **Group 9** involved a supplemental maxillary second incisor, and in the second case from **Group 13**, the supplemental mandibular second incisor was so normal in appearance that it was necessary to measure all five incisors in order to determine which was the extra tooth. In both cases, the alveolar process had survived intact, with all the incisors *in situ*.

In three further cases, sockets for small supernumerary teeth were observed in the alveolar bone buccal to the maxillary molars. The supernumeraries had been lost post-mortem and their morphology remains unknown. In several other cases, small teeth which may have been supernumeraries were found with articulated specimens, but no socket was present in the jaw fragments and in some instances the tooth had most probably derived from another dentition. A conical supernumerary of the type found in the midline of the maxilla and known as 'mesiodens' was observed with the dentition of a 10-year-old child from **Group 5**, but there is no evidence to show whether it belonged to this dentition. Two tiny molariform teeth found with other dentitions may be supernumerary teeth, but the diagnosis cannot be made with certainty, since no sockets were present for them. The issue is further confused by the observation of very tiny maxillary third molars in two dentitions and the presence of a peg-shaped third molar in another

dentition. The molariform teeth could be microdont third molars or supernumeraries.

Most unusual of all is the developing deciduous supernumerary found with the dentition of a two-year-old child from **Group 10**. The alveolar bone is damaged and the crypt of the supernumerary cannot be identified. Its crown is conical and appears to be closest in morphology to a canine. Deciduous supernumerary teeth are rare.

3.2.5. Gemination

A rare developmental anomaly known as gemination occurs when two developing teeth fuse. Gemination may occur between two members of the normal dentition, or between a normal tooth and a supernumerary element. (Occasionally it may be that a single normal tooth germ has been partially split; the resulting anomaly is usually indistinguishable from gemination with a supernumerary.)

No examples of gemination between two normal teeth were observed in the Whithorn material, but three cases were found of gemination between a supernumerary and a normal tooth. This condition differs from the presence of an additional cusp, not infrequently seen, in that the supernumerary element has its own root, fused to that of the normal tooth. Two of the cases involved maxillary permanent molars, one a second molar and the other a third molar. In the third case, a small supernumerary was fused to a deformed, twisted maxillary lateral incisor.

3.2.6. Embedded teeth

Teeth may develop in an apparently normal manner, but fail to erupt into a functional position. In the majority of cases, the tooth remains embedded deep in the bone of the jaw. Occasionally the tooth may undergo partial emergence into an abnormal position. The teeth which most commonly remain embedded are permanent canines and mandibular third molars.

Maxillary

	U3	U4	U5	U8l
Group 1				
Group 2			1	1
Groups 4–8	5			
Group 9	10	1		
Groups 10–12	3	1	3	2
Groups 13–14	7		1	2
Groups 15–17	6		3	
Total	31	2	8	5

Mandibular

	L2	L3	L4	L5	L6	L8	Total
Group 1		1					1
Group 2						1	3
Groups 4–8			1			2	8
Group 9	1	4		1	1	1	19
Groups 10–12		2				2	13
Groups 13–14		2		3		9	24
Groups 15–17		3				1	13
Total	1	12	1	4	1	16	81

Table 11.44: Distribution of Embedded Teeth in all Phase groups.

Embedded teeth were observed in specimens from all phases at Whithorn. The numbers of embedded teeth are shown in Table 11.44 by tooth class and phase. The tooth most frequently found embedded was the maxillary canine. In the mandible, almost equal numbers of third molars and canines had failed to erupt. Smaller numbers of maxillary second premolars, maxillary third molars and mandibular second premolars were embedded, and there were isolated examples of embedded maxillary and mandibular first premolars, a mandibular second incisor and a mandibular first molar. In six cases, several canines and premolars in the same individual were embedded. The largest number of teeth found to be embedded in a single dentition was five: both maxillary canines, both maxillary second premolars and a mandibular canine.

Embedded third molars are often lying at such an angle that their crowns are impacted against the root of the neighbouring second molar and the pressure from the third molar may cause resorption of the second molar root. Three embedded maxillary third molars in the Whithorn material were slightly impacted under the second molars. The degree of impaction is often more severe in the case of mandibular third molars. In the Whithorn specimens, four mandibular third molars were horizontally impacted, three were in mesio-oblique impaction and four showed slighter degrees of vertical impaction. Radiographs suggested that in several of the horizontal or mesio-oblique impactions, there was early resorption of the root of the second molar, though no cases of gross resorption were seen.

3.2.7. Eruption, other complications

Problems are sometimes encountered during tooth eruption. Infection of the soft tissues around the erupting crown may cause an inflammatory condition known as pericoronitis. In other instances, a fluid-filled cyst known as a dentigerous cyst may develop around the crown of an erupting tooth. One young adult from **Group 14** had had considerable trouble with both mandibular third molars. The teeth had begun to erupt but movement had ceased before they had emerged and the fully formed root apices showed that they could move no further. The crown of one tooth had been enveloped in a dentigerous cyst. On the other side, the tooth had moved a little further and broken through the soft tissues. Infection had then set in and there was clear evidence of a pericoronitis.

There may be evidence of dentigerous cyst in connection with an embedded maxillary canine in an adult from **Group 7**. A dentigerous cyst may also have been present in the position of a mandibular second molar in an adolescent from **Group 9**.

During the shedding of deciduous teeth and eruption of their permanent successors, the roots of the deciduous teeth sometimes fail to resorb completely, leaving tiny fragments, usually of the root apices, embedded in the alveolar bone. For reasons which are not understood, these fragments of deciduous root apex often fail to resorb and may be observed in the alveolar bone many years later. Small fragments of retained deciduous root were observed in five specimens from Whithorn, ranging from **Group 1** to **Groups 15–17**.

Anomalies in the timing of eruption may also be observed. In many of the Whithorn juveniles, slight variations in the sequence of tooth emergence were noted, but in two juveniles, one from **Group 7** and one from **Group 13**, the eruption of canines and premolars had been seriously delayed.

3.2.8. Anomalies in tooth position

Although in many of the Whithorn dentitions the teeth were regularly arranged in the dental arches, minor degrees of crowding of the teeth were not uncommon. Crowding most often affected the mandibular incisors, but may be observed in any part of the dentition. Spacing of the teeth was less common, but noticeable gaps between the teeth (without *in vivo* loss) were observed in eight specimens from Whithorn. In two cases there was a marked midline diastema in the maxilla, and in one instance a diastema existed between two mandibular permanent molars, while in four cases the spacing occurred in the premolar areas. In one adult from **Group 15**, there was spacing of the maxillary incisors and crowding of the mandibular incisors.

In dentitions where teeth had been lost *in vivo*, those teeth on either side of the missing tooth were often tilted over the gap. In the Whithorn material, teeth were sometimes observed to be slightly tilted buccally or lingually, sometimes because of crowding in the dentition but often without obvious cause as there appeared to be sufficient room for them in the arch.

Eleven specimens showed torsoversion of a single tooth, i.e. rotation of the tooth such that the surfaces of the crown were facing in the wrong direction. Most of the teeth affected by this anomaly were second premolars, but a few canines and first premolars, and a mandibular third molar also showed the condition.

Occlusal relationships in the dentitions could not be studied as the cranial base carrying part of the temporomandibular joint was in virtually all cases absent and the jaws could not be brought together in the relationship which had existed in life.

3.3 General (systemic) conditions affecting the jaws

It has been our experience that pathological conditions observed in the jaws in skeletal material have almost always been of dental origin and conditions of a more general nature are rare. This is true of the Whithorn material. No tumours of the jaw bones were observed and there were very few lesions of the jaws which could be attributable to other than dental causes. Parts of two deformed mandibles were found among the individuals from **Group 9**. In one of these, it appeared that there had been inadequate development at the left condylar growth site and the left condyle may have been ankylosed to the base of the skull. The deformity in the other case may have been of developmental origin or due to a fracture. Both specimens were too fragmentary to permit a precise diagnosis.

In fact, there are few general systemic diseases which leave specific recognisable traces in the jawbones or teeth. One systemic disease which may attack the jaws and leave diagnostic signs is leprosy. In this condition, there may be lesions of the soft tissues around the nose and palate which cause a highly characteristic erosion of the bone of the anterior nasal spine and of the palate, and loss of the alveolar bone supporting the maxillary incisors and canines, to the extent that these teeth may be lost *in vivo*. These features are known as facies leprosa and, especially when seen in an individual where alveolar bone has not been lost in other parts of the jaw, are diagnostic for leprosy. No case of facies leprosa was found among the Whithorn jaws. However, in a case of facies leprosa from Hallowhill, St Andrews, an unusual appearance of the mandibular incisors (which in themselves were normal) was also noted, in the form of over-eruption and labial splaying of the incisors, perhaps due to a large mass of lepromatous soft tissue in the upper jaw. One of the mandibles from Whithorn showed a very similar over-eruption and splaying of the mandibular incisors, and it is possible that the missing maxilla to which this mandible belonged may have been a case of facies leprosa. However, the appearance of the mandibular incisors may have been due to some other unknown condition of the maxilla.

Congenital syphilis may cause characteristic developmental defects in the permanent first incisors (Hutchinson's incisors) and permanent first molars (Mulberry or Moon molars). No Hutchinson's incisors were observed among the Whithorn teeth. Among the loose teeth were two permanent first molars, one maxillary and one mandibular, with severe hypoplastic defects of the occlusal surfaces. These teeth are exactly similar in appearance to a mulberry molar in an attested modern case of congenital syphilis and probably indicate the presence of the condition in an individual from Whithorn. The two molars are similar in size and general appearance, and it seems most likely that they have derived from the same dentition.

4. SUMMARY

The aims of the present study have been: to assess dental age in the entire skeletal material from Whithorn; to record all examples of dental or other disease, and dental or bone anomalies; to examine dental age distribution in the skeletons; to assess the prevalence of the commoner dental conditions in the Whithorn population; and to investigate possible differences between the 17 groups to which a large part of the articulated skeletal material has been assigned. In all, 972 articulated specimens, 693 disarticulated jaw fragments and 5506 loose teeth were examined.

There have been problems in the investigation of the Whithorn material, due to its extremely fragmentary state.

Age distribution did not appear to be markedly different for males and for females. Differences between groups consisted mainly in variations in the proportions of juveniles. The proportions of adult age categories varied slightly, but most adults fell within the 25–35 and 35–45 age groups. The overall age distribution showed that in the total articulated material, 34% were juveniles and 66% adults. This may be compared with the medieval population from Kirkhill, St Andrews, where 24% of the specimens were juveniles and 76% adults (Lunt, 1986).

The commonest dental pathological condition observed in the Whithorn dentitions was dental caries, which was studied separately in permanent and deciduous dentitions. Combining data from right and left sides, and from both sexes increased the quantity of data available for comparisons between phases. However, the quantity of data for some of the smaller groups was still insufficient, and some phases were combined, resulting in seven phase groups: **Group 1, Group 2, Groups 4–8, Group 9, Groups 10–12, Groups 13–14** and **Groups 15–17**.

In permanent teeth, caries prevalence in general showed an increase with age within each phase group. The pattern of caries prevalence was similar in **Groups 4–8, 9, 10–12** and **13–14**, while some differences were noted in **Group 1** and **Groups 15–17**. The largest age group, adults aged 25–35, showed a consistent increase in caries from the earliest level of the main site, **Group 1**, to the latest level, **Groups 13–14**, but this was not repeated consistently for all age groups and the question whether there may be any real increase in caries prevalence with time at Whithorn must remain open. It has not been possible within the time available to carry out a full statistical analysis of differences observed between phases.

The overall caries prevalence for all phases, 6.4% of permanent teeth at risk being affected by the disease, has been compared with figures published for other sites in Scotland and England.

Caries prevalence in permanent teeth by tooth class was examined in the main group of later medieval skeletons, **Groups 4–14**. The teeth most frequently attacked by caries were the molars, followed by premolars. The incisor and canine teeth were much less often involved. The results for Whithorn are in some respects similar to those published for Aberdeen medieval skeletons (Kerr *et al.*, 1988), though some differences were also noted.

Caries prevalence in the total articulated material from Whithorn was compared with prevalence in the disarticulated fragments and loose teeth from the site. The general pattern of caries prevalence was similar in the three categories of material, though there were some apparent differences in the level of carious attack, probably resulting from fragmentation of the material.

The occurrence of dental calculus and periodontal disease has been briefly discussed, though there were considerable problems in the accurate recording of these conditions. The formation of dental calculus was widespread in the Whithorn population and may suggest a lack of hygiene. About a third of the dentitions showed some evidence of the earlier stages of periodontal disease and 15% were severely affected by the condition.

In a few cases there was some evidence to suggest that a tooth had been subjected to trauma during life and in several of these a dental abscess had formed at the apex of the tooth.

Developmental conditions affecting the teeth have also been studied. Enamel hypoplasia was assessed in juveniles and young adults. Teeth affected by the gross pitted form of enamel hypoplasia were found in 4.5% of dentitions in **Groups 4–17**, while 17% of the dentitions were affected by linear hypoplasia.

Congenital absence of teeth involved chiefly the permanent third molars, though some mandibular second premolars had failed to form and there were isolated examples of congenital absence of other teeth.

Some cases of supernumerary teeth, gemination between a normal tooth and a supernumerary tooth, and embedded permanent teeth were observed in the Whithorn material, and various complications of the eruption process had affected a few individuals.

Evidence of general systemic conditions affecting the jaws was minimal. There may be some slight indirect evidence of a case of leprosy, but this cannot be confirmed. Two molars show a specific type of enamel hypoplasia (mulberry molars) and probably indicate a case of congenital syphilis. In two cases there was evidence of a deformity of the mandible, whose cause could not be ascertained, though in one case it probably indicated a severe developmental defect of mandibular growth.

Acknowledgments

We are indebted to Mr Peter Hill, director of the Whithorn excavation, for the approximate dating of the medieval phases and other information concerning the excavation, to Ms Amanda Cardy for the detailed lists of phasing of individual skeletons and information concerning sexing of the skeletons, and to Dr A. Watt for considerable assistance with the computer analysis of the data. We wish to thank Mr J. B. Davis, Glasgow Dental Hospital, who photographed the specimens and are grateful to Mr Richard Foye, Department of Oral Sciences, for assistance in radiographing specimens, and to the Department of Radiology, Glasgow Dental Hospital, for processing the radiographs.

The Ninth-Century Carbonised Plant Remains

J. P. Huntley

1. INTRODUCTION

Burnt deposits were uncovered during excavation of the Northumbrian church in 1990 and 1991. The building had opposed doors at the chancel end, and coin evidence from within the demolition debris suggests a tight date range (*c*. 840–845 AD) during which these burnt deposits accumulated. Charred and carbonised plank fragments sealed these deposits. One deposit clearly consisted of cereal grains with other burnt debris underlying it.

Two whole earth samples were received for analysis. One, 90/12356, remained as excavated, the other, 91/15363, had been covered in P.E.G. to consolidate it. Sample 91/15363 was therefore soaked in hot water and repeatedly washed in hot water to remove the P.E.G. Only small volumes of material were present and the samples were thus manually floated to 500μ. After drying, the flots were sorted under a binocular microscope at magnifications of up to ×50 and all identifiable plant remains removed. These were identified by comparison with modern reference material held in the Biological Laboratory, Department of Archaeology, University of Durham.

2. RESULTS AND DISCUSSION

Plant remains were preserved through carbonisation only. Table 1 presents the data in terms of numbers counted per sample.

90/12356

Material to the total of 700g was floated. The resultant flot was more or less pure cereal grain consisting of barley with the occasional oat grain. Twisted and straight embryos were seen and therefore the crop contained at least the 6-row *Hordeum vulgare*. Preservation was not excellent and many of the grains were fragmentary, and presented abraded surfaces. The impression is that the grain was varied in size although very small grains were not clearly apparent. Too few measurements could be taken to fully test this impression. No chaff and no weed seeds were present. It is suggested that the oats were probably weeds growing amongst a barley crop rather than being a crop in their own right. This suggestion is based upon the small quantities recovered.

It would seem that this deposit was fully processed barley grain. Its relatively poor preservation could indicate either that it had lain on the surface for some time prior to burial or that it had been moved around somewhat.

91/15363

A total of 2.1 kg of material was floated. The flot consisted of chunks of wood, charcoal and burnt monocotyledonous material with grass stems, and culm nodes, but not cereal straw. A variety of seeds

			A	B	C	D	E	F	G
Crops									
Hordeum vulgare		Hulled barley			c 200	30			
Avena		Oats			c 10	6			
Cerealia indet		Cereal grain frags			c 200	4	2	5	
culm node		straw				10			
bran			A						
Weeds									
Bromus sp.		Brome-grass				2			
> 4mm Gramineae		large grass				4			
Brassica sp	2	'cabbage'				1			
Brassica cf. napus	4	Rape							
Anthemis cotula	1, 3	Stinking Mayweed				3	6	2	
Atriplex sp.	2	Orache							
Chenopodiaceae undff..	2	fat-hen type				12			
Chenopodium album	2	Fat Hen	3				22	25	14
Chenopodium cf. murale		Nettle-leaved Goosefoot					2		
Chrysanthemum segetum	1	Corn Marigold					35	17	5
Galleopsis tetrahit/speciosa agg	1	Hemp Nettle							1
Labiatae undiff.		labiate flower						1	
Lapsana communis	3	Nipplewort					10	7	8
Polygonum lapathifolium	1,2	Red shank/Pale Persicara	1				1	15	9
Polygonum aviculare	2	Knot Grass							2
Polygonum persicaria	2	Persicara					1	3	
Raphanus raphanistrum	1	Wild Radish							2
Rumex sp.	6	dock					c 100	c 60	7
Rumex acetosella agg.	5	Sheep's Sorrel						1	
Rumex obtusifolius		Docken				2			
Sieglingia decumbens		Heath-grass				3			
Solanum nigrum	2	Black Nightshade						1	
Sonchus asper	10	Prickly Sow Thistle							3
Stachys arvensis		Woundwort			64				
Stellaria media	1, 2, 3	Chickweed	1				3	3	8
Urtica dioica	2	Stinging Nettle					26	16	1
Urtica urens	1, 2	Small Nettle		450					9
Heath and Moor									
Calluna vulgaris		Heather							1
Sagina sp.		Pearlwort							1
Grassland and Meadow									
Leontodon autumnalis		Autumn Hawbill					2		
Linum catharticum		Fairy Flax							1
Potentilla type		Tormentil				1			
Potentilla arentea/erecta/anglica		Cinquefoil or tormentil						1	
<2mm Gramineae		small grasses				4			
<4mm legume		vetch				1			
Plantago lanceolata		Ribwort Plantain				1			
Ranunculus repens-type		buttercups				2			
Ranunculus acris/repens/bulbosa		buttercups						1	3
Ranunculus acris		Field Buttercup			1				
Viola cf canina		Heath Violet						1	
Wet Ground									
Carex (trigonous)		Sedge				7			
Carex spp.		Sedges	2				1	1	
Carex (lenticular)		Sedge				4			
Conium maculatum		Hemlock			2				1
Filipendula ulmaria		Meadow Sweet							1
Eleocharis palustris		Spikerush				2			
Eriophorum angustifolium		Common Cotton Grass					1		
Eriophorum vaginatum		Cotton grass				3			
Ranunculus flammula	7	Crowfoot/Lesser Spearwort				1	1		
Ranunculus hederaceus	8	Ivy-leaved Water Crowfoot					1	1	
Ranunculus sceleratus	7, 8	Celery-leaved Crowfoot					1	3	
Possible Economic/Medicinal									
I Pteridium aquilinum frond frag		Bracken	1			+	P	A	A
Corylus avellana frag.		hazlenut				3	10	21	3
Coriandrum sativum		Coriander	18						
Anethum graveolens		Dill	5						
Brassica nigra		Black mustard	1						
Woodland and Shrub									
crataegus monogyna		Hawthorn						15	
Prunus spinosa		Sloe						1	
Rosa cf. canina		Dog rose	1						
Rubus fruticosus		Bramble	2	3682			2	1	
Rubus idaeua		Raspberry					1		
Sambucus nigra		Elder			49				

						A	B	C	D	E	F	G
Mosses	A	B–D	E	F	G	**Habitat**						
Dicranum majus				p		Upland woods, characteristic of Quercus petraea woodland. Calcifuge						
Eurynchium sp	9											
Eurynchium praelongum			P			Highly shade tolerant. e.g. woodland						
Pleurozium schreberi	6					Coniferous woodland, heathlands						
cf. Rhytidiadelphus triquetrus	4					Woodlands						
cf. Hylocomium flagellare	3											
Hylocomium splendens				P	A	Heath, moors, upland woods. Calcifuge or leached soil if basic						
Hypnum cupressiforme	2					Hedgebanks, heathland soils						
Isothecium myurum				P		On rocks and trees in shaded habitas, especially woodland						
Thuidium tamariscinum			P	P		Woodland and damp turf						
Unspecified mosses					1, 9							

Table 11.45: Species identified in samples from **Period II** church (above), **Period I** pits and **Period IV** ditches and pits after Cameron (1985), Groves (1990), Elliott (1990) and Heaton (1994).

1. Weeds of cultivation **2.** Nitrophilous species appropriate to habitation sites and cultivation **3.** Favour heavy soils **4.** Could have been a weed or a crop **5.** Favour light sandy soils **6.** Abundance suggests was growing *in situ* **7.** Favour damp meadows and pastures **8.** Favour shallow water with mineral rich muddy substrate

A: Period I South Sector Pit 1 **B: Period I** South Sector Pit 9 **C: Period II/7** Cereal on floor of nave **D: Period II/7?** Sieving residue under earth floor in chancel **E: Period IV.6b** hollow cutting floor of Building IV/7 **F: Period IV.6** Pit 7 to east of Building IV/7 **G:** Upper fill of main **Period IV** drainage ditch (417) pertaining to **Period IV.7**.

were present, although not in abundance, representing taxa from a range of habitats. In terms of concentrations of seeds, however, the deposit was quite rich – with about 50 seeds per litre this can be compared with Roman-aged material from elsewhere in northern Britain where values of 20–30 seeds per litre are common.

Cereal debris again dominated the plant remains – predominantly barley grains but with some oats. The culm nodes may have been from cereal or from large grasses given that their seeds, too, were recovered. No clear cereal chaff was present.

Seeds representing weedy taxa are the next most abundant but, even here various more specific habitats are indicated. The *Chenopodiaceae* and *Brassica* seeds suggest a nitrophilous/nutrient-enriched community whereas the *Sieglingia* indicates a more nutrient-poor acidic soil. *Anthemis* is indicative of heavy clay soils. It would suggest a range of soil types were being utilised.

Grassland taxa suggest neutral to acidic grassland communities possibly merging into some of the wet ground communities where there are also indications of stream-edge vegetation.

The only other possible economic species are the hazelnuts, which probably represent opportunistically collected nuts, and the bracken frond fragments which could represent bedding material.

Other than these last two, a likely explanation for this range of seeds with grain is that they were mostly, in fact, growing amongst the cereals which were themselves being grown on a variety of local soils. Whilst many of the plants are not weeds today they could easily have been growing on the edges of fields at a time when monoculture was not the order of the day.

The presence of the monocotyledonous stem fragments could then be explained by the presence of grasses growing amongst the crops.

3. DISCUSSION

The two samples analysed contain very different botanical assemblages and it is suggested that the more or less pure grain sample is just that – fully processed grain. The other material could represent winnowings or fine sievings from a crop being processed. Winnowing would be suitable for indoors with ventilation at opposed ends, as we have at this site. During this process light weed seeds and chaff would be removed from a cereal crop. The fine sieving is the final stage in processing a free-threshing cereal such as barley, although the glumes remain tightly attached to hulled barley when the final weed seeds are removed.

The argument against winnowing is that the seeds present are not particularly lightweight and that chaff is absent; however, neither are the seeds particularly small as suggestive of fine sieving. Overall it is suggested that the second sample represents processing debris but probably from various stages of processing.

What is clear from these samples is that material from further excavations at Whithorn has the potential of providing evidence of crop husbandry from a period which otherwise remains in the 'Dark Ages'. Few other, similarly dated sites in northern Britain have produced any material – even when samples have been taken – leaving a major block of time blank. There are differences in cereal crops and weed assemblages between the Romano-British and early medieval periods in the region but when these changes occurred remains elusive. Whithorn provides an opportunity to redress this imbalance but only when more and larger environmental samples are collected.

PH Comments. The samples came from distinct parts of the former church. The sample of cleaned grain (90/12356) came from the floor of the former nave, while the putative sievings (91/15363) came from the hollow to the east of the screen (Figure 4.21a).

Table 11.45 includes the results of Jacqui Huntley's analysis (**C** and **D**), and of separate studies by Rachel

Groves (1990), Christine Elliott (1990), Maria Heaton (1994), and Nigel Cameron (1985) undertaken as undergraduate projects at the Universities of Leeds and Durham. Grove and Heaton's analyses of samples from **Period I** pits in the **southern sector** are discussed above (pp 124, 127–8). Both studies favour environmental explanations for the majority of species present, and my ethnobotanical interpretations have been questioned by some palaeobotanists and accepted by others. Cameron and Elliott's studies relate to samples from **Period IV** deposits in the **southern sector** (p 222), probably dating to the later-twelfth and later-thirteenth centuries respectively. Both identify a wide range of habitats in the catchment area feeding the **Period IV** drains, and there are marked similarities with the habitats indicated by the putative sievings from the **Period II** church. This group of analyses indicate the potential of the waterlogged deposits in the **Glebe Field**, and it is to be hoped that future work will enlarge upon these preliminary findings.

The dendrochronological evidence: a tree-ring chronology from Whithorn, Dumfries and Galloway

B.A. Crone

1. INTRODUCTION

Nineteen samples of oak (Quercus sp.) were selected for dendrochronological analysis. The samples were taken from *in situ* planks, stakes and posts, or from structural debris, all of which had been fashioned from radially split timber (Table 11.48).

Preparation and measurement of the samples was initially conducted at the dendrochronology laboratory at Sheffield University following standard procedures (see Hillam 1985, for more detail). The samples were frozen for 48 hours and the surfaces then planed, while frozen, to produce a smooth, clear surface for measurement. However, many of the samples suffered in varying degree from belts of severely compressed rings making measurement difficult. These occur when there has been little or no deposition of summerwood usually because of either defoliation by insects or poor weather during the growing season. The large springwood pores are consequently compressed against each other, and it becomes very difficult to determine where each annual ring starts or ends (for example, see Baillie 1982, Plate 2a).

The samples were consequently prepared anew in the dendrochronology laboratory at Queen's University, Belfast, using procedures developed there

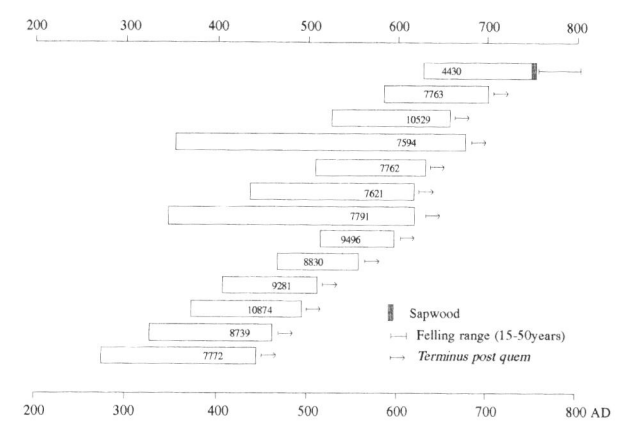

11.49 Dendrochronological samples: relationships of the dated sequences.

by D. Brown. The samples were allowed to dry out overnight and then a selected radius was pared using a razor blade to achieve a smooth glassy surface. Powdered chalk was rubbed into this surface; by filling up the cellular structure of the wood are highlighted, the springwood vessels, thus clarifying the ring pattern.

Using this method of surface preparation positive dating results were achieved.

	4430	7594	7621	7762	7763	7772	7991	8739	8830	9281	9496	10529	10974
4430	0												
7594	-	0											
7621	\	6.1	0										
7762	\	\	\	0									
7763	-	-	3.8	-	0								
7772	\	7.4	\	\	\	0							
7991	\	8.3	7.0	-	4.2	6.2	0						
8739	\	4.0	-	\	\	5.0	5.5	0					
8830	\	-	3.8	-	\	\	-	\	0				
9281	\	3.4	8.0	\	\	4.9	3.0	-	\	0			
9496	\	5.6	3.7	-	\	\	3.6	\	5.5	\	0		
10529	-	4.8	4.3	-	6.3	\	3.1	\	3.8	\	-	0	
10974	\	4.3	-	\	\	-	4.0	3.8	3.9	3.8	\	\	0

Table 11.46: Matrix of t-values for dated samples.

\ = overlap < 15 years
- = t-value < 3.0

Name of Master	T-Val
Teeorry (N. Ireland)	11.37
Carlisle Anglo-Saxon	5.85
Britim (British Isles Master)	7.55
Tamworth	4.26

Table 11.47: T-values between Whithorn and other master chronologies.

2. RESULTS

The results are presented in Table 11.48 and the chronological relationships of the dated sequences are illustrated in Figure 11.49.

Thirteen samples were successfully dated. Table 11.46 shows the t-values for the correlations between the samples; the majority display significant internal cross-correlations. Two samples, 4430 and 7762, do not cross-match well against any of the Whithorn samples but give significant correlations against Irish master chronologies.

Eleven samples, dated in an earlier batch, were averaged together to form a master chronology, WHITHORN, 475 years in length. Extremely significant and consistent matches were found between this master and several Irish, and English chronologies dating WHITHORN to AD 278–AD 752 Table 11.47.

All the samples have been converted in some way from the round (see Table 11.48) and the majority have been heavily trimmed, removing many of the outer growth-rings. Sapwood survives on only two samples, and on many samples much of the heartwood appears to have been trimmed off as well. Consequently, with the exception of Sample 4430, the calendrical date for the outermost year-ring of the other samples provides a TPQ for the felling of the tree. While this means that dendrochronological analysis cannot provide any evidence for structural phases at Whithorn, the samples have produced the first robust, well-replicated chronology for Dark-Age Scotland.

PH Comments. The interpretative strictures in the final sentence are somewhat severe. The samples all come from the **southern sector**, and fall into three main stratigraphic groups. The first comprises two samples from early **Period I** contexts. An offcut (10874) came from Pit 12 (*Stage 7*), and an undated stake (10360) was not ascribed to a specific structure. The main group comprised thirteen samples from *Stage 12* and *13* contexts, of which nine (7594, 7599, 7627, 7762, 7763, 7772, 7773, 7791 and 7827) came from Building I/24 (212.02, Figure 3.43), one (8739) from the floor of the adjacent pit (53.07, Figure 4.30), one (8830) from the adjacent ditch (230.01), one (8738) from waterborne debris abutting the stone boundary (232), and one (10529) from the structure (213.01) in the south-east corner of the trench. These samples (and particularly 7594, 10529 and 7763) provide a valuable *terminus post quem* for this structural phase (p 130). The third group comprises three samples (4430, 8741, 9281) from structures ascribed to **Period II**. The stake (4430) from Building 11/17 (Figure 4.32) suggests it was constructed in the second half of the eighth century (pp 130, 138). The others were less helpful. A final sample (9496) from the **Period IV** ditch (417.02) probably derived from the **Period I** or **II** deposits through which it was cut.

Sample	Context	L	W	T	Code	Function	No of rings	H/S	Dating results	Comment
4430	234	52.0	9.5	3.0	D1	stake	110	6?	AD 643–752	felling date AD 756–801
7593	212.02	17.0	18.0	7.0	D	planking	233	/		problems in early rings
7594	212.02	33.0	20.0	8.0	D	planking	317	/	AD 365–681	
7621	212.02	-	15.0	2.25	D1	plank	191	/	AD 440–630	
7762	212.02	47.0	20.0	7.0	D	planking	124	/	AD 513–636	re-used?
7763	212.02	-	8.0	1.5	D1	offcut	118	/	AD 589–706	
7773	212.02	32.0	9.0	11.0	C/D	stake	131	/		problems in first 50 rings
7791	212.02	39.0	19.0	6.0	D	planking	274	/	AD 350–623	
7827	212.02	60.0	26.0	11.0	B	stake	133	?		
8738	232	-	9.0	3.5	D1	plank	67	/		too short
8739	53.07	15.0	16.0	3.0	D	debris	138	/	AD 329–466	
8741	213.03	43.0	10.0	9.0	D1	post	78	/		too short
8830	230.01	13.5	9.0	5.0	D	planking	93	/	AD 469–561	
9281	234	-	7.0	4.0	D1	offcut	105	/	AD 410–514	
9496	417.02	-	6.0	1.5	D1	lath	84	/	AD 517–600	
10360	57	22.0	6.0	3.5	D/E	stake	54	/		too short
10529	213.01	32.0	15.0	10.0	D	post	130	/	AD 533–662	+ 33 damaged, unmeasured rings
10874	234	43.5	10.0	3.0	D1	offcut	123	/	AD 376–498	

Table 11.48: Dendrochronological samples and results.

The Radiocarbon Dates

Peter Hill

Radiocarbon dates were obtained from nine samples recovered during the trial excavation in 1984 (GU-2050–2058) and from a skull with syphilitic lesions recovered in 1987 (OxA-4873). Calibrated dates are listed in Table 11.49 and illustrated in Figure 11.50.

No. 1 (GU-2052) came from mixed alder, birch, hazel, oak and willow twig charcoal scattered over

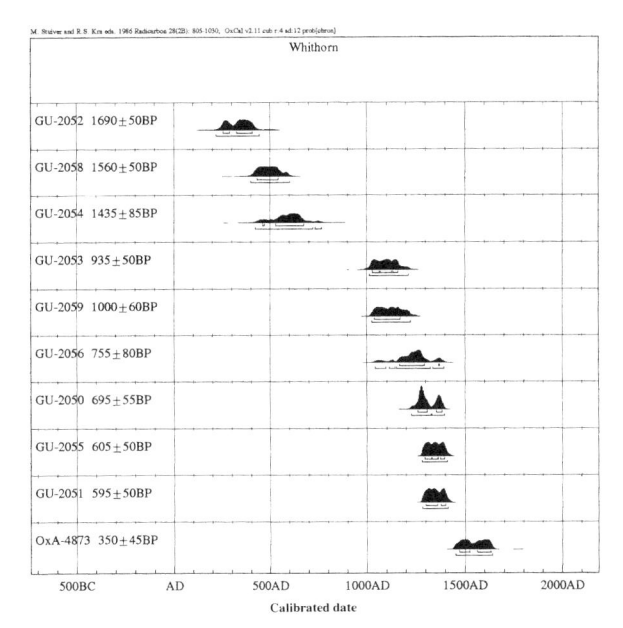

11.50 Calibrated radiocarbon dates (after Stuiver and Kra 1986).

Group E vessel glass, and was probably part of the **Period I/2** rubbish spread (89). This deposit postdated the deposition of B and A ware, and the earliest sherds of E ware, and has been ascribed tentatively to the third quarter of the sixth century (p 101). This lies outside the 1σ range of confidence, but well within the 2σ level.

No. 3 (GU-2054) came from an oak stake exposed in the side of a **Period IV** pit, but probably forming part of the east wall of **Building 1/18** (Figure 3.40). The relatively large standard deviation limits the value of this date, but the later age range at 1σ (533–675AD) accommodates the inferred seventh-century date of this building, and spans an earlier period than the earliest dendrochronological dates from the overlying **Period I.12** deposits.

No. 4 (GU-2053) came from an hazel stake from the east wall of **Building IV/7**, which is ascribed to the mid- to late-twelfth century on the basis of shoe fragments from the adjacent ditch (p 222). This is significantly later than the first of the three 1σ ranges, later than the second, and compatible with the third. It lies happily within the 2σ range.

No. 5 (GU-2059) came from mixed alder, birch, elder, gorse, hazel and ling charcoal from a group of burnt deposits in the east corner of Trench 5, subsequently identified as part of a possible building (IV/15), and ascribed to the later-twelfth/earlier-thirteenth century. It was thus probably later than the upper margin of the 1σ date range, but within the 2σ range.

Nos. 6–9 (GU-2056, 2050, 2055 and 2051) came from human skeletal remains. The first, No. 6 (GU-2056), came from a burial in Trench 4 oversailed by

the floor of **Building I/2**, and associated with a sherd of a B*i* amphora. The fourth century dates are incompatible with the inferred site chronology at both the 1 and 2σ levels of confidence, and could reflect the presence of old wood, possibly the oak.

No. 2 (GU-2058) came from a spread of alder, ash, birch, hazel, oak and pomoidene twig charcoal on the floor of Trench 4, which produced two sherds of

1. DATE GU-2052:
1690±50BP
  68.2% confidence
    259AD (0.27) 291AD
    327AD (0.73) 408AD
  95.4% confidence
    222AD (1.00) 446AD

2. DATE GU-2058:
1560±50BP
  68.2% confidence
    434AD (1.00) 544AD
  95.4% confidence
    401AD (1.00) 604AD

3. DATE GU-2054:
1435±85BP
  68.2% confidence
    464AD (0.03) 472AD
    533AD (0.97) 675AD
  95.4% confidence
    424AD (0.97) 723AD
    736AD (0.03) 767AD

4. DATE GU-2053:
935±50BP
  68.2% confidence
    1029AD (0.29) 1063AD
    1070AD (0.49) 1126AD
    1134AD (0.22) 1159AD
  95.4% confidence
    1013AD (1.00) 1212AD

5. DATE GU-2059:
900±50BP
  68.2% confidence
    1040AD (1.00) 1170AD
  95.4% confidence
    1025AD (1.00) 1224AD

6. DATE GU-2056:
755±80BP
  68.2% confidence
    1168AD (0.98) 1294AD
    1368AD (0.02) 1371AD
  95.4% confidence
    1043AD (0.07) 1097AD
    1116AD (0.04) 1144AD
    1153AD (0.78) 1323AD
    1338AD (0.11) 1394AD

7. DATE GU-2050:
695±55BP
  68.2% confidence
    1262AD (0.69) 1308AD
    1356AD (0.31) 1383AD
  95.4% confidence
    1228AD (0.66) 1327AD
    1334AD (0.34) 1396AD

8. DATE GU-2055:
605±50BP
  68.2% confidence
    1297AD (0.38) 1328AD
    1333AD (0.37) 1363AD
    1376AD (0.25) 1396AD
  95.4% confidence
    1283AD (1.00) 1410AD

9. DATE Gu-2051:
595±50BP
  68.2% confidence
    1301AD (0.74) 1360AD
    1379AD (0.26) 1400AD
  95.4% confidence
    1284AD (1.00) 1414AD

10. DATE OxA-4873:
350±45BP
  68.2% confidence
    1472AD (0.44) 1523AD
    1563AD (0.56) 1630AD
  95.4% confidence
    1452AD (1.00) 1639AD

Table 11.49: Calibrated radiocarbon dates after Stuiver and Kra, 1986.

paving and burnt debris, and ascribed to **Period IV.5** (Figure 6.19 inset). The latter deposits were not well-dated, but finds of white gritty wear commend a date in the earlier-thirteenth century. The earlier 1σ range of the radiocarbon date from the underlying grave is compatible with this. The next three dates came from burials in the middle stages of the **Period V** graveyard, ascribed on imperfect stratigraphic grounds to the fourteenth century. The narrow ranges of the probability curves (Figure 11.50) correspond with a pronounced wiggle in the calibration curve. The sample (GU-2050) from the earliest grave (V/1.5, 535/Gr254) shows two peaks. The earlier is unlikely on archaeological grounds. The other two samples came from **Period V/2** graves (GU-2055, 538/Gr48 and GU-2051, 537/Gr21), and produced closely comparable results. In both instances the later 1σ ranges fit most readily with the circumstantial evidence, while the upper limits of the 2σ ranges provide a valuable terminus for these burial phases.

The most recent date (OxA-4873) came from a fragmentary cranium with syphilitic lesions, found among displaced human bone from the surface of the **Period V** graveyard. This was included with a batch of syphilitic remains studied by Charlotte Roberts (forthcoming) to assess the possible prevalence of the disease in Britain before the rediscovery of America by Columbus in 1492 (pp 542-3). It is difficult to reconcile the three strands of evidence. The final burials (**Period V/3**, 540) were almost all undamaged, and the skull should thus have been displaced from an earlier phase of burial. The final burials are ascribed to the mid-fifteenth century and so coincide with the lower date range at both 1 and 2σ levels of confidence. Earlier burials were probably rather earlier, and so beyond the range of probable dates. The archaeological evidence presented in Chapter 7 indicates that the sample is unlikely to be later than 1492.

Soil Samples

Dr Donald A. Davidson
Department of Environmental Science, University of Stirling

WHITHORN W1

This material was sampled in order to establish the depositional environment of the sediment. The hypothesis was that the fine-grained material had been deposited in a shallow lake. The following types of analysis were performed: particle-size analysis, soil micromorphology and diatom analysis.

1. Particle-size analysis

3 determinations.
Average % clay	23
Average % fine silt	13
Average % medium silt	23
Average % coarse silt	22
Average % sand	20
% organic matter	16

Cumulative frequency graphs were drawn in order to examine the sediment size distribution. Comparison of the graphs with those from known evironments indicated that the sediment was of fluvial origin. The dominant sediment size is silt (58%) and the sediment is high in organic matter.

2. Thin-section micromorphology

Emphasis is given to selected attributes of the sample as seen under the microscope given the geomorphological rather than pedological nature of the material. The outstanding features of the sediment are its apedal structure, uniformity of particle size (grains dominantly quartz with a few felspars and rock fragments) and the very high concentration of organic debris. The organic material consists of root fragments, seeds, leaf residues, fragments of wood and charcoal, plant stems, moss and fungal spores, diatoms, and unidentified fauna. Some of the organic debris occurs in thin layers laid down parallel to the surface. Inwashing of this material and its subsequent incorporation into the sediment is thus indicated.

3. Diatoms

Dr S. Metcalfe (University of Hull) examined one sample for diatoms and her results are presented below (pp 600-1). In outline she proposes the assemblage of diatoms is indicative of a shallow, probably muddy pool or sluggish stream. This accords with the nature of the sediment – its size, sorting and laminations of organic debris. Also of note is the suggestion that the water was neutral to slightly alkaline.

Conclusion

There is no evidence to support the interpretation of the sediments as lake deposits; instead a much shallower water environment is proposed – a muddy pool or slow-flowing stream. Vegetation disturbance upstream is suggested by the high concentration of organic debris.

For comparison with W1, two similar deposits were sampled (W2 and W4).

WHITHORN W2

A thin-section slide was examined and the overall micromorphology was similar to W3. Again a very high organic debris content is evident though less moss remains are present. In contrast to W3, rock fragments (from 25 mm to 0.1 mm) are frequent. The deposit is again of fluvial origin, but higher flow rates must have occurred at certain times to transport the rock fragments.

WHITHORN W3

The thin section again proved very similar to W2 and W3, but with more distinct stratification of organic debris. Variation in water-flow rate is indicated by deposits ranging from very well stratified organic debris to rock fragments (up to 7 mm). Periods of very sluggish or non-existent flow must have occurred for deposition of wood fragments.

Particle size results: clay 22%, fine silt 4%, medium silt 19%, coarse silt 22%, sand 33%. Organic matter: 10%.

PH Comments. Three samples (1–3) were taken to examine water-borne deposits in the **southern sector**. The first (1) came from the thick silty layer (415.01) that accumulated in the later twelfth/earlier thirteenth century. The other two came from similar, though shallower, **Period I** deposits ascribed to the later-seventh and earlier-eighth centuries. The earlier (3) came from the waterborne deposit (58) which probably accumulated in the mid- to late-seventh century. The later (2) came from material which accumulated to the north of the **Period I.12** boundary (232).

WHITHORN W4

This sample was collected for soil micromorphological examination since the hypothesis from field excavation was that this material had accumulated by earthworm activity. Results from particle size analysis are as follows: clay 17%, fine silt 2%, medium silt 17%, coarse silt 15%, sand 41%.

Soil thin-section description

MICROSTRUCTURE

Aggregate types Dominant moderately developed very fine angular blocky aggregates, with partially accommodated undulating walls, showing random unreferred distribution; small area of clustered well-developed angular blocky structure.
Inter-Aggregate Voids Few inter-aggregate normal, strongly oriented coarse meso channels with straight plane walls and rounded shape, showing random unreferred distribution.

Very few inter-aggregate unrelated, unoriented medium macro compound packing voids with rough walls and angular shape, showing clustered unreferred distribution; channels are at right angles to soil surface.
Intra-Aggregate Voids Very few intra-aggregate unrelated, unoriented coarse macro vughs with smooth walls and rounded shape, showing random unreferred distribution.
Microstructure Vughy and channel microstructures.

ORGANIC MATERIAL

Occurrences of reddish-brown concentrations of amorphous organic matter; a few fragments of charcoal (*c.* 0.5 mm), bone (*c.* 0.5 mm) and wood (*c.* 1.0 mm); notable absence of plant remains though some occurrences of highly decomposed roots.

MINERAL COMPONENTS

Coarse Grains Frequent moderately sorted fine sand-size blocky anhedral subangular quartz showing class 0 alteration; also two fine sand-sized grains of plagioclase.
Rock Fragments Frequent rock fragments which are more abundant in lower half of slide; fragments aligned with soil surface.
Fine Mineral Components Speckled material, brown in plane-polarised light and grey in cross-polarised light.

GROUNDMASS
Coarse Fabrics Random coarse fabric with undifferentiated b-fabric showing porphyric distribution.

PEDOFEATURES
Excrement Very few intact moderated rough medium meso weak disintegrating organic-mineral ageing *possible* excremental pedofeatures with porphyric internal fabric.

Interpretation of the slide

The outstanding feature of the sample is the lack of plant remains as well as no evidence for disturbance as expressed in coatings. Thus it is suggested that this soil was not subject to significant inputs of waste materials as W6; furthermore, there is no evidence for this soil having been cultivated. The channel patterns are distinctive and these are likely to have been formed by earthworm activity, though root formation cannot be excluded. The occurrence of excrement pedofeatures is open to question. The suggestion is that this soil once constituted a shallow, stony topsoil which evolved by natural processes, especially earthworm activity.

PH Comments. The sample came from a deposit originally interpreted as a thick worm-sorted soil, but subsequently identified as the earth floor of Building III/3 (Figure 5.6). This identification is tentative, but it may account for the absence of plant remains, and other distinctive features.

WHITHORN W5

This sample was collected for micromorphological examination to determine if there was evidence for plaggen soil formation. Particle size results are as follows: clay 22%, fine silt 18%, medium silt 19%, coarse silt 13%, sand 27%. Organic content: 8%.

MICROSTRUCTURE
Aggregate Types Frequent moderately developed, fine, clodish aggregates, with unaccommodated rough walls, showing random unreferred distribution.
Inter-Aggregate Voids Few inter-aggregate unrelated, unoriented medium macro compound packing voids with rough walls and angular shape, showing random unreferred distribution.
Intra-Aggregate Voids Very few intra-aggregate unrelated, unoriented coarse meso channels with zigzag plane walls and subrounded tubular shape, showing random unreferred distribution.
Microstructure Vughy and channel microstructures.

ORGANIC MATERIAL

Charcoal fragments from 100 μm to 13 mm, common in lower part of slide and few in upper part; random distribution of charcoal; reddish-brown areas of amorphous organic matter ranging in size from 0.2 mm to 2 mm occasionally with some organic structures still evident; very few bone fragments ranging in size from 0.4 mm to 2 mm.

GROUNDMASS
Coarse Fabrics Random coarse fabric with undifferentiated b-fabric showing porphyric distribution.

MINERAL COMPONENTS
Coarse Grains Frequent unsorted silt-size blocky anhedral subangular quartz showing class 0 alteration; quartz sized particles from 20 μm to 500 μm.
 Medium sand size k-feldspar; one grain of microline (200 μm).
Rock Fragments Frequent rock fragments from 0.1 mm to 23 mm.
Fine Mineral Components Speckled material, brown in plane-polarised light and dark brown in cross-polarised light.

PEDOFEATURES
Textural Intact textural coatings; coatings of groundmass on quartz grains and fragments of bone rock, and charcoal.

Interpretation

This is a highly disturbed soil as expressed in the very high charcoal content, the many bone fragments and the coatings of groundmass. Earthworm activity is likely to have formed the channels; no root remains are present. The best way to describe this material is as a cultivated midden soil. No evidence was found to support a plaggen soil interpretation which implies the use of turves as bedding before application to fields. Instead the application of general domestic refuse is suggested as a means of waste disposal as well as an aid to soil fertility.
 PH Comments. The sample came from a thick layer of soil overlying the paved 'floor' of Structure I/2 (Figure 3.8) and sealing a sherd of B*i* amphora. This soil must have been introduced from elsewhere, and in light of the pedological interpretation (below), may indicate a garden within the **Period I** settlement.

Analysis of the diatoms in Sample 1

Dr. S. Metcalfe

University of Hull

Summary

The sample was prepared by drying, then treating with HC1 and H_2O_2 to remove carbonate and organic matter. The suspension was then washed thoroughly in distilled water. The diatoms were mounted on a slide using naphrax resin and examined under a Zeiss photomicroscope at ×1250 magnification. Valves were reasonably abundant in the sample, although many of the larger specimens were broken. The flora was a diverse one (Table 11.50). In general, the assemblage suggests shallow, circumneutral to slightly alkaline water, possibly of quite high conductivity. There does not seem to have been much aquatic vegetation, many of the forms are benthic or epipelic. Occasional desiccation at the site seems a possibility. Overall, the assemblage may represent either a shallow, probably muddy, pool or a shallow, sluggish stream.

Ecology of the major species

Achnanthes lanceolata var. *dubia*
Quite common and widely occurring. Observed in

Major Species:

	%
Achnanthes lanceolata var. *dubia*	32.5
Navicula digitoradiata	11.2
Achnanthes lanceolata	6.0
Navicula heufleri	5.3
Navicula minima	4.6
Pinnularia viridis	3.3
Navicula tantula	3.3
Hantzschia amphioxys	2.0
Navicula cincta	2.0
Caloneis ventricosa var. *minuta*	2.0
Gomphonmena angustatum	2.0

Also present:

Navicula heufleri var. *leptocephala*
Pinnularia borealis
Pinnularia brebissonii
Navicula absikoensis
Fragilaria brevistriata
Surirella ovalis
Pinnularia abaujensis var. *subundulata* (or *P. microstauron*)
Fragilaria pinnata
Navicula elginensis var. *rostrata*
Navicula acceptatea
Navicula sp.
Navicula dicephala
Diploneis puella
Frustulia vulgaris
Navicula accomoda
Pinnularia appendiculata
Navicula seminulum
Diploneis ovalis
Navicular anglica var. *subsalsa*
Caloneis alpestris
Fragilaria construens var. *venter*
Navicular pupula
Fragilaria capucina var. *mesolepta*
Amphora ovalis var. *affinis*
Pinnularia biceps
Pinnularia sp.
Navicular pupula var. *rectangularis*

Some phytoliths and chrysophyte cysts (statospores) were also present.

Table 11.50: Diatom species list for Sample 1.

well aerated flowing water, neutral to alkaline pH. Epipelic or epiphytic. Can also occur in stagnant water.

Navicula digitoradiata
Basically a brackish water form, which can occur in freshwaters of high conductivities (>1000 uS cm^{-1} according to Gasse, 1986).

Achnanthes lanceolata
Ecology similar to var. *dubia*. Described by Gasse as pH indifferent and tolerant of quite high TDS.

Navicula heufleri
Prefers alkaline to slightly brackish water. Benthic or aerophilous.

Navicula minima
Widely distributed, usually regarded as oligohalobous and alkaliphilous. Occurs in lake periphyton and in rivers. May be benthic, epiphytic or aerophilous.

Pinnularia viridis
Tolerates higher mineral content than most Pinnularia spp. Circumneutral pH.

Navicula tantula
Occurs in rivers, marshes and springs, epipelic or epiphytic. May be aerophilous. pH optimum probably 6–7, but also occurs in weakly alkaline water.

Hantzschia amphioxys
Aerophilous species, tolerant of desiccation. Tolerant of a wide range of pH, EC, salinity and ionic composition.

Navicula cincta
Slightly brackish to slightly alkaline waters. Occurs in the periphyton of marshes and lakes, also epipelic in rivers.

Caloneis ventricosa var. *minuta*
Found on the bottom of pools, springs and rivers (still), also near the margins of larger rivers. Tolerant of a wide range of conditions.

Gomphonema angustatum
Found under a wide range of conditions, epiphytic or epipelic. Seems to prefer circumneutral to slightly alkaline freshwater.

The Bird and Fish Bones

Sheila Hamilton-Dyer
University of Southampton

1. INTRODUCTION

The methods used for identification and recording were based on the FRU (Faunal Remains Unit, Southampton) method 86 system, with some modifications (see FRU archive, and SH-D archive file BONESTRU). Identifications were made primarily using the modern comparative collections of the FRU and S. Hamilton-Dyer. Bird measurements follow von den Driesch (1976). Fish bone measurements follow Morales and Rosenlund (1979) in the main. Archive material includes metrical and other data not in the text, and is kept on paper and disc.

The total of 630 fragments was composed of 403 fish-bone fragments and 227 bird-bone fragments. Fish were present in at least one block from each period group, but there were no bird bones from

Period I (Group 1). The largest concentration of both was from **Period II** (Group 2).

There were also two amphibian bones from Block 417 (**Period IV**).

In general the preservation of the bird bones was good. The fish-bone fragments varied from good to poor.

2. THE FISH

Ten species of fish were positively identified and a further two provisionally identified (Tables 11.51 and 11.52). Over half of the fish bones, 250 fragments of a total of 403, were small fragments and fin rays which

Birds
Greylag (or domestic goose), *Anser anser*
Mallard (or domestic duck), *Anas platyrhynchos*
domestic fowl, *Gallus gallus*
buzzard, *Buteo buteo*
Raven, Corvus corax
other Corvidae: include jackdaw, *Corvus monedula*, and jay, *Garrulus glandarius*, or magpie, *Pica pica*
small passerines of blackbird and sparrow size
incompletely identified, includes probable lapwing, *Vanellus vanellus*
unidentified bird fragments

Fish
shark or ray (Elasmo)
thornback ray, *Raja clavata*
common eel, *Anguilla anguilla*
conger eel, *Conger conger*
herring, *Clupea harengus*
Salmonidae, probably all salmon, *Salmo salar*
cod, *Gadus morhua*
pollack, *Pollachius pollachius*
ling, *molva molva*
Gadidae, cod family, includes probable rocklings
ballan wrasse, *Labrus bergylta*
flatfish, probably all plaice, *Pleuronectes platessa*
unidentified fish fragments

Table 11.51: Bird and fish species list.

were not identified to species. Of the remainder, herring constituted the highest fragment count of 57. Frequency of occurrence was, however, equal between herring and shark/ray at nine occurrences. The reason for this difference is due to the frequency in individual contexts: eel, for example, had a high fragment count of 19, but all of these were from Block 320.

Period I (Group 1)
Few fragments were recovered from this period. Salmon was identified from a vertebra from Block 82.05, the other 41 fragments were unidentified fragments and fin rays.

Period II (Group 2)
The only fish species positively identified from the Northumbrian midden (303) was salmon in the form of two vertebrae. The other 63 fish fragments consisted mainly of unidentified fin rays. The presence of salmon is in contrast with the previously reported assemblage from the midden which contained probable *Gadidae* only.

The present assemblage also contained fish bone from other contexts of this period. There were 19 bones of eel, one of herring, one of shark or ray, and three further salmon vertebrae, in addition to 71 unidentified fragments. The eel bones were from at least two fish of approximately 30 cm total length.

Periods III and IV (Group 3)
Only 17 bones were recovered from these periods. These included a shark or ray vertebra and three pharyngeal bones of ballan wrasse.

Period V Graveyard (Group 4)
Although only 14 bones were recovered, these are of a wide range of species: shark or ray, herring, cod, ballan wrasse, and flatfish, probably plaice.

Period V/4–5 (Group 5)
This group contained 47 bones and contributed the greatest range of species: shark, thornback ray, conger, herring, cod, ling, ballan wrasse and flatfish, probably all plaice. Once again, however, the numbers are still extremely low in comparison with many urban assemblages which may contain many thousands of fish bones.

Period VI (Group 6)
There were 68 fish bones from this period including shark or ray, conger, herring, salmon, cod, pollack, probable rockling, and flatfish.

Recent (Group 7)
These modern and mixed contexts contained just ten fragments, no new species were identified.

Discussion

The small numbers prevent detailed spatial and temporal analysis. It is, however, interesting to note that ling, a member of the cod family, and also conger, which occur in several post-medieval blocks are not present prior to the fifteenth century. None of the cod family are present until **Period V** (Group 4). The cod and ling were medium to large fish. They compare with modern specimens of one metre and larger. Both vertebrae and head bones are present. These large *Gadidae* may have been fresh caught or, alternatively, traded as preserved stockfish. Excepting ling, all the fish species would have been readily available from the nearby coastal waters. Ling is today obtained by long-lining mainly from depths of 300–400 metres, the nearest suitable fishing ground would be off Islay.

3. THE BIRDS

The majority of the bird bones (Tables 11.51, and 53) are of domestic fowl, 104 fragments of a total 227.

	elasmo	ray	eel	conger	herring	salmo	cod	pollack	ling	Gadidae	wrasse	flatfish	unid.	Total
PERIOD I														
82.05	–	–	–	–	–	1	–	–	–	–	–	–	–	1
85	–	–	–	–	–	–	–	–	–	–	–	–	31	31
109	–	–	–	–	–	–	–	–	–	–	–	–	10	10
Total	0	0	0	0	0	1	0	0	0	0	0	0	41	42
Percentage	0	0	0	0	0	0	0	0	0	0	0	0	100	
PERIOD II														
303	–	–	–	–	–	2	–	–	–	–	–	–	63	65
206	–	–	–	–	–	–	–	–	–	–	–	–	1	1
214	–	–	–	–	–	–	–	–	–	–	–	–	1	1
251	1	–	–	–	1	–	–	–	–	–	–	–	3	5
316	–	–	–	–	–	–	–	–	–	–	–	–	1	1
320	–	–	19	–	1	3	–	–	–	–	–	–	65	88
Total	1	0	19	0	2	5	0	0	0	0	0	0	134	161
Percentage	0.6	0	11.8	0	1.2	3.1	0	0	0	0	0	0	83.2	
PERIOD IV														
417	–	–	–	–	–	–	–	–	–	–	3	–	1	4
422	–	–	–	–	–	–	–	–	–	–	–	–	4	4
424	–	–	–	–	–	–	–	–	–	–	–	–	4	4
425	–	–	–	–	–	–	–	–	–	–	–	–	2	2
445	1	–	–	–	–	–	–	–	–	–	–	–	2	3
Total	1	0	0	0	0	0	0	0	0	0	3	0	13	17
Percentage	5.9	0	0	0	0	0	0	0	0	0	17.6	0	76.5	
PERIOD V/1–3														
612.02	–	–	–	–	–	1	–	–	–	–	–	–	–	1
Graves	2	–	–	–	2	1	2	–	–	–	1	1	5	13
Total	2	0	0	0	2	2	2	0	0	0	1	1	5	14
Percentage	14.3	0	0	0	14.3	14.3	14.3	0	0	0	7.1	7.1	35.7	
PERIOD V/4–5														
601	2	–	–	1	–	–	1	–	–	–	–	–	4	8
604	1	–	–	–	–	–	–	–	–	–	–	–	–	1
605	–	–	–	–	–	–	–	–	–	–	–	–	1	1
630	–	1	–	1	–	–	–	–	2	–	–	1	2	7
705	–	–	–	1	–	–	–	–	–	–	–	–	–	1
729	1	–	–	–	–	–	1	–	7	–	–	–	5	14
607.05	–	–	–	1	–	–	–	–	–	–	1	–	–	2
615	3	–	–	–	5	–	–	–	–	–	1	4	–	13
Total	7	1	0	4	5	0	2	0	9	0	2	5	12	47
Percentage	14.8	2.1	0	8.5	10.6	0	4.3	0	19.1	0	4.3	10.6	25.5	
PERIOD VI														
621	–	–	–	–	24	1	3	–	–	10	–	–	20	58
608	–	–	–	–	–	–	–	1	–	–	–	–	–	1
708	–	–	–	1	–	–	–	–	–	–	–	–	–	1
712	–	–	–	–	–	–	–	–	–	–	–	1	–	1
715	–	–	–	–	2	1	–	–	–	1	–	2	9	15
722	–	–	–	–	14	–	–	–	–	–	–	–	6	20
724	–	–	–	–	3	–	–	–	–	–	–	1	7	11
728	–	–	–	–	5	–	–	–	–	–	–	–	–	5
Total	0	0	0	1	48	2	3	1	0	11	0	4	42	112
Percentage	0	0	0	0.8	42.9	1.8	2.7	1.8	0	9.8	0	3.5	37.5	
RECENT														
738	–	1	–	–	–	–	1	–	–	–	–	–	–	2
743	–	–	–	1	–	–	–	–	–	–	–	–	–	1
744	1	–	–	–	–	–	–	–	1	–	1	–	1	4
760	–	–	–	–	–	–	–	–	–	–	–	–	1	1
764	–	–	–	–	–	–	–	–	1	–	–	–	–	1
770	–	–	–	–	–	–	–	–	–	–	–	–	1	1
Total	1	1	0	1	0	0	1	0	2	0	1	0	3	10
Percentage	10	10	0	10	0	0	10	0	20	0	10	0	30	–
Grand total	12	2	19	6	57	9	8	1	11	11	7	10	250	403
Percentage	3	0.5	4.7	1.5	14.1	2.2	2	0.2	2.7	2.7	1.7	2.5	62	

Table 11.52: The chronological distribution of fish bones.

Several of the unidentified fragments, probably also of fowl, domestic goose or wild Greylag (*Anser anser*), constituted most of the remainder. The other seven species were sporadic in occurrence. Some of the fowl bones were from female birds in lay, as evidenced by the presence of medullary bone (Driver 1982). Others were from mature males with spurs. One probably male tarsometatarsus from Block 415.01 was pathological.

Period I (Group 1)
No bird bones.

Period II (Group 2)
The proportions of fowl and goose in the Northumbrian midden group (303) are almost equal, differing only slightly from the previously reported material where goose was a little more frequent. Like the previously analysed bird material the bones were mostly the larger meat-bearing bones of the leg and wing. The present material does differ slightly in having a small number of vertebrae, toes, carpometacarpi and a synsacrum present. A complete femur had a greatest length of 66.9 mm and a radius was 55.1 mm in length.

Bird bones were recovered from two other blocks in this period group. Block 249 contained two bones only, a single bone each of fowl and goose. The fowl bone was a femur with a greatest length of 75.9 mm. Block 320 contained 27 bones, eleven of fowl, fourteen of goose and two unidentified fragments.

Periods III and **IV** (Group 3)
Most contexts in this period group contained only a few fowl bones, if any bird at all. Block 417, the ditch (pp 222-3), contained a greater variety including fowl, raven, jay or magpie, and buzzard. The seven raven bones are almost certainly from a single bird. Measurements of the fowl bones include two femora of 68.6 mm and 69.2 mm greatest length, a humerus of 74.6 mm and two tibio-tarsi of 114.5 mm and 111.3 mm. A group from Block 415.01 included four fowl bones, one goose bone and a corvid ulna, probably jackdaw. One of the fowl bones, a tarsometatarsus, was pathological. This bird was probably male as there is a spur scar; above this is a large pit of about 8 mm with a built-up smooth rim. The greatest length of this bone is 73.5 mm.

	fowl	goose	duck	wader	raven	corvid	passer.	buzzard	unid.	Total
PERIOD II										
303	37	27	2	–	–	–	–	–	36	102
249	1	1	–	–	–	–	–	–	–	2
320	11	14	–	–	–	–	–	–	2	27
Total	49	42	2	0	0	0	0	0	38	131
Percentage	37.4	32.1	1.5	0	0	0	0	0	29	
PERIOD III/IV										
417	25	–	–	–	7	1	–	1	1	35
410	2	–	–	–	–	–	–	–	–	2
422	1	–	–	–	–	–	–	–	–	1
424	4	–	–	–	–	–	–	–	–	4
430	1	–	–	–	–	–	–	–	–	1
438	1									1
415.01	4	1	–	–	–	1	–	–	–	6
Total	38	1	0	0	7	2	0	1	1	50
Percentage	76	2	0	0	14	4	0	2	2	
PERIOD V										
546	–	–	–	1	–	–	–	–	–	1
PERIOD V/4–5										
601	4	1	–	–	–	–	–	–	–	5
607.05	–	1	–	–	–	–	–	–	–	1
630	10	7	2	–	–	–	–	–	3	22
729	1	–	–	–	–	–	–	–	1	2
Total	15	9	2	0	0	0	0	0	4	30
Percentage	50	30	6.6	0	0	0	0	0	13.3	
PERIOD VI										
712	–	–	–	–	–	–	–	–	1	1
715	2	–	–	–	–	–	1	–	–	3
Total	2	0	0	0	0	0	1	0	1	4
Percentage	50	0	0	0	0	0	25	0	25	
RECENT										
751	–	–	–	–	–	–	11	–	–	11
Grand total	104	52	4	1	7	2	12	1	44	227
Percentage	45.8	22.9	1.8	0.4	3.1	0.9	5.3	0.4	19.4	

Table 11.53: The chronological distribution of bird bones.

Period V/1–3 (Group 4)
The only bird bone from **Period V/1–4** was a wader carpometacarpus, comparable with lapwing, from Block 546.

Period V/4–5 (Group 5)
As before most of the 30 bones were of fowl and goose, but there were also two fragments of mallard or domestic duck.

Period VI – the Manse (Group 6)
Only four fragments were recovered, these were two of fowl, one sparrow-sized small passerine and one unidentified fragment.

Recent (Group 7)
A single associated group of small passerine bones was recovered from Block 751. These were comparable with mistle thrush or fieldfare.

Discussion

In view of the small sample it is difficult to give a detailed interpretation of the material. The species represented are, however, similar to those at other mainland sites in Scotland. The prevalence of domestic fowl and goose is common throughout Britain from the Romano-British period onwards. There are bones from immature fowl (but not chicks), some large in comparison with the more mature bones, perhaps indicating culling of surplus young cockerels. Although egg production would not have been at the modern level, a few birds may have been kept to provide fresh eggs in season. The few butchery marks are consistent with removal of the foot, probably before cooking.

The Animal Bones

Finbar McCormick and Eileen Murphy
Department of Archaeology, The Queen's University of Belfast

INTRODUCTION

The excavation at Whithorn provided a large quantity of animal bone but several factors severely limited its potential for study. Firstly, much of the bone survives in poor condition and differential survival provided a potential source of error in many of the samples. Secondly, many of the samples were extremely small. Of the seventy samples examined, fewer than ten provided 100 or more identifiable fragments. Finally, there was considerable evidence of disturbance of the material as evidenced by the presence of human remains in many of the samples. In the present instance consideration will be limited to those contexts that produced in excess of 100 fragments (Tables 11.54 and 11.55). These date from the seventh to the sixteenth centuries. The largest sample from the site was from the Northumbrian midden (Tr4). This was examined by Lynn Barnetson and the discussion presented here is based on her report. Summary tables are provided in the text report while more detailed tables are included in her archive report. The minimum numbers of individuals is based on the most frequently recurring bone element, taking left and right into consideration but not the size of the bones or the state of epiphyseal fusion. The epiphyseal fusion ageing data is based on Silver (1969) while the tooth eruption data is based on Silver quoted in Higham (1967), also using the methodology of Grant (1982). The abbreviations used for the animal-bone measurements are those of von den Driesch (1974).

General results

The samples from Whithorn are generally small and consequently need to be treated with caution. Certain observations can, however, be made with confidence. Cattle, in terms of meat weight, always remained the dominant species throughout the periods under study. Assuming the estimated carcass weights outlined by Luff (1982, 35) in which the value for cattle is 408 kg, sheep are 56.7 kg and pig 90.7 kg, it can be calculated that beef constituted at least 80% of the meat consumed prior to the twelfth or thirteenth century. Even during the later-medieval period (Block 607) cattle provided 86%, compared with 11% in the case of sheep/goat and 3.8% in the case of pig. The distribution of the main meat-bearing species from the largest contexts are shown in Tables 11.54 and 11.55. The problems of differentiation between sheep and goat are well known, and most of the samples provided some evidence for the presence of goat. In general, however, goat was of minor importance, although they tended to become more numerous during **Period IV**.

The largest sample from **Period I** came from Block 85, which can be dated to the seventh century AD. The most striking feature of the sample is the extremely low incidence of sheep. There are few contemporary animal bones from southern Scotland, but the low incidence of sheep has also been noted at other southern Scottish sites (Table 11.56).

The table clearly demonstrates the low importance of sheep in the middle of the first millennium AD. This distribution is quite at odds with the distribution noted on English Anglo-Saxon period sites where caprovine remains were generally more numerous than either cattle or pig (Clutton-Brock 1976, 377). Data from Wales is rather scarce but at Dinys Powys 4, which dated from the fifth to eighth centuries AD, sheep were again a minor species constituting 21% of the fragments total compared with 35% in the case of pig and 42% in the case of cattle (Alcock 1987a, 82).

Period	Block	Cattle	Sheep/goat	Pig	Total
Period I	85	82.0	2.6	15.4	1079
Period II	Tr4 midden	49.8	37.6	12.6	2039
Period II	303 midden	64.1	23.0	12.9	1237
Period II	320	53.6	32.0	14.4	125
Period III	309	80.4	6.5	13.1	398
Period IV	417	65.3	15.9	17.7	679
Period IV	415.01	83.3	7.0	9.6	923
c. 1500	607	21.0	71.0	8.0	124
c. 1500	630	52.6	42.1	5.2	382

Table 11.54: Fragments distribution (%) of the main meat-providing species.

Period	Block	Cattle	Sheep/goat	Pig	Total
Period I	85	68.0	8.0	24.0	25
Period II	Tr4 midden	41.8	33.0	25.3	91
Period II	303 midden	56.4	25.6	17.9	39
Period II	320	44.4	33.3	22.2	9
Period III	309	54.5	27.3	18.2	11
Period IV	417	45.0	25.0	30.0	20
Period IV	415.01	66.7	16.7	16.7	18
c. 1500	607	20.0	60.0	20.0	10
c. 1500	630	47.6	42.9	9.5	21

Table 11.55: MNI (minimum numbers of individuals) distribution (%) from the main meat-providing species.

	Date	Cattle	Sheep/goat	Pig	N.
Whithorn **Period I**	Earlier 7th century	82.0	2.6	15.4	1079
Dundurn	6–7th century	70.9	6.3	22.8	619
Iona Vallum	Late 7th century	90.9	6.4	2.7	187
Edinburgh Castle Ph3–4	3–7th century	59.6	13.6	26.8	1759

Table 11.56: Distribution of fragments (%) from main domesticates from southern Scottish sites after Alcock *et al.* (1989) and McCormick (1981 and in press).

Much data is available from early Christian period sites in Ireland but the chronological problems of the period make it difficult to identify specific assemblages as being contemporary with **Period I** at Whithorn. At Knowth, Co. Meath, Phase 1 of the early Christian occupation can be approximately dated from the second or third to fifth centuries AD. Sheep again play a minor role comprising 13% of the fragments compared with 21% in the case of pig and 66% in the case of cattle. An almost identical distribution (12%–22%–66%) was noted from a seventh to eighth-century context (Sample D) at Moynagh crannog, Co. Meath (McCormick 1987).

The samples from Whithorn clearly indicate that sheep were by far the least important of the main domesticates present. This accords well with the low status of sheep, that has been demonstrated on contemporary sites in Ireland, Scotland and Wales, but not in England. Tables 11.54–11.55 also make it clear that there is a significant expansion in sheep rearing during the subsequent Northumbrian period, an expansion that is also paralleled in Ireland. Possible factors that could account for the increase of sheep in the late-eighth and early-ninth century need to be considered.

Sheep can be exploited for their meat, hides, and wool, but only the latter is a product that is exclusive to the animal. It is not known when wool was first exploited in Scotland. Woolen textile is known in England since the earlier Bronze Age (Henshall 1950, 158; Jorgensen 1993, 197), but the only surviving Bronze Age textiles from Scotland are of flax. The earliest evidence for wool in Scotland is from the Iron-Age broch at East Shore, Pool of Virkie, Sumburgh, Shetland (J. Barber Pers. Comm.), and spindle whorls, and so-called loom weights also appear during this period. Unfortunately most of the textile from Iron-Age to Viking period Scotland has not been identified at fabric level (Jorgensen 1993). It can be assumed, however, that from the Iron Age onwards the processing of wool was widespread if not common in Scotland.

The expansion of wool production from a purely self-sufficient or local-market economy to an export 'industrial' economy based on the production of a large surplus, necessitated the concentration of a large number of skills, equipment, and raw material. The latter two could be reflected in the archaeological record by an increase in the material remains associated with wool production and processing, and by an increase in the amount of sheep remains present. It seems likely that this can be identified at Whithorn. Although difficult to quantify there is a clear and definite increase in the numbers of spindle whorls and wool/heckling combs between **Periods I** and **III** (pp 425, 450, Table 10.18), and sheep numbers increase in **Period II**. Jorgensen (1993, 147) has found that at an organised textile industry continued in north-west Europe after the dissolution of the Western Roman Empire. This textile industry would have been enhanced by the establishment of a large number of emporia along both sides of the English channel from the early-eighth century. It is perhaps this increase in trade that provided the catalyst for the increase in the wool trade that is reflected at Whithorn and many Irish sites at about this time.

There is little change between **Periods II** and **IV**. While the fragments distribution of F309 might suggest a decline in sheep-keeping this is not borne out by the MNI distribution. Such apparent contradictions are a result of using small samples. The **Period III–IV** levels date to the later-ninth to thirteenth centuries, but there are very few rural sites with which to compare such material. In tenth to eleventh century deposits in Dublin pig was the dominant (59%) animal present in terms of MNI (McCormick 1991), although they accounted for only 29% of the fragments total. Sheep played a minor role constituting only 5% of the fragments and 10% of the MNI. In Anglo-Scandinavian York, however, both the fragments and MNI date indicate a dominance of cattle, although pig played an unusually important role in a few instances (O'Connor 1989, 1251–3). The evidence at Whithorn suggests that cattle clearly dominate, and that sheep and pig were present in roughly equal numbers, a situation more comparable with York. The distribution of animals at Whithorn, therefore, conforms more to that noted in Scandinavian York than Dublin. It is possible that the high incidence of pig at Dublin is a reflection of the fact that the poor relationship between Dublin and its agricultural hinterlands might have necessitated its inhabitants to become more self-reliant by breeding large numbers of pigs in the town. Such a situation may not have existed at Whithorn.

The **Period IV** deposits show some features that are an indication of a commercial basis to the settlement. Large-scale antler working is present and the exploitation of cats for their skins at this time is a phenomenon that had previously only been noted on urban sites.

The later medieval samples survived in very poor condition, and were especially susceptible to disturbance by burials. By the fifteenth–sixteenth century sheep had clearly predominated, accounting for 71% of the fragments in an admittedly very small sample. Whether this distribution is representative or not, however, is difficult to say, but it is at variance with the general national trend, as the wool trade went into steep decline after 1400 (Lynch 1988, 269).

The Northumbrian Midden (303)

This sample of bones lent itself to detailed analysis of its composition. The midden consisted of two groups, Tr4 and B1 303. The midden sample B1 303 is contiguous with Tr4, but the sample is in poor condition, and contains a slightly different distribution of species and bones. The groups will therefore be considered separately with the emphasis placed on the bones from Trench 4.

The sample from Tr4 is a very large discrete assemblage which appears to have accumulated very rapidly, perhaps in less than a year, and the evidence clearly indicates that it was predominately discarded kitchen refuse. In terms of both fragments and MNI cattle were the dominant species present (Table 11.54). Table 11.57 contrasts the survival rates of the cattle bones from the two parts of the **Period II** midden with that from the **Period IV** ditch, and it can be seen that there is a much lower proportion of waste parts of cattle skeleton in the Tr4 sample. Skull fragments, including mandible fragments and loose teeth, account for only 17.4% of the fragment total compared with 38.2% in the B1 303 midden sample, and 39.7% in the **Period IV** ditch. Feet bones such as the metatarsals and metacarpals are also less common in the Tr4 sample. This could either imply that more than usual of the refuse parts were being discarded elsewhere, or that one is dealing with a high-status assemblage where less of the poorer carcass parts would be expected. The latter observation could also be supported by the high incidence of femur fragments present, although it must be admitted that there is not a corresponding higher incidence of pelvis in the sample.

All the deer bones found in the Tr4 midden were roe deer, while in some other contexts both roe and red deer were present. Again, this could be interpreted as supporting the hypothesis that this is a high status sample as Hargreaves (1976, 136) notes that 'from the gastronome's point of view, the best deer is the roe deer, followed by the fallow deer, then the red deer'.

	Midden Tr4	*Midden B1 303*	*Period IV 417*
Horn	–	1.1	1.6
Skull	1.8	2.7	4.6
Mandible	4.6	2.2	7.8
Teeth	11.3	32.4	25.7
Scapula	5.3	3.4	12.2
Humerus	8.2	4.2	8.7
Radius	7.8	3.5	5.3
Ulna	3.1	2.3	1.6
Metacarpal	0.8	1.9	2.1
Pelvis	5.4	5.9	3.6
Femur	12.7	5.0	4.1
Patella	4.0	1.2	0.4
Tibia	17.3	9.8	8.2
Astragalus	6.5	7.2	1.1
Calcaneus	7.2	7.2	0.9
Metatarsal	0.9	3.3	6.7
Phalanges	3.1	5.5	5.0

Table 11.57: Distribution of cattle parts from three contexts where the number of cattle fragments present is expressed as a % of the overall cattle total.

The Tr4 sample also contained a sample of bird bone with the majority of the identifiable fragments (N = 130) being goose (50%) and domestic fowl (42%). The remainder included duck and gull. Some twenty-three fish bones were present. These were unidentifiable but most likely to have been of cod. The midden sample Block 303 produced two fish-bone fragments, both of salmon (above p 602). Again in this sample the majority of the bird bones were goose (56%) and fowl (41%) with a few duck fragments also present.

Despite the fact that sample Tr4 contained a small number of horse, cat and dog bones (Table 11.62), the general impression is that it reflected an affluent diet with waste parts, for cattle at least, being generally under-represented. The majority of the cattle and sheep were killed between the ages of one and four years, suggesting the selection of prime livestock. Selectivity of this nature may reflect the status of the ecclesiastical community which must have had access to extensive herds and flocks, either through estate management, or receipt of tithes. Although there are no contemporary charters for Galloway, records of other Anglo-Saxon areas indicate that ecclesiastical sees were generally endowed with land, often quite richly so, and rents were paid in food (bread, honey, fish), livestock (bullocks and wethers) and drink (ale and mead) (Stenton 1947). Fowl were also items of rent, and it is possible that the geese and chickens at Whithorn were acquired as such rather than by being raised by the community. The roe deer may also have been provided as rent. It is interesting to note that both roe and red deer were amongst the sixth and seventh century deposits on the monastery at Iona (McCormick 1981, 315–316). It was unlikely that deer herds were raised on such a small island as Iona, and it is more likely that the venison was given to the monks by outsiders.

Cattle

Ageing

The ageing data from Whithorn was obtained both from epiphyseal fusion data based on Silver (1969), and the state of mandibular tooth eruption based on Higham (1967), and Grant (1982). Ageing cattle by epiphyseal fusion is extremely problematical and, indeed, unreliable, but in the absence of good samples of mandibulae this method had to be used. The epiphyseal fusion quantification method devised by Chaplin (1971, 132–133) is used in archive tables 10–15, and summarised in Table 11.58. While this produces rather crude results, it does allow us to compare the data from the different periods on the site. The main problems with using this data is that the fusion of bones occurs over a relatively long period of time rather than at a point, while differential preservation also leads to the under-representation of unfused epiphyses.

The data from the **Period I** deposits suggests that the great majority of the cattle were mature or old animals. The extremely limited quantity of tooth eruption data supports such an extreme pattern, with three of the six mandibulae present being of semi-mature cattle (archive table 16). The tooth wear data demonstrates, however, that more very old cattle were present than in any of the other periods. The three mandibles with worn third lower molars all displayed 'K' stages of wear (Grant 1982, 92). In a large sample (N = 262) of mandibulae from tenth and early eleventh century contexts in Scandinavian Dublin some 53% of the cattle were at a stage when the third lower molar's third cusp was in secondary wear (stage G) or beyond (McCormick 1987). There were two peaks in the wear stages of these mature and older animals the first at stage G (23.2%) and the second at stage K (15.6%). It is tempting to think that the G group were animals that were bred specifically for the urban meat market, while the K group represents old animals that had come to the end of their useful lives for other purposes. The old animals from the **Period I** levels at Whithorn should be regarded in this capacity. The ageing sample from the group is, however, too small to allow any interpretation of general livestock economy of the period.

The fusion data for both the **Period II** samples (Tr4 and BL 320) show a much lower incidence of older cattle than in the **Period I** sample. The Tr4 sample, especially, contains a high proportion of young cattle that could be regarded as prime meat-providing cattle. The possible reasons for this have already

Approx % of animals killed in each age group

Age range – in months approx.	0–10	10–18	18–36	36–42	42–48	>48	no.
Period I Block 85	11%	–	11%	10%	–	68%	182
Period II midden Tr4	9%	5%	30%	33%	–	23%	231
Period II midden Block 320	–	33%	–	30%	–	37%	95
Period IV Block 417	–	–	28%	12%	–	60%	86
Period IV Block 415.01	–	6%	3%	1%	23%	66%	72

Table 11.58: Summary of cattle epiphyseal fusion age slaughter pattern based on Archive tables 10–15.

been discussed above. No comparable tooth eruption data was retrieved from the Tr4 material, and the data from Block 320 was too small for comparative purposes (archive table 17).

The **Period IV** fusion data (417 and 415.01) show a return to a high incidence of mature cattle. This is not, however, supported by the eruption data where only 33% (N = 9) of the lower third molars are of G stage or greater. As in all the other contexts, the evidence is at best limited, and sometimes contradictory.

Sex distribution

In the absence of adequate samples of complete metacarpals one is generally restricted to using the metacarpal distal widths (Bd) as an indicator. Analysis of large samples of complete metacarpals from Irish early-Christian and Viking period sites (McCormick 1992) suggests that Bd measurements of less than 55.5 mm are female, while those above 57.5 mm are male. It was not possible to differentiate between bulls and castrates.

Samples from Whithorn were again disappointingly small, especially due to the fact that metapodials were under-represented in the Northumbrian midden sample, where they may have been removed for industrial usage. The **Period I** levels, however, produced a comparatively large sample with nine out of ten being female according to the above criteria. The Northumbrian levels produced one male and one female, while two **Period IV** deposits produced four females and no males (417), and three females and two males (415.01). At Whithorn, therefore, it can be seen that in most phases where there are adequate samples present the majority of the mature cattle present are cows. This can reflect a situation were dairying played a predominant role in the livestock economy, but on its own cannot be taken as unequivocal evidence for dairying (McCormick 1992).

Size

A summary of the cattle measurements from the **Period I–IV** is provided in archive table 29. Analysis of the results suggested a slight decrease in cattle size after **Period I**, but the decline was probably not significant. Table 11.59 shows the dimension of the complete metacarpals from the site and the estimated withers' heights using the multiplication factors of Fock (quoted in von den Driesch and Boessneck 1974). These are especially useful as different multiplication factors are provided for male and female.

Comparative data for complete cattle metacarpals are virtually non-existent for Scotland at this time, and elsewhere, generally, male and female metacarpals are not differentiated. Comparative material is, however, available from Ireland and these data along with data from Dorestad, show little difference in the size of the cattle from the different sites (Table 11.60). It is interesting to note, however, that the cattle at the important royal site at Lagore are, on average, larger than those noted elsewhere.

Only one complete horn core was present and this was from **Period IV** levels. It was of the short-horned type having a length along its outer curve of 187 mm.

Period	GL	Bp	Bd	SD	Sex	Withers' height
Period I	175.8	47.1	49.8	25.8	F	105.5
	176.0	–	52.5	32.8	F	105.6
	177.0	49.9	53.7	27.6	F	106.2
	177.9	46.7	46.9	26.0	F	106.7
	182.0	50.2	53.6	28.1	F	109.2
	192.0	51.1	52.2	30.0	F	115.2
Period II	178.9	–	52.7	29.9	F	107.3
Period IV	172.1	49.6	51.4	25.5	F	103.3
	173.1	47.9	49.9	27.0	F	103.9
	173.1	45.9	50.2	26.0	F	103.9
	188.3	–	58.8	–	M	117.6

Table 11.59: Estimated cattle withers' heights (in cm) based on metacarpals.

Site		N	Min.	Max.	Mean
Dublin	Hib-Nor	124	97.2	115.2	108.2
Moynagh crannog	EC	35	102.0	117.6	109.6
Lagore crannog	EC	30	105.0	117.6	111.4
Whithorn	**Periods I & II**	7	105.5	115.2	108.0
Dorestad	8th–9th century	27	103.1	117.9	109.6

Table 11.60: Estimated shoulder size of cows from Whithorn compared with Irish sites and Dorestad, Netherlands (after McCormick, 1987, and Prummel, 1983).

Palaeopathology

Palaeopathology was limited to cattle bones from the **Period I** and **Period IV** deposits. Photographs of these were sent to Dr John Baker of Liverpool University and his comments form the basis to much of what follows. X-ray photographs of the pathologies usually confirmed the original diagnosis.

Both a **Period I** metacarpal and metatarsal displayed a mid-shaft lump which was interpreted as indicating that either the animal had been hit or, more likely, that it had struck its leg rather severely against a hard surface. This led to haemorrhaging below the periosteum which then became ossified to produce a visible lump. A metatarsal from the **Period IV** levels displayed spavin which can be associated with either the use of the animal for draught purposes or, in certain instances, keeping the animal tied up and unable to move for long periods. A **Period IV** vertebra displayed osteoarthritis and eburnation.

Sheep/Goat

The difficulties of differentiating between sheep and goat need not be rehearsed here. It is sufficient to say that the great majority of the caprovine bones could not be identified at species level but of those that could, the great majority were generally sheep. In the **Period II** midden (Tr4) no definite goat remains were present, although two goat horn cores were found elsewhere in Northumbrian deposits. Goat seems to become more important during **Period IV**, but the sample is too small to be quantified. The low incidence of goat is paralleled on the few other Scottish sites of this period. Goat was incidental in a Dark Age sample from Edinburgh Castle (McCormick in press), while none were noted at Clatchard Craig or Dundurn, although no attempt was made to differentiate between the two at the latter site (Alcock *et al.* 1989). In Ireland, too, goat is extremely rare on early Christian rural sites, but is much more numerous in urban Hiberno-Norse Dublin. The Irish pattern is therefore similar to that noted at Whithorn.

In general it is assumed that the great majority of the ageing and metrical data at Whithorn represents sheep, and the caprovine bones will, in general, be referred to as sheep.

Ageing

It has been suggested that the increase in sheep at Whithorn between **Periods I** and **II** was a result of an expansion in wool trade. The only samples that have produced a reasonable sample of fusion data are the two Northumbrian samples (Tr4 and Block 303). Both provide contrasting results. In the case of the better-preserved Tr4 sample only 14% of the sheep are greater than 3½ years (after Silver 1969) while in the case of Block 303 some 38% are in this group (archive tables 19 and 20). It could be argued that the higher incidence of old animals in the B1 303 sample is simply due to the poorer preservation of that sample. Again, however, we could return to the hypothesis that Tr4 was an unusually high-quality assemblage, and that the high incidence of prime younger sheep is simply a reflection of this. Whether or not the 38% is more representative of a wool-producing regime than mutton production is, however, difficult to evaluate. On the basis of the fusion data the distribution from B1 303 is very similar to Viking urban Dublin (42% greater than 3½ years) where one would expect the sheep age/slaughter pattern to reflect the production of mutton for an urban meat market.

Tooth eruption and wear data were extremely limited in Whithorn. There was none from **Period I** and **II** deposits, while the **Period IV** samples provided only six mandibulae. Of these, five were of less than about two years old at the time of death (archive table 22).

Size

The problems of considering sheep size are complicated by the possible inclusion of goat bones, but the metrical data from the different phases is summarised in archive table 30. Table 11.61 provides the dimensions of the complete metatarsals and metacarpals that can definitely be identified at species level, but the samples are too small to compare with other sites.

Palaeopathology

A sheep/goat tibia from a **Period IV** deposit indicated that it had suffered severe strain or possibly a dislocation of the joint leading to the expansion of the distal end.

Pig

Pig played a relatively consistent role between **Periods I** and **IV**, accounting for between 21% and 18% of the main species fragments totals, after which their role

Phase	GL	Bp	Bd	SD	Withers' height
Metacarpal					
Period II	111.0	22.5	25.1	14.0	53.4
	119.6	22.5	25.1	14.0	58.4
Period IV (goat)	107.0	24.1	28.0	16.1	61.1
Metatarsal					
Period II	129.0	23.6	20.0	9.5	58.6
	134.4	21.5	25.2	12.5	61.0
Period IV	142.9	22.8	27.3	19.1	64.8

Table 11.61: Estimated sheep, unless otherwise stated, withers' heights (in cm) based on metacarpals using the multiplication factors of Teichert (quoted in von den Driesch and Boessneck 1974). The multiplication factor for goat is after Scramm (quoted in ibid.).

seems to decline (Table 11.55). This may be associated with the decline in beech or oak woodland in the areas, as mast can play an important role in their diet.

Ageing

The pig ageing data is summarised in archive tables 24–28. Virtually all the useful epiphyseal fusion and tooth eruption data is confined to the **Period IV** ditch (417), and this is characterised by an extremely high incidence of young pigs present. The epiphyseal fusion data suggests that the great majority of the pigs are less than one year with a smaller number being between one and two years. There are no older animals present. The sample is small, but the same acute pattern can also be seen in the mandibular data where five of seven mandibulae are of less than one year. The distribution from other small **Period IV** deposits is more like that observed elsewhere with the majority of them being killed between about eighteen and twenty four months, i.e. just as the animal is reaching full size. This was the most economic age at which to kill pigs. An age slaughter pattern similar to the B1 417 sample was noted in a late-thirteenth/early-fourteenth century assemblage from Waterford, a site founded as a Hiberno-Norse town. The rich assemblage of pottery present indicated that the bones represented the refuse of an extremely affluent group of people who were consequently able to kill the more palatable, but less economic, young pigs. It is also possible that the refuse represented by the Block 417 group also represents an affluent group.

Size

The small sample of measurable pig bones is summarised in archive table 31. Little can be said other than that they are similar in size to the small domesticated pig noted elsewhere during the first millennium AD. Wild pig was probably represented by a very large, male canine from Block 424.

Palaeopathology

A pig mandible from **Period I** possessed an extra cusp on its third lower molar. The presence of extra cusps is thought to be a result of genetic or congenital defects.

Other domesticates

Horse

Small quantities of horse bone were found in all the principal contexts and many of the minor assemblages. All parts of the skeleton were present. A high incidence of loose teeth was noted, but this is not unusual as teeth were generally the most frequent bone of the other species found. It is difficult to know how the horse remains should be interpreted. They may be incidental bones like those of dog and cat which did not represent food refuse. On the other hand many of the bones showed a breakage pattern consistent with the exploitation of marrow, e.g. a femur and tibia fragment from Block 417 and a metacarpal fragment from Block 309. Faint knife marks, probably representative of boning, were present on a radius fragment from Block 630.

All of the horse remains were of old or mature individuals, implying that they may have been slaughtered after their usefulness for other purposes drew to an end. Their presence in an ecclesiastical context during **Periods I** and **II** is unexpected seeing that Pope Gregory II's early-eighth century letters to St Boniface make it clear that such a practice was unacceptable for Christians. The letter states

> 'You say, among other things, that some have the habit of eating wild horses and very many eat tame horses. This, holy brother, you are in no wise to permit in future but are to suppress it in every possible way, with the help of Christ and impose suitable penance upon the offenders. It is a filthy and abominable practice' (Emerton 1940, 58).

We know that in Scotland also the eating of horse flesh was considered a lowly practice because in *Adomnan's Life of Columba* it is regarded as fitting only for thieves (Anderson *et al.* 1961, 251–253). Yet there were butchered bones in the primary vallum fill at Iona (McCormick 1981, 315). Is it possible that instead of horse bones representing the conscious consumption of horse flesh, it instead may represent the selling of such flesh by unscrupulous dealers who were passing it off as beef or venison.

Context	Cattle	Horse	Sheep/goat	Pig	Dog	Cat	Red deer	Roe deer
Period I BL 85	885	9	28	166	8	1	2	10
Period II BL 320	67	–	40	18	–	–	–	–
Period II BL 303	793	7	284	160	–	1	–	–
Period II TR4	1016	23	766	257	1	2	–	20
Period III BL 309	320	6	26	52	–	–	4	–
Period IV BL 417	443	8	115	120	19	95	–	–
Period IV BL 525	769	13	65	89	12	2	–	–
c. 1500 BL 607	26	2	88	10	6	–	–	–
c. 1500 BL 630	201	5	161	20	11	–	–	–

Table 11.62: Distribution of fragments from main contexts.

No complete bones were present so it was not possible to estimate the height of the horses present. The few useful measurements available consist of a tibia Bd 70.6 (B1 417), a metacarpal Bd 44.8 mm (B1 415.01) and a radius Bd of 67.2 mm (B1 630).

Dog

Dog, in general, tended to be more common than cat at Whithorn. Small fragments of dog bone are a feature of nearly all sites and it is unlikely that they represent discarded food refuse. The dogs present were almost all mature animals. Most of the bones were broken but the available measurements are provided in Tables 11.63 and 11.64. A complete dog skull from the **Period IV** ditch (417) had a length of 192 mm which corresponds in size to a modern red setter. The long bones from the seventeenth century correspond to the post-early Christian medium-sized group outlined by McCormick (1991). They would have been similar in height to a modern whippet.

generally account for between 0.1% and 4% of the fragments total. Individual features occasionally contain a much higher incidence. In a late-thirteenth/early-fourteenth century stone-lined pit from Waterford, Ireland, cat constituted 10% of the assemblage. It may be purely a coincidence that both this Waterford assemblage and the present Block 417 provided the unusually high incidence of young suckling pigs discussed above.

The second feature of interest in the assemblage is that the **Period IV** cats at Whithorn are the small cats associated with urban settlement rather than the larger cats found on rural sites. Due to the immature age of most of the cats present at Whithorn the metrical data was extremely limited. A complete femur had a GL of 85.6 mm, while a complete humerus had a GL of 83.1 mm. Several cat humeri had a Bd range of 14.2 mm–15.0 mm with a mean of 14.5. The humerus was smaller than any noted on an early Christian rural site in Ireland, and lay at the lowest end of the scale of those from Hiberno-Norse urban Dublin (McCormick 1988, but note that the

Bone	Date	GL	Bp	Bd	SD	EWH
Calcaneus	**Period IV**	35.2	–	–	–	–
Calcaneus	17th century	–	–	–	–	–
Femur	**Period I**	–	24.1	–	–	–
Humerus	**Period IV**	–	32.5 (Dp)	–	–	–
Humerus	17th century	138.1	34.9 (Dp)	26.1	19.8	46.5
Humerus	17th century	143.2	34.6 (Dp)	26.6	–	44.7
Humerus	17th century	–	–	21.8	21.0	–

Table 11.63: Whithorn dog measurements. The estimated withers' heights are based on the factors provided by Harcourt (1974).

I	II	III	IV	IX	X	XI	XII
192.0	100.4	98.1	98.8	94.9	49.0	67.9	25.2

Table 11.64: Dog skull measurements (Block 417) in mm using the abbreviations of Harcourt (1974).

Cat

The earliest incidence of domesticated cat in Scotland is during the first few centuries AD at the Howe, Orkney (Smith 1995), and it is also present in the **Period I** deposits at Whithorn. Most of the cat remains, however, came from the **Period IV** ditch sample (417). Cat remains there constituted an MNI of six individuals or 12% of the fragments total, although many of these came from the semi-complete skeleton of one individual. This assemblage is extremely unusual for several reasons.

In the first instance the cats constitute a very large proportion of the assemblage both in terms of fragments total and minimum numbers of individuals. High incidences of cat bones are not usually a feature of rural sites, the phenomenon being generally confined to urban settlements. McCormick (forthcoming) has surveyed the incidence of cat in several late-first and early-second millennium towns including Southampton, York, Dorestad, *Haitabu*, Exeter, Dublin and Waterford, and found that they

captions of Figures 1 and 2 have been transposed). The femur dimensions confirm the small size of the cats at Whithorn.

Finally, it can be seen on the basis of Table 11.65 that most of the cats present at Whithorn were juvenile. This too is a feature of urban sites and has been noted both in English and Irish sites (McCormick 1988; O'Connor 1992). It seems most likely that such a pattern reflects the deliberate breeding of cats for their skins. The animals were allowed to grow to full size and were then slaughtered and skinned. Proof of this hypothesis is provided by two skull fragments that display cut marks incurred during skinning. The small size of the cats probably reflects the poor way in which they were fed in contrast to the large, well-fed cats on other rural sites where the cats were treated as prized pets rather than simply as economic objects. The affluent diet of young suckling pigs in Block 417 suggests that trading in cat pelts may have been a lucrative business and, as noted above, this affluent diet was also noted amongst a group of cat skinners in Waterford, Ireland.

Bone	Context	Fused	Unfused	Age at fusion (in months)
Humerus p.	417	1	3	15–20
Humerus d.	417	6	0	4–7
Radius p.	417	5	2	4–7
Radius d.	417	0	4	15–20
Ulna p.	417	0	7	8–14
Femur p.	417	0	2	8–14
Femur d.	417	0	2	15–20
Femur P.	414	1	0	8–14
Femur D.	414	1	0	15–20
Tibia p.	417	0	1	15–20
Tibia d.	417	1	2	8–14

Table 11.65: Cat epiphyseal fusion data using ageing data of Habermehl quoted in O'Connor (1992).

Wild animals

Deer

Most of the deer fragments from the site consisted of red-deer antler, but the presence of post-cranial deer bones showed that venison played an occasional role in the diet. The antler was clearly being used as a raw material for industrial usage and is discussed elsewhere in the report. The non-antler cervid remains consisted of red- and roe-deer. The roe-deer remains were confined to **Period I** and **II** deposits, the largest sample having come from the 'high-status' Northumbrian midden Tr4. It has been suggested above that, since roe venison is superior to that of red deer, their carcasses might reflect tribute. Other roe-deer remains consisted of some teeth from Block 85 and a metatarsal from Block 88. Since roe deer generally prefer a more densely wooded environment than the red, it is possible that their absence after the Northumbrian period reflects the destruction of such a habitat. The disappearance of red-deer bones, as opposed to antler, after the **Period IV** might imply that all the forest had disappeared at this time. Roe deer have never been present in Ireland but the presence of some roe deer amongst a large assemblage of red-deer antler in a twelfth century context in Waterford indicated that they were importing the antler from abroad, probably from England or Wales.

The only metrical data available was a red-deer radius from **Period I** (BL 85) which had a Bp of 52.9 mm. This lies at the lower end of the range of large prehistoric deer (53 mm–65 mm), but is larger than those of island populations such as Oransay at 44.5 mm and Cnip, Harris at 45.1 mm (Grigson and Mellars 1987, 259).

Fox and hare

Only a small sample of other wild mammals were noted in the samples and none were present in the main samples listed in Table 11.59. An unfused hare femur was present in a **Period II** deposit (B1 319) while a hare humerus (Bd 12.1 mm) from a poorly defined medieval context (Bl 525). A small number of fox bones were present in two adjacent **Period I** contexts (B1 89 and 94), a complete femur having the following dimensions: GL 131.1, Bp 25.9, Bd 19.8, SD 9.7 mm.

The evidence at Whithorn clearly indicated that wild game played an incidental role in the diet.

APPENDIX 1

The Provenance of the Early Christian Inscriptions of Galloway[1]

Derek Craig

The 'Latinus' stone

This slab was discovered during William Galloway's excavations at Whithorn Priory in the 19th century. It is first mentioned and discussed in a letter dated 8 November 1890, from Galloway to General Pitt-Rivers, then Inspector of Ancient Monuments, in which he states that it was found 'on the site of the Priory', but without giving details. He had apparently already received comments on the inscription from Hübner and other correspondents (SRO/MW.1/17). J. Rhys, who saw it in August 1891 and was the first to publish it, simply stated that it had been found 'some time ago' (Rhys 1891, 201). Romilly Allen's erroneous date of 1891 for the discovery is apparently based on the date of Rhys' visit or article, which he cites (Allen & Anderson 1903, 496–7).

Galloway died before his excavations could be published, but in the schedule to the 1891 Deed of Nomination, which lists thirteen stones from Whithorn, No. 12 (this stone) is said to have been 'found about the same time and in the same locality as No. 11' (i.e. Whithorn Museum 19). No. 11 is stated to have been found 'in December 1888, within the area of what in all probability was the Priory Chapter House' (SRO/MW.1/17). This indirect evidence for the date of discovery seems a year too early, as it is difficult to believe Galloway waited two years to contact Pitt-Rivers, with whom he was in regular correspondence; or that an inscribed stone would have been ignored by the Dumfries and Galloway Archaeological Society on their visit in July 1889, when several other carved stones were noted (Dickie 1887–90, 164). However, the Chapter House was part of the East Range of the Priory, and lies under the path to the 1822 parish church. A few years later, P. M'Kerlie, who died in 1900, wrote that 'when the gravelled walk in front of the parish church was opened up under the direction of the late Mr Galloway, an ancient monument to Latinus and his daughter was discovered lying close behind the north wall of the old cathedral' (M'Kerlie 1906, 435; see also E. M'Kerlie 1916, 83). This siting would therefore agree with the evidence of the 1891 list. The position of W. Galloway's trench is shown in Figure 12.2 (see Hill below, p 619).

Radford thought that the Latinus stone was 'found at the east end of the church', in or near his early building (Radford 1957, 171), and he has been followed in this by Thomas in his recent publications (Thomas 1992a, 3; Thomas 1992b, 3). Neither of these opinions appears to derive from the evidence discussed here, since Radford's early building lies to the east of the quire, and the path to the present parish church crosses the site of the transept.

The slab is oblong, tapering slightly at the top and damaged on the upper left-hand corner. The lower third of the slab is rough and unworked, and indented on the left side (see RCAHMS 1912, Fig. 109 A, for the complete stone). Two-thirds of the back on the left side appear to have been restored with cement and embedded chippings of stone. The upper half of the other face is roughly flat, with chamfered edges, and is worn at the top. Beneath this are twelve horizontal lines of an inscription in pocked and incised Latin capitals. This extends the full width of the chamfered area of the face, and measures approximately 70 cm high by 34 cm wide, extending 82 cm below the summit of the stone. The letters vary between 4 and 7 cm high. The inscription has been damaged at the top and on the right edge.

---

[1] This section summarises material treated in somewhat greater detail in my thesis (Craig 1992, III): the Latinus stone, pp 285–9; the Peter stone, pp 188–98; the Kirkmadrine inscriptions, pp 115–34; Low Curghie, p 1824). The inscriptions themselves have recently been analysed by Charles Thomas in his fourth Dalrymple lecture (Thomas 1992b) and his Whithorn lecture (Thomas 1992a), and are not dealt with here.

> Whithorn, Wigtownshire, N.B.
> November 8th, 1890.
>
> Dear Sir,
>
> As you have taken so much interest in our Romano-British Stones here, especially those bearing the chrisma, I herewith forward a drawing based on rubbing of the inscription, which I have just been deciphering on a stone found on the site of the Priory here. I have been, or rather am, in communication with the Earl of Southesk, and Prof: Hubner of Berlin, as to the precise intrepretation, and in so far as the major portion goes, I think this is settled, reading as follows :-
>
> The remaining five lines are much more uncertain, owing to injury to, or defects in, some of the letters. Save for the initial I-C which may be ICIC Professor Hubner gives up line 9, reads line 10 as FECERV[N]T.
>
> TE·DOMINV[M]
> LAVDAAAVS
> LATINVS
> ANNORVM
> XXXV ET
> FILIA SVA
> ANNI V

12.1 Opening part of the letter from William Galloway to General Pitt-Rivers illustrating the Constantinian chi-rho above the inscription.

TE[DOMI]NV[.]
LAVDAM[V.]
LATINV[S]
ANN[OR]V[.]
XXXVE[T]
FILIA SV[A]
ANNI V
[I]C[S]INVM
[FI]CERVT
N[I]PVS
BA[R]ROV[A]
DI

Above the inscription and directly below the summit in the centre of the slab is a small incised chi-rho of the six armed Constantinian form (*c.f.* Frantz 1929, 10; Thomas 1981a, 87–8), measuring 10 cm high. This chi-rho has not been noted since the first record of the stone by W. Galloway in 1890 (letter in SRO/MW.1/17; drawing in SRO/DD.27/821).[2] It is very worn. In his letter to Pitt Rivers cited above, Galloway refers to this stone as 'bearing the chrisma' (Figure 12.1). And in the list of crosses attached to the 1891 Deed of Nomination, No. 12 is described as a 'massive unhewn block of greywacke ... with an inscription of the Romano-British period having the chrisma at the top, with twelve lines of an inscription in Roman characters and Latin language ...' (SRO/MW.1/17).

Constantinian chi-rhos have not been found on carved stones in Britain anywhere north of Cornwall, except for two from the Roman forts at Maryport on the Cumbrian coast and Catterick in Yorkshire (Wall 1965, 213–4, Fig. 3; Thomas 1981a, 106–7, Figs 4.1; 5.11). A distribution map is given in Hamlin 1972, Fig. 3, with references to the two Cornish examples at Phillack and Cape Cornwall (Langdon 1893, 1015, Pl. I, no. 1, 1a, 2; Wall 1968, 175–6, nos 14 and 15, Figs 1.14, 1.16). Thomas (1981a, 86–8, Fig. 3) has shown that the six-armed Constantinian type is generally earlier than the four-armed monogram, as seen at Kirkmadrine. But the use of a chi-rho to preface an inscription is also found in the dedication stone at Jarrow, dated to 685 (Cramp 1984, 113–14, Pl. 58.524), as well as on Continental examples of earlier date.

It is therefore possible that this chi-rho is the '*sinum*' referred to in the inscription, despite Thomas' reservations about the spelling (Thomas 1992a, 6). The chi-rho became a universal Christian symbol after Constantine's vision of the cross in 312/3, which was accompanied by the words '*In hoc signo vince*' (in this sign conquer), in Rufinus' Latin translation of Eusebius (Thomas 1981a, 87). A 7th/8th century cross-slab from Jarrow has been shown to carry the inscription '*In hoc singulari signo vita redditur mundo*' (in this unique sign life is

---

[2] The file in which Galloway's drawing is found is still closed to public inspection under the Official Secrets Act, but it is reproduced by permission of the SDD in my thesis (Craig 1992, Pl. 171 D), where photos of the chi-rho may also be seen (Pls. 171 A-C). Galloway's letter is reproduced here by permission of Historic Scotland.

restored to the world) (Levison 1943, 121–6; Cramp 1984, 113, no 16). In both cases the term '*signum*' refers to the cross or chi-rho symbol, as had become common practice after the 4th century (Levison 1943, 125). It has been shown above that this pillar slab was not found at the east end of the later priory church near Radford's early building, but under the path which crosses the transept. It is therefore less likely that earlier churches on the site were focused on this stone. But the present excavations have shown that the earliest burials in the sixth century were focused on an enclosure that may have had a pillar stone at the centre (pp 91-2).

The 'Peter' stone

The earliest description of the location of Whithorn Museum 2 appears to be that given in a letter of Bishop Richard Pococke, written in 1760 but not published until 1887: 'A little way out of town, towards the isle of Whithern, is a stone like a boundary, with a cross on it in a wheel. As the name of Peter is on it, the common people say St. Peter was buried there. It was probably put up in memory of some like event' (Kemp 1887, 17).

The stone was also noted in the late 18th century in the Statistical Account of Scotland, but its location is not made clear. Following a discussion of Whithorn Priory and parish church, and a ruined church and burial ground near the Isle of Whithorn, the author simply states: 'Between these places there is a stone, upon which is inscribed, "*Hic est locus Petri Apostoli*" (Davidson 1795, 287). But in 1863, when first described by Mitchell (1870–72, 579), and subsequently Stuart (1867, 53), it was clearly standing by the west side of the road leading to the Isle of Whithorn, just south of Enoch farm, and ⅔ of a mile (1.07km) south of Whithorn Priory, and its position is marked on the 1895 25-inch Ordnance Survey map, sheet XXXV.4, at NX 4431 3921, although the stone had been transferred to the Priory in 1889 (Dickie 1887–90, 165). This site has therefore been accepted as its earliest known location by the majority of later writers.

However, in 1877 the local historian and genealogist P. M'Kerlie, after quoting Stuart (op. cit.), stated: '... and we have to add that the stone in question was brought to its present site' (i.e., by the roadside) 'from the farm of Mains, which is partly within the burgh' (M'Kerlie 1877, 418; 1906, 419). And there is independent confirmation of this in a letter from Sir Herbert Maxwell to General Pitt Rivers, then Inspector of Ancient Monuments. In an earlier letter Maxwell had argued that the stone should remain by the roadside at Enoch farm rather than being removed to the Priory. But on 23 December 1886 he announced: 'When I wrote to you about it before I was under the impression that the stone was standing on its *original site*' (his emphasis). 'I have since ascertained without any doubt that it formerly stood on Mains farms ½ mile from its present position and that the tenant, being annoyed by visitors crossing his farm in search of it, had it removed to the road-side.[3] Under these circumstances the objection to its removal disappears' (SRO/MW.1/17).

High Mains and Low Mains are farms lying to the east of the present road to the Isle at NX 446 395 and NX 447 390 respectively. Both are marked on the 1850 Ordnance Survey 6 inch map, but High Mains is shown as lying just south of the parliamentary boundary around the town of Whithorn, and about 730 metres from the Priory. It may therefore be suggested that this is the farm described by P. M'Kerlie as 'partly within the burgh'. But although in existence by 1849, neither High Mains nor Low Mains is marked on J. Ainslie's 1782 map of Wigtownshire (Stone 1967, 188–9). On this there is a completely different farm called 'Mains' which appears on none of the later OS maps. This lies due east of a point halfway between the two later farms, and S.S.W. of High Skeog. It is situated at approximately NX 452 393, where un-named buildings are marked on the 1850 OS map near a well.

Unfortunately neither Maxwell nor M'Kerlie seem to have known when the removal took place, so it is not entirely clear whether the site named as 'Mains' in 1877 referred to the earlier farm of that name, or to High Mains, though perhaps the latter seems more likely if the removal to the roadside took place within living memory, and probably after the Ordnance Survey's fieldwork in 1849. It is likely that the stone was not yet standing beside the road at Enoch when the first edition of the Ordnance Survey 6-inch map, Wigtownshire sheet 34 (1850), was surveyed, as it is neither marked here on the map nor mentioned in the Name Books for Whithorn parish, despite references to other sculpture.

It is therefore possible, as implied in the earliest accounts, that the stone initially stood by the old road to the Isle of Whithorn, which ran S.E. from Whithorn Priory and lay to the N.E. of High and Low Mains farms. It survives as a street in Whithorn itself called the King's Road, and a footpath across the fields still marked on recent OS maps. The buildings identified as possibly the 1782 'Mains' farm lie adjacent to it. This road appears to have gone out of use before the first edition of the OS map in 1850, being supplanted by the road running farther south, to the side of which the stone was moved.

Radford suggested that the stone marked the site of an early oratory, or even the boundary of Whithorn monastery (Radford 1957, 178–80; Radford & Donaldson 1953, 8; 1984, 4); but it is perhaps more likely that it stood in a cemetery of dug or stone-built graves, as has been shown in the case of the pillar stone at Kilnasaggart, Co. Armagh (Hamlin 1982, 291, 294, Pl. 17.4 A,B), which also carries an inscription dedicating the place to Peter the Apostle (Macalister 1949, 114–5, no. 946, Pl. XLVI).

The stone was removed from the roadside in 1889

---

[3] I have not been able to trace any records made by such visitors before the stone was moved.

under the supervision of William Galloway, and is now in Whithorn museum (Radford & Donaldson 1984, 27–8, no. 2, plate). But the initial letter 'L' recorded in early drawings (Muir 1864, 45; Stuart 1867, Pl. LXXVII.2; Mitchell 1870–72, Fig. 2) had been flaked off before this move (see Harper 1876, 247, fig).

The stone is an oblong pillar of rectangular section, damaged on one side. This face is dressed at the top and bottom and on the upper left side, but the area between, adjacent to the decorated face, has been gouged back, leaving a stepped area at the base. The damaged area measures 90 cm high.

This damage, which postdates the dressing of the stone, appears to predate the inscription and cross-of-arcs on the adjacent face.[4] The foot of the stone is now stepped outwards on the left edge, due to the damage to the upper part of this face (see RCAHMS 1912, Fig. 109 B, for the complete stone), but the outer circle of the cross, which extends the full width of the stone, is intact on both sides, and the stem of the cross and the outer letters of the inscription are equidistant from both the damaged and undamaged edges of the stone. It is therefore possible, as Macalister suggested, that an earlier inscription had been deliberately obliterated on the left face before the cross-of-arcs was carved (Macalister 1935–36, 320; 1945, 499), but there is no evidence of any surviving lettering.

The type of cross-of-arcs on the Peter stone is almost unknown in Wales, but common on the west coast of Ireland and at Maughold in the Isle of Man. This cross-of-arcs with a double ring is a form found at Maughold on four examples (Kermode 1907, nos 21, 25, 26, 117), and one of these also carries a chi-rho (Trench-Jellicoe 1980, 202, Pl. XIa). The P letter form also occurs at Maughold, and it is likely that there was close contact with Man at this date. It is notable that this connection is not visible in the later sculpture (Craig 1992, I, 265).

A fragmentary cross of this type, though with circumference arcs as on Maughold 46 (26) and Ronaldsway (Kermode 1907, no 26; Megaw 1939, Pl. 173.5) was found in the present excavations reused in a later building (pp 437-9, No 14), and a simpler example (No 16) was found in a 7th-century grave. Subsequently, slabs with compass-drawn designs forming marigold and cross patterns were recognised on paving slabs in the Northumbrian period ecclesiastical buildings (pp 155, 187-8, Nos 17–19). On the reverse of Whithorn Museum 36 (Craig 1992, Pl. 174b), there are three interlocking circles with two crudely drawn crosses with expanded terminals in the outer circles. It is therefore clear that the cross-of-arcs on the Peter stone is not as isolated in this area as it appeared a few years ago, and it is suggested here that it may have been the basis for a regional form of cross within a circle with expanded terminals, as on Whithorn Museum 4 (Collingwood 1922–23, Fig. 8; Craig 1992, Pl. 173c) and the crosses above an indented stem on St Ninian's Cave C.3 (Collingwood 1922–23, Fig. 6; Craig 1992, Pl. 162a) which, the St Ninian's Cave evidence suggests, may have been the basis for the Whithorn School disk-head type (Collingwood 1922–23, 218–27; Radford & Donaldson 1984, 257).

Kirkmadrine 1–3

The three inscribed stones at Kirkmadrine were first recorded at the beginning of the 19th century in a drawing made by William Todd, parish schoolmaster at Kirkmaiden. This drawing, made in about 1810,[5] remained unpublished for sixty years. A note by Todd at the top of it reads: 'The three following figures are faithful representations of three stones with inscriptions on them (as below) as they stand in the Old Burial ground at Kirkmadrine Parish of Stoneykirk and Estate of Ardwell' (Mitchell 1870–72, 569-70, Pl. XL).

The three stones appear to have been still standing in the burial ground in 1839, when the New Statistical Account was written: '... And Kirkmadrine, with its church-yard, still preserved as a burying-place, contains some grave-stones, with antique inscriptions' (Anderson 1845, 164). However, during the incumbency of the Rev. Robert M'Neil, who was minister from 1840 to 1844 (Scott 1917, 355), the previously unenclosed burial ground was walled in (Robertson 1916–18, 139), and Kirkmadrine 1 and 2 were reused as gateposts at the entrance. At the same period, following the Disruption of the Church of Scotland in 1843, Kirkmadrine 3 was removed to the new Stoneykirk Free Church manse (NX 096 488), 1.7 km to the east, and built into the gate pillar (Maxwell 1916–17, 203).[6]

Kirkmadrine 1 and 2 were noted in their new position by the Ordnance Survey a few years later: 'Kirkmadrine: This name applies to the ruins of an old church and its adjoining grave yard. The latter is still used as a burying ground which has recently been rebuilt by the proprietor ... Note. the pillars to which the grave yard gate is hung has some antique inscriptions thereon' (OS Name Book, Wigtown No 70 (1847-8), p 18).

Approximately a decade later Dr A. Mitchell first

---

[4] Mitchell appears to be mistaken in suggesting that the stone has been squared since the inscription was cut (Mitchell 1870–72, 579).

[5] Romilly Allen dates this drawing to 1822 (ECMS iii 1903, 495), but Mitchell only stated that Todd had made the drawing fifty years before its recovery (Mitchell 1870–72, 569). It is therefore probable that Allen assumed the drawing to have been made fifty years before the date of its publication in 1872, rather than fifty years before Mitchell's meeting with Todd, which took place c. 1860. Todd was born in 1774 (Donaldson 1924, 20).

[6] The Rev. M'Neil, who was apparently responsible for the reuse of Kirkmadrine 1 and 2 as gateposts, was probably also responsible for authorising the reuse of Kirkmadrine 3 in the gate pillar of the new manse, as he threw in his lot with the breakaway Free Church in 1843 (Scott 1917, 355; Brown 1884, 800).

noted the two inscribed gate pillars, and subsequently arranged for casts to be made (Mitchell 1870–72, 568–9). The date of Mitchell's visit is not recorded, as he did not publish his findings for another ten years, but the casts were donated to the National Museum in June 1861 (Donations 1860–62, 293).[7] Mitchell saw Todd the year after his first visit, and was given the drawing of the three stones. For reasons discussed under Low Curghie, it is possible that this meeting took place shortly before 1860. Todd died in May 1863, aged 89 (Donaldson 1924, 22).

Mitchell's discovery brought the two stones to general attention, and they were scheduled under the Ancient Monuments Protection Act of 1882. However, they remained in use as gateposts until 1890 (see Starke 1887–90, 170; Harper 1896, 361), when an open alcove was built at the end of the restored burial chapel, and all the known stones were placed behind an iron railing (SRO/MW.1/1060). But the abraded 'W' of the Alpha and Omega inscription on Kirkmadrine 1, which is visible on the cast taken in 1861, had already been chipped off by the time of this move (see memo by Pitt Rivers in SRO/MW.1/1060, dated December 22 1886). Both pillars had also had holes bored in them in order to hang the gates, as shown in a drawing of the same date in SRO/MW.1/1060 (Craig 1992, Pl. 134a).

Todd's drawing of the missing stone was published by Mitchell in 1872 (Mitchell 1870–72, Pl. XL), but the stone itself was not recovered until the autumn of 1916, when the gate pillar at Stoneykirk manse was repaired. This gate pillar was a conical drum-like construction 6ft high and 11ft in circumference (Brown 1921, Pl. I, 2). The inscribed stone was placed horizontally and ran the full width of the pillar. It is probable that this stone was originally of similar length to Kirkmadrine 1 and 2, but the lower part had been removed and an iron staple inserted into the foot, on which the upper part of the gate was hung (see elevation in SRO/MW.1/1060; Craig 1992, Pl. 134b). The inscription was on the lower face, and only noticed by the mason after he had started to break up the stone for building material (Robertson 1916–18, 140; Maxwell 1916–17, 202–4).

It should be noted that this sequence has not previously been established in detail (though see Brown 1921, 30–3). Therefore C. Thomas was able to say: 'The Kirkmadrine stones were not found *in situ*' (Thomas 1968, 118, fn 40), whilst giving a reference to Maxwell 1916–17, 99, which only mentions the stones as gateposts. His assumption therefore that the Kirkmadrine stones came from the same site as Low Curghie (Thomas 1981a, 284), which was found 12 km (7 miles) to the south, must be questioned. Both Kirkmadrine 1 and 2 are about 2 metres in height and weigh at least 450 kg (1000 lbs) each. But as he says: 'Kirkmadrine itself shows no signs at all, either from the air or on the ground, of any form of enclosed cemetery of early type' (Thomas 1968, 102; see also Thomas 1981a, 388, fn 48). The present burial ground is a raised mound situated on the crest of a low ridge.

Kirkmadrine 1 and 2 are both about 2 metres high, expanding in width at the base; Kirkmadrine 3 was probably about the same height, as suggested in Todd's drawing, before being cut down for use in the gate pillar. An elevation of it in this position shows the remnants of an expanded foot (SRO/MW.1/1060; Craig 1992, Pl. 134b). It is therefore possible, as Baldwin Brown argued in detail (Brown 1921, 43–8), that the base of each stone was embedded in a mound, such as a cairn or barrow.[8]

It is not clear if the phrase 'as they stand' on Todd's drawing implies that the three stones were placed side by side, with Kirkmadrine 3 in the middle, as shown in the published engraving (Mitchell 1870–72, Pl. XL). M'Neil suggested that the Todd drawing might be used to fix the original position of the stones in the graveyard (M'Neil 1952, 177), but this is not possible using Mitchell's version, though Todd's original sketch may have been more detailed.[9] That these stones acted as foci for subsequent burial at Kirkmadrine is demonstrated by the later series of carvings from this site, which despite a lack of excavation, has produced about ten cross-slabs (RCAHMS 1912, 156–7; Radford & Donaldson 1984, 30–2; Craig 1992, III, 135–47).

These three stones have recently been seen as separated over a period of several hundred years, with Kirkmadrine 1 being dated to the 5th century, and Kirkmadrine 3 to the early 7th (Radford & Donaldson 1984, 31). But given that all three stones appear originally to have been of the same type, despite the damage to the base of

---

[7] There are also brief references to Kirkmadrine 1 and 2 in articles by Prof. J.Y. Simpson dated January 28 and February 11 1861, five months earlier (1860–62a, 17; 1860–62b, 130). Simpson was the first person to be informed of the find, and he donated the casts (Mitchell 1870–72, 569).

[8] The Welsh Penmachno inscription, which also carries a chi-rho cross, refers to burial 'in hoc congeries lapidum' (Nash-Williams 1950, 92, no 101). The Manor Water stone, Peebles (Macalister 1945, 486, no 511) was taken from a cairn (Macdonald 1935–36, 36). Similarly the Catstane, Midlothian (Macalister 1945, 486, no 510), which originally stood on the edge of a low circular mound (Simpson 1860–62b, 126; Rutherford & Ritchie 1972–74, 185–6), and the Yarrow Stone, Selkirk (Macalister 1945, 493, no 515; RCAHMS 1957, 110–3, no 174), both refer to burial 'in hoc tumulo' (see also Nash-Williams 1950, nos 41, 289, 294, 409). Radford's argument against this reading of the word 'tumulo' does not distinguish between cairn and barrow burial (RCAHMS 1957, 112). See also the evidence from Wales cited by Davies (1982, 186–8).

[9] Although Todd appears to have given the sketch to Mitchell in about 1860 (Mitchell 1870–72, 570–3), and despite a statement by Reid that it is 'now in the library of the Society of Antiquaries, Edinburgh' (Reid 1957–58, 184), enquiries at the RMS, the NMRS, the SRO, and the National Library of Scotland, have failed to locate the original sketch. It does not appear in the RMS catalogue of Society of Antiquaries of Scotland manuscripts.

Kirkmadrine 3 resulting from its horizontal reuse in the gate pillar, it is possible, despite the use of insular majuscule on Kirkmadrine 1 and 2, and the introduction of half-uncial letters on Kirkmadrine 3, that Radford's chronology is excessively extended, and that all three stones were carved within a single generation, as R.G. Collingwood implied (1936–38, 285–9). It is noticeable that all three inscriptions use the same form of ligature in the word ET, which occurs on all three stones (Collingwood 1936–38, 28–67), and is also found in the inscription on the Peter stone. The omega on Kirkmadrine 1 is of minuscule type, also found on Maughold 41 (21), in the Isle of Man, a stone which carries a chi-rho of cross-of-arcs type (Trench Jellicoe 1980, 202, Pl. XIa). Chi-rho crosses of any form are rare in Wales, with only two examples (Nash-Williams 1950, 16), yet in Ireland where the monogram form is found on at least seven examples (Hamlin 1972, Fig. 3, with additions), horizontal Latin inscriptions are extremely rare (Nash-Williams 1950, 7; Higgitt 1986b, 128). It is therefore possible that these stones with open rhos are the result of direct Mediterranean influence and contacts, as Frantz (1929) would imply, and as Charles Thomas has recently shown (1992b, 7; 1992a, 9–13). Evidence for long-range contacts with this area is provided by the discovery of Type A table ware and Type B amphorae in the Whithorn excavations (pp 315-9). It is evident this site is of such potential interest that, as Thomas noted in his recent Whithorn lecture (1992a, 20), survey and excavation at Kirkmadrine appear to be an essential research project.

Low Curghie

This stone was first noted in 1860 by William Todd, the schoolmaster at Kirkmaiden who originally recorded the Kirkmadrine inscriptions: 'Nigh to the house of Low Curghie, a grave was lately opened up, covered with a flag of slaty stone, on which was a Latin inscription; but so wasted by time that nothing could be gathered from it further than that the person's name was Ventidius, and that he was a subdeacon of the Church. The inscription shows that this grave was not one of the most ancient kind, being evidently made after Christianity was professed in the land' (Todd 1860, iii–iv). But the significance of this passage was only noticed a century later by R.C. Reid (1957–58, 184–5). The inscription has more recently been discussed by C. Thomas (1968, 103; 1981a, 284–5; 1992b, 3, 7; 1992a, 8-9).[10]

At an unspecified date ('some years ago') Todd informed Dr A. Mitchell about the missing Kirkmadrine stone (Kirkmadrine 3) which he had drawn fifty years before (Mitchell 1870–72, 569). He also gave him one version of the history of the Drummore slab (*op. cit.*, 582). It is therefore difficult to understand why he did not also draw his attention to the Low Curghie find if it had been discovered recently. Reid is mistaken in thinking that Mitchell saw him shortly before 1872, and that Todd, a very old man, had therefore forgotten the find (Reid 1957–58, 184–5). In fact Todd died in 1863, aged 89 (Donaldson 1924, 22), three years after the Low Curghie pamphlet was published. But following Mitchell's initial undated discovery of the Kirkmadrine stones, sufficient time elapsed for casts to be made and donated to the National Museum in June 1861 (Donations 1860–62, 293; see also Mitchell 1870–72, 569). It therefore seems possible that the Low Curghie inscription was discovered after Mitchell's visit to Todd. But since Todd himself died shortly afterwards, the reference in his pamphlet to an inscribed stone went almost unnoticed, possibly because Todd's pamphlet is a history of Kirkmaiden parish: Kirkmadrine is in Stoneykirk parish, 7 miles (12km) to the north. There is no evidence that the slab was retained after its discovery. The grave and its cover were probably re buried.[11]

A possible contemporary record of the find-spot of the 'Latinus' stone

Peter Hill

The excavation of the **Museum Garden** in 1989/90 was preceded by a watching brief during the clearance by Historic Scotland of the stairwell to the north of the crypts, excavated by P R Ritchie. This entailed the examination of his photographic archive then held by Historic Scotland, which includes a print (Historic Scotland Photographic Archive, A 2208–4) of a plan made by William Galloway in July 1886 (Figure 12.2).[12] The plan includes details of features to the south of the church dated 1889, and the features exposed during the excavation of the pathway leading to the parish kirk may thus be an addendum to the original drawing. The area now identified as the north transept of the cathedral (e.g. Radford and Donaldson 1984, 16), was then labelled as the Chapter House, and the plan records a 'frag of cross' lying against the north wall, and a 'Site of pillar' lying some 15' to the south. Although either could mark the find-spot of the 'Latinus' stone, the

---

[10] Reid left out the word 'Low' in his quotation from Todd. As a result Thomas refers to this stone as 'Curghie'. This is slightly confusing as High and Low Curghie are separate farms 1 km apart. The site (RCAHMS 1985, 29, no 181; c. NX 129376) is farther south than shown on Thomas' map (1968, 101).

[11] A number of cist burials have been recorded S.W. of Kilstay cottage, 600 m to the N. of Low Curghie (c NX 125381). There is also a supposed church site in the field 150 m S.S.W. of this cottage. See RCAHMS 1985, 11, no 42; 27, no 168.

[12] I am grateful to Historic Scotland for permission to reproduce this photograph.

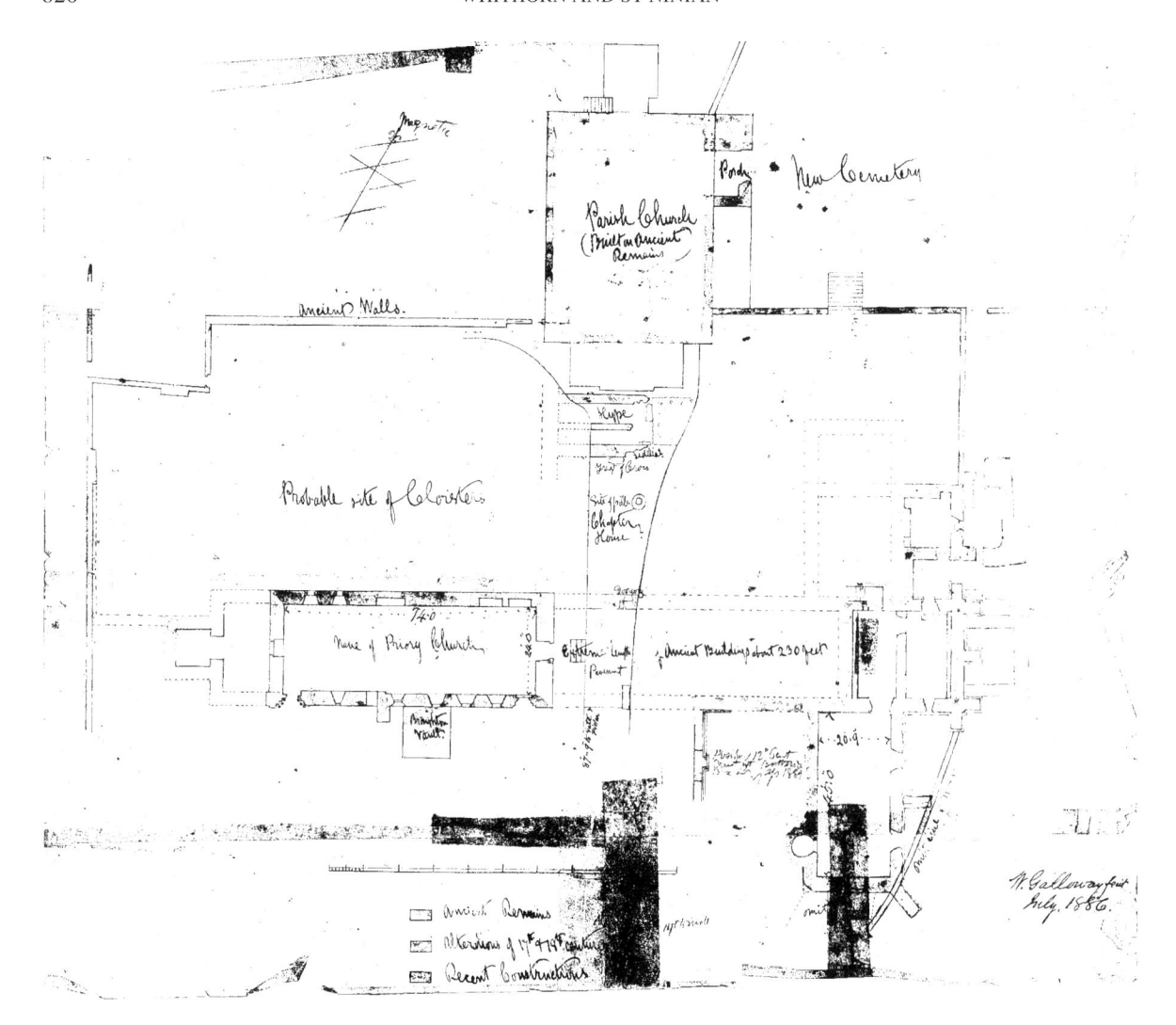

12.2 William Galloway's plan of Whithorn Priory showing probable find-spot of the 'Latinus' stone.

'frag of cross' is marked by an outline of appropriate size (*c.* 5' by 2'6"), and its position corresponds well with M'Kerlie's description (above). William Galloway's interest in the putative Constantinian chi-rho is evident from his letter to Pitt-Rivers (above), and it is thus plausible that he would have described the stone as a 'frag of cross', despite the relative invisibility of the chi-rho. This is thus likely to mark the position from which the stone was recovered in the nineteenth century, and it may have been incorporated in the foundations or floor of the north transept of the twelfth century church. Its original position remains unknown.

APPENDIX 2

Metalwork and Sculpture: Design and Patronage in *c*. 900 AD

Andrew Nicholson

Five late-ninth/earlier-tenth century artefacts from the excavation establish important links with a group of 'Celtic-Norse' objects from the Isle of Man and the Western Isles. Details of their design suggest they were made by Scandinavian craftsmen, but drew on Hiberno-Saxon and Celtic motifs. This group of copper-alloy objects can be linked with some of the sculptures of the Whithorn School, while the designs on harness mounts associated with one of the buckles are closely comparable to the hexafoil cross incised on a slab from the floor of the **Period III/3** church. These multiple links (Figure 12.3) suggest that the Machars contributed to the development of these objects, and that one workshop was probably located at Whithorn.

The three principal objects are a putative leather motif piece (**a**, LR16.1), a copper-alloy buckle (**b**, BZ18.4), and the hexafoil design from the **Period III/1** church (**c**, SE14.17, Figures 5.4 and 10.108). Two ring pins (BZ15.3 and 4) help to correlate the Whithorn finds with the related material from the Isle of Man. An arciform design on an ingot mould (**d**, SE45.3) of the later-seventh or earlier-eighth century helps to establish the ancestry of arciform designs in the area.

The Whithorn buckle belongs to a series of copper-alloy objects, primarily buckles and bridle fittings, whose distribution is otherwise confined to Ireland, the Isle of Man and the Western Isles of Scotland. These are characterised by attached, hollow, hemispherical bosses set within incised circles, frequently with adjacent panels of interlace design. Michelli, in discussing the contemporary bossed penannular brooches, suggested that while the type, material, and possibly the iconography and overall style of an artefact give information about the patron; the technique, style and internal structures of the decoration reflect the craftsman's professional origin; and the detail of the decoration indicates his professional history (Michelli 1991, 18–23). Engraving, the form of decoration on the copper-alloy objects, is seen as a Scandinavian tradition rather than an Insular one, if used as the primary means of decoration. Interlace is not culturally specific, nor is there any indication that the use of bosses is, either. However it is possible to suggest some affinities between Whithorn material and the group of copper-alloy objects.

The decorated leather offcut (**a**) makes most sense as a trial or motif piece, and is thus likely to have been made at Whithorn, although the buckle could have been imported. It bears a design matched on the Whithorn buckle (**b**) and on a strap-end (**j**) from the Udal (Graham-Campbell 1973, Fig. 51), which was also used in the plain interlace on the sculptured stones Whithorn 6 (**q**) and 15 (**ri**), and the lower panel of Glenluce 1 (**hi**).[13] The main panel of Glenluce 1 (**hii**) utilises a closed ring around the crossover of the interlace, and this design is also found on one of the harness mounts (**k**) from the Viking burial at Balladoole,[14] Isle of Man (Bersu and Wilson 1966, Pl. 5a), as well as on one of the carved slabs (**f**) from Kirk Andreas, Isle of Man (Cubbon 1926, 29), and the Machars sculptures Wigtown 1 (**g**) and Whithorn 9 (**e**) and 13 (**p**).

The raised boss motif is shared by the Whithorn buckle (**b**) and two set of bridle mounts from burials at Balladoole, Isle of Man (including **k** and **l**) and Kiloran bay, Colonsay, but they differ in the treatment of the terminals of the adjacent interlace. The interlace on the Whithorn buckle ends in two closed loops, and this style is also used on a strap end (**i**) from Cronk Moar, Isle of Man (Bersu and Wilson 1966, Pl.VIb), and on a recently-discovered strap end from Ashaig, Skye (Miket 1994, 43–4). The terminals of the interlace on the Balladoole pieces have an outer strand following the convex curvature of the edge of the decorative zone as it interfaces with the concentric rings around the boss. This design is also used in the relationship of the interlace panel and the head of the cross on the stone sculpture Whithorn 9 (**e**), which also utilizes the closed ring at the crossover. Whilst other mounts from Colonsay have specifically Celtic motifs, the piece with interlace (**t**) utilises a knotwork pattern (Adcock's

---

[13] The numbering follows Craig (1992).

[14] The Balladoole finds have been interpreted as a possible bridle harness decorated with strip and six or eight circular mounts (Bersu and Wilson 1966, Fig. 16). Although the designs on the strips and circular mounts are dissimilar, they are likely to have been the product of the same workshop.

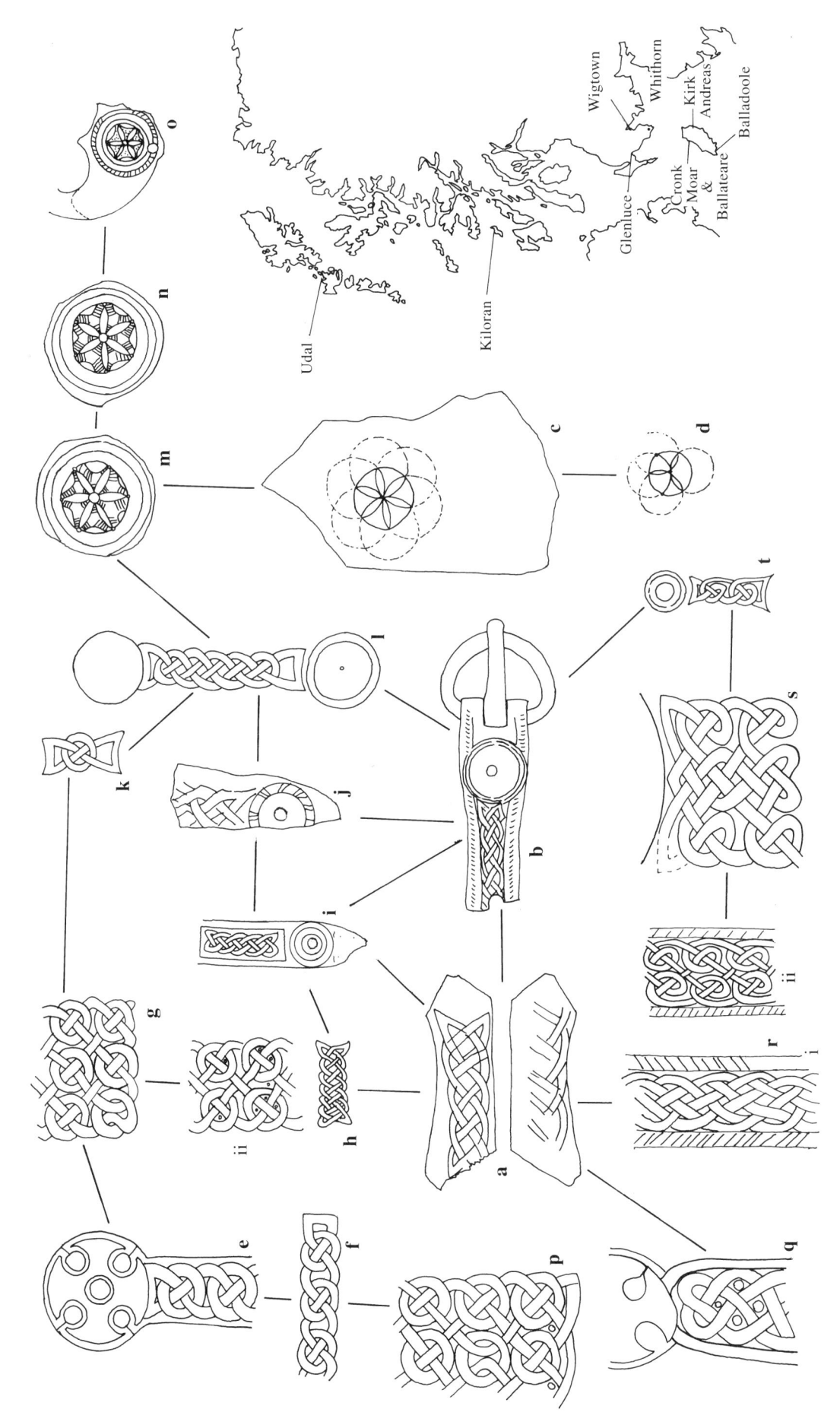

12.3 Design features linking late-ninth and tenth century objects from Whithorn with metalwork from Man and the Western Isles, and sculpured stones from the Machars. **a-e** Whithorn excavations, **f** Kirk Andreas, **g** Wigtown, **h** Glenluce, **i** Cronk Moar, **j** The Udal, **k-n** Balladoole, **o** Knock y Doonee, **p-s** Whithorn Museum, **t** Kiloran Bay Colonsay.

Type A asymmetrical loop; Adcock 1978, 34) matched on Whithorn sculptures 12 (**s**) and 15 (**r** ii), with the terminal outer strand again following the curvature of the rings around the domed boss.

The metalwork group has been ascribed to the period 850–950 AD (Bersu and Wilson 1966, 85; Graham-Campbell 1973, 128), but two of the Manx assemblages (Balladoole and Ballatear) included ring-headed pins of *c*. 870–920 AD (Fanning 1983b), and a polyhedral-headed ring pin from the Cronk Moar burial is closely comparable with the Whithorn pin (BZ15.4) stratified over the **Period III/1** church, and is unlikely to have been deposited prior to 925 AD (Fanning 1994). Current thinking suggests that the sequence of pagan burials which produced the majority of the copper-alloy objects probably spans no more than a couple of generations.[15] Given the dating of the pins this would place the graves in a date bracket of *c*. 890–930 AD. The metalwork is thus slightly earlier than the generally accepted date of the Whithorn School sculptures,[16] but shows the cultural milieu within which the Whithorn craftsmen were working, whilst the leather fragment shows that the local craftsmen were *au fait* with contemporary styles.

Five circular bridle mounts (including **m** and **n**) from Balladoole (Bersu and Wilson 1966 Pls. Vf and VIc) and a penannular brooch (o) from another Viking burial at Knoc y Doonee, Isle of Man (Cubbon 1986, 31) bear incised hexafoil motifs, with emphasis placed on the central point and six circumferential points. These designs are similar to the hexafoil cross (**c**) incised on a paving slab in the **Period III/1** church, where the circumferential points are indented, as the rotational point for the scribing compasses, and found on other arciform designs. Craig points to the development of the cross-of arcs into the later cross styles (pp 441, 617), and to the sculptural links between Whithorn and Maughold, Isle of Man (above). An unfinished hexafoil design (**d**) scribed on an ingot mould of the later-seventh or earlier-eighth century, links back to the cross slab of *Inruit* from Maughold (Harrison 1986, 26), and to Irish metalwork of the sixth and seventh centuries (Youngs 1989, 42–4). The distinction between the earlier Irish hexafoils, and the later sculptural stonework and metalwork, is the absence of indented points on the first, and their emphasis on the later pieces. This suggests that the later metalwork may have been derived from extant visible stone models, rather than ascribed a direct link with the Irish metalwork which precedes it by a good two centuries.

The group of copper-alloy buckles and mounts from the western seaboard stands clearly linked into the sculptural sequence, reflecting a transitional period unrepresented in the current corpus of carved stone. Such close links between sculpture and metalwork are also reflected in both earlier and later sculptural works from the area (Bailey, forthcoming). These stylistic links suggest the bronze buckle from Whithorn and the related objects from elsewhere belong within an ongoing artistic tradition, which also produced the Whithorn School sculptures. The use of incised ornament on these pieces suggests that the craftsmen were trained in Scandinavian workshops, while the use of the hexafoil motif from Whithorn suggests British or Anglo-British patronage. The leather offcut gives a hint that at least one of these Celtic/Norse craftsmen was working at Whithorn, and the copper-alloy artefacts, such as the buckle, or the harness fittings, may have been the product of a Whithorn workshop.

This provides an added dimension to the toponymic evidence of Scandinavian settlement in the Machars (Figure 2.17 pp 52-4). Four of the related metalwork groups come from pagan burials, of which one, Balladoole, is in a formerly Christian burial ground, and another, Kiloran Bay, evidences Christian links (Crawford 1987, 162–3), and all are apparently Norse. The craftsmen were apparently of Scandinavian origin, and their workshops must have been established some time before these burials. It is thus likely that they were established by the end of the ninth century, and that their market extended to the pagan Norse settlements on the Isle of Man and the Hebrides. Their presence in Dublin at a later date (P. Wallace and O. Owen, Pers. Comm.) suggests that Ireland was not the point of origin. The sculptural links show at least access to a common repertoire of patterns, although the shared approaches to linking panels of interlace to circles (the disk-heads of the crosses and bosses of the metalwork) suggest a somewhat closer connection.

---

[15] Rynd lecture 1996.
[16] Collingwood proposed a floruit post 950 AD, others have been more reticent. Some of the sculptural parallels for the metalwork use plain interlace, rather than the stopped plait style which should post-date 925 AD.

Abbreviations

BMC	*Catalogue of English Coins in the British Museum. Anglo-Saxon Series*, C.F. Keary and H.A. Grueber. 2 vols., 1887–93.
BMS	*SCBI-British Museum Anglo-Saxon Coins V*, M.M. Archibald and C.E. Blunt, 1986.
CDS	*Calendar of Documents relating to Scotland*, J Bain (ed), 1881-8, Edinburgh.
CPL	*Calendar of Entries in the Papal Registers relating to Great Britain and Ireland: Papal Letters*, W.H. Bliss *et al.* (eds), 1893-, London.
R. and M. (1984)	(*The late*) S.E. Rigold and D.M. Metcalf, 'A revised check-list of English finds of sceattas', *SEC* (1984), 245–68.
RMS	*Registrum Magni Sigilli Regam Scotorum*, J.M. Thomson *et al.* (eds), 1882-1914, Edinburgh.
SCBI	*Sylloge of Coins of the British Isles*.
SCBI Chester I	Grosvenor Museum, Chester, I, E.J.E. Pirie, 1964.
SCBI Cop. IIIA	*SCBI, 13: National Museum, Copenhagen IIIA*, G. Galster, 1970.
SCBI Cop. I	*SCBI, 4: National Museum, Copenhagen I*, G. Galster, 1964.
SCBI Merseyside	*SCBI, 29: Merseyside County Museums*, M. Warhurse, 1982.
YC	Yorkshire Collections (York and Leeds).

ASNI = Archaeological Survey of Northern Ireland
ONB = Original Name Books of the Ordnance Survey (NMRS/SRO MSS)
RCAHMS = Royal Commission on the Ancient and Historical Monuments of Scotland
RCHME = Royal Commission on Historical Monuments (England)
SRO = Scottish Record Office

Bibliography

Adkins, G 1978 'The theory of interlace and interlace types in Anglian sculpture' *in* Lang, J (ed), 33–45.

Alcock, E A 1992 'Burials and cemeteries in Scotland' *in* Edwards, N and Lane, A (eds), 125–30.

Alcock, L (ed) 1963 *Dinas Powys: an Iron Age, Dark Age and Early Medieval settlement in Glamorgan*. Cardiff.

Alcock, L 1987a *Economy, Society and Warfare among the Britons and Saxons*. University of Wales Press, Cardiff.

Alcock, L 1987b 'Pictish studies: present and future' *in* Small, A (ed) 80–92.

Alcock, L 1988a 'The activities of potentates in Celtic Britain, AD 500–800: a positivist approach' *in* Driscoll, S T and Neike, M R (eds), 22–46.

Alcock, L 1988b 'The Rhind Lectures 1988–89: a synopsis. An heroic age: war and society in northern Britain, AD 450–850', *Proc Soc Antiq Scot 118*, 327–34.

Alcock, L 1993 *The Neighbours of the Picts: Angles, Britons and Scots at war and at home* (= Groam House Lecture). Dornoch.

Alcock, L forthcoming *Cadbury Castle, Somerset: the early historic archaeology*. University of Wales Press, Cardiff.

Alcock, L and Alcock, E A 1990 'Reconnaissance excavations on Early Historic fortifications and other royal sites in Scotland, 1974–84: 4, Excavations at Alt Clut, Clyde Rock, Strathclyde, 1974–5', *Proc Soc Antiq Scot 120*, 95–149.

Alcock, L, Alcock, E A and Driscoll, S T 1989 'Reconnaissance excavations on Early Historic fortifications and other royal sites in Scotland, 1974–84: 3, Excavations at Dundurn, Strathearn, Perthshire, 1976-7', *Proc Soc Antiq Scot 119*, 95–149.

Alcock, L, Alcock, E A, Bateson, J D and Webster, P V 1992 'Excavations at Alt Clut, 1974–5: catalogue of coins, metal object and Romano-British pottery', *Proc Soc Antiq Scot 122*, 289–93.

Allen, J R, and Anderson, J 1903 *The Early Christian Monuments of Scotland*. Edinburgh.

Almqvist, B and Greene, D (eds) 1976 *The Seventh Viking Conference*. Dundalk.

Ambrosiani, K 1981 *Viking Age Combs, Comb Making and Comb Makers in the Light of finds from Birka and Ribe* (= Stockholm Studies in Archaeology 2). Stockholm University.

Anderson, A O 1908 *Scottish Annals from English Chroniclers*. London.

Anderson, A O and Anderson, M O 1961 *Adomnan's Life of St Columba*. London.

Anderson, J 1845 'Parish of Stoneykirk' in *The New Statistical Account of Scotland, 4 (Wigton)*, 162–7.

Anderson, J R 1985 *Muir's Textbook of Pathology* (12th edn). Edward Arnold.

Anderson, M O 1978 *Kings and Kingship in Early Ireland*. Edinburgh.

Anderson, R S G 1925–26 'Three crosses in the south-west of Scotland', *Proc Soc Antiq Scot 60*, 266–8.

Anderson, R S G 1926–27 'Crosses and rock sculptures recently discovered in Wigtownshire', *Proc Soc Antiq Scot 61*, 115–22.

Anderson, R S G 1935–36 'Sculptured stones of Old Luce church, Wigtownshire', *Proc Soc Antiq Scot 70*, 139–45.

Archibald, M M *et al.* 1985 'The coinage of Beonna in the light of the Middle Harling hoard', *Brit Numis J*, 55, 10–54.

Archibald, M M and Blunt, C E 1986 *Sylloge of Coins of the British Isles – British Museum Anglo-Saxon Coins V*. London.

Armelagos, G J and Chrisman, O D 1988 'Hyperostosis frontalis interna: a Nubian case', *Am J Phys Anthrop 76*, 25–8.

Armit, I (ed) 1990 *Beyond the Brochs*. Edinburgh.

Armstrong, P and Ayres, B 1987 'Excavations in High Street and Blackfriargate. Hull' (= Old Town Report Series, No 5), *East Riding Archaeologist Vol 8*.

Armstrong, P, Tomlinson, D, Evans, D H (eds) 1991 *Excavations at Lurk Lane Beverley, 1979–82* (= Sheffield Excav Rep 1.)

Armstrong, E C R 1922 'Irish bronze pins of the Christian period', *Archaeologia 72*, 71–86.

Arnold, C J 1988 *An Archaeology of the Early Anglo-Saxon Kingdoms*. London.

Arnold, T (ed) 1882 *Symeonis Monachi Opera Omnia. I Historia Ecclesiae Dunhelmensis* (= Rolls Series, No. 75 i). London.

Arnold, T (ed) 1885 *Symeonis Monachi Opera Omnia. II Historia Regum* (= Rolls Series, No. 75 ii). London.

Arwidsson, G and Berg, G 1983 *The Mästermyr Find. A Viking Age tool chest from Gotland*. Stockholm.

ASNI 1966 *An Archaeological Survey of County Down*. Belfast.

Backhouse, J 1981 *The Lindisfarne Gospels*. London.

Bailey, R N 1974 'The Anglo-Saxon metalwork from Hexham' *in* Kirby 1974 (ed), 141–67.

Bailey, R N 1980 *Viking Age Sculpture in Northern England*. London.

Bailey R N forthcoming *Ambiguous birds and beasts: three sculptural puzzles in south-west Scotland* (= Fourth Whithorn Lecture) Friends of the Whithorn Trust, Whithorn.

Baillie, M G L 1982 *Tree-Ring Dating and Chronology*. Croom Helm.

Baillie, M G L 1986 'A sherd of souterrain ware from a dated context', *Ulster J Archaeol 49*, 104–5.

Barber J W (ed) 1981a 'Excavations on Iona, 1979', *Proc Soc Antiq Scot 111*, 282–380.

Barber, J W 1981b 'Wooden objects' *in* Good, G L and Tabraham, C J (eds), 116–23.
Barber, J W 1990a 'Burnt mound material on settlement sites in Scotland' *in* Buckley, V M (ed), 92–6.
Barber, J W 1990b 'Scottish burnt mounds: variations on a theme' *in* Buckley, V M (ed), 96–105.
Barclay, K, and Biddle, M 1990 'Stone and pottery lamps' *in* Biddle 1990, 983–1000.
Barley, M W and Hanson, R P C (eds) 1968 *Christianity in Britain 300–700*. Leicester.
Barnes, R P 1989 *Geology of the Whithorn District*. HMSO, London.
Barrow, G W S 1973 *The Kingdom of the Scots*. London.
Barrow, G W S 1981 *Kingship and Unity*. Edinburgh.
Bateson, J D and Mayhew, N J 1987 *Scottish Coins in the Ashmolean Museum, Oxford, and the Hunterian Museum, Glasgow* (= Sylloge of the Coins of the British Isles 35). Oxford.
Bateson 1973 'Roman material from Ireland: a re-consideration', *Proc Roy Ir Acad 73C*, 21–97.
Baumgartner, E and Kreuger, I 1988 *Phönix aus Sand und Asche; Glas des Mittelalters*. München.
Bayley, J 1988 'Non-ferrous metalworking: continuity and change' *in* Slater, E A *et al.* (eds), 193–208.
Bayley, J 1992 *Anglo-Scandinavian non-ferrous metalworking from 16–22 Coppergate* (= The Archaeology of York 17/7). Counc Brit Archaeol, London.
Bayley, J 1987 'Viking glassworking; the evidence from York', *Annales du 10 Congrès de l'Association internationle pour l'Histoire du Verre*, 245–53.
Beeley, J G and Lunt, D A 1980 'The nature of the biochemical changes in softened dentine from archaeological sites', *J Archaeol Sci 7*, 371–7.
Beresford G 1975 *The Medieval Clay-land Village: Excavations at Goltho and Barton Blount*. (= Soc Medieval Archaeol Monogr Ser 6). London.
Bersu, G and Wilson, D M 1966 *Three Viking Graves in the Isle of Man* (= Soc Medieval Archaeol Monogr Ser 1). London.
Biddle, M 1976 'The towns' *in* Wilson, D M (ed), 99–150.
Biddle, M (ed) 1990 *Object and Economy in Medieval Winchester*, (= Winchester Studies 7). Oxford.
Biddle, M and Hunter J, 1990 'Early medieval window glass' *in* Biddle, M (ed), 350–85.
Bieler, L (ed) 1979 *The Patrician Texts in the Book of Armagh*. Dublin.
Bieler, L 1963 *Ireland: harbinger of the Middle Ages*. London, New York, Toronto.
Bieler, L and Binchy, D A 1963 *The Irish Penitentials* (= Scriptores Latiniae Hiberniae vol. V). Dublin.
Binchy, D A 1962 'Patrick and his biographers, ancient and modern', *Studia Hibernica 2*, 7–123.
Blackburn, M A S 1984 'A chronology for the sceattas' *in* Hill, D and Metcalf, D M (eds), 165–74.
Blackburn, M A S (ed) 1986 *Anglo-Saxon Monetary History*. Leicester.
Blair, J 1992 'Anglo-Saxon minsters: a topographical review' *in* Blair, J and Sharpe, R (eds), 226–66.
Blair, J and Ramsey, N (eds) 1991 *English Medieval Industries: Craftsmen, Techniques, Products*. London.
Blair, J and Sharpe, R (eds) 1992 *Pastoral Care before the Parish*. Leicester
Blunt, C E, Stewart, B H I H and Lyon, C S S 1989 *Coinage in Tenth-Century England from Edward the Elder to Edgar's Reform*. London.
Bogdan, N Q and Wordsworth, J W 1978 *The Medieval Excavations at the High Street, Perth 1975–76, an interim report*. Perth.
Boon, G C 1966 'Roman window glass from Wales', *J Glass Stud 8*, 41–5.
Booth, J 1984 'Sceattas in Northumbria' *in* Hill, D and Metcalf, D M (eds), 71–112.
Booth, J 1987 'Coinage and Northumbrian history, c.790–c.810' *in* Metcalf, D M (ed), 57–90.
Boudeau, E 1970, *Monnaies Françaises (Provinciales)*. repr. Barcelona.
Bradley, J 1982 'Medieval' samian ware – a medicinal suggestion', *Ulster J Archaeol 44–5*, 196–7.

Bradley, J (ed) 1990 *Settlement and Society in Medieval Ireland; Studies presented to F X Martin, o.s.a.* Kilkenny.
Bradley, J 1993 'Moynagh Lough: an insular workshop of the second quarter of the 8th century' *in* Spearman, MR and Higgit, J (eds), 74–81.
Brady, N D K 1988 'The plough pebbles of Ireland', *Tools and Tillage VI:1*, 45–60.
Breeze, D J 1982 *The Northern Frontiers of Roman Britain*. London.
Briggs, G S 1985 'A neglected Viking burial with beads from Kilmainham, Dublin, discovered in 1847', *Medieval Archaeol 29*, 94–108.
Brill, R H 1992 'Chemical analyses of some glasses from Frattesina', *J Glass Stud 34*, 11–22.
Brisbane, M 1988 'Hamwic (Saxon Southampton): an 8th-century port and production centre' *in* Hodges, R and Hobley, B (eds), 101–8.
Brock, S and Ruff, 1988 'Diachronic patterns of change and structural proportions of femora in the prehistoric American South-West', *Am J Phys Anthrop 75*, 113–27.
Brooke, C N L 1982 'Rural ecclesiastical institution in England: the search for their origins', *Settimane ... di studi sull'alto medioevo xxviii*, 685–711.
Brooke, D 1983 'Kirk-compound place-names in Galloway and Carrick', *Trans Dumfriesshire Galloway Natur Hist Antiq Soc 58*, 56–71.
Brooke, D 1987a 'The Deanery of Desnes Cro and the Church of Edingham', *Trans Dumfriesshire Galloway Natur Hist Antiq Soc 62*, 48–65.
Brooke, D, 1987b *The Medieval Cult of St Ninian*. Friends of the Whithorn Trust, Whithorn.
Brooke, D, 1989 'St Ninian and the Southern Picts: speculations as to topography and personnel', *Trans Dumfriesshire Galloway Natur Hist Antiq Soc 64*, 21–42.
Brooke, D 1990 *The Search for St Ninian*. Friends of the Whithorn Trust, Whithorn.
Brooke, D 1991a 'Gall-Gaidhil and Galloway' *in* Oram, R D and Stell, G P (eds), 97–116.
Brooke, D 1991b *Fergus the King*. Friends of the Whithorn Trust, Whithorn.
Brooke, D 1991c 'The Northumbrian settlements of Galloway and Carrick', *Proc Soc Antiq Scot 119*, 295–327.
Brooke, D 1995 *Wild Men and Holy Places: The Ancient Realm of Galloway AD 82–1513*. Edinburgh.
Brothwell, D R (ed) 1963 *Dental Anthropology*. Oxford.
Brothwell, D R 1972 *Digging up Bones*. London.
Brothwell, D R 1981 *Digging up Bones* (3rd edn). Oxford.
Brothwell, D R and Higgs, E (eds) 1969 *Science and Archaeology* (2nd edn). London .
Broun, D 1994 'The origins of Scottish identity in its European context' *in* Crawford, B E (ed), 21–32.
Brown, D 1974 'So-called needle cases', *Medieval Archaeol 18*, 15–14.
Brown, C G and Harper, A E T 1984 'Excavations on Cathedral Hill, Armagh, 1986', *Ulster J Archaeol 47*, 109–61.
Brown, G B 1921 *The Arts in Early England, 5, the Ruthwell and Bewcastle Crosses, the Gospels of Lindisfarne, and other Christian monuments of Northumbria*. London.
Brown, G B 1937 *The Arts in Early England, 6(ii), Anglo-Saxon Sculpture*. London.
Brown, T 1884 *Annals of the Disruption, 1843*. Edinburgh.
Bruce, M F 1986 'The skeletons from the cists' *in* Shepherd, I A G, 17–23.
Bruce, M F, Cross, J F and Kerr, N W 1990 *Human Skeletal Remains from Kirkhill, St Andrews*. Scottish Urban Archaeological Trust, unpublished report.
Bruce-Mitford, R L S, 1960 'Part IV. Decoration and miniatures' *in* Kendrick *et al.*, 107–260.
Brunskill, R W 1985 *Timber Building in Britain*. London.
Bryant, R and Hare, M 1990 'The Lypiat Cross', *Trans Bristol Gloucestershire Archaeol Soc 108*, 33–52.
Buckley, V M (ed) 1990a *Burnt Offerings: International Contributions to Burnt Mound Archaeology*. Dublin.
Buckley, V M 1990b 'Experiments using a reconstructed fulacht with a variety of rock types; implications for the petromorphology of fulacht fiadh' *in* Buckley, V M (ed), 168–74.

Burgess, C and Miket, R (eds) 1984 *Between and Beyond the Walls: Essays on the Prehistory and History of North Britain in Honour of George Jobey*. Edinburgh.

Burns, E 1887 *The Coinage of Scotland*. Edinburgh.

Butler, L A S and Morris, R K (eds) 1986 *The Anglo-Saxon Church. Papers on history, architecture and archaeology in honour of Dr H M Taylor* (= Counc Brit Res Rep, 60). London.

Buxton, D L H 1938 'Platymeria and platycnemia', *J. Anat 73*, 31–8.

Byrne, F J 1973 *Irish Kings and High-Kings*. London.

Caldwell, D H 1981 'Metalwork' *in* Good and Tabraham 1981, 106–16.

Callander, J G 1916 'Notice of a jet necklace found in a cist in a Bronze Age cemetery, discovered on Burgie Lodge Farm, Morayshire, with notes on Scottish prehistoric jet ornaments', *Proc Soc Antiq Scot 50*, 201–40.

Callander, J G 1924 'Fourteenth-century brooches and other ornaments in the National Museum of Antiquities of Scotland', *Proc Soc Antiq Scot 58*, 160–84.

Callander, J G 1932 'Earth-houses at Garry Iochdrach and Bac Mhic Connain, in North Uist', *Proc Soc Antiq Scot 66*, 32–67.

Cameron, N 1985 *Plant Remains from Excavations at Bruce Street, Whithorn 1984*. Unpublished third year dissertation, University of Leeds.

Campbell, E 1988 'The post-Roman pottery' *in* Edwards, N and Lane, A (eds), 124–36.

Campbell, E 1989 'New finds of post-Roman imported pottery and glass from South Wales', *Archaeol Camb 137*, 59–66.

Campbell, E 1990 'A blue glass squat jar from Dinas Powys, South Wales', *Bull Board of Celtic Stud 36*, 239–45.

Campbell, E 1991 *Imported Goods in the Early Medieval Celtic West: with special reference to Dinas Powys*. Unpublished PhD thesis, University of Wales, College of Cardiff.

Campbell, E 1995 'New evidence for glass vessels in western Britain and Ireland in the 6th/7th centuries AD' *in* Foy, D (ed), 35–40.

Campbell, E forthcoming a 'The archaeological evidence for contacts: imports, trade and economy in Celtic Britain AD 400–800' *in* Dark, K R (ed).

Campbell, E forthcoming b 'A review of glass vessels in western Britain and Ireland AD 400–800' *in* Price J (ed).

Campbell, E forthcoming c 'Early medieval artefacts' *in* Kissock, J *et al*.

Campbell, E forthcoming d 'Dark Age pottery and glass from Hen Gastell, Britton Ferry, West Glamorgan', *Medieval Archaeol*.

Campbell, E and Lane, A 1988 'The pottery' *in* Haggarty, A (ed), 208–12.

Campbell, E and Lane, A (eds) 1993 'Excavations at Longbury Bank, Dyfed, an early medieval settlement in South Wales', *Medieval Archaeol 37*, 15–77.

Campbell, J 1979 'Bede's words for places' *in* Sawyer, P H (ed), 34–54.

Campbell, J (ed) 1982 *The Anglo-Saxons*. London.

Campbell, M 1991 'Gold, silver and precious stones' *in* Blair, J and Ramsey, N (eds), 107–66.

Cardy, A H and Hill P H 1992 'In the shadow of St Ninian: life and death in medieval Whithorn' *in Medieval Europe 1992 4*. York.

Cardy, A H 1993 *Report on Human Skeletal Remains from Logies Lane, St Andrews*. Scottish Urban Archaeological Trust, unpublished report.

Cardy, A H 1996 *The Human Skeletal Remains from excavations at The Green, Aberdeen, 1994*. Aberdeen City Council Archaeology Unit, unpublished report.

Carson, R A G (ed) 1971 *Mints, Dies and Currency: Essays in Memory of Albert Baldwin*. London.

Carver, M O H (ed) 1992 *York Minster Excavations I*, HMSO, London.

Casey, J 1984 'Roman coinage of the fourth century in Scotland' *in* Burgess, C and Miket, R (eds), 295–304.

Cayon, J R and Castan, C 1991 *Monedas Espanolas*. Madrid.

Chadwick, N K 1950 'St Ninian: a preliminary study of sources', *Trans Dumfriesshire Galloway Natur Hist Antiq Soc 34*, 9–53.

Chadwick, N K (ed) 1954 *Studies in Early British History*. Cambridge.

Chadwick, N K (ed) 1958 *Studies in the Early British Church*. Cambridge.

Chadwick, N K 1970 'Early literary contacts between Wales and Ireland' *in* Moore, D (ed), 66–77.

Chaplin, R E 1971 *The Study of Animal Bones from Archaeological Sites*. London.

Charles-Edwards, T 1992 'The pastoral role of the church in the early Irish laws' *in* Blair, J and Sharpe, R (eds), 63–80.

Cherry, J 1992 *Medieval Craftsmen: Goldsmiths*. London.

Christison, D and Anderson, J 1905 'Report of the Society's excavations of forts on the Poltalloch Estate, Argyll, in 1904–5', *Proc Soc Antiq Scot 39*, 259–322.

Christopherson, A 1980 'Raw material, resources and production capacity in early medieval comb manufacture in Lund', *Meddelanden från Lunds Universitets Historika Museum* new ser. 3, 150–65.

Clarke, D 1972 'A plough pebble from Colstoun, East Lothian, Scotland', *Tools and Tillage II:1*, 50–1.

Clarke, H B and Simms, A (eds) 1985 *The Comparative History of Urban Origins in Non-Roman Europe: Ireland, Wales, Denmark, Germany, Poland and Russia from the Ninth to the Thirteenth Century* (= Brit Archaeol Rep, Internat Ser, 255). Oxford.

Clarke, H and Carter, A 1977 *Excavations in King's Lynn 1963–70* (= Soc Medieval Archaeol Monogr Ser, 7). London.

Clogg, P forthcoming 'Monkwearmouth coffin fittings' *in* Cramp, R J (ed) forthcoming.

Close-Brooks J and Maxwell S 1974 'The Mackenzie Collection', *Proc Soc Antiq Scot 105*, 287–93.

Clutton-Brock, J 1976 'The animal resources' *in* Wilson, D M (ed), 373–92.

Coad, J G and Streeten, A D (eds) 1982 'Excavations at Castle Acre Castle, Norfolk, 1972–77', *Archaeol J 139*, 138–301.

Coatsworth, E 1978 'The four cross-heads from the Chapter House, Durham' *in* Lang, J (ed), 85–96.

Collingwood P D 1982 *The Techniques of Tablet Weaving*. London.

Collingwood, R G 1938 'The Kirkmadrine inscriptions', *Trans Dumfriesshire Galloway Natur Hist Antiq Soc, 3 ser, 22*, 275–89.

Collingwood, W G and Reid, R C 1928 *Whithorn Priory, Wigtownshire*. London.

Collingwood, W G 1909 'Anglian and Anglo-Danish sculpture at York', *Yorkshire Archaeol J 20*, 149–213.

Collingwood, W G 1922–23 'The early crosses of Galloway', *Trans Dumfriesshire Galloway Natur Hist Antiq Soc, 3 ser, 10*, 205–31.

Collingwood, W G 1927 *Northumbrian Crosses of the Pre-Norman Age*. London.

Cormack, W F 1965 'Northumbrian coins from Luce Sands, Wigtownshire', *Trans Dumfriesshire Galloway Natur Hist Antiq Soc 52*, 149–50.

Cormack, W F 1989a 'Two recent finds of exotic porphyry from Galloway', *Trans Dumfriesshire Galloway Natur Hist Antiq Soc 64*, 43–7.

Cormack, W F 1989b *Fifth Interim Report on Excavations at Barhobble, Mochrum 1984–9* (privately printed).

Cormack, W F 1990 *Sixth Interim Report on Excavations at Barhobble, Mochrum 1984–90* (privately printed).

Cormack, W F 1993a 'Barhobble (Mochrum parish), 12th-century church on earlier ecclesiastical site', *Discovery Excav Scot 1993*, 26.

Cormack, W F 1993b 'Kirkmadrine (Sorbie parish), compass-inscribed circles on church wall', *Discovery Excav Scot 1993*, 26.

Cowan, E J 1991 'The Vikings in Galloway: a review of the evidence' *in* Oram, R D and Stell, G P (eds), 63–75.

Cowan, I B and Easson, D E 1976 *Medieval Religious Houses: Scotland* (2nd edn). London.

Cowgill, J 1994 'Lead vessel from Riby Crossroads', unpublished Site Archive report.

Cowgill, J, de Neergaard, M and Griffiths, N 1987 *Medieval Finds from Excavations in London: 1, Knives and Scabbards*. HMSO, London.

Cowie, T E 1978 'Excavations at the Catstane, Midlothian 1977', *Proc Soc Antiq Scot 109*, 166–201.

Cox, E, Haggarty, G and Hurst, J G 1984 'Ceramic material' *in* Tabraham, C J (ed), 381–98.

Crabtree, P J and Ryan, K (eds) 1991 *Animal Use and Cultural Change* (= MASCA Research Papers in Science and Archaeology, Supplement to Vol 8).

Craddock, P T 1989 'Metalworking techniques' *in* Youngs, S (ed), 170–213.

Craig, D J 1991 'Pre-Norman sculpture in Galloway: some territorial implication' *in* Oram, R D and Stell, G P (eds), 45–62.

Craig, D J 1992 *The Distribution of Pre-Norman Sculpture in SouthWest Scotland: Provenance, Ornament and Regional Groups.* Unpublished PhD thesis, 4 vols, Durham University.

Cramp, R 1969 'Excavations at the Saxon monastic sites of Wearmouth and Jarrow, Co. Durham: an interim report', *Medieval Archaeol 13*, 21–67.

Cramp, R J, 1970a 'Decorated window-glass and millefiori from Monkwearmouth', *Ant J 50*, 327–35.

Cramp, R J, 1971 'The position of the Otley crosses in English sculpture of the eighth to ninth centuries' *in* Milojcic, V (ed), 55–63.

Cramp, R J 1974 'Early Northumbrian sculpture at Hexham' *in* Kirby 1974, 115–40, 172–9.

Cramp, R J, 1975 'Window glass from the monastic site of Jarrow', *J Glass Studies 17*, 88–96.

Cramp, R J 1976 'Monastic sites' *in* Wilson, D M (ed), 201–52.

Cramp, R J 1984 *Corpus of Anglo-Saxon Stone Sculpture, I, County Durham and Northumberland.* Oxford.

Cramp, R J 1993 'A reconsideration of the monastic site at Whitby' *in* Spearman, M R and Higgitt, J (eds), 64–73.

Cramp, R J (ed) forthcoming *The Excavations of the Monastic Sites of Jarrow and Wearmouth.* English Heritage.

Cramp, R J, and Douglas-Home, C 1978 'New discoveries at the Hirsel, Coldstream, Berwickshire', *Proc Soc Antiq Scot 109*, 223–32.

Craw, J H 1930 'Excavations at Dunadd and at other sites on the Poltalloch Estates, Argyll', *Proc Soc Antiq Scot 64*, 111–27.

Crawford, B E 1987 *Scandinavian Scotland.* Leicester.

Crawford, B E 1994 (ed) *Scotland in Dark Age Europe.* St Andrews.

Cross, J F and Bruce, M F 1989 'The skeletal remains' *in* Stones, J A (ed), 119–42.

Crowdy, A 1986 'The pottery' *in* Dixon, P (ed), 38–55.

Crowe, C 1982 'A note on white quartz pebbles found in Early Christian contexts on the Isle of Man', *Isle of Man Natur Hist Antiq Soc 7.4*, 413–15.

Crowe, C 1987 'Excavations at Ruthwell, Dumfries, 1980 and 1984', *Trans Dumfriesshire Galloway Natur Hist Antiq Soc 62*, 40–7.

Cruden, S 1951 'Glenluce Abbey: finds recovered during excavations. Part 1', *Trans Dumfriesshire Galloway Natur Hist Antiq Soc 29*, 177–94.

Cruden, S 1963 *The Scotsman Weekend Magazine*, 4 May 1963.

Cruwys, E and Foley, R A (eds) 1986 *Teeth and Anthropology.* Oxford.

Cubbon, A M 1983 *The Art of the Manx Crosses* (3rd edn) Douglas.

Cubbon, A M 1986 'Digging up the past' *in* Harrison, S (ed), 28–57.

Cubbon, W 1952 *Island Heritage.* Douglas.

Cunliffe, B 1976 *Excavations at Portchester Castle, Volume II: Saxon* (= Rep Res Comm Soc Antiqs London, 33). London.

Curle, A O 1914 'Report on the excavation in September 1913 of a vitrified fort at Rockcliffe, Dalbeattie, known as the Mote of Mark', *Proc Soc Antiq Scot 48*, 125–68.

Curle, A O 1924 'A note on four silver spoons and a fillet of gold found in the nunnery at Iona; and on a finger-ring, part of a fillet, and a fragment of wire, all of gold, found in St. Ronan's Chapel, the nunnery, Iona', *Proc Soc Antiq Scot 58*, 102–11.

Curle, A O 1935 'An account of the excavations of a dwelling of the Viking period at 'Jarlshof' Sumburgh, Shetland, carried out on behalf of H.M. Office of Works', *Proc Soc Antiq Scot 69*, 265–321.

Curle, A O 1939 'A Viking settlement at Freswick, Caithness', *Proc Soc Antiq Scot 77*, 71–110.

Curle, J 1932 'An inventory of objects of Roman and provincial Roman origin found on sites in Scotland not definitely associated with Roman construction', *Proc Soc Antiq Scot 66*, 277–397.

Danachair, C O (ed) 1976 *Folk and Farm: essays in honour of A T Lucas.* Dublin.

Daniels, R 1988 'The Anglo-Saxon monastery at Church Close, Hartlepool, Cleveland', *Archaeol J 145*, 159–210.

Dannenberg, H and Cohn, S, 1877 'Der Münzfund von Lübeck', *Zeitschrift für Numismatik iv* (Berlin), 50–124.

Dark, K R 1992 'Epigraphic, art-historical, and historical approaches to the chronology of Class I inscribed stones' *in* Edwards, N and Lane, A (eds), 51–61.

Dark, K R (ed) forthcoming *External Contacts and the Economy of Celtic Britain AD 400–800.* Woodbridge.

Darwin, C 1881 *The Formation of Vegetable Mould through the Action of Worms.* London.

Dauzat, A 1934 'Araire et charrue, les anciens instruments aratoire: origine et repartition', *La Nature 29–30, I–VIII*, 482–6.

Davey, P J (ed) 1977 *Medieval Pottery from Excavations in the North West.* Liverpool.

Davey, P (ed) 1978 *Man and Environment in the Isle of Man* (= Brit Archaeol Rep, Brit Ser, 54(ii)). Oxford.

Davey, P and Hodges R (ed) 1983 *Ceramics and Trade.* Sheffield.

Davidson, I 1795 'Parish of Whithorn' *in* Sinclair, J (ed), *The Statistical Account of Scotland, 16*, 275–98.

Davies, W, 1982 *Wales in the Early Middle Ages.* Leicester.

Davies, W, 1994 'Ecclesiastical centres and secular society in the Brittonic world in the tenth and eleventh centuries *in* Ritchie, A (ed), 92-101.

Davis, M 1993 'The identification of various jet and jet-like materials used in the Early Bronze Age in Scotland', *The Conservator 17*, 11–18.

Dawes, J D 1980 'The human bones' *in* Dawes, J D and Magilton, J R (eds), 19–82.

Dawes, J D and Magilton, J R (eds) 1980 *The Cemetery of St. Helen-on-the-Walls, Aldwark* (= The Archaeology of York, 12/1). Counc Brit Archaeol, London.

De Hammel, C 1994 *A History of Illuminated Manuscripts.* London.

De Paor, L 1976 'The Viking towns of Ireland' *in* Almqvist, B and Greene, D (eds), 29–37.

Demirjian, A, Goldstein, H and Tanner, J M 1973 'A new system of dental age assessment', *Hum Biol 45*, 211–27.

Demirjian, A and Goldstein, H 1976 'New systems for dental maturity based on seven and four teeth', *Ann Hum Biol 3*, 411–21.

Dickie, W, 1887–90 'Field meeting, 6th of July', *Trans Dumfriesshire Galloway Natur Hist Antiq Soc, ser 2, 6*, 162–9.

Dilworth, M 1994 *Whithorn Priory in the Late Middle Ages.* (= 2nd Whithorn Lecture). Friends of the Whithorn Trust, Whithorn.

Dixon P 1986 *Excavations in the fishing town of Eyemouth 1982–84* (= Border Burghs Archaeology Project Monogr Ser, 1).

Doherty, C 1980 'Exchange and trade in early medieval Ireland', *J Roy Soc Ant Ir 110*, 67–89.

Doherty, C 1985 'The monastic town in early medieval Ireland' *in* Clarke, H B and Simms, A (eds), 45–76.

Dolley, R H M 1966 *Sylloge of Coins of the British Isles: The Hiberno-Norse Coins in the British Museum.* London.

Dolley, R H M 1968 'The Irish mints of Edward I in the light of the coin hoards from Ireland and Great Britain', *Proc Roy Ir Acad 66, C*, 235–97.

Dolley, R H M and Cormack, W F 1967 'A Hiberno-Norse penny of Dublin found in Wigtownshire', *Trans Dumfriesshire Galloway Natur Hist Antiq Soc 44*, 122–5.

Donaldson, A, 1924 'William Todd, parish schoolmaster of Kirkmaiden, 1799–1845', *The Gallovidian Annual 1924*, 20–2.

Donaldson, G 1950 'The bishops and priors of Whithorn', *Trans Dumfriesshire Galloway Natur Hist Antiq Soc 34*, 127–54.

Donations, 1860–62 'Donations to the museum', *Proc Soc Antiq Scot 4*, 293.

Donations, 1969–70 'Donations to and purchases for the museum, 1969–70', *Proc Soc Antiq Scot 102*, 296.

Donnachie, I 1971 *The Industrial Archaeology of Galloway.* Newton Abbot.

Driesch, A von den 1976 *A guide to the measurement of animal bones from archaeological sites* (= Peabody Museum Bulletin 1). Harvard.

Driesch, A von den and Boessneck, J A 1974 'Kritische Anmerkungen zur Widerristhohenberechnung aus Langenmassen vor- und fruhgeschichtlicher Tierknochen', *Saugetierkundliche Mitteilungen 22*, 345–48.

Driscoll, S T and Nieke, M R (eds) 1988 *Power and Politics in Early Medieval Britain and Ireland.* Edinburgh.

Driscoll, S T (ed) forthcoming 'Excavations at Edinburgh Castle'.

Driver, J C 1982 'Medullary bone as an indicator of sex in bird remains from archaeological sites' *in* Wilson, B, Grigson C and Payne S (eds) 251–4.

Dümmler, E (ed) 1895 *Epistoli Karolini Aevi* (= Monumenta Germaniae Historica II). Berlin.

Dumville, D N 1977 'Sub-Roman Britain: history and legend', *History 62*, 173–92.

Dumville, D N 1984 'Gildas and Uinniau' *in* Lapidge, M and Dumville, D N (eds), 207–14.

Dumville, D N 1987 'Textual archaeology and Northumbrian history subsequent to Bede' *in* Metcalf, D M (ed), 43–55.

Dumville, D N 1993 *Saint Patrick A.D. 493–1993*. Woodbridge.

Duncan, A A M 1975 *Scotland: The Making of the Kingdom*. Edinburgh.

Dunlevy, M 1988 'A classification of early Irish combs', *Proc Roy Ir Acad 88C*, 341–422.

Dunning, G C, Hodges, H M W and Jope, E M 1957–8 'Kirkcudbright Castle, its pottery and ironwork', *Proc Soc Antiq Scot 91*, 117–38.

Duns, J 1894 'Antiquarian notes', *Proc Soc Antiq Scot 28*, 126–35.

Edwards, B J N 1992 'The Vikings in north-west England: the archaeological evidence' *in* Graham-Campbell, J (ed), 43–62.

Edwards, N 1990 *The Archaeology of Early Medieval Ireland*. London.

Edwards, N and Lane, A (eds) 1988 *Early Medieval Settlements in Wales AD 400–1100*. Cardiff and Bangor.

Edwards, N and Lane, A (eds) 1992 *The Early Church in Wales and the West*. Oxford.

Egan, G and Pritchard, F 1991 *Dress Accessories c. 1150–c. 1450* (= Medieval finds from excavations in London: 3). London.

Eisenstein, S 1978 'Spondylolysis', *J Bone Jt Surgery 64B(4)*, 488–94.

El Najar, M Y and McWilliams, K R 1978 *Forensic Anthropology*. Charles Thomas.

Elliott, C 1990 *Analysis of Plant Remains from a Hiberno-Norse Ditch at Whithorn*. Unpublished honours dissertation, Durham University.

Emerton, E (ed) 1940 *The Letters of St Boniface*. New York.

Eogan, G 1974 'Report on the excavations of some passage graves, unprotected inhumation burials and a settlement site at Knowth, Co. Meath', *Proc Roy Ir Acad 74C*, 13–112.

Everson, P (ed) 1977 'Excavation in the Vicarage Garden, Brixworth, 1972', *J Brit Archaeol Assoc 130*, 55–122.

Evison, V I 1967 'The Dover ring-sword and other ring-swords and beads', *Soc Antiq London*, Oxford.

Evison, V I 1972 'Glass cone beakers of the 'Kempston' type', *J Glass Stud 14*, 48–66.

Evison, V I 1982a 'Anglo-Saxon glass claw-beakers', *Archaeologia 107*, 43–76.

Evison, V I 1982b 'Bichrome glass vessels of the seventh and eighth centuries', *Studien zur Sachsensforschung 3*, 7–21.

Evison, V I 1983 'Some distinctive glass vessels of the post-Roman period', *J Glass Stud 25*, 87–93.

Evison, V I 1987 *Dover: The Buckland Anglo-Saxon Cemetery*. London.

Evison, V I 1988a 'Vieux-Marché, Place Saint-Lambert, Liège – The glass' *in* Otte, M (ed), 215–9.

Evison, V I 1988b 'Some Vendel, Viking and Saxon glass' *in* Hardh, B et al. (eds), 237–45.

Evison, V I 1990 'Red marbled glass, Roman to Carolingian', *Annales du 11e Congrès de l'Association pour l'histoire du Verre, B,le, 1988*, 217–28.

Evison, V I 1991 'Le verre carolingien' *in* Foy and Sennequier 1991, 137–48.

Ewart, G 1980 'Excavations at Stirling Castle, 1977–1978', *Post-Medieval Archaeol 14*, 23–51.

Ewart, G 1985 *Cruggleton Castle: Report of excavations 1978–81* (= Dumfriesshire Galloway Natur Hist Antiq Soc Occasional Paper). Dumfries.

Fairhurst H 1939 'The galleried dun at Kildonan Bay, Kintyre', *Proc Soc Antiq Scot 123*, 185–228.

Fanning, T 1975 'Some bronze ringed pins from the Irish Midlands', *J Old Athlone Soc 1, 4*, 211–18.

Fanning, T 1969 'The bronze ringed pins from Limerick City Museum', *North Munster Antiq J 12*, 6–12.

Fanning, T 1983a 'Some aspects of the bronze ringed pin in Scotland' *in* O'Connor, A and Clarke, D V (eds), 324–42.

Fanning, T 1983b 'The Hiberno-Norse pins from the Isle of Man' *in* *The Viking Age in the Isle of Man*, Viking Society for Northern Research, University College, London, 27–36.

Fanning, T 1990 'Three ringed pins from Viking Dublin and their significance' *in* Bradley, J (ed), 161–75.

Fanning, T 1992 'Ringed pins, the Hiberno-Norse and the discovery of Vinland', *Archaeology Ireland 6*, 1, 24–6.

Fanning, T 1994 *Viking Age Ringed Pins from Dublin* (= Medieval Dublin Excavations 1962–81 Ser B, Vol. 4). Roy Ir Acad, Dublin.

Fawcett, R 1985 *Scottish Medieval Churches*. Edinburgh.

Fellows-Jensen, G 1991 'Scandinavians in Dumfriesshire and Galloway: the place-name evidence' *in* Oram, R D and Stell, G P (eds), 77–95.

Fellows-Jensen, G 1992 'Scandinavian place-names of the Irish Sea province' *in* Graham-Campbell, J (ed), 31–42.

Fenton, A 1963 'Early and traditional cultivating implements in Scotland', *Proc Soc Antiq Scot 96*, 264–317.

Ferembach, D, Schwidetzky, I and Stloukal, M 1980 'Recommendations for age and sex diagnoses of skeletons', *J Hum Evol 9*, 517–49.

Fernie, E 1983 *The Architecture of the Anglo-Saxons*. London.

Finberg, H P R 1964 *Lucerna: Studies of some problems in the early history of England*. London.

Fleming, D H 1931 *St Andrews Cathedral Museum*. Edinburgh and London.

Foot, S 1992 'Anglo-Saxon minsters: a review of terminology' *in* Blair, J and Sharpe, R (eds), 212–25.

Foote, P G and Wilson, D M 1970 *The Viking Achievement: the society and culture of early medieval Scandinavia*. London.

Forbes, A P 1874 *Lives of S. Ninian and S. Kentigern* (= Historians of Scotland vol. 5). Edinburgh.

Foreman, M 1991a 'The nails' *in* Goodall, 133–5.

Foreman, M 1991b 'The lead and lead alloy' *in* Armstrong, P et. al. (eds), 155–64.

Foreman, M 1991c 'The bone and antler' *in* Armstrong, P et. al. (eds), 183–97.

Foreman, M 1991d 'The objects of stone and fired clay' *in* Armstrong, P et. al. (eds), 105–14.

Foster, J 1958–60 'The Ballantrae cross', *Ayrshire Archaeol Natur Hist Collect, 2 ser, 6*, 9–11.

Fowler, E 1963 'Celtic metalwork of the fifth and sixth centuries A.D.', *Arch. J 120*, 98–160.

Foy, D (ed) 1995a *Le Verre de l'Antiquité tardive et du Haut Moyen Age*. Association Française pour l'Archaeologie du verre/Musée Archeologique du Val D'Oise.

Foy, D 1995b 'Verres du Ve au VIIIe siècles en France méditerranéenne: essai de typo-chronologie' *in* Foy, D (ed), 187–242.

Foy, D and Sennequier, G (eds) 1991 *A travers le Verre du moyen âge à la Renaissance*. Rouen.

Frantz, M A 1929 'The provenance of the open rho in the Christian monograms', *American J Archaeol, ser 2, 33*, 10–26.

Fulford, M G 1989 'Byzantium and Britain: a Mediterranean perspective on post-Roman Mediterranean imports in western Britain and Ireland', *Medieval Archaeol 33*, 1–6.

Fulford, M G and Peacock, D P S 1984 *Excavations at Carthage: the British mission. Vol. 1(2) The Avenue du President Habib Bourguiba, Salammbo: the pottery and other ceramic objects from the site*. Sheffield.

Gailey, A 1984 *The Rural Houses of Northern Ireland*. Edinburgh.

Gaimster, D R M, Margeson, S, and Barry, T 1989 'Medieval Britain and Ireland in 1988', *Medieval Archaeol 33*, 161–41.

Galloway, P 1990 'Combs of bone, antler and ivory' *in* Biddle, M (ed), 665–78.

Galloway, P and Newcomer 1981 'The craft of comb making, an experimental enquiry', *Instit Archaeol Bull. 18*.

Galster, G 1964 *Sylloge of Coins of the British Isles, 4: National Museum, Copenhagen I*. London.

Galster, G 1970 *Sylloge of Coins of the British Isles, 13: National Museum, Copenhagen IIIA*. London.

Garrad, L S 1977 'Was pottery made in the Isle of Man in medieval times?' *in* Davey, P (ed), 109–12.

Garrad, L S 1978 'Medieval pottery in the Isle of Man' *in* Davey, P (ed), 357–65.

Gasse, F 1986 *East African Diatoms*. Cramer.

Gelling, P S 1969 'A metalworking site at Kiondroghad, Kirk Andreas, Isle of Man', *Medieval Archaeol 13*, 67–84.

Gelling, P S 1975 'Ballacraine' *in* Webster, L E and Cherry, J (eds), 230–1.

Germain, H 1981 *Flore des Diatomees, eaux douces et saumatres*. Edition Boubee.
Gilbert, E 1974 'Saint Wilfid's Church at Hexham' *in* Kirby D P (ed), 81–113.
Gilmour, S 1993 EDXRF *Analysis of Whithorn 6th–7th Century A.D. Stone Moulds, Ceramic Moulds and Crucibles*. Unpublished 3rd year project, Edinburgh University.
Good, G L and Tabraham, C J 1981 'Excavations at Threave Castle, Galloway, 1974–78', *Medieval Archaeol 25*, 90–140.
Goodall, I H 1975 'Metalwork from Goltho' *in* Beresford, G (ed), 79–6.
Goodall, I H 1991 'The ironwork' *in* Armstrong *et al*. (eds), 132–46.
Goodall, I H 1982 'Metalwork', 227–240; *in* Coad, J G and Streeten, A D (eds), 138–301.
Goodall, A 1991 'The copper alloy and gold' *in* Armstrong, P *et al*. (eds), 148–55.
Gooder, J W 1993 EDXRF *Analysis of Whithorn Anglian and Hiberno-Norse crucibles*. Unpublished 3rd year project, Edinburgh University.
Goodman, C N and Morant, G M 1939 'The human remains of the Iron Age and other periods from Maiden Castle, Dorset', *Biometrika 31*, 295–312.
Goodman, A H and Rose, J C 1991 'Dental enamel hypoplasias as indicators of nutritional status' *in* Kelley, M A and Larsen, C S (eds), 279–93.
Graeme A S 1914 'An account of the excavation of the Broch of Ayre, St. Mary's Holm, Orkney', *Proc Soc Antiq Scot 48*, 31–51.
Graham-Campbell, J 1973a 'The ninth-century Anglo-Saxon hornmount from Burghead, Morayshire, Scotland', *Medieval Archaeol 17*, 43–51.
Graham-Campbell, J 1973b 'A fragmentary bronze strap-end of the Viking period from the Udal, North Uist, Inverness-shire', *Medieval Archaeol 17*, 128–31.
Graham-Campbell, J 1976 'Viking-age silver and gold hoards from Scotland', *Proc Soc Antiq Scot 107*, 114–35.
Graham-Campbell, J 1980 *Viking Artefacts: a select catalogue*. London.
Graham-Campbell, J (ed) 1992 *Viking Treasure from the North West: the Cuerdale Hoard in its context*. Liverpool.
Grant, M A and Murison D D (eds) 1956 *The Scottish National Dictionary Vol. 4*. Edinburgh.
Grant, A 1982 'The use of tooth wear as a guide to the age of domestic ungulates' *in* Wilson, B, Grigson, C and Payne, S (eds), 91–108.
Greig, D C 1971 *British Regional Geology: The South of Scotland* (3rd edn). Edinburgh.
Grierson, P and Blackburn, M A S, 1986 *Medieval European Coinage, 1*. Cambridge.
Griffiths, D 1992 'The coastal trading ports of the Irish Sea' *in* Graham-Campbell, J (ed), 63–72.
Grigson, C and Mellars, P 1987 'The mammalian remains from the middens' *in* Mellars, P (ed), 243–79.
Grove, R 1990 *Analysis of Plant Remains from an Early Christian Pit at Whithorn*. Unpublished honours dissertation, Durham University.
Guido, C 1978 *Glass beads of the Prehistoric and Roman periods in Britain and Ireland* (= Rep Res Comm Soc Antiqs London, 35). London.
Habermehl, K-H 1961 *Die Altersbestimmung bei Haustieren, Pelztieren und beim jagdbaren Wild*. Paul Parley, Berlin.
Haddan, A W and Stubbs, W (eds) 1871 *Councils and Ecclesiastical Documents Relating to Great Britain and Ireland. Vol III*. Oxford.
Haggarty, A 1988 'Iona: some results of recent work', *Proc Soc Antiq Scot 118*, 208–12.
Haggarty, G R 1980 'The pottery' *in* Ewart 1980, 36–46.
Haggarty, G R 1981 'Pottery: coarsewares' *in* Good, G L and Tabraham, C J (eds), 129–31.
Haggarty, G R 1985 'The pottery' *in* Ewart, G (ed), 56–63.
Haggarty, G and Haggarty, A 1983 'Excavations at Rispain Camp, Whithorn 1978–81', *Trans Dumfriesshire Galloway Natur Hist Antiq Soc 58*, 21–51.
Hald, M 1972 *Primitive Shoes* (= Nat Mus Denmark Archaeol Hist Ser I), 13.
Hall, R A 1984 *The Viking Dig*. London.
Hall, R A (ed) 1978 *Viking Age York and the North* (= Counc Brit Archaeol Res Rep 27). London.
Hall, R A and Wyman, M 1986 'Ailcy Hill, Ripon', *Bulletin C.B.A. Churches Committee 24*, 17–20.
Hamilton, J R C 1956 *Excavations at Jarlshof, Shetland*. Edinburgh.
Hamilton, M 1906 *Incubation; or, the cure of disease in pagan temples and Christian churches*. St Andrews.
Hamilton, N E S A (ed) 1870 *Willelmi Malmesbiriensis Monachi – De Gestis Pontificarum Anglorum* (= Rolls Series No 51). London.
Hamlin, A 1972 'A chi-rho-carved stone at Drumaqueran, Co Antrim', *Ulster J Archaeol, 3 ser, 35*, 22–8.
Hamlin, A 1982 'Early Irish stone carving: content and context' *in* Pearce, S M (ed), 283–96.
Harbison, P 1982 'Early Irish churches' *in* Lowe, H (ed), 618–29.
Harbison, P 1991 *Pilgrimage in Ireland*. London.
Harcourt 1974 'The dog in prehistoric and early historic studies', *J Archaeol Sci I*, 151–75.
Harden, D B 1956a 'Glass vessels in Britain and Ireland, AD 400–1000' *in* Harden, D B (ed) 1956b, 132–67.
Harden, D B (ed) 1956b *Dark Age Britain*. London.
Harden, D B 1961 'Domestic window glass: Roman, Saxon and medieval' *in* Jope, E M (ed), 39–63.
Harden, D B 1963 'The glass' *in* Alcock, L (ed), 178–88.
Harden, D B 1971 'Ancient glass III: post-Roman', *Archaeol J 128*, 78–117.
Harden, D B 1974 'Window-glass from the Romano-British bath-house at Garden Hill, Hartfield, Sussex', *Antiquaries J 54*, 280–1.
Harden, D B 1976 'The glass' *in* Cunliffe, B (ed), 232–4.
Hardh, B *et al*. (eds) 1988 *Trade and Exchange in Prehistory. Studies in honour of Berta Stjernquist*. Lund.
Hare, M and Hamlin, A 1986 'The study of early church architecture in Ireland: an Anglo-Saxon viewpoint, with an appendix on documentary evidence for round towers' *in* Butler, L A S and Morris, R K (eds), 131–45.
Hargreaves, B 1976 *The Sporting Wife: A guide to game and fish cooking* (1987 edn). H and G Witherby, London .
Harper, M M'L 1876 *Rambles in Galloway – topographical, historical, traditional, and biographical* (1st edn). Edinburgh.
Harper, M M'L 1896 *Rambles in Galloway* (2nd edn). Dalbeattie and London.
Harrison, J R 1990 'The 'slow' method of construction of traditional wet mixed and placed mass subsoil walling in Britain' *in Adobe 90 Preprints* (= 6th International Conference on the Conservation of Earthen Architecture). Getty Conservation Institute, Los Angeles.
Harrison S (ed.) 1986 *100 Years of Heritage. The work of the Manx Museum and National Trust*.
Hartgroves, S and Walker, R 1988 'Excavations in the Lower ward, Tintagel Castle, 1986', *Cornish Studies 16*, 9–30
Hartley, B R 1972 'The Roman occupations of Scotland: the evidence of samian ware', *Britannia III*, 1–55.
Hartley, B R and Dickinson, B M 1980 'Samian ware' *in* MacIvor, I *et al*. (eds), 243–7.
Hattatt, R 1989 *Ancient Brooches and Other Artefacts*. Oxford.
Hawkes, S C and Dunning, G C 1961 'Soldiers and settlers in Britain, fourth to fifth century: with a catalogue of animal-ornamented buckles and related belt-fittings', *Medieval Archaeol 5*, 1–71.
Hawthorne, J G and Smith, C S (trans) 1979 *Theophilus' On Divers Arts*. New York.
Heaton, M 1994 *An Analysis of the Plant Remains from Pit Context Number 9144 from Whithorn*. Unpublished honours dissertation, Durham University.
Heawood, R and Nicholson, A J in prep. 'Northumbrian Chests from Whithorn'.
Heawood, R 1990 *Iron Coffin Fittings from Northumbrian Period Whithorn*. Unpublished MA thesis, Durham University.
Hedges, J 1982 'Fabric types from Lloyds Bank' *in* MacGregor, A (ed).
Heighway, C M 1979 'Miscellaneous small find' *in* Heighway, C M *et al*., 201–3.
Heighway, C M, Garrod, A P and Vince, A G 1979 'Excavations at 1 Westgate Street, Gloucester', *Medieval Archaeol 23*, 159–213.
Heighway, C and Bryant, R 1986 'A reconstruction of the 10th century church of St Oswald, Gloucester' *in* Butler L A S and Morris, R K (eds), 188–95.

Henderson, I B 1987 'Early Christian monuments of Scotland displaying crosses but no other ornament' *in* Small, A (ed), 45–58.

Henderson, J 1991 'The glass' *in* Armstrong, P *et al*. (eds), 124–30.

Henderson, J 1993 'Scientific analysis of the glass' *in* Campbell, E and Lane, A (eds), 46–9.

Henry, F 1937 'Early Christian slabs and pillar stones in the west of Ireland', *J Roy Soc Antiq Ir 67*, 265–79.

Henry, F 1945 'Remains of the Early Christian period on Inishkea North, Co Mayo', *J Roy Soc Antiq Ir 75*, 127–55

Henry, F 1965 *Irish Art in the Early Christian Period to AD 800*. London

Henshall, A S 1950 'Textile and weaving appliances in prehistoric Britain', *Proc Prehist Soc 16*, 130–57.

Henshall, A S 1982 'The finds' *in* Taylor, D B (ed), 225–44.

Herity, M 1984 'The layout of Irish Early Christian monasteries' *in* Ní Chatháin, P and Richter, M (eds), 105–16.

Heyworth, M P 1991 *An Archaeological and Compositional Study of Early Medieval Glass from North-West Europe*. Unpublished PhD thesis, University of Bradford.

Higgitt, J (ed) 1986a *Early Medieval Sculpture in Britain and Ireland* (= Brit Archaeol Rep, Brit Ser, 152). Oxford.

Higgitt, J 1986b 'Words and crosses: the inscribed stone cross in early medieval Britain and Ireland' *in* Higgitt, J (ed), 125–52.

Higham, C F W 1967 'Flock rearing as cultural factor in prehistoric Europe', *Proc Prehist Soc 33*, 84–106.

Higham, N J 1992 'Northumbria, Mercia and the Irish Sea Norse, 893–926' *in* Graham-Campbell, J (ed), 21–30.

Higham, N J 1993 *The Kingdom of Northumbria AD 350–110*. Stroud.

Hill, D and Metcalf, D M (eds), 1984 *Sceattas in England and on the Continent* (= Brit Archaeol Rep, Brit Ser, 128). Oxford.

Hill, P H 1984 *Excavations at Bruce Street, Whithorn 1984: interim report*. SDD: AM, Edinburgh.

Hill, P H 1985 'Whithorn', *Curr Archaeol 96*, 27–9.

Hill, P H 1986 'Whithorn', *Scottish Archaeol Gazette*.

Hill, P H 1987a *Whithorn 1: 1986 excavations*. Whithorn Trust, Whithorn.

Hill, P H 1987b 'Whithorn Priory: multi-period ecclesiastical and secular remains', *Discovery Excav Scot*, 9–12.

Hill, P H 1988a *Whithorn 2: Excavations 1984–1987: interim report*. Whithorn Trust, Whithorn.

Hill, P H 1988b *Whithorn Supplement: 1988 Excavation*. Whithorn Trust, Whithorn.

Hill, P H 1988c 'Whithorn', *Curr Archaeol 110*, 85–91.

Hill, P H 1988d 'Whithorn: multi-period ecclesiastical and secular remains', *Discovery Excav Scot*, 10–11.

Hill, P H 1990 *Whithorn 3: Excavations 1988–1990: interim report*. Whithorn Trust, Whithorn.

Hill, P H 1991a 'Whithorn: the missing years' *in* Oram, R D and Stell, G P (eds), 27–44.

Hill, P H 1991b *The Whithorn Excavation: 1990 Supplement*. Whithorn Trust, Whithorn.

Hill, P H 1991c *The Whithorn Trust 1991 excavation*. Whithorn Trust, Whithorn.

Hill, P H 1992a *Whithorn 4: Excavations 1990–1991: interim report*. Whithorn Trust, Whithorn.

Hill, P H 1992b 'A thousand years of contact: the economy of Whithorn from 450 –1450', *Medieval Europe 1992 5*, York.

Hill, P H and Kucharski, K 1990 'Early medieval ploughing at Whithorn and the chronology of plough pebbles', *Trans Dumfriesshire Galloway Natur Hist Antiq Soc 65*, 73–83.

Hill, P H and Pollock, D C 1992 'The Northumbrian Church at Whithorn', *Medieval Europe 1992 6*. York.

Hillam, J 1985 'Theoretical and applied dendrochronology: how to make a date with a tree' *in* Phillips, P (ed), 17–23.

Hills C 1977 *The Anglo-Saxon Cemetery at Spong Hill, North Elmham. Part 1* (= East Anglian Archaeology, Report No.6). Gressenhall.

Hillson, S 1986 *Teeth*. Cambridge.

Hilton, R C, Ball, J and Benn, R T 1976 'Vertebral end-plate lesions (Schmorl's nodes) in the dorsolumbar spine', *Ann Rheum Dis 35*, 127–32.

Hinton, D A 1980 'The bone and antler objects' *in* Holdsworth, P (ed), 76–7.

Hirata, K 1990 'Secular trend and age distribution of cribra orbitalia in Japanese', *Hum Evol 5*, 375–85.

Hoare, F H 1980 *The Western Fathers*. London.

Hochuli-Gysel, A 1995 'Le verre du IVe-VIe siècles en Aquitaine; un état de la question' *in* Foy (ed).

Hodges, H W M and Jope, E M 1956 'The medieval pottery from Castle Street' *in* Hogg, R (ed), 79–107.

Hodges, R 1982 *Dark Age Economics: The origins of towns and trade A.D. 600–1000*. London.

Hodges, R and Hobley, B (eds) 1988 *The rebirth of the towns in the west AD 700–1050* (= Counc Brit Archaeol Research Rep, 68). London.

Hodges, R and Jennings, S 1981 'Continental medieval imports' *in* Jennings, S (ed), 26–59.

Hoffman, D 1990 *The New Holistic Herbal* (rev edn). Shaftesbury and Rockport, Massachusetts.

Hogg, R (ed) 1956 'Excavations in Carlisle, 1953', *Trans Cumberland Westmorland Antiq Archaeol Soc 55*, 59–107.

Hold, A G 1991 *The Study of the Anglian Vessel and Window Glass from Whithorn using ICPS Analysis*. Unpublished 4th year dissertation, University of Bradford.

Holdsworth, P 1975 'Saxon Southampton; a new review', *Medieval Archaeol 20*, 26–61.

Holdsworth, P 1980 *Excavations at Melbourne St., Southampton 1971–6* (= Counc Brit Archaeol Res Rep, 33). London.

Holdsworth, P (ed) 1987 *Excavations in the Medieval Burgh of Perth 1979–1981* (= Soc Antiq Scot Monogr Ser, 5). Edinburgh.

Holdsworth, P 1992 'A multi-period settlement on the Lothian coast', *Medieval Archaeology 1992 8*, 41–6.

Holmes, N M McQ 1983 'A fifteenth-century coin hoard from Leith', *Brit Numis J 53*, 78–107.

Hooke, B G E 1926 'A third study of the English skull with special reference to the Farringdon Street crania', *Biometrika 18*, 1–55.

Huggins, P J 1970 'Excavation of a medieval bridge at Waltham Abbey, Essex, in 1968', *Medieval Archaeol 14*, 126–48.

Huggins, P J 1976 'The excavation of an 11th-century Viking hall and 14th-century rooms at Waltham Abbey, Essex, 1969–71', *Medieval Archaeol 20*, 75–134.

Hughes, K 1966 *The Church in Early Irish Society*. London.

Hughes, K and Hamlin, A 1977 *The Modern Traveller to the Early Irish Church*. London.

Hunter, F J, McDonnell, J G, Pollard, A M, Morris, C R and Rowlands, C C 1993 'The scientific identification of archaeological jet-like artefacts', *Archaeometry 35*, 69–89.

Hunter, F J 1994 'Dowalton Loch Reconsidered', *Trans Dumfriesshire Galloway Natur Hist Antiq Soc 69*, 53–72.

Hunter, J R 1977 'Glass fragments' *in* Everson, P (ed), 104–7.

Hunter, J R 1980 'The glass' *in* Holdsworth, P (ed), 59–72.

Hunter J R 1986 *Rescue Excavations on the Brough of Birsay 1974–82* (= Soc Antiq Scot Monogr Ser, 4). Edinburgh.

Hurley, M 1988 'Recent archaeological excavations in Waterford City', *Archaeol Ireland 2 (1)*, 17–21.

Hurst, J G 1961 'The kitchen area of Northolt manor, Middlesex', *Medieval Archaeol 5*, 211–300.

Hurst, J G 1966 'Imported flasks' *in Kirkstall Abbey Excavations 1960–1964*. Publ Thoresby Soc LI, 112, 54–9.

Hurst, J G 1977 'Spanish pottery imported into medieval Britain', *Medieval Archaeol 21*, 68–105.

Hurst, J G, Neal, D S and van Beuningen, H J E 1986 'Pottery produced and traded in North-West Europe 1350–1650', *Rotterdam Papers 6*.

Hurst, J G and Haggarty, G R 1981 'Imported finewares and stonewares' *in* Good, G L and Tabraham, C J (eds), 131.

Hustedt, F 1927–1966 *Die Kieselalgen Deutschlands, Oesterreich und der Schweiz*.

Iscan, M Y and Kennedy, A R K 1989 *Reconstruction of Life from the Skeleton*. Alan R Liss.

Isings, C 1957 *Roman Glass from Dated Finds*. Groningen and Djarkata.

Ivens, R J 1989 'Dunmisk fort, Carrickmore, Co Tyrone: excavations 1984–1986', *Ulster J Archaeol 52*, 17–110.

Jorgensen, L B 1993 *North European Textiles until AD 1000*. Aarhus University Press.

Jackson, K H 1955 'The Britons in southern Scotland', *Antiquity 29*, 77–88.

Jackson, K H 1958 'The sources for the life of St. Kentigern' *in* Chadwick, N K (ed), 273–357.

Jackson, R 1988 *Doctors and Diseases in the Roman Empire*. London.

James, E 1988 *The Franks*. Oxford.
James, H 1992 'Early medieval cemeteries in Wales' *in* N Edwards and A Lane (eds), 90–103.
James, S, Marshall, A and Millett, M 1984 'An early medieval building tradition', *Archaeol J 141*, 151–279.
Jarman, A O H 1990 *Aneirin: Y Gododdin. Britain's Oldest Poem*. Wales.
Jennings, S 1981 *Eighteen centuries of pottery from Norwich* (= East Anglian Archaeology, Report No. 13). Gresenhall.
Johanson G 1971 'Age determination from human teeth', *Odont Revy 22* suppl. 22, 27–39.
Jope, E M (ed) 1961 *Studies in Building History. Essays in recognition of the work of B H St J O'Neil*. London.
Jope, E M, Jope, H M, Stewart, I H, and Thompson, J D A 1959 'A hoard of 15thth-century coins from Glenluce sand-dunes and their context', *Medieval Archaeol 3*, 259–80.
Julkunen, H, Heinonen, O P and Pyorala, K 1971 'Hyperostosis of the spine in an adult population', *Ann Rheum Dis 30*, 605–12.
Jurmain, R D 1977 'Stress and the aetiology of osteoarthritis', *Am J Phys Anthrop 46*, 353–66.
Karkov, C and Farrell, R (eds) 1991 *Studies in Insular Art and Archaeology* (= American Early Medieval Studies I). Oxford, Ohio.
Karkov, C 1991 'The decoration of wooden architecture *in* Ireland and Northumbria' in Karkov, C and Farrell, R (eds), 27–48.
Keary, C F and Grueber, H A, 1887–93, *Catalogue of English Coins in the British Museum. Anglo-Saxon Series* (2 vols). London.
Kelley, M 1982 'Intervertebral osteochondrosis in ancient and modern populations', *Am. J Phys Anthrop 59*, 271–9.
Kelley, M A and Larsen C S (eds) 1991 *Advances in Dental Anthropology*. New York.
Kemp, D W (ed) 1887 *Tours in Scotland 1747, 1750, 1760, by Richard Pococke, Bishop of Meath* (= Scottish Historical Society, 1). Edinburgh.
Kendrick, T D 1939 'Gallen Priory excavations, 1934–5', *J Roy Soc Antiq Ir 69*, 1–20.
Kendrick, T D, Brown, T J, Bruce-Mitford, R L S, Roosen-Runge, H, Ross, A S C, Stanley, E G and Werner, A E A 1960 *Evangeliorum Quattuor Codex Lindisfarnensis, II*. Olten and Lausanne.
Kendrick T D 1933 'A gaming board of the Viking period found in Ireland', *Acta Archaeol 4*, 85.
Kermode, P M C 1907 *Manx Crosses, or the inscribed and sculptured monuments of the Isle of Man*. London.
Kerr, N W 1988 'A method of assessing periodontal status in archaeologically derived skeletal material', *J Paleopath 2*, 67–78.
Kerr, N W, Bruce, M F and Cross, J F 1988 'Caries experience in the permanent dentition of late Mediaeval Scots (1300–1600 A.D.)', *Archs Oral Biol 33*, 143–8.
Kilbride-Jones, H E 1938 'Glass armlets in Britain', *Proc Soc Antiq Scot 72*, 366–95.
Kimbell, G S and Stone, P 1992 'Geophysical evidence for a concealed Caledonian intrusive body at Sandhead, Wigtownshire', *Scott J Geol 28 (1)*, 19–25.
King, M D 1992 'Ladywell (Kilspindie parish), cross-slab; spring; quernstones', *Discovery Excav Scot 1992*, 78–9.
Kirby, D P (ed) 1974 *Saint Wilfrid at Hexham*. Newcastle upon Tyne.
Kirby, D P 1987 'Northumbria in the ninth century' *in* Metcalf, DM (ed), 11–25.
Kirby, D P 1991 *The Earliest English Kings*. London.
Kissock, J et al. forthcoming 'Excavations at Llanelen, West Glamorgan', *Archaeol J*.
Knight, I 1984 *The Heights and Weights of Adults in Great Britain*. HMSO, London.
Krogman, W M and Iscan, M Y 1986 *The Human Skeleton in Forensic Medicine* (2nd edn). Charles C Thomas.
Lacaille, A D 1944 'Stone basins', *Glasgow Archaeol Soc Trans 62*, 1953, 41–93.
Laing, L R 1973 'The Mote of Mark', *Curr Archaeol 4/4*, 121–4.
Laing, L R 1974a 'Picts, Saxons and Celtic metalwork', *Proc Soc Antiq Scot 105*, 189–98.
Laing, L R 1974b 'Cooking pots and the origins of the Scottish medieval pottery industry', *Archaeol J 130*, 183–216.
Laing, L R 1975 *The Archaeology of Late Celtic Britain and Ireland c.400–1200 AD*. London.

Laing, L R 1976 'People and pins in Dark Age Scotland', *Trans Dumfriesshire Galloway Natur Hist Antiq Soc 51*, 53–71.
Laing, L R 1985 'The Romanization of Ireland in the fifth century' *Peritia 4*, 261–78.
Lane, A 1990 'Hebridean pottery: problems of definition, chronology, presence and absence' *in* Armit, I (ed), 108–30.
Lane, A 1994 'Trade, gifts and cultural exchange in Dark-Age western Scotland' *in* Crawford (ed), 103–15.
Lang, J T (ed) 1978 *Anglo-Saxon and Viking Age Sculpture and Its Context* (= Brit Archaeol Rep, Brit Ser, 49). Oxford.
Lang, J T 1991 *Corpus of Anglo-Saxon Stone Sculpture, III, York and Eastern Yorkshire*. Oxford.
Langdon, A G 1893 'The chi-rho monogram upon Early Christian monuments in Cornwall', *Archaeol Camb, 5 ser, 10*, 97–108.
Lapidge, M and Dumville, D N (eds) 1984 *Gildas: New Approaches*. Woodbridge.
Larsen, C S, Shavit, R and Griffin, M C 1991 'Dental caries evidence for dietary change: an archaeological context' *in* Kelley, M A and Larsen, C S (eds), 179–202.
Lawlor, H C 1925 *The Monastery of St Mochaoi of Nendrum*. Belfast.
Leahy, K 1995 'The Flixborough hoard', *Curr Archaeol 141*, 352.
Lee, C 1984 *An Investigation into a Lateral Flange of Proximal Medieval Femora*. Unpublished BSc thesis, University of Aberdeen.
Lerche, G 1970a 'The ploughs of medieval Denmark', *Tools and Tillage I:3*, 131–49.
Lerche, G 1970b 'Pebbles from wheelploughs', *Tools and Tillage I:3*, 150.
Levison, W 1940 'An eighth-century poem on St. Ninian', *Antiquity 14*, 280–91.
Levison, W 1943 'The inscription on the Jarrow cross', *Archaeol Aeliana, 4 ser, 21*, 121–6.
Lewis, J M and Evans, D H 1982 'Southern European imported pottery in Wales', *Bulletin of the Welsh Medieval Pottery Research Group, No. 5*, 76–95.
Lionard, P 1961 'Early Irish grave-slabs', *Proc Roy Ir Acad 61C*, 95–169
Lith, S M E van 1977 'A Romano-British glass bangle from Valkenburg ZH', *Ex Horreo IPP 1951–1976*, 130–4.
Liversage, G D 1968 'Excavations at Dalkey Island, Co Dublin', *Proc Roy Ir Acad 66C*, 53–233.
LMMC 1940 *Medieval Catalogue (London Museum Catalogue No 7)*. Reprinted Anglia Publishing, Suffolk, 1993.
London Museum 1954 *Medieval Catalogue* (rev edn). London.
Lowe, C E 1991 'New light on the Anglian 'Minster' at Hoddom', *Trans Dumfriesshire Galloway Natur Hist Antiq Soc 66*, 11–35.
Lowe, H (ed) 1982 *Die Iren und Europa im fruheren Mittelalter. I*. Stuttgart.
Luff, R M 1982 *A zooarchaeological study of the Roman Northwestern Provinces* (= Brit Archaeol Rep, Internat Ser 137). Oxford.
Lunt, D A 1974 'The prevalence of dental caries in the permanent dentition of Scottish prehistoric and mediaeval populations', *Archs Oral Biol 19*, 431–7.
Lunt, D A 1986 'Mediaeval dentitions from St Andrews' *in* Cruwys, E and Foley, R A (eds), 215–24.
Lynch, M 1988 'The social and economic structure of the larger towns, 1450–1600' *in* Lynch, M, Spearman, M and Stell, G (eds), 261–86.
Lynch, M, Spearman, M and Stell, G (eds) 1988 *The Scottish Medieval Town*. John Donald, Edinburgh.
Lynn, C J 1974 'Ballywee', *Excavations 5*, 4–6.
Lynn, C J 1985 'Excavations on a mound at Gransha, County Down, 1972 and 1982: an interim report', *Ulster J Archaeol, 3 ser, 48*, 81–90.
Lynn, C J 1988 'Excavations at 46–48 Scotch Street, Armagh 1979–80', *Ulster J Archaeol 51*, 69–84.
Lyon, C S S 1957 'A reappraisal of the sceattas and styca coinage of Northumbria', *Brit Numis J 28*, 227–42.
Lyon, S 1987 'Ninth-century Northumbrian chronology' *in* Metcalf, D M (ed), 27–41.
M'Kerlie, E M H 1916 *Pilgrim Spots in Galloway*. London and Edinburgh.
M'Kerlie, P H 1877 *History of the Lands and Their Owners in Galloway, illustrated by woodcuts of notable places and objects, with a historical sketch of the district, II*. Edinburgh.
M'Kerlie, P H 1906 *History of the Lands and Their Owners in*

Galloway, with historical sketches of the district, new edn, *II*. Paisley.

M'Neil, C 1952 'The lost stone of Kirkmadrine', *University of Edinburgh J*, 16(3), 174–7.

Mac Niocaill, G and Wallace P (eds) 1988 *Keimelia: Studies in medieval archaeology and history in memory of Tom Delaney*. Galway University Press.

Macalister, R A S 1935–36 'The ancient inscriptions of Kirkmadrine and Whithorn', *Proc Soc Antiq Scot 70*, 315–25.

Macalister, R A S 1945 *Corpus Inscriptionum Insularum Celticarum, I*. Dublin.

Macalister, R A S 1949 *Corpus Inscriptionum Insularum Celticarum, II*. Dublin.

MacDonald, A 1981 'Notes on monastic archaeology in the Annals of Ulster' *in* O'Corráin, D (ed), 304–19.

MacDonald, A 1984 'Aspects of the monastery and monastic life in Adomnáns's Life of Columba', *Peritia 3*, 271–302.

Macdonald, G 1935–36 'On two inscribed stones of the Early Christian period from the Border district', *Proc Soc Antiq Scot 70*, 33–9.

Macdonnell, W R 1904 'A study of the variation and correlation of the human skull, with special reference to English crania', *Biometrika 3*, 191–244.

Macdonnell, W R 1906 'A second study of the English skull, with special reference to the Moorfields crania', *Biometrika 5*, 86–104.

MacGregor, A G 1974 'The Broch of Burrian, North Ronaldsay, Orkney', *Proc Soc Antiq Scot 105*, 63–118.

MacGregor, A G 1978 'Industry and commerce in Anglo-Scandinavian York' *in* Hall, R A (ed), 34–57.

MacGregor, A G 1982 *Anglo-Scandinavian finds from Lloyds Bank, Pavement and other sites* (= The Archaeology of York 17/3). Counc Brit Archaeol, London.

MacGregor, A G 1985 *Bone, Antler, Ivory and Horn; the technology of skeletal materials since the Roman period*. London.

MacGregor, A G 1989 'Bone, antler and horn industries in the urban context' *in* Serjeantson, D and Waldron, T (ed), 107–28.

MacGregor, A G and Currey, J D 1983 'Mechanical properties as conditioning factors in the bone and antler industries of the 3rd to 13th Centuries AD', *J Archaeol Science 10*, 71–7.

MacKenzie, W 1841 *A History of Galloway from the Earliest Period to the Present Time, in two volumes*. Kirkcudbright.

Mackerrel, A 1950 'The Kintyre properties of Whithorn Priory', *Trans Dumfriesshire Galloway Natur Hist Antiq Soc 34*, 183–192.

MacQuarrie, A 1987 'The date of St Ninian's mission: a reappraisal', *Records of the Scottish Church History Society 23*, 1–25.

MacQuarrie, A 1992 'Early Christian religious houses in Scotland: foundation and function' *in* Blair, J and Sharpe, R (eds), 110–36.

MacQueen, J 1961 *St Nynia*. Edinburgh.

MacQueen, J 1990 *St Nynia*. Edinburgh.

MacQueen, J 1991 'The literary sources for the life of St Ninian' *in* Oram, R D and Stell, G P (eds), 17–25.

MacQueen, W 1960 'Miracula Nynie Episcopi', *Trans Dumfriesshire Galloway Natur Hist Antiq Soc 38*, 21–57.

Magnusson, M and Palsson, H 1960 *Njal's Saga*. Penguin.

Mahr, A 1932 *Christian Art in Ancient Ireland, Vol.1*. Dublin.

Manchester, K 1983 *The Archaeology of Disease*. Bradford.

Mann, J E 1982 *Early medieval finds from Flaxengate, I: objects of antler, bone, stone, horn, ivory, amber and jet* (= The Archaeology of Lincoln, XIV 1). London.

Maxwell, H E 1885 'St Ninian's Cave, Glasserton', *Hist Archaeol Coll Wigtownshire/Galloway Assoc 5*, 18.

Maxwell, H E 1916–17 'The crosses of Kirkmadrine: discovery of the missing third stone', *Proc Soc Antiq Scot 51*, 199–207.

Mayr-Harting, H 1991 *The Coming of Christianity to Anglo-Saxon England* (3rd edn). London.

Mays, S A 1991 *The Medieval Burials from the Blackfriars Friary, School Street, Ipswich* (= Ancient Monuments Laboratory Report 16/91). London.

McArthy, M R (ed) 1990 *A Roman, Anglian and Medieval site at Blackfriars Street, Carlisle: Excavations 1977–9* (= Cumberland Westmorland Antiq Archaeol Soc Research Series No 4). Kendal.

McCormick, F 1981 'The animal bones from Ditch 1' *in* Barber J (ed), 313–18.

McCormick, F 1987 *Stockrearing in Early Christian Ireland*. Unpublished PhD thesis, the Queen's University of Belfast.

McCormick, F 1988 'The domesticated cat in early Christian and medieval Ireland' *in* Mac Niocaill, G and Wallace, P (eds), 218–28.

McCormick, F 1991 'The effect of the Anglo-Norman settlement on Ireland's wild and domesticated fauna' *in* Crabtree, P J and Ryan, K (eds), 40–52.

McCormick, F 1992 'Early faunal evidence for dairying', *Oxford J Archaeol 11*, 201–9.

McCormick, F in press 'The mammal bones from Edinburgh Castle' *in* Driscoll, S (ed).

McCormick, F forthcoming 'The mammal bones from Waterford'.

MacIvor, I, Thomas, M C and Breeze, D J (eds) 1980 'Excavations on the Antonine Wall fort of Rough Castle, Stirlingshire, 1957–61', *Proc Soc Antiq Scot 110*, 230–85.

McWhirr, A, Viner, L and Wells, C 1982 *Romano-British Cemeteries at Cirencester* (= Cirencester Excavations II). Cirencester.

Megaw, B R S 1939 'Seven crosses and an unusual carved slab found since 1932', *J Manx Museum 4(61)*, 163–4.

Megaw, B R S 1950 'The monastery of St Maughold', *Proc Isle Man Natur Hist Antiq Soc 5(2)*, 169–80.

Megaw, J V S 1961 'An end-blown flute or flageolet from White Castle', *Medieval Archaeol 5*, 176–81.

Mellars, P (ed) 1987 *Excavations on Oronsay*. Edinburgh University Press.

Merbs, C F 1989 'Trauma' *in* Iscan, M Y and Kennedy, K A R (eds).

Metcalf, D M 1984 'Estimation of the volume of the Northumbrian coinage, c. 738–88' *in* Hill, D and Metcalf, D M (eds), 113–6.

Metcalf, D M, Merrick, J M and Hamblin, L K, 1968 *Studies in the Composition of Early Medieval Coins*. Newcastle Upon Tyne.

Metcalf, D M (ed) 1987a *Coinage in Ninth-Century Northumbria* (= Brit Archaeol Rep, Brit Ser, 180). Oxford.

Metcalf, D M 1987b 'A topographical commentary on the coin finds from ninth-century Northumbria (c.780–c.870)' *in* Metcalf, D M (ed), 361–82.

Metcalf, D M 1992 'The monetary economy of the Irish Sea province' *in* Graham-Campbell, J (ed), 89–106.

Michelli P 1991 'Migrating ideas or migrating craftsmen? The case of the bossed penannular brooches' *in* Spearman, M and Higgitt, J (eds), 182–7.

Miles, A E W 1963 'The dentition in the assessment of individual age in skeletal material' *in* Brothwell, D R (ed), 191–209.

Miles, A E W 1989 *An Early Christian Chapel and Burial Ground on the Isle of Ensay, Outer Hebrides, Scotland, with a study of the skeletal remains* (= Brit Archaeol Rep, Brit Ser, 212). Oxford.

Milojcic, V (ed) 1971 *Kolloquium über spätantike und frühmittelalterliche Skulptur, 2*. Mainz.

Mitchell, A 1870–72 'Inscribed stones at Kirkmadrine, in the parish of Stoneykirk, county of Wigton', *Proc Soc Antiq Scot 9*, 568–86.

Moore, D (ed) 1970 *The Irish Sea Province in Archaeology and History*. Cardiff.

Moore, M J 1984 'Irish cresset-stones', *J Roy Soc Antiq Ir 114*, 98–116.

Moore W J and Corbett, M E 1971 'The distribution of dental caries in ancient British populations I. Anglo-saxon period', *Caries Res 5*, 151–68.

Moore W J and Corbett, M E 1973 'The distribution of dental caries in ancient British populations II. Iron Age, Romano-British and Mediaeval periods', *Caries Res 7 (1973)*, 139–53.

Moore W J and Corbett, M E 1975 'The distribution of dental caries in ancient British populations III. The 17th century', *Caries Res 9*, 163–75.

Moorrees, C F A, Fanning, E A and Hunt, E E 1963 'Age variation of formation stages for ten permanent teeth', *J Dent Res 42*, 1490–502.

Morales, A and Rosenlund, K 1979 *Fish Bone Measurements*. Steenstrupia, Copenhagen.

Morant, G M and Hoadley, M F 1931 'A study of the recently excavated Spitalfields crania', *Biometrika 23*, 191–248.

Morris, J 1973 *The Age of Arthur*. London.

Morris, J 1980 *Nennius: British History and Welsh Annals*. London and Chichester.

Morris, R W B and Van Hoek, M A M 1987 'Rock carvings in the Garlieston Area, Wigtown District', *Trans Dumfriesshire Galloway Natur Hist Antiq Soc* 62, 32–9.

Morrison, I A, 1991 'Locality and landscape evolution' *in* Oram, R D and Stell, G P (eds), 1–16.

Mortimer, J R 1905 *Forty Years' Researches in British and Saxon Burial Mounds of East Yorkshire*. London.

Mould, Q 1986 'Medieval and early post-medieval leather from three excavations', *Archaeological Leather Group Newsletter, 1*.

Muir, T S 1864 (nd) *The Lighthouse: a sketch addressed to my landlady in Limbus Patrum*. Edinburgh (privately printed).

Muir, T S 1885 *Ecclesiological Notes on Some of the Islands of Scotland*. Edinburgh.

Munro, R 1899 *Prehistoric Scotland*. Edinburgh.

Munro, 5 1882 'Notice of the excavation of a crannog at Buston, near Kilmaurs', *Hist Archaeol Coll Ayr Wigtownshire/Galloway Assoc* 3, 19–51.

Murray, H 1983 *Viking and early medieval buildings in Dublin* (= Brit Archaeol Report, Brit Ser, 119). Oxford.

Mytum, H 1992 *The Origins of Early Christian Ireland*. London and New York.

Nash-Williams, V E 1950 *The Early Christian Monuments of Wales*. Cardiff.

Ní Chatháin, P and Richter, M (eds) 1984 *Irland und Europa: Die Kirche im Frühmittelalter/ Ireland and Europe: the Early Church*. Stuttgart.

North, J J 1989 *Edwardian English Silver Coins, 1279–1351* (= Sylloge of the Coins of the British Isles 39). Oxford.

North, J J 1991 *English Hammered Coinage, vol. 2*, 3rd edition. London.

Nowakowski, J and Thomas, C. 1990 *Excavations at Tintagel parish churchyard, Cornwall, spring 1990, interim report*. Truro.

Nowakowski, J and Thomas, C. 1992 *Grave news from Tintagel, an account of a second season of archaeological excavation at Tintagel churchyard, Cornwall, 1991*. Truro.

O'Brien, E 1992 'Pagan and Christian burial in Ireland during the first millennium AD: continuity and change' *in* Edwards, N and Lane, A (eds), 130–7.

O'Connor, A and Clarke, D V (eds) 1983 *From the Stone Age to the 'Forty-Five; Studies presented to R B K Stevenson*. Edinburgh.

O'Connor, S 1992 'Conservation of the Coppergate Ironwork' *in* Ottaway P (ed), 466–71.

O'Connor, T P 1989 *Bones from Anglo-Scandinavian Levels at 16–22 Coppergate*(= The Archaeology of York 15/3). Counc Brit Archaeol, London.

O'Connor, T P 1991 'Pets and pests in Roman and medieval Britain', *Mammal Review* 22, 107–13.

O'Corráin, D (ed) 1981 *Irish Antiquity*. Cork.

O'Kelly, M 1962 'Two ring-forts at Garryduff, Co Cork', *Proc Roy Ir Acad* 63C, 17–124.

O'Kelly, M 1976 'Plough pebbles from the Boyne valley' *in* Danachair, C O (ed), 165–76.

O'Kelly, M 1978 'Three passage graves at Newgrange, Co. Meath', *Proc Roy Ir Acad* 78C, 249–53.

O'Meadhra, U 1979 *Early Christian, Viking and Romanesque art: motif-pieces from Ireland*. Stockholm.

O'Meadhra, U 1987 *Early Christian, Viking and Romanesque art: motif-pieces from Ireland, 2, a discussion on aspects of find-context and function*. Stockholm.

O'Rahilly, C 1973 *A Catalogue and Classification of Bronze Stick Pins from the Excavations in Dublin 1962–72*. Unpublished MA thesis, University College, Dublin.

O'Riordain, B 1971 'Excavations at High Street and Winetavern Street, Dublin', *Medieval Archaeol* 15, 73–86.

Oakley, G E 1979a 'The copper alloy objects' *in* Williams, J H (ed), 248–65.

Oakley, G E 1979b 'The lead alloy objects' *in* Williams, J H (ed), 265–68.

Oakley, G E 1979c 'The worked bone' *in* Williams, J H (ed), 308–18.

Oakley, G E 1979d 'The nails' *in* Williams, J H (ed), 275–7.

Oakley, G E and Hall, A D 1979 'The spindle whorls' *in* Williams, J H (ed), 286–9.

Oram, R D 1988 *The Lordship of Galloway c. 1000–c. 1250*. Unpublished PhD thesis, University of St Andrews.

Oram, R D 1991a 'Fergus, Galloway and the Scots' *in* Oram, R D and Stell, G P (eds), 117–30.

Oram, R D 1991b 'In obedience and reverence: Whithorn and York c. 1128–c. 1250', *Innes Rev* 42 No. 2, 83–100.

Oram, R D and Stell, G P (eds) 1991 *Galloway: Land and Lordship*. The Scottish Society for Northern Studies. Edinburgh.

Ottaway, P (ed) 1992 *Anglo-Scandinavian ironwork from 16–22 Coppergate* (= The Archaeology of York 17/6). Counc Brit Archaeol, London.

Ottaway, P forthcoming 'Iron coffin fittings from Dacre, Cumbria'.

Otte, M 1988 'Les Fouilles de la Place Saint Lambeert à Liège 2 La Vieux Marché', *Etudes et Recherches Archéologiques de l'Université de Liège, 13*.

Owen, O A 1992 'Eildon Hill North' *in* Rideout *et al*. (eds), 21–72.

Owen-Crocker G R 1986 *Dress in Anglo-Saxon England*. Manchester.

Pagan, H E 1969 'Northumbrian numismatic chronology in the ninth century', *Brit Numis J* 38, 1–15.

Parsons, D 1986 'Sacrarium: ablution drains in early medieval churches' *in* Butler, L A S and Morris, R K (eds), 105–20.

Patrick, R and Reimer, C 1966 *The Diatoms of the United States, Vol. 1*.

Patrick, R and Reimer, C 1975 *The Diatoms of the United States, Vol. 2. no.1*.

Patte, E 1952 'Les 'galet-clous' de la gatine de Deux-Sèvres', *Gallia* 9, 56–9.

Pearce, S M (ed) 1982 *The Early Church in Western Britain and Ireland: studies presented to C A Ralegh Radford* (= Brit Archaeol Rep, Brit Ser, 102). Oxford.

Peltenburg, E J 1982 'Excavations at Balloch Hill, Argyll', *Proc Soc Antiq Scot* 112, 142–214.

Pennick, N 1984 *Pagan Prophecy and Play in Northern Europe*. Cambridge.

Perin, P 1991 'Le verre merovingien' *in* Foy and Sennequier (eds), 125–36.

Philips, S 1960 *The material evidence from Nendrum monastery, Co Down, 1922–1924*. Unpublished BA thesis, The Queen's University, Belfast.

Phillips, C 1938 'Pebbles from early ploughs in England', *Proc Prehist Soc* IV:2, 338–9.

Phillips, P (ed) *The Archaeologist and the Laboratory* (= Counc Brit Archaeol, Res Rep, 58). London.

Pindborg, J J 1982 'Aetiology of developmental enamel defects not related to fluorosis', *Int Dent J* 32, 123–34.

Pirie, E J E 1964 *Sylloge of Coins of the British Isles Chester I Grosvenor Museum, Chester, I*. London.

Pirie, E J E 1981 'Northumbrian coins at auction, 1981', *Brit Numis J* 51, 32–51.

Pirie, E J E 1984 'Some Northumbrian finds of sceattas' *in* Hill, D and Metcalf, D M (eds), 207–16.

Pirie, E J E 1986 'Finds of 'sceattas' and 'stycas' of Northumbria' *in* Blackburn, M (ed), 67–90.

Pirie, E J E 1987a 'Phases and groups within the styca coinage of Northumbria' *in* Metcalf, D M (ed), 257–328.

Pirie, E J E 1987b 'Adamson's Hexham plates' *in* Metcalf, D M (ed), 257–328.

Pirie, E J E 1992 'The seventh-century gold coinage of Northumbria', *Yorkshire Numis* 2, 11–15.

Pirie, E J E 1996 *Coins of the Kingdom of Northumbria, c. 700–867*. Llanfyllin.

Pirie, E J E with Archibald, M M and Hall, R A (*et al*.) 1986 *Post-Roman Coins from York excavations, 1971–81* (= The Archaeology of York, 18/1). Counc for Brit Archaeol, London.

Pirie, E J E and Archibald, M M 1995 '6.7. coins' *in* Carver, M O H (ed), 527–30.

Platt, C and Coleman-Smith, R (eds) 1975 *Excavations in Medieval Southampton, 1953–1969. Vol. 2: The Finds*. Leicester.

Plummer, C 1896 *Venerabilis Baedae Opera Historica, 2 vols*. Oxford.

Pollock, D C 1993 *Whithorn 5: Interim Report on the 1992 Excavations at Whithorn Priory*. Whithorn Trust, Whithorn.

Pollock, D C 1993 *Whithorn 6: Interim Report on the 1993 Excavations at Whithorn Priory*. Whithorn Trust, Whithorn.

Powicke, F M (ed) 1950 *Life of Aelred of Rievaulx*. London and Edinburgh.

Preston-Jones, A and Rose, P 1986 'Medieval Cornwall', *Cornish Archaeol* 25, 135–85.

Price, J 1988a 'Romano-British glass bangles from east Yorkshire' *in* Price, J and Wilson, P R (eds), 339–66.

Price, J 1988b 'The glass' *in* Hartgroves, S and Walker, R, 25–6.

Price, J 1990 'Roman vessel and window glass' *in* McArthy, M R (ed), 163–79.

Price, J 1992 'Report on the vessel and window glass' *in* Rahtz, P et al. (eds), 132–43.

Price, J 1995 'Glass vessels with wheel-cut, engraved and abraded decoration found in Britain in the fourth and fifth centuries' *in* Foy (ed), 25–34.

Price, J (ed) forthcoming *Glass in Britain, AD 350–800*. British Museum Press, London.

Price, J and Cottam, S forthcoming 'Glass' *in* Alcock, L forthcoming.

Price, J and Wilson, P R (eds) 1988 *Recent Research in Roman Yorkshire* (= Brit Archaeol Rep, Brit Ser, 193). Oxford.

Price, L, 1959 'Rock-basins, or 'bullauns', at Glendalough and elsewhere', *J Roy Soc Antiq Ireland* 89, 161–88

Pritchard, F 1989 'Small finds' *in* Vince, A G (ed).

Proudfoot, V B 1961 'The economy of the Irish rath', *Medieval Archaeol* 5, 94–123.

Prummel, W 1983 *Excavations at Dorestad 2. Early medieval Dorestad, an archaeozoological study*. Nederlandse Oudheiden 11, Rijksdienst voor het Oudheidkundig Bodemonderzoek, Amersfoort.

Pryce, H 1992 'Pastoral care in early medieval Wales' *in* Blair, J and Sharpe, R (eds), 41–62.

Radford, C A R 1935 'Tintagel; the Castle and Celtic Monastery, Interim Report', *Antiq J* 15, 401–19.

Radford, C A R 1942 'Tintagel in history and legend', *J Roy Inst Cornwall* 25, 25–41.

Radford, C A R, 1950 'Excavations at Whithorn, First Season, 1949', *Trans Dumfriesshire Galloway Natur Hist Antiq Soc*, 3 ser, 27, 85–126.

Radford, C A R 1951 'St Ninian's Cave', *Trans Dumfriesshire Galloway Natur Hist Antiq Soc* 28, 96–8.

Radford, C A R 1952–53 'Hoddom', *Trans Dumfriesshire Galloway Natur Hist Antiq Soc* 31, 174–97.

Radford, C A R 1957 'Excavations at Whithorn (Final Report)', *Trans Dumfriesshire Galloway Natur Hist Antiq Soc* 34, 131–94.

Radford, C A R 1958 'The excavation at Glastonbury Abbey, 1956–7', *Somerset and Dorset Notes and Queries* 27, 165–9.

Radford, C A R 1967 'The early church in Strathclyde and Galloway', *Medieval Archaeol* 11, 105–26.

Radford, C A R 1968 'The archaeological background on the continent' *in* Barley, M W and Hanson, R P C (eds), 19–36.

Radford, C A R 1971 'Christian origins in Britain', *Medieval Archaeol* 15, 1–12.

Radford, C A R, and Donaldson, G 1951 'The post-Reformation church at Whithorn', *Proc Soc Antiq Scot* 85, 117–33.

Radford, C A R, and Donaldson, G 1957 *Whithorn and Kirkmadrine Wigtownshire* (= Ministry of Works Official Guide Book: second impression). Edinburgh.

Radford, C A R, and Donaldson, G 1984 *Whithorn and the ecclesiastical monuments of Wigtown District*, rev edn. Edinburgh.

Radley, J 1971 'Economic aspects of Anglo-Danish York', *Medieval Archaeol* 15, 35–57.

Radnor, J N 1978 *Fragmentary Annals of Ireland*. Dublin.

Rahtz, P 1971 'Excavations on Glastonbury Tor, Somerset, 1964–6', *Archaeol J* 127, 1–81.

Rahtz, P, Woodward, A, Burrow, I, Everton, A, Watts, L, Leach, P, Hirst, S, Fowler, P and Gardener, K 1992 *Cadbury Congresbury 1968–73 A Late/post-Roman Hilltop Settlement in Somerset* (= Brit Archaeol Rep, Brit Ser, 223). Oxford.

Rahtz, P A 1993 *Glastonbury*. London.

Raine, J (ed) 1864 *The Priory of Hexham. Its Chroniclers, Endowments, and Annals. Vol I* (= Surtees Society XLIV). London.

Randoin, B 1981 'Essai de classification chronologique de la céramique de Tours du IVe au IXe siècle', *Recherche sur Tours* 1, 103–14.

RCAHMS 1912 *Fourth Report and Inventory of Monuments and Constructions in Galloway, I, County of Wigtown*. Edinburgh.

RCAHMS 1956 *An Inventory of the Ancient and Historical Monuments of Roxburghshire*. Edinburgh.

RCAHMS 1957 *An Inventory of the Ancient and Historical Monuments of Selkirkshire*. Edinburgh.

RCAHMS 1971 *Argyll. An Inventory of the Monuments, I, Kintyre*. Edinburgh.

RCAHMS 1982 *Argyll. An Inventory of the Monuments, IV, Iona*. Edinburgh.

RCAHMS 1985 *The Archaeological Sites and Monuments of Scotland, 24, West Rhins, Wigtown District, Dumfries and Galloway Region*. Edinburgh.

RCHM(E) 1975 *An inventory of the historical monuments in the city of York, IV, Outside the city walls east of the Ouse*. London.

Reece, R 1981 *Excavations in Iona 1964 to 1974*. London.

Reid, R C 1957–58 'The Ventidius stone, Kirkmaiden', *Trans Dumfriesshire Galloway Natur Hist Antiq Soc* 36, 184–5.

Reid, R C 1960 *Wigtownshire Charters* (= Scot Hist Soc 51). Edinburgh.

Reimann, F 1978 'Metopism in iron deficiency disease – a roentgenological investigation', *Fortschritte auf dem Gebiete der Rontgenstrahlen* 129, 246–9.

Renaud, J G N (ed) 1968 *Rotterdam Papers*.

Resnick, D and Niwayama, G 1978 'Intravertebral disk herniations: cartilaginous (Schmorl's) nodes', *Radiology* 126, 57–65.

Revell, P A 1986 *Pathology of Bone*. Berlin.

Reynolds, S 1977 *English Medieval Towns*. Oxford.

Rhys, J 1891 'Some inscribed stones in the north, II', *The Academy* 40, 201.

Richey, J E, Wilson, J V and Anderson, E M 1925 *The Economic Geology of the Ayrshire Coalfields; Area 1, Kilbirnie, Dalry and Kilmaurs*. HMSO, Edinburgh.

Riddler, I D 1980 *Structural Fittings from Anglo-Saxon Graves in Kentish Cemeteries*. Unpublished MA thesis, Durham University.

Rideout, J S, Butler, S, Owen, O A, Halpin, E 1992 *Hillforts of southern Scotland*. Edinburgh.

Rigoir, J 1968 'Les sigillées paléochretiénnes grises et oranges', *Gallia* 26, 177–244.

Rigoir, J, Rigoir, Y and Meffre, J-F 1973 'Les dérivées paléochrétiennes du groupe atlantique', *Gallia* 31, 364–409.

Rigold, S E 1977 'The principal series of English sceattas', *Brit Numis J* 47, 21–30.

Rigold, S E and Metcalf, D M 1984 'A revised check-list of English finds of sceattas' *in* Hill, D and Metcalf, D M (eds), 245–68.

Ritchie, A 1977 'Excavation of Pictish and Viking-age farmsteads at Buckquoy, Orkney', *Proc Soc Antiq Scot* 108, 174–227.

Ritchie, A 1993 *Viking Scotland*. London.

Ritchie, A (ed) 1994 *Govan and its early medieval sculptures*. Stroud.

Rivet, A L F and Smith, C C 1979 *The Place-Names of Roman Britain*. London.

Roberts, C 1987 'Possible pituitary dwarfism from the Roman period', *Brit Med J* 295, 1659–60.

Roberts, C and Wakely, J 1992 'Microscopical findings associated with the diagnosis of osteoporosis in palaeopathology', *Internat J Ostearchaeol* 2, 23–30.

Robertson, G P 1916–18 'The lost stone of Kirkmadrine', *Trans Dumfriesshire Galloway Natur Hist Antiq Soc* 5, 136–41.

Robertson, J 1853 *On Scholastic Offices in the Scottish Chirch in the Twelfth and Thirteenth Centuries*. Privately printed.

Rodwell, W J 1985 *Rivenhall: investigations of a villa, church, and village, 1950–1977* (= Counc Brit Archaeol Res Rep, 55). London.

Rodwell, W J, 1986 'Anglo-Saxon church building: aspects of design and construction' *in* Butler, L A S and Morris, R K (eds), 156–75.

Rodwell, W J 1989 *Church Archaeology*. London.

Roes, A 1963 *Bone and Antler Objects from the Frisian Terpmounds*. Haarlem.

Roesdahl, E 1982 *Viking Age Denmark*. London.

Roesdahl, E, Graham-Campbell, J, Connor, P and Pearson, K 1981 *The Vikings in England*. London.

Rogers G B 1974 *Poteries sigillées de la Gaule centrale* (= Gallia Supplement XXVIII).

Rollins, J G 1981 *Needlemaking*. Shire Album 71.

Rothschild, B M, Woods, R J and Ortel, W 1990 'Rheumatoid arthritis 'in the buff': erosive arthritis in defleshed bones', *Am J Phys Anthrop 82*, 441–9.

Russell-White, C J 1990 'The East Rhins' *in* Buckley, V M (ed), 70–6.

Rutherford, A and Ritchie, J N G 1972–74 'The Catstane', *Proc Soc Antiq Scot 105*, 183–8.

Ryan, M 1973 'Native pottery in early historic Ireland', *Proc Roy Ir Acad 73C*, 619–45.

Ryan, M (ed) 1987 *Ireland and Insular Art, AD 500–1200*. Dublin.

Rynne, E 1980 'Slate medals and amulets from the Aran Islands', *J Galway Archaeol Hist Soc 35*, 78–84.

Sachs, C 1942 *The History of Musical Instruments*. London.

Saluja, G et al. 1986 'Schmorl's nodes (intervertebral herniations of intervertebral disc tissue) in two historic British populations', *J Anat 145*, 87–96.

Samson, R 1982 'Finds from Urquhart Castle in the National Museum, Edinburgh', *Proc Soc Antiq Scot 112*, 465–76.

Sanderson, D C W and Hunter, J R 1981a 'Compositional variability in vegetable ash', *Science and Archaeology 23*, 27–30.

Sanderson, D C W and Hunter, J R 1981b 'Major element glass type glass type specification for Roman, post-Roman and medieval glasses', *Revue d'Archeometrie III*, 255–64.

Sanderson, D C W, Hunter, J R and Warren, F E 1984 'Energy dispersive X-ray fluorescence analysis of 1st millennium AD glass from Britain', *J Archaeol Sci 11*, 53–69.

Savory, H N 1960 'Excavations at Dinas Emrys, Beddgelert, Caernarvonshire', *Archaeol Camb 109*, 13–77.

Sawyer, P H 1970 'The Vikings and the Irish Sea' *in* Moore, D (ed), 86–92.

Sawyer, P H 1979 (ed) *Names, Words and Graves: Early Medieval Settlement*. Leeds.

Schofield, J 1976 'Excavations south of Edinburgh High Street, 1973–4', *Proc Soc Antiq Scot 107*, 155–241.

Schour, I and Massler, M 1941 'The development of the human dentition', *J Am Dent Assn 28* (1941), 1153–60.

Schultz, A H 1939 'Notes on diseases and healed fractures of wild apes', *Bull Hist Med 7*, 571–82.

Scott, H (ed) 1917 *Fasti Ecclesiae Scoticanae: the Succession of Ministers in the Church of Scotland from the Reformation*, new edn, *II, Synods of Merse and Teviotdale, Dumfries and Galloway*. Edinburgh.

Scott, J G 1983 'A note on Viking settlement in Galloway', *Trans Dumfriesshire Galloway Natur Hist Antiq Soc 58*, 52–5.

Scott, J G 1988 'The Origins of Dundrennan and Soulseat Abbeys', *Trans Dumfriesshire Galloway Natur Hist Antiq Soc 63*, 35–44.

Scott, R G 1990 *Early Irish Ironworking*. Belfast.

Serjeantson, D and Waldron, T (eds) 1989 *Diet and Crafts in Towns* (= Brit Archaeol Rep, Brit Ser 199). Oxford.

Sharpe, R 1992 'Churches and communities in early medieval Ireland: towards a pastoral model' *in* Blair, J and Sharpe, R (eds), 81–109.

Sherlock, S J and Welch, M G 1992 *An Anglo-Saxon Cemetery at Norton, Cleveland* (= Counc Brit Archaeol Res Rep, 82). London.

Shepherd, I A G 1986 *Powerful Pots*. Aberdeen.

Silver, I A 1969 'The ageing of domestic animals' *in* Brothwell, D and Higgs, E (eds), 283–302.

Simpson, J Y 1860–62a 'Address on archaeology', *Proc Soc Antiq Scot 4*, 5–51.

Simpson, J Y 1860–62b 'On the Catstane, Kirkliston', *Proc Soc Antiq Scot 4*, 119–65.

Simpson, W D 1935 *The Celtic Church in Scotland*. Aberdeen.

Simpson, W D 1950 'The Ninianic controversy', *Trans Dumfriesshire Galloway Natur Hist Antiq Soc 34*, 155–62.

Skene, W F 1887 *Celtic Scotland: a history of ancient Alban*. Edinburgh.

Skinner, W C 1931 *Candida Casa; the Apostolic Centre of Scotland*. Dundee.

Slater, E A and Tate, J O (eds) 1987 *Science and Archaeology* (= Brit Archaeol Rep Brit Ser 196). Oxford.

Small, A 1966 'Excavations at Underhoull, Unst, Shetland', *Proc Soc Antiq Scot 98*, 225–48.

Small, A (ed) 1987 *The Picts: a new look at old problems*. Dundee.

Small, A, Thomas, C and Wilson, D M 1973 'St. Ninian's Isle and its Treasure', *Aberdeen Univ Studies Ser 152*, 2 vols.

Smith, B B 1995 *The Howe: four millennia of Orkney prehistory* (= Soc Antiq Scot Monogr Ser). Edinburgh.

Smith, B H 1991 'Standards of human tooth formation and dental age assessment' *in* Kelley, M A and Larsen C S (eds), 143–68.

Smith R A 1993 *British Museum Guide to Anglo-Saxon Antiquities 1923*. Republished, Ipswich.

Smyth, A P 1984 *Warlords and Holy Men: Scotland AD 80–1000*. London.

Spearman, R M and Higgitt, J (eds.) 1991 *The Age of Migrating Ideas: Early Medieval Art in Northern Britain and Ireland*. Edinburgh and Stroud.

Spearman, M R 1988 'Early Scottish towns: their origins and economy' *in* Driscoll, S T and Neike, M R (eds), 96–110.

Spencer, B W, 1968 'Medieval pilgrim badges' *in* Renaud, J G N (ed), 137–53.

Stanfield, J A and Simpson, G 1958 *Central Gaulish Potters*. London.

Starke, J G H 1887–90 'The Kirkmadrine crosses (note)', *Trans Dumfriesshire Galloway Natur Hist Antiq Soc, 2 ser, 6*, 170–1.

Steensberg, A 1963 'Indborede sten og traeplokke som erstatning for beslag', *Varbergs Museum arsbok*, 69–76.

Steinbock, T D 1976 *Palaeopathological Diagnosis and Interpretation*. Illinois.

Stenton, F M 1947 *Anglo-Saxon England* (2nd edn). Oxford.

Stevenson, R B K 1951 'A hoard of Anglo-Saxon coins found at Iona Abbey', *Proc Soc Antiq Scot 85*, 170–5.

Stevenson, R B K 1955 'Pins and the chronology of brochs', *Proc Prehist Soc 21*, 282–94.

Stevenson, R B K 1956 'Native bangles and Roman glass', *Proc Soc Antiq Scot 88*, 208–21.

Stevenson, R B K 1966 *Sylloge of Coins of the British Isles 6 National Museum of Antiquities of Scotland, Edinburgh, I. Anglo-Saxon Coins*. London.

Stevenson, R B K 1976 'Romano-British glass bangles', *Glasgow Archaeol J 4*, 45–54.

Stevenson, R B K 1990 'The Bawbee Issues of James V and Mary', *Brit Numis J 59* (1989), 120–56.

Stewart, I 1984 'The early English denarial coinage, *c*. 680–*c*. 750' *in* Hill, D and Metcalf, D M (eds), 5–26.

Stewart, I 1991 'A Northumbrian coin of King Ethelwald and Archbishop Ecgberht', *Numis Chron 151*, 223–5.

Stewart, I H 1959 'The Glenluce hoard, 1956', *Brit Numis J 29*, 362–81.

Stewart, I H 1967 *The Scottish Coinage* (revd edn). London.

Stewart, I H 1971 'Scottish Mints' *in* Carson, R A G (ed).

Stewart, I H and North, J J 1991 'Classification of the single-cross sterlings of Alexander III', *Brit Numis J 60* (1990), 37–64.

Stewart, T D 1979 *Essentials of Forensic Anthropology*. Charles Thomas.

Stewart, T D 1980 'Responses of the human skeleton to changes in the quality of life', *J Forensic Science 25 No.4*, 912–21.

Stone, J C 1967 'The early printed maps of Dumfriesshire and Galloway', *Trans Dumfriesshire Galloway Natur Hist Antiq Soc 44*, 182–95.

Stones, J A (ed) 1989 *Three Scottish Carmelite Friaries: Excavations at Aberdeen, Linlithgow and Perth 1980–86* (= Soc Antiq Scot Monogr Ser 6) Edinburgh.

Strecker, K (ed) 1923 *Poetae Latini Aevi Carolini* (= Monumenta Germaniae Historica IV/II–III). Berlin.

Stuart, J 1867 *Sculptured Stones of Scotland, II* (= Spalding Club, 35). Edinburgh.

Stuart-Macadam, P 1985 'Porotic hyperostosis: representative of a childhood condition', *Am J Phys Anthrop 66*, 391–8.

Stuart-Macadam, P 1992 'Porotic hyperostosis: a new perspective', *Am J Phys Anthrop 87*, 39–47.

Stuiver, M and Kra, R S (eds) 1986 Calibration issue. Proceedings of the 12thth International 14C conference, *Radiocarbon 28 (2B)*, 805–1030.

Sugden, K F and Warhurse, M 1979 'An unrecorded parcel from the Hexham hoard of 1832', *Numis Chron 139*, 212–17 .

Swan, L 1985 'Monastic proto-towns in early medieval Ireland: the evidence of aerial photography, plan analysis and survey' *in* Clarke, H B and Simms, A (eds), 77–102.

Tabraham, C J 1979 'Excavations at Whithorn Priory, Wigtown District, 1972 and 1975', *Trans Dumfriesshire Galloway Natur Hist Antiq Soc 54*, 28–38.

Tabraham, C J 1984 'Excavations at Kelso Abbey', *Proc Soc Antiq Scot 114*, 365–404.

Tarter, S 1988 *A study of of medieval grave orientation with applications to the Whithorn Priory cemetery.* Unpublished senior honours thesis, Cornell University.

Tattersall, I 1968 'Dental paleopathology of Mediaeval Britain', *J Hist Med 23*, 380–5.

Taylor, D B (ed), 1982 'Excavation of a promontory fort, broch and souterrain at Hurly Hawkins, Angus', *Proc Soc Antiq Scot 112*, 215–76.

Taylor, M 1981 *Wood in Archaeology.* Shire.

Tempel, W-D 1969 *Die Dreilagenkämmen aus Haithabu: Studien zu den Kammen der Wikingerzeit im Nordseekustenbiel und Skandinavien.* DPhil thesis, University of Göttingen.

Thomas, C 1966 'Ardwall Isle; the excavation of an Early Christian site of Irish type', *Trans Dumfriesshire Galloway Natur Hist Antiq Soc 34*, 84–116.

Thomas, C 1967 'An early Christian cemetery and chapel on Ardwall Isle, Kirkcudbright', *Medieval Archaeol 11*, 127–88.

Thomas, C 1968 'The Evidence from North Britain' *in* Barley, M W and Hanson, R P C (eds), 93–121.

Thomas, C 1971 *The Early Christian Archaeology of North Britain.* Oxford.

Thomas, C 1981a *Christianity in Roman Britain to AD 500.* London.

Thomas, C 1981b *A provisional list of imported pottery in post-Roman western Britain and Ireland* (= Inst Cornish Studies Special Rep 7). Redruth.

Thomas, C 1982 'East and west: Tintagel mediterranean imports and the early insular church' *in* Pearce, S M (ed), 17–34.

Thomas, C 1985 *Christianity in Roman Britain to AD 500* (2nd edn). London.

Thomas, C 1986 'Recognizing Christian origins: an archaeological and historical dilemma' *in* Butler, L A S and Morris R K (eds), 121–5.

Thomas, C 1987 'The earliest Christian art in Ireland and Britain' *in* Ryan, M (ed), 7–11.

Thomas, C 1988a 'Tintagel Castle' *Antiquity 62*, 421–34.

Thomas, C 1988b 'The context of Tintagel: a new model for the diffusion of post-Roman mediterranean imports' *Cornish Archaeol 27*, 7–25.

Thomas, C (ed) 1988c 'Tintagel Papers', *Cornish Studies 16*.

Thomas, C 1990 '"Gallici nautae de Galliarum provinciis" – a sixth/seventh century trade with Gaul, reconsidered', *Medieval Archaeol 34*, 1–26.

Thomas, C 1992a *Whithorn's Christian Beginnings* (= 1st Whithorn Lecture). Friends of the Whithorn Trust, Whithorn.

Thomas, C 1992b 'The early Christian inscriptions of southern Scotland', *Glasgow Archaeol J 17*, 1–10.

Thomas, C 1993 *Tintagel: Arthur and Archaeology.* London.

Thomas, C 1994 *And Shall These Mute Stones Speak?* University of Wales.

Thomas, M C 1981 'The leather' *in* Good and Tabraham (eds), 123–6.

Thomas, M C 1986 'Medieval leather artefacts in Scotland', *Archaeological Leather Group Newsletter, 1*, 4–9.

Thomas, M C 1987 'The leather' *in* Holdsworth, P (ed), 174–189.

Thomas, M C nd *The Leather from High Street, Perth.* Scottish Development Department, unpublished archive report, Perth Museum.

Thompson, F H 1960 'The deserted medieval village of Riseholme, near Lincoln', *Medieval Archaeol 4*, 95–109.

Thompson, M W 1967 *Novgorod the Great; Excavations at the Medieval City 1951–62, directed by A V Artsikhovsky and B A Kolchin.* London.

Thoms, L M 1976 'Coarse pottery' *in* Schofield 1976, 190–206.

Thoms, L M 1982 'Trial excavation at St Ann's Lane, Perth', *Proc Soc Antiq Scot 112*, 437–57.

Thornton, J H 1973 'Excavated shoes to 1600' *in* Doughty, P S (ed) *Transactions of the Museum Assistants' Group 12.*

Thornton, J H 1990 'Shoes, boots and shoe repairs' *in* Biddle, M (ed), 591–621.

Thorpe, C M 1988 'Incised pictorial slates from Tintagel' *in* Thomas, C (ed) 1988c, 69–78.

Thorpe, W A 1935 *English Glass.* London.

Todd, W 1860 *The Clerical History of the Parish of Kirkmaiden.* Glasgow.

Torgerson, J 1951 'Hereditary factors in the sutural pattern of the skull', *Acta Radiologica 36*, 374–82.

Trench-Jellicoe, R 1980 'A new chi-rho from Maughold, Isle of Man', *Medieval Archaeol 24*, 202–3.

Trench-Jellicoe, R 1985 *A Re-definition and Stylistic Analysis of P M C Kermode's Pre-Scandinavian Series of Sculptured Monuments.* Unpublished PhD thesis, 4 vols, Lancaster University.

Trotter, M and Gleser, G C 1952 'Estimation of stature from longbones of American Whites and Negroes', *Am J Phys Anthrop 10*, 31–58.

Trotter, M and Gleser, G C 1958 'A re-evaluation of estimation of stature taken during life and long-bones after death', *Am J Phys Anthrop 16*, 79–123.

Truckell, A E 1989 'A proto-history of Galloway', *Trans Dumfriesshire Galloway Natur Hist Antiq Soc 64*, 48–57.

Truckell, A E and Williams, J 1967 'Medieval Pottery in Dumfriesshire and Galloway', *Trans Dumfriesshire Galloway Natur Hist Antiq Soc 44*, 133–74.

Turner, W E J 1956 'Studies in ancient glasses and glassmaking processes part v: raw materials and melting processes', *J Soc Glass Tech 40*, 276–300.

Tweddle, D 1986 *Finds from Parliament Street and other sites in the city centre* (= The Archaeology of York 17/4). Counc Brit Archaeol, London.

Tylecote, R F 1986 *The Prehistory of Metallurgy in the British Isles.* London.

Ubelaker, D H 1978 *Human Skeletal Remains.* Washington DC.

Ulbrich, I 1978 'Die Geweihverarbeitung in Haithabu', *Die Ausgraungen in Haithabu 7*, Neumünster.

UNICEF 1993 *The State of the World's Children 1993.* Oxford.

Vince, A G (ed) 1989 *Aspects of Saxo-Norman London II: Finds and Environmental Evidence* (= Middlesex Archaeol Soc Special Paper 12). London.

Waldron, T 1989 'The effects of urbanisation on human health: the evidence from skeletal remains' *in* Serjeantson, D and Waldron, T (eds), 55–73.

Walker, P L, Johnson, J R and Lambert, P M 1988 'Age and sex biases in the preservation of human skeletal remains', *Am J Phys Anthrop 76*, 183–8.

Wall, J 1965 'Christian evidences in the Roman period: the northern counties, part I', *Archaeol Aeliana, 4 ser, 43*, 201–25.

Wall, J 1968 'Christian evidences in Roman south-west Britain', *Trans Devonshire Assoc 100*, 161–78.

Wallace, P F 1985 'The archaeology of Viking Dublin' *in* Clarke, H B and Simms, A (eds), 103–46.

Wallace, P F and O Floinn, R 1988 *Dublin 1000. Discovery and Excavation in Dublin, 1842–1981.* Dublin.

Walton, P and Eastwood, G 1988 *A Brief Guide to the Cataloguing of Archaeological Textiles.* IAP, London.

Warhurse, M 1982 *Sylloge of Coins of the British Isles, 29: Merseyside County Museums.* London.

Warner, R 1976 'Scottish silver arm-rings: an analysis of weights', *Proc Soc Antiq Scot 107*, 136–44.

Warner, R 1979 'The Clogher yellow layer', *Medieval Ceramics 3*, 37–40.

Warwick, R 1968 'Part II. The skeletal remains' *in* Wenham, L P (ed), 111–76.

Waterman, D M 1956a 'The excavation of a house and souterrain at Whitefort, Drumarood, Co. Down', *Ulster J Archaeol 19*, 73–86.

Waterman, D M 1956b 'An excavation of a house and souterrain at Craig Hill, Co. Antrim', *Ulster J Archaeol 19*, 87–91.

Waterman, D M 1959 'Late Saxon, Viking and early medieval finds from York', *Archaeologia 97*, 59–105.

Watkins, J G 1987 'The pottery' *in* Armstrong, P and Ayres, B (eds), 53–181.

Watson, W J 1926 *The History of the Celtic Place-names of Scotland.* Edinburgh.

Watt, D E R 1991 *Series Episcoporum Ecclesiae, Catholicae Occidentali, Series VI: Britannia, Scotia et Hibernia, Scandinavia.* Stuttgart.

Webb, J F and Farmer, D H (trans) 1983 *The Age of Bede* (revd edn). Penguin.

Webster L 1991 'The new learning: metalwork, bone, wood and sculpture' *in* Webster, L and Backhouse, J (eds), 47–62.

Webster, L and Backhouse, J 1991 *The Making of England: Anglo-Saxon Art and Culture, AD 600–900.* London.

Webster L and Cherry J 1973 'Medieval Britain in 1972', *Medieval Archaeol 17*, 138–88.

Webster, L E and Cherry, J 1975 'Medieval Britain in 1974', *Medieval Archaeol 19*, 220–60.

Wells, C 1982 'The Human Burials' *in* McWhirr *et al.* (eds), 135–202.

Wells, L H 1969 'Stature in earlier races of mankind' *in* Brothwell, D R and Higgs, E (eds), 453–67.

Wenham, L P (ed) 1968 *The Romano-British Cemetery at Trentholme Drive, York*. HMSO, London.

Wessels, W I 1986 *A Catalogue and Discussion of Stone Worked Vessels from Monkwearmouth, Jarrow, and Lumley Street, Hartlepool*. Unpublished MA dissertation, Durham University.

Wheeler A, 1978 *Key to the Fishes of Northern Europe*. Frederick Warne, London.

White, R B 1972 'Excavations at Arfryn, Bodedern, long cist cemeteries and the origins of Christianity in Britain', *Trans Anglesey Antiq Soc, 19–51*.

White, W J 1988 *The Cemetery of St Nicholas Shambles*. London and Middlesex Arch Soc.

Whittaker, D K, Molleson, T, Daniel, A T, Williams, J T, Rose, P and Resteghini, R 1985 'Quantitative assessment of tooth wear, alveolar-crest height and continuing eruption in a Romano-British population', *Archs Oral Biol 30*, 493–501.

Wiles, P 1960 *Fractures, Dislocations and Sprains*. London.

Williams, A, Smyth, A P and Kirby, D P 1991 *A Biographical Dictionary of Dark Age Britain*. London.

Williams, J 1966 'Some spindle whorls from early ecclesiastical sites', *Trans Dumfriesshire Galloway Natur Hist Antiq Soc 43*, 149–50.

Williams, J H (ed) 1979 *St. Peter's Street, Northampton; Excavations 1973–1976*. Northampton.

Wilson, A 1989 'Roman penetration in West Dumfries and Galloway: a field survey', *Trans Dumfriesshire Galloway Natur Hist Antiq Soc 64*, 7–20.

Wilson, B, Grigson, C and Payne, S (eds) 1982 *Ageing and Sexing Animal Bones from Archaeological Sites* (= Brit Archaeol Rep, Brit Ser, 109). Oxford.

Wilson, D M 1964 *Anglo-Saxon Ornamental Metalwork 700–1100 in the British Museum* (= Catalogue of Antiquities of the Later Saxon Period, 1). London.

Wilson, D M (ed) 1976 *The Archaeology of Anglo-Saxon England*. London.

Wilson, P A 1964 'St Ninian and Candida Casa: literary evidence from Ireland', *Trans Dumfriesshire Galloway Natur Hist Antiq Soc 41*, 156–85.

Wooding, J M 1987 'Some Evidence for Cargoes in Trade on the Western Coast of Europe 400–900 AD', *Sailing Ships and Sailing People, Proceedings, Section 3*, Perth, Western Australia, 1–17.

Workshop of European Anthropologists 1980 'Recommendations for age and sex diagnosis of skeletons', *J Hum Evol 9*, 517–49.

Wright, A 1991 *Craft Techniques for Traditional Buildings*. London.

Yorkshire Archaeological Society 1986 'Thwing, Excavation and Fieldwork in East Yorkshire 1986, The Anglo-Saxon Cemetery'. Y.A.S. Prehistory Research Section.

Young, A 1956 'Excavations at Dun Cuier, Isle of Barra, Outer Hebrides', *Proc Soc Antiq Scot 89*, 290–327.

Youngs, S (ed) 1989a *The Work of Angels*. London.

Youngs, S 1989b 'Fine metalwork to *c* AD 650' *in* Youngs, S (ed), 20–71.

Youngs, S M, Clark, J, and Barry, T 1987 'Medieval Britain and Ireland in 1986', *Medieval Archaeol 31*, 110–91.

Youngs, S M, Clark, J, Gaimster, D R M, and Barry, T 1988 'Medieval Britain and Ireland in 1987', *Medieval Archaeol 32*, 225–314.

Zivanovic, S 1982 *Ancient Diseases, the Elements of Paleaopathology*. Methuen.

Concordance of stratigraphic units (Blocks)

P = Period, **PI/1** = Period I Phase 1, **P.1** = Period I Stage 1, **P/1.1** = Period I Phase 1 Stage 1. Capital letters in brackets indicate excavation areas in the main trench. The **Period IV** matrix has independent branches for the *inner precinct* and for two areas of the *outer zone*. These are distinguished as IP (*inner precinct*), OZE (eastern part of the *outer zone*) and OZS (southern part of the *outer zone*). NS distinguishes a similar stratigraphic branch of **Period III** buildings in the northern sector. Blocks in the Museum Garden (Area M) and Fey Fields (Areas H and J) are so designated.

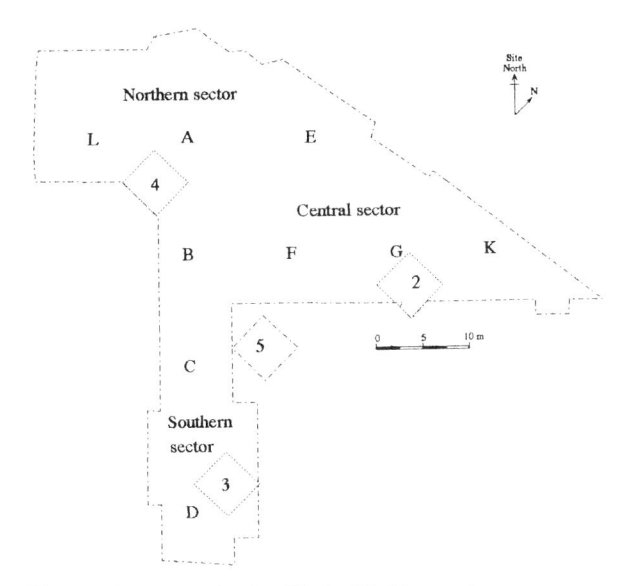

Excavation areas in the Glebe Field trench

50.01–06 Structural features in southern part of southern sector: 50.01 gullies (**PI.5**, D); 50.02 Structure I/16 (**PI.6**, D); 50.03 gully and paving (**PI.7**, D); 50.04 trampled surface (**PI.7**, D); 50.05 Building I/19 (**PI.8**, D); 50.06 construction slot (**PI.9**, D)
51 Charcoal spread and metalworking waste (**PI.4**, D)
52 Unphased **Period I** structural features (**PI**, D)
52.01–05 Buildings in central part of southern sector: 52.01 Building I/12 (**PI.5**, D); 52.02 Building I/15 (**PI.6**, D); 52.03 Building I/17 (**PI.7**, D); 52.04 Building I/18 (**PI.8**, D); 52.05 Building I/20 (**PI.9**, D)
53.01–15 **Period I** pits in the southern sector; 53.01 Pit 1 (**PI.5**, C); 53.02 Pit 2 (**PI.7**, D); 53.03 Pit 3 (**PI.7**, D); 53.04 Pit 4 (**PI.7**, D); 53.05 Pit 5 (**PI.7**, D); 53.06 Pit 6 (**PI.7**, D); 53.07 Pit 7 (**PI.12**, D); 53.08 Pit 8 (**PI.7**, D); 53.09 Pit 9 (**PI.11**, D); 53.1 Pit 10 (**PI.4**, D); 53.11 Pit 11 (**PI.5**, D); 53.12 Pit 12 (**PI.7**, D); 53.13 Pit 13 (**PI.7**, D); 53.14 Pit 14 (**PI.6**, D); 53.15 Pit 15 (**PI**, D)
54 Subsoil and residual early soil (D)
55 Waterborne silts: middle of area (**PI.10**, D)
56 Early ploughsoil in southern sector: 56.01 south part of area (**PI.3**, D); 56.02 central part of area (**PI.3**, D)
57 Unphased stakes and stakeholes (**PI**, D)
58 Waterborne silts: south part of area (**PI.10**, D)
59 Building I/22 (**PI.11**, D)
60 Building I/23 (**PI.11**, C)
61 **Period I.7** ditch: 61.01 west–east ditch (**PI.7**, D); 61.02 gravel upcast from ditch (**PI.7**, D)
64 Early deposits in northern part of southern sector: 64.01 early plough-soil (**PI**, C); 64.02 cultivated soil cutting **Period I/0** roadway (**PI.3**, C); 64.03 wormed soil over ploughing (**PI.3–10**, C); 64.04 sondage and poorly-stratified deposits (**PI**, C)
66 Plough-soil in central sector (**PI/1.1**, EF)
67 Enclosure and related deposits: 67.01 soil and debris under **Period I/1.5** graveyard (**PI/1.4**, EF); 67.02 graveyard enclosure (**PI/1.5**, EF)

69 Early debris in eastern part of northern sector: 69.01 dumped material, including clastic lime (**PI/1.2**, E); 69.02 soil and debris (**PI/1.3**, E); 69.03 builders' waste and metalworking debris (**PI/1.4**, E)
70 Hollow (=97) and overlying charcoal and debris (**PI/1.6**, EF)
71 Surfaces and deposits in hollow: 71.01 shale path on floor of hollow (**PI/2.1**, E); 71.02 cobbled surface on east side of trench (**PI/2.3**, E); 71.03 worm-sorted silt over cobbling etc (**PI/2.4**, E)
72 Paved roadway (=98, **PI/2.7**, E)
73 Soil accumulations over and flanking paved roadway: 73.01 accumulation of soil and mud to north of roadway (**PI/3.1**, E); 73.02 mud and soil over **Period I/4** graves (**PI/4.34**, E); 73.03 wormed soil over **Period I/2** roadway (**PI/3**, E); 73.04 wormed soil and stones over north side of **Period I/2** 'shrine' (**PI/3**, E)
74 Early features in eastern part of central sector: 74.01 boundary ditch on east side of trench (**PI/1**, G); 74.02 Building I/1 (**PI/1**, G)
75 **Period I/4** roadway: 75.01 gravel roadway (**PI/4.5**, EF); 75.02 wormed soil over gravel roadway (**PI/4.67**, EF)
76 Low mound or platform (**PI/4.5**, E)
77 Band of rocks on north edge of **Period I/2–3** roadway (**PI/3.2**, E)
78 **Period I/2** 'shrine' in central sector: 78.01 truncated ditch (possible 'shrine') (**PI/2.4**, G); 78.02 shale surface oversailing ditch (**PI/2.2**, G); 78.03 paving and surfaces in 'shrine' (**PI/2.3**, EG); 78.04 annulus of paving and overlying vein quartz (**PI/2.4**, EG); 78.05 ditch defining north side of 'shrine' (**PI/2.6**, E); 78.06 rubble band and overlying stone kerb on north side of 'shrine' (**PI/2.7**, E); 78.07 soil overlying and interleaved with paved annulus (**PI/2**, E)
79 Early graves in **Period I/1.5** graveyard: 79.01 lintel graves (**PI/1.5**, F); 79.02 Log coffin burials (**PI/1.5**, F)
80 **Period I/2** graves: 80.01 south-east row of graves (**PI/2.5**, G); 80.02 middle row of graves (**PI/2.3**, FG); 80.03 north-west row of graves (**PI/2.67**, FG); 80.04 outlying **Period I/2** graves abutting possible boundary ditch (**PI/2**, F)
81 **Period I/3** graves: 81.01 **Period I/3.1** lintel graves (**PI/3.1**, AEFG); 81.02 **Period I/3.2** log coffin burials (**PI/3.2**, AEFG)
82 **Period I/4** log coffin burials: 82.01 first row of graves. (**PI/4.1**, E); 82.02 second row of graves. (**PI/4.2**, BE); 82.03 third row of graves. (**PI/4.3**, ABE); 82.04 fourth row of graves. (**PI/4.6**, B); 82.05 fifth row of graves. (**PI/4.7**, L); 82.06 unlocated finds from **Period I/4** graves (**PI/4**, ABEFG
83 Platform shrine (**PI/4.5**, L)
84 Pit and hollow cutting early features: 84.01 pit cutting **Period I/1** ditch (**PI/1.5**, E); 84.02 shallow hollow cutting **Period I/1** deposits on north side of 'shrine' ditch (**PI/2**, E)
85 Rubbish deposits and related features in western part of northern sector: 85.01 early rubbish spread (**PI/2.41**, AL); 85.02 large rubbish spread (**PI/3.21**, L); 85.03 rubbish spread (**PI/3–4**, L); 85.04 workshop debris abutting **Period I/4.5** shrine (83) (**PI/4.6**, AL); 85.05 worm-sorted soil over shrines and adjacent rubbish spreads (**PI/4.7**, L); 85.06 debris scattered under **Period II/1** enclosure wall (**PI/4.7**, AL); 85.07 miscellaneous **Period I/4** features at west end of northern sector (**PI/4**, L); 85.08 unphased early postholes in north-west corner of northern sector (**PI** or **II**, L)
86 **Period II** enclosure wall (**PII/1**, AL): 86.01 enclosure wall fabric (**PII/1**, AL); 86.02 rubble abutting enclosure wall (**PII/1**, AL)
88 Structural features in northern sector: 88.01 Building I/9

(**PI/2.21**, AL); 88.02 extension to platform of Building I/9 (**PI/2.31**, AL); 88.03 possible 'shrine' overlying Building I/9 (**PI/3**, AL)
89 Rubbish spread including vessel glass fragments (**PI/2.21**, AL)
90 Rubble over graves in western part of northern sector (**PI/4.4**, AL)
91 Gateway and Building I/8 (**PI/1.5**, AL)
92 Building I/5 and underlying cultivated soil (**PI/1.3**, AL)
93 Early deposits, structures and possible buildings in western part of northern sector: 93.01 early cultivated soil: (**PI/1.1**, AL); 93.02 rubble terrace and stake revetment (**PI/1.3**, AL); 93.03 Building I/3 (**PI/1.3**, AL); 93.04 Building I/4 (**PI/1.3**, AL); 93.05 possible original ground surface between Buildings I/6 and 7 (**PI/1.3**, AL)
94 Buildings, deposits and surfaces in northern sector: 94.01 possible quarry spoil to south of Building I/7 (**PI/1.3**, L); 94.02 possible quarry spoil to south of Building I/6 (**PI/1.4**, AE); 94.03 redeposited builders waste between Buildings I/6 and 7 (**PI/1.4**, L); 94.04 Building I/6 (**PI/1.4**, AE); 94.05 Building I/7 (**PI/1.4**, L); 94.06 shale path abutting Building I/7 (**PI/1.4**, L); 94.07 paving and shale flanking Building I/6 (**PI/1.4**, AE)
95 Paved surface and overlying burnt debris (**PI/1.5**, AL)
96 Organic soil adjacent to Building I/6 (**PI/2.11**, AL)
97 Hollow (=70) and overlying path and rubbish spreads (**PI/1.6**, AL)
98 Paved road (=72, **PI/2.7**, AL)
99 Gravel roadway (=75, **PI/4.5**, AL)
100 Rubbish spread in **Phase 1/6** hollow (**PI/2.11**, AL)
101 Post-holes associated with Grave 1/1 (**PI/4**, F)
102 Metalled roadway (**PI/0**, BCFG)
103 Early features in Trench 2: 103.01 Structure 1/2 (**PI/1**, 2); 103.02 Charcoal and soil overlying Structure 1/2 (**PI/1**, 2)
104 Unphased **Period 1** deposits in southern sector (**PI**, CD)
105 Early soil in central part of central sector, (**PI**, B)
106 Early soil in western part of central sector, (**PI**, F)
107 Early pits and postholes in central part of central sector, (**PI**, F)
108 Unphased **Period I** or **II** features in central and eastern parts of central sector, (**PI** or **II**, F)
109 Hollow and rubbish filling it (**PI/3.21**, AB)
110 Notional dump of **Period I** metalworking debris reused as levellng material at start of **Period II**
112 Unphased **Period I** deposits in southern sector (**PI**, D)
113 Unphased **Period I** deposits in northern sector (**PI**, AL)
114 Rubbish spread (**PI.6**, D)
115 Debris and paving in Building I/21 (**PI.11**, D)
116 Stake lines including putative boundary fences. (**PI.11**, D)
117 Linear cut on west side of southern sector (**PI.11**, CD)
118 Poorly-stratified rubbish spread to north of Building I/5 (**PI/2–4**, B)
119 **Period I/2** hollow: 119.01 **Period I/2** hollow and the soil filling it (**PI/2.2**, EF); 119.02 possible building (I/10) over 119.01 (**PI/2.3**, EF)
120 Shallow ditch separating inner precinct from outer zone (**PI/2**, BC)
121 Building I/14 (**PI.5**, 5)
122 Shale pathway (**PI.12**, 5)
203 **Period II** surfaces and related deposits: 203.01 shale path from Hall 6 to chapel (**PII/1**, BE); 203.02 shale surface over 203.01 to south of kerb (**PII/2**, B); 203.03 shale surface of main **Period II/2** E/W path (**PII/2**, BEF); 203.04 shale path in eastern part of central sector (**PII**, G); 203.05 resurfacing and wormed soil over 203.03 (**PII/3**, BEF)
206 Surfaces to south of chapel: 206.01 levelling material under paving (**PII/4**, E); 206.02 paving to south of chapel (**PII/4**, E); 206.03 wormed soil over paving (**PII/4.7**, E); 206.04 shale surface (**PII/4**, E)
207 Fire debris inside chapel (**PII/7**, E)
212 Timber buildings in southern sector; 212.01 Building I/21 (**PI.11**, D); 212.02 Building I/24 (**PI.12**, D);
213 Possible gateway and related deposits at south end of southern sector: 213.01 possible gateway (**PI.12**, D); 213.02 fence, mud and shale (**PI.13**, D); 213.03 possible timber gateway (**PI.13**, D)
214 Building II/12 (**PII** early, C)
215 Building II/14 (**PII** intermediate, C)
216 Curving ditch (**PI.11**, CD)
217 Building II/13 (**PII** early, C)
218 Building II/15 (**PII** late, C)
219 Building I/13 (**PI.5**, C)
220 Construction of primary oratory and platform (**PII/1**, AL)
222.01 Construction of orthostatic terrace revetment (**PII/3**, ABEL); 222.02 construction of new wall and rubble buttress (**PII/3**, ABEL)
224 Second phase chapel and related deposits: 224.01 construction of second phase chapel (**PII/2**, E); 224.02 levelling to south of new chapel, and overlying surface (**PII/2**, E); 224.03 wormed soil over 224.02 (**PII/2**, E)
225 Coffin burials in chapel: 225.01 earlier coffin burials in chapel (**PII/1**, E); 225.02 later coffin burials in chapel (**PII/3**, E)
226 Fence and structures to east of chapel: 226.01 fence line to east of chapel (**PII/3**, E); 226.02 Structure II/5a (**PII/4**, E); 226.03 Structure II/5b (**PII/5**, E)
227 Features to south of chapel: 227.01 surface, gate and boundary (**PII/3**, BE); 227.02 wormed soil over 227.01 (**PII/3**, BE)
228 North doorway of chapel; 228.01 construction features (**PII/2**, E); 228.02 burnt debris in doorway (**PII/7**, E)
229 Structure II/18 (**PII** late, D)
230 Drains in southern sector: 230.01 large drainage ditch (**PI.12**, D); 230.02 recut ditch (**PI.13**, D); 230.03 recut drain (**PII** late, D)
232 Stone boundary, path and adjacent silt deposits (**PI.11**, D)
233 Earth floor in chapel: 233.01 secondary floor (**PII/3**, E); 233.02 primary floor (**PII/2**, E)
234 Structure II/17 (**PII** intermediate, D)
235 Waterborne silts on west side of trench (**PI.10**, CD); 235.01 to north of baulk (**PI.10**, CD); 235.02 to south of baulk (**PI.10**, CD)
236 Roadway and fence line: 236.01 possible fence line (**PI.12**, D); 236.02 shale road surface abutting fence (**PI.12**, D); 236.03 paving on road and around building I/24 (**PI.13**, CD)
237 New building encompassing two earlier oratories (**PII/3**, AL)
238 Construction of second oratory (**PII/2**, AL)
239 Original 'altar' (**PII/3**, AL)
240 Robbing pits in 'chancel' (**PII/3**, AL)
241 Shale path and kerb (=203.03, **PII/2**, AL)
245 Partitions in nave (**PII/3**, AL)
246 Grave and charnel pit (**PII/1**, E)
247.01 Enclosure wall, levelling deposits and path (**PII/1**, E); 247.02 wormed soil over 247.01 (**PII/1**, E)
248 Partial demolition of enclosure wall (**PII/1**, E)
249 Primary chapel: 249.01 construction of primary chapel/enclosure (**PII/1**, E); 249.02 south doorway of primary chapel (**PII/1**, E)
250 Clay-puddling pits: 250.01 small clay-puddling pit (**PII/3**, E); 250.02 small clay-puddling pit (**PII/5**, E); 250.03 large clay-puddling pit (**PII/4**, EF)
251 Wormed soil adjacent to chapel (**PII/4.7**, EF)
252.01–6 Alignment of posts and stones (**PI/4–PII/1–4**, BEFG)
253 Hall II/9a and b (**PII** early and intermediate, F)
254 HallII/6: 254.01 Hall II/6a (**PII** early, B); 254.02 Hall II/6b (**PII** intermediate, B); 254.03 Hall II/6c (**PII** late, B)
255 Miscellaneous **Period II** features in central part of central sector (**PII**, F)
256 Unphased **Period II** deposits in western part of northern sector (**PII**, AL)
258 Soil east of Halls II/7 and 9 (**PII**, FG)
259 Structure II/11 (**PII** late, F)
260 Surfaces between Buildings II/6 and II/12–15 (**PII**, BC)
261.01 Building II/13 (**PII** early, 5); 261.02 Building II/16 (**PII** intermediate, 5)
262 Halls II/8 and 10 (**PII** early and intermediate, 2)
263 Hall II/7 (**PII** early, F)
264 Shale surfaces to north of church (**PII**, AL)
300 Structural features and demolition deposits in **Period III** church (**PIII/2.1**, AL): 300.01 Building III/12 (**PIII/2.2**, AL); 300.02 demolition rubble in **Period III** church (**PIII/2.3**, AL)
301 Building III/20 (**PIII/2.3**, B)
302 Weathered shale over rubbish spread (**PIII/1.1**, B)
303 Rubbish spread abutting terrace (**PII/4.7**, B)
305 **Period II** and **III** burials to east of chapel: 305.01 primary phase of children's graveyard (**PII/1.3**, E); 305.02 main phase of children's graveyard (**PII/3**, E); 305.03 two late coffin burials (**PII/4**, E); 305.04 **Period III** burials (**PIII/1**, E); 305.05 cremated human bone over children's graveyard (**PIII/1**, E); 305.06 disarticulated bones and grave fill from children's graveyard. (**PII**, E); 305.07 ditch cutting children's graveyard (**PII/3**, E)
306 **Period III** chapel and related features: 306.01 rebuilt chapel (Building III/2, **PIII/1**, E); 306.02 boundary wall to east of chapel (**PIII/1**, E)

CONCORDANCE

307 Debris from collapse of chapel (**PIII/3**, E): 307.01 clay and stone (**PIII/3**, E); 307.02 weathered clay (**PIII/3**, E)

308 Compass-drawn graffiti on path by chapel (**PII** late, E)

309 Waterborne silts in southern sector: 309.01 miscellaneous disturbances to Buildings II/16 etc (**PIII**, CD); 309.02 waterborne silts and rubbish (**PIII**, CD)

310 Construction of final 'arcades' (**PII/6**, AL)

311 Modification of 'arcades' and doors of church (**PII/5**, AL)

312 Extension to chancel (**PII/4**, AL)

313 Relocation of 'altar' in church (**PII/4**, AL)

314 Replacement of wooden church walls on stone plinths (**PII/4**, AL)

315.01 Burnt debris in church (**PII/7**, AL); 315.02 Floor and burnt debris (**PII/7**, AL)

316 Building III/1 (**PII/1**, AL)

318 Fire debris to east of chapel (**PII/7**, AL)

319 Final terrace (**PII/4**, ABEL)

320 Pits and other poorly-phased features in church. (**PII** late, AL)

321 Early surface and pits (**Ph 1.1**, Museum Garden)

322 Part of north wall of timber hall (**Ph 1.2**, Museum Garden)

323 Soil abutting hall wall (**Ph 1.2**, Museum Garden)

324 Shale surface and possible structure (**Ph 1.3**, Museum Garden)

325 Path and scattered debris (**Ph 1.3**, Museum Garden)

326 Pit and gullies (**Ph 1.2**, Museum Garden)

327 Cobbled surface, possibly road (**Ph 1.4**, Museum Garden)

328 Pits (**Ph 1.4**, Museum Garden)

329 Rock-cut pit, possible building (possibly 13th C, Fey Field)

330 Surfaces and buildings, (possibly 13th C, Fey Field)

333 Probable mid-ninth century ploughsoil (**PIII/1.2**, G)

334 Probable mid-ninth century ploughsoil (**PIII/1.2**, G)

336 Unphased features in western part of northern sector (**PII**, AL)

337 Unphased post-holes in western part of northern sector (**PII**, AL)

339 Burnt debris to south of chapel; 339.01 clay and burnt clay (**PIII/1.1**, E); 339.02 wormed soil over burnt debris (**PIII/1.1**, E)

399 Mid-ninth century ploughing: 399.01 in west part of central sector (**PIII/1.2**, B); 399.02 in central part of central sector (**PIII/1.2**, F); 399.03 in east part of central sector (**PIII/1.2**, G)

400 Rubble and soil banked against terrace (**PIII/2.1**, B)

401 Building IV/27 (**PIV.2** [IP], B)

402 Building III/18 (**PIII/2.2**, B); 402.01 earth floor (**PIII/2.2**, B)

403 Building III/34 (**PIII/3.1**, B)

404 Fragmentary paving, possibly building remains (**PIII**, B)

405 Buildings III/27a and b (**PIII/3.1**, B)

406 Building IV/1 (**PIV.2** [OZS], C)

407 **Period IV** structures and deposits in northern sector: 407.01 possible ploughsoil over Buildings III/13 etc (**PIII/3**, AL); 407.02 Building IV/28 (**PIV.5**[IP], AL); 407.03 post-holes (**PIV.5** [IP], AL); 407.04 soil and debris over Stage 5 buildings (**PIV.6** [IP], AL); 407.05 isolated pebble surface and fire debris (**PIV.5** [IP], AL); 407.06 shallow ditch (**PIV.5** [IP], AL); 407.07 Pit cutting into **Period II** terrace (phase uncertain) (**PIV.5** [IP], AL)

408 Scattered debris and deposits in Museum Garden: 408.01 burnt debris over 326 (**Ph 1**); 408.02 surfaces and structures (**Ph 1.5**)

409 Building IV/8 (**PIV.6** [OZS], CD)

410 Building IV/6 (**PIV.5** [OZS], CD)

411 Superimposed **Period IV** buildings and adjacent features and deposits: 411.01 Building IV/2 (**PIV.2** [OZS], D); 411.02 Building IV/3 (**PIV.3** [OZS], D); 411.03 Building IV/7 (**PIV.6** [OZS], D); 411.04 organic debris surrounding Buildings IV/7 and IV/8 (**PIV.6** [OZS], D); 411.05 late hollows cutting Building IV/7 (**PIV.6** [OZS], D); 411.06 paving beyond Building IV/7 (**PIV.6** [OZS], D); 411.07 upcast from ditch cleaning abutting Building IV/7 (**PIV.6** [OZS], D); 411.08 Pit 1 (**PIV.6** [OZS], D); 411.09 Pit 2 (**PIV.6** [OZS], D); 411.10 Pit 3 (**PIV.6** [OZS], D); 411.11 Pit or post hole 4 (**PIV.6** [OZS], D)

412 Building IV/4 (**PIV.4** [OZS], CD)

413 Building IV/16 (**PIV.9** [OZS], CD)

414 **Period IV.7** structures: 414.01 bank of rubble to south of Buildings IV/9–12 (**PIV.7** [OZS], CD); 414.02 Building IV/12 (**PIV.7** [OZS], C); 414.03 Building IV/9 (**PIV.7** [OZS], C); 414.04 Building IV/10 (**PIV.7** [OZS], C)

415 Waterborne deposits and overlying structure: 415.01 waterborne deposits and rubbish spreads (**PIV.7** and **8** [OZS], CD); 415.02 Building V/2B (**PV.2**, CD)

416 **Period IV/9** ditch (**PIV.9** [OZS], D)

417.01 Cut for main drainage ditch (**PIV.1** [OZS], D); 417.02 fill of main drainage ditch (**PIV.6** [OZS], D)

418 Possible building and fence line (probably 13th C, Fey Field)

419 Possible building (probably 13th C, Fey Field)

420 Building III/9 (**PIII/1.4**, G)

421.01 Burnt cobbles (**PIII/1.3**, EFGK); 421.02 wormed soil over burnt cobbles (**PIII/1.4** (?), EFGK)

422 Burnt debris in and around **Period III/1** buildings: 422.01 Building III/11 (**PIII/1.4**, EF); 422.02 ash over Building III/11 (**PIII/1.4**, EF); 422.03 debris outside Building III/11 (**PIII/1.4**, EF); 422.04 burnt debris between Buildings III/5 and 6, and in 4 (**PIII/1.4**, EF); 422.05 burnt debris, probably same as 422.01–04 (**PIII/1.4** (?), F)

423.01 Building III/7 (**PIII/1.4**, G); 423.02 Building III/8 (**PIII/1.4**, G)

424 Ground surface and large shallow pits (**PIV.1** [IP/OZE], G)

425.01 Fragmentary midden, predominantly antler and bone (**PIV.1** [IP], EF); 425.02 insecurely stratified 'midden' assigned to **Period IV** (**PIV**, EF)

426 Scattered pits and post-holes, probably associated with **Period III** buildings (**PIII**, F)

427 **Period III** and **IV** deposits in Trench 2: 427.01 Building III/10 (**PIII/1.4**, 2); 427.02 Building III/24 (**PIII/2.3**, 2); 427.03 mixed soil, probably **Period IV** debris displaced by **Period V** graves (**PIV**, 2)

428 **Period III** and **IV** deposits in Trench 4: 428.01 two burials (**PIV.4** [IP], 4), 428.02 Building IV/30 (**PIV.5** [IP], 4)

429 Fragmentary paving, probably associated with **Period III** buildings (**PIII**, EF)

430 Rubble spread in west part of central sector (**PIV.3** [IP], BFE)

431 Building III/38 (**PIII/3.1**, F)

432 Cobble surface (**PIV.1** [IP], B)

433 Building III/4 (**PIII/1.4**, F)

434.01 Building IV/29 (**PIV.5** [IP], A); 434.02 truncated pit (**PIV** [IP], A)

435 Building III/5 (**PIII/1.4**, F)

436.01 Inner boundary ditch (**PIII/3.1**, BEF); 436.02 outer boundary ditch (**PIII/3.2**, CF)

437 Cobbling under Building III/24 (**PII** or **III**, K)

438 Cobbled surface and overlying silt (**PIII/3.2**, K)

439 Building IV/17a (**PIV.1** (**OZE**), K)

440 Building IV/18 (**PIV.1** (**OZE**), K)

441 Building IV/17b (**PIV.1** (**OZE**), K)

442 'Building' IV/20 (**PIV.2** (**OZE**), K)

444 Building IV/19 (**PIV.1** (**OZE**), K)

445 Building IV/21 (**PIV.3** (**OZE**), K)

446 Building IV/19 (**PIV.1** (**OZE**), K)

447 Building IV/19b (**PIV.1** (**OZE**), K)

448 Building IV/22 (**PIV.3** (**OZE**), K)

449 Building IV/24 hearth (**PIV.4** (**OZE**), K): 449.01 Building IV/24, part (**PIV.4** (**OZE**), K); 449.02 Building IV/24, part (**PIV.4** (**OZE**), K)

450 'Buildings' IV/25 and 26 (**PIV.4** (**OZE**), K)

451 Miscellaneous deposits, region of Building III/40 (**PIV** [IP], BC)

452 Stone-lined drain (**PIV.1–6** [OZS], D)

453 Disturbed soil under Commendator's House, possibly including grave fill (probably **PIV/V**, K)

454 Building III/22 (**PIII/2.3**, K)

455 Building IV/23 (**PIV.4** (**OZE**), K)

456 **Period III** and **IV** deposits in Trench 5: 456.01 pond silts and debris (**PIII**, 5); 456.02 Building IV/5 (**PIV.4** [OZS], 5); 456.03 part of Building IV/10 and other ash layers (T5) (**PIV.7** [OZS], 5)

457 Fragments of **Period IV** debris in central part of central sector (**PIV** [IP], F)

458 Building IV/5 (**PIV.4** [OZS], 5)

459 Building III/40 (**PIII/3.2**, BC)

460 Building III/39 (**PIII/3.2**, B)

461.01 Building III/13a (**PIII/2.4** [NS], A); 461.02 Building III/13b (**PIII/2.4** [NS], A)

462 Building III/14 (**PIII/2.4** [NS], L)

463 Building III/15 (**PIII/2.4** [NS], A)

464 Building III/16 (**PIII/2.4** [NS], A)

465 Stone reveted platform to south of burial chapel **PIII** (**PIII/1.5**, E)

466 Building III/41 (**PIII/3.2**, F)

467 Possible building IV/11 (**PIV.7** [OZS], 5)

468 Building III/21 (**PIII/2.3**, F)

469 Building III/29 (**PIII/3.1**, F)

470 Building III/33 (**PIII/3.1**, FG)
471 Building III/43 (**PIII/3.2**, F)
472 Building III/30 (**PIII/3.1**, F)
473 Building III/44 (**PIII/3.2**, EG)
474 Building III/31 (**PIII/3.1**, E)
475 Building III/36 (**PIII/3.1**, EF)
476 Building III/35 (**PIII/3.1**, BF)
477 Building III/32 (**PIII/3.1**, E)
478 Building III/3. (**PIII/1.2**, E)
479 Structure III/19 (**PIII/2.2**, BF)
481 Building III/23 (**PIII/2.3**, F)
482 Building III/25 (**PIII/2.3**, K)
483 Building III/26 (**PIII/2.3**, F)
484 Building III/42 (**PIII/3.2**, F)
485 Building III/37 (**PIII/3.1**, EA)
486 Fragmentary walls in inner precinct (**PIV.4** [IP], BF)
487 Ditch south of Building IV/1 (**PIV.2** [OZS], C)
488 Building IV/13 (**PIV.8** [OZS], C)
489 Building IV/14 (**PIV.8** [OZS], C)
490 Possible building IV/15 (**PIV.8** [OZS], 5)
491 Building III/6 (**PIII/1.4**, EG)
492 Building III/17 (**PIII/2.4** [NS], E)
493 Building III/28 (**PIII/3.1**, BF)
494 Lowest excavated deposits at eastern end of central sector, probably **Period III** (**PIII** (?), K)
495 **Period IV** deposits in south part of central sector (**PIV**, F)
500.01 Lower courses of boundary wall (**PV.1**, D); 500.02 silt abutting boundary wall (**PV.1**, D)
502 Boundary ditch to west of graveyard (**PV/2**, L)
504.01 Shale path to south of Building V/1 (**PV/1**, L); 504.02 pits cutting path (504.01) (**PV/1**, L)
505 Floor deposits in Building V/3 (**PV.4**, D)
506 Building V/3: 506.01 probable foundations of Building V/3 producing contemporary and displaced finds. (**PV.4**, CD); 506.02 west, north and east walls of Building V/3 and floor deposits (**PV.4**, CD); 506.03 cobbling to north of Building V/3 (**PV.4**, C); 506.04 possible founds of south wall of Building V/3 (**PV.4**, D)
507 Building V/1: 507.01 construction of Building V/1 (**PV/1**, L); 507.02 floor deposits in Building V/1 (**PV/1**, L); 507.03 demolition deposits in Building V/1 (**PV/1**, L)
508 Band of large stones, possibly boundary to west of graveyard (**PV/1**, L)
511.01–10 Stage 1–9 burials, and unphased graves (**Ph 2**, Museum Garden)
512 Stage 10 burials (**Ph 2**, Museum Garden)
513 Rough surface (**PV.5**, CD)
514 Demolition deposits in Building V/3 (**PV.5**, CD)
515 Structure (**PV.5**, CD)
516.01 Oven to south of boundary wall (**PV.3**, D); 516.02 burnt deposits overlying oven (516.01) and adjacent wall (**PV.3**, D)
517 **Period V.5** surfaces: 517.01 shale surface overlying burnt deposits and Building V/2a (**PV.4**, D); 517.02 shale surface on west side of trench, possibly same as 517.01 (**PV.4**, D); 517.03 surfaces on east side of trench, possibly same as 517.01 (**PV.4**, D)
518 Stone lined drain to north of Building V/2a (**PV.3**, D)
519 Paving and narrow stone-lined drains to south of boundary wall (**PV.2**, D)
520 Building V/2a and related features: 520.01 sub-rectangular building (V/2a) with paved floor (**PV.2**, D); 520.02 clay spreads and other late features in Building V/2a (**PV.3**, D); 520.03 burnt deposits overlying Building V/2a, probably same as 516.02 (**PV.3**, D); 520.04 sinuous stone-lined drain underlying paving at west end of Building V/2a (**PV.3**, D); 520.05 isolated ash patches to west of Building V/2a (**PV.2**, D)
521 Stone-lined and -capped drain to north of Building V/3 (**PV.4**, C)
522 Hearths and related features oversailing possible south wall of Building V/3 (**PV.5**, CD)
523 Putative stake-lined pit at south end of trench and disturbed organic debris (**PV.5**, D)
524 Repair of **Period V/1** boundary wall (**PV.5**, D)
525.01 Rough surface (**PV.4**, D); 525.02 putative earth bank (**PV.5**, D)
526 Cultivation furrow and upcast layers (probably 13th C, Fey Field)
527 Surfaces and fragmentary wall (probably 13th C, Fey Field)
528 Surface and layers of clay and silt (probably 13th C, Fey Field)
529 Mixed deposits (13th C and later, Fey Field)
530–535 **Period V** graveyard: Stage 1–5 burials (**PV/1**, ABEFGK)
536–539 **Period V** graveyard: Stage 6–9 burials (**PV/2**, ABEFGK)
540 **Period V** graveyard: Stage 10 burials (**PV/3**, ABEFGK)
541 Unphased articulated skeletons (**PV/1–3**, ABEFGK)
542 Unphased graveyard deposits (**PV/1–3**, ABEFGK)
543 Graveyard cleaning contexts (**PV/1–3**, ABEFGK)
544 Graveyard soil (**Ph 2**, Museum Garden)
546 Cultivation furrows to west of graveyard (**PV/1**, L)
547 Thick spread of shells displaced by later graves in north part of trench (**PV/2**, A)
548 Remains of two buildings V/5a and b in east corner of trench (**PV/4**, K)
549 Late medieval post setting (**PV**, B)
550 Ground surface to west of graves (**PV/1–3**, L)
551 Severely-disturbed shallow ditch between graves and cultivation furrows (**PV**, L)
560 Disturbed deposits on east side of trench (**PV.5**, A)
600.01–05 Trampled stony surface overlying (**Period V** graves (**PV/3**, ABEFKL)
601 Soakaway pit to west of Building V/4, and debris filling it (**PV/4**, K)
602 Small pits and post-holes cutting surfaces on north side of trench (**PVI/2**, L)
603 Building V/4 east, south and north walls (**PV/4**, K)
604 Late 'surfaces', probably masons' waste inside and beyond Building V/4 (**PV/4**, K)
605 Construction debris and overlying 'surfaces' (masons' waste) to west of Building V/4 (**PV/4**, K)
606 Surfaces inside Building V/4, possibly masons' waste (**PV/4**, K)
607.01–4 Robbing pits over and to north of Building V/1 (**PV/2**, AL)
607.05–9 Probable quarry-pits and smaller holes to north of Building V/1 (**PV/4**, AL)
608 Plough soil (**PVI**, AL)
610 Excavated segment of field wall: 610.01 original wall (**PVI/1**, AL); 610.02 rubble to west, possibly from demolition and rebuild (**PVI/1**, L); 610.03 rebuilt wall and flanking deposits (**PVI/1**, L)
611 Worm-sorted soil (**PVI/1**, L)
612.01 Two robbing pits cutting the **Period II** terrace (**PV/2**, L); 612.02 a hollow cutting the earlier robbing pits (**PV/2**, L); 612.03 soil over the hollow (612.02) (**PV/4**, L); 612.04 possible path over 612.03 (**PV/4**, L)
613 Four troughs (**PVI/1**, L)
614 Dark soil separating two phases of cultivation (**PVI**, L)
615.01–05 Worm soil (**PV/3**, BEFKL)
616.01–07 Cobbled surface (**PV/3**, AKL4)
617 **Period V/3–5** surfaces and structures in centre of trench: 617.01 cobbles (**PV/3**, E); 617.02 worm soil (**PV/4**, F); 617.03 cobbles (**PV/5**, EF); 617.04 possible structure (**PV/5**, E); 617.05 stone kerb (**PV/5**, F)
618 Structure V/7 – parallel trenches packed with rubble and clay (**PV/4**, E)
619 Building V/9 619.01 original stone walled building (**PV/5**, E); 619.02 successive earth floors (**PV/5**, E); 619.03 secondary modifications: doorway blocked and partition wall built (**PV/5**, E); 619.04 demolition deposits of rubble and clay (**PV/5**, E)
620 Building V/6: 620.01 gullies/construction trenches marking walls (**PV/4**, E); 620.02 successive earth floors and related deposits (**PV/4**, E)
621 Cobbled roadway surface severely disturbed by cultivation (**PVI/2**, L)
622 Construction of new crypt (**Ph 2**, Museum Garden)
623 Stage 11 burials (**Ph 2**, Museum Garden)
624 Soil, probably upper horizon of graveyard (**Ph 2**, Museum Garden)
625 Stony soil, probably upper horizon of graveyard (**Ph 2**, Museum Garden)
630 Rubbish, including builders' waste, banked against west wall of Building V/4 (**PV/4**, K)
631 Cobbling, silt and rubbish over **Period V** roadway in north part of trench (**PVI/1**, E)
632 Rough cobbling or stone spread (**PV.5**, D)
633 Wormed soil over rough cobbling (632), possibly same as 709 (**PV.5**, D)
634 Late pits containing disarticulated human bone (**PV/4**, 4)

CONCORDANCE

635 Possible smithy structures and debris overlying quarry pits (**PV/5**, A)
700 Fragmentary walls of Building V/8, possibly Commendator's House (**PV/5**, GK)
701 Reconstruction of inner face of main block (700) of Building V/8 (**PVI/2**, GK)
702 Paved sunken yard to east of Building V/8 (**PV/5**, GK)
703 Floor in main block of Building V8 (**PVI/2**, GK)
704 Rubbish spreads to south of Building V/8 (**PV/5**, GK)
705 Fragmentary wall of southern extension to Building V/8 (**PV/5**, GK)
707 Hollow to south-west of manse, probably dug during construction of west wing (**PVI/2**, FGK)
708 Soil and rubbish accumulation in hollow 707 (**PVI/2**, FGK)
709 Soil accumulation in southern sector (**PVI/1**, D)
710 Stone-walled and -capped field drain (**PVI/2**, D)
711 Narrow cultivation trenches (**PVI/2**, C)
712 Western extension of manse (**PVI/2**, G)
713 External stone-filled drains (**PVI/2**, G)
714 Probable rebuild of manse internal wall (**PVI/2**, G)
715 Soakaway and floor of west wing (**PVI/2**, G)
716 Stone surface over cultivation furrows (**PVI/2**, C)
717 Broad cultivation trenches (**PVI/2**, C)
718 Soil accumulation over field-drain 710 (**PVI/2**, D)
719 New corridor and floors in main block of manse (**PVI/2**, G)
720 New floor surfaces in north room of manse (**PVI/2**, G)
721 Soakaway pits beyond west wing of manse (**PVI/2**, G)
722 Patchy surfaces to south of west wing of manse (**PVI/2**, G)
723 Revetment wall to north-west of manse (**PVI/2**, G)
724 Refurbishment of fireplace (**PVI/2**, G)
725 Large stone-filled land drain (**PVI/2**, ABEFL)
726 Stone filled land-drains in southern sector (**PVI/2**, D)
727 Demolition of west wing of manse (**PVI/2**, G)
728 Refurbishment of original manse building (**PVI/2**, G)
729 Rubble and rubbish spreads filling courtyard of Commendator's House, (**PV–VI**, GK)
730 Box drain to east of manse (**PVI/2**, GK)
731 Yard and enclosure to west of manse (**PVI/2**, G)
732 Fragmentary cultivation trenches in southern sector (**PVI/3**, D)
733 Broad wall foundation at southern end of manse (**PVI/2**, GK)
734.01 Possible late field drain to south of manse (**PVI/2**, D); 734.02 late pit cutting remains of manse (**PVI/3**, K)
735 Shallow scoop in western part of central sector, and the material filling it (**PVI/2**, BF)
736 Spread of rubble in southern sector (**PVI/2**, D)
737 Late cultivation furrow or pit at south end of southern sector (**PVI/2**, D)
738 Demolition of old manse and adjacent yard (**PVI/3**, G)
739 Late ploughing over remains of old manse (**PVI/3**, G)
740 Ploughing to west of old manse (**PVI/3**, EF)
741 Recent disturbances (**PVI/3**, EF)
742 Recent disturbances cutting Old Manse (**PVI/3**, GK)
743 Backfill of previous excavations (**PVI/3**, GK); 743.01 1972 Trench E (**PVI/3**, EF); 743.02 1984 Trench 2 (**PVI/3**, GK); 743.04 1984 Trench 4 (**PVI/3**, AB); 743.05 temporary backfill of northern part of northern sector (**PVI/3**, A); 743.06 Fey Field Trench (**PVI/3**, Fey Field)
744 Topsoil in main trench (**PVI/3**, A–K)
745 Late cultivation to west of field wall (**PVI/3**, L)
746 Late cultivation to east of field wall (**PVI/3**, L)
747.01 Construction of original greenhouse (**PVI/3**, L); 747.02 rebuilding of field wall (**PVI/3**, L)
748.01 Internal path in greenhouse (**PVI/3**, L); 748.02 pit within greenhouse (**PVI/3**, L); 748.03 planting bench supports (**PVI/3**, L); 748.04 path surfaces and related deposits (**PVI/3**, L); 748.05 fire debris in original furnace (**PVI/3**, L)
749 Demolition or repair debris to east of field wall (**PVI/3**, L)
750.01 Construction of new furnace (**PVI/3**, L); 750.02 reconstruction of west wall (**PVI/3**, L); 750.03 construction of internal water tank (**PVI/3**, L); 750.04 external wall by furnace entrance (**PVI/3**, L)
751 Ashy fill of later furnace (**PVI/3**, L)
752 Fill and blocking of disused furnace (**PVI/3**, L)
753.01 Construction of overflow pipe from water trough (**PVI/3**, L); 753.02 construction of internal planting bed (**PVI/3**, L); 753.03 fill of planting bed (**PVI/3**, L)
754 Demolition of greenhouse (**PVI/3**, L)
755 Posthole in internal greenhouse path, possibly much earlier (**PVI/3**, L)
756 Gravel path alongside to greenhouse (**PVI/3**, L)
757 Large pits possibly associated with new buildings (**Ph 3.2**, Museum Garden)
758.01 Fragmentary kirkyard boundary wall (**Ph 3.3**, Museum Garden); 758.02 probable gatepost sockets (**Ph 3.3**, Museum Garden); 758.03 roadway surfaces, charnel pit and infant burial. (**Ph 3.3**, Museum Garden) 758.04 late stone revetment to roadway surfaces 758.03 (**Ph 3.3**, Museum Garden)
759 Late graves (**Ph 3.3**, Museum Garden)
760 Land drains (**Ph 3.4**, Museum Garden)
761 Large pit, possibly for winch base (**Ph 3.4**, Museum Garden)
762 Builders debris (**Ph 3.4**, Museum Garden)
763 New boundary wall and paths around the crypts (**Ph 3.5**, Museum Garden)
764 Recent paths (**Ph 3.5**, Museum Garden)
765 Possible boundary wall and collapsed material (c 1300 and later, Fey Field)
766 Ploughsoil and topsoil (14th C–Present, Fey Field)
767 Recent rubble abutting field wall (**PVI/3**, L)
769 Cobbled path beside greenhouse (**PVI/3**, L)
770 Topsoil and path in Museum Garden (**Ph 3.5**, Museum Garden)
771 Late quarry pit with shaley fill (**PVI/3**, L)
772 **Period V/4–6** surfaces severely contaminated with recent finds (**PVI/3**, BF)
773 Field wall of Glebe Field (**PVI**)
774 Miscellaneous recent construction trenches, pole sockets etc (20th C)
901–928 Unstratified and poorly-stratified deposits and finds: 901 General cleaning of excavated areas; 902 Finds from section cleaning; 903 Finds from spoil, including some from spoil of known origin retained for metal detection; 904 Finds from known area, but uncertain context; 906 Finds from trampled surfaces; 909 Finds recovered from baulks; 910–923 Unphased deposits: various areas; 924 Unlocated finds; 926 Mislabelled finds

Plate I General view of Whithorn from the north-west with the Isle of Whithorn in the upper right corner.

Plate II Aerial view of the excavation in the Glebe Field from the south-west with the parish church and ruined priory to the left and the town to the right.

Plate III   The *Latinus* stone.

Plate IV **Period I** features in the eastern part of the Glebe Field viewed from the north. The special grave (**I/18**) is in the lower left corner and the hearth of Building I/1 in the centre.

Plate V Experimental reconstruction of a twelfth century house based on the evidence from Building IV/7.

Plate VI   Excavation in progress in 1991 with the pebble covers of Graves I/68 and I/80 in the foreground, and log-coffin burials (Graves I/74–78) cutting the **Period I/3** roadway beyond.

Plate VII   The **Period II** burial chapel from the east, during the excavation of the coffins in the internal graves.

Plate VIII The **Period II** church from the west showing the foundation trenches of the two oratories (1 and 2) framed by the sockets of the later arcade posts, and with the Period II/1 enclosure wall to the right.

Plate IX   Early medieval window glass.

Plate X   Early medieval vessel glass.

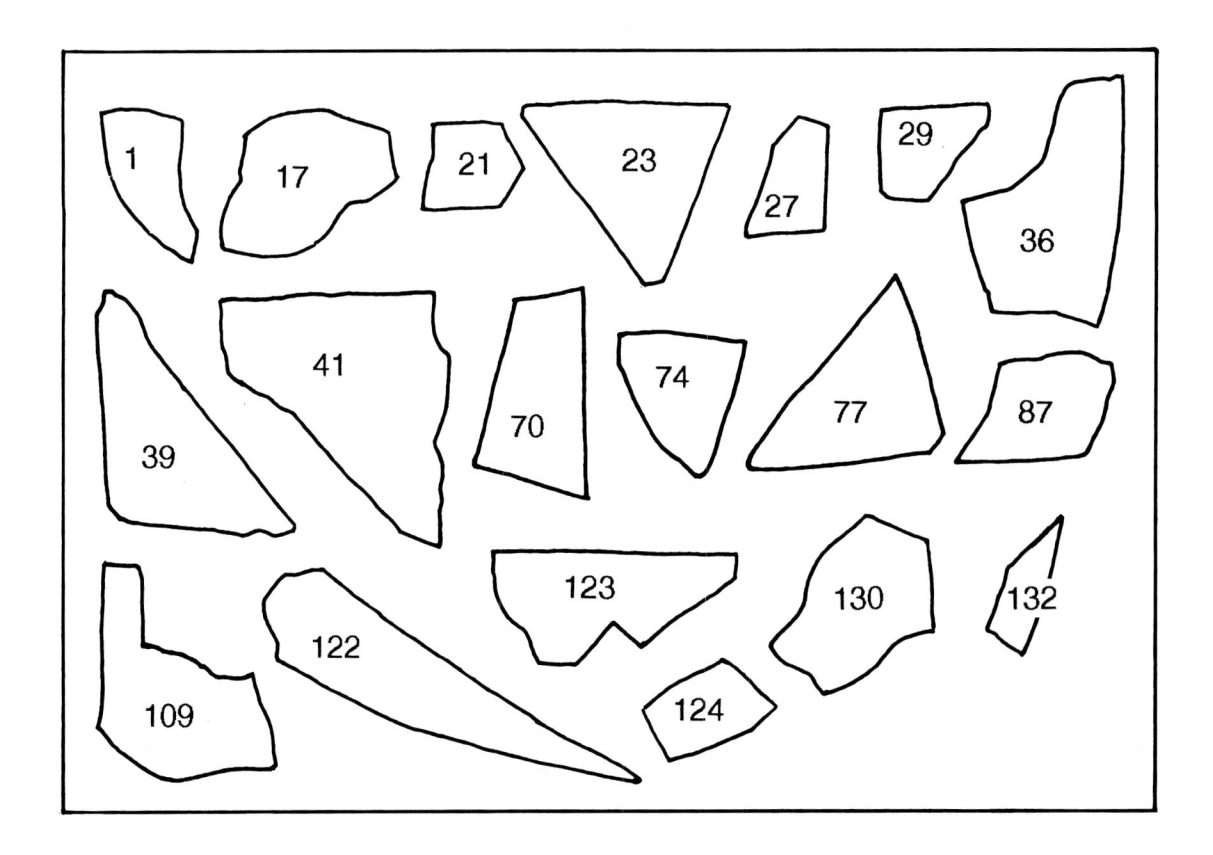

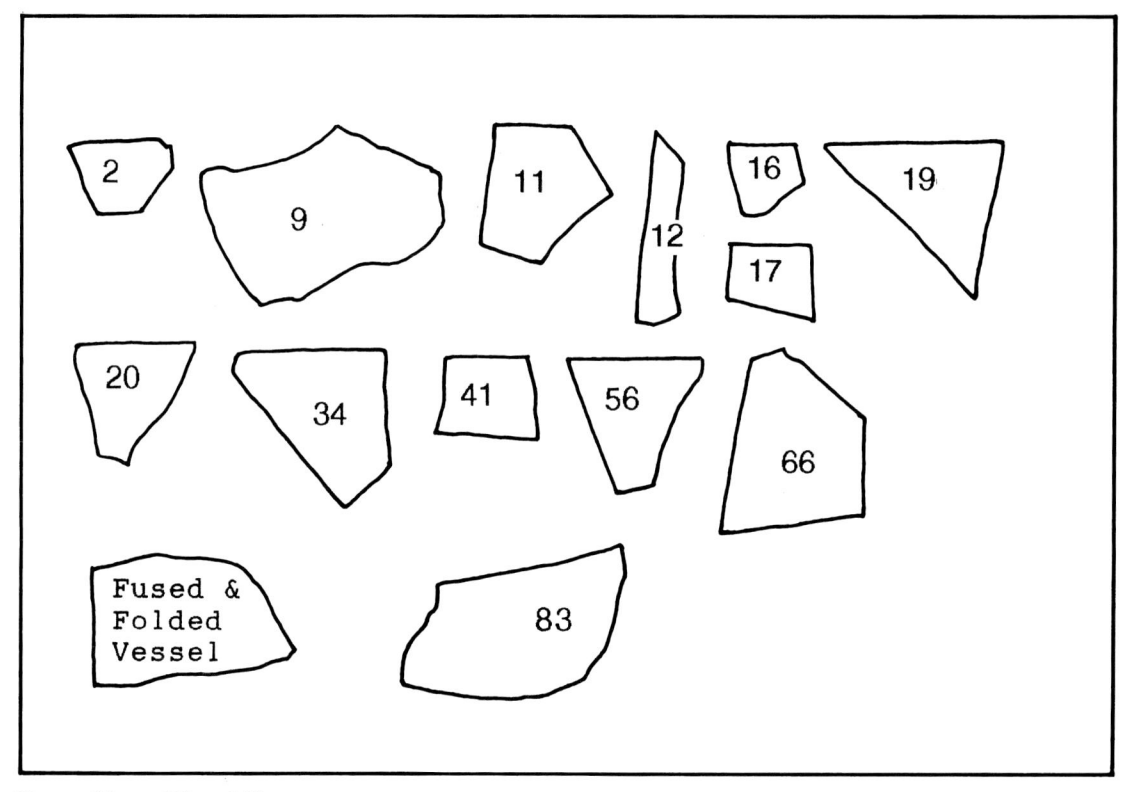

Key to Plates IX and X